THE COMPLETE LIBRARY
OF
CHRISTIAN WORSHIP

THE COMPLETE LIBRARY
OF
CHRISTIAN WORSHIP

Volume 4, Music and the Arts in Christian Worship

ROBERT E. WEBBER, EDITOR

Book 1

HENDRICKSON PUBLISHERS

The Complete Library of Christian Worship, Vol. 4, Music and the Arts in Christian Worship, Book 1.

Hendrickson Publishers, Inc.
P. O. Box 3473
Peabody, Massachusetts 01961-3473

Printed in the United States of America

Hendrickson Publishers edition
ISBN 1-56563-189-7
Hendrickson edition published by arrangement with Star Song Publishing Group, a division of
Jubilee Communications, Inc.
2325 Crestmoor, Nashville, Tennessee 37215

Unless otherwise indicated, all Scripture quotations taken from the HOLY BIBLE, NEW INTERNATIONAL VERSION. Copyright © 1973, 1978, 1984 by International Bible Society. Used by permission of Zondervan Publishing House.

Scripture quotations marked (KJV) are from the HOLY BIBLE, KING JAMES VERSION.

Scripture quotations marked (NASB) are taken from the NEW AMERICAN STANDARD BIBLE. Copyright © 1960, 1962, 1963, 1968, 1971, 1972, 1973, 1975, 1977, the Lockman Foundation. Used by permission.

Scripture quotations marked (RSV) are taken from the REVISED STANDARD VERSION of the Bible. Copyright © 1946, 1952, 1971, 1973 by the Division of Christian Education of the National Council of Churches of Christ in the U.S.A. Used by permission.

Scripture quotations marked (NRSV) are taken from THE HOLY BIBLE: NEW REVISED STANDARD VERSION. Copyright © 1989 by the Division of Christian Education of the National Council of Churches of Christ in the U.S.A. Used by permission.

Scripture quotations marked (TEV) are taken from TODAY'S ENGLISH VERSION of the Bible, Third Edition. Copyright © 1966, 1971 American Bible Society. Used by permission.

CONTENTS

Part 2: MUSIC IN WORSHIP

Part 3: THE VISUAL ARTS IN WORSHIP

List of Illustrations and Tables

Board of Editorial Consultants

The Board of Editorial Consultants is made up of leaders in worship renewal from major Christian denominations. They have functioned as advisors, often through letter and telephone. Every attempt has been made to include material on worship representing the whole church. For this reason, different viewpoints are presented without any attempt to express a particular point of view or bias. A special word of thanks is due to the executive and consulting editors for their helpful input. Their ideas, suggestions and contributions have strengthened the *Complete Library of Christian Worship*. Omissions and weaknesses in all seven volumes are the sole responsibility of the compiler and editor.

Editor

Robert E. Webber, Professor of Theology, Wheaton College, Wheaton, Illinois
Th.D., Concordia Theological Seminary

Executive Editors

Darrell A. Harris
President, Star Song Distribution Group

Stan Moser
Chief Executive Officer, Star Song Distribution Group

Matthew A. Price
Vice President, Star Song Publishing Group

David R. West, Jr.
National Sales Director, Star Song Publishing Group

Project Editors

James C. Galvin, The Livingstone Corporation
Ed.D., Northern Illinois University

J. Michael Kendrick, The Livingstone Corporation
Ph.D. (candidate) University of Wisconsin-Madison

Larry Nyberg, Liturgy and Education Consultant, Diocese of Chicago
Ph.D. (candidate) Drew University

John D. Witvliet
Ph.D. (candidate), Notre Dame University

Substantive Editors

John Finley (Music)
M.A., University of California, SBC

David Gillaspey (Leading Worship)
M.A., University of Missouri

Richard Leonard (Scripture)
Ph.D., Boston University

Dennis Martin (Sacraments)
Ph.D., University of Waterloo

Jack Mercer (Preaching)
D.Min., Princeton Theological Seminary

Douglas Morgan
Ph.D., University of Chicago

William Mugford (Bibliography)
Ph.D. (candidate) University of Chicago

Carol Nyberg (Children's Worship)
B.A., Trinity College

Phillip Beggrov Peter
Ph.D., Northwestern University

Rebecca Slough (Arts)
Ph.D., Graduate Theological Union

Grant Sperry-White (History)
Ph.D., Notre Dame University

Consulting Editors

Douglas Adams
Pacific School of Religion, Berkeley, California

William Barker
Westminster Theological Seminary, Glenside, Pennsylvania

Paul Bassett
Nazarene Theological Seminary, Kansas City, Missouri

Harold Best
Wheaton College Conservatory of Music, Wheaton, Illinois

Donald C. Boyd
Asbury Theological Seminary, Wilmore, Kentucky

Emily Brink
***Reformed Worship**, Grand Rapids, Michigan*

Donald Bruggink
Western Theological Seminary, Holland, Michigan

John Burkhart
McCormick Theological Seminary, Chicago, Illinois

John W. Morris
   _St. George Antiochian Orthodox Church, Cedar
   Rapids, Iowa_

John P. Mossi
   North American Academy of Liturgists

Richard J. Mouw
   Fuller Theological Seminary, Pasadena, California

William Mugford
   University of Chicago, Chicago, Illinois

May Murakami
   _Christ United Presbyterian Church, San Francisco,
   California_

Carol Myers
   Hope College, Holland, Michigan

Loni McCalister
   Lee College, Cleveland, Tennessee

William B. McClain
   Wesley Theological Seminary, Washington, D.C.

Richard McDaniel
   _Steward of the Word Ministries, Chapel Hill, North
   Carolina_

Killian McDonnell
   Order of St. Benedict, Collegeville, Minnesota

William K. McElvaney
   Perkins School of Theology, Dallas, Texas

Gary B. McGee
   _Assemblies of God Theological Seminary,
   Springfield, Missouri_

Martha McIntosh
   St. Patrick's Church, Tampa, Florida

Elsie McKee
   _Princeton Theological Seminary, Princeton, New
   Jersey._

Jean McLaughlin
   St. Joan of Arc Parish, Toledo, Ohio

Francis McNutt
   _Christian Healing Ministries, Inc., Jacksonville,
   Florida_

Philip D. Needhan
   The Salvation Army, Atlanta, Georgia

David R. Newman
   Emmanuel College, Toronto, Ontario, Canada

Kathryn L. Nichols
   _Paxton Presbyterian Church, Harrisburg,
   Pennsylvania_

Stanley E. Niebruegge
   _Presbyterian Church USA, Franconia, New
   Hampshire_

Charles Nienkirchen
   Rocky Mountain College, Calgary, Alberta, Canada

James Notebaart
   _Our Lady of Mt. Carmel Parish, Minneapolis,
   Minnesota_

David Noy
   _Austin Presbyterian Theological Seminary, Austin,
   Texas_

Celeste Marie Nuttman
   _Worship, Art, and Music Commission of the
   Archdiocese of San Francisco, California_

Carol Nyberg
   Episcopal Diocese of Chicago, Chicago, Illinois

Larry Nyberg
   Episcopal Diocese of Chicago, Chicago, Illinois

Mark Olson
   The Other Side, Philadelphia, Pennsylvania

Dennis Okholm
   Wheaton College, Wheaton, Illinois

Hughes Oliphant Old
   _Princeton Theological Seminary, Princeton, New
   Jersey_

Gilbert Ostdiek
   Catholic Theological Union, Chicago, Illinois

Richard N. Ostling
   Time, _New York, New York_

Jerome T. Overbeck
   Loyola University, Chicago, Illinois.

Chris Stoffel Overvoorde
   Calvin College, Grand Rapids, Michigan

Dean Palermo
   Bethlehem Baptist Church, Minneapolis, Minnesota

Lloyd Patterson
   _Episcopal Divinity School, Cambridge,
   Massachusetts_

Robert W. Pazmiño
   _Andover Newton Theological Schoool, Newton
   Center, Massachusetts_

Jim Peck
   Wheaton College, Wheaton, Illinois

Steve Pederson
   _Willowcreek Community Church, South Barrington,
   Illinois_

Hayim Perelmuter
   Catholic Theological Union, Chicago, Illinois

Edward Phillips
   Union College, Barbourville, Kentucky

Tim Phillips
   Wheaton College, Wheaton, Illinois

Mary Alice Piil
   _Seminary of the Immaculate Conception,
   Huntington, New York_

List of Cooperating Publishers

BOOK PUBLISHERS

Abbott-Martyn Press
2325 Crestmoor Road
Nashville, TN 37215

Abingdon Press
201 8th Avenue South
Nashville, TN 37202

Agape
Hope Publishing
Carol Stream, IL 60187

Alba House
2187 Victory Boulevard
Staten Island, NY 10314

**American Choral
Directors Association**
502 Southwest 38th
Lawton, Oklahoma 73505

**Asian Institute for
Liturgy & Music**
P.O. Box 3167
Manila 1099 Philippines

Augsburg/Fortress Press
426 S. Fifth Street
Box 1209
Minneapolis, MN 55440

Ave Maria Press
Notre Dame, IN 46556

Baker Book House
P.O. Box 6287
Grand Rapids, MI 49516-6287

Beacon Hill Press
Box 419527
Kansas City, MO 64141

Bethany House Publishers
6820 Auto Club Road
Minneapolis, MN 55438

The Brethren Press
1451 Dundee Avenue
Elgin, IL 60120

Bridge Publishing, Inc.
200 Hamilton Blvd.
South Plainfield, NJ 07080

Broadman Press
127 Ninth Avenue, North
Nashville, TN 37234

C.S.S. Publishing Company
628 South Main Street
Lima, OH 45804

Cathedral Music Press
P.O. Box 66
Pacific, MO 63069

**Catholic Book
Publishing Company**
257 W. 17th Street
New York, NY 10011

CBP Press
Box 179
St. Louis, MO 63166

Celebration
P.O. Box 309
Aliquippa, PA 15001

Channing L. Bete Company
South Deerfield, MA 01373

Choristers Guild
2834 W. Kingsley Road
Garland, TX 75041

Christian Literature Crusade
701 Pennsylvania Avenue
Box 1449
Ft. Washington, PA 19034

Christian Publications
3825 Hartzdale Drive
Camp Hill, PA 17011

**The Church
Hymnal Corporation**
800 Second Avenue
New York, NY 10017

The Columba Press
93 Merise
Mount Merrion
Blackrock, Dublin

Concordia Publishing House
3558 S. Jefferson Avenue
St. Louis, MO 63118

Covenant Publications
3200 West Foster Avenue
Chicago, IL 60625

Cowley Publications
980 Memorial Drive
Cambridge, MA 02138

CRC Publications
2850 Kalamazoo SE
Grand Rapids, MI 49560

**Creative Communications
for The Parish**
10300 Watson Road
St. Louis, MO 63127

**Crossroad Publishing
Company**
575 Lexington Avenue
New York, NY 10022

Crossroad/Continuum
370 Lexington Avenue
New York, NY 10017

Dominion Press
7112 Burns Street
Ft. Worth, TX 76118

Duke Univesity Press
Box 6697 College Station
Durham, NC 27708

Faith and Life Press
724 Main Street
Box 347
Newton, KS 67114

The Faith Press, Ltd.
7 Tufton Street
Westminster, S.W. 1
England

Fleming H. Revell Company
184 Central Avenue
Old Tappen, N.J. 07675

Folk Music Ministry
P.O. Box 3443
Annapolis, MD 21403

Franciscan Communications
1229 South Santee Street
Los Angeles, CA 90015

Georgetown University Press
111 Intercultural Center
Washington, D.C. 20057

GIA Publications
7404 S. Mason Avenue
Chicago, IL 60638

Great Commission Publications
7401 Old York Road
Philadelphia, PA 19126

Grove Books
Bramcote Notts
England

Harper & Row Publishers
Icehouse One-401
151 Union Street
San Francisco, CA 94111-1299

Harvard University Press
79 Garden Street
Cambridge, MA 02138

Harvest Publications
Baptist General Conference
2002 S. Arlington Heights Road
Arlington Heights, IL 60005

Hendrickson Publishers, Inc.
P.O. Box 3473
Peabody, MA 01961-3473

Herald Press
616 Walnut Avenue
Scottdale, PA 15683

Hinshaw Music Incorporated
P.O. Box 470
Chapel Hill, NC 27514

Holt, Rinehart & Winston
111 5th Avenue
New York, NY 10175

Hope Publishing Company
Carol Stream, IL 60188

Hymn Society of America
Texas Christian University
P.O. Box 30854
Ft. Worth, TX 76129

Indiana University Press
10th & Morton
Bloomington, IN 47405

Integrity Music
P.O. Box 16813
Mobile, AL 36616

J.S. Paluch Company, Inc.
3825 Willow Road
P.O. Box 2703
Schiller Park, IL 60176

**The Jewish Publication
Society of America**
1930 Chestnut Street
Philadelphia, PA 19103

Judson Press
P.O. Box 851
Valley Forge, PA 19482-0851

**Light and Life Publishing
Company**
P.O. Box 26421
Minneapolis, MN 55426

Liguori Publications
One Liguori Drive
Liguori, MO 63057

Lillenas Publishing Company
Box 419527
Kansas City, MO 64141

The Liturgical Conference
1017 Twelfth Street, N.W.
Washington, D.C. 20005-4091

The Liturgical Press
St. John's Abbey
Collegeville, MN 56321

Liturgy Training Publications
1800 North Heritage Avenue
Chicago, IL 60622-1101

**Macmillan Publishing
Company**
866 Third Avenue
New York, NY 10022

Maranatha! Music
25411 Cabot Road
Suite 203
Laguna Hills, CA 92653

Mel Bay Publications
Pacific, MO 63969-0066

Meriwether Publishing, Ltd.
885 Elkton Drive
Colorado Springs, CO 80907

Michael Glazier, Inc.
1723 Delaware Avenue
Wilmington, Delaware 19806

Morehouse-Barlow
78 Danbury Road
Wilton, CT 06897

Multnomah Press
10209 SE Division Street
Portland, OR 97266

**National Association
of Pastoral Musicians**
25 Sheridan Street, NW
Washington, DC 20011

NavPress
P.O. Box 6000
Colorado Springs, CO 80934

New Skete
Cambridge, NY 12816

**North American
Liturgical Resources**
1802 N. 23rd Avenue
Phoenix, AZ 85029

Oxford University Press
16-00 Pollitt Drive
Fair Lawn, NJ 07410

The Pastoral Press
225 Sheridan Street, NW
Washington, D.C. 20011

Paulist Press
997 McArthur Boulevard
Mahwah, NJ 07430

The Pilgrim Press
132 West 31st Street
New York, NY 10001

Psalmist Resources
9820 E. Watson Road
St. Louis, MO 63126

Pueblo Publishing Company
100 West 32nd Street
New York, NY 1001-3210

Regal Books
A Division of Gospel Light
  Publications
Ventura, CA 93006

Resource Publications, Inc.
160 E. Virginia Street #290
San Jose, CA 95112

The Scarecrow Press
52 Liberty Street
Box 416
Metuchen, NJ 08840

Schocken Books
62 Cooper Square
New York, NY 10003

**Schuyler Institute for
Worship & The Arts**
2757 Melandy Drive, Suite 15
San Carlos, CA 94070

SCM Press Ltd.
c/o Trinity Press International
3725 Chestnut Street
Philadelphia, PA 19104

Servant Publications
P.O. Box 8617
Petersham, MA 01366-0545

The Sharing Company
P.O. Box 2224
Austin, TX 78768-2224

Sheed & Ward
115 E. Armour Boulevard
P.O. Box 414292
Kansas City, MO 64141-0281

Shofar Publications, Inc
P.O. Box 88711
Carol Stream, IL 60188

SPCK
Holy Trinity Church
Marylebone Road
London, N.W. 4D4

St. Anthony Messenger Press
1615 Republic Street
Cincinnati, OH 45210

St. Bede's Publications
P.O. Box 545
Petersham, MA 01366-0545

St. Mary's Press
Terrace Heights
Winona, MN 55987

St. Vladimir Seminary Press
575 Scarsdale Road
Crestwood, NY 10707-1699

Thomas Nelson Publishers
P.O. Box 141000
Nashville, TN 37214

Twenty Third Publications
P.O. Box 180
Mystic, CT 06355

Tyndale House Publishers
351 Executive Drive
Carol Stream, IL 60188

United Church of Christ
Office of Church Life and
  Leadership
700 Prospect
Cleveland, OH 44115

United Church Press
132 West 31st Street
New York, NY 10001

**The United Methodist
Publishing House**
P.O. Box 801
Nashville, TN 37202

**United States
Catholic Conference**
Office of Publishing and
  Promotion Services
1312 Massachusetts Avenue, NW
Washington, DC 20005-4105

University of California Press
1010 Westward Blvd.
Los Angeles, CA 90024

**University of Notre
Dame Press**
Notre Dame, IN 46556

The Upper Room
1908 Grand Avenue
P.O. Box 189
Nashville, TN 37202

Victory House Publishers
P.O. Box 700238
Tulsa, OK 74170

Westminster John Knox Press
100 Witherspoon Street
Louisville, KY 40202-1396

**William B. Eerdmans
Publishing Company**
255 Jefferson S.E.
Grand Rapids, MI 49503

**William C. Brown
Publishing Company**
2460 Kerper Boulevard
P.O. Box 539
Dubuque, IA 52001

William H. Sadlier, Inc.
11 Park Place
New York, NY 10007

Winston Press
P.O. Box 1630
Hagerstown, MD 21741

Word Books
Tower-Williams Square
5221 N. O'Conner Blvd. Suite
  1000
Irving, TX 75039

**World Council of
Churches Publications**
P.O. Box 66
150 Route de Ferney
1211 Geneva 20, Switzerland

**World Library
Publications, Inc.**
3815 N. Willow Road
P.O. Box 2701
Schiller Park, IL 60176

**The World
Publishing Company**
Meridian Books
110 E. 59th Street
New York, NY 10022

Yale University Press
302 Temple Street
New Haven, CN 06510

Zion Fellowship
236 Gorham Street
Canadagina, NY 14424

**Zondervan Publishing
Company**
1415 Lake Drive S.E.
Grand Rapids, MI 49506

PERIODICAL PUBLISHERS

The American Center for Church Music Newsletter
3339 Burbank Drive
Ann Arbor, MI 48105

American Organist
475 Riverside Drive, Suite 1260
New York, NY 10115

ARTS: The Arts in Religious and Theological Studies
United Theological Seminary of
  the Twin Cities
3000 5th Street, NW
New Brighton, MN 55112

Arts Advocate
The United Church of Christ
  Fellowship in the Arts
73 S. Palvuse
Walla Walla, WA 99362

The Choral Journal
American Choral Directors
  Association
P.O. Box 6310
Lawton, OK 73506

Choristers Guild Letters
2834 W. Kingsley Road
Garland, TX 75041

Christians in the Visual Arts
(newsletter)
P.O. Box 10247
Arlington, VA 22210

Church Music Quarterly
Royal School of Church Music
Addington Palace
Croyden, England CR9 5AD

The Church Musician
Southern Baptist Convention
127 9th Avenue N.
Nashville, TN 37234

Contemporary Christian Music
CCM Publications
P.O. Box 6300
Laguna Hills, CA 92654

Diapason
380 E. Northwest Highway
Des Plaines, IL 60016

Doxology
Journal of the Order of St. Luke in
  the United Methodist Church

1872 Sweet Home Road
Buffalo, NY 14221

Environment and Art Letter
Liturgy Training Publications
1800 N. Hermitage Avenue
Chicago, IL 60622

GIA Quarterly
7404 S. Mason Avenue
Chicago, IL 60638

Grace Notes
Association of Lutheran Church
  Musicians
4807 Idaho Circle
Ames, IA 50010

The Hymn
Hymn Society of the United States
  and Canada
P.O. Box 30854
Fort Worth, TX 76129

Journal
Sacred Dance Guild
Joyce Smillie, Resource Director
10 Edge Court
Woodbury, CT 06798

Journal of Ritual Studies
Department of Religious Studies
University of Pittsburgh
Pittsburgh, PA 15260

Let the People Worship
Schuyler Institute for Worship and
  the Arts
2757 Melendy Drive, Suite 15
San Carlos, CA 94070

Liturgy
The Liturgical Conference
8750 Georgia Avenue, S., Suite
  123
Silver Spring, MD 20910

Liturgy 90
Liturgy Training Publications
1800 N. Hermitage Avenue
Chicago, IL 60622

Modern Liturgy
Resource Publications
160 E. Virginia Street, Suite 290
San Jose, CA 95112

Music in Worship
Selah Publishing Company
P.O. Box 103
Accord, NY 12404

Newsnotes
The Fellowship of United
  Methodists in Worship, Music,
  and Other Arts
P.O. Box 54367
Atlanta, GA 30308

Pastoral Music
225 Sheridian Street, NW
Washington, D.C. 20011

PRISM
Yale Institute of Sacred Music
409 Prospect Street
New Haven, CT 06510

The Psalmist
9820 E. Watson Road
St. Louis, MO 63124

Reformed Liturgy and Music
Worship and Ministry Unit
100 Witherspoon Street
Louisville, KY 40202

Reformed Music Journal
Brookside Publishing
3911 Mt. Lehman Road
Abbotsford, BC V2S 6A9

Reformed Worship
CRC Publications
2850 Kalamazoo Avenue, SE
Grand Rapids, MI 49560

Rite Reasons
Biblical Horizons
P.O. Box 1096
Niceville, FL 32588

St. Vladimirs Theological Quarterly
757 Scarsdale Road
Crestwood, NY 10707

Studia Liturgica
Department of Theology
University of Notre Dame
Notre Dame, IN 46556

Today's Liturgy
Oregon Catholic Press
5536 NE Hassalo
Portland, OR 97213

Worship
The Liturgical Press
St. John's Abbey
Collegeville, MN 56321

Worship Leader
CCM Communications, Inc.
107 Kenner Avenue
Nashville, TN 37205

Worship Today
600 Rinehard Road
Lake Mary, FL 32746

Preface to Volume 4

The authors and editors of this series recognize that modern society is in the midst of a communications revolution involving a shift from print to multisensual media. Not surprisingly, contemporary worship renewal is caught in this tension between the older written and more verbal forms of communication and the proliferation of newer multimedia communication. This shift needs to be seen in the context of the history of communication, particularly communication in worship. The Old Testament descriptions of tabernacle and temple worship portray a worship that was highly visible, sensual, and tactile. The presence of God's beauty and majesty was expressed in vibrant colors, motions, gestures, and sounds. The space in which worship took place was like the vault of heaven.

This setting of worship was changed by the destruction of the temple and the introduction of a simpler synagogue worship. Christian worship began in synagogues and in the home, so it naturally followed the simpler pattern of the synagogue. But after the conversion of Constantine, the Roman world of the West and the Byzantine world of the East restored art, architecture, icons, frescos, and various styles of music and motion to congregational worship.

Nearly a millennium later, Reformation Protestants, influenced by the innovation of print, shifted worship away from the visual. They emphasized plain buildings and a less ornate worship setting but continued to develop music, particularly hymns and songs for worship. Still, the importance of the visual was largely lost to Protestant worship, in contrast to Eastern Orthodox and Roman Catholic churches, both of which retained highly visual elements. Many of these differences continue to this day.

The communications revolution of the twentieth century has challenged all Christians to reevaluate their position toward music and the arts in worship. Today's worship leaders are investigating the history and tradition of music and the arts in worshipping communities and are contributing new creations and compositions. Fittingly, *Music and the Arts in Christian Worship* addresses the issues of worship in a multisensual society and explores the communication between God and the worshiping community through imaginative and effective means. In keeping with the other volumes of *The Complete Library of Christian Worship,* this volume addresses music and the arts from a biblical, historical, and theological view with an eye toward their effective use in contemporary worship.

I hope you will find *Music and the Arts in Christian Worship* to be informative, challenging, inspirational, and above all useful in your efforts to renew worship.

The Lord be with you.

Robert E. Webber, Editor

Introduction

The *Complete Library of Christian Worship* has been designed to meet a need in the church. Christian leaders and congregations are becoming increasingly interested in the subjects of worship and worship renewal in the local church. Often, however, they lack adequate biblical and historical perspective or the necessary materials and resources to engage in the renewal process.

To fulfill the demand for worship resources, publishing houses, particularly those of specific denominations, have been producing materials for the local church. While these materials may find use within the constituency of a particular denomination, only a few break across denominational barriers and become known throughout the church at large.

The Complete Library of Christian Worship draws from more than one hundred publishing houses and the major Christian denominations of the world in order to bring those resources together in a seven-volume work, making them readily available to all.

The purpose of this introductory material is to acquaint the reader with *The Complete Library of Christian Worship* and to help him or her to use its information and resources in the local church.

First, the reader needs to have some sense of the scope of worship studies and renewal that are addressed by *The Complete Library of Christian Worship* (see section 101 below). Second, it is important to learn how to use the *Library* (see section 102). Finally, there is a need to understand the precise content of Volume 4, *Music and the Arts in Christian Worship*.

These three introductory entries are a key to the whole concept of the *Library,* a concept that brings together instruction in worship and vital resources for use in worship. The *Library* also directs the reader to a vast array of books, audio tapes, videotapes, model services, and resources in music and the arts. It seeks to provide direction and inspiration for everything the church does in worship.

101 • INTRODUCTION TO *THE COMPLETE LIBRARY OF CHRISTIAN WORSHIP*

The word *library* implies a collection of resources, together with a system of organization that makes them accessible to the user. Specifically, *The Complete Library of Christian Worship* is a comprehensive compilation of information pertaining to the worship of the Christian church. It draws from a large pool of scholars and practitioners in the field, and from more than two thousand books and media resources in print.

The purpose of *The Complete Library of Christian Worship* is to make biblical, historical, and contemporary resources on worship available to pastors, music ministers, worship committees, and the motivated individual worshiper. The *Library* contains biblical and historical information on all aspects of worship and numerous resource materials, as well as suggested resource books, audio tapes, and video instructional material for every worship act in the local church.

The twentieth century, more than any century in the history of Christianity, has been the century for research and study in the origins, history, theology, and practice of Christian worship. Consequently there are seven broad areas in which worship studies are taking place. These are:

1. the biblical foundations of worship;
2. historical and theological development of worship;
3. resources for worship and preaching;
4. resources for music and the arts in worship;
5. resources for the services of the Christian year;
6. resources for sacraments, ordinances, and other sacred acts; and
7. resources for worship and related ministries.

The Complete Library of Christian Worship is organized around these seven areas of worship renewal. In these seven volumes one will find a wide variety of resources for every worship act in the church, and a select but broad bibliography for additional resources.

102 • HOW TO USE *THE COMPLETE LIBRARY OF CHRISTIAN WORSHIP*

The Complete Library of Christian Worship differs from an encyclopedia, which is often organized alphabetically, with information about a particular subject scattered throughout the book. The *Library* does not follow this pattern because it is a work designed to educate as well as to provide resources. Consequently, all the material in the *Library* is organized under a particular theme or issue of worship.

The difference between the *Library* and an encyclopedia may be illustrated, for example, by examining the topic of environmental art in worship. Some of the themes essential to environmental art are banners, candles, stained glass windows, lighting, pulpit hangings, table coverings, and Communion ware. In a typical encyclopedia these entries would be scattered in the B, C, S, L, P, and T sections. Although this is not a problem for people who know what environmental art is and what needs to be addressed in environmental art, it is a problem for the person whose knowledge about the subject is limited. For this reason *The Complete Library of Christian Worship* has been organized—like a textbook—into chapters dealing with particular issues. Therefore, all the matters dealing with environmental art can be found in the chapter on environmental art (see Volume 4, *Music and the Arts in Christian Worship*). In this way a reader becomes educated on environmental art while at the same time having the advantage of in-depth information on the various matters pertaining to this aspect of worship.

Therefore, the first unique feature of *The Complete Library of Christian Worship* is that each volume can be read and studied like a book.

The second unique feature of the *Library* is that the materials have been organized to follow the actual *sequence in which worship happens.*

For example, Volume 1, *The Biblical Foundations of Christian Worship,* looks at the roots of Christian worship in the biblical tradition, while Volume 2, *Twenty Centuries of Christian Worship,* presents the development of various historical models of worship along with an examination of the theology of worship. Next, Volumes 3 through 7 provide re-

sources for the various acts of worship: Volume 3, *The Renewal of Sunday Worship,* provides resources for the various parts of worship; Volume 4, *Music and the Arts in Christian Worship,* presents resources from music and the arts for the different aspects of worship. Volume 5, *The Services of the Christian Year,* branches out to the services of Advent, Christmas, Epiphany, Lent, Holy Week, Easter, and Pentecost, providing resources for those special services that celebrate the saving acts of God in Jesus Christ. Volume 6, *The Sacred Actions of Christian Worship,* deals with Communion, baptism, funerals, weddings, and other special or occasional acts of worship. Finally, Volume 7, *The Ministries of Christian Worship,* deals with evangelism, spirituality, education, social action, children's worship, and other matters impacted by Christian celebration.

Each volume contains an alphabetical index to the material in the book. This index makes desired information readily available for the reader.

The resources in these volumes are intended for use in every denomination and among all groups of Christians: liturgical, traditional Protestant, those using creative styles, and those in the praise-and-worship tradition. Resources from each of these communities may be found in the various volumes.

It is difficult to find material from the free churches (those not following a historic order of worship) and from the charismatic traditions. These communities function with an oral tradition of worship and therefore do not preserve their material through written texts. Nevertheless, a considerable amount of information has been gathered from these oral traditions. Recently, leaders in these communities have been teaching their worship practices through audio tapes and videotapes. Information on the availability of these materials has been included in the appropriate volumes.

The written texts have been the easiest to obtain. Because of this, *The Complete Library of Christian Worship* may give the appearance of favoring liturgical worship. Due to the very nature of written texts, the appearance of a strong liturgical bent is unavoidable. Nevertheless, the goal of the *Library* is not to make free churches liturgical. Rather, it is to expand the perspective of Christians across a wide range of worship traditions. In this way, liturgical resources may serve as guides and sources of inspiration and creativity for free churches, while insights from free traditions may also enrich the practices and understanding of the more liturgical communities.

In sum, the way to use *The Complete Library of Christian Worship* is as follows:

1. *Read each volume as you would read a book.* Each volume is full of biblical, historical, and theological information—a veritable feast for the curious, and for all worshipers motivated to expand their horizons.

2. *Use the alphabetical index for quick and easy access to a particular aspect of worship.* The index for each volume is as thorough as the listings for an encyclopedia.

3. *For further information and resources, order books and materials listed in the bibliography of resources.* Addresses of publishers may be found in your library's copy of *Books in Print.*

4. *Adapt the liturgical materials to the setting and worship style of your congregation.* Many of the worship materials in *The Complete Library of Christian Worship* have been intentionally published without adaptation. Most pastors, worship ministers, and worship committee members are capable of adapting the material to a style suitable to their congregations with effective results.

103 • INTRODUCTION TO VOLUME 4: MUSIC AND THE ARTS IN CHRISTIAN WORSHIP

Throughout the history of the church, the use of music and the arts in worship has fluctuated considerably. There have been times when music and the arts have flourished, and other times when they have been ignored or even disdained. We now live in a period of history where people are both challenging classical forms of music and the arts in worship and introducing pathbreaking compositions and innovative art forms.

Volume 4 of *The Complete Library of Christian Worship* has set out on a bold and adventurous journey to include all the forms and styles of music and the arts from both the past and the present. This comprehensive volume—which includes the subjects of music, the visual arts, drama, dance, mime, and the literary arts—also combines three very important features: historical background, theological understanding, and practical application.

First, with regard to history, the authors of all the articles have made a special effort to detail the historical development of music, the visual arts, drama, dance, and mime. In these articles, the reader will grasp that the wide range of arts used in contemporary worship is based on precedent.

Then there is the theological issue. Why do music and the arts have a place in worship? One would think that the "why" of music and the arts in worship would need no explanation. Yet there are those who have real questions about the validity of the arts, particularly drama, dance, and mime. For this reason the authors have carefully delineated the theology or philosophy of the arts in worship.

A final question remains: How do we properly use the arts in worship, and how do the arts contribute to worship renewal? These matters have also been addressed, providing the reader with sensitive and detailed guidance for implementing or reintroducing music and the arts in his or her own worship community.

PART ONE

Music and the Arts Among the Churches

ONE

Music and the Arts Among the Contemporary Churches

The essays which follow offer an overview of the current worship practices of most of the major denominations in this country, each prepared by a person active in that particular church. Read individually, they furnish a wealth of fresh ideas; collectively they give evidence that, while each denomination remains theologically focused on its tradition and centers its worship on the familiar, there is hardly one which is not actively re-examining its worship philosophy and experimenting with new forms, music, and visual art. Insularity and Rigidity (and their offspring Routine and Passivity) have given way to a flowering of creativity which fosters commitment. Earlier labels such as Liturgical, Praise, Full Gospel, and Evangelical are no longer definitive. Each denomination appears to be eager to learn from the practices of others as a stimulus to their own worship rather than looking only to the past, only inward, or only to other churches within their denomination. Narrowness is out, and features once thought the special province and mark of a particular group are being fruitfully and joyfully embraced by others. The variety is so widespread that it is almost more appropriate to focus on the specific practices of an individual congregation, rather than to make generalizations about a denomination as a whole. As Philip Begrrov Peter notes, "Style is becoming more and more eclectic and there is a healthy regard for the special contribution that every individual may make. Worship, once almost the property of the officiating clergy rigorously hewing to a prescribed pattern, has rightly become the responsibility of Everyperson."

104 ✦ ADVENTIST CHURCHES

Gospel song is prominent in the music of Adventist churches. However, the range of music used spans the centuries from traditional masterpieces to contemporary choruses. Churches rely on a variety of instruments, from large pipe organs to electronic synthesizers. The other arts are not generally used in worship, but among a few leading churches banners, hangings, and drama have been introduced.

— Music —

From its very beginnings, the Seventh-day Adventist Church has witnessed a fascinating polarity in music preferences and practices. The church was forming during the period of revival and camp-meeting enthusiasm in the mid-nineteenth century. A considerable portion of music in the emerging church consisted of the white spirituals and gospel songs that one would expect from that background. Wesleyan hymns were significant, and people coming to the Adventist church from other denominations brought their hymns with them. Early Adventist leaders published hymnals and worked diligently to teach the people how to understand and use music from the great traditions of hymnody. This work continues. It would be difficult to define a Seventh-day Adventist music tradition because of the eclectic use of music in worship, although gospel song is the most prevalent genre.

Given this background, it is perhaps surprising that the use of the guitar in worship has been resisted in many places. However, a number of Adventist churches intent on renewing worship use not only guitars, but synthesizers, electric basses, drums, and various other instruments. Use of such instruments was almost negligible prior to the mid-1980s. Since the late 1970s many churches have added handbells to their worship programming. During this same period, though beginning earlier, Adventist college campus churches, as well as various other large Adventist churches have increasingly used brass ensembles and chamber groups in worship.

During the 1970s and 1980s several Adventist churches, mostly on college campuses, installed large mechanical action organs. The Rieger organ at Pacific Union College Church (Angwin, California, north of San Francisco) is the largest such organ on the West Coast, and the Brombaugh organ at the Collegedale Church (Southern College, near Chattanooga, Tennessee) is one of the largest in the United States. A number of Adventist churches also have large Casavant organs. Most Adventist churches, however, use a small electronic organ and often a piano for the accompaniment of worship.

One finds considerable musical variety within Seventh-day Adventist churches. Most typical is the standard fare of hymns and gospel songs which may be used for both congregational singing and service music. In the churches emphasizing renewal, particularly those with a celebrative type of worship, most of the music consists of Scripture songs and praise choruses. The great masterpieces of music are also heard regularly in the largest Adventist churches. Christian rock music, however, is rare.

——— Visual and Performing Arts ———

A growing, though still very small, number of Seventh-day Adventist churches are using banners to enhance worship. For example, beginning in 1987 in Waynesboro, Virginia, and in 1990 in Lakeside, California, the author introduced banners, an artistic medium that had never before been used. Although the congregation first questioned their use, they soon recognized their great benefit. In Lakeside we have produced banners for Advent, Christmas, the Easter Season (Triumphal Entry, Crucifixion, Resurrection), Pentecost, Adventist Heritage Sabbath, and Thanksgiving.

Beginning at the Sligo Church (near Washington, D.C.), and then in Waynesboro and the author's church in Lakeside, the author has introduced table displays to illustrate, complement, or expand the morning worship theme. A few Adventist churches, including the Sligo church, have commissioned artistic wall hangings. A limited number of Adventist churches have flexible seating, and only a few of those have varied the seating from time to time to enrich worship.

Chancel drama is a recent addition to Seventh-day Adventist worship and is used in only a very small

number of churches. However, its use increased notably during the 1980s, to the point where several of the renewing churches are using drama almost every week.

In 1985 the Seventh-day Adventist *Hymnal* (Hagerstown, Md.: Review and Herald Publishing Association, 1985) was published. It is the first Seventh-day Adventist hymnal or liturgical book of any kind to include extensive worship aids. Prior to that, the most recent hymnal had been published in 1941. *A Companion to the Seventh-day Adventist Hymnal* by Wayne Hooper and Edward E. White was published in 1988 (Hagerstown, Md.: Review and Herald Publishing Association, 1988).

Merle J. Whitney

105 • AFRICAN METHODIST EPISCOPAL CHURCHES

Music has always been central to the worship of the African Methodist Episcopal Church. Richard Allen, the founder of the denomination, provided a hymnal filled with selections that were popular among his people and that reflected the African-American heritage. Subsequent editions of the hymnal have included a wide variety of material. The visual and performing arts have also become a hallmark of worship in the AME church. Colorful robes and stoles and vibrant liturgical dance have contributed significantly to worship.

——————— Music ———————

Richard Allen, the founder of the African Methodist Episcopal Church, knew and appreciated the importance of music to his people. Because of this, one of his first official acts as an AME minister was to publish a hymnal for the exclusive use of his congregation. This hymnal, published in 1818, was compiled by Bishop Allen, Daniel Coker, James Champion, and Jacob Tapisco. The importance of this first hymnal designed exclusively for an all-black congregation cannot be overemphasized. Whereas Bishop Allen might have used the official Methodist hymnal, instead he consciously set about to collect hymns that would have a special appeal to the members of his congregation. These were undoubtedly long time favorites of American blacks. Thus the hymnal provides an index to the hymns popular among black congregations (the AME in particular) of the new nation. These hymns represented the black worshipers' own choices and not those of white missionaries and ministers. This hymnal contained three hundred and fourteen hymns and spirituals carefully chosen to nourish the church in doctrine and spiritual content. Subsequent editions of the hymn book with some minor changes were published between 1818 and 1872.

In 1984, the Commission on Worship and Liturgy, chaired by Bishop Vinton R. Anderson, compiled the Bicentennial Edition of the AME Hymnal which paid honor to the contributors of all past and present efforts. The latest edition of this hymnal and future reprintings will be known as *The Hymnal: African Methodist Episcopal Church.* It is the major worship instrument as we begin the third century of the church. The four musicians that were on this commission include Daisy N. Brown of Dayton, Ohio; William Melvin Campbell of Newark, New Jersey; Josephine Howard of Georgetown, South Carolina; Jimmie James, Jr. of Jackson, Mississippi; and Edith W. Ming of Cape Town, South Africa. The Bicentennial Hymnal is the most hymnologically advanced black denominational hymnal currently being used in this country. It also represents the culmination of one of the richest hymnological histories of any black denomination, a history that resonates with the great events of African-American history and with the musical philosophy of the AME Church.

Range of Music. The extensive range of music in the African Methodist Episcopal Church includes hymns, anthems, spirituals, and gospel songs, embracing traditional works as well as those unique to African-American congregations. At present the scope of music used in AME Churches continues to expand, and in some instances it is selected and performed differently than traditional AME Church music. However, in recent years many district choirs including those in the fifth and eighth districts have shown a resurgence in selecting traditional anthems, hymns, and spirituals used in worship in the AME Church. It is hoped that this renaissance will also manifest itself within the general church through a mammoth effort to improve the quality of service music used in AME worship services.

Use of Music. Music used in the AME Church ministers to the various aspects of worship including the liturgical and theological needs of pastors and congregations. Service music such as introits, response, chants, doxologies, benedictions and the amens are used traditionally and consistently in every service.

Introits, responses, and chants may be selected to coincide with the church season.

The Use of Instruments. In addition to traditional service instruments such as the organ and piano, other instruments, including handbells, are used at Wayman AME Church in Dayton, Ohio. The synthesizer, guitar and orchestral instruments, in addition to rhythm band and Orff instruments, are used for Sunday services by the Children's Choir at Pearl Street AME Church in Jackson, Mississippi. And in the First Episcopal District, the traditional use of organ, piano, and orchestral instruments is increasingly supplemented with synthesizers.

Instrumental music has a distinctive character that makes it particularly desirable for special occasions. In the AME Church, this is true for Christmas, Easter, and other religious holidays, dedication ceremonies, religious festivals, sacred music concerts, and other services. However, instrumental music is also a valuable part of regular church services. Naturally there is variety in the mood and atmosphere in the different services of the church, which influences the kind of instrumental music used.

Instrumental music is not easily classified into formal or informal categories. Appropriate selections are usually planned for those occasions which are more dignified, as well as for those times when lighter, less serious music is desired. A stringed instrument or flute playing a devotional song will tend to create one mood, the noble sound of a brass quartet playing a stately hymn will evoke a different quality of feeling, and a guitar or tambourine accompanying a bright, tuneful folksong will have still another effect. Thus, the decisions regarding which instrumental music is best suited to a given service is made based on different considerations, both practical and philosophical.

The Visual Arts

Sacred Monograms. The Alpha and Omega appear often on AME church altars and pulpit hangings. The Alpha and Omega represent Jesus Christ "the same yesterday and today and forever" (Heb. 13:8). Another popular symbol, IHS, consists of the first three letters of Jesus' name in Greek.

Flags. Many AME Churches have both a Christian and an American flag which demonstrates warmth because of their beautiful color, design, and the realities which they signify. The Christian flag represents Christianity in its entirety, including its faith, worship, tradition, responsibilities, and many other blessings.

Vestments. The practice of wearing robes and stoles in the AME Church is more prevalent than in former years. Robes signify humility in leading an orderly and dignified worship service. When robes are worn, the attention of the worshipers is more easily focused on the religious messages conveyed by the words spoken or sung, and the feelings that are associated with the public service of divine worship are naturally sustained by their use.

The stole represents the ordination of the clergyman and marks the sacredness of the sacraments. The minister's five differently colored stoles are used in conjunction with the liturgical colors of the church year. But because the stole is becoming more prevalent, it is no longer symbolic only of the clergyman's ordination. The stoles for choirs are symbolic of the yoke of obedient service to the Master while rendering music to his glory.

Art for the Church Year. In the AME Church the changing colors of the church year attract, add variety, and point to the significance of the season or the festival. The same colors of the church year are used for bookmarks and for stoles.

White is the symbol of created light, joy, purity, innocence, glory, and perfection. Violet denotes mourning and penitence, and is also symbolic of humility, suffering, sympathy, and fasting. Purple is used in different ways. It is the regal color that refers to the triumphal entry of the King of Kings, who was of royal descent. As the color of penitence, purple also refers to the purple garments put on the Lord when they mocked him. Red depicts divine zeal on the Day of Pentecost, and refers to the blood of the martyrs of the church. Green is the universal color of nature, signifying hope. Black is the color of grief and sorrow. To these five colors we may add gold. Gold refers to worth, virtue, the glory of God, and Christian might.

——— Liturgical Drama and Dance ———

Musical dramas, dramatic liturgies, and storytellings are included in special programming and workshops for youth and adults in the First Episcopal District. In the Eighth Episcopal District, special presentations during African-American History Month feature monologues and other dramatic presentations. Visual arts, including sculpture by black artists and fashions from the African continent, re-

flect the African-American heritage of the African Methodist Episcopal Church.

In recent years, liturgical dance has become more evident as a medium of worship and praise in the AME Church. This should not, however, be too surprising since dance simply paraphrases the music in a different interpretive medium, while emulating the physical movement embodied in the worship service. Critics, including some in the AME Church, often condemn liturgical dance because they feel it is too sensual. But as dance authorities point out in response, dance is sensual only in that it flows from the senses and is similarly experienced through the senses of others. This should not suggest nor be confused with eroticism. Finally, if music is the spirit of worship, singing articulates the message and dance merely brings that message to life through movement.

In the First Episcopal District, liturgical dance is included in workshop classes, worship services, and special programs. Styles cover a broad spectrum with an emphasis on African and interpretative genres created by a choreographer on the district music staff. In the Eighth Episcopal District, liturgical dance has been performed as part of Robert Ray's *Gospel Mass* and on other occasions at Pearl Street AME Church in Jackson, Mississippi, and in the Third Episcopal District at Wayman AME Church in Dayton, Ohio.

Jimmie James, Jr.

106 ✦ AFRICAN METHODIST EPISCOPAL ZION CHURCH

Zion Methodism continues to use hymn singing as its chief expression of music in worship. Congregational hymnody ranges from traditional hymns to spirituals and gospel hymns. These hymns, along with choral responses, are carefully integrated into the liturgy. Although not traditionally important, banners and dramatic presentations are now included in some worship services.

——————— Music ———————

Worship usually has four main congregational hymns, sung in their entirety with the congregation standing: the processional hymn, the hymn of praise, the invitational hymn, and the recessional hymn. These hymns are supplemented with the following traditional choral responses:

1. The Call to Worship: "The Lord is in His Holy Temple"
2. The Invocation: "Hear Our Prayer, O Lord"
3. The Responsive Reading: the "Gloria Patri"
4. The Apostles' Creed: "Three Fold Amen"
5. The Pastoral Prayer: "Let the Words . . . Our Father . . ."
6. The Offering: "All Things Come of Thee . . ."
7. The Benediction: "Three-Fold Amen" or a chant

Additionally, the doxology is used either near the beginning of worship or in a later portion of the service.

Zion's Great Celebration, the sacrament of the Lord's Supper, uses the same basic format as regular worship services. There is usually the addition of the Communion hymn, prior to the Communion ritual. That hymn helps to shift the emphasis from the regular worship service to the Communion service.

Zion's first hymn sets forth the chief theological focal point of the denomination: "Holy, Holy, Holy"—the praise of the Triune God by the Church Triumphant in union with the Church Militant. This hymn is the normal processional hymn for Zion's monthly Communion service.

Most churches replace the responsive reading on this Sunday with the reading of the Decalogue and our Lord's summary of the Law. The choral response to this is "Lord, have mercy upon us." Throughout the Communion portion of the service, hymns point to our thankfulness for Christ's atonement. The congregation chants the Sanctus with preface and the Lord's Prayer during the ritual. As worshipers participate in communion, hymns are sung by the choir and congregation. At the conclusion of the sacrament, all stand and extend to one another Zion's right hand of fellowship, singing "What a Fellowship."

In addition, this writer promotes the inclusion of the Introit, using the French carol "Let All Mortal Flesh." The first stanza, found in Zion's hymnal, is used generally, with the second stanza used for Communion, the third for Advent and Epiphany, and the fourth for Eastertide. This writer, as pastor, sings this after calling on the congregation to stand. This is the announcement that we are ready to begin the formal act of worship and the adoration of our God.

A number of nontraditional selections, sung to familiar tunes, are becoming more popular. "Old Hundredth" is used, for example, when singing "All People that on Earth Do Dwell." The congregation now served by this writer has become familiar with the West Indian version of the Lord's Prayer, and the songs "Majesty," "We Have Come into This House," and "They'll Know We Are Christians." These new selections are used to increase the ways a congregation can express their praise to God.

A commission has been appointed to compile Zion's bicentennial hymnal, but has not yet begun this work. This will be an important step in documenting the inclusion of hymns and other music Zion borrows from others and uses regularly.

Visual Arts

Art, in the broader sense, is not an integral part of worship enhancement in Zion. Most of our edifices, old and new, have stained glass windows with a Caucasian Jesus as Good Shepherd among the most popular illustrations. More ethnically oriented churches are using a black Jesus in their windows and paintings in the church edifice.

Zion is increasingly embracing the use of banners as a means of education. We are using seasonal banners to emphasize the Christian year and special banners for groups like the _Missionary's Buds of Promise._ The banner provides a tool to teach about the corresponding color and theme of a season, complementing the paraments of the pulpit area. Clergy are using kente cloth for vestments, paraments, and banners in increasing numbers.

Drama and Dance

Christian education plays and dramas are supplementing traditional Easter/Christmas "sentence readings" where there is a liturgical emphasis in the local church. Litanies for special days also provide a vehicle for broader expression. The editor of Zion's _Church School Herald,_ Ms. Mary Love, has published an original play, _The Passion Symbols Speak,_ and a volume on banners to broaden Zion's awareness.

Dance, in any form, has not been accepted generally by Zion. The traditional Methodist view that dancing, in any form, is not appropriate remains the predominant view.

Andrew Foster

107 • THE AMERICAN BAPTIST CHURCHES IN THE USA

As a result of both the autonomy of their local churches and the ethnic diversity among member congregations, diversity is the dominant adjective used to describe the use of music and the arts in American Baptist churches. The size, theological orientation, and geographical location of individual congregations are all factors that influence the music and arts used in individual congregations. National conferences are important in providing vision and leadership for music and the arts.

The traditional practices, theological history, and ethnic orientation of individual congregations are the dominant factors shaping the worship experiences of each American Baptist church in the last decade. Music, though regarded as an essential part of worship in many Euro-American churches, is also often viewed as being preliminary and subsidiary to preaching, whereas it would usually have a much more dynamic place within Latino and African-American congregations. The latter have traditionally included more music in worship, both congregational and choral, and have long used instruments in addition to organ and piano.

To some extent the factor of size is significant in the type of music used in ABC/USA churches. Prominent, large churches have more classical, formal musical styles in contrast to the less classical forms found in smaller churches. This is related in some measure to the presence of trained musicians on staff. Such paid musical leadership is usually limited to the organist and choir director, with a strong emphasis on volunteer lay musicians in all other aspects of a church's music ministry. A limited number of churches also employ section leaders for their choirs. Some large churches have, for many years, used brass and tympani for the festivals of Christmas and Easter, or organized string orchestras for special musical presentations within the context of worship. In recent years smaller churches are more likely to have introduced recorded accompaniments for choir presentations as a means of instrumental variety.

Another major factor in music within each church is the hymnbook in use. The last hymnal published by the denomination, the *Hymnbook for Christian Worship,* which was issued in 1970, includes mostly classical and traditional hymns, reflecting very little of the gospel song tradition significant in many

ABC/USA congregations. Therefore, in congregations with an evangelical theological tradition or in African-American congregations, the hymnals of other publishers, such as other Baptist groups or independent houses, have had long currency. Some churches supplement a traditional hymnbook with a contemporary collection (in some cases, not only to add newer songs, but also to provide ethnic variety), or, by means of cooperative copyright access, print supplementary music for the weekly worship order.

Openness to new expressions is dependent upon pastoral leadership and, to some extent, upon geographical location. Churches on the West Coast have adopted the use of synthesizers and electric guitars much more commonly and have incorporated new musical styles to a greater extent than those east of the Rockies. Openness to new musical styles often does not mean openness to the full range of the church's musical heritage. Contemporary praise choruses, hymns, and gospel songs may be introduced, but historic chants, psalm singing, or antiphons would not necessarily—or likely—be embraced in the same context.

As an example of a church committed to renewal in worship, First Baptist Church of Bakersfield, California, known as the Christian Life Center, regularly uses a convergence of musical styles and worship traditions from the whole range of the church, both past and present. Philip Dodson, the Pastor of Worship and Music and a classically trained organist, oversees the worship plan for each service, seeking creativity and balance in a blend of styles that gives every service its unique design. Congregational singing is led by a worship team of musicians and singers, using a combination of guitar, bass, drums, and piano, along with organ. Music is a dominant part of the service from beginning to end. Banners, processions (especially for Advent and Christmas, Easter and Pentecost), and antiphonal speaking are all used with the intention of using the entire space of the sanctuary. Dance and drama are also incorporated on occasion into the worship plan.

Many other churches in the denomination are highly attentive to worship planning and will use a variety of elements both from music and the other creative arts, primarily for special occasions. Banners are frequently found; dance and drama are less common, but are used. Many churches have exquisite stained glass windows and architecture that is aesthetically significant in the worship environment. Good examples of this include First Baptist Church of Washington, D.C. and First Baptist Church of Columbus, Indiana.

Since 1962 the Fellowship of American Baptist Musicians (FABM) has provided leadership in the networking and education of musicians of the denomination. Its mission has been to improve the quality of music ministry, emphasizing good music as a means of enriching the worship experience. The philosophy guiding the annual national conferences at the American Baptist Assembly in Green Lake, Wisconsin, has been to use and enhance the musical talents and gifts of each congregation by exposing American Baptist musicians to excellence in a variety of styles, while encouraging each congregation to do what is appropriate for its local context. The programs of these annual conferences are organized according to the following areas: adult, youth, children, organ, handbells, and worship. From this structure it is evident that many church music programs have graded choirs, that organ and handbells are predominant instruments, and that church musicians have a significant interest in the subject of worship. In fact, the worship seminars are the most popularly attended, attesting to a felt need and concern for growth in that area. Jay Martin, Executive Secretary of FABM, has also observed that there is a growing interest among American Baptist musicians in the use of orchestral instruments in conjunction with church music, noting that a seventy-member orchestra was part of the 1992 conference.

As a means of observing trends and forecasting possible future developments, one can also reflect upon worship services planned for national gatherings of the denomination. At a national convocation on evangelism, held in May 1992 at First Baptist Church of Washington, D.C., daily worship was designed to be the integrating focus of the week. _Alleluya: Songs of Renewal_ (ed. Corean Bakke and Tony Payne) was produced as a conference hymnal. It was multicultural and multilingual with songs in Karen (Burmese), Russian, Kiowa (Native American), Spanish, Japanese, Chinese, and English. All the proceedings were signed for the hearing impaired. As a visual expression of the spoken word, this became a kind of dance for at least some of those with hearing. Processionals with flags and banners, banners hung in the sanctuary, and hangings on the lectern and the pulpit contributed to visual impact,

along with the cathedral setting of First Baptist Church and, for one service, the National Cathedral. Dramatic monologues were presented in many services. A booklet for private devotional use directed attention to the windows of First Baptist as a point of reference. As a counterpoint to the banquet that had opened the conference, the closing communion service focused on the heavenly banquet of the Lamb with a beautifully appointed banquet table as a centerpiece between the pulpit and the lectern. Thus, creative use of music and the fine arts provided a major impact at this significant national conference.

Current plans for the 1993 biennial meeting of the denomination call for similar worship services that are multicultural and multilingual, that balance a variety of musical styles and instruments, and that will seek to use visual and other arts as part of the worship experience. As such meetings provide opportunities for exposure of church leaders to creative possibilities in the use of music and the arts, the impact of such events may extend throughout the denomination in the worship experiences of local churches.

Jeannette F. Scholer

108 • ANGLICAN AND EPISCOPAL CHURCHES

Anglican and Episcopal Churches inherit a rich liturgical tradition that is the product of many periods of worship renewal in the history of the church. Worship renewal in Anglican and Episcopal churches today seeks both to maintain the vitality of the historic liturgy and to use the best of contemporary musical and artistic expressions.

Augustine, the saint credited with planting Christianity in Britain, purportedly said "Singing is to pray twice" and "A Christian is an Alleluia from head to toe." It is in this spirit that the substance of renewal in worship within Anglicanism finds its origins and continuing inspiration. The Anglican church's tradition has been marked by the sights and sounds of the great cathedrals with their choirs' singing wafting through their sacred arches. Complacency, however, can often turn tradition to stone and quench the Spirit's ardor in worship. Yet Anglicanism, by nature of its beginning, was always a church of "renewing" worship and is a leader in renewal today.

Renewal in the History of the Church

The English church, after its own reformation, became the instrument of translating the Roman Mass into the vernacular. This is embodied in Cranmer's triumph, *The Book of Common Prayer*, of which the 1662 version is still in active use in the Church of England. (While retaining the substance of the original book, most Provinces of the Anglican Communion use an updated version. The most recent version was approved in the United States in 1979). With the advent of worship in the English language, the creation of a musical setting of the Ordinary of the Communion service was deemed necessary. The first musical setting of the English liturgy was composed by John Merbecke in chant-like simplicity, establishing a new expression of music in worship. The *Hymnal 1982* (USA) and the *New English Hymnal* (UK) both contain revised versions of the Merbecke setting.

The Evangelical revival in the Church of England in the eighteenth century brought new life and energy to worship in the hymns and music of the Wesleys, all of whom were Anglicans. Charles Wesley's hymns epitomize the excellence and depth of the Anglican spirit of worship, warming heart and mind. Where can one find a higher expression of love and praise than in Wesley's classic hymn "Love Divine, All Loves Excelling," a hymn which has found use in many denominations?

Plainsong is another type of music that is used in Anglican worship. Although it was replaced in the period following the Reformation by four-part Anglican chant (originally TTBB, but now SATB in most cases) as a means of singing psalms and canticles, plainsong made its way back into the church's music with the Oxford Movement in the 1850s. Its renewing power and simplicity have continued to be incorporated actively in today's worship, along with four-part Anglican chants.

The arts in general have always found great acceptance within Anglicanism. Its cathedrals have been centers for all the activities in a city, including theater and dance. The liturgy in its richness has always dictated that movement and drama are integral to the rite. The movements of the sub-deacon, deacon, and celebrant have been carefully choreographed to express the emotion of a certain portion of the service. Bowing, signs of the cross, and kneeling have spoken to the need to express physically a reaction to significant moments of the Eucharist, such as at the elevation of the host.

The English Reformation, with its wave of Puritan clamor, often subdued or abolished music in worship, replacing musical expression with the rhetoric of lengthy sermons and arduous spoken liturgies (though there was the inclusion of unaccompanied metrical psalms). Sunday worship at a cathedral or parish church found the faithful in their pews for hours for the litany, exhortations, Matins, and Holy Communion. The congregation returned for Evensong that same afternoon for another round of Scripture and preaching without the benefit of music.

The Anglo-Catholic revival, another stage of worship renewal, saw the emergence of vested choirs in a prominent setting and a wealth of new anthems and hymns. Organs were once again heard and the starkness of the Puritans gave way to the splendor of a renewed Anglican liturgy, despite the destruction of many cathedrals, shrines, and abbeys that the Puritans had accomplished. In our day of renewed emphasis on the senses and emotion in worship, we can still tour these great Christian ruins and wish that they could be restored.

Thus renewal, restoration, and recovery have always been the key to the Anglican expression of worship. These constitute the essence of the historical experience of the church that brought the English translation of the scriptures and liturgy into our Christian experience.

Contemporary Renewal

Today the charismatic movement has had considerable influence on worship, much like earlier renewal movements. Like the Anglo-Catholic revival, renewal today seeks to enliven an already expansive tradition. Linking practices to scriptural times, dance, and posture have been used to emphasize the actions of the Holy Spirit within the context of a community at worship. Music such as that used at Taizé, a unique ecumenical center in France, has broadened our senses with the haunting repetition of phrases of prayer and praise. Taizé attracts thousands of people, particularly the young, who are drawn to its holiness and simplicity. The monks there come from Protestant, Roman Catholic, and Anglican backgrounds. The music, created to meet the needs of the international multilingual participants, is the work of Jacques Berthier. It is distributed by Collins in the United Kingdom and by GIA

Publications in Chicago. Taizé music can be effectively used in the Sunday liturgy at the intercessions and during Communion.

Churches now often have several minutes of praise hymns prior to worship, instead of an organ prelude or voluntary. Responsorial psalms and alleluia verses heighten the attention given to the role of Scripture in the service.

Renewal tends to make the assembled congregation more inclusive. An example of this may be experienced at the prestigious St. Bartholomew's Episcopal Church of Park Avenue in New York. Here the rich and famous as well as the poor and homeless gather for worship, with everyone receiving a warm and personal greeting. Above is a banner proclaiming: "St. Bart's 9 A.M. Worship—Sing, Dance, and Pray." The Eucharist is lively, with a loose-leaf hymnal ready to be enlarged when someone finds an appropriate new song or hymn. Instruments and song-leaders, as well as powerful preaching, mark the service.

Contemporary renewal worship in the Episcopal Church was born in Houston (USA) at the Church of the Redeemer. Under the leadership of the Rev. Graham Pulkingham, Betty Pulkingham, and George Mims, a new genre of musical style has found its place in American and now international Anglicanism. Always performed with professional musical quality, the use of various instruments brought life to this charismatic Eucharistic community. The organ, enhanced by oboes and flutes, is used along with guitar and strings to make an inclusive offering to God. The Fisherfolk, a group of singers active in Episcopal renewal, has been influential in spreading the experience of this unique style of worship throughout the church. Likewise, publications coming from the Church of the Redeemer and the Fisherfolk have inspired others in their worship. _Sounds of Living Waters_ is a particularly fine mixture of new and traditional music.

In London, All Souls Church, Langham Place, in the heart of the city's shopping district, abounds with fine music and worship in the evangelical Anglican tradition. The church currently is responsible for _Prom Praise,_ an annual event gaining in popularity. This event is modeled after the _Proms Concerts_ that are so much a part of the English heritage, but features the texts and music of Christian writers and composers from all ages. A few blocks away one finds the brilliant music of All Saints, Margaret Street, likely the most well-known

of the Anglo-Catholic churches in the Anglican Communion. Polyphony, chant, and a professional choir all contribute to a liturgy that has a vitality of its own. Its current musical director is the head of the Royal School of Church Music.

Other churches uniquely involved in the renewal of worship include Truro Church, Fairfax, Virginia; St. Barnabas Church, Glen Ellyn, Illinois; Holy Trinity Brompton, London, England; St. Paul's, Darien, Connecticut; St. Michael's Chester Square, London, England; St. Nicholas, Durham, England; St. Luke's, Atlanta, Georgia, and many more.

Michael Marshall, speaking of music in the church in his book _Renewal in Worship,_ says, "Using all its differing dimensions, music is once again becoming central in authentic worship. The good news of the Christian gospel was heralded by a chorus of angels singing. The handmaid of the Lord herself broke into words that have subsequently and significantly become the gospel song of the redeemed, who, like her, acknowledge 'the greatness of the Lord.' From the vast choirs with major orchestral accompaniment to simple folk tunes as setting for scriptural texts, music has formed the texture of Christian witness and worship through the ages. Doubtless it will continue to do so until all our earthly worship is finally subsumed into the worship of heaven, where surely music in some form or another—a form appropriate to its resources and environment—will have its eternal place."

Regarding the other arts, both drama and dance have been used profitably. Dramatic storytelling or mime can effectively replace or complement the sermon and the message can be proclaimed in mime such as that done by the Rev. Steven Woodward of Madison, Wisconsin. Dance, along with festive processions, recall something of the medieval as well as the biblical tradition.

Inculturation throughout the Anglican Communion is giving a tradition once bound by the experiences of the white missionaries a chance to incorporate other ethnic expressions into worship practices that are rich with the symbols and ceremonies of other cultures, yet expressed in a very Anglican way. The consecration of eight missionary bishops in the Anglican Church of Nigeria was celebrated with a liturgy proud of its Anglican roots that also incorporated elements of local dance, costumes, and spontaneity. Thus, in these cases, art and music can be understood as natural expressions of who we are as God's creatures and as a response to that which we encounter in life, both in and outside of the church.

Such expressions of renewal in music and the visual arts help Anglicans remain true to their origins as an English-speaking church. There is a thread that runs through all of worship, weaving Scripture, hymns, anthems, and the like into a complete drama unfolding the theme presented in the assigned Scriptures. This theme may be as simple as that of the Upper Room or as complex as that of the Book of Revelation. Although Anglicans have their share of people claiming "we never did it that way before" and bolting because of the change, a majority prays that the church will remain the light that shines on from age to age, expressing itself in ways that are both old and new.

The Episcopal Church and the Anglican Communion have begun a "Decade of Evangelism." For many years the care and beauty of worship in this tradition was one of its chief evangelistic tools. People came to church and felt God's presence through the Word preached and the sacrament celebrated. This brought them back and led them to fuller participation in the Church community. Our worship must express the vibrancy and expression that compels one *in* worship *to* worship. Our human senses can then respond with an outpouring of thankfulness as we offer back to God, through the talents of music and art, the gifts so freely given to us.

J. M. Rosenthal

109 • Assemblies of God Churches

Assemblies of God churches have always maintained a highly pragmatic approach in their use of music, always making use of a secularized and popular style of church music. In recent years this has extended to the inclusion of Christian music derived from rock music. They believe that matters of artistic style are secondary to moral purity or doctrine.

The current use of music and the arts in the Assemblies of God is a continuation of the pattern established by the fellowship in its formative years. Organized in the spring of 1914 in Hot Springs, Arkansas, the fledgling Pentecostal church developed a highly pragmatic attitude toward music and the arts.

Though the Assemblies adopted the holiness posture of separation from the worldliness of secular culture, Pentecostals nevertheless embraced a comparatively secularized and popular church music style. Indeed, according to Assemblies of God historian William Menzies, "Pentecostals were among the first to engage 'worldly' rhythm as a medium in religious music." (William Menzies, *Anointed to Serve* [Springfield, Mo.: Gospel Publishing House, 1971], 350). They gradually developed a lively, boisterous style of singing, often accompanied by strong, rhythmic handclapping. Gospel songs provided the movement with music which appealed to the musical taste of both members and the unevangelized alike. The simple repetitive lyrics and music of the refrains were frequently sung from memory without the stanzas. Freed from having to hold a songbook, worshipers could raise both hands and with eyes closed focus without distraction on the adoration and praise of the Almighty. Gospel songs, of course, were neither unique to Pentecostals nor used to the complete exclusion of traditional hymnody. But accompanied by piano and any instruments indigenous to the local Assembly, the exciting manner in which they were sung advanced the new movement's cause. The Assemblies had found what worked for them—a popular musical style.

Pragmatic musical standards kept Pentecostals from connecting their Christian faith with much of the artistic tradition in music, especially that which was most esoteric. They were literalists who best understood the tangible and clearly observable. Their condemnation of dancing, for example, did not extend to dance music. For Pentecostals, music was a language beyond aesthetic, let alone theological, judgment. Music was simply a matter of taste, having no right or wrong. Spontaneity, freedom, and popular appeal (rather than craftsmanship, integrity, and creativity) were hallmarks of the new movement's music.

The results of the die cast in the first decades of their history caused some concern. As early as 1937 the fellowship was admonished in its official publication, *The Pentecostal Evangel,* to avoid songs in fast "pump-handle" time, and "words that may carry but little depth of meaning" (Clinton H. Patterson, "Why, How, and What Shall We Sing?" *The Pentecostal Evangel* [May 15, 1937]: 2). In 1956 musical "lightness and irreverence" in the fellowship caused R. A. Brown to write: "We have noticed in many Pentecostal meetings that sacred songs are now put to ragtime music, and that people work themselves into a frenzy playing and singing in the effort to please the listeners." ("Jazz at Church," *The*

Pentecostal Evangel [March 4, 1956]: 29). He explained that such entertainment caters to the flesh, producing a superficial faith. Nevertheless, the trend continued.

The advent of rock 'n' roll in the 1950s was the single most important influence on the music of the Assemblies of God in the second half of the twentieth century. Initially Pentecostals avoided this music. But eventually the secular cultural milieu produced a tolerance in the constituency that gradually eroded the church's anti-rock defenses. The allure of Christian contemporary music (CCM), a derivative of rock, was irresistible. Not everyone gave in without a fight. But by the mid-1980s one of the denomination's leaders argued that "we shouldn't waste our ammunition or energies fighting each other on an issue that is often more a matter of musical taste than moral purity or doctrine" (Lowell Lundstrom, "Contemporary vs. Traditional Gospel Music," _The Pentecostal Evangel_ [April 26, 1987]: 22). The pragmatic belief that any art form is able to accommodate the gospel to culture gave little hope that conservatives could prevail. Currently, based upon what church musicians and pastors now program in their churches, the religious form of rock of one type or another has finally become entrenched as an accepted musical language in the Assemblies of God.

Another phenomenon related to early Pentecostal beginnings is the increasing popularity of chorus singing and the decreasing popularity of the hymnal. At the publication of the fellowship's second hymnal (the first was in 1924), chorus singing was established well enough to warrant inclusion of 30 separate choruses (in addition to the choruses attached to every gospel song). Influenced by the relatively recent charismatic movement, chorus singing eventually became the preponderant congregational music. Many such choruses feature strong rhythms and up-beat tempos useful for energizing a congregation in demonstrative actions such as handclapping, swaying, and other physical manifestations. An abundance of more meditative choruses (many of them quotations or paraphrases of Scripture) are used to intensify corporate devotion and worship.

In spite of the fact that some churches use the hymnal minimally and others not at all, hymn singing has not become obsolete. The last two hymnals, _Hymns of Glorious Praise_ (Springfield, Mo.: Gospel Publishing House, 1969), and _Sing His Praise_ (Springfield, Mo.: Gospel Publishing House, 1991), indicate that the leadership of the Assemblies is committed to providing the constituency with a substantial selection of traditional and gospel hymns for their use. Hymns such as "Holy, Holy, Holy, Lord God Almighty!" used to open the 1919 General Council are part of the fellowship's heritage. Nevertheless, the real ministry of congregational music is now largely believed to lie with the chorus, not the hymn.

Currently, the larger churches feature beautifully robed choirs which continue to sing arrangements of gospel or contemporary music. The Christmas or Easter cantata has given way to a full-blown dramatic musical production in the popular vein. Independence Day may be celebrated with a special musical presentation. Worship teams, each member with a microphone, often provide congregational musical leadership in the singing of seamless strings of choruses. Accompanying instruments such as drums, electric guitars, and synthesizers are widely used. The custom of singing in the Spirit (singing in tongues) is not practiced as much as it once was. Well-rehearsed vocal solos are almost invariably sung in the style of secular or religious pop music. Technology such as amplification, accompaniment tracks, and rote learning tapes have mechanized much music-making. Larger churches may spend half a million dollars on special-effects systems, lighting, and stage paraphernalia.

The music pragmatism of more concern for ends (results) than means (method) is a key to understanding Assemblies of God practice in the other arts. In literature, the movement has shown great concern for moral content but less for artistic form; in architecture, more consideration for practicality than for theological statements; in drama, more attention to quality of presentation than to quality of writing. Interestingly, when it came to music, many texts were sung which did not reflect the collective theological understanding of the fellowship. A religious song was prized more for its being a musical outlet than a repository for finely reasoned theological truth.

For the most part, constituents are content to move in the direction of secular pop music culture. Being strongly pragmatic, Assemblies of God churches contextualize the gospel in the preferred musical language of the unchurched and make it their own.

Calvin M. Johansson

110 • BAPTIST (EVANGELICAL DENOMINATIONS AND INDEPENDENT BAPTIST CHURCHES)

Music in evangelical Baptist churches derives largely from interdenominational hymnals, but also calls on a wide variety of sources ranging from choruses and pop gospel to Anglican chant. Many Baptist churches are also making use of dramatic arts and the structure of the Christian year to enhance worship, as does the congregation described here.

Evangelical Baptist churches use the hymn books published by interdenominational publishing houses which have in recent years included music from all periods with an emphasis on the eighteenth and nineteenth centuries. Chorus singing has become important in many of their churches as well. An increasing use of drama and the creative use of space have also found their way into Evangelical Baptist churches.

The music employed in Baptist churches is generally taken from mainline evangelical traditions. The majority of hymns are of the gospel type from the late nineteenth century, but a few hymns as old as Luther's, as well as traditional Christmas carols are included. Contemporary Christian music in a more popular style is also widely used and enjoyed. As most of our churches make use of untrained volunteers in their music, taped accompaniments are frequently used. Choral music might include examples from Gabrieli to Gaither. There is an abundance of gospel hymn choral arrangements and vocal solos as well as frequent use of small ensembles. Still, there is a strong emphasis on congregational singing, and four or five hymns are sung in each service. Some of the largest churches enjoy sizable pipe organs with excellent organists, while the smaller churches usually have only a piano or small electronic organ with a pianist-turned-organist at the keyboard.

In the author's own church we do not have a beautiful building to help us focus our worship and thus need to work to provide a suitable environment. We worship in a square, low-ceilinged building and sit on folding chairs under cold fluorescent lighting. There is a concrete beam ceiling only ten feet above us and blue indoor-outdoor carpeting on the floor. During quiet moments in the service we are able to hear the children upstairs participating in the children's service. We have no stained glass, a dry acoustic environment, no gold or silver vessels, no sound system, no grand piano, and no orchestral instruments. We do, however, have an excellent electronic organ that provides sounds of great majesty during the singing of hymns of praise. We draw congregational hymns from our usual hymnal as well as many other sources, reproducing them in our order of worship, securing the appropriate permission from the copyright owners where necessary. The hymns selected speak the same message as will be preached by the pastor. The main theme expressed each Sunday is stated in one sentence in the opening portion of the printed order of worship. Everything we do in our service is there for a reason, and each action ties into and helps reinforce the spiritual truth or theme.

In this context we strive to prompt each worshiper to come to, pray to, and listen to God. Our congregation understands that worship of God is something we do, not something we leave to worship leaders. We sing the Scriptures both in choral and congregational form. Our choir often sings choral descants on certain verses of hymns. We also use alternate harmonizations for organ accompaniment for many hymns, and it is not unusual to sing a verse unaccompanied. In addition to a broad spectrum of Christian hymnody, we sing both praise choruses as well as more traditional Anglican psalm chants, the latter having become a very comfortable experience because of its simple, repetitive nature. This allows worshipers to concentrate easily on the scriptural text, enabling them to offer praise directly to God.

Music is never used as a filler or warm-up for something else. The account in 2 Chronicles 5 shows something of the power that music might have in the worship of Almighty God. The dedication of the temple provided a strategic opportunity for the Holy Spirit to move among people, and it was the ministry of music that ushered in the presence of the Holy Spirit. The glory of God was so apparent that the priests could not proceed. While this is not the experience every week in our church, it is also not uncommon.

The first attribute we see of God in the opening of Genesis is creativity. Since the Scriptures declare that humankind is made in God's image, our expression of creativity should be important in our worship. A portion of this expression for us is the use of original musical compositions by members of our parish and other local composers. God gifts us with the ability to not only to use traditional elements in worship, but also to approach him with new styles and fresh approaches. To those whose worship remains relatively unchanged each week, our more creative worship efforts might seem highly unusual.

One order of worship we use comes directly from the Scriptures. We simply do together what the Scriptures tell us to do. For example, when we use Psalm 95 as a foundation for worship, we read the psalm aloud as if it were being expressed for the first time by God himself. In response, we all sing a joyful and majestic hymn. We then note in the psalm a passage which suggests thanksgiving, which leads us to express our thanks or even celebrate the Great Thanksgiving, the Eucharist, kneeling before the Lord our maker again as detailed in the psalm.

Sometimes we use short dramatic presentations that communicate truth about the theme of the particular service, finding visual depiction of an idea to be particularly powerful. We design and fabricate banners that express and support our focus for worship. These are sometimes mounted in full view and are sometimes used in processionals at the beginning of the service.

The physical arrangement of the worship area is also determined by the theme of the service. For example, if we want to emphasize that God is in our midst, we might celebrate Holy Communion with the table in the center rather than at one end of the space. Similarly, if we wish to emphasize our membership in the church family, we might arrange all of our chairs around the table. We might also arrange the chairs in a semicircle with ten or fifteen chairs removed from the center and celebrate the Eucharist there. If we want to emphasize that we are each individually responsible to God for our own sin, we might place the chairs somewhat farther apart rather than immediately next to each other in order to evoke a sense of isolation. Different arrangements communicate specific truths and reinforce the preaching of the word. While we at times explain why we have arranged the chairs as they are, most often we do not.

We find that using all of our senses is very helpful in assisting us experience God's presence and the truth of Scripture. Relying only on preaching and

reading of the Scriptures is unnecessarily restrictive. One meaningful practice is to have each person write down their sins on a sheet of paper and then lay the paper on the table as an act of confession to God and plea for forgiveness. Later in the service the pastor and an elder would go to the table and pick up the papers, tear them into tiny pieces, and then discard them in view of the congregation while the passage of Scripture that promises forgiveness is read. In another service, wishing to emphasize the importance of hunger for God, we had fresh bread baking nearby and the aroma of the yeast filled the room, giving reinforcement to the theme. At the close of the service we ate the bread, experiencing the benefit of its nourishment and acknowledging the strength that comes from knowing God.

We also celebrate the changing seasons and feast days of the Christian year. The arrival of Advent immediately reminds us not only about the coming of our Savior as a child in the manger but also of his second coming. The celebration of Epiphany encourages us to learn about the gifts given to our Lord by the Magi, but also calls us to examine and act responsibly in response to those many gifts that God has given us. The Lenten season calls us to reflect upon the great sacrifice that Jesus made for our redemption, challenging us to seek God's guidance in living sacrificially to his glory. We celebrate Ascension Sunday with the presence of hundreds of brightly colored helium filled balloons. At the end of the service during the final hymn we all process outside the building carrying the balloons. We gather outside and close with the worship leader saying "He is risen!" The congregation responds "He is risen, indeed!," releasing the balloons that float high into the sky. This graphic experience will always help us remember the reality of Jesus' ascension to be with the Father. These are but a few of the spiritual truths and doctrines that must be brought to our attention year after year. The Christian year is a tremendous structure in which these truths can systematically fit.

Our goal in worship is to assist people in communicating with God. While this may take many different forms, we always include the reading of Holy Scripture, prayer, praise, and thanksgiving, and a quiet time for listening to and responding to God. Worship is an act in which we focus on God. We talk and sing to him and not for each other. We believe that this brings strength and blessing to his people and great joy to the Lord.

Larry Ellis

III • BAPTIST GENERAL CONFERENCE

The Baptist General Conference has been influenced by contemporary music and arts. Many of its churches sing praise choruses as well as hymns and gospel songs. The popular arts of drama, storytelling, and banners are used in many churches.

The Baptist General Conference is composed of dozens of large congregations in major metropolitan areas of the United States and Canada and hundreds of small congregations in both cities and rural areas. Many of these are very open to creativity in worship, especially in music, drama, Scripture reading, and preaching. This is true not only of the larger, metropolitan churches, but also of the smaller, even rural congregations where one might not expect an openness to change.

Although many congregations approach worship in the same way as their predecessors did years ago, the majority are moving beyond the exercise of defining worship and into the joy of doing it with an openness that allows a wider range of expression. There is great diversity of style across the United States and Canada within the denomination, with no universal pattern for the worship service. Although there are many similarities, each church is free to express itself in the way it prefers and to design the worship experience as it sees fit. While the following observations are generalizations, one would find them to be true of a great number of Baptist General Conference churches.

Dance and Drama

Many Baptists would associate such art forms as interpretive movement and environmental art with other mainline denominations. Very few of our churches will ever use dance in worship. Many allow choreography by their children and youth (and even adults) in musical presentations, but denounce interpretive movement which they could categorize as "dance." A more acceptable form of interpretation is signing. Many music groups include some of this beautiful movement in their presentations. But dance in any of its forms is rarely acceptable.

The use of drama is much more prevalent than interpretive movement. Due partially to the support of drama in contemporary creative congregations like Willow Creek Community Church in South Barrington, Illinois, drama has enjoyed a resurgence among hundreds of congregations across America. Vignettes and even full-scale plays are popular. Drama has been most helpful in preparing worshipers for subsequent activity, such as the sermon or even music related to the dramatic theme.

Many young preachers, and veterans as well, have been honing their craft in recent years, delivering much better sermons. I have experienced "illustrated sermons," in which a biblical character or the writer of a certain biblical passage is portrayed. By this means, I have met the Apostle Paul, Peter, and even John Wesley in Baptist General Conference churches. I saw one "living sermon" in which the preacher was depicting the broad way to destruction spoken of in so many biblical passages. Some of the predicaments he faced along his way were easily recognized by his hearers. They identified with the preacher and realized quickly that he might have been portraying any one of them. Thus, the use of drama has found its way into preaching as well as other aspects of the worship service.

I have also experienced various forms of storytelling, including some wonderfully exuberant "children's sermons." Storytelling is becoming more popular, with emphasis on making a biblical narrative become alive to the hearers, often by a creative modernization of the biblical passage. I believe this practice has been fostered by the increase of modern paraphrases and translations of Scripture, and also by sensitivity to unchurched people who do not respond easily to complex theological terminology.

Visual Arts

More careful thought has been given recently to design of the worship space, including such aspects as seating, platform shape and size, banners and wall hangings, and seasonal art. Although this might be termed environmental art, it is approached more in terms of functional necessity than artistic expression. Pulpits are smaller than they once were, as preachers are concerned about not separating themselves from the people. Current design of worship centers emphasizes helping the worshipers to be participants rather than spectators. Banners have been used by some churches as a visual aid during missions conferences or other celebrations. Some churches have banners on the walls at all times. Few have a weekly processional, although some do so on occasion, especially at high festivals.

Music

The greatest area of both change and discussion has been in the field of church music. The Baptist General Conference has long been a stalwart in evangelical church music, having produced many writers and leaders in the field. The range of acceptable musical style has always been quite wide, from the traditional music of yesterday's masters to the contemporary styles of today. Hymns, gospel songs, contemporary praise choruses, anthems, classical literature—all of it is acceptable in the Baptist General Conference. Although this wide variety of musical styles is not necessarily practiced in any specific church, it can be seen across the denomination as a whole. The singing of psalms has been absent, including the use of antiphons which have been more associated with mainline denominations. But this is beginning to change. Today many congregations are becoming acquainted with a whole new range of musical styles. Most stay with more contemporary styles, using anthems and classics sparingly, but there is at least an understanding that "old" does not mean "not good." Members of the Baptist General Conference would agree that "musical style is negotiable, the message is not."

The appearance of a few new hymnals in the late 1980s and early 1990s has been an important influence, coming at a time during which many congregations were in the market for a new book. The denomination has not produced its own hymnal. Two hymnals finding wide acceptance are _The Hymnal for Worship and Celebration_ (Waco, Tex.: Word Music, 1986) and _The Worshiping Church_ (Carol Stream, Ill.: Hope Publishing Company, 1990). Many churches are using transparencies for congregational singing, with positive results. It seems the singers can hear each other better when their heads are lifted up to sing, causing increased joyful participation. There is also a growing acceptance of different instruments used to accompany music, including synthesizers, guitars, and drums, along with the typical acoustical piano, organ, and orchestral instruments.

There are two major reasons for this acceptance of creativity and change. First, Baptist General Conference churches are becoming open to "outsiders," whereas many years ago it was seen as a group only

for the Swedish. There is great concern about unchurched people and in order to evangelize effectively we believe that we must be open to a variety of styles. We do not attempt only to attract people to our church, but to present to them the Lord Jesus Christ and we must therefore become willing to accept and adopt new methods, including change in musical style and in other areas.

The second reason for growth in worship is rise of education and teaching on the subject over the past few years. Bethel College and Seminary, both schools of the Baptist General Conference, have been at the forefront of this effort for many years. As the Director of Worship Resources for the entire denomination for several years, it was my privilege to do seminars and workshops, helping raise the consciousness of the churches to worship, music, creativity, etc., for the layperson as well as the seminarian, pastor, or church music director.

Some of these issues have been addressed in writings by people within the Baptist General Conference, either explicitly for a Baptist General Conference publication, or for some other publisher. Over the years the award-winning denominational periodical, _The Standard,_ has included many helpful and even provocative articles. Books and resource materials, including music and other worship aids, are offered to pastors and laypersons through a mail-order catalog produced by Harvest Publications, a branch of the BGC. This is an eclectic compilation, aimed primarily at pastors, church musicians, educators, and other leaders. There is a formal paper available on worship planning, dealing with philosophy and style as well as offering many specific suggestions and creative ideas. (Tim Mayfield, _Leader's Guide for Planning Worship Services_ [1990]; available through the Baptist General Conference, 2002 S. Arlington Heights Road, Arlington Heights, Ill. 60005.)

An Example of a Baptist General Conference Congregation

A good example of how music and the arts may be used in a typical Baptist General Conference church is found in the following comments by Dean Palermo, the associate pastor of Music and Worship at the Bethlehem Baptist Church in Minneapolis:

Music. In the last decade, music in worship has undergone a significant change at Bethlehem Baptist Church, the most noteworthy being the introduction of a philosophy of music in the church by my predecessor and mentor, Dr. Bruce H. Leafblad: "The purpose of music in the church is nothing more than, nothing less than, and nothing other than the work of the church—which is ministry." The ministry finds expression in the threefold priorities of the church: worship, nurture, and outreach. That is, music is the means to the end of our stated purposes of ministry as a church in which we exist to:

1. Savor our vision of God in Worship;
2. Strengthen our vision of God in Nurture; and
3. Spread our vision of God in Outreach.

As a result of this change, music has undergone a shift from being considered a mere "preliminary" to the main event of the sermon, to being seen as a point of significant encounter or communion between the church and her Lord.

Another change in the use of music has been in the area of musical style. Whereas many churches have adopted an "either/or" approach to musical style, Bethlehem has grown to appreciate and adopt a "both/and" approach. That is, we have chosen to incorporate an eclectic range of music that includes classical, historical, traditional, and contemporary forms of music. Therefore, use of music includes classical literature (vocal and instrumental), traditional hymnody, occasional use of gospel songs, chants, antiphons, and psalm singing, as well as spirituals and contemporary praise choruses.

Because of the nature of these different styles of music, it also follows that we incorporate an array of instrumental accompaniment. Sunday mornings tend to feature the traditional use of organ (although in our new sanctuary we are currently using a grand piano until we raise enough funds for a pipe organ), brass, woodwinds, strings, and choir. Sunday evenings feature contemporary instruments such as piano, flute, acoustic guitars, electric bass, drums, and four or five vocalists. We also tend to use hymnals (that include musical notation) in the morning, and professional quality slides (words only) in the evenings. The use of both forms includes the best qualities of both genres: the ability to teach our children (and adults!) how to read music, and the freedom that comes from lifting our heads and hands up toward the heavens as we sing to the Lord (through the use of slides).

The Arts. It has been encouraging to see the growing influx in the use of other art forms in worship. The past decade has seen the introduction of several art forms: paintings, large banners, liturgical dance, drama, storytelling, pulpit tapestries, liturgical candle holders, and sculpture.

One of the exciting developments in the last few years has been the design and building of a new sanctuary. Right from the beginning, there was a concern and commitment regarding how the design of the sanctuary would be affected by visual and material elements. Care was taken to design a room where there would be a lot of natural lighting (as well as sufficient artificial lighting for evening); where the colors of the materials were bright and neutral enough to enhance liturgical colors when they are introduced through flowers, banners, choir stoles, etc.; where there was enough reverberation to enhance congregational singings (as well as the vocal and instrumental music of the church); where there was sufficient flexibility for drama; where there were places to hang and see large liturgical banners; and where there were large liturgical candle holders that could be easily seen from anywhere in the room.

Tim Mayfield and Dean Palermo

112 • BRETHREN (PLYMOUTH) CHURCHES

Plymouth Brethren worship is characterized by a commitment to austerity and simplicity. Music in worship has traditionally been limited to unaccompanied hymn singing. Musical and artistic creativity is most prevalent in Open Brethren churches in worship services other than the breaking of bread service. In some cases, instrumental accompaniment, contemporary music, and dramatic presentations of portions of Scripture are now used.

The (Plymouth) Brethren Movement began as a reaction to the strict sectarianism and clericalism evident in England and Ireland in the 1820s. Among the early leaders were George Müller, Henry Craik, Anthony Norris Groves, J. G. Bellett, John Nelson Darby, and Edward Cronin. Its high goals included a return to a spirit of simplicity, catholicity, and equality of all believers in the worship and remembrance of the Lord, in anticipation of his imminent return.

As a result, artistic expression in worship among the Brethren was not held in high esteem. What was considered simple worship was more highly valued, that is, a type of worship that is "in spirit and truth" (John 4:24). The first Brethren believed that such simplicity allowed for only that which is Spirit-guided and otherworldly and not that which is influenced by the trappings of this world or is used to stir the emotions and sensibilities. Austerity in individual and corporate lifestyles was encouraged as a demonstration of this simple, otherworldly faith. And, since the Lord was expected to return soon, there was no need to involve oneself in any lasting cultural expression. Simplicity and even barrenness of architecture and interior decor was cherished so as to keep the focus otherworldly in worship.

The only area of artistic expression considered acceptable to the early Brethren was hymn writing, but even hymns were regularly sung without instrumental accompaniment, and nonbiblical imagery was infrequent in their composition. Any extant hymns adopted by the movement were carefully reviewed, and lyrics were corrected to ensure doctrinal purity. With the split of the movement into Open and Exclusive branches over the issue of reception (1845–48), the Darbyite Exclusives began developing their own hymnology, culminating in the many editions of *Hymns for the Little Flock.* The Open Brethren under the influence of Groves, Muller, and Craik, developed and used a number of other hymnbooks, though some among the Opens also use the Exclusive book.

John Darby, the chief Exclusive theologian, also wrote several well-used hymns for the Brethren. He capsulized the Brethren perception of the arts in his preface to the 1881 edition of *Hymns for the Little Flock,* where he stated that although a hymn did have something of the spirit of poetry, poetry itself was to be rejected as "merely the spirit and imagination of man." In addition to Darby, the earliest of Brethren hymnwriters included S. P. Tregelles (of Greek/Hebrew concordance fame), J. G. Deck, Robert Chapman, and Sir Edward Denny. The central theme of many of these Brethren hymns is devotion to Christ and his sacrificial death. These hymns fit well within the weekly Brethren focus of the breaking of the bread. This concentration on one theme is also a reason why so few Brethren hymns have made their way into non-Brethren hymnbooks.

In the last decade or so, a number of leaders in both England and North America began to recognize the numeric and spiritual decline of the move-ment and spawned various calls and structures for renewal. The Open Brethren movement in particular has begun to see some renewal in the area of worship, although this is still not widespread and is viewed with suspicion in many Brethren quarters.

In the area of musical accompaniment, the Open Brethren have increasingly included in their central Breaking of Bread meeting the use of musical instruments (most often the piano, but also occasionally the flute and guitar), although a cappella singing was originally preferred. This preference grew from the desire to minimize or remove any form of human leadership, in deference to the Holy Spirit. The meeting was understood to belong under the leadership of the Holy Spirit alone, and the use of instruments or any other form of prearranged leadership was felt to be contrary to the Spirit's ownership. But many newer Brethren have felt free to allow for the guidance of the Spirit in the planning and execution of certain elements of the meeting as well. Further, many newer worship choruses have been written and used, although there is a strong desire to use them only alongside of more didactic, traditional hymns.

Traditionally, Brethren have tended to treat the weekly Breaking of Bread meeting as the true locus of worship and have kept it separate from the preaching/teaching service (often called the *Family Bible Hour* in North America) and any gospel preaching services they may hold. A more integrative approach has been tried in some assemblies so that the entire morning has been considered a worship experience. One assembly placed the Breaking of Bread as the final meeting of the morning, and an extension that is climactic to the preaching session. But this practice is rare among the Brethren, since the Breaking of Bread is customarily a separate meeting held either first on Sunday mornings or later on Sunday evenings.

Because the Breaking of Bread meeting has been deemed sacrosanct by the Brethren, it is the other meetings of the assembly, especially the *Family Bible Hour,* which have seen most of the creativity in music and the arts. Some younger music leaders and participants have come to believe that their work is very much a part of the worship experience as well, and have put much planning, practice, and prayer into the coming Sunday's meeting. They have begun to employ newer hymns and choruses, synthesizers, electronic and traditional drums, acoustic and electric guitars, violins and cellos, and back up vocalists to enliven the musical participation of the congregation. Dramatic life-presentations, creative dance, and creative signing to contemporary music have also been used in some assemblies. Newer choruses are often projected by an overhead projector rather than sung from a chorus book to lend greater corporate involvement. Occasionally Scripture has been read dramatically, such as in an oral interpretation of an entire biblical book that might be used in the place of a traditional Bible message.

In keeping with the Brethren commitment to simplicity in worship, the arts historically have not found expression either in architecture or interior decoration. Most Brethren meeting rooms, halls, or chapels have tended toward being very simple, functional, and unadorned. Decoration is often limited to a modestly adorned biblical text hanging behind the pulpit. Rarely a cross or other form of symbolism may be seen on their buildings or in their meeting rooms. Seating arrangement does have, in a number of instances, a certain symbolic element to it. Often the seating arrangement for Breaking of Bread is circular, with the table and elements in middle, to symbolize the centrality of the Lord's Supper to this group. More progressive Open Brethren have been more sympathetic toward aesthetic concerns in their building design, but buildings still have a far more functional than aesthetic orientation.

Thus, as far as the arts are concerned, the Brethren are still in search of an identity that does not violate the essence of their weekly focus on Christ and his work, and yet may incorporate a more creative approach to the Spirit's living presence among the people of God. The younger leaders among the Open Brethren are leading the way toward a greater incorporation of the artistic in worship. It remains to be seen whether they will be successful in integrating these newer ideas with traditional Brethren practices.

Rex A. Koivisto

113 • CALVARY CHAPEL

Calvary Chapel uses contemporary music in worship but does not emphasize the visual arts.

Music. Music has always played a significant role in the life of Calvary Chapel. When the first Jesus' people visited the Chapel in the late sixties, they brought a style of music with them that could relate to that generation. Through the ministry of Calvary Chapel, this music touched the world. Groups such as *Love Song,* as well as many solo artists, emerged from the chapel and began to perform concerts, minister on the streets, and travel to other churches. Their music was captured on paper and published through a fledgling arm of the church called Maranatha! Music, which became the first publisher to specialize in worship songs. Marantha grew very large over the next twenty-plus years and was eventually sold. Another publishing resource, Asaph Publishing, is now affiliated with Calvary Chapel.

The Arts. The area of the arts in worship, especially visual arts, has never been strongly emphasized by those within leadership of the Calvary Chapel. While some Calvary chapels around the country may use certain aspects of visual arts, the use of banners and pageantry, liturgical dance, and other expressive forms in worship is not common.

Randy Sly

114 • CHARISMATIC CHURCHES

With its roots in the Pentecostal movement, which had rejected most of the fine arts as worldly, the charismatic movement has only more recently begun to explore the full range of artistic activity in worship. Although the visual and literary arts largely await development, both dance and drama have found increasing acceptance in some charismatic circles. Most importantly, charismatics have become leaders within the Christian community in the creation of contemporary worship music.

Music

Whether or not music is the universal language, it is the one art form universally found in the charismatic churches of North America. A virtual explosion of new worship music has taken place over the past two decades, sparked by the charismatic renewal of the 1960s and the "Jesus movement" that followed, especially among young people on the west coast. These new believers' search for ways to express their love and devotion to the Lord became the seedbed for a musical revolution. Reacting to a perceived irrelevance of the worship style of most churches to their quest of the living Jesus, the young men and women of the Jesus movement abandoned more traditional musical forms in favor of shorter choruses that described in contemporary idiom their personal relationship with the Lord. Simultaneously, the Catholic charismatic movement began to produce its own variety of contemporary musical settings for the increasingly popular folk masses.

The charismatic Jesus movement took the gospel out of the church and into the world through street witnessing, concerts, festivals, coffee houses, Christian communities, and home groups. The music for this movement had to be portable, accompanied by the acoustic guitar. As the influence of the Jesus movement was felt in charismatic churches, the guitar displaced the traditional organ and piano as the instrument of choice in accompanying worship. Jesus bands and soloists began to emerge everywhere, especially through the local coffee houses and Jesus communities.

Another revolution began with the work of Ralph Carmichael, a popular composer-arranger. Noting the gap between youth and the church, he wrote several contemporary musicals, introducing drums, guitars, electronic keyboards, and rock style to the music of local churches, in order to attract and hold a younger generation. Others followed Carmichael's lead.

The last decade has seen the emergence of the worship team or praise band, an ensemble modeled after the instrumental groups which back up popular recorded music, consisting usually of guitar, keyboard, bass, and drums. Within this model the synthesizer has emerged as the preferred keyboard. Along with this development, a much broader range of instruments, from the orchestral to the ethnic, has become not only acceptable but popular for accompanying worship music. Some larger charismatic churches have been able to form symphony orchestras to accompany worship. An increasing musical sophistication is evident in the use of music by Bach, Handel, or other classical composers.

The advent of "praise marches" or "public praise," taking worship outside the walls of the church as a means of evangelistic outreach, has called for a type of song suitable for marching. Many songs written for this purpose have been incorporated in charismatic worship, giving it an often militant stamp. In addition, the melodically and theologically simplistic songs of two decades ago, such as "Father, I Adore You" (Terrye Coelho) and "God Is So Good" (traditional) are now accompanied by more sophisticated newcomers such as

"Shine, Jesus, Shine" (Graham Kendrick) and "Let There Be Praise" (Dick and Melodie Tunney).

Another trend is the rise of "prophetic praise." In this act of worship, an individual either sings spontaneous praise to God or sings a prophecy under the inspiration of the Holy Spirit. This is more frequently heard in churches affiliated with the "restoration" or "Davidic worship" movement, as well as churches that have been more active in prophecy in general, such as the Vineyard churches.

The publishing and recording industry has helped to raise the professional level of musical activity in charismatic circles. Worship songs, musical dramas such as Steve Fry's _Thy Kingdom Come,_ and other types of music have been disseminated through cassettes and compact discs. Prominent in this industry are firms which originated within the charismatic community, such as Integrity's Hosannah! Music or Maranatha! Music. Maranatha was the first publishing company to focus exclusively on contemporary worship music. Integrity has made contemporary praise and worship music available to the public through recordings of actual worship settings that feature congregational singing as directed by a prominent worship leader and backed by professional singers and instrumentalists. Through these recordings, together with lead sheets, chorus books, and other products, fresh worship resources have been made available even to individuals and fellowships in rural areas or other places remote from the influence of contemporary worship. Christian Copyright Leasing, Inc., and other organizations provide copyright clearance to local churches for this new music and supply overhead transparencies and other aids.

In the evangelical church at large, it has been charismatics who have taken the lead in creating a style of music reaching a wider audience. The work of composers such as Bill and Gloria Gaither or Twila Paris and of performers like Sandi Patti or Larnell Harris, has become standard fare in the spiritual life of the evangelical community. Music by composers and performers of charismatic background is widely featured in Christian broadcasting, even by stations representing points of view theologically opposed to the charismatic movement.

Dance

If music is virtually universal, the art form of dance may be almost as universally divisive—at least among charismatic churches. Positions toward this expression range from the highly positive to the highly critical. Outstanding dance ministries such as those of Randall Bane (interviewed on CBN's "Heart to Heart" in November 1991) and *Ballet Magnificat* spend much of their time in charismatic churches. Both of these were featured in the cover story "Praise Him with the Dance" in *Charisma,* March 1989. At the other extreme, the Assemblies of God published a negative position paper on dance in the November 1986 issue of *Pentecostal Evangel.* That article, written by T. Burton Pierce, both acknowledged the continued practice of dance among some Assemblies of God churches and took a strong position against such practice.

At least some of the disagreement is related to the difference between spontaneous, individual "dancing in the Spirit," and orchestrated, rehearsed "dancing before the Lord" (a distinction made by Kenneth Hagin, and quoted in the *Charisma* article). Some large and influential churches have championed worship dance. However, many charismatic groups, such as charismatic Baptists, while not being as critical of dance as the Assemblies of God, nevertheless have taken a cautious attitude. There is some uneasiness about dance in charismatic circles and tension over this issue may increase before consensus is reached. In any case, dance is growing in acceptance, largely through workshops sponsored by charismatic churches and led by nationally or regionally recognized talent such as Mikhail Murnane or Pamela Smith. Special resources for the movement arts in worship, including costuming, flags, and streamers, are produced by *Pazaz,* a ministry in the greater St. Louis area.

Interestingly, outside of North America the charismatic church is using worship dance effectively in evangelism and outreach. Dance in this context has been particularly well received in Mexico and in many nations of Europe and Asia. In these areas, evangelistic teams of Youth with a Mission (YWAM) often use dance to make contact with the unchurched. When asked the reason for its effectiveness, Kirk Dearman, who headed Project Exalt in Europe, explained that because dance is perceived as a cultural or fine arts event, it is much better attended than an event billed as an evangelistic rally. More people are then open to hear what the artists have to say. The annual Christian Feast of Tabernacles in Jerusalem reaches an Israeli audience, as well as Christian attendees from around the world, with

the worship dance ministry of artists such as Randall Bane and Valerie Henry.

The South African arts group Friends First is another example of an organization that uses dance both inside and outside of the walls of the church. During the mid-1980s this eclectic and interracial ensemble became widely known for its impact in worship in its own country, and traveled to England and the United States as well. This group successfully combined traditional dance movements from the heritage of several tribes in their region with original, more contemporary, choreography.

Visual Arts

While the realm of the visual arts (including painting, sculpture, and architecture) yields less to consider within charismatic circles, this also has been an area of controversy. Divergence of opinion is found even in one area where charismatics have been most active: the creation of banners.

Banner making, which began to impact the mainline churches about three decades ago, has now become a popular art among the charismatic churches. Banners, which may depict sacred symbols such as a cross or crown, or carry verses of Scripture or ascriptions of honor to the Lord, are often displayed in the place of worship. They may also be carried in procession, as in the "praise marches" that have become quite well known in England. However, Anne Gimeneyz of the Rock Church went on record as equating them with the paganism of the Israelites' golden calf, arguing that the antecedent for banners was the flag making in ancient Egypt (*Ministries Today,* May/June 1990). The use of banners as a vehicle for pageantry seems to be growing, however, as part of the movement to apply artistic expression to the exaltation of the Lord. Through their use in worship conferences such as the International Worship Symposium, some outstanding works of banner-making art have become regionally well known.

Occasionally one does hear of charismatic churches commissioning works of visual art for their worship environments, such as a multimedia mural by a sculptor/parishioner at Church in the City Vineyard Fellowship, Houston, Texas, and the series of ten-foot-square paintings at Cathedral of the Holy Spirit in Decatur, Georgia. Thus far, these seem to be isolated instances, only the precursors of a possible trend. The demographics of the charismatic movement have been such that professional artists in the visual media, such as painting and sculpture, are less often found in these circles than within the orbit of the mainline or sacramentally oriented churches. However, one popular form, T-shirt art, has flourished since being taken up by the Jesus movement.

In the realm of church architecture, two observable trends seem to emerge. One trend is toward the low-cost, high-utility warehouse-_cum_-auditorium structure favored by groups impacted by the church growth movement. The other trend is to the more opulent theater setting, evident especially among the "faith" churches. The classic Pentecostal denominations (Assemblies of God, Pentecostal Church of God, Foursquare Gospel, and similar groups) tend to erect buildings not dissimilar from those of their noncharismatic Protestant siblings, but often reflecting one of the trends mentioned above. In erecting new places of worship, charismatic congregations show a growing tendency, shared with Christians of other traditions, to arrange the worship area in a more open in-the-round or semicircular fashion, as opposed to the older lecture-hall style of church construction. Many charismatic churches started meeting in rented quarters such as school gymnasiums, often with the worshipers facing the long wall instead of the end. The ambiance of this arrangement, which brought the worship leaders closer to the congregation, affected worship style and may have motivated architectural preferences.

Drama and Mime

Drama was one of the fine arts that did flourish at an early stage in the charismatic movement. David Watson, a charismatic Anglican from London, had a strong drama group in his church called Riding Lights. In North America, national ministries such as The Lamb's Players, Covenant Players, and Jeremiah People influenced many churches, both charismatic and mainstream, to incorporate both drama and comedy skits into their worship. The medium of drama was also used by parachurch organizations such as Youth with a Mission in their outreach and street ministries.

In the ongoing life of charismatic churches, the greatest amount of dramatic activity occurs in connection with the seasonal Christmas and Easter pageants. These presentations, for which some congregations are locally famous, may involve elaborate lighting, costuming, sound systems, and the other trappings of professional dramatic productions, along with extensive orchestral and choral resources. Easter pageants are especially common and function as the charismatic equivalent of the passion play, the stations of the cross, or other traditional ways through which Christian worshipers have participated in the reenactment of the drama of salvation. In this sense, when performed with a high degree of Christian commitment and the anointing of the Holy Spirit, they may have a "sacramental" quality. Where a church has a tradition of these productions which attract the larger community, this fact may influence the architecture of the church auditorium. Short skits are occasionally used in charismatic churches, usually to publicize an upcoming event (a week of prayer, Vacation Bible School) or to promote a special emphasis (world missions, evangelism).

Related both to dance and to drama, the art of mime (or pantomime) is coming into wider use in charismatic circles, propagated through national and regional worship conferences. Mime is usually a visual accompaniment to music recorded by Christian artists, especially where the song tells a story. A high professional standard has been set by artists like Todd Farley, a student of the famed French mimist Marcel Marceau.

Film and Video

Film and video works that employ the dramatic arts are rarely used in the context of the worship service. They are more often used in the Christian education program with specialized groups such as youth ministries or for evangelistic outreach. Most of these resources are not specifically targeted toward a charismatic audience, but are produced by ministries or firms serving the greater Christian public. Examples include James Dobson's Focus on the Family productions, _Chariots of Fire, China Cry,_ or music videos by popular Christian recording artists. Occasionally a film shown to the entire congregation may substitute for the regular Sunday evening or midweek service.

The Pentecostal movement of a generation ago was opposed to motion pictures, in reaction to the values propagated by the film industry and the on- and off-screen excesses of Hollywood personalities. The charismatic movement, as it evolved among non-Pentecostals, exhibited a more relaxed attitude. Charismatic leaders also eagerly embraced the video medium for the broadcast of worship services or for programs in evangelistic, talk-show, or guest-artist format. However, there was never a great artistic thrust to such programming, and its influence (with some exceptions) has recently been in decline due to the well-publicized excesses of some of the major figures involved.

─────────── **Literary Arts** ───────────

In North America, expression by charismatics through the literary arts (fiction, poetry, essay) has not been a major factor in the worship setting. Again, the historic demographics of the charismatic community do not suggest that one would normally encounter the degree of literary activity found in churches long associated with institutions for higher learning and the intellectual community in general. However, this would be an area to watch for future trends as the charismatic church continues to mature. Colleges and universities such as Oral Roberts University and Regent University have developed largely from within the charismatic community, and scholars associated with these and other institutions have begun to make significant contributions in the fields of biblical and systematic theology and in other academic disciplines. Writers and publishers with charismatic backgrounds are now producing important material in the field of worship studies.

Darrell A. Harris,
Richard C. Leonard, Randolph W. Sly

115 ◆ CHRISTIAN AND MISSIONARY ALLIANCE CHURCHES

A. B. Simpson, the founder of the Christian and Missionary Alliance Churches, first articulated the need for a spirit of renewal in worship, and this approach has marked its practices ever since. While avoiding extremes, some congregations, such as the one described here have been open to new music, using guitars, synthesizers, and drums along with the organ, and regularly includes drama and banners as examples of the other arts.

In the closing decade of the nineteenth century, A. B. Simpson gave visionary leadership to a new movement known today as the Christian and Missionary Alliance. He was deeply concerned that men and women hear the message of God's love, a concern that resulted in the birth of a unique missionary society. Simpson united groups of Chris-

tians in the United States with men and women called to serve on foreign fields. He believed that healthy, local Christian bodies could provide ongoing support, both spiritual and financial, for overseas missions. Thus, an alliance of Christians and missionaries was formed.

Simpson maintained that there were three essentials for good health in Christian groups committed to serving missionaries. These priorities were certainly reflected in the ministry of worship in early Alliance services. Stated briefly they were, first, the centrality of the person and work of Jesus Christ. Simpson was consumed by the person of Jesus Christ, reflected today in the centerpiece of Alliance theology and practice, the "Fourfold Gospel": Jesus as Savior, Sanctifier, Healer, and Coming King. A. B. Simpson felt that the message and music of the denomination should reflect this priority.

Secondly, Simpson was concerned that local Christians experience, particularly in worship, the dynamic presence of the Holy Spirit. It was the Holy Spirit's fire that ignited a passion within him that he then encouraged others to seek. Worship in the earliest days of the Alliance was alive with the Spirit's presence, and as a result people were transformed.

A third and practical concern focused on keeping the ministry and message of salvation relevant to contemporary society. Nowhere was this more evident than in the music in A. B. Simpson's meetings. He wanted lyrics that reflected God's Word and melodies that were "of the people." As a result, he personally wrote over one hundred and eighty gospel songs with music that would appeal to the people of his day.

Turning back to the 1890s will help us understand worship renewal among Alliance congregations in the 1990s. Local churches hungry for dynamic worship are in reality re-embracing concerns articulated by A. B. Simpson over one hundred years ago. At the heart of Christian and Missionary Alliance worship renewal is a desire to be Christocentric, spiritually vital, and relevant to the contemporary context. In the purest sense Alliance congregations are always in the midst of renewal.

Attention given to music and the arts in Alliance worship services is rooted in the threefold concern outlined above. To illustrate let us look at one Christian and Missionary Alliance congregation as an example. North Seattle Alliance Church has been for years one of the strongest congregations within the denomination. It has been characterized by strong preaching, excellent Bible teaching, and evangelistic concern.

In 1986, Rev. David Klinsing was called as senior pastor of North Seattle Alliance. Almost immediately Klinsing set into motion the process of positively and patiently renewing worship within the congregation. His philosophy of worship was faithful to Simpson's three-fold concern. He desired to have educated worshipers led each week to celebrate vibrantly the person and work of Jesus Christ in forms relevant to the 1990s and in an atmosphere that welcomes the presence and power of the Holy Spirit. Klinsing hired a pastor of worship committed to the same ideals, willing to work with him toward renewal.

Music, previously traditional at North Seattle Alliance, today reflects a more contemporary style. In the first of two Sunday morning services worship ensembles have replaced choirs. Guitars, synthesizers, and drums are as standard as the organ was in the past. Scripture songs and choruses are the predominant form of music, including a balanced number of those addressed to God and those extolling his acts and attributes. Particular attention is given to those songs and choruses that seem to unleash the power of the Holy Spirit in the midst of worship. Hymns are still used in the service, preceded by an explanation of their history, theology, and importance. Klinsing is concerned that music draws people into a celebrative and intimate encounter with the living Christ, in a style that is appealing to the contemporary worshiper.

Like other churches in renewal, North Seattle Alliance recognizes that sight as well as sound engages people in a vital experience of adoration. Two ways this has been expressed are through drama and banners. Worship services at North Seattle Alliance often include dramatizations. They serve either as illustrations to the morning message or the rehearsing of some biblical theme set apart from the sermon in the worship service. Klinsing noted that traditionalists often find drama out of place, claiming that it is unspiritual. But newcomers regularly comment that dramatizations touch them deeply, slipping in their message through the emotions when a direct assault on the mind is ineffective.

The North Seattle Alliance congregation, committed to celebration, has chosen to develop banners as an aid to worship. Festive in design, the intention is to employ liturgical themes which will highlight the positive motifs of the ecclesiastical year. These banners will serve to change the frequently noted funereal atmosphere experienced in many evangelical worship services.

The North Seattle Alliance church sanctuary has pews which are placed in straight rows facing the pulpit. The chancel area is high, designed to illustrate the transcendent nature of God. As part of renewal, architectural changes are being suggested that will reflect the new understanding of worship. Pews will be arranged semicircularly to create a more communal and participatory atmosphere. The platform will be extended into the congregation, a statement of the immediacy and intimacy of the Living Word. The architectural centerpiece, according to Klinsing, will be the Table of the Lord, highlighting the redemptive act of God that keeps on happening in the midst of his people.

What is occurring at North Seattle Alliance is to greater or lesser degree happening in many congregations in the Christian and Missionary Alliance. In the decade to come scores of other churches eager to experience the dynamic power of worship will join the journey to renewal. It is important that denominational leaders prepare resources that will help congregations along this path. Local churches should be aided in the development of a balanced philosophy of worship. Likewise, it is essential that changes be made with a keen sensitivity to the century-old concerns of the denomination. Worship renewal in the Christian and Missionary Alliance is not some new fad or fancy. It is a return to priorities articulated by the denomination's founder, A. B. Simpson, over one hundred years ago.

Terry Wardle

116 • Christian Church (Disciples of Christ)

Since they have always adhered to the principle of freedom in those things which were considered nonessentials, it may come as no surprise that diversity marks the worship practices of the Christian Church (Disciples of Christ). Because music and the other arts are not essential elements of belief and because there is no extensive musical heritage, the denomination has always felt free to leave the development and implementation of worship practices to local leaders. Unlike the Church of Christ, the Disciples of Christ permits the use of the organ and other instruments in congregational worship.

A Symbol of the Four Evangelists. This symbol was found among the catacombs of the early church.

As a denomination, a theme heard more generally and more often than any other during the decade of the 1980s was "diversity." This theme expresses both a growing reality as well as an increased awareness of what has been true of the denomination. Diversity is increasing within the church in most respects, including ethnic make-up, theological perspective, the nature of church or nonchurch backgrounds, family and lifestyle choices, tastes, and sociological variety. This is not unlike the experience of most denominations during this period, excepting perhaps those church bodies which seek a specific and intentional homogeneous grouping, such as some Pentecostal and some fundamentalist sects. All these factors influence the practice of the arts in congregations.

However, diversity has always been a facet of the denomination. A frequently quoted saying of the church's founding father, Alexander Campbell, is: "In essentials unity; in nonessentials liberty; in all things, charity." Disciples of Christ have fiercely adhered to liberty in nonessentials as an inalienable right.

Music

Among the Disciples, music and the arts have never been considered an essential area in which unity be sought. Opinions continue to range widely.

A fair percentage of the church—perhaps even a broad majority—would concur that music is a necessary aspect of worship. Beyond this simple acknowledgment, however, there immediately springs a myriad of contradictory thoughts about particulars. Disciples of Christ do not have a musical heritage that informs and guides its leadership, no Martin Luther or Samuel Wesley to look to and claim.

Two historic events which are uniquely within the denomination's history have made a significant impact on the musical life of congregations. The first is the rift that occurred at the close of the nineteenth century between those who ardently pursued the restoration of biblical worship forms and those who favored a more pragmatic or modern approach to worship. As this battle raged, the organ and other musical instruments became a symbol of this argument, with the restorationists insisting that organs were not used by the biblical church in worship and should not be used by modern-day congregations. Pragmatists disagreed. The ideological split eventually produced in 1910 two denominations: the Church of Christ (noninstrumental) and the Christian Church (Disciples of Christ). While Disciples of Christ publicly voiced no objection to using organs and other instruments, the scars of battle have had a lasting effect on the use of music in general within congregations, seminaries, and the national level of the church. To this day there is no staff for sacred music in national, regional, or area structures of the church. Only a very few congregations employ musicians with specific education in sacred music. And over the past decade, the number has declined.

The second historically significant event was the formation of the Association of Disciple Musicians, established in 1962. The principal activity of this group has been to sponsor annual church music workshops. Each year, major personalities in choral, organ, children's choir, handbells, and worship leadership are attracted to lead five-day classes. A significant number of the denomination's musical leaders come together each year for study and fellowship. This annual event has remained the only denominationally sponsored opportunity for the encouragement and growth of church musicians. While its impact continues to be felt in specific congregations, it has not had broad influence across the denomination. The national church structure (the "General Church") provides administrative support, but there is no paid staff which directs the organization. It does enjoy official recognition within the denomination.

Given its "nonessential" status and an absence of direction from the denomination's leadership and seminaries, the practice of music and other arts within congregations have been left entirely to local leadership. With a pervasive lack of trained leadership in church music in local churches, the practice of music within the denomination has been left to the winds and wiles of secular culture.

In the decade of the 1980s, musical practice also followed the general theme of "diversity." Each local congregation practices the art of church music as they see fit. The trend in the past decade was to respond to popular (uninformed) opinion and commercial tastes of music which increasingly have replaced traditional church music and music of historical source and practice. Pianos are increasingly used; organs less so. Popular styles of music increasingly replace traditional choral anthems and solo singing and small vocal ensembles sing popular songs and new "Gospel" music with increasing frequency.

The *Hymnbook for Christian Worship* of 1970 was not broadly accepted, and churches have largely moved to nondenominational hymnals. Supplemental hymn publications have grown in popularity, typically including youth camp-style choruses and gospel songs. Instrumental groups have grown in popularity, primarily as ensembles of youth who perform folk and modern gospel music. Handbell choirs for all ages are common and are used mostly as replacements for organ preludes and offertories and as accompaniments to choral groups. Modern interests in psalm singing, chanting, antiphons, and other "liturgical" forms have not gone unnoticed in Christian churches.

The Other Arts

Interest in banners, vestments, and other environmental art has been very modest. Some products of the 1960s and 1970s, the period when popular interest peaked, are still being used. Art expressions within the Disciples of Christ are more of a social experience. Members of churches are sometimes given opportunities to display their crafts, amateur secular photography, and painting. Displaying children's art is common. Liturgical dance is practiced in a handful of congregations.

Disciples rely on the publication efforts of others in all areas of the arts. The church's publication house, the Christian Board of Publication, has contributed an occasional resource in the past, but not in recent times. The church's recent worship resource, *Thankful Praise,* makes only an occasional suggestion for musicians. The Association of Disciple Musicians offers no publications or journals beyond a promotional newsletter.

Dale E. Ramsey

117 • Christian Churches (Independent) and Churches of Christ (Instrumental)

Independent Christian Churches and instrumental Churches of Christ have historically showed a hesitant attitude toward incorporating the arts in worship, believing evangelism to be more important than corporate worship. In recent years, some congregations have moved away from this position and now actively promote the development and use of dramatic and visual components in worship services. All congregations continue to be shaped by a century of singing both traditional hymns and gospel songs.

The development of music and the arts among Christian Churches and Churches of Christ demonstrates the dichotomy of their background. They are the centrist group of the Stone/Campbell Movement of the early nineteenth century. From the beginning the movement was a fragile coalition. Churches joined the brotherhood in the interest of unity but came from a wide variety of backgrounds. On one side of the fence were noninstrumental Churches of Christ, and on the other were the Disciples churches. Each side had its own ideas about the arts. Independent Christian Churches and instrumental Churches of Christ, which are the topic of this article, came from both sides of the fence and met somewhere in the middle.

Hymns or Gospel Songs

By the 1860s, a clear distinction arose between the churches that used hymns only and those that were adopting the new gospel songs. Disciples Churches generally preferred hymns only while Churches of Christ were adding evangelistic gospel songs. The majority of independent Christian Churches probably sided with the noninstrumental churches in using evangelistic gospel songs, but was not the case with all. The battle of hymns versus gospel songs has long been over, but the differing approaches to Sunday morning worship linger on.

Around the middle of the twentieth century, most Christian Churches used hymns for Sunday morning worship services and gospel songs for Sunday evening evangelistic services and for revivals. By the second half of the century many of the churches (but certainly not all) were also using gospel songs on Sunday morning (perhaps more to liven up the service than to sing to the lost).

It was almost universal among these churches that there was virtually no singing of chants or the Psalms, although occasionally service music (calls to worship, prayer response, etc.) was sung by a volunteer choir. Several of the churches used responsive readings; but the clear consensus of the churches was that they wanted to avoid anything that smacked of liturgical worship (i.e., both Roman Catholicism and mainline denominationalism). Use of electric organ and piano was considered pretty upscale for most of the rural churches.

Evangelism or Icons

Christian Churches also have historically avoided the arts, devoting their energies instead to evangelism and seeking primitive biblical simplicity. Some are strictly iconoclastic, but that position is seen more frequently in noninstrumental Churches of Christ. Most churches are built as inexpensively as possible. The churches have tended to emphasize evangelism above worship. Also, any investment in something that is associated with Roman Catholicism or denominationalism is suspect. Hence, when some of the larger churches started erecting "Family Life Centers" (gymnasiums) or installing pipe organs or fountains in their buildings in the 1970s, they were met with some criticism.

Even today, functional art is suspect of being too showy and of evidencing poor stewardship of church resources. The term of choice for a church's meeting center seems to be "auditorium," and the buildings are generally designed for study and prayer, not ceremony. A simple Table and pulpit are typically placed front and center, with the only other noticeable symbolic image perhaps being a plain cross on the wall behind the pulpit. In the hallways there might be an occasional reprint of a painted portrait of Jesus or of some biblical scene, and some of the baptisteries have a mural of a river or water scene painted by a volunteer artist. Pews tend to be in straight rows, facing the elevated platform.

Changes of Renewal

When the Christian Churches began to experience worship renewal in the 1980s, they began to expand their use of music and the arts. While maintaining an interest in evangelism and missions, many of the growing churches are discovering a new appreciation for other worship traditions. Other congregations have had no conscious change in worship philosophy, yet are finding that their traditional assemblies need a new approach for the purpose of evangelism.

Larger churches are designing more lavish buildings, and are including some architectural symbolism. Seating is often in a fan shape, with some sort of architecturally balanced focus on three items: the baptistry, the pulpit, and the Table. Icons are still subtle, perhaps including a dove or a flame set in the brick design over the baptistry, or a rising ceiling going to a steeple behind the pulpit, over the baptistry. Banners are becoming fairly common. These banners are not designed based on the church seasons, but are designed instead to highlight a sermon series or to serve a more general purpose. Drama is used in some of the churches, as a short slice-of-life skit to illustrate the sermon. Liturgical dance is attempted in very few churches, although songs performed with stylized sign language are common, even in churches without an organized ministry to the hearing impaired.

Musically, the larger churches have broadened from a staple diet of gospel anthems to include every kind of music, from gospel to contemporary to classical, with an emphasis on majestic inspirational music from nondenominational publishers. Generally, Christian Churches avoid the "classical" publishing houses and those used by the mainline denominations. Reasons for this include concern for theological differences, concern for relevance to unchurched visitors, and the associations of such music with high church denominations. However, many of the larger churches (in which over 400 persons gather for worship on a Sunday morning) are adding band and orchestral instruments to their Sunday mornings. Many are forming worship teams consisting of "praise bands" of contemporary rhythm sections with a few vocalists to provide leadership to congregational singing and a smooth blending of "special music" with the congregational song. Ironically, although the Christian Churches have been slow in associating with other evangelicals, they do not have their own representative music publisher, so they must purchase music from outside their own group. They have not had their own hymnal for years. The most popular hymnals are _The Hymnal for Worship and Celebration_ and other nondenominational, evangelical hymnals.

Christian Churches and Churches of Christ live in a loose coalition of hesitant artistic progression. Some are progressive contemporary churches, such as Belmont Church in Nashville, where many of the Nashville musicians attend. Others explore "high" art, with full orchestra, pipe organ, and elaborate facilities, such as East 91st Street Christian Church in Indianapolis. Most of the churches are somewhere in between. They are moderate in creative expression, committed to evangelism, and of the conservative evangelical tradition.

Kenneth Read

118 ✦ CHRISTIAN REFORMED CHURCH IN NORTH AMERICA

Strong congregational singing has long marked common worship in the Christian Reformed Church. Psalms only were sung in the Christian Reformed Church until 1934. Since then the Psalter Hymnal _has included hymns from every period of history. Today, congregations are using a greater variety of song and instrumental accompaniment in services designed with flexible liturgical forms. And once-austere buildings and liturgy are now characterized by an increasing use of visual and decorative arts._

———— Music ————

Music in the Christian Reformed Church (CRC) is guided by a Statement of Principle found at the beginning of the denominational _Psalter Hymnal_ (1987), which reads in part: "The music of the church should be appropriate for worship—that is, it should be liturgical and have aesthetic integrity. The music of worship should serve the dialogue between God and his people."

Congregations in the CRC continue a heritage of hearty and solid congregational singing accompanied by organ as the primary music in worship. On a typical Sunday, from three to six hymns and/or metrical psalms are sung from the _Psalter Hymnal_ in both the morning and evening services. The or-

ganist may be a paid staff member helping to plan worship, but is more often a volunteer who accompanies the hymns and plays a prelude, offertory, and postlude.

The heritage of the CRC was one of exclusive metrical psalmody until 1934, when it added hymns in the first edition of the _Psalter Hymnal._ Since 1975, freedom to choose congregational songs beyond the denominational hymnal has resulted in great variety. A 1990 survey showed 78 percent of congregations printing additional songs in bulletins and 37 percent using overhead projectors at least occasionally. Informal song services in the evening are also common.

Beyond congregational singing, choirs are common in congregations in the United States, but are rare in Canadian congregations, where exclusive congregational singing is still the norm. Yet most choirs function as anthem choirs, not service choirs participating every Sunday. Children's choirs and bell choirs are growing in popularity.

Congregations seeking worship renewal have often begun with changes in music, with recent changes in music being evident in three areas:

Repertoire. The 1987 edition of the _Psalter Hymnal_ introduced great stylistic variety, with songs both new and old, European-based and from around the world, challenging and childlike. Though the complete Psalter is present, hymns by far predominate in practice. Most congregations supplement the hymnal with contemporary hymns and choruses, especially in the "praise and worship" style. In a few congregations, hymnals have disappeared in favor of songs projected on overheads.

Instrumental and Vocal Variety. A growing number of congregations have adopted a more contemporary style of music; some have replaced the organist with a variety of instrumentalists, sometimes forming "praise teams" with pianos and/or synthesizers and drums as well as wind and stringed instruments. The traditional anthem choir is shifting its role by more often enhancing congregational singing and helping the congregation learn new songs. There is a growing desire to use members' gifts and to increase congregational participation in worship.

Liturgical Role. Rather than hymns, and perhaps an anthem, filling the same slots in an unchanging liturgical structure, congregations are increasingly making varied musical choices on the basis of a more flexible structure. There is a growing interest in thematically designed worship, in which every action flows in a unified structure so that the people of God understand their role in the meeting between God and his people. The church year is followed most carefully during Advent/Christmas, and increasingly in the Lent/Easter cycle.

The Arts

The traditional CRC building is plain, stained glass windows and carpeting perhaps offering the only variety in color. Even flowers are unusual, except those kept after a wedding or funeral. The typical CRC resembles an auditorium, with fixed pews in rectangular sections facing a raised platform containing a large pulpit with pulpit Bible, baptismal font, Communion table, and a couple of chairs—often all matched in style and containing visual symbols as part of the furniture design. A few have divided chancels or a pulpit and lectern. Flags are sometimes still found in local churches. More affluent churches have added carpeting and padded seats, most often with detrimental acoustical effect.

But the traditional reluctance to visual symbols beyond pulpit, font, and Table—a reluctance rooted in the iconoclastic reforms of the sixteenth century—has faded significantly in the past generation. The most common additional symbol is the cross. A 1990 survey reveals that 82 percent of CRCs use banners for special occasions, 44 percent use banners for the church year, and 24 percent use paraments or Communion table runners. Most ministers wear business suits, a few wear robes, a very small minority wear clerical collars. Vestments are even more rare.

Many churches are designing more flexible worship spaces, with less of a division between platform and pew. With a growing emphasis on gathering around the Word and Table, moveable chairs or pews curving in sections more nearly facing each other are replacing the straight lines and rectangular shapes.

Drama in worship is beginning to grow, especially in evangelistically designed "seeker services." But even in congregations which have not introduced drama, greater attention is paid to dramatic readings directly from the Scriptures. Children's messages, found in over 80 percent of congregations, often include a dramatic component.

Liturgical dance is rare, but growing insofar as it is used as a visual accompaniment to congregational singing of the praise-and-worship style.

Resources

The primary resource for congregational worship in the CRC is its denominational *Psalter Hymnal,* for which many supporting resources are also published, including instrumentations, recordings, a bibliography of organ music, and concordance. A handbook/companion to the *Psalter Hymnal* is in progress. A new children's hymnal and an accompanying leaders' guide for a church education program are also in progress.

The main resource for music and the arts produced by the CRC is *Reformed Worship,* a quarterly journal designed to provide worship leaders with guidance and practical assistance in planning, structuring, and conducting congregational worship in the Reformed tradition. Although produced by the CRC, *Reformed Worship* enjoys both authorship and readership from many different denominations.

Emily R. Brink

119 • Church of God, Anderson, Indiana

A diverse collection of hymns and increasing interest in instruments, graded-choir programs, and new architectural designs mark these Church of God congregations. The visual arts and drama are also more frequently being used in worship. Use of the arts is often determined by the size, location, and leadership of individual congregations.

Diversity is a popular label used to describe trends and practices within many church groups today. The Church of God is no exception to this phenomenon as evidenced by an assessment of the general trends of music and the arts in local congregations.

Music

Since the birth of the Church of God in the late 1800s there has been a gradual move from an exclusive diet of "native" hymnody to a very ecumenical body of hymnody, though a significant number of hymns unique to the Church of God continue to be sung regularly and widely. Church of God hymnody today is significantly influenced by the hallmark of evangelical churches, the gospel song, with its experiential-testimonial emphasis. Traditional hymns are also widely used, especially in metropolitan settings where many denominational backgrounds may be represented in a single church setting. The voluminous increase of praise or Scripture chorus material has also made its mark, especially in newly planted churches and in congregations with a strong outreach ministry to the unchurched.

Any of these categories of hymns may predominate in a given congregation. Numerous factors heavily influence the nature of a congregation's hymnody, including the size, geographical location, and nature of the church's leadership. There does seem to be a commitment, though, in many Church of God settings, to preserving and using the best of all types of hymns.

The Church of God, though characterized as "a singing people," has not historically had many full or part-time persons providing professional leadership to music and arts development. Nor are there national or regional leaders charged with providing full-time direction to this aspect of the church's life. As a result, resources and general publications to support these ministries have been minimal.

However, a strong commitment both to maintain a sizable body of the treasured heritage of hymnody and also to nurture a relevant and unique voice in evangelical Christianity prompted the publication of a new hymnal in 1989 entitled _Worship the Lord—Hymnal of the Church of God._ It has been widely accepted as a worthy successor to its 1971 predecessor. It is a comprehensive volume with generous representation of classic hymns, gospel songs, Church of God heritage hymns, and praise/Scripture choruses. It, too, is a reflection of diversity. A hymnal companion has subsequently been released. Its content focuses on basic reference material and practical instructions for persons involved in worship planning and leadership, whether they be ordained clergy, full or part-time staff, or committed volunteers.

There is an increasing interest in the use of instruments in worship. This is seen as an additional dimension to congregational singing and an avenue for meaningful inclusion of budding or gifted instrumentalists. Orchestral instrumentalists, guitarists, and drummers are represented in solo or duet settings, small ensembles, and occasional (or regular in a few churches) full orchestras. Handbells are frequently used as well.

An increasing number of churches are establishing graded choir programs. Adult choirs are present in most congregations, though in many they may not sing on a weekly basis. The small membership of many Church of God congregations combined with, in most cases, the volunteer nature of leadership often causes the age-groupings for children's choirs to be larger than what might be considered ideal. Their participation is also more likely to be limited to a predetermined program or a selected musical rather than ongoing involvement in worship leadership and music education. However, the focus on children and youth in this regard certainly has merit.

Environmental Art

Numerous churches have engaged in construction programs in recent years, often resulting in new settings for corporate worship. It is not uncommon to see new worship centers designed with flexibility to accommodate the varied set-up needs of diverse programming. Flexible seating (i.e., chairs instead of pews) are frequently included in part, if not all, of the worship center.

The fan-shaped worship center (as opposed to the more traditional long and narrow sanctuary design) is predominant. An increasing trend is a move away from the use of the pulpit. It is not uncommon for a preacher to stand in front of the congregation without a pulpit. These trends, along with other developments, are efforts to foster participation and a sense of "family" among clergy and laity alike.

There is a gradual move to elevate the service of the Table in the worshiping life. This is evidenced by the centrality of the Table itself as well as by a trend toward more frequent observance of Communion. Altar rails continue to be a central part of architectural design and function in many churches, though they are not always visibly prominent in new churches whose target ministry is to the unchurched.

Other worthwhile traditions that for years have been labeled "high church" are being revisited and considered as local congregations try to find appropriate balance between both being part of the historic church and also being a unique, contemporary voice in today's world. The use of banners, liturgical colors, and other art expressions (such as stained glass) are readily found in many churches. It is not uncommon for vestments to be used in some settings, though there is some polarization on this issue. New churches with stated goals of reaching the unchurched tend to shy away from the use of vestments, while established urban congregations and particularly some black churches are very open to their use.

Drama and Dance

Drama in small and large scale form is being increasingly used in worship. Drama presentations are typically short, contemporary, and focused on a single thought, perhaps underscoring a central biblical or preaching theme. In a few isolated places, liturgical or interpretive dance is being included in the worship context. It is seldom used in and of itself, but is typically used in concert with a choral or other musical selection.

A growing interest in worship resources and a renewed commitment by the church's publication arms indicate that an increasing number of related publications may be on the horizon. All of these relevant resources will better enable a diverse church to meet a needy world with the eternal and changeless Christ.

Lloyd Larson

120 • Church of God, Cleveland, Tennessee

Praise choruses with accompanying instrumental support give emotional impact to the proclaimed message in these Church of God congregations. While the decorative arts are used minimally, drama is often featured. Dance, however, remains controversial.

Music

Traditionally, music in the Church of God has been used as a vehicle for worship rather than as an end in itself. The expectation is that the worshiper will engage in worship by relating to the music on an emotional level rather than a cerebral level. This expectation calls for a type of music that speaks to the individual in a direct way. Inasmuch as the denomination grew out of a desire for a personal intimate relationship with God, it follows quite naturally that its music would be rather informal. For many years gospel songs, convention songs, hymns and a few anthems filled the need for worship music.

In recent years music in the Church of God has undergone significant changes. The use of praise choruses has made a tremendous impact on music ministry. In almost every church one will find these choruses used. In some cases, they are used as a means of worship to the exclusion of all other types of music. These choruses meet the need of Pentecostal worship for several reasons. Texts are often taken directly from or are adapted from Scripture. They are usually short and simple, making them easy to learn and easy to sing. It should be noted, however, that these choruses seem to be becoming increasingly more complex in their harmonies and rhythms.

During the past ten years, significant changes have occurred in the area of instrumental music in the Church of God. Many churches of only moderate size and resources have an "orchestra" that provides music for postlude, prelude, offertory and choral accompaniment. In larger churches use of an orchestra is expected. The instrumentalists in these groups are most always amateur musicians, high school and college students, as well as older individuals who have maintained an interest in instrumental music that they acquired in high school.

Central to the orchestra is the rhythm section consisting of piano, trap drum set, bass, and guitar. Added to this core group will be trumpets, trombones, flutes, saxophones, and other wind instruments. Although string parts are included in most arrangements, it is unusual to find strings in most church orchestras. String parts are often covered by the use of synthesizers. Obviously in a volunteer situation such as this, flexibility and adaptability regarding instrumentation are very necessary. Use of electronic organ is common in Church of God worship services. With the advancement of orchestral music however, there is less dependency on this instrument. The pipe organ is not a part of the musical heritage of the Church of God.

The Other Arts

Just as music used in the Church of God leans toward the utilitarian, so does the overall application of the arts in worship. Even in congregations of great resources the use of environmental art is limited to modest displays consisting of stained glass and seasonal decoration. The architecture of the typical Church of God is simple and functional in its design. In the past ten years banners have been added as a part of the decor in some churches. Drama is used often as a part of musical presentations especially at Easter and Christmas. These presentations are of the pageant variety and can be quite lavish in costuming and staging. Drama groups exist as a part of many youth programs in the

Church of God. These groups use drama as a means of addressing contemporary issues as well as outreach.

Liturgical dance remains a controversial issue in the Church of God. It is utilized in only a few churches. There are many congregations that do not accept this art form as a means of worship expression.

The denomination as a whole does not give much attention to the arts. There are no publications that deal with the arts directly. The greatest amount of activity is seen in the area of music publishing where song collections are regularly produced and distributed by the denominationally sponsored publishing house.

Lonnie McCalister

121 • CHURCH OF GOD IN CHRIST

Congregations of the Church of God in Christ have a vibrant tradition of praise singing and free-flowing worship. Music styles range from the traditional call-and-response songs to contemporary gospel music made famous by a variety of recording artists. Both congregational singing and gospel choir music have strong roots in the Church of God in Christ. Church leaders are concerned about keeping music focused on the gospel message of Jesus Christ.

The music tradition of the Church of God in Christ had its origin in the worship services of rural people in the deep South. The early members of the Church were people who were close to the land and did not have much wealth or education. What they did have was a desire to praise God. Therefore, with feet, hands, and voices (often joyously and at high volume), their services featured praise, songs, shouting, and dancing in the spirit. From this very genuine start has developed a unique musical tradition. From its inception, the Church of God in Christ has spawned some of the pioneering giants of religious music, and many of the current recording artists and choirs of today are affiliated with the denomination. Today's Pentecostal worship services offer the same dynamic free-flowing spirit which made the fledgling organization ideal for African-American people.

The history of music in the Church of God in Christ can be appreciated better if one understands the corporate nature of Pentecostal worship. Pentecostals have a time for individual serene and quiet meditation. But when it comes to singing, Pentecostals enjoy the presence of the group. Pentecostals find great pleasure in seeing the demonstration of personal talents being used for God and believe that after one is saved, one's gifts and talents must be used exclusively for the Lord. It is in worship that one's personal fulfillment should be manifested. Thus, a converted jazz singer would quit singing jazz in the ballrooms and bars and give his or her talent back to God exclusively. There was a lot of creative power being channeled through those early local churches and the beat, the melodies, and the harmonies brought into the church approached the contemporary music of the times. The early saints did what they knew how to do while making music, and this created a foundational difference between the Church of God in Christ and others. This free influx of talented people produced what possibly was one of the major influences on the development of the denomination's music. Hence, sacred music for the emerging Church of God in Christ was a mixture of established Negro spirituals and elements of secular origin.

The majority of the saints were simple people without means, and the purchase of song books was not a primary concern. People basically sang what they could remember of songs from their former religious associations. These memories were possibly the second great foundation of the denomination's musical traditions. Often the saints didn't sing the verses of a song, but repeated the refrain over and over. This singing method was referred to as "congregational singing." All of this lent itself well to the spontaneous and free-flowing style of Pentecostal worship. So, the congregational song tradition, in which the song was offered by whoever wanted to sing with the congregation responding, is thoroughly representative of Church of God in Christ worship.

After a time, the exclusive use of those traditional hymns gave way to a spirit of originality. The founder of the Church of God in Christ, Bishop C. H. Mason composed numerous songs. The converted field hands, jazz singers, and blues entertainers were often inspired to write songs compatible with their religious experience. Following the example set by Bishop Mason, people would announce to the congregation that the Lord gave them a song.

The fact that the Church of God in Christ is basically African-American in its origin suggests that the music fits the heritage of the people and was purely Pentecostal in essence. Songs like "I'm A Soldier" have been standards of power and inspiration. For years the call-and-response was the standard method for singing in corporate worship. The call-and-response method is one thing that could be attributed to the African heritage of the Church of God in Christ.

The genuine Pentecostal essence easily conformed to the African experience of the saints. In 1982 the publishing board of the Church of God in Christ published the *Yes Lord Hymnal* and offered a broad song selection representative of the Church's total experience. The hymnal offers everything from "Joyful, Joyful, We Adore Thee" (a text of Henry Van Dyke set to Ludwig Van Beethoven's "Ode to Joy") to Andrae Crouch's "My Tribute." But the richest and most meaningful music in the hymnal is found in the last pages, where the old call-and-response songs are listed.

To understand truly the music of our church's worship, one must appreciate the call-and-response method, which is the standard for congregational singing. The call-and-response song was largely used before choirs became the norm. Handclapping and foot-stomping Pentecostal worship always carried the saints into a fully committed style of corporate worship. The hymnal includes this third category of songs because of its importance in the life of the church. The authors of the hymnal further established that the musical accompaniment for the call-and-response songs specifically and musically fit three basic patterns of lyrics. This means that numerous songs were basically arranged to three scores of music. If a piano player could manage to play three standard tunes he or she could play hundreds of songs. Therefore, "Have You Tried Jesus?" had basically the same music as "If You Call On Jesus." Likewise, "I'm a Soldier" and "Just Life Fire," could be sung to the same music and rhythm. The original composers, teachers, and instrumentalists were the pioneering saints who for the most part were untrained but understood what worked. Bishop Mason would also make up little songs from Scripture and life's experiences. Most of his songs fit the three musical patterns that characterized most call-and-response songs. Bishop Mason's most well-known contribution was the praise song "Yes Lord!" for which the official church hymnal is named. This composition was different from the usual call-and-response song and promoted the singing of the same word in unison. The entire song has the two words: "Yes Lord!" The preface in the song book offers the following about what the praise means to the Church of God in Christ.

"Yes Lord!" The sound of this phrase bespeaks a high exaltation found in God. Since the inception of the Church of God in Christ, the praise "Yes Lord!" has carried a wealth of spiritual meaning. Bishop C. H. Mason sang this quite free, dynamic, and spiritually lifting praise to pull the congregation together in commitment and spiritual communion. When the saints sing, "Yes Lord!" we are saying "Yes" to God's will; "Yes" to God's way; and "Yes" to God's direction in our lives.

In a Church of God in Christ worship service one will hear hymns, gospel songs, praise choruses, and psalms. The variety of musical instruments is ever-expanding. At one point, the saints simply had clapping hands and stomping feet to go along with simplicity of verse. Possibly one of the first musical instruments that was seen in the brush harbors and store fronts of long ago was the spoons and washboard. Then the saints graduated to the tambourine. Now nearly every local church has a Hammond organ, drums, guitars, and horns, along with beautifully robed choirs that grace the Sunday morning services.

To appreciate the importance of a choir in the present Church of God in Christ, one must make a comprehensive study of the nature and function of choirs. Dr. Mattie Moss Clark, National President of the Church of God in Christ Music Department has shared her views. Dr. Clark is responsible for recording the very first gospel choir and is the recipient of three gold albums. The Southwest Michigan State Choir was a landmark group and an award-winning trend setter in the music industry. Dr. Clark is credited with improving the singing skills of choirs when she introduced formal parts for the tenor, alto, and soprano sections of the choir. She initially began writing songs in order to create a standard of music for holiness-Pentecostal churches. Her desire was to reflect the experience of Pentecostal people in music, but more importantly, to present clear scriptural and descriptive lyrics which pointed to a loving relationship with God. Dr. Clark reflected, "The music must be Christ centered and provide the sense of ministry to which one is motivated." Choirs are a standard part of the local church.

Dr. Clark has said that she fashioned the choir as the veil upon the face of the bride of Christ. If the

Church is the body of Christ, then the choir is the veil, symbolizing innocence. In the words of Dr. Clark, "Choir members need to be saved and able to sing with conviction about matters of faith and salvation. Just as the veil means a type of purity, so too the choir should be made of righteous individuals." In the Church of God in Christ choirs are a vital source of evangelism and a help in stabilizing and developing youth in the church. Singing gives youth something tangible to do and a significant role to play in the ministry of the church.

When asked about modern trends in music, Dr. Clark stated that a large amount of the artists are interested in the money. With the exceptions of "Oh Happy Day" by Edwin Hawkins, and "You Brought the Sunshine" by the Clark Sisters, contemporary music has largely ventured into the crossover market with gospel music. One strange fact is that many current contemporary artists never mention the name Jesus. This leads many traditional artists to believe that some record companies produce music for a market, not ministry, and money becomes the chief aim of many contemporary groups. Real gospel music is about Jesus and his saving grace in the life of people. It is not merely "music with a message" as many artists of inspirational music state. "Gospel music must be Christ-centered." She further stated that gospel music's greatest challenge is to remain sacred. "Churches everywhere must draw the line about the form and expressions gospel music will take," stated Dr. Clark. She is fearful that the art form and sacredness of gospel could be jeopardized by attempting to meet market demands, especially if those markets are not serious about Christian standards.

Dr. Clark's desire for choirs everywhere is to train them to deliver music that will help the Pentecostal message reach the masses. In the International Holy Convocation of the Church of God in Christ, the founder's day worship service begins with an antiphon, hymns, and gospel selections. The instruments such as guitars, synthesizers, horns, and string instruments are all incorporated into the body of music. The origins and trends in music in the Church of God in Christ are representative of the Pentecostal focus of the saints and typifies the experience of the cultural blend that religion in America truly is.

David Hall

122 • CHURCH OF THE BRETHREN

Singing has always been a central aspect of Church of the Brethren worship. A recently published hymnal promises to sustain this tradition while expanding the repertoire, musical styles, and instruments used by most congregations. In recent years, the use of the visual arts in worship have increased, and the variety of banners and symbols is now more widespread in Church of the Brethren worship than ever before.

Music

When Brethren first came to North America, they sang in German and made a gradual switch to English. Various hymnals were published in the nineteenth century for congregational worship. During the twentieth century four hymnals have been published for congregation use, the most recent being _Hymnal: A Worship Book_. Published in 1992, it is the result of a cooperative project by the Church of the Brethren, the General Conference Mennonite Church, and the Mennonite Church.

Until near the end of the nineteenth century, hymns were lined, with the minister reading a line and a chorister setting the tune. The congregation would respond in unison or four-part a cappella singing. No musical instruments were allowed until the twentieth century at which time the piano and organ were slowly and reluctantly brought into the sanctuary.

Today various instruments are heard in many congregations. The piano and organ are the most familiar, although strings and brass are also occasionally used. The guitar has also become more common and in the newest hymnal, guitar chord markings are included with folk songs and choruses. Handbell choirs are heard in a small percentage of churches. With the introduction of shared-culture hymns in _Hymnal: A Worship Book,_ more rhythm instruments undoubtedly will find their place in worship. At the same time that the greatest variety of instruments has been incorporated in the history of Brethren worship, there also is a resurgence of a cappella singing.

For Brethren, music is considered not only an aid to worship but an act of worship itself. Some brethren consider congregational singing as important as preaching. Many styles of music are sung, including chorales, gospel songs, Scripture songs, spirituals, ethnic, and classical hymns. Contemporary hymnody in the style of a melody line and a flowing accompaniment requires Brethren to sing some hymns in unison, although historically their preference has been four-part harmony. Antiphons and psalmody, which have had only token representation in past Brethren hymnals, enjoy more exposure in the most recent hymnal. Whether Brethren are willing to sing hymns in the style of chant has yet to be tested.

Themes in hymnody range from praise of God, Jesus Christ, and the Holy Spirit, to peace, social justice, discipleship, stewardship, and personal salvation. Hymns with themes based on the Brethren ordinances, such as anointing, laying on of hands, Believers' baptism, love feast, and footwashing, have also been written by Brethren. Brethren authors and composers continue to be represented in the denominational hymnal, not merely because they have been loved and respected, but because their hymns help Brethren identify with our Anabaptist/pietist roots.

The Arts

Traditionally the visual arts have not been as important as music in Brethren worship. For most of their history, Brethren have worshiped in very simple buildings with nothing of artistic appeal to catch the eye. According to one historian,

> Neither inside nor outside was a dollar spent for any sort of ornamentation. The style of architecture was bare in its simplicity, and far removed from such vanities as spires, towers, stained windows, painted or cushioned pews, ornamental pulpits, or anything else which could not show the passport of indispensable utility . . . (Henry R. Holsinger, *History of the Tunkers and the Brethren Church* [Oakland, Calif.: Pacific Press Publishing Co., 1901], 243–244)

In a recent publication, *Sign and Symbol in the Church of the Brethren,* author Patricia Kennedy Helman agrees, as she states:

> It is noted often in the writings of the mystics that one can have a religious experience by either feasting or fasting. The members of the Church of the Brethren chose to fast in their style of worship in the plain meetinghouse, with no statuary, no paintings or stained glass, no incense or candles, no musical instruments, nothing to command the senses. Nothing but the sounds of their own voices rising and falling in cadence. Nothing but the hope that when the presence of God was invoked they would

sense affirmation! ([Elgin, Ill.: Brethren Press, 1991], 19)

At the 1971 Annual Conference a small group of persons organized together into what has become known as The Association for the Arts in the Church of the Brethren (AACB). This group encourages and recognizes artists, writers, dramatists, and musicians within the denomination. Since 1971 the Association has actively influenced art at Annual Conference by submitting designs for the conference logo, by sponsoring annual quilting and a quilt auction, and by sponsoring *Art for Hunger.* In addition, AACB publishes a newsletter for its members, holds workshops, and creates worship resources. Above all, "their main contribution has been the liberating of the artistic spirit within the church." (Ibid., 74).

Today's worship environment is very different from that of early Brethren worship. Early Brethren churches had a plain table for the ministers, on the same level as the congregation. Later, Communion tables were introduced. Today, the term altar or worship center is used, signifying a more liturgical style of worship. The worship environment may include banners, worship centers designed around a given theme, candles, an open Bible, and a cross. Symbols are used on the church's letterhead and denominational materials. The cover of the 1992 *Hymnal: A Worship Book* includes an Anabaptist symbol of the lamb in the midst of briars, denoting "the suffering lamb of God who calls the faithful to obedient service." (The cover symbol of *Hymnal: A Worship Book* is described on the fly leaf of the book.)

Vestments are worn by some pastors, as are robes by some choirs. Although there is a strong feeling that the pastor and choir ought not to be separated from the congregation, the decision is made according to local practice.

Liturgical dance has encountered skepticism because to some it symbolizes undisciplined and worldly living. In the past decade, many congregations have found meaning in chancel drama and storytelling. The core of Brethren heritage is the charge that calls members to radical discipleship to Christ. Any sound or sight which would deter them from that faithfulness would be seriously questioned for its appropriateness in both worship and daily living.

Nancy Rosenberger Faus

123 ✦ CHURCH OF THE NAZARENE

Worship services in Church of the Nazarene congregations feature an extensive amount of music, most of which consists of nineteenth-century gospel songs and contemporary praise choruses. Choral and vocal solo selections are as important as congregational singing. Many congregations are currently eagerly seeking worship renewal, often borrowing practices from either liturgical or charismatic traditions.

From prelude to postlude, Nazarene worship is replete with music. Congregations are led in spirited singing of hymns, gospel songs, and choruses, often in succession and usually accompanied by piano, organ, or both. Choirs are fairly common and special music such as vocal or instrumental solos, duets, trios, and ensembles are routine. Vocalists generally prefer to use taped accompaniment, guitar, or synthesizer and tend to mimic contemporary Christian entertainers in terms of selections and style. Guest artists or visiting choirs are occasionally employed to offer a concert in lieu of the traditional worship service.

Since the Church of the Nazarene was organized at the turn of the twentieth century, its worship understandably bears the influence of both frontier worship and the camp-meeting tradition. It is fair to say that Nazarene worship has an evangelistic flair. Gospel songs and choruses tend to overshadow hymns and anthems. Scripture songs and other praise choruses are especially popular, and music done *for* the congregation is just as likely as music done *by* the congregation.

While services almost always end with some kind of choral response to the sermon, some services end with an altar service. Standard "invitational songs" such as "Just As I Am" or "Softly and Tenderly" are sung, sometimes repetitiously, by the congregation while the pastor invites seekers to come to the altar for prayer.

Perhaps *Worship in Song* (Kansas City, Mo.: Lillenas Publishing Company, 1972), the denomination's official hymnal since 1972, best reflects Nazarenes' music preference. Of the 510 entries, only 37 are designated as "worship" hymns or songs. The bulk of the hymnal is given to gospel songs, Wesley tunes, and songs unique to the holiness movement of which the Church of the Nazarene is a part.

In the past ten years, the Nazarene's Lillenas Publishing Company has produced two hymnal supple-

ments that have been well received by the denomination. The 1984 edition of *Exalt Him* and the 1987 release of *Master Chorus Book* included new hymns, gospel songs, and a heavy dose of praise music, the genre of choice. The more popular selections from the 1972 hymnal and the two hymnal supplements were significant in the preparation of the new Nazarene hymnal, *Sing to the Lord*, scheduled for release in 1993.

Historically, Nazarenes have not been inclined to use the arts in worship. Many Nazarene churches have pulpit-centered sanctuaries accented with stained glass windows, a cross, and the Communion table. In contrast, banners celebrating the Christian year, baptismal fonts, and liturgical dance are generally foreign to Nazarene worship. While drama has long played a role in congregational life, only of late has it enjoyed a more routine role in some parts of the country.

Three divergent trends in Nazarene worship renewal are evident. Olivet College Church of the Nazarene, Kankakee, Illinois, bears the influence of Bill Hybel's Willow Creek model. "Seeker sensitive" services feature dramatic readings, mini-dramas, and upbeat praise music lead by a worship team.

A second approach in Nazarene worship is evident at the Fairibault Church of the Nazarene, Fairibault, Minnesota. There, Christ-centered worship often begins with the unison reading of the Psalms, an Entrance hymn, and the Lord's Prayer prayed in unison or sung by the congregation. The *Gloria Patri* follows. Obvious is the use of the lectionary, the Apostle's Creed, and doxology. Congregational participation is preferred over special individual offerings. Though other examples of this liturgical bent are recognized, it barely qualifies as a trend among Nazarenes.

The rapidly growing Grove City Church of the Nazarene, Grove City, Columbus (Ohio), exemplifies the more popular trend in Nazarenes committed to renewal. On the heels of pastoral greeting, the congregation sings, without interruption, five choruses, one hymn and the verse of yet another hymn, all of which is followed by the choir, special music, offertory, prayer chorus, prayer, more special music, and the sermon. Newsworthy events in the life of the church are offered in the worship folder in lieu of a printed order of service.

Though traces of worship renewal can be documented, Nazarenes tend to be fond of their near century-old tradition of free worship. Accordingly, they have never insisted on uniformity in worship style, a practice that fosters a spirit of toleration and that allows for both diversity in renewal and the retention of tradition.

Randall E. Davey

124 • CHURCHES OF CHRIST (NONINSTRUMENTAL)

Worship services of the Churches of Christ are marked by the complete absence of musical instruments. All of the music is unaccompanied singing. The music heard most frequently is, nevertheless, quite diverse and includes a wide range of classic hymns and gospel songs. While congregational singing is the foundation of worship music, choirs and special singing groups are sometimes included. Many congregations now use modern songs that speak more directly to younger people in place of older texts, with their agricultural and seafaring metaphors. The visual arts are not emphasized, although increased attention is being given to the worship setting. Drama is slowly being introduced in some churches.

Music

Music in Churches of Christ is unique among evangelical churches. The first thing most visitors notice when they attend a worship service is the absence of musical instruments. Churches of Christ sing a cappella (without instrumental accompaniment). This practice is based upon the belief that musical instruments were not used in Christian worship until around 1600 A.D. Feelings surrounding the use of instruments in worship were so strong that the introduction of a piano in worship was one of the primary factors that split the American Restoration Movement of the nineteenth century into the Disciples of Christ (who chose to use instruments) and Churches of Christ.

There is a great diversity of music in Churches of Christ, including great classic hymns in the Watts-Wesley genre, gospel song classics from the nineteenth century Crosby-Doane era, and gospel songs in the twentieth century tradition of R. E. Winsett and Stamps-Baxter. Most hymnals used in this fellowship include time-honored hymn tunes such as "ARLINGTON," "AZMON," "CONSOLATION," "DUKE STREET," "MERCY," "OLD HUNDREDTH," and "ST. PETER." Music scholars within Churches of Christ say there is a body of some 1,000 or more hymns that have endured from generation to generation since the beginnings of the Restoration Movement in the early 1800s.

Although most Christians do not realize it, many religious musical traditions come from secular music on the American frontier. Christian writers frequently adopted favorite recreational tunes and added Christian words to them. Many religious traditions continue to cherish songs that were made popular during this period. For some older church members, any other type of music simply is not "church music."

Churches of Christ have avoided choirs and emphasized congregational singing in the assembly. Although congregational singing remains the predominant musical mode, many congregations committed to worship renewal have begun to make limited use of choirs and special singing groups. Many of them use a variety of methods to encourage singing. Some congregations use a worship team. This team is usually comprised of a quartet (sometimes including two women singing the soprano and alto parts) who lead the congregation in singing. Traditional congregations call on one man to lead the entire congregation, but worship teams allow the congregation to hear the four-part harmony more easily and clearly. This aids in teaching new music. It is not uncommon for renewing churches to employ full-time ministers of music who are trained musicians and who work primarily as worship coordinators and leaders.

Occasionally, congregations have a chorus that sings to the congregation. This is different from the traditional choir in most other religious groups. There are no choir lofts in Churches of Christ. These choruses may stand in front of the people, but more often than not, they stand to the side or in the back or in the balcony. A chorus might sing a new song that teaches an important lesson or that motivates other worshipers to focus on the Lord more clearly. Although a growing number of congregations are experimenting with such groups, there is no reason to believe that Churches of Christ will abandon their love for and commitment to congregational singing.

Renewing churches are making a commitment to music that praises God and causes worshipers to fix their gaze above rather than on one another. There is a place for songs like "Onward, Christian Soldiers," which are primarily designed to help believers encourage one another. Renewing churches, however, believe they should sing more songs that adore the Lord such as "O Worship the King" and "There's Something About That Name." The older hymnbooks contain far more songs with a generally inspiring focus than a God-centered focus. Therefore, renewing churches supplement their hymnals with new songs shown on overhead projectors or distributed on song sheets. Hymnals used in Churches of Christ, such as _Great Songs of the Church_ (Abilene, Tex.: ACU Press), have recently undergone revisions to reflect these concerns. _Praise for the Lord_ (Nashville: Praise Press) is a new hymnal that includes about 80 contemporary hymns along with almost eight hundred well-known standards. The _Singers Worship Series,_ edited by Ken Young and produced by Hallel Music in Irving, Texas, provides new song sheets, music, and cassette tapes to individuals and congregations desiring to learn and use new praise music.

Many of the old songs, while expressing eternal truths, use agricultural and seafaring metaphors that no longer speak to many younger people. Therefore, renewing congregations strive to include music that is contemporary and that reflects the feelings of the worshipers. Although Churches of Christ use no instruments of music in the worship assembly, many of the younger generation have a profound appreciation for modern contemporary Christian music and feel deeply blessed by it.

———— The Other Arts ————

Art has never played a significant role in this tradition. However, a growing number of congregations are beginning to give attention to this aspect of worship. Many assembly halls have semicircular seating where people can see one another and interact more easily. The Garnett Church of Christ in Tulsa, Oklahoma, has a round auditorium with the platform in the center. In many congregations, large wooden pulpits have been replaced with clear plexiglass podiums. Stationary microphones have been replaced with cordless lapel microphones. All of this is designed to remove the barriers that might distance worshipers from those leading in worship.

The Lord's Supper is the central event in worship. Churches of Christ partake of the bread and the cup every Lord's Day. The physical placement of the Lord's Table varies from church to church. Some congregations place it in the front in the most prominent position possible. Usually it sits immediately in front of the pulpit. Occasionally it sits behind the pulpit but is elevated on a platform above it.

No vestments are used in Churches of Christ. A growing number of congregations are using banners and hangings to direct worshiper's minds to spiritual truths. The Madison Church of Christ in Madison, Tennessee, the largest Church of Christ in the world, chose the theme "Victory in Jesus" for its first banners. Each of the two banners is about twenty-five feet long and hangs on either side of the stage.

Drama is slowly making its way into the worship of renewing congregations. The Madison church has begun using drama. Occasionally its preacher will assume the role of a Bible character (even dressed as the person might have dressed in biblical days) and preach a "first-person sermon." However, most of the drama occurs at times other than the Sunday morning assembly. For its "Summer Spectacular" (a new night-time approach to a Family Vacation Bible School), the Madison church has staged rather elaborate productions such as the story of Noah and Jonah and the Great Fish. On Sunday and Wednesday evenings, this congregation has done such events as a dramatic reading of the story of Job. The Madison church has a troupe of teenage actors called the Prime Time Players who perform modern situational dramas, each of which is designed to teach some biblical truth or principle for godly living.

Dan Dozier

125 ✦ CONGREGATIONAL CHURCHES

Congregational meetinghouses of the traditional kind express the early character of Congregationalism, especially in the central location of the pulpit. Subsequent renovations have attempted to embody a variety of theological commitments. Careful consideration has also been given to the appointments of Congregationalist meetinghouses. In addition, several Congregationalist artists have been in the forefront of the liturgical dance movement.

———— The Meetinghouse ————

Congregational church art and architecture focus on the character and appointments of the meetinghouse. The theological statement of a meetinghouse is that followers of Jesus Christ gather to meet with each other and with God. A meetinghouse is not a church; a church is a body of Christ's followers who have voluntarily covenanted with God and with one another and have gathered in a community for Scripture reading and exposition, prayer, praise, preaching, Christian nurture, and service. The design of meetinghouses is directed toward the end of fostering these functions of the community of believers.

Historical Background. Early American meetinghouses were simple, and decoration or embellishment was minimal. The arts, it was felt, needed to be checked because they were so easily turned to the service of idolatry. The meetinghouses and their appointments, however, were not devoid of symbolism. The Old South Meetinghouse in Boston (1720) has a 180-foot wooden steeple, often alluded to as a "finger of God," surmounted by a weather cock, an emblem of the sovereignty of God (Federal Writers Project, Massachusetts [Boston, 1939], 155f.). More overt figurative symbols, banished from the interior of meetinghouses, often flourished just outside the doors in the burial ground. Sculptors such as Nathaniel Fuller turned their imaginations loose on gravestones, depicting skulls, faces, heads, and hearts embellished with wings, geometric patterns, doves, sunbursts, hourglasses, acorns, and inscriptions (Peter Benes, *The Masks of Orthodoxy* [Amherst: University of Massachusetts Press, 1977], 21ff.).

By the time of American independence, a body of principles guiding the construction of meetinghouses had grown up. In witness to the character of worship, architect and carpenter Asher Benjamin published in 1797 *The American Builder's Companion,* in which he suggested proper uses for classical forms such as the Doric, Ionic, Corinthian, and Composite orders (reprint, New York: Dover Books, 1969, 34–37). Successive editions of the *Builder's Companion* were used in the construction of hundreds of meetinghouses.

From about 1870 to 1930 gothic architecture and elaborate orders of worship appeared, signaling a new openness to traditional "catholic" elements of worship and ecclesiastical art. Representative examples are Mount Holyoke College Chapel in brownstone, First Congregational Church of Kalamazoo in brick, and the First Congregational Church of Los Angeles in cement.

The twentieth century produced new plans for meetinghouses and building complexes. Colonial Church of Minneapolis erected a group of buildings replicating a colonial New England village green

(c. 1970). Oneonta Congregational Church in South Pasadena created seven buildings grouped around a central lawn and gardens, designed in accord with the themes of faith, freedom, and fellowship (Henry David Gray, *Guide Book to the Oneonta Congregational Church Buildings* [South Pasadena, Calif., 1950]).

Reconstruction is a centuries-old habit in Congregational meetinghouses. Difficult decisions, both historical and theological, are required, however, in the process of renovating or adding to existing structures. In 1873, for example, the 1827 interior of Second Church in Hartford was virtually made over with new windows, platform, pulpit, pews, and wood paneling in a style which might be called Victorian. "The great window behind the pulpit," says the church's historian, "was walled up and inscribed with the Lord's Prayer, the creed, and other suitable texts" (E. P. Parker, *History of Second Church in Hartford* [Hartford: Belknap and Warfield, 1892]). In 1920, the 250th anniversary of its gathering, Hartford's South Church recreated the original interior and added an enormous chandelier suspended from the 1873 domed, pantheon-like ceiling. Pews were moved to provide for doorways and space for choirs, drama, and sacred dance.

Typically nineteenth and twentieth-century Congregational churches have added facilities to serve many needs, opening a special opportunity to revisit earlier years, learn from them, and seek to reconstruct or to add functions while retaining the architectural and spiritual intent of the meetinghouse. Reconstructions usually demand a central theme, and a favorite among American Congregationalists has been freedom to worship, one of the themes of the Oneonta Meetinghouse in Pasadena.

Furnishings and Symbolism. Although the central symbols of congregational worship have remained constant—Bible, pulpit, and Table—the quantity and variety of symbolic artworks have increased greatly over the last century and a half. The open Bible on central pulpit or table proclaims the right and duty of every member to read and interpret the Scriptures. Harvard and Yale colleges were established to provide educated ministers for the church, and members were also expected to know how to think.

In eighteenth-century meetinghouses the pew arrangement was lengthwise around the pulpit and Table, as in the Old South Meetinghouse in Boston

(1729). Old South pews were family-oriented, square, and elevated, with children facing their parents and with foot warmers provided for relief from winter cold (Henry David Gray, _Old South Congregational Church_ [Hartford, 1970]). In the nineteenth century the pews crossed the narrow width. The pulpit and table were raised at one end of the building with the chief entrance doors at the other. This rearrangement mirrored a change from family-gathered-round-the-pulpit to audience-chamber whose occupants were to observe a civic/religious duty and voluntary attendance.

Old meetinghouses used plain glass or later cathedral glass (frosted clear glass). One of the earliest Congregational churches to use stained glass was Center Church, Hartford, whose memorial windows depicted scriptural and symbolic figures (Rockwell Harmon Potter, _Hartford's First Church_ [Hartford, 1932]). Asylum Hill Congregational Church provided a rationale for memorial windows in its _Systematic Plan for Memorial Windows, 1913_ (L. B. Paton and E. K. Mitchell [Hartford, 1939]). In some churches the original window on the east wall behind the pulpit was bricked up, covered with drapes, or replaced with the tablets of the law.

In pre-1950 meetinghouses, the pulpit was elaborately crafted with motifs from the classical orders and biblical inscriptions relating to the Word of God and featured beautifully wrought spiral stairs. The Communion table in a Congregational church is a true table and not a high altar set apart from the people. Set out from the east wall with the minister behind it and the deacons encircling its sides, it invites and includes the people. One of the chalices of the Old South Church in Boston is dated 1607, the oldest Communion cup in use in America; another is the famous chalice made by Paul Revere (Frederick M. Meek, _Brief History and Guide_ [Boston: Old South Church, n.d.]). Baptismal fonts vary in form from standard circular or octagonal fonts located near entrances to silver vessels held by deacons.

Clothwork has reentered the meetinghouses as weavers and embroiderers have contributed tapestries, pulpit panels, and cushion covers. A beautiful and functional crewel tapestry designed by Pauline Baynes and created by church women adorns Plymouth Congregational Church in Minneapolis, and improves the acoustics. It depicts "the story of congregationalism and its contribution to American history" (Howard Conn, _A Hand Always Above My Shoulder_ [Edina, Minn.: Aberfoyle Press, n.d.], 17).

Dramatic Arts in Worship

The Congregational churches have also been active in incorporating dramatic arts and dance in worship. The beginnings of these practices can be traced to the solemn processions of the Pilgrims into the meetinghouse at Plymouth colony (described in _Three Visitors to Early Plymouth,_ ed. by Sydney V. James, Jr. [Plymouth: Plymouth Plantation, 1963], 76–77). Pioneers in liturgical dance include Ted Shawn; the First Congregational Church, Berkeley; Margaret Palmer Fisk, who inaugurated dance choirs at Dartmouth Congregational Church, Hanover, N.H., from 1938 to 1950; and Helen L. Gray, Ruth St. Denis, and Jerry Green of Oneonta Congregational Church. By 1991 the Sacred Dance Guild, founded in Boston in 1958, had enrolled 770 members in North America. A plethora of books offer manuals, scripts, diagrams, directions and rationales (see Margaret Fisk Taylor, _A Time to Dance,_ revised ed. [Philadelphia: United Church Press, 1981]; Christena L. Schlundt, _Ruth St. Denis, and Ted Shawn_ [New York: New York Public Library, 1950]; Helen L. Gray, _As We Pray Together_ [Los Angeles: Oneonta Congregational Church, 1952]).

The inherent freedom of Congregational churches has encouraged the presentation of Christian faith in choral speech, liturgy with acolytes, crucifer and lay readers, dramas, passion plays, and music. No "authority" is permitted to crib or confine each church's freedom to express the gospel of the God and Father of our Lord Jesus Christ in ways of its own choosing.

Henry David Gray

126 • The Eastern Orthodox Churches

The trend among Eastern Orthodox churches in America is to return to the customs of the ancient church in architecture, icons, and music. However, some churches are writing new music in an American idiom, but always with the ancient tradition in mind. In every case, music, iconography, and architecture are used as servants to the liturgy.

The Orthodox Churches of America share a common faith but a diverse ethnic heritage. There are more than sixteen jurisdictions of churches that call themselves Orthodox, but the form of worship is one, and the faith they hold is one. Three large groups serve as especially important models in America: the Greek Orthodox Church, the Antiochian Orthodox Church, and the Orthodox Church in America, with its Slavic roots.

According to ancient evidence and scriptural tradition, the worship of the Christian church developed around the hours of prayer, as in the synagogue, together with the living remembrance of Christ's sacrifice on the cross, expressed in the Divine Liturgy (the preparation, Word, and Holy Communion service). It was emphasized by the apostle that we are spiritually "seated with Christ in the heavenlies" and "have come to the Mount Zion, and to the City of the Living God, the heavenly Jerusalem, and to innumerable angels in festal gathering, and to the assembly of the firstborn who are enrolled in heaven, and to God, the Judge of all, and to the spirits of the just made perfect, and to Jesus, the Mediator of the New Covenant, whose blood speaks more graciously than the blood of Abel" (Heb. 12:22-23). These texts, along with biblical Psalms, canticles, and descriptions of heavenly worship, formulate both the reality of Orthodox worship and its goal.

Formal Orthodox worship takes place both in the Christian "temple," the sacred space set apart for worship, and the home, likewise consecrated by a yearly dedication. In the home, worship is characterized by prayers, psalms, Bible readings, grace at meals, and the "family altar," whereupon may be displayed sacred pictures (icons), a cross, the Bible, blessed water, and perhaps incense. These are constant reminders that the home is the "little church," often called by the Orthodox "the domestic church," of which Christ is the head to whom the members are subject.

Orthodox worship is, in a certain sense, a continuation of Old Testament temple worship, but more significantly, it is an expression of its fulfillment in Christ. It is not subject to innovation, yet it seeks to adapt itself to the circumstances of modern life. It has been said that the Orthodox church changes only to remain the same. Yet in order to remain the same—faithful to the apostolic tradition—the American church has adapted itself to assure the fuller participation of the faithful in the services, as well as to expand its missionary outreach.

Architecture

The Orthodox church building, or "temple," must reflect the theology that undergirds it, both in its architecture and in its appointments. Typically, the building is square or rectangular in shape and includes three significant areas: an outer narthex or portico, the body of the church in which the faithful gather, and the sanctuary, wherein the celebrants stand for much of the service. The latter area is slightly raised above the level of the rest of the church. In front of the screen or railing separating the sanctuary from the body of the church is the *ambo,* the portion of the platform where the sermon is read, blessings are given, and the congregation comes forward for Communion. Central to the interior is the "throne," or altar table, whereon the Communion gifts are consecrated and the Gospels are kept in honor.

The trend in church architecture is toward functionality, simplicity, and the expression of Orthodoxy within the American culture. For example, there is a desire in many churches to take out the choir loft, in order to restore the sense of "singing with one voice," the Orthodox ideal for worship that promotes the participation of the entire worshiping community. Instead of singing from a loft, the choir sings on the same floor as the congregation, leading rather than representing them in song. In addition, the icon screen, which was formerly built rather like a wall in Slavic churches, is often made less solidly, so that all the participants may see the celebrants clearly. This "innovation" is in fact a restoration of the early ideal—full participation of the people of God in the Divine Liturgy.

Icons

Iconography, the ancient art of sacred painting, plays an important part in Orthodox worship. Although grounded in Scripture, it is often confused with the worship of images, which is strictly forbidden. Within the temple and the home, icons are displayed to direct the mind and heart toward God, and thus are sometimes called "windows on heaven." Fr. John Breck succinctly states the theology of the icon:

> An icon painted on a piece of wood
> Becomes a window on reality
> Through which a man in prayer can see the
> good
> and perfect image of divinity.

Through matter Spirit comes to speak the truth
That unto endless ages yet shall last
And, first proclaimed when faith was in its
    youth,
Unites the present moment with the last.

An icon is not a simple picture or portrait, painted according to the whim of the artist; it is a spiritual statement "written" within strict and ancient guidelines. While they are not in themselves objects of worship, icons are venerated because they represent the timeless and ever-present Kingdom of God present with us as a "great cloud of witnesses" (Heb. 12:1):

The faithful fruit of fasting and of prayers
This hallowed image formed by brush and paints
The message of the Liturgy declares
That we are called to be one with the saints
Whose glory proves that by some sacred plan
The icon of the Unseen God is man.

A widespread trend toward excellence in iconography is encouraged by schools of iconography and associations of iconographers. The availability of superb textbooks, prints, and teachers has brought about a renaissance in this ancient and difficult art.

———— Music ————

The Orthodox church is a singing church, using more music in its worship than any other Christian body of believers. In the Divine Liturgy, for example, almost everything but the sermon (and, in some churches, the Lord's Prayer and creed) is sung, either by celebrants or by the assembly.

Sacred song has been called "the heightened speech of worship." It is "worship, especially when it is Scripture we are singing. It characterizes the body of Christ, as if we are one gathered singing assembly, singing in unison with the angels. It should not be an accompaniment, background, preparation, a moodsetter, filler, or any such thing. It is serious and certainly not a _divertimento_" (Fr. Sergei Glagolev). Following the understanding of the early church, even the Scriptures are chanted, rather than read. That is not because the early Christians did not have good acoustics or electronic enhancement, but because they believed, according to Jewish precedent, that it was disrespectful to the Word of God merely to read the text; it must be proclaimed in song.

In today's church, as in the early church, most music is unaccompanied. There are several reasons for this. First, the instruments available to the first Christians were used in pagan worship and not thought seemly for Christian use. Second, the Jews laid aside their instruments in mourning for the destruction of the Temple, and the Jewish converts to Christianity no doubt followed their lead. But more important than these considerations was (and is) the idea that instrumental music is not worded, as is vocal music, and an instrumental solo or ensemble cannot replace the unified people of God "singing with one voice" in his praise.

Orthodox church music is not meant for performance, with the exception of some elaborate later settings that are more appropriate to the concert hall. Choirs and individual cantors are used, but their music is meant to be a simple expression of praise that elevates the soul and not something sung to elicit an emotional response. The music is based upon a tonal system, that is, upon simple melodies that can be learned by all the people, so that when one might hear, "The _Prokeimenon_ (gospel hymn) is in the eighth tone," one would know what to expect and how to respond antiphonally. This tonal system, along with the practice of "lining" some of the hymns, allows the congregation to sing whether they can read music or not.

Johann von Gardner aptly states the philosophy of Orthodox music in these words:

Since the Church in a sense is timeless, existing both outside of time and encompassing all of time, its singing also must preserve the traditions of the past while maintaining a link with the present. Above all, the singing of the Church must never stray from its central essence: the liturgy. It must avoid at all cost the tendency to pursue exclusively aesthetic or personal, subjective goals. Only a thorough knowledge of the entire system and history of Orthodox liturgical singing will enable this middle ground to be found.

In spite of what may seem to be rigidity in its tradition, the Orthodox church has witnessed a tremendous resurgence of scholarship and creativity in its music for worship. There is the same sense of excitement about the rediscovery of excellent traditional music as there is regarding excellent iconography and architecture.

Research and scholarship have uncovered a treasury of ancient chants, valuable in themselves and as examples for modern composers. In addition, because of a movement toward unity among the various jurisdictions and their continuing efforts to work together in all areas, Orthodox churches and seminaries use and teach music from many ethnic backgrounds. Furthermore, because of an urgent sense of mission, as well as the desire to make itself understood to the faithful (who are less likely to be immigrants than in past generations), the church in her several jurisdictions is proceeding with the painstaking production of translations of the services into English and the task of improving existing translations.

In addition to the rediscovery of the Orthodox musical heritage, there are musicians who are producing original compositions and experimenting with an American idiom in which to continue the Orthodox musical tradition. Some of these have chosen to support their compositions with a light accompaniment; others have not. Some, particularly in the Antiochian Evangelical Orthodox Mission, have used Western hymn melodies as vehicles for Orthodox texts, in the belief that they will be more readily understood here in America than the sometimes exotic-sounding strains of the Eastern chant. These divergent ideas represent the growth of the contemporary church, and underscore the need for continuing adaptation, based on the Orthodox understanding that to be an artist, architect, or musician is first and foremost to be a theologian, a servant of the Word.

Other Uses of the Arts

The worship heritage of the Orthodox church includes the use of incense. Candles illumine the faces of the icons and of the worshipers, who are censed with the icons to remind us that we ourselves are icons, images of Christ, made in the image and likeness of God. The service includes processions, sometimes around the outside of the church (as at the Paschal service), the use of bells, which are unique and joyously rhythmic, banners (usually featuring the patron of the church, who may be a saint—other banners may portray Christ or the cross), and a variety of worship postures. While most Orthodox churches in America now have pews, many prefer the greater freedom of individual movement which the traditional central standing room provides. There are always seats available to the infirm. Visitors are welcome not only at the churches but at the many monasteries throughout the country, as well as at the seminary chapels, which present some of the best examples of Orthodox worship as they train future clergy, musicians, iconographers, and architects to bring their particular talents to the Master for his honor and glory.

Dena and Sue Talley

127 • Evangelical Covenant Churches

The Evangelical Covenant Church eschewed traditional church architecture and use of the arts in its beginning. But in the twentieth century it has produced church buildings built in a variety of architectural styles. Denominational leaders have been influential in the literary and visual arts.

Architecture

The Evangelical Covenant Church was born out of the pietistic renewal movements that swept Sweden in the nineteenth century. It was organized in Sweden in 1878 and in the United States in 1885. Colporteurs distributing tracts and other Christian literature became key links among and between conventicles. Some became gifted preachers. Meeting in homes, halls, and lofts, the setting, often a circle, was open, face to face, and intimate. Place was given to people of low and high birth, tenant and owner, men and women. Great energy, power, and freedom were released, and the emphasis attending a firsthand experience of grace yielded a feeling of immediacy but not necessarily emotionalism.

Early Covenant churches were very simple in design. Often they resembled a rural school building or meeting home. Such simplicity of architecture has several roots. One was legal. Olaf Gabriel Hendengren was a wealthy estate owner and a pietist who built a plain building—his "chapel" as he called it—because he was obliged to design it to be "as unlike the churches as possible." First built as a house of prayer and study for his workers, it would have run afoul of the law if it had resembled a church. Second, such a structure was an ideal setting for fellowship and encounters with each other in Christ through the power of the Holy Spirit. Third, this differentiation became part of the church's identity as a "free"—i.e., non-state—church and a place of open fellowship for those who had found new life in Christ. So while the phrase "unlike the churches as possible" originally described a legal circumvention, it soon became common to appropriate such a phrase to show one's distinction from the Lutheran state church. As such it became an important architectural criterion for Covenant churches.

In the United States, revivalists such as D. L. Moody also made a contribution. Already the emphasis in Covenant life had been placed on reading, discussing, and preaching of Holy Scripture. The pulpit was central and, as Karl Olsson says, the church was a "listening post." American Covenanters were particularly amenable to the "Akron plan" or, in some cases, to a design that resembled a tabernacle. The "wrap-around" seating arrangement gathered people close to and around the pulpit. The intimacy of the conventicle was somewhat retained, but the center became a pulpit and preacher. Churches were built to accommodate listeners.

A change in the approach to church architecture took place in the late 1920s in that a few congregations erected buildings of Gothic design and introduced the divided chancel. Stained glass windows began to include more than biblical scenes. Classical symbols now graced newly built churches, introducing a new language into worship, a language addressed to the imagination more than the language of literal, reproductive art. An editorial in the _Covenant Companion_ of this period remarked that older churches were built for evangelistic services, whereas the newer churches attended more to the devotional aspects of worship. It was further contended that the ritualistic churches retained the children better than free-church congregations because the iconoclasm of the latter took away many things that appealed to children.

This development had earlier roots. In 1900 the Covenant's Committee on Ritual published a volume called _Guide to Christian Worship_. This volume contended that "the outward form of the worship should be _reverent, festive,_ and _beautiful._" Human beings are described as "spiritual-physical beings" who have a continuous interaction between the body and the soul, which are entered through the "Eyegate and Eargate." The symbols present and the forms used kept the gospel perceivable and concrete, thus avoiding sentimentality and abstraction. Formalities, not formalism, awakened and maintained devotion. Thus, the architectural changes and liturgical developments of this period were a natural outgrowth of a document stressing reverence, festivity, and beauty.

There is, however, no uniformity regarding architectural styles in the Covenant churches. In fact, one can find vigorous discussion as to whether or not a "churchly" building may interfere with an outreach to a culture put off by the songs and structures of Zion. The phrase, "as unlike the churches as possible" may again find currency, not because of legal restrictions or antistate church bias, but for cultural reasons. Voiced in particular by the church growth movement and the megachurch philosophy, this phrase is a programmatic criterion used in support of the idea that the alien character of classical church tradition, music, and architecture not only communicates nothing to contemporary Americans, but in fact alienates them. Hence the interface between church and culture, in the form of music, buildings, forms of worship, and the nature of church programming is front and center. Churches with memories of the intimacy of the conventicles, the intensity of evangelistic meetings, and also the impingement of the transcendent through the liturgy and architecture in the "liturgical" churches from which they have come, will struggle incessantly with functionalism. The statement issued by the Committee on Ritual in 1900 refused the "functional only" route by granting an integrity of its own to symbols, festivity, and beauty. With that, early Covenanters granted an intrinsic ecclesiastical identity to churchly matters for the sake of the gospel and its being heard _and_ seen.

Storytelling

Hearing and seeing find expression in an art form intrinsic to pietism, namely testimony and storytelling. In the late 1920s Olga Lindborg (1889–1945), a leader in the educational work of the Covenant, wrote with a sophisticated understanding of the phenomenon of narrative expression in a simple style that gave Sunday School teachers in Covenant churches a highly competent analysis of the power of story and its educational potential. Lindborg pointed out the differences among story, myth, fairy tale, epic, biography, and history. She noted continuities within discontinuities. The hero in a story or epic is a successor to the giant in a fairy tale. What these art forms have in common is that they address the imagination, a most important human faculty. Imaginative people, she argued, are joyous beings, adept at self-expression. Hence she became an advocate of Forebel's idea that education rests on a law of self-expression and thus contended that handwork needed to be a part of Sunday school teaching. By extension, pageants were also a form of handwork because they were imaginative reconstructions of primal events and experiences; through them children became a part of the story they heard—in other words, they saw it and felt it. However valuable this was educationally, many in the church viewed it as worldly, arguing that if pageants were approved, one could also approve the theater. And if one could use moving pictures in church, why could one not approve of the moving picture industry? Lindborg found herself in the midst of controversy, engendered in no small way by pietism's effort to separate from the world. Perhaps its failure to distinguish worldliness from living in the world led to this love/hate relationship with aesthetic expression and consequently to a nearly exclusive emphasis on preaching.

Yet Covenant preachers knew instinctively what Lindborg was exploring in her sophisticated analysis of storytelling. Early Covenant sermons were laden with stories, and conventicles thrived on testimonies of the friendship of God in Jesus Christ with those who were seeking new life and joy. Story writers, said Lindborg, are not in touch with an audience; a storyteller is. Story readers go off alone to read, while a storyteller requires a community. Storytellers are not mere reciters but must appeal to the senses, creating an immediate and interactive event.

Lindborg's attempt to recognize that human beings respond bodily as well as mentally, imaginatively as well as intellectually, is now bearing fruit elsewhere. Some literature in Covenant history virtually repudiates bodily movement to music. "If the tune moves the feet, it is worldly" is an example of one such negative reaction. But in Covenant churches today one can find some use of liturgical dance, mime, and widespread use of musicals, choral readings, pageants, and audio-visuals. Praise music is accompanied by clapping and movement of feet along with drum, synthesizers, bells, pipe organs, and pianos. Lindborg would agree, I think, with poet and critic John Ciardi that if one asks not so much *what* but *how* does a poem mean, one could ask the same about church and education: *how* a service means is as crucial as *what* it means. The "how" issue calls for congregational and/or class involvement, and that calls for ritual, carried out in accordance with the gospel. By implication, pastors, and teachers are choreographers, a high art if there ever was one. The gospel story can be danced, mimed, sung, painted, sculpted, and told—one story in multimedia.

Visual Arts

While relying mostly on musical and verbal arts, Covenant artistic expression includes painting. Well known is the work of Warner Sallman (1892–1968), whose *Head of Christ* has been distributed in hundreds of millions of copies. Sallman, who began his career as an illustrator for a fashion magazine, studied at the Art Institute of Chicago and in several Bible institutes. He was advised by a dean to paint a "masculine" Christ, a rugged Christ of the desert, a Christ whose face had a distant gaze, in light of the events of Good Friday. Sallman focused on the meaning of a face, believing it to be the place where person and character are revealed. He often inscribed his work, with this text from 2 Corinthians 4:6 (Phillips): "We now can enlighten men only because we can give them the knowledge of the glory of God in the face of Jesus Christ." The other person whose painting reached a wide audience was Walter Olson (1893–1974). Also trained as an illustrator, Walter Olson became the artist for the well-known Bethel Bible study program for which he rendered many of the epochal events of salvation history in portrait form.

Sallman and Olson are representative of two major emphases of Covenant life and history: the Word of God and the centrality of Christ. Significantly, Sallman's work is called the *Head of Christ*. Pietism continually does battle with the tendency to flirt with a "Jesusology," which promotes a more romantic than prophetic person of Jesus Christ, in place of a Christology.

The Covenant Archives located at North Park Theological Seminary in Chicago have materials related to Sallman and Olson, as well as bound volumes of the *Covenant Companion, Covenant Quarterly, The Children's Friend,* and the *Covenant Weekly.* Karl Olsson's *By One Spirit* (Chicago: Covenant Press) is the definitive history of the Evangelical Covenant Church, which should be read together with *Into One Body by the Cross,* 2 vols. (Chicago: Covenant Press). "The Mission Covenant Church of Sweden and Art" is published in *Gyllene ljus* (Stockholm: Verbum). *The Covenant Book of Worship* of 1964 contains the formative statement of the Covenant Committee on Ritual of 1900.

John Weborg

128 • EVANGELICAL FREE CHURCHES

Worship in the Evangelical Free Church of America is based on the evangelical revivalist tradition, but in recent years some congregations have shown a remarkable inclination for innovation. Praise singing is now used in addition to traditional gospel hymnody. Some congregations also make use of technological advances in lighting, computers, and sound-system design.

From its inception through the 1950s (the period in which it arrived at its present form), the Evangelical Free Church of America (EFCA) offered worship services in the evangelical-revivalist tradition, with elements from its Norwegian and Swedish heritage. Examples of these services abounded in the Chicago area, where gospel radio station WMBI exerted considerable influence. EFCA pastors-in-training at Trinity Evangelical Divinity School, the EFCA seminary near Chicago, carried the influence throughout the denomination. Consequently, though lacking denominational worship statements or materials, a common approach to worship existed throughout the 1950s, 1960s, and 1970s.

The denomination has continued to be influenced by current trends in music. In response to church music publishers' materials, churches have developed age-graded choirs, orchestras, and handbell choirs. Song repertoire for soloists, choirs, and congregations has mirrored the music of popular gospel recording artists, changing styles with the passing times.

Stirrings toward more radical changes through the 1980s received focus at the 1991 National Conference, when incoming President Paul Cedar announced that worship would be the topic for the 1993 Conference. What previously was uncritically accepted was now to be examined and modeled.

Services of the Lord's Table have been little touched by recent change. They continue primarily as monthly memorials or remembrances, though with increasing variety in the manner of serving the elements. Services of the Word, on the other hand, evidence a growing inclusiveness and variety of content. In a typical seventy-five minute service, a theme derived from the sermon text or Scripture lesson (which may be the only Scripture passage read) will climax in a thirty-five minute Bible teaching. Items frequently mentioned as innovations include:

- Platform leadership provided by a small worship team of singers and occasionally praise bands.
- Increased use of musical instruments and musical styles influenced by the world of entertainment.
- More flexibility in the order of service, often including additional music.
- Scheduling of several related services, sometimes with contrasting styles of expression.
- Inclusion of short dramas or dramatic readings.
- Use of song medleys, often with video projections of the text.

(This information is taken from the tabulation of a one-page questionnaire mailed in April 1992, to seventy-one EFCA churches, forty-eight of whom responded. The churches were selected because they designate worship leaders or are known to be innovative in worship. Thus the response is felt to be an accurate though selective representation of present practices.)

The frequent use of copy machines and video projectors naturally require reliance on Christian Copyright Licensing, Inc. (CCLI) for copyright authorization. Easy reproduction of materials undoubtedly has encouraged more praise singing, which is dependent on a regular supply of new publications. In the survey, churches reported that a total of seventy-six hymns and established gospel songs are widely known and that one hundred and thirty-three praise songs are frequently used.

Many of the changes in worship experienced in the EFCA may be said to derive from modern technology in areas such as lighting, computers, amplified sound, and electronic media effects. Many church services are becoming like the electronic cocoons of rock concerts, presenting all-encompassing media presentations designed to lift people to ecstasy.

In spite of changes such as these, most EFCA congregations still use worship expressions strongly rooted in their evangelical-revivalist tradition. Still, some churches are consciously innovating, and others are imitating worship practices they have experienced elsewhere.

An illustration of the current diversity in worship expression can be shown in the two EFCA churches located in Indianapolis. Services in the newer, younger church use a liturgy held in a "worship center" warehouse and include praise singing led by effective leaders. The older, more established church, on the other hand, retains more elements of the revivalist liturgy, is more dependent on the spoken materials, and is found in a more typical church building sanctuary. The worship style of each church bears a very distinctive character.

Churches throughout the EFCA tend to reflect one or the other of these tendencies. Most accept wide varieties of worship expression as appropriate reflections of the variety God shows in his creation. At the same time, there is an expectation that a new creation may be imminent.

Kerchal Armstrong

129 • EVANGELICAL LUTHERAN CHURCH IN AMERICA

Music and the arts have always played an important role in the worship services of the ELCA, which has reflected Martin Luther's appreciation of the arts. In most churches the entire liturgy is sung. Musical styles range from plainsong and the rich tradition of Lutheran chorales to varieties of contemporary folk music. Considerable thought has also been given to the shape of the worship space and to the use of the visual arts.

— Music —

The Lutheran tradition assigns a very high place to the role of music in worship. Martin Luther wrote that "next to the Word of God, music deserves the highest praise" (*Luther's Works,* vol. 53: *Liturgy and Hymns* [Philadelphia: Fortress Press, 1965], 323; referred to as *LW* 53 below). He fostered congregational participation in worship by encouraging hymn singing. This required hymns, and Luther led the way by writing thirty-six hymns of his own. Choirs were retained in Lutheran churches to provide leadership in singing and, especially in Latin services, to sing polyphonic settings of psalms and canticles. Sometimes choir and congregation alternated in singing the stanzas of hymns and the verses of psalms and canticles. Organs were used to provide intonations and introductions which developed into chorale preludes. Hymns, art music, and organ literature all flourished in the Lutheran churches. This can be contrasted with the Reformed tradition, in which choirs and organs were initially abolished and congregational singing was limited to metrical psalms, and with the Roman Catholic tradition, in which choirs and organs were used but congregational singing was limited.

Lutheran services were and continue to be typically sung throughout by ministers, choirs, and the people. Luther himself provided detailed directions for chanting the Scripture readings, the collects, and the words of institution in his German Mass (1526). He regarded singing as the inevitable eruption of joyful song in the hearts of the redeemed. Music injects an ecstatic quality into worship, enabling the worshiper to move beyond oneself in praise and adoration of the Holy Trinity. Hymns also serve as excellent teaching devices; they make doctrines memorable because they are put in memorizable form. In this way music serves the Word of God. Music also serves an edifying purpose by building up the fellowship of the congregation, since group singing builds bonds between people. Finally, music serves as a bridge between the Christian cult and culture. Lutheran music simultaneously embraced the classical tradition of Gregorian chant, contemporary art music, and folk idioms. Luther himself encouraged the use of both the most sophisticated and the simplest forms of music to embrace the whole people of a society.

The North German Baroque period (1600–1750) constituted the high point of Lutheran church music. Poets allied themselves with reputable musicians, as in the partnership between Paul Gerhardt and Johann Curger, to produce a remarkable corpus of hymnody. The greatest North German composers from Michael Praetorius through Heinrich Schütz to Johann Sebastian Bach provided choral and organ music for worship services. George Frideric Handel was also a Lutheran who composed significant religious music. But unlike Handel's oratorios, the cantatas, passions, and chorale preludes of Bach were used in church services.

The time after Bach was characterized by liturgical deterioration which also included a decline in church music. This was because the best musicians found employment outside the church in the burgeoning concert halls and theaters. Liturgical recovery began in the mid-nineteenth century and also brought about a revival of church music in Germany and Scandinavia. In the twentieth century composers such as Hugo Distler, Ernst Pepping, Hans Friedrich Micheelsen, Jan Bender, and Heinz Werner Zimmerman have led the way in composing church music which is musically respectable and liturgically satisfying. Their efforts have been emulated by capable Lutheran musicians in North America.

Lutheran musicians have been open to a wide range of musical styles, from plainsong to gospel music. Only Christian popular and rock music have found little acceptance in Lutheran congregations. Recent years have witnessed a recovery of psalm singing using responsorial and antiphonal methods. Efforts have been made to emphasize the role of the choir in supporting and enriching congregational singing. New worship resources include settings of proper alleluia and offertory verses for the choir. In addition to the organ, wind instruments and guitars, brass and tympana, as well as handbells and synthesizers have found acceptance and have provided an additional opportunity to use the talents of the members of the congregation.

The Arts

Luther's positive attitude toward church music is also seen in his attitude toward the arts of worship. Vestments could be "used in freedom, as long as people refrain from ostentation and pomp" (*LW* 53, 31). "We neither prohibit nor prescribe candles or incense. Let these things be free" (*LW* 53, 25). Altars could be retained, but they should be pulled away from the east walls so that the priest could preside facing the people "as Christ doubtlessly did in the Last Supper. But let that await its own time" (*LW* 53, 69).

One of the problems with architecture is its permanence. Buildings cannot easily be changed and this undoubtedly contributes to a fair amount of liturgical conservatism. When Lutherans constructed new buildings, these reflected the prevailing architectural styles of the times from the Baroque and neoclassical periods to the neogothic and contemporary American periods. Lutherans were in the vanguard of contemporary church architecture in the 1950s and 1960s.

Since the seventeenth century, Lutheran worship space brought into close juxtaposition the altar, pulpit, and font to emphasize the unity of Word and sacrament. Baroque churches were modeled on the theater or opera house so that people could hear and see. Contemporary church buildings reflect either neogothic design (e.g., the A-frame) or the theater-in-the-round (e.g., the centrum plan popularized by Edvard Sövik of Northfield, Minnesota). The latter reflects the corporate nature of the worshiping community, but loses the former's sense of transcendence.

Contemporary Lutheran church buildings are often characterized by simplicity of design that allows liturgical colors in paraments, vestments, and banners to dominate the environment. While Lutherans have not always retained historic vestments, the alb and stole have become almost universal apparel, and many pastors wear the chasuble for eucharistic celebrations. Banner-making has become common in many congregations as a way of involving people in liturgical art and as a way of advertising the significance of special times and occasions in the church year. Other liturgical art includes candles, crosses, or crucifixes (both stationary and processional), missal stands, chalices and patens, paschal candle stands, and vigil lights (signifying the abiding presence of Christ).

One art form that has been tried but not widely accepted is liturgical dance. Dancing in the worship space is hampered by spatial limitations, liturgical furniture, and also by the inability of the congregation to participate. But it has been used regularly and effectively at St. Peter's Lutheran Church in New York City under the direction of Carla DeSola. Chancel dramas and storytelling have been more popular, especially at Christmas and during Lent and Holy Week.

Frank Senn

130 • FRIENDS (QUAKERS)

Quaker or Friends meetings inherit a tradition of silent worship, which allows no room for congregational music or the arts. In some churches, however, particularly in the Evangelical Friends branch, many aspects of free-church worship are finding their way into Friends services.

Trends in the use of music and the arts by Quaker or Friends churches are best understood against the backdrop of their 350-year history. In classical, silent Quaker worship—also called unprogrammed—there was no pastoral leadership, service planning, or prearranged music. All human elements were carefully avoided to allow the Spirit of God complete freedom to move as he pleased. Worshipers waited in silence for the Spirit's movement and then contributed individually to the service as led by the Spirit's direction.

The face of Quaker worship in America began to

change in the mid to late-nineteenth century as a strong evangelical movement emerged from within the Quaker tradition. The revival and renewal that took place within American Protestantism during that period and the evangelistic success of pulpit-centered churches caused many Quaker churches to adopt a programmed, or structured, approach to worship. More recently, Quaker churches, like many others, have felt the influence of the charismatic and praise-and-worship movements.

Today Quaker worship and use of music and the arts exhibit a synthesis of their own theology and these two historical influences. Lacking a strong musical tradition of their own, Quaker churches seem to have adopted an imitative pragmatism to guide their use of music and the arts. Simply put, they borrow freely from others and adopt what works—that is, those things that "aid" worship or attract outsiders—with the result that they now share much in common with their evangelical, pulpit-centered neighbors from the free-church traditions.

Within the context of their recent heritage, the music used in evangelical Quaker churches ranges from the traditional to popular. Most churches, except perhaps those that have adopted a congregation-centered praise and worship style of worship, have choirs or other vocal ensembles. While they may occasionally sing a "popular" standard anthem like Jane Marshall's "My Eternal King," more often they may be heard singing anthems by composers like Tom Fettke or Robert Clatterbuck or arrangements of hymns and currently popular songs.

Congregational music, likewise, ranges from traditional evangelical hymns and gospel songs to praise choruses. Quaker congregations are increasingly adopting the use of extended periods of singing, for reasons not unlike their historical commitment to silent worship. For these they use projected texts instead of hymnals. Accompaniment varies, ranging from piano and organ, individually or together, to synthesizers and "praise bands." Little use is made of chants, psalm singing (apart from praise chorus texts), or antiphons.

In addition to the instruments referred to above, handbells and brass, woodwind or string instrumental ensembles may be found in Quaker churches. Some maintain small orchestras or assemble them for special occasions, using both members of the congregation and contracted players.

Use of the arts in evangelical Quaker churches

The Symbol of St. Mark. *The winged lion represents Christ's royal character, which St. Mark proclaimed.*

is limited mostly to that found in contemporary musicals and the occasional chancel drama and readers theater group. Little attention is paid to environmental art, except at the holidays, and liturgical dance is virtually nonexistent.

Warren Ediger

131 • International Foursquare Gospel Church

Music and the other arts are essential components of worship in Foursquare Gospel churches. A limitless variety of musical styles, including both traditional and contemporary examples, are included in worship services. Drama and dance also play a very significant role. The following article focuses on music and the arts at The Church on the Way, Van Nuys, California, as an example of Foursquare Gospel worship.

Since the days of our founder, Aimee Semple McPherson, the International Church of the Foursquare Gospel has always endeavored to reach across denominational and cultural barriers to bring the "full gospel" to people. This has never been more true than in the area of music, especially in the last twenty years. Taking our cue from our innovative founder, we have sought to be open to exploring the many avenues of musical and other artistic expressions with which the Lord has blessed us.

Characteristic of a Foursquare Gospel philosophy of music is the belief that God created music as a vehicle for people to praise and worship him, for moving their hearts toward receiving him, for celebration, for instruction and communicating the Word of God, and as a powerful weapon in spiritual warfare. In short, music is an important part of every event, regardless of size, function, or scope of influence. Services, classes, meetings, etc., all have music of some form.

For example, in a presentation of Easter music, The First Foursquare Church of Van Nuys, California (The Church on the Way), explored the jazz and rock idioms to express the timeless truths of a time-honored hymn, "The Old Rugged Cross." Utilizing the cry of an improvised solo on the soprano saxophone to portray the agony of the cross, coupled with the rough-hewn voice of one of our vocally gifted men, resulted in a dynamic, spiritually-rich experience of worship for that congregation.

On Mother's Day Evening in May of each year, this same church releases ministry through many art forms in an evening service dedicated to worshipful expressions through the arts, entitled "A Night of Royal Splendor." Classical music by a string ensemble, dance, and visual art are featured, as well as the presentation of more traditional groups such as a children's chorale and a newly formed adult gospel choir.

Drama has been part of the Foursquare experience from the beginning, when Aimee Semple McPherson wrote operas like *The Crimson Road* and *The Bells of Bethlehem*. She herself was quite dramatic in her approach to public ministry—it is reported that one time she even rode a motorcycle into the sanctuary to make a point. Today, many Foursquare churches are exploring drama as an effective supplement to the worship experience, with everything from small "skits" in services to underscore the message to complete plays and musicals.

Dance has been explored both as a beautiful visual complement to worship (by a dance ministry team) and as a corporate expression of worship by having the congregation literally "dance in the Spirit."

The Sanctuary Choir at The Church on the Way continues to be an "ignition point" to inspire and encourage worship in the congregation. At first, it was a vehicle to launch two musicals in the 1970s: *Come Together* and *If My People*. Later, in 1981, it presented *Majesty*. The philosophy has always been that *the people are the choir*. Consequently, the Sanctuary Choir is not a "performance-oriented" ensemble that substitutes for the congregation's need to be worshipers.

The range of musical styles used in The Church on the Way is limitless. Traditional hymns have been put into classical, jazz, dixieland, contemporary rock, fusion, country, and Latin settings, to name a few. Infants through senior citizens engage in musical activities. Classes are held for infants and mothers to experience music together through games and finger play. Toddlers and their mothers actively participate by singing, marching, and playing rhythm instruments. Organized choirs start at age three and continue through the elderly.

Instrumental support for congregational worship services is provided by a rhythm section consisting of piano, organ, drums, guitar, electric bass, and synthesizer. Rhythm sections are also used for worship by all Sunday school classes. Elementary, junior high, high school, college, and singles each have their own rhythm section. For Communion services (usually once a month), a brass ensemble consisting of three trumpets, two French horns, three trombones, tuba, and percussion is added to the rhythm section. The Communion instrumentation is used to support congregation worship, special choir numbers, and to play preludes. Instrumentation for some seasonal music celebrations usually includes four woodwinds, four trumpets, four French horns, three trombones, tuba, percussion, harp, and rhythm section. There is also a fifty-piece concert band, Jericho, which does other presentations throughout the year. Entire libraries are kept for brass ensembles, string ensembles, dixieland bands, and trombone bands.

While the church has sought to remain sensitive to the ever-changing cultural climate in the area of music and the arts, that change has never been at the expense of the valued and essential traditional music and art forms already resident in the church. The Church on the Way also adheres to a balanced diet of worship choruses coupled with hymns. The purpose is to make and keep worship music available to the people so that they can easily take it and use it for their own personal and corporate times of worship. This approach to worship is borne out of an "undergirding" philosophy of replacing "the ministry of the professional" (which had allowed the individual a growing avoidance of the responsibility of being a worshiper) with "the ministry of the individual believer."

The Church on the Way is an example of a church that has set the pace in the composition of hymns, choruses, and other music, but there are variations of music and art forms throughout the Foursquare denomination depending on locality, taste of its members, and varying philosophies regarding worship service functions. Worship expressions range from specialized music teams such as are being used in the Christian Assembly Foursquare Church in Eagle Rock, California, (which presents four evangelistic concerts per year in addition to its weekly ministry in worship) to more traditional forms of worship, such as found in the Florence Avenue Foursquare Church in Santa Fe Springs, California.

During the Jesus Movement of the late 1960s and early 1970s, many Foursquare churches replaced their organs with guitars and hymns with worship choruses. Many new and "renewed" congregations sought a "full-gospel" experience in worship that was fresh and alive, meaning that many of them abandoned the traditional worship forms of hymnody and organ music. Those congregations that built their new spiritual life on the "rock" of a scripturally based worship foundation and balanced approach to the "new wave" of the Spirit survived. Those that built on the "sand" of "experience only" or "experience-for-its-own-sake" either withered or became cultist in their practices. It is interesting to note the number of those churches that have recaptured the essence of the meaning of old, doctrinally rich hymns (and even organ music in some cases) with an adventurous new sense of purpose.

Today, the International Church of the Foursquare Gospel seeks to maximize the potential of music and the arts to release its people in praise and worship. This is accomplished by a spiritually responsible approach to wise and sensitive stewardship of all resources, both human and God-inspired, human-made tools produced by current technology.

Jim Barnett and Bob Dawson

132 ✦ Independent Fundamentalist and Evangelical Churches

Churches of the Independent Fundamentalist and Evangelical denomination use a wide variety of elements in worship renewal, reflecting the differing backgrounds of the individuals who make up its congregations. Music continues to be an important contribution to worship, and environmental art, dance, and drama are used increasingly. Leadership is often assigned to a minister of fine arts.

A significant trend in the renewal of worship is the new emphasis on music and the visual arts. The trend is so significant that churches are hiring ministers of music and worship, or of music and fine arts, or simply ministers of fine arts. The churches are rethinking the meaning of worship, music, and the liturgy.

Music

Philosophy. Music has often been thought of as a part of heavenly worship. It is one of the few "descriptive" elements of earthly worship that clearly continues in the heavenly realm and expresses both the heart and mind of the worshiper. For music in worship to be authentic it must be embraced by both the heart and the mind. As the congregation comes to understand and experience this, worship can be revitalized. Where worship is dynamic and genuine, music is seen as substantive, theological, and significant. It is not to be merely a decorative addition, but becomes an audible expression of the heart and mind.

Style. One of the contributing factors to revitalized worship that is often cited by members of the congregation is the great variety of musical styles heard during services. In observing creation, we see that the Creator's own handiwork is expressed with considerable variety. Having been made in the image of God, it is reasonable, even expected, that one should express his or her love in a variety of styles and colors appropriate to a specific environment. Worship music ought to reflect the style of each culture and the unique perspective of each ethnic group. Thus, variety enables the worshiper to gain a sense of history (the Independent Fundamentalist and Evangelical churches were not the first to discover authentic worship), a sense of identity (our churches are only a small part of the "holy, catholic church"), and a sense of joy, color, and creativity (there are many ways to express love). The many arts offer a great opportunity to teach breadth of style for the glory of God.

Function of Music. One of the hallmarks of renewal in worship is understanding that music serves many different functions in worship. Just as a service is organized around the several aspects of worship (adoration, confession, thanksgiving, Communion, and so forth), likewise music must be planned to serve each of these components. Music planning should not merely be a matter of plugging in an all-purpose "opener" and "closer," but rather should involve reflecting on what the text of a musical number actually says and from that determining where it might best be placed in the service. Great historical hymns as well as contemporary examples, occasional chant, gospel songs, praise choruses, singing of psalms, and responsorial hymnody all become part of the regular musical expression in worship. Thus, very rarely is the service identical from week to week. There is, however, enough repetition with an ever-expanding body of musical literature so that continuity is maintained.

Contemporary Instrumentals. One of the clear trends in churches marked by dynamic worship is the growth of instrumental programs. It is common for larger churches to hire part-time or full-time instrumental directors. Of particular note is the interest in synthesizers and other high-tech devices. The surge of interest in "discovering the potential within" and meditation have resulted in a whole field of reflective mood music that makes considerable use of keyboard instruments of all kinds and acoustic guitars. The church, which might be criticized for merely following contemporary trends in commercial music, has seen a rise in the use of straight instrumental music in worship. This may not be bad in itself, but is rather to be welcomed, but for different reasons than the usual "this is what the people are listening to and we want to be relevant." A far better reason to use handbells, guitars, strings, brass, winds, synthesizers, pipe organs, pianos, and percussion is that they can help us express the feelings, ideas, and joys we can express in no other way. The minister of music is called upon to create, arrange, or find parts for the available instrumentalists and to foster the development of players within the congregation.

The Arts

Environmental Art. It is common and desirable for churches to be constructed in such a manner as to allow flexibility for the placement in the chancel area of the important items needed for worship (pulpit, font, Table, choir, etc.). Depending on the size and shape of the sanctuary (sadly, often called the "auditorium"), the pews or chairs can be variously arranged to reflect the particular emphasis from week to week. In the larger congregations, of course, there is less flexibility.

It is the practice of some congregations to display Advent and Holy Week banners. While this is usual in certain denominations, others in the free-church tradition have begun to benefit from a more general awareness of the church year and the use of banners and hangings. It is common to find the display of flags and festive processional surrounding mission conferences. One church offers Communion every other month on Sunday mornings, while Communion services in the alternate months are in the evening. The ministers, who normally wear suits, don vestments for these services. It is not uncommon to find a wide variety of liturgical expressions in worship since independent churches often draw from a wide variety of religious affiliations. More importantly, these churches have also discovered that this variety opens whole new vistas of possibilities for worship.

Drama. Another significant movement in recent years is the development of drama in worship and ministry. Numerous Christian drama troupes travel the country, and drama ministries within local churches have flourished. One such local church developed a dramatic rendering of the story of Hannah, Samuel, Elkanah, and Eli at Samuel's dedication to the Lord. The portion from the First Book of Samuel was developed into an eight-to-nine minute vignette suitable for part of a service that included a children's dedication.

Some portions of Scripture are best read dramatically, and others in dialogue with a narrator. Sometimes portions are most effective if the reader is not seen as, for example, when the voice is to be that of God (e.g., the story of the Transfiguration).

In some churches a theater ministry has recently developed with various kinds of outreach productions, particularly in the Christmas and Easter seasons. These are variously approached from the simplest (and perhaps least interesting) use of an already published "canned cantata" to a completely original work. One church works with an entirely new script each year, but uses a wide variety of styles and sources for the Christmas music. This has the benefit of using familiar Christmas music in combination with an original story. Also, the church's resources in talent and vision are given opportunity for expression.

It is also common to find dance, usually a combination of ballet and mime in festive programs, or in special seasons such as Holy Week. There is a growing awareness, albeit reluctant in some quarters of the church, of the great ability to communicate beautifully through dance in worship. In this ministry, it is important that the performers are very good and clearly understand the nature of the offering. The best and most effective source for the dancers is in the congregation itself. It would seem most inappropriate to ask an unbeliever to lead in worship in a dancing role.

The Minister of Fine Arts

One of the clear responsibilities of the minister of fine arts in worship renewal is the great privilege and responsibility of teaching. The church has too often used frustrated performers in leadership positions in worship. This has often led to a clash of egos. This is the great danger in so-called "contemporary worship" led by a Christian band that "performs" or leads worship. Ministers of fine arts, those called upon for leadership in the artistic elements of worship, need to teach both their congregations and their fellow staff members about the nature of worship. Fine arts staffs should include persons who have some training in music education and worship, but not simply those with degrees in music performance, e.g., organists who know only the traditional repertoire. Put simply, much more versatility is required of them, and they must be an active part of the congregation's spiritual life. Sadly, ministers of fine arts are still largely left on their own in developing an appropriate philosophy of art in worship, though there are happily a few exceptions being developed in some seminary programs.

Dan Sharp

133 • THE LUTHERAN CHURCH—MISSOURI SYNOD

Although the Lutheran Church—Missouri Synod is deeply rooted in the Lutheran tradition and continues to use the music and arts from its heritage, it is increasingly affected by the contemporary developments in the various arts. This innovation, however, is most often proposed in order to recapture traditional practice and to complement the historic Lutheran liturgy.

Lutherans possess a rich and varied heritage of music for worship. Each era, guided by values first articulated by Martin Luther, searches for new expressions. Luther saw music as a gift of God to be used in the service of the gospel. He appreciated well-crafted music and gave music a high place, next to theology. While the nineteenth-century Lutheran immigrants to America especially valued hymns, their mid-twentieth century descendants rediscovered and explored the choral and instrumental music from earlier centuries of the church. After the wave of "folk" hymns in the 1960s, congregations often operated with official hymnals and with local selections of hymnody and spiritual songs outside their hymnal. Today they are aided by the photocopier and the personal computer. Any text (hymn, prayer, Scripture) can be customized and printed. Worshipers may never suspect the actual sources. Copyright law, however, puts limits on the use of recently published material. This choosing and editing requires skills not previously envisioned in the training of worship leaders. As more people are drawn into this kind of leadership, the need for careful, pastoral control becomes more and more apparent. The publication of a series like *Creative Worship for the Lutheran Parish* offers resources that reduce some of the editing formerly needed.

Up to now, hymnody has been drawn from the last five to ten centuries of the church. Many congregations now expand this repertory at the local level to include the folk hymn tradition of the 1960s, current "Christian pop" songs, and praise songs. The reprinting is arranged through license clearinghouses and annual fees. Liturgical melodies, even recent ones with refrain features, sometimes are shunned, and nonofficial texts of services are created by musicians who find their own musical considerations more important than the words. In the new hymnal *Lutheran Worship* (Minneapolis: Augsburg, 1982), the singing of psalms was encouraged by providing a variety of melodic formulas to fit any of the texts. Psalms and liturgical texts may be sung by a solo voice, choral groups, or subdivisions of the congregation to lighten the task of singing prose texts.

Choir anthems continue to be used, with special arrangements of hymns (called concertatos) becoming most common. Such concertatos often call for instruments, organ, and choir to support and to alternate with the congregation. Many congregations have established handbell choirs in the last decade. Some congregations use hand and orchestral instruments in small ensembles on special occasions. Some have contemporary ensembles with guitar, bass, drums, and electric keyboard. Synthesizers are increasingly part of instrumental ensembles and sometimes replace the organ in leading the congregation. In some places both piano and organ accompany the singing. Instrumental soloists often draw on music from the Baroque period.

A few parishes find ways to use drama to illustrate teachings, to show the dynamics of faith in action, or to act out a scriptural event, frequently in conjunction with a homily. Ceremonies like removing the altar paraments on Maundy Thursday or a procession of children singing on Palm Sunday provide effective elements which distinguish one service from another. Decorative plants are used at Christmas and Easter, and palms are used on Palm Sunday. A tenebrae service may include the extinguishing of a series of candles. Successive Sundays of Advent may see a new candle lit on a wreath. The processional cross and candles moving into the nave at the reading of the gospel have become a regular part of high festivals in some churches. Entrance processions are also often used at festival services.

The traditional architecture of a long nave with fixed seating and a center aisle frequently is replaced in new structures by an altar on a platform (one or two steps above the main floor) with pews or chairs on three sides. This puts the people in closer proximity to the action of worship, but may also make it difficult for a preacher to face everyone during the sermon. Seasonal colored hangings are placed on the altar, pulpit, and lectern. The 1982 hymnal permits blue for Advent, scarlet for Holy Week, and gold for Easter, colors not previously used. The alb has become the normal vestment for worship leaders in the chancel whether clergy or layperson. The clergy usually wear stoles, and a few wear a chasuble at the Eucharist. Acolytes and banners are widely accepted.

James L. Brauer

134 ✦ MENNONITE CHURCHES

Congregational singing is an especially important aspect of worship in the Mennonite tradition, the most unique aspect of which is unaccompanied four-part congregational singing. A new congregational hymnal and the contributions of many Mennonites in various artistic arenas are important signs of renewed vitality in the Mennonite churches.

Hymnal: A Worship Book, 1992, is the latest Mennonite hymnal, a joint project of the Mennonite Church (MC), General Conference Mennonite Church (GC), and the Church of the Brethren. Its predecessor was _The Mennonite Hymnal,_ 1969, published by the Mennonite Church and General Conference Mennonite Church, the two largest Mennonite groups of North America. To include "worship" in the new book's title indicates growing care about how worship happens. The music and written aids are grouped by worship act: gathering, praising/adoring, confessing/reconciling, proclaiming, affirming the faith, praying, offering, witnessing, and sending. Supplemental materials published with the hymnal are: _Hymnal: Companion, Hymnal: Accompaniment Handbook,_ and related monographs, "A House of Our Hymns," "Planning Worship Services," "The Importance of Music in Worship," and "Our Hymnology Shapes Our Theology."

Enthusiastic, unaccompanied singing in four parts is an earmark of congregational song among Mennonites, especially in Mennonite churches, but the tradition is fading in some places. Along with fine congregational singing, the General Conference Mennonite churches also enjoy a strong heritage of choral and organ contributions to worship. Choruses, Scripture songs, and worship-and-praise songs are used by numerous congregations. As newer styles and concepts of worship are being adopted, some traditional musical elements are being lost. Some congregations, however, are learning to merge the various styles. In addition, as Mennonites carry out their mission to include all peoples, rich musical contributions are being made by African-Americans, Hispanics, and various native American and Asian American groups.

Mennonite worship has been heavily word-oriented with emphasis on the sermon, and until recently that has been acceptable. Some people want change, but not all agree on the nature and extent of the change that may be needed. The artistic expression that has existed has come traditionally through congregational song, seasonal choral programs, and performance of large works by area choral organizations. Mennonite places of worship employ little symbolic art, although examples of fine visual art have been created for worship. Often visual art, such as a banner, is created with little or no artistic understanding. Meanwhile, certain artists hesitate to create art for worship without a clear theological statement to guide them. Drama includes storytelling and Bible sketches. Pageantry and liturgical dance are utilized by various congregations.

Among Mennonites, one finds prominent artists throughout the range of artistic expression from opera house to theater stage, art gallery to dance studio, concert hall to film, and play script to potter's wheel. In 1989 the Association of Mennonites in the Arts was founded to provide a network for encouragement and support of the arts and artists, and to give direction for artists wanting to relate to the church. The Association started a directory of Mennonite-related artists, including those who are professional or amateur, full-time or part-time.

Philip K. Clemens

135 ✦ MESSIANIC SYNAGOGUE

The Messianic Synagogue, true to its direct connection to Judaism, often incorporates musical materials with Israeli motifs. Congregations may have a worship leader called a "cantor," but the art of solo cantorial singing, common in Jewish temples, is rarely encountered. Accompaniment for singing is most often supplied by the guitar, strings, tambourine, and—more recently—electronic equipment such as synthesizers. Drama, the visual arts, and carpentry for such important features as the ark do find ready use in Messianic Synagogue worship.

Music

Singing has frequently been an important part of worship in the synagogue, and the Messianic synagogue is no exception. The use of praise-and-worship choruses and songs has become increasingly common during the past twenty years. Folk songs from Israel, or ones modeled on Israeli motifs, have been popular from the inception of the Jews for Jesus song ministry known as the Liberated Wailing Wall. In the early 1970s the popular duo Lamb continued the trend, and Joel Chernoff, Lamb's lead singer, continues to write music for use in the Messianic synagogue.

Yiddish folk music has also served as a source for occasional ballads, although it has had relatively little impact on contemporary worship materials produced within the Messianic Movement. In addition, songs originally made popular by non-Messianic recording artists have been slightly modified for congregational use in Messianic synagogues. In most of the local congregations, solo vocal music has enjoyed relatively little prominence.

Early in the history of the Messianic Movement, piano accompaniment was supplemented by the guitar. Guitar accompaniment continues to be common, largely because many Messianic congregations do not own their own buildings, which is due primarily to the youth of the movement and the financial instability of many of the congregations. Strings and tambourines have also been traditionally used, with more recent music featuring electronic music, using electronic tapes and synthesizers.

A few congregations include some form of dancing in their worship services, usually, perhaps universally, based on the *hora,* an Israeli folk dance. This dance is often accompanied by clarinet, flute, and recorder. It remains relatively uncommon in liturgical worship services and may be less common now than fifteen or twenty years ago, although statistical evidence is not readily available.

Messianic synagogues, whether liturgical or not, often have a worship leader called a cantor, but Jewish *chazzanut* (the art of cantorial music) is infrequently encountered. Nevertheless, *chazzanut* has a significant influence on the chanting of the liturgical prayers in those congregations where chanting is practiced. From time to time, attempts to develop more traditional *chazzanut* have been made. For example, in the 1970s the cantor of Congregation Adat Hatikvah in Chicago studied the cantorial music of Waldman and Pierce, and utilized Eastern European, rather than Israeli, music in the liturgy of that synagogue. However, there have been few, if any, examples of Messianic cantors following that example during the years since the mid-1970s. For most of the congregations throughout the history of the Messianic Movement, the practices found in Israel have had a far more formative influence than those of Eastern Europe, an influence not limited to music alone.

Drama

In a number of Messianic congregations, especially the less liturgical ones, drama groups have emerged as a significant worship resource. The pervasive influence of Jews for Jesus in non-liturgical congregations has enhanced this trend, although it does not entirely account for its existence. Purim has been traditionally associated with costume and drama, and the building of the Sukkah (the Tabernacle for the Festival of Booths, Sukkot, in the early autumn) lends itself to dramatizations. However, the primary use of drama is in outreach, both in explaining the Messianic Movement to churches and in explaining Yeshua to Jewish audiences. Dramatization is only occasionally a substitute for preaching.

Liturgical efforts, such as the prayer books edited by Michael Becker (_Machzor for High Holy Days_ [Chicago: Congregation B'nai Maccabim, 1986]) and John Fisher (_Messianic Services For Festivals and Holy Days_ [Palm Harbor, Fla.: Menorah Ministries, 1992]), offer the Messianic Movement resources with which to develop creative new liturgies, but the Messianic Movement is handicapped in this area by the relative newness of liturgy in the ministries of many of the older congregational leaders. Lack of depth in Hebrew is another serious problem the movement must seek to overcome, and this has been addressed through the efforts of both the Union of Messianic Congregations and within individual synagogues. However, until the Messianic Movement produces more than minimal familiarity with the Hebrew language and historic _chazzanut,_ it is unlikely that Messianism will be set free to handle liturgical materials creatively.

Visual Arts

The Messianic Movement has made extensive use of the visual arts such as banners, scroll coverings, portable coverings for walls of worship halls borrowed from other institutions, and graphics for printed worship literature, including prayer books of various kinds. Its Hebrew Christian wing (primarily Jews for Jesus) has been extraordinarily creative in developing visual outreach materials for street evangelism. Hineni Ministries (the name Jews for Jesus uses within the Jewish community) has developed a glossy newsletter for apologetic purposes, called _Issues,_ which demonstrates increasing maturity and sophistication.

A final element the cannot be overlooked in a survey of the visual arts in worship of Messianic congregations is the manufacture and care of the arks. The Aron ha-Kodesh (Hebrew for "ark") is a central feature in the synagogue, and is no less a symbol in the Messianic synagogue. It houses the Torah scrolls, and its curtain or door is opened at key points of the liturgy as a symbol of access to God through prayer. The limited budget often available to Messianic congregations has an impact on the sophistication of their _aronim_ (arks), but not on the congregations' commitment to creating or obtaining these important religious artifacts. Often

hand-made, the arks evidence artful design and a high level of carpentry skills.

Kenneth Warren Rick

136 ✦ NATIONAL BAPTIST CONVENTION OF AMERICA

While music has always been among the most important elements in black Baptist churches, there has been little uniformity in practice, largely because local congregations depended mostly on pastoral leadership and lacked professional directors of music. Recent years have seen the introduction of instruments other than the piano and organ and the prevalence of popular music styles. There is a new emphasis on the other arts as well, as reflected in colorful clergy and choir vestments and in the introduction of drama.

Music has always been an integral part of the worship experience in member churches of the National Baptist Convention of America, Incorporated. Prayer, responsive Scripture reading, music, and the proclamation of the Word have comprised the most prevalent format for worship for several centuries. Art, on the other hand, was not considered to be a significant component for enhancing the worship experience, an attitude that dates back to the period when the black Baptist churches were first recognized as official denominations. Art was recognized for the medium that it is. It was appreciated and admired as something to look at, and artists were appreciated for their creativity and their tremendous aesthetic sense. But art was not considered to be a medium of worship. Black Baptists had not bridged the chasm of using the artistic beauty in the worship experience. For the most part, stained-glass windows have always been significant in the building plans of black Baptist churches even though, in many instances, there was little significant recognition of their aesthetic quality. There was, however, recognition of the biblical characters who adorned many of these windows. In contrast to the visual arts, music continues to be the standard element in black Baptist worship.

Music

Hattie L. Wade, director of music in the Galilee Baptist Church of Shreveport, Louisiana, where the president of the National Baptist Convention of America serves as pastor, suggests that evidence seems to support the theory that there is no universal philosophy of music nor music tradition in the black Baptist churches across the United States. Each church community contributes significantly to the formulation and demonstration of its own music philosophy. The formulation of a music philosophy and the variations in music styles are greatly influenced by pastors of churches, the lack of sufficient church staffing, and directors of music who have not been formally trained. The result has been that many varied musical styles and philosophies are imposed upon black Baptist church congregations.

The music philosophy of the Galilee Baptist Church, according to Hattie Wade, is predicated upon the affirmation that all music rendered must be biblically and theologically sound, and rendered to the glory of God. The "Good News" of the gospel through music in the Galilee Baptist Church is centered in the worship experience and not in performance and entertainment. All music at Galilee is incorporated from the black experience, including the hymns, chants, moans, metered hymns, gospel songs (traditional and contemporary), the psalms (rendered through anthems), spirituals (with accompaniment and a cappella), jubilee music, and others. The a cappella music literature rendered in the Galilee church is based upon the scriptural record in Colossians 3:16: "Let the word of Christ dwell in you richly as you teach and admonish one another with all wisdom, and as you sing psalms, hymns, and spiritual songs with gratitude in your heart to God." The pastor and the director of music are the agents for change in the Galilee church. Music rendered in the worship services is planned as an integral part of the worship experience, is presented with quality and dignity, and dedicated to the glory of God. The emphasis, therefore, is not upon choirs singing and instruments playing, but on presenting an act of worship to God.

The emergence of instruments in the member churches of the National Baptist Convention of America does represent a significant change in practice. The organ and the piano have always been fixtures in the black Baptist churches, but within the last twenty years other instruments have been employed to enhance the worship experience. These instruments are as varied as the musical styles that are used. Drums and other percussion instruments, guitars (bass and lead), trumpets, clarinets, and saxophones are now used with regularity in a number of churches in the denomination. These instruments have fostered a popularity among community choirs who also use electronic keyboards and synthesizers. When community choirs sponsor musical concerts, several keyboards may be used. The emergence of these musical instruments has had a tremendous impact upon worship experiences. In fact, sometimes the instruments, the styles, and the sounds can hardly be distinguished from the sounds of the "big bands." The electronic keyboard is used in the Galilee church to heighten the effect of the text and the music.

Bell choirs were extremely popular twenty years ago and could be found in member churches where there was a long-standing and established music ministry, but they later became nearly extinct in member churches. Other band and instrument ensembles have been used less frequently. The dearth of bell choirs and band and instrument ensembles may be attributed to the lack of formal training of music directors, the economics of congregations, the long hiatus from the use of instruments in older congregations, and the fact that they are believed not to appeal to newer members. However, there appears to be a resurgence in the use of bell choirs, band, and instrument ensembles because of efforts at local schools to improve music programs. Moreover, African-American young people are purchasing their own instruments as they enroll in private and public school music programs and as they seek professional opportunities beyond high school.

Most assuredly, the consensus among trained musicians serving member churches of the denomination is that instruments can be used "tastefully" and "tactfully" to enhance worship and special musical presentations. On the other hand, the plethora of instruments in the member churches of the denomination where there is an absence of trained leadership (pastor and director of music) has caused congregations to look askance upon their usage, and trained music directors interpret their use as a display of entertainment, performance, ostentation, and self-gratification.

Suffice it to say then, that the music literature in the member churches of the denomination is in many cases limited to the preferences of the pastors and the directors of music. In some cases, the decisions regarding music are left up to directors who promote the music ministry as top priority, rather than evangelism and mission. This occurs especially when untrained musicians are responsible for the music ministry. The result is that many choirs and individual music artists are "crossing over" into popular styles. These styles are demonstrated in the performances and the music literature sung. The traditional hymns and anthems of the church are often labeled by them as being "old and unexciting." Many congregations have been tremendously influenced by this new approach to music ministry, in which one can hardly distinguish the sound of the popular from the sacred. If pastors of the member churches of the denomination continue to permit this contemporary gospel with its rearrangement of the text and the rhythmic beat of the popular idiom, it will become the standard repertoire for music ministry in member churches of the National Baptist Convention of America.

Nevertheless, there are still member churches of the denomination, like the Galilee church, whose music philosophy focuses upon choirs singing quality music, historically rooted in the witness of the Christian faith, biblically authenticated, and who envision their participation as servants who are partners in leading worshipers to a meaningful relationship with God and Jesus Christ rather than performing and entertaining.

The Arts

Historically, the visual arts have never been perceived as enhancers of the worship experience in the member churches of the denomination. While Baptists, especially black Baptists, have always considered themselves to be a simple people with little or no flare for the spectacular, it does seem that art, especially environmental art, has captured their attention. This is evidenced in clergy and choir vestments, church furnishings, church architecture, and sanctuary ornamentation. This most recent preoccupation with environmental art has been prompted and inspired through the promotional and marketing skills of Christian bookstores and suppliers which have done more to promote art in member churches of the denomination than the power of the spoken Word.

The new trends in colors, fabrics, and pulpit vestments for pastors have inspired a movement from the traditional dark colored, heavy-textured, and conservative vestments to dramatic colors and fabric weights for the seasons of the year. The styles range from the traditional to avant-garde, with tunics, collars, velvet yokes, and velvet stoles. Similarly, choir robes have moved from the traditional black to multiple colors and styles.

Pulpit furniture has always been standard in the member churches of the denomination. Recently, however, the style of pulpit furniture has changed because of architectural changes in some churches. Traditionally, the pulpit desk in black Baptist churches was the central focal point for worship, but many member churches have moved to the split pulpit and the traditional center pulpit chair, with side chairs being replaced by pulpit benches. Bookmarks, pulpit scarves, and Communion table runners with colors that coordinate with the celebrative days of the Christian year are used. The pulpit furniture in many member churches is now adorned with candelabras, Bible stands, vases, and candlesticks. This has prompted many congregants to say that our Baptist freedom has now been usurped by a preoccupation with liturgical church adornments. With these dramatic changes brought about by the emergence of environmental art, pastors have given more attention to the teaching and interpretation of what these changes mean for worship.

Drama in member churches of the denomination has emerged as a result of improved program planning and the recognition that the gospel can be communicated through other means than the proclamation of the Word, the teaching of the Word, and the rendition of the Word through music. The growing concern of young people and young adults for participation in the church's ministry has caused pastors and Christian education directors to introduce innovative ways to witness to the gospel message. Again, it appears that black Baptists have borrowed from the liturgical churches and have made drama a significant medium, especially during the festive seasons of the calendar year.

Dance, on the other hand, still has not been accepted in most of the member churches of the denomination because most black Baptists continue to associate dance with the secular. There also has not been sufficient training and teaching among pastors and Christian education directors to move from the rejection of dance to its use as a teaching and communication vehicle for witnessing to the gospel. As black Baptist pastors and Christian education directors receive more formal training, including instruction in liturgical dance and art forms, a few churches have been bold enough to use them as a part of the worship service and in other aspects of their total ministry. The Galilee church is among the exceptions because it has combined drama, dance, and music to further the presentation of the history of the black church as a significant niche in African-American history and culture.

Richard Rollins and Hattie L. Wade

137 ◆ NATIONAL BAPTIST CONVENTION OF THE USA

Churches of the National Baptist Convention of the USA make extensive use of traditional black music such as spirituals and hymns as well as contemporary music that features modern harmonies and rhythms. The perceived secularity of some varieties of contemporary music presents one challenge to member churches. The dramatic and visual arts are also significant to member churches.

William Black is quoted as saying, "A Poet, A Painter, A Musician, An Architect, the man or woman who is not one of these is not a Christian." According to Scripture, these art forms are not determining factors of who or what we are, but they are a medium through which we can acknowledge who God is. Within the black Baptist community music, drama, and artistic expression are commonly used to declare devotion to God and are central in the worship experience.

Real worship is our response to God's revelation of himself. Musically we respond through spirituals, gospel, hymns, and contemporary music forms. Spirituals link the past to the present and future. Many of these songs were born out of the despair of slavery and social injustice that had denied a real partnership in society and the freedom to experience America. Spirituals not only encouraged the soul but allowed for the passing on of information among slaves who otherwise would not be permitted to converse with each other. "I Couldn't Hear Nobody Pray" reassured field workers that their prayer meeting in the brush harbor went undetected last night and that all was well. "Steal Away" not only spoke of a desire for a better land but indicated that someone was going to escape to freedom. "Go Down Moses," "Wade In The Water," "O Freedom," and "Over My Head" were not only messages of a hope yet alive, but a balm that soothed the black souls as they languished over the unfulfilled specter of their dreams. Today these songs are sung as specialty items or by college choirs.

The hymns of the black church include those tunes in the *Baptist Standard Hymnal* and are com-

mon to most of the Christian community. However, there is a unique form of hymn singing in the black church, a form that has survived every form of social adjustment and environmental change. This form is the meter hymn. Metered hymns were used in worship beginning in the early eighteen hundreds. The first collection of these hymns was published in 1897 by R. H. Boyd after being requested by pastors to provide a suitable list of songs to be shared by the pastor and deacons in prayer meetings. The three standard meters or patterns are long, short, and common. Long meter is represented by a line or verse being sung in a slow, unbroken pattern with the rise and fall of the phrase describing the fervor of pathos of the message. Short meter would require that the pattern be broken or cut off in short phrases allowing a responsive part to be sung in equal time and measurement. The reference to "common meter" simply points to the manner in which a song is most often sung. Originally, the texts of meter hymns were direct quotations from the Psalms and other portions of Scripture. In our more recent history words describing the desires and needs of humanity were incorporated, for example:

I spread my wants before his face and he spreads my rewards abroad.

Father, I stretch my hands to thee; no other I know.
If thou withdraw thyself from me, O whither shall I go.

I know I am a child of God, although I move so slow.
I'll wait until the Spirit comes and move at God's command.

Contemporary music is one of the newer forms of music being developed in the worship of the church. Generally the words fit the style of traditional gospel music but the harmony makes use of the more recent jazz chords. Much of this contemporary music does not fit the traditional mold, but is believed to cater to the younger audience. Urban contemporary music is filled with progressive harmony and nontraditional rhythmic patterns and is considered by many to be an overidentification with the worldly music scene. Many of the urban contemporary songs written for Christian worship are so vague in their verbal message and so lost in tempo and vigorous in meter that MTV and R&B stations play them as dance tunes. This music appeals more to the young but often lacks the soundness of content to serve as an anchor of the faith or as a guide toward spiritual maturity. In far too many instances a clear reference to God and his purposes is nonexistent. These styles are called by some "creative expression." However, as Walter Nathan says, "Creativity is an ingredient in eternity, and time in timelessness. One can see humanity's own creative power to be nothing less than its identification with the divine." Some of the popular performers of contemporary music that have made positive contributions are Rev. Rance Allen, Tramaine Hawkins, and the Wynans.

Drama in the Baptist church has its roots in childhood memorization of Scripture passages for Sunday school, parts in plays and speeches for Easter and Christmas such as _I've Found A New Doctor_ by Mrs. Maxine Vance, the acting out of the parables of Jesus, and creative writing projects of local youth ministries. In addition, oratorical contests sponsored by the National Baptist Convention are designed to increase the knowledge of our youth in the foundational truths of faith and practice.

It is said that "art and artistic experiences should create a deeper awareness of Christian faith, hope and love." Art serves as visible evidence of our religious heritage and heavenly expectation. A good example of effective implementation of art in a church setting can be seen at the Prince of Peace Baptist Church in Akron, Ohio. A series of stained glass windows have been arranged around the sanctuary area depicting the life and ministry of Jesus Christ from his birth to his ascension. Art as seen in the architectural designing of buildings tends to be conservative. There is a strong desire and need to be identified as a traditional place of worship where the ordinances of Christ are still central while progressive programs are being developed to serve our membership and the community. While the building structures remain generally traditional, unique pieces of artwork are being incorporated into the decor, especially when Christ-centered messages can be projected and perceived. Regardless of the wishes of any particular group, religious art and images are given facts in a pluralistic society and cannot be ignored. A religious picture on a calendar may shape a child's mental image of Christ long before he has learned anything definite about the Christian faith. Although there is a great need for an adequate theology of art, the arts are being displayed more and more within the church commu-

nity because we realize that a large percentage of communication is accomplished through the visuals.

Whether singing, dramatizing, or using other forms of artistic expression, our primary purpose is to worship and glorify God. Warren Wiersbe simply says, "Worship is at the center of everything that the church believes, practices and seeks to accomplish." God the Father has given his Son, the apostle Peter has declared him, and we continue to live out the desire of the apostle Paul, to know him:

> For my determined purpose is that I may know him, that I may progressively become more deeply and intimately acquainted with him, perceiving and recognizing and understanding the wonders of his person more strongly and more clearly, and that I may in that same way come to know the power outflowing from his resurrection which it exerts over believers, and that I may so share his sufferings as to be continually transformed in spirit into his likeness even to his death, in the hope that if possible, I may attain to the spiritual and moral resurrection that lifts me out from among the dead even while in the body.

Allen E. Middleton, Sr.

138 • PRESBYTERIAN CHURCH IN AMERICA

Worship in the Presbyterian Church of America is marked by an accent on what are regarded as timeless principles first articulated in the earliest years of the denomination. These principles, however, are most often seen as reflecting the need for maintaining doctrinal standards rather than dictating a need for only traditional artistic expression. Thus, while psalm singing is fostered and traditional hymns are heard, there is, especially in newer congregations, an acceptance of less formal orders of worship and newer musical styles. Most churches observe the passing liturgical year only minimally, and the use of the visual arts is sparing, but on the increase.

The Presbyterian Church in America (PCA) was organized in December 1973. Its 40,000 members were dispersed among 260 churches with 196 ministers. They supported eight foreign missionaries. Twenty years later, the PCA had grown to 240,000 in 1,100 churches with 2,200 ministers. Its foreign mission force currently numbers over 600 in full-time ministry, with several hundred more involved in short-term mission works. In addition, the denomination has nearly 100 military chaplains and a considerable number of people leading campus ministries and national home-mission projects. From its beginning as a regional church in the southeast, it has become truly national in character, with strong presbyteries in the Northeast, Midwest, and Pacific regions.

Virtually all of the leadership and membership of the PCA in 1973 had come out of the Presbyterian Church in the United States (which has since merged with the United Presbyterian Church). Conservatives in that denomination had, throughout the sixties, attempted to redirect the more liberal doctrinal and social trends of their church. By 1973, those liberal trends included rejection of biblical inerrancy, support of abortion, lessening commitment to evangelism, endorsement of liberation theology, and acceptance of ministers who did not believe in the historicity of Adam, the record of biblical miracles, the substitutionary atonement of Christ, or the physical resurrection of the Savior.

The PCA was born out of that controversy, but at its first General Assembly determined not to focus on criticism of its former denominational home. Instead, an aggressive, forward-looking evangelistic spirit was consciously adopted and pursued. Primary attention was given to the support of evangelists and church planters on home and foreign fields as well as for discipling ministries in the Christian education programs of local churches. The historic constitution of American Presbyterianism was adopted. All ordained officers (teaching and ruling elders and also deacons) take vows of agreement with the system of doctrine in the seventeenth century Westminster Confession of Faith (WCF) and the Westminster Larger and Shorter Catechisms.

Matters relating to worship, music, and the arts continue to be answered not by reference to local church preference and tradition. Rather, a concerned effort is made to reach decisions on the basis of clear biblical teaching and example and by constitutional instruction. In addition to the material on worship in the Westminster standards, the PCA also has a "Book of Church Order" (BOCO), third part of which is a "Directory for Worship."

Both documents (WCF and BOCO's Directory for Worship) are products of the seventeenth-century English Puritan reaction to efforts to reintroduce elements of Roman liturgy, sacramentalism, and liturgical conformity. They have their origins in the principles of reform articulated by John Calvin in Switzerland and by John Knox in Scotland, both in the mid-1500s. But as part of the constitution of the PCA, these documents continue to be used for their statement of timeless principles in defining and regulating worship on the contemporary scene.

"The regulative principle of worship" is a phrase often heard in the PCA in discussing matters of worship, music, and the arts. It is firmly planted in WCF and in BOCO, and is familiar to all in the ministry of the PCA. The principle is that since worship is of such prominence in Scripture, it must be of first importance to God. Therefore he has spoken in Scripture (not in tradition or in church council) to define and regulate worship. All that God has said should be done in his worship must be included in our worship. And only that which God said may be done in his worship can be included in our worship.

The elements of worship that God commands in Scripture are generally viewed as being the reading of Scripture, preaching, prayer, the sacraments (baptism and the Lord's Supper), offerings, professing of faith, singing, and receiving God's benediction (blessing). The expressions of these elements will vary according to custom and convenience and will include such issues as the time and order of worship, the architecture and design of the worship center, the style of music, and the frequency of Communion.

While the PCA is "conservative" in its traditional view of Scripture and its maintenance of historic doctrinal standards, it is generally "progressive" in applying Scripture and doctrinal standards to contemporary culture. This is true whether the "culture" is that of Old Downtown First Church, New Community Suburban Church, or one of the many ethnic missions at home or abroad. There is universal agreement as to the "elements" of worship, as defined above, but widespread diversity in implementing the varied "expressions" of those unchanging elements.

In most PCA churches (typically under 150 members), the local pastor has the primary (almost sole) influence on the style of worship. As the church grows, it is typical for staff musicians (usually part-time, often volunteer) to participate in some of the planning. It is unusual to find a music and worship committee of the session (the ruling body of elders) that includes some lay members.

Generally, worship order is traditional and unchanging. Hymns, prayer, an offering, and special music precede Scripture and sermon, which is usually twenty-five to thirty minutes in length. Increasingly, PCA churches, especially newer congregations organized within the last ten years, are adopting a less formal and more flexible order and style of worship. Along with efforts to reach ahead for the new are also efforts to reach back for the old. A concerted effort (with wide support) is underway to encourage the singing of more Psalms than just the twenty-third and one hundredth. Increasing numbers are drawn to this as being not only biblical but also historical. Reformed churches in Switzerland, Holland, England, and Scotland originally sang only the Psalms, not hymns.

Victorian hymns and gospel songs (both nineteenth-century products) were the standard fare in PCA churches in 1973. Only larger churches had pipe organs. Few had paid musicians on staff. Today, many of the newer congregations add a full-time minister of music and worship before adding a youth minister, and even before moving out of rented facilities and into their own building. Increasingly, a more contemporary worship style is being viewed as a primary means of attracting the unchurched. While this has not resulted in a widespread adoption of the Willow Creek model (with its tendency to appeal more to entertainment qualities than to worship), it has resulted in even well-established churches using accompaniment tapes, electric keyboards, and praise choruses on overhead projectors along with traditional hymns, anthems, pianos, and organs.

Still, very traditional small churches continued to play piano-accompanied gospel songs as their primary worship music (although they may add selections in the "pop" style of John W. Peterson or the Gaithers). Then there are very traditional large churches that maintain an excellent "high church" style of worship and music, from anthems to hymnody, with magnificent pipe organs and occasionally even orchestras. But the greater number of churches in the PCA are increasingly using an eclectic approach to style, always within the bounds of the "regulative principle of worship." As would be expected from their "free church" background, PCA churches do not customarily take note of the seasons of the church year. However, most churches do observe an Advent season (sometimes including an Advent candle ceremony) leading up to Christmas Eve candlelight services (frequently with Communion) and Christmas Sunday celebrations. Similarly, one will generally find Palm Sunday, Maundy Thursday or Good Friday, and Easter Sunday services. Rare will be the PCA church with a full Lenten season observance. Liturgical colors, lectionaries, vestments (other than a simple black robe), chants, and antiphons are relatively unknown entities.

Use of the arts (beside music) is spare, but on the increase. Most church buildings reflect a very traditional and functional design that emphasizes simplicity and conforms to budgetary restraints. Decoration in newer buildings is more likely to consist of thematic banners than of stained glass windows. Drama and dance are beginning to find a place in a relatively small number of congregations, but not without objection. Often, these are performed by visiting professional teams, as in a concert series. Where they are utilized "in house," it is with careful definition that these are not additional "elements" in worship (certainly not to replace others, such as the sermon), but rather as varied "expressions" of those elements. For example, a skit may serve as an illustration of a point to be made in the sermon, or a dance might accompany an anthem or solo. These uses of the arts are generally more likely to be found in newly established congregations than in those predating the denomination's 1973 organization. Where they have found a place, drama and dance teams meet regularly as another ministry option alongside rehearsals for handbells, instrumentalists, and choirs. These churches have developed a reputation for a very high standard of excellence in all of the arts.

While there is not a denominational office dealing with worship and music, the subject is one of increased discussion at many levels. In 1991 a denominational hymnal was published through Great Commission Publications, the PCA publishing agency (Horsham, Pennsylvania). The _Trinity Hymnal_ contains seven hundred forty-five selections, including settings of most of the Psalms. Musical styles range from traditional and gospel to folk and contemporary. A number of the hymns give chords for guitar accompaniment. The responsive Psalm readings use the New International Version translation. The full text of the Westminster Confession of Faith and Shorter Catechism, along with very extensive Scripture and topical indexes are included. Two denominational studies are currently underway. A large committee is preparing an extensive manual to define principles and recommend practices in the fields of music, worship, and the arts to assist church planters in the formative stages of a new congregation's life. And another committee is studying ways to encourage more singing of psalms in the church's worship.

Lawrence C. Roff

139 • PRESBYTERIAN CHURCH USA

A renewed interest in psalmody, one of the foundations of Presbyterian worship, and a new hymnal that includes the best of the past as well as appropriate ethnic materials, mark contemporary services in the Presbyterian Church USA. Although Presbyterians have been cautious in introducing the visual and dramatic arts, given their historically conservative use of representational art, there is now widespread use of the visual arts and increasing use of dance and drama in worship.

Music

The twentieth century has been for Presbyterians a time of glad exploration of the ways music and the arts can enhance the individual and corporate experience of worship. Our Reformation heritage has taught us the joy of congregational singing, especially of the Psalms. Shaped by this heritage, we naturally express through music all the aspects of worship present in the Psalms: proclamation, prayer, adoration, confession, thanksgiving, supplication, intercession, self-giving, and benediction.

In the last decade or so, psalmody has been renewed for contemporary worshipers through the work of people like Fred Anderson and Arlo Duba who interpret the Psalms for today. New too is *The Presbyterian Hymnal: Hymns, Psalms, and Spiritual Songs* (Presbyterian Publishing House, 1990), which brings a freshness to worship through selections which not only help us rediscover the best from our past, but also bring rich flavors from other musical and cultural traditions, including the African-American, Hispanic, Native American, Oriental, and African traditions.

Congregations joyously augment traditional music in worship by involving choral groups of all ages, handbell choirs, orchestras and ensembles, guitars, and electronic instruments. Some congregations have initiated an alternative Lord's Day service using contemporary and participatory music forms. And our new hymnal calls for us to celebrate diverse ethnic traditions by using instruments like the tom-tom and maracas.

Visual Arts

The "Directory for Worship," as a part of the constitution for members of the Presbyterian Church (USA), encourages congregations to be open to the Spirit's creative order under the authority of Scripture, cautioning only that "those entrusted with the proclamation of the Word through art forms should exercise care that the gospel is faithfully presented in ways through which the people of God may receive and respond!" This freedom in using visual and dramatic arts in Presbyterian worship has come slowly, because early Reformers feared idolatrous use of representational art, while even in the early years of this century, many Presbyterians viewed theater and the dance as "worldly" or "carnal" congregations.

In recent decades, however, Presbyterian awareness of the potential for involving other arts in worship has burgeoned. Sessions are encouraged to take responsibility for making the worship space a visual expression of what we believe about worship. It is important that the worship space be welcoming, accessible to all, a place for the community to celebrate the priesthood of believers, while the arrangement of pulpit, Table, and font visually presents the integral relationship between Word and sacrament in congregational worship.

While almost all Presbyterian congregations now enhance the worship setting with flowers, candles, and paraments, thoughtful worship committees augment the meaning of these by relating them to current worship themes. Thorns enveloping the chancel cross on Good Friday or red balloons on the narthex ceiling at Pentecost help move worshipers from the secular mode to the sacred.

Banners have burgeoned under the impetus of our recent bicentennial. Many congregations have represented their unique identity and history through a banner, used not only in their own worship place but in larger Presbyterian gatherings. There are also banners evoking theological truths or events in church history, displayed sometimes as a single banner on a stand or over a balcony rail, sometimes as a permanent array carefully planned to enhance the entire setting for worship. And to mark the seasons of the church year, what could be better than an outburst of banners?

——————— **Dance and Drama** ———————

As church leadership becomes more aware of the value of hands-on experience as one of the most important ways people learn and worship, enacted prayer and praise are incorporated into liturgy. The "Directory for Worship" reminds Presbyterians that since earliest biblical times prayer has been expressed in actions like kneeling, bowing, lifting up of hands, dancing, clapping, and laying on of hands. In some settings, these actions are formalized, in others, they are spontaneous. But worship planners now often incorporate opportunities for kinesthetic participation (shaping a prayer-petition from clay, dropping pocketfuls of pebbles into the font as confession, corporately constructing a cross as a Lenten meditation).

From these kinds of activities, it is only a small step to dance and drama. Experiences like the dance-like movements with which a children's choir interprets a hymn and the emotional impact on hearing worshipers of the motions of a signed service encourage churches to train volunteer choirs to interpret both hymns and Scripture texts in rhythmic movements. Other congregations develop liturgical dance troupes who lead in praise, receive and dedicate offerings, or offer the benediction.

Beyond the typical Christmas and Easter pageants, drama teams in some congregations form a group of "chapel players" for a ministry in proclamation, teaching, and celebration through liturgical drama. Some teams use street theater to bring mall spectators into the action with dialog about matters of faith and ethics. Even the smallest congregation can take time once a month to translate the gospel lesson into a format with a narrator and multiple voices reading the Scripture dialog, using a contemporary version of the gospel.

——————— **Resources** ———————

The *Directory for Worship* opens up new ideas for meaningful celebrations of worship. Incorporated in the *Book of Order* published by the Office of the General Assembly, it is available through Distribution Management Services, 100 Witherspoon Street, Room 1A, 1425, Louisville, KY 40202-1396, or by calling 1-800-524-2612.

The Presbyterian Hymnal: Psalms and Spiritual Songs is available in several editions from Presbyterian Publishing House at 100 Witherspoon Street, Louisville, KY 40202-1396, or by calling 1-800-227-2972.

The Supplemental Liturgical Resources (SLR) are prepared by the Joint Office of Worship for the Cumberland Presbyterian Church as well as for the denomination. They include liturgies for and commentaries on various worship services. The series to date includes *The Service for the Lord's Day, Holy Baptism and Services for the Renewal of Baptism, Christian Marriage, The Funeral, Daily Prayer, Services for Occasions of Pastoral Care,* and *The Liturgical Year.*

Reformed Liturgy and Worship is an invaluable resource published quarterly by the Ministry Unit on Theology and Worship of the denomination. As the official journal of the Presbyterian Association of Musicians, it offers significant articles on music and other arts in corporate worship.

The Book of Common Worship (1993) is a comprehensive resource of liturgical texts. It includes complete orders of worship for many services in the liturgical year and a variety of texts for each individual act of worship. Also included are a liturgical psalter, liturgies for daily prayer services, services of Christian marriage, funerals, and other pastoral services.

Mellicent Honeycut-Vergeer

140 ✦ PROGRESSIVE NATIONAL BAPTIST CONVENTION

In the churches of the Progressive National Baptist Convention, the transmission of theology rests heavily upon the sermon and the songs which support it. Worship services feature both European-American and African-American music. More progressive congregations use a wide variety of musical instruments, a popular style of music, and even dance and drama. New publications offer a wide variety of traditional music and folk songs.

Dr. Wyatt T. Walker, in his book *Somebody's Calling My Name,* has stated: "Music is one of the three major support systems in Black Church Worship" ([Valley Forge, Pennsylvania, 1979], 2). Praying, preaching, and music are the three interacting systems. Prayers are often expressed in a moaning or musical manner. Sermons are often preached in a lyrical style. In terms of the time given to the three support systems, music dominates. The sermon hymn before preaching usually prepares the worshiping community for preaching. The sermon, upon completion, has powerful support from the choir. The choir sings a carefully selected song designated to stamp the sermon message upon the hearts of the audience. The transmission of theology is dependent upon both songs and sermon.

Most of the Progressive National Baptist churches are large churches that employ chants, hymns, anthems, gospel, and praise choruses in order to meet the diverse tastes and needs of heterogeneous audiences. A range of Euro-American and Afrocentric music may be heard in a single worship service.

Afrocentric stained-glass windows, priestly vestments, and banners adorn the worship environment. Yet pulpit and Communion table tapestries are not as sharply illustrated as in some churches.

In the recent past, Progressive Baptist churches that have pipe organs have added drums, guitars, and organs that are used to play more jazzy music. Trumpets, saxophones, and stringed instruments play while the choir sings or at times play solos. Large churches also have ensembles and orchestras. The Allen Temple Baptist Church has a children's liturgical dance troupe that performs during the special days and seasons of the liturgical year.

At Christmas time in our church the Cantateers provide music and drama. This group performs Langston Hughes's *Black Nativity* and at Easter time attracts large audiences to hear and see the drama of the Crucifixion and Resurrection. In addition, the national, regional, and state meetings of the Progressive National Baptist Convention always open with a musical. They also have a convention choir and music classes during these sessions.

Black Christian publishing houses are producing hymnals and gospel song books. In August of 1982, the *New Progressive National Baptist Hymnal* was released. This book included responsive readings, calls to worship, benedictions, meditations, and articles of faith, as well as hymns, spirituals, anthems, gospel songs, and praise songs. The purpose of the hymnal was to balance congregational, choral, and individual singing, and to discourage sacrilegious or so-called worldly music in the singing of Christian worship. Another important source of music is *Religious Folk Songs of the Negro* as sung at Hampton Institute (now Hampton University). Hampton University published the book in 1927. Dr. R. Nathaniel Dett of Hampton's Department of Music was the editor.

Alain Locke has given insight on black church music in his *The Negro and His Music* and *Negro Art: Past and Present* (New York: Arno Press, 1969). James Weldon Johnson and J. Rosamond Johnson have given a rich resource in *The Roots of American Negro Spirituals* (New York: Viking Press, 1969). Other sources can be located in New York City's Schomberg Library, at Fisk University of Nashville, and at the National Baptist Sunday School Publishing Board in Nashville.

J. Alfred Smith, Jr.

141 ✦ REFORMED CHURCH IN AMERICA

The RCA originally sang from the Genevan Psalter but in subsequent years adopted music and hymn resources from other denominations. More recently it has published its own hymnbook and musical resources. However, some churches have adopted the praise-and-worship songs and have abandoned the hymnal.

The Reformed Church in America (RCA) includes almost a thousand congregations in the United States and Canada. It was founded in 1628 as a branch of the established church of the Netherlands, but its larger part, found in the Midwest, came out of a conservative Dutch free-church movement. In spite of its nickname, the "Dutch Reformed Church," the RCA has never been exclusively Dutch. Its first recorded service was celebrated in both Dutch and French. By 1776 the Dutch, French, German, and English languages were all in use. From the start, RCA worship styles have been diverse.

For the first century-and-a-half of its existence, the RCA's music was dominated by the Genevan Psalter. In 1767, in order to allow for simultaneous bilingual singing in both Dutch and English, the Collegiate Church of New York published an *English Psalmbook,* an effort that was flawed and unsuccessful. As the whole denomination Americanized, it abandoned the Genevan type of psalmody in favor of Anglican and Presbyterian psalmody. The first denominational book of *Psalms and Hymns* (1789) was mostly "Tate and Brady" (an English Psalter) plus about a hundred hymns arranged to supplement the preaching of the Heidelberg Catechism and the celebration of the Lord's Supper. By 1814 the psalmody was mostly that of Isaac Watts, and the collection of hymns began to grow. The last edition of the *Psalms and Hymns* had seven hundred and eighty-seven hymns!

After 1860 the RCA gave up publishing its own hymnal, and congregations chose from whatever was on the market, the only requirement being that the catechism and liturgy should be bound in. Not one of the books available had any kind of psalmody. Even though Psalm-singing was kept alive by the new wave of Dutch immigrants to the Midwest, the practice has never survived the switch to English. The RCA was gradually being cut off, not only from its own tradition, (the Genevan tunes being the chief loss) but also from the mainstream of Reformed worship worldwide.

The next century saw the denomination uncertain of its direction. It participated half-heartedly in the United Presbyterian Psalter of 1912. Five years later, it teamed up with the (German) Reformed Church in the U.S. to produce _The Reformed Church Hymnal,_ which included very little psalmody. After World War II, it joined the (Southern) Presbyterian Church in the U.S. in the development of _The Hymnbook,_ which appeared in 1955. But these officially endorsed hymnals were not used by even half of the denomination. In the Midwest especially, the revival style of music came to dominate, and Hope Publishing's _Service Hymnal_ and _Worship and Service Hymnal_ were the books of choice. The result was the development of two distinct musical cultures within the RCA, sometimes at war within the same congregation.

To celebrate the RCA's three hundred and fiftieth anniversary, the esteemed hymnologist Erik Routley was invited to edit a new denominational hymnal. It was published in 1985, a year after Routley's sudden death, as _Rejoice in the Lord: A Hymn Companion to the Scriptures._ In its wonderful plan and its noble character, _Rejoice_ is a hymnological landmark, but as a denominational book it must be considered a brilliant failure, for it presumes a level of musical sophistication beyond that of most RCA congregations. Many congregations have taken a good look at it only to decline to purchase it. Others that did get it are already abandoning it. Routley had hoped that _Rejoice_ might find a market in other denominations, but it failed to do so, and it looks instead like the new Christian Reformed and Presbyterian hymnals might find use in the RCA. And the congregations that used the _Worship and Service Hymnal_ are replacing it with such books as _Praise!_ and _Hymns for the Family of God._

If there is any renewal vitality at all, it is in the increasingly popular praise-and-worship move-

ment. Some congregations have abandoned their hymnals for overhead projectors, and their musical diet consists of only choruses and Scripture songs. Although these latter examples, like the old metrical Psalms, have the benefit of allowing people to sing Scripture, they lack the emotional depth of good psalmody. Furthermore, although the RCA confesses "the Holy Catholic Church," the catholicity of church music is lost to a diet of choruses and Scripture songs. The character of this movement cannot fully be reconciled with the official liturgy of the RCA.

One positive development has been the appearance of the magazine _Reformed Worship,_ which is published by the Christian Reformed Church but includes many contributions from RCA members. Primary attention is given to developments in music and liturgy, but visual arts, banners, and even dance are covered as well. Most of the creativity comes secondhand from other English-speaking worship traditions, and the magazine attempts to measure (and temper) these developments from a Reformed viewpoint. Undoubtedly, this magazine has been a boon to local worship committees.

Surprisingly, there has been little impact by Taizé. In the last decade, however, the _Common Lectionary_ has found wide use in the RCA. It remains to be seen whether this will have an effect on the liturgical arts. Another recent development has been the "Young Children in Worship" program, which has brought its own kinds of renewal to those congregations using it. But the wider repercussions of this cannot yet be measured either.

The RCA is wide open when it comes to music and the arts. For the last century, its churches have been borrowing haphazardly from here and there, increasingly so in the last decade. In spite of an obligatory liturgy and a strong doctrinal tradition, anything can happen, and does. Apart from scattered congregations, it cannot be said that there is any significant renewal of worship in the RCA. There is no center for renewal that is serving the whole, and no community of musicians or artists giving creative leadership. The three RCA-affiliated colleges do not act as nurseries for the denomination's liturgical culture. It appears that though the RCA may honor its tradition, it has little confidence in it.

Daniel Meeter

142 ✦ REFORMED EPISCOPAL CHURCH

The churches of the Reformed Episcopal Church stress their connection with the ancient church, fostering psalm singing and hymns that clearly reflect great historical doctrinal truths. In addition, there is a dependence on music associated with the earliest years of the Anglican churches of the Reformation. More modern musical styles and even dance, however, are finding their way into the practice of Reformed Episcopal worship.

Music in the Reformed Episcopal Church reflects the evangelical (Reformation) and the undivided (ancient) church within the Anglican tradition. Each aspect involves several doctrinal and practical commitments.

In the ancient church, music was to be biblical. For this reason, the words and pre-Christian Jewish tunes of the book of Psalms became the primary, although not the exclusive, songs of the New Testament and early church. These texts were chanted in a manner much like Jewish psalm-singing. Music in the early church was also Christological and credal.

The Symbol of St. Matthew. The winged man symbolizes the human nature of Jesus, which St. Matthew proclaimed.

It pointed to Christ, as evidenced in some of the early scriptural hymns. The great creeds of the faith were put to music so that essential theological truths could be preserved. Some of the earliest hymns have become part of an ongoing doctrinal expression, such as the famous *Te Deum Laudamus* (We Praise You, O Lord). The power of doctrine in song is confirmed in a negative illustration by the musical talents of the famous heretic Arius, who pulled the church in the wrong theological direction by his popular heterodox hymn, "There Was a Time When Christ Was Not."

This historic tradition has been maintained in the Reformed Episcopal Church through classical Anglican hymnody. A model church for this is the one-hundred-year-old St. Paul's Reformed Episcopal Church of Oreland, Pennsylvania. With a skilled choirmaster, choir, and organist, the music at St. Paul's reflects the best of historic Anglicanism. The 1940 *Hymnal* of the Episcopal Church, perhaps the finest collection of historic hymnody in the liturgical tradition, is the basic song book of the parish. Portions of the Psalms, called canticles, are chanted as the congregation joins this most ancient form of singing. Special music is often sung from the better-known liturgical composers. In addition, this choir has performed such classical pieces as Haydn's *Creation,* and even other dignified contemporary music to appeal to the community. All of this gives a sense of reaching to the high standard of the best of the liturgical Anglican tradition. St. Paul's is also noted for housing Arthur B. Carle's famous copy of Raphael's *The Transfiguration*, commissioned in 1907 by St. Paul's and now hanging in the chancel behind the sacrament table. The original in the Vatican was left incomplete at Raphael's death even though it was the culmination of his life's work. Art students still come to study Carle's completion of Raphael's work, which sets a tone for the classical tradition of music at this Reformed Episcopal Parish of Oreland.

The other important musical tradition in Anglicanism is the evangelical, which emphasizes the great theology of the Reformation. Several theological themes that were prominent in the Reformation later became the subject for much hymnody. They all generally focus on the doctrine of salvation. The reformational view of justification underscored the truth of salvation and release from sin and death immediately upon the exercise of personal faith. This theme elicited a church music that was and is joyous and quick in pace. Archbishop Cranmer commissioned liturgical tunes that could be sung in such a way as to indicate this immediate conversion and assurance of salvation. The music was no longer only to reflect the dour medieval uncertainty of one's standing with God. The music of the Reformation proclaimed that one could know he or she was truly converted. One no longer had to nag God endlessly, for to do so nearly makes doubt a virtue and admits of a lack of faith; hence, there is no real salvation.

The Reformed Episcopal Church is part of this evangelical heritage in its music and is open to traditional as well as contemporary forms of gospel expression. Model churches, such as Bishop Cummins Memorial Church of Baltimore, Maryland, blend the traditional with contemporary by using appropriate praise music and different instruments, especially the guitar. This parish has also availed itself of artistic expression in the form of ballet at special marriage services and so forth. In addition, the black parishes of the REC manifest other elements of great evangelical and gospel singing. Most of these congregations sing the classic spirituals with great enthusiasm, bodily swaying, and hand-clapping. They represent in their congregational singing an important art form within the Christian Protestant tradition.

Thus, the Reformed Episcopal Church is developing two great traditions of music. In many ways, it is rediscovering its liturgical musical heritage, while at the same time it is learning of new contemporary music. These directions are more and more working to make liturgical form speak to today's culture. The present is not to be sought at the expense of the past. Nor is the past to be held so tenaciously that the present and even the future are lost. The Reformed Episcopal Church, therefore, builds on the great ecclesiastical music of the past along two guiding tracks of ancient and evangelical traditions that continue to propel this denomination through the present into the future.

Ray Sutton

143 • ROMAN CATHOLIC CHURCHES

A revolution has occurred in music and the arts in the Roman Catholic church since Vatican II: Churches have been renovated to styles more conducive to the new liturgy; new music has been written for liturgical texts; and the arts have found a new place in Catholic worship.

Before Vatican II, the rubrics (ceremonial directions) for Roman Catholic rituals were very specific. Documents clearly indicated what was permissible in liturgy and clearly separated the sacred from the secular. During the period when Vatican II council documents were emerging (1963–1975), the nature of liturgical music and visual elements reflected assumptions of a new celebrative spirit. Rubrics were put aside, some of them forever (e.g., the ruling that women could play no role in the ritual in the sanctuary). The influence of life, rather than law, laid the groundwork for renewal.

Worship continued in parishes during the years when the official documents for the renewal of the seven sacrament rituals were being written. Facilities were renovated, some more than once, and new facilities were built. Many new possibilities were attempted in the liturgy itself, including many that proved to be ineffective. For example, the offertory procession sometimes seemed like a parade that interrupted the ritual process. At times an eagerness to keep the Mass celebrational resulted in an overly flamboyant visual and/or musical texture. The use of felt banners that proclaimed "theme" slogans in words distracted from rather than inspired the prayer text. Multimedia presentations, dance, drums, drama, bells, harp, sitar, and balloons all permitted time and space to be explored in the ritual process, but also tended to drain power from the liturgy itself. In retrospect, it seems that music and art had to go through a "throwaway phase," that is, a time when permanence was viewed as negative while flexibility and newness, or eclecticism, were believed to offer the richest access to the spiritual. Many of these innovations were dropped.

Along with the spirit of renewal, social and cultural issues entered sacrament ritual life. The blatant male references in rousing old hymns became offensive rather than conducive to prayer in communities sensitive to inclusiveness, peace, and justice.

It was fortunate that the final documentation for the sacramental rituals coincided with the 1976 bicentennial of the United States. The heightened awareness of our history awakened the interest of church communities in their beginnings. For communities housed in fine examples of historical architecture, the task became not simply renovation, but also restoration. Commitment to both directions led to the mutual enhancement of worship spaces and ritual processes. When these are considered separately, an emphasis on one can be detrimental to the other. For example, the architectural integrity of many turn-of-the-century revival-style church interiors was diluted when they were painted white in the name of "relevance." Fortunately, in many cases this served as an undercoat for the rich Victorian colors of the postmodern period. In music, early efforts to update chant by replacing Latin with English have been preempted by works such as the chants of Taizé.

For anyone assisting a faith community in building new worship spaces or renovating a worship space, it is natural to ask, "Why do you go?" Earlier, the natural Roman Catholic answer would have been "out of obligation"; now the answer tends to be something like "because here I find support for my life . . . a family." From one community to another, the sense of family has become the common element that holds together the communal expression of faith. Although the same approved new texts are used in all churches (the Mass went from one eucharistic prayer to a choice of nine), the climate of liturgical expression varies. Some communities prefer orderly services guided by professional leaders in structured environments. There, ministers of music and art might be on the staff. The music planned for a ritual would be rehearsed; its score and text would be reproduced and handed out by ministers of hospitality as people enter the ritual space. The visual elements, whether permanent or seasonal, are envisioned as architectural environmental art. In such a community, the family is celebrating something special in a special way.

Another community might find the idea of family liturgy better supported by an informal style and setting. The music and art could be disposable, created for the moment of celebration and not meant for critical review or repeated use. To serve the ritual need of such a community, the environment might be loosely structured; there might be chairs instead of fixed pews, a flexible modular platform for the sanctuary, the use of children's art. For this community, the family celebrates something special in a serious playful way. These are the extreme ends of the spectrum. Between them, there are many variations.

The kind of questions that arise today in relation to the texture of liturgical music, art, or architecture are:

- What is the nature of the celebration?
- Does the opening music signify a processional entrance or a call to prayer?

- Is the music presented for or participated in by those present?
- Is the music knitting those present together or merely supporting a text?
- Are the words that accompany the music relevant?
- Are actions or objects the focal elements of the ritual?
- Is the ritual power embodied in the ordained men or in those present who share a common initiation?
- Is the building a withdrawal from the world, or planted in the world?
- Does the building look like a church?
- As one journeys from the parking lot to the sanctuary, what is revealed by what is seen and heard?
- Did the sacrament event provide entertainment or transformation?

These and other related questions will provide stimulus for the continuing renewal of worship practices within the Roman Catholic church.

Willy Malarcher

144 ✦ THE SALVATION ARMY

The Salvation Army, whose long-time commitment to music is particularly well-known given the visibility of its performers, is not restricting itself to its traditional musical repertoire. Rather, for the past ten years it has been introducing new music in its services and its public appearances, including nearly every style of contemporary music.

The Salvation Army has a rich and unique heritage of instrumental and vocal music that reaches back to its earliest days in Victorian England. The Army is currently experiencing a dramatic renewal of its music. This is due both to a systematic emphasis on music education and to a reemphasis on the functional philosophy of music that guided both the initial, rapid development of our music programs and publications during the 1880s and also the growth of Army music in subsequent decades. This philosophy of Salvation Army music was articulated by General Albert Orsborn years later:

We have no wish to be outcasts of the musical world but our music is, and must continue to be functional as distinct from the merely artistic, aesthetic or impressionistic. Our message, our praise, our mission, and our worship all embody our function. (Ronald W. Holz, "A Brief Review of the Function and Administration of Salvation Army Music," in _A History of the Hymn Tune Meditation and Related Forms in Salvation Army Music in Great Britain and North America, 1880–1980_ [Storrs, Conn.: Unpublished Ph.D. dissertation, University of Connecticut, 1981], 6).

In the preface to _Salvation Music,_ Vol. 2, published in London in 1883 for congregational use, the founder of the Salvation Army, William Booth, wrote:

The music of the Army is not, as a rule, original. We seize upon the strains that have already caught the ear of the masses, we load them with our one great theme—salvation, and so we make the very enemy help us fill the air with our Savior's fame.

This radical approach to nineteenth-century church music was reflected in the borrowing of popular ballads, drinking songs, patriotic anthems, and folk songs. American gospel songs and spirituals were also included in this early-day song book.

The popular music of late nineteenth-century England was found at park bandstands and in the music halls. William Manchester in his bibliography of Winston Churchill, _The Last Lion,_ documents the principal venues for popular music during Churchill's youth:

Not counting The Salvation Army and the military, there were over five thousand bands in the country, and on holidays Londoners crowded around the bandstands in their parks. This was the golden age of the music halls. Between 1850 and 1880 about five hundred new ones were built with the city's fifty theaters, meaning that 350,000 Londoners were entertained every night. (William Manchester, _The Last Lion: Winston Spencer Churchill; Vision of Glory: 1874–1932_ [Boston: Little, Brown, 1983], 68).

William Booth echoed Martin Luther's question from the sixteenth century: "Why should the devil have all the best tunes?" Booth's forces conducted many of their early-day meetings in rented music halls, wisely borrowing the tunes of music hall songs and added religious words. The most popular music hall song of the 1880s, "Champagne Charlie Is Me Name," became "Bless His Name, He Sets Me Free" (_The Song Book of the Salvation Army,_ American ed. [Verona, N.J.: The Salvation Army, 1987], 149).

The British "working class" of this period found that the brass band provided a comparatively easy way of participating in a music group. One hundred years ago the Army attracted the poor and underprivileged of the "working class," and new Salvationists were encouraged to bring their instruments to the meetings. This included not only brass instruments, but also banjos, concertinas, and accordions. Within just a few years there were hundreds of Salvation Army brass bands in Great Britain. As the Salvation Army rapidly spread from London to many parts of the world, the British brass band remained a distinctive feature of the Salvation Army whether on the streets of New York or in the parks of Sydney and Adelaide. (Eric Ball, "Salvation Army Bands and Their Music," in _Brass Bands in the 20th Century,_ Violet and Geoffrey Brand, eds. [Baldock, Herts., UK: Egon Publishers, 1979], 184–186.)

The renewal of Salvation Army worship during the past ten years has been strongly influenced by changes in our music publications and music programs. For over 100 years the Salvation Army has published its own band and vocal music as well as its own congregational songbooks. By regulation Army bands and songster brigades (choirs) are limited to performance of only music published by the Salvation Army. This was somewhat relaxed in 1991 when at the same time all Salvation Army music was first marketed to other denominations and schools.

The current generation of Salvation Army composers and arrangers has updated the Army tradition of presenting the gospel message through popular music, and Army music publications now regularly include the full gamut of contemporary music styles. It is no longer unusual for a Salvation Army band to perform jazz-influenced arrangements during a worship service. Collections of contemporary songs written and arranged by Salvationists have been published for the rapidly growing number of contemporary Christian music ensembles. (Stephen Bulla, ed., _The Contemporary Songbook,_ vols. 1 and 2 [Atlanta: The Salvation Army, 1987, 1992].)

In 1987 the Salvation Army published the first revision of _The Salvation Army Song Book_ since 1953 (_The Song Book of the Salvation Army,_ American ed., [Verona, N.J.: The Salvation Army, 1987]). This was followed in 1988 by the total revision of the _Youth Songbook of the Salvation Army_ (Verona,

N.J.: The Salvation Army, 1988). For the first time many Salvation Army worship services included the hymns of Brian Wren, the songs of Bill and Gloria Gaither, Kurt Kaiser, and Ralph Carmichael as well as contemporary hymns and songs by the new generation of Salvationist songwriters.

These changes in music publications have been accompanied by significant growth among Salvation Army music groups. The major factor in this growth during the 1980s has been the employment of full-time music directors at the state level. These professional music educators supervise the developing programs at the local level, provide intensive music instruction at summer music camps and regional music schools, and train local volunteer music leaders. In 1992, there were approximately forty-five full-time music directors working on behalf of Salvation Army music within the United States. Within the Salvation Army in the United States, there are 841 local corps (church) brass bands (adult and youth) with a combined membership of 7,778, and 1,418 local corps choirs (adult and youth) with a combined membership of 19,162. (Data from *The Salvation Army National Composite Statistics* for the year ending December 1990.)

Richard E. Holz

145 ◆ SOUTHERN BAPTIST CONVENTION CHURCHES

Southern Baptists use a wide range of music from the rich tradition of ancient hymnody to the praise chorus tradition. There is an equally wide range in the use of the arts, from relatively unadorned worship services to services that incorporate banners, dance, and drama frequently.

Music

The music tradition in Baptist worship has centered on the hymnbook, with the hymnbook and sermon serving as the dual foci of Baptist worship. Vigorous hymn singing accompanied by piano or organ has been the dominant musical expression. Vocal solos, choral anthems, and instrumental music have come (from the 1960s through the 1980s) to have a more important function, but hymn singing still predominates.

Since the 1950s perhaps the most important contribution of Southern Baptist church music has been the graded choir program. Preschoolers, children,

and youth are actively recruited and trained in age-graded choirs. Music education is the main objective of these choirs; children and youth are taught to sing, to become musicians and to learn the faith expressed in songs, hymns, and anthems. The 1960s and 1970s saw the introduction and growth of musicals for youth and children. Different musical forms (folk, rock, musical stage) and instruments were introduced through these musicals. The philosophy of church music has centered on worship and nurture: music as an aid in the worship of God and music as an educative tool for learning about God.

The range and variety of music in Southern Baptist churches has been enormous: from Stamps Baxter (gospel) to Johann Sebastian Bach, from historic hymnody to praise choruses, from the full range of serious classical music to contemporary "pop" Christian music. Larger and more urban churches tend to use more "classical" music while smaller and more rural churches tend to use more gospel music. Theological differences also influence music choices. The more "conservative" churches tend to sing more gospel music and sing more subjective hymns and songs telling what Christ has done for "me" and how "my" faith is going. The more "liberal" churches use more classical music and sing more objective hymns that tell of God's work in creation, providence, and redemption.

The 1970s and 1980s saw increasing variety in the use of musical instruments in worship, including handbells, guitars, and orchestral instruments. Congregational music continues to center on hymn singing, though praise choruses are growing in popularity in some quarters.

The Arts

Southern Baptists have traditionally ignored the use of arts other than in music. Visual symbolism was identified as being "too Catholic." Until recently, Baptist church sanctuaries were devoid of Christian symbolism, even the cross. Faith was thought to come by hearing; sanctuaries were auditoriums. The eye was an unimportant if not suspect organ in the worship of God.

Since the 1960s, however, the visual arts have been used increasingly. Many churches now have crosses in their architectural design. Banner art is used to present a wider array of symbol and visual communications. Some churches invite the visual artists in the congregation and community to display art in church galleries. The art pieces may be thematically related to seasons of the church year like Advent, Lent, Easter, and Pentecost. Bulletin art is also used to communicate the faith.

Drama has also received increased usage in the past few decades. The 1960s brought youth musicals; children's musicals increased in the 1970s and 1980s. In the 1990s more adult drama groups are being formed that present sacred and secular drama, e.g., *Godspell, Murder in the Cathedral, After the Fall.* Drama is also used in worship services. Dramatic vignettes and sketches are used for biblical and theme interpretation. Dramatic monologues are employed to bring a biblical character alive. Storytelling, mime, and puppetry are also used in chancel drama. Liturgical dance has a small but spirited following in Baptist churches.

Resources

Most state conventions have church music departments. The Southern Baptist Convention Sunday School Board has a church music department which publishes a wide range of educational resources and music. Many Baptist colleges and seminaries have music schools and drama departments which train church musicians and artists. The Sunday School Board also has a church drama department.

In the 1980s, Southern Baptist Theological Seminary created a Center for Religion and the Arts. Headed by William Hendricks, this center encourages the use of a wide range of arts in the service of the gospel. In 1991, *The Baptist Hymnal* was published (the fourth hymnal Southern Baptists have published). It includes an extensive variety of hymns and songs and uses visual art.

Conclusion

Southern Baptist churches are witnessing in some quarters a "liturgical renewal" movement. Worship renewal is happening through increased attention to the Christian year; through borrowing from worship traditions of other denominations; and through an increased emphasis on the ordinances, the Table and pool, as central acts of worship. There is an increased use of visual and dramatic arts in these churches.

In other quarters the praise-and-worship movement is gathering momentum, featuring an extended "praise time" in worship with extensive use of praise choruses. The overhead projector is used more than the hymnal. Church orchestras and

bands are replacing the piano and organ as major instruments.

Many Southern Baptists want worship to be more God-centered. The horizontal experiences of worshipers with each other and the subjective orientation of the faith and life of the worshiper predominate. Too few songs and hymns focus on God and what God is like and has done. The contemporary is used at the expense of the historic church music tradition.

Overall, there is a great expansion of the use of the arts in Southern Baptist worship. In a visually oriented culture, this is an essential aid to the sharing of the gospel.

H. Stephen Shoemaker

146 • United Church of Christ

The congregations of the relatively new United Church of Christ use worship music that includes both traditional hymnody and music from a variety of ethnic and cultural backgrounds. A new hymnal is scheduled for publication in 1995. It will be patterned after the liturgical year as well as the Common Lectionary and will feature texts that use only inclusive language. The denomination is also noted for the variety of the locally appropriate architectural styles used in their churches.

The United Church of Christ was founded in 1957 by the joining of the Evangelical and Reformed Church and the Congregational Christian Church. These two denominations were likewise the result of mergers in the 1930s of the Evangelical Synod with the Reformed Church, and of the Congregational Church with the Christian Church. The present United Church of Christ includes German-rooted Evangelical and Reformed churches, Puritan Reformation-based Congregationalism, and the free-thinking spirit of the southern Christian Church.

As a relatively new denomination, the United Church of Christ has been intentional in its work of providing a body of worship material for the diversity of worship styles that still exist. *The Hymnal of the United Church of Christ,* 1974, and *The Book of Worship,* 1986, are the denomination's first hymnal and service book.

At this writing, a second hymnal is being prepared. Its goal is to continue to mold denominational identity through a blend of core hymnody that would represent not only its European heritage, but also the African-American, Spanish-American, Asian-American and native American roots of the denomination. At the same time it seeks to find the common hymns of the constituency. The spectrum of worship styles will be reflected also. Musical elements of the liturgical order of worship, such as the *Kyrie, Gloria,* and *Sanctus,* will be provided in a variety of multicultural settings. A Psalter will provide the basis for selective usage and will include suggestions for singing and speaking the Psalms that range from chant to responsive reading.

From its beginnings the United Church of Christ has placed strong emphasis on justice issues, and this is reflected not only in its multicultural attitude, but also in the production of printed materials that carefully avoids language which will reinforce cultural, social, and gender biases. The 1995 hymnal was commissioned by the Board for Homeland Ministries of the denomination to feature inclusive language. Consequently, much attention has been paid to hymn language for people and finding new metaphors for the deity.

The liturgical year and *Common Lectionary* readings are in widespread use in the denomination. Consequently, the 1995 hymnal is planned to be lectionary compatible and scripturally keyed. All of the aforementioned features will make the book ecumenically useful. This is often the case with materials produced by the denomination, owing to the diversity upon which it is founded.

Just as great variety exists in worship style, so it is reflected in architecture. People's Congregational Church in Washington, D.C., provides a modern nave in the form of a stylized African hut for its mostly African-American membership. First Congregational Church in Houston, Texas, is a modern edifice based on simple Puritan principles of architecture. Other U.C.C. churches reflect a German Reformation heritage. The Board for Homeland Ministries has developed a process for helping congregations provide new architectural concepts to reflect their heritage.

New curriculum being developed by United Church Press is following a similar direction as the hymnal. Inclusive, ecumenical, multicultural, and diverse, it also attempts to reflect the broad roots of the church. At its core is the use of visual art from Reformation to present. This use of art will provide not only effective illuminations of lectionary subjects, but will give an opportunity for the works of

art to be viewed as documents through which faith and culture can be understood.

Arthur Clyde

147 • United Methodist Churches

The United Methodist Church is a center for the revival of music and the arts in worship. The new hymnal is characterized by an inclusive use of music from different cultures and periods of history. Methodists have also recovered the lively use of the arts as vehicles for worship.

At the heart of United Methodist worship is music. Music is the language of the congregation, and it is widely understood that the function of music in worship is to help the congregation encounter God. Whether a United Methodist church is "high church," "low church," or somewhere between the two, the philosophy of the function of music rarely deviates. Music is the human expression by which we are joined one to another and by which we claim our understanding of God and our relationship to God. Music is the vehicle, the action, of the work of the people.

A renewed interest and emphasis on the Bible and the sacraments has fostered the study and development of worship practices in the United Methodist Church. In turn, a variety of issues related to music have surfaced. At the top of the list are inclusiveness and appropriateness.

With regard to music, inclusiveness refers to the use of a variety of music in the worship service that relates persons of all ages and theological understandings to God. *The United Methodist Hymnal* (1989) has been a tremendous resource for the United Methodist Church in providing a range of music and liturgical resources that is both inclusive and challenging. It allows churches to use hymns, chants, gospel music, praise choruses, spirituals, and metrical as well as pointed psalms for worship as deemed appropriate for a congregation. The range of music found in United Methodist churches has never been greater. The same is true for the use of instruments.

While the organ continues to be the primary worship instrument for United Methodist churches, especially in accompanying congregational singing, piano, guitar, handbells, and drums (of all kinds) are the other instruments often heard in worship. The prevalent reason for using a variety of instruments in worship is using the talents found in the congregation and providing a variety of ways to express praise and thanks to God through vital and exciting singing and music-making.

The appropriateness of music and all liturgical elements are directly linked to the needs and experiences of the congregation. "Appropriate" does not necessarily mean "familiar," but it does take into account whether a given piece of music or liturgical action is relevant to that worshiping community. Appropriateness along with artistic talents found within the congregation are the primary criteria for a variety of arts in worship. Banners and seasonal art (Advent wreaths, crèches, Lenten crosses, and other items) often make up most of the environmental art outside of the architecture itself. Worship and altar guild committees spend much care in providing art that takes into account the color or colors for a specific season as well as the symbols. The congregation seems to take delight in noticing the changing seasons of the Christian year with the textile and symbolic art that is created and displayed. One important piece of textile art for a large church in Nashville is the tapestry banner that was created from pieces of cloth given by the members of the congregation. This banner exemplifies the desire of the worshiping community to be one with each other and one with Christ.

Drama is also mostly a seasonal highlight with processions and dramatic readings happening around Christmas and Easter. Most dramatic readings take place during Holy Week and dramatic enactments take place during the Christmas season. Some churches have discovered that Scripture passages can be dramatic, especially when it is read in dialogue or in chorus.

The most controversial of the arts in worship remains liturgical dance. Here again the issue is appropriateness. In general, dance groups tend to be accepted more readily than solo dancers. Also, dances that are included in special seasonal celebrations, especially when they involve children and youth, are acceptable to most worshiping congregations.

A new document to be published in 1993 will help churches develop programs and standards for the ongoing support of church music and musicians. The main thrust of this document is the development of musical leadership for the support of the singing congregations.

An affiliate organization, the Fellowship of United Methodists in Worship, Music, and Other Arts continues to be a supportive advocate for music and the arts. They are involved in the development of the document on music and lend support to a variety of programs and resources in worship, music, and the arts sponsored by the United Methodist Church.

Among the newest resources in worship is _The United Methodist Hymnal_ and _The United Methodist Book of Worship_. Both support the use of music and the arts not only to enhance worship, but to make it relevant.

Three periodicals that support church musicians in their work are: _Church Music Workshop_ (United Methodist Publishing House), which offers a feature workshop article with a well-known clinician, a music folio, and an audiocassette; _Quarternotes: For Leaders of Music with Children,_ prepared by the General Board of Discipleship and published by The United Methodist Publishing House that provides articles on teaching children's music, a music booklet for children with over a dozen pieces of music, and an audiocassette; and _Jubilate! A Newsletter for United Methodist Musicians,_ produced by the General Board of Discipleship. This six-page newsletter offers a feature article on some aspect of church music, a resource page, and a page of assorted information on upcoming training events in church music held throughout the United States.

Diane Sanchez

148 ✦ VINEYARD

The Vineyard assemblies are marked by contemporary musical forms in a praise-and-worship style. After a period of development along these lines, some Vineyards are rediscovering the hymns and songs of the historic church. Of the other arts in worship, the Vineyards are making a unique contribution to dance in worship, in the form of free and spontaneous dance rather than formal liturgical dance. Vineyard leadership must "release" dancers to perform their ministry, thereby screening out dance that is inappropriate for worship.

Music

In the Vineyard, we believe that all music is created by God and that all forms of music can be used in an expression of worship. God's presence is not wrapped up in one style of music, for music will change in each generation and culture. It is interesting to note that the Psalms consisted of both music and lyrics, but only the words were preserved as Scripture. A major part of renewing worship is the ongoing task of renewing the music through which it is expressed, keeping it relevant in both style and quality to the cultures in which we live.

The primary form of music in the Vineyard is soft rock, as this seems best to reflect the culture of which we are a part. The primary instruments used are acoustic guitar, electronic keyboards, drums, bass guitar, and electric guitars. There is also some quiet, reflective instrumental music using our normal instrumentation as well as some classical instruments such as the cello. The normal size of a Vineyard worship band ranges from five to ten people, including several vocalists.

As the Vineyard continues to grow and to focus on evangelism, our music is changing as well. At present, the Langley (B.C.) Vineyard has four congregations (services). Two of these are traditional Vineyard (soft rock) and meet on Sunday. The other two are quite different. On Friday night we have "God Rock," where the music is more mainstream rock, with some alternative rock as well. The instruments used are similar, including electric guitars, bass guitar, and drums, but the style of music is different and the volume is louder. On Saturday night "God's Country" meets. This service features country music, primarily contemporary country along with some traditional country. At present the instrumentation is similar to the mainstream Vineyard style, but in the future more "country" instruments may be included, including the pedal steel, mandolin, and harmonica.

We believe that the quality of our music in both musical skill and sound reinforcement should be excellent, comparable to music available in the culture that we are trying to reach. Therefore, it is a high priority that our musicians rehearse regularly and be committed to increasing their skill on their instrument. Also, quality sound involves training qualified sound technicians and investing fairly large amounts of money in professional sound equipment.

At this point, virtually all of our music is worship music, directed to God both in lyrics and in our style of presentation. There is very little special music or performance music used in our meetings. The majority of our songs are worship songs, choruses, and songs of praise. Many of them are written out

of Scripture, either paraphrased or directly used (usually from the NIV). Also, many of our songs are based on our experiences and desires in our relationship with God (e.g., "Father, I Want You to Hold Me"). These songs are not only love songs to God, but contain powerful theological statements about who God is and about our relationship with him.

Another way worship is being renewed in the Vineyard is by embracing the historic church and some of its music that has stood the test of time. Occasionally we include a hymn or two in our flow of worship, arranged to fit our contemporary musical context. We generally do not update the words of these hymns so that we can identify with every part of the church (e.g., "My Jesus I Love Thee"), though the vast majority of our other lyrics are culture-current.

The Arts

In regard to the arts, there has been a major resurgence of faith that God does indeed want to use the arts in our expression of worship. An arts support group has begun in Langley, B.C., as well as in Chicago and in other Vineyards. While most of our regular meetings are held in rented facilities that greatly limit our potential use of environmental art, more and more art is being used at special events. At a recent Vineyard Worship Festival, a large backdrop was painted and other props were designed to enhance the atmosphere and environment in which our worship is expressed. Many Vineyards use banners in worship, though not as frequently as other worship traditions.

For the most part the area of drama is still in the vision and desire stage and is not yet openly implemented as part of our service of worship. On one occasion in our congregation, a woman acted out the pouring of perfume at Jesus' feet as part of worship. But such instances of the drama in worship are still quite rare.

Dance has seen the greatest release in the arts as far as worship in the Vineyard is concerned. Desire and vision have become emerging reality in worship in a number of the Vineyards. Introducing dance at our Vineyard was not easy. Several years ago we had a false start. We greatly desired to see dance in worship, but what we saw at that point seemed more like a showcase of individual talent, rather than something that inspired worship in the congregation. We discontinued using dance for a time, which allowed us to learn a great deal more about it. Now as dance has reemerged, it is breathing life into our meetings through the spirit of worship, humility, and joy that permeates it.

There are many forms of dance, and we do not want to limit God in any form of dance. Yet in the context of our worship, we are pulling it away from what the church has known as dance, i.e., liturgical dance, which is highly choreographed, with no room for spontaneity or the leading of the Spirit. Our form of dance is not dance as the world knows it, because there is no specific form, but would appear closest to ballet. In the church, it is non-threatening and pleasant to observe. Sign language is also incorporated.

The purpose of dance is to enhance worship, to allow the Holy Spirit to lead us, flow through us, and to generate from us a participation from the congregation, to enter into praise, adoration, joyful worship, spiritual warfare, intercession. We are not pursuing self-glorification or performance, but dance in brokenness and vulnerability, allowing others to see and experience intimacy with the Father. Heart and motivations must be pure when called to the ministry of dance.

Specifically, we have one individual who oversees dance, and only specific people are released to dance up front, in both choreographed group dances or spontaneous dance. All are free to express their worship in the back of the sanctuary, or in smaller meetings, though there are also times in our larger meetings when the worship leader releases everyone to dance. These occasions are a very joyful, celebrative expression of dance.

We believe that God desires to breathe life into each cultural expression of music, dance, and the arts to inspire worship and to call people to relationship with their Creator.

Brian Doerksen

149 • WESLEYAN CHURCHES

Winds of worship change are blowing in the Wesleyan Church, but not always in the same direction. Different as they may seem, the trends toward celebrative worship on the one hand and a more liturgical framework on the other are both encouraging signs of life in corporate worship, and both emphasize music and the arts as key elements in renewal.

———— Music in Worship Renewal ————

A century ago, Wesleyans were singing "All My Life Long I Had Panted for a Draught," a new gospel song from the pen of Clara Tear Williams, a Wesleyan song evangelist. Gospel music and the Holiness movement grew up together, and in the hundreds of rural and small-town Wesleyan churches, as well as in scores of summertime camp meetings, it is still standard fare.

In the 1960s and 1970s, the contemporary musical scores of Wesleyans Derrick Johnson and Otis Skillings advanced the revolution on the youth scene that Ralph Carmichael had begun. Much of today's popular praise-and-worship music is derived from that sound, and much of the church is singing it, especially in younger congregations.

In every age, Charles Wesley's hymns are at home in churches of the Wesleyan tradition. "O for a Thousand Tongues" opens the Wesleyan hymnal as it opens hymnals worldwide in the Methodist family of churches. A recent gathering of Wesleyan ministers sang only Wesley hymns at a three-day conference, and the response was uniformly positive. The great hymns of the church are alive and well in Wesleyanism—at least in this generation.

The point is, of course, that the music of Wesleyan worship is very eclectic. _Hymns of Faith and Life,_ the denominational hymnal published in 1976 in cooperation with the Free Methodist Church (the third such joint venture this century), may be joined in the pew rack by a gospel songbook, or supplanted entirely by a contemporary hymnal from an independent publisher offering the latest in praise choruses and Scripture songs. For some, the sounds of renewal are a classic hymn, a choral anthem, and the voices of the congregation united in the doxology. For others, a synthesizer has replaced organ and piano, drums and brass accompany congregational singing, and special music relies on taped tracks.

Wesleyans appear to be a people of one heart, but not one ear. (Observation of the broader church scene would seem to indicate that they are not unique in that regard.) The good news is that both wings of the renewal movement are seeing success in restoring worship as a priority of congregational life.

———— The Arts in Worship Renewal ————

Wesleyan architecture and sanctuary furnishing have historically reflected (and probably helped to perpetuate) the simple, free worship style of the church. They still do, but it is also true that art and design are playing a greater role in the church than ever before.

New sanctuaries do not automatically mimic the traditional "concert stage" arrangement, although the central pulpit is almost universally employed as representative of the centrality of the Word. There is a significant trend toward hangings—paraments on pulpit and Table, banners for seasons of the Christian year—and a growing awareness of the significance of liturgical colors. Wesleyan clergy do not wear vestments, but choir stoles may be selected with liturgical colors in mind.

In a related trend, more Christian symbols are likely to grace the sanctuary once reserved for Sallman's head of Christ or Hunt's depiction of Christ at the door. Not all new sanctuaries are designed for fixed furnishings. Many congregations opt for the flexibility afforded by a multipurpose room, where the art is as movable as the seats. Here, too, are alternative renewal movements at work.

Musically, Wesleyan worship is a medley. Artistically, it's a mosaic.

Bob Black

150 • WISCONSIN EVANGELICAL LUTHERAN SYNOD

The Wisconsin Evangelical Lutheran Church has remained quite traditional in its approach to music and the arts. Recent changes include the recovery of psalm singing and, in some churches on particular occasions, the use of choruses. Little use is made of the arts.

Two events, the publication of a new hymnal in 1993 and the installation of an organ in 1991, illustrate the renewal of music in WELS worship.

──────────── **The New Hymnal** ────────────

The publication of *Christian Worship: A Lutheran Hymnal* illustrates not only where we are headed but also where we have been. The WELS is often stereotyped as rigidly conservative, painfully slow to change, and little interested in how anyone else is changing. But the new hymnal belies this stereotype. By convention decision, it is a "new/revised" hymnal. It includes an adaptation of the main service from *The Lutheran Hymnal* of 1941. Another Service of Word and Sacrament offers two composite canticles that have not appeared else-

where. The music is good, solid writing for the liturgy that is intended to wear well even though it can't be learned in one experience.

More significant are psalm singing and encouragement of a heightened "liturgical" use of the choir. The psalm tones are similar to those in the other newer Lutheran hymnals, but with the addition of refrains (antiphons). The ecumenical excitement over responsorial psalm singing had become established enough during the hymnal planning stage that the use of refrains seemed automatic. The psalms do not include verses according to any existing lectionary. They are "psalms for singing," a comfortable length, often condensed from a complete psalm, and a springboard to other ways of singing the Psalms. Twenty years ago sung psalms would have had less chance of success: "too Catholic!" Now, even before the hymnal is published, many congregations as well as worker training schools are using them. A parochial school teacher tells of sixth graders asking with enthusiasm, "Can we sing (i.e., chant) Psalm 16?" At the other extreme, some congregations rarely hear children's choirs singing hymns, even in creative arrangements, as their "choir" piece for worship.

The hymns show a desire to conserve and share the Lutheran heritage and even to bring out more old treasures from the storehouse as did the *Lutheran Book of Worship* and *Lutheran Worship*. This new hymnal includes: "The Only Son from Heaven" ("Herr Christ, der einig Gottes Sohn"); "Break Forth, O Beauteous Heavenly Light" (the Bach setting from the Christmas Oratorio); "O Lord of Light, Who Made the Stars" ("Conditor alme siderum"). The hymnal also welcomes treasures of recent vintage: "Sing a New Song to the Lord" ("Cantate Domino"); "Now" (Carl Schalk and Jaroslav Vajda); "Have No Fear, Little Flock" (Heinz Werner Zimmermann). The newer treasures, though not particularly bold, are a refreshing addition to repertoire built on the 1941 hymnal.

A few churches here and there are using praise choruses and Christian contemporary music, mostly in youth-oriented alternative services and Sunday evening services, although sometimes also in Sunday morning services. The use of this music is restricted because of WELS Lutherans want to avoid worship that resembles entertainment. They are cautious about both overly subjective elements in worship and the use of music not quite worthy of divine worship. The musical arguments generated, in part, by the church growth movement have not been as painful for the WELS as for other Lutherans. But at least we thank the church growth movement for reinforcing the common-sense insight that we must offer quality worship planned with care.

—— Instruments in Worship Renewal ——

A new tracker pipe organ was installed at the synod's only seminary near Milwaukee (Wisconsin Lutheran Seminary, Mequon). The seminary's gymnasium/mass assembly hall already had a large electronic organ. Some might have been content to let this serve as the only instrument for the seminary. But the quality pipe organ just installed will help shape worship renewal for decades as future pastors worship with the present leadership in daily chapel services. The educational impact of a good instrument will be a refreshing change from recent decades when a woefully defective instrument shaped the ears and expectations of the synod's ministerium. The new seminary organ speaks to the future role of the organ in WELS worship renewal.

Within the WELS as elsewhere, overuse of the organ (often a musical monopoly) has contributed to its decline. The first five minutes of pre-service music can use up a great deal of talent and preparation for very few listeners. Few seem to listen in a meaningful way. (Few seem to want to learn how to play in a meaningful way.) Yet in recent years we have used more and more instruments in ways that show continuity with historic liturgical worship. Even the synthesizer (used here and there) has found a place in rather traditional worship, adding special "spice" to the old meat-and-potatoes routine of organ music in worship. This is quite a change from the day when some churches passed resolutions limiting "permissible" instruments. Handbells are used only sporadically; their liturgical uses (e.g., cadences in psalm tones) aren't as well known.

The recently installed seminary organ says something about quality in worship renewal. In the current climate, the old false dichotomy that pits "missions vs. worship," or "missions vs. organs" is no longer advanced. One respected pastor said, "What evangelism was to our Synod in the 70s (in the sense of attention, discovery, and energy), worship will be in the 90s." With a rediscovered sense that worship is the heart and core of our lives together before the Lord, attention to quality in worship will not be viewed as self-centered extravagance. The "old" outlook focused too much

on one axiom: "It's offered to God's glory, and I did the best I can. So it's good enough. Accept the mistakes in Christian charity." The growing balance to that view recognizes, "It's offered for my neighbor's edification (and delight!), so it must be as good as possible." The growing outlook recognizes that music must be of high quality to meet the potential that God put into his gift of music.

The WELS is rediscovering that musical quality isn't a function of quality instruments only. Other quality factors include: (1) the use of hymns; (2) pay and time for musicians; (3) worship planning that deserves more of a pastor's time and of the congregation's budget.

The vast majority of WELS churches are committed to mainstream hymnody. This presents a challenge when many people judge traditional hymns to be boring. Some new musical vigor is growing out of an awareness that for years we've used hymns in an unimaginative fashion. Hymns have a chance to live and sparkle, to burrow more deeply into our consciousness when accompanied by grand or even modest resources. This can't happen when six stanzas are sung by the same people, to the same harmony and (almost) the same organ registration. (The faithful enjoy singing not only out of piety but also because of its art and fun and variety.)

Quality music requires time; quality music is a labor-intensive product. Historically, teachers in WELS parochial schools have had most of the responsibility for church music. Though overworked, many have served as choir directors and organists, squeezing practice and preparation in between coaching, correcting, and family. That may be changing—slightly. But another prospective trend offers encouragement. Two churches have recently called pastors to positions with extensive responsibilities for music and worship planning and leadership. In earlier days that would have been judged unnecessary, a waste of pastoral training and ability. Such calls may be common in other church bodies, but they are not in the WELS, where overworked parochial schoolteachers or marginally capable volunteers have often lead the music.

One more comment related to quality. In the nineteenth century William Schuelke, a WELS member, built respected pipe organs in the upper Midwest. The WELS again has a quality organ builder. Bruce Case completed his Opus 1 in 1991. An engineer by training and with organ-building apprentice experience in England, he has set up shop near Madison, Wisconsin.

The Arts

The arts are not widely used in WELS churches, except for some of the following examples.

- Banners have been used for decades. There is no discernible trend regarding their use, unless it is a scattered graduation from felt and glue to more worthy materials.
- Regarding environmental art, design and placement of baptismal fonts have received only some of the attention they deserve. More new churches are including a free-standing altar or Table, especially if encouraged to think through a theology of design.
- Regarding vestments, perhaps the broadest trend, if one can call it that, is the switch from black Geneva gowns to while albs (and stoles) for pastors. This has not happened out of concern for "historical liturgical correctness," but simply because it seems so much more appropriate to the joy of worship. We do not need to stress penitence quite as much as the black gown would seem to suggest. But the black gown could reappear each year during Lent.

Chancel drama is quite rare, except for children's Christmas services and dramatic readings of the Passion on Palm Sunday or Good Friday.

The Status Quo and Hope for the Future

This picture of music (and the arts) in the WELS has described what one might experience in churches giving renewed attention to worship and music. Perhaps most churches are rather content in various ruts, some comfortable, some complacent. That may not harm their salvation, but neither will their worship have the impact it could. In far too many churches the music is just sort of there, resembling neglected landscaping or well-worn carpet. The music with its mistakes and lack of vigor is neither strongly offensive nor highly inspiring. The choir may fail to approach anything transcendent or even mildly moving, but at least it is a good small-group activity for the nineteen regulars.

And the music from the pews, congregational song? In most places we will have to work to encourage participation that is intentional. Bland ac-clamations of the gospel and vacant stares during the Communion distribution hymn indicate the work we have ahead of us in worship renewal.

Nevertheless, many amateur musicians are quite eager to improve their skills. Their willingness to spend a Saturday at a workshop bodes well for the renewal that comes from heightened vision and new ideas. Participants in these workshops, even those with the lowest level of skill, seem eager for more. "Do this again every year," they say.

Resources

WELS resources are limited. We have tended to rely on others. A *Worship Leader's Manual* will accompany the new hymnal. It will include four sections on the following topics: worship in theology and practice; the services in detail and use; planning for worship (church year and propers); and music in worship.

Focus on Worship, published for many years by the Commission on Worship, ceased publication in 1992. Several other "parish service" publications also ceased when the Board for Parish Services introduced a new journal. This publication, *Parish Leadership,* will address worship concerns along with five other areas of "parish service."

The twelve geographic districts of the WELS have elected "Worship Coordinators." Some of these are assisted by a committee. Some districts organize workshops, some have sporadically published newsletters. Underfunding, lack of training or time, and inadequate direction limit the assistance these coordinators can offer.

The synod convention has approved a worship administrator at the national level. Staffing now awaits funding. This position would be concerned with music and the arts, architecture, and even preaching. Guidance and resources for work on the district level should increase.

Laudate, a relatively new organization within the WELS, consciously addresses the arts beyond music in its newsletter. Though music has been its strongest focus, the first issues have also given attention to architecture and watercolors.

The arts in the broadest sense are part of another newer journal from Wisconsin Lutheran College. *Glory* has addressed visual and graphic arts, literature, jazz, CCM, and film criticism. The second issue, published in March 1992, featured articles on sacred dance and worship renewal. Faculty members of Wisconsin Lutheran College also coordinate the WELS Art Guild.

The WELS elementary school system is not a resource, strictly speaking, but is rather unique in its musical impact. A similar "resource" exists in many Catholic churches and in the Lutheran Church— Missouri Synod. One third of WELS congregations operate a parochial school. These schools often exert a profound (though not always imaginative or energetic) impact on music for worship.

Bryan Gerlach

151 • WOMEN'S AGLOW FELLOWSHIP

Music in Aglow's monthly fellowship meetings, biannual retreats, and annual conventions is as diverse as the cultural differences in the 104 nations of the world where Aglow is located. Voices join to worship God in each national language accompanied by ethnic instruments ranging from guitars to organs, steel drums to violins, accordions to pianos.

If you were to travel to cosmopolitan cities such as Buenos Aires or Singapore, you would find Aglow worshipers singing more contemporary choruses or hymns. Aglow in the outback of Australia or villages in Norway or Germany would probably feature simple choruses being sung either without accompaniment or with a single instrument. Women in the Caribbean often praise the Lord to a calypso beat, while African women may chant their praises accompanied by drums or only the clapping of hands. Koreans worship God in a delightful "sing-song" style of singing, while the American Aglow women's style of worship may range from gospel to jazz, country to classical, Jewish to contemporary.

Our biennial International Conferences reflect the great diversity of praise-and-worship songs as well as the types of instruments better than any other place in Aglow. Here we try to meet the musical styles and tastes of our attendees and feel there is room for them all! Because of the diverse musical education and background of the worship team and orchestra, we are able to enjoy most styles of music in this gathering of 5,000–10,000 attendees.

Our opening ceremonies can range from a call to worship on the Jewish _shofar_ (ram's horn) to the pageantry of everyone's favorite—the "Parade of Flags"—which features women dressed in their national costumes each proudly carrying their nation's flag into the arena while the attendees watch and listen to rousing choruses or majestic hymns played by the conference orchestra. Applause to our God often spontaneously breaks out as we visibly see the results of his mighty works demonstrated. In 1989 we saw two women, East and West German, carrying their two respective nations' flags while walking side by side with hands joined (this was before the reunification of Germany). In 1991 four Soviet women proudly carried their nation's flag in the parade for the very first time. Nowhere else in Aglow is the passage from Revelation 7 so visibly demonstrated as in this setting: "behold, a great multitude from every nation and all tribes and peoples and tongues were standing before the throne and before the Lamb . . . worshipping God . . ."

Many have described our conference worship as a "foretaste of heaven." What began ten years ago with one or two musicians leading in simple choruses has greatly matured as we have sought to become the type of skilled worshipers portrayed in the Scriptures. Our worship team now consists of a whole band of men and women who have traveled with professional groups and are now involved with worship teams in their own various churches. Musicians from the audience who want to participate in the conference orchestra are also included on the last night. The instruments used include piano, synthesizer, drums, bass, electric and acoustic guitar, violin, saxophone, and trumpets.

Our international president, the praise-and-worship leader, and the worship team (singers and musicians) flow together in one accord in leading the people into worship. We have frequently experienced impromptu "prophetic music," that is, worship inspired by the Spirit of God by one or more musicians spontaneously playing unlearned melodies. This will often result in the power of God being dramatically released and people in the audience being "slain in the Spirit" (i.e., falling under the power of God) or healing and deliverance released to individuals. Some of the documented healings include a pastor from England whose heel was healed from an old war injury, another pastor from Washington whose deaf ear was healed, a woman from New Mexico who was healed from blindness, a military wife from the Philippines who was healed from an intestinal parasite that was literally eating her alive because there was no medical cure, and the most dramatic healing of all, at our 1987 International Conference in New Orleans. As our president was speaking, a woman from Canada collapsed in the audience. The paramedics were summoned to revive her and they said "she was gone and had started to turn blue and cold." Our president had the audience pray and sing the praise song "With Healing in His Wings" over and over and the paramedics were astounded when life began to flow back into the woman's body. Later, at the hospital, doctors determined that not only had life returned to her body but she had also been totally healed of a congenital heart disease which had left her with chronic heart pain for over 50 years. The heart condition, scars on the heart, and the pain were totally gone! What rejoicing at the power and compassion of our awesome God!

Also during our worship sessions, the musicians will sometimes play and/or sing prophetically and a "spirit of prophecy" will be released upon the gathering, as intercession takes place for our nation, for other nations, and for women in particular. Sometimes new "songs of the Lord" are spontaneously created that often become praise-and-worship choruses that are used for years afterwards throughout the body of Christ. Dramatic readings and scenic videos have also been used to enhance our worship as well as single or teams of interpretive dancers.

Because of the many denominations and cultures represented in Aglow, we have sought to search the Scriptures regarding praise and worship. We've become more aware of the different Hebrew root words for praise and what God intends to do through the praises of his people. It has caused us to open our hearts to *his* way instead of *our* traditions. A workbook called *Introduction to Praise* was written to spur others on to a more spontaneous, loving, and intimate relationship with God, showing them that praise is *about* God and his characteristics but worship is expressing our love *to* him.

Ruth Collingridge

152 ✦ ALTERNATIVE USE OF MUSIC AND THE ARTS IN THE LITURGICAL TRADITION

Liturgy was once thought to imply prescribed text, music, movement, and environment and the proscription of everything else. Yet many liturgical congregations are attempting to plan powerfully imaginative worship experiences that use both traditional liturgical resources and a variety of contemporary practices from around the world. The following article describes the practice of one such congregation.

Social historians distinguish the Great Tradition of a culture, comprising its high literature, art, music, science, and theology on the one hand; and the Little Traditions, comprising folk legends, art, music, ways, and religion on the other. These periodically cross-fertilize each other, often at periods of great creativity, or in the work of great creators, and especially often in worship. Our own period is pregnant with creative liturgical opportunity. The Christian church ministers today in a world of cultural confluence, where people communicate at both traditional levels on a scale unknown since European armies expelled the Moors in the early Renaissance. In such a confluence, acculturation—that is, sharing the gospel with people on their own traditional terms—inevitably becomes a two-way road. Western worshipers appropriate Eastern Christian icons sprung from roots in Hellenistic Greece, India, and central Asia; Christian monks take up Buddhist meditation methods; Roman popes collect and show African ritual art for church artists to copy—and Christianity shifts irreversibly. All world culture is ours to talk with, and the talk will change us. If we find ways to talk authentically and creatively, we too can hear the gospel anew.

——— Environmental Art ———

St. Gregory Nyssen (Gregory of Nyssa) Episcopal Church in San Francisco joins the arts of Great and Little Traditions from many times and cultures, to celebrate the gospel through architecture, decoration, vesture, music, dance, and drama. Whereas some worship styled "folk" today applies a popular contemporary aesthetic to a conventional theater or lecture format for services, our liturgy format is participatory and incorporates traditional folk expression. Our floor plan, drawn from ancient Jewish and Christian synagogues, serves now as then to enhance congregational involvement. At one end of the building seats surround a raised platform [*bema*] with a preacher's chair ("Moses' Seat," Matt. 23:2) facing a raised lectern [*ambo*] at the church's center, backed by a tree-of-lights [*menorah*] and screen. Here people gather to hear the Bible, sing, comment together on the Scriptures, and offer their own prayers. The platform affords a place in plain view where we baptize, incorporate new members, and celebrate marriages in the midst of the congregation. Beyond the screen stands the eucharistic Table in the center of a wide open floor space. There the whole congregation processes, eats, drinks, and dances together.

We embellish this plan to reflect the ethnic richness of the Christian missionary world through traditional folk art. Our walls bear large folk icons from the largest eastern Christian church, in Ethiopia; the screen behind our lectern is formed of Ethiopian crosses with their customary cloth streamers; our censers, too, are Ethiopian, and ring with little bells when the congregation processes through the church. Our preacher's chair, at the apex of the seating, is a Thai elephant _howdah_. The platform before it, and the furniture round the church, hold drums, bells, and gongs from all over the world. Our vestments and hangings come mainly from west Africa, where they are in daily secular use—as all Christian vestments originally were. These _bubus_, or inexpensive stuff, richly tie-dyed and free of symbolic ornament, represent a living tradition of human clothing, giving our assembly a natural colorfulness. (By contrast, many modern vestments look like donned curtains or upholstery, because that is what the fabric was designed for.) Much as Christians of every sort once wore the chasubles later vestigially relegated to clergy alone, we spread our African chasubles liberally among lay and ordained ministers, marking our presiding clergy by stoles of African stripweave worn over these.

During most of the year we mix these vestments in an intuitive play of colors, following the simplest seasonal scheme, with festal days calling for the brightest cloth. Only in Holy Week do specifically symbolic fabrics appear. At our Maundy service commemorating the Last Supper, we celebrate the Eucharist within a meal, following the second-century _Didache_ ritual. Removing our usual altar table, we fill the open floor with dinner tables. Above these, creating an air of intimate splendor, we suspend a ceiling tent of our richest African cloths, mixing some woven for royal wedding banquets with others made for funerals—a mixture fitting this emotionally complex event. On Good Friday, when we read the story of Christ's universal victory on the cross, we vest all our clergy and lay ministers in black and red folk-weavings made for sacred use by peoples outside the Christian church: Mayan priests' ponchos; Indonesian burial offering cloths; Moslem imams' pilgrimage cloaks. Thus we honor the faith and prayers of all the people with whom Christ's death makes one (cf. Col. 3:11). Then for Easter—a nighttime service with us, as with the early

church—we produce our own folk art, filling the building overhead with a temporary art installation, which our church members create each year under the supervision of a nationally known artist in our congregation. At other seasons our children bring artwork they have made in church school, laying it on the altar with the eucharistic gifts.

Music

But the heart of our liturgical and creative life is music. Whether drawn from Great or Little Traditions, St. Gregory's music chiefly serves participatory worship. A short opening rehearsal allows newcomers to join in freely with the rest. Our congregation sings three quarters of an hour of music altogether each Sunday, nearly all of which is sung a cappella or is accompanied by rhythm instruments. (A modern harpsichord and small organ stand by for occasional support.) We choose high quality music from a wide range of traditions: plainsong; Russian, Greek, Armenian and Arab chant; renaissance polyphonic chant; early American shape-note hymns; European and African folk hymns; white and Negro spirituals; and classic hymns in four-part harmony from the Episcopal church's _Hymnal_ and other sources.

And while singing these hymns the whole congregation dances—twice each Sunday, and for half an hour in our Easter liturgy. Congregational liturgical dance had an honored place in the early church, featured prominently in patristic sermons, and endured vigorously for ages, finally disappearing only in the eighteenth century. We restored it tentatively at first, as an Easter custom and soon found our people asking for it at normal weekly services. Now we dance at every Eucharist. Because patristic and medieval choreography is mostly not recoverable, we adapt traditional folk dances to modern liturgical functions, as early Christians probably did. Following the intercessions, clergy and people process together to the altar table in the ancient tripudium step (three forward, one back) which G. Diekmann brought us from a Luxembourg abbey, where it has been used for this procession since the fourth century. This dance ends with the kiss of peace shared enthusiastically round the church, and the eucharistic prayer, which is sung throughout. Then after hearing choir anthems at Communion and alms-gathering, all circle the altar in a Greek folk step, singing a final hymn to the rhythm of drums, tambourines and Ethiopian sistrum rattles. (Many basic

Greek steps date to the early church period or earlier. They are repetitive and quick for newcomers to learn. Among folk dances they have the advantage of moving sensuously sideways, allowing everyone to feel the whole church dancing together. Roughly a third of the hymnbook tunes will dance easily using only four or five such steps.)

Musicians in the congregation contribute broadly to our musical life. A choir of gifted singers rehearse and sing anthems of the Great Tradition from many periods, often accompanied by harpsichord or small organ; drummers lend a hand; children learn seasonal hymns to share with us. Twice yearly St. Gregory's church sponsors a retreat for writers and composers, and through the year composers and arrangers within the church provide us with new music to try out, and adopt into out liturgy, and publish.

Silence, too, is part of music, and is slowly returning to liturgical use today, though many parishes try it sparingly, finding that worshipers stir uncomfortably after only a short time, or feel uncertain what to do. St. Gregory's Sunday worship includes three two-minute meditative silences, begun with the ringing of Japanese, Tibetan, and Thai temple bells, whose long reverberations help everyone to fall into deep quiet. These bells are our most widely copied innovation; visiting clergy constantly ask us where to buy them. They make the silence work so well it has become the most popular single element in our service.

On Christmas Eve we combine all these arts in a folk nativity play, as children and adults, players and audience act and sing out the ancient story of Jesus' birth. This play is rewritten each year from medieval source, to fit the gifts of those taking part, and forms the synaxis for our Christmas Eucharist. Other such plays may emerge into the liturgy during Eastertide, for example, as our children explore the deep bond between faith and art and life.

At this writing St. Gregory Nyssen Episcopal Church is fourteen years old, and entering a new stage of artistic opportunity. Having outgrown our rented chapel, we have bought land and will soon build a church of our own, where we can give fuller expression to the confluence of liturgical art and music from around the world, and so serve the gospel and the church today.

Richard Fabian

153 • ALTERNATIVE USE OF MUSIC AND THE ARTS IN THE FREE CHURCH TRADITION

Decisions made about the use of music and arts in worship always imply some theological understanding about the nature of worship. The following article describes a congregation in the free church tradition that has gone about the process of liturgical renewal well aware of the theological issues involved. This concern has influenced their choice of liturgical and hymns texts, the role that the choir plays in their services, and the ways in which visual and other arts have been incorporated.

At Grace Fellowship Community Church, we believe that the worship of God is the single greatest call and the single greatest need of our lives. To celebrate who God is and what he has done, to anticipate with the whole body of Christ what he will do at the very end of our deliverance, to give ourselves to adoring Christ in all his mystery and majesty—this is the point of our lives. Our destiny as the people of God is to be worshipers.

The implications of this for the weekly celebration of the church are wide-ranging and numerous. The obvious starting place is that worship cannot be selfish. It must draw us away from the smallness of our lives—the realities of family issues, career decisions, daily headlines, and politics—and point us to the greater reality that Christ has come to invade our world and give our lives Kingdom significance. We ask ourselves the wrong questions when we ask: Was the worship service uplifting to me? Did it inspire me, move me, challenge me, encourage me? Rather, we need to ask: Was God honored by the way I worshiped? Did I enter into worship as if I were indeed addressing the very Center of the universe or did he find me bored, distracted, passive, immovable? Real worship will be encouraging to us only as a result of our abandoning ourselves as we glorify God and seek to enjoy him forever, not when we make our own encouragement the goal.

Music

In our congregation, we view worship as dialogical. It is a dialogue initiated by God, always in grace, and always with a call for response. The same God who spoke creation into being calls us every Sunday morning to worship, to confession, to hear his Word, to meet him at his Table and then back to the world where we join him in his work. Music is one way to answer back to the God who so relentlessly pursues us. Through music, we nurture the conversation that God has been having with his people since Adam, and we anticipate the dialogue of heaven, where day and night they never stop saying, "Holy, holy, holy is the Lord God Almighty, who was, and is, and is to come!" To sing this to him now is to be drawn into heaven, into the presence of God, and that is what worship is all about.

When our congregation began, we were mostly familiar with pietistic gospel hymns that addressed God and called us to commitment in deeply personal and highly individualized ways. In the eight years of life together, we are recovering the whole hymnal and have found such a richness of expression, both in melody and text, from the hymns that have been given to the church throughout the centuries (not just the nineteenth!). Those pietistic hymns are much more potent and meaningful when they do not need to carry the whole weight of our worship. There is something very confirming about singing the fourth-century words and thirteenth-century chant of "Of the Father's Love Begotten," a Christmas hymn, and then reveling in the glorious theological picture of the God who comes with "healing in his wings" in Charles Wesley's "Hark! the Herald Angels Sing," and then finally being driven to pure celebration in "Go Tell It On the Mountain" at the simple and radical truth that Jesus Christ is born.

Good hymns always expand our thinking about God. They are unashamedly theological and they dare us to be. They give us words beyond our common words for him and keep us from addressing God in ways that become too casual and familiar. And, when we are sensitive to the truth they hold, they allow us to make these words of reverence and awe our own. Good hymns link us to history and remind us that the Christian faith is not just our story, but the story of generations and generations of saints who have loved Jesus and have tried to follow him. When we sing the hymns of Bernard of Clairvaux or Martin Luther, we are affirming our oneness with them. We have also been appreciating the contemporary hymn writers—Timothy Dudley-Smith, Christopher Idle, Margaret Clarkson, to name a few—as they have interpreted in fresh ways what it means for us to be God's church in these times. We are very pleased with our hymnal, *The Worshiping Church* (Carol Stream, Ill.: Hope Publishing Co.), for its inclusion of these hymn

writers and for offering what we feel is the best and most enduring of Christian hymnody.

We also incorporate praise choruses from both the Catholic and evangelical traditions. We have found these to give us a greater freedom in expressing our love and gratitude to God and are helpful when used in a supportive, responsive role. In our service, they are usually sung following a hymn or prayer when we want the congregation to focus on a particular truth for a longer period. We use choruses after the prayer of adoration (which follows the call to worship and opening hymn) as a way to elaborate on the prayer we have just prayed and allowed the momentum of worship to grow. This "momentum" has more to do with how the text highlights, interprets, and responds to particular events in worship than with the musical elements of tempo, melody, dynamics—though they are obviously intertwined.

Our choir plays a very substantial role in our service. The choir teaches new hymns to the congregation, serves as a "cantor" for music which is in the style of "musical liturgy," and along with the piano (we do not have a song leader), shares in the task of encouraging and directing the congregational singing. In our service, the choir anthem is not locked into a certain spot every week; the choir might sing the call to worship one week and one of the prayers (confession, preparation for the Word, Communion) the next. The fact that the anthem can be a fluid part of the structure is helpful in two ways. First, it gives the choir director a much greater flexibility in terms of repertoire because the anthem isn't confined to playing one particular role week after week. Secondly, it helps the congregation to appreciate that the choir is not "entertainment" but actually serves, particularly when the choir sings the prayers, to speak on behalf of the whole community to God.

Our desire to follow the church calendar has been the motivation behind much of the work we have done in the arts. The ancient seasons of Advent, Christmas, Lent, Easter, and Pentecost are not only helpful in rooting us in the story of Christ's life and the truths of the gospel—incarnation, redemption, and consummation—but they provide us with a visual way to enter into and celebrate these truths. The symbols, colors, and drama of these different seasons have come to be part of our tradition at Grace Fellowship, and every year they grow in their meaning as we grow in understanding how they give a holy perspective to our lives.

Visual and Dramatic Arts

Most of us had come out of a church background in which the visual arts did not play a significant role in worship, so the first step for us was research. One person on our worship team did a lot of reading on the historic celebrations of these seasons, which inspired much of the rituals and practices we do at these special times. Another person worked on the traditional symbols and Chrismons (Christ's monograms) of the faith, which led to her designing various banners and pulpit hangings for each of the seasons.

We celebrate Advent with the traditional wreath and four candles, each representing a different aspect of Christ's coming. A new candle is lit each week so that by Christmas Eve, as the light grows brighter and our anticipation of Christ's coming is heightened, we light the fifth and final candle, the Christ candle, and that is the sign for us that the longings and expectations of all creation are met in the Light of the world, Jesus Christ. A four-paneled banner is used in a similar way to tell the Advent story. The picture is based on the Isaiah 11 vision of the shoot that springs up from the stump of Jesse. The first panel, brought out on the first week, shows in dark, desert colors of what appears to be a lifeless branch. The second panel adds to this picture one tiny, but vivid green leaf set against the brown and gray background. The third panel shows more leaves and tiny pink buds. By the fourth week of Advent, the picture is complete: at the center a brilliant red rose has blossomed, representing Christ.

During Advent we celebrate the Light who is Jesus Christ growing brighter and stronger as the season progresses, but during Lent we watch that light grow fainter as we journey with Jesus to Calvary. Our practice at Lent is to place seven candles (one for each week in Lent, plus Good Friday) on a table along with a plain, wooden cross that has been draped with a sheer, purple cloth. Each week as we reflect on what it means for Christ to submit himself into the hands of sinners, one light is snuffed out. By Good Friday, a service we hold in almost total darkness, we remove the purple cloth from the cross, sing the words of the Kyrie ("Lord, have mercy. Christ, have mercy. Lord, have mercy.") and snuff out the last flame. This is drama at its simplest,

starkest form, but it tells the story—the world has killed its Deliverer, and all the lights go out.

Often just the simple reading of Scripture provides an opportunity to use drama in the service. Once, in a series on the Psalms, we used as an additional text 2 Samuel 12:1-13, where several characters playing Nathan, David, and a narrator, read through the story of Nathan's confrontation with David after his adulterous relationship with Bathsheba and the murder of her husband. This is a text full of tension ("You are the man!") and poignancy ("I have sinned against the Lord!") as David's sin is exposed and he senses the horror of what he had done. This text was followed by the David character reading Psalm 51, where David pours out his soul in confession to the God who does not despise broken and contrite hearts but redeems them.

In a sense, this kind of drama, not very elaborate or lavish, but simple, typifies our whole approach to music and the arts in worship. Because we are not a large congregation with a big budget for the arts, we must rely on finding beauty in simple things. This "limitedness" has served us well. We are discovering that in the gospel itself, the story of God's loving pursuit of his people, is enough drama and music and beauty and art to continue to renew our worship.

Sharon Huey

154 ◆ ALTERNATIVE USE OF MUSIC AND THE ARTS AMONG PENTECOSTAL/ CHARISMATIC CHURCHES

Music continues to be the most important element in Pentecostal worship. In congregations such as one described here, musicians have been challenged to serve as primary teachers and theologians in the church. Thus, they are composing music that addresses an increasingly wide range of topics. This concern for theological growth is also an important aspect of renewal of the other arts.

Music

Pentecostals are a musical people. If one were to survey the artists of popular American music, secular and religious, country, rock, and rap, one would find that an extraordinary percentage come from Pentecostal origins. American Pentecostalism has two central points of origin: the black church and Appalachian/frontier Methodism. Both of these people groups are noted for their love of music and their ability to pour strong emotion through it. "Soul" music was a standard feature of Pentecostal worship long before Motown ever brought it to the American public.

Pentecostals have traditionally used the frontier hymns of the Holiness movement, southern quartet styles, and black gospel. They learned to put their own twist on it all, and in the last twenty years this "twist" has been arguably the strongest central influence on gospel music, which in turn has had a large impact in certain quarters of the broader evangelical world.

Christ Church in Nashville, Tennessee, stands in the center of the gospel music world. Dozens of the most well-known gospeland country artists and song writers make it their church home, as well as many who are involved in the related publishing and recording industry that supports their distribution. The church is noted for its two hundred voice choir, which was nominated for a Grammy in 1992 in the black gospel choir category, even though the choir is predominately white. To attend a service at Christ Church is to witness a powerful music experience involving everything from Bach to rap. Although the church is unique, it only moves what is already a long Pentecostal musical tradition to a new level.

The church is also involved in liturgical renewal. Several years ago it introduced a catechism to its members that continues to be used, with hundreds having taken the course. The leaders of the church noticed, however, that even though many had taken the course, more did not. They also noticed that it was music which continued to define church life. They decided that for new generations of Americans, information was not primarily communicated through the written word. The new catechists of American evangelicals were gospel songwriters. That was alarming because by and large gospel music is theologically shallow. Christ Church decided to do something.

The writers of the church were encouraged to write new music. Several began to use the _Book of Common Prayer_ and other liturgical sources in their writing. The choir began to perform many of these songs. _We Believe,_ for example, is a modern gospel adaptation of the Apostles' Creed that is sung especially for Communion and ordination services. Steve Green, popular gospel artist, released the song on his album under the same name. Church choirs across the evangelical world have picked it up and

are using it in their services. (Petra, a Nashville-based rock group, released _This is My Creed,_ the same creed set to driving rock.) Christ Church choir now has a collection of songs to fit every part of the liturgy, using styles of music already familiar to the people. (The music can be obtained from Steve W. Mauldin Productions, 1905 Stratford Avenue, Nashville, Tennessee, 37216.)

Visual Arts

Christ Church uses the visual arts as well, though this is in its infancy. The seasons of the church year are announced visually through flower arrangements, sculpture, and banners. There are two very striking permanent pieces of art in the smaller chapel, where Communion is served weekly, on either side of the central cross behind the altar. The subject of one is the lamb with the triumphant cross, the other depicts a eucharistic theme: hands erupt from the bottom of the piece reaching for a piece of bread; a chalice is in the upper left corner, and the entire work has a border that reads "for the life of the world."

Christ Church hosts each spring an annual conference, the Word and Spirit Celebration, that brings together church leaders from the North American continent. This meeting has created quite a network of independent churches, which are mostly but not entirely from Pentecostal roots. Most of these assemblies are sympathetic to the worship and artistic renewal going on at Christ Church, and many of them are doing similar things.

It is safe to predict a growing use of the arts in worship among Pentecostals. In the next few years they are likely to be studying the heritage of Christian art, determining their own theological parameters for the use of the arts in the church, and continuing to build on their own artistic tradition, especially as it relates to music.

Dan Scott

155 • ALTERNATIVE USE OF MUSIC AND THE ARTS IN THE SEEKERS SERVICE

At the Willow Creek Community Church, a production team unites all of the elements of worship (music, the visual arts, drama, elements from the electronic media) into a single powerful experience with styles ranging from the classical to the most recent contemporary innovations.

Over the centuries, the church has used music and the arts to worship God with their beauty and encourage believers with their power. Willow Creek Community Church continues this tradition in new and unique ways. Artistic expression plays an integral part in Willow Creek's outreach to seekers and service to its New Community.

Willow Creek uses music, drama, and to some extent art, to present the gospel and deeper biblical truths in ways that grab attention and provoke a response. They enhance and promote worship and prepare the seeker on the weekends and believers at weekday evening New Communities for the speaker's message. No single ministry is allowed to stand apart from the whole. All play their part in advancing the common goal of the church, which is building bridges to an unbelieving society outside and between Christians inside.

Center to this ministry is the main auditorium, which is large enough to host music concerts and musicals that are part of Willow Creek's outreach to the Chicagoland area. At such times, members can invite friends and family to visit not just a service but something even more narrowly cultural. Able to seat almost five thousand people in the auditorium alone, with room for thousands more in various other rooms and in a large activity center, all linked by video, an impressive impact is assured. Willow Creek is blessed with many and diverse resources, and it has learned to use them wisely and efficiently. An extensive sound and lighting system completes the picture of professionalism.

The music and drama teams are two of the most important creative outlets for Willow Creek to use in its worship services. Their size and scope is unique in America.

Music

Since Willow Creek's founding in 1975, music has been one of its most relevant and innovative tools for ministry. It is contemporary without being superficial, and entertaining and challenging at the same time. The impact of the choice of music is carefully considered, and the music team is free to range over almost the whole spectrum of taste to achieve its worship goals.

With six full and part-time staff members, over one hundred musicians and up to twenty-five vocalists, there is much talent to form small or large bands, string quartets or orchestras, according to what may be needed for a given service. Many members of the team are professionals who produce high-quality performances that are important in maintaining the team's popularity and expertise. The music director is convinced that if the music is good, people will listen to it. Vocalists regularly perform original or popular Christian songs, singing solo or as a group. Occasionally, volunteers from the congregation form a large choir and sing special songs or backup for community worship.

While the team enjoys a generous budget, which allows them to purchase a variety of instruments such as guitars, pianos, and synthesizers, they find that everything need not be state-of-the-art to be effective. Wise stewardship walks a line with innovative ingenuity.

Overall responsibility for planning belongs to the programming team, which determines the sort of music to be played at a service, ranging from country and light rock to jazz to classical music, from traditional hymns to charismatic choruses. They find purpose and appeal in diversity.

Taking full advantage of our society's love of music, Willow Creek has produced a cassette/CD of some of the church's most asked for songs and choruses. Another collection is being prepared. Plans for a recording studio and a music school reach further into the 1990s. Sheet music will be made available also through an agreement with Zondervan Publishing House.

Drama

Dramatic sketches have also been an integral part of Willow Creek's outreach from the beginning. Like the music, drama helps focus attention on the direction of worship and the speaker's message during weekend seeker services. Subject matter is primarily determined by the sermon topic, but its expression can vary from comedy to tragedy. The actors and script writers work at staying fresh and relevant and incorporate easily recognized references to popular TV shows and movies in their work.

The drama team director is also the only full-time staff person. He directs almost thirty volunteer actors and actresses and three writers, who are paid a nominal fee for each script. Props for each of the three-to-five minute sketches can come from anywhere. Some are made at the church or even borrowed from local businesses, such as airline seats from a local training school for a major airline.

Not everyone on the team is as professionally

trained to the extent that most music team members are. While risky, this practice preserves and encourages authenticity as men, women, and children find skills and talents that would have gone unused or untested otherwise. The director provides solid, experienced coaching that helps polish rough edges.

The teaching staff and the programming team provide sketch topics with enough time to prepare and rehearse a script. But the drama director places great emphasis on proper exercise of stagecraft. His technical experience is the groundwork of each production.

A script catalog of most drama sketches from the past several years to the present is available for any church that wants to use drama in its own services. Occasionally, both drama and music teams combine to produce a complete musical for a particular outreach or Christian holiday.

Dramatic readings of Scripture and literature are frequently employed for the same purpose as music and drama, as is interpretive dance to a much lesser extent. Graphic artwork highlights certain message series or Christian holidays and is normally displayed in the main auditorium. As a point of policy, Willow Creek avoids any obvious religious displays, such as crosses or stained glass windows, to promote a nontraditional atmosphere.

Members of both teams find it a struggle to maintain a balanced life between family, work, and church. Creative tension is common because of the stresses arising from their art. Both directors understand that a sense of community, responsibility, and accountability needs to be nurtured and sustained. Character conflicts are not allowed to go unconfronted. Consistent shepherding leads to deeper investment in the lives of volunteer and staff alike.

As Willow Creek expands both its local and national influence, the music and drama teams will be available as resources to churches in the U.S. and abroad. Their innovations and experience are at the service of the church.

Steve Burdan

PART TWO

Music in Worship

TWO

The Theological Foundations of Music in Worship

Music has played a prominent role in nearly every service of Christian worship ever conducted—in any culture, period of history, or worship tradition. Music has accompanied every liturgical act, from Entrance rites to sacramental liturgies; it has been used to express every emotion, from grief to joy. It is no surprise, then, that a major portion of this volume should be dedicated to discussing the role of music in worship. The following chapters include both theoretical and historical considerations regarding music in worship and appropriate suggestions for the practice of music in worship.

Music in worship is not an end in itself. Rather, it is a means by which the gospel is proclaimed and by which the people respond in prayer. It may, in fact, be the most universal way for rendering Christian liturgy. Because of this function, any discussion of music in worship must center on the nature of Christian liturgy as much as any musical considerations. Only on this basis can the varieties of music for worship be understood, whether differences in cultural forms of music-making or differences among liturgical, free, and charismatic churches. The following essays attempt to come to terms with this diversity, examining the appropriate function of music in worship and the theological bases for determining this function.

156 • MUSIC AND MUSICIAN IN THE SERVICE OF THE CHURCH

Music has great power to both reflect and shape human experience. In worship, as in other activities, music is able to express the most profound thoughts and emotions in ways that words cannot. Music in Christian worship is a powerful—even a risky—force that must be used thoughtfully, imaginatively, and prayerfully.

Music soothes, transfigures, opens the fountains of a greater deep and bathes us in a world of victory, which submerges our griefs so that we see them as lovely as ruined towers at the bottom of a clear lake on whose bosom we glide. It has, for the hour, the power that faith has for good and all—to unloose, emancipate, and redeem. When the ransomed of the Lord return to Zion, it is with singing and great joy upon their heads. (P. T. Forsyth, *Christ on Parnassus: Lectures on Art, Ethic and Theology* [London: Hodder and Stoughton, 1911], 225)

———— **The Nature of Music** ————

Music consists of rhythm, pitch, melody, and harmony, but it is not just that, for music has power.

When an evil spirit was tormenting Saul, his servants advised him to let them "seek out a man who is skillful in playing the lyre; and when the evil spirit from God is upon you, he will play it and you will be well" (1 Sam. 16:16). David was the one chosen, and his mellifluous performance caused Saul to be refreshed and made well, whereupon "the evil spirit departed from him" (1 Sam. 16:23).

Through the ages people have been awed and mystified by the power of music. With its changes of pitch, volume, tempo, rhythm, and harmony, music offers a wider variety of expression than words. That which seems intangible, and fades as soon as it is heard, and is different each time it is performed, can express and elicit emotions of great intensity, something that touches the human soul. Further, long after sound waves have vanished, music can live on as it and the emotions it evoked are later aroused by the listener's memory. Of course, musicians can also hear music within themselves while reading a score though no sound waves are produced. Music even exists for those who have become deaf as they, like Beethoven in his later years, conjure up the beautiful sounds within their minds.

Martin Luther, who thought "that next to the Word of God, music deserves the highest praise," (*Luther's Works,* vol. 53 [Philadelphia: Fortress Press, 1965], 323) painted a portrait of the effects music has on human beings:

> Whether you wish to comfort the sad, to terrify the happy, to encourage the despairing, to humble the proud, to calm the passionate, or to appease those full of hate—and who could number all these masters of the human heart, namely the emotions, inclinations, and affections that impel (humans) to evil or good?—what more effective means than music could you find?

Music can comfort, excite, encourage, and call forth a host of other reactions, giving voice to unutterable feelings. It is a gift from God that fosters soundness of mind in temporal confusion and enhances our lives as is reflected in this collect by Erik Routley:

> Almighty God, who gave us music to bring sanity to a distracted world, and to use for the fortifying and beautifying of human life; grant that our learning of it, our interpreting it, and our sharing it may arouse in our own hearts and minds gratitude to you, and in the lives of others a new consciousness of your love which is over all your works: through Jesus Christ, our Lord. Amen. (From the dedication of Lee Hastings Bristol, Jr., Church Music Resource Center, Westminister Choir College, October 13, 1982)

Though music affects us in the realm of emotions, it has been noted that "music can never express a specific grief, always just 'joy, sorrow, grief, horror, jubilation, happiness, peace per se, to a certain extend *in abstracto,* their essence without any accidents'" (Gerardus van der Leeuw, *Sacred and Profane Beauty: The Holy in Art,* trans. David E. Green [New York: Holt, Rinehart, and Winston, 1963], 246; the quotation within is from Schopenhauer). While music may not convey the specific, particular music does become associated with particular emotions so that, for instance, when one hears a hymn which was sung at a loved one's memorial service, or an organ composition which was played at one's marriage service, the grief or joy felt at the time can well up with powerful insistence.

Music dwells in the same realm as love and faith and imagination, intangible and undefinable, but sometimes describable in its effects. Throughout the ages poets have paid tribute to music, revering its mysterious nature and influence, struggling to evoke its beauty and power. In the following pages we will examine some of the ways the church has appreciated and made use of music.

Church Music

> When in our music God is glorified,
> and adoration leaves no room for pride,
> it is as if the whole creation cried,
> Alleluia!
>
> How often, making music, we have found
> a new dimension in the world of sound,
> as worship moved us to a more profound
> Alleluia!
>
> So has the Church, in liturgy and song,
> in faith and love, through centuries of
>   wrong,
> borne witness to the truth in every tongue.
> Alleluia!
>
> And did not Jesus sing a psalm that night
> when utmost evil strove against the Light?
> Then let us sing, for whom he won the fight,
> Alleluia!
>
> Let every instrument be tuned for praise!
> Let all rejoice who have a voice to raise!
> And may God give us faith to sing always:
> Alleluia! (Frederick Pratt Green, 1971)

This brings us into the realm of church music which Vatican II deemed the "treasure of immeasurable value, greater even than that of any other art" (*Constitution on the Sacred Liturgy, 6, 112* in *The Documents of Vatican II,* Walter M. Abbott, ed. [New York: Guild Press, 1966], 171). In the words of Isaac Watts, it is both a duty and a delight to worship God, and marvelous things happen when we find expression for our devotion in music, joining "instrument and voice and sound to make one music for the Lord of all" (Erik Routley, *In Praise of God Meet Duty and Delight* Hinshaw Music, 1977, vol. 2).

> The desert is refreshed by songs of praise,
>   relaxed the frown of pride, the stress of grief;

in praise forgotten all our human spite;
   in praise the burdened heart finds sure relief.
     (ibid)

How does this happen? The inherent powers of language are magnified when married to music and used as a vehicle for praise. And it is in praise of God that we find our proper place as God's children, for our "chief end is to glorify God and enjoy him forever" (*Westminster Shorter Catechism,* question 1).

Martin Luther was certain that the "fathers and prophets wanted nothing else to be associated as closely with the Word of God as music" (*Works,* vol. 53). This is how he explained why the church has so many hymns and psalms "where message and music join to move the listener's soul, while in other living beings (i.e., birds) and bodies (i.e., instruments) music remains a language without words." Luther thought humans had been vested with language so they could "praise God with both word and music, namely by proclaiming (the Word of God) through music and by providing sweet melodies with words" (*Works,* vol. 53).

As hinted above, when music and text are combined, the music "no longer expresses the action or the words themselves, but something which goes much deeper: 'the most secret meaning of the same'" (van der Leeuw, 246). So music is one of the languages of worship. This is the new dimension celebrated by Fred Pratt Green in a hymn exalting the glorification of God through music:

How often, making music, we have found
a new dimension in the world of sound,
as worship moved us to a more profound Alleluia!
(*Hymns and Ballads of Fred Pratt Green*
[Carol Stream, Ill.: Hope Publishing Co., 1982])

A new entity is created when words are put to music. This happens both in hymns (in the words of Erik Routley, "songs for unmusical people to sing together") and in music sung by choirs and soloists where more talent and technical expertise are demanded.

One of the remarkable things about music is that with text it can express more than one emotion or affection at the same time. Examples of this abound, for instance in the works of Bach, one of the ultimate text-painters of all time. Albert Schweitzer has pointed out that in the opening chorus of the *St. John Passion,* which uses the words,

Lord our Redeemer, whose name in all the world is glorious, show us by your passion that you, the true Son of God for evermore, are glorified even in the deepest humiliation

both suffering and glory are depicted. This is done by the accompanying flutes and oboes which "sigh and wail incessantly," and by strings which "in grave and tranquil semi-quavers, symbolize the majesty of the glorified Son of God (*J. S. Bach,* vol. 2, trans. Edward Newman [New York: Dover Publications, Inc., 1966], 184). The organ is similarly involved in supporting the glorification theme. Music is capable of allowing humans more complex expression than speech alone does. It is not just something which provides first-class transportation for words. For in the conjunction of music and words, each is vivified and more is said that either could say alone.

Augustine struggled with this power of music, knowing that it did something to the texts that were being sung, changing them to another reality, at times kindling "an ardent flame of piety," and at others, sinfully overwhelming the truth. Confessing his early iniquitous captivation by the "pleasures of sound," Augustine discussed the snares set by church music and his reaction to them in this description of his journey into the realm of hymn singing:

I admit that I still find some enjoyment in the music of hymns, which are alive with your praises, when I hear them sung by well-trained, melodious voices. But I do not enjoy it so much that I cannot tear myself away. . . . But if I am not to turn a deaf ear to music, which is the setting for the words which give it life, I must allow it a position of some honor in my heart, and I find it difficult to assign it to its proper place. For sometimes I feel that I treat it with more honor than it deserves. I realize that when they are sung these sacred words stir my mind to greater religious fervor and kindle in me a more ardent flame of piety than they would if they were not sung . . .

Sometimes, too, from over-anxiety to avoid this particular trap I make the mistake of being too strict. When this happens, I have no wish but to exclude from my ears, and from the ears of the church as well, all the melody of those lovely chants to which the Psalms of David are habitually sung.

But when I remember the tears that I shed on

hearing the songs of the Church in the early days, soon after I had recovered my faith, and when I realize that nowadays it is not the singing that moves me but the meaning of the words when they are sung in a clear voice to the most appropriate tune, I again acknowledge the great value of this practice. So I waver between the danger that lies in gratifying the senses and the benefits which, as I know from experience, can accrue from singing. Without committing myself to an irrevocable opinion, I am inclined to approve of the custom of singing in church, in order that by indulging the ears, weaker spirits may be inspired with feelings of devotion. Yet when I find the singing itself more moving than the truth which it conveys, I confess that this is a grievous sin, and at those times I would prefer not to hear the singer. (*Confessions,* 10, 33)

At first, Augustine was beguiled by the beauty of music, but believed that God freed him to see that it was the texts to which the music was set that gave it its true significance. We know that St. Paul pledged to sing with the spirit and with the mind also (1 Cor. 14:15). Augustine, however, fearing that his mind would be paralyzed by the gratification of his senses, overreacted and tried to shut out the music. Later he became more trusting and proceeded, with caution, to endorse the singing, at least admitting it on the basis that it indulged the ears of "weaker spirits" to be "inspired with feelings of devotion." In fact, Augustine was perceptive in his suspicion about the place of beauty in worship. For if music is primarily beautiful, then it has betrayed its function as bearer of kerygma:

> Forbid it, Lord, that I should boast
> save in the death of Christ, my God;
> all the vain things that charm me most,
> I sacrifice them to his blood. (Isaac Watts,
> "When I Survey the Wondrous Cross")

Church Music as Event

In the passage from his *Confessions* quoted above, Augustine set up a dichotomy between music and words that is too simple. Indeed, there are those two components, but united, they form a third. At the heart of the matter is the fact that music in combination with text sung to God's glory becomes an event. There is a relationship between this and the dynamics of a service of worship. Corporate worship as the response of the body of Christ to God is central to the church. Here the Word is not just proclaimed, but *heard;* Christ is not just remembered in the celebration of the Eucharist, but is, through the Holy Spirit, *present in reality* in the hearts of the faithful. So more is happening in worship than an uninitiated observer might guess.

Communion with the divine is an all-encompassing experience, and so is the church's music as it swells from the depths of being and bursts forth in praise to God. That music forms an event, a part of the Word proclaimed, whether it is sung by all the people, or by a group of them and *heard* by others, or played by instrumentalists and *heard* by all. What does this mean? To hear the Word is to open our hearts and minds and allow the radiance of the Gospel to shine upon us. This is part of the responsibility of all who worship, something not limited to a response to the reading of the Scriptures and preaching of the sermon, since these are not the sole ways in which the Word is proclaimed. We enter into the event of worship, participating in praise, not just with our minds, not just with our breath, but with our whole beings. Through the power of the Holy Spirit, music provides one of the avenues through which we may respond in faith and allow Christ to be our way, our truth, and our life.

Worship in Wholeness

When we participate in worship in wholeness, we move from observation to participation. Church music is not part of a concert; the sermon is not an exercise in elocution; the Lord's supper is not a snack served by people paid with money received earlier during the service. Worship is classified not in the category of entertainment, but conversation. No empty palaver, it is a conversation with accountability attached. We hear the Word of God proclaimed and respond with praise and thanksgiving and show forth Christ's death until he comes again (1 Cor. 11:26), something which Calvin interpreted as a command to extol God's gifts to others for "mutual edification" (*Short Treatise* 18). We also exhibit the fruits of faith as we "grow and increase daily in the faith which is at work in every good deed" (John Calvin, "Thanksgiving after the Supper," Strassburg Liturgy, *Liturgies of the Western Church,* ed. Bard Thompson, [Philadelphia: Fortress Press, 1961], 208).

In a sermon where he was encouraging the faithful to find oneness in Christ by loving him who first loved us, Augustine exhorted his congregants: "'Sing to the Lord a new song' . . . but let not your life belie your words. Sing with the voice, sing with the heart, sing with the mouth, but sing with your whole life" (*Sermon 34, The New Chant* in *The Paschal Mystery,* ed. Adalbert Hammon [Staten Island, N.Y.: Alba House, 1969], 183).

This is reminiscent of the advice offered by the author of the letter to the Colossians: "Sing psalms and hymns and spiritual songs with thankfulness in your hearts to God" (Col. 3:16). It is significant that this was said in a context in which the Colossians are directed to love and forgive each other, letting the peace of Christ rule in their hearts. The point here and in Augustine's sermon is that the Christ-like life must enter every area of life. It is not something to be donned for the weekend in honor of Lord's Day worship.

Perhaps this was at the root of the prophet Amos' excoriation of the vacuous use of music not grounded in action. He clamored for justice rather than songs:

Take away from me the noise of your songs;
  to the melody of your harps I will not listen.
But let justice roll down like waters,
  and righteousness like an ever-flowing stream.
    (Amos 5:23-24)

There is an ancient prayer asking that what we sing with our lips we may feel in our hearts, and what we feel in our hearts we may show forth in our lives. This captures the essence of worshiping in wholeness.

Church Music as Functional

One presupposition on which church music stands is that it is functional music, a means unto an end, not complete in itself. The beauty and power of music and poetry undergirds worship and lends wings to communication between the human and the divine. Music also promotes the learning of words, and therefore truths, partly by allowing more time for reflection than speech permits, and partly by simply making words easier to memorize. Basil, the fourth century Bishop of Caesarea, noticed this particular power of music and saw it as an advantage, the gift of the Holy Spirit:

The Holy Spirit sees how much difficulty humanity has in loving virtue, and how we prefer the lure of pleasure to the straight and narrow path. What does he do? He adds the grace of music to the truth of doctrine. Charmed by what we hear, we pluck the fruit of the words without realizing. (Homily on Psalm 1, PG 29.211)

One ultimate effect of repetitive singing is that people finally begin to believe what they sing, however subconsciously. This must be respected by all who choose music for corporate worship since untruths, sentimental half-truths, and questionable theological concepts can be ingrained as easily as that which is pure and holy.

Of course, much about faith has been taught through the music of the church. Erik Routley singled out hymnody as being able to convert unbelief, strengthen faith, and bind together "the Christian community in that disciplined charity of which singing together is a symbol" (Routley, *In Praise of God*). The last-mentioned matter of church unity is not a minor one. Of course, all our worship traditions (not to be confused with local customs), handed down through the ages, serve as a means of unifying the body of Christ, whether we recognize it or not. And on a more particular level, in the worship of one congregation, singing binds people together as with one heart they lift their voices in praise. In the late fourth century John Chrysostom, Bishop of Constantinople, commented in a sermon on what he had noticed about congregational singing:

The psalm which occurred just now in the office blended all voices together, and caused one single fully harmonious chant to arise; young and old, rich and poor, women and men, slaves and free, all sang one single melody. . . . All the inequalities of social life are here banished. Together we make up a single choir in perfect equality of rights and of expression whereby earth imitates heaven. Such is the noble character of the Church. (Homily 5, PG 63.486-7)

Certainly one could wish that this "noble character" of the church united in song be carried out into the world with more effect than it usually is. But at least in worship we are given a vision of what it means to be one in Christ, and are confirmed in hope for the day when we all sit down together at the marriage supper of the Lamb. For a while we are changed: "in praise is earth transfigured by the sound and sight of heaven's everlasting feast" (Routley, *In Praise of God*).

People enter a different dimension as they worship together. It is to be hoped that music may lift us to a new realm where we are better able to apprehend God's presence with us.

Church Musicians

Having delved into the nature, power, and function of music in worship, we will here explore the vocation of the church musician, the one who in collaboration with other staff members is primarily responsible for creating the environment where music can make its contribution to worship, where it can do all the above mentioned things and more. Of course, the separation of church musician from church music is an artificial one, for they are inseparable. Equally unnatural is the isolation of the function of church musicians from that of pastors who lead worship and who can, by their understanding of the place of music in the church (or lack thereof), either foster its contributions or thwart them. All that is said here about church musicians should be attended to by pastors.

For this study we will distinguish the work of the church musician from the reprehensible activities of musicians who work in churches, using churches as their concert halls, and also from the activities of those faithful church musicians who serve as choir members and instrumentalists, but who are not in positions of leadership. While this statement obviously raises questions about the first group (whose actions are scrutinized below), it in no way denies the latter people their vocations as they serve God through the use of their talents in music. By the Holy Spirit we are called to ministry, using our gifts for the edification of the body of Christ. But some are called to be leaders in this ministry, particularly as musicians. Sometimes they are ordained, often they are not. It is their work which we will examine, looking, to the extent that has already been delineated above, for its theological basis, and exploring appropriate motivations and ways in which church musicians function best in relation to the people with whom and to whom they minister.

First, we examine the nefarious activities of the "musician in the church," negating that as our model. Through the centuries there have been problems with unscrupulous musicians who have exploited the church as a setting for their own advancement. The seventeenth century German writer, Grossgebauer, complained about this:

Hence, alas, organists, choirmasters, flutists, and other musicians, many of them unspiritual people, rule in our city churches. They play and sing, fiddle and bow to their heart's content. You hear the various noises but do not know what they mean; whether you are to prepare for battle or go your way. One chases the other in their concertizing manner, and they contend in rivalry to see who can perform most artistically and come closest to the nightingale. (Theophil Grossgebauer, *Waechterstimme aus dem verwuesteten Zion Drei Geistreiche Schriften* [n.p., 1667], 208, quoted in Freidrich Kalm, *Theology of Worship in Seventeenth Century Lutheranism,* trans. Henry Hamann [St. Louis: Concordia Publishing House, 1965], 145)

There is no proper place in worship leadership for musicians who have no commitment to the Christian faith. How can one lead that which one is not doing?

Church music is prayer. The leader of this prayer, the church musician, has great responsibility to the congregation both to be firm in the faith, and to choose faithfully the music used, letting theology inform the choices. This is related to Augustine's caveats about the use of music: it can be dangerous; it can be manipulative; it can preach a shallow gospel, proclaiming Christ risen but not crucified. So the church musician must never work apart from theology, always keeping in the forefront the God whose praises are being extolled, the God to whom prayers are addressed, the Christ who mediates salvation, and the Holy Spirit who mediates God's presence in the world, empowering the faithful to live as God's chosen people. The Second Helvetic Confession says that ministers will perform their tasks better if they fear God, are constant in prayer, attend to spiritual reading, are watchful, and maintain purity of life that their light may shine before all (5.164). This is good counsel for all who minister in the church, and certainly for musicians.

Church musicians not only work with music, they work with people. In fact, the effectiveness of music in worship depends, in part, on the relationships built among pastors, church musicians, choir members, instrumentalists, *et alia,* and other congregational members, and upon the resulting mutual ministry that takes place as people mirror the love that God has shown them, caring for one another. Fostering these relationships is as vital a part of the church musician's duties as the high-level preparation of music for public presentation. For choirs are part of the congregation, "the true choir," (*Directory for the Service of God:* Presbyterian

Church, USA, S-2.0700), and by singing they represent the rest, just as the pastor in praying speaks for all. And just as the clergy's prayers in corporate worship become more genuine when they know the needs of their flock, so also can musicians better represent the people if they have struggled through life with them during the week.

Church musicians also help others to make music. This is done by drawing on the innate abilities that every person has at some level, helping people to develop and use their talents to the glory of God. The psalmist did not cry, "Sing praises to God only if you have a trained voice, only if you won't embarrass us." All are encouraged to sing, and it is the church musician's duty to help through thoughtful and sensitive leadership, furthering both the spiritual and the musical growth of the congregation as together they glorify God.

Church musicians do this recognizing that it is possible, not through their own merits, but through God's grace:

No skill of ours, no music made on earth,
no mortal song could scale the height of
heaven;
yet stands that Cross, through grace ineffable
an Instrument of praise to sinners given.

So confident and festive, let us sing
of wisdom, power and mercy there made
known;
the song of Moses and the Lamb be ours,
through Christ raised up to life in God
alone. (Routley, *In Praise of God*)

Thanks be to God.

Kathryn L. Nichols[1]

157 • THE FUNCTIONS OF MUSIC IN WORSHIP

Music in worship serves many purposes and manifests itself in a variety of expressions. It is used both to praise God and to proclaim the Word; it both expresses prayer and relates the Gospel story. This article examines the various functions of music in worship and describes their implication for the church musician, who is the leader of the people's song.

What is the role of the church musician? The question can be answered by looking first at the nature of the church's song. Five headings suggest themselves.

A Song of Praise

The church's song, especially for Protestants, is most obviously a song of praise. Many Psalms—like Psalm 98, "O sing to the Lord a new song"; Psalm 100, which calls us to "Come into [God's] presence with singing"; or Psalm 150, where instruments and "everything that breathes" are all exhorted to praise the Lord—give expression to what is implicit throughout the Bible: God is to be praised, and music is one of the chief vehicles for expressing that praise.

Luther explains how this song of praise comes about. "God has made our hearts and spirits happy through His dear Son, whom He has delivered up that we might be redeemed from sin, death, and the devil. He who believes this sincerely and earnestly cannot help but be happy; he must cheerfully sing . . ." (Foreword to the *Geistlich Lieder of 1545,* quoted in Walter E. Buszin, *Luther on Music* [St. Paul: North Central Publishing Company, 1958], 6). God acts with loving kindness toward us, and we respond with a jubilant song of praise. That is an essential part of the church's song from its most formal to its most informal expression.

Karl Barth, one of the most important twentieth-century Reformed theologians, virtually made the church's song of praise a mark of the Christian community. He wrote,

The praise of God which constitutes the community and its assemblies seeks to bind and commit and therefore to be expressed, to well up and be sung in concert. The Christian community sings. It is not a choral society. Its singing is not a concert. But from inner, material necessity it sings. . . .

What we can and must say quite confidently is that the community which does not sing is not the community. (*Church Dogmatics,* IV.3., second half, trans. G. W. Bromiley [Edinburgh: T. and T. Clark], 866–867)

A Song of Prayer

The song of the church is also a song of prayer. This perspective finds preeminent expression among Roman Catholics and those with more Catholic liturgical forms. The roots of temple and synagogue worship are a sung tradition, as are Christian liturgies of both the East and the West. Gregorian chant, which accompanied much of the Western liturgical tradition, is seen by some as prayer itself (Dom Joseph Gajard, *The Solesmes Method,* trans.

R. Cecile Gabain [Collegeville: The Liturgical Press, 1960], vii). The Solesmes school of thought even calls Gregorian chant "a way of reaching up to God" and "a means of sanctification" (ibid., 85).

While many who live in the heritage of the sixteenth-century Reformers may wince at the Solesmes perspective because it can easily be seen as works' righteousness, John Calvin himself considered church song in the section on prayer in his *Institutes* (ed. John T. McNeill [Philadelphia: Westminster Press, 1960], III:X:31–32.) Luther and the Lutheran church retained the singing of collects and indeed the whole liturgy, and a large body of Protestant hymns are in fact prayers. Though the emphasis may differ, almost all traditions treat music as prayer in some way. That should not surprise us any more than using music as praise should surprise us. Human beings both laugh and weep. Laughter is the incipient form of sung praise, as weeping is the incipient form of sung prayer (cf. Joseph Gelineau, *Voices and Instruments in Christian Worship* [Collegeville, Minn.: The Liturgical Press, 1964], 15–19). The two very often run into one another and cross (see Patrick D. Millar, Jr., *Interpreting the Psalms* [Philadelphia: Fortress Press, 1986], 64–78).

A Song of Proclamation

The church's song is also a song of proclamation. The author of Ephesians expressed this by saying, "be filled with the Spirit, addressing one another in psalms and hymns and spiritual songs" (Eph. 5:18-19).

Here it is clear that music is a means by which the words and word of the gospel are proclaimed. Luther referred to the parallel verse in Colossians (3:16) and wrote,

> St. Paul . . . in his Epistle to the Colossians . . . insists that Christians appear before God with psalms and spiritual songs which emanate from the heart, in order that through these the Word of God and Christian doctrine may be preached, taught, and put into practice. (Preface to the *Geistliche Gesangbuchlein* of 1524, quoted in Buszin, *Luther on Music,* 10)

There is often an element of praise in thoughts of this sort. One can easily move from music as proclamation to music as praise without realizing it. Such a leap removes the distinction between these two motifs and tends to collapse one into the other.

Usually, since praise is so obvious, it takes precedence.

The use of music to proclaim the word, however, needs to be kept separate, even though the connections to praise can be close. This is true not only for theological reasons, but to do justice to the church's musical heritage. Much of that heritage is exegetical or proclamatory: music helps to proclaim, to interpret, to break open the Word of God. That is in part what happens when the congregation sings. That is why, from ancient times, biblical lessons have been sung or chanted. Motets by Schütz and chorale preludes, cantatas, and passions by Bach are more complex examples of the same intent. Without a kerygmatic (proclamatory) understanding of these pieces, they are incomprehensible (see Robin A. Leaver "The Liturgical Place and Homiletic Purpose of Bach's Cantatas," *Worship* 59:3 (May 1985): 194–202 and *J. S. Bach as Preacher: His Passions and Music in Worship* [St. Louis, Concordia Publishing House, 1984]).

The Story

Praise, prayer, and proclamation probably move, for many, from the most to the least obvious definitions of church music. A still less obvious aspect of the church's song is, upon reflection, both the most obvious and the most profound: the church's song is story.

When the people of God recount the history of God's mighty acts, they invariably sing. The morning stars "sang together" at creation on behalf of the people (Job 38:7). After their deliverance from Egypt, Moses and the people sang a song (Ex. 25:1-8). The reason for the psalmist's songs of praise is that God "has done marvelous things" (Ps. 98:1). New Testament canticles like the *Magnificat* (Luke 1:47-55) and the *Benedictus* (Luke 1:68-79) are songs which recount God's mighty deeds. The songs of Revelation tell the story of God's mighty acts in an eschatological frame of reference. From the beginning of the biblical saga to its end, from one end of history to the other, the story is a song to be sung.

The same can be said of the church's hymnody. If you were to lay out the hymns of almost any mainstream hymnal in a sequential fashion, you would find the entire story of God's mighty acts there—from creation through Old Testament history and incarnation, to the church in the world "between the times," to last things. Individual hymns often tell the story by themselves. "Oh, Love, How Deep, How Broad, How High" is a good example. Music is the vehicle by which the community remembers and celebrates what God has done—which leads me to three points about the church's song as story.

First, it is sequentially and logically easy to lay out the story of the Bible from creation to consummation as I have just done in the last two paragraphs. In fact, the story is more sophisticated than that, and sorting it out is more complicated. Like our own stories and those of the psalmist, it often begins in the midst of things, with personal laments and personal songs of thanksgiving and with people who emerge on the stage of history with their own struggles and visions. For the Christian the event of Jesus stands at the center of the story and as its key. It radically alters and fulfills all personal laments, thanksgivings, struggles and visions, and gradually gives meaning to past and present.

Second, music has a peculiar communal and mnemonic character. A group who sings together becomes one and remembers its story, and therefore who it is, in a particularly potent way. Hitler knew this and exploited the demonic potential of that reality. Whenever the church loses its song, a vacuum is created that the Hitlers among us will invariably fill.

Third, music spins itself out through time just like the story which the song recounts, and just like the worship where the song is sung. As the Eastern Orthodox church knows so well, music "is by nature an event. It is dynamic rather than fixed." Like the story and like worship and "more than any other art . . . it carries the possibility of change, of transformation" (Archbishop John of Chicago, et al., _Sacred Music: Its Nature and Function_ [Chicago: The Department of Liturgical Music, Orthodox Church in America, 1977], 2). This means it is peculiarly suited not only to tell the story, but to accompany worship as well.

A Gift of God

Finally, the church's song, like music itself, is a gift of God. Music is a joy and delight with which God graces creation. We do not bargain for it. We do not deserve it. It is simply freely given, there for the hearing, a joyous overflow of creation's goodness.

This gift can be viewed in many ways. One is the way Luther did it. Oskar Söhngen points out that Luther was forever amazed that music, this "unique gift of God's creation," comes from "the sphere of miraculous audible things," just like the word of God ("Fundamental Considerations for a Theology of Music" in _The Musical Heritage of the Church_, vol. 6 [St. Louis: Concordia Publishing House, 1962], 15.) This perceptive insight points to music as gift and to the close relationship between music and words: both are audible, words, amazingly, can be sung, and it is all gift.

A more Catholic approach, like Joseph Gelineau's, is to call music "God's daughter," given to humanity to signify the love of Christ (_Voices_, 27). Viewed this way, music almost takes on the character of a sacramental sign that points beyond itself to pure love. The Eastern Orthodox church often takes a similar view: that music can "reflect the harmony of heaven" and "can provide us with a foretaste of the splendor of the Age to come" (Archbishop John, _Sacred Music_, p. 2, 3).

These views always bring with them music's power to uplift, transform, refresh, and recreate the heart and soul. John Calvin asserts this when he calls music a "gift of God deputed" for "recreating man and giving him pleasure" (Charles Garside, Jr. "Calvin's Preface to the Psalter: A Re-Appraisal," _The Musical Quarterly_ 37 [October 1951]: 570). While Ulrich Zwingli in the sixteenth century related the refreshment of music to secular play, thereby allowing music no relevance at all to worship (Charles Garside, Jr., _Zwingli and the Arts_ [New Haven and London: Yale University Press, 1966]), even liberal Protestantism today may call music "revelatory." Robert Shaw, for instance, when he was installed as minister of music of the First Unitarian Church of Cleveland, Ohio, quoted J. W. N. Sullivan and argued that "a work of art may indeed be a 'revelation'" (_Music and Worship in the Liberal Church_, typescript, September 25, 1960, 8). Many Christians would disagree with what Shaw means by revelation and worship, but his use of the term _revelation_ shows how all worshiping traditions grapple with the gift of music and with its power.

The Cantor's Task

A host of theological issues attend these matters. The intent here is not to explain them in great detail. The point is that defining the church's song under the headings of praise, prayer, proclamation, story and gift offers clues to the dimensions of the cantor's task.

Leading the People's Praise. The cantor is the leader of the people's praise. The explosive response to God's grace, in order to be expressed, needs form and shape. Someone has to take responsibility for that forming and shaping, and this is the cantor's role. He or she has to sense the capacities and resources of a particular congregation, then write or choose music which expresses the praise of God with those capacities and resources. Once the music is composed and chosen, the cantor must then lead the people in actually singing the song of praise.

The song of praise is preeminently vocal. Words are the means by which our praise is articulated, and music is the means by which the articulation is carried aloft so that song gives wings to the words. But not only humanity sings this song of praise. The whole creation is called to join in. Instruments are therefore called to play their part. That part is not only to accompany the voices, but to sound alone where fitting and appropriate. The cantor is called to coordinate this and even to play, as talents warrant, so that instrumental music relates to the people's song of praise. Neither instrumental music nor any other music ought to be an afterthought or an unrelated addendum.

Leading the People's Prayer. The cantor aids the presiding or assisting minister in leading the people's prayer. The presiding and assisting ministers bear the primary responsibility for the proper prayers and petitions of a particular service, and the pastor bears the ultimate responsibility for the prayer life of a people. The cantor assists in this responsibility in the following ways:

First, the cantor provides the leadership for the people's litanic responses, spoken and sung. Corporate responses to a pastor's bids, even when spoken, are incipiently musical—elated forms of speech. The cantor through his or her direct leadership or through training of the choir shapes this response and thereby helps to shape the prayer life of the people.

Second, since some hymns are themselves prayers, the cantor sometimes leads the people in prayer by leading hymns.

Third, the choir also sings some texts that are prayers. In this case the cantor leads a group who prays on behalf of the people just as the pastor does. This is obviously not a performance before the people; it is rather an act of intercession on the people's behalf.

Proclaiming the Word. The cantor aids the readers in the proclamatory work of reading lessons. This may on some occasions involve the use of more or less complex choral or solo settings of lessons in place of readings. That is rare for most of us. It should not be normative, although it deserves more consideration than we normally accord it. Where lessons are sung by a lector, the cantor should obviously aid those who do the singing. For most of us, lessons are read. There too the musician has a role we rarely think about, namely, helping readers read clearly. Musicians understand phrasing and the ebb and flow of a line of words. Choral musicians understand diction and enunciation. These are necessities in good reading, which is close to a lost art in many churches and in the culture at large. Musicians can help repair the breach so that lessons can be understood.

The preacher obviously has the primary proclamatory task of publishing the good news of God's grace and love among us. By careful application to the biblical word and the daily newspaper, the preacher speaks his or her poor human words in the hope that they will be heard as the word of God itself so that the love of God in Christ will be known among us.

The cantor cannot and should not attempt to preach in the same way as the preacher because, first, the composing of text and music and the preparation of music by musicians preclude the preacher's relevance to the moment, and, second, the preacher can examine detailed relationships in spoken prose in a way that is not possible for the musician.

On the other hand, a polyphonic piece of music or the simultaneous juxtaposition of two texts gives the musician an opportunity to proclaim relationships in a way that is not open to the preacher, who must communicate in a stream of monologue. And, while the relevance of the moment is not the responsibility of music, which is of necessity more prepared and formal, music also has the capacity for breaking open a text in a way spoken words cannot do. In singing a hymn or hearing a Schütz motet or a Bach cantata, many Christians have shared William Cowper's experience:

> Sometimes a light surprises
> The Christian while he sings;
> It is the Lord who rises
> With healing in his wings.

Telling the Story

The cantor helps the people sing the whole story and thereby tells the story. The preacher also tells the story, of course, as does the teacher. Some understandings of preaching would even argue that it is at heart storytelling. There is a sense in which that is true: proclaiming the good news is telling the story of God's love. But the preacher is always compelled to apply the story to us in this moment so that the searing edge of God's love can burn its way into our hearts. This requires the context of the whole story, and preaching can only give that context over time or in an ancillary way. The cantor is responsible for the context and the fullness of the story.

This means that the cantor tells the story by seeing to it that the whole story is sung. The lessons, prayers, and sermon for a given service are likely to have a thematic focus. The hymnody, psalmody, and anthems ought to relate to that focus also, but in addition they flesh out the rest of the story and remind us of other parts of the plot. Over the course of a year the whole story should certainly have been sung, from Creation to Last Things. This means that doing the same six or ten hymns over and over does not serve the people well, because it keeps them from singing the whole story and omits much of the context the preacher needs for his or her words.

The Steward of God's Gift

The cantor is the steward of God's gracious gift of music. Since this gift is so powerful, the steward receives tremendous power as the deputy. That power can easily be misused for selfish ends of ego gratification and personal power. The cantor is called, therefore, to the paradox of using the power which is granted, but of using it with restraint on behalf of God in Christ from whom all blessings—including this one—flow.

That paradox brings with it another. The cantor knows that the preacher or lector can stumble over a word here or there, and still the message will have its impact. To stumble over a note is much more dangerous; the message's impact will dissipate much more quickly when there is musical error. So the cantor is constantly constrained to attempt an excellence and perfection that are never humanly possible. That drives the church musician to rehearse and practice every detail until it is right, for without practice there is the certainty that the nec-

essary perfection and excellence will never be achieved. The paradox is that even with disciplined rehearsing, there is no guarantee. The musician who is at all sensitive knows that when she or he finally gets it right, that too is a gift for which the only appropriate response is thanksgiving.

Paul Westermeyer[2]

158 • THE DIFFERENCE BETWEEN CONCERT MUSIC AND MUSIC FOR WORSHIP

Although the technical aspects of music are the same for concert and worship music, the function and purpose of music in these settings is different. Understanding these differences is important for church musicians, ultimately changing the criteria by which music is selected and influencing the way in which music is rehearsed and presented.

In choir lofts and parochial offices, an argument as old as the church goes on today. It focuses on the choice of music to be used in the church. On one side are those who assume that church music is to be judged in the same manner as all "good" music, namely, the music of the conservatory and concert hall. On the other side are those who assume that the criterion should be whether the music moves the people in the pews. In the heat of battle, these two sides are often pitted against one another and caricatured. In reality, both arguments involve false assumptions that obscure the real source of tension.

The Church and the Concert Hall

Although I understand the need to establish aesthetic values in the church, I disagree with some of the basic premises of those who uncritically apply the norms of the concert hall to church music. This practice undermines the integrity of the profession by obscuring the relationship between music and the people of the church and between music and worship.

I can explain my point by making a comparison. The members of the Boston Symphony Orchestra are musicians whose social responsibilities are narrow and well defined: they are part of a cultural institution that performs music drawn largely from the so-called "classical" repertory of western Europe. They are curators of this tradition. Their responsibility—to perform the music of that repertory with integrity—extends to the tradition itself and, beyond that, to those who pay money to hear them.

They keep that tradition alive and support its transmission from one generation to another.

Members of the church music profession share some of the same responsibilities as orchestra members. We are committed to perform good music well. But our relationship to the people who walk in the door of the church is very different from the relationship of the orchestra players to the people who pay to hear them. There are at least four major differences between what happens in church and at a concert.

1. For an important and extensive segment of our repertory, i.e., hymns, psalms, and other liturgical music, the assembled congregation assumes the role of the orchestra. The people to whom we are responsible are not an audience but a congregation.
2. The music performed in church is part of a liturgy, not a concert program, and liturgy is already a very complex art form, in which the music often follows a spoken text rather than other music.
3. The primary purpose of liturgical music is to be a vehicle through which people praise God. As part of worship, music is doxological.
4. Musicians occupy an important place in a community, and explicit ethical commitments underlie their vocations. Albert Camus wrote, "There is beauty and there are the humiliated. Whatever difficulties the enterprise may present, I would like never to be unfaithful to one or the other." (Albert Camus, *Lyrical and Critical Essays,* ed. Philip Thody, trans. Ellen Conroy Kennedy [New York: Knopf, 1968], 169f.)

This article will explore the implications of each of these four differences between liturgical music and concert music.

The Congregation as Orchestra

Hymns, psalms, and settings of the mass ordinary form the core repertory of church music. In her book *Worship,* Evelyn Underhill defines worship as "the response of the creature to the Eternal" (Evelyn Underhill, *Worship,* reprint [Westport, Conn.: Hyperion Press, 1979]). Throughout the ages various art media, especially music, have been used to deepen that response. Thus it is the responsibility of the church musician to train the congregation to express its praise in song.

Church musicians are music educators. To carry out their educational mission, they must understand why people sing and what will promote that activity. They must learn the musical vocabulary of the congregation they serve and use it as the starting point. In some large urban churches, the musical vocabulary may be that of the concert hall, but such is not the case in most local churches. A church musician cannot assume that the music program of the large urban church is a model for the music programs of all churches.

In worship everyone is on stage—everyone performs in the orchestra. If an audience is created by separating the performers from the nonperformers, worship does not take place. The quality of the participation and the status of the participants distinguish ritual from events with distinct audiences.

Worship does not exist apart from the need of the community to engage in it; therefore, there is no such thing as an observer of worship. The more a congregation chooses or is forced to play the role of an audience, the less integrity its worship has. If people sense that the choir and organist are performing a concert series on Sunday mornings, they will settle back and become an audience. When they relinquish the responsibility to raise their voices in song to God and hand this task over to the professionals who do it better, they cease to be worshipers.

The Context of Liturgical Music

To listen to a motet when its text may be included in a subsequent sermon, and to listen to that same motet in the midst of several others in a concert are two distinct experiences. It is a characteristic of our musical culture that the latter is the norm for establishing the musical value of the motet. Church musicians work within the liturgical context, yet for their musical judgment they often revert unconsciously to the experience of the concert.

Working with music in liturgy entails working with a musical form set within a verbal art form of great complexity. Within the context of this art form music takes on the power and meaning of its surroundings. What happens when a motet originally composed for liturgical use is extracted from that context and put into a concert hall program? The absence of its liturgical surroundings, from which it derived its unique power and meaning, causes the wrong kind of pressure to be put on the music. In the concert hall the music is forced to mean something on its own, and to absorb the liturgical context into itself. Thus a motet about Christ as the bread of life has to impart its meaning in an abstract and ethereal way, apart from its original context as a musical accompaniment to the Eucharist. Performed among others of its kind, the feature that attracts attention and is sought after is not the power of the liturgy but its "differentness"—that which distinguishes it from the similar pieces that precede and follow it.

In a liturgical context, on the other hand, the value of the music immediately before the sermon derives from congruence with its surroundings, clarity of text, and expression. The liturgy may be better served by a simple, unison hymn tune that everyone knows by heart than by a complex Renaissance motet. In the concert hall, technique and novelty are often the predominant musical values; in the midst of the Eucharist they may be of secondary concern.

Listening to a musical idea preceded by another musical idea differs from hearing it after the reading of a text, and a musical idea that accompanies an action is heard in yet another way. The dominance of the paradigm of the concert hall with its audience quietly listening to one musical idea after another obscures the variety of uses to which music can be put in worship.

Concert performance of music that originally was scattered through the various liturgical occasions can have alarming results. The current interest in early organs and the music written for them is a case in point. An entire evening of organ music written for liturgical occasions—processionals and hymn improvisations used in alternative congregational singing—can be very tedious, even at the hands of great interpreters. Musical invention in a series of three-minute pieces never becomes complex or varied, or at least not enough to sustain an hour and a half of continuous listening. Consequently, the performer does things to the music to make it more interesting, often negating the very authenticity that motivated the retrieval of the music in the first place.

This caution can be carried too far. The play of the musical imagination is behind every musical endeavor, whether the music is designed for the symphony hall or for eucharistic prayer. The point is that church musicians work within certain limitations that do not constrain other musicians. The drama of liturgy also provides unique opportunities to develop music that enhances its theological and aesthetic power. By approaching the work of the church through the lens of the concert hall, church musicians obscure the nature of their task.

The People's Praise

The primary purpose of music in the church is to enable the people to praise God, but this goal does not fundamentally alter the procedures of the musicians, who must employ the same skills and the same deliberate care, no matter how their music will be used. They must always strive to call forth the highest levels of ability, though their attitudes to learning and evaluation may be affected by the purpose of their music.

In his book *Ministry and Music,* Robert Mitchell speaks of the shift in values that takes place when one works with a musical organization in the church. He is referring specifically to the volunteer church choir, but his words pertain to many situations.

> A kind of conflict of values or priorities is intrinsic to the volunteer church choir situation. The reason for the choir's existence as commonly understood is to create a product—music—which will be used to enhance the worship experience. Very good—until one attempts to evaluate this task in the light of scriptural teaching. The Bible does not directly address itself to matters of music or art or aesthetics. . . .
>
> Viewed, however, from another perspective, from the nature of the process that goes on as the choir works at its task, there is a great deal of Scripture teaching that is relevant. Intrinsic to this process are matters of relationship . . . and matters of attitude. (Robert Mitchell, *Ministry and Music* [Philadelphia: Westminster Press, 1978], 55)

Mitchell goes on to describe how different work becomes when concern for people is the highest value. He decries the tendency on the part of musicians to focus on the final outcome and in the process exploit and harass the people who are trying to provide it.

If church music-makers allowed relationships and attitudes toward people to be their highest values, the choir repertory and its relative importance vis-à-vis the musical life of the congregation would shift. Instead of trying to jam a rocky, hesitant volunteer choir into a practice schedule that would produce an anthem a week or duplicate in dreary mediocrity the repertory of a paid choir, it is better to work on music that is easier to sing and to do less frequent performances. While one should never compromise on the quality of the music undertaken, neither should one use the standards of repertory and performance of an a cappella motet choir of singers from the local conservatory. Good music has vitality at many levels of competence, as anyone who has sat through student recitals knows. Moreover, what constitutes good music varies according to the aesthetic standards of varying repertories: a good motet and a good hymn tune are similar in some qualities, different in others.

——— Accepting Cultural Pluralism ———

Shifting the emphasis from product to process in a church music program is an ethical act. It is not, however, the total ethical commitment of the church musician. We do a great disservice to the musical and religious lives of a congregation when we employ only the values of the concert hall to evaluate the music of worship, because this approach so often leads to the elimination of other viable musical cultures from the life of the church.

Disguised in the various battles about music in the church—old hymns versus new hymns, Bach versus rock, organ versus guitar, gospel songs versus anthems—is a conflict between the "high" culture of the elite and the cultures of the rest of the population. The university and the conservatory, the training ground for so many church musicians, are centers of this elite culture; its precepts and music standards are talked about, written about, explained and transmitted along with an unfortunate disdain for other musical cultures. Often no attempt is made in these institutions to judge other musical cultures on their own terms, for they are considered devoid of aesthetic worth.

A profound ignorance of the purposes and values of musical culture other than high culture pervades the educational institutions that train professional church musicians. This ignorance supports the view that the music of other cultures lacks aesthetic worth. Indeed, ignorance prevents aesthetic judgment from taking place, since that would entail a prior belief that one in is the presence of a work of art (Arthur C. Danto, *The Transfiguration of the Commonplace* [Cambridge, Mass.: Harvard University Press, 1981], 98f). In the same way, musicians

who categorically reject all nineteenth-century hymnody will not undertake the acts of mind and heart requisite to establishing its aesthetic value.

When the attitudes and standards spawned in conservatories are transported without question into the musical life of local churches, they become the norm by which all various and sundry musical cultures are judged as inferior and inadequate vehicles of the holy. Under the guise of such standards, musicians impose their musical tastes on the congregation and risk suppressing the voice that wells up from the hearts of the assembled faithful. Further, they make certain assumptions about the relative importance of their own opinions compared with those of the congregation. If the people's musical vocabularies—their taste and training—are not as elevated as the musician's, the assumption is that they must adjust or conform to his or her superior taste and training.

In *Popular Culture and High Culture,* Herbert Gans tries to provide alternatives to an "either/or" approach to the problem of aesthetic value in art. He argues for cultural pluralism and for the promotion of cultures that do not now find expression in the elite media of the country. He states that "if people seek aesthetic gratification and . . . if their cultural choices express their own values and taste standards, they are equally valid and desirable whether the culture is high or low" (Herbert Gans, *Popular Culture and High Culture* [New York: Basic Books, 1974], 127). One evaluates an aesthetic choice by what it adds to the people's experience, rather than solely by its content. He continues,

> The evaluation of people's choices cannot depend only on the content they choose but must compare what might be called the incremental aesthetic reward that results from their choices: the extent to which each person's choice adds something to his or her previous experience and his or her effort toward self-realization. (Ibid.)

By calling for cultural pluralism in the church, I am by no means proposing to eliminate the music of high culture from the church's repertory, nor to discontinue the use of critical standards in choosing music for worship. Mediocre music can never serve any lasting purpose in worship. To paraphrase Underhill, the responsibility of the church musician is to evoke the congregation's response to their creator. Musicians have long understood that bad music inhibits this response. They are just beginning to understand the extent to which ignoring the musical culture of the congregation also makes it impossible.

If the musician's task is to educate and train the voice of the congregation, then one begins this process by taking seriously the people whose voice it is. Condemning their musical taste out of hand is very poor pedagogical practice, and it insures that one's efforts will meet resentment and resistance. Ideally, church musicians should approach any music, regardless of style or occasion, with understanding and the willingness to judge it on its own terms.

Music That Works

The attitude that any music that moves people is valuable for worship reverses the problem discussed above. Here, liturgical and pastoral norms appear to have primary place, while aesthetic norms are disregarded. Advocates argue that church music is strictly utilitarian; it is fine to use "throwaway" music that dies once its immediate purpose has been fulfilled. Whereas those who subscribe uncritically to concert-hall standards ignore the people who come to church and what they do there, these people ignore the fact that bad art actually suppresses the religious spirit and therefore will never "work" in any correct sense of the term. The continual use of music with no aesthetic worth corrupts the church. In _Feeling and Form,_ Susanne Langer writes:

> Art does not affect the viability of life so much as its quality; that, however, it affects profoundly. In this way it is akin to religion, which also . . . defines and develops human feelings. When religious imagination is the dominant force in society, art is scarcely separable from it; for a great wealth of actual emotion attends religious experience, and unspoiled, unjaded minds wrestle joyfully for its objective expression, and are carried beyond the occasion that launches their efforts to pursue the furthest possibilities of the expressions they have found. In an age when art is said to serve religion, religion is really feeling art. Whatever is holy inspires artistic conception. (Susanne Langer, _Feeling and Form_ [New York: Charles Scribner's Sons, 1953], 402)

Langer's ideas undergird one of the points that Nathan Mitchell makes in his article, "The Changing Role of the Pastoral Musician" (_Reformed Liturgy and Music_ 13 [1979]: 17f.). He argues that a pastoral musician is

> a theologian who confronts us with the immediate raw intensity of the human search for vision, the human search for God. . . . Our task is to hear what the human search for God sounds like and to shape that sound into music that will challenge, provoke, affirm, annoy, encourage, and delight believers."

The attitude that any music will do as long as it works betrays a basic misunderstanding of the aim of art and its use in worship. Art's primary aim is not to be effective, but to allow for insight. The artist creates a form—a symbol—as an embodiment of the life of feeling. To this symbol we react with recognition or clarified experience. This is what Langer means when she says that music, like religion, defines and develops human feeling. If the artist creates a musical form with the idea that it will move people to tears, or that tears are the only appropriate response to it, he or she is working in a closed process and not allowing listeners the freedom to bring their own experience to the symbol.

When the artist assigns a meaning and prearranges a response, the art work is destroyed. As an example, take the scene of Jesus' trial in the _Passion According to Saint John_ by Bach. Bach manages to bring us into the room to witness and participate in the scene. But he does not dictate our reaction to the experience. We may have many possible reactions; some are portrayed in the various characters, but many are not. Since Bach relies on us to complete the symbol, we can return to that room over and over again, bringing ourselves each time. And each time we are different. If tears were the only option, the experience would be the same and we would soon tire of it. If the response were so programmed by Bach, we might never make it to the room at all. We return to the scene of the trial in _St. John's Passion_ because its excess of meaning draws us.

The Musician's Call

Music in the church should show forth what it means to live faithfully at the end of the twentieth century. Music that is derivative or distorted, or that coats over real suffering and pain and joy with sentimentality and cliché, will never really "work." Not all music in the church need be contemporary, but all of it should pertain to the life of the faithful.

Despite their age, Bach's B Minor Mass, the black spirituals, the motets of Gibbons, and the hymns of Watts and Wesley still carry profound insight into the human search for God.

The task of the church musician who works with many kinds of music is to learn the categories of judgment appropriate to each, so as to judge them from the inside out. Setting criteria for good music involves deciding whether or not the symbol adequately portrays what it intends to portray. A Good Friday hymn need not say everything about the crucifixion, but what it does say should be true to that experience and relevant to the people who must use it to express their faith.

We are in a period of great change in our worship styles. Even well-trained and sincere music ministers often feel unsure in their judgments when confronted with new types of music or new ways of using music in worship. It is part of the risk of our calling that sometimes we will find, after several weeks of rehearsal, that music that originally seemed fresh and meaningful is actually flat and lifeless. Yet we cannot evade the responsibility to apply standards of judgment to the music we use. Mistakes are permitted; indolence is not.

Linda Clark[3]

159 • THE PLACE OF PRAISE IN WORSHIP

Worship in the praise-and-worship tradition is based on the assumption that praise is not identical to worship. Praise is the prelude to worship, our entrance into God's presence, which is the locus of true worship. This article describes this distinction.

The phrase "praise and worship" is frequently used by Christians, and yet these two words are rarely mentioned together in the Bible. Is there a distinction between praise and worship? What does it mean to praise the Lord? What place does praise have in our worship of God? Many have different answers. *Webster's New World Dictionary* tells us that one meaning of the verb "praise" is "to laud the glory of [God], as in song."

Hundreds of times throughout the Scriptures, particularly in the Psalms, we are exhorted to praise the Lord. In fact, the whole last segment of the book of Psalms deals with praise to God, and concludes, "Let everything that hath breath praise the LORD/ Praise ye the LORD" (Psalm 150:6, KJV).

The Symbol of St. John. The winged eagle represents the grace of the Holy Spirit that was always on Jesus and proclaimed by St. John.

Because there are so many verses in Psalms on the subject of praise, we may tend to think that praise is Davidic. But praise is divine. We are to follow God's pattern when we praise, not man's. Praise is God's idea, God's command, and also God's pleasure. He loves to hear his people praising him!

—— Praise Is Different from Worship ——

There is a difference between praise and worship. Worship in its broadest sense encompasses thanksgiving and praise, as well as the Eucharist, the act of giving thanks.

Praise is born in faith, is an instrument of war and a method of creating an atmosphere for the presence of the Lord. Worship is born from our relationship with God. We praise him for what he has done and worship him for who he is.

Praise is a sacrifice we give in faith. "Through Him then, let us continually offer up a sacrifice of praise to God, that is, the fruit of lips that give thanks to His name." (Heb. 13:15, NASB)

Praise is our entrance into God's presence. When we find him, we worship. "Let us come before His presence with thanksgiving/Let us shout joyfully to Him with psalms/Oh come, let us worship and bow down/let us kneel before the LORD our Maker" (Psalm 95:2, 6). Praise and worship are likened to rings that are linked together. They overlap, and yet they each have their own identity.

The Importance of Praise

As stated in Psalm 150, God has told us that we are to praise him, that this is his will for his children. Over and over again throughout the Scriptures we are exhorted to praise God and in turn he will communicate with us through praise.

Psalm 81 offers a clear picture of praise and its importance. Verse one (KJV) tells everyone to "sing aloud unto God our strength/make a joyful noise unto the God of Jacob." (This encourages both singers and non-singers to praise God in song). The second verse instructs the musicians to "take a psalm, and bring hither the timbrel, the pleasant harp with the psaltery." The key is in verse 4, which says, "For this was a statute for Israel and a law of the God of Jacob." It is a command. Praise is not an option for a few but a requirement for all.

> All God's creation, from the lowest to the highest, sings praise to him.
>
> Sing, O ye heavens; for the LORD hath done it: shout, ye lower parts of the earth: break forth into singing, ye mountains, O forest, and every tree therein. (Isa. 44:23)

The Scriptures say that the sun, moon, and stars praise the Lord.

> Praise the LORD from the earth / Sea monsters and all deeps / Fire and hail, snow and clouds / Stormy wind, fulfilling His word / Mountains and all hills / Fruit trees and all cedars / Beast and all cattle / Creeping things and winged fowl / . . . Let them praise the name of the LORD / For His name alone is exalted / His glory is above the earth and heaven. (Psalm 148:7-10, 13, NASB)

In the Apocalypse John said, "Every created thing which is in heaven and on the earth and under the earth and on the sea, and all things in them, I heard saying, 'To Him who sits on the throne, and to the Lamb, be blessing and honor and glory and dominion forever and ever'" (Rev. 5:13, NASB).

God's created beings, including angels, are to praise him. "Praise ye Him, all His angels: praise ye Him, all His hosts" (Ps. 148:2, KJV). In Isaiah 6, seraphim are described as praising before the throne of God. The same is true in Revelation 5:12 (NASB), where "myriads of myriads, and thousands of thousands" loudly proclaim, "Worthy is the Lamb that was slain to receive power and riches and wisdom and might and honor and glory and blessing."

If all the ranks of God's creation praise him, how can human beings, the highest of God's creation, do anything else? Praise is not optional; it is obligatory. It is not a preference; it is a prerequisite.

One of the most frequently sung songs of praise sums it up: "Praise God from whom all blessings flow / Praise him, all creatures here below / Praise him above, ye heavenly host / Praise Father, Son, and Holy Ghost!"

Praise Testifies

Praise is a testimony. It speaks forth wondrous things of God and his ways. He is lifted up for all to see and adore when we offer praise to him. The Scripture says, "And He hath put a new song in my mouth, even praise unto our God; many shall see it, and fear, and shall trust in the Lord" (Ps. 40:3, KJV).

Peter declared that we "are a chosen generation, a royal priesthood, an holy nation, a peculiar people; that [we] should show forth the praises of him who hath called [us] out of darkness into His marvelous light" (1 Pet. 2:9, KJV).

People are supposed to see us praise the Lord. Praise is not just for our prayer closet but for public testimony. Praise is a witness of our redemption and new birth. We have been chosen to display the praises of our Savior. God is the center of attention because he is the source and the object of that praise. Our praise reveals God to the world.

Praise Is Associated with God's Presence

It is in praise that God's presence becomes evident. "Yet Thou are holy, O Thou who are enthroned upon the praises of Israel" (Ps. 22:3). God dwells in praise; praise is his habitat. The Bible tells us to enter "his courts with praise" (Ps. 100:4, KJV). Praise is the open door to God's presence.

Praise is appropriate for believers. We read in Scripture that "praise is comely" [becoming, or suitable] (Ps. 147:1, KJV). The glow of God's presence as his children praise him is very becoming to them. As Moses' face shone with the glory of God, so the brilliant light of God's presence will be upon the faces of those who spend time in his presence praising him.

His glory will be revealed in the countenances and lives of those who are close to him, for they will radiate God to the world. Their lives will emit the fragrance of his presence, causing others to realize that they have been with the Lord.

Praise Delivers

There is a power in praise that can bring deliverance. Because the all-powerful and all-knowing One resides in praise (Ps. 22:3), no adversary has a chance. The Lord our God in our midst will save us.

Praise brings deliverance from mourning, depression, and a heavy spirit. The results are as sure as God's promises. Consider the prophetic word given through Isaiah:

The Spirit of the Sovereign Lord is on me, . . . to comfort all who mourn, and provide for those who grieve in Zion—to bestow on them a crown of beauty instead of ashes, the oil of gladness instead of mourning, and a garment of praise instead of a spirit of despair. (Isa. 61:1-3, NIV)

Depression, weighty spirits, heavy burdens, and accompanying worries fall away when praise begins.

Christians who "mount up with wings as eagles" are those who have learned to "wait upon the Lord" (Isa. 40:31, KJV). As they confidently expect God to come, they exchange their own strength for God's. Waiting on the Lord does not mean total passivity.

The House of Praise

In Isaiah 56 God declares that "mine house shall be called a house of prayer for all people" (v. 7, KJV). The word for prayer is the Hebrew word *tephillah* meaning "songs of praise and intercession." God wants his church to be a place where prayers and praise are sung as well as spoken.

However, believers are praisers not because they sing for a half hour on weekends, but because they have a life of singing praise to the Lord. *We* are the house of the Lord; each Christian is a "temple of the Holy Spirit." A temple is a place of worship. Wherever we go as the "house" or "temple" of the Lord, praise is appropriate. The church of the Lord is a fountain of praise to its exalted Head.

Praise Is Joyful and Loud

The Scriptures, particularly the Psalms, describe many kinds of praise. David and the other psalmists speak often of rejoicing and of expressing praise to God in an exuberant or demonstrative manner:

"Praise ye the LORD. I will praise the LORD with my whole heart" (Ps. 111:1).

Quite often praisers are criticized for being too emotional or too loud, but the Bible says, "Let the children of Zion be joyful in their King" (Ps. 149:2, KJV) and "Blessed is the people that know the joyful sound" (Ps. 89:15, KJV). The Hebrew word for joyful actually means "earsplitting." How many of us have ever even come close to that level in our praising? Moreover, John describes heavenly activity "as the voice of many waters, and as the voice of great thunder" (Rev. 14:2, KJV). Praise is the sound that fills heaven—loud spontaneous songs from millions of saints. God desires the earth to be filled with this praise, many voices in chorus singing their own song to the Lord.

Every creature, every nation, and every person in every language will sing glorious, audible praise to our exalted Lord. He delights in the praise of his people and is completely at home in their loud praises.

Praise is a sacrifice of thanksgiving and honor to the Lord. It is a declarative statement and must come from the heart. It must start with God and end with God and speak of God in between.

Lamar Boschman

160 • Philosophy of Music in Roman Catholic Worship

Roman Catholic directives in music have restored a sung liturgy and developed a liturgical role for music. What is true in Catholic circles is also true among other liturgical communities. The goal of music in worship is the text of the liturgical service.

Before 1903, the philosophy of music in liturgical worship existed only in practice, in the making of music. The first official written statement on sacred music by an authority within a liturgical church was the papal letter *Tra la Solicitudine* in 1903. Written as a reform document to correct the abuses of operatic and romantic music of the two preceding centuries, Pope Pius X, who had been the choir director in the seminary in Venice, wanted to reinstate a chant style of music in the liturgy.

Vatican Council

At the Second Vatican Council in 1963–65, the leaders of the Catholic church, with support from all the liturgical churches, affirmed that "full, conscious, and active participation" of the faithful was the aim of the liturgical renewal and should be considered before all else. Specific directives were given to encourage active participation, including, for the Catholic church, the use of vernacular languages throughout the world.

In regard to sacred music, an entire chapter (VI) of the _Constitution on the Sacred Liturgy_ put forth a series of directions that codified some of the philosophical principles for sacred music. Here is a summary of the main points of this document.

1. Sacred music is to be considered the more holy in proportion as it is more closely connected with the liturgical action, whether it adds delight to prayer, fosters unity of minds, or confers greater solemnity upon the sacred rites. The church approves of all forms of true art having the needed qualities and admits them into divine worship (par. #112).

2. Liturgical worship is given a more noble form when it is celebrated solemnly in song (par. #113).

3. Repertoire from the past (the treasury of sacred music) is to be preserved and fostered. Choirs are to be promoted, and the whole body of the faithful must be able to participate (par. #114).

4. Education in music by well trained teachers is encouraged in seminaries, institutes of higher learning, and for composers and singers (par. #115).

5. "The Roman Catholic Church acknowledges Gregorian chant as specially suited to the Roman liturgy; therefore, other things being equal, it should be given pride of place in liturgical services. But other kinds of sacred music, especially polyphony, are by no means excluded from liturgical celebrations" (par. #116).

6. Religious singing by the people is to be skillfully fostered, so that in religious prayer the voices of the faithful may ring out (par. #118).

7. Throughout the world, a suitable place is to be given to music which reflects the diversity of cultures and place. This native music should lead people toward a central unity and reflect the diversity by adapting worship to the native situation (par. #119).

8. In the Latin church, the pipe organ is to be held in high esteem. But other instruments suitable for worship may be used (par. #120).

9. Composers are encouraged to develop new music appropriate to the liturgy, not confining themselves to works which can be sung only by large choirs, but providing also for the needs of small choirs and for the active participation of the entire assembly of the faithful. The texts should be chiefly drawn from Scripture and liturgical sources.

Current Practice

Since the Second Vatican Council (1965–present), the development in sacred music for liturgical worship has been explosive and the philosophy along with it. Every major denomination has issued a revised hymnal, reflecting various stages of development. Some contain sexist language; others incorporate inclusive language. In 1980, an International Study Group, _Universa Laus,_ issued a statement on the philosophy of music in liturgical worship. And throughout this period, The National Association of Pastoral Musicians has reflected the development of the philosophy of church music in the United States, based on the practice of its members. Here are five key principles.

1. Musical liturgy is normative. In the tradition of liturgical worship, the liturgy is supposed to be sung or cantillated. A spoken text is an aberration in liturgical worship. Music, therefore, is the handmaid of the text (words) and the text is already given—e.g., Lord, have mercy; Glory to God; Holy; Psalm texts, etc.

2. The assembly is the primary musician. All others who take a musical role assist the assembly's worshiping role.

3. Music supports a liturgical function. Each section of the liturgy has a ritual function—e.g., procession, blessing, acclamation, etc.—and the role of the music is to enrich that ritual function. When music calls attention to itself, it distracts from the ritual function.

4. Liturgical prayer through music is balanced between performance and participation. Too much exclusive attention to either performance or participation is detrimental to prayer; it is equally true that too little attention to liturgical prayer itself is also detrimental.

5. Liturgical music is a unique art form. In the historical development of music, a musical form for specific use in the liturgy developed first, followed by choral music, symphonic and operatic. Some of the early stages of all of these forms took place first in church, using church texts. But in hindsight, the liturgical movement has judged that, while this musical development was important for music in general, it was detrimental to the basic philosophy of

musical liturgy. Musical liturgy is more like a folk art form because of the diversity of assemblies using it—from small to large, from ethnic based to plural forms, etc. However, liturgical music is a true art form, unique because the principle instrument is the singing assembly.

Trends for the Future

Current trends would indicate that the development of music in liturgical worship will continue into the future. For this development to take place, it will require dropping some of the practices which have recently developed and, of course, developing new practices. Many of these trends are already apparent and are beginning to redefine the philosophy of church music in practice.

From:	To:
Hymnody	Service music
Singing thematically	Singing liturgically
Singing everything, even poorly	Singing less, but well
Sacred treasure	Pastoral music
Praise only	Adoration/thanksgiving/ petition
Song leaders	Cantors
Choirs	More choirs
Parish musician	Musician/liturgist
Central leadership	Pastoral leadership

Hymnody is not native to the Roman liturgy. It entered into the Mass when musicians were seeking quality music immediately after permission was given to sing in the vernacular. More emphasis is now being placed on "service" music, or singing the given text of the Mass.

The principles for selecting repertoire are changing from the misconceived idea that the Scripture readings produced a "theme" for the Mass and therefore the music should reflect this theme. Today, most musicians have abandoned this false principle and have a better understanding of the liturgical year.

With the first flush of enthusiasm following the Second Vatican Council, some amateur musicians were insisting, "Sing anything, just sing." As congregational participation has faced its limitations, musicians are selecting the repertoire more carefully and encourage singing only what can be done well.

Art music is giving way to music which functions in and with the liturgical requirements. Only slowly

have musicians discovered the functional aspects of liturgical worship and the important role which music plays in it.

Music carries a variety of prayerful sentiments, more than simply praise. More musicians are discovering the importance of music in carrying the diversity of positions which human beings hold in relationship to God, from adoration and supplication to praise and thanksgiving.

The musicians themselves are changing; no longer seeing themselves as simply leaders of song, but developing their role as liturgical ministers. As parishes are financing full time musicians, many are becoming liturgists responsible for planning the entire liturgical celebration and assisting in the "performance" aspect of all the liturgical arts, including drama, movement, visual arts, etc.

The greatest overarching influence on church music is the relationship between the clergy and musician, which should be developed and nourished through regular meetings and open communication.

The philosophy of music in liturgical worship exists in these two worlds: the theoretical world of our documents and directives, and, simultaneously, in the practical world of parish life. It has always existed in these two worlds, and it will continue to exist in these two worlds. Hopefully, a working knowledge of this tension will serve to produce better liturgical music in our parishes.

Virgil C. Funk

161 • Philosophy of Music in Lutheran Worship

Among Protestant churches, the Lutheran tradition has the richest heritage of music for worship. It is based on the assumption that music is a profound means by which we enter God's presence and render our liturgy of thanksgiving to God. Bringing together insights first developed by Martin Luther and practices that have grown out of almost 500 years of Lutheran worship, this article describes why and how music is used in Lutheran worship.

The public worship of God's people is only rarely what we know it can or should be. A lack of understanding on the part of pastors, church musicians, and laity alike as to what Lutheran worship really is or might be is all too common. Inadequate experience and education in living the liturgy in colleges, seminaries, and in the local congregation has resulted in confusion and misunderstanding about worship, worship forms, and worship practices on the part of clergy, laity, and church musicians alike. In large part, this confusion is the result of being cut off from the basic understandings that enabled Lutheran worship and church music to achieve such a glorious history.

As more people in our congregations reflect backgrounds, traditions, and practices other than Lutheran, it is increasingly important that basic guidelines be set out that reflect Lutheranism's understanding of its worship, and particularly the role of music in that worship tradition.

Lutheranism has a distinct point of view in matters of worship and church music. It is hoped that this affirmation will help focus attention on this point of view for pastors, church musicians, and laity alike. In this way may it help in fostering a parish practice that is both faithful to Lutheran traditions and, in returning to Lutheranism's roots, help to realize a more vital worship practice in our parishes.

Worship and Music

What place does music have in a Lutheran understanding and tradition of worship?

The answer to that question is rooted in how Lutherans have seen themselves throughout their history. While the sixteenth century ultimately saw a separation of Lutherans from the catholic church of its day, Martin Luther and those who followed him did not see themselves primarily as a new church, but rather as a distinctive confessional movement within a larger Christianity. That understanding is a key one as Lutherans approach the matter of worship—how they see themselves in relation to the larger Christian tradition, and how they view music and its role in their corporate praise and prayer.

The Lutheran church is a worshiping church. Lutherans concern themselves seriously with all aspects of the church's worship life. Particular emphasis, however, is given to corporate, congregational worship, where Christians gather to hear the Word and to share the sacrament. For Lutherans, corporate worship is not simply a pleasant option; it is the indispensable and central work of the gathered Christian community from which all other facets of the church's life and mission, including one's

individual worship life, derive their strength, purpose, and direction.

The Lutheran church is a liturgical church. With much of Christianity it shares a concern for ordered worship. Its worship is characterized neither by eccentricity nor faddishness. Lutheran worship underscores the elements of stability and continuity with worship forms and practices that place Lutherans in the long line of worshipers from the New Testament to the Parousia. They worship not in subjective isolation, but "with angels and archangels and with all the company of heaven," in concert with Christian believers of all times and places.

Lutheran worship offers a richness and variety of forms and practices that give fullness to the celebration of corporate worship. As Lutherans worship with the recurring cycles of the church year, as they hear the Word proclaimed through ordered readings and preaching that recount the full council of God, and as they celebrate the sacraments, Lutherans are united with Christians of other times and places and receive strength for their task in the world.

Lutherans receive their heritage of worship forms and practices with thanksgiving and appreciation. Lutherans understand that their heritage is a meaningful source of continuity with their own past as well as with that of the whole church catholic. Yet Lutherans do not deify, ossify, or accept their heritage uncritically. Lutherans also see their heritage as a basis for moving toward the future. Thus Lutheran worship is simultaneously conservative and open to the future.

As music in Lutheran worship builds on these understandings, as it helps to nourish the faith, as it works to the glory of God and the edification of the neighbor, it has always had a welcome and important role among Lutheran Christians. Where it has fallen short of these understandings, where it has substituted other goals, where it has become man-centered rather than God-centered, to that extent it has ceased to be Lutheran in motivation, realization, and result.

Music in Lutheran worship—whether the music of congregation, choir, pastor, organ, solo voice, or instruments—*finds its most natural and comfortable place in the context of the liturgy.* It is in the liturgy, in all its fullness and completeness, that music in Lutheran worship finds its highest goal and achieves its greatest fulfillment. At its best, Lutheranism upholds this priority. When Lutheran worship forsakes its roots in the liturgy, as it substitutes other priorities, or as it seeks to imitate sectarian practices, it loses its orientation and perverts the role of both music and worship.

For Luther, music was next in importance to theology, a living voice of the Gospel (*viva vox evangelii*), a gift of God to be used in all its fullness in Christian praise and prayer. As the implications of these concepts begin to permeate our understanding and our practice, music in Lutheran worship will move ever closer to a fuller realization of its potential in the hearts and lives of worshipers everywhere.

Luther's View of Music in Worship

Martin Luther, alone among the reformers of the sixteenth century, welcomed music into the worship and praise of God with open arms. For Luther, music was a "noble, wholesome, and joyful creation," a gift of God. For Luther, music was a part of God's creation with the power to praise its Creator, and it found its greatest fulfillment in the proclamation of the Word.

> Therefore accustom yourself to see in this creation your Creator and to praise him through it.
> If any would not sing and talk of what Christ has wrought for us, he shows thereby that he does not really believe. . . . (quoted in Walter E. Buszin, *Luther on Music* [n.p.: Lutheran Society for Worship, Music, and the Arts, 1958])

For Luther, to "say and sing" was a single concept resulting from the inevitable eruption of joyful song in the heart of the redeemed. In contrast to some other reformers who saw music as always potentially troublesome and in need of careful control and direction, Luther, in the freedom of the Gospel, could exult in the power of music to proclaim the Word and to touch the heart and mind of man.

In emphasizing music as God's—not man's—creation and as God's gift to man to be used in his praise and proclamation, and in stressing particularly the royal priesthood of all believers, Luther laid the foundation for the involvement of every Christian—congregation, choir, composer, instrumentalist—in corporate praise at the highest level of ability. In seeing all of music as under God's redemptive hand, Luther underscored the freedom of the Christian to use all of music in the proclamation of the Gospel. The music that developed in this tradition is elo-

quent testimony to the fact that the church's musicians and its people found that Luther's views provided a healthy and wholesome context in which to work, to sing, and to make music in praise of God.

Luther encouraged the most sophisticated forms of the music of his day—Gregorian chant and classical polyphony—to be taught to the young and sung in church together with the simpler congregational chorales. In contrast to both the Latin tradition and that of the Calvinist reformation, it was the Lutheran reformers' understanding of music as a gift of God that successfully encouraged the reciprocal interaction of simple congregational song and art music of the most sophisticated kind. A flourishing tradition of church music was the happy result.

A Lutheran View of Tradition

Because it views itself as part of the one, holy, catholic, and apostolic church, Lutheranism looks to the experience of the church at worship throughout its history as an important source of its way of worship. Its use of forms and practices with which the church has prayed and praised for centuries—forms that have been tested, tried, and found nourishing through the experience of countless Christians—affirms Lutheranism's continuity with the whole church. In its life of worship Lutheranism gives such forms and practices a central place. Luther's view, which sought to retain from the past all that was useful, rejecting only what could not be retained in good conscience, was no flight into a wistful nostalgia; it was rather a pastorally responsible attempt to demonstrate the continuity and unity of Lutheranism with all of Christendom.

Lutheranism, on the other hand, does not hesitate to critically examine its heritage from the past, subjecting it to sound theological, psychological, and sociological examination for its meaning and usefulness for our own time. In doing so, Lutheranism is reminded that a sentimental return to any earlier age, ignoring later history, is no more adequate an answer than to suggest that each age must start anew to fashion structures of worship and prayer.

For Lutherans, the word *tradition*—in the sense of the gathered experience of the church at worship throughout its history—is an important working concept. For Lutherans, their worship tradition is always a living tradition, continuously developing and living in a vital parish practice. Building on the experience of the past, the church moves confidently into the future.

In some places tradition is misunderstood to mean merely conventional practices that may have developed in some place and have no relation to the experience of the whole church. Often it means no more than "what we in this parish are used to" or "how we did it last year." More often than not such "traditions" merely reflect sectarian fads that have become conventional through repetition.

It is a Lutheran conviction that the needs of people at worship are most effectively met by forms and structures of prayer that draw on the collective experience of the whole church at worship. For some, such structures and practices—when used for the first time—will be new and, perhaps, disconcerting. Once they become a normal part of the life of worship, however, their richness, strength, diversity, power to nourish faith and life, and their ability to help Christians praise God and enjoy him forever soon become apparent.

The Music of the Congregation

The chief musical reform of the Lutheran church in the sixteenth century was the establishment of congregational singing as a vital ingredient in corporate worship. It was not enough for Luther that people merely be present at worship—their faith should erupt in song: "God has made our hearts and spirits happy through His dear Son . . . . He who believes this sincerely and earnestly cannot help but be happy; he must cheerfully sing" (Buszin, *Luther on Music*). Thus what was only tolerated in the medieval church—and then only on infrequent occasion—became a central feature of worship in the church of the Lutheran Reformation.

Congregational singing, then as now, centers in the hymnody of the people, particularly in the Lutheran chorale. This unique body of words and melodies, which took shape in the early years of the Reformation, was drawn from the chants of the medieval church, from the many popular pre-Reformation "Kyrie songs," from nonliturgical Latin and Latin-German songs of pre-Reformation times, from secular melodies to which sacred words were adapted, and from newly written texts and melodies. The Lutheran chorale texts spoke clearly of sin and salvation, of death and resurrection; they recounted the story of man's fall into sin and his redemption won through Christ's victory over death and the devil. Its melodies—sung by the congregation in unison and without accompaniment—were vigorous, rhythmic, and truly popular.

The chorale spread rapidly and achieved a remarkable popularity wherever Lutheranism took root. The words and tunes of the chorale have continued to provide strength and comfort to worshipers wherever they have been used, and they have served as the basis for an ever-growing body of church music by composers since that time. There is hardly a Christian hymnbook that has not been enriched through the inclusion of Lutheran chorales, just as Lutheran hymnals have been enriched by the hymnody of others.

This unique wedding of words and melody which is the Lutheran chorale gave rise to the uniquely Lutheran custom of singing hymns in alternation between congregation, choir, and organ. Alternating stanza for stanza throughout the entire hymn, this manner of singing offered not only variety in the musical presentation of the hymn, but also provided opportunity for meditation on the words of the stanzas presented by the alternating groups. Each musical entity had a place in the singing of the chorale; at the heart and center, however, was the congregation.

The uniqueness of Lutheran hymnody lies in the fact that from the very beginning it has been an important part of the liturgy, not—as in most other traditions—a general Christian song loosely attached to worship. It was and continues to be *the* vehicle for congregational song.

Luther himself led the way in encouraging the creation of new texts and melodies through which the congregation could give voice to its faith in corporate song. The result has been the incorporation into Lutheran worship of a large body of hymnody reflecting a wide diversity of origins and musical styles.

For worshiping Lutherans, congregational song centers in the singing of hymns of proclamation and praise, prayer and adoration. And wherever a Lutheran understanding of worship and congregational song prevails, the chorale—among all the many jewels in the treasury of the church's song—continues to hold a place of special prominence.

In more recent history, Lutherans have also encouraged congregational singing of such other portions of the liturgy as the great prose songs of the mass (*Kyrie, Gloria, Sanctus, Agnus Dei*), various canticles (*Venite, Magnificat, Nunc dimittis*), together with a variety of shorter responses in the liturgy. Most of the early ventures in this development consisted of not too successful adaptations for congregations of music originally intended for choral performance. Only in very recent years has the attempt been made to fashion music for the liturgy that is truly congregational in its conception and realization.

Whatever its characteristics may be, true congregational song operates within the musical limitations of largely amateur singers, yet has a musical integrity and character distinctly its own. True congregational song is neither simplistic, undistinguished melody whose only purpose is functional; neither is it essentially choir music simplified for the purposes of group singing. True congregational song is a genre all its own, and its prototype and model—in terms of an accessible unison melody with rhythmic life and variety—is the Lutheran chorale.

The Music of the Choir

In the Lutheran tradition of worship the choir functions liturgically as a helper and servant to the congregation, enlivening and enriching the worship of the entire assembly. It does this in three ways. In order of importance they are

1. The choir supports and enriches the congregational singing of hymns and of the liturgy.
2. The choir brings richness and variety to congregational worship by singing the portions of the liturgy entrusted to it.
3. The choir enriches congregational worship by presenting attendant music as appropriate and possible.

1. *The choir supports and enriches the congregational singing of hymns:* by regularly devoting time in rehearsals to practicing the hymns to be sung in the various services, thus establishing a nucleus of singers who can confidently lead the singing; by helping to enlarge the congregation's repertoire through learning new hymns of worth and introducing them appropriately to the congregation; and by participating with the congregation in the regular festive presentation of the Hymn of the Day.

The choir supports and enriches the congregational singing of the liturgy: by devoting time, on a regular basis, to rehearsing the liturgy, so that the choir can lead the congregation most effectively; by teaching and introducing to the congregation the

portions of the liturgy that have not yet been learned, or learned only incompletely; by helping the congregation enlarge the dimensions of its participation through learning new musical settings of the liturgy or portions of the liturgy as appropriate. By helping the congregation, of which the choir is a part, sing the services it already knows more effectively, and by introducing—over a period of time—several different musical settings of the service that the congregation can use with the changing moods of the church year, the choir will be assuming more fully its role of leader in the liturgical worship of the congregation.

The uniquely Lutheran tradition of the "hymn mass," while not suggested as a norm, might well be used as occasionally appropriate to substitute for the prose texts of the major songs of the service.

2. *The choir also adds variety to congregational worship by singing the portions of the liturgy that have been entrusted to it by the congregation.* In the singing of the liturgy, certain texts, because of their unique appropriateness to the Sunday, festival, or season of the church year, change from week to week. Thus these texts are more suitable for singing by a group that meets regularly for rehearsal. At different times in the church's history these texts have been assigned to various groups; their use, however, is crucially important since they provide part of the variety that is important to liturgical worship.

In the services at which Holy Communion is celebrated, the "proper" texts traditionally assigned to the choir were

- the Introit
- the Gradual
- the Alleluia
- the Tract
- the Sequence
- the Offertory
- the Communion

In the recently revised American Lutheran orders for Holy Communion, the attention of the choir is directed especially toward the following "propers":

- the Entrance Psalmody (or Introit)
- the Psalm (in which the choir may participate in various ways with the congregation)
- the Verse

- the Sequence Hymn
- the Offertory

In the services at which Holy Communion is not celebrated, chiefly matins or morning prayer, vespers or evening prayer, and other services centered on the Word, the chief variable texts are

- the Antiphons
- the Psalms
- the Responsory or Response
- the Canticles

This rich selection of texts provides the basis for the participation of the choir in the varying portions of the liturgy, a participation for which the choir is uniquely suited and through which it can make a contribution of major significance. In certain newer liturgies some of these texts occur in slightly different contexts. They remain, however, the basic texts to which the choir must address itself as it prepares for its participation in the varying portions of the liturgy.

3. _The choir also enriches congregational worship by presenting attendant music as appropriate and as possible._ The term attendant music refers to that entire spectrum of motets, anthems, passions, cantatas, and other music not covered in the preceding discussion. As attendant music is planned for use in worship, three considerations are crucial:

a. Attendant music should be liturgically appropriate to the Sunday, festival, or season of the church year.
b. Attendant music should be appropriately placed in the liturgy. (Here special emphasis should be given the traditional Lutheran practice of music _sub communione_—during the distribution of Holy Communion.)
c. Attendant music should always be within the musical limitations of the choir.

In preparing attendant music, care must always be taken that the time and effort involved does not displace preparation for those other functions of the choir in worship that have prior claim in liturgical worship.

The choir has a unique and significant place in Lutheran worship. It can fill that role with music ranging from the simplest to the most complex; but complexity is never a criterion of liturgical suitabil-

ity. What is important and crucial is that choirmaster and singers together—as well as the pastor and congregation—understand what the real function of the choir in liturgical worship is, and that, understanding their priorities, they work toward carrying them out in interesting, effective, and meaningful ways that will contribute to the worship of the whole congregation.

A Note on the Soloist

The use of the solo voice in Christian worship finds its roots in the Jewish cantorial tradition and the continuation of elements of that practice in the use of solo voices in the Christian chant of the medieval church. In Lutheran worship that practice was continued, and the music of Lutheranism from Luther to Bach in particular reflects the continued development of that tradition.

The soloist in Lutheran worship always functions liturgically. Where a solo voice is used in the service, for example at times when a choir is not available, a Lutheran understanding of corporate worship assumes that the soloist—in reality a "one-person" choir—will provide the liturgical music necessary for the particular service. Then, when possible and desirable, the soloist may present additional attendant music according to his or her ability. The liturgy offers many opportunities for participation by the solo voice in ways—characterized by a spirit of modesty and restraint—that give richness, variety, and greater meaning to liturgical worship.

As a particular matter, soloists drawn from the ranks of choirs where the singing of appropriate liturgical music is the norm will usually see their function as soloists in a liturgical context more readily than will soloists who see their role to be exclusively that of presenting "special" music.

The Music of the Presiding and Assisting Ministers

The corporate worship of Lutheran Christians has traditionally been sung. This is true also of the parts of the liturgy that are the unique province of those leading the service. The singing of the liturgy by those leading in worship and people together adds a beauty and solemnity not possible in any other way. It elevates the doing of the liturgy to a place that moves beyond the personalistic and idiosyncratic to that of truly corporate song.

Certain portions of the liturgy are essentially _li-_

turgical conversation between pastor and people. Such familiar exchanges as "The Lord be with you—And also with you," "Lift up your hearts—We lift them up to the Lord," "Let us give thanks to the Lord our God—It is right to give him thanks and praise" naturally call for singing by both participants in the dialogue. In many other places in the various orders of worship this kind of liturgical conversation is important. When such liturgical conversation occurs, it is the most natural and desirable practice that both portions of the dialogue be sung.

Other parts of the liturgy given to those leading in worship are essentially a kind of monologue. Examples include the Scripture lessons, the collect, and the words of institution. These portions of the liturgy are usually sung on one tone with simple inflections. Luther himself took care to provide such simple recitation formulas for use in these instances. Most musical settings of the liturgy provide such simple recitation formulas, and congregations should encourage their ministers to use them when the rest of the service is sung by the congregation.

Many pastors already sing certain parts of the liturgy. This is a most commendable practice. Pastors and other worship leaders should be encouraged by their congregations—wherever they may be hesitant—to assume their fuller role in the singing of the complete liturgical service whenever the rest of the service is sung by congregation and choir.

The Music of the Organ

The organ has played a significant role in Lutheran worship since Reformation times, even though various aspects of its role have changed since that time. In its unique way the organ, too, can be the "living voice of the Gospel" and its use in Lutheran worship has demonstrated that possibility.

The Lutheran organist is a liturgical organist. This means that the way the organist functions in the service is determined by the movement and requirements of the liturgical action. It is not the function of the organist to entertain, to provide meaningless meanderings at the keyboard, or to fill every quiet moment with music. It is the function of the liturgical organist to lead the congregation in the singing of the hymns and chorales, to accompany, as appropriate, other portions of the liturgy sung by the congregation or choir, and to present other liturgical and attendant music alone or in ensemble.

The most important role of the organist is that of introducing and leading the congregational singing of the hymns and the liturgy. The practice of using the organ to accompany congregational singing was unknown at Luther's time, when the chorales were sung unaccompanied and in unison. But today the common practice is for the organist to accompany most, if not all, the stanzas of the hymns. Effective leadership here can do much to make worship the exciting adventure it is at its best. Through the use of effective introductions, careful choice of tempos, rhythmic playing, appropriate registration, judicious use of varied accompaniments, the occasional singing of a hymn stanza without the organ, and especially through the use of alternation between the congregation, organ, and choir, the organist sets the spirit and carries the momentum of hymn singing from the introduction through to the final stanza. When the organ accompanies other portions of the liturgy sung by the congregation it should do so with a forthrightness and vigor appropriate to the circumstances. In all situations the organ *leads* the congregational singing; it does not merely provide a bland and lifeless accompaniment.

It is customary in many places that the organ play at the beginning of worship, during the gathering of the gifts, and as the congregation disperses at the close of worship. It is most helpful and meaningful if the organ music at these times is based on the hymns or chorales sung in the service. At the least such music should clearly reflect the spirit of the particular celebration.

In general, the Lutheran organist plays less rather than more. When the organist does play it should be liturgically, functionally, and practically to the point. When the organ has no particular liturgical function it should remain silent. While the liturgical organist seeks to avoid a self-centered flamboyance and pretension in his playing, at the same time he uses all his skills in highlighting the inherent drama of the liturgical celebration. Only in this way will the organ's role as a liturgical instrument be more readily apparent.

The Music of Instruments

At its best the Lutheran church has always welcomed the use of a variety of instruments as a particularly festive way of expressing the celebrative aspects of joyful worship. Luther encouraged all Christian musicians to "let their singing and playing to the praise of the Father of all grace sound forth with joy from their organs and whatever other beloved musical instruments there are" (from E. M.

Plass, _What Luther Says_ [St. Louis: Concordia Publishing House, 1959], 982).

The organ has always had a place of special prominence in Lutheran worship. Lutherans have also used a great variety of instruments of all kinds in praise of God. Brass instruments, stringed instruments, woodwinds, bells, percussion—all these and more have been used in Lutheran worship, some of these even being preferred over the organ in the early Reformation era.

A rich treasury of music, intended for use in Lutheran worship using instruments, developed in the centuries after the Reformation. This music includes instrumental pieces intended as preludes, postludes, and interludes, both chorale-based and free compositions for organ and one or more solo instruments, and countless large- and small-scale concerted works for voices and instruments together. Special attention has been given in more recent times to providing a variety of solo and concerted music for small numbers of instruments with organ, or in concert with voices, that can be performed by instrumentalists of modest ability.

Instruments can play an important part in corporate worship, helping us to sing and dance our faith, helping us to express more fully and clearly the changing moods of Christian worship, from the leanness and spareness of such seasons as Advent and Lent to the more exuberant character of the Easter and Christmas seasons. Instruments can help foster communion with God and with our fellow worshipers and can serve as an extension of the human voice in sounding the special joy in the heart of the Christian as—through faith in his Lord—he affirms the totality of God's creation.

— The Pastor and the Church Musician —

It is only when pastor, church musician, and people work together toward the accomplishment of these goals that a truly living and vital parish worship practice in the Lutheran tradition can result. Each participant plays his own distinctive role, yet each complements and reinforces the others.

Regular planning sessions are an important part of this mutual preparation for worship. Pastors and church musicians, especially, need to meet often to exchange ideas and to discuss plans for future services and the role each will play. But whatever the vehicle for planning, pastor and church musician need to work carefully together. Only in that

way will worship be the best we can offer and God's people be truly inspired and edified.

Carl Schalk[4]

162 • PHILOSOPHY OF MUSIC IN REFORMED WORSHIP

Although the Reformed tradition has been more restrictive about the use of music in worship than the Lutheran tradition, it nevertheless highly values the role of music in worship. This article describes emphases important in the Reformed tradition, largely in terms of the writings of Reformer John Calvin.

The comparison is unavoidable: two great reformers of the sixteenth century with two vastly different approaches to reforming public worship. For Luther, it was the reform of the Mass. For Calvin, whatever his debt to the Mass, it was a new service. For Luther, it was the retention of the full musical resources of the church. For Calvin it was only the voice of the congregation. For Luther it was whatever texts were theologically correct. For Calvin, it was only the words of Scripture.

Both Luther's _Formula of Mass_ (1523) and his German Mass (1526), Latin and German Reformation forms of the Roman Catholic Mass, were the stimuli for the writing of numerous musical works for congregation, solo voices, choir, organ, and instruments, not only achieving a culmination in the great works of Johann Sebastian Bach, but also continuing to provide inspiration for composers into the present.

In contrast, Calvin's _The Form of Church Prayers_ inspired an elegant collection of metrical Psalm texts and melodies, a few canticles, and some sixteenth- and seventeenth-century polyphonic vocal settings of these texts and melodies for use outside the church service. These range from simple, familiar-style settings to monumental multi-movement Psalm motets. In spite of this early flowering of polyphonic Psalm settings, the development of a significant body of art music that was distinctively Reformed was frozen in the sixteenth century.

This comparison of the musical results of these two Reformation branches is not intended to diminish the value of the numerous Genevan and non-Genevan metrical settings of the Psalms and other passages of Scripture for congregational singing that have come out of the Reformed tradition of worship. Nor is it intended to diminish the significance of the organ and choral works based on Genevan and other Psalm melodies and metrical texts. Nevertheless, a Psalter is a closed volume once the 150 Psalms and a few canticles are prepared. In contrast, the Lutheran hymnal was an open-ended book, inviting continuing contributions from poets and musicians and providing composers with new texts and melodies as the basis for new compositions.

And the limitation of musical resources for public worship in the Reformed tradition to the voice of the congregation discouraged the writing of works for the full musical resources available to Lutheran composers. In the Reformed churches there was no need to write a cantata for the third Sunday after Pentecost or an anthem for the second Sunday in Epiphany.

The result of this relatively small body of distinctively Reformed music is that not much attention is given to John Calvin or the Reformed tradition when discussing church music. The Psalms and the Reformed services attracted but a few significant composers in the history of music, and most of those were concentrated in a short span of time.

From a musician's point of view, Calvin's reform is, therefore, usually judged negatively. It was he, it is said, who silenced choirs and tore out organs as being unnecessary in and even detrimental to the newly reformed way of worship. And his limitation of worship music to the unaccompanied singing of metrical Psalms and some canticles by the congregation produced rather few polyphonic vocal settings of the Psalms (though by composers of note) and (when organs were restored) some organ settings of those same Psalm melodies.

As a result of the differences in approach to reforming the abuses of the medieval church, the Lutheran churches received the fruits of a long line of distinguished composers from Walter to Distler. Though the Calvinist tradition in its four-hundred year history has produced significant music for voices and for organ based on the melodies of the metrical Psalter of 1562, the shadow cast by the vast and distinguished repertory of Lutheran church music places the Calvinist contribution to church music in a near total eclipse for many music historians. And that eclipse of the music inspired by the Genevan Psalter by Lutheran art music has also, unfortunately, placed Calvin's careful and logical thought for the music of the church in eclipse.

The error is that music historians leave their evaluations of Calvin with complimentary words for the Psalter melodies and for the sixteenth-century polyphonic settings of them. However, as musically valuable as the Genevan Psalter melodies and their polyphonic settings are, Calvin's contribution to the music of public worship is not primarily the 150 Psalms and a few canticles in metrical versions and their settings for voices and for organ that follow, but rather a well thought-out theology of church music.

While Calvin's theological foundations were born out of sixteenth-century thought, their applicability is not limited to a single time. His principles are timeless, clearly based on Holy Scripture and the thought of the early church. They balance sixteenth-century humanism, with its concern for human interests, and Renaissance rebirth of interest in ancient learning: a balance of the tension between the present and the past, between tradition and experience. The keeping of these two foci in creative tension is significant for finding direction for the music of the church in all times and places.

Calvin understood worship to be the most important of all relationships: the relationship between the all-holy God and sinful humans. It is, therefore, not a casual relationship. Neither the texts of worship nor the music that carries them can be casual. Theologically, it is a spiritual relationship between a covenant-making and a covenant-keeping God with his chosen people. At its best, Calvinist worship aims at restoring the ideal of communion with God enjoyed by Adam and Eve before their disobedience, a restoration not to be perfected until the coming of the kingdom.

Given the significance of this relationship of communion with God, worship and its music are approached with care, done only according to God's commands and carried out under the laws of order and decorum of the church, laws based on the Holy Scriptures. Calvin recognizes, however, that worship needs also to be done with concern for human frailty. He understands the reality of sin in human life and its role as impediment to fellowship with God. Therefore there is in Calvin a pastoral concern for the worshiper. External aids, rites, and ceremonies with valid purpose and not for spectacle, are necessary. Their purpose is to inspire reverence for the holy mysteries of sacrament and service, arouse piety in the exercise of worship, encourage modesty so the worshiper comes into the presence of God without presumption, foster gravity in order to worship only with seriousness of purpose, and above all lead the worshiper directly to Christ. In Calvin's thought, music is an important aid for the worshiper.

Given the accumulated quantity and the questionable quality of such aids in the church before the Reformation, Calvin insisted that these aids are to be simple, few in number, of clear value in assisting weakness, and understood by the worshiper. Displays of praying hands, the use of choirs, bands, and banners were not part of Calvin's plan. The question always is "what is necessary and what obscures Christ?" What encourages communion with our actually present Lord in the Holy Supper and what impedes it? For Calvin, it was less music rather than more; simpler music rather than more complex.

Calvin's liturgy, then, is a reformed service rather than a reformed Mass with its tradition of music. Worship needed to be returned to the people in language, in ritual, in clarity of thought, in accuracy of biblical meaning, and in simplicity of music so there could be meaningful physical, intellectual, and spiritual participation. The result is a liturgy reduced to its essentials with that which was judged extraneous and distracting removed. All aspects of the liturgy, including the music, are to serve the central functions of the word read and preached and the sacrament appropriately administered. Visual and aural effects were diminished, so magnificent altar and reredos were replaced by a simple table; elaborate priestly vestments were replaced by the academic gown; images, candles, incense, and bells were replaced by a simple sanctuary and service. Organs and choirs were replaced by an unaccompanied singing congregation.

Evaluation of Calvin's liturgical and musical reform is, therefore, usually concerned with what Calvin "got rid of"; what needs to be considered is what he brought to the service. Priority is given to the Word read and preached over the sacrament (though Calvin preferred weekly Communion). Attention is no longer directed primarily to the altar but to the pulpit from which God speaks through his Scripture. Music is used to enhance Scripture. The Psalms, extolled for their value in the Christian life by all who take time and effort to know them, are put in a form that ensures their assimilation into the thought and life of the singer.

That the Psalms, all 150 of them, should have been given to the people in an easily singable and easily remembered form was an enormously significant contribution to church worship and the Christian life. Testimony to their value in the Christian life can be found in writings from St. Basil and St. Augustine to C. S. Lewis and W. Stewart McCullough in _The Interpreter's Bible_. But perhaps Calvin says it best in his introduction to his _Commentary on the Psalms_.

> There is no other book in which there is to be found more express and magnificent commendations, both of the unparalleled liberality of God towards his Church, and of all his works; there is no other book in which there is recorded so many deliverances, nor one in which the evidences and experiences of the fatherly providence and solicitude which God exercises toward us are celebrated with such splendour of diction, and yet with the strictest adherence to truth; in short, there is no other book in which we are more perfectly taught the right manner of praising God, or in which we are more powerfully stirred up to the performance of this religious exercise.

And later,

> In one word, not only will we here find general commendations of the goodness of God, which may teach men to repose themselves in him alone, and to seek all their happiness solely in him; and which are intended to teach true believers with their whole hearts confidently to look to him for help in all their necessities; but we will also find that the free remission of sins, which alone reconciles God towards us, and procures for us settled peace with him, is so set forth and magnified, as that here there is nothing wanting which relates to the knowledge of eternal salvation.

Can there be any question as to why Calvin gave the Psalms to the people in song?

Calvin finds his foundation and nourishment for reforming the worship of the church in the tradition of the church, of which the Bible is the most significant part, over present experience. Therefore, two principles undergird Calvin's reform: the absolute sovereignty of God over against his human creatures, and the absolute authority of God's Word found in the Bible over human thoughts and experience. Yet, sixteenth-century humanism influences Calvin to make worship the people's offering to God. His respect for Scripture and his knowledge of God keep God and his revelation central in Calvin's reform. But the reform is to make public worship the people's worship.

The result was a service which focused the people's attention on the exalted, enthroned, ruling Christ seated at the right hand of God. The worshiper's heart is to be lifted up "on high where Jesus Christ is in the glory of His father." Public worship puts one in the presence of God and his angels, raises the worshiper to heavenly places. How logical that in the awe-inspiring presence of God the worshiper sings only words received from God himself in his Scriptures.

In keeping with Calvin's high regard for what worship is, the relationship of sinful humans to their all-holy God, the service expresses clearly the posture of adoration for the absolutely sovereign God and the need for purification when entering into the very presence of God. This adoration is possible only when the worshiper is restored to holiness and is acting in obedience to God. The opening invocation from Psalm 124, "Our help is in the name of the Lord, who made heaven and earth" immediately identifies who the worshiper is in relation to God. That realization prompts the worshiper immediately to confess sin as a beginning of the return to holiness of life as essential preparation for fellowship with God. The worshiping sinner confesses before God's holy majesty "that we are poor sinners . . . incapable of any good," but also asks God to "magnify and increase in us day by day the grace of thy Holy Spirit . . . producing in us the fruits of righteousness and innocence which are pleasing unto thee. . . ." Then follows the absolution in which God, through the minister, says "To all those that repent . . . and look to Jesus . . . for their salvation, I declare that the absolution of sins is effected. . . ." Those who have thus been restored to sanctity are fit to commune with God in the Holy Supper, to be raised to heavenly places, to sing his praises.

This lofty understanding of what public worship is leads Calvin to great care in crafting the service and choosing the words to be used. The liturgy is a fixed liturgy. Freedom and spontaneity are restricted, for after learning from Scripture, there is little room for improvisation and certainly none for caprice. Free prayer, so cherished in later Reformed churches, is given little room in Calvin's liturgy, and those prayers that are left for the minister to phrase are prescribed as to content. And when prayer is sung (Calvin regarded church song as a form of prayer), only the words of God, those from the Bible, are permitted.

It is this liturgy which is the context for the music of public worship and which prescribes its role. The essential ingredients of that liturgical context for music are preaching, communion, and prayer. It is important to note here that these are not items merely to be listed. The very nature of worship for Calvin requires that these three essential ingredients be present and that they demonstrate the authority of God's Word, be done corporately by the holy people of God (and not be done for them), and that in each the Holy Spirit is present and active. Without that presence, worship is a purely human and earthbound activity.

Of particular interest in regard to the music of public worship is prayer. Prayer is done according to the rules for right prayer from Scripture, and, whether sung or spoken, prayer in public is a corporate act made effective by the Holy Spirit, who intercedes for us. It is impossible to understand Calvin's seemingly limited church music without the theological foundation and liturgical context for it. The music appointed for the liturgy follows logically from them.

Calvin first insists that music for worship have clear purpose. He does not begin with the assumption that music must be present in public worship. He begins with a theological justification for it. It is essential for Calvin that there be a well thought-out reason for its presence in the public worship of God. That reason must be based on Holy Scripture and the thought and practice of the early church, as well as contemporary experience based on thorough knowledge of the faith. That is, the question must be asked, "What can and should music do to assist the worshiper?" Without clear definition of purpose, there is no demonstrated need for its existence in the public worship of God, and there is very little possibility of its doing what it can do and best ought to do for the worshiper.

For Calvin, music in public worship ought to aid concentration by exercising "the mind in thinking of God and keeping it attentive." It should also inspire reverence, lending "dignity and grace to sacred actions." Further, it should create unity by joining "the faithful in one common act of prayer." It should also rouse zeal, kindling "our hearts to a true zeal and eagerness to pray." And it should provide edification "as each from the other receives the confession of faith" in song. Well might the contemporary churchgoer and the modern church's leadership ask whether prayer and concentration on the thing prayed, reverence in speaking with God, unity in prayer, zeal and eagerness in prayer, and spiritual growth are being served by our church song.

So that the purpose for the music of the church may be realized, Calvin recognized that it is necessary for music to be regulated. This is necessary because music has power "to turn or bend . . . the morals of men. . . . We find by experience that it has . . . incredible power to move our hearts in one way or another." And music being a gift of God "we must be the more careful not to abuse it . . . converting it to our condemnation when it has been dedicated to our profit and welfare." This power of music, particularly with text, has been recognized by all who have reflected on the role of music in human life. Plato, Basil, Luther, and Confucius all knew the power of music. And so does the contemporary church. But Plato and Calvin and others knew that for salutary results in the use of music careful regulation was essential.

This regulation is accomplished, first of all, by the rules for right prayer, since song in the service is a form of prayer. One must sing with reverence, sincerity, penitence, humility and faith. But congregational song is also regulated by the scriptural rules for decorum. It is to be simple, it is to be understood, and it is to be adapted to the age in which it is used.

The purposes and the proper use of music require an appropriateness of text and music to the human response of worship, for only then will its purposes be realized and proper use be respected. As sung prayer, music is not decoration, entertainment, or filler, but it is one of the three essential ingredients of public worship. Calvin therefore understands that it must have weight or significance, and majesty, that is dignity. And the texts associated with the music are to be preeminent and are to represent true doctrine.

In Calvin's own words appropriateness is expressed this way:

When we have looked thoroughly, and searched here and there, we shall not find better songs nor more fitting for the purpose, than the Psalms of David, which the Holy Spirit spoke and made through him. And moreover, when we sing them, we are certain that God puts in our mouths these, as

if he himself were singing in us to exalt his glory. . . . Touching the melody, it has seemed best that it be moderated in the manner we have adopted to carry the weight and majesty appropriate to the subject, and even to be proper for singing in the Church, according to that which has been said.

As is so often true in the realm of the spiritual, the truth of a matter is represented by an ellipse, having two foci. Purposes, proper use, and appropriateness are to be balanced with a pastoral concern. It is a matter of respecting the divine while recognizing the human. That is, the music that results from respect for these three (purpose, proper use, and appropriateness) must be useful to the worshiper. It must serve the worshiper in serving God. It must be usable. Though addressed to God, it is a congregational prayer which, while offered to God, also edifies the worshiper and gives witness to the faith.

In bringing purpose, regulation, and appropriateness to the people, the church's song must be useful and useable so as to be of benefit to them. This results in a music of a particular character. This music is first of all biblical. Only if it is true to Scripture can it be the right worship of God and of true benefit to the worshiper. For in praying in accord with Scripture one comes to know and do God's will in prayer. For Calvin this means sung prayer is by means of the very words God gives us. To be appropriate, the church's song must be biblical. "We shall not find better songs . . . than the Psalms of David, which the Holy Spirit spoke and made through him."

This music must also be decorous, that is, it must have dignity and aptness. It serves an elevated purpose as prayer to God and is therefore to be noble in character as one addresses the song to God. It is to be proper to the subject, the text, so as to be suited to singing in the church "before God and his angels" and in so doing to bring attention to the texts, the thing prayed, and not merely delight the ears. "There is a great difference between music which one makes to entertain men at table and in their houses, and the Psalms, which are sung in the church in the presence of God and his angels." And "such songs as have been composed only for sweetness and delight of the ear are unbecoming to the majesty of the church and cannot but displease God in the highest degree."

In addition, this music is to be sacred for it needs to be a distinctive music if it is intended for a distinctive people engaged in a distinctive activity. It is for the holy people of God engaged in intimate fellowship with their all-holy Creator. It is not music for aesthetic enjoyment nor for entertainment. It is music for the dialogue of worship. In the text of the song, the Psalms, God speaks to the worshiper and the worshiper speaks to God in prayer.

This being music for the people, it must also be popular. That is, it must be easy to sing, it must be understandable, and it must be attractive. Without those qualities it would not likely be used. Note that this popularity is not in the contemporary sense of a music purveyed in enormous quantity so that it becomes popular by hype. It is music that is simply useful and usable.

That Calvin succeeded in a useful and useable body of church music is attested to by the over 60 known editions of the Psalter that were published within three years of its first publication in 1562. The rhymed texts in two simple classic poetic meters, with an entirely original melody type as to rhythm (with its longer notes at the beginning and end and in only two note values) gave them durability and wide dissemination.

These four characteristics properly understood are not merely descriptions of Calvin's music in the sixteenth century but represent a significant contribution to thinking on the music of the church for all ages. These characteristics, biblical, sacred, decorous, and popular, all at the same time, are principles that are also useful in our own age. Music, then, is to be of assistance in the true and spiritual worship of God. This makes Calvin's concerns for defined purpose, regulation, appropriateness, and usefulness the concerns for worshipers in all ages. Only then will music aid concentration, increase reverence, provide unity, rouse zeal, provide edification and in the offering of our worship refresh us in God's grace.

The results of Calvin's careful scriptural thought regarding the worship and worship music of the church resulted in a closed "hymnal." The texts of Calvin's completed "hymnal" of 1562 are limited to the 150 biblical Psalms plus the Decalogue and the Song of Simeon. The completed version of the Psalter consisted of 152 texts and 125 melodies. The authors of the texts were Clement Marot, court poet to Francis I of France. His death in 1544 left the versification of the remaining Psalms to Theodore de Beza, a Reformed theologian. The texts are metrical, rhymed, strophic, in classic poetic meter

(mostly iambic) and set syllabically to the music. They are, therefore, accessible to a singing congregation. They are popular in the most elevated meaning of that word.

The first of the composers is presumed to be Guillaume Franck, musician at St. Peter's church in Geneva, Calvin's church. Louis Bourgeois followed Franck at St. Peters and is *the* musician of the Psalter. His style is stamped on the Psalter since he not only added melodies but edited those already in the collection. His work dates from the 1551 edition. Pierre Dague, Bourgeois's successor at St. Peter's, is thought to have finished the music of the Psalter. As Beza had Marot's work to emulate, so Dague had the work of Bourgeois to emulate. It is generally conceded that the original texts and the Genevan melodies are of superior literary and musical quality.

The melodies are often assumed to be edited from secular sources. However, Bourgeois, in the preface to the *Pseaumes Octant Trois* of 1551 says the source of his work is pre-Reformation melodies, which some commentators take to be Gregorian chant. Whether the source is secular or sacred for any given melody, the style is radically changed, particularly by the schematicized rhythm.

The melodies are characterized by structural simplicity. The settings of the texts are syllabic, the music is strophic, the phrases are arche-shape, melodic movement is mostly stepwise, and the range of a melody rarely exceeds an octave. And while the melodies are modal, they are, for the most part rather major- or minor-like. Only two basic note values are used and these in a schematic design with phrases normally beginning and ending with longer notes with the shorter notes clustered in one or two groupings in the middle of a phrase of melody. The aesthetic character of the melodies develops from the combination of stepwise movement and the schematic rhythm along with the lack of a regularly recurring strong accent. The melodies possess a graceful, rhythmic flow.

By every standard, these melodies are accessible to a singing congregation. However, Enlightenment regularity and symmetry have accustomed us to a consistency of meter and design not possessed by the original Genevan Psalter melodies. The considerable variety of metrical scheme for the music and the absence of classic regularity make these melodies less easy for us to sing than for their sixteenth-century users, though the rewards of learning and using them are enormous.

It should be noted that the melodies of the Genevan Psalter are in a style that was familiar to the sixteenth-century worshiper in France. They are not, however, in the style of folk music or music of the pub, but in the style of cultivated music of the day. The schematicized rhythm sets them apart from even that music, making this truly a distinctive music for a distinctive people engaged in a distinctive activity, the public worship of God.

In summary, Calvin's contribution to the music of the Christian church lies in his carefully reasoned thought regarding the church at worship and the use of music in that worship. In preparing a suitable music for the church's worship, he expresses four concerns: for the purposes that music can and should serve in the worship of God, for its regulation so as to insure the realization of those purposes, for its appropriateness to the subject of the text and the object of our worship, and for its usefulness in serving the worshiper in serving God. These concerns resulted in a music that was biblical, decorous, sacred, and popular.

When thinking about church music, admiration is most likely to appear in the presence of a significant repertory of art music for choir, instruments, and organ—artistic value offered to God in the presence of his people. One stands in much less awe in the presence of a music intended for common worship. Even less consideration is given to a music that is not even intended for the enjoyment of community singing but only as a corporate offering of words by means of music in response to God's words to the worshiper.

However, this seeming tension between art music and congregational music need not be settled on the side either of music beyond the average congregation nor music beneath a suitable level of artistic integrity. And Calvin would not settle the matter of music for use by the congregation on the side of a distinctly secular music. He writes in the Psalter preface that "care must always be taken that the song be neither light nor frivolous: but that it have weight and majesty, as St. Augustine says, and also, there is a great difference between music which one makes to entertain men at table and in their houses, and the Psalms which are sung in the Church in the presence of God and his angels." Calvin achieved this ideal.

Churches in the Reformed tradition were affected by the same cultural influences as every other Christian tradition, but particularly by pietism, the En-

lightenment, and post-Enlightenment thought. The results have been principally in two directions. On the one hand, there has been an increasing openness to new ideas, growing confidence in human gifts, and the desire for a pleasing human experience in public worship. By and large, such openness has meant the abandoning of Calvin's principles for worship reform and for worship music. On the other hand, some Reformed communions have resisted cultural influences and retained Psalm singing to the exclusion of hymns, some even without accompaniment. While the former abandoned Calvin's principles, the latter failed to apply those principles to the present, overlooking Calvin's injunction that "rites and ceremonies," including music, need to be adapted to the age.

Calvin recognized that his application of principles to the practice of the church was conditioned by his time. His practice was adapted to his age. His, however, was a time of a fortuitous combination of humanistic interest in the person and Renaissance interest in the tradition. It put the reformers in a posture of relying on the truth of the past, particularly the Holy Scriptures, and bringing it to the benefit of the people. It is at this point that our own time needs again to examine Calvin, the other sixteenth-century reformers, and the church fathers for balance between the human and the divine, between personal experience and the tradition, between theocratic and democratic forces in church music.

John Hamersma

163 • Philosophy of Music in Free Church Worship

Music in free worship is not bound to the text of worship itself, but appears here and there as separate, special, occasional, and incidental to the order of worship. This approach has led to a wide divergence or practice among churches.

It is almost impossible to arrive at a single philosophy for the music of free worship; the range of practice is extremely wide—from the quasiliturgical, to denominational formalism, to populist evangelicalism and fundamentalism. Theological paradigms vary widely, as do governance systems, ranging from centralized authority to localized sovereignty. Emphases among worship, evangelism, and outreach likewise differ from church to church.

And finally, aesthetic philosophies range all the way from blatant utilitarianism (music's worth lies in its effectiveness) to idealism (music's effectiveness is subject to its intrinsic worth), and back to the middle (when worth and function are properly integrated, the music will be appropriate).

Nonetheless, there are five biblical injunctions and precedents which broadly inform free worship musical practice:

1. Music making, both vocal and instrumental, is not an option but a commandment (Ps. 149:1—Sing [play] to the Lord).
2. Christians are commanded to make music first to God as an act of worship (Ps. 149:1—Sing/play to the Lord), then to each other (Eph. 5:19; Col. 3:16), and before the world (Ps. 57:9).
3. Even if music making were not a commandment, the person and work of God are of such magnitude that the redeemed cannot help but make music (Ps. 51:14).
4. All presentational types of music are acceptable: solo (I will sing/play), the trained ensemble (1 Chron 15;16ff: temple choirs and instrumental ensembles), and the gathered congregation (temple worship, early church).
5. Newness and repetition are equally welcome (Ps. 33:3: Sing/play a new song; Ps. 137:3: Sing us one of the songs of Zion).

Because of the wide variations in practice throughout the free churches, and since there are many ways in which they often borrow from current liturgical practice and retain memories from their several liturgical pasts, it is important to discuss the one difference that distinguishes the musical practice of the truly liturgical church from that of the free church.

In a true liturgical context, musical practice is inseparable from celebrating the liturgy. Musical action, whatever its kind, does not precede, alternate with, bridge, or follow, other parts of the liturgy. There is no separately special, occasional, or incidental place for music. Instead, it is an indivisible part of a larger offering up—one facet of a larger confluence of languages (verbal, sensory, visual, iconographic, vestmental, and gestural) that comprise the whole. And the whole is not just the liturgy itself, but a comprehensive liturgical ethos of which everything comprising the life of the liturgical church is influenced. In this sense, musical practice is informed by thematic, calendrical, and contextual canons. While musical innovation and conservatism, singleness and repetition are equally possible, they are governed by the dynamics of the overall ethos. Liturgical music, by consequence, is probably less subject to whimsical change and the urges of pragmatism than many of its free-church counterparts.

Distinctives and Issues of Free Worship Music

Music Making Fulfills a Commandment. Music is not a luxury but a church-wide obligation from which no one is exempted. It is not something just reserved for the highly trained, nor does professional music- making earn a higher place before God. All is by faith, not by works or their quality, lest anyone should boast. Consequently, congregational song is at the center of free worship, in all its forms: hymns, gospel songs, and Scripture and praise choruses. The range of style and quality—and it is great—is often of less consequence than popularity, for heartfelt accessibility is of the essence.

Music Making Is Primarily Godward. Singing to the Lord clarifies the principle (though, in practice, not always) that music making is first of all an act of worship—an offering. This concept further serves as a safeguard against the all-too-common tendency to judge audience response as the primary evaluative criterion for quality. Singing "to one another" reveals the didactic nature of song; yet while text is doing the teaching, melody still goes Godward ("making melody in your hearts to the Lord"). "To the world" is a primary aspect of free worship music, the strongly evangelistic tenor of which demands no little attention to musical outreach. The tripartite concept of "to the Lord," "to each other," and "to the world" is a complex concept and, historically speaking, not without its philosophical and practitional problems, two of which must be mentioned here: (1) overemphasis on utilitarianism at the expense of quality; (2) the attitude toward music as more of an "aid" to worship than an "act" of worship.

The Redeemed Cannot Help But Make Music. Free church worship is centered in personal redemption. The gospel is for all. It is personally offered, personally received, personally celebrated, and personally spread. The grace of God, lavishly shown in Christ, is there for the faithful asking and taking. Communion with God, whether personal or corporate, is simple, uncluttered, and direct. The joy of the Lord translates quickly into song and the redeemed cannot help but take it up frequently, spontaneously, and above all, corporately. A musical worshiping church is therefore a musical witnessing church.

The Appropriateness of All Types of Music. Little comment is necessary except for three matters. (1) The personal nature of free worship, the primacy of the spoken word (therefore of the pulpit), and the priesthood of all believers contribute, all too often, to an overemphasis on the individuality of music making. There is an ongoing tension between performance as showmanship, in contrast to humble musical servanthood. (2) Instrumental music by itself, outside of preludic, interludic, and postludic actions (not to be confused with the more intrinsic work of congregational, solo, and choral song) is often considered suspect or secondary because it has no text; Scripture, however, mandates prophesying (speaking up) on instruments themselves. (3) Free church music is eclectic and populist. If redemption is personal and the Good News is to be spread with all haste, this must mean that the church is a witnessing church and its music a witnessing music. Witnessing music must be accessible and "in the language of the people" or it might not witness. Consequently, the music of the culture(s) being witnessed to must be incorporated into the church's witness.

The Balance of Newness and Repetition. The free church often ends up confusing novelty with newness, and rejecting it in favor of repetition and stylistic conservatism. Yet its doctrine of faithful sojourn and reckless abandon to the moving of the Spirit—often into uncharted territory—should allow for more musical innovation than is usually the case. In this matter, the free church is guilty of considerable distance between theology and practice.

Harold M. Best

164 ✦ PHILOSOPHY OF MUSIC IN PRAISE-AND-WORSHIP TRADITION

Praise music emerged from the revival atmosphere of the Jesus Movement and the charismatic movement of the mid-1960s. Its purpose is to make singing relevant to the worship experience of the believers. It is designed to express the renewed spiritual fervor of those who are rediscovering their personal faith in a personal God.

Throughout church history, theologians, pastors, and church musicians have struggled to achieve and maintain a balance between revealing the awesomely transcendent nature of God in the worship of the church while at the same time conveying God's relevancy, or his desire for a personal relationship with those who have fully accepted his plan of redemption through Jesus Christ. This struggle becomes particularly apparent in church history during the times of spiritual revival, restoration, and/or reformation, when the need for a personal revelation and relationship with God comes into emphasis.

Even in Scripture, the theme of God's transcendence (e.g., Psalm 104) is often juxtaposed to and always contrasted with the theme of God's relevancy to his creation (e.g., Psalm 103).

Music of the Great Revivals in the Church

Since the worship life of a community is a major means by which it communicates with its Creator, its style of worship during times of renewal takes on a strong character of relevancy and intimacy. During the German Reformation in the early sixteenth century, congregational singing was reestablished after having been discontinued in the church following the Council of Laodicea in A.D. 367. To make the singing relevant to the worship experience of those reformed believers, newly authored texts and Scripture versifications, all in the vernacular of the people, were set to often already familiar, and in some cases, popular melodies. Singing these texts to familiar melodies created a relevancy to the corporate worship of these Christians and helped to engender and nurture their personal faith. During the Great Awakening, the great evangelical revival of the mid-1700s, the newly composed hymnody took on a much more personal quality than the previously authored post-Reformation hymns. The most prolific writers of the day, Charles and John Wesley, often used in their hymnody the concept of personally experiencing the Lord's redeeming love while maintaining worshipful themes and poetic beauty. Later in the mid-1800s another revival broke out, primarily in Great Britain and the United States. This Second Great Awakening, as it is sometimes called, was characterized by an evangelical fervor that found its greatest musical expression in the gospel song. The gospel song can be described as a musically and textually simple song that expresses the Christian experience and salvation.

Because of their simplicity and experiential relevance, these songs became widely popular in such settings as revival services, Sunday school meetings, and camp meetings. The gospel song tradition was also utilized with the Pentecostal revival at the turn of the century.

The Revival of the 1960s

With the advent of the charismatic movement and the Jesus movement in the early to mid-1960s, the need again arose for a new type of music to express the renewed spiritual fervor that was experienced by those who were discovering or rediscovering their personal faith in a personal God. Many worshipers wanted to combine musical styles of the prominent pop culture with words that were of a sacred, worshipful nature, resulting in a culturally relevant yet sanctified genre. A type of worship music, which we will call "praise music," emerged. It was, and continues to be, characterized by generally easy-to-learn and sometimes colloquial texts and fairly simple melodies set to contemporary musical styles. Often Scriptures have been used as texts in praise songs, so the truth and beauty of the Word of God may be confessed as the singer sings. In liturgical churches, parts of the liturgy are sometimes set in a praise-music style to add a contemporary aesthetic relevancy to the text. In recent years, praise music has become extremely popular in congregations of all denominations and has utilized almost all popular music idioms as well as some classical styles. Even many of the hymns and gospel songs in the Christian tradition are being reworked musically with contemporary stylizations.

Cultural Relevancy

Every revival or spiritual awakening in church history has been accompanied by a development of music that reflects the spiritual intimacy (through nurturing a personal relationship with God through Jesus Christ) and cultural relevancy of the movement. In each case there eventually is also a rediscovery of the need to emphasize the awesomeness, transcendence, and majesty of God. Much praise music that is being written currently proclaims the glory of God while still using contemporary musical styles.

As praise music tends to nurture the simple intimacy and sonship of our relationship with God, so hymns tend to help us reestablish our historical and doctrinal foundations of faith. Care must be given by pastors/priests, musicians, and congregations to embrace the intimacy nurtured by praise music while embracing also the timeless heritage of hymns and gospel songs.

James Hart

165 • Philosophy of Music in the Charismatic Tradition

Unique to music in the charismatic worship is what is known as "singing in the Spirit." This form of music is characterized by a spontaneous response to the work of the Spirit in the worship service. It is based on a theology that emphasizes the dynamic and ongoing presence of the Spirit among believers.

A perusal of the songbooks and hymnals published by Pentecostal denominations (including such groups as the Assemblies of God, the Pentecostal Holiness Church, some branches of the Church of God, and other smaller Pentecostal churches) since about 1915 shows them to be repositories of interdenominational hymnody, albeit hymnody of the gospel song variety. Yet there is a small percentage of music which is distinct and unique to Pentecostals. It is called "singing in the Spirit."

Theological and Musical Background

Theologically, the modern-day Pentecostal movement has a Wesleyan ancestry. Pentecostals trace their doctrinal heritage through the Wesleys to Anglicanism. Standing outside the Reformed tradition of such men as Ulrich Zwingli and John Calvin, Pentecostals have more in common with the theology of Anglicans and Methodists than with Presbyterians and Baptists.

Musically, Pentecostals have a somewhat unique heritage. Being fiercely concerned with accommodating the gospel to ordinary culture for the sake of reaching the average person in evangelism and worship, Pentecostals choose to follow the musical practices of those groups who had a similar intensity of concern for popular evangelism. The musical issue has been methodology, not theology.

This pragmatic bent led the fledgling Pentecostal movement to base its music on the music of the frontier camp meeting, the National Holiness Association (Methodist), various Baptist groups, and other strongly evangelistic models. It also attempted to emulate the musical practices of such popular evangelists as Dwight Moody, R. A. Torrey, and Billy Sunday. But in one area Pentecostals were on their own. Without an established denominational precedent, they pioneered the twentieth-century phenomenon known as "singing in the Spirit."

Like most denominations, the Pentecostal church has an eclectic ancestry. Most of its theology and music share a commonality with various branches of the established church. But the theological and musical distinctives that give the movement its uniqueness have been obscured by centuries of corporate neglect. Only in the past twenty-five years have these unique Pentecostal distinctives been experienced among the older established churches in the form of the charismatic movement. In this way Pentecostals have been able to make a theological and musical contribution to the larger church to which they owe so much.

True to their pragmatic heritage, Pentecostals are currently embracing newer musical forms that are designed to reach people in the context of present-day culture. As a result of this commitment to accommodate the gospel to an ever-changing world, the eighty-year-old movement is using fewer gospel songs in favor of such diverse forms as worship choruses, contemporary gospel music, country-and-western songs, and gospel rock music. Pentecostals are continuing the practice of singing in the Spirit, though often in smaller gatherings rather than at the main worship services.

Theological Distinctives

The Pentecostal movement's understanding of the work of the Holy Spirit is its main theological distinctive. Knowledge of this distinctive is very important for comprehending the musical practice of singing in the Spirit.

Pentecostals (1) believe every Christian has available to himself or herself the baptism in the Holy Spirit, with tongues or glossolalia (speaking in an unknown language) as the initial evidence according to Acts 2:4; (2) believe tongues and the interpretations of tongues are special gifts of the Spirit to be used in corporate worship for the edification of the saints (1 Cor. 12:10). All other gifts of the Spirit, such

as the working of miracles, the word of knowledge, prophecy, and gifts of healing, are equally available and valid for today's believer.

The exercise of tongues is an act of the will. The mind maintains control (1 Cor. 14:27, 28). It is similar to praising the Lord or praying in English except that the language used is an unknown language prompted by the Holy Spirit. It produces great emotion, great heartfelt love for Jesus, at times even ecstasy, but all without loss of self-control.

Musical Distinctives

It is obvious to musicians that music and worship go hand in hand. Historically the adage, "He who sings prays twice," has been the experience of most religious movements. Thus it is not surprising that Pentecostals have used music in practicing their theological distinctive of glossolalia. Such a practice results not only from the natural predilection of Christians to sing their worship, but from the biblical material that Pentecostals feel encourages singing in the Spirit.

Paul's "psalms and hymns and spiritual songs" (Col. 3:16) and the lengthy discourse in 1 Corinthians 14 concerning the use of tongues in corporate worship indicate that singing in the Spirit was a frequent practice in the New Testament church. In verse 15 Paul specifically mentions praying and singing with the spirit and with the mind also. Pentecostals, noting that the whole context is about tongues, believe that whatever else Paul intended here, tongues and singing in tongues are normative.

Singing in the Spirit, strictly speaking, is simply singing in tongues. On the other hand "praise singing," which has a similar musical form, contains no tongues. However, when there is a mixture of tongues and the vernacular, as is most often the case, the term "singing in the Spirit" is appropriate.

General Characteristics of Singing in the Spirit

Glossolalia has no written form. It is spontaneous and unrehearsed. Consequently it is not surprising that the music to which tongues is set is likewise spontaneous and unrehearsed. It is an improvised music. One can easily imagine an individual in private prayer singing praise and adoration to God in an unknown tongue with a spontaneously improvised melody. It is harder to imagine a whole congregation caught up in the practice, each member simultaneously singing his or her own different and unique tongue to a melody that he or she is improvising on the spot. But congregational singing in the Spirit is a reality.

Having 10, 20, 100, or 1,000 people simultaneously improvising congregational song dictates that the music of such a congregational practice be extremely simple. It is almost invariably sung unaccompanied, but occasionally the addition of the organ or other instruments is thought to be helpful.

Four Musical Characteristics

The first musical characteristic of singing in the Spirit is the use of reciting notes such as those used in the Gregorian psalm tones. These notes usually carry the bulk of the tongue utterance, be it syllables, words, or sentences. The rhythm is that of ordinary speech.

Second, *melismas* (more than one note to a syllable) are common. However, there are no specific words or syllables, such as "hallelujah," which are routinely sung melismatically. The improvisatory principle at work mandates that there be complete freedom to sing the Spirit-prompted utterances spontaneously as they are felt.

The third characteristic is that usually only one chord forms the harmonic basis on which this congregational improvisation is built. At any given time there will appear in the texture the simultaneous singing of the root, third, and fifth of this solitary chord, each individual choosing whatever notes suit him or her, plus passing tones, neighbor notes, or other embellishments. Most of the words will be declaimed on the root, third, or fifth, while other notes will be used with less frequency. Nonharmonic tones are normally reserved for melismas or for syllabic word setting. The whole effect is not unlike the gentle strumming of a harp, using the diatonic notes of C major (for example) with the tonic chord predominant.

Fourth, there are no prescribed beginnings or endings such as the *intium, mediatio,* and *finalis* of Gregorian psalmody. Spontaneity throughout is the rule.

The Worship Service

The place in the service when singing in the Spirit happens is quite varied. It is usually thought appropriate whenever prayer and praise are appropriate. Often, extended congregational praise will very gradually evolve into singing in the Spirit. Some congregations exercise it after a hymn or chorus,

utilizing the keynote of that song as the harmonic basis of the exercise. Others sing in the Spirit at the congregational prayer times during the service or at the ending altar service. Some churches practice it regularly, others infrequently, and some not at all.

As previously mentioned, singing in the Spirit most often includes the vernacular as well as tongues. It is quite natural, when engaged in intense worship and praise, for the individual to move from glossolalia to English and back again at will. One hears such phrases as "Thank you, Jesus," "Praise the name of Jesus," "I love you, Lord," "Hallelujah," and so forth. Including the vernacular in corporate singing in the Spirit also allows those who do not speak in tongues to participate with praise singing. Thus no one is excluded.

The singing of so many different expressions concurrently might seem at first to be confusing to the uninitiated. For musicians, however, it is but another use of musical and textual counterpoint.

A Pentecostal Development

The return of singing in the Spirit to the life of the church is the result of the young Pentecostal movement's tenacity in pursuing its convictions. Over a period of eighty-some years it has developed, practiced, and popularized this type of song. With 75 million Pentecostals and at least 100 million charismatics worldwide, singing in the Spirit will no doubt continue for the foreseeable future.

Calvin M. Johansson[5]

166 • Philosophy of Music in African-American Worship

Music in black churches an is exuberant celebration of Jesus Christ and realization of the power of the Spirit. It is necessarily shaped by the unique experience of black Christians and emphasizes themes—such as the need for liberation in Christ—important to this experience.

Music has always been a necessary thread in the fabric out of which the human spirit was created. From ancient times to the present day, music has filled the gaps made by humanity's attempt to express the inexpressible. As Debussy observed, music "reaches the naked flesh of feeling."

This is especially true when considering the religious pilgrimage of the human race. Worship forms and practices have been designed to assist in humankind's quest to find meaning and purpose. And music has been part and parcel of deity worship from the dawn of civilization.

The Judeo-Christian heritage attests to the importance of musical expression. It would be impossible to imagine the people of God without a song. Evidence is plentiful that music played an important role in the Hebrew worship of Yahweh. The Psalms attest to the importance of music in the worship of God.

Even though the New Testament church was composed of a variety of forms and practices, all of these expressions sprang from Jewish roots. The New Testament church was a reflection of Jewish forms. Even though the evidence is not as pronounced, we know that the early Christian church emphasized music as an integral part of worship and praise to God. In the early church, music belonged to the congregation, and Scripture makes many references to the practice of singing. Some of the most beautiful passages in the New Testament are ancient hymns, borrowed and recast by the biblical writers to fit a particular theological purpose. . . .

Toward a Better Way

One of the tasks of ministers and musicians is to monitor and examine the music of the church, specifically the music of the black worship experience, and to see whether or not the people of God are giving their best. Traditions must be constantly reexamined. An attempt should be made, not only to reflect the best of the African-American tradition, but also to be true to the biblical model.

One of the purposes of this article then, is to make contemporary black ministers more aware of the issues with which they must deal if they are serious about correcting abuses within the church that relate to music and worship. Such correction is an educational task. To accomplish this task, the reader must glean some understanding of the nature and meaning of music as reflected in the history of Israel and in the churches of the New Testament. The people of God have always been a singing people, and their experiences have always given shape to their song.

Another purpose of this article is to take a closer look at the pastor-musician-choir-congregation relationship. Even though singing is not an end in itself, neither is it a means of filling in the gaps in the worship experience. Music is not to act as a piece of scenic background. Songs should not be sung just because they are on the "top ten" gospel list. The congregation is not ever to be spectator but, through a unique spiritual encounter, is to become participant. The function of the choir is to worship as well as to sing. This article will take a deeper look at this complex set of relationships in order to aid the examination of the issues to be raised.

Still another aim of this article is to take a look at how the state of music in the black church has developed. Usually cultural trends take place over a period of time and cannot be traced to any one cause. In studying the development of these cultural trends, my intention is not to remove from black culture that which has given power, substance, and life to black religion, but to preserve the best of the black faith heritage and to foster continual growth and creativity out of which its music was and continues to be born. One must not only speak of the past relevance of the black church but must also address the question of continuing relevance. The genius of the black slaves was in their ability to apply "contemporary hermeneutic" to the situation in which they found themselves. They did, in effect, "sing the Lord's song in a strange land" (Psalm 137:4). To a large extent the land is still strange. But a song must be sung.

A Black Point of View

When speaking of black religion, it may be an understatement to say that music has always been a necessary ingredient in the religion of the African American. In this case, music has been more than a mere ingredient. It has been the yeast that has given shape, substance, and content to the black religious experience.

First of all, when one stops speaking of religion and begins speaking of black religion, that person immediately risks compartmentalizing the whole of religious experience. However, it must be recognized that societies impose labels that have, to a large extent, defined the parameters of human existence. The people of various societies filter their behavior, view of reality, religious beliefs, and identity through different cultural screens.

Inevitably the question must be asked, "What is black religion?"

Henry Mitchell names some characteristics of black religion. First, he finds a uniqueness of black culture in the freedom of expression observed in the pulpit and the congregation of any given church. A second, closely related characteristic in the black worship experience is what he calls "ritual freedom," that is, the spirit dictates, and not the printed order of worship, who shall participate, when, and for how long. Akin to this second characteristic is the freedom found in the music of black worship. The black church has "melodic license" and makes uninhibited use of improvisation.

African Roots and Influence

Even though much has been written in recent years about African roots, it may be well to identify some characteristics in order to say how the past has shaped the present state of affairs in the black church.

Miles Mark Fisher, in his book *Negro Slave Songs in the United States,* identifies some of the characteristics of African culture, especially as they related to the music and worship practices of the African. It might first be noted that religion, as well as music, was deeply embedded in the whole of African life. African thought was not compartmentalized and fragmented. The African's view of the world was holistic. Even the distinction in Western culture between "sacred" and "secular" did not apply in African culture. Music was part of every event and experience in the life of the African. Music told the unwritten story of the history of a given community.

Eileen Southern describes the style of singing in African culture. "The singing style employed by the Africans was characterized by high intensity and the use of such special effects as falsetto, shouting and guttural tones" (*The Music of Black Americans* [New York: Norton, 1971], 14). In terms of musical form

> The most constant feature of African songs was the alternation of improvised lines and fixed refrains. This form allowed for both innovative and conservative procedures at the same time: the extemporization of verses to suit the specific occasion and the retention of traditional words in the refrains; the participation of the soloist in the verses and of the group in singing the refrains; improvisation or embellishment upon the solo melody and reinforcement of the traditional tune in the refrains.

Dena Epstein seeks to trace African roots and contends that one must look in such places as Jamaica and the West Indies for additional sources. She says that West Indian accounts give valuable information

about the music of slaves that could not be gathered in mainland reports. She concludes that "African musics were transplanted to the New World by the second half of the seventeenth century." Musical instruments in use at the time included drums, rhythm sticks, banjos, musical bows, quills or pan-pipes, and a form of xylophone called the balafo.

African Influence in the New World

The arrival of a few African slaves at Jamestown in 1619 was the beginning of another chapter in the history of the New World. The scars of slavery have already been well documented. The important point to remember is that the African slaves brought with them components of a culture that could not and would not be extinguished in the new land. This was due, in part, to the persistence of an oral tradition. Knowing of this tradition is vital to understanding the continuation of musical forms and practices *during* slavery. (Note that slavery did not destroy these forms and practices.)

Even though slaves in the New World were separated from family and kin and from those of common tongue, the musical forms of African culture were retained. Wyatt Tee Walker (*Somebody's Calling My Name* [Valley Forge, Pa.: Judson Press, 1979], 29) notes that

> with no common tongue, the musical expression was reduced to chants and moans on the rhythm forms and in the musical idioms that survived. As the slaves learned the language of the masters, their verbal commonality became most pronounced in the music that developed in the context of slavery.

The emergence of what E. Franklin Frazier calls the "invisible church" was a logical consequence of the desire of the slaves to maintain continuity with the past, and the form of worship in the "secret meetings" was akin to the forms of worship in the motherland. In these services, the tone was altogether different from the tone of the plantation owners' services.

One of the characteristics of this tone can be identified as "call and response." Southern (*Music of Black Americans,* 18) notes:

> Modern scholars often use the term "call and response" to describe the responsorial or antiphonal nature of African song performance—i.e., the alternation of solo passages and choral refrains or of two

different choral passages. Typically, a song consists of the continuous repetition of a single melody, sung alternately by the song leader and the group, or alternately by two groups. The importance of the song leader cannot be overstressed: it was he who chose the song to be sung, who embellished the basic melody and improvised appropriate verses to fit the occasion, and who brought the performance to an end.

Another feature of the music of the slaves was its improvisational quality. A genius of the slaves was their ability to create new songs from old melodies and to improvise upon various themes. Those who heard the slave melodies found it quite difficult to explain or define what they heard.

In order to understand the culture of black people, one must study African culture. In research done by Miles Mark Fisher, he suggests that music was the means by which the African people commented on their laws, customs, and history. "Folk historians" in every town were "living" encyclopedias. In various life situations there was music: on the battlefield, in secret meetings, at marriages and funerals, at childbirth, in hunting, and in recreation.

Fisher concludes that five statements can be postulated concerning the importance of spirituals as historical documents. First, "the primary function of African music was to give the history of a people." Second, "African Negros were transplanted to the Americas along with their gifts of song." Third, "the first extended collection of slave songs was advertised as historical documents from the Negro people." Fourth, "such an evolution of slave songs was perceived by divers people." And, fifth, "Negro spirituals are best understood in harmony with this historical interpretation."

To deny that there are identifiable characteristics of black culture and religion and, therefore, of its music is to deny that any culture has an identity of its own. No matter how cultures may overlap and the degree to which they are assimilated, each culture has identifiable characteristics. It is also to deny the existence of various forms of witness within the "churches" of the New Testament. To affirm the expression of faith as given to those of African-American descent is to recognize the extent to which cultures have responded to the activity of God in the world.

Black Theology and Black Music

Black theology deals with how black people see God, the world, and themselves from the vantage point of the oppressed.

I have indeed seen the misery of my people in Egypt. I have heard them crying out because of their slave drivers, and I am concerned about their suffering. I have come down to rescue them. . . . (Exod. 3:7-8)

Black religion is a response to God's initiative, articulated through the thought forms, music, art, and customs of African culture. Black music comments on the history of that pilgrimage; a journey of sorrow, joy, despair, hope, frustration, and fulfillment.

The task, then, is to affirm the good in black theology and to offer correctives so that black theology may continue to address the needs of black people in light of their relationship to God and culture.

Historically, as has been shown, the music of the black church has reflected the theology of the pilgrimage of black people. Set within the context of the black church, the religious music of black people has helped to articulate the very soul and substance of the black experience, most especially for those who belong to the family of God.

In many instances, music has not only been shaped by theology but has also shaped theology. Not only may one speak of a theology of music, but one might also speak of the music of theology. There is no doubt that in the black church music is the lifeblood. Among blacks, music is not always compartmentalized into categories such as sacred and secular. In fact, the black church itself does not always see itself in light of such labels. Among African Americans, just as in African culture, religion permeates the whole of life, and so does music.

Here a distinction must be made between the folk religion of the black masses and the religion of those blacks who are part of a more institutionalized form of religion and have been influenced to a greater extent by white culture. It would appear that musical expression is much more significant among blacks who make up the middle- to lower-class structures.

Henry Mitchell also speaks of the "call-and-response" element in black preaching. To a large extent the power of the sermon is determined by how well the black preacher can "sing" the sermon. Such matters as voice intonation, style, and sermonic rhythm help determine the success and popularity of many black preachers. Especially is this true among blacks who have made no attempt to "whiten" their culture.

This is not to suggest that black congregations do not value preparation, both academic and spiritual, and the content of the sermon. The black preacher must preach to the needs of the people. The preaching style only highlights the extent to which music is embedded in the entire worship experience of the black church.

To a large extent, a black church is judged by its spiritual tone, most often reflected in its ministry of music and worship. Often music is the vehicle by which the masses of black people are initially drawn into the community of faith. Many people join a particular church because that church has a "good" choir. Of course, that does not mean that such people, attracted to a church because of the music, are necessarily serious about the church's real ministry, which runs far deeper than superficial attractions.

Evidence of Erosion

Increasingly, music in the black church has been separated from its theological and historical underpinnings. Instead of serving theology as a legitimate response to God and telling the story of hardship, disappointment, and hope, music in the black church has become, in many instances, an end to itself. This often fosters the goal of entertainment rather than the goal of ushering people into the very presence of the Almighty and sending them forth to serve.

J. Deotis Roberts (*Roots of a Black Future: Family and Church* [Philadelphia: Westminster, 1980], 114–115) offers a valuable insight into the proper understanding of the relationship between black theology and music. He says,

> Our theological task is to supply a theological underpinning for meaning in black life. Black churches are now experiencing a great influx of black youth because of the popularity of gospel music. . . . But the underlying reason for the enchantment with the "gospel sound" may be a profound search for purpose and value in life. Gospel music is emotional and otherworldly. It has little if anything to do with finding meaning for life in a hostile world. Unless we are able to anchor the celebration in Biblical faith

and personal and social ethics, our success story will have a short history.

More and more, music in the black church has become commercialized and packaged. Some of its lyrics represent poor theology, which has no place in black churches seeking to present the best of the faith heritage. As a result, the black church runs the risk of misusing this vital and necessary component of the faith.

Two of the responsibilities of the black church are to preserve its rich musical heritage as well as to create new music. One of the forms of this heritage is called the Negro spiritual. In many instances the spirituals, or "stories in music," have been abandoned, and generations of black boys and girls are growing up with no appreciation for black history as recorded in the spirituals. These "social commentaries" are yet relevant, for they speak today in a society in which both despair and hope affect the human spirit.

The music of the black religious experience was born out of struggle and represents genuine emotion and motivation. In many instances what exists today is an attempt to copy what has already been packaged and to bury the gift of the creative spirit behind electronic instruments and assembly-line lyrics.

The singing of hymns has always been a great experience in the black worship idiom, and often hymns sound different when sung in black churches than when they are sung in white churches. Frequently these hymns have been just about removed from the order of worship. Many choirs who sing gospel music loud and clear can hardly be heard when the time comes to sing a congregational hymn. Even when hymns are sung, they have been "gospelized" to a point at which their true beauty cannot be appreciated.

Another evidence of decay is the less frequent use of the old meter hymns, born in England, brought to New England, and adopted by blacks. They are a solid fixture in the black religious heritage, and the preservation of the meter-hymn style of singing should be ensured by our learning them from a dying breed of southern blacks and teaching them to our young.

The Abuse of the Black Heritage

Obviously, the social context of blacks has helped to shape and define their institutions. Systematically barred from full participation in the large society, blacks have had to develop support systems of their own creation. The black church has not only served a religious function but has been an all-purpose institution, providing social as well as spiritual services. Much like the synagogue of Judaism, the black church has been the center of black life. From it came self-help organizations, resources for extended families, educational opportunities, and political organizations. It provided a place for the free display of talent and potential that could not be utilized and appreciated in America's marketplace. Those who were powerless had access to power within the black church. Those who had neither title nor position elsewhere could hold office in the black church. Those who could not release their feelings in the everyday world could be heard on Sunday morning. The black church was and is both a place of temporary withdrawal as well as a place to refuel for the journey.

Even though the sharp distinction between "sacred" and "secular" does not exactly fit the black experience in religion, it can be postulated that the rise of secularism in the larger society has had an effect upon the secularization of music within the black church. When gospel music came into prominence in the 1930s and was popularized by the recording industry in the 1940s, many blacks initially resisted this "honky-tonk" music, as it was called. Even though the advent of pianos and organs was initially seen as profane, the present movement toward drums, guitars, and tambourines has been seen by some as a further contamination of a rich and glorious heritage. During the latter part of this century, the rhythm of the spirituals and meter hymns has been replaced by the beat of the gospel song.

Of course it is not the use but the abuse of this music form that causes such concern. This is not to suggest that other forms cannot or have not been subject to abuse and misuse. It is to suggest, however, that the music prevalent in many black churches today more easily lends itself to the possibility of abuse, if the direction it is taking is allowed to persist unchecked. The worship experience demands discipline as well as freedom, which is a constant theme of the apostle Paul. To paraphrase Cullmann, Paul sought to balance the "free expression of the Holy Spirit" with the "binding character of liturgy."

It is necessary to continue to affirm the power and appeal of music in the black church. Just as the Africans were a musical people, so African-Americans are a musical people. In the black church the two major attractions are still good preaching and good singing, although perhaps not always in that order. Already I have alluded to the way in which the preaching of the gospel is punctuated with musical intonations. The power of worship is in the music, and music's importance must continue to be affirmed. Blacks seem to tolerate poor preaching if the services can be redeemed by good singing.

It must also be recognized that the masses of black people have been attracted to the churches through gospel music rather than hymns. However, it is still necessary to guard against the temptation to give people what we think they want without critical examination of what is offered and of what they need.

Pastoral Leadership

In the black church the pastors have a great deal of freedom to shape, define, and influence the worship experience. More than any other persons, pastors are expected to lead in worship. Their responsibilities include encouraging and insisting that the congregation give its best to God and overseeing the entire ministry of the church. Even though the pastors of black congregations may not be musicians, they must be in touch with the issues relevant to the quality of music that comes forth from the worshiping congregation. Unfortunately, the seminary does not always equip pastors in the development of a theology of church music.

One of the problems is that ministers often take a hands-off policy rather than be intentional as they engage in ministerial transactions within the church. The minister has the responsibility and challenge to define, interpret, and plan those areas that will absorb the resources and energies of the congregation.

Toward a Theology of Music and Worship in the Black Idiom

What, then, is black worship? It is the corporate reflection by black people upon the acts of God, who responds to the theological, sociocultural, and political needs of black people. A theology of worship must, then, reflect the cultural peculiarities of blacks, and at the same time, rest upon the biblical foundations that have historically shaped the direction and destiny of African Americans.

What, then, are some of the characteristics of black worship at its best? To ask further, how can one, in fact, test the following guidelines against the biblical and cultural norm? How does one determine whether the music that enters worship represent the best of the African-American heritage?

First, music in the black church must express the communal nature of the black experience. This does not mean that music expressing the desires of the individual should be rejected. It does mean, however, that the individual finds meaning through identity with co-sufferers, with those who walk the same existential path. James Cone expresses the individual-within-community concept when he says, "Black music is unifying because it confronts the individual with the truth of black existence and affirms that black being is possible only in a communal context."

Cone's understanding is in line with the biblical norm and the apostle Paul's concept of the building up of the family of God (1 Cor. 14:3-4; Eph. 4:12). In the Corinthian passage, Paul tested the value of the diversity of gifts against his norm of edification. He said, "He who speaks in a tongue edifies himself, but he who prophesies edifies the church." (Although New Testament scholars debate the Pauline authorship of Ephesians, Pauline theology in Ephesians is evident.) Music in the black church must edify the family of God as it places the individual within the context of the community.

Second, music in the black church must hold in tension the emphasis on this world and the expectations of the new age. It must be "this worldly" without being materialistic and earthbound. It must be "otherworldly" without being disconnected from the concerns of social justice. Music is to minister to the whole person. This is the task of black churches seeking to be true to their heritage. Some churches are not seeking to be true to their heritage.

Third, music in the black church must balance the freedom of the Holy Spirit with liturgical restriction. Spontaneity must be tempered with a sense of order and meaningful content. Emotion in black worship must be affirmed, but emotionalism must be discouraged.

Fourth, the black church must continue to be a place for celebration, and such celebration must continually be reflected in the music. Blacks have always gathered for worship expecting celebration to happen.

No doubt music will always be a vital component of the religious pilgrimage of black Americans. As it has done in the past, music must continue to comment on the hopes, fears, disappointments, and faith of a people who still must struggle to "sing the Lord's song in a strange land." Just as the early Christians initially gathered each Lord's day to celebrate the Resurrection, so blacks will continue each Sunday morning to share in that victory over the unjust social structures that still need to be dismantled, so that "the kingdom of the world has become the kingdom of our Lord and of his Christ; and he shall reign for ever and ever" (Rev. 11:15).

J. Wendell Mopson, Jr.[6]

167 • A ROMAN CATHOLIC DOCUMENT: *MUSIC IN CATHOLIC WORSHIP*

In 1972, a committee appointed by the Federation of Diocesan Liturgical Commissions examined post–Vatican II documents on worship and music and issued the following document, Music in Catholic Worship, *a revision of the earlier document* The Place of Music in Eucharistic Celebrations. *This document includes a thorough discussion of theological issues related to liturgical music, along with guidelines for planning music for worship, especially for services that include the Eucharist.*

——— The Theology of Celebration ———

1. We are Christians because through the Christian community we have met Jesus Christ, heard his word in invitation, and responded to him in faith. We gather at Mass that we may hear and express our faith again in this assembly and, by expressing it, renew and deepen it.

2. We do not come to meet Christ in worship as if he were absent from the rest of our lives. We come together to deepen our awareness of, and commitment to, the action of his Spirit in the whole of our lives at every moment. We come together to acknowledge the love of God poured out among us in the work of the Spirit, to stand in awe and praise.

3. We are celebrating when we involve ourselves meaningfully in the thoughts, words, songs, and

gestures of the worshiping community—when everything we do is wholehearted and authentic for us—when we mean the words and want to do what is done.

4. People in love make signs of love, not only to express their love but also to deepen it. Love never expressed dies. Christians' love for Christ and for each other and Christians' faith in Christ and in one another must be expressed in signs and symbols of celebration or they will die.

5. Celebrations need not fail, even on a particular Sunday when our feelings do not match the invitation of Christ and his church to worship. Faith does not always permeate our feelings. But the sign and symbols of worship can give bodily expression to faith as we celebrate. Our own faith is stimulated. We become one with others whose faith is similarly expressed. We rise above our own feelings to respond to God in prayer.

6. Faith grows when it is well expressed in celebration. Good celebrations foster and nourish faith. Poor celebrations weaken and destroy faith.

7. To celebrate the liturgy means to do the action or perform the sign in such a way that the full meaning and impact shine forth in clear and compelling fashion. Since these signs are vehicles of communication and instruments of faith, they must be simple and comprehensible. Since they are directed to fellow human beings, they must be humanly attractive. They must be meaningful and appealing to the body of worshipers or they will fail to stir up faith and people will fail to worship the Father.

8. The signs of celebration should be short, clear, and unencumbered by useless repetition; they should be "within the people's power of comprehension and normally should not require much explanation" (Second Vatican Council, _Constitution on the Liturgy_ [_CSL_], No. 34).

If the signs need explanation in order to communicate faith, they will often be watched instead of celebrated.

9. In true celebration each sign or sacramental action will be invested with the personal and prayerful faith, care, attention, and enthusiasm of those who carry it out.

Pastoral Planning for Celebration

10. The responsibility for effective pastoral celebration in a parish community falls upon all those who exercise major roles in the liturgy. "The partic-

ular preparation for each liturgical celebration should be done in a spirit of cooperation by all parties concerned, under the guidance of the rector of the church, whether it be ritual, pastoral, or musical matters" (Congregation of Rites, _Instruction on Music in the Liturgy,_ March 5, 1967, no. 5e; _Roman Missal, General Instruction_ [_GI_], No. 73). In practice this ordinarily means an organized "planning team" or committee which meets regularly to achieve creative and coordinated worship and a good use of the liturgical and musical options of a flexible liturgy.

11. The power of a liturgical celebration to share faith will frequently depend upon its unity—a unity drawn from the liturgical feast or season or from the readings appointed in the lectionary and artistic unity flowing from the skillful and sensitive selection of options, music, and related arts. The sacred Scriptures ought to be the source and inspiration of sound planning, for it is the very nature of celebration that people hear the saving words and works of the Lord and then respond in meaningful signs and symbols. Where the readings of the lectionary possess a thematic unity the other elements ought to be so arranged as to constitute a setting for and response to the message of the Word.

12. The planning team or committee is headed by the priest (celebrant and homilist), for no congregation can experience the security of a unified celebration if that unity is not grasped by the one who presides, as well as by those who have special roles. It should include those with the knowledge and artistic skills needed in celebration: men and women trained in music, poetry, and art, and familiar with current resources in these areas; men and women sensitive to the present-day thirst of so many for the riches of Scripture, theology, and prayer. It is always good to include some members of the congregation who have not taken special roles in the celebrations so that honest evaluations can be made.

13. The planning should go beyond the choosing of options, songs, and ministers to the composition of such texts as the brief introduction, general intercessions, and other appropriate comments as provided in the _General Instruction of the Roman Missal._ The manner of inviting the people to join in a particular song may be as important as the choice of the song itself.

14. In planning pastoral celebrations, the congre-

gation, the occasion, and the celebrant must be taken into consideration.

The Congregation

15. "The pastoral effectiveness of a celebration depends in great measure on choosing readings, prayers, and songs which correspond to the needs, spiritual preparation, and attitudes of the participants" (*GI,* No. 313). A type of celebration suitable for a youth group may not fit in a retirement home; a more formal style effective in a parish church may be inappropriate in a home liturgy. The music used should be within the competence of most of the worshipers. It should suit their age level, cultural background, and level of faith.

16. Variation in level of faith raises special problems. Liturgical celebration presupposes a minimum of biblical knowledge and a deep commitment of living faith. Lacking these conditions, the liturgy may be forced to become a tool of evangelization. Greater liberty in the choice of music and style of celebration may be required as the participants are led toward that day when they can share their growing faith as members of the Christian community. Songs like the Psalms may create rather than solve problems where faith is weak. Music, chosen with care, can serve as a bridge to faith as well as an expression of it.

17. The diversity of people present at a parish liturgy gives rise to a further problem. Can the same parish liturgy be an authentic expression for a grade-school girl, her college-age brother, their married sister with her young family, their parents and grandparents? Can it satisfy the theologically and musically educated along with those lacking in training? Can it please those who seek a more informal style of celebration? The planning team must consider the general makeup of the total community. Each Christian must keep in mind that to live and worship in community often demands a personal sacrifice. All must be willing to share likes and dislikes with those whose ideas and experience may be quite unlike their own.

18. Often the problem of diversity can be mitigated by supplementing the parish Sunday celebration with special celebrations for smaller homogeneous groups. "The need of the faithful of a particular cultural background or of a particular age level may often be met by a music that can serve as a congenial, liturgically oriented expression of prayer" (Bishops' Committee on the Liturgy [BCL],

April 18, 1966). The music and other options may then be more easily suited to the particular group celebrating. Celebration in such groups, "in which the genuine sense of community is more readily experienced, can contribute significantly to growth in awareness of the parish as community, especially when all the faithful participate in the parish Mass on the Lord's day" (BCL, February 17, 1967). Nevertheless, it would be out of harmony with the Lord's wish for unity in his Church if believers were to worship only in such homogeneous groupings. (Congregation for Divine Worship [CDW], *Instruction on Mass for Special Gatherings,* May 15, 1969.)

The Occasion

19. The same congregation will want to celebrate in a variety of ways. During the course of the year the different mysteries of redemption are celebrated at Mass so that in some way they are made present (*GI,* No. 1; *cf. CSL,* No. 102). Each feast and season has its own spirit and its own music. The penitential occasions demand more restraint. The great feasts demand more solemnity. Solemnity, however, depends less on the ornateness of song and the magnificence of ceremony than on worthy and religious celebration (*Instruction on Music in the Liturgy,* No. 11.)

20. Generally a congregation or choir will want to sing more on the great feasts like Christmas and Easter and less in the season through the year. Important events in family and parish life will suggest fuller programs of song. Sundays will be celebrated with variety but always as befits the day of the Lord. All liturgies, from the very simple to the most ornate, must be truly pastoral and prayerful.

The Celebrant

21. No other single factor affects the liturgy as much as the attitude, style, and bearing of the celebrant: his sincere faith and warmth as he welcomes the worshiping community; his human naturalness combined with dignity and seriousness as he breaks the Bread of Word and Eucharist.

22. The style and pattern of song ought to facilitate the effectiveness of a good celebrant. His role is enhanced when he is capable of rendering some of his parts in song and he should be encouraged to do so. What he cannot sing well and effectively, he ought to recite. If capable of singing, he ought, for the sake of the people, to rehearse carefully the sung parts that contribute to their celebration (Ibid., No. 8).

The Place of Music in the Celebration

Music Serves the Expression of Faith

23. Among the many signs and symbols used by the church to celebrate its faith, music is of preeminent importance. As sacred song united to the words, it forms an integral part of solemn liturgy (cf. *CSL*, No. 112). Yet the function of music is ministerial; it must serve and never dominate. Music should assist the assembled believers to express and share the gift of faith that is within them and to nourish and strengthen their interior commitment of faith. It should heighten the texts so that they speak more fully and more effectively. The quality of joy and enthusiasm that music adds to community worship cannot be gained in any other way. It imparts a sense a unity to the congregation and sets the appropriate tone for a particular celebration.

24. In addition to expressing texts, music can also unveil a dimension of meaning and feeling, a communication of ideas and intuitions which words alone cannot yield. This dimension is integral to the human personality and growth in faith. It cannot be ignored if the signs of worship are to speak to the whole person. Ideally, every communal celebration of faith, including funerals and the sacraments of baptism, confirmation, penance, anointing and matrimony, should include music and singing. Where it is possible to celebrate the Liturgy of the Hours in a community, it, too, should include music.

25. To determine the value of a given musical element in a liturgical celebration a threefold judgment must be made: musical, liturgical, and pastoral.

The Musical Judgment

26. Is the music technically, aesthetically, and expressively good? This judgment is basic and primary and should be made by competent musicians. Only artistically sound music will be effective in the long run. To admit the cheap, the trite, the musical cliché often found in popular songs for the purpose of "instant liturgy" is to cheapen the liturgy, to expose it to ridicule, and to invite failure.

27. Musicians must search for and create music of quality for worship, especially the new musical settings for the new liturgical texts. They must also do the research needed to find new uses for the best of the old music. They must explore the repertory of good music used in other communions. They must find practical means of preserving and using our rich heritage of Latin chants and motets (cf. *CSL*, No. 114).

In the meantime, however, the words of St. Augustine should not be forgotten: "Do not allow yourselves to be offended by the imperfect while you strive for the perfect."

28. We do a disservice to musical values, however, when we confuse the judgment of music with the judgment of musical style. Style and value are two distinct judgments. Good music of new styles is finding a happy home in the celebrations of today. To chant and polyphony we have effectively added the chorale hymn, restored responsorial singing to some extent, and employed many styles of contemporary composition. Music in folk idiom is finding acceptance in eucharistic celebrations. We must judge value within each style.

"In modern times the Church has consistently recognized and freely admitted the use of various styles of music as an aid to liturgical worship. Since the promulgation of the Constitution on the Liturgy, and more especially since the introduction of vernacular languages into the liturgy, there has arisen a more pressing need for musical compositions in idioms that can be sung by the congregation and thus further communal participation" (BCL, April 18, 1966).

29. The musician has every right to insist that the music be good. But although all liturgical music should be good music, not all good music is suitable to the liturgy. The musical judgment is basic but not final. There remains the liturgical and pastoral judgments.

The Liturgical Judgment

30. The nature of the liturgy itself will help to determine what kind of music is called for, what parts are to be preferred for singing and who is to sing them.

Structural Requirements

31. The choice of sung parts, the balance between them and the style of musical setting used should reflect the relative importance of the parts of the Mass (or other service) and the nature of each part. Thus elaborate settings of the Entrance song, "Lord have Mercy" and "Glory to God" may make the proclamation of the word seem unimportant; and an overly elaborate offertory song with a spo-

ken "Holy, Holy, Holy Lord" may make the eucharistic prayer seem less important.

Textual Requirements

32. Does the music express and interpret the text correctly and make it more meaningful? Is the form of the text respected? In making these judgments, the principal classes of texts must be kept in mind: proclamations, acclamations, psalms and hymns, and prayers. Each has a specific function which must be served by the music chosen for a text.

In most instances there is an official liturgical text approved by the episcopal conference. "Vernacular texts set to music composed in earlier periods," however, "may be used in liturgical texts" (National Conference of Catholic Bishops [NCCB], November 1967). As noted elsewhere, criteria have been provided for the texts which may replace the processional chants of Mass. In these cases and in the choice of all supplementary music, the texts "must always be in conformity with Catholic doctrine; indeed they should be drawn chiefly from holy Scripture and from liturgical sources" (*CSL,* No. 121).

Role Differentiation

33. "In liturgical celebrations each person, minister or layperson, who has an office to perform, should do all of, but only, those parts which pertain to that office by the nature of the rite and the principles of liturgy" (*CSL,* No. 28). Special musical concern must be given to the roles of the congregation, the cantor, the choir and the instrumentalists.

The Congregation

34. Music for the congregation must be within its members' performance capability. The congregation must be comfortable and secure with what they are doing in order to celebrate well.

The Cantor

35. While there is no place in the liturgy for display of virtuosity for its own sake, artistry is valued, and an individual singer can effectively lead the assembly, attractively proclaim the Word of God in the psalm sung between the readings, and take his or her part in other responsorial singing. "Provision should be made for at least one or two properly trained singers, especially where there is no possibility of setting up even a small choir." The singer will present some simpler musical setting, with the people taking part, and can lead and support the faithful as far as is needed. The presence of such a singer is desirable even in churches which have a choir for those celebrations in which the choir cannot take part, but which may fittingly be performed with some solemnity and therefore with singing" (*Instruction on Music in the Liturgy,* No. 21). Although a cantor "cannot enhance the service of worship in the same way as a choir, a trained and competent cantor can perform an important ministry by leading the congregation in common sacred song and in responsorial singing" (BCL, April 18, 1966).

The Choir

36. A well-trained choir adds beauty and solemnity to the liturgy and also assists and encourages the singing of the congregation. The Second Vatican Council, in speaking of the choir, stated emphatically: "Choirs must be diligently promoted," provided that "the whole body of the faithful may be able to contribute that active participation which is rightly theirs" (*CSL,* No. 114).

"At times the choir, within the congregation of the faithful and as part of it, will assume the role of leadership, while at other times it will retain its own distinctive ministry. This means that the choir will lead the people in sung prayer, by alternating or reinforcing the sacred song of the congregation, or by enhancing it with the addition of a musical elaboration. At other times in the course of liturgical celebration, the choir alone will sing works whose musical demands enlist and challenge its competence" (BCL, April 18, 1966).

The Organist and Other Instrumentalists

37. Singing is not the only kind of music suitable for liturgical celebration. Music performed on the organ and other instruments can stimulate feelings of joy and contemplation at appropriate times. (Cf. *CSL,* No. 120; *Instruction on Music in the Liturgy,* Nos. 63–65; CDW *Third Instruction,* September 5, 1970, No. 3c.) This can be done effectively at the following points: an instrumental prelude, a soft background to a spoken psalm, at the preparation of the gifts in place of singing, during portions of the Communion rite, and the recessional.

In the dioceses of the United States, "musical instruments other than the organ may be used in liturgical services, provided they are played in a manner that is suitable to public worship" (NCCB, November 1967; cf. *CSL,* No. 120). This decision deliberately refrains from singling out specific instruments. Their use depends on circumstances, the nature of the congregation, etc.

38. The proper placing of the organ and choir according to the arrangement and acoustics of the church will facilitate celebration. Practically speaking, the choir must be near the director and the organ (both console and sound). The choir ought to be able to perform without too much distraction; the acoustics ought to give a lively presence of sound in the choir area and allow both tone and word to reach the congregation with clarity. Visually it is desirable that the choir appear to be part of the worshiping community, yet a part which serves in a unique way. Locating the organ console too far from the congregation causes a time lag, which tends to make the singing drag unless the organist is trained to cope with it. A location near the front pews will facilitate congregational singing.

The Pastoral Judgment

39. The pastoral judgment governs the use and function of every element of celebration. Ideally this judgment is made by the planning team or committee. It is the judgment that must be made in this particular situation, in these concrete circumstances. Does music in the celebration enable these people to express their faith, in this place, in this age, in this culture?

40. The instruction of the Congregation for Divine Worship, issued September 5, 1971, encourages episcopal conferences to consider not only liturgical music's suitability to the time and circumstances of the celebration, "but also the needs of the faithful who will sing them. All means must be used to promote singing by the people. New forms should be used, which are adapted to the different mentalities and to modern tastes." The document adds that the music and the instruments "should correspond to the sacred character of the celebration and the place of worship."

41. A musician may judge that a certain composition or style of composition is good music, but this musical judgment really says nothing about whether and how this music is to be used in this celebration. The signs of the celebration must be accepted and received as meaningful for a genuinely human faith experience for these specific worshipers. This pastoral judgment can be aided by sociological studies of the people who make up the congregation: their age, culture, and education. These factors influence the effectiveness of the liturgical signs, including music. No set of rubrics or regulations of itself will ever achieve a truly pastoral celebration of the sacramental rites. Such regulations must always be applied with a pastoral concern for the given worshiping community.

IV. General Consideration of Liturgical Structure

42. Those who are responsible for planning the music for eucharistic celebrations in accord with the three judgments above must have a clear understanding of the structure of the liturgy. They must be aware of what is of primary importance. They should know the nature of each of the parts of the liturgy and the relationship of each part to the overall rhythm of the liturgical action.

43. The Mass is made up of the liturgy of the Word and the liturgy of the Eucharist. These two parts are so closely connected as to form one act of worship. The table of the Lord is the table of God's Word and Christ's Body, and from it the faithful are instructed and refreshed. In addition, the Mass has introductory and concluding rites (_GI_, No. 8). The introductory and concluding rites are secondary.

The Introductory Rites

44. The parts preceding the liturgy of the Word, namely, the Entrance, greeting, penitential rite, Kyrie, Gloria, and opening prayer or collect, have the character of introduction and preparation. The purpose of these rites is to help the assembled people become a worshiping community and to prepare them for listening to God's Word and celebrating the Eucharist (_GI_, No. 24). Of these parts the Entrance song and the opening prayer are primary. All else is secondary.

If Mass begins with the sprinkling of the people with blessed water, the penitential rite is omitted; this may be done at all Sunday Masses (cf. _Roman Missal, Blessing and Sprinkling of Holy Water_, No. 1). Similarly, if the psalms of part of the Liturgy of the Hours precede Mass, the introductory rite is abbreviated in accord with the _General Instruction on the Liturgy of the Hours_ (Nos. 93–98).

The Liturgy of the Word

45. Readings from Scripture are the heart of the liturgy of the Word. The homily, responsorial psalms, profession of faith, and general intercessions develop and complete it. In the readings, God speaks to his people and nourishes their spirit; Christ is present through his word. The homily explains the readings. The chants and the profession of faith comprise the people's acceptance of God's

Word. It is of primary importance that the people hear God's message of love, digest it with the aid of psalms, silence, and the homily, and respond, involving themselves in the great covenant of love and redemption. All else is secondary.

The Preparation of the Gifts

46. The eucharistic prayer is preceded by the preparation of the gifts. The purpose of the rite is to prepare bread and wine for the sacrifice. The secondary character of the rite determines the manner of the celebration. It consists very simply of bringing the gifts to the altar, possibly accompanied by song, prayers to be said by the celebrant as he prepares the gifts, and the prayer over the gifts. Of these elements the bringing of the gifts, the placing of the gifts on the altar, and the prayer over the gifts are primary. All else is secondary.

The Eucharistic Prayer

47. The eucharistic prayer, a prayer of thanksgiving and sanctification, is the center of the entire celebration. By an introductory dialogue the priest invites the people to lift their hearts to God in praise and thanks; he unites them with himself in the prayer he addresses in their name to the Father through Jesus Christ. The meaning of the prayer is that the whole congregation joins Christ in acknowledging the works of God and offering the sacrifice (GI, No. 54). As a statement of the faith of the local assembly it is affirmed and ratified by all those present through acclamations of faith: the first acclamation or Sanctus, the memorial acclamation, and the Great Amen.

The Communion Rite

48. The eating and drinking of the body and blood of the Lord in a paschal meal is the climax of our eucharistic celebration. It is prepared for by several rites: the Lord's Prayer with embolism and doxology, the rite of peace, breaking of bread (and commingling) during the "Lamb of God," private preparation of the priest and showing of the eucharistic bread. The eating and drinking is accompanied by a song expressing the unity of communicants and is followed by a time of prayer after Communion (GI, No. 56). Those elements are primary which show forth signs that the first fruit of the Eucharist is the unity of the body of Christ, Christians loving Christ through loving one another. The principal texts to accompany or express the sacred action are the Lord's Prayer, the song during

the Communion procession, and the prayer after Communion.

The Concluding Rite

49. The concluding rite consists of the priest's greeting and blessing, which is sometimes expanded by the prayer over the people or another solemn form, and the dismissal, which sends each member of the congregation to do good works, praising and blessing the Lord (GI, No. 57).

A recessional song is optional. The greeting, blessing, dismissal, and recessional song or instrumental music ideally form one continuous action which may culminate in the priest's personal greetings and conversations at the church door.

V. Application of the Principles —— of Celebration to Music in —— Eucharistic Worship

General Considerations

50. Many and varied musical patterns are now possible within the liturgical structure. Musicians and composers need to respond creatively and responsibly to the challenge of developing new music for today's celebrations.

51. While it is possible to make technical distinctions in the forms of Mass—all the way from the Mass in which nothing is sung to the Mass in which everything is sung—such distinctions are of little significance in themselves. Almost unlimited combinations of sung and recited parts may be chosen. The important decision is whether or not this or that part may or should be sung in this particular celebration and under these specific circumstances. (GI, No. 19; cf. *Instruction on Music in the Liturgy*, Nos. 28 and 36). The former distinction between the ordinary and proper parts of the Mass with regard to musical settings and distribution of roles is no longer retained. For this reason the musical settings of the past are usually not helpful models for composing truly liturgical contemporary pieces.

52. Two patterns used to serve as foundation for the creating and planning of liturgy: One was "High Mass" with its five movements, sung Ordinary and fourfold sung Proper. The other was the four-hymn "Low Mass" format that grew out of the *Instruction on Sacred Music* of 1958. The four-hymn pattern developed in the context of a Latin Mass which could accommodate song in the vernacular only at certain points. It is now outdated, and the Mass has more than a dozen parts that may be sung, as well as

numerous options for the celebrant. Each of these parts must be understood according to its proper nature and function.

Specific Applications

The Acclamations

53. The acclamations are shouts of joy which arise from the whole assembly as forceful and meaningful assents to God's Word and action. They are important because they make some of the most significant moments of the Mass (gospel, eucharistic prayer, Lord's Prayer) stand out. It is of their nature that they be rhythmically strong, melodically appealing, and affirmative. The people should know the acclamations by heart in order to sing them spontaneously. Some variety is recommended and even imperative. The challenge to the composer and people alike is one of variety without confusion.

54. In the eucharistic celebration there are five acclamations which ought to be sung even at Masses in which little else is sung: Alleluia; "Holy, Holy, Holy Lord;" Memorial Acclamation; Great Amen; Doxology to the Lord's Prayer.

The Alleluia

55. This acclamation of paschal joy is both a reflection upon the Word of God proclaimed in the liturgy and a preparation for the gospel. All stand to sing it. After the cantor or choir sings the alleluia(s), the people customarily repeat it. Then a single proper verse is sung by the cantor or choir, and all repeat the alleluia(s). If not sung, the alleluia may be omitted (*GI*, No. 39). In its place, a moment of silent reflection may be observed. During Lent, a brief verse of acclamatory character replaces the alleluia and is sung in the same way.

Holy, Holy, Holy Lord

56. This is the people's acclamation of praise concluding the preface of the eucharistic prayer. We join the whole communion of saints in acclaiming the Lord. Settings which add harmony or descants on solemn feasts and occasions are appropriate, but since this chant belongs to priest and people, the choir parts must facilitate and make effective the people's parts.

The Memorial Acclamations

57. We support one another's faith in the paschal mystery, the central mystery of our belief. This acclamation is properly a memorial of the Lord's suffering and glorification, with an expression of faith in his coming. Variety in text and music is desirable.

The Great Amen

58. The worshipers assent to the eucharistic prayer and make it their own in the Great Amen. To be most effective, the Amen may be repeated or augmented. Choirs may harmonize and expand upon the people's acclamation.

Doxology to the Lord's Prayer

59. These words of praise, "For the Kingdom, the power and the glory is yours, now and forever," are fittingly sung by all especially when the Lord's Prayer is sung. Here, too, the choir may enhance the acclamation with harmony.

The Processional Songs

60. The two processional chants—the Entrance song and the Communion song—are very important for a sense of awareness of community. Proper antiphons are given to be used with appropriate Psalm verses. These may be replaced by the chants of the *Simple Gradual*, by other psalms and antiphons, or by other fitting songs (*GI*, No. 56).

The Entrance Song

61. The Entrance song should create an atmosphere of celebration. It serves the function of putting the assembly in the proper frame of mind for listening to the Word of God. It helps people to become conscious of themselves as a worshiping community. The choice of texts for the Entrance song should not conflict with these purposes. In general, during the most important seasons of the church year—Easter, Lent, Christmas, and Advent—it is preferable that most songs used at the Entrance be seasonal in nature (NCCB, November 1969).

The Communion Song

62. The Communion should foster a sense of unity. It should be simple and not demand great effort. It gives expression to the joy of unity in the body of Christ and the fulfillment of the mystery being celebrated. Because they emphasize adoration rather than Communion, most benediction hymns, by reason of their concentration on adoration rather than on Communion, are not acceptable. In general, during the most important seasons of the church year—Easter, Lent, Christmas, and Advent—it is preferable that most songs used at the Communion be seasonal in nature. During the remainder of the church year, however, topical songs may be used

during the Communion procession, provided these texts do not conflict with the paschal character of every Sunday (NCCB, November 1969).

Responsorial Psalms

63. This unique and very important song is the response to the first lesson. The new lectionary's determination to match the content of the psalms to the theme of reading is reflected in its listing of 900 refrains. The liturgy of the Word comes to life if between the first two readings a cantor sings the psalm and all sing the response. Since most groups cannot learn a new response every week, seasonal refrains are offered in the lectionary itself and in the *Simple Gradual*. Other psalms and refrains may also be used, including psalms arranged in responsorial form and metrical and similar versions of psalms, provided they are used in accordance with the principles of the *Simple Gradual* and are selected in harmony with the liturgical season, feast, or occasion. The choice of the texts which are not from the Psalter is not extended to the chants between the readings (NCCB, November 1969). To facilitate reflection, there may be a brief period of silence between the first reading and the responsorial psalm.

Ordinary Chants

64. The fourth category is the ordinary chants, which now may be treated as individual choices. One or more may be sung; the others spoken. The pattern may vary according to the circumstances. These chants are the following:

"Lord Have Mercy"

65. This short litany was traditionally a prayer of praise to the risen Christ. He has been raised and made "Lord," and we beg him to show his loving kindness. The sixfold Kyrie of the new Order of Mass may be sung in other ways, for example, as a ninefold chant (cf. *GI,* No. 30). It may also be incorporated in the penitential rite, with invocations addressed to Christ. When sung, the setting should be brief and simple so as not to give undue importance to the introductory rites.

"Glory to God"

66. This ancient hymn of praise is now given in a new poetic and singable translation. It may be introduced by celebrant, cantor or choir. The restricted use of the Gloria, i.e., only on Sundays outside Advent and Lent and on solemnities and feasts (*GI,* No. 31), emphasizes its special and solemn character. The new text offers many opportunities for

alternation of choir and people in poetic parallelism. The "Glory to God" also provides an opportunity for the choir to sing alone on festive occasions.

Lord's Prayer

67. This prayer begins our immediate preparation for sharing in the Paschal banquet. The traditional text is retained and may be set to music by composers with the same freedom as other parts of the Ordinary. All settings must provide for the participation of the priest and all present.

Lamb of God

68. The Agnus Dei is a litany-song to accompany the breaking of the bread in preparation for Communion. The invocation and response may be repeated as the action demands. The final response is always "grant us peace." Unlike the "Holy, Holy, Holy Lord," and the Lord's Prayer, the "Lamb of God" is not necessarily a song of the people. Hence it may be sung by the choir, though the people should generally make the response.

Profession of Faith

69. This is a communal profession of faith in which "the people who have heard the Word of God in the lesson and in the homily may assent and respond to it, and may renew in themselves the rule of faith as they begin to celebrate the Eucharist" (*GI,* No. 43). If it is sung, it might more effectively take the form of a simple musical declamation rather than that of an extensive and involved musical structure.

Supplementary Songs

70. This category includes songs for which there are no specified texts or any requirement that there should be a spoken or sung text. Here the choir may play a fuller role, for there is no question of usurping the people's parts. This category includes the following:

The Offertory Song

71. The offertory song may accompany the procession and preparation of the gifts. It is not always necessary or desirable. Organ or instrumental music is also fitting at this time. When song is used, it is to be noted that the song need not speak of bread and wine or of offering. The proper function of this song is to accompany and celebrate the communal aspects of the procession. The text, therefore, can be any appropriate song of praise or of rejoicing in keeping with the season. The antiphons of the Roman Gradual, not included in the new Roman Mis-

sal, may be used with psalm verses. Instrumental interludes can effectively accompany the procession of preparation of the gifts and thus keep this part of the Mass in proper perspective relative to the eucharistic prayer which follows.

The Psalm or Song after Communion

72. The singing of a psalm or hymn of praise after the distribution of Communion is optional. If the organ is played or the choir sings during the distribution of Communion, a congregational song may well provide a fitting expression of oneness in the eucharistic Lord. Since no particular text is specified, there is ample room for creativity.

The Recessional Song

73. The recessional song has never been an official part of the rite; hence musicians are free to plan music which provides an appropriate closing to the liturgy. A song is one possible choice. However, if the people have sung a song after Communion, it may be advisable to use only an instrumental or choir recessional.

Litanies

74. Litanies are often more effective when sung. The repetition of melody and rhythm draws the people together in a strong and unified response. In addition to the "Lamb of God," already mentioned, the general intercessions (prayer of the faithful) offer an opportunity for litanical singing, as do the invocations of Christ in the penitential rite.

Progress and New Directions

75. Many new patterns and combinations of song are emerging in eucharistic celebrations. Congregations most frequently sing an Entrance song, Alleluia, "Holy, Holy, Holy Lord," Memorial Acclamation, Great Amen, and a song at Communion (or a song after Communion). Other parts are added in varying quantities, depending on season, degree of solemnity and musical resources. Choirs often add one or more of the following: a song before Mass, an offertory song, the "Glory to God" on special occasions, additional Communion songs or a song after Communion or a recessional. They may also enhance the congregationally sung Entrance song and acclamations with descants, harmony, and antiphonal arrangements. Harmony is desirable when, without confusing them, it gives breadth and power to their voices in unison.

76. Flexibility is recognized today as an important value in liturgy. The musician with a sense of artistry and a deep knowledge of rhythm of the liturgical action will be able to combine the many options into an effective whole. For the composer and performer alike there is an unprecedented challenge. They must enhance the liturgy with new creations of variety and richness and with those compositions from the time-honored treasury of liturgical music which can still serve today's celebrations. Like the wise householder in Matthew's Gospel, the church musician must be one "who can produce from his store both the new and the old."

77. The church in the United States today needs the services of many qualified musicians as song leaders, organists, instrumentalists, cantors, choir directors, and composers. We have been blessed with many generous musicians who have given years of service despite receiving meager financial compensation. For the art to grow and face the challenges of today and tomorrow every diocese and parish should establish policies for hiring and paying living wages to competent musicians. Full-time musicians employed by the church ought to be on the same salary scale as teachers with similar qualifications and workloads (BCL, April 18, 1966).

78. Likewise, to ensure that composers and publishers receive just compensation for their work, those engaged in parish music programs and those responsible for budgets must often be reminded that it is illegal and immoral to reproduce copyrighted texts and music by any means without written permission of the copyright owner. The fact that these duplicated materials are not for sale but for private use does not alter the legal or moral situation of copying without permission (BCL, April 1969).

VI. Music in Sacramental Celebrations

79. While music has traditionally been part of the celebration of weddings, funerals and confirmations, the communal celebration of baptism, anointing, and penance has been only recently restored. The renewed rituals, following the _Constitution on the Sacred Liturgy,_ provide for and encourage communal celebrations, which, according to the capabilities of the congregation, should involve song (cf. _CSL,_ No. 27).

80. The rite of baptism is best begun by an Entrance song (Rite of Baptism for Children, No. 5:32 and 35); the liturgy of the Word is enhanced by a sung psalm and/or alleluia. Where the processions to and from the place of the liturgy of the Word

and the baptistry take some time, they should be accompanied by music. Above all, the acclamations—the affirmation of faith by the people, and the acclamation immediately after the baptism, the acclamation upon completion of the rite—should be sung by the whole congregation.

81. Whenever rites like the anointing of the sick or the sacrament of penance are celebrated communally, music is important. The general structure is introductory rite, liturgy of the Word, sacrament, and dismissal. The introductory rite and liturgy of the Word follow the pattern of the Mass. At the time of the sacrament, an acclamation or song by all the people is desirable.

82. Confirmation and marriage are most often celebrated with a Mass. The norms given above pertain. Great care should be taken, especially at marriages, that all the people are involved at the important moments of the celebration, that the same general principles of planning worship and judging music are employed as at other liturgies, and above all, that the liturgy is a prayer for all present, not a theatrical production.

83. Music becomes particularly important in the new burial rites. Without it, the themes of hope and resurrection are very difficult to express. The Entrance song, the acclamations, and the song of farewell or commendation are of primary importance for the whole congregation. The choral and instrumental music should fit the paschal mystery theme.

VII. Conclusion

84. We find today a vital interest in the Mass as prayer, and in this understanding of the Mass lies a principle of synthesis which is essential to good liturgical worship. When all strive with one accord to make the Mass a prayer, a sharing and celebration of faith, the result is unity. Styles of music, choices of instruments, forms of celebration—all converge in a single purpose: that men and women of faith may proclaim and share that faith in prayer and that Christ may grow among us all.

The Bishop's Committee on the Liturgy/
Federation of Diocesan Liturgical Commissions[7]

168 • AN ANGLICAN DOCUMENT ON MUSIC IN WORSHIP: *IN TUNE WITH HEAVEN*

The following paragraphs are selected from the 1992 report of the Anglican Archbishops' Commission on Church Music, *the third such report issued in the twentieth century. These paragraphs, here identified by the paragraph numbers used in the full report, outline theological considerations for the use of music in worship and reflect a convergence of worship styles within the Anglican communion.*

God, Music, and Creation

56. Most people would be hard pressed to produce a satisfying definition of music, yet they know instinctively what is meant by the word. In spite of differences in our ability to recognize, appreciate, and make it, there is music of some kind within every one of us. It is an experience common to all people and all nations. It is identified variously in the rhythms and tunes of human invention, the songs of birds, the sounds of waters and winds, or even the supposed harmonies of the spheres in space. Religious belief is not necessary to accept that music is part of the natural order. It is something that is there, to be enjoyed or not, as we wish, in the same way as the scent of flowers, the colors of the rocks, the taste of honey, or the warmth of the sun.

Creation and Communication

57. For those who believe in a divine Creator, however, the natural order has its origins in God and is no mere chance happening. The beginning of Scripture depicts its being carefully planned and describes everything as being "very good" (Gen. 1:31), from the division of light and darkness to the creation of the human race. No less than the earth and its resources, music is an integral part of God's great act of creation. Like all manifestations of truth, beauty, goodness and love in their many forms, it has its origin in God. With its place in his design, it has a purpose.

58. At the simplest level that purpose may be described as communication. In this music is not alone. Writing, painting, and sculpture also communicate, as do speech, gesture and other means of expression which depend on neither sound nor sight. Each has its place and each its distinctive way of conveying thoughts, ideas, and emotions. But music, which is our concern here, is one of the most accessible and universal languages, being less limited than speech by social, intellectual, national, or religious boundaries. It expresses, often more effectively than words, our feelings and aspirations. It is therefore widely employed in religious rituals,

not only to address God but also to express his reality for the worshipers.

A Revelation of God

59. That which is made reveals something about its maker, as a book its writer or a home its occupants. Music may be seen, therefore, as telling us something not only about its composer and performers but also about the God who has given it. In common with other creative gifts, it expresses something of the mystery, the order, and the glory of creation and its Creator. Music partakes of the goodness of the Creation and reflects varying aspects of the divine nature. It is thus used by God, both within and outside worship, to speak to us of himself. By means of it we may glimpse his majesty and his simplicity, his righteousness and his mercy, his power and his gentleness, his mystery and his love. One might even suggest that the revelation of God as Trinity is reflected in different kinds of music. So for some the triumphant last movement of a Beethoven symphony conveys the power and transcendence of God the Father; the gentle plaintiveness of an Irish folk song may speak of the humanity and solidarity in suffering of the incarnate Son; and the cheerful appeal of a Strauss waltz might reflect for some people the warmth and encouragement of the indwelling Holy Spirit.

Uses and Abuses of Music

60. In addition to speaking to us of God, music has other uses, including that of simple enjoyment. Indeed, it is not improper to suggest that God may have given it to us largely for that purpose. The fact that most people respond positively to music indicates that it is among those things of this world which are provided for our pleasure. Not surprisingly, therefore, it is widely employed to help people, and even animals, relax. It can also be of great assistance in the process of healing; David was employed to play in order to soothe the demented Saul (1 Sam. 16:23). It can challenge, too. Thus, Elisha summoned a minstrel to enable him to prophesy (2 Kings 3:15). Shakespeare describes it as "the food of love" (_Twelfth Night_, I, i) and it is without doubt a potent means of stirring emotions at their deepest level. By music people are easily moved, inspired, and uplifted.

61. Like all God's good gifts, music can be trivialized, as it is so often when it is employed as background noise for gatherings of people. More serious is its actual abuse. For, as a "language," it is quite capable of being used to express that which is evil, as well as that which is good. The views and state of mind of those who compose and perform it will influence its content and its effect. Association of ideas is a strong element in musical language; if the ethos of some music is too much associated with a way of life in conflict with the Gospel, its use could even have harmful results. This might be true not only of the more extreme forms of "pop" music, but also of the very secular and pagan ideas found in some of the music of Wagner, for example. The close connection between some kinds of music and the drug culture may not be coincidental. The use of music as a kind of anaesthetic is well known, even in religious gatherings.

62. The manipulation of feelings through music is not new, and because of this many of the church fathers regarded music as part of our lower nature. St. John Chrysostom, for example, believed it to be sensual and pagan, obstructing our progress towards the "real world" of the Spirit. There was a concern that people might be moved more by the music than by the Reality for whose worship it is used. Such concern was not without foundation, and Erasmus in the sixteenth century anticipated the view of the Protestant Reformers when he complained that the English were obsessed with the performance of fine music in church. Calvin allowed only "utility" music in the Genevan Psalm tunes. Lutheranism generally encouraged much fuller artistic expression and created a climate in which great music could flourish. There were nevertheless those who objected to the liturgical pieces of composers such as Bach and Buxtehude, because of their being too "elaborate."

63. Certainly it was, and is, possible for people to be drawn more to the means than to the End. But even St. Augustine, who worried a good deal about the worldly nature of music, had to admit to a profound experience as a result of it:

> How I wept to hear your hymns and songs, deeply moved by the voices of your sweet singing in church. Their voices penetrated my ears, and with them truth found its way into my heart; my frozen feeling for God began to thaw, tears flowed and I experienced joy and relief. (_Confessions_ IX.6.14)

64. Nevertheless, it has to be recognized that music, and our use of it, is not perfect. It is part of a universe which waits with "eager longing" for

redemption, in which all humans and their gifts are to find their fulfillment in Christ, together with their physical environment (Rom. 8:18-23). Until that time, we recognize the imperfections of a "fallen" creation. Whilst acknowledging the dangers of allowing his many gifts to interrupt the direct relationship between God and his children, we use those gifts as responsibly as we can. To do otherwise would be to reject without gratitude what God has provided for us.

The Necessity of Music

65. As gifts of God, therefore, music and the other arts should not be seen as luxuries or optional extras, to be indulged only when all the other needs of daily living have been met. Even in times of hardship, danger or oppression, people paint the walls of caves, whittle pieces of wood, make up prison poems, tell and act stories, create simple musical instruments or sing songs of freedom. We need, as those made in the likeness of God (Gen. 1:27), an outlet for that creative instinct which all of us share with our Creator. To regard music as an unnecessary indulgence not only denigrates one of God's gifts, but also suppresses human creativity.

66. Since the church has a concern for the redemption of the whole human person, physical, spiritual, intellectual, emotional and aesthetic, it has the responsibility to encourage to the full the cultivation of musical and other artistic gifts. Indeed, our western culture is the result of such encouragement in the past. But there needs to be the recognition that different people have different gifts and that musical tastes vary widely. As Jesus asserts, each person has individuality and unique worth within the vast complexity of the universe (Luke 12:6-7).

Music and Worship

67. A further reason why the church has the responsibility for encouraging the arts arises from our understanding of worship. In that activity everyone offers to God a personality whose gifts are artistic and creative as well as spiritual. The offering of music as one of these gifts rests upon a firm biblical foundation. The Christian church has been singing since the time of Jesus and the Apostles (Mark 14:26). They in turn were within a long Jewish musical tradition in which the Song of Moses (Exod. 15:1-18) and the Song of Deborah (Judg. 5) are among the oldest parts of Scripture. Hymns of praise are found within the Psalter, too, but that also contains outpourings of sorrow, complaint, and

anger. Indeed, the whole gamut of human emotion had its poetic and musical expression in the worship of the Jewish people. However, references to music in Scripture and quotations from early Christian hymns in the New Testament Epistles, as well as the songs of the redeemed in Revelation, show music mostly as a means of giving glory to God. It communicates the thanksgiving and joy of the created to their Creator.

Sacred and Secular

68. The Fathers believed that in order to be acceptable in worship the music had to be "purified" and "seized" by the life-giving power of the Spirit. This belief is not widely held today, any more than the view that music is irretrievably tainted as part of fallen creation. But there is considerable debate, and much prejudice, as to what music is suitable for use in church. For example, there is common disagreement between those who believe that the only appropriate music is that which is instantly communicable to all the faithful, and others who hold that an insistence on vocal participation by everybody underrates the use, demanded by much music of the European classical tradition, of the mind and senses.

69. For many of the latter the music preferred by proponents of "full participation" is not properly "religious" in its feel. It has too much of the world about it. But that is true also of much of the more traditional repertoire, even if it does not reach the proportions of Gounod's somewhat operative *Messe Solennelle*. If a secular musical idiom is compatible with a Christian view of life, there seems no reason why it should not be used and consecrated in worship as part of a whole human offering. Given the belief that music itself is part of a fundamentally good creation, and not merely a means of understanding it, and given that it is capable of enhancing rather than detracting from the bond between God and his people, it is difficult to draw a line between what is sacred and what is secular. It is dangerous to make too clear-cut a separation of life inside and outside a church building. Too great a concern to have only "religious" music in church may limit the worshiper's response to God's goodness in creation. It is understandable that people whose life and work is largely "secular" should wish to use the world's idioms at least occasionally in their worship. What is acceptable secular activity for the Christian surely

becomes sacred through its conscious offering to God.

70. The ability to discern is listed as one of the gifts of the Holy Spirit (1 Cor. 12:10). It is as necessary for church musicians as for anyone else to seek that gift, in their choice of music. Moreover, God's Spirit is mentioned in Scripture as having part both in the Creation, and in the bestowal of artistic talents on human beings (Gen. 1:2; Exod. 35:30-35). From him we derive our many and varied abilities, including the gift of music which is commonly regarded as being amongst the highest manifestations of human creativity. Whether or not music is used in the context of worship, it remains a gift of God to the world. Its pervasiveness in every human society is indicative of its importance.

Worship, Prayer and the Liturgy of the Church

71. We have referred to worship several times in the preceding pages, but there is more to be said. Worship provides the context for the music which is the concern of this Report. It is an activity which expresses an attitude fundamental to human life. Many people experience, deep within themselves, the need to give glory to God and an urge to have communion with him. St. Augustine identifies the reason for this in his oft-quoted words: "Thou hast made us for thyself, and the heart of man is restless until it finds its rest in thee" (*Confessions* I, i). It is not, however, only a matter of instinct. We worship God because we know him to be worthy of worship, and because he both desires and enables us to offer it. This is a truth which all Christians believe, even though their responses to it vary according to differing traditions.

72. The most common form of response is to praise God and to thank him because of the salvation which he offers us in Jesus Christ. Thanksgiving is indeed the characteristic form of corporate worship, both in the Eucharist and on other occasions. So the Ephesians were enjoined to be "filled with the Spirit . . . always and for everything giving thanks in the name of our Lord Jesus Christ to God the Father" (Eph. 5:18-20). Whilst other forms of devotion may be helpful in taking us deeper into the mystery of prayer, thanksgiving marks Christian liturgical worship at its best. In it we give glory to God in response to his mighty acts. The act of thanksgiving reminds us that even in worship the initiative lies not with us but with God.

The Purpose of Worship

73. In its proper sense worship is not confined to an activity in church, or to when one seeks to be consciously "religious." Genuine faith expresses itself in the worship of one's whole life, as is suggested by St. Paul when he writes, "I appeal to you . . . by the mercies of God, to present your bodies as a living sacrifice, holy and acceptable to God, which is your spiritual worship" (Rom. 12:1). Nevertheless, the worship of daily life is expressed and focused in the liturgical worship of the church. That worship not only reflects the worship of everyday living but also helps to form it. For this reason it is vital that the church's services be services of *worship* before they be anything else.

Teaching, Fellowship, and Evangelism

74. Often, however, there would seem to be other priorities in the minds of those responsible for the worship in our churches. Three are common. The first is when a service is used for "teaching," so that the Sunday liturgy is principally a time to communicate the faith. Thematic lectionaries, and hymn lists to complement them, encourage such thinking, and the structure of the traditional morning and evening prayer of Anglicanism seems to lead towards a climax of the expounding of the Word. For some people it is the preaching which determines their attendance at a particular church. Yet the public reading and exposition of the Scriptures, which themselves give glory to God, are as much directed towards him in worship as towards the people for their edification. There are other occasions and contexts for the latter.

75. Another, and increasingly popular, view is that of worship as a means of promoting fellowship within the Christian community. Appropriate hymns and songs bind the people together in solidarity and love, which may be further expressed and fostered by movement and ritual. The whole atmosphere speaks of welcome, of belonging and friendship. There is no denying the enormous gain that has been brought by the rediscovery of church services as the normative context for Christian fellowship, but that is not the primary purpose of worship.

76. Nor is its purpose chiefly one of evangelism, even if a service and its music have the undeniable power to convert or inspire. For whilst it is perfectly proper to expect people to be drawn by worship into a first experience of the living God, or to be

reconverted in that context, the overriding purpose of worship is not one of mission.

Thanksgiving

77. There is no doubt that worship does instruct, promote fellowship, and present the Gospel to those who have not before been touched by it and to those whose faith has weakened. It does all these and does them well. But that is because God chooses or allows it for one or more of these purposes. It is his prerogative and activity, not ours. Our responsibility is first and foremost to offer to him ourselves, "our souls and bodies" in thanksgiving. Nothing matters for us except to give glory and to seek communion with him. The *raison d'etre* of the whole enterprise is that worship is for God. In it we consciously stretch up towards heaven, seeking to get in tune with the angels and archangels. We strive to latch on to that worship of the whole company of the redeemed which is depicted in Revelation as being unceasing. For this reason the central part of authentic worship is the offering of thanksgiving, adoration and praise. By this means, above all others, we help people to catch a glimpse of God's glory.

— Public Worship and Personal Prayer —

78. Part of the difficulty in achieving this purpose arises from a widely held belief that we have lost a sense of the numinous. It is sometimes suggested that this is a result of "abandoning" *The Book of Common Prayer*, or of the fact that the celebrant no longer has his back to the people at a distant east end. But whatever the effects of particular liturgical texts or of architectural and choreographic arrangements, the difficulty in capturing a glimpse of heaven has much to do with the spiritual condition of those who worship.

79. The quality of the devotional life of the faithful is important, not least because many people see little connection between private prayer and public worship. This is true of some who practice both, but is even more true of the large number of people who either go to church or say their prayers, but do not do both. Yet the liturgy is seriously weakened by such disconnections, since it needs above all to be prayed. Below the level of hymns, psalms, readings and prayers there needs to be an undercurrent or reservoir of prayerfulness. This is not the kind of praying which is turned on by "Let us pray," and off again by the saying of the Grace. It is a deep spirit of

longing for God. It is also rather different from the once popular custom of offering one's own personal prayers, often from a little holy book, at certain points during the liturgy. A private supplement to public worship, or an alternative approach to God in parallel, is not helpful. What is required is a prayerfulness in all who are present, which is wholly integrated with the action of the liturgy and which deepens it at every point.

Music and Silence

80. Music is one aide recovering this undercurrent of prayerfulness. An opportunity is provided, for example, by the singing of an anthem during the liturgy. It may well be used by God as a "word" for people, as they sit quietly and let the music wash over them. Many of those who go to Evensong in a cathedral have learned to use the singing of the choir in just this way. There is no justification for a piece of music's intrusion into the flow of the service, however, unless worshipers are drawn into a deeper sense of God and a closer communion with him. It is not uncommon to find the singing of an anthem which rings more of "performance" than prayerfulness, as the people sit back after the "act" has been announced to enjoy (or endure) the result. Anthems should bring us to our knees, but it is not always so. The provision of a text can help people to unite themselves fully with what the choir is doing.

81. More telling as an aid to prayerfulness, however, is silence. For prayer in worship is not what the minister does, or even what the people do when they join in the set-piece texts. It is what continues when the speaking or the singing stops and the silence starts. The loss of this sense is illustrated in the way in which the collect of the day is commonly used. In the classic start to the liturgy, after the presider's greeting, the words "Let us pray" introduced a lengthy silence before the praying of the collect. However, "Let us pray" has come to be understood as an instruction about posture, instead of expressing an attitude of mind and heart. No longer does it allow silent prayer by the people to take place during a substantial pause. The collect, no longer a collective summing up of all the individual praying, is left on its own to "collect" something which has not happened. All that remains of the people's praying is the "amen" at the end of it.

82. The loss of silence has been a serious impoverishment of the liturgy for a thousand years and we

need to recover its use, together with music, as a means of deepening the prayerfulness of worshipers. For participation in worship does not consist of being singled out to do something apart, or even in joining vocally in as much of the service as possible, whether singing or saying. Our profoundest offering is often to be silent and still. In such apparent passivity, we may contribute that undercurrent of prayer which is absolutely crucial and which gives worship its authenticity. This is as true of public liturgy as it is of private devotion. The recovery of this truth will help significantly in regaining a sense of the numinous.

Transcendence and Immanence

83. In speaking of the numinous (and some would prefer to speak of catching a glimpse of heaven as being more concrete and biblical), it needs to be remembered that in the Incarnation we have an expression of the numinous in human form. Unlike those who belong to nonincarnational religions, Christians believe that in Jesus Christ the transcendent has been embodied and that we have received a full revelation of the God who has made heaven and earth. For this reason there is danger in drawing too sharp a distinction between the vertical and the horizontal in our faith and worship. In Jesus they have come together. A blessing used at Christmas expresses it: "Christ . . . by his incarnation gathering into one things earthly and heavenly." In trying to catch a glimpse of heaven, we do so as those who have in a sense received it and are surrounded by it. In reaching up to God in our worship we respond to the one who has reached, and continues to reach, down to us.

God's Use of Our Worship

84. In our worship God often takes what we are trying to give him, no matter how inadequately, transforms it and makes of it a gift to us. We think we are doing one thing, only to find that God has turned the tables on us and given us much more than we have been able to give him. This is his nature and character. So worship is after all a means of teaching. The whole experience, including the readings and preaching, teaches us of God, not because of our plans but because God chooses to accept what we offer and to use it in this way. Similarly, we do not set out to use worship as a means of fostering fellowship. But it develops into that, and at a level as deep as the reality and quality of the worship which is being offered. In the same way,

we seek to worship rather than intend to evangelize at a Sunday Eucharist. But we often find that God so fills the assembly with grace that people can discover him, either for the first time or more deeply than before.

Giving Glory to God

85. In the end, therefore, worship *is* a means of teaching, fellowship, mission, and much else besides (for example, encouragement—Hebrews 10:25), but the *reason* for our worship nevertheless matters. Giving glory to God is not just one, or even the first, of a long string of reasons. It is the fundamental, deepest and truest reason, all-sufficient in itself. All the other reasons that are given for worship are to be seen, not as products of our own contriving, but as the gifts of God in return for our response of giving him the glory.

86. This means that in the preparation for the Sunday liturgy there needs to be (especially on the part of those who lead it) a desire above all to worship God. They will long to experience a glimpse of heaven and have communion at a level that is only in part about bread and wine. In response to such yearning of the soul, God is able to work the miracle which makes it possible to speak of worship in terms of teaching, fellowship, and mission.

87. The primacy of praise and adoration remains, however, and is well expressed in Bishop Thomas Ken's familiar doxology:

> Praise God, from whom all blessings flow,
> Praise him, all creatures here below.
> Praise him above, ye heavenly host,
> Praise Father, Son, and Holy Ghost.

Music and Worship

88. Almost all Christian traditions include the use of music in their worship. Worship can happen without it, but the recognition that music is one of God's gifts which we have to offer in worship has ensured its place in the services of the church from biblical times onwards. There are many examples and exhortations in Scripture, and those who employ music in worship belong in the mainstream of Christianity, both East and West. We are able to draw on a rich tradition.

89. If the fundamental purpose of worship is to give glory to God, this must be the overriding reason for the use of music within that context. However, as has been noted, what begins as our offering

to God often becomes his giving to us. Thus he accepts the offering of our hymns, songs, anthems, and settings and returns it to us transformed and enriched for our benefit. This may be so as to reveal something of himself, and in order that we may have a glimpse of heaven. It may also be for blessings of other kinds. Two in particular, unity and evangelism, were mentioned in the previous chapter, and are dealt with more fully here.

Unity

90. Music, as has been said, may be a means of creating, fostering, and deepening the fellowship of the congregation. Those who have experienced the singing of a crowd at a World Cup final or of the audience at the Last Night of the Proms know that music binds people together more deeply than almost anything else. It is, perhaps, part of St. Paul's concern for unity amongst his readers that leads him to urge them, whilst singing in their hearts to the Lord, to use "psalms and hymns and spiritual songs" to address one another, and even to teach and admonish (Eph. 5:19; Col. 3:16). Whilst some may find it a strange notion, it may not be inappropriate for those singing in church to look one another in the eye, and even to smile as they do so. By such means God not only enlarges our awareness of his Word and deepens our confidence in the faith; he also blends widely differing people together in mutual joy, encouragement and acceptance.

91. In some traditions this is the more real when the exchange of the peace in the Eucharist is accompanied by singing, and sometimes dancing as well. The corporate encouragement that may be derived from music sends the worshiper out with a deeper sense of security and a renewed hope. There is something to "take away" for the facing of the demands of daily life. It is thus valuable in encouraging people in the many areas of mission and Christian caring in society, as well as having important implications for ecumenism.

Evangelism

92. No less significant is God's use of worship and music to confront those present with the Gospel, with all its promises and demands. For some, his way into their hearts is through music and they are brought to faith, or have their commitment renewed or deepened, because of what they hear or sing.

93. This is not always an instant process and it may be spread over a long period of time. There are very many people, for instance, who have been brought to Christ, and sometimes to ordained ministry as well, as a result of many year's membership in a choir. Equally, people who attend services because they enjoy the music can one day find that they are there for more than that. God has used it to draw from them their love and obedience to himself. A consequence of such "conversion" is that a person who has been blessed in this way may be enthused to share a new-found faith with others. Music has considerable potential for evangelism both in itself and through its devotees.

Our Responsibility

94. Precisely how or when, or even if, the use of music will move worshipers is something that cannot be foreseen, planned, or guaranteed. It remains part of the mystery of God's gift. We may neither anticipate nor dictate the ways and occasions on which he will use it. The important and well-planned service does not always "take off," no matter how great the care that has been lavished upon its preparation. A "routine" service, on the other hand, sometimes quite unexpectedly catches fire, and people experience something of the numinous. Like the wind, the Spirit blows where he wills (John 3:8), whatever the results we hope for from our planning.

95. We are not, however, absolved from the work of planning. Our receptiveness to the "miracle" to be performed by God is perhaps in direct proportion to the quality of the material we offer him through careful preparation. This makes considerable demands on those who are responsible for the choice and performance of music. Perhaps their chief concern should be to create the right mood, both for the service as a whole and for its constituent parts.

Music and Mood

96. Filmmakers and broadcasters know well the unsurpassable power of music to set a mood, and church musicians may learn much from them. What happens before a service, for example, is important, whether it be silence or the use of worship songs or the playing of an instrumental voluntary. Erik Routley once said that the organ music before a service does for Anglicans what the smoke of incense does (or used to do) for Catholics: "It lifts you over the threshold and into worship." Thereafter the average congregation responds well to a well-known and lively piece in which all can join to-

gether. This generally gets the service off to a better start than when most of those present are silent, either because they do not know the music or because it is for the choir alone.

97. At other points in the worship the mood will be different. Something quiet and gentle is called for during those parts of the service which are reflective; or strong, affirmative music for a confession of faith and commitment; or merry and boisterous pieces where the mood is one of celebration and praise. The final piece or the final voluntary is important, too, in influencing the morale of worshipers as they leave the service.

98. A valuable defense against monotony, prejudice, and personal idiosyncrasies is in the themes for the day or season provided by the liturgical year. Even so, one of the Commission's members heard of a church which on Easter Day 1990 had one Easter hymn, two for Passiontide, and one for Ascension Day.

99. The importance of music for setting the appropriate mood, both for and within an act of worship, cannot be overemphasized. Those who are responsible for its choice and performance wield an influence which is awesome indeed. They are perhaps helped by the fact that most of the music that is used is written for the enrichment of words. These provide a more concrete vehicle for the expression of human emotion, and most people use words as the primary means of expressing their feelings for God. Music is for the enhancement of their offering.

Singing in Tongues

100. Something of the same might be said about the phenomenon known as singing in tongues. Particularly used by the Pentecostal churches, this is one of the marks of the charismatic movement which has emerged in some churches within the mainline denominations during the past few decades. It has its theological roots in the New Testament, where it is commonly associated with praising God and is a spontaneous improvisation in a "language" not previously known by the worshiper. It conveys a depth of worship literally beyond description.

101. Because of its unfamiliarity, the sound of singing in tongues at first strikes some people as eerie; however, it is not long before most appreciate its beauty and its simplicity. Often it begins by one person singing a melody, either quietly during a silence or at the height of praise which follows joyful hymns and songs. Other people begin to join in, each in an individual given "language," and they contribute to variations on a common chord with the occasional passing note, or to harmony and counterpoint which may rise and fall in different parts of the church. If there are instruments, they may add their individual melodies, weaving in and out in improvisation.

102. After a continuous time of worship through music someone may sing in a tongue, either a song of praise to God or a prophecy. In this case, since the solo involves only voice, the leader is likely to pray for an interpretation to be given. This may be received either by the original singer or by some other person, and is usually a paraphrase rather than a literal translation of the original tongue. It may be spoken or sung. When it is sung it is often an exact repeat of the original melody, in spite of its usually being too long or complicated to be memorized on one hearing even by a trained musician. Or the interpretation is given in music which decorates, answers, or complements the original.

103. Neither the leader of the worship nor the director of music plans, initiates or terminates the period of "worshiping in the Spirit." Nor is there any question of the congregation being out of control, since each individual can start or stop at will. Not all people have the ability or wish to sing in tongues, although many of those who desire this particular gift of the Spirit may well receive it at some time in their lives.

104. The musician observing this phenomenon might well expect chaos to be the result of such spontaneity by those who are not particularly musical. They seem to be largely unaware of key, rhythm, occurrence of notes and pitch, and other "technical" considerations. Yet many people who cannot normally sing in tune do so perfectly when singing in tongues and produce a pleasing vocal sound. Moreover, the melodies that are sung are normally well-constructed and interesting. Far from there being discords and cacophony, there is such harmonious blending and unity that some would see it as an anticipation of the worship of heaven.

105. The practice of singing in tongues need not divide a congregation. A sensitive leader will invite all to join together in singing, if not in tongues then in familiar words and phrases such as "Alleluia," "Hosanna," or "We praise you, O God." What matters is not so much the language used as that a whole

congregation offers their spontaneous and heartfelt worship to God.

Liturgical Dance

106. Words are not the only form of expression for which music provides an accompaniment, for with the introduction of many new songs since the charismatic renewal of the 1970s, there has been an increasing use in church of liturgical dance. It was to be expected that "folk" music should find additional expression through movement, and its ethos is more one of corporate participation than of "performance." Those who present dance in worship are usually amateur enthusiasts rather than highly trained "balletic" professionals.

107. Liturgical dance has been described as a "descant in movement" and that indicates both its subordination to, and its embellishment of, a theme. Frequently it accompanies the spoken word, such as a reading from Scripture. It can also take the form of a silent mime. Most commonly, however, it is accompanied by music. This may be prerecorded or live, instrumental or vocal.

108. The appropriate context for liturgical dance is an atmosphere of worship, sharing and prayer, and the ideas and vision for its use arise naturally from the regular meetings of a committed membership. The underlying principal is that it should fit comfortably into the service. With or without words, it is as much an interpretation or expression of worship as the music which accompanies it.

Performance and Participation

109. In common with dancers, musicians are commonly described as giving a performance. When this is applied to those who sing in church, it can give rise to misunderstanding. For whether or not all those who are present *perform* the music which is employed in worship, it is *for* the *use* of everyone. When an anthem is sung, that music is offered for use by those who are listening silently to it, quite as much as by its performers. The announcement that "the choir will sing an anthem" is an invitation to worshipers, not to sit back and relax but to do some "praying with their ears," as Cardinal Basil Hume has suggested.

110. Today there is an increasing emphasis on active musical "participation" by the whole congregation. It should not be forgotten, however, that performance by a smaller number of people is a valid means of participation, which brings its own advantages. It encourages the employment of special musical skills, whilst allowing those who cannot or do not wish to sing to enjoy and meditate upon what is being done by others. Both are part of the worshiping congregation. The word "performance" is not necessarily a pejorative one. Full participation does not, properly understood, demand speaking or singing by everybody all the time.

Musicians without Faith

111. Those who accuse choirs of giving "performances" in church sometimes find justification in the seeming attitude of those whom they criticize. But it is dangerous to make assumptions concerning the quality of their Christian commitment. God alone is the judge of the human heart, and some reticence is required before judging the motives or spiritual qualifications of players and singers.

112. Nevertheless, not all church musicians are believing Christians, and a good musical tradition often attracts those whose interest is more in the music than in the worship. Some argue that only believers should be involved (and perhaps quote John 4:24), whilst others see God as accepting and using a musical contribution for the benefit of the whole community, whether it is offered by a believer or not. There are many architects, painters, sculptors, and embroiderers, as well as musicians, who are not believers but who want to make a contribution to the church's worship. Dare we say that God does not wish to make his gifts available to us through them?

113. Music as a means or vehicle for worship is not the sole preserve of those who gather in church. Its use in a service clearly makes it an offering to God by those who are there on that occasion. But it may also be an expression of worship by those who are not present who are responsible for its composition and even perhaps its publication. God gives music as much to those who write and propagate it as to those who perform and listen to it in church. There are composers for whom the writing of a piece of music is an act of response to God; there are secular musicians who regard their performances in terms of glorifying God. People can encounter God within a concert hall as well as in a church building. There is always a danger when we restrict God and his power to our own preconceptions.

Conclusion

114. The attempt to describe the role of music in worship can be neither tidy nor precise. It is

impossible to define the point at which our offering of music to God becomes his offering to us, since both usually happen at the same time. *We* use it to create an atmosphere helpful to worshipers and as a vehicle to express our feelings for God, with or without words or dance. *He* uses it simultaneously to reveal something of his nature to us, or in some other way to "speak" to his people, or to draw people to himself, or to bring the congregation together. What is important is that we hold to our belief that music is a gift from God. As we offer the other gifts of creation to him in worship, so we offer and use this one. It is a gift which communicates chiefly in the area of human emotion, as well as being immensely satisfying to the intellect. There is nothing wrong with that. As Spurgeon, the great Baptist preacher, said in reply to a question about what kind of music should be used in church, "Why, music which gives the *heart* the most play."

Words and Music

115. In almost all Christian traditions speech predominates in church services. Consequently, music in worship is nearly always used in conjunction with words and is commonly seen as subordinate to the words to which it is set. There is no doubt that an appropriate musical setting can greatly enhance the power of speech. As has been said, "he who sings prays twice."

Language and Expression

116. The emphasis on verbal communication is understandable in a society as dependent as ours upon speech. Words are plentiful and are employed cheaply. They are necessary for philosophical thought, for the exchange of ideas and for the formulation and definition of anything beyond the vaguest feeling.

117. Words are also used both for the creation of beauty and to allow the feelings of awe and wonder, joy and laughter, to be discovered and refined. The practice of poetry is the discovery of human ability to give language to what was hitherto inexpressible, and T. S. Eliot describes it as "a raid on the inarticulate" (*Four Quartets*).

118. So, although music has perhaps a greater capacity for expressing the subtleties of human emotions, we need words on most occasions in order to express what we hope or feel. Used in worship, they can exalt and proclaim, excite and delight. They allow our souls to express themselves,

"Till we cast our crowns before thee/Lost in wonder, love and praise."

119. But speech can also oversimplify issues, and ill-chosen words can debase them by their coarseness, their lack of finer feelings, their insensitivity, their use of cliché, or their sheer quantity. When the mind and spirit flag because of words ill-used in worship, music, as well as silence, provides blessed relief. It may also heighten the value and significance of the surrounding speech.

Variety and Flexibility

120. Many of the traditional patterns of worship (associated for Anglicans with matins, Evensong, and the 1662 service of Holy Communion) have disappeared, taking with them much of the fine language of former days, and have made way for styles which give greater emphasis to spontaneity, variety, and freedom of choice. Congregations differ in their styles of worship and "churchmanship" and in their composition, according to age, ethnic make-up or social situation. Consequently, the same language is made to sound different in different contexts, by pronunciation and rhythm. The English of BBC 1 or 2 sounds different from that broadcast on BBC 3 or 4, and the kind of music used with that language differs as well.

121. Those who adopt the idiom of BBC 1 or 2 and of the tabloid newspapers do so because these are the media with which their congregations are familiar. However, there is danger in any approach which aims for what is most widely acceptable. To hold to the level of the popular press and radio is liable in the long run to lead to the debasing of worship. But the cultural and intellectual approach of the other radio stations and "quality" newspapers clearly has its dangers as well. For many, the language of *The Book of Common Prayer* is unsurpassed in its beauty, but for others it is antiquated and out of touch with contemporary needs. For that reason there is widespread support for those who, like the Jubilate Group, set out to provide "modern words for modern people."

122. As with music, so language has to meet the varied demands of different styles of worship. There are registers and styles for prayer and reflection, for celebration and adoration. There are languages for sermons and for hymns. There are biblical languages of many kinds: prophetic, poetic, narrative, philosophical and mystical. The words used in church, therefore, have to satisfy a number

of needs. They have to be clear, literal, and down to earth in order to express the doctrines and grounds of belief; to be metaphorical and beautiful in order to express mystery and holiness; to be familiar in order to provide a right kind of security; to be fresh in order to offer a challenge; to be gentle for prayer and joyful for praise.

123. All this underlies the need to be flexible in the use of language in worship and to take account of every occasion and every mood. It is no longer assumed that worship can or should be the same for all cultures and communities, or for all time, in a society which is multicultural and multiracial and in which words and their meanings are continually changing. For this reason words, as well as music, have to be more adaptable today than in the past. Modern and experimental language in worship has to exist side by side with that which is traditional.

Sexism in Language

124. One of the most significant agreements among those writing texts today is the recognition that exclusively masculine language is no longer satisfactory. To the widespread recognition of the equality of the sexes has been added an awareness that attitudes toward women continue to be influenced by the traditional language of a patriarchal society. Religious and official documents seem to imply that women are less important than men. Inclusive language is a necessary corrective. Sometimes the traditional language also has militaristic overtones (an example is "Soldiers of Christ, Arise," based on Ephesians 6:10-17) which compound the offense.

125. Awareness of this poses little problem for present-day writers, but some people find difficulty using hymns which refer in masculine terms to the human race. There are those who find it offensive to refer even to the Persons of the Holy Trinity as male. Whilst it is possible to make simple amendments to some texts, collects, and hymns without doing violence to the language or musical setting, there are many which cannot be altered appropriately. In such cases it is preferable to recognize the language as being normal in the age in which they were written. It would be a pity if our sensitivities caused them to fall into disuse.

The Psalms

126. The oldest form of hymnody is the Psalter. This is one of the greatest treasures of Christian worship inherited from Judaism, in which human yearning and a full range of emotions are powerfully expressed in noble words. The Reformers valued the Psalms because, "whereas all other Scriptures do teach us what God saith unto us, these praises . . . do teach us what we shall say unto God." Calvin described them as "the anatomy of all parts of the soul."

127. Use of the Psalms in church is common to all traditions. Although the quality of their poetry and the range and depth of their feeling ensure their effectiveness when spoken, they are commonly used with music. This usage varies in difficulty and appropriateness, ranging from plain song, metrical and Anglican chants to Gelineau, Taizé, responsorial, and polyphonic settings, and modern song. Of these, Anglican chant is one of the harder forms to master, and unless it is sung fluently, the music may be a hindrance rather than a help to devotion.

Hymnody

128. Of all the new writing of texts for the church today, that of hymns and worship song is the most common and important. It is an art form which seems more readily accessible to both writer and singer than any other. So recent years have seen what is commonly called a hymn explosion, with a boom in the publishing of new books which shows no sign of abating.

129. Hymns have been part of Christian worship since the earliest times. They feature at the Last Supper, in St. Paul's writings (for example, Ephesians 5:14, Philippians 2:5-11), and are mentioned by Pliny the Younger (early second century). The *Didache,* of the first or second century, includes some prayers written in rhythmical prose. In the Western church, the *Te Deum* (traditionally ascribed to St. Ambrose) was one of the earliest Latin hymns. Almost every part of the Christian world had its hymns, written by poets and monks such as Venatius Fortunatus and Rabanus Maurus (who probably wrote *Veni Creator Spiritus*), by Prudentius in Spain, and by St. Patrick and St. Columba among the Celts. St. Augustine says:

> If you praise God, and do not sing, you utter no hymn. If you sing, and praise no god, you utter no hymn. If you praise anything which does not pertain to the praise of God, though in singing you praise, you utter no hymn.

130. To this day, through the Reformation and with high periods during the eighteenth and nine-

teenth centuries, hymns have retained their popularity. It is not difficult to see why. They provide opportunities for varieties of self-expression by the worshipers, in verse as against prose, sound as against silence, singing as against saying. They draw upon the Psalms or other passages of Scripture, which they paraphrase, versify, and expound. They articulate personal spiritual experience, with its difficulties as well as its joys. They reveal the inner weather of the human heart.

131. Hymns are used to complement lessons, prayers, and sermon. They allow the congregation to be vocally active in standing and expressing their praise, thought, and emotion in words and music. They help worshipers to experience a deeper unity through making music together and singing the same words simultaneously. For preachers they can be a valuable resource in supplementing their message, in quotations from their statements of doctrine and ideas about belief.

132. Dr. Johnson thought hymns to be restricted in their expression. Although they are written within the strict constraints of tempo and meter, they are capable of great variety in the hands of craftsmen such as Watts and Wesley. Congregations have come to accept that their style and deviations from normal speech are part of a special rhetoric. They sing, without a flicker of hesitation, inversions of normal word order such as "To his feet thy tribute bring." Distortions of syntax and unusual juxtapositions were a marked feature of the metrical psalms (especially the 'Old Version' of Sternhold and Hopkins) which had a long dominance in the worship of this century.

133. Whatever the origin of this trait, the linguistic and stylistic organization of hymns has worked well for centuries and has become part of the consciousness of ordinary people in worship. Hymns provide a rich resource for personal devotion and can be recited as poetry. However, inasmuch as they are written for corporate singing, many of them feel rather flat when spoken; they need to be sung if they are to come to life. For they are what Roland Barthes would call "Image-Music-Text," the unique combination of words and music which exists in a hymnbook but which only truly exists when it is performed in worship. The hymn is written down, but the writing does not come off the page until the congregation sings it and it enters the body, the lungs, and the blood. Through the sound made by the mouth and breath the writing becomes "speech" again.

Music's Significance

134. "Church music" means hymns for very many people, not so much because the music enhances the words as because music and words are inseparably linked. Indeed, a hymn tune is sometimes more memorable than its words, since associations are generally more readily evoked by music than by a text. Consequently, some hymns and songs retain their place in collections, in spite of words of doubtful literary or theological merit, because their tunes are popular.

135. This situation is seldom reversed, although one sometimes comes across a hymn in which both text and music are of poor quality but which nevertheless keeps its place in the repertoire, perhaps for "old times sake." In such cases it is often the familiarity of the tune which carries the day. Further evidence of the significance of the music of hymns and songs is that few things upset regular worshipers more than changing the traditional partnership of words and music in a particular piece. This suggests the need for great sensitivity in the increasingly common practice of either "borrowing" a well-known tune for new words or introducing a new tune to a familiar text.

136. Music is also of service to hymns because it is an aid to memory. Many a former cathedral chorister know how a particular Anglican chant brings to mind at least some of the words to which it was set when he was a boy. Opera singers are able to cope with a long and complex libretto because of the wedding of the words to music. So the music used in church on Sunday can provide material for the worshiper during the week. A snatch of a canticle may be hummed and pondered or a fragment of a chorus, or a phrase from a hymn. Familiar music may well be the major factor in the enormous popularity of television programs such as "Songs of Praise." People take the opportunity to hear their long-loved favorite tunes again and again.

The Independence of Music

137. Before leaving the question of the words, it should be pointed out that on occasions music in church has a life of its own, and even a significance greater than words. As has been suggested, it is capable of expressing the full variety of human emotions, without verbal undergirding. A piece played by a music group, a voluntary on the organ, or a

Mozart symphony may "speak." It may express what we want to "say" to God as much as "Rejoice, Rejoice, Christ is in you" or Nunc Dimittis or *Messiah*. To stress overmuch the importance of words is to forget that music is an effective form of communication in its own right. It has the power to create an atmosphere for prayer and contemplation, and to set the tone for a celebration.

138. Nevertheless, words will continue to have priority in our worship. Music will be used primarily for their enhancement. There can be no more powerful partnership than these two forms of expression, but that depends on their being used with imagination and awareness of their creative potential.

139. Words and music are important as symbols in themselves, but they need to become more than that and to *live*. To cite Coleridge's use of the imagery of Ezekiel, "The truths and symbols that represent them move in conjunction and form the living chariot that bears up (for *us*) the throne of the Divine Humanity." Those concerned with the use of language in worship need to remember that words are capable of bearing such imaginative charge. For God reveals himself through them, as he does through music.

Quality, Styles, Standards, and Choice

164. The choice of music in worship is a responsibility greater than is often recognized. It does not always rest alone with those who direct its use or performance in church; in many situations it involves the clergy and musical director in consultation. Increasing use is made of worship subcommittees which include "ordinary" members of the congregation as well as those with musical or liturgical expertise. Circumstances differ greatly from place to place, but a healthy church should have no difficulty in achieving a proper balance between its specialists and the rest of the worshiping community, where the expertise of the specialist will be recognized and the wishes of the nonexperts will be respected by the specialist. When there is a lack of acceptance on either side, or a failure to recognize the right of all to participate in worship, there will probably be trouble.

Only the Best

165. Perhaps the least satisfactory discussion in connection with any art form is in reply to the question, "What is good art . . . painting . . . sculpture . . . poetry . . . music?" Except in a few cases, there is unlikely to be a conclusion with which all will agree, and it has to be recognized that judgment depends primarily on personal taste. We may not expect too definite an answer in reply to "What is good church music?" There is difficulty even in trying to define exactly what we mean by saying that only the best is good enough for God. Of course it is, but how do we know what is best in his eyes? Who dare presume to describe the aesthetic tastes of the Almighty? Who other than he can finally judge the quality of our offering in worship?

166. Yet some judgment of quality has to be made by the people responsible for the choice of music. Such discernment is highly subjective. Deciding on pieces of music by merit or quality is often difficult. It is always subject to the danger of arbitrariness based on prejudice or preference. But it is some comfort to recognize that often that which is really good stands out just as clearly as that which is of poor quality. Moreover, the bad does not on the whole survive. Publishers' catalogues in the last century contained quantities of dross, together with the gems that are still part of the standard repertoire.

167. In the end the choice is best based not on personal preferences but on asking the question, "Within the style which is suitable, comprehensible and helpful to my congregation, is this piece of the best quality that I can find?" The answer to that question may not always be easy. But there should never be a suspension of sensible critical judgement because the music is for use in church.

Appropriate Styles

168. The question of quality is further complicated because the church musician is faced with an almost bewildering variety of musical styles. The point has already been made that none of these can safely be said to be outside God's inspiration. Potentially, any of them might be appropriate for a particular act of worship. In addition, to "church" music, folk music (real or imitation), classical music, rock, pop, and jazz have all been used with varying degrees of success.

169. As well as being an offering to God, the particular musical style adopted in a church is intended to help people in their worship, rather than obtrude or be a source of irritation and dissatisfaction. Consequently most churches have a repertoire which is limited, and, some would say, unimaginative. That each church and cathedral should de-

velop its own musical tradition is to be expected. Some will find rock music offensive in church, whilst others are bored or even alienated by the more traditional forms.

The Needs of People

170. Diversity of preferences is explained by the fact that people differ enormously in their temperaments and personalities and therefore in their responses to different kinds of music. The significance of these differences has long been known to those interested in the relationship of psychology and spirituality. In recent years it has become more widely known through the Jungian Myers-Briggs Type Indicator.

171. This suggests that there are sixteen basic personality types with many subtle differences within each type. Broadly, each person is somewhere on a continuum between extroverted and introverted, sensing and intuiting, thinking and feeling, judging and perceiving. Consequently, in a congregation some people will not want to change anything in their worship; for others, the more change there is the happier they will be. Some long for more silence and know how to use it creatively; others find silence difficult and need to have their minds and their worship channelled. Some will happily accept what is offered them; others will want answers to innumerable theological and liturgical questions before making up their minds. Some will be drawn to worship through the power and beauty of a performance of Bach's _St. Matthew Passion;_ others will be reached through Christian pop music.

172. People therefore differ in temperament as well as according to any temporary state of happiness, anxiety, grief, anger, depression, or exhilaration. They differ, too, in their preferences and needs according to where they are in their spiritual journey. As an individual moves from one stage to the next it is normal to enjoy a different kind of musical expression. Progress in maturity may well be marked by a greater catholicity of taste.

173. It is not a question of one way being superior to another. Different people have their own preferred ways of worshiping, in which they can feel at ease. Such differences have to be taken seriously, not only by church musicians but by all who plan and lead worship. All of us are created in the image of God. But each is a unique personality, with the need to respond to the worth and love of God as oneself and not as a stereotype. This is obviously more possible in the context of individual devotion than that of public worship. Knowledge of the many temperamental differences within a congregation, however, explains why a particular musical piece attracts some but repels others. It calls for greater sensitivity on the part of those responsible for the music.

174. We have also to accept that what once appeared to be a common musical language in which all could participate has been curtailed. Thus, familiar hymns and psalms which were part of most church people's upbringing before 1950 are not known by a younger generation. In any case the congregation will probably contain people of significantly differing tastes.

175. In the large town or city, there are enough places for people to find the kind of worship which is most helpful or congenial to them. But in small centers of population and rural communities, where there is only one place of worship, the question of musical styles has to be faced particularly sensitively and imaginatively. There is no reason why all the music in all the services should have the solemnity popularly associated with church music. It should be possible to use varying styles, either on the same occasion or at different services. People may need to learn that their indifference or antipathy to a particular style does not mean that it is unsuitable for others. Preferences will be expressed, but there has also to be a tolerance of other tastes. One style of hymn is not necessarily "better" or "worse" than another.

Standards of Performance

176. In the performance of a musical piece, no matter what the quality and style of the writing and whether it be simple or complex, there should always be the aim of achieving the highest possible standard. This is because music in worship is part of the church's offering to God. It is also because a poor performance can distract the congregation and be destructive of worship. Poorly played hymns, strident singing, insensitive amplification, poor intonation, or insecure part-singing can all intrude and will unsettle the worshiper no less seriously than an unsatisfactory sermon. Moreover, performers are likely to be judged increasingly by the standard of the many recordings of the church and other music which are widely available today.

177. Because perfection is unattainable here on earth, there is bound to be some falling short of the ideal. Worshipers readily forgive minor blemishes,

but this should not be made an excuse for shoddy performances. Nor is there any justification for a popular notion that the standard of performance does not matter as long as it is sincere. It is not sincerity before God on the part of musicians if they ignore the right notes or do not attempt to fulfill the intentions of the composer. After all, the skills of performers and composer alike are God-given, and it is no glory to him to be musically careless. God may not be glorified by a congregation which has been set on edge by a needlessly low standard of singing or playing.

Making the Choice

178. Standards are dictated in the first place by the choice that is made of the music to be performed. That choice is determined by a number of factors, but it is always subject to the overriding consideration that worship is first and foremost an offering to God, whether it be in the simplicity of a country church with a "reluctant organist" and no choir, or in the grandeur of a Perpendicular cathedral with a team of thirty-six professional musicians. The music is neither community singing nor is it a concert performance. It is the raising of the hearts and minds of the congregation, whether they take part silently or with their voices.

179. Of the other considerations which guide the choices to be made, the most important is the necessity of tailoring one's selection to the resources which are available. Pieces which are beyond the skill of players or singers, or an over-ambitious anthem can seriously detract from an otherwise admirable service. Although it is often stated, it remains true that a simple piece well or even adequately performed is much more effective than one which is too difficult for the performers and leaves performers and listeners alike with a feeling of dissatisfaction.

180. It is important to take account both of the styles of music which meet the requirements of that particular congregation, and of the quality of music within those styles, if there is to be a worthy act of worship. There is also the need to be sensitive to the moods of the seasons of the year, of the service as a whole and of the different parts of the service. Moreover, it is essential to have some understanding of the effect that music can have upon the human being.

Music's Power

181. The power of music to heal is familiar to those who use it for therapy. The wide range of people helped in this way includes those with mental, physical, or emotional handicaps, sufferers from disease, and those with other disadvantages. There is a biblical precedent in the story of David's playing for Saul when he was under the influence of an "evil spirit from God" (1 Sam. 16:23). The therapist "uses music, in a therapeutic environment, to influence changes in the patient's feelings and behavior" (Flashman and Fryear, *The Arts in Therapy* [Chicago: Nelson Hall, 1981]). It is also used for self-enrichment.

182. Therapists analyze the effects on their clients of the basic components of music, such as pitch, duration, loudness, and timbre. Most people, for example, are most comfortable with the middle range of pitches. A high range creates tension and a lower one brings relaxation. Tempi of 70–80 beats per minute echo the average beat of the human heart. An accelerating tempo may speed up the pulse-rate and provide stimulation, but a lower one will relax the listener. Loud music may give the client a sense either of being safe or surrounded or of being excluded or of feeling frightened. Reactions differ widely, too, to timbre and tone color. The sound of a bagpipe, for example, affects different people in very different ways. Moreover, individual associations, such as the words of a song or the familiarity of a piece, will determine the response of the listener. If music can be used to heal and help, it can also, therefore, be harmful.

183. The implications of this for church musicians are obvious. Because music is a powerful tool which can affect people deeply, even when this is not perceived or intended, those responsible need to be aware of its influence. It may not be realistic to incorporate instruction on the psychology of music, or the basic principles of music therapy, in the training of musicians and clergy. But it should be possible to observe the reactions of congregations during worship. Also, members of the congregation might be given some opportunity to respond to the choice of music, and even to have some part in it. This is one of the principles of music therapy, and it would provide for greater cooperation and participation in the planning of services, which in turn could bring benefits to the worshiping life of the church.

Censorship

184. From time to time the suggestion is made that "the church" should ban certain pieces of

music from use in worship. Apart from being practically difficult, such prohibition is highly undesirable. For congregations differ in their ethos and tradition and they need to address God through the music of their choice. Furthermore, if God can reveal something of himself through many styles of music, whether it be Mozart or the Beatles, we might be in danger of limiting both God and church musicians were we to compile an index of forbidden pieces. We could also be in danger of creating a musical elite with the right to bind or loose.

185. But it is important that neither within a congregation nor within the wider Church should there be a single group which assumes that it alone has the right approach. In this area, as in many, no one has the authority finally to judge others. Tolerance of different approaches is essential. We are, unhappily, accustomed to condemning or despising the forms of worship unfamiliar to us but it can be deadly to the life of the church. Whilst preferences are both allowable and necessary, judgmentalism is not.

Conclusion

186. Every effort should be made to educate fully those who are responsible for music in church. It is so important an ingredient of worship that the greatest care needs to be taken over its choice, in order to ensure that the varying temperamental, spiritual, and cultural needs of the congregation are respected. Above all, the quality and style of music must assist the community to worship in a way that will lift their hearts and minds as an offering to God.

The Archbishops' Commission
on Church Music[8]

169 ✦ THE RELATIONSHIP OF CHURCH MUSIC AND CULTURE

Throughout history, the church has related to the culture in which it exists in very different ways, choosing in some cases to oppose cultural developments and in others to adopt them to a greater or lesser extent. Such variety is certainly evident with regard to the contemporary church's response to cultural developments in music. Understanding these relationships and the special demands of contemporary culture is essential in developing a thoughtful approach to church music.

To say there is a diversity in church music at the end of the twentieth century is an understatement.

The Symbol of St. Luke. The winged calf testifies to the sacrificial nature of Christ, so clearly and simply put forth by St. Luke.

One can visit church services and find almost anything: Gregorian chant; a Mozart mass—either for the ordinary of the mass itself or in pieces as anthem material; a cappella singing and singing with every kind of instrumental accompaniment—from organs to percussion to electronic; instrumental and choral music from virtually every period—of the highest quality and the most banal; classic hymn tunes and new hymn tunes—some carefully crafted, some poorly crafted; Broadway hits and popular tunes; hymns meant to appeal to "outsiders," performed by choirs and electronic media with little congregational participation; high decibels and low decibels; psalm settings in all styles—with and without congregational participation; African-American and Southern white spirituals; and a variety of Asian, African, Native American, and Hispanic materials. Any of this may be executed ably or abysmally, may follow the latest performance practice standards or ignore performance practice issues altogether, may engage congregations or bore them.

When one looks at this massive variety, the first impression is confusion. The tendency is to see no order whatsoever. That tendency is increased when one realizes that denominational boundaries do not necessarily provide help in sorting out musical matters. Two Baptist, Methodist, Presbyterian, Roman Catholic, or Lutheran churches may be as different musically from one another as they are like their sisters and brothers in another denomination. Careful listening and looking can usually reveal roots that differ, but, depending upon the congregation, the musical practice of two parishes in different denominations often can be deceptively similar.

Old alignments may be breaking down. We may be in a period of fundamental shifts, not unlike the time of the reformation. We certainly are fashioning an expanded musical syntax in worship, simply because families, communities, schools, and churches now have numerous ethnic, confessional, and musical memories in their midst—as well as increasingly perplexing personal and social challenges to face. This is very painful: the promise of rebirth is here, but so is the reality of death.

Though old alignments may be breaking down, enduring problems have not changed. Making sense of them is one way to sort out the confusion. H. Richard Niebuhr's typological framework in *Christ and Culture* provides a helpful grid for the sorting.

The Polar Types

In the United States, groups called evangelicals or fundamentalists—often identified with some Southern Baptist churches, the Assemblies of God, television evangelists, megachurches, and those who choose these as their models—appear to live at the polar extremes of Niebuhr's types: in both the "Christ of culture" and "Christ against culture" folds. They hold these poles together not in paradox or schizophrenic confusion; they simply apply them to different areas.

In order to appeal to a popular mindset and thereby "bring people to Christ," they use popular musical styles without hesitation or embarrassment. There is no concern here about whether or not the musical medium is superficial or whether (since "the medium is the message") it communicates less than the fullness of the faith or something different from the faith. The point is to utilize what the people know and hear in their daily lives—for example, in popular music or in television or radio commercials. This is a Christ of culture position.

At points of moral teaching, however, these same groups tend to argue against any "liberal" drift. They are therefore likely to oppose anything that would appear to accommodate moral ambiguity or a pluralism which might challenge, say, prayer in schools. This is Christ against culture.

Holding these two poles together is no sleight of hand or devious trick. (There is hypocrisy in this camp, of course, as the recent debacle of television evangelists has indicated; but there is hypocrisy everywhere, and its presence or absence does not make or break a position.) It works because these people locate sin only at certain points in the culture. Musical syntax and associations do not fall at those points so long as the music is put into "saving" purposes. That means people in this group can use radio and television and all the modern electronic technical wizardry available, while at the same time attacking the media and even popular music for its godless slant. It means they can use the sounds of popular culture while attacking the immorality of the culture. It means they are not so concerned about an assembled and singing body of Christ as they are about decisions for Christ and the emotive power to propel these decisions—whether that happens in huge throngs carried along in a wash of electronic sound, or through watching such events in living rooms on television screens.

The Mediating Types

The three mediating types—traditionally identified with Roman Catholics as "Christ above culture," Reformed bodies as "Christ the transformer of culture," and Lutherans as "Christ and culture in paradox"—live in states of deeper complexity and ambiguity. They and their concerns require people gathered in one place in order to be nourished by Word and sacraments, and in different ways they all require a gathered body that sings. They cannot therefore embrace radio and television the way the more "evangelical" groups can. They are also nervous about sound that submerges the people or substitutes amplified decibels for congregational singing. (It should be noted that similar concerns have been expressed in the past about organs or other instruments, so this is not a new issue. Now, however, the increase in the perception or actuality of loudness, coupled with the artificiality of speakers rather than acoustic instruments, divorces what is heard even farther from the natural human voice.)

1. *Christ above culture.* The Christ-above-culture folk use sounds from the popular culture in such a way that they lead beyond themselves to something like the purity of Gregorian chant and its polyphonic progeny. Sound itself is not even an end, however. It is a means of entry into the "salvific mystery," or it points beyond itself to the silence of pure love. The congregation may therefore not sing vigorously (there is a theological reason why Catholics don't sing), or they may participate in the music by listening to a choir. But they need to assemble to

do this, and sound that might submerge them or substitute for them is only a passing cultural accommodation to get to what is of more value.

2. *Christ the transformer of culture.* Those who take this position may be understood at one level to identify with what is popular in music. Music for Calvin was like a funnel through which words "pierce the heart more strongly." But Calvin emphasized the necessity of "weight" and "majesty" in church music, and he distinguished it carefully from the music one uses "to entertain" people "in their houses." Here the issue is not that music leads beyond itself, but that the music transforms (actually the Holy Spirit transforms, by means of the Psalms dressed in moderated melody). As Francis Williamson recently suggested to me, Psalm singing for Calvin was a sanctifying action. This makes the singing of the people extremely important, and the absence of instruments in Geneva and Reformed practice more generally was no accident. Those who stand in this tradition (though today they may have accepted instruments) still find anything that substitutes for the people's song to be misguided, and their major concern is clearly the people's transformation.

3. *Christ and culture in paradox.* For those who see Christ and culture in paradox there is no possibility either of a wholesale embrace of the culture or a wholesale rejection of it, because it is fully sin-soaked and yet the object of God's grace. Like Luther, they know about the possibility of perverting the gift of music with "erotic rantings," and, also like Luther, they regard music as one of God's greatest gifts, which is to be used with gratitude from any source—as long as well-crafted and durable creations result. Today, however, they do not have Luther's luxury. Luther could carve out a setting of Psalm 46 or Psalm 130 from the hardy quarry of German folk song, but to attempt the same thing in our commercial culture from the idiom of a Coca-Cola or Honda jingle or a popular song is quite a different thing.

Additional Matters

1. *Faceless public.* It is true there is great diversity; any group may sound like any other group: Roman Catholics and Reformed resemble Methodists or Episcopalians, and so on. People in any group also look over their shoulders and seek to imitate the Christ-of-culture type because it seems to be able to appeal to our mass culture. The mediating

types are currently under attack, therefore, because they are seen to be ineffective, at least as far as numbers are concerned; and in a capitalistic mass culture, numbers are the means by which we norm ourselves.

The Christ-of-culture appeal is also its liability. One of our current cultural tendencies is to treat people like a faceless public. Shopping malls bring many people together, but we gather there not in dialogue or contact. We gather there as unrelated pieces of jetsam or flotsam with no relation or responsibility to one another; our only value is that we are bearers of money which we may be convinced to part with.

To adopt the culture as a model means appealing to it with music that manipulates the hearer the way commercials manipulate us to part with our money. When the church does this it too treats people like a faceless public. Such a posture poses a serious problem for the mediating types because baptism and the Lord's Supper imply a different notion of humanity. Baptism immerses us into Christ's death and resurrection, and the drenching propels us into the world on behalf of others. The bread and wine of the supper are "for you." These realities mean it is not possible to treat people like a faceless public; people are persons for whom Christ died, not to be manipulated by music or anything else, but to be treated with the utmost value and respect with which Christ treats us. So for the mediating types the music we use must value the hearer and singer.

2. *Violence and the sweet sound.* Our society is violent. Each day we hear reports about someone else who has been violated, abused, or killed. My daughter recently told me she learned in her college psychology class that television gives us five acts of violence per hour at prime time, twenty acts of violence per hour during cartoons, and the average young person will see 13,000 television murders during the elementary and junior high years. My point here is not to bash television, but to indicate how deep the tentacles of violence reach.

The society often uses sweet and sentimental sounds to insulate us from the violence. The church has in many ways, across the various types but especially where the culture provides the norm, responded similarly with music that is sweet. Sweet sounds, in conjunction with other sounds, certainly have their place. The problem is that too much that is sweet and confectionery insulates us from society's violence and provides an escape that keeps us from trying to confront the horror. The result is a fairyland that in the final analysis avoids the gospel, its realism, and its ethical fervor. As Joseph Sittler once told me, "It is not hard like the Word of God."

3. *Reductionism.* As one listens to discussions about music in worship, arguments are being made for minimalist participation by the people by using music that imitates popular styles. For those who embrace historic liturgical forms, this leads to arguing that the people's part is essentially brief acclamations. For those who reject historical liturgical forms, this leads to arguing that the people's part is essentially what George Shorney and others have called "teeny hymns."

The argument here is buttressed by four presuppositions: the culture is making a shift from the intellectual to the emotive; this is a new thing in American religion; we live in a post-literate age; and popular and rock music are in the ear of the culture—not classical music.

The first three of these propositions are inaccurate. In pre-marital counseling and other contacts I encounter more and more people who, though they have appreciated worship earlier in their lives, now stay away from it because they find the preaching and the music so shallow and superficial, even vapid. They indicate anything but a turning away from the life of the mind. As to the emotive being new, while American religion has had its thinkers like Jonathan Edwards and Reinhold Niebuhr, much of popular American religion has been essentially emotive, and the dialogue between the intellect and the emotions is hardly new: revivalism and both Great Awakenings generated it again and again. What we have today looks pretty much like a variation of what we have had in the past, varied, of course, by concerns about minority rights and patriarchy, interpretive modes that center in the "I," and the pluralism of the global village—all of which enlarge the debate, but which do not make the emotive something new. Third, if we live in a post-literate age, where is the memory that marked pre-literate humanity, and why do we have so many books that are supposed to be things of the past? Even more important, is the point of this argument that the church ought to support the absence of literacy? It is surely true that television is a visual medium, that it has generated a visual memory, and that we no longer live in the Reformation's love affair with moveable type or even Wesley's world of words. But

that is not the same as presuming a literary absence; it simply means the field of play is larger.

The fourth presupposition, that popular and rock sounds are in the ears of the culture, is probably accurate, but it begs the question. It assumes that, in Christ of culture fashion, worship can or should merely imitate the culture. That does not necessarily follow. In part, our worship must use the culture's sounds because, in order to sing, we have to employ what is in our ear's memory bank. But the memory bank of the church extends beyond the culture's current fads. It has in it sounds that are primeval and archaic because the story they carry reaches before our period, back to God the Alpha, before the Creation, even before the morning stars sang together. And it searches out sounds that are perpetually new, pushing beyond our period, because they carry a story that reaches to God the Omega at the end of history.

These observations simply question the accuracy of the analysis that is currently taking place in many churches. In part they take themes from H. Richard Niebuhr's mediating types or from his Christ-against-culture type and apply them to music. Taken together, they suggest we are tilted toward neglecting the life of the mind. This is not to say that recent right-brain and left-brain discussions or broader categories like aural-verbal and symbolic-visual are not helpful, or that we should neglect the emotive, intuitive, and psychomotor parts of our being. It is to say that reductionism is dangerous and that a balance, not an imbalance, is necessary.

Concluding Observations

The mediating types have often assumed a stance of maintenance rather than mission. They have also sometimes succumbed to another Christ-of-culture type than the one described above, one which identifies a common spirituality or undefined love and mystery with a Christ principle. The current challenges to the mediating types are therefore healthy.

But that does not mean the enduring problems have gone away. We delude ourselves if we think they have. No matter what our configurations and context may look like at the moment, the issues remain and cannot be avoided. If we avoid them, we will be poorer, and future generations will have to confront the truncated creations we bequeath to them.

Our task as a church, it would seem, is to get some perspective on the whole of the gospel and allow our music to reflect that wholeness and authenticity on behalf of the world. Simply celebrating the diversity we are experiencing or allowing everything to be pulled to a Christ of culture position seems ill-advised.

As we expand our musical syntax, a better approach would be to take our various traditions seriously, not for the sake of tribalism or warfare, or because we want to replicate some past of our futile imagining, but precisely for responsible evangelicity and for the contributions we each have to make to the ecumenical mosaic. This is not to suggest that Methodists suddenly restrict themselves to Charles Wesley, Calvinists to metrical Psalters, Lutherans to chorales and pieces built on chorales, Roman Catholics to Gregorian chant and Palestrina, African-Americans to spirituals, Southern whites to shaped notes, Welsh to William Williams and Welsh tunes, and Episcopalians to Tallis and Tye—though we all would be well-advised to use our traditions and treat them with respect rather than beat up on them. The fundamental point, however, is not only to use them with a muscular humility, but to understand them and embody what lies behind them—for our own sake, for the sake of the whole body of Christ, and for the sake of the world.

Of course we need to use what is contemporary as well, and we need to expand our own traditions for the sake of the wholeness of the message among the people we serve in specific places. But we need to do that in the context of who we are and what we each have to offer the whole. In spite of the fact that many people live in mixed marriages and have crossed denominational boundaries or that communities are a mix of multiple memories, we still live in churches with confessional histories and loyalties. To collapse everything into a mindless diversity as a norm or thoughtlessly to embrace a fleeting cultural moment is to treat ourselves, the people we serve, and the world beyond with a contempt that flies in the face of Christ's example. The gospel speaks a different message. So should our music.

Paul Westermeyer[9]

170 • POPULAR CULTURE AND CONGREGATIONAL SONG

Over the past generation, congregational song has been influenced by developments in popular music in an unprecedented way. This article describes this phenomenon and raises some important philosophical questions that arise out of it.

On a dimly lit stage, several musicians go through their routine of preparation. The pianist carefully arranges the music to be played so the transitions can be negotiated smoothly. The guitarists tune their instruments and check the volume controls. The percussionist insures that all parts of the trap set are in good working order. And the four singers—the lead singer and three back-up vocalists—go through sound-level checks. Within minutes the crowd will have gathered, and these musicians will begin a fifteen- or twenty-minute set of music that might be described as rhythmically energized, upbeat, and intended to promote a general feeling of enthusiasm among those in the audience. Indeed, audience participation is an important part of the agenda. In the prevailing format, the leader provides verbal introductions and transitions, at times sings—along with the back-up vocalists—to introduce a new selection, and coaxes the audience to ever-heightened levels of energized participation. And all the while, the instrumentalists lay down their accompanying riffs, lending support to the proceedings.

The scene just described is neither a nightclub, a rock concert, nor a warm-up for a concert by a leading performer in that genre usually identified as Contemporary Christian. It is the beginning of a worship service. The time might be Sunday morning, Sunday evening, or even Saturday evening. The location could be Florida, Texas, Illinois, California, or any state. The denominational context might be Pentecostal, Baptist, Methodist, Lutheran, or a variety of others.

The reality of the occurrence of scenes such as the one just described, the frequency of their occurrence, and the diversity of geographical locales and denominational contexts in which they occur make unnecessary the question, "Has popular culture—in its musical expressions—had any impact upon congregational song?" For anyone with an ear to hear or an eye to behold, the answer is emphatically, "yes!" Some of the pertinent questions that then emerge include:

1. Are there historical precedents for this phenomenon that has unfolded over the past three decades?

2. Are there substantive differences between contemporary reflections of popular culture in congregational song and the appearance of populist influences in congregational song in earlier eras?

3. What have been the principal sources or manifestations of the influence of the music of popular culture upon congregational song during this time period?

4. How has the content of hymnal compilations been affected by the new songs, choruses, and hymns produced by the movement?

5. How do we, as persons both interested in and concerned about the music of the congregation, respond?

It is these questions that I shall attempt to address. But at the outset it is necessary to offer one caveat. The subject is too big and too complex for this article to be considered more than an introduction to it. Furthermore, opinions on the matter tend to be strong on both sides—those who argue vigorously for the value of the "music of the people" (as they describe the new songs influenced by popular music styles) and those who oppose them with equal vigor. In the course of this presentation I will attempt to be objective and allow my own personal biases to show as little as possible.

The setting of texts for congregational song to music drawn from styles that might be described as "music for the people" rather than "high art" was not an invention of the mid-twentieth century. As Donald Hustad has pointed out, this practice has been almost normative for those periods in the history of the Christian church that could be described as times of renewal [Donald P. Hustad, *Jubilate! Church Music in the Evangelical Tradition* (Carol Stream, Ill.: Hope Publishing Company, 1981), 120]. It has been speculated that during the Arian controversies of the fourth century both orthodox and heretical groups used popular tunes as settings for their hymn texts to make them more attractive. The use of popular tunes from secular origins as one of the early sources for Lutheran chorale melodies has been well documented. Some of the tunes initially used for Wesleyan hymns were adaptations of popular songs and familiar operatic airs (Nelson F. Adams, "The Musical Sources for John Wesley's Tune-Books: The Genealogy of 148 Tunes" [New York: Unpublished D.S.M. dissertation, Union Theological Seminary, 1973]). The music of the nineteenth-

century gospel song reflects not only the influence of the camp-meeting song, but also the stylistic traits of popular secular song of the time. (Indeed, some of the familiar Stephen Foster melodies were adapted as hymn tunes.) It has been the pattern of the church to assimilate the "new sounds" (at times begrudgingly) until, over a period of years, they have become part of the accepted "sacred" musical language.

If the practice of drawing upon popular music, whether specific melodies or general styles, from the surrounding culture as a source of tunes for congregational song is not new, is there something about the use of this practice in the latter decades of the twentieth century that differentiates this period from earlier ones? There are a number of contemporary writers who would offer an emphatic "yes" to that question. The difference lies in the use and meaning of the term "popular culture," or "mass culture," as it is often called. One critic of popular culture has stated his case in this manner:

Mass culture [popular culture] is imposed from above. It is fabricated by technicians hired by businessmen; its audiences are passive consumers, their participation limited to the choice between buying and not buying [or, in our case, singing or not singing]. The lords of *kitsch* ["*Kitsch*," a word derived from German that means "trash," is sometimes used by art critics as a pejorative reference to the aesthetic norms of popular culture], in short, exploit the cultural needs of the masses in order to make a profit [Dwight Macdonald, "A Theory of Mass Culture, " in *Mass Culture: The Popular Arts in America,* ed. Bernard Rosenberg and David Manning White. (Glencoe, Ill.: The Free Press, 1985), 60]

Here is another perspective, drawn from one of the manifestations of popular culture, the newspaper comic strips. The speaker is Calvin, the juvenile miscreant, who, along with his sometimes inanimately stuffed, sometimes alive companion, the tiger, Hobbes, are the central characters of "Calvin and Hobbes," drawn by Bill Watterson. In a frame that appeared recently, Calvin says: "But *popular* art knows the customer is always right! People want more of what they already know they like, so popular art gives it to 'em!"

The above two perspectives represent some of the arguments presented by proponents of the thesis that today's popular culture as it relates to the church does, indeed, differ from the way in which the church has been influenced by "popular" elements from the surrounding culture in past eras. The first view speaks for those persons who consider that today's popular culture has been manufactured and imposed upon an unwitting populace by business enterprises interested solely in their own gain. From its perception, the "recipients" of popular culture have little choice in the matter; they simply receive passively what the purveyors of popular culture have decided they should accept. The second view is representative of the notion that popular culture is a phenomenon driven by consumer tastes. As Calvin says, "people want more of what they already know they like," so the market responds to the broadest prevailing taste and gives the people what they want. In both of the perspectives just presented, the emphasis is upon consumer-producer relationships as the primary determinant of popular culture, even in its expressions in artistic realms. In earlier eras, the proponents of both perspectives would contend, the prevailing culture of the people was more "honest" or "authentic"—less determined by the power of consumerism in an affluent society.

On the other hand, there are those who would argue passionately that culture embraces the sum total of those factors of human environment that influence human existence. Therefore, in a commercialized, technological society, technology and commercialization join other factors—on an equal footing and without bias—in shaping culture. Hence, popular music today is _still_ the "music of the people"—because the people allow it to be so. The issues are complex—far more so than can be explored in this article. So, for the moment, we shall leave this thorny question unresolved. (See Kenneth A. Myers, _All God's Children and Blue Suede Shoes: Christians and Popular Culture_ [Westchester, Ill.: Crossway Books, 1989].)

Let us instead explore the sources and manifestations of popular culture in congregational song, as they have been expressed over the past three decades. Let me try an analogy. Consider the broad field of congregational song influenced by popular culture as a river—an ever-expanding river fed by many streams or tributaries. These streams will represent the diverse genres in which the music of popular culture has influenced the music of the church, particularly in congregational song. If American pop-influenced congregational song can be considered such a river, its fountainhead might

be traced, not to developments in this country, but to the experiments of Geoffrey Beaumont and the 20th Century Church Light Music Group in England during the late 1950s and early 1960s. The publication and promotion by Paxton Music, Ltd. and Josef Weinberger, Ltd. of hymn tunes by Beaumont, other members of the Light Music Group, and Malcolm Williamson assisted in their gaining popularity, and some notoriety, rather quickly. The performance instructions that appeared with many of these tunes suggested their stylistic origins. Placed above the opening measures were phrases such as "with a lilt," "with a beat," "waltz time," "blues tempo," and "medium rock." The tunes were written for unison singing with piano accompaniment. The musical style was imitative of stage musicals and more conservative popular music from earlier in the twentieth century.

The primary approach of both Geoffrey Beaumont and Malcolm Williamson was to write new tunes for traditional texts. Other members of the Light Music Group wrote both texts and tunes. The most widely used tune to come from this group of composers was Beaumont's "Gracias," which was paired with Catherine Winkworth's translation of Martin Rinkart's "Nun danket alle Gott." In the United States, this combination of text and tune was included in the _Hymnbook for Christian Worship,_ jointly published in 1970 by the Christian Church (Disciples of Christ) and the American Baptist Convention.

The hymn tunes of Geoffrey Beaumont and his British contemporaries did not gain wide acceptance in this country, but their innovations were mirrored by several developments in America. Because the American developments were in many ways inter-related, it will be more useful to consider them categorically rather than chronologically.

With the nation's increased "youth consciousness" of the 1960s came a deluge of music for Christian young people that, in broad categorization, might be classified as "folk-pop." Encompassing a variety of substyles, all of which would fit comfortably under that umbrella label, folk-pop (or "Christian pop," as it was sometimes called) became the intended musical panacea for curing youth's disenchantment or boredom—take your pick—with the church. It was sung in liturgical settings, in evangelical churches, and at informal religious gatherings, particularly those associated with various expressions of the "Jesus Movement." We shall return to its liturgical use later, particularly in relation to the Roman Catholic church, but for now I will focus on the renewal of interest in chorus singing. This product of YMCA and Youth for Christ gatherings had never completely faded into disuse; it was perpetuated by use at campfire devotionals and "singspirations." But in the 1960s the practice was rediscovered with new fervor, and there began the production of a stream of new "teenie hymns," as my colleague Don Hustad calls them, that continues to this day. They soon came to be known as "praise choruses," although the subject matter was seldom restricted to that aspect of Christian faith and worship. Of course, the more formal evangelical churches, as well as the liturgical ones, had long had their "praise choruses." They called them "Doxology" and "Gloria Patri." But the new "praise choruses" were in a different style, usually combining short, simple texts with easily remembered, singable melodies in one of the prevailing folk-pop styles.

Many of those early texts have been criticized—and in some cases justifiably so—for both their superficiality and self-centeredness. But those traits were not new to the "praise chorus." Have you discovered the following text, cited by Henry Wilder Foote in his *Three Centuries of American Hymnody*, which purportedly was sung in nineteenth-century America?

> The bells of hell go ting-a-ling-a-ling
> For you, but not for me.
> The blessed angels sing-a-ling-a-ling
> Through all eternity.
> O death, where is thy sting-a-ling-a-ling?
> O grave, thy victory?
> No ting-a-ling-a-ling, no sting-a-ling-a-ling,
> But sing-a-ling-a-ling for me [Henry
> Wilder Foote, *Three Centuries of
> American Hymnody* (Cambridge,
> Mass.: Harvard University Press, 1940),
> 269].

Superficiality and self-centeredness, indeed!

The chorus genre proved to be particularly suited to the needs of the charismatic movement and youth organizations such as Campus Crusade for Christ. At first, the choruses were published in paperback collections produced by both denominational and commercial music publishers. Maranatha! Music, in particular, brought into print a number of choruses that were to become popular far beyond

charismatic circles. But in recent years they have made their way into hymnals intended to have a longer life span, and so form one of those streams that feed the river of pop-influenced congregational song today.

Relatively few of the first generation of folk-pop choruses survived—a commentary, perhaps, upon the ephemeral, transitory nature of the form. However, the second generation is well represented in recent hymnal compilations. Many of these second-generation choruses are less "folksy" than their ancestors; certainly, many of them do not lend themselves easily to accompaniment only by acoustical guitar. One of the most popular of the new choruses is "Majesty," written by Jack Hayford in 1977. It first appeared in a hymnal in 1986 in *The Hymnal for Worship and Celebration*. In addition to its several hymnal appearances, for the past year and a half it has held the number-one position in the "Top Twenty-Five Songs" listing compiled from the biannual surveys conducted by Christian Copyright Licensing, Inc.

If the praise choruses were the most ubiquitous aspect of the folk-pop movement, the youth musicals—the second stream of influence—rivaled them in popularity. Evangelical and mainline churches that had been suspicious of the folk-pop idiom and the jazz idiom when they were used to set liturgical texts suddenly welcomed the same idioms with open arms when they appeared in musico-dramatic form—or at least *some* of them did. The rapid growth in enrollment in youth choirs, including the recruitment of teenagers who had not previously been active in church life, provided a compelling argument for allowing the new styles into the church, to the dismay of some persons from the more conservative older generations.

The youth musicals did not yield an extensive body of materials that eventually made their way into congregational use, but there were a few notable examples. The genre was primarily choral and soloistic, but in some of the musicals the congregation was given an opportunity to participate, usually near the end. One of the more attractive new tunes to emerge from this source was "Tabernacle," written by Phillip Landgrave for the conclusion of his youth musical *Purpose,* composed in 1968. Taking his cue from the practice of Geoffrey Beaumont and his contemporaries of writing new tunes in pop style for traditional texts, Landgrave wrote "Tabernacle" as a setting for "Just As I Am" by Charlotte Elliott.

What was to become the most widely used congregational song to come from the youth musical genre appeared the following year, 1969, in _Tell It Like It Is,_ a musical written by Ralph Carmichael and Kurt Kaiser. Kaiser's "Pass It On" not only appeared in six of the hymnals surveyed for the "Selected List of Illustrative Hymns and Choruses" that follows this article, but I know of at least four other hymnals not included in the survey in which it is included, as well as numerous paperback collections.

A third tributary that has supplied our ever growing waterway of pop-influenced congregational song with new materials is African-American gospel music. The roots of this genre extend back into the late nineteenth century, but its initial popularization occurred in the 1920s with the work of Thomas A. Dorsey, often called the "Father of Gospel Music." Whereas the stylistic origins of most of the tunes that emerged from the British experiments, the praise choruses, and the youth musicals can be traced to stage musicals, various styles of mid-century popular music, and imitations of folk music, black gospel music has for its heritage the blues. In an article that appeared in the Spring 1989 issue of _The Journal of Black Sacred Music,_ Jeremiah Wright suggested that Dorsey "brought into the gospel idiom the chord progressions and rhythmic syncopations of blues. Not only did he attempt to bring the music of the secular stage into the sacred sanctuary, he also brought an instrumental style that flew in the face of everything 'trained' musicians had been taught to revere" (Jeremiah A. Wright, Jr., "Music as Cultural Expression in Black Church Theology and Worship," _The Journal of Black Sacred Music_ 3:1 [Spring 1989]: 4).

Though Dorsey's music initially faced opposition in affluent black congregations, it has endured. One of his songs, "Precious Lord, Take My Hand," which for years has been a staple of paperback collections of choruses, has been included in several recently published hymnals.

The most widely sung composer of gospel music over the past two decades has been Andrae Crouch. His more than three hundred songs, which represent a variety of styles in addition to black gospel, have brought him several Grammy and Dove awards (Paul A. Richardson, "Crouch, Andrae," in _Handbook to the Baptist Hymnal_ [Nashville, Tenn.: Con-

vention Press, 1992], 323). (Parenthetically, it is worth noting that the existence of categories for popular Christian music in the Grammy competition and the creation of a set of awards solely for the Contemporary Christian recording industry may be considered symptoms of the way in which at least one aspect of sacred music has been influenced by popular culture.) Indicative of Crouch's impact upon trends in congregational song is the fact that five of his songs are included in the "Selected List of Illustrative Hymns and Choruses," a collection that represents those selections most widely published in hymnals over the past seventeen years. Crouch's most frequently published and recorded song is "My Tribute," but his style of gospel music is better represented by "Soon and Very Soon," which seems to be catching up with "My Tribute" in popularity.

As noted above, contemporary African-American gospel music has come to be considered one of the branches of the Contemporary Christian industry, so it is appropriate to look at that phenomenon in its broader expression as yet another source that feeds pop-influenced congregational song today. The branch of the recording industry specializing in Contemporary Christian music and the proliferation of radio stations that have adopted that format almost exclusively have combined to form one of the most, if not _the_ most, pervasive influences upon the musical tastes of church-attending young people over the past two decades. The ubiquitous presence of the "Contemporary Christian sound" in homes, over car radios, over the sound systems in Christian bookstores, and in churches has, by sheer weight of frequency, molded the listening and singing tastes of teenagers and many young collegians. The appearance of these sounds in churches in recent years reflects both the desire of church members to appeal to youth and young adults and the collective impact of two decades of the influence of this musical style. Remember, the young people who sang those folk musicals and choruses in the 1960s and 1970s are today's young adults, many of whom are approaching middle-age status.

It is not surprising, then, that many of the songs that have been made popular by Amy Grant, David Meece, Twila Paris, Michael W. Smith, Sandi Patti, and Dottie Rambo, along with a host of others, are now beginning to find their way into hymnal collections that include both hymns and choruses. For most of the songs in this genre, it is the choruses that have been claimed as vehicles for congregational singing. And, in truth, many of the Contemporary Christian songs consist of several repetitions of chorus-like material. In the "Selected List of Illustrative Hymns and Choruses" there appear six songs in this category written since 1980, and there are several others listed which appeared before that date. The list includes a variety of substyles within the genre, but it would not be particularly helpful at this time to pursue the subtleties of differentiation.

There is one body of material—of the stream, to remain faithful to my analogy—which I have some difficulty categorizing stylistically. The commercialization with which it has been promoted places it within the umbrella of the overall topic that this article addresses, but in terms of musical style it does not fit convincingly. Musically, it seems to be a continuation of the line established by the late nineteenth- and early twentieth-century gospel song. Therefore, I shall label this genre the "contemporary gospel song." Its primary progenitor around mid-century was John W. Peterson, but the most prolific and influential proponents of this style since that time have been William J. and Gloria Gaither. Though in recent years the Gaithers have moved toward a style that would fit within the Contemporary Christian umbrella, most of their songs that appear in current hymnals date from the 1960s and early 1970s and resemble earlier gospel songs more than those of the folk-pop styles.

It is now time to return to that body of material to which allusion was made earlier—music written for the Roman Catholic worship tradition. Soon after the dissemination of the Second Vatican Council's *Sacrosanctum Concilium* (*Constitution on the Sacred Liturgy*) in 1963, American parishes were flooded with both settings of the liturgy and congregational songs in the folk-pop idiom. "Michael, Row the Boat Ashore," "Kum Ba Yah," "Blowin' in the Wind," and other similar songs were claimed by American Catholics as their own as they found their collective voices—to the delight of many and the dismay of others. It was not long before new songs written specifically for the Catholic community were appearing in print. Missalettes published with the intent of having a short lifespan fed the collective appetite for a continuing supply of new materials, and published collections of hymns in the new folk-pop style proliferated.

One of those early songs, "They'll Know We Are Christians by Our Love," written by Peter Scholtes in 1966, rather quickly gained widespread popularity extending far beyond Catholic circles. It has subsequently appeared in a few hymnals outside that tradition, and would probably have been included in more if some hymnal editors had not experienced difficulties in negotiating copyright clearance for its use.

A second generation of Catholic composers of hymns and songs in the diverse substyles of the folk-pop idiom has continued to supply Catholic congregations with an abundance of new materials. Bob Dufford, Dan Schutte, Michael Joncas, and Marty Haugen have been among those composers whose songs have been particularly well-received.

There has been one somewhat curious feature of the use of the folk-pop idioms in the Catholic tradition—it has been rather self-contained, at least on the basis of materials included in hymnal compilations. The only Catholic hymnal that I have found to contain materials from the broader ecumenical expression of folk-pop idioms in congregational song to any noticeable degree is *Lead Me, Guide Me,* the African-American Catholic hymnal published in 1987. That collection, not surprisingly, includes several songs by Andrae Crouch, but it also contains selections by Kurt Kaiser and the Gaithers. The third edition of *Worship,* published in 1986 by GIA Publications, included Karen Lafferty's chorus, "Seek Ye First the Kingdom of God," first published by Maranatha! Music in 1972.

Conversely, until the release of *Hymnal: A Worship Book* (1992) there had been very limited appearance of materials in popular styles written by composers of music for Catholic congregations in hymnals outside that tradition, with the exception of "They'll Know We Are Christians by Our Love," mentioned earlier. An "Amen" by Marty Haugen and "Here I Am, Lord" by Dan Schutte were included in the 1990 *Presbyterian Hymnal.* The only songs to make multiple appearances are Schutte's "Here I Am, Lord," which also appeared in *The United Methodist Hymnal* published in 1989, and "On Eagle's Wings" by Michael Joncas, which appears in *The United Methodist Hymnal* and in *The Baptist Hymnal* of 1991. In contrast, *Hymnal: A Worship Book,* a joint publication of Brethren Press, Faith and Life Press, and the Mennonite Publishing House, has thirteen hymns or songs by six different contemporary Catholic composers in the various folk-pop styles, including six by Marty Haugen.

Having surveyed the primary sources of congregational song influenced by popular music culture, it is now appropriate to look at their assimilation, or lack thereof, into published hymnals. There have been a variety of approaches. Two hymnals—the 1978 _Lutheran Book of Worship_ and _Rejoice in the Lord,_ published in 1985 by the Reformed Church in America—ignored this style of congregational song entirely. _The Hymnal 1982,_ published for the Episcopal Church, included Karen Lafferty's chorus, "Seek Ye First the Kingdom of God," and "I Am the Bread of Life" by Suzanne Toolan. _The Presbyterian Hymnal: Hymns, Psalms, and Spiritual Songs,_ published in 1990, contains seven selections by composers who wrote in the popular music styles, and the 1987 _Psalter Hymnal_ of the Christian Reformed Church in North America has fourteen, including three by Andrae Crouch.

Among denominational hymnals published in recent years that I have surveyed, the two which reflect most extensively the impact of popular music are _The United Methodist Hymnal_ of 1989 and _The Baptist Hymnal_ of 1991, with the latter collection having the largest number of entries. _The Worshiping Church,_ published by Hope Publishing Company in 1990, contains a similar proportion of music from the various streams influenced by popular song as _The Baptist Hymnal._

Among all recently published hymnals, the two which most reflect the influence of the recent trends are _The Hymnal for Worship and Celebration,_ published by Word Music in 1986, and _Worship His Majesty,_ published by the Gaither Music Company in 1987. If one discounts the preponderance of songs by William J. Gaither in the latter collection (a total of 46), then _The Hymnal for Worship and Celebration_ is clearly the hymnal most representative of the diverse expressions of popular music style in congregational song. Of the 628 musical selections in the hymnal, 99 were classified by the author of a recent thesis devoted to this hymnal as fitting into the broad outlines of popular music style (Judy Marlene Flathers, "An Analytical Study of Contemporary Christian Music in _The Hymnal for Worship and Celebration_ (Word Music, 1986)" [Seattle: Unpublished M.A. thesis, Seattle Pacific University, 1988)]. Is there any significance to the fact that this hymnal, without a specific denominational constituency to promote it, recently passed the two million mark in number of copies sold?

Among hymnals published to serve the needs of a Roman Catholic constituency, the third edition of

Worship retained that publication's pattern of utilizing traditional hymnody. However, that 1986 edition contains two selections by Marty Haugen, including his increasingly popular "Gather Us In." Two hymnals produced for Catholic worship which strongly emphasize materials in the folk-pop idioms are _Gather,_ a joint collaboration of GIA and North American Liturgy Resources published in 1988, and the various editions of _Glory and Praise_ published by North American Liturgy Resources, the most recent of which was issued in 1990.

The sources have been surveyed, the impact upon hymnal compilation has been quickly scanned, and the question that now remains is, "So what?" How do persons whose lives are deeply invested in the music of the church, and _particularly_ in the congregational music of the church, respond? The pattern has often been to respond at one of two extremes—either an abject rejection and denunciation of pop-influenced church music as being totally unworthy of the high calling of worship or an unquestioning acceptance of it as the new wine of musical expression for the needs of the contemporary church. Following are a few examples. Rather soon after the introduction of the folk-pop idioms into Catholic liturgy, one observer wrote:

> In the name of the "People of God," the amorphous mass of Catholic humanity for whom, ostensibly, the liturgists commit their Puritanical depredations, we have now been reduced to a non-community of non-singers performing non-music. We have made two artistic compromises in our church music: we have tried cheap vernacular settings of Mass texts and vernacular hymns; and we have tried, in the name of youth, rock and folk music. Both compromises have been found invalid, because both have failed as the vaunted panacea for our musical and liturgical woes (Ralph Thibodeau, "Threnody for Sacred Music, or The People of God Have Been Had," _Commonweal,_ Dec. 13, 1968. Reprinted in _Church Music_ 69:2, p. 14).

Do you remember that critique of popular culture presented earlier that suggested that it is something imposed upon passive consumers by commercial interests? It is echoed in this excerpt from Thomas Day's _Why Catholics Can't Sing:_

> The congregation at St. Wil's [a fictitious parish created by Day to illustrate his concerns], most of the time, is only permitted to hear or sing famous con-

temporary music by famous composers and famous groups. . . .

St. Wilbur Catholics have been trained to live lives of obedient, unquestioning consumers. Society teaches them that the latest contemporary product will give them powers and freedoms that their parents never knew. The media guarantees, absolutely, that, if you buy the latest designer jeans, modeled by beautiful and skinny youths, you too will become beautiful and skinny. If you sing the latest designer songs, you too will attain the same level of piety attained by the designer composers. Today's designer song can quickly become yesterday's passing fad. [Thomas Day, *Why Catholics Can't Sing* (New York: Crossroad, 1990), 77.]

Contrast that perspective with this retrospective evaluation of those same developments that appeared in an issue of *Pastoral Music* in 1990: "The strongest positive influence on sung participation from American culture was the introduction of the folk idiom into worship." [Lawrence J. Madden, "Is the Folk Mass America's Only Contribution to Liturgy?" *Pastoral Music* 14:4 (April–May 1990): 54.]

At times the embracing of church music styles strongly influenced by models from popular music is accompanied by the exclusion of more traditional styles. A recent article in *The Wall Street Journal* quoted the pastor of a large church in Southern California who referred to pipe organs, traditional hymns, and the music of the classicists as "passé" [R. Gustav Niebuhr, "So It Isn't Rock of Ages, It Is Rock, and Many Love It," *The Wall Street Journal,* Thursday, December 19, 1991]. That same article estimated that approximately one thousand Lutheran churches had taken up contemporary songs and instruments over the past three years.

In contrast to these samplings of strongly polarized opinions, in recent years more moderating views have been sounded by persons trying to move beyond responses based upon liking or disliking or evaluating the new idioms primarily on the basis of aestheticism on one hand or pragmatism on the other. Such developments are welcome. An insightful article by Paul Westermeyer that sought to explore the issues from a balanced perspective appeared last March in *The Christian Century* (Paul Westermeyer, "Beyond 'Alternative' and 'Traditional' Worship," *The Christian Century* [March 18–25, 1992]: 300–302).

It is time for us to wrestle with the theological issues inherent in the matter. For example, what does an incarnational theology have to say about the way the church uses familiar cultural forms to communicate important matters of faith? Or what does our understanding of creation and creativity say to us about the restrictedness or inclusiveness of the ways in which persons express their creative impulses within the church as one reflection of *imago Dei?* And how does making music in church reflect our understanding of offering or sacrifice? Is it possible that in order to symbolize musically the paradox of a God who is both transcendent and immanent, we need *both* the traditional, more "classical" congregational song *and* the accessible, familiar "music of the people"? These are representative of some of the questions that we need to be asking as we decide what we are to do with elements of the music of popular culture in our congregational song. They are far more important than "Do I like this music?" or "Do I dislike it?" May the reflections, discussions, and wrestling continue!

Milburn Price[10]

171 • The Issue of Contemporary Christian Music in Worship

One of the largest repertories of Christian music developed in recent years is the genre known as Contemporary Christian Music (CCM). This music unites texts that express aspects of the Christian faith with a variety of popular musical styles, including rock. This article describes some philosophical perspectives relating to this genre and its use in worship.

Jesus Music, Gospel, and CCM as Terms: Style vs. Genre

To attempt to categorize or describe the musical phenomenon in the church over the last half century or so by applying the term *Contemporary Christian Music* to it is imprecise at best, and also, as is often the case, misleading and oversimplified. The history of music in general, and sacred music in particular, is best viewed through the image of a long river: At times it moves slow and the current is fairly uniform; in other places the movement is swifter and marked by swirling, overlapping, and even crossing currents.

The debate over the "content" of one kind of music very often overlooks the fluid nature of musical style and genre. Even worse, many cultural critics paint with broad brushes, invoking broad terms by which they seek to represent the many styles and forms of a certain genre. The danger is in confusing the terms *genre* or *type* with *style*. Let's consider these two points a bit further.

First, those who criticize popular music, and particular derivatives such as folk, country, or gospel, often fail to take into account the overwhelming evidence throughout history of the mutual sharing of musical forms, materials, lyrics, melodies, and styles that occurs between these and the so-called "fine-art" types of music. To even try to argue for the exclusivity of one type of music from another is a lost cause. If the native folk music of the Hungarian people was worth incorporating into the compositions of such masters as Haydn, Liszt, and Bartok, or the often secular-based chorale tunes into the Passions and cantatas of Bach, then they must contain some enduring qualities. Nearly every acknowledged musical "master" from Machaut to Stravinsky has taken stock—in varying degrees—of the music of his or her surroundings, or of his or her homeland.

The music of the common people in nearly every age and in every land is marked by characteristics of directness, genuine expression, and unashamed ethnicity, locality, or nationalism. It is also marked by spontaneity, simplicity, and lively improvisation. It is meant to be played or sung by nearly everyone in the village at almost any time or place, to communally express its various emotions, beliefs, rhythms, and sounds. It is out of such circumstances that spirituals and gospel music themselves were born.

There is no generic style of popular music, no single formula. It is an amalgamated and cumulative genre passed from one generation of a culture to the next. There is certainly no inherent lack of goodness or artistry in it. Wherever it is found it generally possesses the positive qualities of artlessness: unaffected, honest, unselfconscious, straight-forward, and accessible. It can be poorly performed or masterfully and genuinely performed. Those who hear and participate in it can, despite the impression given by many critics, tell the difference keenly and quickly. If this seems hard to believe, watch "Live at the Apollo" once, or listen to a recording of The Chieftains playing live in Belfast, Ireland, or to Paul Simon playing with his ethnic band in South Africa.

Why has the term *popular music* become essentially a pejorative term in the mouths of the cultural establishment? To hold that popular music, as such, needs to be redeemed, or refined, or even worse, silenced in favor of the high art forms, is highly pretentious. Such a "highbrow" attitude (a term never known before the turn of this century), only fosters the very contempt and subsequent backlash that began the relatively recent countercultural movement in the first place:

Whatever cogency and effectiveness rock and roll may have as an expression of political or social protest, it is certainly a powerful and profound expression of middle-class rebellion against the cultural authority of Western bastions of fine art and taste—and all the artifacts and privileges associated with them. Rock attempts more than anything else to break down the walls protecting "elite" culture from the savaging masses. It seeks not to build bridges, but to destroy barriers. . . . It was a fast music for fast times for youth caught in a staid and regimented society . . . [it] gave the youth of America an authoritative and distinctive voice with which to challenge the gatekeepers of the cultural establishment.

Rock and roll continues to challenge symphonic music, opera, art museums, Shakespeare and the literary canon, and even the pop music of the twenties, thirties, and forties. Although today's rock music is not so much feared as it is despised by the establishment, it is not loathed because of its [negatively viewed qualities]. Rather, it is despised because it subverts the authoritative hold that the middle and upper social classes supposedly have on mainstream American culture. In that sense, rock is protest that genuinely challenges society. (Quentin Schultze, et al., *Dancing in the Dark: Youth, Popular Culture, and Electronic Media* [Grand Rapids, Michigan: Eerdmans, 1991], 173–74).

This powerful analysis reveals that there may be more behind the heated debate over the place and legitimacy of popular music than an argument about aesthetic purity and value. The motives of popular musicians, particularly those who are Christian brothers and sisters, are no more or less suspect as a whole than the motives of those who tout the cause of the fine arts. Some humility and forbearance are thereby cautioned for any who would try to tame the awesome forces that are the currents of musical evolution.

This leads to the second point: This culture war is fought too often through the use of sweeping terms that are more effective in stigmatizing and alienating a type of music and the people associated with it than they are at clearing up and resolving ignorance and confusion.

Consider the term *classical,* for example, and how it is applied in music. The word is used to describe a whole genre of music that is alternately referred to by the somewhat more loaded term *fine art.* It is also used to describe an era in Western musical history that can somewhat loosely be thought of in terms of a "style". The composers and writers of that era—roughly the second half of the eighteenth century—themselves thought of yet another era described as "classical". At the sound of that word, they thought of ancient Greece and Rome, of the qualities of the art of that age: ordered, sharply delineated, structured, and created according to universal and enduring standards. It is ironic that the term *classical* has become so imprecise in application—the very antithesis of what the word inherently means. Almost anything that hangs onto the public consciousness for more than a decade or so can be referred to as "classical" or a "classic": a classic cola, a classic car, a classical argument, even classic rock music.

Imprecision also adds to the confusion over a description like "Contemporary Christian Music." How will it be referred to a few decades from now? Classic Contemporary Christian Music as opposed to Contemporary Christian Music? This absurdity shows that anyone who uses the term CCM to lump together all of the music produced and performed by Christians over the last few decades knows little about its content, or does know and is deliberately trying to mislead others in some attempt to dismiss the whole genre.

Christian rock as a term similarly fails to take into account the diversity of styles and types of music composed and played by Christians of all kinds. "Jesus Music" is more meaningful as a term, but it is used primarily to tag the music of the late 1960s and early 1970s that arose as the main vehicle of the Jesus Movement. Clearly, the music "contemporary" with that decade sounds different in style than the music being performed today. So, can that term be applied more generally to encompass the whole? Not without sacrificing some meaning and clarity, as has become the case with the word *classical.*

Whatever terms we may use, we must begin to be more honest and clear in this debate about what the content of a "type" of music is and how it influences people either for good or ill. We need to realize that the terms we use to label music can be more divisive and confusing than clarifying and helpful. *Popular music* is simply a generic term for music of the people, or, more specifically and historically, the common people. *Folk music* is music of the common folk of a given culture. *Country* and *blues* are terms that refer to the popular music of a certain ethnicity or geographical location. Even a term like *rock* refers not to a style of music, but to an indigenous genre popular generally with the youth of America, and now the world, over the last forty years.

Contemporary Christian Music, as it is presently called and however it may come to be called in the future, is likewise a broad genre of music that incorporates all the other musical genres—including classical—but it is created and mostly appreciated by yet another specific group of people: those who follow Jesus Christ as Lord.

In the introduction to his book, Don Cusic makes the point clear as he poses and answers his own question: "What is Gospel Music?"

> The twentieth century answer is that "there is no such thing as gospel music." There is such a thing as a gospel song, which depends primarily upon the lyric to express its Christian message. The song carries the gospel, or "good news" in music, which qualifies it as a gospel song. But the vehicle—the music itself—may be rock, country, r & b, folk, classical, jazz or any other kind of music. Because Christianity always seeks to be contemporary, it adapts its structure to the music of the day (today's being the music of popular culture) to carry its message. . . . This has been the history of music in religious revivals from Martin Luther's day to the Jesus Movement of the 1970s (Don Cusic, *The Sound of Light* [Bowling Green, Ohio: Bowling Green State Univ. Press, 1990]).

What makes music "Christian," in other words, is not a distinct technique or specific style; it is Christian mainly because it reflects the beliefs and worldview of those who create it. As Franky Schaeffer emphatically points out:

> There is no particularly Christian style. . . . An imposed Christian style becomes stifling and rigid, which leads to redundance in the area of creativity. Creativity needs freedom. . . . [T]here is no secular or Christian world. There is only one world, the whole world as God has made it. . . . The terms "secular" and "Christian" are only words. Reality cannot be compartmentalized. If we Christians have lost our influence in part of the world's activities, we must reclaim it. (Franky Schaeffer, *Addicted to*

Mediocrity: Twentieth Century Christians and the Arts [Westchester, Ill.: Crossway Books, 1985], 104–110)

The Substance of Contemporary Christian Music— Content and Critique

The drive to "reclaim" the artistic activities of a misguidedly "secularized" culture is the fuel that has fanned the flames of so-called Christian music and arts in the last few decades. While the methods may be different, all truly committed Christians share the same goal: to know the Lord and to further the kingdom. In this quest, as always, there have been triumphs and pitfalls, greedy charlatans and those of true commitment.

A particularly modern pitfall is that commercialism has unfortunately beset the movement to a degree that both stifles and formalizes some of its musical output. When a song or album is seen primarily as a product to be sold, and certain bands or individuals put themselves into hock to a point where they have to play it safe and maximize revenue, they write only what the majority of people want to hear—what is catchy or follows the fad of the day—rather than what has artistic merit. This is particularly the case with some of the large Christian record labels. The only way out of this or around it is for a musician to sign for a smaller company that has built itself on artistic risk-taking, to do it all himself, or to play the corporate game long enough to gain enough personal recognition and artistic clout to be able to do things more and more according to his own vision.

To pretend, imply, or even flatly state that this is only a problem unique to the popular music industry is dead wrong. Just ask someone who plays in or conducts a municipal symphony or chorus. Attend a whole concert season and count how many new works are performed, how many risks of programming are taken. The most successful ones are those that strike that precarious balance between artistic integrity and adventurousness on the one hand, and fiscal responsibility along with realistic views of meeting basic life needs on the other. This is true of popular music, symphonic music, and Christian music equally in a modern world that is run by democracy and the free market rather than nobility and patronage.

True musical artists of great artistic and spiritual integrity do exist, create, produce, and perform in the Christian music industry. As is stated above, these people share the same vision and goal, but their modus operandi vary as widely as the individuals themselves.

One can view the activities of these people as through a spectrum: At one pole would be those who are musically talented and love to perform and entertain, but who also happen to be Christian or have been converted at some point in their careers. This will obviously affect what they do and say, what they write, or what they choose to sing about, but they still primarily consider themselves entertainers. Examples of groups and individual artists who fall at or near this end are U2, Allies, Bob Dylan, Kerry Livgren (formerly of the band Kansas), Bruce Cockburn, Amy Grant, Michael W. Smith, and Take 6.

At the other end are those who have a strong call to ministry, both to evangelize and to aid in shepherding the fold. Rather than writing books, lecturing, or going into pulpit ministry, they use music as a primary tool. Their format is often similar to a concert, but incorporated are aspects of a worship service: Scripture readings and quotations, testimonies and homilies, altar calls, sometimes even an offering for a chosen cause. These people see what they do as primarily music ministry through an entertainment medium. Musicians such as Steve Green, Carman, Sandi Patti, Bill Gaither, Michael Card, and Larnelle Harris are among the most respected and accomplished at this end of the spectrum.

There are those who blend all these characteristics equally and stand near the middle: groups such as Whiteheart, Petra, 4 Him, and DeGarmo & Key; individuals such as Steven Curtis Chapman, Connie Scott, Margaret Becker, BeBe and CeCe Winans, Wayne Watson, and Charlie Peacock.

The musical activities of any one artist or group often do encompass nearly the whole of this spectrum, however, including many of those mentioned above. Almost no one can be pigeonholed when one considers the entire output of his or her work. What places someone on a certain point in the spectrum, then, is essentially a matter of personal calling and relative amounts of gifts from the Holy Spirit. For instance, some have tremendous singing voices, and can speak effectively and persuasively to crowds, but write little or no music of their own. Others can't sing technically well and don't like to speak much at all, but their songwriting and instrumental proficiency is so great that the music speaks for itself. Other combinations occur as well in any given individual.

As numerous as the gifts are the personal styles: some are versatile and relish eclecticism, while others work from a solid core. For example, the band U2 has a "sound" all its own both as a band, and in the distinctive voice of its lead singer, Bono. There is no "formula" to their writing, but their sound is unique and instantly recognizable to anyone even somewhat familiar with their music. Take 6, a newer group on the scene, uses no instruments at all, but just the six voices of its members to create a tremendous variety of acoustic effects and instrumental imitations mainly in a vocal jazz idiom. Their songs range from jazz arrangements to old gospel quartet tunes and spirituals to fresh, striking original compositions. Theirs is also a "core sound" with almost instant recognizability.

Those who are more versatile and eclectic are found mainly in the music ministry sphere. Their versatility is often a tool to make themselves and their message relevant and accessible to a wide audience. Sandi Patti, for example, will switch from a rousing orchestral arrangement, to a beautiful, stirring ballad, to a pop song, to a children's song, to a hymn arrangement or medley, to gospel, to jazz, and even to some unique and fresh style of song written by someone with her voice in mind. She is the stature of singer, along with her colleagues and friends Steve Green and Larnelle Harris, that inspires some gifted and willing songwriters to tailor some of their work to suit their voices. What holds the concert or album together for this type of musician is usually not a personal style, but a theme or a purpose. Sandi Patti's latest album *Le Voyage* is a prime example, as is Steve Green's *A Mighty Fortress*.

Bill Gaither, who pioneered this format and helped launch the ministry careers of the three singers just mentioned as well as Take 6 and many others, himself offers grand revival-type concerts that can last a whole weekend or more—officially called "Praise Gatherings." He uses singers, groups, instrumentalists, preachers, seminar speakers, and his own Vocal Band and Trio to offer Christians a workshop-type motivational and inspirational mass-media event. Gaither, however, does not presume to replace Sunday worship. In fact, the event culminates in a Saturday night concert gala so that those who are residents in the city of the given event, as well as those participating and performing, can get to their home parishes on Sunday.

Michael W. Smith is an artist who began as a songwriter and performer for others, most notably Sandi Patti and Amy Grant, and gradually made a name for himself. He is an example of one whose musical endeavors run through the spectrum, but who is nearer the pole that describes those who consider themselves more as musicians and less as evangelizers or ministers. A typical Smith concert features almost nonstop music with little or no talking. The emphasis is on entertainment, albeit with a wholesome message and atmosphere.

His is a unique style that thrives on rather arresting compound rhythms and complex harmonies, a natural gift for melody, all wedded to intriguing, challenging lyrics. His compositional skill is immense. One album of his can contain a wide range of ensembles and styles: from rap to the American Boy Choir, ballads to orchestral arrangements, countrified rock to Latin/jazz influenced styles. His brand of rock is all his own as well; he copies or follows no one in "secular" music. This versatility and originality have brought him respect from a wide field of musicians and critics. He has mustered the clout to cross over his distribution and airplay to the mainstream of popular music without sacrificing spiritual content (an incredible feat, considering the contemporary environment of hostility in the media towards anything Christian). Listen to his albums *Eye 2 Eye, Go West Young Man,* and his Christmas album to get a good representation of his recent, and most acclaimed, work.

Another arena of fresh musical output is found in hymnody and psalmody. Again, many of the names already encountered offer some of the richest supply: Bill Gaither and his wife Gloria (who writes many of the lyrics) have written hundreds of hymns and praise songs. "Because He Lives" is perhaps the most widely known. Michael W. Smith and his wife, also a gifted poet, have contributed substantially to the pool of praise songs. Interest in original, contemporary music for the church has caused a wave of inspired composers to publish songs for choirs, soloists, and congregations.

The praise song is usually in the form of a memorable refrain or chorus with corresponding verses, which are often optional or intended for a soloist/worship leader. It can be based on original texts, such as the song "Shine, Jesus, Shine", or quite often taken verbatim from Scripture. Psalms, Wisdom literature, the prophets, and pithy, musical verses from the New Testament are frequent sources. The melodies and chord structure are usually simple and repetitive, yet tuneful and moving when at their best. This allows the words, be they Scriptural or conceptual, to "hook" into the mind quickly and indelibly. These types of songs also foster wide participation in terms of congregational singing and instrumental accompaniment. Guitars, various rhythm instruments, and piano, each alone or in ensemble, are sufficient and appropriate to carry the song. They tend to be more intimate and personal in tone, even when they are most exuberant. The repetition and simplicity offer opportunity for spontaneity and improvisation.

Some churches tend to overuse these songs in worship, all but replacing what are perceived by them as archaic and staid hymns. It is true that these praise songs offer some refreshing newness to the music of worship, but if they are accompanied by a negative reaction to traditional hymns and liturgical music, a house that is built upon a rock has been traded for one on shifting sand. Better to renovate and add on to a tried and true foundation than to fall headlong into the worldly sweep of a counter-cultural, anti-establishment current that would see all moorings destroyed.

It is only right for the church to adapt itself to the times and the surroundings in which it finds itself to keep its message relevant. While the importance of passing on the accumulated knowledge and integrity of the church, especially its music, cannot be denied, contemporary believers must be wary of inhibiting the movement of the Holy Spirit and quenching the blaze of true revival. In our zealousness to further the Kingdom and spread the Good News, we must humbly allow for the grace and will of our Lord. Christ guaranteed that a bad tree could never bear good fruit, and that a good tree could not help but bear good fruit. Paul assures believers that God's ways are mysterious in that he demonstrates his power through the use of "earthen vessels." John lovingly encourages believers to "test the spirits to see whether they are from God" (1 John 4:1). Only that which is truly of God will endure; the rest, it can be certain, will be pruned away. The development of music has proven true to this axiom: the best survives and carries on. What is shallow and insubstantial passes into insignificance and even oblivion.

Responses to Typical Criticisms of the Genre

It is a testimony to the tremendous power of music that it engenders such controversy and divided feelings in all walks of life, particularly when it comes to the life of the church. Battles over the proper place and kind of music for worship have been around since the Old Testament days and have embroiled the Christian church from its inception. The early church fathers argued as fiercely over this issue as any theological heresy, and it was once considered out of place for any instrument to be used in the sanctuary but the human voice. Singing more than one line of music at a time was once thought of as cacophony. Psalm 150 was interpreted away as allegory instead of being considered literally as a call to loud and multiphonic musical praise.

The Reformation and Counter-Reformation was likewise a period of intense struggle over, among other things, liturgical uses for music. Congregational singing of hymns was once unheard of, while Luther was ridiculed and condemned for his use of "worldly" tunes and vernacular language to inspire the collective voice of the laity to worship God from their own hearts. To this he replied, with his characteristically sardonic wit, "Why should the Devil have all the good tunes?" Also, organs were once literally being smashed apart by some Protestant zealots who considered them the "Devil's bagpipes."

The fruit of these controversies has nevertheless become some of Christendom's most glorious and inspiring music. Vernacular worship, congregational singing, instruments, and organs are now staples for worshipers, even Catholics, who resisted these changes for centuries. Luther at first had to plant choir singers in the congregation to encourage them to engage in the strange new phenomenon of hymn singing. Today it has become fundamental to the life and worship of believers everywhere. How far we have come over the millennia, yet the struggles over music remain. The current battle in the church looks and sounds much like those in the past. Even the criticisms have a familiar ring.

One of the lingering controversies regards music and worldliness. The argument of nonconformity to the world is as old as the Church. Perhaps no other issue has caused more division and denominational strife in Christendom than this one. Romans 12:2, "Do not conform any longer the pattern of this world" and 1 John 2:15, "Do not love the world or anything in the world" are often invoked when the relationship of Christianity to culture is discussed. The intermingling of the Gospel with "secular" music is seen as a clear trespass of these scriptural injunctions.

Steve Miller, in his article "In Defense of Contemporary Christian Music" (*CCM Magazine* 15:10 [April 1993]: 32-38), boils the critics' arguments down to three main areas of contention: "Charges of Worldliness," "Bad Associations," and "Questionable Motives." Miller begins by insightfully juxtaposing John 3:16 with 1 John 2:15. In the former verse, we read, "God loved the world so much that he gave his only Son." Yet, in the latter verse, believers are admonished not to "love the world." The confusion lies in what "world" (*kosmos* in the original Greek) connotes according to these texts. As with many words, there are alternative meanings that can only be derived from the context. In the Pauline and Johannine epistles, *kosmos* takes on a distinctly moral tone, referring to things that are sinful and apart from God. *Kosmos* in the former sense, the *kosmos* God loves, is Creation: that which he declared "good" in Genesis, that *kosmos* which "groans" toward rebirth according to Paul in another context.

Worldliness, then, is an attitude distinctly human. Inanimate objects cannot rightly be thought of as sinful or "worldly." Sinfulness is a condition of the heart of a moral agent. Worldliness is properly understood as a skewed attitude toward the things of the world, living in the world without recognition of its Creator, or believing falsely that there is a secular or neutral arena between God's activity and Satan's in which we act without moral consequence.

Music, it is certain, is a powerful phenomenon in the world, but of itself cannot be bad or good in a moral sense. "After all, we need to ask ourselves, does a musical scale differentiate between a secular C and a spiritual C? Can we find at the piano both an evil C and a righteous C? Is there such a thing as a secular guitar and a Christian guitar?" (Dan Peters, et al., *What About Christian Rock?* [Minneapolis: Bethany House, 1986], 41.) What is it, we might add, that makes syncopation evil when Madonna incorporates it, but glorious in the hands of Mozart and Beethoven?

People are evil, not things or materials. A musical composition is the product of a creative human mind intended to communicate with other minds. Our ear drums do not distinguish between music conveyed for evil or good, nor do stereo speakers, microphones, or instruments. A discerning soul bears such responsibility, not the artifacts.

Christian musicians are condemned for the tools that they use to ply their trade while other human endeavors are not held to the same standard. A Christian bricklayer does not use "Christian" bricks, nor does a Christian car mechanic use a "Christian" wrench. Why, then, is a Christian musician admonished to use only godly, Christian music in their trade, as if such a thing existed in distinction from others? Remember that Christian music is not a particular style, technique, or a certain arrangement of musical materials; the heart of the one writing or performing the music makes it so.

Miller notes a similar charge to worldliness, that of "bad associations." It is said that nowadays one cannot distinguish a Christian musician from a secular one by their appearance or their style of playing. Once again, however, critics are selective in their judgment. Can one discern the Christians in an orchestra or choir, or a Christian businessman by the shade of gray suit that he wears? One must observe the individual in action within his or her environment to make such determinations.

The argument that Christian musicians are indistinguishable from secular ones is one based either in ignorance, or a faulty, limited frame of reference. Even for those musicians who do not proselytize, but simply play their music, the difference between a concert of theirs and that of a typical rock band is quite striking. Besides the absolute contrast in the message conveyed, there is a distinct otherness to the environment in which the music is performed, the least of which is the absence of drugs and drunkenness. As Miller observes: "Transport any Motley Crüe groupie from a secular rock concert to a Petra concert, and he or she would immediately sense the contrast in both the performance and the atmosphere" ("In Defense of Contemporary Christian Music," 37).

Critics also focus their judgment to the inward motivations of a Christian popular musician. Charges of charlatanism run rampant against any Christians who use modern media to convey their message. Certainly some do exist, and are justifiably chastised. Materialism, however, is a matter of attitude toward money, not a matter of how successful one becomes financially. Much of the money made by Christian musicians goes toward equipment and recording facilities. Total resources will remain scarce, despite the growing market for Christian performing venues, radio play, and recordings. It can be assured that most are not in Christian music to "make money," because it doesn't happen very easily, even when one achieves a certain amount of success. The market, while it has grown, is still too small, while the pool of talent overflows. For the most part, musicians in the Christian music industry must be quite frugal in order to maintain maximum quality production while avoiding financial trouble through overextending resources. Those who would make baseless or wildly generalized accusations of "questionable motives" among Christian artists must check their own, as well as checking out the facts. As Miller states: "We must be careful not to judge another . . . when we have no solid evidence of his or her fault" (1 Cor. 4:5). (Ibid.)

By using the modern media, many Christians today hope to engage in what Lutheran theologian Martin Marty has called "cultural jujitsu": to use the force of opponents and their weapons against them by giving with them enough to return the impact of the blow back upon the source. One may argue against the method from a theological standpoint, or criticize the ability and technical mastery of a given individual, but the motivation is generally pure: to change the world for Christ, meeting the enemy where he is found. Christ was not above being found among sinners within their environment, and so it should be for us, think Christian musicians and radio/television broadcasters.

Conclusion: Accepting the Cycles of Change

Miller points out that the history of music in the church follows a cyclical pattern involving four stages. The first stage, which he calls separation, "finds the old forms of music firmly entrenched. . . . These styles communicate almost exclusively to those who have grown up in the church, alienating the uninitiated. What was once effective salt has lost its savor, and the stage is set for Phase 2: Integration." (Ibid.) He continues:

Bold innovators, convinced that outdated forms are stifling heartfelt worship, adopt the musical language (often the actual tunes) of the common per-

son, much to the chagrin of diehard traditionalists. The guardians of the past counter, ushering in Phase 3: Conflict.

At this point, innovations are bitterly denounced as compromise with the world, sub-biblical, use of the devil's music . . . and a host of other concerns. Enter Phase 4: Renewal.

Worship is again in the language of the people, and church music becomes an integral part of the believers' everyday lives as they carry their heartfelt songs outside the church walls into the factory and marketplace.

Finally, what was once new and fresh becomes standard. What was once condemned as secular finds its way into the hymnbook and is considered sacred. At the same time, the popular style of the common person has continued to change so that there is once again a dichotomy between the traditional and the popular. . . . And so we find ourselves back at Phase 1, and history repeats itself (Ibid., 37–38).

Especially when it comes to music, the innovations of one generation become the traditions of the next. This is Miller's driving point. In seeking to promote peace and avoid controversy, some insist that we cling to what has been well established and resist what is changing. However, must Christianity continue to lag behind culture, to be reactionary rather than revolutionary? It has not always been so. There have been relative glory days in the past when Christianity was the culture.

In our offering our message to the world, ought we not call it to something rather than merely beckoning it back from somewhere, to ask it to join the journey toward the light instead of merely shouting at it to avoid the darkness?

Music is a powerful medium for changing hearts and minds. Luther placed it next to theology and the Scriptures in importance and effectiveness as a means of persuasion, education, and edification. He believed music could reach to places in the human condition that the others could not. Music, to him, was a power to be respected, but not shackled. His was an attitude toward music that can be emulated to this day, for we still bask in the effects of the revolution he ushered in over five centuries ago. He emphasized and unleashed music's positive qualities, always humbly aware and out of the way of God's grace and activity in it. Nothing more or less can be asked of the church today.

Of all the joys upon this earth
None has for me a greater worth
Than this I have from my singing,
To set my voice sweetly ringing.
There cannot be an evil mood
Where good fellows sing,
There is no envy, hate, or ire,
Gone is through her all sorrow dire;
Greed, care, and lonely heaviness:
No more do they the heart oppress.

Each man can in his mirth be free
Since such joy no sin can be,
But God in her more pleasure finds
Than all the joys of earthly minds.
Through her bright power the devil shirks
His sinful, murderous, evil works . . .
   (Martin Luther, *Frau Musica*)

Michael Burgess, Jr.

172 • Music in the Multicultural Church

Many congregations today consist of people from a wide range of ethnic and cultural backgrounds. Music in worship is one means by which this rich cultural diversity can be expressed. This article challenges congregations to sing the music of many cultures in worship.

The challenges that face many of our urban and large suburban churches are complex and multifaceted. Some congregations find their membership increasingly drawing from racially and ethnically diverse groups of individuals, often creating upheaval and a sense of division between the new and old members of the parish. Other congregations seem to be on the verge of extinction because they fail to attract members from the changing neighborhoods that envelop their parish. Both types of congregations face challenges that will require patience, love, and the will to be servants of the Lord.

Music has long been called the universal language, transcending the barriers of different races and ethnic tongues. Thus as we seek ways to find common ground in the rapidly changing congregations of our cities and suburbs, music seems a logical building block for developing such a sense of unity.

However, before exploring ways in which music can be a force for reconciliation and renewal in our changing congregations, what do we mean by a multicultural church? In an article discussing the implications of the Christian Reformed Church becoming a truly multicultural denomination, author Gary Teja writes:

> In a multicultural church we don't just start churches for other ethnic groups or share our facilities when we're not using them. We go further—we make a genuine attempt to be one body of people of many different languages, customs and life experiences, worshiping together, praying together, singing together in the same service at the same time.
>
> A multicultural church encourages all of its members to appreciate the ethnic heritage that each person brings with himself or herself. Becoming multicultural doesn't mean rejecting your heritage; it means learning to appreciate the cultural backgrounds of others! (*The Banner,* 125:34 [October 1, 1990])

I strongly concur with this wonderful model of a multicultural church as described by Mr. Teja. However, I believe that a large majority of our urban and suburban churches can be characterized at best as multiracial congregations. Typically these congregations are dominated in membership by an aging Caucasian population with smaller populations of African-Americans, Hispanics/Latinos, or Asian-Americans. These racial/ethnic minorities are tolerated to the degree that they assimilate into the traditional style of worship that has been the norm for that particular congregation. Consequently, these churches deceive themselves when they believe they are multicultural simply by the mere presence of one or more ethnic groups. Another erroneous concept of multicultural ministry occurs when "outreach" programs are developed by a congregation for a neighboring area of "disadvantaged" people, without the people of the program ever really being invited into full fellowship with the "mainstream" congregation. Only when these folks are made equal partners in the faith mission of that congregation may we begin to call that congregation multicultural.

On the positive side, there are many congregations who may quite properly call themselves multicultural. There are also an increasing number of churches who are in the process of evolving from multiracial/multiethnic congregations into truly multicultural bodies of believers. I strongly hold that the music ministry of the church may be a powerful means of establishing a strong foundation for building a multicultural congregation. The new United Methodist, Presbyterian, Christian Reformed, and Brethren hymnals, as well as many other recently published collections, provide churches with new and wonderful treasuries of ethnic hymnody. We may begin a process of creating a multicultural church by singing of our shared faith in these new songs of God's people. Worship committees, ministers of music, and clergy and educational leaders can explore ways to incorporate these new songs of God's mighty acts in our lives through congregational hymns, liturgical music for choirs, and music for church school.

Another idea to consider is the need for urban churches to share worship experiences with congregations who may be able to offer some innovative perspectives to expand their style of worship. These exchanges should include worship in both parish sites and the sharing of worship traditions. These services should seek to affirm and enrich the lives of all those who attend.

The increasing demand for after-school childcare affords the imaginative urban congregation the opportunity to develop a creative after-school music ministry. Weekday afternoon choir schools that include children of the congregation as well as neighborhood youngsters are a marvelous means of evangelism and go far in establishing an atmosphere for teaching musical literacy, healthy singing technique, improvisation, and movement while also teaching the fundamentals of our Christian faith. Also, by initially involving the children, parents and other adults are often drawn back into a worshiping lifestyle.

Let us take the leap of faith that will enable us to sing out in voices of hope, love, and peace:

> In Christ there is no east or west
> He breaks all barriers down;
> By Christ redeemed, by Christ possessed,
> In Christ we live as one.

Anton E. Armstrong[11]

173 • A Paradigm for the Church Music of the Future

This chapter has presented a variety of ideas and ideals about music for use in worship. This article describes one approach for synthesizing many of these ideas, an approach especially suited for charismatic churches. Based on Paul's references to "psalms, hymns, and spiritual songs," _this article argues for a balanced and visionary approach to the use of music in worship._

All of us have personal preferences. Some prefer blue over green. Some prefer a trip to the beach over a trip to the mountains. Some favor grits over hash browns, country music over rock. And almost everyone favors the home team over the visitors.

But while we smile at some of our preferences, our religious preferences are often quite a different matter. For some reason, our own particular religious traditions and experiences tend to color our ideas of what God's preferences are and aren't. Nowhere is this more true than in the area of worship styles. How quickly our preferences become biases. And how easily our biases become walls that keep us from the larger body of Christ and from fuller expressions of worship.

The sum total of these distinctives and preferences is termed _culture_. Every individual and group is part of a culture. Worship and culture are closely related. It is interesting that the root word for culture is _cult_, which is, in its simplest definition, a system of worship or devotion. You could say our culture reflects our worship. We should neither despise nor deny our culture, for it helps to give us the initial parameters for personal identity, but we must thoughtfully evaluate all our ways in light of God's ways. When God says that his ways are higher than our ways (Isa. 55:9) he is saying that his divine culture is higher than our human culture. The Lausanne Covenant of 1974 appeals for churches to be "deeply rooted in Christ and closely related to their culture."

> Culture must always be tested and judged by Scripture. . . . The gospel does not presuppose the superiority of any culture to another, but evaluates all cultures according to its own criteria of truth and righteousness. . . . Churches have sometimes been in bondage to culture rather than to the Scripture."

Denominations within the church are typically cultural divisions before they are theological. They have to do with conflicting folkways. A Presbyterian pastor made this observation: "Part of the problem in coming into unity is that we have recruited people into personality distinctives of our own congregations and traditions, rather than into Christ. As a result, their loyalties are more to these distinctives than to Christ's Kingdom." In the spirit of Lausanne, we need to evaluate our traditions of worship—whether historic traditions or more recent renewal traditions—in light of Scripture to see if we are adherents of an approach to Christ or of Christ himself.

Toward Understanding Divine Preferences

Music powerfully communicates culture. That's why the church's music is so vital in communicating its life. Even the effects of a vibrant sermon can be canceled out by lifeless music. Some would observe that the music more accurately reflects the life of the congregation than do the words spoken.

What are we communicating culturally? What kinds of songs should we be singing? What are the parameters of biblical worship? Do our biases keep us from a fuller expression of worship? The easy answer to these kinds of questions goes something like this: *"God is only concerned with the attitude of our hearts, not the forms of our expressions."* Granted, the heart's disposition is primary, but should we not allow God to transform and enlarge our forms as well as our hearts? It's not that our worship traditions are intrinsically wrong . . . just incomplete.

Consider these three statements as beginning points in this discussion of biblical patterns of worship:

1. True worship is both spiritual *and* intellectual. *"True worshipers will worship the Father in spirit and in truth"* (John 4:24).
2. Heavenly worshipers worship the God of the past, present, and future. *"Day and night they never stop saying: Holy, holy, holy is the Lord God Almighty, who was, and is, and is to come"* (Rev. 4:8, see also Rev. 1:4, 8).
3. In the New Testament, God endorses three primary song forms: psalms, hymns, and spiritual songs. *"Let the word of Christ dwell in you richly as you . . . sing psalms, hymns, and spiritual songs with gratitude in your hearts to God"* (Col. 3:16, see also Eph. 5:19-20).

Spirit and Truth

Today some segments of the church specialize primarily in spirit. Favorite teaching topics in the churches would likely include "Hearing God" and "Being Led by the Spirit." Leaders encourage fol-

lowers to develop intuitive skills. Worship is generally spontaneous and Spirit-led.

Other segments of the church specialize primarily in truth. Among these groups, biblical scholarship and critical thinking are held in high esteem. Here worship is more orderly and structured.

Each tradition is suspicious of the other and often reinforces its own uniquenesses to justify its existence. Facing these tendencies is very difficult but very necessary. But Jesus said that true worshipers must worship in spirit and truth . . . not one or the other. If we love to "flow in the Spirit" but are impatient with the process of making careful observations, we are not yet the kind of worshipers God is looking for. If we are diligent students and yet we can't make room for someone to base a claim on revelation, we are not yet the worshipers that please God.

If the worship in our congregation only attracts the critical thinkers, it's time to do some critical thinking about our own cultural preferences. If our congregation is attracting only the intuitive or feeling types, it's time to ask the Spirit to lead us into all truth. Biblical worship is to be spiritual and thoughtful. These two components are implied in Romans 12:1 in the phrase *logikos latreia,* which is translated in the NIV as either "spiritual act of worship" or "reasonable act of worship."

Past, Present, and Future

Some of us are more familiar with what God is saying than what God has said, to the point that we disdain any reference to history. I have heard this referred to as "the cult of contemporaneity." Others are well versed in what has gone on before us and yet out of touch with what is going on now. One pastor confidently told me that nothing of any significance has happened in the church in the last 250 years. Most likely the church he pastors will be populated with those who are friendly to that point of view.

Still others of us are so future-oriented that we fail to worship the God of the past and the present. We must not try to confine God's kingdom exclusively to past, present, or future reality. Each are only partial reflections of God's glory.

Psalms, Hymns, and Spiritual Songs

Some charismatic churches tend to sing choruses to the exclusion of hymns. Some traditional churches sing hymns to the exclusion of choruses.

And a very small percentage of churches have any significant experience with spiritual songs. In contrast, God's Word invites us all to express our gratitude through all three song forms.

To sing a psalm is not necessarily the equivalent of singing from the book of Psalms. A psalm is a song. The term _psalm,_ like _song,_ can be used in a general or a specific sense. In the general usage it would include a hymn, just as there are hymns included in the book of Psalms.

In the specific sense however, a psalm would contrast with a hymn. Similar to what we today call choruses, a psalm, or song, is generally simpler, shorter, more testimonial, and less theological than a hymn. A hymn would usually carry a greater sense of reverence; a song would be more personal. The psalm is more contemporary and has a shorter life span.

The spiritual song is even more of a song-of-the-moment. The spiritual song that consists of spontaneous melodies around a chord or a slowly moving chord progression, has been referred to as the "song of angels" because of its mystical, otherworldly quality. Even as the Spirit is the believer's down payment on the future age, the spiritual song must be a foretaste of heavenly worship itself.

The genius of these three song forms is that each is uniquely appropriate to express a dimension of God's nature and each will speak for a different kind of personality, as well as the different facets of the individual. The hymn corresponds to the God who was—the God of history; the psalm corresponds to the God who is—the God of the now; and the spiritual song corresponds to the God who is to come—the God of the future. The hymn will satisfy our hunger for truth and depth of understanding; the psalm will speak to our need for encounter and experience; and the spiritual song will stimulate the prophet and visionary in us.

The command to employ psalms, hymns, and spiritual songs requires a greater cultural flexibility than we have had in order to enjoy the variety of worship expressions. For instance, the youth of the church will probably prefer a more contemporary style of worship than the older members. The common solution to this cultural problem is to segregate the youth church from the adult church. But the psalms-hymns-and-spiritual-songs paradigm begs for a different solution: diversity within unity. This new paradigm allows the contemporary and the historic to stand side by side and challenges our hearts to greater love. It means being both reverent and celebrative, objective and subjective, structured and spontaneous, testimonial and theological.

Instead of affirming our own strengths and acknowledging the limitations of other traditions, we must begin to recognize the limitations of our own traditions and affirm the strengths of the others. The result will be that our own preferences will be enjoyed by others, as well as enlarged by others. Like an onion in the stew, we will both flavor the other ingredients and be flavored by them—all the while, remaining an onion.

Paradigm for the Future

The church of the future must become transcultural. The evangelical church must learn to sing spiritual songs; the charismatic church must rediscover the hymns; and the traditional church must begin to sing a new psalm. The young church must respect the older church and vise versa. Bridges of cooperation and counsel must be built between black and white churches. The stagnating pools of our cultural prejudices must be flooded by the river of God's divine purposes. Accepting and practicing God's standard of psalms, hymns, and spiritual songs in our worship is a simple but challenging exercise designed to break us loose from our idols of ethnocentrism.

Where will all of this lead us? To the most exciting celebration imaginable: the international, interdenominational, multilingual, multiethnic celebration of Christ Jesus, the Son of God!

> After this I looked and there before me was a great multitude that no one could count, from every nation, tribe, people, and language, standing before the throne and in front of the Lamb. (Rev. 7:9)

Dare we look upon what John saw: representatives from every culture, nation, tribe, people, and language, declaring their praises together with a loud voice, overwhelmed with gratitude for this majestic King who has made them into one people (Rev. 5:9-10)? If we can see that, we can see our destination. The heavenly vision is that of worshipers of many different stripes who are more conscious of the greatness of Jesus Christ than of their cultural distinctions.

If worship styles have been the source of divisions among us, let's turn the tables and allow God's design for worship be a source of unity among us.

Let's pray that heaven's worship will overtake earth's as we sing psalms, hymns, and spiritual songs.

Gerrit Gustafson

174 ✦ BIBLIOGRAPHY ON THE THEOLOGICAL FOUNDATIONS OF MUSIC IN WORSHIP

Archbishops' Commission. *In Tune With Heaven: The Report of the Archbishops' Commission on Church Music.* London: Hodder and Stoughton, 1992. A comprehensive statement about the nature and place of music in worship and the state of church music in England, along with suggestions for the future directions for church music in England. See also Jane Sinclair, *Keeping in Tune with Heaven: A Response to the Report of the Archbishops' Commission on Church Music* (Bramcote, U.K.: Grove Books, 1992).

Berglund, Robert. *A Philosophy of Church Music.* Chicago: Moody Press, 1985. Discusses in broad terms the role of a church music program in the life of the church, with chapters on the participants in a church music progam and the institutional structures to such a program.

Best, Harold. *Music Through the Eyes of Faith.* San Francisco: Harper San Francisco, 1993. A work that seeks to answer the questions of how Christians should appropriate the musical arts. The book is not primarily concerned about church music, though one chapter is devoted to the subject. Best argues for a thoughtful acceptance of a variety of musical styles, a musical pluralism rooted in a high view of creation.

————. "Schaeffer on Art and Music," in R. W. Ruegsegger, ed. *Reflections on Francis Schaeffer.* Grand Rapids: Zondervan, 1986. A detailed critique of Schaeffer's theological and aesthetic position on the roles of music and art in the believer's life. Important as a recent assessment of still-current controversies among evangelicals regarding music in worship and life.

Boschman, Lamar. *The Rebirth of Music* (1986) and *The Prophetic Song* (1990). Shippensburg, Pennsylvania: Destiny Image Publications. Two books by a leader in the praise-and-worship tradition, describing the role and importance of music in charismatic worship.

Collins, Mary, David Power, and Mellonee Burnim, eds. *Music and the Experience of God.* Edinburgh: T. and T. Clark, Ltd., 1989. A collection of essays that examine the role of ritual music in a variety of cultural settings, emphasizing the socio-cultural dimensions of music.

Day, Thomas. *Why Catholics Can't Sing: The Culture of Catholicism and the Triumph of Bad Taste.* New York: Crossroad, 1992. A famous book that analyzes the cultural and liturgical forces that have shaped worship in the twentieth century. As such, it is valuable, thought-provoking reading for Christians from any tradition.

Davison, Archibald. *Church Music: Illusion and Reality.* Cambridge, Mass.: Harvard University Press, 1960. An older but well-presented discussion about the nature of church music in traditional Protestant worship.

Deiss, Lucien. *Spirit and Song of the New Liturgy.* Cincinnati: World Library Publications, Inc., 1976. A work that describes the theological foundations of music in worship in the Roman Catholic tradition, the role of the various music participants in the liturgy, and an extended discussion of the role of music in each portion of the eucharistic liturgy.

Ellsworth, Donald Paul. *Christian Music in Contemporary Witness: Historical Antecedents and Contemporary Practices.* Grand Rapids: Baker, 1979. A history of church music that concentrates on music in evangelical churches and on theological foundations of current practice. In particular, the book attempts to analyze and critique music used in evangelistic services and music composed in contemporary styles.

Eskew, Harry, and Hugh McElrath. *Sing with Understanding: An Introduction to Christian Hymnology.* Nashville: Broadman Press, 1980. The standard introduction to the study of hymns that also includes chapters on the role of hymns in proclamation, worship, education, and related ministries.

Foley, Edward. *Music in Ritual: A Pre-Theological Investigation.* New York: Paulist Press, 1984. Surveys the function of music as communication, symbol, and language from the perspective of ritual studies.

Funk, Virgil C. *Music in Catholic Worship: The NPM Commentary.* Washington, D.C.: National Association of Pastoral Musicians, 1982. A collection of essays previously published in Pastoral Music Magazine that are organized following the outline of the document _Music in Catholic Worship_ (printed in this volume) and describe the implications of this document.

———. _The Singing Assembly._ Washington, D.C.: The Pastoral Press, 1991. Fifteen essays that discuss the role of the congregation in the music of worship, arguing that the congregation should be a primary participant in the music of worship.

———. _Sung Liturgy: Toward 2000 A.D._ Washington, D.C.: The Pastoral Press, 1991. Six essays that deal with current issues in church music, especially in light of inculturation and liturgical education issues.

Gelineau, Joseph. _Learning to Celebrate: The Mass and its Music._ New York: Paulist Press, 1985. A basic introduction to the role that music plays in worship in the liturgical tradition, written by one of the most respected Roman Catholic church musicians of this century. Useful for all worshiping communities.

———. _Voices and Instruments in Christian Worship._ Trans. Clifford Howell. Collegeville, Minn.: The Liturgical Press, 1964. Principles about the role of vocal and instrumental music in worship derived from theological, liturgical, and historical perspectives.

Hannum, Harold B. _Music and Worship._ Nashville: Southern Pub. Association, 1969. An overview of the proper role of music in worship in traditional Protestant worship.

Hatchett, M. J. _A Manual for Clergy and Church Musicians._ New York: Church Hymnal Corp., 1980. A guide to the terminology in the field of church music. Written and published in the Episcopal tradition, but generally useful for musicians and worship planners in any worship tradition.

Hoelty-Nickel, Theodore, ed. _The Musical Heritage of the Church._ St. Louis: Concordia, 1944–1981. A multivolume series of essays on the theology of music in worship, spanning the 1940s through 1980s.

Hoffman, Lawrence, and Janet R. Walton, eds. _Sacred Sound and Social Change: Liturgical Music in Jewish and Christian Experience._ Notre Dame, Ind.: University of Notre Dame Press, 1993. Scholarly essays that discuss music for worship in light of its social context. Essays cover both historical and philosophical subjects.

Hustad, Donald. _Jubilate: Church Music in the Evangelical Tradition._ Carol Stream, Ill.: Hope Publishing, 1981. The single most complete volume on music in worship in the evangelical tradition. Chapters cover the nature of worship, the role of music in worship, the history of music in worship, and the proper place of various types of music in worship.

Huijbers, Bernard. _The Performing Audience._ Phoenix: North American Liturgical Resources, 1974. Some very thought-provoking essays on music and song in liturgy by a Roman Catholic church musician from the Netherlands. These essays cover a broad range of historical and liturgical topics, arguing for greater participation on the part of the worshiping community.

Johansson, Calvin M. _Music and Ministry: A Biblical Counterpoint._ Peabody, Mass.: Hendrickson Publishers, 1984. This work gives a thoroughgoing theological rationale for the nature and role of music in worship, discussing church music in light of creation, the image of God, the Incarnation, faith, and others. It also includes a perceptive analysis of contemporary culture and suggestions for how the church should respond to it.

Johnson, Lawrence J. _The Mystery of Faith: The Ministers of Music._ Washington, D.C.: National Association of Pastoral Musicians, 1983. A comprehensive presentation of new ministries of music since Vatican II. Discussions of assembly, presider, deacon, cantor, choir, instrumentalists, organist, dancer, composer.

Leaver, Robin. _Church Music: The Future._ Westminster Choir College, 1991. Essays on composing for the church, the use of instruments in worship, and other questions currently being discussed in the area of church music.

———. "The Theological Character of Music in Worship." In _Duty and Delight: Routley Remembered,_ edited by Robin A. Leaver and James Litton, 47–64. Carol Stream, Ill.: Hope Publishing Company, 1985. Thoroughgoing discussion on the musician as liturgical theologian; the function of proclamation; music and Christology; music and doctrine; eschatology.

Lovelace, Austin C., and William C. Rice. _Music and Worship in the Church._ Rev. ed. Nashville: Abingdon Press, 1976. Particularly designed for seminary use. Covers all aspects of the music ministry of the church.

Maries, Andrew. *One Heart, One Voice: The Rich and Varied Resource of Music in Worship*. London: Hodder and Stoughton, 1986. A complete discussion of the field of church music from an English evangelical.

Miller, Steve. *The Contemporary Christian Music Debate: Wordly Compromise or Agent of Renewal?* Wheaton: Tyndale House, 1993. Discusses the appropriate response to the genre of Christian popular music.

Mitchell, Robert H. *Ministry and Music*. Philadelphia: Westminster Press, 1978. A description of the practice of church music in traditional Protestant worship, along with arguments about the proper role and use of the organ, choir, and congregation within a worship service.

————. *But I Don't Like That Music*. Carol Stream, Illinois: Hope Publishing, 1992. A book directed to the center of present discussions about the use of contemporary musical styles in worship, as well as the issue of musical eclecticism in worship.

Mopson, J. Wendell, Jr. *The Ministry of Music in the Black Church*. Valley Forge, Pa.: Judson Press, 1984. An overview of the contributions of African-American worship to the Christian church and insights about the role of music in African-American worship.

Pass, David B. *Music and the Church*. Nashville: Broadman, 1989. Discusses the role the music in worship, focusing on issues regarding contemporary Protestant worship.

Pottie, Charles S. *A More Profound Alleluia*. Washington D.C.: The Pastoral Press, 1984. An essay on the life and thought of arguably the two greatest thinkers and practitioners of music in worship in this century, Joseph Gelineau and Erik Routley.

Pulkingham, Betty. *Sing God a Simple Song*. San Francisco: Marshall Pickering, 1986. An essay by a leader of the worship renewal movement in the Episcopal church about the importance of relevant and direct music that does justice to the liturgy.

Rock, Judith. *Performer as Priest and Prophet: Restoring the Intuitive in Worship Through Music and Dance*. San Francisco: Harper and Row, 1988. Explores the intuitive, affective dimensions of music in worship, along with a discussion of liturgical dance.

Routley, Erik. *Church Music and the Christian Faith*. Carol Stream, Ill.: Agape, 1987. A classic philosophy of church music that uses historical and theological insights to argue for music that does justice to the nature of liturgy and the all-encompassing nature of faith.

————. *Words, Music, and the Church*. Abingdon, 1968. An early classic by this respected scholar and pastor that seeks to understand the dramatic and textual dynamics of music in worship, especially in light of the new musical styles that were introduced in the late 1960s.

Review and Expositor 87:1 (Winter 1990). "The Song of the Church." An entire issue devoted to the theological foundations of church music within the Baptist tradition.

Schalk, Carl, ed. *Key Words in Church Music*. St. Louis: Concordia, 1978. This compilation of essays remains at present an excellent survey of most of the controversial or problematic terminology in the worship music field. Not so much a glossary as a series of extensive annotations.

Schmidt, Orlando. *Church Music and Worship Among the Mennonites*. Newton, Kans.: Faith and Life Press, 1981. A brief essay describing the history of church music in the Mennonite/Anabaptist tradition along with guidelines for current practice.

Schmitt, Francis P. *Church Music Transgressed: Reflections on Reform*. New York: The Seabury Press, 1977. An essay describing and critiquing trends in Roman Catholic church music since Vatican II.

Schultze, Quentin, Roy M. Anker, et al. *Dancing in the Dark*. Grand Rapids: Eerdmans, 1991. The best single work on the growth of a youth culture in America, including a discussion of popular music that has serious implications for the practice of church music.

Spencer, Jon Michael. *Protest and Praise: Sacred Music of Black Religion*. Minneapolis: Fortress Press, 1991. A history of black sacred music in America that explains the cultural background that shaped it and the rich diversity of genres and styles it represents.

Topp, Dale. *Music in the Christian Community*. Grand Rapids: Eerdmans, 1976. An analysis of the many ways in which music shapes the Christian lifestyle and community, including its role in church, school, and home. This viewpoint provides a holistic framework in which to consider the role of music in the life of the church.

Wienandt, Elwyn A. *Opinions on Church Music.* Baylor University Press, 1974. An anthology of writings by leading church musicians and liturgists throughout the history of the church.

Winter, Miriam Therese. *Why Sing? Toward a Theology of Catholic Church Music.* Washington, D.C.: The Pastoral Press, 1984. A comprehensive discussion of the implications of Vatican II reforms for the practice of music in worship.

Wohlgemuth, Paul W. *Rethinking Church Music.* Chicago: Moody Press, 1973. Ideas about the function of church music in light of contemporary Protestant worship.

THREE

A Brief History of Music in Worship

Throughout its history, the Christian church has used music to proclaim the gospel and to return thanks and praise to God. The history of this musical expression teaches us a great deal not only about the culture and everyday life of earlier Christians, but also about their unique experience of and insights into the Christian faith. These lessons can, in turn, enlighten, emend, and inspire our own worship of God.

The history of the church's song teaches us, for example, how embedded in culture this song has always been. It inspires us by pointing us to Christians who have dedicated their whole lives to the artful craft of rendering musical prayers and proclamation for the service of God in worship. And it reminds us of the tremendous power of music to either enrich or corrupt our faith and the witness of the church.

As Christians living today, we have the rare privilege of learning about Christians in faraway lands and times. While not nearly complete, this chapter tells the story of a host of Christians, Eastern and Western, European, African, and American. Hearing this story deepens our appreciation of the universal Church and whets our appetites for hearing stories yet untold of Christians on other continents and in other eras.

175 • MUSIC IN THE WORSHIP OF THE OLD TESTAMENT

Music was an important element of both temple and synagogue worship. Undoubtedly this music and its forms influenced the form and use of music in the early Christian church. Both Jews and Christians revere a transcendent God and both give honor to Scripture. For these reasons and others, Jewish synagogue worship and modern Christian services are similar in content and spirit.

Through almost three thousand years of Hebrew/Christian history, music has been inseparable from worship, and the Bible contains much of our early heritage of worship song. The Psalms come from many periods of the ancient Jewish culture, and they were augmented by canticles that date back to Israel's deliverance from Egypt.

Synagogue worship probably developed among the Jews as a result of their dispersion in the fifth century before Christ. With its emphasis on the reading and explanation of Scripture, prayers, and the singing of psalms and canticles, it was very significant in the framing of early Christian worship. Music in the synagogue was led by cantors—soloists who may have been trained in the temple Levitical ministry—and included some congregational participation.

The New Testament era began with the canticles surrounding Christ's birth, recorded in the Gospel of St. Luke. The new faith and its expression were supported with several types of music—"psalms and hymns and spiritual songs" according to the apostle Paul. The epistles do contain some general principles: the Scriptures were to be read and the gospel was to be preached, certain types of prayer were encouraged, and believers were expected to celebrate the Eucharist, or Communion.

The Early Traditions

The first biblical reference to musical experience is a narrative of musical thanksgiving, led by Moses and his sister Miriam, after the Israelites had been delivered from the Egyptians:

Then Moses and the Israelites sang this song to the Lord: "I will sing to the Lord, for he is highly exalted. The horse and its rider he has hurled into the sea. . . ." Then Miriam the prophetess, Aaron's sister, took a tambourine in her hand, and all the women followed her, with tambourines and dancing. Miriam sang to them: "Sing to the Lord, for he is highly exalted. The horse and its rider he has hurled into the sea" (Exod. 15:1, 20-21).

This performance was both instrumental and vocal, involved both men and women, and was accompanied by expressive movement. The song was a prototype of the expressions of praise to God that are found throughout the Old Testament, particularly in the Psalms.

Erik Routley has reminded us that there are two musical worship traditions in the Old Testament: one was spontaneous and ecstatic, the other formal and professional (_Church Music and the Christian Faith,_ p. 6). The first of these is mentioned as part of Saul's preparation to become king of Israel; the prophet Samuel was giving the instructions:

After that you will go to Gibeah of God . . . as you approach the town, you will meet a procession of prophets coming down from the high place with lyres, tambourines, flutes and harps being played before them, and they will be prophesying. The Spirit of the Lord will come upon you in power, and you will prophesy with them; and you will be changed into a different person. (1 Sam. 10:5-6)

In this early period, music was apparently expected to assist the worshiper's experience of God. The same idea is expressed in connection with an occasion when the Prophet Elisha foretold God's judgment: "But now bring me a harpist." While the harpist was playing the hand of the Lord came upon Elijah and said, "This is what the Lord says" (2 Kings 3:15-16). The expectation that music can affect human behavior (ethos) was common in Scripture times and has persisted through history. The Bible also records an early use of music in therapy: whenever the spirit from God came upon Saul, David would take his harp and play. Then relief would come to Saul; he would feel better, and the evil spirit would leave him (see 1 Samuel 16:23).

Music in the Temple

The second Old Testament musical tradition—the music for the temple—was formal and professional, and was initiated by Israel's shepherd-king who was himself a musician and hymn composer: David told the leaders of the Levites to appoint their brothers as singers to sing joyful songs, accompanied by musical instruments: lyres, harps and cymbals (1 Chron. 15:16).

As priest-musicians, these performers gave full time to their musical service. They were chosen on the basis of their talent (1 Chron. 15:22) and were thoroughly trained, serving five years of apprenticeship before being admitted to the regular chorus. The Jewish choir was organized under at least three composer-conductors—Asaph, Herman, and Jeduthun (2 Chron. 5:12). The singing was accompanied by many kinds of instruments—lyres, pipes, harps, trumpets, and cymbals—and was also associated with dance (Ps. 150:4).

The Musical Sound

In ancient Hebrew worship, the words of Scripture were never spoken without melody; to do so was considered to be inappropriate. They were always sung in a fervent cantillation. ("Shout to God with loud songs of joy!" Ps. 47:1). They were accompanied by instruments in what is believed to have been a sort of heterophony, in which the instruments provided embellishments of the vocal melody. As in most early cultures, Hebrew instruments were of three basic types:

- String—_kinnor_ ("lyre," related to the Greeks' _kithara_) and _nebbel_ ("harp" with up to ten strings, sometimes called "psaltery" in KJV).
- Wind—_shophar_ (a ram's horn), _halil_ (a double-reed, like the oboe), _hazozerah_ (a metal trumpet), and _ugabb_ (a vertical flute, used mainly in secular music).
- Percussion—_toph_ (tambourine, or hand drum), _zelzelim_ (cymbals), and _mena an im_ (a sistrum). (See _The New Oxford History of Music,_ vol. 1, 295–296, and footnoted references.)

In Old Testament worship antiphonal singing was probably the norm, as evidenced by the fact that many of the Psalms are couched in a responsorial pattern. In modern liturgical church practice, each verse is divided into a _versicle_ and _response._

V: God be merciful unto us, and bless us;
R: And cause his face to shine upon us. (Psalm 67:1, KJV)

V: O give thanks unto the Lord; for he is good:

R: For his mercy endureth for ever. (Psalms 136:1, KJV)

It is natural for us to try to guess what this ancient music sounded like. Some Jewish worship musicians insist that they still retain much of the original character of their chants, even though they may have been originally preserved only by oral tradition. Recent musicologists have reasoned that the early Christian chant styles were patterned after Jewish antecedents. It is probable that certain traditions in the Byzantine chant of the Greek, Antiochian, and Palestinian churches carry some remnants of the original sounds. Eric Werner says that all the foremost authorities (Curt Sachs, A. Z. Idelsohn, and R. Lachman) agree that the chants were based on four-note (tetra-chordal) melodic motives, and that "the archetype of chant was similar to ancient Gregorian tunes, which means that they were based upon small melodic patterns of a rather narrow range, usually not exceeding a fourth or a fifth" (Eric Werner, *Jewish Music*, 623).

Within the last few years, French musician and scholar Suzanne Haik Vantoura released the results of her four years of research in the book *La Musique de la Bible Revelee* (The Music of the Bible Revealed). She is convinced that mysterious signs scattered throughout the Hebrew scriptures, both above and below the letters, are actually a system of musical notation, and not punctuation or accent marks as has been traditionally believed. Furthermore, she has reduced these signs to a system of notation, and has transcribed and recorded the melodies for approximately three hours of Bible music.

Werner also describes the musical performance in the Jews' Second Temple:

> The morning sacrifice was accompanied by three trumpet blasts; the cymbals clashed, signaling the beginning of the Levitical chant. At the end of each portion the trumpets joined the singing to indicate to the congregation the moment when they were to prostrate themselves. Every song was probably divided into three portions. (Werner, 623)

Most scholars agree that music in the temple was almost completely professional and sacerdotal (performed by priests). The Jewish people participated principally as listeners. It is reasoned that they may have frequently joined in the traditional responses "amen" and "alleluia," and possibly in an antipho-

nal refrain like "for his steadfast loves endures for ever" (Ps. 136).

The book of Psalms has been called the "hymnal of Israel." The Psalms were sung in regular sequences following the morning and evening sacrifice on specified days of the week, and were accompanied by instruments which occasionally indulged in an interlude indicated by the word *Selah*.

Psalms offered three types of worship expression:

1. Praise
   - Praise the Lord!
   - For it is good to sing praises to our God; for he is gracious, and a song of praise is seemly (Ps. 147:1).
2. Petition
   - Give ear, O Shepherd of Israel, thou who leadest Joseph like a flock! Thou who art enthroned upon the cherubim, shine forth before Ephraim and Benjamin and Manasseh! Stir up thy might, and come to save us! (Ps. 80:1-2).
3. Thanksgiving
   - I love the Lord, because he has heard my voice and my supplications (Ps. 116:1).

There were special psalms associated with festival occasions—royal psalms to honor the kings (e.g., 21, 45, 101), processional psalms (e.g., 24, 95, 100), and penitential psalms for periods of national repentance (e.g., 130). The "Egyptian Kings" Psalms (113–118) were very significant in the observance of the Passover and other times of national penitence.

There were at least four different modes of presentation:

1. A simple psalm (e.g., 46:1), sung by one person alone.
2. A responsive psalm (e.g., 67:1, 2), in which a choir answers the solo chant.
3. An antiphonal psalm, with several lines beginning or ending with the same phrase (e.g., 103:1, 2, 20-22), sung by two choirs in alternation.
4. A litany (e.g., 80:2, 3, 6, 7, 18, 19), which included a repeated refrain (Werner, 621–623).

Eric Werner also gives four design types: (Eric Werner, *The Sacred Bridge*, p. 133.)

1. The plain, direct psalm—no strophic arrangement.
2. The acrostic psalm—phrases in alphabetical sequence (e.g., 119).
3. The refrain psalm—each verse ending with the same refrain (e.g., 136).
4. The Hallelujah psalm—begins or closes with the ecstatic exclamation (e.g., 145–150).

In addition to the Psalms, a number of important biblical canticles were used regularly by the Hebrews in worship, and have been carried over into many Christian traditions as well. These are the best known:

1. Moses' (and Miriam's) song of victory over Pharaoh (Exod. 15).
2. Moses' prayer before his death (Deut. 32).
3. The song of Hannah (1 Sam. 2), a prototype of Mary's song in Luke 1:46-55.
4. The song of Habakkuk (Hab. 2).
5. Isaiah's song (Isa. 26).
6. The prayer of Jonah in the fish's belly (Jonah 2).
7. The prayer of Azariah—*Benedictus es, Domine* (Daniel 3, Douay version; Vulg., 3:26-49, Apocrypha).
8. The song of the three Hebrew children in the furnace—*Benedicite omnia opera Domini* (Dan. 3, Douay version; Vulg. 3:52-90, Apocrypha).

Worship and the Calendar

Historic Jewish worship acknowledged that God is the Lord of times and seasons in the ebb and flow of life. The sacrifices were observed in both the morning and evening every day in the tabernacle and later, in the temple. In addition, the Jewish family regularly offered prayers at home at stated hours and at mealtime. The Sabbath was a time for more exacting expressions of worship; it commemorated God's rest from the acts of creation and was observed in obedience to his command. Finally, there were times of intensely celebrative or penitential worship: Passover, to commemorate their deliverance from Egypt; the Day of Atonement, at the beginning of the New Year; Pentecost, associated with the giving of the Law, at the corn harvest; and the Feast of Booths (tabernacles) as "harvest home." As we will see later, most of these practices based on the calendar have been fulfilled in Christ and transformed into Christian worship.

Worship Music and the Experience of God

The Hebrews shared a richly symbolic worship that appealed strongly to the senses. The music which accompanied the sacrifices was a conspicuous part of the sensory experience. Musical sound revealed the presence of God, as evidenced in the accounts of the ecstatic moments of Saul and Elisha, and also in the requirement that song-chant would always be the vehicle of the holy scriptures.

One occasion when God was pleased to reveal his presence through musical performance was the dedication of Solomon's temple:

> Now when the priests came out of the holy place (for all the priests who were present had sacrificed themselves, without regard to their divisions; and all the Levitical singers, Asaph, Heman, and Jeduthun, their sons and kinsmen, arrayed in fine linen, with cymbals, harps, and lyres, stood east of the altar with a hundred and twenty priests who were trumpeters; and it was the duty of the trumpeters and singers to make themselves heard in unison in praise and thanksgiving to the Lord), and when the song was raised, with trumpets and cymbals and other musical instruments, in praise to the Lord, "For he is good, for his steadfast love endures for ever," the house, the house of the Lord, was filled with a cloud, so that the priests could not stand to minister because of the cloud; for the glory of the Lord filled the house of God (2 Chron. 5:11-14).

Worship in the Synagogue and the Jewish Home

The tradition of synagogue worship is of uncertain origin. Some scholars surmise that Jewish laypersons gathered in remote parts of Palestine at the time of the regular sacrifices in the temple at Jerusalem; others guess that the practice may have begun among Jews who were captives in other lands. Because the traditional sacrifices could only be offered in the temple, "sacrifices of praise and prayer" were substituted for offerings of animals and grain. Synagogue worship was in full flower during the lifetime of Jesus and the early days of the Christian church. It is not surprising then that early Jewish Christians modeled their worship partly on what they had experienced in the synagogue.

Synagogue worship was essentially a Service of

the Word; it centered in the ceremonial reading of the Scripture, especially the Torah and the prophets, followed by an explanation of their meaning in a homily. It should be understood that the synagogue service was essentially congregational; though the position of the rabbi (teacher) developed in its context, it was essentially a meeting of laypersons, who probably participated in the prayers, and also in the free discussion which might follow the Scripture lection (see Acts 17:17).

These then are the component parts of synagogue worship, most of which have come down to us from the earliest traditions.

- Scripture Readings (Torah; the Prophets)
- Homily, followed by discussion
- Psalmody
- The *Kedusha,* "Holy, Holy, Holy," (Isa. 6:3)
- Prayers (The Yotzer and the Ahabah, emphasizing the creative acts of God and his love for his people, ending with the Shema—"Hear, O Israel; the Lord our God is one Lord," etc., a declaration of faith and a glad benediction, from Deut. 6:4-9, 11:13-21; Numbers 15:37-41)
- The Eighteen Benedictions (expressions of praise, petitions for material and spiritual blessings, and intercessions for many people, concluded with a united "amen")

It is not known when music entered synagogue worship, but it is surmised that certain Levitical singers may have continued to practice their art in the lay-oriented gathering. We do know that only one or two solo singers (cantors) were involved in a service. They chanted the Scripture readings, the Psalms, the post-biblical prayers (Benedictions) and, according to some scholars, certain "melismatic" songs which may have been similar both to the ecstatic music of earlier days and to the "spiritual songs" mentioned in Colossians 3:16 and Ephesians 5:19. The musical style must have been related to that of temple worship, though presumably no instruments were involved, since they were associated only with animal sacrifices. It is also surmised that, in the congregational character of this gathering, all the worshipers joined in the psalms which they knew, and very frequently in a repeated refrain, a "Hallelujah" and an "amen."

We make this latter assumption partly on the witness of Mark (14:26): "And when they had sung a hymn, they went out to the Mount of Olives." On the occasion of the last supper of our Lord with his disciples, the hymn sung was possibly one of the "Egyptian Kings" Psalms (113–118), traditionally used in the observance of Passover. In the custom of a typical Jewish home, Jesus pronounced a blessing over a loaf of bread, broke it, and gave portions to all those around the table. Similarly, at the end of the meal, a Jewish host would take a cup of wine mixed with water, give thanks, and then pass it around for all to drink. So it was that at the Upper Room supper, Jesus transformed this traditional act of thanksgiving and made it new, instituting the Lord's Supper, or Eucharist, which many Christians believe to be the most significant single act of worship. The full order of historic Christian liturgy was developed by uniting the pattern of Jewish synagogue worship with the Eucharist.

Modern Jewish services continue in synagogues, without significant change in the basic elements. (In the orthodox Jewish tradition, the singing is still largely cantoral and unaccompanied.) The feasts are still observed as in ancient times, with one significant addition: Hanukkah, "the festival of lights," is celebrated in December to commemorate the rededication of the temple in the second century B.C., following the victory over the Syrians under Antiochus IV. In connection with the cycle of annual worship centering in the festivals, a regular schedule of Scripture readings (the lectionary), psalms, and prayers was developed to support the emphasis of each season. (The close relationship between Jewish and early Christian activity in the developing of "propers" for daily worship is related in Werner, 50–101.)

Donald P. Hustad

176 • MUSIC IN THE WORSHIP OF THE NEW TESTAMENT

From the beginning of the New Testament experience, the believer's response to Jesus Christ has included song. Most of the New Testament songs or hymns have found their way into the enduring liturgy of the church, including the Magnificat, the Benedictus, the Gloria, and the Nunc Dimittis. New Testament music in worship included psalmody, hymns composed in the church, and spiritual songs—alleluias and songs of jubilation or ecstatic nature. Further, many of the elements characteristic of later liturgical practice are rooted in New Testament actions and elements of worship.

Early Christian Worship

It is not just coincidence that the birth of Christ was announced by an outburst of song which is recorded in the first two chapters of Luke. Since that time, the Christian faith has been expressed with joyful music that has not been matched by any religion in history. The four canticles found in Luke are psalmodic in style and are traditionally known by the first words of their Latin translation.

- *Magnificat.* And Mary said, "My soul magnifies the Lord, and my spirit rejoices in God my Savior" (Luke 1:46-55)
- *Benedictus.* Zechariah was filled with the Holy Spirit, and prophesied, saying, "Blessed be the Lord God of Israel" (Luke 1:67-79)
- *Gloria in excelsis Deo.* And suddenly there was with the angel a multitude of the heavenly host praising God and saying, "Glory to God in the highest, and on earth peace among men with whom he is pleased!" (Luke 2:13,14)
- *Nunc Dimittis.* He (Simeon) took him up in his arms and blessed God and said, "Lord, now lettest thou thy servant depart in peace, according to thy word; for mine eyes have seen thy salvation" (Luke 2:28-32).

The Song of Mary, the Song of Zechariah (father of John the Baptist), the Song of the Angels, and the Song of Simeon have been used more in historic Christian worship than any other biblical passages, outside of the Psalms.

After the resurrection and ascension of Christ, the disciples (later including the apostle Paul) continued to meet in the synagogues on the Sabbath as was their custom, giving witness to their faith in the risen Christ as the Jewish Messiah. At the same time, they met on the first day of the week to "remember their Lord" in the celebration of the Eucharist, followed by an agape meal, or love feast. Eventually, it became apparent that their presence would no longer be tolerated in the synagogues, and they began to meet for their own "Christian synagogue" service. In the final evolution of full Christian worship, the synagogue and the Upper Room experiences were united in one two-part service.

Regarding music, it seems clear that first century Christians used three different types of songs: "psalms and hymns and spiritual songs." It is little short of amazing that Paul delineates three different genres of music for worship, mentioning them in two different letters to young churches. We must believe that they were contrasting—in origin, in subject matter, and possibly even in performance practice. This is substantiated by Egon Wellesz, one of the leading authorities on the music of this period.

St. Paul must certainly have been referring to a practice well known to the people to whom he wrote. We may therefore assume that three different types of chant were, in fact, used among them, and we can form an idea of their characteristics from the evidence of Jewish music and later recorded Christian chant:

1. Psalmody: the cantillation of the Jewish psalms and of the canticles and doxologies modelled on them.
2. Hymns: songs of praise of a syllabic type, i.e., each syllable is sung to one or two notes of the melody.
3. Spiritual songs: Alleluia and other chants of a jubilant or ecstatic character, richly ornamented (Egon Wellesz, "Early Christian Music," in *The New Oxford History of Music,* vol. 2, p. 2).

Whether or not Wellesz is correct about the musical character of these forms, the nature and source of the texts seem well established. "Psalms" no doubt included all the psalms and canticles that were common to Jewish worship, in the tabernacle, the temple, and the synagogue. "Hymns" were probably new expressions in song, presenting the doctrine and theology of the church. There are a number of these hymns in the letters of Paul, written in the patterns of classical Greek poetry, and it is reasonable to assume that they were quickly adopted as "Christ songs" by the churches which read the epistles. One is in the form of a simple creed, or statement of faith:

> Great indeed, we confess, is the mystery of our
>   religion:
>   He was manifested in the flesh,
>   vindicated in the Spirit,
>   seen by angels,
>   preached among the nations,
>   believed on in the world,
>   taken up in glory. (1 Tim 3:16)

The poetic (and possibly antiphonal) form is obvious in another:

> The saying is sure:
>   If we have died with him, we shall also live
>   with him;
>   if we endure, we shall also reign with him;
>   if we deny him, he also will deny us;
>   if we are faithless, he remains faithful—
>   for he cannot deny himself. (2 Tim. 2:11-13)

The koine Greek phrase for "spiritual songs" is *odaes pneumaticaes*—"pneumatic odes," or possibly "odes upon the breath" since the same word was used for "breath" and "spirit." Some have conjectured that these were melismatic songs based on acclamations such as "alleluia", "glory", or "holy."

Wellesz connects it with the common practice of most Near Eastern cultures at the beginning of the Christian era. Furthermore, he suggests that it was perpetuated in later Christian worship in the *jubilus* of the mass, the (originally improvised) melismatic prolongation of the final syllable of the "Alleluia." As St. Augustine said of this type of Jewish-Christian song

> It is a certain sound of joy without words . . . it is the expression of a mind poured forth in joy. A man rejoicing in his own exultation, after certain words which cannot be understood, bursteth forth into sounds of exultation without words so that it seemeth that he . . . filled with excessive joy cannot express in words the subject of that joy. (*Nicene & Post-Nicene Fathers,* ser. 1, vol. 8, 488)

We presume that early Christian worship was strictly vocal, since instrumental music was primarily associated with Hebrew temple sacrifices, was probably not used in synagogues, and was abandoned even by the Jews when the temple was destroyed in A.D. 70.

The Functions of Music in the Early Church

The New Testament emphasizes both the human and the divine sources of song. Music flows from human experience, and it no doubt also affects that experience. James seem to suggest that it is most logically associated with the emotion of Christian joy. "Is any one among you suffering? Let him pray. Is any cheerful? Let him sing praise" (James 5:13). In Paul's first letter to Christians at Corinth, one

verse (when read alone) seems to be saying that all musical worship should be equally emotional and cerebral. "I will sing with the spirit and I will sing with the mind also" (1 Cor. 14:15). However, the scriptural context reveals that he is talking about two different experiences. Relating the verse to Ephesians 5:19 and Colossians 3:16, it may be Paul is suggesting that he would sing "hymns" with the mind and "spiritual songs" with the spirit. In any experience of worship, our minds are engaged, no doubt, at different levels at different times; on occasion, perhaps most persons hear music more emotionally than rationally.

All of these functions of music in the early Christian community may be seen to support the expression of Christian faith. One passage in the Authorized Version, "teaching and admonishing one another in psalms" (Col. 3:16), seems to be a clear biblical injunction to use song to learn doctrine and to teach Christian ethics.

The early church sang of the divinity and the work of Christ to express their new faith; at the same time, they were teaching those doctrines to the catechumens, those who were still being trained in the faith but had not yet been baptized.

Finally, and perhaps primarily, we should see Christian song as an offering to God in worship. Paul mentions this specifically in Hebrews 13:15: "Through him [Jesus] then let us continually offer up a sacrifice of praise to God, that is, the fruit of lips that acknowledge his name." This is also emphasized in the two verses in which Paul says so much about musical worship: "singing and making melody to the Lord with all your heart" (Eph. 5:19), and "sing . . . with thankfulness in your hearts to God" (Col. 3:16).

Worship Elements Mentioned in the New Testament

The following is a brief outline of early Christian worship taken from various excerpts of Scripture:

Liturgy of the Word

1. Singing (of various types)—"psalms and hymns and spiritual songs" (Col. 3:16), probably without instrumental accompaniment
2. Prayers—"And they devoted themselves to . . . prayers" (Acts 2:42).
3. Congregational amen—"how can any one in the position of an outsider say "amen" to

your thanksgiving when he does not know what you are saying?" (1 Cor. 14:16).

4. Scripture readings (especially the prophets, and including letters from Paul)—"Till I come, attend to the public reading of Scripture" (1 Tim . 4:13).

5. Homily (exposition)—"On the first day of the week, when we were gathered together to break bread, Paul talked with them . . . and he prolonged his speech until midnight" (Acts 20:7).

6. Physical action—"I desire then that in every place the men should pray, lifting holy hands" (1 Tim. 2:8).

7. Intercession (following the example of Christ in the Upper Room)—"When Jesus had spoken these words, he lifted up his eyes to heaven and said . . . I am not praying for the world but for those whom thou hast given me" (John 17:1, 9).

8. Collection (alms)—"Now concerning the contribution for the saints . . . On the first day of every week, each of you is to put something aside and store it up, as he may prosper, so that contributions need not be made when I come" (1 Cor. 16:1, 2).

Liturgy of the Body and the Blood

9. The kiss of peace (evidently a Jewish practice, continued by early Christians)—"So if you are offering your gift at the altar, and there remember that your brother has something against you, leave your gift there before the altar and go; first be reconciled to your brother" (Matt. 5:23, 24). The phrase "kiss of love" or "holy kiss" is found in Rom. 16:16, 1 Cor. 16:20, 1 Thess. 5:26, and 1 Pet. 5:14.

10. A confession of faith—"take hold of the eternal life to which you were called when you made the good confession in the presence of many witnesses" (1 Tim. 6:12).

11. Thanksgiving (Eucharist)—"And he took bread, and when he had given thanks" (Luke 22:19).

12. Remembrance (*anamnesis,* Gr.)—"Do this, as often as you drink it, in remembrance of me" (1 Cor. 11:25).

13. The anticipation of Christ's return—"For as often as you eat this bread and drink the cup, you proclaim the Lord's death until he comes" (1 Cor. 11:26).

——————— **Summary** ———————

One of the Bible's most significant contributions to church music is the broad spectrum of texts it has left for Christian worship. The psalms and canticles of the Old Testament and of Luke 1 and 2 have been the basis for liturgical expression for almost two thousand years. In addition, the New Testament hymns and many other passages in both Testaments have been used verbatim in anthems, motets and cantatas, and have provided the inspiration for many of our extrabiblical hymns and Christian songs. The Scriptures will always be our best source for worship material; that which is not directly quoted or paraphrased is rightly expected to conform to Bible truth.

By inference, the scriptures also suggest proper functions for today's church music. Both Old and New Testaments reveal a transcendent God who is the object of our adoration. From the New Testament, we understand more of the believer's personal relationship with God through Christ, and also of his fellowship with other saints.

Donald P. Hustad

177 • MUSIC IN THE WORSHIP OF THE EARLY CHURCH

Very little can be said with certainty about the music of the first three centuries of the church beyond texts used and liturgical forms followed. Judging from later music in the Eastern churches and in Gregorian chant in the West, the musical settings of these texts probably shared characteristics with much Eastern music, including tunes in various modes. Ecstatic song continued in the practice of the thanksgiving of the "prophets" in some early liturgies.

It is evident that a set pattern of liturgy emerged at a very early date. In a letter to the Corinthian church (A.D. 96), Clement of Rome included a long, noble prayer which is closely related to eucharistic prayers of later centuries; it also refers to the *Sanctus* (Holy, holy, holy, Lord of hosts . . .), which was a common feature of both Jewish and early Christian worship. The *Didache* (c. A.D. 100) records that the Communion celebration was combined with a common meal (an agape or love feast) and that it was preceded by the confession of sins. It also gives the set prayers that were to be used, along with the encouragement to the "Prophets" to continue in prayer "as much as they desire" (*Didache* X, 7).

At about the same time, the pagan historian Pliny (Governor of Bithynia, *c.* 111–113), in a letter to the Roman emperor Trajan, referred to Christians as "meeting on a fixed day before daylight and reciting responsively among themselves a hymn to Christ as a god, and that they bound themselves by an oath not to commit any crime. . . . When they had performed this it was their custom to depart and to meet together again for a meal, but of a common and harmless kind." The hymn mentioned may well have been one of the New Testament Christological hymns (such as Col. 3:16), or an extrabiblical hymn of the same type.

The Second Century

The first definitive worship order is contained in Justin Martyr's *First Apology* (to the Emperor Antoninus Pius, *c.* 150) in which he describes a typical Christian worship service "on the day called the Feast of the Sun." This outline can be traced clearly:

The Liturgy of the Word
  Readings from the Prophets, and "memoirs of the Apostles" (Gospels and Epistles)
  Sermon (instruction and admonishing)
  Common prayers (the congregation standing, all participating)

The Liturgy of the Eucharist
  Kiss of peace
  Offertory (Alms, bread and wine)
  Prayer of thanksgiving ("at great length" and improvised "according to his ability") followed by a common "amen"
  Communion

The Third Century

Beginning with the third century, we have much more information about the practice of worship in the church. Primary sources of this information include the writings of Clement of Alexandria (d. *c.* 220), Tertullian (d. *c.* 240), and Cyril of Jerusalem (*c.* 313–*c.* 386). One of the most significant records is by Hippolytus of Rome (d. *c.* 236) in a Greek document known as *The Apostolic Tradition.*

The significant feature of this compilation is a complete eucharistic prayer which is suggested as a model for Christian worship, though each leader is encouraged to "pray according to his ability." It is interesting to note that the prayer begins with the Salutation and the Sursum Corda, which were traditional Jewish forms long before they were used by Christians. The *Sanctus* (Holy, holy, holy) is not indicated, though it was in common use by this time. Music (psalms and hymns) are also not mentioned, but were undoubtedly included.

This then is the outline of worship as recorded by Hippolytus, including the biblical concepts mentioned in the eucharistic prayer (see R. C. D. Jasper and G. J. Cuming, eds., *Prayers of the Eucharist: Early and Reformed,* 2d ed. [New York: Oxford University Press, 1980], 22-23):

Liturgy of the Word
  Psalms
  Lessons
  Sermon
  Intercessory Prayers
  Kiss of Peace

Liturgy of the Table
  Offertory (the bread and wine are brought to the table)
  Salutation (responsory, between leader and people)
    The Lord be with you: And with your spirit.
  Sursum Corda
    Lift up your hearts: We lift them up to the Lord.
    Let us give thanks to the Lord: It is meet and right.
  Eucharistic prayer (thanksgiving)
    Salvation history (the Incarnation; Jesus' life, death, and resurrection)
    Words of institution ("He took bread, and giving thanks, . . .")
    Remembrance (Gr. *anamnesis*) ("Remembering therefore his death and resurrection")
    Oblation ("We offer to thee the bread and the cup, . . .")
    Invocation of the Holy Spirit (Gr. *epiklesis*) ("We beseech thee that thou shouldst send thy Holy Spirit, . . .")
    Doxology to the Trinity, with congregational amen
  The Communion
    Presbyter's post-Communion prayer; people's amen
  Bishop's benediction and dismissal

According to the presbyter's closing prayer, the "Holy Mystery" was received, "not for guilt or condemnation, but for the renewal of soul and body and spirit."

The Fourth Century

In the early decades after Christ, the Christian religion was practiced in secret, in adherents' homes, or even in underground catacombs for fear of persecution by Roman authorities. Once the emperor Constantine decreed that Christianity should be tolerated throughout the empire (A.D. 313), the new faith spread like wildfire. It is evident that by this time Christian worship was already developed considerably. The Christian faith was now free to develop its practices openly and to record them in detail for posterity. Larger and larger buildings were erected for the growing congregations, and worship was organized and disciplined to meet the challenge. More and more of the activity (including some of the singing) was given to the clergy, partly to control the occasional outcropping of heresy.

We shall look at one more early worship form, recorded in the Apostolic Constitutions (A.D. *c.* 380). It is called the Clementine Liturgy, since the anonymous book is written "in the name of" Clement, Bishop of Rome at the end of the first century. From Books II and VIII of the Constitutions, this complete service may be reconstructed (see Ibid., 70–79):

The Liturgy of the Word

Scripture Readings (several, from Old and New Testaments, especially the Epistles and Gospels)

Psalms, interspersed with the above (some sung by cantors, some with responses by the congregation)

Sermons (by several of the presbyters)

Dismissal of the catechumens (those under instruction but not yet baptized), the possessed, and the penitents with a Litany and people's response ("Lord, have mercy")

The Liturgy of the Eucharist

Prayers of the faithful

Salutation and response (a Trinitarian benediction, or "The Lord be with you, etc.")

Kiss of peace

Offertory

Washing of hands of the bishop and presbyters

Offering of the bread and wine and of alms

"Fencing" of the table (to forbid participation by the unworthy)

Robing of the bishop in "a splendid vestment"; he then makes the "sign of the cross" on his forehead.

The eucharistic prayer (*Anaphora*)

Sursum Corda ("Up with your mind . . .")

Preface: Thanks for all of God's providence, beginning with creation, the provision of all things for life on earth, and the history of God's dealings with his people

Sanctus ("Holy, holy, holy, Lord God of hosts . . .")

Thanksgiving for the incarnation and redemption

The words of institution: "For on the night he was betrayed, he took bread in his holy and blameless hands and, looking up to you, his God and Father, he broke it. . . . Likewise he also mixed the cup of wine and water and sanctified it. . . . Do this for my remembrance . . . until I come."

Anamnesis and oblation

Epiklesis: ". . . send down your Holy Spirit upon this sacrifice, the witness of the sufferings of the Lord Jesus, that he may make this bread body of your Christ, and this cup blood of your Christ; that those who partake may be strengthened to piety, obtain forgiveness of sins, be delivered from the devil and his deceit, be filled with the Holy Spirit, become worthy of your Christ, and obtain eternal life."

Prayer of intercession (ten sections)

Doxology and people's amen

The Lord's Prayer

Bidding prayers led by the deacon, and bishop's prayer

The call to Communion: "Holy things to the holy people" with response: "One is holy, one is Lord, Jesus Christ, to the glory of God the Father, blessed to the ages. Amen."

Gloria in excelsis: "Glory to God in the highest, and peace on earth, goodwill among men."

Hosanna and benedictus qui venit (Matt. 21:9): "Hosanna to the Son of David: Blessed is he who comes in the name of the Lord. God is Lord and is manifested to us: Hosanna in the highest."

Communion, with the singing of Psalm 34 ("O taste and see that the Lord is good")

Bishop's thanksgiving for communion and intercession followed by prayer and blessing

Dismissal

It is apparent here that the Liturgy of the Eucharist was a highly significant part of public liturgy, although it may not have taken as long to perform as the Liturgy of the Word (with its multiple Scripture readings, a number of psalms, and several sermons).

A spirit of fear and dread connected with receiving holy Communion unworthily eventually discouraged worshipers from participation in Communion. Over the next few centuries, participation dwindled, and most people took Communion only once a year, as they were obliged to do.

The Church Year

In the most ancient expressions of the church's worship, God is revealed through Scripture and sermon in the Liturgy of the Word, and in Communion in the Liturgy of the Eucharist. Furthermore, the macrocosm of God's revelation throughout history is shown in the shape of the liturgical year recorded in the liturgical calendar.

In the West, the church year begins with Advent (starting four Sundays before Christmas), a time of penitence in anticipation of the coming of Christ, a time when believers remember God's acts in creation, in the history of the Jewish people, and in the prophecies and the events leading up to Christ's incarnation. Christmas (December 25) and Epiphany (January 6) celebrate God's self-revealing in Christ; the first of these is undoubtedly related calendrically to the Jewish Feast of Lights (Hanukkah) and the Christian transformation of the pagan celebration of the winter solstice into Christmas. The season of Lent (forty days before Easter) beginning with Ash Wednesday, is a high period of penitence in preparation for Holy Week, recalling Christ's forty days of temptation, and Israel's forty years of wandering in the desert. Holy Week (Palm Sunday through Easter) follows the last days of Christ's earthly ministry, including his triumphal entry, death, and resurrection. Easter is often called the "Christian Passover" (*Pascha*) because of its similarity to the Jewish holiday, revealing the Christian's deliverance from the bondage of sin and death. Pentecost (a name taken directly from the Jewish festival of "first fruits") commemorates the sending of the Holy Spirit and the establishing of the church; this event begins the second half of the church year. In this final season (called variously "The Weeks after Pentecost," "The Season of the Holy Spirit," "The Church Season," "Ordinary Time," or in England—where the season is reckoned from the Sunday after Pentecost, Trinity Sunday—"Trinity Season") the emphasis is on God's purposes for the church in this "age of grace" through the empowering of the Holy Spirit.

In each period and on each particular day of the church year, the Scripture readings (lections), the prayers, and the sermons are different to match the theological emphasis of that season and day.

Witness Music in The Early Christian Era

Post-biblical writings of the early church fathers suggest that Syrian (Antiochian) churches may have been first to develop a corpus of Christian hymnody. In the conflict over the teaching of Arius (c. 250–366), both orthodox and heterodox used popular hymns to support their arguments. In the East in northern Mesopotamia, Ephraem Syrus (born c. 307), so successfully advanced the anti-Arian cause that he was called "the cithern of the Holy Spirit." In the West, Ambrose of Milan (c. 340–397) countered the Arian hymns with his own doctrinally pure texts. He also developed a simple, rhythmic, and syllabic chant which had strong appeal to the masses of unsophisticated worshipers.

Perhaps the only overt reference to musical evangelism in the early church is a statement about Nicetas of Remesiana (c. 335–c. 414), a missionary to Dacia (now part of Yugoslavia), who is given credit for writing the immortal Latin hymn *Te Deum laudamus.* Jerome (c. 340–420) says that Nicetas spread the gospel among fourth century European pagans "chiefly by singing sweet songs of the cross."

Donald P. Hustad

178 ◆ The Orthodox Churches

Christians in North America are often unaware of one of the largest and most devoted segments of the Christian church, the Orthodox churches. During the first few centuries A.D., the church remained largely unified. But eventually, a variety of doctrinal and political disputes led to the separation of the church into roughly two main divisions, East and West. The following article traces the history of the Eastern church.

It is impossible not to be profoundly moved by the liturgy of our own Orthodox church. I also love vespers. To stand on a Saturday evening in the twilight in some little country church, filled with the smoke of incense; to lose oneself in the eternal questions, whence, why and whither; to be startled from one's trance by a burst from the choir; to be carried away by the poetry of this music; to be thrilled with quiet rapture when the Royal Gates of the Iconostasis are flung open and words ring out, "Praise the Name of the Lord!"—all this is infinitely precious to me! One of my deepest joys! (Peter Tchaikovsky, letter to Nadejda von Meck, quoted in V. Volkoff, _Tchaikovsky_ [London, 1975], 169–170.)

So wrote the composer Tchaikovsky in 1877. To enter an Orthodox church, to experience its music, is to enter another world. The Orthodox have a long and sometimes turbulent history, full of divisions and schisms, yet their music has a timeless quality and a changeless beauty.

Constantine and Christianity

It was the new status of Christianity as a state religion in the fourth century that first caused serious problems. The conversion of the Emperor Constantine and the spread of Christianity as a "state religion" throughout the Roman Empire brought into focus issues of doctrine and uniformity. This led to the setting up of the Council of Nicaea (325), and further councils in the fourth and fifth centuries, eventually leading to the division of the Roman church from the Orthodox.

Following the Emperor Constantine's adoption of Byzantium as the center of his new Christian empire (he renamed the city Constantinople), the city quickly became the center of Orthodox Christianity. Relations with neighboring Armenia (whose king Tiridates III was converted to Christianity even earlier than Constantine, in 301) were good until the Chalcedon Council of 451, to which the Armenians were unable to send representatives. The Armenians disagreed with the decisions made in their absence and were thereafter branded as heretic by the Orthodox bishops. The same council failed to reconcile the Coptic and Ethiopian churches to orthodoxy, and they also broke away.

The Five Patriarchs

By the fifth century authority in the Christian world was in the hands of five patriarchs whose centers were Rome, Constantinople, Alexandria, Antioch and Jerusalem. Their jurisdiction extended to numerous districts presided over by metropolitans. The intention was for the patriarchs' authority to be equal, but the constant rivalry between them strengthened their frontiers, particularly between East and West. Through the turbulence in the East— the many divisions and sects, the adherence to heresy—Rome, by contrast, proved to be a center of some stability, to whom other patriarchs could appeal for dispassionate advice over local disagreements.

The patriarchs of Rome grew ever more aware of the importance of their apostolic succession through St. Peter and believed more and more in the additional authority that this gave them over the other patriarchies. This supremacy was eventually claimed to be absolute, but this claim has never been recognized by the East.

The saddest aspect of this most serious division is the issue that lay at its heart. As before at the earlier councils, it was a question of creed. John's Gospel states that the Holy Spirit, the third member of the Trinity, "comes from the Father." Western Christians were required to accept a creed which stated that the Holy Spirit proceeds from the Father "and the Son" _(filioque)_. On this difference and the question of authority was built a controversy which finally (in 1054) became the chief justification of a permanent schism between the church of Rome and the churches of the East.

The Crusades

The incessant arguments over doctrinal matters may seem trivial, but they had very real consequences in the appalling suffering of the common people caught up with one faction or another.

The Crusades proved to be a further disaster both to the credibility and unity of the Christian faith. They began both as pilgrimages and holy wars, bent on rescuing the most precious Christian sites from the Muslims. In the First Crusade of 1095, a Christian army from the West wrested control of Jerusalem from the Muslims after great bloodshed in 1099. But the Fourth Crusade (1202–04) was disastrously directed against Constantinople—Western Christian fighting Eastern Christian. During Holy Week of 1204, Constantinople was sacked and looted by a Christian European army. Many of the spoils found their way back to Europe, where they contributed to the fabulous wealth of such cities as Venice.

Although the reunion of East and West was discussed again, the Eastern Church was too exasperated by the forcible occupation of Constantinople to be able to negotiate. Such carnage, based ultimately on greed, turned the gospel on its head.

The Strength of Orthodoxy

Constantinople was restored as the center of Eastern Christendom and the Byzantine Empire in 1261, but it was much weakened and gradually gave way to the Turks over the next two centuries. During the fourteenth century the emperor unsuccessfully implored the assistance of the West, hoping that the offer of reunion with Rome could be exchanged for the Western church's help. Nothing was forthcoming. The gradual decline of the Byzantine Empire led eventually to the conquest of Constantinople by the Turks in 1453.

Curiously enough, the downfall of Constantinople temporarily increased the authority of the Orthodox church under its patriarch, for the Turks who now ruled allowed them freedom to worship, if not to make converts or to display Christian symbols (like the cross) on their churches. And the Turks naturally identified religious leadership with national identity.

Under these conditions the patriarchs of Constantinople retained—and even gained—power and respect. But on the other hand they lived through five centuries of Turkish rule which proved to be perilous. Many patriarchs were driven from their thrones by the Turks, some abdicated, some were murdered. But the Christians clung to the faith with remarkable tenacity through their example and through the pastoral care of the country priests.

The people of the Orthodox church have also had the advantage of a liturgy which has remained in a language well understood by them and of a church in which they feel truly at home.

Orthodoxy Today

Of the four ancient Orthodox patriarchies, only that of Constantinople has been discussed so far. But the other three, established at the very beginnings of the Christian faith, are still in existence, though their sphere of influence is not what it once was. The Orthodox patriarchy of Alexandria (established by St. Mark) is now small (perhaps 250,000) as most Christians in Egypt are members of the independent Coptic church. The region of this patriarchy also covers countries like Saudi Arabia and Libya, which are nowadays almost wholly Muslim.

Antioch at the time of its conversion was an immensely important center, politically and economically. Its patriarchy was established at a very early stage in Christian history (earlier than A.D. 45) but down the ages Christians in the region have become independent (such as the church of Cyprus) or heretical (such as the Jacobites and Nestorians). Many Christians in the region are now Uniate (that is, they owe their allegiance to Rome). All this has eroded the influence of Antioch as a center of Orthodoxy.

Jerusalem is such a vital and emotive center for Jews, Christians, and Muslims that its Orthodox patriarchy has inevitably seen great turbulence. This is the church whose traditions Egeria described at the start of the fifth century. Even then the city was a center of pilgrimage for many faiths. The church in Jerusalem has striven to keep the peace under these most difficult circumstances.

The Orthodox church also consists of a number of other branches, all of whom are now independent, though they use a very similar liturgy in their appropriate languages. The church of Cyprus became independent in 431, the church of Russia in 1589. Greece remained under Turkish rule with only interruption (1684–1718) from the fifteenth century to the nineteenth. Modern Greece came into being in 1829, following the defeat of the Turks by Britain, France, and Russia in the naval battle of Navarino. Shortly after, in 1833, the independent Orthodox Church of Greece was created, with its metropolitan in Athens. Later in the nineteenth century the Orthodox churches of Bulgaria, Yugoslavia, and Romania also became independent.

Andrew Wilson-Dickson[12]

179 • MUSIC IN THE BYZANTINE TRADITION

Music for worship in the Byzantine Orthodox tradition is thought to be a direct descendent of the music used in the synagogues during the life of Jesus. The Orthodox have a very high, almost sacramental, view of music, believing that it is a "window to heaven." Music is intrinsic to the liturgy of the church, for it is frequently used to express the liturgical text.

Historical Development

While some scholars would speculate that the music of the ancient church was a survival of the old classical Greek music, most have taken the position that the music of the ancient church is primarily a legacy from the music of the synagogue.

This affirms the conviction that Christ handed down to his apostles not only the rule of faith (the Doctrine of the Apostles) but also the rule of prayer (the Worship of the Apostles). We find in the Gospels that Christ and his disciples regularly attended the synagogue, and that after Pentecost, the disciples continued to attend the synagogue until they were no longer allowed to attend because of persecution. The melodies sung in the synagogue were near, no doubt, to the hearts of Christ's disciples, and they took these melodies with them into the Christian gatherings which followed a similar order of worship.

The best scholarship indicates that the ruling principle of church music of the early Byzantine era was formulary rather than modal. This means that the music was grouped by melodic characteristics or formulas (motives) rather than by scale or mode. This music of the ancient church was most likely preserved through the oral transmission of melodies from one generation to another until the eighth century, at which time a system of eight tones (or modes) was developed by St. John of Damascus as a basis for collecting these melodies into eight major groups.

Theological Foundations of Byzantine Music

The hymnody of the Byzantine church is theologically the richest in the world. One can learn a great deal about the church's doctrine and life by carefully and prayerfully singing or contemplating the hymns of the church. In his essay, _Sacred Music,_ Constantine Cavarnos explains the purpose of Byzantine sacred music in worship.

The aim of this music is not to display the fine voices of the chanters, or to entertain the congregation, or to evoke aesthetic experience. Indeed, the chanters who sing it must have good voices. . . . Good execution [is not sought for its] own sake; and the pleasure it evokes is not an end it deliberately seeks, but something incidental, and further, is not mere aesthetic pleasure but something much richer and higher. The aim of Byzantine sacred music is spiritual. This music is, in the first place, a means of worship and veneration; and in the second place, a means of self-perfection, of eliciting and cultivating man's higher thoughts and feelings, and of opposing and eliminating his lower, undesirable ones.

The use of this music as a means of worship consists in employing it to glorify God, and to express feelings of supplication, hope, gratitude, and love to Him. Its use as a means of veneration consists in employing it to honor the Holy Virgin and the rest of the saints. Its use as a means of cultivating higher thoughts and feelings and opposing the lower ones is inseparable from these. There is not one kind of music employed as a means of worshiping God and honoring the saints, and another kind employed for transforming our inner life, but the same music while having as its direct aim the former, incidentally leads also to the fulfillment of the latter. For while glorifying God and honoring the saints by means of psalms and hymns, or while listening to others chant while we do so in our hearts, feelings such as sadness, hatred, anger, and torpor [laziness] subside, and feelings such as contrition, love, peace, and spiritual joy and aspiration are aroused." (Constantine Cavarnos, "Sacred Music," in _Byzantine Thought and Art_ [Belmont, Mass.: The Institute for Byzantine and Modern Greek Studies, 1968, reprint 1980], 97–98)

In his book _Russian Church Singing,_ Johann Von Gardner points out the inseparability of worship and singing: "The Russians of past centuries referred to worship as 'singing.' 'To go to sing' meant the same as 'to go to worship.' 'It's the time for singing, it's the hour for prayer! Lord Jesus Christ, our God, have mercy on us!'" (Johann Von Gardner, "Orthodox Worship and Hymnography," in _Russian Church Singing,_ vol. 1 [Crestwood, N.Y.: St. Vladimir's Seminary Press, 1980], 25).

The Music of Heaven

Byzantine composers worked within the framework of Orthodox theology, which taught that the prototypes of the melodies were the songs of praise of the angels, inaudible to human ears, but transmitted and made audible by the inspired hymnographers. For instance, we know from Scripture that the continual worship around the throne of God includes the song of the angels: "Holy, Holy, Holy, Lord of Hosts. Heaven and earth are filled with Your glory" (Isa. 6:3). The role of the composer was to make audible that inaudible melody of heaven. Such a task was accomplished through prayer and supplication, and revealed by God to the pure in heart.

But even then, the composer was not left merely to ecstatic or spontaneous inspiration. He worked within the system, that is, within the context of melodic formulas that had been passed down by his predecessors. To work within the framework of traditional melodic formulas was to take an ultraconservative view of one's function as a composer. It implied a deep-seated respect for tradition, but was at the same time an enormously sophisticated way of working, susceptible to infinite refinement.

The beauty and spirituality of such music must have surpassed anything we can imagine. The account of the followers of Prince Vladimir who visited the Moslem Bulgars of Volga, the Christian church in Germany and Rome and finally, the Church of the Holy Wisdom (*Hagia Sophia*) in Constantinople in search of a true religion for their people, illustrates the point:

> There is a story in the Russian Primary Chronicle of how Vladimir, Prince of Kiev, while still a pagan, desired to know which was the true religion, and therefore sent his followers to visit the various countries of the world in turn. They went first to the Moslem Bulgars of the Volga, but observing that these when they prayed gazed around them like men possessed, the Russians continued on their way dissatisfied. "There is no joy among them," they reported to Vladimir, "but mournfulness and a great smell; and there is nothing good about their systems." Traveling next to Germany and Rome, they found the worship more satisfactory, but complained that here too it was without beauty. Finally they journeyed to Constantinople, and here at last, as they attended the Divine Liturgy in the great Church of the Holy Wisdom, they discovered what they desired. "We knew not whether we were in heaven or on earth, for surely there is no such splendor or beauty anywhere upon earth. We cannot describe it to you: only this we know, that God dwells there among men, and that their service surpasses the worship of all other places. For we cannot forget that beauty." (Timothy Ware, *The Orthodox Church* [New York: Penguin Books, 1963], 269)

Cultural Influences

The modern system we hear today in churches that are rooted in the Byzantine tradition is radically different from the medieval system. Medieval Byzantine chant was wholly diatonic, that is, it could be played with sufficient accuracy on modern keyboard instruments. The Gregorian system, which is also diatonic, was derived from the medieval Byzantine system, but used different names for the eight tones and developed along different lines.

The modern Byzantine (Chrysanthine) system de-veloped in 1821 includes chromatic and enharmonic scales in addition to the diatonic. The whole fabric is not Greek at all but is Oriental, i.e., Arabo-Turkish. Yet the church accepted these cultural influences as appropriate and beneficial. For instance, the Russian eight-tone system began with the Byzantine eight-tone system as a basis, but developed over a period of 200 years into its own cultural and national expression of church music.

In our day, it would seem profitable to study and learn the Byzantine system of eight tones since it dates back to biblical times and finds its roots in the music of the synagogue and temple worship. Further, it would be important to analyze its development in different cultural settings through the ages. Such a study would undoubtedly find its application in adapting and developing this system of church music that truly reveals the worship of heaven to our present cultural situation.

John David Finley

180 • CHURCH MUSIC IN THE GREEK ORTHODOX CHURCH

Almost the entire Orthodox liturgy is sung, most often to centuries-old melodic formulas. In addition to chanted liturgical texts, hymns play an important role in Greek Orthodox worship. Over 60,000 hymns, following one of a variety of prescribed patterns, have been written for use in these churches. Though local custom may influence the way in which this music is chanted, most singing follows traditional practice.

Music is uniquely integrated into the worshiping traditions of the Eastern churches. In the Orthodox churches music and liturgy are interdependent. In well-endowed churches the singing is by choirs; in a humble village church, the priest and people sing. Following the injunctions of the church fathers, musical instruments have never been accepted. The sound of the human voice raised in song is central. As Basil the Great wrote as far back as the fourth century:

> A psalm is tranquillity of soul and the arbitration of peace; it settles one's tumultuous and seething thoughts. . . . A psalm creates friendships, unites the separated and reconciles those at enmity. Who can still consider one to be a foe with whom one utters the same prayer to God! Thus Psalmody provides

the greatest of all goods, charity by . . . joining together the people into the concord of a single chorus. (J. McKinnon, _Music in Early Christian Literature_ [Cambridge, U.K.: Cambridge University Press, 1987], 65–66)

The church year and its fasts, feasts and celebrations dominates national and home life in a way that is difficult for the Westerner to appreciate:

Nobody who has lived and worshipped among Greek Christians for any length of time has but sensed in some measure the extraordinary hold which the recurring cycle of the church's liturgy has upon the piety of the common people. Nobody who has kept the Great Lent . . . who has shared in the fast which lies heavy on the nation for forty days . . . who has known the desolation of the holy and great Friday, when every bell in Greece tolls its lament and the body of the Saviour lies shrouded in flowers in all the village churches . . . who has been present at the kindling of the new fire and tasted the joy of a world released from the bondage of sin and death—none can have lived through this and not have realised that for the Greek Christian the Gospel is inseparably linked with the liturgy that is unfolded week by week in his parish church. (R. Hammond, _The Waters of Marah_ [London, 1956], 51–52)

Monastic traditions of worship are very strong in the East, and the twenty monastic foundations on Mount Athos in Greece form its cornerstone. For them, life is governed by Daily Offices similar to those of the Western monastic tradition, but for churches in towns and villages only extracts from the full monastic liturgy are celebrated. The most important of these is the Divine Liturgy (that is, Mass or Communion), the central act of worship on Sundays and feast days. The people do not receive Communion without initial preparation and fasting.

The Divine Liturgy

There are three liturgies used by the Orthodox churches today. The Liturgy of St. John Chrysostom is in common use throughout the year; the Liturgy of St. Basil is rather more elaborate and is used only on Christmas Eve and at Epiphany; the Liturgy of St. James (the oldest of the three) is heard only rarely.

The Divine Liturgy of the Orthodox church follows the pattern of worship that has changed little in 1,500 years. It may be interesting to compare its outline with that of Egeria's experience of Mass in fifth-century Jerusalem and the outline of the later Roman Mass.

It cannot be stressed enough how important a role music plays in the liturgy. Apart from the sermon, the silent prayers and perhaps the creed, everything is sung.

Chanting

The simplest type of chanting can be heard in the Scripture readings, declaimed to a single note with deviations related to the punctuation. Between about the eighth and thirteenth centuries a simple but unique method was used to indicate the way in which the pitch of the reader's voice had to be raised or lowered. This _ekphonetic_ (exclamatory) notation consisted of signs written above the beginnings and endings of sentences, although their meanings are still not completely understood. Today ekphonetic notations are still used in some Eastern churches and in the Jewish synagogue.

The psalms used in the Divine Liturgy and those which also form the backbone of the Daily Office are sung to chants belonging to one of eight modes. These modes are similar to those of Western medieval music, being scale-systems whose finals (like key-notes) are the notes D, E, F and G.

Psalm-singing is elaborated to a similar degree to Western chant. More interestingly, the eight modes are incorporated into the church's year.

For symbolic reasons buried in antiquity the modes of Byzantine chant are governed by an eight-weekly cycle, the eight modes being changed Sunday by Sunday until the cycle is begun afresh. The systematic organization of all chants into the eight modes is called the _oktoechos_.

Perhaps the most interesting feature of the modes is the tendency of music written in any one mode to develop a unique character through the use of stock melodic ideas or formulae, a practice known as centonization. This is a feature of many types of music which are created aurally rather than composed on paper.

There is evidence of centonization in Gregorian chant and it is an essential part of Indian classical music, where a _rag_ is given its character not just by the notes of the scales used, but by the melodic ideas used as the basis for improvisation. African master-drumming is based on the same principle, and it is inherent in contemporary jazz.

Hymns

One of the most striking musical features of Orthodox worship must be its hymns, which have been composed in huge numbers from the fourth century onwards. One compilation lists at least 60,000 (Follieri, *Initia Hymnorum Ecclesiae Gracae,* quoted in the *New Grove Dictionary of Music and Musicians* [London, 1980], under the entry "Byzantine Rite"). Byzantine hymns have traditional structures which all have their proper place in the liturgy.

The simplest hymns are one verse long and called *troparia* (singular *troparion*). Originally these were short poetic prayers inserted between the verses of a psalm and set to simple music easily memorized by a congregation.

Kontakia are much more extended hymns, being built up of many verses—perhaps thirty or more. They are based on a number of traditional patterns (called *hirmoi*) which govern the numbers of lines for each verse and the number of syllables and their stresses in each line. The beginning letters of each verse make an acrostic that may spell out the name of the author, or the day and feast for which the *kontakion* was intended, or perhaps the musical mode to which it was sung. Each verse has a short refrain suitable for participation by choir or congregation. Many *kontakia* were composed by Romanus in the sixth century.

Kanones became the most complex of all Byzantine hymns and replaced *kontakia* around the eighth century. In full they consist of nine sections (called odes), the subject of each being based on nine biblical songs:

- Exodus 15:1-19
- Deuteronomy 32:1-43
- 1 Samuel 2:1-10
- Isaiah 26:9-19
- Daniel 3:26-45 and 52-56 (including the deuterocanonical section)
- Daniel 3:57-88 (including the deuterocanonical section)
- Jonah 2:3-10
- Habakkuk 3:2-19
- Luke 1:46-55 (Magnificat)
- Luke 1:68-79 (Benedictus)

As with the *kontakia,* the odes consist of a verse from a traditional source (the *hirmos*) followed by a number of *troparia* modeled on it.

Each ode is sung to a different melody. In practice, *kanones* in their full form are very long and are only heard nowadays at the important yearly feasts and then only in monasteries and cathedrals. They are sung during the Morning Office and split into three parts (odes 1 to 3, 4 to 6, and 7 to 9). (A glance at the subject matter will suggest why it is included only during Lent.) Between these parts are inserted hymns and a reading. Usually *kanones* are drastically shortened so that only the initial *hirmoi* are sung.

Stichera were a later development of the *troparia*—hymns sung after a verse of a psalm. In this respect they are similar to Western antiphons. They are divided into different categories according to their subject and the feast for which they are appropriate.

In the last few centuries of the Byzantine Empire, expert singers and composers—*maistores*—developed a highly elaborate style of *kalophonic* singing, beautifying the already elaborate chant. The names and compositions of these *maistores* are known today, Joannes Koukouzeles (about 1280–1370) being the most revered (he is a saint of the Greek Orthodox Church). This unique singing tradition even had a competitive element, *maistores* rivaling each other in their spectacular elaborations of a given text. The *kalophonic* tradition lasted until the nineteenth century, when Chrysanthos of Madytos revised and simplified the chant to bring it back into closer touch with the common people.

The Byzantine Chant Today

How is Byzantine chant performed today? The answer of course depends on where it is performed, but under no circumstances will it be heard with musical instruments. In a village church there may very well be no choir, and the chanting will be undertaken by the local priest. If the priest himself is not available, a lay reader will be able to take the role of *psaltes* (cantor), for the music will be very familiar to regular churchgoers.

In a few city churches in Athens it is still possible to hear Byzantine chant harmonized in a manner developed in the seventeenth and eighteenth centuries, but in most monasteries and cathedrals this is not the case. Here the music will be sung in the long-established manner by two choirs standing on either side of the chancel, the left-hand choir led by the *lampadarios* and right-hand by the *protopsaltes.* The right-hand choir tends to have the more skilled singers and handles more complex music, though much of the music is antiphonal, the music moving from one choir to the other and back again. Highly skilled cantors will sing the most complex chants (such as the _prokeimenon_) as solos.

In many monastic choirs (such as that of the Monastery of Saint Simon on Mount Athos) a tradition of two-part singing is preserved. In reality the second part is not melodic but consists of held notes rather like a drone, a practice dating from about the seventeenth century. The upper part keeps to the traditional chant.

The language used by the church for its traditional music is the Greek of the very earliest years of Christianity, very different from modern Greek, but nonetheless understood and revered by churchgoers.

The music of course has changed since its creation in those early times. How much it still resembles the music of the ancient Byzantine Empire is a difficult question which cannot be answered easily (see M. P. Dragoumis, "The Survival of Byzantine Chant" in E. Wellesz, ed. _Studies in Eastern Chant,_ vol. 1 [Oxford, 1966], 9). But considering the enormous time span from their composition to modern times, the correspondence between ancient manuscripts and the present-day chant is remarkable.

Andrew Wilson-Dickson[13]

181 ✦ CHURCH MUSIC IN THE RUSSIAN ORTHODOX CHURCH

While small segments of the Russian Orthodox Church have continued to use only traditional Byzantine chant in their worship, the larger portions of the church have allowed music that is a hybrid between traditional liturgical chants and the popular art music of a given historical period. This music has remained distinctively liturgical and Russian, but has led many to lament the loss of traditional forms.

The history of Christianity in Russia began properly with the baptism of Vladimir, Emperor of Kiev, into the Orthodox Christian faith in 988. As did the Roman Emperor Constantine long before him, he proclaimed: "Whosoever he be, who will not come to the river tomorrow to be baptized, be he rich or poor, will fall into disgrace with me" (N. Zernov, _Eastern Christendom_ [London, 1961], 112). In the following year he married the Byzantine emperor's

sister, cementing a relationship with the empire at the height of its power.

The History

For some time the metropolitans of the Russian church were mostly Greeks appointed by the patriarch of Constantinople. Only in the fifteenth century did the Russian church begin to make decisions for itself.

By this time, the Byzantine liturgy was firmly established with little alteration except for its translation into Slavonic, which is the language still used by the Russian Orthodox Church today.

During the period of the Tartar occupation of Russia (1240–1461) Christianity survived. In 1272 the Tartars had embraced the Islamic faith, but—like the Turks who later occupied Byzantium—they were tolerant of Christian "People of the Book" (the Old Testament). A century after the fall of Constantinople and the end of the Byzantine Empire, the Russians appointed their first patriarch in Moscow in 1589.

From that time the Russian church had to face constant difficulties. Among them was the Time of Troubles, a civil war which followed the death of the Emperor Boris Godunov in 1605. Worse, perhaps, were the failed ambitions of Nikon (patriarch from 1652-66) for the supremacy of the church over the state, resulting in the Great Schism and leaving the church under the thumb of Tsarist rule.

The most recent catastrophe was the Bolshevik Revolution of 1917. The long history of the church's allegiance to the Tsar inevitably marked it out for special treatment by the Bolsheviks, who worked hard to diminish the church's authority as much as possible. Sadly, they were assisted by some church leaders prepared to further the Communist cause.

The patriarch Tikhon was arrested in 1923, and determined attempts were made to undermine the church economically (church valuables and buildings were confiscated by the state) and spiritually (monasteries were dissolved, restrictions were placed on religious gatherings, religious teaching in schools was forbidden, and more than a thousand priests were martyred in the first years of the Revolution).

The Second World War gave the Communists a short-lived awareness of how the church could be used to stir up patriotism, but the Khrushchev era renewed the pressures and penalties on those who openly confessed the Christian faith. In spite of the constant oppression, the recent collapse of Communism has revealed the churches of Russia and Eastern Europe to be very much alive and rejoicing in a new-found freedom of worship.

The Music of the Russian Orthodox Church

The liturgy of Russian Orthodoxy is very closely allied to that of the Byzantine church; many of the general remarks made about the worship of Greek Orthodox Christians in the previous article apply equally to the Russians.

The music, however, is very noticeably different. The reasons often cited include the loss or corruption of early chants and the church's current perception of traditional or "canonical" music, as it is termed.

The ancient chant of the Russian church, like the Greek, was written down in a notation similar in principle to the Byzantine, and manuscripts go back as far as the eleventh century. From these it is clear that the chant was a single melody just like Gregorian or Byzantine chant, and to begin with (according to the scholar Preobrazhensky) the melodies were Byzantine, too. The translation of the Greek liturgy into the Slavonic language and its transplantation into a different culture rapidly changed its music to something unlike any other tradition. The name given to this collection of chant was *znamenny raspev* (chanting by signs), now known simply as *znamenny*.

Although the old books still exist in great numbers, the symbols used in the notation are ambiguous, and the earliest versions of these ancient melodies cannot yet be sung with accuracy. During the seventeenth century the now-familiar Western notation was brought to Russia (together with many other Western innovations) and a few of the traditional melodies were copied out. Unfortunately, the incentive at the time was for drastic reform, imposed by the Patriarch Nikon.

The changes included the adoption of a new Western style of music, sung in a Baroque harmonic style. This so incensed a number of Christians that they separated themselves from the church altogether in order to continue the old traditions. (The transition to the new music during the seventeenth century is well-documented in A. J. Swan, *Russian Music and Its Sources in Chant and Folksong* [London, 1973], 48ff. For a study of *znammenny*, see J. Gardner, *Russian Church Singing* [New York,

1980], and J. L. Roccasalvo, *The Plainchant Tradition of Southwestern Rus'* [New York, 1986].)

Miraculously, adherents to the old way are still worshiping today and are known as the Old Believers. They have no priests but worship together in isolated parts of the Ural mountains and in Siberia. They have also emigrated to Canada and the United States and continue their worship there.

The Old Believers are the only Christians who still sing the *znamenny* chant in anything like its true form. Another type of chant, now even less accessible than *znamenny*, was *demestvenny*, a highly decorative chant for solo voice used for special feast days. In its elaboration it paralleled the *kalophonic* chant of the Byzantine church.

From the seventeenth century on, Russian church music is much more akin to the West than the East. Nikolai Diletsky (about 1630–90) was a musician from Kiev who had studied in Poland (where Italian music was well known). He promoted Western styles of church music through his own compositions and text books.

The following generation of Diletsky's pupils included Kalashnikov, who wrote sumptuous settings of texts for Vespers which he called Sacred Concertos. These are pieces for up to four choirs and in as many as twenty-four parts; their imitative effects are reminiscent of the polychoral music of Gabrieli and Monteverdi in Venice a century earlier. In such pieces all connection with the tradition of *znamenny* chant was lost.

By the close of the eighteenth century Italian opera had been firmly established in Russia with its consequent importation of skilled and professional foreign musicians. Conversely, Russian musicians of the Court Chapel such as Berezovsky (1745–77) and Bortniansky (1751–1825) had the opportunity to study in Italy. While they did not use Italian operatic styles in their Christian music, they nonetheless brought the technical skills of counterpoint and harmony to bear on it. Many of their works are settings of psalm texts and are masterpieces of concentrated economy and intensity in choral writing.

But the character of Russian church music today owes more to the nineteenth century than to any other period. It was dominated by Fyodor L'vov and his son Alexy (1798–1870 and musical director of the Court Chapel for twenty-five years), Pyotor Turchaninov, and many others. They created the sonorous and sometimes sentimental style of singing associated with Russian liturgical music, sometimes dubbed the "St. Petersburg style."

The chants used in the Court Chapel were simplified and shortened versions of traditional melodies and these romantic and rhetorical harmonizations of them were published in an edition of the *obikhod* (Canticles of the Ordinary) in 1848. They were thus disseminated throughout Russia and are still the basis of Russian Orthodox music today. It is most unfortunate that the Russian church has come to identify its musical traditions so closely with these chants (and, even worse, with the wooden and uninspiring contributions of Bakhmetyev).

At that time Russian art music was beginning a most exciting period of natural development, beginning with Glinka and culminating in the music of the Russian Five—Rimsky-Korsakov, Borodin, Cui, Balakirev, and Mussorgsky. Tragically, none of these composers made any impact on the music of their national church.

The difference between the sentimental harmonies of L'vov and the spectacular world of Russian symphonies and ballets must have seemed an unbridgeable gap. Only one great composer of that time made a serious and single-minded contribution to Orthodox church music, and he was taken to court for doing so.

———— Tchaikovsky's *Liturgy* ————

On 30 April 1878, Tchaikovsky wrote to his confidante Nadejda von Meck:

> If the favourable mood lasts long enough, I want to do something in the way of church music. A vast and almost untrodden field of activity lies open to composers here. I appreciate certain merits in Bortiansky, Berezovsky and others; but how little their music is in keeping with the Byzantine architecture, the ikons, and the whole spirit of the Orthodox liturgy! . . . It is not improbable that I shall decide to set the entire liturgy of St. John Chrysostom. (R. Newmarch, ed., *The Life and Letters of P. I. Tchaikovsky* [London, 1906], 298–299)

The Court Chapel held a monopoly on the publication of all church music (a fact that contributed greatly to its musical sterility) so, having gained approval from the Ecclesiastical Censors of his new setting of the *Liturgy of St. John Chrysostom,* Tchaikovsky published abroad. Bakhmetyev, the director of music of the Court Chapel, immediately protested and the publisher Jurgenson was taken to court. After two years, Tchaikovsky and his publisher won the case and litigation finally forced Bakhmetyev to resign.

Tchaikovsky's *Liturgy* is a work of simplicity and restraint, artistically far in advance of anything of which the Chapel composers were capable. At the same time it takes no imaginative steps outside the conventionally rhetorical world of diatonic harmony nor does anything distinctive "in keeping with the Byzantine architecture." Certainly Tchaikovsky used none of the old *znamenny* chant, nor showed that he was aware of its true nature.

Rachmaninoff's *Liturgy* ———— of *St. John Chrysostom* ———— and *All-Night Vigil*

Only one composer of the following generation and of similar stature to Tchaikovsky in the world of art-music made musical settings of the Orthodox liturgy—Sergei Rachmaninoff (1873–1943). This might come as a surprise, not least because his legendary reputation as a pianist and the popularity of his own music for the instrument have given a distorted impression of the breadth of his talent.

Although Rachmaninoff had expressed an interest in setting the liturgy of St. John Chrysostom in 1897, it was not until 1910 that he composed his *Liturgy,* opus 31. He too, was deeply attracted to the traditions and the music of Russian Orthodox worship, a sympathy which spills over into his music for the concert hall. Like Tchaikovsky, he wanted to write music specifically for use in worship. His setting of the *Liturgy* accordingly sets all the required passages and makes due allowances for the cantillation of readings and prayers.

Like Tchaikovsky's *Liturgy,* though, the music has been ill-fated, and for similar reasons. Unaccompanied choral music lacks the dramatic rhetoric that concert-hall audiences expect and is a taste they are rarely encouraged to acquire. On the other hand, the Orthodox church found the music too compelling, too reminiscent of opera. Early concert-hall performances of the music generated considerable enthusiasm, but for one perceptive observer of the time, the music was "absolutely wonderful, even too beautiful, but with such music it would be difficult to pray; it is not church music" (quoted in B. Martyn, *Rachmaninoff* [Aldershot, Hants, 1990], 222).

Rachmaninoff seems to have recognized these unsolved (and perhaps insoluble) difficulties but was drawn once more to the liturgy, this time that of Vespers and Matins—known collectively as the *All-Night Vigil,* as they run together as a preparation for Divine Liturgy the following day. His profound respect for the old *znamenny* chant prompted him to use a number of ancient melodies as the basis for his settings and they give a unique character to the music, a flexibility that is hard to describe.

Rachmaninoff must have realized that liturgical use of his music was unlikely (it seems that the *Liturgy* was never used in worship) and perhaps wrote his *All Night Vigil* (opus 37) more as an expression of personal faith. This puts the work (apart from extracts like *Nyne Otpushchayeshi,* the *Nunc Dimittis*) into the category of art-music. For some, its restraint effaces the composer's public identity (a hindrance to an artist in an age of individualism) and as a result its extraordinary beauties are only now beginning to be discovered.

The first performances of the *All-Night Vigil* took place in 1915, only two years before the Russian Revolution completely overturned the world of the arts (Rachmaninoff was among many artists forced to flee to the West). As the church was forced into hiding, Christian music could no longer enjoy any creative life.

Andrew Wilson-Dickson[14]

182 • CHURCH MUSIC IN THE COPTIC AND ETHIOPIAN CHURCHES

Millions of Christians who live in Egypt and Ethiopia have inherited a rich tradition of worship practices. Each of these churches maintain a variety of ancient worship customs, including the use of music. In Egypt, the congregation participates in the music of worship. The most striking feature of Ethiopian worship is the contribution of the priests, who spend up to several decades mastering the music, poetry, and dance that are used in worship.

The churches of the East can be divided into three groups: first, the Orthodox Churches of the four ancient patriarchs (Constantinople, Alexandria, Antioch and Jerusalem), together with the now independent churches still in communion with each other: Cyprus, Greece, Russia, Bulgaria, Yugoslavia, and Romania. Second are the Uniate Churches, in union with the church of Rome although following an Eastern rite. These owe their existence to Roman Catholic missionary work in the seventeenth and

eighteenth centuries and are to be found in small numbers all over Eastern Europe and the Middle East, including the Melkite and Maronite Christians.

The third group of Churches are what the Orthodox church would call heretical. That is, they broke away from the Orthodox, mostly at the time of great doctrinal struggles in about the fifth century. These are the Nestorian church (the Church of East Syria) and the Monophysite Christians consisting of the Jacobite church of Antioch, the Armenian church, the Coptic church, and the Ethiopian church. These last two are particularly good illustrations of the wonderful riches in the Christian music of the area.

The Coptic Church

The words *Egypt* and *Copt* have the same basic root and refer to the geographical area around the Nile. The older form, Copt, has become attached to the language spoken in Egypt before Arabic became commonplace about six centuries ago. It is therefore a language that dates back, through the Bohairic dialect, to the ancient Egyptian period.

There may be as many as 7 million Coptic Christians in Egypt today, living in reasonable harmony among at least 40 million Muslims. Some Muslims are becoming more militant and look for an Islamic revolution as a reaction to the increasing poverty and hardship in the country. On the other hand, the Muslim and Christian communities in Egypt have lived in mutual cooperation for centuries and at present that seems set to continue.

Coptic Christians are keenly aware of their ancient ancestry. They revere the apostle Mark as the saint who established the Christian church in Alexandria before his martyrdom there in A.D. 68. They particularly treasure the story of Joseph and Mary's flight to Egypt with the young Jesus. Many ancient Coptic churches were built to commemorate the various resting places of the Holy Family.

Egypt became one of the great centers of Christian monastic life from the fourth century onwards. Antony (about 251–356) is held to have been the first and finest example of a Christian following a world-renouncing life in the desert.

Many others followed. By the fifteenth century there may have been as many as 300 monasteries and nunneries in Egypt. At present there are seven, supporting some 300 monks.

When the Coptic church separated from the Orthodox in the schism of 451, its sense of spiritual and national identity was brought into a sharp focus which has never been lost. As a consequence, the traditions of worship have been less subject to change than in most other Eastern churches.

A visitor to a Coptic church today is immediately aware of being put in touch with very ancient customs which words can only attempt to describe:

> Perhaps nowhere in the world can you imagine yourself back in so remote an age as when you are in a Coptic church. You go into a strange dark building; at first the European needs an effort to realise that it is a church at all, it looks so different from our usual associations. . . . In a Coptic church you come into low dark spaces, a labyrinth of irregular openings. There is little light from the narrow windows. Dimly you see strange rich colours and tarnished gold, all mellowed by dirt. . . . Lamps sparkle in the gloom [and] before you is the exquisite carving, inlay and delicate patterns of the *baikal* (chancel) screen. All around you see, dusty and confused, wonderful pieces of wood carving. Behind the screen looms the curve of the apse; on the thick columns and along the walls . . . are inscriptions in exquisite lettering—Coptic and Arabic. (A. Fortesque, *Lesser Eastern Churches* [London, 1913], 288)

As with the Orthodox churches, the Divine Liturgy is central to Coptic worship—even services of baptism will end with Communion. The liturgy generally used is that of St. Basil the Great, the liturgies of St. Gregory of Nazianzus and St. Mark being reserved for special occasions. There is a dramatic shape to the service that is made very evident by the involvement of everyone present. The participation is practical, too.

As in the Orthodox church, music is an inseparable part of the liturgy and the whole service is sung from beginning to end—the music being not so much a *way* of worshipping, but worship itself. Unlike the Orthodox however, the congregation are emotionally and vocally involved in the refrains of the litanies.

The pace of the liturgy can be very slow (depending on the priest) and the intonations have a hypnotic quality, using a very narrow range and intervals of a semitone or smaller. The responses are congregational and vocally strongly committed.

A choir, or *schola,* will lead the singing at large gatherings. Choirs are made up of theological students, for knowledge of the music is inseparable from study of the liturgy. They accompany some chants with cymbal and triangle, a practice introduced during the Middle Ages and somewhat akin to the vocal drones of the Greek monks. The chanting is always in unison and the percussion instruments keep time with a fairly fast and syncopated beat. The *Sanctus,* an emotional high point in the Divine Liturgy, is much enhanced by this style of accompaniment.

This very ancient liturgical music is quite different from the popular music of modern Egypt, which is often played by Western instruments such as the electric guitar and synthesizer. It can also be something of an endurance test for the younger generation—but they still attend. In Sunday School, though, there is music of a more relaxed and folk-song style. Here the children and young people sing a different collection of Christian songs, some of which may be chants adapted from the liturgy. Instruments can be used that could never be brought into church, such as violin, flute, piano and drums. As with much Middle Eastern folk music, the instruments decorate and play along with the vocal melody but do not provide additional lines or harmonies.

Since most Christians attend church three times a week, the liturgy and its music becomes very familiar and much treasured. It is at once one of the most ancient of all musical traditions but at the same time a vital and living force in Christian music, remarkable for its variety and richness.

The Ethiopian Church

The instruments of Musick made use of in their rites of Worship are little Drums, which they hang about their Necks, and beat with both their Hands; these are carried even by their Chief Men, and by the gravest of their Ecclesiasticks. They have sticks likewise with which they strike the Ground, accompanying the blow with a motion of their whole Bodies. They begin their Consort (that is, music-making) by Stamping their Feet on the Ground, and playing gently on their Instruments, but when they have heated themselves by degrees, they leave off Drumming and fall to leaping, dancing, and clapping their Hands, at the same time straining their Voices to the utmost pitch, till at length they have no Regard either to the Tune, or the Pauses, and seem rather a riotous, than a religious, Assembly. For this manner of Worship they cite the Psalm of David, "O clap your Hands, all ye Nations." (Father J. Lobo, *A Voyage to Abyssinia,* trans. by Samuel Johnson [London, 1735])

So wrote a Jesuit priest, Jerome Lobo, in 1627. By any standards, Ethiopia is an inhospitable place to live. In the last ten years or so it has been beleaguered by catastrophic famine due to repeated failures of the rains, a disastrous locust plague in 1986, and a malaria epidemic in 1988. The government is constantly in conflict with groups fighting for their independence. It is not surprising that Ethiopia is described as "economically one of the least developed countries in the world."

In spite of all this, it is a country of lively culture and strong spirituality, both of very long standing. The story goes that the Ethiopians adopted the Christian faith in about A.D. 328 after the shipwreck of two Coptic Christians, Frumentius and Aedesius, on their shores. From this very early stage they have maintained strong links with the Coptic church, siding with it in the Chalcedonian schism of 451.

The Ethiopian church also developed a desert monastic tradition from the fifth century onward. Many of the Ethiopian monks were highly educated and by the seventh century had translated the Bible from Syriac, Coptic, and Greek into the language of Ge'ez, which is still used in the Ethiopian church today. Like Coptic, this liturgical language is now quite different from the locally spoken Amharic language.

In its Christian history, Ethiopia has had very little contact with the West. Although it has been evangelized by Jesuits and more recently by Protestant missionaries, it is unique among African countries in having a Christian church which was established before the conversion of most of Europe. That church is strongly supported by at least 22 million members, divided among 20,000 parishes and led by about 250,000 priests! This represents nearly half the population, the rest being Muslims or members of traditional animist religions.

The statistics alone show a support for the Christian faith unmatched by any European country. If the number of priests suggests that their title is a nominal one, then the intensity and thoroughness of their training tells a different story. As well as priests there are deacons, monks, and *dabtaras*. All of these have a knowledge of their Christian music, for it is bonded to the liturgy as closely as in other Eastern churches. To the *dabtaras* is given the responsibility of preserving the artistic traditions of church worship. After an elementary schooling, a *dabtara* undergoes an intense training in traditional music *(zema)*, dance *(aquaquam)*, poetry *(qene)*

and perhaps in theology and church history, too. The task is a huge one and may take twenty years.

In music, the *dabtara* faces a rigorous study of the traditional hymns and anthems, of which there are many hundreds. The study is sufficiently intensive, for the *dabtara* must memorize them all. As part of this process he must make his own copy of the whole vast collection, manufacturing his own parchment and coloured inks, binding the books and making leather cases to preserve them. This task alone may take him seven years, during which time he must also practice the chant daily.

Then the *dabtara* must study the sacred dances and how to accompany them.

The third study, ecclesiastical poetry, is by all accounts a highly sophisticated art, resembling (and probably surpassing) the most demanding of Western disciplines. The poems first and foremost have to be a perfect fit to one of the traditional chants, for they will be heard in worship as a commentary on Scripture. The poem has to be written in the ancient church language of Ge'ez and conform to strict rules of grammar. Most important of all, the poems use a host of scriptural symbols that the congregation understands very well. The poet is judged on how subtly and deftly he handles these symbols and all the technicalities of their expression.

Ethiopian Christians treasure their faith and its traditional expression. By this rigorous training it is handed down accurately from generation to generation, but at the same time there is room for creativity and a place for new work within its confines.

The reverence in which these traditions are held is delightfully illustrated by the legends which describe their origin. Ethiopian Orthodox Christians believe that all their sacred chant was created by Yared, a saint of the sixth century:

> At this time, there were no rules for the famous *zema*, or liturgical chant. The offices were recited in a low voice. But when the Saviour wanted to establish sacred chant, he thought of Yared and sent three birds to him from the Garden of Eden, which spoke to him with the language of men, and carried him away to the heavenly Jerusalem, and there he learnt their chant from twenty-four heavenly priests.

Back on earth, Yared set to work composing and singing the sacred chants:

And when the king and queen heard the sound of his voice they were moved with emotion and they spent the day in listening to him, as did the archbishop, the priests and the nobility of the kingdom. And he appointed the chants for each period of the year . . . for the Sundays and the festivals of the angels, prophets, martyrs and the just. He did this in three styles: in ge'ez, 'ezl and araray; and he put into these three nothing far removed from the language of men and the songs of the birds and animals. (M. Powne, _Ethiopian Music_ [Oxford, 1968], 91)

These stories are recorded in a fourteenth century _synaxarium_ (Lives of the Saints) called the _Senkessar,_ but in reality the chant is likely to be even older than the time of Yared. It is probable that some direct link exists with the temple music of Jerusalem.

This connection is reinforced by some remarkable circumstantial evidence. For instance, the characteristic shape of many of the churches is circular and inside are three sections, one inside the other. The outer passage is open to anyone and is where the _dabtara_ sings. The middle section is where the baptized take communion, but the innermost chamber is only for the priests; it houses the _tabot,_ an altar very much like the ark of the covenant, made of wood and draped with highly decorated cloth. Even the name of the innermost chamber _(keddusa keddusan)_ is clearly connected to the Hebrew _kodesh hakkodashim_—the holy of holies.

The dance is of course the most striking link with the Old Testament:

The veneration accorded to the _tabot_ in Abyssinia [Ethiopia] up to the present day, its carriage in solemn procession accompanied by singing, dancing, beating of staffs or prayer-sticks, rattling of sistra and sounding of other musical instruments remind one most forcefully of the scene in 2 Samuel 6:5, 15, and 16, when David and the people dance round the ark. The entire spectacle, its substance and its atmosphere, has caused all who have witnessed it to feel transported into the times of the Old Testament. (Quoted in M. Powne, _Ethiopian Music,_ 98–99.)

Andrew Wilson-Dickson[15]

183 • CHURCH MUSIC IN MISSIONARY AND INDEPENDENT AFRICAN CHURCHES

Missionaries from Europe and North America brought to Africa many Western forms of music and worship. In the _last several years, especially after Vatican II, Africans have developed more indigenous approaches to music in worship. The fascinating diversity of current musical practices is documented in this survey of independent African churches._

The Influence of Western Music in African Churches

The Christian ancestry of Ethiopia is unique in Africa, but in the last few decades Christianity has blossomed in many other areas of the continent. Some African countries have a higher percentage of followers than the Western European nations that first evangelized them. Africa is a huge continent, and a survey of its Christian music here cannot even begin to be exhaustive. Through brief and selective views, therefore, the following chapters trace the steady climb that Christianity is making—away from Western trappings and dogma to a faith which expresses African priorities, fully absorbed into African life. The musical consequences of this change are dramatic.

It is comparatively recently (around 150 years ago) that Western missionaries became fired with the task of converting "pagan" Africa to the Christian faith:

However anxious a missionary may be to appreciate and to retain indigenous social and moral values, in the case of religion he has to be ruthless . . . he has to admit and even to emphasise that the religion he teaches is opposed to the existing one and one has to cede to the other. (D. Westermann, _Africa and Christianity_ [Oxford, 1937], 94)

The traditional religions have certainly ceded. In Kenya estimates are that in 1900, 95.8 percent of the population adhered to traditional religions and only 0.2 percent were Christian. By 1962 the figures were respectively 37 percent and 54 percent: by 1972, 26.2 percent and 66.2 percent. Although these figures refer to one country, they reflect the general trend dramatically.

Western Lifestyle

Along with these changes in religious persuasion have come imported lifestyles which have found their natural habitat in the big cities. With them come all the trappings—good and bad—of Western lifestyle: the cars, the clothes, the fast food, the ghetto-blasters. It is in such surroundings that churches with a European style of worship are to be found in great diversity, with their Western liturgies, languages, and music.

But unlike Europe and North America, the majority of Africans still live in a rural setting, where traditions established over centuries, even millennia, continue to exert a powerful influence. In the cities an adapted Western culture has long been accepted and has replaced many local customs, but it is in village life that the collision of European Christianity and local customs is still an issue.

The place of music in these societies provides one indication of the cultural gulf to be bridged, for it plays a far more active part in the consciousness of Africans, penetrating deeply into traditional upbringing:

> The African mother sings to her child and introduces him to many aspects of music right from the cradle. She trains the child to become aware of rhythm and movement by rocking him to music, by singing to him in nonsense syllables imitative of drum rhythms. When he is old enough to sing, he sings with his mother and learns to imitate drum rhythms by rote. . . . Participation in children's games and stories incorporating songs enables him to learn to sing in the style of his culture, just as he learns to speak its language. His experience, even at this early stage, is not confined to children's songs, for African mothers often carry children on their backs to public ceremonies, rites and traditional dance arenas . . . sometimes the mothers even dance with their children on their backs. (J. H. Kwabena Nketia, *The Music of Africa* [London, 1982], 60)

Early missionaries seem to have been blind to these qualities of life and to the strong religious awareness of African peoples. As the nineteenth-century missionary Robert Moffat wrote:

> Satan has employed his agency with fatal success, in erasing every vestige of religious impression from the minds of the Bechuanas, Hottentots and Bushmen; leaving them without a single ray to guide them from the dark and dread futurity, or a single link to unite them with the skies. (E. W. Smith, *African Ideas of God* [London, 1961], 83)

Europeans believed that the minds of Africans were empty of any sense of religion or culture and were waiting to have these instilled into them. Desmond Tutu summarizes the result:

> These poor native pagans had to be clothed in Western clothes so that they could speak to the white man's God, the only God, who was obviously unable to recognise them unless they were decently clad. These poor creatures must be made to sing the white man's hymns hopelessly badly translated, they had to worship in the white man's unemotional and individualistic way, they had to think and speak of God and all the wonderful Gospel truths in the white man's well proven terms. (Desmond Tutu, "Whither African Theology?" in *Christianity in Independent Africa*, ed. by Fashole-Luke, Gray, et al. [London, 1978], 365)

Establishing trade with Africa was high on the European agenda in the nineteenth century and a prime reason for converting the continent to Western ways:

> In the Buxton expedition of 1841 . . . the first aim was to discover the possibilities of legitimate trade with Nigeria. . . . But the spreading of the Gospel was regarded as essential and integral to this. It was widely believed that, in order to have legitimate trade, one must have a people of developed culture, reliable and industrious habits. . . . Christianity was

St. Jude. This apostle, also known as Thaddaeus, traveled far with St. Simon on missionary journeys. Consequently his symbol is a sailboat with a cross-shaped mast.

confidently regarded as the foundation for all of these and all the virtues of social and commercial intercourse. . . . (A. D. Galloway, "Missionary Impact on Africa," in *Nigeria* [Independence Issue of *Nigeria Magazine,* Lagos, Nigeria, October 1960], 60)

The signs of a change of attitude among the missionary churches is evident in a hymnbook like *Africa Praise,* published in 1956 for use in English-speaking schools. It contains many of the best-loved Protestant hymns of the past two centuries, but also a large number of African songs to English words in tonic *sol-fa* (very few Africans have a musical training which allows them to read Western notation). The hymnbook is an indication of a desire to narrow the gap between the African and European cultures, but it was only a first step.

The Western Legacy

In a few city cathedrals, resources are channeled to the provision of printed books and to musicians who know how to get the best out of them; outside their walls the music of the many churches founded by the West is in a sorry state. Without the provision of music books with stimulating contents of high quality and without the training to use such material, the Western legacy of Christian music has become a dead weight, even a millstone. Norman Warren described his experience of Christian music in Uganda after a visit in 1985:

Generally speaking, we found the life of the church at a low ebb. All too common was the desire to ape the West. . . . I was disappointed in coming across so little original music in worship. In most instances the music was rather formal and old-fashioned . . .

He noted the use of *Hymns Ancient and Modern* (standard version) at Kampala Cathedral, Moody and Sankey in a suburban church in Kusoga, and *African Praise* at Arua Church in the north. The musical facilities available even in Mukono Cathedral were very slender:

The organ is a pedal harmonium that has not worked for months. All the music was unaccompanied and led with great gusto by a small choir. The hymn tunes were, without exception, Victorian . . . and, quite frankly, I would never want to hear them again. (*Music in Worship* 33 [September/October 1985]: 6-7)

The Language of the People

The musical legacy of the missionary churches in Africa is not wholly depressing, however. The Roman Catholic church worldwide adopted a dramatic and new attitude to its liturgy in Vatican II (the Second Vatican Council) of 1962. The abandonment of Latin and the adoption of the language of the people was its most radical step.

A Coming-of-Age

Vatican II coincided with the independence of many African countries and a powerful awareness of national identity and heritage. The feelings of Catholic African bishops were summarized in a report in 1974:

The "coming-of-age" of the Churches signifies a turning point in the history of the church of Africa. It is the end of the missionary period. This does not mean the end of evangelization. But it means, in the words of Pope Paul VI during his visit to Uganda: "You Africans may become missionaries to yourselves." In other words, the remaining task of evangelization of Africa is primarily the responsibility of the African church itself. This fact implies a radically changed relationship between the church in Africa and . . . the other Churches in Europe and North America. (*Report on the Experiences of the Church in the Work of Evangelism in Africa;* the African Continent's report for the 1974 Synod of Bishops on *The Evangelization of the Modern World,* 16)

One important consequence of this new attitude is the reduction of the numbers of missionaries from the traditional societies and churches working in Africa and alongside that, the development of new styles of worship more in harmony with African culture and lifestyle.

Church Music in the Independent Churches of Africa

Another development in the recent history of African Christianity is the pronounced and dramatic growth of indigenous independent churches. The Kimbanguist Church of Zaire is one of hundreds founded as the result of the inability of the established missionary churches to understand African needs and aspirations in the faith. As a member of the Kimbanguist Church has written:

The arrival of the missionaries, accompanied by colonisation, obscured the new knowledge of Christianity. The preaching of Christ was seen as another means of helping colonisation to alienate men completely from their African identity. It was in this situation that Christ turned his face towards his people and chose the prophet Simon Kimbangu as his messenger . . . (D. Ndofunsu, "The Role of Prayer in the Kimbanguit Church," in *Christianity in Independent Africa,* ed. Fashole-Luke, Gray, et al. [London, 1978], 578)

Kimbanguist Music

In common with many indigenous churches in Africa, the Kimbanguists value the Bible and its teachings highly and their practices are founded on biblical principles. They also denounce the traditional animist religions with vigor, but remain close to many local customs. Music is an important aid to worship, from the simple unison singing of the thrice-daily services of prayer through to the choral and instrumental sounds of Sunday worship and the colorful festivals of the church year. The beginning of the Kimbanguist musical traditions is indicative of the failure of the established missions in colonial times to understand the needs of the Christian community in Africa:

> At the start of the prophet's mission at N'Kamba, the songs utilized to accomplish the work of Christ were those of Protestants. But the Protestants refused to sell their hymnbooks to the followers of the prophet. Saddened, Simon Kimbangu went apart to pray, laying before God this poverty, so deeply felt by his congregation. From that was born the gift of "catching" the songs. (D. Ndofunsu, "The Role of Prayer in the Kimbanguit Church," 590)

The musical tradition that has developed is perfectly attuned to a society where it is memory rather than the written word that provides cultural identity and continuity:

> Kimbanguists catch songs in various ways: in dreams, and in visions in which they hear angels singing. As a general rule, once they have been caught, the songs are sent to an office set up by the church, called the Directorate of Kimbanguist Songs, where they are studied and to some extent modified to give them a good meaning. Other songs are deleted, if the meaning of the song is not clear. The songs have to be examined to avoid those that

> may be inspired by the Devil. (D. Ndofunsu, "The Role of Prayer in the Kimbanguit Church," 590)

The songs have all sorts of functions—some are songs of praise, others are "living lessons, explaining and clarifying biblical teaching, still others are prophetic." After approval these songs are learnt by a regional choir of leaders whose members then pass them on to the local choirs. One regional choir, the Kimbanguist Theatre Group, travels round the churches using singing and drama to bring Bible stories and the church's history to life.

Aladura Churches

The Kimbanguist Church is only one of the hundreds of indigenous Christian organizations thriving in Africa today. Because there are no Europeans involved and little sign of Western culture, they can make an impact in areas hardly touched by the older missionary churches. The Aladura Churches, for instance, which are very popular among the Yoruba and Ibo people in southern Nigeria, have also become established in the Muslim north of that country. In political terms, these churches have generally been treated in a friendly manner by emerging nationalist governments, in contrast to the previously open suspicion toward colonial churches.

Among people of all walks of Nigerian life, the Aladura Churches are supported enthusiastically. Where the Kimbanguists are reminiscent of seventeenth-century Puritans in their restrictions on smoking, drinking, and dancing, the Aladura celebrate their faith with hand-clapping, dancing, and traditional instruments. They have incorporated other elements of traditional worship, too—instantaneous healing of the sick, raising of the dead, prophecy, and exorcism. As one Aladura Christian puts it, it is in their liturgy that "the unfulfilled emotional needs in the Western-oriented churches have found ample fulfillment" (A. Omoyajowo, "The Aldura Church in Nigeria Since Independence," in *Christianity in Independent Africa,* ed. by Fashole-Luke, Gray, et al. [London, 1978], 110).

An indication of the popularity of the Aladura Churches in city and country is provided by their choirs' and solo singers' great following; an American-style network of gospel music is developing fast. The guitarist Patty Obassey is one of the best known, scoring an enormous success with *Nne Galu* in 1984. Among the many choirs who have produced a number of albums are Imole Ayo and the Christian Singers, the Choir of the Eternal Sacred Order of Cherubim and Seraphim, and Erasmus Jenewari and his Gospel Bells.

The balance of European and African influences on the practice of Christianity is still on the move in favor of the African, but this does not mean a wholesale eradication of Western culture. The style of vestments worn by Aladura priests is only one element borrowed from the Protestant and Catholic Churches. On the other hand, the independent churches have taught the older mission churches valuable lessons in liturgy and Christian music.

Ecstatic Music

There are a growing number of indigenous churches where the style of worship is difficult to distinguish from the traditional animist religions. The African Apostolic Church, founded in 1932 by John Maranke, is an example. It is based in Eastern Zimbabwe but its influence has spread far and wide. Where the Kimbanguist Church approves and disseminates its songs in a highly organized manner, spontaneity and improvisation are the most striking elements of Apostolic worship.

The main meeting of the African Apostolic Church is held on Saturday—the Sabbath—and may last several hours. Worship begins with an invocation—_kerek! kerek!_—which is the name given to the ecstatic state the group will later experience. Then hymns are sung, which are formal not in the sense of being read out of a book, but by being commonplace among many churches in Africa:

> Mwari Komborera Africa, Alleluia Chisua yemina
>   matu yedu Mwari
> Baba Jesu utukomborera Jesu, turi branda bako
> Refrain: O mueya, boanna mueya utukomborera

In translation, this means:

> God save Africa, Alleluia, Hear our prayers God,
>   Father, Jesus, bless us
> Jesus, we are your servants
> Refrain: O come Holy Spirit, bless us

The words are in Chishona, a language reserved for religious ceremony. The invocation of Father, Son, and Holy Spirit (the last is emphasized) is a sign to the people of a spiritual presence among them which is to become almost tangible.

The men are seated on the open ground sepa-rately from the women and all are addressed by preachers (there may be three or more) and the chief evangelist. Between them they will have agreed beforehand on the biblical topics most appropriate for the day.

After the opening hymns the preaching begins, but members are free to interrupt with songs of their own choosing at any point. They are particularly likely to jump in and lead off with a song whenever the preacher hands over to a reader. As in the Kimbanguist Church, instruments and dancing are not allowed, but their place is taken by the use of _ngoma_—vocal sounds which imitate drumming—and swaying while standing or sitting.

The call-and-response form so commonplace in African music demonstrates the relationship between a song leader and the rest of the congregation, who respond with their refrain even before the leader's improvised verses have ended.

These songs exert a powerful emotional influence on the meeting and may very well develop into the repetitive chanting of a short refrain, such as "God in Heaven" (_Mambo wa ku denga_):

> During chanting, the rhythmic shape of the song is transformed as worshippers put increasing emphasis on strongly accented beats. . . . While the rhythm is accentuated, the harmonies of the chorus tighten. The loose collection of voices (of the call-and-response) becomes a tight, single unit. The overall effect is hypnotic. The rhythmic and harmonic ramifications push the singers into a state of maximum spiritual involvement. As the change proceeds, individuals moan, yodel, and insert _ngoma_ . . . and glossolalic utterances (the gift of tongues). The entire congregation sways to the rhythm . . . (B. Jules Rosette, "Ecstatic Singing: Music and Social Integration in an African Church" in I. E. Jackson, ed., _More than Drumming_ [London, 1985], 134)

It is sometimes difficult for the preacher to regain control of the service unless the chanting dies out naturally. If it does not, then he may attempt to break the spell by shouting a greeting. These songs are nevertheless regarded by the preachers as a valuable reinforcement of their message and the value of the meeting depends on the degree to which the members have experienced "possession" by the Holy Spirit.

The congregation's sense of participation is absolute, even extending to the improvisation of songs expressing discontent—perhaps expressing disagreement with one of the church leaders or with the way in which a decision has been made. Even if problems are aired through song during the service, the sense of peace of unity after a long *kerek* is very evident.

Andrew Wilson-Dickson[16]

184 • MUSIC OF THE MEDIEVAL ERA IN THE WESTERN CHURCH

The Middle Ages in the West saw the gradual dominance of the Roman rite over the local rites that had developed before the ninth and tenth centuries. Musically this entailed the spread of Gregorian chant. Later centuries saw the development of polyphony. In the late Middle Ages, the preaching service of Prone became the model for Reformed worship.

The Standardizing of Worship

In the early years following Christianity's recognition, each metropolitan center developed its own liturgy and practices within the sphere of its cultural influence and under the leadership of the bishops of Antioch, Alexandria, Byzantium, Jerusalem, Milan, and Rome. Later developments of the Mozarabic liturgy in Spain, the Gallican liturgy of northern Europe, and the Celtic liturgies in Britain resulted from the missionary expansion of the Western church centers. Each liturgy was sung with its own traditions of cantillation, so that we have historical records of the development of Antiochian chant, Coptic chant (Egypt), Mozarabic chant (Spain), Ambrosian chant (Milan), and so forth. All the early churches used the Greek language in worship, even the church at Rome. Latin began to be used in the fourth century, and eventually displaced the Greek in the Western churches.

After the year A.D. 400, the Roman Empire was permanently divided into Eastern and Western empires. The imperial court at Byzantium exerted strong influence toward conformity in doctrine and worship practice in the Eastern churches in order to strengthen the bonds of the empire. By the seventh century two Byzantine liturgies became standard throughout the domain: the Liturgy of St. Basil (used during Lent, on Christmas and Epiphany and on St. Basil's Day), and the Liturgy of St. Chrysostom (a shortened form, most commonly used). Orthodox liturgies have not changed essentially since that time, except that there was no hesitation to translate

them from the Greek into the vernacular. Orthodox liturgy is always sung, partly in chant and partly in more contemporary music forms (e.g., Russian Orthodox music).

The Roman Mass

In the West, Rome was the center of the church and the Roman (Gregorian) rite eventually became the universal liturgy. Early important revisions were made by Pope Gelasius I (492–496), St. Gregory the Great (590–604) (who also founded the *Schola Cantorum* which standardized Western chant), the emperor Charlemagne (742–814) and his associate Alcuin (c. 735–804). Even so, there were many differing practices throughout the Middle Ages until the Council of Trent (1562) and the resultant *Missale Romanum* (Roman Missal) of 1570 brought liturgical uniformity.

Historically, before Vatican II (1962) there were three modes of mass celebration: (1) The Low Mass (*Missa Lecta*), which was spoken only and which became most popular in the Middle Ages when it was traditional for every priest to celebrate the Mass once a day and when many individuals celebrated in the same church (at different altars) at the same time; (2) The Sung Mass (*Missa Cantata*), which was the principal Sunday or holy day celebration in a parish church; and (3) High Mass (*Missa Solemnis*), which was sometimes called a Festival Mass and included assisting celebrants, and frequently a choir.

The musical masses were commonly sung in Roman (Gregorian) Chant, which included psalm tones (basically the use of a single reciting tone, followed by prescribed cadences). In addition, the high masses could feature composed settings of the five great prayer-songs of the mass (*Kyrie, Gloria in excelsis Deo, Credo, Sanctus et Benedictus, Agnus Dei*). The oldest extant settings of these mass forms are from the twelfth century composers Leonin and Perotin in Paris. Through the centuries, mass settings (the five songs only) have been written by such great composers as Machaut, Josquin des Prez, Palestrina, Haydn, Mozart, Beethoven, Schubert, Bruckner, Vaughan Williams, and Stravinsky, each in his own distinctive musical style.

The *Schola Cantorum* was established by Gregory the Great (c. 540–604) to standardize and to teach the official chant of the church. As Christianity spread throughout the Western world, and as the various cultures developed during the Middle Ages, the cathedrals, monasteries, abbeys, and collegiate churches developed choir schools where boys received their general education and were trained in music for the church's worship.

The early church fathers forbade the use of instrumental music in worship because of their association with mystery cults, the Greek theater, and pagan rituals. Nevertheless, rudimentary organs began to appear in churches by the sixth century, and their use in the Mass was widespread by the twelfth century. In the fifteenth century, some German churches boasted organs with all the essential tonal resources of modern instruments. Evidently the use of the organ was limited, however. Basically it was a means of setting the pitch ("intonation") for the unaccompanied chant or choral setting. It was also featured in what is known as an _alternatim_ practice, in which portions of liturgical music were shared by choir and organ, with the instrument performing sections (or stanzas) in alternation with the choir.

Non-Eucharistic Worship Through the Medieval Period

During this long period of Christian history, certainly for the millennium 500–1500, eucharistic liturgy was considered to be the highest form of worship. But it was not the only mode.

The Offices. The "Services of the Hours" constituted another form of worship designed to sanctify the time in which Christians live. It probably stemmed from the Jewish custom of regular prayer at stated hours of the day. Early Christians commonly prayed privately at the third, sixth, and ninth hours (Acts 3:1) and eventually this became a public practice, following the Roman division of the day into "hours" (prima, tertia, sexts, and nona) and the night into four "watches." Office worship, so-called because participation was the duty ("office") of the celebrants, was developed and perpetuated in the monasteries, but also observed in cathedrals and collegiate churches.

The full cycle of eight "offices" consisted of Matins (between midnight and dawn), immediately followed by Lauds ("cockcrow"), Prime (6:00 A.M.), Terce (9:00 A.M.), Sext (noon), None (3:00 P.M.), Vespers (6:00 P.M.), and Compline (before retiring). The principal component of office worship consisted of the reading and chanting of Scripture; thus in the total "Hours" the Psalms were completed (sung responsively) once each week, the New Testament

was read through twice in a year, and the Old Testament once. In addition, special place was given to the biblical Canticles, especially the Song of Zacharias, father of John the Baptist (_Benedictus Dominus Deus Israel_), The Song of Mary (_Magnificat_), The Song of Simeon (_Nunc Dimittis_), The Song of the Three Hebrew Children (_Benedicite,_ from the Apocrypha), and the fourth-century extrabiblical hymn attributed to Niceta of Remesiana, _Te Deum laudamus_. Finally, this form of worship also included hymns, versicles and responses, prayers, and sometimes a homily. The offices of Matins and Lauds in the morning, and Vespers and Compline in the evening, were the major services in which the most music was featured. In the Roman tradition, the psalms, canticles, and hymns were sung in Gregorian chant exclusively, except in the office of Vespers when contemporary, "composed" settings might be used. It is in this latter tradition that Monteverdi composed his "Vespers of 1610."

One office characteristic has been carried over as a conspicuous part of evangelical worship to the present day. Beginning in the second century it was the custom to follow each psalm (and later each canticle) with the _Gloria Patri_. This ascription of praise to the eternal trinity served to bring the Old Testament psalm into a New Testament context:

Glory be to the Father, and to the Son and to the Holy Ghost; as it was in the beginning, is now, and ever shall be, world without end. Amen.

Preaching Services. Also in the medieval period, a sermon was occasionally featured in the Office of Lauds. Furthermore, "preaching missions" were common throughout Christian history, for which congregations met in the naves of the cathedrals and large churches. This explains the location of a pulpit in the middle of a sanctuary far from the altar, as modern tourists will observe in historic European churches. From this tradition, a basically vernacular worship form developed known as the Prone, first inserted as a part of the mass and later featured as a separate service. It is significant because of its resemblance to the worship form adopted by John Calvin in the sixteenth century, a form which has carried over into common evangelical worship. The following is an advanced form of the Prone that was used in Basel (Eberhard Weismann, "Der Predigtgottesdienst und die verwandten Formen," in _Leiturgia,_ vol. 3, 23–24; cited by Eugene L. Brand, "The Liturgical Life of the Church," in _A Handbook of_

Church Music, ed. Carl Halter and Carl Schalk [St. Louis: Concordia, 1978]):

Call to worship ("In nomine Patri, . . .")
Sermon Scripture in Latin (for the intellectuals)
German Votum with congregational "amen"
Sermon text in German
Invocation of the Holy Spirit
Sermon
Parish announcements
Prayer of the Church
Lord's Prayer and *Ave Maria*
Apostles' Creed
The Ten Commandments
Public Confession
Closing Votum

Donald P. Hustad

185 • FROM GREGORIAN CHANT TO POLYPHONY

Music in early Christian worship consisted of melody only. Toward the end of the Middle Ages, more complex music, featuring the simultaneous singing of more than one melodic line, was composed for use in worship. For several centuries, this complex—or polyphonic—music was composed by many of Europe's most famous and skilled composers.

For the first eight hundred years of Christian worship the musical vehicle for the liturgy was melody. It might take the form of a cantillated prayer of extreme simplicity or of an ornate Gradual for a solemn occasion. But whatever its complexity, monody—the single line of melody untainted by any accompaniment—was the most perfect and satisfying symbol for the unity of Christian believers. It was the advent of notation that allowed polyphony—many melodies together—to develop, in directions that have since made Western music unique.

When buildings are constructed on land which is plentiful, the area they occupy is not a critical factor in their design, and conurbations can be made up of low-story houses, spreading outwards from a center. But as soon as space becomes restricted, then the cost of land rises and economics dictate that buildings must become taller if housing expansion is to continue. So it was with Gregorian chant. The limits of human endurance meant that solemn chant had developed to its greatest practical length. But a continuing desire for its adornment on special occasions led musicians to consider embellishing the

chant in another way altogether; by singing different melodies simultaneously.

The first steps towards a new concept of singing, known as *organum,* came mostly from France. For a long time France had favored a special quality of ceremony in worship. The choir at the Abbey of St. Martial at Limoges for instance, gradually took to singing certain items of the Mass by splitting the choir into parts, one group singing the original chant and others (perhaps the basses) singing four or five or eight notes below. The idea (called *organum*) was a simple method of introducing a further degree of decoration into the chant, but one which nonetheless needed no writing down.

Other possibilities were explored too, especially those which allowed the two parts to become more independent. This freer type of *organum* required one part to sing the original chant and a second line to supply a more florid part against it. One of the most valuable collections of these two-part pieces, the Winchester Troper, was compiled during the tenth and eleventh centuries at Winchester Cathedral in southern England. This precious manuscript contains all the different sorts of troping (interpolations and additions to the chant) as well as the two-part "florid" *organum.*

The Beginnings of Polyphony

The great Cathedral of Notre Dame is perhaps the best known of all Gothic cathedrals. Considering its immense size and complexity, it was built with considerable speed between 1163 and 1250, the bulk of it being complete by 1200.

The creation of such a magnificent structure is evidence that France was beginning to enjoy a period of stability and affluence, becoming a country in whose towns culture and learning could flourish as never before. During the building of the new cathedral, composers working at its music school were notating a type of *organum* more lavishly decorated than anything yet heard.

An anonymous treatise reveals the names of two famous composers from Notre Dame at this period, both canons at the cathedral:

Leonin was the best composer of *organum.* He wrote the *Great Book of Organum,* for Mass and Office, to augment the Divine Service. This book was used until the time of the great Perotin, who shortened it and rewrote many sections in a better way . . . with the most ample embellishments of harmonic art. (Anonymous IV, quoted in the _Pelican History of Music,_ vol. 1 [London, 1982], 224.)

This once again draws attention to the continuing delight of Christians in elaborating the liturgy, and luckily the Great Book itself survives. Corroborative evidence shows that the florid _vox organalis_ added to the chant was sometimes improvised from a number of stock musical phrases. Certainly the special expertise of the musicians was rewarded accordingly:

And to each clerk of the choir who will attend Mass, two deniers, and to the four clerks who will sing the Alleluia in _organum,_ six deniers . . . (Quoted in C. Wright, _Music and Ceremony at Notre Dame, 500–1500_ [Cambridge, 1989], 339.)

As in the music of the Winchester Troper, Leonin's pieces (compiled between about 1150 and 1170) supplied an extra vocal line. This was added to sections of chants which in themselves were already decorative—such as Graduals or Alleluias at Mass or Responsorial chants at Matins.

The extra line that Leonin added (called the _duplum_ or second part) needed considerable singing skill. It had to be sung quite fast, not least because as many as forty notes of the _duplum_ fitted to just one of the original chant. As a result, some parts of the chant became greatly stretched out, with its singers spending perhaps twenty seconds or half a minute on a single note. The words, of course, progressed even more slowly.

No wonder then that Perotin, Leonin's successor, shortened parts of these compositions. At the same time he enriched the harmony still further by adding new voice-parts: a _triplum_ (third part) and sometimes even a _quadruplum_ (fourth part). The independence of the vocal lines can now properly be called polyphony.

Another feature of this remarkable music was the presence of a regular pulse in triple time. The perfection of the number three was inherent in the medieval worldview. As the theorist Jean de Muris wrote in 1319:

That all perfection lies in the ternary number is clear from a hundred comparisons. In God, who is perfection itself, there is singleness in substance, but threeness in persons; He is three in one and one in three. Moreover: [there are] . . . in individuals generation, corruption and substance; in finite timespans beginning, middle and end; in every curable disease onset, crisis and decline. Three is the first odd number and the first prime number. It is not two lines but three that can enclose a surface. The triangle is the first regular polygon. (Quoted in P. Weiss and R. Taruskin, _Music in the Western World_ [London, 1984], 69.)

The rhythm of this early polyphony soon resolved itself into the quick triple time so characteristic of medieval music of this period. Until this time there had been little need for written guidance to the singers concerning rhythm, but the complexity of the Notre Dame _organum_ for the first time necessitated a system for notating rhythm as well as pitch. (The complexities of modal rhythmic notation are described in W. Apel, _The Notation of Polyphonic Music,_ 5th ed. [Cambridge, Mass., 1961].)

The startling effect of the choir suddenly changing from the lone and sinuous melody of the chant to three- or even four-part music did not please everyone. There are records of an increasing number of complaints from churchmen about this elaborate music. John of Salisbury, a contemporary of Perotin, wrote a particularly vitriolic criticism:

Music sullies the Divine Service, for in the very sight of God, in the sacred recesses of the sanctuary itself, the singers attempt, with the lewdness of a lascivious singing voice and a singularly foppish manner, to feminise all their spellbound little followers with the girlish way they render the notes and end the phrases . . . (Quoted in P. Weiss and R. Taruskin, _Music in the Western World_ [London, 1984], 62.)

But such criticism cannot have represented the majority in the liturgical corridors of power, as the practice quickly spread to a number of monasteries and cathedral churches across Europe.

The Motet

Where the original plainsong melody had a melisma—a number of notes sung to one syllable—the composers of Notre Dame felt it appropriate in their _organum_ settings to make the chant move along faster and in rhythm. Strange though it may seem, they took to writing these sections (called _clausulae_) separately from the main piece, so that one could be substituted for another, like engine spare parts.

Before long, these sections were soon being performed as separate pieces in their own right. What is more, composers started to add completely new sets of words to the upper parts (yet another example of troping), creating what they called a motet, that is, a piece with words to the added lines (from the French *mot,* meaning "word").

The result is the most sophisticated musical form known to the Middle Ages, a piece in two, three, or even four parts, whose foundation (the so-called *tenor*) is a fragment of chant, snipped out, as it were, from the middle of a traditional melody. The tenor had a regular pulse imposed on it, while around it were added between one and three freely composed voice-parts with new texts. By this means it was perfectly possible for up to four different sets of words to be sung together.

Motet technique was developed in a number of ways in the thirteenth century, which were not by any means always pleasing to the church. Such pieces became popular for secular ceremonies (at banquets for instance) and popular tunes would be incorporated in them. Some of these found their way back into church motets, and Pope John XXII in 1323 was compelled to issue a papal bull, in which he made some very significant complaints:

> Certain disciples of the new school . . . prefer to devise new methods of their own rather than to sing in the old way. Therefore the music of the Divine Office is disturbed with these notes of quick duration. Moreover, they . . . deprave it with discants and sometimes pad out the music with upper parts made out of profane songs. The result is that they often seem to be losing sight of the fundamental sources of our melodies in the Antiphoner and Gradual. . . . The consequence of all this is that devotion, the true aim of all worship, is neglected, and wantonness, which ought to be shunned, increases. We hasten to forbid these methods . . . (Quoted in P. Weiss and R. Taruskin, *Music in the Western World* [London, 1984], 71.)

The Conductus

Not all medieval part-music had the complex structure of the motet, for the church initiated another type of polyphony in its continuing pursuit of the "embellishment of harmonic art." During the twelfth century it became customary in services of solemnity to lead the lesson-reader to the lectern with a short song called a *conductus* (from the Latin *conducere,* to lead).

Once again, more complex and lengthy chants of this processional type developed as musicians delighted in the addition of as many as three extra parts against the original. The result was a piece of music newly composed in all parts (not usually based on traditional chant or other tunes) and with all voices singing the same text.

Franco of Cologne, a composer and theorist of the later thirteenth century, described how such pieces were written:

> He who wants to write a *conductus* should first invent as beautiful a melody as he can, then using it as a *tenor* is used in writing discant (in other words, writing another melody against it, the *tenor* being the original "beautiful melody"). He who wishes to construct a third part *(triplum)* ought to have the other two in mind, so that when the *triplum* is discordant with the *tenor,* it will not be discordant with the discant, and vice versa. (Franco of Cologne, *Ars Mensurabilis Musicae,* chapter 11. Further extracts from this important treatise can be found in O. Strunk, *Source Readings in Music History* [New York, 1990], 139–159.)

This method of composition is very different from classical music of the last few hundred years. If a choir sings a four-part hymn or anthem, for instance, all voices fill in a particular harmony. If one is missing, or breaks down, the effect on the composer's intentions is probably fatal. But in medieval times polyphonic music was perceived as a number of layers. The composing process began with the *tenor,* then the *discant* or *duplum,* then the *triplum,* then the *quadruplum*—as many layers as circumstances required.

A composer (like Perotin) would feel quite at liberty to add another layer to pre-existing music, or to perform a piece with one of the upper layers missing. Such methods would produce truly appalling results if applied to classical music, but make good sense in the field of Western popular music today. In jazz especially, the "tenor," in the form of popular song "standards," is common property, to be surrounded by other musical lines depending on the occasion.

Like the motets, medieval songs in *conductus* style became fashionable outside the church as well as within, and courtly musicians used the idiom to create part-songs about the Crusades, about politics, and about love.

The Ordinary of the Mass

In the late thirteenth century, polyphonic settings during the celebration of Mass extended for the first time to the Ordinary, those unchanging texts which had at one time been opportunities for the expression of faith of the whole Christian community. In well-endowed cathedrals and monasteries, the Ordinary texts were left more and more to the choir, who sang on behalf of those present (and perhaps even of those absent). It is a poignant irony that much of the outstanding Christian music of the Middle Ages, and the superb cathedrals that echoed to it, can be understood as monuments to the vaingloriousness of the church during this period.

The life of Guillaume de Machaut illustrated well the blend of secular and sacred that was common in this period. Born in about 1300, he took holy orders and was made a canon of Rheims and of St. Quentin, attached to the cathedral. He had also, from 1323, been secretary to John of Luxembourg, King of Bohemia, who had taken him on his military campaigns all over Europe before Machaut became canon. King John was killed at Crecy in 1346, and from that time Machaut was patronized by the Kings of France, Cyprus and Normandy, his fame as a poet and musician spreading throughout the European courts.

In spite of his holy orders and with a few notable exceptions, his creative energies were devoted to writing long, elegant, and sophisticated love-poems, some of which he set to music. Some of the love lyrics he wrote in his sixties were inspired by his relationship with a nineteen-year-old girl. The poetry of this ''jolly and worldly ecclesiastic'' was known and admired by a younger contemporary of his, Geoffrey Chaucer (1340–1400).

Apart from some motets with sacred texts, Machaut's outstanding music for the church was his *Messe de Notre Dame,* a comprehensive setting of the Ordinary of the Mass for four voices. Settings of the Ordinary already existed by this time, but they seem to be compilations of pieces from various sources and not always complete. His setting is ornate and written with extreme care and great creative energy—it was probably created for some special occasion, though whether it was for Mass at the coronation of Charles V of France in 1364 is now disputed.

Machaut's Mass is the first setting of the type that countless composers have written since, consisting of a *Kyrie, Gloria, Credo, Sanctus Agnus Dei* and a final *Ite, Missa Est.* Machaut uses the composing techniques of both motet and conductus, moving from music of intellectual sophistication and artistry (such as the *Amen* to the *Credo)* to a simpler style that suggests that he may have taken some heed of Pope John XXII's bull of a few years earlier. As a monument to the Middle Ages' expression of spiritual truth, it is outstanding.

Andrew Wilson-Dickson[17]

186 ✦ Music of the Reformation

The reforms in music which attended the reform of worship in the Reformation ranged widely from the rejection of all instruments and the restriction of singing solely to the Psalms to the choral Eucharists of the Anglicans. This article traces musical developments in the Lutheran, Anglican, Reformed, Puritan, and early free church traditions.

Christian Worship in the Reformation

During the Middle Ages, worship had developed into an elaborate ritual which evidenced serious distortions of apostolic standards, according to the Reformers, in both theology and practice. The following five developments were especially troubling to the Reformers.

(1) The Liturgy of the Word had little significance. Although provision was made for Scripture reading and a homily in the vernacular, a sermon was rarely heard since most local priests were too illiterate to be capable of preaching.

(2) Typical worshipers understood little of what was being said or sung, since the service was in Latin. Their own vocal participation was almost nonexistent.

(3) The Eucharist was no longer a joyful action of the whole congregation; it had become the priestly function of the celebrant alone. The congregation's devotion (mixed with superstition) was focused on the host (the bread) itself, on *seeing* the offering of the sacrifice, or on private prayers (e.g., the rosary).

(4) Each celebration of the Mass was regarded as a separate offering of the body and blood of Christ. The emphasis was limited to Christ's death, with scant remembrance of his resurrection and second coming. Furthermore, the custom of offering votive

masses for particular individuals and purposes became common.

(5) The Roman Canon was not a prayer of thanksgiving, but rather a long petition that voiced repeated pleas that God would receive the offering of the Mass, generating a spirit of fear lest it not be accepted. As a result, most of the congregation took Communion only once a year. On many occasions, only the officiating priests received the bread and the cup.

Our look at the worship of the Reformation churches will include a consideration of the German, English, and French-Swiss traditions. However, none of these was the first expression of rebellion against Rome. The Unitas Fratrum (United Brethren), which began under John Hus in Bohemia, had its own liturgical and musical expressions. However, the reforms that were begun in this movement were aborted because of the death of Hus, who was burned at the stake in 1415.

The Lutheran Reformation

Martin Luther's quarrel with Rome had more to do with the sacerdotal interpretation of the Mass and the resultant abuses which accompanied it than with the structure of the liturgy itself. For him, the Communion service was a sacrament (God's grace extended to man). A musician himself, he loved the great music and the Latin text which graced the mass. Consequently, in his first reformed liturgy—*Formula missae et communionis* (1523)—much of the historic mass outline remains. Luther (1483–1546) is remembered as the individual who gave the German people the Bible and the hymnbook in their own language in order to recover the doctrine of believer-priesthood. He also restored the sermon to its central place in the Liturgy of the Word. But in the *Formula missae,* only the hymns, Scripture readings, and sermon were in the vernacular; the rest continued to be in Latin. He achieved his theological purposes relating to the communion by removing many acts of the Liturgy. All that remained were the Preface and the Words of Institution.

The German Mass (*Deutscher messe,* 1526) was more drastic in its iconoclasm and may have been encouraged by some of Luther's more radical associates. In it, many of the historic Latin songs were replaced by vernacular hymn versions set to German folksong melodies.

Throughout the sixteenth century, most Lutheran worship used a variant of the Western liturgy. The *Formula missae* was the norm for cathedrals and collegiate churches, and the German Mass was common in smaller towns and rural churches. Twentieth century Lutherans tend to agree that Luther was excessively ruthless in the excisions made in the Communion service. Consequently, in recent service orders, they have recovered much of the pattern and texts of the third and fourth century eucharistic prayers, while still retaining their Reformational and Lutheran theological emphasis.

We have already mentioned Luther's love of the historic music of the church. In the *Formula missae,* the choir sang the traditional psalms, songs, and prayers in Latin to Gregorian chant or in polyphonic settings. They also functioned in leading the congregation in the new unaccompanied chorales. Later, they sang alternate stanzas of the chorales in four- and five-part settings by Johann Walther, published in 1524 in the *Church Chorale Book*. In the seventeenth and eighteenth centuries, the choir made significant new contributions to worship in the singing of motets, passions, and cantatas.

The treble parts of the choral music were sung by boys who were trained in the "Latin" (parochial and cathedral) schools. The lower parts were sung by Latin school "alumni" or by members of the *Kantorei*—a voluntary social-musical organization that placed its services at the disposal of the church. Where there was no choir, the congregation was led by a "cantor." That title, meaning "chief singer," was also given to a musical director of large churches such as J. S. Bach, whose career culminated with service to churches in Leipzig from 1723 to 1750.

Luther seems to have been indifferent to (and occasionally critical of) the organ in divine worship, as were most Roman Catholic leaders of that period. As in the Roman church, the organ gave "intonations" for the unaccompanied liturgical singing and also continued the *alternatim* practice in the chorales. The "intonation" for the congregational chorales developed into what we know as a "chorale prelude." Later, as composing techniques moved toward homophonic styles with the melody in the soprano, the organ took over the responsibility of leading the congregation in the chorales.

Luther felt that the multiple services of the medieval offices had become an "intolerable burden." Since monasteries had been abolished, he prescribed that only the most significant morning and evening "hours"—Matins and Vespers—would be observed daily in local churches. However, office worship never really caught on among Lutherans. The practice soon died out and has only recently been revived, with moderate success. For non-eucharistic worship, Luther's followers have preferred a shortened Mass called an "ante-Communion," which simply omits the Lord's Supper observance from the regular liturgy.

The Reformation in England

The early impetus for the Reformation in England was more political than spiritual. This was partly evident in the fact that for years after Henry VIII broke with the pope (1534) and assumed himself the leadership of the English (Anglican) church, the Latin Roman Mass continued to be used without change. However, during the ensuing years, evangelical thought became more widespread and after Henry's death in 1547, Archbishop Cranmer (1489–1556) set about to devise a truly reformed English liturgy.

The first *Book of Common Prayer* was released in 1549, the title ("common") indicating that worship was now to be congregational. This vernacular Mass retained much of the form of the Roman rite, with drastic revision only in the Canon (eucharistic prayer), because of the rejection of the concepts of transubstantiation and sacrifice. A significant number of Anglicans (especially Anglo-Catholics) still express regret that this rite never became the norm for the Church of England. As was true in Lutheran Germany, popular opinion seemed to demand even more drastic revision, and three years later another prayer book was published. Much of the influence for the more radical trend came from the Calvinist movement in Strasbourg and Geneva.

In the Prayer Book of 1552 the word *Mass* was dropped as the title of the worship form, vestments were forbidden, and altars were replaced by Communion tables. The Agnus Dei, the Benedictus, and the Peace were all excised from the liturgy, and the Gloria in excelsis Deo was placed near the end of the service. Thus the beginning of the ritual became basically personal and penitential, losing the corporate expression of praise and thanksgiving. The introit, gradual, offertory song, and Communion song were replaced by congregational psalms in metrical versions and later by hymns. In comparison with the "Liturgy of the Eucharist" that Roman Catholics used *c.* 1500, the greatest difference lies in the very-much shortened eucharistic prayer.

During the brief reign of "Bloody Mary" (1553–1558) the Roman Catholic faith and worship were reinstated, and many Protestant leaders were burned at the stake or beheaded. Others fled to such European refuges as Frankfort and Geneva, where they came under the influence of John Calvin and John Knox. When they returned to their native country, they brought with them an even more radical revisionist attitude that eventually showed itself in the Puritan movement within the Church of England and the emerging of Nonconformist churches (Presbyterian, Independent, and Baptist). With the death of Mary, Queen Elizabeth I sought to heal the wounds of her broken country and to bring papists, traditionalists, and Puritans together. Under her leadership, the prayer book was revised in 1559. Some worship practices found in the 1549 version were restored, though the changes were slight. Vestments, for example, were once again permitted.

The Puritan movement gathered increasing momentum during the close of the sixteenth and the beginning of the seventeenth century. In worship, its emphasis was on "scriptural simplicity"—no choral or instrumental music, no written liturgy, and no symbolism (vestment, liturgical movement, etc.), much after the pattern of John Calvin's Geneva. Eventually, the group developed enough political strength to overthrow the king and set up a republic. In 1645 the Prayer Book was replaced by the *Directory for the Plain Worship of God in the Three Kingdoms.* For a brief period, the choral and instrumental worship of the church went into complete limbo.

In 1660 Charles II was placed on the throne. He immediately brought the prayer book back into use. Soon a new revision (1662) was brought out; it made no substantial changes in the old version, retaining basically the 1552 worship outline, and that book became the norm for the Church of England for the next 300 years. It remains basically the same today, though there is considerable sentiment for a thorough revision.

We have already noted Luther's purpose pertaining to the continuance of the two "offices" Matins and Vespers as public, daily services of non-eucharistic worship. This practice was also adopted by Archbishop Cranmer for the English church, and liturgies for these services appeared in each of the prayer books mentioned above. As in the old Roman tradition, the emphasis was on the reading and singing of Scripture; the Psalter was to be sung through each month, the Old Testament read through each year, and the New Testament twice each year. In making this service completely "English," the revisions of 1552 and 1662 had changed the titles of the services to "Morning Prayer" and "Evening Prayer," placed a general confession and absolution (assurance of pardon) at the beginning, added the *Jubilate Deo* (Psalm 100) as a regular canticle plus an anthem, with four collects and a general thanksgiving as the prayers. In common practice a sermon is also included, and this service has been for many Anglicans the "preferred" option for typical Sunday worship.

The 1549 Prayer Book had stressed the requirement that Communion was not to be celebrated unless communicants were present and participating, and specified that members in good standing would receive Communion at least three times a year. The 1552 prayer book indicated that "ante-Communion"—the same service but omitting the eucharistic prayer and Communion—would also be observed on Sundays and "holy days." Because, like Lutherans, most Anglicans retained the medieval sense of awe and fear in receiving Communion, non-eucharistic services tended to be the most popular in Anglican worship until recent times.

We have already noted that congregational hymns became the norm of Protestant musical worship under Luther. In the early development of the English reformation church, this possibility was considered, and Bishop Myles Coverdale made an English translation of certain German and Latin hymns together with metrical versions of psalms and other liturgical material in a volume *Goostly psalms and spiritual songs* (1543), intended for use in private chapels and homes. But, eventually the Lutheran example was rejected in favor of the Calvinist standard—metrical psalms. In 1549, a Thomas Sternhold, the robe-keeper to Henry VIII (Albert E. Bailey, *The Gospel in Hymns* [New York: Scribner, 1950], 7) published a small collection of nineteen psalms without music. By 1562, with the help of J. Hopkins, Sternhold completed the entire Psalter, which was named for its compilers. "Sternhold and Hopkins" remained in use (along with others) for more than two hundred years.

Psalm singing received added impetus during the exile of English Protestants in Geneva during the reign of Mary, Queen of Scots. There they produced a number of versions of the Anglo-Genevan Psalter, with tunes, beginning in 1556. This book was based on Sternhold and Hopkins with certain additions of texts (and especially tunes) from the French psalters of Calvin. In the early eighteenth century English Nonconformists began to write and sing psalm paraphrases and "hymns of human composure," beginning with Isaac Watts (1674–1748). But free hymns were not widely accepted in Anglicanism until well into the nineteenth century.

Particularly in the services of morning and evening prayer, the Psalms were regularly sung in prose version; this was also true of the Canticles (*Benedictus, Te Deum, Magnificat, Nunc Dimittis*). For this purpose, in the seventeenth century a new "Anglican chant" was produced, based on small snatches of Gregorian melody and sung in four-part harmony.

Despite its rejection of Luther's hymns, the English church followed the example of the Lutherans in adapting the choir to its new Protestant patterns, particularly in the "cathedral tradition." From almost the beginning of Anglicanism, the choir was retained to lead the congregation, but also to sing alone, as in a *Choral Eucharist*. In the sixteenth century the Tudor composers who had produced Latin masses (e.g., William Byrd, John Merbecke, Thomas Tallis, Richard Farrant) began to set portions of the new prayer book services. A complete "service" included music for Holy Communion as well as for the canticles of morning and evening prayer. Anglican services have been written by British (and other) composers in every generation. These services are not performed in their entirety in one service as is the Latin mass, but they are published together for liturgical use in larger Anglican (including Episcopalian) churches.

In addition, the Anglican heritage made a unique contribution to church music in the anthem—originally an English motet, whose name is derived from "antiphon." So-called anthems existed before 1550, but they remained in disfavor until the Restoration. In the prayer book of 1662, they are acknowledged to be a regular part of worship in churches that boasted a choir.

In the English tradition it may be said that provision is made for a wide variety of musical tastes. In the parish church, congregational singing is central even though a modest choir may in some instances be available to sing an anthem and to lead the hymns and chants. In the cathedral setting, certain services are essentially choral, with less congregational participation. These services give opportunity for the very finest examples of the choral art to be used.

Both Anglicans and Lutherans continued to observe the liturgical calendar with its festivals and holy days. In both the eucharistic services and the offices, the "Ordinary" remained fairly constant throughout the year. The "Propers" provided Scripture readings, prayers, responses, and "sermon emphases" which changed according to the season and the day involved.

—— Worship in the Calvinist Tradition ——

In Reformation times, the most severe reaction to traditional Roman Catholic worship came in the Calvinist tradition; for this reason, it is closely related to modern evangelical practice. But first, we must look briefly at some of John Calvin's predecessors.

Ulrich Zwingli (1484–1531), whose reform leadership centered in Zurich, was more of a rationalist-humanist than Luther or Calvin, both of whom shared the medieval scholastic tradition. Consequently, Zwinglian worship tended to be more didactic than devotional. His typical morning service resembled the ancient Prone liturgy, consisting of Scripture reading (Epistle and Gospel), preaching, and a long prayer. In the first German liturgy of 1525, music was eliminated completely (although Zwingli himself was an accomplished musician); however, psalms and canticles were recited responsively. The Communion service was celebrated four times a year, with the congregation seated as for a family meal. The Eucharist service had no true eucharistic prayer and no prayer of intercession; it consisted of an exhortation, "Fencing of the Table," the Lord's Prayer, prayer of "humble access," words of institution, ministers' Communion, Communion of the people, psalm, collect, Dismissal. According to Zwingli, the Eucharist was only "the congregation confessing its faith in obedience to our Lord's command."

Martin Bucer (1491–1551), a follower of Zwingli, developed quite a different tradition when he was put in charge of Reformed worship in Strasbourg in 1535. Prior to that time, the city had been dominated by Lutheranism. Consequently, Bucer's liturgy of 1537 seems to combine Lutheran and Zwinglian elements. He retained the optional *Kyrie* and *Gloria in Excelsis,* though in time these were replaced by psalms or hymns. The Communion service included intercessions as well as a Prayer of Consecration.

When John Calvin (1509–1564) first preached and taught at Geneva, he evidently followed no set form of worship, and the service was entirely without music. When he was banished from Geneva in 1538, he went to be pastor of the French exiles in Strasbourg. He was quite impressed with Bucer's German rite and, according to his own admission, "borrowed the greater part of it" for his own French liturgy of 1540. Later when he returned to Geneva, this liturgy was simplified slightly, becoming the Geneva rite of 1542 and the basis for Calvinist worship in all of Europe—Switzerland, France, Germany, Netherlands, and Scotland.

The medieval eucharistic vestments were discarded. (The traditional black cassock now worn by Presbyterian ministers is essentially a reminder that Calvin preached in his overcoat because the cathedral at Geneva was unheated!) Indeed, all the traditional Roman symbolism was stripped from the building. A Calvinist "processional" (particularly in Scotland) is headed by a deacon carrying the Bible into the sanctuary to place it on the pulpit. Calvin ignored the church calendar (except for the principal feast days) and with it the lectionary of readings. The Scripture was read only to serve as a basis for the sermon.

Calvin's ideas about the Eucharist were not radically different from those of Luther, though he rejected the idea of "consubstantiation." He too saw the Eucharist as a sacrament and desired that it would be celebrated weekly as part of a full service of Word and Eucharist. But this was not to be, because many of the French Reformed leaders (including the magistrates at Geneva) had a more narrow view of Communion. Indeed, they restricted its observance to four times a year, despite Calvin's persistent objections.

Calvin is most frequently criticized for his actions restricting music in worship. He discarded the choir and its literature completely, and Calvinist iconoclasts removed the organs from the formerly Catholic churches. As mentioned earlier, worship in Geneva had no singing at all, and Calvin complained about the resultant "cold tone" in the services. When he went to Strasbourg, he was pleased with the German Psalm versions he found in the congregations there, whereupon he set several Psalms himself in metrical French to tunes of Mattheus Greiter and Wolfgang Dachstein. These were included with his Strasbourg service book, *The Form of Prayers and Manner of Ministering the Sacraments According to the Use of the Ancient Church* (1640).

Later he commissioned the French court poet

Clement Marot to set all the Psalms in meter, which resulted in the historic Genevan Psalter (1562). The Psalms were sung by the congregation in unison and without accompaniment. (Four-part settings of the Marot Psalms were composed by Sweelinck, Jannequin, and Goudimel, but they were heard only in the home and in educational circles.) Music editor for the volume was Louis Bourgeois (c. 1510–c. 1561), who adapted tunes from French and German secular sources and no doubt composed some himself.

This is not the place to debate Calvin's decision for the Psalms and against hymns, in the light of his dictum "Only God's Word is worthy to be used in God's praise." No doubt he was reacting strongly to the complex, verbose Roman liturgy, with its many "tropes" and "sequence" hymns. He did not have all the writings of the early church fathers at his disposal, from which he might have learned the significance of the New Testament "hymns and spiritual songs" (which in the early patristic period were not part of the biblical canon) and of the successors of those forms in the early church. The Calvinist tradition of singing Psalms was also inherited by the Anglican church and by early free churches in both England and America. It has persisted in some places to the present day.

Worship in the Free Church Tradition

In the closing years of the sixteenth century, the passion for religious reform was most intense in the most radical of the English Puritans. They are known historically as the Separatists, since they intended to part company with the established Anglican church. When they did so, they were more iconoclastic than Calvin himself, reducing worship to something less than the essentials! They rejected all established liturgical forms. When they met together (in barns, in forests and fields, or in houses on back alleys, as such gatherings were forbidden by law), their services included only prayer and the exposition of Scripture. Prayer was always spontaneous; not even the Lord's Prayer was used, since it was considered to be only a model for Christian improvising.

The early Separatists evidently had no music, but eventually they began to sing unaccompanied metrical psalms. When it was possible for them to celebrate Communion, the appointed pastor broke the bread and delivered the cup, which was then passed to every member of the group while the leader repeated the words of 1 Corinthians 11:23-26. There is also record that on such occasions an offering was received at the end of the service, by men who held their "hats in hand."

The Separatists followed several traditions under a number of dynamic leaders, and eventually formed the churches known as Presbyterian, Independent (Congregational), and Baptist. Their negative attitude about earlier music is expressed in a quote from John Vicar in 1649, who was speaking as a convinced Puritan, but still an Anglican:

> . . . the most rare and strange alteration of things in the Cathedral Church of Westminster. Namely, that whereas there was wont to be heard nothing almost by Roaring-Boys, tooting and squeaking Organ Pipes, and the Cathedral catches of Moreley, and I know not what trash, now the Popish Altar is quite taken away, the bellowing organs are demolished and pull'd down; the treble or rather trouble and base singers, Chanters or Inchanters, driven out, and instead thereof, there is now a most blessed Orthodox Preaching Ministry, even every morning throughout the Week, and every Week throughout the year a Sermon Preached by the most learned grace and godly Ministers.

Anabaptists ("re-baptizers," who insisted that baptism was only for adult believers) appeared both on the Continent and in Great Britain in the late sixteenth century. Records of a group in Holland in 1608 indicate that a typical service consisted of the following.

- Prayer
- Scripture (one or two chapters, with a running commentary on its meaning)
- Prayer
- Sermon (one hour, on a text)
- Spoken contributions by others present (as many as would)
- Prayer (led by the principal leader)
- Offering

It is not surprising that such a service often lasted as long as four hours. Sunday worship ran from about 8 A.M. to noon, and again from 2 P.M. to 5 or 6 P.M. (See Horton Davies, *Worship and Theology in England,* vol. 2 [Princeton: Princeton University, 1975], 89)

English Baptists were by no means of one mind

theologically. They divided into General Baptists (more Arminian in theology), Calvinistic Baptists (John Bunyan belonged to this group), Seventh-day Baptists (who worshiped on Saturday) and Particular Baptist (radically Calvinist). For all of them, the typical worship consisted of ministry of the Word (reading and exposition), extemporized prayer (lengthy—no collects) with a congregational "amen," and possibly metrical psalms sung to open and to close the service.

There is evidence that in some churches the only music was sung by a single individual "who had a special gift." John Bunyan once argued that open congregational singing could not fulfill the standard of Colossians 3:16 because some might participate who did not have "grace in the heart." As late as 1690, Benjamin Keach (1640–1704) had difficulty persuading his own congregation to sing in unison. However, he did prevail, and it is said that he was the first to introduce hymns (in addition to psalms) to an English congregation. He wrote the first hymn to be sung at the conclusion of the Lord's Supper, "following the example of Christ and his disciples in the upper room." Beyond this, we have little indication of how Baptists celebrated Communion, except, ironically, that it was a weekly occurrence.

Evangelicals are in large part the successors of the Separatist movement, and in many instances have inherited the anti-Romanist, anti-liturgical, and anti-aesthetic attitudes of their forebears. It may help one understand why these prejudices are so deeply ingrained to remember that our forefathers were moved by a strong spiritual commitment to evangelism. Furthermore, as dissenters they endured constant persecution by the Puritan/Anglican regime (or the Lutheran or Calvinist) under which they lived. To disobey the law by leading in clandestine worship was to risk a heavy fine and lengthy imprisonment.

───────── **Summary** ─────────

This article, along with the others that have preceded it, has traced our worship-practice roots, from New Testament times through 1600 years of the history of the Christian church, ending with the Reformation and finally, the emergence of free churches. The purpose has been to show our universal Christian heritage, as well as the unique tradition of each individual fellowship.

To be sure, there is common, universal heritage. We have seen that material from Scripture was the basis of musical worship in all medieval services. We have also traced the evangelical emphasis on preaching from New Testament times and the early church fathers, through the medieval Prone, the reformed services of Luther and Calvin, and the worship of the Separatists. All Christians continue to experience a Liturgy of the Word and a Liturgy of the Eucharist, though most Reformed and free churches have perpetuated the medieval reluctance to participate in Communion on a frequent basis. Furthermore, particularly in the free-church tradition, occasional observance tends to give the impression that the Lord's Supper is an appendage that is not central to full-orbed worship. Most evangelical scholars agree that the early church celebrated the Eucharist each Lord's Day. It may be that the free churches should face up to the question as to whether or not, in this matter, they are living up to their claim to be the New Testament church.

All the changes brought by the Reformation were responses to the sincere desire to be more "evangelical." Obviously, the reaction of the free (Separatist) bodies was the most radical, but it tended to be tempered (as in the matter of the use of music) within a few years. Nevertheless, some of the attitudes and practices which began at that time have haunted certain free church groups ever since. It is important that we distinguish true evangelical reform from blind iconoclasm. In recent years, many Christian groups have taken a new look at their heritage and have tended to reinterpret those reforms.

Donald P. Hustad

187 ✦ MUSIC IN THE MODERN REVIVALIST TRADITION

The revivalist tradition is rooted in pietest hymnody. It is characterized by an emphasis on the relationship of Christ (the bridegroom) to the church and to the individual believer (the bride). It is commonly held that Isaac Watts combined most successfully the expression of worship with that of human devotional experience. The Wesleys developed what we know today as "invitation" songs. When transported to America, this tradition gave rise to the modern revival movement.

The Pietist Movement in Germany

In the late seventeenth and early eighteenth centuries, an important movement flowered in the German Lutheran church known as pietism. Its first leader was Philipp Jakob Spener (1635–1705), who called the church from its obsession with dry scholasticism and cold formalism to an emphasis on personal study of the Scriptures and experiential "religion of the heart."

Pietists rejected all art music in worship because of the "operatic tendencies" of the time. Johann Sebastian Bach was in constant conflict with the pietists, though his cantata texts show the influence of their theology. The movement inspired a flood of subjective hymnody, much of which was set to tunes in dance-like triple meter, in sharp contrast to the older, rugged chorale style. Some of the best-known hymnists were Johann Freylinghausen (1670–1739), Ludwig von Zinzendorf (1700–1760), Benjamin Schmolck (1672–1737), and Erdmann Neumeister (1671–1756). It is interesting to note that Neumeister wrote cantata texts used by J. S. Bach and also the original version of the gospel hymn "Sinners Jesus Will Receive" (Christ Receiveth Sinful Men).

One of the favorite images of pietest hymnody—the relationship of Christ (the bridegroom) to the church and to the individual believer (the bride)—appears in even earlier hymns, such as "Jesu, meine Freude" by Johann Franck (1618–1677). The following is a rather literal translation of the first stanza and part of the last.

Jesus, meine Freude,	Jesus, my joy
Meines Herzens Weide,	My heart's longing,
Jesu, meine Zier,	Jesus, my beauty.
Ach, wie lang, ach lange	Oh, how long, how long
Is dem Herzen bange	Is the heart's concern
Und verlangt nach dir!	And longing after you.
Gottes Lamm, mein	Lamb of God, my
Brautigam,	bridegroom,
Ausser dir soll mir auf	May nothing on earth
Erden	become dear
Nichts sonst Liebers	To me except you.
werden.	
Weicht, ihr Trauergeister,	Get out, spirit of
	sadness!
Denn mein Freuden-	For my Lord of
meister,	gladness—
Jesu, tritt herein.	Jesus, enters in.
Denen, die Gott lieben	To those who love God,
Muss auch ihr Betruben	Even their sorrows
Lauter Zucker sein.	Are purest sweetness
	("sugar").

Franck had modeled his hymn on the love song of H. Alberti, "Flora, meine Freude" (Flora, my joy). English translations have ignored much of the original anthropomorphic imagery, and current German versions have changed the word Zucker (sugar) to Freude (joy).

Dissenters in England

We have already noted that it was a Dissenter—Benjamin Keach, a Baptist—who first introduced a hymn of "human composure" into the psalm-singing culture of seventeenth-century England. Isaac Watts (1674–1748), a Congregational minister, had the most profound influence on his country's transition to hymn singing and thus became known as the "father of English hymnody." It is significant that hymn singing flourished in the "renewal-born" free churches (Congregational, Baptist, and Presbyterian) for a hundred years while it was still being rejected in the established Church of England. Watts has been said to combine most successfully the expression of worship with that of human devotional experience, and it is best illustrated in his well-known hymn "When I Survey the Wondrous Cross," of which the first and last stanzas are quoted here.

> When I survey the wondrous cross,
>   On which the Prince of glory died,
> My richest gain I count but loss,
>   And pour contempt on all my pride.
>
> Were the whole realm of nature mine,
>   That were a present far too small;
> Love so amazing, so divine,
>   Demands my life, my soul, my all.

The Wesleyan Revival

Evangelistic hymns in the modern sense were one of the glorious by-products of Britain's Great Awakening in the eighteenth century. It was the preaching of John (1703–1791) and Charles Wesley (1707–1788), and the underlying tenets of the Dutch theologian Jacob Arminius (1560–1609) that led to the creation of the first "invitation" songs. Hard-line "hypercalvinism" based on covenant theology and the doctrine of predestination had rarely generated widespread, enthusiastic evangelism. In contrast, the Wesleys' Arminian theology emphasized that an individual may say either yes or no to a seeking God. To press the claims of Christ while still admitting human free will, Charles Wesley wrote:

> Come, sinners, to the Gospel feast:
>   Let every soul be Jesus' guest;
> Ye need not one be left behind
>   For God hath bidden all men sing.
>
> This is the time; no more delay!
>   This is the Lord's accepted day;
> Come thou, this moment, at his call,
>   And live for him who died for all.
>   (_Methodist Hymnal_ [1964], no. 102)

The Wesleys must be credited with rescuing hymn singing from the bondage of the two-line meters—common long and short. Their sources were the newer psalm tunes, opera melodies, and folk songs of German origin. An example of this type of tune is "Mendenbras" (which was actually first used with a hymn text by Lowell Mason in 1839), which we commonly sing with the text "O day of rest and gladness," although it may still be heard with its historic popular words in the beer gardens of Germany. The Wesleys' texts were fundamental for early Methodist theology. They also covered almost every conceivable aspect of Christian devotional experience and may be said to be the progenitors of the modern gospel song.

In any period of spiritual renewal, old symbols frequently lose their meaning and new ones must be sought. Obviously, they will be found outside the church, and because they must be "common" or "popular," they will come from folk songs and even from commercial entertainment music. In the evangelistic thrust of renewal, these fresh melodies become an effective vehicle for witness to the uncommitted. The newly adopted modern language eventually gains a new sacralization and becomes the norm for divine worship. It remains so until another spiritual revival displaces it.

In a theological rationale, one might say that this process demonstrates the church's willingness to be forever incarnational, to identify with "the world" and to transform it for Christ. It is certainly not a new concept in church music.

The American Scene

The early colonies took their worship and evangelism cues from Mother England. America's first worship music consisted of metrical psalms, and these were still the norm during the thundering revival preaching of Jonathan Edwards, best remembered by the title of one of his famous sermons, "Sinners in the Hands of an Angry God." When the Great Awakening came to America in the mid-eighteenth century—largely through the preaching sorties of the Wesley's associate George Whitefield—singing broke the bonds of strict psalmody and the hymns of Isaac Watts came to these shores. In the late 1700s, rural Baptists in New England were singing "old country"; the tunes were perpetuated through such books as _Kentucky Harmony_ (1825) and _The Sacred Harp_ (1844), and have come to be known as "white spirituals" or "Appalachian folk hymns."

The Camp Meetings. In 1800 the camp meeting movement began with an outbreak of revival in an outdoor encampment in Caine Ridge, Logan County, Kentucky. The music which characterized the camp meetings was very simple with much repetition, evidently very emotional and frequently improvised. These are typical texts which are little more than refrains:

> Come to Jesus, come to Jesus, Come to Jesus just
>   now,
>   Just now come to Jesus, Come to Jesus just
>   now.
> He will save you, he will save you, He will save
>   you just now,
>   Just now he will save you, He will save you
>   just now. (_The Revivalist_ [1872], 142)
>
> O get your hearts in order, order, order,
>   O get your hearts in order for the end of time.
> For Gabriel's going to blow, by and by, by and
>   by,
>   For Gabriel's going to blow, by and by.
>   (_The Evangelical Harp_ [1845], 40)

Much has been said about the relationship between black spirituals and camp meeting music, with the general impression that the latter may have copied the former. However, at that time in history, particularly in the revival context, blacks and whites worshiped together. It is possible that both cultures contributed to the spontaneous singing in the "brush arbor" meetings, and that blacks continued the tradition after the interest of the whites had diminished and they had moved on to new forms of more traditional, "composed" music. The similarity between camp meeting songs and black spirituals is shown by Ellen Jane (Lorenz) Porter in her lecture

"The Persistence of the Primitive in American Hymnology." She points out that the song "Where Are the Hebrew Children?" is found in both the North and the South and among the blacks.

1. Where, O where are the Hebrew children*
   (repeat)
   Who were cast in the furnace of fire?
   Safe now in the promised land.

*2. good Elijah, 3. prophet Daniel, 4. weeping Mary, 5. martyred Stephen, 6. blessed Jesus, etc.

By and by we'll go home to meet them, (repeat)
By and by we'll go home to meet them,
   Way over in the promised land.
                              (*Oriola* [1862], 236)

Many of the camp meeting songs also used popular melodies. According to Mrs. Porter, "Where Are the Hebrew Children?" has many parodies, including the Ozark song, "Where, O Where Is Pretty Little Susie?" and the college song "Where, O Where Are the Verdant Freshmen?"

It is evident that refrains were the most important element in camp meeting music, and some songs were little more. In other instances, favorite refrains were attached to many different hymns. In the *Companion to Baptist Hymnal* (p. 48), William J. Reynolds cites a quotation of P. P. Bliss in which "I will arise and go to Jesus" is identified as "one of the old-fashioned camp meeting spirituals" which could be sung as a response to Joseph Hart's "Come ye sinners, poor and needy" or after each stanza of an anonymous paraphrase of the prodigal son story, "Far, far away from my loving Father." Note also that the refrain "Blessed be the name of the Lord" appears with Charles Wesley's "O for a Thousand Tongues to Sing" (*Baptist Hymnal* [1975], no. 50) and with William H. Clark's "All praise to Him who reigns above" (*Hymns for the Living Church* [1974], no. 81). In the same tradition, Ralph E. Hudson added the lilting testimony refrain "At the cross, at the cross, where I first saw the light" to the sober, devotional "Alas! And Did My Savior Bleed?" of Isaac Watts. In another example, the final stanza commonly sung to John Newton's "Amazing Grace," by an unknown author, was also appended both to Isaac Watts's "When I Can Read My Title Clear" and to the sixteenth-century anonymous hymn "Jerusalem, My Happy Home," despite its grammatical weaknesses.

When we've been there ten thousand years
   Bright shining as the sun;
We've no less days to sing God's praise
   Than when we first begun. (sic)

The Finney Revival. The Second Great Awakening was an urban phenomenon in Eastern seaboard states in the early nineteenth century. Charles Granville Finney, a Presbyterian with a pronounced Arminian theological bent, was the central preacher. He frequently worked with the music educator-composer Thomas Hastings. Their association marks the first recorded instance of a songbook published specifically for a revival campaign. The following hymn was reputed to have been in one of Hastings's compilations and to have been used by Finney at the conclusion of the sermon as part of a protracted, emotional "altar call."

Hearts of stone, relent, relent,
   Break, by Jesus' cross subdued;
See his body, mangled—rent,
   Covered with a gore of blood.
Sinful soul, what hast thou done!
   Murdered God's eternal Son.

Yes, our sins have done the deed,
   Drove the nails that fixed him there,
Crowned with thorns his sacred head,
   Pierced him with a soldier's spear;
Made his soul a sacrifice,
   For a sinful world he dies.

Will you let him die in vain,
   Still to death pursue your Lord;
Open tear his wounds again,
   Trample on his precious blood?
No! with all my sins I'll part,
   Savior, take my broken heart.

Sunday School Hymns and the Gospel Song

Beginning in the 1840s, the Sunday school hymns of William B. Bradbury and others had the same musical form as camp meeting songs—catchy melody, simple harmony and rhythm and an inevitable refrain. Eventually these children's hymns were picked up by adults and the "gospel hymn" or "gospel song" was born, so named by Philip Phillips, "the Singing Pilgrim." It was the evangelistic missions of Moody and Sankey in Great Britain and

America that launched the gospel song on its century-long career that is still going strong. The gospel song also received a great impetus by its association with the "sing schools" conducted by itinerant music teachers in the middle of the nineteenth century. The most successful of the teachers—J. G. Towner, P. P. Bliss, and George F. Root, and many others—wrote and published both sacred and secular music, and in much the same style as Stephen Foster, composer of "My Old Kentucky Home" as well as many sacred selections. The hallowed Fanny Crosby, author of perhaps 9,000 gospel song texts, had achieved earlier success writing popular secular songs in collaboration with George F. Root, an associate of Lowell Mason in public school music, who taught at New York's Union Theological Seminary and also supplied music for the original Christy Minstrel Singers.

It should not be thought that these were unlettered, uncultured individuals who lacked recognition in their own society. Phoebe Palmer Knapp, composer of the music for "Blessed Assurance," was married to the president of the Metropolitan Life Insurance Company, and William Howard Doane, the most frequent collaborator of Fanny J. Crosby, was an extremely wealthy industrialist and civic leader. William Bradbury, George F. Root, and Charles Converse (_What a Friend We Have in Jesus_) all studied in Europe, and were acquainted with Robert Schumann, Franz Liszt and Louis Spohr. Fanny Crosby was well known by five American presidents and many other government leaders. The music these individuals wrote was highly successful in nineteenth-century America, and often made a great deal of money for them and their publishers.

We must also note that "experience hymns" continued to appear in evangelical settings the world around. For one thing, American hymns in this style were translated into every language in which Protestant worship was conducted, both in Europe and in mission lands. In addition, other countries produced their own versions. In Sweden, for example, a renewal movement developed in the Lutheran church during the 1840s under the lay preacher Carl Rosenius (1816–1868). Lina Sandell (1832–1903) supported the movement with her hymns to such an extent that she became known as the "Swedish Fanny Crosby." Music for many of her songs was written by Oscar Ahnfelt, who was called the "Swedish Troubadour" because of his itinerant ministry of singing and playing his own accompani-

ments on a guitar. The Sandell/Ahnfelt songs were published in a series of books with the help of the famous coloratura soprano, Jenny Lind, "the Swedish Nightingale." This is the first stanza of one of Lina Sandell's best-known hymns, many of which were brought to America by Swedish immigrants and are now sung by many evangelicals.

> Day by day and with each passing moment,
>   Strength I find to meet my trials here;
> Trusting in my Father's wise bestowment,
>   I've no cause for worry or for fear.
> He whose heart is kind beyond all measure
>   Gives unto each day what He deems best—
> lovingly, its part of pain and pleasure,
>   Mingling toil with peace and rest.
>   (Lina Sandell, 1865, Trans. by A. L. Skoog)

There have been many attempts to define a "gospel song" in order to differentiate it from more traditional hymn forms. Frequently it has been argued that hymns are "objective" (about God, the "object" of our thought) and gospel songs are "subjective" (about the thinking "subject" and his or her experience of God). However, many historic hymns are simultaneously both "objective" and "subjective" (e.g., Watts's "When I Survey the Wondrous Cross") while some acknowledged gospel songs are quite thoroughly objective (e.g., "Praise Him, Praise Him, Jesus Our Blessed Redeemer," by Fanny J. Crosby). Even metrical psalms have been set to gospel song music (e.g., E. O. Sellers's adaptation of Psalm 119, "Thy Word Is a Lamp to My Feet").

The title gives some cue as to the norm. "Gospel" suggests that it is usually concerned with a simple gospel: the message of sin, grace, and redemption, and a person's experience of them; "song" indicates a nontraditional origin—that is, it is not a hymn. Basically, the poetry was simpler than that of a hymn—less theological and less biblical, less challenging to the imagination, sometimes even inane. The musical structure was characterized by a refrain—a novelty in hymns, a simple lyric melody, inconsequential harmony, and a sprightly rhythm.

The Moody-Sankey Campaigns

Early in his ministry in the slums of Chicago, the untutored lay preacher Dwight L. Moody (1837–1899) sensed the power of the new songs to motivate men and women to spiritual action. When he embarked on a wider ministry, he chose Ira D. Sankey (1840–1908), a civil servant and amateur musician, to accompany him. Sankey led the congregational hymns and sang his solos while seated at a little reed organ. He was also a prominent composer and publisher of gospel songs. The story of Sankey's experience as he accompanied Mr. Moody to Scotland in 1873 is told in his own book, *My Life and the Story of the Gospel Hymns and of Sacred Songs* (New York: Harper, 1907). On one particular occasion, he was concerned because the illustrious hymn writer Horatius Bonar was in the audience:

> Of all men in Scotland he was the one concerning whose decision I was most solicitous. He was, indeed, my ideal hymn writer, the prince among hymnists of his day and generation. And yet he would not sing one of his beautiful hymns in his own congregation . . . because he ministered to a church that believed in the use of the Psalms only.
>
> With fear and trembling I announced as a solo the song, "Free from the law, oh, happy condition." Feeling that the singing might prove only an entertainment and not a spiritual blessing, I requested the whole congregation to join me in a word of prayer, asking God to bless the truth about to be sung. In the prayer my anxiety was relieved. Believing and rejoicing in the glorious truth contained in the song, I sang it through to the end.
>
> At the close of Mr. Moody's address, Dr. Bonar turned toward me with a smile on his venerable face, and reaching out his hand he said: "Well, Mr. Sankey, you sang the gospel tonight." And thus the way was opened for the mission of sacred song in Scotland. (Ibid., pp. 61–62)

In the Moody-Sankey meetings, England and America witnessed the advent of "Jesus" preaching and singing. Along with the biblically-strong "Free from the law," which was a good choice for the theologically minded Scots, there were many simple expressions of the love of God through Christ:

> I am so glad that our Father in heaven
> Tells of His love in the book He has given;
> Wonderful things in the Bible I see:
> This is the dearest, that Jesus loves me.
> (P. P. Bliss)

It is characteristic of the best witness songs that they are always couched in contemporary language. In Moody's day the idea of "being lost" or "saved" was often expressed in nautical terms:

> Pull for the shore, sailor, pull for the shore,
> Heed not the rolling waves, but bend to the oar;
> Safe in the lifeboat, sailor, cling to self no more;
> Leave that poor old stranded wreck, and pull for the shore. (Author unknown)

> I've anchored my soul in the haven of rest,
> I'll sail the wide seas no more;
> The tempest may sweep o'er the wild, stormy deep,
> In Jesus I'm safe evermore. (H. L. Gilmour)

The idea of conflict and challenge in spiritual living probably took images from the Civil War.

> Ho, my comrades! See the signal waving in the sky!
> Reinforcements now appearing! Victory is nigh!
> Hold the fort! for I am coming;
> Jesus signals still.
> Wave the answer back to heaven;
> "By thy grace, we will!" (P. P. Bliss)

Since the days of Sankey, the solo singer has been a distinctive part of musical mass evangelism in America. Philip Phillips (1834–1895) was perhaps the first in a long line of illustrious soloist-song leader-publishers, which includes Sankey's contemporaries Robert Lowry (1826–1899), P. P. Bliss (1838–1876), James McGranahan (1840–1907), P. P. Bilhorn (1865–1936), and Homer Rodeheaver (1880–1955). The strong contribution of the gospel singer is the "person to person"—often layperson to person—witness of Christian experience. In this ministry, the gospel message acquired an intensity of emotional communication that is acknowledged by both its proponents and its detractors. This was true even in the earliest days when the songs were not characteristically soloistic, but were sung by soloists and congregations alike. It is even more so now that styles of writing and performing solo music are fully developed. The gospel singer's appeal and popularity may be surpassed only by the singer of secular popular music—whether Rudy Vallee, Bing Crosby, Frank Sinatra, Elvis Presley, Johnny Cash, or Olivia Newton-John. It was this same personal, emotional communication of common human experience that gave Sankey equal billing with Moody.

"Charlie" Alexander and Gospel Choirs

In the early twentieth century, it was Charles Alexander (1867–1920), song leader for evangelists R. A. Torrey and J. Wilbur Chapman, who brought the "gospel choir" to its apex. Not an outstanding soloist himself, Alexander specialized in the leading of massed choirs and congregations around the world for more than twenty-five years. Once again, the significance of a ministry in music gave the song leader equal billing with the evangelist. Earlier it had been Moody and Sankey. Now it was Torrey and Alexander as well as Chapman and Alexander. One is tempted to discount the laudatory reports of Alexander's conducting successes in newspapers of that day.

Mr. Alexander is a conductor of the first order, and he exercises a curious spell over an audience. He drills a thousand people with the precision and authority of a drill-sergeant. He scolds, exhorts, rebukes, and jests. And the amusing feature is that the great audience enjoys being scolded and drilled. . . . They seem at first an audience for whom music has ceased to have any ministry. But as the singing goes on, the tired faces relax, the eyes brighten, the lips begin to move. . . . Music, as the servant and vehicle of religion, has fulfilled its true and highest office. It has set a thousand human souls vibrating in gladness. No one need doubt that the gospel can be sung as effectively as it can be spoken. (A statement by W. H. Fitchett, editor of *The Southern Cross,* describing a midday meeting in Melbourne, Australia's Town Hall, quoted in Helen C. Alexander and J. Kennedy Maclean, *Charles M. Alexander: A Romance of Song and Soul-Winning* [New York: Marshall Bros., 1921], 51–52)

I have watched the methods and the triumphs of the most famous baton-wielders of the time—Colonne, Nikisch, Mottl, Weingartner and Henry J. Wood. Never have I been so much impressed as I was by this bright-faced, energetic young evangelist. As the leader of a choir he has an amazing and almost magical influence, not only over the trained choir; he simply makes everybody sing, and sing as he wants them to. "Watch my hand!" he calls, and the men's unaccompanied voices rise and fall in crooning cadences with an effect any conductor might be proud of. Watch his hands? Why, we are watching every part of him; we cannot take our eyes off him; we are fascinated, hypnotized, bewitched . . . (Ibid., p. 106. The article is by H. Hamilton Fyle, music critic, in

the London *Daily Mirror,* February 6, 1905, reporting on a meeting in Royal Albert Hall.)

This kind of entertaining genius may help to account for the physical stamina which was demonstrated by audiences of that day. A "Festival of Song"—shared equally by congregation, choir, and soloists—was expected to last for three hours. In a report of the meetings in Royal Albert Hall, London, it was said that the audience came at two o'clock in the afternoon and stayed until six. Torrey preached for about forty-five minutes and the rest of the time was consumed by song, with the audience calling for one favorite after another.

It is apparent that the revival choir was expected to share the prophetic/evangelistic ministry of the evangelist; its materials consisted of the "basic gospel," and it was seated with the evangelists behind the pulpit, not in a "divided chancel" or in the balcony in the tradition of Old World churches.

"Charlie" Alexander was responsible for one more innovation in revivalist music—the use of the piano. Earlier leaders had used the pipe organ when it was available, or else a harmonium, a reed organ. Alexander found that the percussive piano was more helpful in leading the livelier songs of his day. Robert Harkness was his best known pianist. Harkness also wrote a number of songs in a more distinctively "soloistic" style (e.g., "Why Should He Love Me So?") It is said that Harkness was recruited from a "music hall" before he was a committed Christian, and that Alexander led him to personal faith in Christ.

The Team of Billy Sunday and Homer Rodeheaver

It is a popular misconception that "gospel music" did not change much from 1850 to 1950. Each generation has contributed its own theological, poetic, and musical flavor. From 1890 to 1910, the scene was dominated by teachers and students of the Moody Bible Institute, where D. B. Towner had become the mentor of gospel music. Songs of that period were intensely biblical and theological. Between 1910 and 1920, Billy Sunday came to the fore as an evangelist, with his song leader-soloist-trombonist, Homer Rodeheaver. Both men had gifts suited to the theater—Sunday was the dynamic, compulsive, athletic spellbinder, and Rodeheaver was the genial, suave, relaxed, joking "master of ceremonies." They brought evangelistic crusades to a new level, with crowd-pleasing mannerisms of entertainment.

> "Rody" was a master at getting people to sing. He used every gimmick at his disposal to break down the traditionally staid approach to religious music. Neither "Rody" nor Sunday would tolerate glumness in the Gospel, and the tabernacle crowds soon learned to expect the unexpected. Delegations that came were asked to sing their favorite song; railroaders, for instance, stood to sing "I've Been Working on the Railroad." College groups could count on a chance to sing their Alma Mater and give a victory cheer. (D. Bruce Lockerbie, *Billy Sunday* [Waco, Tex.: Word Books, 1965], 58)

Seafaring imagery was still around in those days because memories of the "Titanic" tragedy were still vivid.

> I was sinking deep in sin, Far from the peaceful
>   shore . . .
>
> Love lifted me, love lifted me,
> When nothing else could help, Love lifted me.
>   (James Rowe)

Other expressions were more serene, if not strongly theological:

> What a wonderful change in my life has been
>   wrought,
>   Since Jesus came into my heart;
> I have peace in my soul for which long I had
>   sought,
>   Since Jesus came into my heart.
>   (C. H. Gabriel)

The early twentieth century had its own "physical" music, as well. I remember singing one in the 1920s that was obviously inspired by stories of the First World War.

> Over the top for Jesus, Bravely we will go,
> Over the top for Jesus, Routing every foe;
> Never delaying when we hear the bugle blow,
> We'll fight for the right with all our might
> As over the top we go. (Author unknown)

Radio Renewal

During the "roaring twenties" mass revivalism went into a decline. It continued to be practiced in the local church, but there was no commanding evangelist to capture the nation's attention for a pe-riod of almost thirty years. Southern Baptists showed the most interest in continuing the tradition in the local church or community, and their most gifted songwriter, B. B. McKinney, composed words and music of some of the most important gospel hymns of the period. For many, the interest in outreach shifted to radio. The music of "gospel radio" was colored by the demands and the traditions of the new medium. Like television twenty-five years later, radio contributed much to the "spectator complex" in the recreation habits of our culture, and undoubtedly it encouraged spectatorism in church life. Much of the new gospel music had been "special," never intended for congregational use. Undoubtedly the voicing (the ladies' trio, for instance), the choral and instrumental arranging techniques, and the more advanced harmonic and rhythmic patterns were all borrowed from the entertainment world.

At the historic, radio-conscious Chicago Gospel Tabernacle, Merrill Dunlop wrote and published *Songs of a Christian* (Chicago: Van Kampen Press, 1946). He says that he was first inspired by the "different" harmonies and styles of Robert Harkness's songs. In his own advanced, jazz-related rhythm and harmony, Dunlop foreshadowed the present day. On one occasion he wrote a missions hymn in rhumba rhythm; to him this was perfectly logical because his special interest in foreign missions was South American. At about the same time and in the same city, Moody Bible Institute began gospel broadcasting in 1926; their radio director, Wendell Loveless, wrote gospel songs and choruses in a pseudo-Broadway style.

Youth for Christ

In the 1940s, evangelism was frequently associated with Youth for Christ, one of the parachurch organizations that have become so common on the evangelical scene. Traditionally YFC rallies met on Saturday evening for a pleasant blend of entertainment, fellowship, and religious challenge. Their norm for congregational singing was the gospel chorus. This return to the camp-meeting emphasis of the 1800s seemed to indicate that they agreed that the refrain was the only significant part of a gospel song, or that it was all the text that an audience could be expected to assimilate. When traditional gospel songs were sung, frequently the stanzas were completely omitted. In addition, many independent choruses were composed and collected in a huge proliferation of "chorus books."

> Into my heart, into my heart,
>   Come into my heart, Lord Jesus.
> Come in today, come in to stay,
>   Come into my heart, Lord Jesus.
> (Harry D. Clarke, 1922, copyright renewal
> 1952 by Hope Publishing Co. Used by
> permission.)

> Altogether lovely, He is altogether lovely,
>   And the fairest of ten thousand, this
>   wonderful Friend divine;
> He gave Himself to save me, now He lives in
>   heaven to keep me,
>   He is altogether lovely, is this wonderful
>   Savior of mine.
> (Wendell P. Loveless, 1931, copyright
> renewal 1959 Hope Publishing Co.
> Used by permission.)

In the late 1940s a new gospel hymn writer appeared. John W. Peterson (b. 1921), a pilot in World War II, first came to national attention about 1950 when his song "It Took a Miracle" began to be played on jukeboxes. His music was generally designed to be sung by soloists, choirs, and small ensembles, and only recently has begun to appear in hymnals. Peterson later found that he had a talent for composing "cantatas" for churches that had not traditionally used that form; he has now written more than a score of them and reportedly has sold more than a million copies!

In general, his lyrics show his strong biblical roots, particularly his postwar study at Moody Bible Institute in Chicago. His music varies from a typical gospel song style to an imitation of Broadway show tunes and was sufficiently creative to capture the attention of a large section of the evangelical public.

The Era of Billy Graham

The world-famous evangelist Billy Graham began his ministry with Youth for Christ, and in 1949, thanks to publicity by Hearst newspapers, he came to the attention of much of the world. The music of the Billy Graham crusades has largely depended on materials developed since 1850, borrowing some items from each period. A doctoral dissertation (George Stansbury, _The Music of the Billy Graham Crusades, 1947-1970_ [Louisville, Ky.: Unpublished Ph.D. dissertation, Southern Baptist Theological Seminary, 1971], 311–312) points out that, unlike

its revivalist predecessors, the Graham ministry has neither produced nor promoted a large body of new musical material. This may be partly due to the fact that, unlike Sankey, Alexander, and Rodeheaver, song leader Cliff Barrows is not a publisher. However, this unique phenomenon in the history of evangelism more likely reflects the "establishment" image which characterized revivalism in the mid-twentieth century. Dr. Graham evidently purposes to be conservative—fresh and appealing, but shunning the sensational and overemotional. Consequently Barrows has used materials that have been already proven to be widely popular, choosing them from the compositions of Ira Sankey, Fanny Crosby, Charles H. Gabriel, Haldor Lillenas, Merrill Dunlop, John Peterson, and finally, Bill Gaither. The Billy Graham films have made their own contribution to contemporary music through the folk/ballad songs of Ralph Carmichael (e.g., "He's Everything to Me" and "The New 23rd"), who composed the musical scores for several releases. Pianist Tedd Smith has also written some very significant music. The new musical feature in Graham crusades, however, has been the use of show-business talent like Johnny Cash and Norma Zimmer—as well as the best-known contemporary gospel singers—to attract the unchurched.

In the 1980s, the music of John Peterson came to be considered sophisticated and even elitist. In the typically "gospel song" style, it was Bill and Gloria Gaither from central Indiana who captured the imagination and the approval of much of the evangelical public. The Gaithers write songs that are much less theological and overtly biblical than Peterson's. They get their inspiration, they say, by listening to the latest pop songs; their songs, then, are "religious" reply. There is just enough contemporary freshness in the title and the principal refrain-phrase to appeal to modern evangelicals, many of whom are drawn to country music. Among the best-known Gaither songs are "He Touched Me," "Get All Excited," "The King Is Coming," "Just Because He Lives," and "The Old Rugged Cross Made the Difference."

As in all experience songs, the new gospel music reflects the thought patterns of our day. A modern person's need of God will not be expressed well in such frontier language as "I've wandered far away from God; Now I'm coming home," or "Would you be free from your burden of sin? There's power in the blood." Sin and lostness must be redefined for each succeeding generation. An individual's estrangement from God may be better described today in one of the favorite solos of Graham's gospel singer, George Beverly Shea: "Tired of a life without meaning / Always in a crowd, yet alone."

In a time when psychologists remind us that love is sometimes best expressed in physical contact, it should not be surprising that Bill Gaither will ignore all the traditional fears of anthropomorphism (attributing to God the characteristics of mortals) and write these words:

> He touched me, oh, He touched me,
>   And O, the joy that floods my soul.
> Something happened, and now I know,
>   He touched me, and made me whole.
>   (Copyright 1963 by William J.
>   Gaither. Used by permission.)

Both psychiatrists and sociologists tell us that the prevailing illness of our culture is loneliness. When "relational theology" is in vogue and we emphasize the "fellowship" aspect of Christian life and worship, it was inevitable that somebody would write about Christian fellowship:

> There's a sweet, sweet Spirit in this place,
>   And I know that it's the Spirit of the Lord;
> There are sweet expressions on each face,
>   And I know they feel the presence of the
>   Lord.
> (Doris Akers, copyright 1962 by Manna
> Music, Inc. All international copyright
> secured. All rights reserved. Used by
> permission.)

Other Musical Styles

Of course, the gospel song has not been the only variety of witness music known in recent years. In the 1930s, perhaps recalling the heyday of barbershop quartet singing, the Stamps-Baxter "gospel quartet" emerged to present all-night gospel sings and to publish scores of small songbooks which became popular, particularly in rural churches of the South. Most of these Southern hymns were uptempo, combining the call-and-response techniques of spirituals with the word-repetition common to the quartet song. In later years, the singing groups have varied in size and in voicing (including women as well as men), have adopted several different musical styles, and communicate both in "sacred concerts" and on television.

Even more startling varieties of gospel music were yet to come. In the wake of the Beatles and Geoffrey Beaumont's *Twentieth Century Folk Mass*, "gospel folk" and "gospel rock" appeared in Great Britain in the early 1960s. It was quickly transported to America, where its first appeal was strongest in the liturgical and more liberal ecclesiastical communities. It was heralded as a renewal in communication by churches whose attendance and financial support were falling off, and where young people were conspicuous by their absence.

The first reaction of the traditionally evangelical groups was a little amusing when one remembers their long-time heritage of borrowing secular tunes for sacred purposes. Horrified protests that "this worldly, entertainment music [was] not worthy of the message of Christ" poured in from many denominations. However, most evangelicals soon recovered their equilibrium, and their young people eagerly joined the crescendo of drums, guitars, and voices. At first they were not allowed to indulge their new musical tastes in the church sanctuary; the folk musicals had to be performed in the fellowship hall or in an outside auditorium. But in the last ten years, gospel rock and gospel folk music have become common, and many other styles have been added. It is already apparent that we have seen the most complete invasion of religious expression by popular music in history. Music leaders change formats almost monthly to keep up with the latest trends in secular popular music.

Summary and Evaluation

Much criticism has been leveled at modern day evangelism. What can we say then about the effectiveness of revivalism with its music in the history of America and of the world? Since we believe that the Holy Spirit has been present and creatively active in the world since Pentecost, we must acknowledge that the extra-ecclesiastical, personality-centered ministry of revivalists has contributed to the growth and the renewing of the church, from Francis of Assisi to John Hus to the Wesleys to D. L. Moody to Billy Sunday to Billy Graham and Barry Moore. Whatever their personal weaknesses—of character or theology or method—these individuals have been used by God to accomplish some of his purposes.

It would be difficult to separate the musical expression of revivalism from the preaching; the two seem to belong to each other, though both have tended to be anti-establishment. In sixteenth-century Germany, Luther was both preacher and hymn writer, and it would be hard to prove that one role was more significant than the other in advancing the cause of the Reformation. In the history of Great Britain in the 1870s and 1880s, the names of Moody and Sankey are forever linked, for the musician seemed as important as the preacher in accomplishing God's work. It was the same with Chapman and Alexander and later with Sunday and Rodeheaver. Furthermore, each period of renewal has been characterized by a flowering of new hymnody; it is as a result of these stimuli that hymnology textbooks are written.

We need both the transcendent and the immanent in music, because that is the God we know—the God who is above all his creation, whom we cannot see except "through a glass darkly" (1 Cor. 13:12), and yet One who dwells within the believer, closer than hands and feet. It is expressed well in one verse from the Old Testament:

> For thus says the high and lofty One who inhabits eternity, whose name is Holy: "I dwell in the high and holy place, and also with him who is of a contrite and humble spirit, to revive the spirit of the humble, and to revive the heart of the contrite. (Isa. 57:15)

This theological paradox is argument enough for a twofold purpose in church music. The church requires music that expresses both the perfections of the "high and holy" God, and also the personal, religious experience of the "broken and humble."

Donald P. Hustad

188 • Church Music in the American Colonies

The preceding article traced the outlines of the revivalist music tradition in both Europe and America. The following article looks more closely at the church music in the period of American colonization and revolution. Church music during this period was based on European models, especially the Psalm singing of the Calvinists. Later, the rise of singing schools and the presence of groups such as the Moravians and Shakers produced church music that was distinctively American.

A census of citizens of North America in 1790 revealed that only 5 percent professed any religious affiliation. Today that figure is 95 percent, of whom nearly half worship regularly in a Christian church. These simple statistics represent a growth that might be the envy of Christians in Western Europe, whose numbers have suffered a steady decline over the same period.

The story of the development of Christian music in the United States is a complex and colorful one, additionally important for the impact that it has had on the world at large. For North Americans do not keep their faith to themselves. In 1985, Protestant Christian missionary societies alone spent more than $500 million in supporting overseas missions and that figure is rising yearly. The 20,000 missionaries that the sum sends out worldwide take the hymns and songs of America with them.

———— The American Heritage ————

Compared with Europe, Christianity in the United States has developed over a mere few hundred years, without the support of the wealth and traditions of an established church. These two facts may have some bearing on the present strength of faith in the United States.

The first Christian settlement, in Jamestown, Virginia, was established only in 1607. These English settlers and the immigrants who followed them from other parts of Europe arrived with none of the resources that those they had left behind could take for granted. Their life in the New World began with the poverty and hardship that had driven them there in the first place. There was no church wealth built up over centuries, no Christian traditions of worship. They had nothing except what they carried with them, probably no more than a Bible and a metrical psalter.

Christianity in North America has grown since those times as a fire grows from a spark. But a healthy suspicion of ecclesiastical power has remained. The style of worship still valued most highly is one of directness and simplicity, without undue ceremony.

Life in North America is too easily known by its urban side, the extraordinary blend of decadence and deprivation that is supported by the technology of instant communication. For between the huge cities there are vast and sparsely populated areas of countryside in which small communities enjoy a continuity of traditions in life and faith. Here the true Christian music of North America is to be found. It is a folk art, which in its formative years had no chance of being influenced by music as an art form, for classical music remained undeveloped in North America until the mid-nineteenth century. Even today it remains largely untouched by the sophistication of European traditions.

Establishing a New Tradition

The Christian music sung by the early white settlers was that of the metrical psalms. Indeed, the pilgrims left their European homes with the psalm tunes ringing in their ears:

> They that stayed at Leyden feasted us that were to go at our pastor's house, being large; where we refreshed ourselves, after tears, with singing of Psalms . . . and indeed it was the sweetest melody that ever mine ears heard. (Edward Winslow, "Hypocrisie Unmasked," and quoted in W. S. Pratt, *The Music of the Pilgrims* [Boston, 1921], 6.)

For the French Huguenots in Florida or the English and Dutch Puritans of New England, psalm singing was at the heart of their musical expression of faith. Its importance to the early Christian communities is evident from the first publication of any kind in America, the *Bay Psalm Book*. Remarkably, it was published in Boston as early as 1640 and its pioneering spirit is evident from the preface:

> God's altar needs not our pollishings: for wee have respected rather a plaine translation . . . and so have attended Conscience rather than Elegance, fidelity rather than poetry . . . that soe wee may sing in Sion the Lords songs of prayse according to his own will; untill hee take us from hence, and wipe away all our tears, & bid us enter into our masters joye to sing eternall Halleluiahs.

The *Bay Psalm Book* did not contain any music, but recommended the tunes of Ravencroft's *Whole Book of Psalms* "collected out of our chief musicians."

The practice of "lining out" (described in some detail in Chapter 19) was established early in America, as the Rev. John Cotton made clear in 1647:

> For the present, where many in the congregation cannot read, it is convenient that the minister, or some other fit person . . . do read the psalm line by line before the singing thereof. (Cotton Mather, *Singing of the Psalms a Gospel Ordinance* [1647],

and quoted in P. Scholes, *The Puritans in Music* [London, 1934], 265.)

The results for American psalmody were as extraordinary as for the Old World:

> The same Person who sets the Tune, and guides the Congregation in Singing, commonly reads the Psalm, which is a task too few are capable of performing well, that in Singing two or three Staves, the congregation falls from a cheerful pitch to downright Grumbling, and then some to relive themselves mount an Eighth above the rest, others perhaps a Fourth or Fifth, by which Means the Singing appears to be rather a confused noise, made up of Reading, Squecking and Grumbling . . .

> In many places, one Man is upon this Note, while another is a Note before him, which produces something so hideous and disorderly, as is beyond Expression bad . . . and besides, no two Men in the Congregation quaver [decorate the tune with extra notes] alike, or together; which sounds in the Ears of a good Judge, like Five Hundred different Tunes roared out at the same time . . . (T. Walter, *The Grounds and Rules of Music Explained* [Boston, 1721])

By the early eighteenth century, some ministers were beginning to clamor for a more "Regular" way of singing, causing "Heats, Animosities and Contentions" among the old guard. Typically, it was the country areas that resisted any suggestion of change:

> Tho' in the polite city of Boston this design [the new way] met with general acceptance, in the country, where they have more of the rustic, some numbers of elder and angry people bore zealous testimonies against these wicked innovations, . . . not only . . . call the singing of these Christians a worshipping of the devil, but also they would run out of the meeting-house at the beginning of the exercise. (K. Silverman, *Selected Letters of Cotton Mather* [Baton Rouge: Louisiana State University Press, 1971], 376)

In New England, new ways of singing eventually supplanted the old, but not in other parts of North America. Extraordinarily enough, there are still isolated parts of Appalachia and the Southeast where the old practice of lining-out is still practiced, particularly among remote Baptist churches. It is an oral tradition—just as it was 300 years ago—where the congregation relies on its memories of the tunes and sings in heterophony ("500 different tunes roared out at the same time") and at an extremely slow pace.

The Singing Schools

The new way of singing was really only a return to what today's church musicians would call normality; the Americans called it "singing by note." But education had to be provided for such a change. As a minister observed as early as 1720:

> Would it not greatly tend to promote singing of psalms if singing schools were promoted? . . . Where would be the difficulty, or what the disadvantages, if people who want skill in singing, would procure a person to instruct them, and meet two or three evenings in the week, from five or six o'clock to eight, and spend their time in learning to sing? (Quoted in H. W. Hitchcock, _Music in the United States_ [New Jersey, 1974], 7.)

These singing schools sometimes provided more than they were originally intended, as a student at Yale revealed in a letter to a friend:

> At present I have no inclination for anything, for I am almost sick of the World & were it not for the Hopes of going to the singing-meeting tonight & indulging myself in some of the carnal Delights of the Flesh, such as kissing, squeezing &c. &c. I should willingly leave it now. (Quoted in I. Lowens, _Music and Musicians in Early America_ [New York, 1964], 282.)

These singing schools had their parallels in English country parishes. They were set up on a temporary basis in a schoolhouse or a tavern with the blessing of the local church, and worshipers were encouraged to enroll for a course of singing lessons (provided that they brought their own candles with them). The lessons were based on instruction in solmization, a system of pitching adapted from the invention of Guido d'Arezzo whereby the notes of a scale are identified by names. Where Guido used a different name for each note of the scale, the pioneers of the singing schools used a simplified system using only four: _fa, sol, la_ and _mi._ Thus an upward major scale would have been sung to the note names _fa, sol, la, fa, sol, la, mi, fa._ Such a system might seem oversimplified to the point of confusion, but the standard of singing in many churches improved noticeably. As Samuel Sewall wrote in his diary in

the early 1720s: "House was full, and the Singing extraordinarily Excellent, such as has hardly been heard before in Boston" (M. H. Thomas, ed., _The Diary of Samuel Sewall,_ New York, 1973, Vol. 3, p. 285).

Gradually, other systems to help people to read notation developed, from the crude system of the Rev. John Tufts, which placed letters indicating the _sol-fa_ names in the appropriate positions on a five-line stave, to the shape-note systems of the turn of the eighteenth century, where shapes corresponded with the four _sol-fa_ names—a triangle for _fa,_ a circle for _sol,_ a square, _la,_ and a diamond, _mi._

The many new tune-books appearing from the 1750s onward catered to the developing interest in part-singing: _Youths Entertaining Amusement_ (1754), _Urania_ (1761), _Royal Melody Complete_ (Boston, 1767, containing music by the British composer William Tans'ur) and others. The music of some of these books contained pieces complicated enough to be called anthems rather than psalm tunes.

Such pieces testify to the musical ambitions and even the success of some of the singing masters who, when their course of lessons was complete, would move on to the next town to start again. Nonetheless, the instructors themselves were self-taught. There were no colleges teaching the rudiments of music, let alone the conventions of counterpoint and harmony. All that was picked up by the very imperfect example of oral tradition and through printed music.

Changing tastes in the expanding urban populations gradually ousted this rough-hewn music from city churches, but in the South and at the westward-advancing frontiers it remained popular. Nineteenth-century music collections continued to print the music of the singing-school pioneers of a century before: _Virginia Harmony, Kentucky Harmony_ (1816), _Knoxville Harmony_ (1838), _Union Harmony_ (Tennessee, 1837), _Southern Harmony_ (1835), and many others.

These collections also show quite clearly how folk tunes, originally wedded to secular words, came to be accepted in church worship with Christian texts. From these sources come a number of folk hymns whose tunes have penetrated the consciousness of the English-speaking world: in _Southern Harmony,_ for instance, can be found _Wondrous Love_ and a hymn by Isaac Watts put to the tune of "Auld Lang Syne." The best-loved of all, perhaps, is

Amazing Grace, originally set to "There is a land of pure delight" in *Virginia Harmony.*

A collection of 1844 called *The Sacred Harp* has a special significance, having given its name to the annual Sacred Harp Conventions which still meet today to celebrate this Christian folk-music—clear evidence that it is still known and well-loved in the Southern states.

Moravians and Shakers

Two traditions of worship established in North America in the eighteenth century created Christian music of particular richness. The cultures from which they sprang were opposites, but both for a while chose isolation rather than integration with the societies around them. Such insularity was necessary for something exceptional to grow, but it also prevented such Christian music finding its way into the worship of other denominations.

As they traveled to North America on an evangelistic mission in 1737, John and Charles Wesley found that they were sailing with a group of Moravian Brethren with the same intentions. These Moravians had come from Herrnhut, a settlement in north Germany, but the origins of their movement, the Unitas Fratrum, lay in the reforming zeal of Jan Hus in sixteenth-century Bohemia. The revival of the Moravian Church in 1722 sent missionary expeditions to the Virgin Islands, then to Greenland, South Africa, Jamaica, and North America. Communities of Moravians were founded in Bethlehem in Pennsylvania and in parts of North Carolina.

For the German-speaking Moravians, as for the Lutherans, music generally held a treasured place in life. They brought instruments with them from north Germany, and there were instrument-makers among them. Thus bands were available for ceremonial occasions of all kinds—weddings, christenings and so on.

The Moravians had a knowledge of the European music they left behind them, a knowledge that was rare in eighteenth-century America. Their Christian music lay at the center of this activity and only quite recently has the true extent of this music been uncovered. Not only did they have their own hymn writers, but they also boasted choirs which, judging by the music composed for them, must have possessed skills quite beyond those of the New Englanders.

The Shakers, "The United Society of Believers in Christ's Second Appearing," started life as a small English sect to which Ann Lee had been attracted at the age of twenty-two in 1758. She was a humble woman from the slums of Manchester who became convinced that she was "Ann the Word" and "the Bride of the Lamb." Some of her converts emigrated to North America, where, in the early years of the nineteenth century, the Society's membership grew to about 6,000, settling mostly in areas of the Northeast such as New York, Massachusetts, and Connecticut. One of her converts described Mother Ann Lee:

> Mother Ann Lee was sitting in a chair, and singing very melodiously, with her hands in motion; and her whole soul and body seemed to be in exercise. I felt, as it were, a stream of divine power and love flow into my soul, and was convinced at once that it came from Heaven, the source and fountain of all good. I immediately acknowledged my faith, and went and confessed my sins. (S. Y. Wells, ed., *Testimonies Concerning the Character and Ministry of Mother Ann Lee and the First Witnesses of the Gospel* [Albany, 1827], 101, and quoted in D. W. Patterson, *The Shaker Spiritual* [Princeton, 1979], 18.)

The believers lived in small, exclusive, and self-sustaining villages. Their very strict moral sense kept the sexes apart, even by providing separate entrances and staircases in homes and meetinghouses—though women and men had equal status. They built their own dwellings and churches, grew their own food, made their own furniture (now highly prized and much copied), everyone covenanting their wealth to a central fund.

Most Shaker songs were created as a spontaneous act of praise and under the control of the Holy Spirit, whether in a worship meeting or outside. A Shaker pamphlet of 1782 described the spontaneity of their worship, clearly related to charismatic meetings today:

> One will begin to sing some odd tune, without words or rule; after a while another will strike in; and then another; and after a while they all fall in, and make a strange charm—some singing without words, and some with an unknown tongue or mutter, and some with a mixture of English . . . (*Some Brief Hints, of a Religious Scheme, Taught and Propagated by a Number of Europeans, Living in a Place called Nisquenia, in the State of New York*

[Salem, Mass., 1782], quoted in E. D. Andrews, *The Gift to Be Simple* [New York, 1940], 10.)

In the earlier days these songs were passed down in oral tradition, as the Shakers initially resisted the idea of notating their music. The first printed collections of Shaker tunes did not appear till the 1830s, but surviving manuscripts and notebooks show the true scale of their creativity and contain as many as 10,000 tunes.

Shaker music is a uniquely refreshing reminder of the simplicity of much Christian music in America. In country areas around and beyond the Shaker communities, where education was even harder to come by and illiteracy was high, music was still being handed down orally from one generation to the next. It was largely a folk art, recalled as much as read, each performer adding new flavor to an old song.

Andrew Wilson-Dickson[18]

189 • CHURCH MUSIC OF AFRICAN-AMERICANS

One of the richest contributions to church music in America has undoubtedly come from the heritage of the African-Americans who came to America as slaves. Their hymns and spirituals, which are sung today across the world, give evidence of both the extreme hardships and the fervent faith that was a part of their experience in America.

Africans in America

A glance down the "for sale" columns of eighteenth-century American newspapers would reveal dozens of small ads such as this:

TO BE SOLD a valuable young handsome Negro Fellow about 18 or 20 years of age; has every qualification of a genteel and sensible servant and has been in many different parts of the world. . . . He lately came from London, and has with him two suits of new clothes, and his French horn, which the purchaser may have with him.

Slavery had begun two centuries earlier—the first slaves were brought to America by Sir John Hawkins in 1563. The plantations that developed in America's middle colonies in the eighteenth century increased the demands for slaves enormously, bringing the number by the 1750s to 300,000. By the end of that century this figure had tripled. One

St. Philip. The most common shield for this apostle depicts a tall, slender cross and a basket, recalling Philip's words when Jesus fed the multitudes (see John 6:7).

estimate suggests that altogether 15 million black slaves were brought to the continent (including the West Indies and South America) before Abraham Lincoln's Emancipation Proclamation in 1863.

The Music of Africa

The wonderful musicality of Africa came with the slaves. It could be heard even in the appalling and life-threatening conditions of the slave ship:

[The slaves on the ship] sang songs of sad lamentation. . . . They sang songs expressive of their fears of being beat, of their want of victuals, particularly the want of their native food, and of their never returning to their own country. (Ecroyd Claxton, *Minutes of the Evidence . . . Respecting the Slave Trade*, 34, pp. 14–36, House of Commons, quoted in D. J. Epstein, *Sinful Tunes and Spirituals: Black Folk Music to the Civil War* [Urbana, Illinois, 1987].)

The slaves on board had to make music whether they liked it or not, being forced to dance for the entertainment of the sailors:

and if they do not, they had each of them [the boatswain and his mate] a cat to flog them and make them do it. (Ibid., p. 8)

The many musical traditions brought over from Africa were transformed by the conditions of slavery and by the arbitrary mixing of peoples of differing cultures (this was a specific policy believed to make the slaves less rebellious) but they were not eradicated. On the contrary, music and dance remained, as in Africa, far more than a diversion from the hardship and injustice of slavery. They were vital expressions of identity occasionally permitted in a life of almost unremitting labor.

Dancing and music-making using traditional instruments were celebrated at festivals such as Pinkster Dagh (a corruption of "Pentecost Day") when white spectators could look on at a great carnival of ecstatic dancing and music lasting several days.

It was also possible to hear the musical expression—the hollers—of black slave-workers in the fields and open spaces:

Suddenly one raised such a sound as I never heard before, a long, loud, musical shout, rising and falling, and breaking into falsetto, his voice ringing through the woods in the clear, frosty night air, like a bugle call. As he finished, the melody was caught up by another, then by several in chorus. (F. L. Olmstead, *Journey in the Seaboard Slave States,* vol. 2 [New York, 1856], 19, and quoted in E. Southern, *The Music of Black Americans,* 2d ed. [New York, 1983], 156.)

The conversion of the blacks to the Christian faith went ahead slowly, for not all whites felt it appropriate for their slaves to know for themselves the privileges of their faith. But in such scraps as the slaves could pick up, they discovered the God who ignores human barriers, who delivers people from oppression, and in whose sight everyone is equal. These were messages of hope and eventual liberation that came to be celebrated in music and dance of great power:

it was musicking and dancing . . . with their unique power to weld into a higher unity the contradictory experiences of sorrow, pain, joy, hope and despair, that were at the center of their religious expression. (C. Small, *Music of the Common Tongue* [London, 1987], 87)

Hymns

So when the slaves adopted Christianity and began to sing the Psalms and hymns in the white churches (albeit segregated) they brought a life and vigor to the music which the whites could not fail to notice:

. . . all breaking out in a torrent of sacred harmony, enough to bear away the whole congregation to heaven. (S. Davies, *Letters from the Reverend Samuel Davies and Others . . . ,* quoted in C. Hamm, *Music in the New World* [New York, 1983], 128.)

The skill and passionate sincerity in Christian music-making was brought into the homes of white Christians. In 1755 the Rev. Samuel Davies described the slaves singing from their Psalters and hymnbooks:

Sundry of them have lodged all night in my kitchen, and sometimes when I have awaked about two or three o'clock in the morning, a torrent of sacred harmony has poured into my chamber and carried my mind away to heaven. . . . I cannot but observe that the Negroes, above all the Human species that I ever knew, have an Ear for Musicke, and a kind of extatic Delight in Psalmody . . . (S. Davies, quoted in C. Hamm, *Music in the New World,* 128.)

By now it will be evident how significant are those last few words, for through their continued celebration of "extatic delight," the black community in America has proferred a great gift to the legacy of Christian music.

It was not until the 1770s that blacks were permitted to form their own churches. The first hymnal for black churches was published in 1801, the *Collection of Spiritual Songs and Hymns Selected from Various Authors*. The hymns, with texts by Isaac Watts, Charles Wesley, and others, were selected by Richard Allen, minister of one of the first independent black denominations, the African Methodist Episcopal Church (his church was in Philadelphia). The many editions of this influential hymnbook (even up to recent times) have been a touchstone for the changing tastes of hymn singing in many black congregations. The early editions, for instance, contain simple, folklike tunes popular at the revival meetings of the late eighteenth century. Subsequent editions contained the most popular contemporary spirituals.

The folk tunes of the early editions were not to

everyone's taste. A Methodist Minister, J. F. Watson, wrote in 1819 of

> a growing evil, in the practice of singing in our places of public and society worship, merry airs, adapted from old songs, to hymns of our (the whites') composing: often miserable as poetry, and senseless as matter . . . most frequently composed and first sung by the illiterate blacks of the society. (J. F. Watson, _Methodist Error_ [Trenton, 1819])

Spirituals

Camp meetings were an important basis for the growth of what are now known as spirituals. These songs, whether sung by blacks or whites, were essentially music of the countryside. The blacks brought special qualities to their spirituals, namely, a background of field hollers (see above) and the ecstatic character of their African musical heritage.

The words of the spirituals were directly biblical, drawn especially from passages which speak of liberation (Moses, Daniel, and the Book of Revelation were favorites) and perhaps adapted from popular English hymns, for example, the popular hymn by Isaac Watts:

> When I can read my title clear
> to mansions in the skies,
> I'll bid farewell to ev'ry fear,
> And wipe my weeping eyes.

This became the basis for several spirituals, such as the following:

> Good Lord, in the mansions above,
> Good Lord, in the mansions above,
> My Lord, I hope to meet my Jesus
> In the mansions above.
>
> My Lord, I've had many crosses, and trials here
>   below;
> My Lord, I hope to meet you,
> In the mansions above.

The music tended to be of the call-and-response type. This simple structure, so common in African traditional music, allows great freedom: no books are needed, for the chorus is easy to pick up and the solo calls can be improvised on the spot. All this was accompanied by hand-clapping and foot-stamping, creating a Christian protest music of distilled and concentrated ecstasy.

White spirituals of the same period often adapted the texts of hymns in the same kind of way, perhaps repeating lines or adding a short refrain (like "Glory, hallelujah!') between them, just like the black spirituals. The music was often borrowed or adapted from well-known folk-melodies.

Conversely, black Christians were well aware of the songs that the whites were singing in the camp meetings and were happy to sing tunes from white traditions. There were more pragmatic reasons for white ministers' disapproval of the wild conduct of black worship in the South. The words of their songs had layers of meaning which could be as temporal as they were spiritual, such as the following lines from the spiritual "Dere's No Rain,": "no more slavery in de kingdom/no evil-doers in de kingdom/all is gladness in de kingdom." (Quoted in E. Southern, _The Music of Black Americans,_ 159.) Besides being a spiritual home in "the heavens above," "de kingdom" could have also meant the North, where an escape from the bondage of slavery was possible.

One organization to assist slaves to flee their masters was called the Underground Railroad. A black slave, Frederick Douglass, became involved with it in 1835 in an attempted escape and later explained the coded messages embedded in spirituals:

> We were, at times, remarkably buoyant, singing hymns and making joyous exclamations, almost as triumphant in their tone as if we had reached a land of freedom and safety. A keen observer might have detected in our repeated singing of "O Canaan, sweet Canaan," something more than a hope of reaching heaven. We meant to reach the North—and the North was our Canaan. (F. Douglas, _My Bondage and My Freedom_ [New York, 1855], 87, quoted in E. Southern, _The Music of Black Americans,_ 143.)

Many whites felt that the preaching of the Christian gospel of justice and liberty for all men was dangerous. It seems they were right.

The Period of the Civil War

The population of the industrial areas of North American grew rapidly during the nineteenth century. With the inexorable move towards the abolition of slavery, more and more black churches were established that did not have to suffer the strict control of the white Episcopal church. They reflected a number of traditions, from an orderliness which emulated the atmosphere of many white congregations, to an ecstatic and physical abandon characteristic of African tradition.

African Worship

Frederika Bremer visited some black churches in Cincinnati in 1850. The Episcopal church there left her with the impression of a service that was "quiet, proper and a little tedious." But the African Methodist church was quite a different matter:

> I found in the African Church African ardor and African life. The church was full to overflowing, and the congregation sang their own hymns. The singing ascended and poured forth like a melodious torrent, and the heads, feet and elbows of the congregation moved all in unison with it, amid evident enchantment and delight in the singing. . . . (A. B. Benson, ed., *American of the Fifties: Letters of Frederika Bremer* [New York, 1924])

Another report comes from William Faux who visited a black church in Philadelphia in 1820:

> After sermon they began singing merrily, and continued, without stopping, one hour, till they became exhausted and breathless. . . . While all the time they were clapping hands, shouting and jumping and exclaiming, "Ah Lord! Good Lord! Give me Jesus! Amen." (W. Faux, *Memorable Days in America . . .* [London, 1823], 420)

Such descriptions are evidence that informal dance was a central part of much black worship. Paradoxically, it was the suppression of dance by influential Puritan whites in the eighteenth century that encouraged its development when the black churches became independent.

The Abolition of Slavery

By the 1840s the ideological split between the Northern and Southern states was affecting every aspect of life. The white Southerners no longer holidayed in the North, nor sent their sons to be educated in the famous Northern universities of Yale, Princeton, and Harvard. The issue that polarized North and South was slavery. The Northern states, better educated and more liberal than the South, had long accepted its abolition as inevitable, but the Southern states refused to comply. The issue split the church: in 1840 the Methodists in the South were unable to agree with those in the North over

the morality of slavery; Baptists divided on the same issue a year later. (The rift between the Methodists was not formally settled until 1936.)

The issue was finally settled in the Civil War, where the eventual defeat of the Southern forces allowed Congress to bestow freedom on slaves in all states in 1865. Tragically, this victory did not necessarily improve the lot of the ex-slaves, many of whom found themselves worse off than before. In an atmosphere of vengeance the South established Black Codes and Jim Crow laws that made segregation almost universal. Blacks were still dependent on whites for their livelihood and given no chance to improve their position. The deprivation and suffering of ex-slaves was made worse still by the activities of white gangs such as the Ku Klux Klan, which attempted to preserve white supremacy by merciless terrorism.

The exodus of liberated slaves from the South therefore continued for the rest of the century. Gradually the spirituals of the countryside were replaced in the minds of migrant freedmen by music of the growing city churches. A schoolteacher in Tennessee noted this change after the Civil War:

> How I wish you could hear my children sing their strange, wild melodies, that bring back so vividly the old slave life with its toil and servile ignorance. Yet their old plantation songs are falling into disuse, and in their stead we hear chanted daily the hymns and psalms so familiar to Northern ears. (L. W. Slaughter, *The Freedmen of the South* [Cincinnati, 1869], 134)

But the spirituals were preserved in invaluable collections, the first and most important of which was *Slave Songs of the United States*. They were also popularized worldwide by black singing groups, such as the Fisk Jubilee Singers, at a time when the slave culture that produced their music was rapidly disappearing.

But true folk music (like the original spirituals) is a delicate plant. Its transportation away from its natural surroundings and the popular acclaim that follows inevitably changes and probably diminishes it. It seems that the essential qualities of the slave spiritual cannot be sensed from even the earliest collections of the music, let alone from more recently published versions. Its clearest evocation may only lie in the recorded eyewitness accounts of the culture that produced it.

Andrew Wilson-Dickson[19]

190 • MUSIC IN TRADITIONAL CHURCHES DURING THE MODERN ERA

Through much of the nineteenth century, worship in liturgical churches followed largely low-church convictions. In the mid-nineteenth century and continuing into the twentieth, many of these churches began recovering ancient patterns of worship. In music, this meant the recovery of Gregorian chant in the Catholic church, the return of Lutherans to sixteenth-century liturgy forms, a movement in some Anglican churches away from a Puritan-influenced worship to the recovery of catholic forms, and the trend in some free churches from revival-style worship to quasi-liturgical practices.

Worship Forms and Music in Diverse Churches

It has already been noted that, in its frontier culture, early American worship practices were exceedingly primitive. Concurrent with advance in education and in the arts, there was pressure in the older churches for the development and the standardization of worship forms. Following the War for Independence, all Protestant bodies severed their Old World connections. Nevertheless, worship design was frequently influenced by liturgical movements abroad as well as at home. At the same time, this interest in patterned worship came into direct conflict with the repeated outbreaks of revivalism. Through the years, there has been continuing tension between these two forces—formal versus spontaneous worship.

In the twentieth century, we have seen "thesis, antithesis and synthesis" in the outworking of the struggle. Some groups are clearly "formal" or clearly "spontaneous" in worship habits. In other churches, a new interest in liturgy and liturgical symbolism has been coupled with a concern for Christian fellowship and a desire for spontaneity in worship. In the next few pages we will consider the historical developments in both the liturgical and the free churches, since they have tended to interact, sometimes in imitation and sometimes in reaction.

The Liturgical Communions

Roman Catholic. Roman Catholic worship in America is not appreciably different from that in other parts of the world, and it did not change its basic patterns from the Council of Trent (1562) until the Second Vatican Council (1962). Nevertheless, there has been considerable diversity in the music which accompanies the liturgy.

Little is known about Roman Catholic music in the thirteen colonies. In 1787, *A Compilation of the Litanies, Vespers, Hymns and Anthems As They Are Sung in the Catholic Church* was published in Philadelphia by John Aitken, containing litanies, historic hymns, psalms, anthems, a Mass of the Blessed Trinity, a requiem mass (in plainsong), and a Solemn Mass with musical settings in both Latin and English. In the nineteenth century, new waves of Catholic immigrants came to these shores, mostly from very humble circumstances in Europe. Consequently their musical expectations were very limited, and in most churches there was no singing at all.

In those that supported choral music, the preference was for nineteenth-century operatic styles, in many instances performed by a quartet choir. In a few dioceses, beginning in the late nineteenth century, the influence of John B. Singenberger (1848–1924) and his Cecilian Society led to musical reform. Like the parent Cecilian movement in Germany, this group espoused the revival of Gregorian chant, a return to a cappella polyphonic forms, and vernacular congregational singing. However, its influence was chiefly felt in the German communities of Cincinnati, Chicago, and Milwaukee. Most Catholics in typical parish churches continued to favor the spoken mass, and singing occurred only in the popular novena services.

Lutheran. Lutherans have brought many different national and regional traditions to this country. Those who found homes in the East lost their ethnic language and identity more quickly than those who settled later in the Midwest. Consequently, Lutheran worship (and especially its hymnody) along the Atlantic seaboard was more Anglo-American than German or Scandinavian. Many adherents had been identified with the pietist movements within European Lutheranism, and in this country that influence was intensified by revivalist activity. In the mid-nineteenth century, a growing disaffection with revival-influenced worship was fed by the sentiments of new European immigrants. The widespread desire to recover their confessional roots resulted in a conference of all Lutheran groups which adopted a Common Service in 1888, based on "the common consent of the pure Lutheran liturgies of the sixteenth century." Nevertheless, there continued to be considerable variation in Lutheran worship, since conformity was not obligatory. In the late twentieth century, there seems to be a growing preference for a completely vernacular version of Martin Luther's *Formula missae* as evidenced in the ecumenical *Lutheran Book of Worship* (1978).

American Lutherans inherited the European preference for an ante-Communion service. Through the nineteenth century, the full Eucharist was observed only a few times each year. In recent years, Holy Communion has been offered more frequently, and the historic Lutheran Matins service has also been used, perhaps once each month. In the nineteenth century, congregational singing was the musical norm. In the East, Anglo-American hymn traditions prevailed, while the Midwest churches perpetuated their German or Scandinavian hymnody. In recent years, Lutherans countrywide have shown a desire to share their unique ethnic traditions while preserving their common Reformation heritage. In addition, thanks largely to the efforts of Concordia Publishing Company, choirs are using plainsong, as well as polyphonic styles, in singing the "propers" of the liturgy.

Anglican. Established in the colony of Virginia in the early seventeenth century, the Church of England in America was organically united to the bishoprics of Canterbury and York. The church grew rapidly and by the time of the American Revolution was the dominant religious force in this country. After the Declaration of Independence, Anglicans in the United States formed an independent Protestant Episcopal Church, linked only in heritage and in fellowship with the Anglican Communion worldwide. In colonial days, and even much later, Anglicans used the services of morning and evening prayer almost exclusively, with Communion being observed only three or four times a year. The American *Book of Common Prayer* was derived from Cranmer's Prayer Book of 1549 (through the Scottish *Book of Common Prayer*) and was less Calvinistic than the 1552 and 1662 books that were commonly used in England.

According to Leonard Ellinwood, the music of colonial Anglican worship was scarcely different from that of the Puritans in New England and consisted mostly of metrical psalms sung with the aid of a precentor. Anglican chant was introduced during the last two decades of the eighteenth century, and its use became common within a short time. There is further record that organs began to be used in the 1700s, playing a voluntary following the "Psalms of the day" and an offertory for receiving the collection. A few choirs (with boys singing the treble parts) also appeared during the eighteenth century. All of the extant music from that period is related to the services of Matins and Vespers.

In the mid-nineteenth century the Episcopal church was influenced by the ideas of the Oxford Movement, which brought back much of orthodox theology and liturgy into a number of British churches—reviving the ancient Greek and Latin hymns in English translations, Gregorian chant, and the use of symbolism in vestments, furnishings, and liturgical action. This worship revolution, together with the advent of liberal theology in another group of Anglican churches, eventually resulted in the development of three Anglican parties in England in the late nineteenth century: (1) the Anglo-Catholics, who were closest to Rome in theology and worship practice; (2) the Low churchmen, many of whom were strongly evangelical in emphasis, rejecting the Oxford movement as "popish," and (3) the Broad churches, who tended to be moderate in liturgy but liberal in theology, emphasizing social reform rather than personal salvation. In America, Episcopal churches have tended to be high or low in liturgy, but only a few are as evangelical as their British counterparts. Beginning in the late 1970s, however, a significant number of evangelicals from free church traditions have entered the Episcopal church, in some cases influencing parishes in a low-church direction, in others uniting evangelical theology with high liturgical practice.

After 1850, a number of American churches adopted the principles of the Oxford movement, using vested choirs (of boys and men) and substituting plainsong for Anglican chant. However, the quartet-choir was more common—a volunteer group of men and women led by four soloists, which often degenerated into just a quartet, singing mostly romantic services and anthems by European, and later, American composers. The most-used compositions were written by such well-known musicians as Mendelssohn, Gounod, Gaul, Mozart, Boyce, Stainer, Parker, Shelley, Rossini, and Buck, and others who are now forgotten—Hodges, Naumann, Larkin, Bridgewater, Hatton, and Gilbert.

In the early twentieth century, Anglican churches outside the United States experienced a musical renaissance under the influence of such composers as Charles Stanford, Hubert Parry, Charles Wood, Ralph Vaughan Williams, Walford Davies, and the Canada-based Healey Willan. Increasingly, their music (both service music and anthems) has also been favored in American Episcopal churches, along with the works of American composers Leo Sowerby, T. Tertius Noble, David Mck. Williams, Thomas Matthews, and others. During this century, the outstanding leader in Episcopal church music has been Charles Winfred Douglas (1867–1944). An ordained priest in the church, he was long a member of the Episcopal Joint Commission on Church Music and the Hymnal Commission, serving as music editor for the denomination's hymnals of 1916 and 1940. A frequent lecturer on church music, he founded the Evergreen Conference in Colorado, and presided over its annual School of Church Music.

In very recent times, the Episcopal church has adopted a new liturgy which, while retaining its essential Anglican character, has returned to the basic outline of the historic mass. For example, the *Gloria in excelsis* has been returned to the early part of the service, and much of the evangelical text of the eucharistic prayer has been restored.

Nonliturgical Churches—Revivalist vs. "Pseudo-Liturgical" Worship

Methodism in England resulted from an eighteenth-century schism in the Anglican church, precipitated by the preaching of John and Charles Wesley. Worship among Methodists varied from group to group, from the low-church style of the Church of England to the unstructured pattern of Baptists. Although many of the Calvinist and Wesleyan groups in Europe and Great Britain followed traditional worship patterns, their American successors—Presbyterian, Methodist, Evangelical, and Reformed—tended to adopt the freedom of the nonliturgical Congregationalists and Baptists. For some this meant a revivalist format; others developed what I choose to call a "pseudo-liturgical" pattern. These two styles are still common in many American churches.

We have already narrated in detail the story of American revival movements and the resultant wor-

ship tradition which lingered in many churches. Following is their basic service outline, although the most significant feature was a sense of freedom and spontaneity generated by the leadership of "charismatic" personalities.

- Hymns (a group, often not related to each other or to the sermon, led by a "song leader")
- Prayer (brief)
- Welcome and announcements
- Special music (choir, solo, or small group)
- Offering
- Solo
- Sermon
- Invitation (Hymn)
- Dismissal (Benediction)

Revivalist free churches in the nineteenth century tended to favor gospel songs for congregational singing, with a sprinkling of traditional hymns from English and American authors. If the choir literature developed beyond those same hymnic boundaries, they tended to use "chorus choir" selections—two-page settings (found in the hymnal or songbook) in the style of extended hymns or abbreviated anthems.

Other free churches evidenced a broader concept of worship, particularly as the influence of revivalism waned and liturgical movements abroad and at home came to their attention. They moved toward a pattern that has some kinship to the ante-Communion service of Lutheranism or the Liturgy of the Word in an Anglican Eucharist.

Choral and solo literature in the early twentieth century tended to fall into the same mold as that of Episcopal (and even Roman Catholic) churches of that period. Congregational singing was often limited to one or two selections in a service and tended to use the standard hymns of British and American authors; gospel hymns were often standard fare on Sunday evening, for Sunday School, and in other informal services. Until later in the twentieth century, organists relied heavily on the music of romantic composers, including transcriptions of popular orchestral works.

Like the liturgical fellowships, free churches tended to use the quartet-choir when their budget permitted it; their choices in literature were also similar. Instrumental music varied according to the size and affluence of the individual group: pipe organs with trained performers for the larger, wealthier congregations and reed organs and amateur organists for the smaller and less prosperous.

As the twentieth century progressed, free churches broadened the scope of their music—congregational, choral, and instrumental—though there is marked variance within both traditional and revivalist groups. Hymnody now includes materials from the entire Christian heritage, American and European. Choral and organ performance covers the entire historic literature, from the Renaissance period through the contemporary. In addition, our century has encouraged the emergence of a large group of "functional" church music composers, who supply materials in every conceivable style for every possible taste. Nowadays only a few evangelical churches employ a quartet of professional singers, partly because of the high musical competence of many members in the congregation. In the early twentieth century, following the example of revivalists of that day, pianos replaced the reed organ in small churches and joined forces with the pipe organ in the larger. With the advent of electronic organs in 1935, many small congregations were financially able to add that sound to their worship experience for the first time. All in all, American churches today have more music activity—with more choirs and instruments, and larger budgets—than those in any other country in the world.

Donald P. Hustad

191 ✦ Music in Twentieth-Century Worship

The trend toward a return to primal traditions in theology and worship practice was intensified in the mid-twentieth century, partly due to the influence of the "New Reformation." Along with a return to biblical authority, we have seen a revival of Reformation worship forms and practice, including even neobaroque organ design. The total result is a blend that includes three traditions: the apostolic heritage, historic medieval contributions, and Reformation distinctives.

The Liturgical Movement

The liturgical movement includes a renewed interest in liturgical symbolism, especially in vestments, church design, and furnishings. The liturgical movement has had considerable influence on Calvinist and free churches, some of whom have been guided by the same objectives mentioned above: to unite their own distinctives with the tradi-

tions of the apostles and the medieval church. To illustrate, the *Worshipbook* (1974) of the United Presbyterian Church contains a Communion service which can be said to combine the early form of John Calvin with elements of eucharistic worship from earlier centuries. The text of the service is an amplification of Calvin's Geneva service of 1542. In the music section of the book, the historic songs of the mass (*Kyrie, Gloria, Credo, Sanctus, Agnus Dei*) are included so that they might be added to that service.

Though some evangelicals may doubt that they have been influenced by the liturgical movement, these trends will be noted in many groups:

1. Increased interest in more sophisticated church architecture and furnishings, whether or not it includes the consideration of theological principles in symbolism.
2. Development of more complete worship forms, with more congregational participation.
3. More frequent observance of the Communion. Many evangelicals do so once each month, rather than quarterly—the historic norm.
4. Increased observance of the liturgical year, especially as related to Advent and Holy Week.

The Evangelical Influence of Vatican II

Eugene L. Brand describes the liturgical movement as "the label given to efforts across the breadth of the Western church to restore full and vital corporate worship that centers in a eucharistic celebration where Sermon and Supper coexist in complimentary fashion" ("The Liturgical Life of the Church," in *A Handbook of Church Music,* ed. by Carl Halter and Carl Schalk, 53). As such, much of its impetus came from encyclicals of Pius X and Pius XII and from other church leaders both in Europe and America. The Second Vatican Council of 1962 marked the climax of the movement for Roman Catholics with the release of the *Constitution on the Sacred Liturgy.* All observers agree that its reforms have been "evangelical" in nature. These are some of the most significant:

1. Worship is to be social and rational, not personal and mystical.
2. A return to vernacular languages.

3. Full congregational participation, including the use of "Protestant" hymns.
4. Inclusion of several Scripture readings from both Old and New Testaments.
5. Inclusion of a sermon on a regular basis.
6. "Concelebration" of the mass—the people with the priest.
7. A retreat from extremely sacerdotal theology. (The revised _Sacramentary_ includes four versions of the eucharistic prayer; only one closely resembles the old Roman Canon.)

There is now more similarity between the services of Lutherans and Episcopalians (even of liturgical Presbyterians) and those of Roman Catholics than there has been at any time since the Reformation.

As a result of their new freedom, many Roman Catholics now participate in the worship services of evangelicals. Some regularly attend small Bible study groups, and even extraliturgical, charismatic worship services.

The New Pietism

What we identify as "celebration" today may be partly a reaction to the liturgical movement of yesterday. Laypersons who are expected to take a larger part in worship may well insist that it should consist of activities that they enjoy. For this reason we may call the contemporary style "the new pietism" (the emphasis is on religious experience), or even "the new worship hedonism" (the emphasis is on enjoyable experience).

There are other contributing influences which should be noted:

1. Existentialist philosophy—emphasis on the "now" experience which may sometimes be suprarational.
2. McLuhanism—"the medium is the message." McLuhan foresaw the weakening of words as communicative symbols and noted increased interest in audio-visual media.
3. Secular theology—a decline in the significance of traditionally sacral expressions in the awareness that the church is sent forth "into the world."
4. Roman Catholic reforms—Vatican II encouraged its communicants to be rational, social, and joyful in worship.

5. Relational theology—the importance of our relationships with other persons, both in and out of the church.
6. The philosophy of "linguistics"—a consideration of the meaning of words.
7. A reappearance of the aesthetic concept of music as "revelation" (see Mellers, _Caliban Reborn_).
8. The growth of Pentecostalism.

The resultant expressions in contemporary worship can also be listed:

1. Emphasis on celebration—a total experience in which there is appeal to all the senses by means of new worship forms and expressions, more emotional music, multimedia, drama, new symbolism, physical movement, etc.
2. Updated translations of Scripture; fresh, more personal language in liturgy, hymns, prayers, and sermon.
3. Congregational participation not spectatorism.
4. Renewed emphasis on Christian fellowship in worship (in the tradition of the "kiss of peace") and in daily life.
5. Cross-fertilization of the sacred by the contemporary, in text as well as music.

"The new pietism" appeared first among the liturgical churches and more liberal communions, and its total impact may have been more revolutionary among them. After all, the movement simply validated the ancient heritage—of joy in worship and in fellowship with other persons. Furthermore, it was moving counter to the interest of some evangelicals who were seeking to develop a greater sense of reverence in public worship.

One of the first expressions of the new music in contemporary worship was Geoffrey Beaumont's _Twentieth Century Folk Mass,_ which appeared in 1957. As a member of the Light Music Group of the Church of England, he stated their philosophy succinctly and boldly: Worship should include not only the timeless music of master composers, but also the popular styles of the day, which are so much a part of people's lives. Soon thereafter, youth musical ensembles were appearing among evangelicals in Great Britain, patterning their styles after those of the Beatles and other folk and rock groups. Their objectives were to communicate the gospel and to express Christian response in word/music languages that were comprehensible to young people, both inside and out of the organized church. Before long, liturgical churches and traditional denominational bodies in America were following these examples in an endeavor to make worship services more relevant and celebrative.

Among typical American evangelicals, popular expressions in witness music had not changed dramatically since the advent of the gospel song about 1850. To be sure, there had been modest variations in style in the mid-twentieth century—including "Southern quartet" forms, "western" hymns, a few songs in a mild Broadway-musical style, and the beginning of a country ballad hymnody. But, by and large, evangelicalism had not shown great interest in new music since the days of Billy Sunday and Homer Rodeheaver.

There was, however, considerable awareness of the need of fresh expressions in the church, and considerable (but not universal) support for new translations of the Bible and new phraseology in prayer. Evangelicals used the available new Scripture versions and even sponsored some of their own. The musical breakthrough came with a few gospel folk songs by Ralph Carmichael that appeared in Billy Graham films and with the youth musical *Good News,* released by the Southern Baptists in 1967. The latter was soon followed by a flood of similar works, written for various age groups, using contemporary popular music forms and frequently performed with the recorded accompaniment of a full professional orchestra.

Soon shorter musical works began to be published in the same idioms. Older titles (and even new works in older forms, like Bill Gaither's gospel songs) continued to appear, but in upbeat arrangements—with strong syncopated rhythms, a goose-bump-raising orchestration, and a series of "half-step-up" modulations—which added up to strongly-emotional expression.

In the last ten years, we have also seen an unparalleled rise in the number of professional performances of popular religious music by traveling artists. A large number of youth groups are on the road, like *Re-Generation* (with Derek Johnson) or the *Continentals* (sponsored by Cam Floria). Older professional singers (e.g., Hale and Wilder, the Bill Gaither Trio, Andrae Crouch, Ken Medema, Bill Pearce, Suzanne Johnson, Jimmy McDonald, and Evie Tornquist) give full programs of music, some-times in churches and sometimes in auditoriums. And there is a new breed of professional Christian musician, some of whom have crossed over into the pop market, most notably Amy Grant and Michael W. Smith. Many of these young performers write their own songs and perform them almost exclusively. All of this activity has been a great boon to the religious music publishing and recording businesses and has created a multimillion dollar market centered largely in Nashville, Tennessee. It is safe to say that we have just witnessed the most significant new development in Christian witness music since Ira Sankey popularized the gospel song more than 100 years ago.

No doubt there is much that is good in the new spirit and expressions of worship. But, as in so much of life, every plus is a potential minus if we do not maintain a healthy balance. It is well to give vent to emotional expression, providing it does not lead to emotionalism and irrationality. The new humanism is good when it helps us be more aware of ourselves and our neighbors in full-orbed worship and fellowship, but bad if we substitute transcendent human experience for a full understanding of the transcendence of God. The creativity that new forms offer may lead to a loss of meaning and identity if we forsake completely the historic expressions that are part of our religious roots. Finally, the "new enjoyment" may lead to a worship hedonism that is another form of idolatry—worshiping the experience instead of God.

Donald P. Hustad

192 • BIBLIOGRAPHY ON THE HISTORY OF MUSIC IN WORSHIP

———— **Historical Surveys** ————

A recent single work to attempt to encompass all of the music of the church from the beginning to the present is Andrew Wilson-Dickson's *The Story of Christian Music: From Gregorian Chant to Black Gospel: An Illustrated Guide to All the Major Traditions of Music in Worship* (Oxford, U.K.: Lion Publishing, 1992), portions of which are reprinted in this chapter. It is necessarily brief on any given subject and is written for a general audience, but it is enlightening on many topics, especially trends in the last ten years, and covers technical matters of music, church worship practice, and theology. The book is a great pleasure to browse. Full of sidebars and color illustrations, its aim of comprehensiveness is fulfilled in its sympathetic treatment of the immense variety of the church's expression of worship in song.

There are also a number of older histories of church music that provide helpful ways of organizing the history of church music, even if they have been surpassed by musical scholarship. These include Russel N. Squires's _Church Music: Musical and Hymnological Developments in Western Christianity_ (St. Louis: The Bethany Press, 1962), Edward N. Dickinson's _Music in the History of the Western Church_ (New York: Scribner's, 1902), and Charles Winfred Douglas's _Church Music in History and Practice_ (Irvine, Calif.: Reprint Services Corp., 1937, 1992).

For a survey of the history of **Roman Catholic** worship, see K. Fellerer's _A History of Catholic Church Music_ (Baltimore: Helicaon, 1961), which covers the period up to Vatican II, and the more recent _Twenty Centuries of Catholic Church Music_ by Erwin Esser Nemmers (Westport, Conn.: Greenwood Press, 1978). Also significant is the comprehensive volume, _Papal Legislation on Sacred Music, 95 A.D. to 1977 A.D._ by Robert F. Hayburn (Collegeville, Minn.: The Liturgical Press, 1979), a volume that includes both translations of important documents and helpful background information and analysis.

Discussion of music in the **Orthodox** churches includes H. J. W. Tillyard's _Byzantine Music and Hymnography_ (London: Faith Press, 1923); Constantine Cavarnos's _Byzantine Sacred Music_ (Belmont, Mass: Institute for Byzantine and Modern Greek Studies, 1956); Egon Wellesz's _A History of Byzantine Music and Hymnography,_ 2d ed. (Oxford, U.K.: Clarendon Press, 1961); Johann von Garner's _Russian Church Singing_ (Crestwood, N.Y.: St. Vladimir's Press, 1980); Dimitri E. Conomos's two recent works: _Byzantine Hymnography and Byzantine Chant_ (Brookline, Mass.: Hellenic College Press, 1984) and _The Late Byzantine and Slavonic Communion Cycle: Liturgy and Music_ (Washington, D.C.: Dumbarton Oaks Research Library and Collection, 1985); and the variety of scholarly essays included in the 5 volumes of _Studies in Eastern Chant_ (1970–1990, early volumes published by Oxford, later volumes by St. Vladimir's Press).

The single most comprehensive treatment of **Protestant** worship music is F. Blume's _Protestant Church Music_ (New York: W. W. Norton, 1974). Other helpful, though less comprehensive overviews include Robert Stevenson's _Protestant Church Music in America_ (New York: W. W. Norton, 1970) and Edwin Liemohn's _The Organ and Choir in Protestant Worship_ (Philadelphia: Fortress Press, 1968). See also the collection of essays found in Johannes Riedel's _Cantors at the Crossroads_ (St. Louis: Concordia, 1967), which includes histories of a variety of subjects related especially to Protestant church music not treated elswhere.

The history of **Choral music** used in Christian worship is amply covered in Elwin A. Weinandt _Choral Music of the Church_ (New York: The Free Press, 1965). For a study of the choral anthem, see Elwin Weinandt·and R. H. Young _The Anthem in England and America_ (New York: The Free Press, 1970).

Congregational singing, including hymnody and psalmody are covered by a large number of sources described in the bibliographical essay at the end of chapter 4.

In addition, general resources for music research provide very helpful entries on history of church music. The best encyclopedic sources are _The New Grove Dictionary of Music and Musicians,_ 20 vols. (London, Washington, D.C., 1980), which is topically arranged, and the historically organized _New Oxford History of Music,_ 10 vols. (New York: Oxford University Press, 1943–1990). For other resources, consult Richard Chaffey von Ende, _Church Music: An International Bibliography_ (Metuchen, N.J.: Scarecrow Press, 1980).

Music in the Early Church

One of the foremost scholars of the earliest writings on Christian music is James McKinnon. His helpful volume _Music in Early Christian Literature_ (Cambridge, U.K.: Cambridge University Press, 1987) is an inclusive research tool for studying the views of early Christian authors on music in worship from the era of the Apostolic Fathers through the early fifth century. It includes 398 passages from writers of this period, which are printed in translation together with original source identification and relevant biblical passages. Because of its clarity of presentation, the book is suitable to nearly any serious worship leader or pastor/teacher in the field. See also J. Quasten, _Music and Worship in Pagan and Christian Antiquity_ (Washington, D.C.: Catholic University Press, 1983); Herbert M. Schueller,

The Idea of Music: An Introduction to Musical Aesthetics in Antiquity and the Middle Ages (Kalamazoo, Mich.: Medieval Institute Publications, 1988); and ErikWerner, *The Sacred Bridge* (New York: Columbia University Press, 1959).

The Middle Ages

Music in the later portion of the Middle Ages is helpfully explained by a variety of sources. Standard musical histories of this period are largely devoted to church music. They include Richard Hoppin, *Medieval Music* (New York: W. W. Norton, 1978) and Gustave Reese, *Music in the Middle Ages* (New York: W. W. Norton, 1940). See also the section on medieval music in Richard Crocker's *A History of Musical Style* (New York: McGraw Hill, 1966; reprint, Dover Books, 1991).

Plainchant, including Gregorian chant, is an area for a substantial amount of continuing research. A helpful though somewhat dated overview of the subject is Willi Apel's classic, *Gregorian Chant* (Bloomington, Ind.: Indiana University Press, 1966). See also Alec Robertson, *The Interpretation of Plainchant* (Westport, Conn.: Greenwood Press, 1970) and Marie Pierik's works *Dramatic and Symbolic Elements in Gregorian Chant* (Rochester, N.Y., 1989) and *The Spirit of Gregorian Chant* (Boston: McLaughlin and Reilly, 1989). More scholarly studies include Peter Jeffery, *Re-envisioning Past Musical Cultures: Enthomusicology in the Study of Gregorian Chant* (Chicago: University of Chicago Press, 1992); Hendrick Vander Werf, *The Emergence of Gregorian Chant* (Rochester, N.Y., 1989); and Finn Egeland Hanson, *The Grammar of Gregorian Tonality* (Copenhagen, 1979). A comprehensive index to chant tunes and texts is *An Index of Gregorian Chant*, 2 vols., edited by John R. Bryden and David G. Hughes (Cambridge, Mass.: Harvard University Press, 1969).

In addition, the following works treat specific topics in the study of medieval music: Richard Crocker, *The Early Medieval Sequence* (Berkeley: University of California Press, 1977); Susan Rankin, *The Music of the Medieval Liturgical Drama in France and England* (New York: Garland, 1989); Thomas Forrest Kelley, *The Beneventan Chant* (Cambridge, U.K.: Cambridge University Press, 1989); and Craig Wright's comprehensive *Music and Ceremony at Notre Dame of Paris, 500–1500* (Cambridge, U.K.: Cambridge University Press, 1991). The bibliographies included in almost any of these books will list the many other classic works in this field.

A helpful survey of the revival of interest in Gregorian chant in the past 150 years is included in Noritan Lanner's *Chant: From Guerganger to Gelineau* (Washington, D.C.: The Pastoral Press, 1984).

The Period of the Reformation

Standard music histories are helpful in this period as well, the classic of which is Gustav Reese, *Music in the Renaissance* (New York: W. W. Norton, 1954).

Works on the music of the Lutheran Reformation include Paul Netll, *Luther On Music* (New York: Russell, 1967) and Carl Schalk, *Luther on Music: Paradigms of Praise* (St. Louis: Concordia, 1971).

Many fine works describe English music during this period, including John Caldwell, *The Oxford History of English Music. Volume 1: From the Beginnings to c. 1715* (Oxford, U.K.: Clarendon Press, 1991); Peter Le Huray, *Music and the Reformation in England 1549–1660* (Cambridge, U.K.: Cambridge University Press, 1967); Peter Phillips, *English Sacred Music, 1549–1649* (Oxford, U.K.: Gimell, 1991); and Denis Stevens, *Tudor Church Music* (New York: W. W. Norton, 1961).

Works on the Calvinist and Zwinglian Reformation include Charles Garside, *Zwingli and the Arts* (New Haven: Yale University Press, 1966) and other resources listed in the bibliography on hymnody.

Church Music in Europe

Church music today throughout the Western church remains significantly influenced by music in the European church since the Reformation. Church music in **Germany** can be studied by examining the biographies and descriptions of the music of any of its most famous church musicians, including Johann Walther, Johann Pachelbel, Dietrich Buxtehude, and Johann Sebastian Bach. Of particular interest in the study of Bach is Gunther Stiller, *Johann Sebastian Bach and Liturgical Life in Leipzig* (St. Louis: Concordia, 1984); J. A. Westrup's *Bach Cantatas* (London: British Broadcasting Corporation, 1966); W. Murray Young's *The Cantatas of J. S. Bach: An Analytical Guide* (London: McFarland and Company, 1989); and Robin Leaver's *J. S. Bach as Preacher: His Passions and Music in Worship* (St. Louis: Concordia, 1984).

Church music in **Russia** is covered in J. Gardner's *Russian Church Singing* (Crestwood, N.Y.: St. Vladimir's Seminary Press, 1980).

Church music in **England** is described in a number of fine works, in addition to those already mentioned. The history of English cathedral music is told in Edmund Fellowes, _English Cathedral Music,_ 5th ed., edited by Jack Westrup (New York: W. W. Norton, 1982), and in Kenneth Long's extensive _The Music of the English Church_ (London: Hodder and Stoughton, 1991). The history of English parish music is told in Nicholas Temperley, _The Music of the English Parish Church_ (Cambridge, U.K.: Cambridge University Press, 1983). A brief, but well-organized account of English church music can be found in Erik Routley's _A Short History of English Church Music_ (London: Mowbrays, 1977).

Music in specific periods can be studied by biographies of famous English church musicians, such as Thomas Tallis, William Byrd, Henry Purcell, and Samuel Sebastian Wesley, as well as by the following descriptions of various periods: Christopher Dearnley, _English Church Music, 1650–1750_ (New York: Oxford, 1970) H. Watkins Shaw's _Eighteenth Century Cathedral Music_ (London: Hodder and Stoughton, 1970); Arthur Hutchings's _Church Music in the Nineteenth Century_ (London: Herbert Jenkins, 1967); Bernard Rainbow's _The Choral Revival in the Anglican Church 1839–1872_ (New York: Oxford University Press, 1970); William J. Gatens's _Victorian Cathedral Music in Theory and Practice_ (Cambridge, U.K.: Cambridge University Press, 1986); and Erik Routley's _Twentieth Century Church Music_ (New York: Oxford, 1964) and also his book _The English Carol_ (London: Herbert Jenkins, 1958).

Church music in Ireland is described in Gerard Gillen and Harry White, eds., _Irish Musical Studies. Vol. 2: Music and the Church_ (Dublin: Irish Academic Press, 1993).

——— **Church Music in America** ———

Many standard music histories of American music include significant discussions of music in worship, particularly in the earlier periods of American history. See Gilbert Chase, _America's Music: From the Pilgrims to the Present_ (Urbana: University of Illinois Press, 1987, reprint); H. Wiley Hitchcock's _Music in the United States: A Historical Introduction_ (Englewood Cliffs, N.J.: Prentice Hall, 1988); and Daniel Kingman's _American Music: A Panorama_ (New York: Schirmer, 1990).

Works that treat church music exclusively include Leonard Ellinwood's _The History of American Church Music_ (New York: Da Capo, 1970). Treatment of specific periods include Ralph T. Daniel's _The Anthem in New England before 1800_ (Evanston, Ill.: Northwestern University Press, 1966); Jane Rasmussen's _Musical Taste as a Religious Question in Nineteenth Century America_ (Lewiston, N.Y.: Edwin Mellon Press, 1986); William Lynwood Montell's _Singing the Glory Down: Amateur Gospel Music in South Central Kentucky, 1900–1990_ (Lexington, Ky.: University of Kentucky Press, 1991); Talmage Dean's _The History of Protestant Church Music in America in the Twentieth Century_ (Nashville: Broadman Press, 1988); and Charles J. Evanson, _Evangelicalism and the Liturgical Movement and their Effects on Lutheran Worship_ (St. Louis: Morning Star Publications, n.d.).

Shape note singing is treated in Dorothy D. Horn's _Sing to Me of Heaven_ (Gainesville, Fla.: University of Florida Press, 1970); Buell E. Cobb, Jr., _The Sacred Harp: A Tradition and Its Music_ (Athens, Ga.: The University of Georgia Press, 1978); and by George Pullen Jackson's writings from the 1930s to the 1950s.

Music in the African American tradition is well described in Jon Michael Spencer's _Protest and Praise: Sacred Music of Black Religion_ (Minneapolis: Fortress Press, 1991); Don Cusic's _The Sound of Light: A History of Gospel Music_ (Bowling Green, Ohio: Bowling Green State University Popular Press, 1990); Paul Oliver, Max Harrison, and William Bolcom, eds., _The New Grove Gospel, Blues, and Jazz_ (New York: W. W. Norton, 1986); and Anthony Heilbut's _The Gospel Sound: Good News and Bad Times_ (New York: Limelight Editions, 1985).

A variety of specific topics, including the music of several denominational traditions can also be found in the _New Grove Dictionary of American Music._

FOUR

A Brief History of Congregational Song

From the earliest times, the people of God have raised their voices in song to praise the living God of creation and redemption. These never-ending expressions of faith have been tremendously varied, both in textual content and musical style. At times these heartfelt songs have been but simple, brief responses of affirmation by the gathered congregation. At other times, congregational songs of praise and prayer have been both lengthy and complex.

Regardless of the text and tune, everyone takes part, because congregational singing is for everyone. No one is to be silent. Indeed, all who are capable of speech are called upon to sing their praise to God.

In order to promote wholehearted participation, the texts that are sung need to be understood by the members of the local congregation. The music which accompanies each text must also be accessible. Only when the text and tune are understood by those who sing them does the song truly become congregational. Each singer in the congregation is then freed from misunderstanding and distraction and thus is able to sing with conviction. In order to achieve this, some education is needed.

In early biblical times the chanting of liturgical texts was taught to the boys and young men of the worshiping community. In later biblical times the surrounding Greek cultural influences were purified and incorporated into the forms of sung praise to Christ. In Europe during the Middle Ages, the Latin hymns that were written adopted the poetic form familiar to those who sang them. Furthermore, when Cyril and Methodius took the Orthodox faith from Constantinople to Russia in the tenth century, they formed an alphabet for the Russian people and translated the services and hymns into Slavonic. When Martin Luther established the chorale, he, too, wrote and encouraged the use of language and music understood by the people of his country and his time.

Similarly, the words and music of the Psalters used in the English-speaking world for over two hundred years were well known and loved by those who sang metrical psalms. The advent of the hymns of Watts and the Wesleys brought about another bonding between song and singer, with new textual content and spirited music. Moreover, the hymns of the Oxford movement provided many in England with suitable congregational resources, while the gospel song gave others in America material for evangelism.

This is rightly so. Each culture, at any given time, has a need for its own congregational song. According to Donald P. Hustad, congregational song is the tribal music of the church. Likewise, the late Erik Routley called it "the folk song of the church." And even though these expressions change from place to place and from time to time, they are living expressions of a common love for God and vital statements of relevant Christian experience.

In America, it generally makes little difference to most worshipers whether a hymn was written by a German pastor, an Anglican priest, or an African-American singer. It matters little whether the text is an original work by a Methodist or a Baptist or if the words are translated from another language. It is not so important to the singer that the music comes from the eighteenth century or the twentieth century. It is the meaning of the text and the feeling of the music that have become most important.

Thus, a multiplicity of texts and a variety of musical styles best serve the contemporary worshiper, giving meaningful expression to belief and emotional release to the deepest longings of the heart.

The following articles trace the history of congregational song. Special attention is given to the origin and development of hymns that are still commonly sung today.

193 ⬥ BIBLICAL SONGS

Biblical songs for corporate singing are to be found throughout both the Old and New Testaments. The earliest recorded song is the Song of Moses (Exod. 15:1-18), and the last song is found in the book of Revelation (Rev. 19:1-8). This article lists the most important biblical songs, which are sometimes called canticles, *and notes how these biblical songs are sung in the contemporary church.*

The Old Testament repertoire includes the Song of Hannah (1 Sam. 1:1-10), the Song of Jonah (Jonah 2:2-9), the First Song of Isaiah (12:2-6), the Second Song of Isaiah (26:9-21), and the Song of Habakkuk (Hab. 3:2-19), as well as the Psalter and other poetic passages.

The Psalter itself is made up of texts that are sung corporately by all of God's people. These one hundred and fifty selections probably represent many other unrecorded psalms which were sung responsively by a leader and the congregation or antiphonally by two groups of singers. Thus, from Old Testament times singing was a part of the public praise of God.

Several New Testament songs were sung in Christian worship. This repertoire includes the Song of Mary (the *Magnificat,* Luke 1:46-55), the Song of Zacharias (the *Benedictus,* Luke 1:68-79), the *Gloria in Excelsis* or Greater Doxology (Luke 2:14), and the Song of Simeon (the *Nunc Dimittis,* Luke 2:29-32).

Other New Testament songs or fragments of songs are found in Ephesians 5:14; Philippians 2:6-11; Colossians 1:15-20; 1 Timothy 1:17, 3:26, and 6:15-16; and 2 Timothy 1:11-13. These passages are chiefly doctrinal and didactic. However, in the case of Ephesians 5:14, the baptismal phrase, "Awake, thou that sleepest," is liturgical. Moreover, the devotional songs of the book of Revelation discussed in Robert E. Coleman's inspirational text *Songs of Heaven* (Old Tappan, N.J.: Fleming H. Revell Company, 1980) usually include a doxological stanza of praise.

Three of the best known songs of this type are the Song of the Creator (Rev. 4:11), the Song of Judgment (Rev. 11:17-18) and the Song of Moses and the Lamb (Rev. 15:3-4).

—— Contemporary Use of Biblical Song ——

All of these biblical songs are still in current use as translations or paraphrases of the original text. Their use is a part of the current renewal of interest in biblical songs in many Christian churches, liturgical and nonliturgical, traditional and contemporary, charismatic and noncharismatic.

An early impetus to this increasing use of biblical song for congregational singing came from a number of English hymn writers in the 1970s. These concerned writers participated in an effort to provide relevant material, hoping to make psalm singing more accessible to participants in Anglican worship and informal gatherings alike. *Psalm Praise* (Chicago: GIA Publications, 1973) contains contemporary texts based upon scriptural passages and new music by the editor Michael Baughen and committee members Timothy Dudley-Smith, Christopher Idle, Michael Perry, Michael Saward, James Seddon, Norman Warren, and others.

Their efforts were also evident in *Psalms for Today* (Michael Perry and David Iliff, eds. [London: Hodder & Stoughton, 1990], available from Hope Publishing Company, Carol Stream, Ill.) designed to provide contemporary communal worship songs based upon what they called the basic hymnbook of the Christian church—the Psalms. This superb collection includes psalm texts for chanting, metrical versions for singing, special arrangements for choral speaking, along with popular known hymn tunes and new tunes.

Although psalm singing has been a form of congregational song in churches for centuries, it has had a significant revival throughout America during the latter part of the twentieth century. Always a part of Orthodox and Reformed worship, the practice of psalm singing continues in the worship services of the various Presbyterian and Reformed churches in America. This is quite evident in the 1987 *Psalter Hymnal* (Emily R. Brink, ed. [Grand Rapids, Mich.: CRC Publications, 1987]) of the Christian Reformed Church, with its clearly defined section of one hundred and fifty psalm selections, and in the 1990 edition of the *Presbyterian Hymnal: Psalms and Spiritual Songs* (Linda Jo McKim, ed. [Louisville, Ky.: Westminster/John Knox Press, 1990]), with its section of one hundred psalm paraphrases and hymns based upon selected psalm texts.

Scripture Songs

These same two volumes of the Reformed tradition also contain a number of non-psalmodic biblical songs. For example, the *Psalter Hymnal* offers a versification of the Song of Hannah, settings of the Song of Mary and the Song of Simeon, and a text based upon the Song of Zacharias. Likewise, the "Service Music" section of the *Presbyterian Hymnal* includes musical settings of the songs of Mary, Zacharias, and Simeon. Finally, the nondenominational hymnal, *The Worshiping Church* (Donald P. Hustad, ed. [Carol Stream, Ill.: Hope Publishing Company, 1990]), has a designated section of "Psalms and Canticles." Here the reader will discover the First Song of Isaiah in a version by an American, Carl P. Daw, Jr., and the Second Song of Isaiah paraphrased by an Englishman, Michael Perry. Of particular interest in this section is the inclusion of eight separate Scripture readings divided by the repeated singing of a musical phrase. For example, the text of Psalm 98 is divided into three sections, with each spoken section concluding with the singing of a musical setting of the first verse by Hal Hopson, a noted American church music composer.

Besides this, contemporary versions of numerous scriptural songs and others based upon Scripture are to be found in recent publications, of which the following are representative. A British publication, *Come Rejoice* (Michael Perry, ed. [Carol Stream, Ill.: Hope Publishing Company, 1989]) contains Brian Black's setting of the Song of Christ's Glory (Phil. 2) along with Christopher Idle's version of the Song of Mary. In *Go Forth for God,* a collection of hymns by J. R. Peacey (Carol Stream, Ill.: Hope Publishing Company, 1991), "Awake, awake: fling off the night!" is offered as a paraphrase of Ephesians 5:14 according to the New Revised Standard Version of the Bible. In this same genre of music, eighteen

metrical canticles can be found in *A Year of Grace* (Carl P. Daw, Jr., ed. [Carol Stream, Ill.: Hope Publishing Company, 1990]). These canticles have been published separately under the title *To Sing God's Praise* (Carl P. Daw, Jr. [Carol Stream, Ill.: Hope Publishing Company, 1992]).

William Lock

194 ◆ Greek and Latin Hymnody

The very word hymn *comes from the Greek* hymnos, *which means a song of praise to a god or hero. Adapting this pagan practice for their own use, early Christians wrote many hymns that have become models for hymn writers over the centuries. The hymns of both early Greek and Latin Christians are represented in the most recent American hymnals by the inclusion of five to eighty selections. These hymns reflect the faith and thought of many of the most well-known early Christian leaders and theologians.*

Early Greek Hymnody

The Christian hymn of the New Testament church and the early church was distinctively a song of praise to Christ as God. This fact has been verified in the well known letter of Pliny the Younger to Emperor Trajan in which Pliny, speaking of the Christ followers, states that "they were accustomed to come together on a regular day before dawn and to sing a song alternately to Christ as a god" (M. Alfred Bishsel, "Greek and Latin Hymnody," in *Hymnal Companion to the Lutheran Book of Worship* [Philadelphia: Fortress Press, 1981], 4).

Moreover, the Apostolic Constitutions of the fourth century mention a number of Greek hymns for morning and evening services. One such liturgical morning hymn was an expansion of the Greater Doxology, with one stanza which was later included in the *Te Deum.* And one of the evening hymns combined the opening of Psalm 113, a paraphrase of the *Gloria in Excelsis,* and the text of the Song of Simeon. Another Greek hymn found in the liturgies of Clementine, St. Mark, St. James, and St. John Chrysostom and which is still sung today is the *Trisagion* (Thrice Holy Hymn) based upon the opening verses of Isaiah 6. Of particular importance to early Christians was the hymn *Doxa Patri,* which is identical to the Latin *Gloria Patri*—"Glory be to the Father, and to the Son, and to the Holy Spirit, now and ever and unto ages of ages. Amen." This Trinitarian statement came to be used in both Greek and Latin liturgies in order to give a Christian interpretation to the reading and singing of psalms.

This first period of Greek hymnody took place during the time of St. Clement of Alexandria, who lived from about A.D. 170 until about A.D. 220. His work combined the ideals of Greek poetry and Christian theology. An example from this period, which is still in common usage, is the devotional song "Lord Jesus, Think on Me", written by Synesius (*c.* A.D. 375–*c.* 414). The most familiar song of the Liturgy of St. James of Jerusalem is the Christmas hymn "Let All Mortal Flesh Keep Silent." Another hymn that is still sung at evening services is "O Gladsome Light" (*Phos Hilaron*), composed by an anonymous poet of the Alexandrian School.

During the second period of Greek hymnody (the most brilliant period) St. John of Damascus (*c.* A.D. 670–*c.* 780) was the leading writer of Greek canons. Each canon consisted of nine odes (eight in actual practice), and each ode consisted of from three to twenty stanzas. It was not until the nineteenth century that St. John of Damascus' brilliant poems were translated into English. After twelve years of work, John Mason Neale, the first and leading translator of Greek hymns, published in 1862 his collection, *Hymns of the Eastern Church.* In that book we find "The Golden Canon" or "Canon for Easter Day," which is still sung today on Easter Sunday.

Latin Hymnody

The number of hymns in current American hymnals representing the development of the Latin hymn ranges from five to eighty. The earliest of these hymns were written after the Council of Nicaea (A.D. 325) and the adoption of the Nicene Creed. They became the means of combating Arian theology, which was propagated in the sermons, poems, and hymns of Arius of Alexandria, who had been excommunicated from the church by the Council of Nicaea.

One early hymn writer was St. Hilary, the Bishop of Poitiers (*c.* A.D. 310–366), who became familiar with the singing of hymns by Greek Orthodox believers during his four-year exile in Asia Minor. Upon his return to Poitiers he immediately began to write hymns in a decided effort to combat false doctrine and to reinforce Trinitarian theology.

It was also the goal of Ambrose, Bishop of Milan (A.D. 341–397) to use hymn singing to combat Arianism. Sensitive to the need for immediate acceptance of the hymns, he chose the popular folk rhythm, long meter form. This, too, followed the practice of hymn singing in Eastern churches. His work is represented in a number of contemporary hymnals by the Trinitarian hymn, "O Splendor of God's Glory Bright."

Another prolific writer of Latin hymns was the lawyer Prudentius (A.D. 348–413). He, too, was determined to fight Arianism and to present the Orthodox doctrine of the two natures in Christ. In his retirement, he devoted much of his time and energy to the writing of spiritual songs in Rome. Many Christians know and love his magnificent Christmas hymn, "Of the Father's Love Begotten."

During the succeeding centuries there appeared other accomplished Latin poets. Fortunatus (A.D. 530–609), later Bishop of Poitiers, wrote four hymns still in current usage. "The Royal Banners Forward Go" and "Sing My Tongue" are often sung during Lent. His two Easter hymns are the lengthy "Welcome Happy Morn" and the triumphant "Hail Thee Festival Day." The familiar Palm Sunday text, "All Glory, Laud, and Honor," was the work of Theodulph of Orleans (*c.* 760–821), a student of Prudentius. The hymn of the Holy Spirit, "Come Holy Spirit, Our Souls Inspire," has been attributed to Maurus (d. 856). And finally, one morning hymn by St. Gregory (540–604), "Father, We Praise Thee," also is also incorporated in some contemporary hymnals.

In the latter part of the Middle Ages a number of monasteries that exerted an enormous influence on religious life throughout Europe for some three hundred years were established. The most influential leader at the beginning of this important movement was Bernard of Clairvaux (*c.* 1091–1153). In his own lifetime, some 162 monasteries were established, and within the next eighty-five years the number rose to five hundred. The chief emphasis of Bernard's texts was his own personal cry for holiness. The highly reflective and deeply devotional character of these texts is quite evident in a thoughtful reading of "O Sacred Head Now Wounded," "Jesus the Very Thought of Thee," and "Jesus, Thou Joy of Loving Hearts," subjective prayers arising out of his personal relationship with the Savior.

In contrast to the devotional focus of these hymns, Bernard of Cluny's 3,800-line poem, "Jerusalem the Golden," spoke out against the many evils of his time. The thirteenth century is represented also by Saint Francis of Assisi's hymn of praise, "All

Creatures of Our God and King." Three other Latin hymns still widely known and treasured are the Advent prayer "O Come, O Come Emmanuel," the Christmas hymn "O Come All ye Faithful," and the Easter song, "O Sons and Daughters."

William Lock

195 • THE CHORALE

The chorale was Martin Luther's important contribution to church music. Featuring strong rhythmic tunes and vernacular texts, the early chorales were songs for all worshiping people to sing. Since the Reformation, a long line of hymn writers, especially in Germany and Scandinavia, has contributed to this genre, leaving behind one of the richest bodies of music in the Christian church.

——————— **Martin Luther** ———————

Although more than five hundred years have passed since the birth of Martin Luther in 1483, the influence of this reformer continues to affect congregational singing today. He was the greatest preacher in all of Germany, a thorough biblical scholar, and an influential theologian. He was also both an author and translator, musician and composer.

In writing thirty-seven song texts in German, Martin Luther intended to provide Christians with the truths of Scripture that he himself had worked so hard to recover. He believed that it was imperative for believers to know the Scriptures, to "hide God's word in their hearts." Largely because of his experience in singing in a choir as a boy, he was convinced that this should be accomplished through the singing of hymns.

It was the Bohemian Brethren who had earlier adopted the practice of congregational singing for worship and issued their songbook of 1501 with its eighty-nine hymns. However, it was the writings and publications of Luther which firmly established the practice. His strong desire to have musically literate teachers and preachers is evident in his comment:

I have always loved music; whoso have skill in this art, is of a good temperament, fitted for all things. We must teach music in schools; a schoolmaster ought to have skill in music or I should reject him; neither should we ordain young men as preachers unless they have been well exercised in music. (William Hazlett, ed., *The Table-Talk of Martin Luther*

[Philadelphia: United Lutheran Publishing House, n.d.], 416)

In addition to this, Luther wrote the following in the foreword to the first edition of the 1524 *Wittenberg Gesangbuch:*

St. Paul orders the Colossians to sing Psalms and spiritual songs to the Lord in their hearts, in order that God's word and Christ's teaching may be thus spread abroad and practiced in every way. Accordingly, as a good beginning and to encourage those who can do better, I and several others have brought together certain spiritual songs with a view to spreading abroad and setting in motion the holy Gospel. (*Luther's Works*, vol. 53: *Liturgy and Hymns* [Philadelphia: Fortress Press, St. Louis: Concordia Publishing House, 1955], 316)

Because congregational singing in worship services had been banned by a decree of the Council of Laodicia in A.D. 367 and by the Council of Jerusalem in A.D. 1415, there was a need for hymns in the vernacular to be used in the services that Luther conducted. The songs sung in the vernacular at that time were sacred songs for processions and pilgrimages.

At first Luther struggled in an attempt to fit the newly written German texts to existing chant melodies, and his efforts ended in frustration. Thus he was forced to create his own texts and to restructure existing melodies to fit the new words. Using this method, he finished four songs in 1523. They appeared early in 1524 in the famous little leaflet, *Achtliederbuch*. Very soon thereafter, another nineteen texts were in print. Amazingly, in the next two decades, until his death in 1546, another one hundred new collections of German chorales were published. Five of these were completed under Luther's own personal supervision.

He began to understand the language of the people more fully when he went among them asking how they would express certain phrases. This increased his own understanding of the type of syllabic singing which the people enjoyed. Previously, several notes of a chant melody were attached to a single syllable of the text. Luther's chorale tunes however, were written with one note given to each syllable of the text. His famous battle hymn, *Ein feste Burg* ("A Mighty Fortress Is Our God"), based on Psalm 46, is a superb example of his style of writing and composing.

Luther's new songs for worship services were taught to the children in the school. They in turn sang them in the sanctuary for the adults to learn. Thus, the children would lead the congregation in the singing of the hymns. The melody was always sung by all in unison without accompaniment, as the strength of the melodies and the vitality of the original rhythms required no harmony.

Other Chorale and Hymn Writers

Others followed Luther's lead. Among the important contributors of this first period were Paul Speratus (1484–1551), Nicolaus Hermann (c. 1480–1561) and Nicolaus Decius (c. 1458–1546). The resources which they used for both texts and tunes were chants of the Mass, the office hymns, sacred German folk hymns, Latin spiritual songs, and popular melodies. Decius' well-known "All Glory Be to God on High" is an example of a translation of a Latin liturgical text (the _Gloria_) into the vernacular. In other cases, new original texts were attached to pre-existing melodies. Yet other chorales were completely original works, textually and musically.

The next generation of chorale writers/composers continued to compose melodic/rhythmic tunes without harmony. Two outstanding chorales of this form by Philipp Nicolai (1536–1608) are "Wake, Awake for Night is Flying" and "O Morning Star, How Fair and Bright." The first is often referred to as the "King of Chorales" and the second, the "Queen of Chorales." These chorales were sung to tunes later used by J. S. Bach, Handel, and Mendelssohn in a variety of works for organ and choir.

A pattern of alternation evolved in which the organist played or the choir sang a harmonized version of the chorale music in between the singing of the stanzas which were sung by the congregation. It was only later that harmony was played and sung simultaneously with the singing of the people. And with the addition of harmony, the music became isorhythmic, each note of the melody having the same time value as the other notes.

It was the work of Lucas Osiander (1534–1604) which brought together the congregational singing of the melody and the harmonized version of the choir. In 1586 he published an unusual hymnal in Nuremberg in which the melody of the chorales was put in the soprano part and simple chordal harmony was added underneath. The title of his book makes his purpose clear: _Fifty Sacred Songs and Psalms arranged so, that an entire Christian congregation can sing along._ This work inspired expressive works by Hans Leo Hassler (1564–1612) such as "O Sacred Head Now Wounded" and by Melchior Teschner (1584–1635), who composed "All Glory Laud and Honor."

Other changes became evident during and after the Thirty Years War of 1618–1648. Paul Gerhardt (607–1676) became the leader of a movement to change the emphasis of chorale texts. The former, more objective viewpoint, gave way to a subjective emphasis, leading to the pietistic period of the latter part of the seventeenth century. With the aid of composers Johann Cruger (1598–1662) and Johann Georg Ebeling (1637–1676), Gerhardt's texts grew in popularity. Two of his followers were Martin Rinkart (1586–1649), author of "Now Thank We All Our God," and Georg Neumark (1621–1681), author of "If You Will Only Let God Guide You."

Cruger provided tunes not only for Gerhardt but also for Rinkart and Johann Franck (1618–1677) in his famous hymnal _Praxis Pietatis Melica (The Practice of Piety Through Music)_ which first appeared in 1644. By 1736 it had passed through forty-four editions. Christians everywhere still raise their voices together to sing his tune, JESUS MEINE FREUNDE, for the text, "Jesus, Priceless Treasure."

The Paul Gerhardt of the Calvinists was Joachim Neander (1650–1680), a close friend of Jakob Spener, founder of the pietistic movement, and of Spener's associate, Johann Jakob Schutz (1640–1690). Although a Calvinist, Neander supported pietism. His hymns and those of the prolific writer Gerhard Tersteegen (1697–1769) made increasing use of personal pronouns. The mood of the hymns became more subjective, and they were often used not only in church services but also in private devotions.

By the time of J. S. Bach (1685–1750) hymnals were much larger. The resources at hand were staggering. With great skill he reharmonized the simpler harmonic structures and provided singers with full and rich new harmonies.

During the sixteenth, seventeenth, and eighteenth centuries a large number of hymns were also written by Anabaptists, later known as Mennonites and Bohemian Brethren (the Moravians). The current hymnals of these groups have a generous supply of translations and music from their own rich heritage.

Scandinavian Hymns

During the nineteenth and twentieth centuries a large number of chorales by Scandinavians were published. Much of Denmark's contribution to contemporary hymnology comes from three great hymnists. Denmark's first great hymnist, Thomas Kingo (1634–1703), known as the "Poet of Eastertide" because of his many hymns on the theme of Christ's resurrection, contributed the texts, "Print Thine Image, Pure and Holy" and "Praise to Thee and Adoration." The second great hymn writer was the pietist Hans Adolf Brorson (1694–1764), known as the "Poet of Christmas." Children everywhere enjoy singing his song, "Thy Little Ones, Dear Lord, Are We," and adults in the Lutheran faith (as well as other communions) hold dear his inspiring hymn, "Behold a Host Arrayed in White," along with its Norwegian folk tune. The third member of this celebrated trio of Danish hymn writers was the "Poet of Whitsuntide," Nikolai F. S. Grundtvig (1783–1872). For Christmas he wrote "The Happy Christmas Comes Once More" and "Bright and Glorious is the Sky." Moreover, in his struggle to revive the life of the church, he wrote the well known hymn of the church, "Built on a Rock."

Johan Olof Wallin (1770–1839), considered to be Sweden's leading hymn writer, made numerous contributions to Swedish hymnals. And now some translations have found their way into American Lutheran hymnals. However, none of his hymns are as familiar as Caroline Vilhelmina Sandell-Borg's (1832–1905) "Children of the Heavenly Father." And certainly, no other Swedish song has been so popularized in the United States as Carl Boberg's (1859–1940) "How Great Thou Art."

William Lock

196 ◆ PSALMODY

Whereas Martin Luther would admit any suitable text to be sung in worship unless it was unbiblical, John Calvin would allow only those texts which came from Scripture. Calvin commissioned poets to write metrical settings of the Psalms for the congregations in Strassburg and Geneva. Calvinist churches throughout Europe developed large repertories of psalmody, especially churches in England and Scotland.

By about 1532 the French court poet Clement Marot (*c.* 1497–1544) had already translated some

St. Andrew. *The most common shield of St. Andrew shows a cross saltire with its ends reaching the border of the shield. Andrew is believed to have died on a cross of this sort while preaching in Greece.*

of the Psalms into French verse. These translations were shared at court and sung by an ever increasing circle of admirers. John Calvin selected twelve of Marot's metrical translations along with five of his own to be printed in his first Psalter, the *Aulcunes Pseaulmes et Cantiques Mys En Chant.* This was published in Strassburg in 1539. After Marot's death, the work of translation was continued with the expert aid of Theodore Beza (1519–1605), who moved to Geneva in 1547. A complete Psalter of 150 translations was published in Paris in 1562. It had 125 tunes, 70 of which were composed by Louis Bourgeois (*c.* 1510–1561), a capable musician and music editor. Today, his best known tune is OLD HUNDREDTH, which is now sung to the text "Praise God from Whom All Blessings Flow" and commonly known in many churches as the "Doxology." This 1562 Genevan Psalter was widely accepted and often imitated in the 225 similar publications that appeared within the following one hundred years.

In England the first Protestant hymnal was Myles Coverdale's *Goostly Psalms and Spiritual Songes*

Drawn Out of the Holy Scripture (c. 1539). However, this book, with its translations of German chorales, was prohibited by Henry VIII. Thus, the adoption of chorale singing in England was thwarted, while the practice of psalm singing found acceptance. At first the metrical psalms of Henry VIII's wardrobe attendant, Thomas Sternhold (d. 1549), gained the king's favor. After Sternhold's death, his disciple, John Hopkins (d. 1570), carried on the work. In 1547, the first edition of nineteen psalms was printed. This was followed by an edition with music in 1556. Intended to be sung to familiar ballad tunes of the day, most of the texts were written in common meter of two or four lines of fourteen syllables each (8686 or 8686 doubled).

Eventually, the complete Psalter, published in 1562 as *The Whole Book of Psalms,* came to be known as the Sternhold and Hopkins Psalter. At least one edition or revision appeared each year for the next one hundred years, the first harmonized version being the one by John Day (1563), with sixty-five harmonized tunes.

The Sternhold and Hopkins series was replaced by *A New Version of the Psalms of David* by the poets Nahum Tate and Nicolas Brady. The former was the Poet Laureate to William III, and the latter was a Royal Chaplain. The *New Version* was published in 1696 and became, in spite of some fierce opposition, a tremendously influential work over a period of more than one hundred years.

Other English and Scottish Psalters

A number of publications retained the metrical psalms of the older Sternhold and Hopkins Psalter with different music. The 1579 edition by William Damon contained a large number of common meter (8686) tunes as well as the short meter (6686) tune, SOUTHWELL, often used for the text, "Lord Jesus Think on Me." Among the composers represented in Thomas Este's musical edition were the leading composers John Dowland, John Farmer, and Giles Fornaby. This volume also included George Kirbye's harmonization of the familiar tune, WINCHESTER OLD, sung today with the Nahum Tate text, "While Shepherds Watch Their Flocks by Night." An even more extensive collection of tunes, sung throughout England, Scotland, Wales, and the Continent, was Thomas Ravenscroft's 1621 *The Whole Book of Psalms.* From this book modern hymnbook editors have selected the popular tune, DUNDEE, and placed

it with William Cowper's profound text, "God Moves in a Mysterious Way."

After John Knox returned from Geneva in 1559, he gave oversight to the publication of the Scottish Psalter in 1564. This particular Psalter had the distinction of including more French psalm tunes than any of the English Psalters. By the time the 1615 *Scottish Psalter* came into print, the practice of including psalm tunes without a designation to any specific psalm was accepted. This was in contrast to the German custom of assigning one "proper" tune to each text. Thus, the English and Scottish Psalters allowed any given "common" tune to be used with many different texts in the same meter. In the 1635 *Scottish Psalter* more tunes were provided by Scottish musicians. Finally, the authorized 1650 *Scottish Psalter* appeared without any music. It introduced the most beloved of all English metrical psalms, the twenty-third Psalm, "The Lord's My Shepherd, I'll Not Want."

William Lock

197 • ENGLISH HYMNODY TO 1950

Over a period of time the writers of metrical psalms turned to fashioning free paraphrases of psalm texts. Eventually, in the seventeenth century, several English authors began to write hymn texts independent of the specific words of Scripture. Nineteenth-century fervor for hymn singing culminated with the publication of the most famous and influential of all hymnbooks, Hymns Ancient and Modern. The first half of the twentieth century witnessed growth in the study of hymnology, which led, in turn, to a variety of carefully planned hymnals that have had great influence to the present day.

Foremost among the early English hymn writers was Benjamin Keath (1640–1704). In 1668, he became the pastor of the Particular Baptist Church in Southwark. Then, as early as 1674, he published some hymns for use in his church—in particular, hymns written to be sung at the close of the Lord's Supper. His second collection of 300 original hymns appeared in print in 1691 under the title *Spiritual Melody.* By this time those in favor of singing hymns each week prevailed over the opposing minority.

Similarly, another Baptist pastor, Joseph Stennett (1663–1713) of London began writing hymns to be used by his congregation at the service of the Lord's Supper. In 1697, his significant collection of *Hymns in Commemoration of the Sufferings of Our Blessed*

Saviour Jesus Christ, Compos'd for the Celebration of His Holy Supper appeared.

Isaac Watts

However, it was another pastor, Isaac Watts (1674–1748), who was to become the "Father of English Hymnody." A Nonconformist, he felt no obligation to follow the Church of England ordinance that only the inspired psalms of scripture were to be sung in corporate worship services, a rule that was held in effect until 1821. Nor did he feel limited by the adherence of the Calvinists to the literal Scripture text.

In order to gain acceptance of his ideals, he published *The Psalms of David imitated in the language of the New Testament* in 1719. In this collection he versified and paraphrased 138 psalms in hymn form. He had decided to treat the majority of these psalms using the three best known meters—the common meter, long meter, and short meter. In this process, Watts strove for two primary goals: to interpret psalms in the light of Christ and to write in a language readily acceptable to those who would sing his paraphrases. His first goal was particularly well accomplished. This is evident to the careful reader who will compare any Watts paraphrase with the psalm text on which it is based. Compare, for example, the text, "Jesus Shall Reign," with the text of Psalm 72, the stanzas of "O God, Our Help in Ages Past" with Psalm 90, "Joy to the World" with Psalm 98, and "Give to Our God Immortal Praise" with Psalm 136.

His contribution to hymnody is even more significant, beginning with his 1707 collection of *Hymns and Spiritual Songs*. The 210 hymns of this collection appear under three headings: (1) hymns based upon Scripture, (2) hymns composed upon divine subjects, and (3) hymns for the Lord's Supper. Subsequently, an additional 135 hymns were added in the 1709 edition. Among these was his model hymn, "When I Survey the Wondrous Cross." Here, he ideally combines objective realities and subjective sensitivities, expressing thoughts and feelings common to all Christians. This hymn and so many others by Watts are still in regular use throughout America. In fact, apart from Charles Wesley, it may well be that there are more hymns by Watts in current American hymnbooks than by any other single author.

There are ten hymns by Watts in the *Psalter Hymnal* (1987). The *Lutheran Book of Worship* (1978) and *The Presbyterian Hymnal* (1990) each have thirteen. *The Baptist Hymnal* (1991) lists fourteen, *The United Methodist Hymnal* (1989) has fifteen. Seventeen are indexed in the Episcopal *Hymnal 1982;* there are eighteen hymns in *The Worshiping Church* (1990), and *Rejoice in the Lord* has an amazing thirty-nine!

The contemporaries of Watts who lived in his shadow are also represented in the collections of hymns used by various denominations today. Joseph Addison (1672–1719) is remembered by "The Spacious Firmament on High" and Joseph Hart (1712–1768) by "Come, Ye Sinners, Poor and Needy." Philip Doddridge (1702–1751) a pastor of the Congregational Church, had seven hymns in the Episcopal *Hymnal 1982* and eight hymns in the Reformed Church in America's *Rejoice in the Lord.* The best known of these hymns might well be his jubilant Advent hymn, "Hark, the Glad Sound! The Saviour Comes."

The Wesleys

The two brothers, John (1703–1791) and Charles (1707–1788) Wesley, were inseparable. From their days at Oxford and the *Holy Club,* John, the great organizer, had the support of his younger brother Charles, "the first Methodist." Together they boarded the *Simmonds* in 1735 and sailed for America, John to serve as a missionary to Native Americans, and Charles to serve as personal secretary to the Governor of Georgia, General James Oglethorpe.

During a storm at sea, John was deeply impressed by the conduct of the twenty-six Moravians traveling with them. While the English cried out in fear of being drowned, the Moravians—men, women, and children—calmly prayed and sang hymns. So impressed with their confident faith, John eagerly began his study of the German language and earnestly sought to translate their hymns into English. After his return to England, he journeyed to Hernhut where he made the acquaintance of the founder of the Moravian Church, Count Nicolaus Zinzendorf (1700–1760), himself a hymn writer. Back in London, John pursued an association with the Moravians there.

However, while John was still in America, he edited the first hymnal to be published in America, including in it some of his own translations of Moravian hymns. This Charles Town book of 1737 was entitled *A Collection of Psalms and Hymns.* A second collection was printed in London in 1738. In 1739, the Wesley brothers began their cooperative work of compiling hymnals, a work that was to include some fifty-six publications within fifty-three years. The culminating book was the famous and influential work of 1780, *A Collection of Hymns for the Use of the People Called Methodists.* Arranging hymns according to Christian experience instead of by the church year, they placed Charles' "O for a Thousand Tongues to Sing My Great Redeemer's Praise" first. More than two centuries later, this same hymn was accorded the honor of being the first hymn in *The United Methodist Hymnal* (1989).

This hymn is at once personal, evangelical, and scriptural. The nine stanzas, printed in 1780, were selected from eighteen stanzas previously written in 1739 "for the Anniversary Day of One's Conversion." The original text begins with the words "Glory to God, and praise and love". However, the stanzas in the 1780 collection were rearranged and are, in reality, stanzas 7–10, 12–14, 17 and 18 of the original work. The first line echoes the words of Moravian Peter Bohler to Charles: "Had I a thousand tongues, I would praise him with them all." The song was likely sung to the tune BIRSTALL at the time of its publication.

This and other music that the Wesleys used in their open air meetings and field preaching was collected in the 1742 *Foundry Collection,* named after the main Methodist meeting house in London, an abandoned foundry. Only a few psalm tunes from the music editions of the *New Version* were included. Only four years later, in 1746, their friend, J. F. Lampe (1703–1751), the London bassoonist and composer, issued a collection of twenty-four tunes. And later in 1753, another friend, Thomas Butts, published a complete collection of all of the tunes used by the Methodists at that time. John Wesley compiled an additional collection of tunes in 1761, which appeared ten years later in a second edition.

The tunes were popular in character and were sung at a lively tempo. Old tunes were refashioned and made to sound contemporary. And whereas the older psalm tunes were communal music in which everyone sang the melody together in unison, the new tunes, written out as melody and bass, were better suited for a soloist with accompaniment. They were the ideal vehicle to accompany the evangelical preaching of the two brothers and their associates. They were tuneful, catchy melodies adapted from the opera entertainments heard in London at that time. *The Beggar's Opera* and other light operas cast in a more simple style than the Italian operas of the day provided the reservoir which the Methodists tapped for new materials. This adapted music had instant appeal.

Contemporaries of the Wesleys

An early associate of the Wesleys, the evangelistic preacher George Whitefield (1714–1770), is still represented in the current *United Methodist Hymnal* by his alteration of Charles Wesley's Christmas song, "Hark! The Herald Angels Sing," as is John Cennick by his table grace, "Be Present at Our Table, Lord." Moreover, the work of Augustus Toplady (1740–1778) is signaled by the popular song, "Rock of Ages, Cleft for Me." Toplady, one of several Calvinist preachers who with Whitefield were a part of Lady Huntingdon's (1764–1865) "Connexion," was appointed one of her chaplains. Although she wrote no hymns herself, she encouraged a number of hymn-writing friends in their efforts and promoted the publication of their works. Edward Perronet (1726–1792) had already left the Wesleys when he wrote "All Hail the Power of Jesus' Name." William Shrubsole, composer of the tune MILES LANE used for the hymn, was organist of one of the chapels established by Lady Huntingdon.

The Olney Hymns

Within the Church of England the ban on hymn singing in worship services continued. Only psalm singing was allowed. However, the evangelical influence grew within the ranks of the clergy, and hymn singing was permitted at meetings held outside the sanctuary. Beginning with publications issued in 1760 by Martin Madan (1725–1790) and in 1767 by Richard Convers, new texts became available. However, it was not until 1779 that a truly significant book appeared. That book was *Olney Hymns* by John Newton (1725–1807) and William Cowper (1731–1800). The two men lived close by each other in the village of Olney, where Newton was the Church of England curate. Together they prepared hymns for the meetings held in the "Great House," which included weekday services, children's activities, and prayer meetings.

Cowper is still remembered for his hymns, "God Moves in a Mysterious Way," "O For a Closer Walk with God," and "There Is A Fountain Filled with Blood." Newton, who at one time had been employed in the slave trade, is remembered by his autobiographical hymn, "Amazing Grace," the most popular of all hymns in America. He was also the author of "How Sweet the Name of Jesus Sounds" and "Glorious Things of Thee are Spoken."

During the transition period which followed the publication of the *Olney Hymns*, James Montgomery (1771–1854) wrote the Christmas favorite, "Angels From the Realms of Glory," and Thomas Kelly (1769–1855) wrote "The Head That Once Was Crowned With Thorns."

The Nineteenth Century

The new literary style of the nineteenth century was established by Reginald Heber (1783–1826). Consecrated as Bishop of Calcutta in 1823, he died only three years later. His work, *Hymns, Written and Adapted to the Weekly Church Service of the Year,* was then published posthumously. It included the familiar text, often placed first in hymnals of the past, "Holy, Holy, Holy! Lord God Almighty!" The romantic style is also evident in Charlotte Elliott's (1789–1871) "Just As I Am" and Robert Grant's (1779–1838) "O Worship the King." The musical style changed as well. Harmonic enrichment of the melodies became the distinguishing characteristic of English congregational music.

The Oxford Movement. The Oxford Movement was originally known as the "Tractarian Movement" because of the numerous tracts or pamphlets written between 1833 and 1841 by John Henry Newman (1801–1890), John Keble (1792–1866), and others. It all began in 1833 when Keble preached his famous "Assize Sermon" in the church of St. Mary in Oxford. His public stand against national apostasy came to be printed and widely distributed, serving to rally a response in the Church of England to the growing influence of evangelicalism.

This response included bold attempts at the reformation of the worship services of the Church of England and a renewed interest in reviving the ideals of the pre-Reformation Catholic church. With great respect for the sacraments, clergy of the church began to counteract the obvious abuses seen in worship services. They also nurtured personal piety. Moreover, with the re-examination of the *Book of Common Prayer,* the liturgical hymn gained prominence. Whereas the evangelical hymn of personal experience had been read and sung at home and sounded in the fields and meeting houses, the new hymns (which followed the church year), were de-

signed for corporate worship within the sanctuary. Of particular interest was John Keble's collection of hymns, *The Christian Year* (1827).

Much of the repertoire was resurrected from the past and was the work of translators of Greek, Latin, and German Hymns. From John Mason Neale's *Translations of Medieval Hymns and Sequences,* modern hymnbook editors have retained the Advent song, "O Come, O Come Emmanuel," the Christmas chant, "Of the Father's Love Begotten," and the Palm Sunday hymn, "All Glory, Laud, and Honor". From Edward Caswell's (1814–1878) 1849 collection of translations, *Lyra Catholica,* many still sing "Jesus, the Very Thought of Thee", and from Catherine Winkworth's 1855 edition, *Lyra Germanica,* several hymns have been preserved: "If You Will Only Let God Guide You," "Now Thank We All Our God", "Praise to the Lord, the Almighty" and the two great chorale texts, "O Morning Star, How Fair and Bright" and "Wake, Awake, for Night is Flying."

All of this laid the groundwork for the amazing success of *Hymns Ancient and Modern.* Although the Church of England had not authorized a hymnal (and would not until 1921), the wide acceptance of this English companion to the liturgy influenced congregational singing in profound ways. Fully 131 of its 273 hymns were by English men and women and were already in use. Another 132 were translations of Latin hymns and another ten of German hymns. The first edition, under the guidance of Henry Williams Baker, was published in 1860. The next year the music edition was released, having been edited by William Henry Monk (1823–1889). For the first time text and music were printed together. And although sales records were destroyed in the war years of 1939–1945, it is estimated that 150 million copies of this hymnal have been sold. Since the first editions in the 1860s, a variety of editions and revisions of *Hymns Ancient and Modern* has been issued, including the 1969 supplement *100 Hymns for Today* (London: William Clowes and Sons, Ltd., 1969).

The new hymns called for appropriate music, and it was decided by the musicians who formed the committee that new tunes needed to be written. Speaking in the musical language of Victorian England, John Bacchus Dykes (1823–1876) contributed NICAEA ("Holy, Holy, Holy, Lord God Almighty") and Henry Thomas Smart (1813–1879) composed REGENT SQUARE ("Angels from the Realms of Glory"). Sir Arthur Seymour Sullivan (1842–1900) contributed ST. KEVIN ("Come, Ye Faithful, Raise the Strain"), George Job Elvey (1816–1893), ST. GEORGE'S WINDSOR ("Come Ye Thankful People Come"), Samuel Sebastian Wesley (1810–1876), AURELIA ("The Church's One Foundation"); and W. H. Monk contributed the more than 16 tunes and harmonizations which are now in the _Hymnal 1982,_ one of the most familiar tunes being EVENTIDE ("Abide With Me, Fast Falls the Eventide").

During the remainder of the century, efforts in evangelism accompanied by enthusiastic singing increased in England, Scotland, and Wales. The singing generally was focused on the hymns of Watts, Wesley, and Newton. Then in 1873, the American evangelist Dwight L. Moody (1837–1899) and his song leader, Ira D. Sankey (1840–1908), introduced the gospel song of America to the English populace. About this time Elizabeth Cecilia Clephane's (1830–1869) beloved song, "Beneath the Cross of Jesus," and Joseph Parry's (1841–1903) tune ABERYSTWYTH ("Jesus, Lover of My Soul") became well known.

The Twentieth Century. The two most influential hymnbooks of the first quarter of the twentieth century, _The English Hymnal_ (1906) and _Songs of Praise_ (1925), set new textual and musical standards for congregational singing. The scholarly effort that editor Percy Dearmer (1867–1936) brought to these outstanding collections was appreciated by the cooperating musicians. The 1906 hymnal is famous because of the efforts of music editor Ralph Vaughan Williams (1872–1958) to improve the quality and variety of its hymn tunes. His search took him to the wealth of British folk song which he both recorded and adapted. One highly successful merger was the tune FOREST GREEN and the text "O Little Town of Bethlehem." In addition, his own original tunes, SINE NOMINE ("For All the Saints") and DOWN AMPNEY ("Come Down, O Love Divine") have continuously increased in popularity. The 1925 collection followed the lead of _The English Hymnal_ but contained more adventurous music that was written or selected by Martin Shaw (1875–1958) and his brother Geoffrey (1879–1943).

In addition to new tunes, a number of new texts came into common usage during the first half of the century. In 1906, Canon Henry Scott Holland (1847–1918) of St. Paul's in London, and author of only one hymn, penned "Judge Eternal, Throned in Splendor." In the same year Gilbert Keith Chesterton

(1874–1936) contributed "O God of Earth and Altar" to _The English Hymnal._ In 1908, "In Christ There is No East or West" by John Oxenham (1852–1941) was borrowed from _Bees in Amber._ Finally, in 1931 Jan Struthers (1901–1953) wrote the inspiring text, "Lord of All Hopefulness."

William Lock

198 ✦ AMERICAN CONGREGATIONAL SONG TO 1950

The three hundred year span of time from 1640 to 1940 saw the development of great variety in congregational singing throughout America. Beginning with the Psalters of the first colonists, Americans contributed widely varying styles of songs and hymns, culminating with the popular and influential gospel song.

In the mid-sixteenth century, the Huguenot settlers brought their French metrical psalms and psalm tunes with them to South Carolina and Florida. In the early years of the seventeenth century, the settlers of Jamestown carried their "Sternhold and Hopkins" with them, singing the tunes of the 1592 _Este Psalter._ Following this, the Pilgrims settled at Plymouth, Massachusetts, in 1620; they sang from the familiar _Ainsworth Psalter_ of 1612 along with its accompanying thirty-nine tunes. But it was left to the Puritans, who settled around Boston, to produce their own Psalter, the first book printed in America. That book, _The Whole Booke of Psalms Faithfully Translated in English Metre,_ came to be commonly called the _Bay Psalm Book._ From its appearance in 1640 until the printing of the first music edition in 1698, the tunes to be sung were borrowed from the _Ravenscroft Psalter._ When the music edition finally became available, it contained only 12 tunes, chiefly in one meter (common meter), taken from the eleventh edition (1687) of Playford's _Introduction to the Skill of Music._

As the repertoire of psalm tunes dwindled, the practice of "lining out" the psalms by the cantor became more and more tedious and confusing. The deacon or _precentor_ appointed to line out the psalm would read the first line of the psalm or would sing the first phrase of the psalm tune. This was repeated by the members of the congregation before the leader gave out the second line and so forth. Over a period of time the tempo of the singing would become excessively slow. In order to keep the congregation attentive during lengthy periods of psalm singing, the precentor would add some additional notes, thus ornamenting the melody. The result was that psalm singing became chaotic. One of the early reformers, the Rev. Thomas Walter, described congregational psalm singing in this manner:

> Our tunes are left to the Mercy of every unskillful Throat to chop and alter, to twist and change, according to their infinitely divers and no less Odd Humours and Fancies. I have myself paused twice in one note to take breath. No two Men in the Congregation quaver alike or together, it sounds in the Ears of a Good Judge like five hundred different Tunes roared out at the same Time, with perpetual Interfearings with one another. (Edward S. Ninde, *The Story of The American Hymn* [New York: Abingdon Press, 1921], 76)

Intent on correcting the situation, Walter published a book of music instruction, *The Grounds and Rules of Musick Explained,* in 1721, one year after the printing of the Rev. Thomas Symmes's pamphlet, *The Reasonableness of Regular Singing or Singing by Note.* By these means the two enlightened ministers proposed a "shocking" new way of congregational singing that necessitated musical instruction. The "old way" of singing by rote without music was about to be changed. This change, however, did not come without considerable resistance, even though interest in the new method was particularly high in urban centers. From this growing interest in learning to sing by note rather than by rote, numerous singing schools were begun in the middle of the eighteenth century. The psalm tunes used in those music classes were printed in oblong tune books, with each tune printed in three or four parts with one stanza of the text. Additionally, the books contained some longer anthems at the back of the book and instructions for reading music at the front of the book.

The first significant book of this kind was James Lyon's (1735–1794) *Urania* (1761). This collection was the first to feature some fuging tunes, along with the expected psalm tunes, hymn tunes, and anthems. The fuging tunes had two homophonic chordal sections separated by a central polyphonic section in which the various voice parts, imitating each other, began at different times. The best known singing teacher/composer of the time was William Billings (1746–1800) who published his first tune book, *The New England Psalm Singer,*

in 1770. The other volumes which followed this important work provided material for the singing schools, which he successfully conducted in the areas in and around Boston.

Oliver Holden (1765–1844) composed the earliest American tune still in common usage. His hymn tune, CORONATION, which was printed in his *Union Harmony* in 1793, is still associated with the stirring text "All Hail the Power of Jesus' Name."

———— Moravian Hymns ————

The year was 1735. The group numbered only twenty-six. But on their way to Savannah, Georgia, the Moravians aboard the *Simmonds* gave clear testimony to their faith in the singing of their hymns. John Wesley, a fellow passenger, was deeply impressed. Drawn to them, he began his study of German and the first of his attempts at translating their German chorales into English. These actually became the first English hymns to be written and published in America. They appeared in his *Charlestown Collection* of 1737.

At about the same time, many witnessed the beginnings of the Great Awakening. An early leader in the movement, Jonathan Edwards, was pastor of the Congregational Church in Northampton, Massachusetts. It was in 1739, during the first visit of George Whitefield to America, that the itinerant evangelist demonstrated his keen support for the hymns of Watts by using them to accompany his preaching. Later, Benjamin Franklin and others published Watts's *Psalms and Hymns,* which went through fifty editions within fifty years.

Church of England parishioners in America continued to use the "Old Version" of the Psalter along with the "New Version" by Tate and Brady, often having a copy bound to their *Book of Common Prayer.* Meanwhile, within the Presbyterian church, the "Great Psalmody Controversy" over singing on the "Old Side" from the Psalters of Rous and Barton, or on the "New Side" from the "New Version," or Watts, caused great division.

After the pioneer settlements on the frontier were affected by the Great Revival of 1800 (which had its beginning in Logan County, Kentucky), outdoor meetings and extended camp meetings grew in popularity among the Presbyterians, Methodists, and Baptists. At these meetings, the simple repetitive style of the song was taught by rote, because most of the audience, both black and white, could not read music. However, they enthusiastically sang their songs day and night. Thus, a new folk hymnody emerged. Songs of repentance, death, and judgment as found in Joshua Smith's collection _Divine Hymns or Spiritual Songs_ were similar to selections found in Samuel Holyoke's (1762–1820) _The Christian Harmonist_ (1804) and Jeremiah Ingall's (1764–1828) _Christian Harmony_ (1805).

The "shaped note" tunes which appeared in William Smith and William Little's book, _The Easy Instructor_ (1809), used various symbols for the _fa, sol, la,_ and _mi_ degrees of the scale: a right angle triangle for _fa,_ a circle for _sol,_ a square for _la,_ and a diamond shape for _mi._ Between the introduction of Davisson's _Kentucky Harmony_ in 1816 and the year 1850, about thirty-eight tune books were printed, the majority of them being used in the Southern states.

The two most popular books of this period were _The Southern Harmony_ (1835) by William Walker (1809–1875) and _The Sacred Harp_ (1844) by B. F. White (1800–1879) and co-editor E. J. King. From such books came the folk hymn tunes of contemporary hymnbooks: FOUNDATION ("How Firm A Foundation, Ye Saints of the Lord"), BEACH SPRING ("Come All Christians, Be Committed"), LAND OF REST ("Jerusalem, My Happy Home"), HOLY MANNA ("Brethren, We Have Met to Worship"), PROMISED LAND ("On Jordan's Stormy Banks I Stand") and RESTORATION ("Come Ye Sinners, Poor and Needy").

Lowell Mason

Lowell Mason (1792–1872) single-handedly exerted the greatest influence on congregational singing in American churches in the early nineteenth century. One of the most outstanding American musicians of his day, he first settled in Boston in 1827 where he developed the choir of the Bowdoin Street Church that gained national recognition. While at the church, he also conducted music classes for children, publishing _The Juvenile Psalmist_ and _The Child's Introduction to Sacred Music_ (1829) for them. Then, in 1832, he founded the Boston Academy of Music. By 1838 he had gained approval to teach vocal music in the Boston public schools. His efforts at promoting music education led to the establishment of the first music institutes for the training of music teachers. He was truly the great pioneer of music education. He was also very eager to improve congregational singing in the churches. By fashioning tunes from European sources, he provided churches everywhere with a different, more sophisticated style of congregational song. Most Christians are familiar with his adaptations, including ANTIOCH ("Joy to the World"), AZMON ("O For a Thousand Tongues to Sing"), and HAMBURG ("When I Survey the Wondrous Cross").

Throughout much of the same century many Mennonite, Moravian, and Lutheran congregations continued to use their own repertoire of German hymns and chorales. At the same time, various denominations developed distinctive hymnbooks in English, promoting their preferred song forms. In particular, the Episcopalians, Methodists, Baptists, and Congregationalists retained a large number of English hymns by Watts, Charles Wesley, Newton, and Cowper.

The Gospel Song

Several significant developments in the middle of the nineteenth century resulted in the birth and development of a uniquely American congregational song form, the gospel song.

One such development was the beginning and growth of the Sunday school movement. The idea of Sunday school was first introduced by the Methodists following the Revolutionary War. The lack of public schools had created a pressing need for instruction in reading and writing, a need that was met by the Sunday schools. Instructional materials for these schools were later published by the American Sunday School Union, which was founded in 1824.

The Sunday school hymns of William B. Bradbury (1816–1868) became the amazing success story of sacred popular song. A member of Lowell Mason's Bowdoin Street Church choir and a student of Mason at the Boston Academy of Music, Bradbury became organist at the Baptist Tabernacle in New York City where he conducted free singing classes for young people and where he was instrumental in having music instruction introduced into the public schools. He supplied the music to Charlotte Elliott's text, "Just As I Am," and the simple melody for "Jesus Loves Me, This I Know." Today his music for the text "My Hope Is Built on Nothing Less Than Jesus' Blood" is well known still, as is the attractive melody he wrote for the words, "Savior, Like A Shepherd Lead Us." Two other equally well known melodies are settings for "Sweet Hour of Prayer" and "He Leadeth Me, O Blessed Thought."

The second important development was the founding of the Young Men's Christian Association in England in 1844 and the establishment of a branch in Boston in 1851. By 1870, the annual conventions of the Y.M.C.A. attracted thousands of young men who were caught up in the spirited singing, many of the songs being selected from Bradbury's 1867 Y.M.C.A. collection.

Third, about 1857, in the midst of desperate economic conditions, a widespread movement of evangelical revivalism erupted. Daily interdenominational noonday prayer meetings in churches and theaters became commonplace.

The fourth development of great significance was the Civil War, during which the soldier's hymnbook was used extensively. Nothing could have been more stirring than the singing of patriotic songs and hymns by a large group of men.

Finally, the influence of the "Singing Pilgrim," Philip Phillips (1834–1895), must not be overlooked. At the age of twenty-one years this singer, composer, and publisher was on the road singing the simple songs of his own composition, accompanying himself on the reed organ, and selling copies of his music at every stop. And although his travels took him around the world, he became best known in America, especially for his exceptionally popular "services of song."

Another very influential musician was Philip Bliss (1838–1876). It was 1857 when Bliss attended a music convention led by the famous teacher and composer Bradbury. This experience prompted the young Bliss to enter a music education institute. Following his studies, he became a music teacher and, later still, a representative for the Chicago music publishing company Root and Cady, for whom he gave concerts and organized conventions. In 1869 he met Dwight L. Moody, who persuaded him to leave his job and serve as soloist and song leader for Major D. W. Whittle. Bliss was one of the first major leaders in the creation and use of gospel songs. Widely recognized as an outstanding leader in music education and as a promoter of gospel songs at musical conventions, by the 1870s he was associated with the John Church music company of Cincinnati, the company which published his *Gospel Songs* in 1874. A number of his songs may be found in some contemporary hymnals. *The Worshiping Church,* for example, has four: (1) "Hallelujah! What a Savior," (2) "Wonderful Words of Life," (3) "I Will Sing of My Redeemer" (text only), and (4) "It is Well With My Soul" (music only).

Meanwhile, Ira D. Sankey was a song leader and soloist for Dwight L. Moody, beginning this work in 1870, after he had led music in Sunday School, the Young Men's Christian Association, and for the soldiers in the Civil War. While on his first trip to England with evangelist Moody, he used both Philip Phillips' *Hallowed Songs* (1865) and his own collection of songs, which he kept in a scrapbook. The demand for these new songs in manuscript became so great that the English publisher R. C. Morgan volunteered to print a pamphlet of twenty-three songs in 1873. The first five hundred copies were sold in a day. This special collection, *Sacred Songs and Solos,* passed though several editions and was enlarged to twelve hundred selections. So great was the demand for these popular songs that over eighty million copies were sold within fifty years.

Back in Chicago Sankey was successful in arranging a merger of his collection with the 1874 *Gospel Songs* collection of the singer/composer Bliss. This joint venture, *Gospel Hymns and Sacred Songs* was published in 1875. Subsequently, five editions were printed between 1876 and 1891. Finally, the entire series was published in one volume in 1894 as *Gospel Hymns, Nos. 1–6, Complete.* It included a total of 739 hymns.

Although during his lifetime his texts and music for "Faith is the Victory," "Hiding in Thee," "A Shelter in the Time of Storm," "The Ninety and Nine," and "Under His Wings I Am Safely Abiding" became well known, only one of Sankey's songs, "Trusting Jesus" (music only), is to be found in the modern hymnal, *The Worshiping Church* (1990).

The efforts of the two compilers, Bliss and Sankey, and their two publishers, the John Church Company and Biglow and Main, proved to be immensely successful. Furthermore, a large number of men and women as well as music publishers became involved in the writing and composing of gospel songs, promoting the sales of countless other volumes.

Sankey was not only known to Phillips and Bliss, he was also, as the president of Biglow and Main, the publisher of gospel songs by James McGranahan (1840–1907), George C. Stebbins (1846–1945), and George F. Root (1820–1895).

The most familiar music of McGranahan today is set to the Daniel W. Whittle texts, "I Know Not Why God's Wondrous Grace" and "There Shall Be Showers of Blessing", and Phillip P. Bliss's "I Will Sing of My Redeemer."

The music of Stebbins that has become the most

beloved includes the tunes written for Adelaide A. Pollard's "Have Thine Own Way, Lord," William T. Sleeper's "Out of My Bondage, Sorrow and Night," and William D. Longstaff's "Take Time To Be Holy." The work of George F. Root is represented by the music of "Jesus Loves the Little Children."

Later, the texts of the blind poetess Fanny Crosby (1820–1915) became most prominent. A prolific writer, she stored many texts in her mind and dictated them at various times to a secretary. Her amazing output of 9,000 poems rivals that of the famous Charles Wesley. With the kind and supportive friendship of her publisher, Ira D. Sankey, she made weekly contributions which were immediately set to music.

The nine selections by Fanny Crosby to be found in _The Worshiping Church_ focus on Jesus and our redemption and life in him: "Praise Him! Praise Him!" with music by Chester G. Allen; "Tell Me the Story of Jesus" with music by John R. Sweney; "Redeemed, How I Love to Proclaim It!" with music by William J. Kirkpatrick, but here set to the tune ADA by Aubrey L. Butler; "Blessed Assurance, Jesus is Mine" with music by Phoebe P. Knapp; "To God be the Glory," "I Am Thine, O Lord," "Jesus, Keep Me Near the Cross," and "Rescue the Perishing"— all with music again by William H. Doane; and "All the Way My Saviour Leads Me" with music by Robert Lowry.

These and other gospel songs possess several distinctive characteristics which made them functional pieces for mass evangelism. The very content of the text was the simple gospel story of the experience of sin and God's grace and redemption through Christ, the pleading Savior. The words used were readily understood, often using metaphors from everyday life. Also, there were many repetitions of phrases of the text. The music was often in two parts with a lyric melody and spirited rhythm. The combination of an engaging melody, lively pulse, and simple harmonies made these songs ideal for group singing. At times the verses were sung by a soloist or the choir and the refrain sung by all present from memory.

Multitudes found these subjective testimonials inspiring and thus encouraged their use in worship services. With a focus textually upon salvation, these songs found a sympathetic ear in all those seeking an individual Christian experience. Others considered them inappropriate for corporate worship services. Thus, another period of division took place.

The Twentieth Century

During the first half of the twentieth century, many denominational hymnbooks became both scholarly and ecumenical. For instance, the Episcopal hymnal of 1916 was followed by the music edition in 1918, edited by Canon Winfred Douglas (1867–1944). An authority on Gregorian music, Douglas crowned his achievements with _The Hymnal 1940,_ for which he also served as music editor.

Another distinguished expert on hymns was the Presbyterian minister Louis Benson (1855–1930). Editor of several hymnals, he contributed significantly to the study of hymnology through his definitive work _The English Hymn: Its Development and Use in Worship._

The two branches of American Methodism, the Methodist Episcopal Church and the Methodist Episcopal Church, South, had published separate hymnals in the late nineteenth century but combined their endeavors in 1905 with the help of music editor Peter Lutkin (1858–1931). Another united effort of three Methodist groups took place in 1935. The editor was the distinguished hymnologist Robert G. Cutchan (1877–1958).

The Presbyterian Church (U.S.A.) produced a high quality book, _The Hymnal 1933,_ which reflected the expert assistance of music editor Clarence Dickinson (1873–1969).

In 1941 the joint effort of the Disciples of Christ and the American Baptist Church resulted in _Christian Worship._ The Southern Baptist had their own hymnal in _The Broadman Hymnal_ of 1940, compiled by B. B. McKinney.

From this period also come the hymns of such writers as Julia Cady Cory (1882–1963)—"We Praise You, O God, Our Redeemer, Creator"; Frank Mason North (1850–1935)—"Where Cross the Crowded Ways of Life"; and Harry Emerson Fosdick (1878–1964)—"God of Grace and God of Glory."

In addition to the above, the important efforts of the leaders of the _Hymn Society in the United States and Canada,_ which began in 1922, have encouraged the writing of new texts and music and the enthusiastic singing of many forms of congregational song throughout the United States and Canada.

William Lock

199 • CONGREGATIONAL SINGING IN ENGLAND, CANADA, AND THE UNITED STATES SINCE 1950

Since 1950, there has been more music published for congregational singing than at any other time in the history of the church. Nearly every major denominational body, as well as many independent congregations and publishing companies, have produced official and supplementary hymnals and related collections of songs. In almost every case, these collections evidence a recovery of traditions once lost and relentless pursuit of contemporary music that is both faithful to the gospel and representative of the languages—both verbal and musical—of modern culture.

The 1950s

Several trends continued throughout the decade of the 1950s. Many new publications indicated an increase in the use of some one hundred to two hundred common historic hymns which later became the basic repertoire of congregational songs found in most hymnals. At the same time, the multiplication of simple choruses, sung chiefly in evangelical gatherings, made differences in the musical styles used in the church more pronounced.

Most hymn singing of the 1950s came to sound all the same, almost always sung to organ accompaniment. With the development of technology for sound amplification, numerous sanctuaries were "remodeled" to nullify the distraction of any sound except that which originated from the preacher or singer stationed behind a microphone. This discouraged wholehearted congregational hymn singing.

However, during the same period of time a new working of God's Spirit was evidenced in the phenomenon of glossolalia (i.e., speaking in tongues). This new movement claimed participants in the mainline denominations as well as churches of Pentecostal persuasion.

By the end of the decade criticism against traditional forms of worship and musical styles increased. And, although it was most intense among the youth, adults too voiced concern against archaic language and what seemed to them to be medieval music.

The 1960s

The great divide between the past and the present in congregational singing erupted in England with the publication of Geoffrey Beaumont's *Folk Mass* in 1957. Written for young people, this work was composed in an innovative manner, calling for a cantor to sing a phrase of the text, which was then repeated by the congregation. This responsive form, along with the popular style of its melodies and harmony, made this work an instant success.

Similarly, in the early 1960s, Michael Baughen, later Bishop of Chester, along with some friends, sought to provide new songs for a new generation. Even though no publisher would support their first endeavor, they published *Youth Praise* (Michael A. Baughen, ed. [London: Falcon Books, 1966]). The Church Pastoral Aid Society subsequently published *Youth Praise 2* (Michael A. Baughen, ed., [London: Falcon Books, 1969]) and *Psalm Praise* (Michael A. Baughen, ed. [Chicago: GIA Publications, 1973]). This cluster of friends, known as the Jubilate Group, includes such outstanding writers and composers as Timothy Dudley-Smith (b. 1926), Christopher Idle (b. 1938), Michael Perry (b. 1942), and Norman Warren (b. 1934). It has grown to forty members, becoming well known in the United States due to the consistent effort of George Shorney, Chairman of the Hope Publishing Company. Their modern language hymnal, *Hymns for Today's Church* was published both in England (by Hodder and Stoughton, London) and in the United States (by the Hope Publishing Company, Carol Stream, Ill.).

Fred Kaan, at one time pastor of Pilgrim Church in Plymouth, England, also wrote contemporary hymns for his congregation which were used far beyond those sanctuary walls. His first collection of 50 texts was called *Pilgrim Praise* (Plymouth, England: Pilgrim Church, 1968). After moving to Geneva, Switzerland, where he collaborated with composer Doreen Potter, he published twenty new hymns under the title *Break Not The Circle* (Carol Stream, Ill.: Agape, 1975). Later, in 1985, Hope Publishing Company issued the complete collection of his work, *The Hymn Texts of Fred Kaan* (Carol Stream, Ill.: Hope Publishing, 1985).

Other publications appeared with new texts and music. In London, Josef Weinberger became the publisher of a series of supplemental books beginning in 1965. These contained representative works written in a pop style by the *Twentieth Century Church Light Music Group*. Some of these songs also became available in the United States in the 1970s. In addition, Gailliard (London) published the Sydney Carter song, "Lord of The Dance," in 1963, followed by a collection of other songs by Carter which were recorded and made available in the United States.

Continuing in the tradition of _Hymns Ancient and Modern, 100 Hymns for Today_ (John Dykes Bower, ed., [London: William Clowes and Sons, 1969]) was published as its supplement. Some years later, a similar supplement to _The English Hymnal_ was completed with the title _English Praise_ (George Timms, ed. [London: Oxford University Press, 1975]).

The United States. The earliest work in the United States similar to Beaumont's _Folk Mass_ was Herbert G. Draesel, Jr.'s immensely popular _Rejoice_ (New York: Marks Music Corp., 1964). Later recorded, this sacred folk mass promoted the use of electric guitars and drums in the regular worship services of churches. Then soon after Vatican II, young Roman Catholic musicians introduced a large number of folk masses intended for unison singing with guitar accompaniment. Each of these was made available both in print and on records, which accelerated their popularity.

The great success of F.E.L. (Friends of English Liturgy) Publications widened the acceptance of these and other new songs into Catholic and non-Catholic circles. Their _Hymnal for Young Christians: A Supplement to Adult Hymnals_ (Roger D. Nachtwey, ed., Chicago: F.E.L. Church Publications, 1966) was released in Roman Catholic and ecumenical editions in 1966. A second volume appeared in 1970. Songs such as "We Shall Overcome," "Allelu," "Sons of God," and "They'll Know We Are Christians by Our Love" were commonly sung by Christian young people.

At the same time, many Methodists sang songs found in _New Wine_ (Jim Strathdee, ed., 2 vols. [Los Angeles: Board of Education of the Southern California–Arizona Conference of the United Methodist Church, 1969,1973]), and some Presbyterians adopted Richard Avery and Donald Marsh's _Hymns Hot and Carols Cool_ (Port Jervis, N.Y.: Proclamation Productions, 1967).

In evangelical churches the rapid development of the youth musical (such as Buryl Red's _Celebrate Life_ [Nashville: Broadman Press, 1972]) coincided with the popularity of compositions for youth by Ralph Carmichael that appeared in films and on record. A number of these songs were printed in the little pocket edition (melody line and texts) of "He's

Everything To Me" (Los Angeles: Lexicon Music, 1969).

More traditional in its orientation, the most important Protestant hymnal published in 1960s was _The Methodist Hymnal_ (1964), released under the expert supervision of editor/composer Carlton R. Young.

The 1970s

In the 1970s, ecumenical and denominational hymnals continued to be published. A staggering number of smaller supplemental books, often experimental in nature, also appeared.

The continuing ecumenical emphasis of earlier years was evident in the fourth edition (1970) of The Lutheran World Federations Hymnal, _Laudamus_ (a fifth edition was published in 1984). And the more comprehensive work of hymnologist Erik Routley was evidenced in the 1974 _Cantate Domino_ (Oxford: Oxford University Press, 1980), compiled for the World Council of Churches. In 1971 the impressive _Hymn Book_ (Toronto: Anglican Church of Canada and the United Church of Canada, 1971) drew together quality selections from past centuries as well as some of the finest new songs, such as Sydney Carter's imaginative "Lord of the Dance." During the following year, 1972, the Presbyterian Church in Canada issued its own revision of an earlier book, _The Book of Praise_ edited by William Fitch (Ontario, Canada: The Presbyterian Church in Canada, 1972). This collection adopted the more modern practice of placing all stanzas of the text between the staves of music. The Baptist Federation of Canada followed with their 1973 book, _The Hymnal_ (Carol M. Giesbrecht, ed.) And a joint American/Canadian venture, the General Conference of the Mennonite Brethren Churches, published the _Worship Hymnal_ (Hillsboro, Kans.: Mennonite Brethren Publishing House, 1973) with Paul Wohlgemuth as chairman/editor. _The Covenant Hymnal_ (Chicago: The Covenant Press, 1973) of the Evangelical Covenant Church of America was the result of a careful search for the finest hymns of the past as well as new works, particularly hymns written in response to requests of the Hymn Society in the United States and Canada. Its supplement _The Song Goes On_ (Glen V. Wiberg, ed. [Chicago: Covenant Publications, 1990]) was issued in 1990. Meanwhile, Donald P. Hustad served as editor for one of the more scholarly books to be published by the Hope Publishing Company. That book, _Hymns for the Living_

Church (Carol Stream, Ill.: Hope Publishing Company, 1974) proved itself to be a valuable resource for churches with a broad musical taste. At the same time William J. Reynolds, another outstanding national leader in the area of church music, served as editor of the new edition of the *Baptist Hymnal* (Nashville, Tenn.: Convention Press, 1975).

In the middle of the decade the editors of the Roman Catholic *Worship II* (Robert J. Batastini, ed. [Chicago: GIA Publications, 1975]) were free to admit that

> the Roman Catholic Church has its own sacred music tradition, but that tradition does not include a long history of singing in the English language. Unlike their fellow Americans of the same American "melting pot" culture, Catholic parishes for the most part have yet to experience the same vitality of song that echoes from their neighboring Christian Churches.

That vitality of song had already existed in the worldwide Lutheran church for over 450 years. Lutheran immigrants to America sang their chorales in their original languages. However, by the time of the 1960 and 1962 Lutheran church mergers, those various nationalistic branches had become "Americanized," adopting a larger number of English hymns, along with translations of their ethnic songs. *The Lutheran Book of Worship* (Minneapolis: Augsburg Publishing House, 1987) is a culminating work which includes these translations and a number of contemporary texts and hymn tunes by recognized American Lutheran authors and composers such as Charles Anders (b. 1929), Theodore Beck (b. 1929), Jan Bender (b. 1909), Paul Bunjes (b. 1914), Donald Busarow (b. 1934), Gracia Grindal (b. 1943), Richard Hillert (b. 1923), Frederick Jackisch (b. 1922), Carl Schalk (b. 1929), and Jaraslav Vajda (b. 1919). Members of the committee which produced this book represented all of the participating American and Canadian churches in the Inter-Lutheran Commission on Worship.

Also of importance was the innovative and highly influential collection *Hymns for the Family of God* (Fred Bock and Brian Jeffery Leach, eds. [Nashville: Paragon Associates, 1976]). A new era in congregational singing was proclaimed in its preface:

> Whereas it used to take decades or centuries for a hymn or song-style to become an established part of the Christian's repertoire, today this can happen in a

matter of a few month's time. For example "Alleluia" and "They'll Know We Are Christians by Our Love" are sung almost everywhere by almost everyone.

In addition to the appearance of these new hymnals, there was a flurry of publications of a quite different nature, published to fill the need for more contemporary songs with updated language, and using a greater variety of popular musical styles.

In England the work of the *Hymn Society of Great Britain and Ireland* introduced the newest texts of Albert Bayly (1901–1984), Fred Pratt Green (b. 1903), Fred Kaan (b. 1929), and Brian Wren (b. 1936) as well as the most current music by Peter Cutts (b. 1937) and Michael Fleming (b. 1928). Galliard of Norfolk had a continuing series of books which were made available in the United States, such as *Songs for the Seventies* (James D. Ross, ed. [New York: Galaxy Music Corporation, 1972]). This collection contained Sydney Carter's controversial "Friday Morning."

In America, Hope Publishing Company's subsidiary, Agape, and editor Carlton Young had their own series of imaginative and innovative books. In both a pocket size edition and a larger spiral bound edition, they presented a collection of seventy eclectic songs called *Songbook for Saints and Sinners* (Carol Stream, Ill.: Agape, 1971). The Avery and Marsh folk-song pieces were printed next to Catholic Ray Repp's "Allelu," Lutheran John Ylvisaker's "Thanks be to God," Southern Baptist William Reynold's "Up and Get us Gone," Episcopalian Herbert G. Draesel's "Nicene Creed" and numerous black spirituals. The *Genesis Songbook* (Carol Stream, Ill.: Agape, 1973) which followed in 1973 contained such popular songs as Stephen Schwartz's "Day by Day," Bob Dylan's "The Times They Are A-Changin'," James Thiem's "Sons of God," Sy Miller and Jill Jackson's "Let There be Peace on Earth," and Gene MacLellan's "Put Your Hand in the Hand."

The *Exodus Songbook* (Carlton Young, ed. [Carol Stream: Agape, 1976]) was next in 1976 with an amazingly different gallery of songwriters: Burt Bacharach, Leonard Bernstein, Duke Ellington, George Gershwin, Paul Simon, Kurt Weil, Malcolm Williamson, and Stevie Wonder. Some of the titles indicated the unusual nature of the group of songs in this collection: "We've Only Just Begun," "What the World Needs Now," "It Ain't Necessarily So," "A Simple Song," "Raindrops Keep Fallin' On My Head," "Come Sunday," "He Ain't Heavy, He's My

Brother," "Somewhere," and "Bridge Over Troubled Water."

By 1977 editor "Sam" Young had turned his attention to a uniquely adventuresome supplement project. _Ecumenical Praise_ (Carlton Young, ed. [Carol Stream, Ill.: Agape, 1977]) came to be the most experimental and influential work of its kind. The list of its contemporary composers was quite impressive: Samuel Adler, Emma Lou Diemer, Richard Dirksen, Richard Felciano, Iain Hamilton, Calvin Hampton, Austin C. Lovelace, Jane Marshall, Daniel Moe, Erik Routley, Ned Rorem, Carl Schalk, Malcolm Williamson, Alec Wyton, and Carlton R. Young.

In addition, the evangelical "youth" booklets came forth in a steady and seemingly endless stream. Many had only lyrics, melody line, and guitar chords. They were intended to be used for unison group singing in Sunday school, at camp, in youth meetings and in coffee houses. The youth in the Lutheran church used a number of books such as David Anderson's _The New Jesus Style Songs_ (Minneapolis: Augsburg Publishing House, 1972) while those in evangelical churches sang the songs in Ralph Carmichael's _He's Everything to Me Plus 103_ (Los Angeles: Lexicon Music, 1972). Those who participated in Young Life or Campus Life on high school and college campuses sang from Yohann Anderson's _Songs_ (San Anselmo, Calif.: Songs and Creations, 1972). In time many larger, independent hymnals included other songs of the seventies, such as Andre Crouch's "My Tribute" (1971), Kurt Kaiser's "Oh, How He Loves You and Me" (1975), the Gaithers' "There's Something About That Name" (1970), Jimmy Owen's "Clap Your Hands" (1972), and a large number of spirituals that had been revived during the years of civil unrest.

The 1980s

Ecumenical efforts in the publication of hymnbooks continued. The successor to the 1933 English _Methodist Hymn Book_ was the 1983 _Hymns and Psalms: A Methodist and Ecumenical Hymn Book_ (Richard G. Jones, ed. [London: Methodist Publishing House, 1983]) Prepared by representatives of the Baptist Union, Churches of Christ, Church of England, Congregational Federation, Methodist Church in Ireland, United Reformed Church, and the Wesleyan Reform Union, it produced one hymnbook for several denominations, not unlike the idea of the unified _Korean Hymnal_ of 1984 and similar efforts in Sweden. The contemporary British au-

thors represented in this large (888 items) Methodist book include Albert Bayly, Sydney Carter, Timothy Dudley-Smith, Fred Pratt Green, Alan Luff, Erik Routley, and Brian Wren. Some of the notable hymn tune composers are Geoffrey Beaumont, Sydney Carter, Peter Cutts, Erik Routley, Norma Warren, and John Wilson.

The "hymn explosion" that had taken place in Great Britain became the "hymnal explosion" of the 1980s in the United States. This was due in part to the exceptional efforts of George Shorney, chairman of America's largest publisher of nondenominational hymnals, the century-old Hope Publishing Company. As host to visits of leading English hymnwriters and the publisher of single author books of texts, he did more than any single person to promote the use of those new texts on this side of the Atlantic.

One of the early volumes contained _The Hymns and Ballads of Fred Pratt Green_ (Bernard Braley, ed. [Carol Stream, Ill.: Hope Publishing Company, 1982]), complete with notes on each text. This collection contained "General Hymns," "Hymns for Special Occasions," "Ballads," "Translations," "Early Hymns," and "Anthem Texts." It seems as though every new American hymnal has adopted his oft-quoted "When in our Music, God is Glorified" (_Later Hymns and Ballads and Fifty Poems,_ Bernard Braley, ed. [Carol Stream, Ill.: Hope Publishing Company, 1989]).

In 1983 _The Hymns & Songs of Brian Wren, with Many Tunes by Peter Cutts_ was published in the United States as _Faith Looking Forward_ (Carol Stream, Ill.: Hope Publishing Company, 1983). "Christ is Alive!," one of his innovative works, found its way into a number of hymnals during the eighties. Another collection followed in 1986. Then in 1989 thirty-five new Wren hymns were issued under the title _Bring Many Names_ (Carol Stream, Ill.: Hope Publishing Company, 1989).

The following year the collected hymns of Timothy Dudley-Smith were published as _Lift Every Heart_ (Carol Stream, Ill.: Hope Publishing Company, 1984). And in a very short period of time a number of his widely accepted texts were printed in a variety of denominational and nondenominational books. Likewise, the work of Canada's leading hymnwriter, Margaret Clarkson, was collected in _A Singing Heart_ (Carol Stream, Ill.: Hope Publishing Company, 1987), while American counterpart Jane Parker Huber had her texts published in _A Singing_

Faith (Philadelphia: The Westminster Press, 1987). In the same year, Lutheran Jaraslav J. Vajda had his hymns, carols, and songs published in a volume entitled *Now The Joyful Celebration* (St. Louis, Mo.: Concordia Publishing House, 1987). In the early 1990s, New Zealander Shirley Erena Murray's work was introduced in the United States by the collection *In Every Corner Sing* (Carol Stream, Ill.: Hope Publishing Company, 1992).

A few years later the collected hymns for the church year (after the model set in Keble's *Christian Year*) were assembled in Carl P. Daw, Jr.'s *A Year of Grace* (Carol Stream, Ill.: Hope Publishing Company, 1990). Eighteen of the metrical canticles from this significant work were published subsequently, each with two musical settings, in *To Sing God's Praise* (Carol Stream, Ill.: Hope Publishing Company, 1992).

Finally, the single author collection *Go Forth for God* (Carol Stream, Ill.: Hope Publishing Company, 1991) introduced the complete hymnwriting opus of English clergyman J. R. Peacey to editors and worship leaders in the United States. The British "hymn explosion" had become a significant part of the "hymnal explosion" in the United States.

This decade of the hymnal began with the publication of *Lutheran Worship* (St. Louis: Concordia Publishing House, 1982), the authorized hymnal for the Lutheran Church–Missouri Synod. It restored original unequal rhythms to a number of the early chorales and included important contributions by such contemporary Lutheran composers as Anders, Beck, Bender, Bunjes, Busarow, Manz, Sateren, and Schalk.

However, it was *The Hymnal 1982* (Raymond F. Glover, ed. [New York: The Church Hymnal Corporation, 1985]) which set the standard for future denominational hymnals. A revision of *The Hymnal 1940* (New York: The Church Pension Fund, 1940), it had several noticeable differences: (1) the use of guitar chord symbols; (2) added instrumental parts; (3) metronome markings; (4) black note notation, and (5) music within the musical staff.

In 1985 the Reformed Church in America issued its own book, *Rejoice in the Lord: A Hymn Companion to the Scriptures* (Erik Routley, ed. [Grand Rapids: Eerdmans, 1985]). It is chiefly the work of editor Erik Routley and it bears the stamp of his genius.

A year later two very different collections of congregational songs were published. In *Worship III* (Robert J. Batastini, ed. [Chicago, Ill.: GIA Publications, 1986]), Roman Catholics made an effort to move into the mainstream of congregational hymnody. Distinguished composers included in this new revision of the 1971 and 1975 editions were Marty Haugen, Howard Hughes, and Michael Joncas.

Remarkably different was *The Hymnal for Worship and Celebration* (Tom Fettke, ed. [Waco, Tex.: Word Music, 1986]). Its brief services (and medleys) with choral introductions and codas and the complete orchestration of its contents made this a distinctively new collection. Moreover, the eclecticism of its contents may best be illustrated in the titles of some of the songs: the "Hallelujah Chorus" (*Messiah*); Timothy Dudley-Smith's setting of the *Magnificat,* "Tell Out My Soul"; Andre Crouch's solo song "My Tribute"; the country/western song, "I'll Fly Away"; the spiritual, "He's Got the Whole World in His Hands"; Ralph Carmichael's hit song, "He's Everything to Me"; and Jack Hayford's praise chorus, "Majesty."

Another pair of hymnals was published in 1987. The carefully constructed Christian Reformed *Psalter Hymnal* (Emily R. Brink, ed. [Grand Rapids: CRC Publications, 1987]) featured metrical versions of all 150 psalms, settings of biblical songs from Genesis to Revelation, and hymns for every act of worship and season of the Christian year.

This may be contrasted with the evangelical Gaither Music Company publication, *Worship His Majesty* (Fred Bock, ed. [Alexandria, Ind.: Gaither Music Company, 1987]). Here the reader will find Christian contemporary solos by Paul Stookey, Dottie Rambo, and Bill and Gloria Gaither, along with nineteenth-century gospel songs by Fanny Crosby and Ira D. Sankey. The Church of God also used contemporary Christian songs in their new hymnal, *Worship The Lord* (Alexandria, Ind.: Warner Press, 1989).

Until the publication of their new hymnal in 1989, the United Methodists used the 1982 *Supplement to the Book of Hymns* (Carlton R. Young, ed. [Nashville: The United Methodist Publishing House, 1982]) as well as a 1983 Asian-American collection, *Hymns from the Four Winds* (Nashville: Abingdon Press, 1983) edited by the distinguished ethnomusicologist, I-to-Loh.

At the end of the decade a superb collection of congregational songs was completed by the members of the Hymnal Revision Committee of the

United Methodist Church under the editorship of Carlton Young. This 1989 book was the result of a careful review of traditional and contemporary materials. Well-known hymns from Greek, Latin, German, Scandinavian, Wesleyan, English, and North American traditions were placed alongside representative and meaningful evangelical songs. Selections from the contemporary popular repertoire were printed with English and American hymns of the "hymn explosion" period. A wide variety of ethnic songs were also given some prominence.

Apart from these large collections of congregational songs, a large number of supplemental books appeared during the eighties—books of every possible kind, many with accompanying cassette recordings. And with the recording of the songs in these very diverse books, the adoption of the new music became increasingly rapid.

Roman Catholics purchased cassette tapes of single artist/composers such as John Michael Talbot as well as the music and tapes of _Gather to Remember_ (Michael A. Cymbala, ed. [Chicago: GIA Publications, 1982]). Moreover, the many cantor-congregation publications encouraged an easy form of responsive singing. The _Music of Taize_ (Robert J. Bastastini, ed. [Chicago: GIA Publications, 1978]), a Protestant community in France, was promoted by Robert Bastastini, editor of GIA Publication.

Episcopalians made a significant contribution to the growing repertoire of ethnic hymnody in the publication of _Lift Every Voice and Sing: A Collection of Afro-American Spirituals and Other Song_ (New York: Church Hymnal Corporation, 1981), and the Catholics followed with _Lead Me, Guide Me : The African-American Catholic Hymnal_ (Chicago: GIA Publications, 1987).

The Hope Publishing Company, Agape division, published a 1984 _Hymnal Supplement_ (Carol Stream, Ill.: Agape, 1984) followed by _Hymnal Supplement II_ (Carol Stream, Ill.: Hope Publishing Co., 1987) with new material from leading British and American writers and composers. Then in 1989, Tom Fettke compiled and edited _Exalt Him_ (Waco, Tex.: Word Books, 1989) which was issued in a words-only edition, a music edition, and a piano/rhythm book, and was recorded on cassette and CD, along with a variety of accompaniment tapes.

Three major groups emerged as leaders in the publication of praise-and-worship music. Maranatha! Music had early been the leader with its famous _Praise_ (Costa Mesa, Calif.: Maranatha! Music,

1983). Integrity's Hosanna! Music also developed a continuing stream of both printed and recorded materials, while the Vineyard Ministries spread both their style of worship and their musical repertoire to a number of countries. All three repertoires have been used extensively.

One of the most unusual series of publications of the late 1980s came from the Iona Community in Scotland. The wild goose, a Celtic symbol of the Holy Spirit, was adopted as the symbol of this community of prayer, which is made up of ordained and lay men and women of all denominations sharing a common rule of faith and life. The chief author of each collection of unaccompanied songs was John Bell. Some sixty percent of the fifty songs in each volume were his own compositions. The remainder were mostly British folk tunes such as "O Waly Waly," "Sussex Carol," "Scarborough Fair," and "Barbara Allen." The first collection, _Heaven Shall Not Wait_ (Costa Mesa, Calif.: Maranatha! Music, 1987), was issued in 1987 and revised in 1989. The second volume, _Enemy of Apathy_ was issued in 1988 (John Bell and Graham Maule, eds. (Chicago: GIA Publications); _Heaven Shall Not Wait_ was revised in 1990. The third in the series, _Love from Above_ (John Bell and Graham Maule, eds. [Chicago: GIA Publications, 1989]) was published in 1989. The main themes here pertain to the Trinity, Jesus as a friend, creation, and the oneness of worship and work. A recording of each compilation was also made available.

The 1990s

The publishing of new hymnals continues and shows no sign of abatement. Under a directive to develop a hymnal using inclusive language with an awareness of the great diversity within the church, the Presbyterian hymnal committee included 695 selections in its _Presbyterian Hymnal_ and its ecumenical edition _Hymns, Psalms & Spiritual Songs_ (Linda Jo McKim, ed. [Louisville, Ky.: Westminster/John Knox Press, 1990]). Their aim—"to provide a book for congregational singing with the expectation that all who use it may be enriched by hymns from gospel, evangelical, Reformed, and racial and ethnic traditions in the church"—is clearly stated in the preface (p. 7). True to the Presbyterian heritage, the book includes one hundred musical settings of selections from the Psalter, including six settings for Psalm 23. And there are 157 congregational songs included in the Christian Year section, indicating the continuing interest in the denomination to observe the Christian year. The remaining 347 songs in the Topical Hymns and Service Music sections comprise a varied selection including music provided for Spanish, Korean, Chinese, and Japanese texts.

The leadership of George H. Shorney and the enthusiastic efforts of hymnal editor Donald P. Hustad, one of America's leading church musicians and hymnologists, resulted in *The Worshiping Church: A Hymnal* (Donald P. Hustad, ed. [Carol Stream, Ill.: Hope Publishing Company, 1990]). Of particular interest in this important book are its several adjunct volumes. The three accompaniment books have been published for keyboard, brass, and handbells. The *Worship Leader's Edition* contains helpful articles related to worship and congregational singing as well as a brief analysis of each song printed. The concordance tabulates the texts which contain any important word that the user wishes to find. Moreover, the dictionary companion contains complete historical information about all texts and tunes.

The latest *Baptist Hymnal* (Wesley L. Forbes, ed. [Nashville, Tenn.: Convention Press, 1991]) is a magnificent contribution to the ongoing development of heartfelt congregational singing in the churches of the Southern Baptist Convention, America's largest Protestant denomination. A hymnal for people of the Book, each text has been carefully examined as to its theological content. From the beginning of congregational singing in Benjamin Keach's London church (1691) until 1991, the published books for Baptist congregations have included a wide variety of forms and styles. This book features the greatest variety to date, including traditional hymns and gospel songs as well as contemporary classical hymns, contemporary gospel songs, renewal songs, choruses, and ethnic selections.

Likewise, the 1992 Mennonite *Hymnal* (Kenneth Nafziger, ed. [Scottdale, Pa.: Mennonite Publishing House, 1992]) contains a wide variety of texts. There are twenty by Watts and twenty-three by Wesley, fifteen by Brian Wren, and eight by Fred Pratt Green. The music is also varied. There are fourteen American folk tunes here and thirteen Afro-American songs, ten tunes by Lowell Mason, and thirteen by Vaughan Williams. Ethnic songs are represented by Swahili, Swedish, Taiwanese, Welsh, South African, Slavic, and Spanish melodies.

In England the work of the early church music reformers continues in the endeavors of the *Jubilate*

group. *Hymns for Today's Church* (Michael Baughen, ed. [London: Hodder and Stoughton, 1982]), *Carols for Today, Church Family Worship,* and *Songs from the Psalms* were followed by *Psalms for Today* (Michael Perry and David Ibiff, eds. [London: Hodder and Stoughton, 1990]), also available in the United States from Hope Publishing Company. Intended for Anglican worship, this volume is certain to be widely used in both England and America. Extensive use has been made of folksong-like tunes, as well as newly composed melodies to supplement those selections which continue the use of familiar traditional music.

The printing of supplemental books continues and is well illustrated by *Come Celebrate!: A Hymnal Supplement* (Betty Pulkingham, Mimi Farra, and Kevin Hackett, eds. [Pacific, Mo.: Mel Bay Publications, 1990]) with its very singable songs. Written for the *Community of Celebration* of the Episcopal Diocese of Pittsburgh, a community drawn together for daily worship, this collection, which is a supplement to *The Hymnal 1982,* is intended to be "a resource for enriching parish family worship with simple songs and hymns, on Sundays, at home, at work, and in the dailiness of life" (Preface). Here one will find unison and part songs (with piano or guitar accompaniment and other instruments, including a bass instrument and percussion) for the Daily Office and for celebrations of the Holy Eucharist and the Church Year.

An additional 1992 book of hymns from the Hope Publishing Company is *100 Hymns of Hope* (George H. Shorney, ed. [Carol Stream, Ill.: Hope Publishing Company, 1992]) commemorating the company's 100-year history. Its contemporary hymn texts and music are by English, American, and Canadian authors such as Michael Baughen, Margaret Clarkson, Peter Cutts, Carl P. Daw, Richard Dirkson, Timothy Dudley-Smith, Fred Pratt Green, Hal Hopson, Alan Luff, Jane Marshall, J. R. Peacey, Michael Perry, Richard Proulx, William Reynolds, Erik Routley, Jeffery Rowthorn, Carl Schalk, John W. Wilson, Brian Wren, and Carlton Young, all members of congregational song's "Hall of Fame."

Finally, Word Music has issued a comprehensive collection of *Songs for Praise and Worship* (Ken Barker, ed. [Waco, Tex.: Word Music, 1992]), an anthology of 253 songs and choruses providing material from a number of praise-and-worship-style music catalogs to serve as either a stand-alone collection or a supplement to any hymnal. The several editions include the pew edition, the singer's edition, a worship planner's edition, a keyboard edition, and fifteen instrumental editions. Transparency masters and slides are also available. Its table of contents reveals a growing sensitivity to the need for topical songs and includes sections such as God Our Father, Jesus Our Savior, The Holy Spirit, The Church, The Believer, Opening of Service, and Closing of Service.

────────── **Conclusion** ──────────

Because so many materials are available for congregational singing, and since only a small fraction of the various texts and song forms can be assimilated by any one congregation, worship leaders are constantly required to make difficult choices. Also, because there is such rapid change taking place in American society and within the church itself, worship leaders must be sensitive to the needs and requests of a shifting multigenerational and sometimes multicultural membership.

Lyle E. Schaller says it well in his descriptive work, _It's A Different World!_:

> The increase in the range of available choices has made the task of being a leader in the church more complex and more difficult than it was in the 1950s. Being able to recognize that every choice has a price tag, encouraging people to understand the matter of trade-offs, and being able to identify those trade-offs makes the responsibility of serving as a leader in the church today far more difficult than it ever was in 1955. ([Nashville, Tenn.: Abingdon Press, 1987], 239)

One of the major problems which emerged from the church music renewal movement of the 1960s and 1970s is the division between those churches which chose to continue singing traditional songs and those assemblies which adopted praise-and-worship-style music exclusively. Also, there are those church leaders who opted for both by scheduling two services, one traditional and one contemporary. However, this practice has been just as divisive, though confined to the local church. Congregational song, however, is for all of the people of God in united acts of worship. Thus, the convergence so wonderfully advocated by Robert Webber and Chuck Fromm is the most rational and pragmatic response to the problem. In _Signs of Wonder_

(Nashville: Abbott Martyn, 1992) Webber points out the following:

> There is a movement among the people of the world to find out each other's traditions and to share from each other's experiences. We the people of the church have even more reason to learn what is happening in other worship cultures and to draw from each other's spiritual insights and experiences. After all, there is only one church, and although there are a variety of traditions and experiences within this church, each tradition is indeed part of the whole. The movement toward the convergence of worship traditions and the spiritual stimulation which comes from borrowing from various worship communities are the results of the worship renewal taking place in our time.

In the final analysis, those responsible for leading congregational singing are required to know the entire repertoire of congregational song appropriate to the culture in which they live. They need to know the most meaningful and relevant songs from the past, and they must exercise a growing sensitivity to the heartfelt needs of those whom they lead. And they primarily must seek the mind of God—together with pastoral leaders in their churches—in making the crucial decisions of what is to be sung.

William Lock

200 • BIBLIOGRAPHY ON THE HISTORY OF CONGREGATIONAL SONG

────────── **Surveys** ──────────

There are several outstanding surveys of the history of congregational song. One of the most complete discussions is in Erik Routley's twin volumes _A Panorama of Christian Hymnody_ (Chicago: GIA Publications, 1979) and _The Music of Christian Hymns_ (Chicago: GIA Publications, 1981). Both volumes include extensive anthologies: the first volume, an anthology of hymn texts, the second, an anthology of hymn tunes. Routley also published a less extensive history of hymnody: _Christian Hymns Observed_ (Princeton: Prestige Publications, 1982). Two other well-written introductions to the history of hymnody are William J. Reynolds and Milburn Price, _A Survey of Christian Hymnody_ (Carol Stream, Ill.: Hope Publishing Co., 1987) and Harry Eskew and Hugh McElrath, _Sing With Under-_

standing (Nashville: Broadman, 1980). For brief summaries of the history of a variety of individual hymns, see Austin Lovelace, *Hymn Notes for Church Bulletins* (Chicago: GIA Publications, 1987).

A broad overview of the history of hymnody is also found in the article "Hymns and Hymnals" in *The New Catholic Encyclopedia* (Washington, D.C.: Catholic University of America, 1979, Vol. 17, pp. 284ff.) and in the *New Grove Dictionary of Music and Musicians,* ed. Stanley Sadie (London: Macmillan, 1980).

Yet another fine source of historical information are the handbooks that have been printed as companion volumes to almost every major hymnbook printed in the past several decades.

Greek and Latin Hymnody

For discussion of the sources of early hymnody, J. Julian's monumental *Dictionary of Hymnology,* 2d ed. (London: John Murray, 1907; reprint ed., Grand Rapids: Kregel Publications, 1985) is the standard reference available to lay readers.

Scholarly sources include G. M. Dreve's and C. Blume's *Analecta Hymnica medii aevi,* 55 vols. (Leipzig: Reisland, 1886–1922; reprint ed., New York: Johnson Reprints, 1961), a nearly complete collection of medieval hymn texts, including those of Ambrose. Much of the Latin and Greek hymn legacy can be traced in some detail through W. K. Lowther Clarke's *A Hundred Years of Hymns, Ancient and Modern* (London: Clowes, 1961), which presents a summary of the many editions of *Hymns, Ancient and Modern* from its first appearance in 1861 as one of the most comprehensive hymn-tune anthologies of its genre. Other valuable sources include Ruth Messenger's *The Medieval Latin Hymn* (Washington, D.C.: Capital Press, 1953); J. Mearns' *Early Latin Hymnaries* (Cambridge: University Press, 1913); Perdue-Davis's *A Primer of Ancient Hymnody* (Boston: E. C. Schirmer, 1968); and Denis Steven's *Plainsong Hymns and Sequences* (Surrey: Royal School of Church Music, n.d.).

Discussions of Eastern hymnody can be found in H. J. W. Tillyard's *Byzantine Music and Hymnography* (London: Faith Press, 1923); Constantine Cavarnos's *Byzantine Sacred Music* (Belmont, Mass.: Institute for Byzantine and Modern Greek Studies, 1956); Egon Welesz's *A History of Byzantine Music and Hymnography,* 2d ed. (Oxford: Clarendon Press, 1961).

The Chorale

For sources on the chorale, the single most important citation is the German study of Johannes Zahn, *Die Melodien der evangelischen Kirchenlieder* (Gutersloh: Bertelsmann, 1889–1893), a six-volume collation of 8,600 chorale tunes together with complete texts and a complete concordance networking all tune and text interrelations. A more accessible overview of the topic can be found in Edwin Liemohn's *The Chorale Through Four Hundred Years* (Philadelphia: Muhlenberg Press, 1953) and Johannes Riedel's *The Lutheran Chorale: Its Basic Traditions* (Minneapolis: Augsburg Publishing House, 1967). See also "Chorale" in *Encyclopedia Brittannica* (Chicago, 1961), Vol. 5, pp. 682ff. The article on "Chorale" in *The New Grove Dictionary of Music and Musicians* (1980) updates much information regarding current scholarship from the earlier important sources. *The Lutheran Book of Worship* (Minneapolis: Augsburg, 1978) includes several examples of Reformation chorales as they are used in worship today.

Psalmody

The best overview to psalmody in the Reformation period is found in the *New Grove Dictionary of Music and Musicians,* with articles by Nicholas Temperley, Howard Slenk, Margaret Munck, and John Barley.

Discussions of the history of psalmody in Geneva can be found in *Le Psaultier de Geneve: 1562–1865* (Geneva: n.p., 1986). Written in French, this cutting-edge history of the Geneva Psalter from its 1562 printing through 1865 is published in a facsimile format. Intended as a celebration of the 450th anniversary of the Reformation, it is illustrated with full-color prints of earlier versions and gives an annotated checklist of all complete editions (Geneva-printed) currently known to be extant or classified. It is one of the most valuable resources for the history of Reformation psalmody. See also Waldo S. Pratt's The Music of the French Psalter of 1562 (New York: Columbia University Press, 1939), which includes both historical analysis and a transcription of the Psalter itself.

History of psalmody in England and Scotland is discussed in Maurice Frost, *English and Scottish Psalm and Hymn Tunes* (London: Oxford University Press, 1953), Millar Patrick, *Four Centuries of Scottish Psalmody* (London: Oxford University

Press, 1949), Edna Park's *The Hymns and Hymn Tunes Found in the English Metrical Psalters* (New York: Coleman Ross, Inc., 1966), Rikvah Zim's *English Metrical Psalms: Poetry as Praise and Prayer, 1535–1601* (Cambridge, U.K.: Cambridge University Press, 1987), which deals exclusively with the texts of metrical psalms, and Robin A. Leaver, *Goostly Psalmes and Spirituall Songes: English and Dutch Metrical Psalms from Coverdale to Utenhove, 1535–1600* (Oxford: Clarendon Press, 1991), which discusses Reformation psalmody in both America and the Netherlands.

Psalmody in colonial America is discussed in Percy Scholes's *The Puritans and Music in England and New England* (London: Oxford University Press, 1934).

English Hymnody

In addition to the general sources cited above, the best scholarly discussions of English hymnody are found in Nicholas Temperley's comprehensive *The Music of the English Parish Church,* 2 vols. (Cambridge, U.K.: Cambridge University Press, 1979). See also Louis F. Benson, *The English Hymn* (Richmond: John Knox Press, 1962); Susan S. Tamke, *Make a Joyful Noise Unto the Lord: Hymns as a Reflection of Victorian Social Attitudes* (Athens, Ohio: Ohio University Press, 1978); as well as a variety of works on the hymns of Watts and the Wesleys that may be available at local libraries.

American Hymnody

Albert Christ-Janer, Charles W. Hughes, and Carleton Sprague Smith's *American Hymns, Old and New* (New York: Columbia University Press, 1980) covers American hymnody in a selective but comprehensive collection of 600 hymns intended for study. A "historical singing book," *American Hymns* traces hymns in this country from the beginnings in psalmody to 1980. Excerpts from the early Psalters include Sternhold and Hopkins, Scottish Psalters, the Ainsworth Psalter, Tate and Brady, and the Bay Psalm Book. The contents proceed chronologically and include Psalters, devotional verse, denominational hymns, patriotic hymns, and ethnic hymns in each century. The coverage for the nineteenth century adds folk hymns and spirituals, missionary hymns, carols, Sunday school hymns, and revival and gospel songs. The twentieth century section contains forty hymns commissioned for the book, many with texts by contemporary American poets. The collection is notable for the recovery of some forgotten hymns by the likes of Anne Bradstreet. Published along with the hymnal is a companion volume, *American Hymns, Old and New: Notes on the Hymns and Biographies of the Authors and Composers.* For a history of pre-Vatican II Roman Catholic hymnals in America, see J. Vincent Higginson, *A Handbook for American Catholic Hymnals* (Springfield, Ohio: Hymn Society of America, 1976). For hymnody in African-American traditions, see Jon Michael Spencer's *Black Hymnody: A Hymnological History of the African-America Church* (Knoxville: University of Tennessee Press, 1992). In addition, most of the books listed under the bibliography to chapter 3 contain large sections on the history of American hymnody.

Congregational Singing Since 1950 in Canada, England, and the United States

For this period, which has not yet been described comprehensively, the single most important source is *The Hymn,* the official journal of the Hymn Society of the United States and Canada. In this journal, denominational repertories, ethnic hymnody, and new hymns and hymnals are all considered, along with further bibliographical aids. Its counterpart in England is the *The Bulletin of the Hymn Society of Great Britian and Ireland.* Also helpful in understanding recent developments in congregational song is George H. Shorney's *The Hymnal Explosion* (Carol Stream, Ill.: Hope Publishing Company, 1987).

A Brief History of Jubilation

The phenomenon of jubilation, or wordless song and prayer, was part of the worship practice of the ancient church, as attested in the writings of the church fathers. During the Middle Ages, it was a common popular expression of devotion to Jesus; and it formed an important component in the devotional expression of the great mystics of the Western church. Jubilation has many features in common with the "tongues" of the New Testament church, and its practice in Christian worship appears to have been a continuation of New Testament usage. The recovery of the tradition of jubilation could have significant impact upon the renewal of worship in the contemporary church.

201 • Jubilation in the Patristic Era

The time from the conversion of Constantine until the dawning of the second millennium was the formative period of the church, the era of the church fathers. It was a time of lively faith but also a time of controversy. During this period the expressive worship tradition of the church was shaped and formed and given the roots it needed to grow in richness in the following centuries. An important aspect of this worship tradition was a form of wordless prayer known as jubilation, which the church fathers understood as a natural human response to the mystery of God.

The period of the fathers was a time of a rich variety of styles of expressive prayer and worship. Congregations could be quite spontaneous in calling out phrases of praise and thanksgiving. Sighs, tears, and laughter played an important role in worship. Perhaps the most significant form of spontaneous prayer during the formative period was prayer without words, or *jubilation,* which closely resembles the "tongues" of present-day charismatic renewal. Jubilation was a way of singing and praying aloud without using words. Although the last hundred years have seen even the memory of wordless prayer ebb from the Catholic church's consciousness, it played a vital role in the formation of the liturgy until the ninth century, and was important in private prayer until the late Middle Ages. Traces of it can be found in the mystical tradition as late as the nineteenth century.

Origin of the Term *Jubilation*

The word *jubilation* (or *jubilus*) comes from the classical Latin word *jubilatio* which means "loud shouting, whooping." In classical usage, a jubilation was the pastoral call of a farmer or shepherd. It has been the age-old custom of country people to call to one another or to animals by using special calls or yodels. St. Hilary of Poitiers (d. 368) referred to the peasant origins of the term jubilation:

> And according to the custom of our language, we name the call of the peasant and agricultural worker a *jubilus,* when in solitary places, either answering or calling, the jubilation of the voice is heard through the emphasis on the long drawn out and expressive rendering. (*Ennarationes in Psalmos 65,* as quoted in George Chambers, *Folksong-Plainsong* [1956], 23–24)

This jubilation of the peasant was probably much like a yodel. In fact, the word *yodel* comes from the medieval usage of the word jubilation (*Die Musik in Geschichte und Gegenwart* [1958] vol. 7, p. 74). Alpine shepherds still employ the yodel to call to one another. Western ranch hands of North America herd cattle with a form of yodel. There seems to be a natural human trait, which was much more pronounced in preindustrial societies, to improvise wordless calls and songs. When human muscle power exerted in concert was still a vital source of energy, men regulated the rhythm of their lifting and moving together through the use of wordless calls.

Christians of the late Roman Empire and Middle Ages were well acquainted with a variety of wordless expressions. They saw their wordless prayers as the same type of activity that farmers and shepherds engaged in. They recognized the singing and speaking of wordless phrases as a natural human activity, much more than people of the twentieth century would.

If they saw a great identity between their jubilation and the natural jubilation of the secular world, they also saw profound differences. For them, Christian jubilation was a natural human activity given over to a profoundly Christian and spiritual use. Augustine could call Christian jubilation miraculous (J. P. Migne, *Patrologia Latina,* vol. 40, p. 680). Contrasting secular jubilation with its Christian counterpart, he wrote: "They jubilate out of confusion, . . . we [Christians] out of confession" (*Ennarationes in Psalmos 99*).

Thus, jubilation was viewed as a natural human expression which was given profound spiritual and mystical significance. George Chambers writes of this change of use: "[Jubilation] is the expression of the soul in a higher sense; it ceases to be merely a subconscious utterance and becomes part of the spirit's yearning for the inner things of God" (Chambers, *Folksong-Plainsong,* 5).

Types of Jubilation

The term *jubilation* has a wide range of meanings. Essentially it was understood as the spontaneous outward expression of inner spiritual experience. Such expression might come through wordless songs or sounds, but could also be manifested by bodily expressions such as gestures and laughter. As we survey what the church fathers have to say about it, we note references to three major types of jubilation. First, musical jubilation was a form of spontaneous, wordless singing. Second, congregational jubilation was musical jubilation in a liturgical setting. It was the custom of congregations to sing an *alleluia* before the reading of the gospel, and to extend the last "a" of the *alleluia* into a long, spontaneous, wordless song. Third, mystical jubilation was the flow of wordless sounds, musical or nonmusical, along with laughter and gestures, which accompanies intense spiritual experience. The following is a more complete discussion of these three types of jubilation.

Musical Jubilation. Musical jubilation is singing aloud on vowel sounds as an expression of joy or yearning for God. One of the best definitions of this practice has been provided by music historian Albert Seay, who writes that it is "an overpowering expression of the ecstasy of the spirit, a joy that could not be restricted to words. . . . It occupied a peculiar place in the liturgy, for it carried implications of catharsis, a cleansing of the soul" (*Music in the Medieval World* [1965], 38). In a major work dealing with the jubilus, Théodore Gérold emphasizes its improvisation: "One notes the more or less spontaneous impulse. . . . In [jubilations] [the people] exhaled joy to some extent without control" (*Les pères de l'église et la musique* (*Études d'histoire et de philosophie Réligieuse,* XXV, 1931], 122).

Most major thinkers of the Christian church in the late Roman Empire and early Middle Ages mention the practice of jubilation. We will examine some of their statements.

St. Augustine of Hippo, whose writings were a major influence on Western thought for nearly one thousand years after his death, mentions jubilation several times. In his *Expositions of the Psalms,* Augustine writes:

> Where speech does not suffice . . . they break into singing on vowel sounds, that through this means the feeling of the soul may be expressed, words failing to explain the heart's conceptions. Therefore, if they jubilate from earthly exhilaration, should we not sing the jubilation out of heavenly joy, what words cannot express?"

He urges his people to jubilate, saying:

> You already know what it is to jubilate. Rejoice and speak. If you cannot express your joy, jubilate: jubilation expresses your joy, if you cannot speak; it cannot be a silent joy; if the heart is not silent to its God, it shall not be silent to his reward. (*Ennarationes in Psalmos 97,* in *Patrologia Latina,* vol. 37, pp. 1254-1255)

Augustine speaks of the highly spontaneous and wordless character of jubilation:

> He who sings a jubilus . . . pronounces a wordless sound of joy; the voice of his soul pours forth happiness as intensely as possible, expressing what he feels without reflecting on any particular meaning. . . . He simply lets his joy burst forth without

words. (*Ennarationes in Psalmos 99:4,* in *Patrologia Latina,* vol. 37, p. 1272)

St. Jerome, who translated the Bible into Latin, says:

> By the term *jubilus* we understand that which neither in words nor syllables nor letters nor speech is it possible to express or comprehend how much man ought to praise God. (*Patrologia Latina,* vol. 26, p. 970)

In his translation of the Psalms, Jerome translates the Greek word *alalgma,* which means "shout of joy," as *jubilus.* In this use of the term he probably refers to the experience of wordless singing which was common in his day (Chambers, *Folksong-Plainsong,* 8).

St. John Chrysostom (c. 347–407), the bishop of Constantinople, encouraged his people to sing without words. He says, "It is permitted to sing psalms without words, so long as the mind resounds within" (*Eis ton Psalmon 41:2,* in *Patrologiae Graecae et Latinae,* vol. 55, p. 159; *Prothe ria eis tous Psalmous,* in *PGL,* vol. 55, p. 538).

M. Aurelius Cassiodorus (450–583) wrote a massive commentary on the Psalms in which he mentions jubilation several times. It is not clear from his references whether he is speaking of musical or nonmusical jubilation. He writes:

> The jubilation is called an exultation of the heart, which, because it is such an infinite joy, cannot be explained in words. (*Complexiones in Psalmos 65:1* [66:1 in English versions], in *Patrologia Latina,* vol. 70, p. 451)

He further writes, "Jubilation is the joy expressed with fervor of mind and shout of indistinct voice." Cassiodorus describes jubilation as a response to the incarnation of Jesus through the "new song" referred to in Psalm 33:3. He believed that the entire universe has been filled "with saving exultation" because of that event (*Complexiones in Psalmos 32:3* [33:3 in English versions], in *Patrologia Latina,* vol. 70, p. 226). Again, Cassiodorus asserted that jubilation can teach praise. It is a "helping," a "delighting,"

> . . . for those for whom the exultation of words was not able to be sufficient, so they might leap forth into the most overflowing and unexplainable joy, . . .

teaching rejoicing souls that they ought to give thanks to the Lord, not to sing confused by some anxiety. (*Complexiones in Psalmos 80:1* [81:1 in English versions], in *Patrologia Latina,* vol. 70, p. 586)

St. Isidore of Seville (d. 636) passed on much of the wisdom of the Latin fathers to later generations. Concerning jubilation, he writes:

> Language cannot explain, . . . words cannot explain. . . . It is an effusion of the soul. . . . When the joy of exultation erupts by means of the voice, this is known as jubilation. (*Opera Omnia,* vol. 5, p. 43)

Jubilation was a common form of prayer for believers in the medieval period. Sometimes wordless singing was an extension of vowel sounds after the singing of an *alleluia;* sometimes the jubilation was sung without the *alleluia.* Jerome mentions farmers in the field and even little children praying in this way. Others mention Christian sailors and boatmen on the Loire praying the jubilation. The practice was so widespread that the historian of music Marie Pierik has stated, "This ejaculation, modulated on all forms, became the refrain of gladness which accompanied the daily occupations of the peaceful population converted to the new faith" (Marie Pierik, *Song of the Church*).

Congregational Jubilation. Congregational jubilation is musical jubilation in the context of worship. Most of the descriptions of musical jubilation in general in the writings of the church fathers and music historians also apply to jubilation in congregations. Improvised prayer singing was practiced in a period when church worship incorporated a high degree of spontaneity. In addition to the jubilation, psalm-singing and hymns could be improvised. Congregations might react spontaneously with laughter, tears, and sighs and by shouting phrases such as, "Glory to God!"

It appears that most of the music in the patristic era, and at least some until the time of the ninth-century liturgical scholar Amalarius of Metz, was of an improvisational nature. *L'encyclopédie de la musique* includes this comment:

> From these sources (i.e., the church fathers) one senses clearly that the music of the Christian era was originally improvised. The first Christians expressed their religious ecstasy in a purely emotional and

spontaneous fashion by means of music. According to the terminology of Tertullian all the members of an assembly were invited to participate in the praise of God by words from Scripture or by "songs of their own invention." The first Christian authors, Hilary of Poitiers (315–366), Jerome (340–420), and Augustine (354–430), until Amalarius (ninth century), describe the rich, exuberant coloraturas sung without a text and the alleluia songs as overwhelming melody of joy and gratitude sung upon the inspiration of the moment. A large number of the melodies that have come down to us still have traces of improvisation. (article, "Improvisation," in _L'encyclopédie de la musique_)

St. John Chrysostom suggests that it is the work of the Holy Spirit that makes improvised singing in churches possible. He states, "Though men and women, young and old, are different, when they sing hymns, their voices are influenced by the Holy Spirit in such a way that the melody sounds as if sung by one voice." Chrysostom refers to the cantor as the "prophet" and to music as "prophecy." Of the singing at the Church of Holy Peace in Constantinople, Chrysostom writes: "The prophet speaks and we all respond to him. All of us make echo to him. Together we form one choir. In this, earth imitates heaven. This is the nobility of the Church" (quoted in _L'encyclopédie des musiques sacres_ [1968–1970], vol. 2, p. 15).

Improvised body movements could accompany congregational singing. Theodoret (c. 386–457) has left a report of "hymns being accompanied by clapping of hands and dance movements" (J. P. Migne, _Patrologia Graeca_, vol. 83, p. 426).

Congregational jubilation was a part of the total picture of improvised music. The jubilation came after the singing of the alleluia, just before the gospel during mass. As the congregation and choir sang the last _alleluia,_ the people moved into exuberant wordless singing on vowel sounds, which could last for up to five minutes. In a real sense it was a preparation for the hearing of the gospel. It could also occur in melismatic portions of the graduals and offertories. Cassiodorus writes:

The tongue of singers rejoices in it; joyfully the community repeats it. It is an ornament of the tongue of singers . . . like something good of which one can never have enough. It is innovated in ever-

varying jubilations. (_Complexiones in Psalmos 104,_ quoted in Chambers, _Folksong-Plainsong,_ 7)

It was during the ninth century that improvisation of the jubilus ceased to be an expected part of the liturgy. From the period of Pope Gregory I ("the Great") in the sixth century until the eleventh century, the church was in the process of absorbing new nations and barbarian tribes, often converting them _en masse._ While these were real conversions, it could take generations for a vital Christianity to filter down to the ordinary people. This situation inhibited the practice of improvisation, which relied to some extent on the spiritual sensitivity of congregations. Church music began to be performed more and more by trained choirs; this resulted in the writing of church music in notation, causing it to lose much of its improvised character.

Eventually the jubilation was largely replaced by the sequence. In the year 860, Norsemen sacked the cloister of Jumièges in Normandy, and a monk carried with him the written musical notation for the mass to the safety of the monastery at St. Gall. There a young monk named Notker noticed that words had been written in place of the jubilations after the final _alleluia._ Adopting this suggestion, Notker composed other words to replace jubilations. At first this was a device to help singers remember melodies, but soon it replaced the jubilation entirely (Henry Osborn Taylor, _The Medieval Mind_ [1911], vol. 2, p. 201).

Although jubilation ceased to be an expected part of the liturgy, large groups of ordinary people improvised expressive jubilations well into the Middle Ages, and mystically oriented small groups did so into the seventeenth century and perhaps later.

Mystical Jubilation. Mystics are men and women who feel the pull of eternity in a special way. Their lives are marked by a hunger for God and a close union with him. As a result of the constant quest for a bold experience of God, their lives are often characterized by dark tunnels and moments of indescribable ecstasy, resulting in a radical transformation of their existence. Examples are the ascetics of the desert, who often emerged from long years of prayer as men of great tenderness whose very presence brought healing to disturbed souls.

Part of the prayer experience of these mystics was the outward physical expression of the deep inward moving of the Spirit, sometimes involving jubilation. Traces of the practice can be seen in the patristic era. Later in the medieval period mystical jubilation becomes much more common. Pope Gregory the Great, in his commentary on Job, describes it as an immense interior joy that is manifested outwardly by the voice, physical gestures and laughter. He says:

> What we mean by the term jubilation is when we conceive such a great joy in the heart that we cannot express it in words; yet despite this the heart vents what it is feeling by means of the voice what it cannot express by discursive speech. (*Expositio in Librum Iob,* 8, 88)

Gregory writes that jubilation can also be expressed in bodily gestures: "What we call jubilation is an unspeakable joy which can neither be concealed nor expressed in words. It betrays itself, however, by certain gestures, though it is not expressed in any suitable words" (*Expositio in Librum Iob,* 24, 10). He pictures the heavenlies as a place of jubilation: "The mouth is rightly said to be filled with laughter, the lips with jubilation, since in that eternal land, when the mind of the righteous is borne away in transport, the tongue is lifted up in praise" (*Expositio in Librum Iob,* 8, 89).

John Cassian, the early fifth-century monk, helped to interpret the experience of the desert holy men for the Western church. He refers to monks waking with "a sacrifice of jubilations." Sometimes the delight of this experience is so great that the monk breaks out into shouts. Cassian describes this experience:

> For often through some inexpressible delight and keenness of spirit the fruit of a most salutary conviction arises so that it actually breaks forth into shouts owing to the greatness of its uncontrollable joy; and the delight of the heart and the greatness of exultation make themselves heard even in the cell of the neighbor.

Sometimes this experience of God is felt in profound quiet; sometimes it is expressed by "a flood of tears." Prayer without words, whether shouts, quiet or tears, has great value, according to Cassian: "That is not a perfect prayer . . . wherein the monk understands himself and the words which he prayed" ("Praying in a Transport of Mind," unidentified quote in Reinhold, *The Soul Afire* [1973], 362–363).

Other Styles of Expressive Prayer and Worship

The picture one gets from reading the literature of the early church is that people could be quite expressive both in private and public worship. St. Augustine, pastor and bishop of the Christian church in Hippo during the early fifth century, has left us many interesting accounts of the spontaneity of his congregation. One Augustinian scholar has noted that "Augustine's congregation was in the habit of reacting to whatever was read or preached with all the liveliness of their temperament. They shouted comments, sighed, and laughed, like children at a cinema" (F. Van Der Meer, *Augustine the Bishop* [1961], 339).

Another account of expressive worship comes from *Egeria, the Diary of a Pilgrimage,* the story of a woman from Gaul who made a pilgrimage to Christian Palestine in the early fifth century. She writes that the people of Jerusalem were quite devout and that the houses of the city were emptied on Sundays because people flocked to church. They loved ceremony and candlelight processions.

One of their customs was to gather in the church well before daybreak on Sunday to hear a special reading of the account of Jesus' resurrection. Egeria says, "During the reading of the passage [about the arrest of the Lord] there is such moaning and groaning with weeping from all the people that their moaning can be heard practically as far as the city" (*Egeria, The Diary of a Pilgrimage,* trans. George E. Gingras [1970], 109).

The type of experience described by Egeria appears to be a kindred response to jubilation. Both the "moans" and "groans" of Egeria and the joyful wordless sounds of jubilation are in a real sense glossolalia prayer: wordless, spontaneous prayer that is spoken aloud.

"How sweet," Augustine said in his commentary on the Psalms, "are the sighs and tears of prayer" (*Ennarationes in Psalmos 125*). It was common for members of his congregation to employ such gestures as outstretched hands, prostrations, kneeling, loud beating of the breast, and a person's throwing himself on the floor in contrition.

The Spiritual Significance of Jubilation for the Church Fathers

The church fathers believed that praying with both body and voice was normal and natural for

Christians. They knew that much in God is mysterious; therefore, our encounters with him are also filled with mystery. One way in which believers could respond to God's mystery was through singing and praying without words. The fathers conceived of a rhythm in the heart of God, a beautiful and mysterious song into which Christians can enter by means of jubilation.

In our own day we have witnessed a rebirth of voiced, wordless prayer, most often referred to as "speaking in tongues," or glossolalia. Under the inspiration of the Spirit, the person prays or sings aloud without words, expressing things which cannot be spoken in words. The importance for charismatics is not that it is a language or "unknown tongue," but that it is a means whereby the Holy Spirit prays through the believer, expressing things that are beyond conceptual language. George Montague, a leading theologian of the charismatic renewal, views glossolalia not as a language but as preconceptual prayer (_The Spirit and His Gifts_ [1974], 18–29).

Most Bible scholars consider New Testament tongues to be ecstatic speech, wordless sounds rather than actual spoken language. Significantly, modern culture has recently rediscovered what preindustrial societies knew instinctively, that communication and expression are much broader than the vocabulary and syntax of language. Examples of phrases which indicate this understanding are "body language," "good vibes," and "bad vibes." Thus one can conceive of glossolalia as real communication, even if it does not use syntax and vocabulary.

If both glossolalia and jubilation can be classified as preconceptual prayer, perhaps jubilation qualifies as a form of glossolalia. Indeed, the definition of glossolalia in a major study by Morton T. Kelsey sounds much like the definitions of jubilation given by the church fathers. Kelsey calls glossolalia "a spontaneous utterance of uncomprehended and seemingly random speech sounds" (_Tongue Speaking_ [1968], 1).

A major difference between the church fathers' understanding of glossolalia and the understanding prevalent in Pentecostal and charismatic circles is that the fathers saw it as a natural human activity. There is a tendency among Pentecostals to understand tongues as somehow separate from normal human experience. Analogies are rarely drawn with similar human activities such as yodeling, humming

in the shower, and the like. In fact, one wonders if the reaction of misunderstanding and occasional fear on the part of some Christians to glossolalia does not come from this dichotomy.

Although the church fathers conceived of jubilation as a natural human activity, they also saw it as a form of prayer with profound spiritual significance. As such it was a natural human activity given over to Christian use. An analogy can be made with the Eucharist. Sitting down to a meal is one of the most ordinary of human activities. The Eucharist is also a meal; it is also ordinary and human. The difference between the Eucharist and a family meal is that the Eucharist is a meal given over to a real and profound encounter with Christ.

The same can be said of glossolalia as an ordinary human activity, that of giving over one's voice to a flow of sounds from the subconscious. The fathers viewed it as an experience similar to battle cries, yodels, and humming. Yet among Christians this ordinary activity is given over to the deep movement of the Spirit within the person—a physical, vocal giving of oneself to the movement of the Spirit.

Part of the spiritual significance of jubilation for the church fathers was the understanding that jubilation is essentially God praying through the believer. Augustine clearly delineates this view in his commentary on Psalm 32 (33 in English versions), where he asserts that human beings do not know how to pray or sing to God properly. God himself intervenes through jubilation, even helping to form the tune. Augustine writes, "Lo and behold, he sets the tune for you himself, so to say; do not look for words, as if you could put into words the things that please God. Sing in jubilation: singing well to God means, in fact, just this: _singing in jubilation._" In an apparent paraphrase of Paul's statement in Romans 8:26, Augustine continues: "The jubilus is a melody which conveys that the heart is in travail over something it cannot bring forth in words. [When you cannot say what you want to say] what else can you do but jubilate?" (_On the Psalms_ [1961 edition], 111–112).

This same sentiment is expressed in beautiful, imaginative imagery by St. Peter Chrysologus. He hears the jubilation as God's own song and relates it to the call of the Good Shepherd. In his commentary on Psalm 94 (95 in English versions) St. Peter Chrysologus writes thus:

The Shepherd with sweet jubilus, with varied
    melody,
leads the flock to pasture,
keeps the tired flock at rest under shaded
    grove.
This jubilus urges the flock to climb lofty
    mountains,
there to graze on healthful grasses.
Also it calls them to descend to the low
    valleys
slowly and without hurry.
How happy are those sheep that join their
    voices
to the voice of the Shepherd,
that follow when he calls to feed and gather.
They truly jubilate to their Shepherd. . . .
In [singing] psalms let us jubilate. (*Sermo VI
in Psalmos 94*)

Christians of this period considered jubilation to be an entering into the music of the angels. "Heaven," said St. Isidore, "functions under the rhythm of jubilation" (Chambers, *Folksong-Plainsong*, 8). This was also suggested by Pope Gregory the Great when he described jubilation as the praise of the blessed in heaven.

Augustine viewed jubilation as a confession, Cassiodorus as a "declaration." It was an acknowledgment that much of God is beyond us, and a witness that he prays through his people and unites their voices. Even today the traces of jubilation that remain in Gregorian chant and plainsong eloquently describe that mystery.

Although jubilation was often described as a spontaneous expression of joy, it was also to be engaged in regardless of one's feelings. Augustine, Chrysologus, and others used the imperative form when they admonished the people to jubilate; in short, they commanded the congregation to do so. Improvised jubilation was a regular part of the liturgical life of the people. They engaged in it regardless of circumstance, both in times of dryness and of spiritual blessing. This act of obedience opened up a channel through which God could work and pray through them. They thought of jubilation as entering into the praise of heaven.

202 • Jubilation in the "Age of Faith"

The medieval world at its high point was far from a time of dry metaphysics, religious rigidity and conformity, or darkness and superstition. In actuality, it was a time of creative intellectual ferment, and of tender and warm faith. The age that produced the great cathedrals and inspired scholastic theology was also a time of spontaneous worship that produced many charismatic movements. Ordinary Christians expressed their wonder in much the same way that modern charismatics express theirs: by praying aloud without words and by singing inspired songs. This tradition continued for several hundred years after the end of the Middle Ages.

The years 1050–1350 were a springtime for the Christian church. It emerged from the long night of bloody barbarian invasions to a remarkable period of life. From the fifth century until the eleventh, Europe had been overwhelmed by successive waves of barbarian invaders. However, the church's willingness to convert barbarian tribes and princes, its faithfulness in preserving small embryos of learning and culture in Christian communities, and the openness of a great many young children to seeking union with God in contemplative prayer brought about an era of blessing.

This three-hundred-year period produced universities and great works of scholastic theology and, to some extent, succeeded in humanizing and Christianizing an entire society. Church historian H. Daniel Rops writes:

> For three long centuries . . . society enjoyed what may be considered the richest, most fruitful, most harmonious epoch in all the history of Europe, an epoch which may be likened to spring after the barbarian winter. (*Cathedral and Crusade* [1957], 2)

People possessed a childlike but deeply rooted faith that allowed them to discover new dimensions of human love and charity. This faith and wonder found expression in the lofty spires of cathedrals and in remarkable works of music and art. Faith in miracles, sometimes to the point of excessive credulity, abounded. Men of the stature of St. Bernard of Clairvaux and St. Francis were produced in this fertile ground. Saints were many, and nearly every city or village could claim its share of holy persons and mystics who had lived there.

Wonder and praise also found an outlet in expressive prayer and worship. The glossolalia/jubilation tradition received from the early church continued and flourished, as did other forms of expressive prayer and worship. Although improvised jubilation was no longer a regular part of the liturgy, it remained part of the prayer experience of common people. Jubilation began to include spontaneous body movements and dance-like gestures.

In the medieval period an even closer resemblance to the tongues of the New Testament and of the Pentecostal movement becomes apparent. Evelyn Underhill, who has done what is probably the most significant work on understanding the jubilation of the medieval period, suggests a close kinship between jubilation and the tongues of the New Testament. She writes:

> Richard Rolle, Ruysbroeck, and others have left us vivid descriptions of the jubilus, which seems to have been in their day, like the closely related "speaking with tongues" in the early church, a fairly common expression of intense religious excitement. (Underhill, _Jacopone da Todi_ [1919], 77–78)

—— Personal Devotion to Jesus ——

A warm devotion to a personal Jesus flourished. The movements of Francis, Bernard, and Dominic encouraged love for a very human Jesus. Bernard of Clairvaux, who lived in the twelfth century and perhaps influenced the popular devotion of the "age of faith" more than any other man, could say:

> Hail, Jesus, whom I love. Thou knowest how I long to be nailed with thee to the cross. Give thyself to me. . . . Draw me wholly to thee, and say to me: "I heal thee, I forgive thee. . . ." I embrace thee in a surge of love. (quoted in Rops, _Cathedral and Crusade,_ 48)

St. Bernard's words tremble with tenderness as he repeats the name of Jesus. To his monks he says: "Your affection for your Lord Jesus should be both tender and intimate" (_On the Song of Songs,_ trans. by Kilian Walsh [1971], vol. 1, p. 150). Bernard's sermons are known to have taught healing for both body and soul in the name of Jesus. After describing the healing of the cripple by Peter and John, he continues:

> Write what you will, I shall not relish it unless it tells of Jesus. Talk or argue about what you will, I shall not relish it if you exclude the name of Jesus. Jesus to me is honey in the mouth, music in the ear, a song in the heart. Again, it is a medicine. Does one of us feel sad? Let the name of Jesus come into his heart, from there let it spring to his mouth, so that shining like the dawn it may dispel all darkness and make a

cloudless sky. (_On the Song of Songs,_ vol. 1, p. 110)

Many hymns were written to the name of Jesus. Such hymns as Bernard's _Jesu, Dulcis Memoria_ (known in English hymnals as "Jesus, the Very Thought of Thee") were the songs sung by the average peasant and townsperson.

St. Francis of Assisi, a "friend of Jesus," along with the brothers who followed him, sent this same kind of devotion to Jesus ringing through the cities and villages of Europe. The God-man was not simply Christ, or the Incarnation, or the "Word made flesh." "Jesus"—his personal name—was the "one most loved." People commonly prayed and sang little poems known as "jubilations" which included a repetition of the name of Jesus with a short descriptive phrase. A word frequently used in these descriptions was _dulcis,_ or "sweet."

A fourteenth-century English preacher and mystic, Richard Rolle, writes:

> I cannot pray, I cannot meditate, but in sounding the name of Jesus, I savor no joy that is not mingled with Jesus. Wheresoever I be, wheresoever I sit, whatsoever I do, the thought of the savor of the name of Jesus never leaves my mind. . . . Verily the name of Jesus is in my mind a joyous song and heavenly music in mine ear, and in my mouth a honeyed sweetness. (_Selected Works of Richard Rolle,_ ed. by C. C. Heseltine [1930], 81)

This devotion to the name of Jesus bears remarkable similarity to the constant use of this name in charismatic renewal. Perhaps it marks a shift in emphasis from Jesus the concept to Jesus the person.

—— Theologians and Scholars ——

Jubilation was not simply the experience of peasant folk and a few saints and mystics. It was also described and probably experienced by most of the major theologians and intellectual figures of the Middle Ages. The theologians and scholars had a great sense that jubilation was a heritage received from the early church. They often quote and paraphrase the church fathers on jubilation, and at the same time they add new insight to the work of the fathers on the subject.

In 1490, at the close of the Middle Ages, an excellent description of jubilation was given in a Spanish-Latin dictionary, the _Universal Vocabulario._ It paraphrases Gregory on jubilation when it says that jubilation is a joy that one cannot express in words, yet a joy which cannot be contained; and it places much greater emphasis on gestures than do the patristic definitions:

> Jubilation is when such a great joy is conceived in the heart that it cannot be expressed in words, yet neither can it be concealed or hidden. . . . It manifests itself with very happy gestures. . . . The voice is excited to song. (*Universal Vocabulario en Latin y en Romance,* Reproduccion Facsimilar de la Edicion de Sevilla, 1490 [1967], vol. 1, col. ccxxvii)

One senses in both the writings of the church fathers and in those of the Middle Ages that jubilation was rarely controversial. Parts of the church's doctrine that are controversial or disputed—such as the Trinity, the person of Christ, the Eucharist, and the Assumption—receive very precise definitions, and much has been written about them. Other practices and doctrines, not as controversial but perhaps almost as important, do not receive the same sort of definition and prominence in the theological literature of the church. One finds references to jubilation primarily in folk literature; there is a wealth of material on jubilation in the mystical writings and the medieval chronicles which describe the daily life of faith. We find no long theological definitions of this practice in the Middle Ages like those which exist on doctrines such as the Trinity. Yet we do have significant references to jubilation by the major scholars of this period in their devotional writings, sermons, and biblical commentaries. These were people of fervent faith, and in writings which discuss devotion and inspire to faith they include references to jubilation.

Thomas Aquinas. The best-known theologian of the Middle Ages was St. Thomas Aquinas, whose work has profoundly influenced the Catholic church in subsequent centuries. His devotional writings and hymns, such as *Pange Lingua* and *Lauda, Sion* present a Thomas who was deeply in love with Jesus. It is said that his sermons brought congregations to tears.

In his commentary of Psalm 32 (33 in English versions) he suggests that jubilation is the new song which Christians sing because of their renewal in grace:

> That man truly sings in jubilation who sings about the good things of glory. . . . the jubilus is an inexpressible joy which is not able to be expressed in words but even still the voice declares this vast expanse of joy. . . . Moreover the things which are not able to be expressed, they are the good things of glory. (*In Psalterium David,* Ps. 32:3 [33:3])

In his commentary on Psalm 46 (47 in English versions) Thomas writes:

> Jubilation is an unspeakable joy, which one cannot keep silent; yet neither can it be expressed. The reason that [this joy] cannot be expressed in words is that it is beyond comprehension. . . . Such is the goodness of God that it cannot be expressed, and even if it could be expressed, it could only imperfectly be expressed. (*In Psalterium David,* Ps. 46:1 [47:1])

Thus we are aware that St. Thomas believed that part of human knowledge of God goes beyond conceptual language and cannot be expressed in words. Yet the good things of God are so marvelous that the Christian cannot keep silent. It is for this reason that people enter into jubilation.

Bonaventure. Next to St. Thomas Aquinas, the theological works of St. Bonaventure were the most influential of the medieval period. Bonaventure's writings reflect both the rigor of a competent theologian and the simple love of a mystic. They are filled with a sense of wonder at the mystery of God and of God's creation. On jubilation he quotes Gregory, describing it as an "inexpressible joy of mind which is not able to be hidden nor to be expressed; nevertheless it is betrayed by certain movements." He goes on to compare jubilation to the joyful expression of a bridegroom, "not being able to express the cheerfulness of his mind, however perceiving it about himself" (St. Bonaventure, *In Psalterium 46:3* (47:3 in English versions).

Perhaps above all else Bonaventure was spiritual and a theologian of spirituality. In *The Triple Way,* one of his major works on the subject, he formulates a sequence for relationship with God. First the soul is cleansed through sorrow and tears, then a perfecting of the soul comes through praise, thanksgiving and jubilation. Bonaventure says:

> Perfecting through gratitude implies an awareness that rises to a hymn of thanksgiving for the quality of graces that are offered, a joy that rises to jubilation for the value of the gifts we have received, and a delight that culminates in an embrace because of the

Giver's bounty. (*The Works of Bonaventure,* trans. by Jose de Vinck [1960], 90)

Jean Gerson. Jean Gerson was rector of the University of Paris and a renowned scholar of the Middle Ages. He was also a popular preacher whose sermons were enjoyed by the masses. Gerson describes a particularly exuberant form of jubilation, contrasting it with the unruly noise of the streets and theaters:

> The hilarity of the devout . . . in a certain wonderful and unexplainable sweetness seizes the mind . . . so that now it does not contain itself. There happens some sort of a spasm, ecstasy, or departure. . . . The mind springs forth; it leaps, or dances by means of the gestures of the body, which are comely, and then it jubilates in an inexpressible way. . . . The praise is pleasant, the praise is comely, since the purity of the heart sings along with the voice. (*Oevres Complètes,* vol. 5, p. 284)

The Early Franciscans. In the early part of the thirteenth century, in the thriving town of Assisi, Italy, a young man began acting in an unaccustomed manner. Normally a likable, fun-loving playboy, he began to spend time away from friends and family. The townspeople noticed a fresh, bright glint in his eye and suspected that he was in love. "Are you going to take a wife?" they asked him. "Yes," he answered. "I am marrying a bride more beautiful and more noble than any you have ever seen." The young man was Francis Bernadone, and the bride he was taking, as the people would later discover, was "the kingdom of heaven," "the life of the gospel" (*Early Franciscan Classics* [1962], 15).

This was St. Francis of Assisi. Many of us think only of his love for animals; to some he is just the saint who is found in birdbaths. But Francis was much more than a lover of animals. Most of all he was a "friend of Jesus." An early biographer, Thomas of Celano, says of him: "He was always taken up with Jesus: he ever carried Jesus in his heart, Jesus on his lips, Jesus in his ears, Jesus in his eyes, Jesus in his hands, Jesus in all his members" (quoted in *Early Franciscan Classics,* 43–44). The simple love and joy of Francis was to change the church. Through him the Lord built a community that was to touch countless thousands before his death and millions more in the centuries to come.

Within a few years of his conversion, thousands of people had joined Francis's order. They spread throughout the known world preaching the simple message of the gospel. These early Franciscans had a strong sense of community. God became intimately close in the presence of a brother or sister. Thomas of Celano describes their sense of love for one another:

> What affection for the holy companionship of their fellows flourished among them! Whenever they came together at a place, or met along the road, and exchanged the customary greeting, there rebounded between them a dart of spiritual affection, scattering over all their devotion the seed of true love. And how they showed it! Gentle tenderness . . . delightful converse, modest laughter, a joyous countenance, a sound eye, a humble heart, "a soothing tongue," "a mild answer," unity of purpose, a ready devotedness, and an unwearied hand to help. (*Early Franciscan Classics,* 43–44)

The source of the wonder and tenderness which they felt toward their Lord, one another and all of creation was prayer. Franciscans were constantly praying, both alone and together. They prayed on hilltops, in abandoned churches, along the streets and roads. They often struggled in prayer with sighs and tears.

For them, jubilation was apparently a very important way of praying. It is referred to in a number of writings, and in some passages is equated with contemplation. The followers of Francis practiced it both publicly and privately. Generally it was described as the speaking of wordless phrases as prayer, or the spontaneous singing of wordless phrases or inspired songs.

In a quaint legend from the *Little Flowers* (*Fioretti*), the words of a jubilus are actually written out. The description is amazingly like descriptions of present-day glossolalia within the charismatic renewal:

> Brother Masseo remained so filled with the grace of the desired virtue of humility and with the light of God that from then on he was in jubilation all the time. And often when he was praying . . . he would make a jubilus that sounded like the cooing of a gentle dove, "Ooo-Ooo-Ooo." And with a joyful expression, he would remain in contemplation in that way. . . . Brother James of Fallerone asked him why he did not change the intonation in his jubilation. And [Masseo] answered very joyfully: "Because when we have found all that is good in one

thing, it is not necessary to change the intonation." (*Fioretti,* chapter 32)

Another Franciscan writing compared Francis's jubilations to utterances in French:

Intoxicated by love and compassion for Christ, Blessed Francis sometimes used to act like this. For the sweetest of spiritual melodies would often well up within him and found expression in French melodies, and the murmurs of God's voice, heard by him alone, would joyfully pour forth in French-like jubilations. (*Speculum,* chapter 93)

Large groups of people are said to have entered into jubilation together. Thomas of Celano tells of a Christmas Eve celebration in Greccio, attended by men and women from all over the region, coming to join the friars in celebration of the birth of the Savior. Here is his amazing description of this tender and exuberantly joyful occasion:

A manger has been prepared, hay has been brought, and an ox and an ass have been led up to the place. . . . The people arrive, and they are gladdened with wondrous delight at the great mystery. The woods resound with their voices and the rocks re-echo their jubilations. The friars sing and give due praise to the Lord, and all the night rings with jubilation. The saint of God [Francis] stands before the manger, sighing, overwhelmed with devotion and flooded with ecstatic joy. The sacrifice of the Mass is celebrated over the manger, and the priest experiences a new consolation. (Thomas of Celano, *Vita Prima, Acta Sanctorum Octobris,* Tomus Secundus, 706)

Perhaps the most beautiful description of expressive worship ever written is the account of the canonization of Francis, a man whose life had been like a lyric poem, touching tens of thousands with his love, strength, and tenderness before his death. When the announcement came that Pope Gregory IX was to declare him a saint, people danced in the streets.

When the Pope arrived in Assisi, the city was "filled with gladness." The crowd of people marked the occasion "with great jubilation, and the brightness of the day was made brighter by the torches they brought. The Pope lifted up his hands to heaven and proclaimed Francis enrolled among the saints" (*Early Franciscan Classics,* 127). Thomas of Celano describes the scene thus:

At these words the reverend cardinals, together with the Lord Pope, began to sing the *Te Deum* in a loud voice. Then there was raised a clamor among the many people praising God: the earth resounded with their mighty voices, the air was filled with their jubilations, and the ground was moistened with their tears. New songs were sung, and the servants of God jubilated in melody of the Spirit. Sweet-sounding organs were heard there and spiritual hymns were sung with well-modulated voices. There a very sweet odor was breathed, and a most joyous melody that stirred the emotions resounded there. (*Vita Prima,* 718)

This story contains amazing similarities to group singing in the Spirit, as practiced in the present-day charismatic renewal. Those familiar with medieval literature know that this was not an isolated incident; during times of religious exultation whole cities and towns could enter into this type of praise.

Renewals and Revivals

The "age of faith" was a time of many renewals and revivals. Jubilation and exuberant praise were frequently a vital part of those revivals. Wandering preachers went through the countryside admonishing people to turn to God. This sometimes resulted in entire towns laying aside their implements of war and joining orders such as the Franciscans and the Dominicans. One of these revivals, which took place in northern Italy in 1233, was known as the "Alleluia." This is how the Franciscan chronicler Sambilene describes what happened:

This Alleluia, which lasted for a certain length of time, was a period of peace and quiet, in part because the weapons of war had been laid aside. It was a time of merriment and gladness, of joy and exultation, of praise and jubilation. During this time men of all sorts sang songs of praise to God—gentle and simple people, townspeople and farmers, young men and young women. Old people and young people were of one mind. This turning to God was experienced in all the cities of Italy, and they came from the villages to the town with banners, a great multitude of people, men and women, boys and girls together, to hear the preaching and to [gather together] to praise God. The songs that they sang were of God, not of man, and all walked in the way of salvation. And they carried branches of trees and lighted torches. Sermons were preached in the evening, in the morning and at noon. . . . Also, men took their places in churches and outdoors and lifted up their hands to God, to praise and bless him for ever and ever. They [wished] that they would never have to stop from praising God, they were so drunk with his love. How happy was the man who could do the most to praise God. (*Monumenta Germaniae,* vol. 23, Scriptores, 70)

The style of many of the wandering preachers was amazingly similar to preaching styles among modern Pentecostals. Some of the preachers, such as Benedict of Parma, did not belong to orders. Others were Dominicans and Franciscans. John of Parma often carried a trumpet as he went about "preaching and praising God in the church and the open places." Sambilene describes John's preaching thus:

I myself have often seen him preaching and praising God. He often did this standing upon the wall of the bishop's palace which was at that time in the process of being built. He began his praises by saying in the vulgar tongue, "Praised and blessed and glorified be the Father." Then the children would repeat the same words. A second time he would repeat the phrase, adding "be the Son," and the children would repeat the same and sing the same words. For the third time he would repeat the phrase, adding "be the Holy Ghost," and then "Alleluia, alleluia, alleluia!" Afterward he would blow his trumpet. Then he would preach, adding a few words in praise of God. (*Monumenta Germaniae,* vol. 23, Scriptores, 70)

The spontaneous song of these thirteenth-century Christians, their great love of praising God, and their use of banners and torches is remarkably similar to the large processions at charismatic conferences which often include the use of banners, candles, and inspired songs.

— Charismatic Prayer and Cathedrals —

One of the best examples of religious renewal in the Middle Ages was the building of cathedrals. These magnificent edifices were often constructed as the result of a wave of religious zeal that would grip whole towns, cities, and regions. Much of the work was done by volunteers in an atmosphere of group charismatic prayer. It has been suggested that if all we knew of the Middle Ages were the churches and the cathedrals that have been passed down to us, we would know practically all that we need to know about the faith of the people. Richly carved altars, statues, and windows illuminated with light filtering through stained glass moved worshipers to a deep experience of God.

The queen of cathedrals was Chartres. Its many windows beautifully depicted the place of Jesus in redemption. Scenes of his infancy, his life, and his crucifixion give a pictorial testimony to the deep devotion to their Lord that filled the people of that time. The first part of the cathedral at Chartres, begun in 1145, was built as a result of a revival that swept Normandy. Contemporary accounts indicate that the awakening began in Chartres and spread to Dives and then throughout the whole country. Abbot Haimon of St. Pierre-sur-Dives in Normandy vividly describes this revival in a letter, and the accuracy of his story is attested by other sources from that period (see G. G. Coulton, *Life in the Middle Ages* [1930] vol. 3, p. 18). Charismatic worship, healing services, and a greater call to conversion were all a part of this revival.

The renewal which led to the building of the cathedral was viewed as an act of God's grace. Because people had become "estranged from God" and "sick with sin," "the loving Lord looked from heaven . . . and then he drew to himself those who had moved away from him, and recalled the wandering." In so doing, God showed the populace at Chartres "a new manner of seeking him." A great amount of the work on the cathedral was done by volunteers who numbered in the thousands, an astounding figure when one remembers that the entire population of Chartres was only ten thousand at the time.

Conversion was a major element of the revival; Haimon says that in order to join the voluntary association of those who were building the cathedral, both men and women were required to go to confession, put away grudges and be reconciled with their enemies. During the actual building, priests exhorted the crowds to greater conversion of heart. Members of the nobility worked side by side with common serfs as equals, doing the manual labor so important to the sacred building project. Haimon's words leap across the centuries as he describes the spirit of love and conversion that permeated the work on the cathedral:

For who ever beheld, who ever heard, in all the ages past that kings, princes, the powerful men of this world, proud of their birth and their wealth, used to a life of ease, harness themselves to a wagon and haul a load of stone, lime, wood or some other building material. The load was so heavy that sometimes more than a thousand people were required to pull the wagon. . . . When they stopped to rest nothing was heard but confession of sins and pure prayer to God. . . . The priests encouraged the group to be of one mind; hatreds ceased, grudges disappeared . . . and men's hearts were united.

Charismatic prayer and prayer for healing were important during this renewal. Trumpets and banners accompanied the work of moving stone to the cathedral. Haimon speaks of "blasts of trumpets and waving of banners . . . too marvelous to tell of." When the priests encouraged the people to repent and seek mercy, they would "lift up their sobs and sighs from the inmost recesses of their hearts with the voice of confession and praise." Many would be so overcome with God's presence that they would "fall to the ground, then lie there with outstretched arms and kiss the earth again and again."

According to Haimon, innumerable healings accompanied the prayer and the work: "If I would tell all that I have been allowed to see, even in a single night, my memory and my tongue would utterly fail me," he writes. In the process of moving the stone the wagons would be stopped and the sick prayed for. "You may see the dumb open their mouths to praise God. Those troubled by demons come to sounder mind. . . . The sick and those troubled by various diseases get up healed from the wagons on which they have been laid."

Night was a time for rest and for spontaneous prayer and healing services. The wagons pulled up around the building site. Torches and lights of all sorts were ignited on the wagons. The sick were set apart in groups while the people sang "psalms and hymns" and implored the Lord to heal them. If some were not healed immediately the crowd became even more exuberant in its praying. Cries and tears rose to heaven. People were seen to throw themselves on the ground and crawl toward the high altar. Many were moved to a deep penance. Haimon describes the results of these prayer meetings thus:

Soon all the sick leap forth healed from wagon after wagon. The crippled throw away the crutches on which they had leaned their crippled limbs, hurrying to give thanks at the altar. Blind men see and move about with ease.

St. James. A shield of St. James shows a pilgrim's staff upon which is hung the pilgrim's wallet.

After each healing there was a procession to the high altar and bells were rung. Throughout the night "nothing is heard but hymns, praises and thanks!" (Coulton, *Life in the Middle Ages,* vol. 3, p. 18–22).

Abbot Haimon's remarkable letter reveals that charismatic prayer and worship were a part of the renewal that produced what is perhaps the best Christian art and architecture in the history of the church. The letter also attests to the connection between fervent expressive prayer and healing. The resolution of the crowd to continue praying until all were healed is similar to "saturation prayer" in the current charismatic renewal, during which people are prayed over for healing at length. The atmosphere created by this kind of expectancy generates faith in those who participate.

203 • MYSTICS: SINGERS OF A NEW SONG

Jubilation, the wordless prayer of ordinary worshipers in the "age of faith," occupied an even greater place in the prayer lives of mystics during that period and the centuries that followed. The writers speak of jubilation and spiritual inebria-

tion in referring to the entire spectrum of spontaneous bodily and vocal prayer which might include glossolalia, inspired songs, dancing, and intense bodily movement. Until the seventeenth century, this kind of prayer was mentioned by the majority of religious writers and was experienced by most of the well-known mystics.

Many people misunderstand the term _mystic_ as it is applied to Christian experience. A mystic is a person who is given to deep spirituality and seeking after God. Although some mystics practice silence and solitude, most do not. According to original sources, mystics of earlier centuries were warmly involved in intimate human contact. More often than not they possessed an extraordinary sense of humor, and some—like St. John Gosco, St. Philip Neri and St. Francis of Assisi—elevated the art of clowning to a prayer form.

Until the siege mentality developed in the Catholic church after the sixteenth century, mystics were a vital part of the life of the church. Their hunger for God and their evident freedom, tenderness, and joy were startling signs of God's kingdom being lived out among his people.

Mystic Jubilation

Because mystics were persons who focused their entire beings on the heart of God they were often in the process of radical transformation. Their lives produced great joy and hope, and lent a sense of purpose to the whole Christian church. A mystic's growth toward union with God and with fellow human beings was usually marked by excruciating cleansing and purging, as well as times of incomparable wonder. It is not surprising that jubilation, the prayer of many ordinary Christians in the "age of faith," should have played an even more important role in the prayer lives of mystics then and during the following centuries.

The works of several nineteenth-century scholars present an overview of the part jubilation played in the lives of these holy men. Albert Farges gives this description:

> There are even more violent transports, such as those so often observed in St. Francis of Assisi, St. Philip Neri, St. Joseph of Cupertino, St. Mary Magdalene de Pazzi, and many other holy mystics, whose jubilation or spiritual inebriation showed itself outwardly in actions which astonished and even scandalized the weak and ignorant. Such were their

> sighs, cries, ardent and broken exclamations, abundant tears, and even laughter, songs, improvised hymns, tremors agitating every limb, leapings, impetuous movements, the violent outward expression of enthusiasm and love. (Albert Farges, _Mystical Phenomena_ [1926], 155)

One of the more thorough studies made on the subject is _Die christliche Mystik_ by John Joseph Gorres. Written in the early nineteenth century, the book's purpose is to defend the Catholic faith and Catholic mysticism against rationalism. A part of Gorres's defense is to explain and describe mystical phenomena. He compiled numerous examples from several sources and used science and philosophy to help explain them.

A problem with Gorres's research is that he was not sufficiently critical and was too prone to accept the authenticity of some of the more bizarre accounts of mystical phenomena. Nevertheless, Gorres rendered the church an important service in describing and attempting to explain mystical jubilation. One chapter is devoted to describing the effects of spiritual experience on the vocal apparatus. Spiritual experience, he asserts, affects the voice by enabling it to sing heavenly melodies in a person's own language, or even in a language unknown to the one praying; the same process produces prophetic words. Gorres writes:

> The forces which contribute to the formation of [ordinary speech] can also submit to a transformation in ecstasy, and the sounds produced in this state carry a character which is much different from ordinary sounds. . . . The spirit itself is articulated in these sounds, words which the spirit of man had not thought. The voice then produces sounds which seem to belong to someone else. Or if this is really the voice of the one speaking, it is like elevated or winged thoughts which are spoken. (John Joseph Gorres, _La Mystique_ [French translation of _Die christliche Mystik_, 1854], vol. 2, p. 149)

The effect of spiritual experience on the voice could enable a person to speak a foreign language. Gorres gives the example of St. Mary Magdalene de Pazzi, who was able to speak Latin, a language she had never learned. He adds that predictive prophecy is another effect of religious experience on the voice. Gorres tells a story about St. Humiliane, who was known to sing by the inspiration of the Holy Spirit. The other sisters in her convent would hear her singing musical glossolalia, "a beautiful song with a voice so delicate that when they did not have their ears right up to her mouth, they heard the song but were unable to distinguish words" (*La Mystique,* 150–158).

Christine the Admirable also sang in the Spirit, according to Gorres. He writes that Christine would "turn around like a doll agitated by several children." Then from her lips would issue

> a marvelous song which nobody was able to understand or imitate in spite of all efforts. There was in this song a very fluid element . . . and the succession of these sounds. But the words of these melodies, if one wants to call them words, were sometimes incomprehensible.

After her spiritual song Christine was overcome by spiritual drunkenness. Gorres's account reads, "Little by little she appeared to be drunk—she was drunk in effect, but with a holy and divine drunkenness." She then led the other sisters in the singing of the *Te Deum.*

The jubilation of Christine was so entrancing, writes Gorres, that "it seemed to be the voice of an angel rather than the song of a mortal. It was so beautiful to hear that it surpassed not only the sounds of the most beautiful instruments but even the most pleasant human voice." Christine was also able to sing in Latin, a language she did not understand and had never learned, as well as to pray with glossolalia. Gorres says, "This was the jubilation of her soul which came out in unarticulated sounds" (*La Mystique,* 14, 158–159).

Invisible choirs were sometimes heard accompanying those who sang. This is Gorres's account of that phenomenon:

> Often during the divine service—especially Mass—one often heard invisible choirs making sounds around one of the holy people singing the Sanctus or some other chants. The examples are . . . frequent . . .

Jubilation: An Entrance into Deeper Spiritual Life

The gift of tongues is often looked upon in charismatic renewal as an entrance to a deeper spiritual life. The same appears to be true in the spiritual experience of the mystics. Evelyn Underhill makes this point in her biography of Jacopone da Todi. She calls jubilation "the characteristic phenomenon of the beginner in the supersensual life," and adds:

> These acute emotional reactions, often accompanied by eccentric outward behavior, are a normal episode in the early development of many mystics, upon whom the beauty and wonder of the new world of spirit now perceived by them, and the Presence that fills it, have often an almost intoxicating effect (*Jacopone da Todi,* 76, 78).

This suggestion of Underhill is borne out in the writings of many of the mystics. John Ruysbroeck calls jubilation the "first and lowest mode whereby God inwardly declares himself in the contemplative life" (*The Book of the Twelve Bequines,* chapter 10, as quoted in Underhill, *Jacopone da Todi,* 78). Richard Rolle received the gift of heavenly song early in the development of his spiritual life as a definite experience.

The same is true of the English mystic Gordic. On a pilgrimage to the Holy Land he spent whole nights praying on the mountains and visiting the Holy Sepulcher. Afterward he had an experience which his biographer describes as follows:

> In his heart there was a gentleness greater than anything else, in his mouth a sweetness sweeter than honey on the honeycomb, and his ears were filled with the melody of a great jubilation. (Eric Colledge, *The Medieval Mystics of England* [1961], 39)

It appears, then, that for many contemplatives, entering into the wonder of God with one's voice and body was a natural part of moving into a deeper spiritual life. There is a strong similarity between this form of initiation and tongues as a form of initiation among charismatics in the present-day charismatic renewal.

Jacopone da Todi

One of the more exciting mystics in the history of the church was Jacopone da Todi (1228–1306), a Franciscan friar. Before his conversion Jacopone enjoyed a happy life as a jurist and as the husband of a pretty, young wife whom he passionately loved. At a wedding celebration he and his wife were attending the floor suddenly collapsed during a dance, and Jacopone's wife was killed. When her party dress was removed, a hair shirt was found on her body, a sign that she was a woman of prayer who had been praying for the conversion of her husband. Jacopone, profoundly shaken, sold all of his possessions and eventually joined the Franciscans (Karl Vossier, *Medieval Culture* [1929], vol. 2, pp. 83–84). After many years of soul searching and purging, he entered into a period of overflowing spiritual joy. He describes his mystic journey in a number of songs and poems.

An entire period of his development is related to jubilation, as brought out by Evelyn Underhill in her biography of Jacopone. She records that during this time he "babbled of love with 'tears and laughter, sorrow and delight,' and with gestures that seemed foolishness to other men" (*Jacopone da Todi,* p. 76). In his poem "La Bontade se lamenta," Jacopone paints a vivid picture of the state of a soul in the joyous abandon of jubilation:

> Now a new language doth she speak,
> "Love, Love," is all her tongue can say.
> She weeps, and laughs; rejoices, mourns,
> In spite of fears, is safe and gay;
>
> And though her wits seem all astray,
> —So wild, so strange, her outward mien—
> Her soul within her is serene;
> And heeds not how her acts appear.

Another of Jacopone's poems describes the experience of singing in the Spirit:

> Abundance cannot hide herself apart;
> And jubilation, from out her nest within the heart,
> Breaks forth in song, and in sibilant sound
>   [*sibilare*]
> Even as did Elias long ago.

The subject of a third poem is the intoxicating nature of the love of God which a believer can share in times of jubilation:

> For since God's wisdom, though so great,
> Is all intoxicate, with love,
> Shall mine not be inebriate?
> And so be like my Lord above?
> No greater honour can I prove
> Than sharing His insanity, (*Jacopone da
>   Todi,* pp. 77–79)

In the following poem Jacopone personifies and addresses the jubilus directly. This is the most significant of his jubilation poems; in it he describes the power of the jubilus to overwhelm a person's being with love songs and joy, even when he carries pro-

found sorrow in his heart, so that observers think he has lost his senses:

> Of the Jubilus of the Heart
> That Breaks Forth in the Voice:
>
> Thou, Jubilus, the heart dost move;
> And madest us sing for very love.
>
> The Jubilus in fire awakes,
> And straight the man must sing and pray,
> His tongue in childish stammering shakes,
> Nor knows he what his lips may say;
> He cannot quench nor hide away
> That Sweetness pure and infinite.
>
> The Jubilus in flame is lit,
> And straight the man must shout and sing;
> So close to Love his heart is knit,
> He scarce can bear the honeyed sting;
> His clamour and his cries must ring,
> And shame for ever take to flight.
>
> The Jubilus enslaves man's heart
> —A love-bewildered prisoner—
> And see! his neighbours stand apart,
> And mock the senseless chatterer;
> They deem his speech a foolish blur,
> A shadow of his spirit's light.
>
> Yea, when thou enterest the mind,
> O Jubilus, thou rapture fair,
> The heart of man new skill doth find
> Love's own disguise to grasp and wear,
> The suffering of Love to bear,
> With song and clamour of delight!
>
> And thus the uninitiate
> Will deem that thou art crazed indeed;
> They see thy strange and fervered state,
> But have not wit thy heart to read;
> Within, deep-pierced, that heart may bleed,
> Hidden from curious mortal sight.
>   (Underhill, *Jacopone da Todi,* 279–281)

Words such as "stammering" and "chatterer," which Jacopone uses to describe his experience of jubilus, bear a remarkable resemblance to the descriptions of present-day Pentecostal glossolalia.

John Ruysbroeck

The Black Death, the rise of nationalism in the fourteenth century, and other factors began the unwinding of the medieval spiritual synthesis. Spirituality lost much of its unselfconscious innocence as religious writers became more and more introspective and speculative. Even so, mysticism continued to flourish during this time. Best-known and most revered of mystics in the Rhineland School, a tradition of mystics in the low countries of Europe, were John Ruysbroeck and Henry Suso.

Ruysbroeck mentions jubilation a number of times in his writings. His description of its physical manifestations makes most Pentecostal and charismatic worship appear tame by comparison.

> Spiritual inebriation is this: That a man receives more sensible joy and sweetness than his heart can either contain or desire. Spiritual inebriation brings forth many strange gestures in men. It makes some sing and praise God because of their fullness of joy, and some weep with great tears because of their sweetness of heart. It makes one restless in all his limbs, so that he must run and jump and dance; and so excites another that he must gesticulate and clap his hands. . . .
>
> Other things sometimes happen to those who live in the fierce ardour of love; for often another light shines into them . . . and in the meeting with that light, the joy and the satisfaction are so great, that the heart cannot bear them, but breaks out with a loud voice in cries of joy. And this is called the *jubilus* or jubilation, that is, a joy which cannot be uttered in words. (John Ruysbroeck, *The Adornement of the Spiritual Marriage*, Book 2, chapters xix and xxiv, as quoted in Underhill, *Jacopone da Todi*, 78)

Note that Ruysbroeck repeats the classic definition of the *jubilus:* "joy which cannot be uttered in words."

Jubilation is a means by which God makes his friends "happily foolish." Spiritual experience seizes the believer with such power that

> he scarcely knows how to contain himself, and knows not how he should bear himself. For he thinks that no one has ever experienced the things that he is experiencing and from thence arise jubilee because he cannot restrain himself. . . . Such an impatience possesses him outwardly and inwardly with so great a vehemence, that in all his powers and members there is so joyous an experience. . . .
>
> God makes his friends to be happily foolish. Sometimes this ecstasy is wont to grow to so great a height that the matter becomes serious, and more frequently he is compelled to break out into shouting whilst he is being spiritually touched or pricked.

(John Ruysbroeck, *The Kingdom of the Lovers of God,* trans. by T. Arnold Hyde [1919], 89)

For Ruysbroeck, jubilation was part of a deeply personal relationship with God. The Spirit of the Lord says to the heart: "I am yours, O man, and you are mine: I live in you and you live in me." Such interaction with God causes "great joy and pure pleasure to occupy body and soul," and the joy is so great that the person cannot endure it. This exultation "is called the *jubilus,* which no one can express in words." Says Ruysbroeck: "Hence arises the jubilation, which is the love of the heart, and the burning flame of devotion with praise and thanksgiving and constant reverence and veneration toward God" (*On the First Method of True Contemplation,* in *Opera Omnia Ioannis Rusbrochii,* 436).

In *Contemplatione Opus Praeclarum,* Ruysbroeck describes jubilation as the ebb and flow of reciprocal relationship with the Lord. "This same mutual touch, whether so in turn to touch and be touched, effects the *jubilus.*" In this state the "free and generous emotion pours back everything unto God" (*Opera Omnia,* 469).

——— Henry Suso ———

Henry Suso (1300–1366) also speaks of intense intimacy with the Lord. "I had certain tender conversations with my Creator in which only my spirit talked," he writes. "I wept and sighed; I laughed and cried" (John G. Arintero, *The Mystical Evolution in the Development and Vitality of the Church* [1951], vol. 2, p. 276).

In his autobiography, Henry writes a stirring account of his experience with inspired singing:

> One day . . . while the Servant [Henry's word for himself] was still at rest he heard within himself a gracious melody by which his heart was greatly moved. And at the moment of the rising of the morning star, a deep sweet voice sang. . . . And this song which he heard was so spiritual that his soul was transported by it and he too began to sing joyously. . . . And one day—it was in carnival time—the Servant had continued his prayers until the moment when the bugle of the watch announced the dawn.
>
> And while his senses were at rest, behold! angelic spirits began to sing the fair response. . . . And this song was echoed with a marvelous sweetness in the depths of his soul. And when the angels had sung for some time his soul overflowed with joy; and his feeble body being unable to support such happi-

ness, burning tears escaped from his eyes. (quoted in Evelyn Underhill, _Mysticism_ [1911; reprinted 1962], 277)

Richard Rolle

Probably no one person has probed the richness of the gift of heavenly song more than Richard Rolle of Hampole, England. Rolle (1300–1349) was a mystic and writer whose work left an indelible impression on English literature. An educated man, Rolle studied at the University of Oxford and the Sorbonne in Paris, where doubtless he was exposed to the literature of many mystical traditions.

At the age of eighteen, after finishing his work at Oxford and prior to beginning at the Sorbonne, he became a hermit. Thousands of people visited him at his hermitage because of his sanctity and wisdom (C. C. Heseltine, _Selected Works of Richard Rolle_ [1930], viii). Rolle's writings have much of the warmth and tenderness of Bernard and the early Franciscans.

Jubilation was a central concept in Rolle's understanding of spiritual experience. He used the word hundreds of times in his writings—one hundred twenty-four times in the _Melody of Love (Melos Amoris)_ alone. He also uses such words as "song," "chant," and "melody" when referring to jubilation.

The gift of heavenly song, occurring four years after his conversion, was an event in the life of Richard Rolle that marked an entrance into a deeper spiritual life. Here is his description of the experience:

Whilst I sat in the same chapel in the night, before supper, I sang psalms, as I might, and I heard above me the noise as it were of readers or rather singers. Whilst I took heed, praying to heaven with all desire, in what manner I know not, suddenly I received a most pleasant heavenly melody dwelling within my mind. Indeed, my thought was continuously changed into mirth of song, and I had, as it were, praises in my meditation, and in saying prayers and psalms I gave forth the same sound. (_Selected Works of Richard Rolle_, introduction, pp. xvi–xvii)

Rolle's use of the psalmic phrase _Beatus vir qui scit jubilationem_ (Ps. 89:15, English versions) indicates that he was familiar with the church's teachings on jubilation; that phrase is often used as a starting point for discussing jubilation in the tradition. Rolle writes:

To me it seems indeed that contemplation is the joyful song of the love of God taken into the mind, with the sweetness of angelic praise. This is the joy which is the end of perfect prayer, of honest devotion in this life. This is the mirth to be had in the mind for the everlasting lover, breaking out with a great voice into spiritual songs. This is the final and most perfect of all deeds in this life. The psalmist, therefore, says "Beatus vir qui scit jubilationem," that is to say, "Blessed is the man who knows jubilation," in the contemplation of God. (_Selected Works of Richard Rolle_, 144)

Rolle also wrote about spiritual inebriation in the context of jubilation as other mystical writers have done:

A man is carried above himself, "panting with desire only for the Creator." . . . Lifted up to the melody of song, he is inebriated with divine pleasure.

He describes jubilation as the overflowing of the life of God within the believer which unites body and soul:

Then I may say that contemplation is a wonderful joy of God's love, which joy is the praise of God that may not be told. That wonderful praise is in the soul, and for abundance of joy and sweetness it ascends into the mouth so that the heart and the tongue accord as one, and body and soul rejoice, living in God. (_Selected Works of Richard Rolle_, 50)

In _Contra Amores Mundi,_ Rolle describes the same experience in this way:

Wherefore, too, one who has been made a contemplative man . . . is perpetually raised to such great joy that he is even permitted to hear the song of the angels. Hence he sings his prayers to God, in a wonderful and indescribable way, because, just as now the heavenly sound descends his spirit, so also, ascending in a superabundance of joy to his own mouth, the same sound is heard. . . . Therefore jubilation is taken up brightly in his mind, and with resonant voice he sings the divine praises. . . . The more ardently he loves, the sweeter is his jubilation. (_Contra Amores Mundi_, ed. and trans. by Paul Theiner [1968], 160–161)

Jubilation, says Rolle, is a gift of God made possible by the passion of Jesus. "O good Jesus . . . you endured torments that I might experience the symphony of heaven (*Le chant d'amour* [*Melos Amoris*] [*Sources chrétiennes,* 1971] 93.5).

This intense spiritual experience is not conversion, but takes place subsequently as a result of fervent seeking after God:

> Moreover, although we do not receive this gift in the beginning of our conversion, if we seek continually in our love for Christ for peace of mind and body, we shall receive it presently as a gift from God. In that state I have indeed learned to sing the divine praises in exultation and to jubilate in the mellifluous fervor of singing. (*Contra Amores Mundi,* 71–72)

At least some of the time, Rolle sang his jubilation in the known language. Scholars report that his songs arose naturally from a life of prayer. In *Amending of Life* he writes:

> Our heart being kindled with a fervent love, our prayer also is kindled and offered from our mouth in the savour of sweetness in the sight of God, so that it is a great joy to pray. For whilst in prayer a marvelous sweetness is given to him who prays, the prayer is changed into song. (*Selected Works of Richard Rolle,* 130)

Repetition of the name of Jesus was important to Rolle's prayers. The phrase "jubilation in Jesus" often occurs in his writings. He explains:

> I cannot pray, I cannot meditate, but in sounding the name of Jesus. . . . The name of Jesus has taught me to sing. . . . Jesus, my Dear and my Darling! My delight is to sing to thee! Jesus, my Mirth and my Melody! (*Selected Works of Richard Rolle,* 81, 82, 95)

Rolle's experience of the gift of song seems to have transcended the gift of tongues. His song allowed him to penetrate heaven, to more fully enter the heart of God. Many of the wondrous, the indescribable aspects of God are known in the rhythms and movement of music and sound. Jubilation, the gift of song, was a way of knowing that deep part of God.

St. Teresa of Avila

In the sixteenth century, mysticism took a bright new turn in the lives and writings of St. Teresa of Avila and St. John of the Cross. Close friends, these Spanish mystics explored with heart and intellect the experience of union with God. These two saints did not develop their mysticism in a vacuum. They were both well educated and acutely aware of the mystical writings that had preceded them.

Both Teresa and John were influenced by Luis of Granada, a Spanish writer of the early sixteenth century. Luis was one of St. Teresa's Dominican confessors, as well as a popular preacher whose aim was to formulate a practical spirituality for ordinary people. In his *Guide for Preachers,* he quotes Gregory the Great's classic definition of jubilation: "a joy of the inner man so great that it cannot be expressed in words but is expressed in exterior actions" (Louis De Granada, *Oeuvres Complètes* [1894], vol. 10, p. 199). Luis writes that the joy of jubilation is so great that

> neither Plato the prince of the philosophers, nor Demosthenes the greatest of orators, were liften up to this good thing. . . . God is the author and principle of this joy that we call jubilation. (*Oeuvres Complètes,* vol. 10, p. 199)

St. Teresa is one of the most widely read of the mystical writers on prayer. She exuded happiness and wanted everyone around her to be happy. "I won't have nuns who are ninnies," she said. "Gloomy saints" were not to her liking. It is said that her joy was so infectious that when she laughed, the whole convent laughed with her. Dance, inspired song, and group jubilation were a part of the worship of the reformed Carmelite Order which Teresa founded and headed (Marcelle Auclair, *St. Teresa of Avila* [1953], 220).

She and her nuns enjoyed a warm sense of community and would frequently enter into exuberant praise and worship. In his biography of Teresa, Marcelle Auclair brings together original source material on this expressive worship:

> While they got on with their spinning, they chatted and composed *coplas* [little songs] which the young ones sang very charmingly. Teresa improvised poems that her nuns memorized. . . . One can feel the rhythm of the music. . . . Even at recreation, fervour would take possession of her and she was incapable of resisting the urge of the spirit. She would begin to dance, turning round and round and clapping her hands as King David danced before the ark; the nuns accompanied her "in a perfect

transport of spiritual joy." (Auclair, _St. Teresa of Avila,_ 220–221)

After some of her nuns had gone to France to found Carmelite convents, the French nuns, to their great surprise, saw the Mother Superior

more like a seraphim than a mortal creature executing a sacred dance in the choir, singing and clapping her hands in the Spanish way, but with so much dignity, sweetness and grace that, filled with holy reverence, they felt themselves wholly moved by divine grace and their hearts raised to God. (Ibid.)

It is interesting to note that the dancing was sometimes done "in choir," that is, in a liturgical setting.

One Easter, Teresa asked one of the nuns to sing an improvised song. The nun sang:

May my eyes behold thee,
Good and sweet Jesus. . . .
Let him who will, delight his gaze
With jasmine and with roses.
If I were to see thee,
A thousand gardens would lie before my eyes.

Teresa was so overwhelmed with this song that she fell unconscious in ecstasy. After regaining her senses she herself sang an improvised song. From then on whenever she would go into ecstasy, her nuns would surround her and sing softly (Auclair, _St. Teresa of Avila,_ 222–223).

Teresa makes significant references to jubilation in her writings. She devotes several pages to the subject in her mystical treatise _Interior Castle._ Following are some excerpts:

Our Lord sometimes bestows upon the soul a jubilation and a strange kind of prayer, the nature of which it cannot ascertain. I set this down here, so that, if he grants you this favour, you may give him hearty praise and know that such a thing really happens. . . .

The joy of the soul is so exceedingly great that it would like not to rejoice in God in solitude, but to tell its joy to all, so that they may help it to praise our Lord. . . . She would like to invite everybody and have great festivities. . . . [In such a state of transport, the soul] cannot be expected to keep silence and dissemble. . . . Oh, what a blessed madness, sisters! If only God would give it to us all!

May it please his majesty often to bestow this prayer upon us since it brings us such security and

such benefit. For as it is an entire supernatural thing, we cannot acquire it. It may last for a whole day, and the soul will then be like one who has drunk a great deal, but not like a person so far inebriated as to be deprived of his senses; nor will it be like a melancholiac, who, without being entirely out of his mind, cannot forget a thing that has been impressed upon his imagination, from which no one else can free him either. These are very unskillful comparisons to represent so precious a thing, but I am not clever enough to think out any more: the real truth is that this joy makes the soul so forgetful of itself, and of everything, that it is conscious of nothing, and able to speak of nothing, save of that which proceeds from its joy, namely, the praises of God. (St. Teresa of Avila, _Interior Castle,_ trans. and ed. by E. Allison Peers [1961], 167–169)

In her autobiography, Teresa uses the metaphor of spiritual inebriation to describe this state of prayer. She writes that during jubilation the soul

knows not whether to speak or be silent, whether to laugh or to weep. This state is a glorious folly, a heavenly madness, in which true wisdom is acquired, and a mode of fruition in which the soul finds the greatest of delight. . . . I often used to commit follies because of this love, and to be inebriated with it, yet I had never been able to understand its nature. . . . Many words are spoken, during this state, in praise of God, but, unless the Lord himself puts order into them, they have no orderly form. The understanding, at any rate, counts for nothing here; the soul would like to shout praises aloud, for it is in such a state that it cannot contain itself—a state of delectable disquiet. . . . O God, what must that soul be like when it is in this state! It would fain be all tongue, so that it might praise the Lord. It utters a thousand holy follies, striving ever to please him who thus possesses it. (_The Autobiography of St. Teresa of Avila,_ trans. and ed. by E. Allison Peers [1960], pp. 163–165)

The writings of Teresa demonstrate that spontaneous and fervent praise of God are a result of a deep and living relationship with the Lord. At the same time, it is a behavior that can be encouraged and developed. For Teresa, jubilation in community was a proclamation that God was truly in the midst of his people. Congregational praise is just such a declaration today.

St. John of the Cross

John was a less practical mystic than his friend Teresa. His spirituality has a more speculative note. At the same time, in sublime and poetic ways he plumbs the height and depth of spiritual experience.

In his references to jubilation John, like Teresa, uses the analogy of festivity. He says:

> In this state of life so perfect, the soul always walks in festivity, inwardly and outwardly, and it frequently bears on its spiritual tongue a new song of great jubilation in God, a song always new, enfolded in a gladness and love arising from the knowledge the soul has of its happy state. . . . There is no need to be amazed that the soul so frequently walks amid this joy, jubilance, fruition, and praise of God. (*The Collected Works of St. John of the Cross,* trans. by Kieran Kavanaugh [1973], 609)

John presents a beautifully poetic description of jubilation in his *Spiritual Canticle.* He depicts the soul as a nightingale which

> sings a new and jubilant song together with God, who moves her to do this. He gives his voice to her, that, so united with him, she may give it to him. . . . Since the soul rejoices in and praises God with God himself in this union . . . it is a praise highly perfect and pleasing to God. . . . This voice of jubilance, thus, is sweet both to God and to the soul. (*The Collected Works of St. John of the Cross,* 560)

Like Crysologus and Rolle, John understood jubilation as the very voice of God with which the worshiper blends his own song in response. He also wrote a long passage in which he discusses spiritual inebriation and its effects upon the soul.

St. Philip Neri

Philip Neri, who lived in the tumultuous sixteenth century, was one of the most human mystics in the history of the church. As a layman he formed a household of laymen to help serve the many pilgrims who were flocking to his native Rome. Ordained late in his life, he was the founder of the Oratory.

Philip strove to keep those around him happy and cheerful, to teach them in his "school of merriment," as he called it. His biographer Bacci describes this:

Even when he had reached an advanced age, and his strength was nearly exhausted by his great labors, the holy man was still to be seen going about the streets of Rome with a train of young men, conversing with them on all sorts of subjects according to their different professions, making them affectionate one toward another and winning their reverence and love toward him. . . . Sometimes he left his prayers and went down to sport and banter with the young men and others who flocked to him, as we learn from Cardinal Crescenzi, and by his sweetness and the allurements of his conversations to keep them cheerful and win their souls. He very often took them to some open ground and there set them playing together at ball or some other game. He could have a playful style with those in his charge, going up to people, boxing their ears, and saying, "Be merry." (Bacci, *The Life of St. Philip Neri* [1902], vol. 1, pp. 194–195)

Philip could also feel people's sorrows. He had an amazing ability to enter into the feelings of those to whom he ministered. His expressive style with his fellow human beings was paralleled with expressive worship toward his Lord. With great intensity he entered into prayer. Bacci describes this:

> In those places Philip often was surprised by such an abundance of spiritual consolations that, unable any longer to endure so great a fire of love, he was forced to cry out, "No more, Lord, no more," and throwing himself down he used to roll upon the ground, not having strength to endure the vehement affection which he felt in his heart. . . .
>
> While he prayed he felt the incentives of divine love multiply with such power within him, and kindle such a flame in his breast, that besides continually weeping and sighing, he was often obliged, in order to moderate the fire, to throw himself on the ground, to bare his breast, and use other means to relieve his spirit which was overpowered by the impetuosity of the flame. . . .
>
> Fabrizio de Massimi, going one morning to confession to him, found the door of his room closed and, opening it very softly, saw the saint in the act of praying, standing up with his eyes raised to heaven and his hands uplifted, making many gestures. (Bacci, *The Life of St. Philip Neri,* vol. 1, pp. 21, 19, 338)

The spirituality of Philip and his friends exhibited itself in an intense devotion to the name of Jesus. Bacci tells of a scene of spontaneous worship which occurred at the deathbed of a young man:

Then in an outburst of joy, he began to sing the hymns which were sung at the Oratory, and particularly the one which begins, "Jesus! Jesus! Jesus! let everyone call on Jesus!" (Bacci, _The Life of St. Philip Neri,_ vol. 1, p. 202)

Thus we see that well into the sixteenth century hymns were sung to the name of Jesus, and devotion to him was very much a part of the religious expression of the period.

Other Mystics

One finds accounts and descriptions of expressive worship, often including glossolalia-style prayer, in most of the major mystics until the end of the sixteenth century, and some significant accounts beyond this period. Let us look at some of these.

Father Hoyos, a priest, describes an intensity of prayer that cannot be expressed in language:

> Now one breaks forth in groans and tears; now one would wish to be in a desert place in order to cry out and to give vent to the vehement feelings in his breast. (Arintero, _The Mystical Evolution in the Development and Vitality of the Church,_ vol. 2, p. 282)

The Spanish writer on prayer, **Juan de Jesus Maria,** defines jubilation in this way:

> Sometimes a joy is felt in the interior and it surpasses all the joys of this world, and those new to the service of God break forth into outward acts of jubilation because they cannot restrain themselves. This is usually called a spiritual intoxication or inebriation. (Arintero, _The Mystical Evolution in the Development and Vitality of the Church,_ vol. 2, p. 263)

St. Alphonsus Liguori describes it this way:

> Spiritual intoxication causes the soul to break forth in, as it were, delirium, such as songs, cries, immoderate weeping, leaping _et cetera._ (_Homo Apostolicus,_ Appendix I, 15)

St. Catherine of Genoa experienced jubilation in the form of laughter. Her biographer describes it as follows:

> [During a serious illness] she fixed her eyes steadily on the ceiling; and for about an hour she seemed all but immovable, and spoke not, but kept laughing in a very joyous fashion. . . . Greater interior jubilation

expressed itself in merry laughter; and on the evening of September 7 her joy appeared exteriorly in laughter which lasted, with but small interruptions, for some two hours. (Baron Von Hugel, _The Mystical Element of Religion,_ 13)

Like Catherine of Genoa, **Catherine of Siena** knew laughter as a form of prayer. According to her biographer, she "was always jocund and of a happy spirit . . . full of laughter in the Lord, exultant and rejoicing" (Underhill, _Mysticism,_ 438). This doctor of the church could also break into wordless sounds in her prayer:

> What then shall I say? I will do as one who is tongue-tied, and say: "Ah, Ah" for there is nought else I can say, since finite speech cannot express the affection of the soul which desires thee infinitely. (_St. Catherine of Siena_ [1907], 365)

St. Mary Magdalene de Pazzi is described as another whose behavior, under mystic impulse, could appear bizarre:

> Then she was restless and could not be still. To pour out this fervor that she could no longer contain, she was forced to bestir herself and she was strangely impelled to move about. And so, at such times, one saw her moving quickly from place to place. She ran through the convent as if crazed with love, and cried in a loud voice: "Love, love, love!" . . . And she said to the sisters who followed her: "You do not know, beloved sisters, that my Jesus is nothing but love, yes, mad with love. You are mad with love, my Jesus, as I have said and as I shall always say. You are very lovely and joyous, you refresh and solace, you nourish and unite. You are both pain and slaking, toil and rest, life and death in one." (Reinhold, _The Soul Afire_ [1973], 342–343)

A Fuller Reality

In the jubilation of both common Christians and mystics one finds an apprehension of a wonderfully fresh and joyful reality. Jubilation was an entering into a wondrous song that came forth from the heart of God. This theme is repeated over and over. Richard Rolle described heavenly music entering his ears and his heart and coming out through his voice. Medieval legends describe monks and friars being caught up in ecstasy, hearing the wondrous sound of heaven and then singing it on earth.

Dante, whose work sums up the medieval world, describes laughter and great joy in God at the heart of the Christian universe. Evelyn Underhill summarizes this view:

> Moreover, the most clear-sighted among the mystics declare such joy to be an implicit of reality. Thus Dante, initiated into paradise, sees the whole universe laugh with delight, as it glorifies God, and the awful countenance of Perfect Love adorned with smiles. Thus the souls of the great theologians dance to music and laughter in the heaven of the sun; the loving seraphs, in their ecstatic joy, whirl about the being of God. (*Mysticism,* p. 438)

Mystics were people who possessed a childlike gaiety, a perpetual gladness of heart. Deeply in touch with God, they shocked the world with a delicate playfulness that emanated from an experiential knowledge that they were children of a loving Father. A hymn from the medieval period illustrates their vision:

> There in heaven one hears sweet songs of birds in harmony, angels, too, sing fine melodies; Jesus leads off the dance with all the maiden host. (Anna Croh Seesholtz, *Friends of God* [1933], 12)

Breakdown of the Mystical Tradition

The jubilation tradition of expressive worship and glossolalia prayer continued as a vital force within western Christianity at least until the end of the sixteenth century. Yet today this tradition has been almost completely forgotten. While more research is required into the causes for the virtual demise of jubilation in the Catholic church, we can distinguish several factors which probably played a role in the diminishing of this long tradition.

End of the Medieval Synthesis. The Middle Ages at its height was a period of extraordinary faith. Beginning with the fourteenth century, however, this remarkable Christian synthesis began to unravel. The rise of nationalism, the bubonic plague which wiped out nearly half the population of Europe in a short time, and a growing superstition within the church were all factors.

In fact, much of Catholic history until Vatican II can be seen as a winding down of the medieval synthesis. The Protestant Reformation of the sixteenth century sent shock waves through the Catholic world. It challenged the church to set its house in order. This was accomplished at the Council of Trent, but the result was that the Catholic church also began a move toward ever-increasing rigidity. Additional assaults on the position of the Roman Catholic church came with the French Revolution and the end of cultural Christianity. The scientific revolution, the growth of secular philosophy, and the loss of church privilege all led to the development of a siege mentality within the Catholic church.

Though one can find examples of great holiness, new religious orders, and new inspiration during this time, a growing formalism and moralism began to arise within Catholicism. There was a tendency to reduce the faith to a set of formulas and rules. This was not a time for rich traditions to continue and flourish.

Abandonment of Mysticism. Mysticism, from the beginning, had been at the heart of the life of the church. The healing and transforming power of the love of God was central to the Catholic tradition. Even the end of the "age of faith" did not mark the end of the mystical tradition. In the midst of political and theological turmoil, wave after wave of genuine mystical movements preserved this vital stream of the church's life.

In the seventeenth century, however, two opposite heretical traditions grew up: quietism and Jansenism. Quietism replaced mysticism with an emphasis on extraordinary phenomena and interior peace, but neglected active love and repentance. Quietism was often accompanied by immorality. In contrast, Jansenism emphasized the sinfulness and unworthiness of human beings. A priest of Jansenist orientation once boasted that there had not been one unworthy Communion in his church in a year. The reason was that he had not permitted *any* Communion during the year. The influence of this philosophy was not confined to those who openly espoused Jansenism, and its effects are still with the Catholic church today.

Jansenists and their fellow travelers had little use for mysticism. True mysticism was for them a rare occurrence. An emphasis on unworthiness and a sense of spiritual pride both have the effect of preventing people from moving in a mystical and spiritual direction.

It was necessary for the Catholic church to correct the false mysticism of the quietists, but in so doing it adopted a Jansenist orientation, and true mystical tradition was severely damaged in the process. Henri Daniel-Rops describes what took place:

> A large field of religious experience, the whole spiritual tradition of St. Bernard, of Tauler and Suso, of St. Teresa and St. John of the Cross . . . was suddenly abandoned. And that loss was not without harmful effects upon the vitality of the faith. (_The Church in the Eighteenth Century_ [1964], 292)

Knowledge of the mystical tradition had diminished to the point that in the eighteenth century Father de Caussade lamented:

> Prejudice and an almost absolute ignorance of mystical writers, especially of the matter contained in their works, has gradually made [mysticism] and its ideas so absurd that I am at a loss to describe them. . . . Since these wretched prejudices have prevented men from reading the true mystics of later times, it is noticeable, even in the cloister, that there has been a decrease in the number of interior souls—souls totally detached, dead to the world and to themselves. (quoted in Pierre Pourrat, _Christian Spirituality_ [1955], vol. 4, pp. 263–264)

Continuing Traces. The experience of jubilation and the recognition of jubilation as part of the mystical tradition did not cease all at once. There seems instead to have been a slow winding down of this style of prayer. The tradition continued in the mystical experience of the Catholic church, at least to some extent, until the nineteenth century. John Bosco, a saint of this period, is said to have experienced jubilation in his prayers.

Catholic culture has maintained traces of the expressive worship tradition. The colorful festivities on saints' days and feasts, such as Corpus Christi in Latin countries, are remnants of these practices. A number of Catholics from Slavic backgrounds have reported that they remember older parishioners singing, making long extended sounds, and rocking back and forth while at their devotions. Leonids Linauts, Professor of Stained Glass at Rochester Institute of Technology and an expert on Latvian folklore, affirms that jubilation still existed before World War II in Latvia. He relates that it was the custom in some regions of that nation, particularly the Aswege region, for parishioners to arrive an hour or so before mass for singing and prayer. At times during this period the group would improvise wordless sounds and songs to express their devotion.

It is certainly possible that in rural areas, jubilation and other expressive styles of worship have been preserved. This is a matter for further and more precise investigation.

204 • Jubilation and Speaking in Tongues

Both the tongues or glossolalia of the New Testament and the jubilation of tradition were wordless sounds. Both were a response, an entering into the gospel in ways deeper than conceptual language would allow. There is every reason to assume that jubilation and tongues—ancient and modern—refer to the same phenomenon.

A question arises whether the tongues of Scripture, the tongues of present-day charismatic renewal, and the jubilation tradition are in fact the same experience. Was jubilation the same as glossolalia, a continuation of the tongues of the New Testament?

——— Tongues in the New Testament ———

The issue of New Testament glossolalia has been dealt with by a number of biblical scholars. In general, most do not consider the glossolalia of the New Testament to be foreign languages but, rather, "ecstatic utterance," a speaking forth of wordless sounds as an expression of spiritual fervor. Richard Kugelman writes:

> The gift of tongues was an extraordinary manifestation of the Spirit's presence and activity (Acts 2:4-6; 10:46; 19:6). The precise nature of the gift remains obscure. Many exegetes think that it consisted in incoherent shouting; seized by a religious emotionalism under the impulse of the Spirit, a Christian would begin to shout in a fervid improvisation the praises of God. ("The First Letter to the Corinthians," _The Jerome Biblical Commentary,_ 272)

It must be added that present-day glossolalia is usually a spontaneous liturgical response rather than fervent emotionalism; still, this description has much in common with Egeria's comments on the church in Jerusalem in the fifth century and Augustine's account of the spontaneous worship in Hippo.

The tongues passages in Acts seem to indicate ecstatic utterance. Malcolm Cornwell summarizes the opinion of biblical scholars on the matter:

Accordingly, nearly all commentators today regard the references to tongues in Acts to be similar to the experience of the believers at Corinth. This view would provide a description of glossolalia as the utterance of unknown words or sounds as a consequence of the exuberance of a newly acquired faith of Jesus. (*The Gift of Tongues Today* [1975], 21)

Tongues in the Contemporary Church

Modern-day glossolalia has come under the scrutiny of linguists such as William Samarin. Samarin says that glossolalia as practiced in the present time is not language, although it has many of the features of language. The sounds are taken, for the most part, from the native language of the speaker. He concludes: "When the full apparatus of linguistic science comes to bear on glossolalia, this turns out to be only a facade of language-although at times a very good one indeed (*Tongues of Men and Angels* [1972], 127–128). According to Samarin, glossolalia bears close similarity to chant, mimicry, jingles, and nonsense or baby-talk. In other words, it is similar to other created speech patterns.

Augustine and the other church fathers saw a kinship between jubilation and the yodels and wordless sounds of the broader culture. The work of modern linguists points to the same correlation between normal wordless expressions in the culture and present-day glossolalia.

The Continuity of Jubilation from Apostolic Times

Indications are that jubilation is a continuation of the glossolalia of the New Testament. For one thing, descriptions of the two practices are similar. Also, the first references to jubilation are from the fourth century, an early date. Before this period the church was persecuted and often worshiped in private. Little is known either of the daily worship and life of ordinary Christians or of their liturgy until the fourth century. During the period of the persecutions only the extraordinary and controversial received note. The lack of mention of glossolalia during this period may indicate that it was not controversial but an ordinary part of the fabric of Christian life.

Scholars of music history suggest that jubilation was a continuation of New Testament and apostolic practice. *L'encyclopédie des musiques sacres* contains this comment:

That which concerned the Fathers, just as it had the apostles, was that one sing "in the spirit" ("with one's heart"). This is the advice St. Paul repeated to the Corinthians (1 Cor. 14:15)—"I will sing a song with the spirit"—and to the Ephesians (Eph. 5:18-19)—"Sing in the Spirit . . . from your fullness. Recite psalms and hymns among yourselves, and inspired songs; sing and praise the Lord with all your heart." To the Colossians he said: "Sing to God with all your heart." St. Jerome recalled this long tradition when he wrote about the jubilus, saying: "By the term *jubilus* we understand that which neither in words nor syllables nor letters nor speech is it possible to comprehend how much man ought to praise God." (*L'encyclopédie des musiques sacres* [1968–1970], vol. 2, p. 26)

This point of view is confirmed by George Chambers, who states:

It is a life of "rapture" which the apostle looks for, quite possibly acquired through the ecstatic medium of the "jubilation." . . . It may also be well to refer to the incident in Acts 16:25 when Paul and Silas, chained in prison, were "praying and singing to God," and apparently amazing phenomena followed from their action. (*Folksong-Plainsong* [1956], 11)

The *New Catholic Encyclopedia* (1967) concurs: "The improvised, charismatic song—associated especially with the Alleluia—continued in Christian worship" (vol. 10, pp. 105-106).

Werner Meyer, a German scholar, suggests that plainsong and the musical parts of the liturgy emerged from the early practice of glossolalia:

The glossolalia of the early Eastern Church, as the original musical event, represents the germ cell or the original form of sung liturgical prayer. . . . In the sublime levitation and inter-weaving of the old church tones, and even in Gregorian chant to some extent, we are greeted by an element that has its profound roots in glossolalia. (*Der erste Korintherbrief: Prophezei* [1945], vol. 2, pp. 122ff)

The church fathers, however, did not see their experience as "tongues" or relate it to the New Testament phenomenon. They were either confused by the relevant passages in the New Testament or interpreted them to mean speaking in languages that one had not learned.

On the other hand, they did see a profound relationship between their experience of jubilation and the Scripture. The strongest correlation for them was with the *jubilate Deo* passages in the psalms. It appears that they understood the use of the word *jubilus* in the psalms to refer to wordless singing similar to their own. Because jubilation was non-controversial and devotional, the mystical tradition saw a number of scriptural images in it: the festivity of the father upon the return of the prodigal son, the joy of the bridegroom in the Song of Songs, and imagery from Job, to name a few instances.

The question must be asked why the church fathers and the tradition fail to connect their experience with that of tongues. There is no clear answer. Perhaps the problem is primarily one of semantics. The terminology used in the church to describe glossolalia was different from that used in the Bible. Accepted folk-piety often has fluid and evolving terminology. Already in the New Testament there are several terms that seem to be used synonymously to describe the experience, such as "praying with the Spirit," "blessing with the Spirit," and "singing with the Spirit" (1 Cor. 14). The Ephesians (5:19) and Colossians (3:16) passages concerning "spiritual song" may well refer to glossolalia, as may Paul's reference to the sighs or groans of the Spirit in Romans 8:26. Thus we see varied terminology developing within the New Testament itself.

The jubilation tradition of the church is harmonious with the view of modern biblical exegetes that New Testament glossolalia was an expression of spiritual response to the gospel. The church fathers and the tradition conceived of jubilation in the same way. The "sighs and groans" of the Jerusalem church which Egeria describes were a response to the reading of the gospel during the liturgical celebration, just as the tongues of Acts were a response to the word about Jesus. During the first millennium of the church, the liturgical jubilation came just before the reading of the gospel during Mass and served as a preparation for the Gospel.

205 ᪥ JUBILATION AND THE RENEWAL OF WORSHIP

An important aspect of contemporary worship renewal is the recovery of ancient church practice. The tradition of jubilation has much to contribute to the renewal of Christian worship, in both corporate liturgy and personal worship. An understanding of this tradition helps to place the worship of the modern charismatic renewal into its historical context.

Our inquiries into the way Christians have prayed in the past have yielded strong confirmation of the authenticity of today's glossolalia and expressive worship as found in the charismatic renewal movement. Until very late in the Catholic worship tradition, glossolalia in a variety of forms was a basic response both for groups and for individuals. Improvised group jubilation was a regular part of the liturgy for almost the entire first millennium of the church. Most major mystical traditions before the seventeenth century actually describe this form of prayer, and records can be found well into the nineteenth century of expressive prayer and glossolalia among contemplatives.

The existence of this tradition demonstrates that the present-day charismatic prayer forms and expressive worship are essentially harmonious with the rich tradition of early Christian spirituality. At the same time, the tradition challenges charismatics of today to come to a richer theological understanding of their worship experience and to learn new ways and better language with which to describe it.

This is an era that is rediscovering tradition. The legacy of the centuries just prior to Vatican II was one of increasing rigidity. Though the forms of this pre–Vatican II period are often called traditional, it was a period completely out of touch with tradition. Tradition is the memory of Jesus, the experience of the original apostolic church finding increasing depth and resonance as the church grew in experience. Deepening understandings of the gospel continued for hundreds of years after the New Testament was completed. The doctrine of the Trinity, the understanding of the divinity and humanity of the Lord, and eucharistic devotion all developed in greater fullness as the church lived out its faith through the centuries.

When the Roman Catholic church reacted in panic by convoking the Council of Trent, much of the flow of tradition began to cease. In many areas such as Scripture, spirituality, and liturgy, the church lost vital contact with its sources. The liturgical and biblical movements that led to the Second Vatican Council have once again opened a door to tradition so that the church can creatively face its future by drawing on the resources of its past. Events in the Catholic church have been paralleled by renewal movements in the Protestant community as well.

In many ways, charismatic renewal complements the liturgical renewal and the scriptural renewal of the Catholic tradition. The liturgical movement involved a massive amount of research and study. The scriptural roots of the liturgy, various liturgical practices in different eras, the tradition of the Eastern churches, and the experience of the Protestant churches were all sources that contributed to the renewal of the liturgy.

Yet we have neglected to consult sources in the area of spirituality. In a much more significant way than in the biblical and liturgical renewals, the renewal of spirituality involves *experience*—the experience of God, the church, and the decisions of those who chose to follow the gospel. Both charismatic renewal and the church need again to hear the original stories of Francis and Bernard, of the revivals of the Middle Ages, the stories of faith powerful enough to change cultures. Original accounts of the lives of the saints and the teachings of the mystics need to be heard in our midst once again. We need to return to sources not only with our heads but also with our hearts.

New Understandings of Expressive Worship

A recovery of the tradition of jubilation will have a telling effect upon the renewal of Christian worship, in its human and spiritual dimensions. It will also help to provide a new conceptual framework for understanding tongues within the charismatic experience.

The Human Dimension. One reason that Pentecostal glossolalia has frightened some people is because it has been viewed as something other than a human response. The idea of speaking in unknown tongues through the power of the Holy Spirit is understandably difficult even for many Christians to accept. The experience of the church suggests that wordless prayer and expressive worship can be understood in their natural and ordinary dimensions, as basic human activity given over to a spiritual use. St. John of the Cross compared the gladness of jubilation to the expressions of a bridegroom's joy. St. Teresa of Avila likened jubilation to the festivity of a party. A young man in love hums a new tune and does cartwheels in the park because of the joy of his new relationship. Families hold reunions amidst much laughter and back-slapping. People enjoying one another express their happiness with a variety of spontaneous gestures, movements, and happy noises. Likewise, sorrow and pathos are often marked by the wordless sound of sighs, sobs, and cries.

The Scriptures present God as totally other and transcendent, and at the same time profoundly intimate and immanent. Believers can know their greatest intimacy with God himself. It is natural that spontaneous human response should be part of the intimate human encounter with the Lord and with his people.

Expressive worship reinforces the Christian principle of the unity of body and soul. Jubilation as practiced in groups can bring together separate individuals and form them into a community. Just as secular wordless cries and calls unite a work crew, so spontaneous harmonizing binds Christians in worship and prayer.

The glossolalia experience encompasses broader manifestations than simply speaking in tongues or, as the tradition describes it, vocal praying without words; jubilation also includes inspired song, laughter, tears, and bodily gestures. The Word of God community in Ann Arbor, Michigan, pioneered many areas of expressive worship in the early days of the charismatic movement. During prayer meetings the music group would enter into the melody of jubilation with improvisations on their instruments; others might express the rhythm in dance and gesture. "Praying in the Spirit" with guitars and bodily movement, as well as with the voice, was also a common practice in personal prayer. These shared worship experiences united the community.

The Spiritual Dimension. The fact that the church fathers and the mystical tradition view jubilation and expressive worship as ordinary and natural to human beings does not mean that they do not also see them as having profound spiritual significance. In fact, the emphasis placed upon these worship forms by writers such as Augustine and the fourteenth-century English mystic Richard Rolle is even greater than the importance given to them in the present-day charismatic renewal. The mystics visualized heaven as a place of laughter and joyous spontaneity; they believed that the practice of jubilation is a reflection of heaven in the midst of God's people on earth.

Contemplatives have always contended that the deepest prayer is prayer without words, prayer that God himself gives as a gift. Jubilation is entering into God's gift of prayer with one's entire being—voice, body and heart. In the jubilation tradition, both the human and spiritual sides of expressive prayer are beautifully blended. Jubilation is very human and ordinary; at the same time, it is a mystical encounter with God.

A New Conceptual Framework for Tongues. The tradition of jubilation and the accompanying forms of expressive prayer provide a new conceptual framework for understanding glossolalia and its demonstrative aspects. In order to help Christians comprehend the human processes involved, it might be helpful to employ descriptive language from historical sources. Terms such as jubilation, free-style harmonization, and "sounds of wonder" can be used alongside standard Pentecostal words for glossolalia. Such terms indicate the broad traditional base that exists for this experience. They also reinforce its human and ordinary nature.

The Catholic tradition also emphasizes the spiritual significance of glossolalia as a means of mystical communion with God. Writings from the church fathers and later mystics can be used to clarify that jubilation is a learned response as well as a gift, thus removing some of the trepidation with which some Christians approach the phenomena of the charismatic renewal.

Jubilation in Liturgy and Personal Prayer

Historically, the practice of jubilation has had a place in both the public worship of the church and the personal devotional life of Christian worshipers. Its recovery in the contemporary setting has implications both for renewal of the liturgy and for personal prayer.

The Liturgy. The proper home for jubilation is the liturgical setting. As we have seen, throughout history expressive worship was linked with the liturgy and liturgical celebrations. The *alleluia-jubilus* that was improvised by church congregations until the ninth century was a standard preparation for the reading of the gospel. Egeria described the loud wordless response of the fifth-century Jerusalem church to the reading of Scripture and the praying of the liturgical hours. Today the spontaneous response of charismatic Christians needs to become progressively more integrated with their liturgical and paraliturgical life.

Liturgists and musicians can teach improvised jubilation to the people as they themselves become more familiar with the tradition and with the present-day renewal. The tradition offers a variety of ways in which jubilation can be incorporated into the regular worship life of the people of God. Jubilation and expressive worship can also be taught to children in church schools and training classes, and to adult converts as a part of their faith response to Christ and the gospel. Both the church and its individual members will be enriched as a result.

Personal Prayer. Jubilation also has strong implications for personal prayer. Because it is a way for God to pray through the believer, it can be a means of experiencing the gift of contemplative prayer. Cassiodorus (450–583) called it a "teacher" of prayer.

Revisiting the tradition can open Christians to "mystical jubilation," the spiritual drunkenness that results in expressions of joyful abandon. Familiarity with the tradition of the saints, mystics, and doctors of the church can provide a framework for believers in which they might give expression to laughter, tears, and all manner of physical movements in their personal prayer.

It is important to note, however, that jubilation is simply one style of prayer. Silence, liturgical prayer, intercession and other forms are equally important, and all should be integrated into a healthy prayer life.

The Broader Context. Charismatic renewal has been a great gift to the church, a "stream of grace," as Cardinal Suenens put it. It is an important part of the spiritual renewal of the church, bringing with it the spiritual gifts and a new sense of community.

Any renewal, however, faces the danger of myopia, of looking inward and focusing exclusively upon its own particular areas of emphasis. The broader church needs to be refreshed by the charismatic element, but charismatics also need to be revitalized by the church as a whole. A willingness to listen to tradition, to the biblical and liturgical movements, and other renewals within the church can call the charismatic community to grow out of itself and become more truly the gift to the church it is meant to be.

The church is moving toward a more personal and intimate Christianity, a faith with a more human face. It is also moving toward community and an increasingly informal and expressive worship to help establish that community. There is a strong return to the elements of mysticism and jubilation. Expressive worship has a role to play in this recreation and rebuilding by making spiritual realities personal and visible and by becoming a means through which Christians can celebrate them with one another and with God.

Eddie Ensley

[Note: The articles in chapter 5 have been excerpted and rearranged by Janice and Richard Leonard from Eddie Ensley's *Sounds of Wonder: Speaking in Tongues in the Catholic Tradition* (New York: Paulist Press, 1977).]

Singing in Worship

No act is more integral to worship than singing. The Psalms frequently challenge us to sing to the Lord. The Bible also records numerous songs that the Lord's people sang. At every juncture of the church's history, God's people have sung in worship. At times, the song of the church arose from common experience as folk music. At other times, master composers crafted fine works of art to sing in worship. In each case, singing in worship has expressed the deepest emotions of God's people as they gather to worship, from joyful thanksgiving to sorrowful lament. The articles in this chapter describe the variety of songs that have been and are currently used in common worship. In addition, they give practical suggestions for making singing in worship imaginative, inspiring, and faithful to the Scriptures.

206 ◆ THE THEOLOGICAL SIGNIFICANCE OF THE PSALMS IN WORSHIP

The biblical Psalter is the most important prayer book in both Jewish and Christian worship. The Psalms have shaped both the language used in Christian worship and the very idea of what worship is. This article describes the conception of worship implied in the Psalms. The Psalter can help a Christian community realize its full potential for worship in Jesus' name.

Christ, the Sacrifice of Praise, the Reign of God

In quoting from Psalm 110, the author of the Letter to the Hebrews demonstrates that this ancient, messianic psalm has been fulfilled in Jesus. At the same time we are given here a "liturgical theology" that provides a threefold framework for understanding the place of the Psalms, the liturgy, and all Christian prayer in the economy of salvation. The framework consists of (1) a Christology (who is this Christ?), (2) a doxology (what does it mean to offer praise?), and (3) an eschatology (where is all this leading?): All Christian prayer is offered through the Messiah *who has taken his seat at God's right hand.* Although *his offering* has already perfected those who are *being sanctified,* we continue to offer the *sacrifice of praise* while *he waits until his enemies are placed beneath his feet.* Until that time, all acceptable worship, including the liturgical praying of psalms, is a sacrifice of praise offered through Christ.

Psalms in Israel's Worship. This liturgical theology may have roots in the worship of Israel where the Psalter originated. Walter Brueggemann, in summarizing the work of Sigmund Mowinckel, notes that in the early period of the Jerusalem temple, the king supervised an annual festival in which "Yahweh was once again enthroned as sovereign for the coming year." The Davidic king "played the role of Yahweh and was enthroned on his behalf," legitimizing the Davidic monarchy "which was also liturgically renewed in the festival." Eschatology, as "a projection of hope into the future out of a cultic enactment that never fully met expectations," was also manifest in this liturgy:

> The cultic act, which is an act of liturgic imagination in and of itself, opens to a future that is in tension with "business as usual." . . . Cult and eschatology together mediate an alternative that critiques the present world and invites liberation from it. (*Israel's Praise: Doxology against Idolatry and Ideology* [Minneapolis: Augsburg/Fortress Press, 1988], 4–5)

Brueggemann suggests that Mowinckel's insight here is of paramount importance: worship is "world-making"; liturgy is "*constitutive* and not merely *responsive*" (Ibid., 6–7). This has immediate relevance for the use of the Psalms in the Christian liturgy: "If the subject of the liturgy is kingship—of Yahweh, of David, or derivatively of Jesus—then the liturgy serves to authorize, recognize, acknowledge, coronate, legitimate the ruler and the order that belongs to that ruler." While the world may look upon this as "subjective self-deception," nevertheless "the assembly . . . knows that the reality of God is not a reality unless it is visibly done in, with, and by the community" (Ibid., 10).

Fulfilled in the Paschal Mystery. Since for Israel the Psalms derived from liturgical acts in which the praise of God, Davidic (Messianic) sovereignty, and eschatological expectation all converge, it was only natural that the earliest Christian communities should see in Jesus the fulfillment of all these things of which the psalms speak: he is the Messiah *who sits at God's right hand.*

In Matthew 22:41-46, Jesus himself fulfills the messianic interpretation of Psalm 110:1 that was common in his day when he asks, "If the Messiah is David's Son, why does David call him 'Lord'?" Hebrews 10 goes further: Jesus is not only Messiah (David's son and LORD); he is also the fulfillment and perfection of all worship in the old dispensation— its sacrifices, its priesthood, its singing of the Psalms. Christ himself is the new liturgy. In the perspective of the Letter to the Hebrews, we can now comprehend all the Psalms—indeed the whole of the Hebrew Scriptures and worship—within their "truest" setting, that of the paschal mystery. When the Christian community prays the psalms, Christ is in our midst glorifying the Father and sanctifying us who have already been perfected. All prayer in Christ is praise of God, which transforms us and the whole world.

——— The Psalms and Liturgical Prayer ———

Thus far, only a single verse of a single psalm has been considered, but the whole Psalter can be understood from the Christological, doxological, and eschatological perspective that we have seen in the Letter to the Hebrews. The Psalms concretize for us what it means to pray through, with, and in Christ; to offer praise to God; to acknowledge and be transformed by the order of God's reign. Worship, as Brueggemann noted, is both responsive and constitutive, a reply to God's self-revelation and a "world-making" event. In prayer, we respond to God and in so doing are transformed—whole and entire—into the image of Christ.

Through, with, and in Christ. The Psalms, as part of sacred Scripture, are the Word of God, God's revelation to us. Responsorial psalmody—"receiving" the refrain and giving it back—gives sacramen-

tal form to this theological dynamic. We can only return what God has first given to us as utter gift: "How shall I make a return to the LORD for all the good he has done for me? The cup of salvation I will take up, and I will call upon the name of the LORD" (Ps. 116:12-13, NAB). The recognition that God is the prior, original mover of all prayer is the essence of every act of praise and thanksgiving: "O LORD, open my lips and my mouth shall declare your praise" (Ps. 51:17, NAB). In the words of the *General Instructions on the Roman Missal and on the Liturgy of the Hours,* "Through the chants the people make God's word their own" (*General Instructions on the Roman Missal,* 33 hereafter referred to as GIRM). "Our sanctification is accomplished and worship is offered to God in the liturgy of the hours in such a way that an exchange or dialogue is set up between God and us, so that 'God is speaking to his people . . . and the people are responding to him both by song and prayer'" (*General Instructions on the Liturgy of Hours,* 14, hereafter referred to as GILH; cf. *Constitution on the Sacred Liturgy,* 33, hereafter referred to as SC). But Christ himself—God's perfect word to humanity and the perfect human response to God—is the incarnation of this divine-human dialogue who "introduced into this land of exile the hymn of praise which reechoes eternally through the halls of heaven" (Paul VI, *Laudis Canticum*). Our participation in the Psalms is nothing short of our participation in the eternal, divine-human dialogue of Christ and the Father. We pray *through* him as the one high priest, the only mediator; we pray *with* him as head of the body whose members we are; we pray *in* him since his offering alone is acceptable once and for all.

Offering the Sacrifice of Praise. The many psalms of praise and adoration are what Thomas Merton calls "psalms par excellence. . . . They are more truly psalms than all the others, for the real purpose of a psalm is to praise God" (*Bread in the Wilderness* [New York: New Direction, 1953], 27). "I will praise your name for ever, my king and my God" (Ps. 145:1). "My soul give praise to the Lord and bless his holy name" (103:1). "Let the peoples praise you, O God, let all the peoples praise you" (67:4). "Alleluia! Praise God in the holy dwelling-place! Praise God with timbrel and dance, strings and pipes! Let everything that lives and that breathes give praise to the Lord. Alleluia!" (Ps. 150). The doxological character of all the Psalms—even the laments—must have been uppermost in the minds of the ancient temple liturgists who collected them into the Psalter which in Hebrew is *tehellim,* "songs of praise" and in Greek, *psalmoi,* "songs to be sung to the psaltery (lute or harp)" (see GILH, 103). Doxology—the praise and glorification of God and acknowledgment of God's reign—is the origin and the fulfillment, the "primary theology" of all Christian life and prayer. In singing the Psalms with Christ, we articulate explicitly that sacrifice of praise that is the fruit of lips that acknowledge his name.

The Transformation of Ourselves and the World. While "we wait in joyful hope" for all things to be subjected to him, put under his feet, (i.e., to acknowledge and be transformed by the order of God's reign) the Psalms give us the words with which we subject or surrender ourselves—mind, heart, body—to God, that we may participate ever more fully in the dialogue of Christ and his Father, the praise which is sung forever.

Our **minds**—our cognitive powers—our intellects are freely submitted to Christ in the many psalms which focus on the law, the "way of life": "O search me, God, and know my heart, O test me and know my thoughts; See that I follow not the wrong path and lead me in the way of life eternal" (Ps. 139:23-24); "Lord, make me know your ways, teach me your paths; Make me walk in your truth and teach me for you are God my savior" (Ps. 25:4-5); "I will ponder all your precepts and consider your paths; teach me the demands of your statutes and I will keep them to the end" (Ps. 119:15, 33). But Christ is the Way and the fulfillment of the law. Pondering the precepts of his Gospel means training our minds to think as Christ thinks.

Our **hearts** and feelings, too, must come under his rule. The great variety of psalms permit us first to admit the entire array of emotions that are ours as human beings and then express them before God: "The Lord has done great things for us; we are filled with joy" (Ps. 126:3); "Be merciful, O Lord, for I have sinned" (Ps. 51:3); "My God, my God, why have you abandoned me?" (Ps. 22:2); "Like a deer that longs for running streams, my soul thirsts for you" (Ps. 42:2); "I am afflicted and in pain; let your saving help, O God, protect me" (Ps. 69:30); "O Lord, my heart is not proud, nor are my eyes haughty" (Ps. 131:1); "How great is your name, O Lord, our God, through all the earth!" (Ps. 8:1).

Jesus, who shared fully in our humanity, shared likewise all our emotions. Yet his feelings and the expression of them were free from sin—that is, they were kept within the sphere of his loving, obedient relationship to God. It is precisely our expressing of these emotions in prayer that transforms them into Christian affections. Our surrender of anger, frustration, sinfulness, fear, hope, joy, or wonder to God is itself an act of faith. I can pray, "I hate them with a perfect hate and they are foes to me" (Ps. 139:22), and I can pray, "May the Lord bless you from Zion all the days of your life! May you see your children's children in a happy Jerusalem!" (Ps. 128:5-6) with equal honesty because, in prayer, my desire for either revenge or blessing is surrendered to God; in prayer, it is transformed into praise. This holds true even for the liturgical psalms that do not happen to match our personal feelings at any particular time; for in the liturgy, we pray the prayer of Christ whose heart embraces the affections of the entire human race: "Those who pray the psalms in the liturgy of the hours do so not so much in their own name as in the name of the entire Body of Christ" (GILH, 108). With him we articulate the frustrations, hopes, sorrows, and joys of everyone, and we offer this "world-transforming" sacrifice "for the life of the world."

Our **bodies** and senses are not excluded; they are caught up together with mind and heart in the surrender of praise: "Therefore my heart is glad and my soul rejoices, even my body shall rest in safety" (Ps. 16:9); "Let my prayer arise before you like incense, the raising of my hands like an evening oblation" (Ps. 141:2); "All peoples, clap your hands . . ." (Ps. 47:1); "Come in, let us bow and bend low, let us bend the knee before him" (Ps. 95:6); "Let them praise his name with dancing and make music with timbrel and harp" (Ps. 149:3); "Look towards him and be radiant, let your faces not be abashed" (Ps. 34:6); "Taste and see the goodness of the Lord" (Ps. 34:9); "Your robes are fragrant with aloes and myrrh" (Ps. 45:9); "O that today you would hear his voice!" (Ps. 95:7).

Even our ability to pray must be handed over. The Psalms dispose us to move beyond cognitive, affective, and physical activity to contemplation: the absolute stillness of being, awaiting God's self-manifestation. Merton writes:

The psalms are theology. That means that they place us in direct contact with God, through the assent of faith to His Revelation. It is because of this theological and dynamic effect that the psalms are steps to contemplation. This theological effect depends ultimately on a free gift of God. . . . If we chant the psalms with faith, God will manifest himself to us; and that is contemplation (*Bread in the Wilderness*, 14–15).

The Psalms "rehearse" us in the attitude of absolute faith, openness to God's will, total surrender to God's presence: "The Lord is my shepherd, there is nothing I shall want . . . he leads me near restful waters to revive my drooping spirit" (Ps. 23:1-2); "I have set my soul in silence and peace; a weaned child on its mother's breast" (Ps. 131:2); "Lord, you search me and you know me, you know my resting and my rising, you discern my purpose from afar" (Ps. 139:1-2); "What else have I in heaven but you? Apart from you I want nothing on earth" (Ps. 73:25); "You do not ask for sacrifice and offering, but an open ear . . . not holocaust and victim, instead here am I" (Ps. 40:7-8). God gives us the ability to pray; we respond in prayer. God enables us to surrender even our response; we find God waiting there for us.

The **whole of creation**, the tangible, physical world is also involved with us in being transformed, placed under his feet. In the praying of the Psalms, we are "tuned in" to the silent song in which "the heavens declare the glory of God and the firmament shows forth the work of God's hands . . . no speech no word, no voice is heard yet their span extends through all the earth, their message reaches the utmost bounds of the world" (Ps. 19:2-5). We hear too, "The Lord's voice resounding on the waters . . . the Lord's voice shattering the cedars of Lebanon . . . shaking the wilderness . . . rending the oak tree and stripping the forest bare . . . the God of glory thunders, in his temple they all cry 'Glory!'" (Ps. 29:3-10). In return, we lend our voices to the praise of "sea creatures and all oceans, fire and hail, snow and mist, stormy winds that obey his word; all mountains and hills, all fruit trees and cedars, beasts wild and tame, reptiles and birds on the wing" (Ps. 148:7-8) and articulate creation's wordless groaning for the fulfillment of all that has been promised.

For the Sake of the World. Our surrender of self and our voicing of the praise of creation is not without repercussions for the rest of humanity. We celebrate the liturgy and "make music to our God Most High"

(Ps. 92:1) in order that all peoples may come to acknowledge the glory of God: "O sing to the Lord, bless his name. Proclaim God's help day by day, tell among the nations his glory, and his wonders among all the peoples" (Ps. 96:2-3); that "the gentiles themselves should say, 'What marvels the Lord worked for them!'" (Ps. 126:2) and "all nations learn your saving help" (Ps. 67:3). Our sacrifice of praise is accepted as one with the sacrifice of Christ.

These ancient, inspired, liturgical songs thus concretize the deepest truths of Christian prayer. Like the liturgy itself, the Psalms invite and enable us and the world in which we live to "authorize, recognize, acknowledge, coronate, legitimate the ruler" of the universe "and the order that belongs to that ruler." When all peoples and all creation join us together with all the angels and saints in that hymn of endless praise which Christ introduced and sings forever, then all opposition to his rule will be *placed under his feet*.

In the meantime, we would do well to follow the advice of St. Benedict: "Let us consider how we ought to behave in the presence of God and his angels, and let us stand to sing the psalms in such a way that our minds are in harmony with our voices (*Regula* 19.6-7).

We can paraphrase the words of Benedict in light of the Christological, doxological, and eschatological perspective with which we have examined the liturgical use of the Psalms: "Let us consider who we are in the midst of those who praise God unceasingly; we should conform all our gestures, words and actions to the voice of the liturgy—its psalms in particular—so that ours may be the mind, heart, and body of Christ."

David A. Stosur

207 • WAYS OF SINGING THE PSALMS IN WORSHIP

The Psalms have been traditionally sung two ways in worship, to metrical paraphrases of the Psalms paired with hymn tunes and to the literal prosaic translations of the Psalms paired with plainchant melodies or psalm-tones. The following article explains these two approaches in more detail.

Psalm-singing Christians basically fall into two categories: those who chant the Psalms directly from the Bible and those who sing metrical para-phrases of the Psalms, in which the biblical text is reworked in poetic meter and (often) rhyme.

Metrical Psalmody

Churches with Reformed and Presbyterian roots traditionally are part of the second group, the tradition known as "metrical psalmody." They have sung the Psalms almost exclusively in metered, para-phrased stanzas, and they have done so for obvious reasons. Congregations find metrical psalms easy to learn. And when a psalm is well translated into verse and set to an appropriate tune of regular rhythmic structure, it can be a joy to sing.

Yet there are some perils involved in the use of metrical psalms. First of all, a paraphrase is a para-phrase. The demands of meter and rhyme often necessitate changing a given text and even stretching its meaning somewhat. Worse yet, a rigid metrical pattern may require that such psalms be rendered in an extremely awkward form. In the Scottish Psalter of 1650, for example, the metrical paraphrase of Psalm 23 includes lines such as the following: "He leadeth me the quiet waters by."

Fortunately, contemporary versifiers of metrical psalmody have felt free to depart from even such conventional patterns as rhyme and generally have been more successful in communicating a psalm's original meaning in comprehensible form. A well-known collection of these "freer" metrical psalms is *Psalm Praise* (London: Church Pastoral Aid Society, 1973), a book that was published to popularize psalm-singing among Anglicans in the United Kingdom.

Second, singing the Psalms to conventional hymn tunes can cause confusion, especially if the hymn tunes are well known. Hearing the same tune sung to both a hymn text and a psalm text tends to rein-force the notion that psalms and hymns are largely interchangeable—a notion that may be responsible (at least in part) for the historical tendency of hym-nody to replace psalmody in most Protestant com-munions. Recovery of the Genevan tunes, most of which have not been attached to other texts, may be one way to combat this confusion.

Third, rendering the Psalms in conventional West-ern meters usually means losing the Hebrew poetic forms. For example, the Psalms were written in ac-cordance with what has come to be called "parallel-ism," whereby a certain thought is repeated twice but in different words:

Save me, O God, by thy name, and vindicate me by thy might.
Hear my prayer, O God; give ear to the words of my mouth. (RSV)

In these first two verses of Psalm 54 the second line echoes the first, and the fourth restates the third. This parallelism is easily retained in a standard translation such as the RSV or NIV but is often diffi-cult to manage in a metrical paraphrase.

Chanting the Psalms

Pointed Psalms. In contrast, chanting the Psalms permits the use of a standard translation that not only is more faithful to the Hebrew but also retains the Hebrew poetic patterns. The *Lutheran Book of Worship* (Minneapolis: Augsburg, 1978) offers one of the simplest patterns for chanting the Psalms (us-ing the translation in the 1979 *Book of Common Prayer*); the pattern involves a limited number of chant tones that a congregation will find easy to master. *Lutheran Worship* (St. Louis: Concordia, 1982), the hymnal of the Lutheran Church–Missouri Synod, offers a similar method of chanting the Psalms (as translated in the NIV), using chant tones that are more modal in flavor.

The prose psalm texts are "pointed" for congrega-tional chanting. Each psalm verse is divided by an asterisk (*). The first note in each part of the verse is a reciting tone to which one or more syllables are sung. At the "point" (asterisk), singers move from the reciting tone to the black notes. A vertical mark (|) indicates one syllable per black note; a horizontal mark (–) indicates one syllable per two black notes.

Gelineau Chant. One of the more interesting ways of singing the Psalms was developed by Joseph Geli-neau of France. Of all the methods of singing the Psalms, Gelineau's chant best preserves the Hebrew poetic style, retaining both the parallelism and the metrical structure of the original. Ancient Hebrew meter is somewhat like early English meter (e.g., nursery rhymes) in that it focuses on the number of stresses within a line rather than on the number of syllables. Gelineau psalmody is often sung to the Grail translation, which was produced specifically for this purpose. Gelineau psalmody also takes into account the different number of lines within each stanza—something that is not possible with other methods of psalm-chanting.

Gelineau psalms are usually sung responsively.

The soloist or choir begins by singing the refrain; then the congregation repeats it. The psalm then proceeds responsively with a soloist or choir chanting the verses and the congregation responding with the refrain. Many Roman Catholics, who have recently begun congregational singing, have found this "responsorial" style of psalm-singing very helpful. A refrain (or *antiphon,* an older term) is much easier to learn than the whole psalm. Among Protestants who are used to exclusive metrical psalmody, the responsorial style has the advantage of making a clear distinction between psalms and hymns. Rather than simply reading the psalm directly from the Bible or singing a paraphrased version of it metrically, the congregation can sing the actual words from Scripture.

Other Methods of Singing the Psalms. Other ways of singing the Psalms include the *Anglican chant,* which involves a choir (though not necessarily) singing in harmony to speech rhythms, and the *Gregorian chant,* which is the more ancient method of psalm-chanting, simple enough to be used by either cantor or congregation. Examples of these can be found in the service music section of many denominational hymnals.

David T. Koyzis[20]

208 • Contemporary Developments in Responsorial Psalmody

Recent years have witnessed increased commitment to singing psalms at each worship service. As a result, composers of church music have produced a wealth of psalm settings for congregational use. These range in style and manner, but all intend to restore psalm singing as a significant aspect of common worship.

One of the happier effects of the liturgical movement and the subsequent renewal of worship in this century is the revived interest in singing the Psalms. While it can be rightly argued that some Protestant traditions never abandoned the practice (principally through the use of metrical psalmody), the period following Vatican II and the nearly simultaneous charismatic renewal gave rise to a resurgence of interest in the ancient practice of responsorial psalmody. Spanning the denominational spectrum, the Psalms once again comprise a major component in the sung praise of the church.

This is as it should be. The Psalms, after all, are the church's first hymnbook, and hymns are meant to be sung. To appreciate just how much this is so, one might consider the implications of reciting, rather than singing, congregational hymns in the context of corporate worship. While the poetry of hymnody can certainly convey something of the author's intention for authentic praise, there can be little question that singing would be highly preferable.

Biblical and Early Christian Practice

The scriptural record makes it clear that sung praise was a regular part of ancient Hebrew worship, and psalms were a primary source of repertoire. Though it is not specifically stated in Scripture, it is reasonable to assume that some of the Judaic musical practice of the day was adopted by the early Christian community. Evidence of this can be seen in both the regular Jewish hours of prayer, which eventually evolved into the monastic canonical hours; and in the early eucharistic rites, with the implicit echoes of the Jewish *seder,* the use of the *hallel* (Psalms 113–118) to recount the saving acts of God in history, and the now-stylized four-fold action of the Eucharist.

What Scripture does not make clear are the specific musical or liturgical practices of biblical times, but with regard to the use of psalmody, the Mishnah (c. A.D. 200) gives some insight to the liturgical use of the Psalms in worship at the temple, adapted for synagogue usage: after each verse was chanted by a cantor (or at the temple, a choir), the people in turn responded (hence the name of the form) with an antiphon or refrain. On festival days that employed the *hallel* Psalms, the people responded with "hallelujah."

The responsorial method had much to commend it in a society where access to education was limited and extremely hierarchical. That is to say, at the top of the pyramid were a very few men who could read and write with great facility (the priests, the teachers of the law, many of the Pharisees and Sadducees—the Apostle Paul would be found in this tier). At the next lower level of proficiency were a larger number of men who had some formal education and were reasonably literate (rabbis such as Jesus, for instance), and beneath them were a still larger number of uneducated men who could neither read nor write. At the bottom were the women of the day, who had virtually no opportunity for education.

The use of a repeated refrain that encapsulated the essence of a psalm was an extremely effective way to ensure that a specific element in the greater story of God's dealing with humanity was committed to memory. Functionally, the cantor served as a storyteller, not unlike a balladeer recounting the saving acts of God, giving the people a means of recollection in the refrain. As a pedagogic and catechetical device, the usefulness of this form can scarcely be overplayed, even today in highly literate cultures.

As the church grew and spread beyond the Jewish community, sung praise using the Psalms became a hallmark of its worship. Eusebius, Bishop of Saerarea (260–340), describes the practice: "The command to sing psalms in the name of the Lord was obeyed by everyone in every place: for the command to sing is in force in all churches which exist among the nations, not only the Greeks but also the barbarians throughout the whole world, and in towns, villages and in the fields." At the very least, this suggests that the faith experience and singing praise to God with the Psalms permeated the affairs of daily life.

The musical idiom for the singing of the Psalms gradually developed into what is known today as chant (sometimes called plainchant or plainsong, meaning sung without accompaniment). The melodic sources of these psalm-songs included fragments of ancient Hebrew chants and melodies, borrowed bits of local folk song, and probably some original composition (though it would not have been regarded as such at the time). Eventually, a set of melodies known as tones became the vehicle by which psalms were offered to God in corporate worship.

Within monastic communities, daily repeated exposure to the Psalter using the psalm-tones enabled even illiterate monks and nuns to commit them to memory. In this "closed" setting, chant gradually became more and more complicated, with florid melismas and technical subtleties beyond the capabilities of ordinary people. A largely uneducated laity still relied on the use of the simple antiphon, if they sang anything at all. As a music form, chant reached its pinnacle in the seventh century, when it was codified and became known as Gregorian chant (after Pope Gregory the Great). In addition to psalmody, settings for the Mass, the offices, and hymns had become part of the church's repertoire.

The fortuitous development of a more-or-less standard musical notation during this same period served at least two important positive functions: (1) it provided the means for truly common repertoire, recorded in written form, and (2) it preserved for future generations a priceless body of Christian song with roots firmly in biblical soil.

Today, plainchant as a vehicle for responsorial psalmody (and other sung praise) survives in many religious communities and is used in some parish settings. Beautiful as plainchant is, however, its successful execution depends on sensitive and knowledgeable leadership. Sadly, it is an idiom that is foreign to the ears of many modern worshipers. Thanks to the important work of Charles Winfred Douglas, Healy Willan, Richard Crocker, Mason Martens, Howard Galley, and James Litton, and others, much of this repertory is still accessible for congregational use; *Gradual Psalms* and *The Plainsong Psalter,* to name but two resources, are both available from the Church Hymnal Corporation, New York.

Modern Developments in Responsorial Psalmody

During the latter half of the twentieth century, psalmody specifically, and church music generally has enjoyed a period of unparalleled creativity. Renewal in liturgy, language, and music spawned a pressing need for new material to liberate the faithful in praise. Before Vatican II, before the charismatic renewal, Fr. Joseph Gelineau, S.J., was pioneering a return to the practice of responsorial psalmody for congregational worship. His work was a harbinger of the creative outburst that was to follow a few years later.

Gelineau used the rhythmic strictures of the original Hebrew poetry in his fresh translations: each line has a specified number of accented syllables, with varying, intervening unstressed syllables. This principle governed the composition of both his antiphons and the chant tones. Published in English by GIA Publications, Chicago, his work has entered the mainstream of liturgical song. One notable example is his setting of Psalm 23, recently published in both *The Presbyterian Hymnal* and *The United Methodist Hymnal.* His settings sound very traditional, but it must be remembered that during the 1950s, combining a tuneful, melodic antiphon with a traditional, albeit modern, chant form was thoroughly innovative. Gelineau's work could be rightly called the first fruits of liturgical renewal. Vatican II, and its dictum that the faithful should be active participants rather than spectators in worship, coincided with an outpouring of the Holy Spirit upon the church (now called the charismatic renewal). With renewal of worship as the tenor of the age, the responsorial form provided an obvious way to reinstitute sung prayer and praise by the faithful who had hitherto been willingly or unwillingly silent.

The times were ripe for experimentation and expansion into new realms. The troubadour with a guitar was a pervasive and persuasive cultural image at the time: in the secular sphere, folk music, personified in performers like Peter, Paul, and Mary, Joan Baez, Simon and Garfunkel, Bob Dylan, and Judy Collins to name but a few, gave voice to the troubles and triumphs of the day. The folk style was quickly appropriated by Christian composers eager to meet the demand for material suitable for corporate worship.

Ray Repp and Jo Wise (writers of "I am the Resurrection" and "Take Our Bread," respectively) were two of the more prominent folk composers from this period. Very little of their music is found in use today, but they paved the way for the work of subsequent composers and groups including the St. Louis Jesuits, the Dameans, Cary Landry, and the monks of Weston priory. The St. Louis Jesuits, particularly, drew heavily on the Psalms for material, imitating the various current styles in secular popular music, from folk to country and western to rock. Their songs were cast in a verse/refrain format, a popular restatement of the responsorial method. Some of their more effective and accessible works are "The Cry of the Poor" (Psalm 34), "For You Are My God" (Psalm 16), both from the pen of John Foley, S.J., and "To You, Yahweh, I Lift Up My Soul" by Tim Manion, S.J.

The generally higher musical standard for the St. Louis Jesuits set the stage for three composers who have since dominated the contemporary Roman Catholic music scene: Marty Haugan, David Haas, and Michael Joncas. Their work is broad in its scope, from service music to religious folk/pop to modern traditional hymnody (with some especially fine offerings from Haugan) to psalmody. Their psalmody is in the characteristic popular style, with tuneful refrains and verses that are often through-composed rather than strictly strophic.

A small sampling of their more popular work would include: from Haugan, "Shepherd Me, O God" (Psalm 23), a haunting setting using inclusive language, though that is not immediately apparent; "Your Love is Finer Than Life" (Psalm 63); and "Your Love is Never Ending" (Psalm 136); from Haas, "We Are His People" (Psalm 100), cast in a Taizé-style form with an ostinato refrain, is arguably his best; and from Joncas, "On Eagle's Wings" (Psalm 136), written in an unashamedly sentimental style, has crossed many a denominational line, having found a place in the Methodist, Baptist, and Mennonite/Brethren hymnals. While it remains to be seen whether any of their creative efforts are ultimately durable, Haugan's music particularly is finding a place in more and more denominational hymnals.

The paucity of suitable psalmody for congregational use has engaged a host of other composers, writing in more traditional, though no less innovative, styles. A very partial listing of those making significant contributions in this field today would include James Quin, S.J., Jay Hunstiger, and Howard Hughs, S.M., in the Roman Catholic church; George Black, Peter Hallock, Richard Proulx, and Betty Pulkingham from the Anglican/Episcopal traditions; Carleton Young and Jane Marshall in Methodism; Hal Hopson from the Presbyterian church; and Richard Hillert representing the Lutheran church.

Melodies for their antiphons range from plainchant style to hymn fragments to twentieth-century "serious" music to popular. Accompaniments vary from a cappella voices to organ to hand bells to guitars and tambourine (and any combination of the same). The verses are almost always in a chant form, intended to be sung by a cantor or choir. In this regard, these composers are children of Gelineau, passing on to those who follow the rich legacy of biblical song set to modern music.

Stylistically, the scope among these composers is varied and wide. Hallack's work, for instance, found in his own publication *The Ionian Psalter,* comes from his years of service at St. Mark's (Episcopal) Cathedral in Seattle. Composed to complement the cavernous space in that building, his settings have a decidedly ethereal quality and could be described as somewhat esoteric. Scored for organ, choir, and congregation, they require musical leadership of a very high caliber for satisfying performance. By contrast, *The Basilica Psalter* (Collegeville, Minn.: The Liturgical Press) by Jay Hunstiger features alternate settings for many psalms, one intended for use with a full complement of musical resources, and one for use where musical leadership is more modest.

Hymn fragments (one or two phrases of a hymn) have been effectively used by Hal Hopson in his small collection _Psalms, Refrains, and Tones_ (Carol Stream, Ill.: Hope Publishing Company) and by George Black, a Canadian musician, in his _Music for the Sunday Psalms_ (Toronto: Anglican Book Center) and in _The United Methodist Hymnal_. Charles Smith, editor for the Psalter in the Methodist book, drew heavily on well-known tunes in devising an immediately accessible collection of antiphons. Also featured are antiphons by Young, Marshall, Proulx, and many others. A similar Psalter, utilizing hymn fragments exclusively, is currently in preparation in the Episcopal church.

Betty Pulkingham, a composer from the Community of Celebration noted for her labors in renewal music, has done important work in bridging the gap between "serious" church music and more contemporary expressions of praise. _The Celebration Psalter_ (St. Louis: Cathedral Music Press) showcases her psalmody, which is intentionally eclectic in style. The significance of this collection is in its pairing of traditional chanted psalm tones with antiphons set in more contemporary idioms. Though they are not particularly difficult, adequate preparation is essential for their successful execution.

Finally, a survey of modern trends in responsorial psalm singing would not be complete without acknowledging the music that has emerged from the charismatic movement. Filled with a desire to "sing a new song to the Lord," composers (often people with little or no music training) from every denomination, turned to the Psalms—and Scripture, generally—for texts that taught, encouraged, and exhorted the faithful in praise. Companies like Maranatha! Music, Word, and more recently, Integrity's Hosanna Music, fill a need by publishing and recording new music for worship.

Historically and stylistically, this music shares much with that which emerged from Vatican II (indeed, in places like the Word of God Community, Ann Arbor, Michigan, the two streams of renewal flowed together, and it was not possible to separate one from the other). Significant early contributors include Tommy Coombes, David and Dale Garrett, Betty Pulkingham, and Andre Crouch (whose setting of Psalm 103, "Bless the Lord, O My Soul" has

found a place in the Baptist and Christian Reformed hymnals).

As a genre, these psalm-songs often feature the familiar verse/refrain format, though many are simpler still, utilizing one or two psalm verses in a complete song. While the form cannot be strictly described as responsorial, it achieves the same end: The song gives the people a selection of Scripture set to a memorable tune. The musical integrity of much of this literature is hotly debated, and it remains to be seen if any will survive for use by future generations of Christians.

—— Summary ——

Responsorial psalmody has enjoyed a phenomenal resurgence in popularity during the latter half of the twentieth century. Significant factors include Vatican II; the liturgical movement, generally; and the charismatic renewal.

Based solidly on biblical and historical practice, modern composers of virtually every denomination are stretching creative boundaries for innovative and effective ways to sing the psalms. Whether their work is enduring will be for others to decide, but the benefit to the people of God today—singing the word of God, letting it "dwell in them richly"— cannot be overestimated.

Kevin Hackett

209 • HOW TO INTRODUCE RESPONSORIAL PSALM SINGING

The following article elaborates on a form of responsorial psalmody described in the preceding articles, describing how the Psalms can be sung responsorially and how this practice can be introduced to a congregation not familiar with this practice.

The Psalms may be thought of as honest response to God by humankind. In this frame of reference they are particularly appropriate in corporate worship as a sung response to the reading of Scripture, particularly after the reading from the Hebrew Scriptures.

The singing of the Psalms has been given impetus within recent decades by the establishment of the three-year lectionary with its three prescribed Scripture readings plus an appropriate psalm for each Sunday of the year. The form widely used in singing the Psalms is that of the responsorial psalm. As the name suggests, responsorial psalmody is typified by a short response (refrain, often called an antiphon) sung by the congregation with a cantor or choir singing the verses in a free-speech rhythm. This form is valuable for several reasons. It allows the congregation to be involved in singing the psalm at a comfortable level by singing a repeating refrain. The chanting of the verses as opposed to a metrical rendition allows the subtleties of the text to be communicated in a more convincing manner.

Let us assume that one is serving a church that has never experienced responsorial psalmody. Where does one begin to introduce this form of congregational participation in the liturgy? The prescribed teaching plan, "Easy steps toward congregational participation in responsorial psalm singing," is printed at end of this article. It is carefully developed, graduated approach that has proved to be useful in many churches. It takes the congregation from where they are very comfortable, i.e. reading the psalms responsively, through the singing of a bona fide responsorial psalm. When first introducing psalm singing, the refrains can be phrases from familiar hymns that correlate with the thought of the psalm or the season of the church year. Some suggested refrains in this regard could be "O Come, O Come Emmanuel," "Joy to the World!" The Lord has Come!" "A Mighty Fortress is Our God, a Bulwark Never Failing," or "Lift Up Your Head, Ye Mighty Gates."

The six steps have a logical progression always stretching the congregation from the known to the unknown.

- **Step 1** simply establishes the interspersing of a refrain between the verses (generally after every other verse).
- **Step 2** provides an opportunity for the congregation to sing a familiar hymn refrain.
- **Step 3** makes use of a refrain sung by the congregation other than a familiar hymn phrase. The short antiphonal phrase is easily sung.

- **Step 4** is one in which the choir sings the refrain as a teaching device for the congregation so that the latter is prepared to sing the same refrain at step five.
- **Step 5** provides the opportunity for the congregation to sing a bona fide refrain.
- **Step 6** completes the process with a cantor singing to a psalm tone, and the choir and congregation singing the refrain.

Any psalm text may be easily pointed to accommodate the simple psalm tone B on the "Easy Steps" sheet. Simply divide each psalm verse in two half-verses and place an asterisk at the end of the first half-verse. Locate the last stressed word or syllable in each half-verse and count back two syllables, placing a mark over that syllable. Each measure of the psalm tone is sung to a psalm half-verse. The first part of each half-verse is chanted to the whole note of the tone, moving to the second note of the tone on the syllable with the point. The third and fourth notes of the tone accommodate the remainder of each phrase of the text.

The amount of time spent on each step will vary from congregation to congregation. It is conceivable that all the steps could be accomplished in consecutive weeks, using different psalms with a common theme such as praise of God. Another possibility would be to choose a season such as Advent or Lent and develop a graduated approach based on the six steps to teach the congregation to participate in singing the Psalms.

Obviously, our effectiveness in helping the congregation to participate will be enhanced by an atmosphere of trust and respect for the congregation's ability to enter into such a project. With this in place and a carefully organized approach, responsorial psalm singing can likely become a vital musical and spiritual expression on the part of the congregation. By experiencing the psalms week by week in this overt participatory manner we are able to establish a strong link to the faithful, stretching all the way

---

Easy Steps Toward Congregational Participation in Responsorial Psalm Singing

Step 1: A reader and the congregation read the verses responsively with the choir interjecting a refrain after each pair of verses. The refrain should be a phrase from a well-known hymn. This first step gets the congregation accustomed to having a refrain as a part of the psalmody in the service.

(from "For the Beauty of the Earth")

REFRAIN: Lord of all, to Thee we raise / This our hymn of grateful praise.

Psalm 100:1-4

1 All the lands make joy to you, O God;
2 **We serve you with gladness! We come into your presence with singing!**

REFRAIN

3 You are the Lord our God! You made us, and we are yours; we are your people, and the sheep of your pasture.
4 **We enter your gates with Thanksgiving, and your courts with praise! We give thanks to you, we bless your name!**

REFRAIN

Step 2: A reader and the choir read the verses responsively with everyone (the choir and congregation) singing the refrain after each pair of verses. Again, the refrain should be a phrase from a well-known hymn.

Step 3: A reader and the congregation read the verses responsively with the choir and congregation singing an antiphonal refrain.

REFRAIN: Sing with joy! Sing with joy! Praise the Lord! Praise the Lord!

Step 4: A reader and the congregation read the verses responsively with the choir singing the refrain. (See A below)

Sing, O sing with gladness!

Step 5: A reader reads the verses; the choir and congregation sing the refrain (See A above)

Step 6: A cantor chants the verses on a simple tone (See B above) with the choir and congregation singing the refrain (See A above).

Hal H. Hopson

back to the temple in Jerusalem, "Sing to the Lord a new song."

210 • POETIC ASPECTS OF HYMNODY

Hymns are essentially poems set to music. The following article describes the poetic qualities of hymn texts, defines several of the technical terms used to categorize hymns texts, and then discusses how hymn tunes need to be sensitive to the poetic qualities of the text. Studying the examples provided in this article will help the reader to better understand and use hymns for congregational singing.

——— Meter ———

For many people looking through a hymnal, the use of such letters as SM, CM, LM, CMD and strange numbers such as 77.77., 87.87.D, and 14 14. 4 7 8. are complete mysteries or at best intriguing puzzles. But for anyone seriously concerned with writing hymn texts or setting them to music, they are very important, for they are related to the thoughts and means of expression which are chosen consciously or unconsciously. Artists usually do things more by instinct than by cerebral machination; yet there is plenty of historical evidence to indicate that there are certain poetical rhythms that fit particular types of texts, for the poet has words, sounds, poetic devices, rhythms, and rhyme as tools. Combining these is no easy task, for as the great American poet Robert Frost indicated, writing poetry is like running easily in the harness.

Poetry is organized into "feet," which indicates that poetry "walks" or "marches." A "foot" consists of a group of two or more syllables with one accented and others not. In classical poetry the number of feet was counted. For example, iambic pentameter (a favorite of Shakespeare) was ten syllables arranged in five groups of feet of iambic movement. In hymns we count the number of syllables in a line, rather than the feet. The most common movement is iambic (V /), consisting of an upbeat followed by an accent. Thus it is called the rising foot, and this means that the mind is constantly being propelled forward to the final climactic accent on the last important word or syllable of the line. Trochaic (/ V) is called the falling foot, with the accent first, then falling away to an un-accent on the second pulse. This means the poet must capture interest on the very first word. For example, "Hark! the Herald Angels Sing" gets your attention immedi-

ately. By adding an unaccented syllable to each of these (iambic and trochaic) we have anapaestic (/ V V) or dactylic (V V /). Pure classical dactylic is rarely found because there are few English words which end with two unaccents (e.g., holiness). And anapaestic often begins with only one upbeat sound (e.g., "Immortal, Invisible,"), but it always ends with a final accent. The tripping triplet sounds of these meters is exuberant and infectious, with the feel of the dance. (For a discussion of other meters such as the sapphic, elegia, alcaic, cretic, and spondee, see Austin C. Lovelace, *The Anatomy of Hymnody* [Chicago: GIA Publications] 15, 16). For all practical purposes most hymns will fall into the four basic patterns listed above.

To appreciate the importance of iambic movement, one need only look at the Scottish and English Psalters. There you will find only Common Meter, Short Meter, and Long Meter. Of these, Long Meter (88.88.) is the most ancient, having been used by Bishop Ambrose in the first hymns written using meter. Most LM texts tend to be related to praise or to stating lofty themes about God as Creator and Sovereign Lord. A study of Isaac Watts's use of this meter will be helpful in understanding this form.

Common Meter (86.86.) is the workhorse of hymnody. It was most commonly used for psalm texts that tell a story. With its first eight syllables, it states the beginning of an idea, which is then completed in the second set of six syllables. It can be read in the sing-songy style of a small boy reciting poetry. When Common Meter is doubled (CMD) it becomes what is called "fourteeners"—the tempo is quick enough to make the 8 and 6 into a long line of 14 syllables. Since it flows along rapidly there are seldom words of more than two syllables, and most will be only one. This meter has been used most successfully for teaching and story telling, and is called the ballad meter. Closely related to CM is 76.76.D. which ends lines 1, 3, 5, 7 with what is called a feminine ending (e.g., "The Church's One Foundation"). It is less virile, and the need for double rhyming the last two syllables and using multi-syllabled words tends to more obvious: foundation, creation, nation, salvation, tribulation, consummation.

Short Meter (66.86.) was once called the poulter's measure because of the custom of giving 12 eggs for the first dozen, and thirteen or fourteen for the second. It is made up of two couplets, the first containing 12 syllables and the second 14. It has been used fewer times than LM and CM, because it demands that the poet state the thesis in six syllables, which can then be reinforced in the second line and developed in the last fourteen. Because of its abrupt directness, it is successful for exhorting and admonishing (e.g., "Come, Sound His Praise Abroad" and "Stand Up, and Bless the Lord." Short Meter Double (SMD) was a favorite of Charles Wesley, his "Crown Him with Many Crowns" being an excellent example. Another fine one is George Matheson's excellent use of paradox in "Make Me a Captive, Lord." This meter poses many problems for a hymn tune writer. There is no space for verbosity or rambling melody. DIADEMATA is perhaps the most successful tune in this meter.

Since 8's and 6's are so basic to hymn writing, it is not surprising that there are many other combinations of the two. 66.66.88. was known as HM or Hallelujah Meter. F. Bland Tucker in his hymn for the family, "Our Father, By Whose Name," added an extra 8, possibly to fit it to RHOSYMEDRE. The new _United Methodist Hymnal_ (1989) lists twelve combinations of the two numbers.

Just as Common Meter Double (CMD) is sometimes reduced to 76.76. by having feminine endings in lines 1, 3, 5, 7,. the meter of 87.87. is similar except that the feminine ending is in lines 2 and 4. "The King of Love My Shepherd Is" is the most famous example, but this meter has never been very widely used. However, German hymnody has been successful in 87.87.887., with its added line 6, having been developed from the music and texts of minnesingers.

Hymns having 10 syllables per line are quite common, with 10 10.10 10. being the most popular. It is interesting to note that most examples come from the nineteenth century and were written by ministers. (Does this mean that they tend to be long winded?)

Among trochaic hymns the most common patterns are 65.65. and 65.65.D. ("Onward, Christian soldiers"), and all of the combinations of 7's (77.77., 77.77.77., 77.77.D.). "For the Beauty of the Earth" is typical, with all of the lines being relatively short, and with one idea per line of poetry. Equally or more popular are the 87.87.D. hymns. A look at any metrical index will show a large number of these hymns, all of which are very familiar.

The rhythm of anapaestic (and dactylic) is infectiously exuberant, with its dancing movement in triplets. Wesley's 55.55.65.65. use in "Ye Servants of God, Your Master proclaim" is a classic example. Some exotic combinations found in early American tune books are 5 5 5.11., 6 6 9.D., and 11 8.11 8. However, the most popular texts are put into four 11's, and the ultimate in dactylic treatment is "Praise to the Lord, the Almighty" in 14 14. 4 7 8.

An interesting study is to consider the use of mixed meters, where a hymn uses both iambic and trochaic ("Praise the Lord Who Reigns Above"). "Infant Holy, Infant Lowly" looks and sounds like it is dactylic, but is actually trochaic—an anapaestic tune with a trochaic text. The most famous (and historical) of combined meters is found in the Sapphic (11 11 11.5.). The first three syllables of each line of poetry are dactylic, and then the poetry moves to trochaic for the rest of the line. A good example is the German hymn, "Ah, Holy, Jesus, How Hast Thou Offended."

This is a very sketchy overview of the basic patterns with which poets begin to express their thoughts. The variety of meters is overwhelming. The new _United Methodist Hymnal_ lists 195 different meters! And as if this were not enough, there is another category called IRREGULAR—which means that each hymn is different and can only be sung to its one given tune. In old books such hymns were marked PM, which meant Peculiar Meter or Particular Meter.

One of the features about contemporary hymn writers is the large number of meters used. Fred Kaan of England, one of the jump-states of contemporary hymnody, has written in 86 meters. Timothy Dudley-Smith, an Anglican bishop, has used 87. Jaroslav Vajda (American) also has 86, while the greatest hymn writer of this century, Fred Pratt Green of England, has used an amazing 124. Since only two of Brian Wren's collections of hymns include a metrical index, it is difficult to determine how many meters he has used, but his later works seem to be more poems than hymns with exotic meters which are better read than sung.

Rhyme Schemes

In addition to the importance of the meter matching the material, there is also the matter of rhyming schemes that are aids to the memory. Spelling does not always determine rhyme, but it is sound that must be the same. There are eye rhymes, identities, false rhymes, almost rhymes, consonance (or off rhymes), and assonance. Rhymes may be in couplets (AABB), cross (ABAB), outer-inner (ABBA), internal rhymes ("above thy *deep* and dreamless *sleep*"), and other more complicated patterns, including no rhymes at all. The danger for a hymn writer is the temptation to let the necessity for rhyme determine the thought. A hymn may be admired for its poetry, but its true purpose is as a book of devotion for the people. Chapter 6 of Lovelace's *The Anatomy of Hymnody* lists a variety of poetic devices which are further working tools of the poet.

——— Hymn Tunes and Poetic Texts ———

Just how is the composer affected by all this? In working on the Hymn Tunes Committee for the revision of the 1935 Methodist hymnal, our committee was in complete agreement that the tune PENTECOST in 3/4 time was not right for the text "Fight the Good Fight," written in Long Meter. (Can you really fight in waltz time?) We looked at all sorts of tunes in this meter, such as DUKE STREET and TRURO, but they didn't seem right. So we commissioned a tune called GRACE CHURCH, GANANOQUE by the Canadian composer Graham George. While it is nicely crafted, it did not turn out to be a successful tune for congregational singing. It was this problem hymn which prompted the writing of *The Anatomy of Hymnody* (Chicago: GIA Publications). There were two problems: (1) the hymn begins with a choriambus, which forces the composer to have an accent on the first word "fight", which is awkward in iambic meter. (2) Long Meter is the wrong one for admonishing—this should have been written in Short Meter. Years later I discovered that the only suitable tune for this text is DEO GRACIS (The Agincourt Song) written in 3/4 with the possibility of using either upbeats or downbeats to fit the appropriate accents.

There are always problems for the composer with Long Meter, with its constant movement of 8 syllables per line of poetry. When does the singer have time to breathe? TALLIS' CANON, unless it is sung at a very moderate pace, leaves the singer breathless. OLD 100TH probably has the most effective and successful solution to the problem by starting with a gathering note and ending each phrase with notes of double value, which gives a strong steady pulse and plenty of time for breathing. A study of any hymnal will reveal from 15 to 20 different rhythmic treatments of LM, including 3/4. GERMANY in 3/4, which is sung to "Where Cross the Crowded Ways of Life," was arranged from Beethoven by William Gardiner of England to begin with a downbeat for phrases 1 and 2, with upbeats for 3 and 4, which gives variety and a powerful climax. Unfortunately, the new *Presbyterian Hymnal* (1990) has altered the original to begin all phrases with an upbeat, which defeats the purpose of the tune.

Writing a hymn tune suitable for congregational singing is one of the most difficult of all jobs, for the composer must try to be distinctive and neutral at the same time. The tune must be memorable after a few times of singing, but it must be able to stand up to repetition without losing its freshness. At the same time it must fit the scansion and mood of all stanzas, which usually have many different themes and moods. If the lines of poetry are short, there is not much room to get a musical idea moving very far. If the lines are long, there is the problem of keeping motion and life in a lot of notes. The balance of note values is important, as well as the choices of cadences. For example, a line with ten syllables is very difficult to write unless the composer breaks it down into two small parts, such as a 4 and a 6. (See OLD 124TH.) The hymn "God of Our Life, Through All the Circling Years" (10 4.10 4.10 10.) by Hugh T. Kerr was written to be sung to SANDON, which fits it nicely even if there is a static feel to the harmony. *The Worshipbook* (1972) tried to substitute the tune WITMER by Richard D. Wetzel, which spun out 14 notes in each of the first two lines, and then floundered rhythmically for the last two, with no matching patterns. No wonder that Presbyterians refused to accept the change! 65.65.D. is an awkward meter, for the most obvious pattern is four quarters and two half notes, followed by four quarters and one whole note. The tune dies at the end of every two lines unless an oom-pah bass is used to cover the hole, as in ST. GERTRUDE for "Onward, Christian soldiers." But Ralph Vaughan Williams solved the problem for "At the Name of Jesus" by putting the tune in 3/2 with a magnificent rhythmic change for the last line which matches the climax of the melody.

So which is the more important: the text or the tune? I believe that they are equal, except that the text is more equal. We sing hymns because of what the words say, and if they are our thoughts we join in heartily and agree. However, if the tune does not give wings to the words and make them lyrical, they remain nothing but a poem. So in the long run, the tune turns out to be of ultimate importance, proving the biblical message that the last shall be first. It does pay to pay attention to the "anatomy of hymnody."

Austin C. Lovelace

211 • HOW TO COMPOSE A HYMN TUNE

As the previous article observes, a well-crafted hymn tune is essential for expressing the meaning of a text. Composing hymn tunes, then, is an important task that ultimately makes a hymn text singable and "pray-able." To write an effective tune, the composer must meet poetic, musical, and liturgical criteria.

"Sing to the Lord a new song" proclaims the Psalmist in Psalm 98. Ever since the days of the Psalmist, composers and poets have been faithful to this command and have been inspired to write "new songs" to praise God and edify the church. The following thoughts reflect how I have been motivated and what methods I have used to provide the church with a "new song" to sing.

I began writing hymn tunes the same year that I began directing my first church choir. I was looking for hymns that would serve as choral closings for a service, and I grew frustrated. Although I found some excellent evening hymns, they were set to some very disappointing tunes. Brashly thinking that I could do better, I composed my first hymn tune to the evening hymn "The Day Is Past and Over," which I found in _The English Hymnal_. It served well as a choral closing for my church choir and its use in worship inspired me to continue the search for "serviceable" texts and to compose new tunes for them. Before long I had composed my first five hymn tunes, which were all choral closings written for my church choir. Since then my interest in hymn tune composing has broadened beyond close-of-worship hymns, and I have composed hymn tunes for a wide variety of hymn texts.

My greatest inspiration for composing hymn tunes is the desire to fulfill a liturgical need. Knowing that what I write will be used by eager choir members is further motivation for bringing to worship something fresh and new. However, after the need has been identified and a suitable text has been found, the question of how one composes a hymn tune must be addressed.

The _first_ step in the process of composing a hymn tune begins with the hymn text. Only after a hymn text has been studied and the structure and meaning of the text is fully understood can the composer begin to write a hymn tune that reflects an inevitable and necessary union between text and tune. When the purpose and focus of the text is fully understood, only then can the composer begin to make decisions that reflect a similar purpose and focus in the hymn tune. Items such as the mood of the text, poetic accents, and significant words are considered, and then musical decisions such as the choice of mode (major, minor, etc.), the choice of meter (3/4, 4/4, etc.), and the placement of the musical climax are made.

The _second_ step in the process is the actual composing of the hymn tune. It involves a continuous process of rejecting, rewriting, and accepting musical ideas. Each composer establishes a routine and finds a comfortable place for doing the composing. I myself prefer to do my composing away from a keyboard, just singing various musical ideas while composing—after all, a hymn is essentially _sung_ music. Only later when refining the harmony do I go to a keyboard.

This entire process is governed by certain rules of composition, not to be held as absolute, but to be used as guidelines. These rules, or guidelines, provide a fairly predictable framework, and they separate the composer of the hymn tune from other composers. All composers, of course, follow guidelines. But the guidelines a hymn composer follows are unique, partly because of the audience. As a group, these people—a congregation largely made up of untrained singers—has neither the skill nor the training to sing music that is too complicated. The composer must keep that in mind while, at the same time, giving the congregation a hymn that will challenge them.

Four major guidelines which I consider important for the hymn tune composer are as follows:

1. The _melody_ must be simple enough for a congregation of untrained singers to sing after just one hearing of the tune. A predominantly stepwise melody with a judicious use of leaps and unisons is the norm. The range of the melody must be a comfortable one (usually from middle C to the second D above middle C). One of the strengths of the tune HYFRYDOL can be attributed to the natural flow of the predominantly stepwise melody.

2. The *harmony* must support the melody, not overwhelm it. If the tune is intended to be sung in unison, then the keyboard harmony may be slightly more elaborate. If the tune is intended to be sung with other voices singing harmony, the harmonic lines should possess some melodic interest of their own. Sydney Nicholson's CRUCIFER ("Lift High the Cross") is a good example; it has a unison refrain with a very active but supportive harmony. The refrain is followed by the stanza, which is usually sung in four-part harmony.

3. The *rhythm* of the melody should closely match the rhythm of the hymn text. A reading of the hymn text using the rhythm of the hymn tune should result in an effortless rhythm that propels the text forward. This works very well when the text "Praise to the Lord, the Almighty" is read to the rhythm of the tune LOBE DEN HERREN. The rhythm contains mostly quarter notes, but the occasional dotted quarter, eighth, and dotted half notes bring attention to the melody and the text at those points.

4. The *climax* of the text should coincide with the climax of the melody. After the climax of the text has been determined (ideally in the same place in each stanza), the composer must try to create a climax in the same place in the tune. The climax of the text could be set to a note that is higher (tonic accent) or longer (agogic accent) than any other note. Often the note that marks the climax of the text and tune is both the highest and longest note of the melody. The climax of the tune VENI IMMANUEL ("O Come, O Come, Immanuel") is clearly the second note of the refrain. This note is its highest and longest note and also coincides with the climax of the text at that point: "Rejoice!"

The *third* step in the process is the critical stage of self-evaluation. After the hymn tune has been written, I have found it valuable to set it aside for several days. I then come back to it and review what I've written. Sometimes I'm confronted with some unsatisfactory composing that needs major revision, but usually I find that just a note or two requires change.

After its completion I find that having my choir sing the tune will give me a good indication if the tune has any future life. I listen to what they have to say to me about the tune, and just as important, I listen to their singing of the tune. I can usually get a very good indication of whether the tune will have any use beyond the initial trial run with my choir. If it passes the test, I may use it during worship if its singing fulfills a liturgical need.

Composing a successful hymn tune is not an easy task. It requires a creative mind, a thorough knowledge of the craft of composition, a sensitivity to the hymn text, a knowledge of the capabilities of the singing congregation, a great deal of discipline, and a good measure of patience. If you can coordinate all of these attributes into the creative effort of composing a hymn tune, your rewards will be great. You will be numbered among the thousands of composers and poets who gave to the church and to the Lord a "new song" to sing.

Roy Hopp[21]

212 • HOW TO IMPROVE CONGREGATIONAL HYMN SINGING

Most congregations' repertoire of hymns and songs is relatively small. This article shows the church musician how to introduce and teach new hymns and songs and thus broaden the spectrum of music in the local congregation.

Members of the congregation need and appreciate assistance in singing hymns and responses. Their hymnal provides them with a collection of perhaps 600 hymns, but they probably know only forty to sixty of these. And all too frequently these are "old favorites" that have been worn threadbare through overuse through the years. Members would like to know more about how to sing these favorites with greater understanding and enjoyment. But they also can be conditioned to anticipate with pleasure the prospect of learning some new hymns.

But when a brand new hymn appears in the bulletin, the organist plays a tune never heard before by this congregation. Consequently there is often a negative reaction—"Why don't we sing some familiar hymns?" Suppose it is the new hymn by Jeffrey Rowthorn, the last stanza of which is:

Indwelling God, your gospel claims one family
   with a billion names;
let every life be touched with grace until we
   praise you face to face.

Without singing, everyone could read this splendid text aloud with no hesitancy and with comprehension of what the words mean. But, in a hymnal, texts are accompanied by music. Suppose worshipers are confronted not only with these three stanzas but also with this lovely old folk tune KEDRON:

"Spirit of God, Unleashed on Earth"

```
1. Spir - it of God, un - leashed on earth   With
2. You   came  in power, the  church was  born;  O
3. With  burn - ing words of  vic - tory won  In -

rush of wind  and  roar of flame! With  tongues of fire saints
Ho - ly Spir - it,  come a - gain! From  liv - ing wa - ters
spire our hearts grown  cold with fear.  Re - vive  in  us  bap -

spread good news;  Earth,  kin - dling, blazed  its  loud ac - claim.
raise  new saints,  Let  new tongues hail  the  ris - en Lord.
tis - mal grace,  And  fan our smol - dering  lives to flame.
```

Some members can readily sing this tune at first reading. But many people are either partially or totally illiterate when it comes to reading a music score. They do not know that the tune is in the key of C minor, or that the melody begins on the third of the scale. The half note as the unit of beat would probably mean nothing to them. The subtle rhythms have to be read and interpreted. These and many other aspects of the notation are ingrained in the consciousness of able music readers but are Greek to music amateurs.

When a new hymn and tune are announced without proper introduction, your congregation will experience discomfort when faced by musical language they cannot interpret. So we will discuss the introduction of these two components of a hymn— words and music—and how to improve your congregation's skill in understanding and interpreting them.

Hymn Texts

Reading Hymns. It is a fact that the meaning of hymns can be grasped more readily by reading than by singing the texts. Therefore worshipers should be encouraged to read the texts of hymns as they sit in the pew and prepare for public worship. Also this habit of reading hymns can be further ingrained by urging members to purchase a copy of the hymnbook for use at home. Or you could consider providing a small free booklet of hymn texts, printed in the church office, which can be taken home and used in private devotions. Any hymns which are in public domain could be included.

Singing Hymns Intelligently. John Wesley realized that one's mind can wander during hymn singing and so he advised his followers: "Have an eye to God in every word you sing. Aim at pleasing him more than yourself, or any other creature. In order to do this, attend strictly to the sense of what you sing, and see that your heart is not carried away with the sound, but offered to God continually. . . ." One simple way to concentrate on the hymn texts while you sing is to be aware to whom you are singing—being aware who is being addressed as you sing.

If you see that the hymn is "Fight the Good Fight With All Thy Might," you realize that you are encouraging everyone in the congregation to fight the battle of life in the strength of Christ. Hymns like "Joyful, Joyful, We Adore Thee" and "Holy, Holy, Holy, Lord God Almighty" are obviously addressed to God. This habit of focusing your attention will lead to intelligent hymn singing.

Memorizing Hymns. If a hymn has been memorized and repeated scores of times as needed in daily life, you may be sure that the text has been comprehended and appropriated. Hymns thus become a means of grace. John Calvin commented on the importance of memorizing in the preface to his 1542 Psalter:

> We must remember what Saint Paul has said, that the spiritual songs can only be sung from the heart. Now the heart seeks after understanding, and in that, according to Saint Augustine, lies the difference between the songs of men and that of birds. For a finch, a nightingale, a parrot may sing well, but they do so without understanding. Now the proper gift of man is to sing, knowing what he says, since the intelligence must follow the heart and the emotions, which can only be when we have the song impressed in our minds in order to never cease singing.

Hymn Music

If the majority or all of the congregation knows how to read music notation, then there is no problem in introducing a new hymn from the musical standpoint. But the average congregation probably has a majority of people who would say that they "couldn't carry a tune in a bucket." How do you teach these people to learn a new tune?

You can hardly hope for much success simply by printing the number of an unfamiliar hymn (text and tune), having the organist play it over once, and expecting these music amateurs to sing it with ease. Some may even give up and close the hymnal.

Since they can't read the notes, they must learn the tune by rote—by repetition—by hearing the melody over and over. So considerate organists can play the new tune as a part of the prelude, having informed the people somehow that this is the new tune of the service. Also the choir could sing the hymn the preceding Sunday as an anthem with the congregation having been told that this hymn is to be sung the following Sunday. The people are also urged to turn in the hymnal to the particular hymn.

I have heard a pastor give a brief introduction to a new hymn in which he said that, since the tune was unfamiliar, he suggested that the congregation listen to the organist play the tune and to the choir sing the first stanza in unison. Then the people could join in the remaining stanzas.

The ideal occasion for learning new hymns is in the informal atmosphere of a hymn sing or congregational rehearsal. At these events the leader can give the group some general information about the hymn and its origin and especially some facts about the structure of the tune.

For example, ask the congregation to sing the first stanza of a favorite hymn, say "Come, Thou Fount of Every Blessing." When they have finished, ask if they noticed any repetition of melody from line to line. Someone may have noticed that the first, second, and last lines are identical. Affirm this and then tell them that the third line also has some repetition of musical theme. Have them sing the line. They probably will observe that the two halves of this line are almost identical. If we labeled the lines alphabetically, the pattern of this tune would be A A B¹B²A.

It might be helpful if you told the people that one way hymn music is unified is by the exact repetition of a group of notes as in the tune to "Silent Night," where the first four-note theme is repeated three more times. Then tell them that in many hymn tunes a brief musical phrase is repeated but at a higher or lower pitch and that this device is called a sequence. A familiar tune with two sets of sequences is "Fairest Lord Jesus." The Welsh tune BRYN CALFARIA has three in the third line.

This kind of insight may whet your people's appetite to pay attention to hymn tune shapes, and consequently, to be more eager to tackle new tunes.

James Rawlings Sydnor[22]

213 • CREATIVITY IN HYMN SINGING

Hymns come in a variety of musical and textual styles. Yet often hymns are sung blandly, with no regard to their variety. The following article describes how hymns can be sung creatively, how the differences in hymns can be reflected in how they are sung, and how this approach can increase the potential for expressing the textual and musical ideas contained in a given hymn.

The fact that a hymnal contains some 1500 years of musical, poetic, and theological expressions of faith should be argument enough against boredom ever setting in upon hymn singing. The situation in many congregations, however, is that people have come not to expect much musical satisfaction from their own congregation's hymn singing. The singing of many congregations is characteristically gray: not too fast, not too slow, not too loud, not too soft, and, often, not too interesting. In spite of our low expectations for music in our churches, we still hang on to the belief that singing together is one of the most important things we do when we come together to worship.

It is increasingly apparent that greater attention must be paid to the ways in which we sing in worship. We must resist the ease of singing every hymn as if it had been written in the same style, thus making all hymns and all languages generic. With the availability of recorded sound, it is not difficult, even for those who have had little or no formal education in music, to surround themselves with sounds of medieval Christian singing, mountain shape-note hymn singing, and percussion-and-dance-accompanied African hymns. These source materials are readily available; it is incumbent upon those who are responsible for music to lead their congregation to experience all these musical languages.

In paying attention to the distinctive qualities of the musical languages contained in a hymnal, variation in the sounds of our singing is already addressed. Variety for its own sake has no particular value in worship, but for reasons of textual and musical expressivity it has much to offer. However, one needs to approach the use of variation cau-

tiously, being certain that there is reason for introducing variation, using it as one uses seasonings in cooking—a small amount to enhance the flavor of the whole dish.

Caring for the subtleties of the languages suggests cultural and historical sensitivity, and will of itself create a varied sound for congregational song. Ideas from the poetry may also suggest ways of varying the sound which will more clearly communicate the text. Ignoring the characteristics of the sonorities included in a hymnal reflects a deafness to the movings of the Spirit in sounds other than those to which our ears have grown accustomed, and the implication is that God's praises and our praying and proclamation are heard only when their sound matches our assumptions about sacred sound.

Ultimately the importance of care for the sounds of our singing is that the intention of music is to demand that the ear pay attention. Meister Eckhart said that it is the eye through which we see God and through which God sees us. Likewise, it may well be the ear through which we hear God, and through which God hears us. The gift of sound is a sacred gift of the Creator; it ought to be handled and used with respect. When the gamut of music, from Gregorian chant to contemporary Christian hymnody and from African music to chorales, is allowed its full expression in worship, music becomes an important means by which we know God, the giver of this priceless gift. If one listens carefully, one may hear not only the beauty of the music itself, but may also hear beyond the music, and there discover something of the eternal made audible.

Questions for Reflection

Those who lead music in the congregation must assume responsibility for the sound of all the music which is used in worship. For congregational music, there are questions which we may ask of a hymn concerning its nature. For example, a first question should be: what is its origin? Is the original context for this psalm tune an intimate group of singers who wanted parts written so that they could enjoy the fellowship of singing and playing them together in their homes? What might have been the nature of an outdoor or tent-revival setting with a large group of singers who were enthusiastic and responsive to the spontaneity of the moment? Where might this spiritual have been sung, and what might the singers have been doing when they sang it?

As one begins to ask questions of the origin of our

hymns, one begins to imagine differentiated sounds; matters of dynamics, tempo, and articulation begin to make themselves apparent. The fine print on the page, either above the hymn or below the hymn, can give the first clues about where to look for more help. Nowadays, most hymnals have handbooks which provide a great deal of historical information about the places and times from which our hymns come.

A second question, nearly as important as the first, is: what is the primary musical element of the melody? Alice Parker, in her many fine workshops on hymn singing, often asks people to identify in order of importance the elements of melody, rhythm, and harmony as they sing a hymn tune. The ordering is not so much to find a "right" answer, but to explore the nature of melodies. Some tunes may, on different occasions, have a differing ordering of the elements. The link between this quick analysis and the singing of the hymn itself is that one's understanding of the inherent nature of the melody will affect questions of tempo, dynamics, and articulation. If a hymn is primarily a "melody" tune, then the lyricism of that hymn will likely receive first attention. If the hymn is primarily a "rhythm" tune, the physical, dance-like elements will suggest how the hymn could be sung or moved. If the hymn is primarily a "harmony" tune, then time will be required to allow the harmonies to sound.

The broader question in which this discussion finds a home is this: to what aspect of our singing (or playing) is the appeal of this hymn directed? For the singer in the congregation, a giving over of one's self to the hymn is a necessary element of the circle that unites composer, poet, sound, thought, and the singer. This surrender can occur, completely apart from one's private tastes, as easily and naturally in the abstract coolness of Gregorian chant as in the concrete heat of danced African hymns. Those who lead, be it from a keyboard, with the assistance of a choir, or with the voice, are called upon to be a shepherd of the sound which their congregations are asked to create in worship. Those who lead must sing and play responsibly in order to let the congregation know, without long spoken instructions, the kind of sound into which they are invited to sing. Their responsibility is to set the sound in the room in motion, and do so in such a way that the singers of the congregation will find their surrendered energies worthy of their time and their spiritual devo-

tion. Those who lead must lead with courage and patience and encouragement, like a shepherd who senses the immediate needs of the flock, and they must, also like a shepherd, lead us to fresh water and green pastures and allow us to experience that better place.

A third question, never separable from the first two, is one of context: what is the occasion, the moment for which this hymn is being sung? Here complex links between text and music come into play, sung text being significantly different from either text or music. Connections between the hymn and other ideas and moments of the service add other important considerations. The juxtaposition of a hymn next to what precedes or follows it must also be kept in mind so that the parts of a service form a community of relationships rather than a sequence of interesting events. These considerations are the truly difficult aspects of choosing hymns for worship, rather severely summarized by the question: Why choose *this* hymn for *this* moment anyway?

Beyond questions of sensitivity to the various characteristics of the musical and poetic languages represented in a hymnal, the increasing quantity of musical styles produces other points of stress as they seek to find place in our corporate worship. It comes as a great relief to many people to experience worship in which differing styles of music have found a comfortable home. One may choose to bless or to curse diversity, which seems to be the disposition of our time. For those who bless it, diversity can be a wonderful enrichment of our worship experience, analogous to walking around to another side of a free-standing sculpture and experiencing the same thing from a differing point of view. Most any style of music can find appropriate space in worship if, in the planning of worship, those who lead can imagine the contribution of a specific sound to a moment of time in worship. Completely contrasting styles of music have been used successfully juxtaposed next to each other because each has contributed to the integrity of the other. The use of differing styles for the sake of making sure that everyone's individual tastes are satisfied rarely contributes to the wholeness of worship. The important questions to raise about any music of any style in worship are: what does *this* music contribute to the point of worship at which it will occur, and how does *this* music affect and relate to the other elements of worship which immediately surround it?

One of the richest and most playful sources for introducing variation into a congregation's music is in the textures of hymn singing. If we were randomly to ask people on the street to describe the sound of congregational singing, they would likely (after suggesting that it's not particularly interesting) identify elements of a melody, a supporting harmony, usually with an accompaniment of an organ. Various denominations have their own individualized versions of this stereotype, but everyone _knows_ what congregational singing sounds like! Our hearing, as well as the ears of our souls, can be awakened and quickened now and then by varying the textures of the congregational sound. The choices of when to introduce textural variation will respect the musical language of the hymn and will support and illuminate ideas from the text. Here are some possibilities:

Some Practical Applications

1. It is not necessary that all voices sing all the time in all stanzas, either in unison or in parts. There are many ways of varying the sound, based on which voices sing: women, or men, or children, or one section of the congregation, or solo and congregation combinations (a time-honored, intercultural way of singing), or choir and congregation combinations, to mention several choices. For example, there are times when a stanza might cry out for the sound of children's voices; they ought to be allowed to make such a contribution to worship. The choices must be made to support the nature of the hymn text.

Invariably, the part of the congregation which does not sing while others sing a stanza hears the hymn with different ears, ears that are invited to hear something very familiar in a new way. This _not singing_ during a stanza is different from _sitting out_ for a stanza. Neither is this an arbitrary matter or an exercise in symmetry such that a men's stanza must be balanced by a women's stanza.

An important contribution to the repertoire of choir and congregational hymn settings is the hymn concertato. An arrangement of a hymn for choir, instrumental accompaniment, and congregation, a hymn concertato gives everyone opportunity to add their own color to the experience. These are usually festive and rich settings of hymns, and could become wearisome with overuse. But for an occasional bold stroke of color in a service, little exceeds the effect of a hymn concertato.

It would come as a surprise to many singers in the congregation if only one stanza of a hymn were selected for singing at some point in a service. Or, it would signal to the worshipers that the time is running late, and they must cut out something to gain a few minutes! Johann Sebastian Bach used single stanzas of hymns powerfully at the conclusion of his cantatas. His selection of a single stanza from among many choices of the hymns which were familiar to his congregation succinctly summarizes the entire cantata's exposition and proclamation of the gospel for the day.

2. The number of parts need not be restricted to four. Many hymns, without any additions, make lovely two-part textures. Three-part harmonies, a common feature of many of the early singing school books, work well in many instances. In the singing school books, the tenors sang the melody, the basses sang the bass line, and all the women sang the tenor line an octave higher as a descant to the melody. Many folk hymns, psalm tunes, and eighteenth-century hymns work well this way. To ask women to sing all four parts, or men to do likewise, offers additional color. One can increase the number of parts by having men's and women's voices double each others' lines. Switching voice parts is another choice. Antiphonal and responsorial singing, both ancient ways of singing, might aid in calling attention to the structure of the poetry or the music of a hymn.

These are all choices for the singers of the congregation. Most congregations have instrumentalists among their numbers who could further enrich the choices of sounds. In all cases, the point of variety is not for the sake of variety itself, but rather for helping worshipers hear what they sing with attentive ears and souls.

3. The old techniques of canon, pedal and ostinato, characteristic of much of the folk music of the world, are useful in worship as well. Pentatonic melodies work as canons; some of the current hymnals include listings of hymns that can be sung in canon. If one is not sure about a hymn's usefulness as a canon, one should try it in the company of a few friends before the congregation is asked to try it! The sustained singing of one pitch (a pedal) to support the singing of a melody requires a different kind of attention to the sound—the tension between the changing pitches and the one fixed pitch creates an aural awareness which, for its simplicity, produces profoundly moving effects. The addition

of ostinatos (simple repeated patterns of rhythm or melody or harmony) can also lend a wonderful vitality to the singing of some hymns.

4. Another very old musical device, improvisation, has been temporarily lost for many of us because we have heeded the Western push toward more exact notation of music and to doing things correctly. Improvisation is not a lost art in many of the folk cultures of the world, and is indeed *the* way in which much music continues to be created, in near or complete absence of notation. Those of us who "read" music would do well to recover the ability to improvise. The connection between the spirit and the sound that is so critical to the whole art of music cannot be notated. To learn only the notation gives us partial knowledge of the art and craft of music.

Improvisation, contrary to what many might think, is not simply doing whatever one feels like. Those who improvise well work very hard to achieve a polished and satisfying level of improvisation. In the setting of congregational music, there are opportunities for many to add their own little improvisations: melodic ornaments, harmonic elaborations, conversational elements, or percussive unpitched play with sounds from the text. This is essentially the way many of us sing in the shower when we think no one can hear us! Not all hymns lend themselves equally to improvisations, for some hymns need to be sung more or less exactly as they were notated.

Improvisation is play. It is play with the elements already contained in or suggested by a tune. The ear will become a reliable guide, helping us as we improvise to find that which is appropriate to the particular style. First attempts at improvisation will of course be timid, but with time, both courage and imagination will develop satisfying and rewarding ways of singing hymns for which improvisation is in order. The freedom which is granted to the singer in the pew to add something of his or her own invention may seem very small in many respects, but it goes a long way to offer encouragement to all to sing according to the nature of the gifts they have been given.

There are a nearly infinite number of ways of accompanying hymns that can introduce vitality into our hymn singing. The organ is not, of course, the only instrument which should accompany hymns, but it does have within its power and at the hands of skilled players an enormous range of choices and colors. It is often surprising that with so many choices available, there still seems to be a standard generic sound for accompanying the singing of the congregation. The Psalms are filled with references to rich sounds of strings (bowed and plucked), brasses and winds, and percussion instruments for music in worship. Our music ought to be no less barren in its sound. In our day, with the significantly increased access to hymns from the international Christian community in modern hymnals, we ought to broaden the choices of sounds for accompaniments to include the glorious instrumental colors of Hispanic and African and Asian and native American sources. As we learn to worship surrounded by this musical wealth of the world, we learn indeed that the gospel is greater than culture, that knowing and experiencing God need not be restricted to the harmonic or pitch systems of the West or the rational thought patterns of the post-Renaissance era.

With so many choices for varying the sounds of our hymn singing, there is no reason why anyone should ever become bored. To worship in an environment that calls upon the quality and the significance of every sound honors its Creator and brings us all into that place where, as when Solomon dedicated the temple and the ark was brought in, the "house of the Lord was filled with a cloud, so that the priests could not stand to minister because of the cloud; for the glory of the Lord filled the house of God." To settle for less is not enough.

Kenneth Nafziger

214 ◆ SINGING HYMNS IN CANON

One way of singing hymns creatively involves singing in canon. This article defines what a canon is and how it can be used to foster imaginative congregational singing.

Canons are now appearing frequently in the new hymnals and materials related to congregational singing. There is a resurgence of interest in this age-old system of organizing part-singing. The canonic principle has been a part of our musical tradition for over 700 years, and most of us have had experience performing and hearing canons in both instrumental and choral music. Imagine life without the Pachelbel canon, "Row, Row, Row Your Boat," or "Three Blind Mice." There is a surprising versatility in canons that ranges from the seemingly simple stringing together of a half-dozen notes or so to very complex arrangements that pose riddles to be solved.

——— Nature and History of Canons ———

A good working definition of a canon is "imitation of a complete subject by one or more voices at fixed intervals of pitch and time" (Don Michael Randal, ed., *The New Harvard Dictionary of Music* [Cambridge, Mass.: Harvard University Press, 1986], 128). The term *canon* also refers to law; canons have always been designed so that the harmonic and rhythmic logic works as succeeding voices imitate the original voice. The challenge to a composer of a canon is to create a good melody that can stand alone, but then can be recombined with itself at certain points to produce an agreeable and logical harmony. A good canon is a balanced affair, with melodic sensibility and harmonic logic.

The earliest extant canon is the polished and elegant "Sumer is icumen in." It dates from around 1250, has a refined four-part structure, and is designed to be performed over a two-voice ostinato (or *pes,* "foot"). This canon is of English origin. Because of the preference for thirds and sixths and a major-like tonality, it has been very popular in modern times. It is one of those pleasant cases of a "first" in music that can also lay claim to being a genuine masterpiece. Students of music history and early music performing groups regularly perform this canon. The text deals with the joys of spring and is written in early English.

Since the thirteenth century, the canon has had an influence in every subsequent century. Almost every major composer has produced canons of one kind or another. The canon has been used as an academic exercise, with entire textbooks being devoted to it alone. Canonic writing is regarded as a first step in the study of counterpoint. An intellectual character dominates many canons, but the simpler canons must still exhibit good melodic and harmonic principles.

For our purposes, we are dealing with simple canons that are imitated at the unison or the octave, and with canons in which all rhythmic values remain the same. These are the vocal canons that have social interest—that is, they are canons for a group of singers to perform. There is an English tradition running from the sixteenth through the nineteenth centuries of singing "catches" and "glees," as canons and rounds were once called. These lively (and often

bawdy) canons were performed in men's clubs and were quite popular. Some of these compositions were quite demanding vocally, with ranges of a twelfth not uncommon.

A colonial American variant of this English tradition may be observed in the visual frontispiece of *The New-England Psalm Singer* of William Billings (1770; in *The Complete Works of William Billings.* Vol. 1: *The New-England Psalm Singer,* ed. by Karl Kroeger [Boston: The American Musicological Society & the Colonial Society of Massachusetts, 1981]). Here we have six men and a leader seated at a table, singing from tune-books. The six-voice canon is printed in a circle as a musical decorative wreath. In this visual presentation we may observe the seriousness of purpose and the idea of social singing. Note the presence of a leader. Billings wrote only four canons, and all are presented in this volume. One canon, "When Jesus Wept," is remarkable for its hauntingly beautiful modal melody. It is a canon that deserves modern attention.

One canon, the Tallis Canon, has been included for many years in hymnals of all sorts. It first appeared in print in the metrical Psalter of Archbishop Matthew Parker in 1567 (*The Whole Psalter Translated into English Metre* [London: Matthew Parker, 1567]; for a full and interesting account, consult Leonard Ellinwood, "Tallis' Tunes and Tudor Psalmody," *Musica Disciplina* 2 (1948): 189–195). The conventions of that time had the leading melody in the tenor and the other three parts providing a suitable harmony. In the 1567 version, the tune shows a canonic relationship between the tenor and soprano (treble). In our modern hymnals, this arrangement has been switched to allow our preference for the soprano to initiate the melody. The Parker Psalter repeats each two-measure unit, but our modern versions omit this practice. The original hymn, "God Grant We Grace, He Us Embrace," has been abandoned in most modern hymnals for "All Praise to Thee, Our God, This Night."

The canon is rich in symbolism. As an example of wholeness, each voice is fully individual, yet in combination with the other voices an ordered and meaningful pluralism emerges. The sum of the individual parts is the result of a harmonious working together and of a greater order and design. In performing canons, the circle is emphasized, and the very term *round* indicates this quality. The individuality of each voice is heightened not by isolation, but by cooperation and contrast. In performance, one hears the anticipatory refrain, as well as the echoing of the melody just completed when the canon gets underway. Finally, canons may be infinite in that they are designed to operate indefinitely. Of course there is no practicality in this, but the concept is there and has an attractive subtle implication.

Performing Canons

Turning now to the practical matter of performing canons in a church setting, three categories suggest themselves: (1) informal "sings," (2) congregational performance of canons, and (3) choir performance of canons.

Informal Sings. In the first category, informality prevails, and the best advice is to make certain that the starting pitch is more or less accurate. Picking a pitch out of the sky can lead to some uncomfortable ranges and can jeopardize the overall effectiveness. On the other hand, an impromptu singing of a well-known canon can be very meaningful in a prayer or meditation group, and as long as the pitch is reasonably set, the canon will work its own charm.

Congregational Performance. The second category deals with using canons in congregational singing. A congregation that is accustomed to a song leader has a certain advantage in that the song-leader instructs, rehearses, and directs the whole enterprise. The song leader divides the congregation into various parts, and then proceeds to perform the canon. What we have here is an expanded version of the situation depicted in *The New-England Psalm Singer.* In a congregation of men and women, one can expect the melody to be sung in octaves, creating a richness of timbre and range as the canon unfolds in its full form of all parts singing. Depending upon the proficiency of the congregation, the song leader can distribute the parts in quartets, trios, and so on, so that there is a situation in which each member of the congregation is surrounded with parts leading and parts following him or her.

A congregation that does not utilize a song leader has a unique challenge in singing canons. In this case, the music director must work within the traditions of the congregation and use resourcefulness to introduce the concept. At some point, the congregation will need instruction and rehearsal for new materials. Assuming that there is a choir, one approach is to have the choir strategically placed throughout the congregation, reinforcing each section of the canon. The choir provides the leadership necessary for encouraging each designated section of the congregation. The conclusion of canons is crucial, and care must be taken to avoid a wilted last entry.

Choir Performance. In the third category, using canons for the choir, there is a great opportunity for creativity. No hard and fast rule says that sopranos must sing the opening statement, or that tenors must then respond with the second entry. Adjusting the entries for the best effect can draw upon the resources of the choir. Singing the entire canon through in unison (and octaves) is a common practice for choirs performing canons. The opening of the canon requires strength and certainty, and the ending of the canon is critical so that the piece concludes with a balance of strength and clarity. Some canons are designed to end at a certain designated spot so that the "stringing-out" effect is avoided. Singing canons is excellent practice for choirs that are not too proficient in contrapuntal music.

With the long and distinguished history of the canon in our musical tradition, it is refreshing to see evidences of continued use of this device. With renewed attention to the canon, we can anticipate invigorated congregational singing; since the canon is the traditional gateway to counterpoint of all kinds, we can expect church choirs to enjoy and profit from singing canons. There is a rich repertoire already in existence, and this repertoire and tradition will stimulate the creation of new materials. We salute those creative musicians of the thirteenth century that laid the ground rules and those musicians in subsequent centuries that have given us a good working corpus of canons.

Carl Reed[23]

215 • How to Select a Hymnal

The hymnal that is used in worship is one of the most important elements in shaping the faith and worship of a given congregation. Therefore, great care must be given to selecting the very best hymnal for use in a congregation. The following article describes some of the most important considerations that should be considered when a congregation selects a new hymnal.

Choosing a hymnal for corporate worship is *one of the most important theological decisions a church ever makes.* If that seems an exaggeration, consider the facts: compare the number of people in a congregation who read theology to the number who sing hymns on Sunday. Week after week the hymns of your church are giving people the basic vocabulary of their faith. Hymns shape the landscape of the heart, planting images that bring meaning and order to people's understanding of life. Hymns keep congregations in touch with the history from which they have sprung, reinforcing their identity as Christians and directing their understanding of how they are to live in the world. Hymns do all of this with extraordinary power because they are coupled with music which opens the heart to the more profound resonances of reality, those motions of the Spirit that move through us in "sighs too deep for words" (Rom. 8:26).

In choosing a hymnal, we are doing more than selecting a book of songs. *We are deciding how the faith, theology, and values of the church will be celebrated and transmitted to others in the worshiping community.* Therefore, our decision must rest on something greater than personal preference. Our selection is *an act of discipleship* whose guiding goal is the praise of God.

How much easier this is to state in principle than to carry out in practice! We recall seeing at the International Hymn Convocation in Bethlehem, Pennsylvania, a video tape of Erik Routley doing a presentation on the new hymnal that he edited, *Rejoice in the Lord.* After he had carefully explained the theological basis of the selection process, the first response from someone in the audience was to ask if his favorite hymn was in the book. That is an understandable human reaction, and one that is all the more prevalent in our highly personalistic culture in which most people are "limited to a language of radical individual autonomy" (Robert N. Bellah, et al., *Habits of the Heart* [Berkeley: University of California Press, 1985], 81).

The sense of theological responsibility and corporate identity required in choosing a hymnal cannot be taken for granted. They must be consciously claimed by the selection committee before individual books are considered. Rather than assume that the committee shares a mutual understanding of your church's tradition and a common vision for your community's worship life, *begin by identifying the essential principles and characteristics of your liturgical life.* Here are two important questions to guide you:

1. What hymns and liturgical materials must be preserved (or regained!) for you to maintain your historical identity?
2. What new concerns and needs have arisen in the church and in the world that you need to incorporate into your worship?

By historical identity we mean more than simply the denomination you grew up in as children. Who are the founders of your tradition? What was at the core of their belief and practice? What were the important movements and developments in your worship tradition that have given it a distinctive shape and character? Without this knowledge you are *not* ready to begin considering a hymnal. Do not be embarrassed if you do not know this information. Many churches do not. Instead, use this opportunity to do some research. Part of your work can involve looking into the history of hymns that are central to your tradition. How did they get there? What were the movements in society or in the church that they reflect? This will raise the committee's consciousness of how hymns have functioned through history and give you a sense of the cloud of witnesses that is with you in this process. Share your new knowledge with the whole congregation through reports and education so that the selection of the hymnal becomes an occasion for the church to reclaim and strengthen its corporate spiritual identity.

Our hymnal selection process has begun by clarifying the theological nature of our task and by locating ourselves in history. We are now ready to establish criteria that will guide our decisions and become a basis for reasoned discussion about conflicting judgments. Of course, people will always have different perspectives and opinions. But if the selection committee covenants to discipline its deliberations by mutually acknowledged theological and historical criteria, it can avoid the tyranny of imposing individual and transitory preferences upon the congregation.

Although each tradition and congregation has needs that are unique, our work on worship renewal with many different denominations and parishes reveals a number of criteria that are essential to the selection process in all churches. We now want to explore these criteria and suggest how they can make the selection committee's work more incisive.

Historical, Pastoral, and Liturgical Considerations

The first major criterion that flows from our theological understanding is that a hymnal, assuming it is not a supplemental work but the major collection of congregational song for a church, must have a historical, pastoral, and liturgical breadth.

Our culture has a low historical consciousness. We are immersed in the present with little or no sense of our connection to the past. We tend to "talk of socialization rather than of tradition" (Bellah, *Habits of the Heart,* 60). But a church that loses its tradition will lose its identity. Therefore, in choosing a hymnal we must resist the temptation of reducing the church's corporate members to what we remember personally. We need to sing the hymns of our ancestors in order to recall the "dangerous memories" of history "which make demands on us." Such memories remind our generation of the sacrifice and struggle that have kept faith alive through the ages (Johann Baptist Metz, *Faith in History and Society* [New York: The Seabury Press, 1980], 109).

Sometimes people object to the ancient hymns because they are not instantly engaging and accessible. But to break our connection with history on these grounds is to accept uncritically the culture of mass media in which we are "amusing ourselves to death" by replacing the enduring values of our traditions with a "supra-ideology" of "entertainment" (Neil Postman, *Amusing Ourselves to Death* [New York: Viking Penguin, 1985], 87). It is ironic that many Christians who are upset about the loss of values in society settle for a range of congregational song whose lack of historical depth reinforces the cultural shallowness they deplore.

In our own congregation we recently sang a hymn attributed to Augustine. At first we struggled a little with the words and the setting, but quite quickly we mastered them. Then the sound filled the chapel and we sensed the cloud of witnesses (cf. Hebrews 11–12) that surrounds us as we worship. We left the service ready to face the present difficulties of our lives because of the strength that had been poured into us from the past. How wise the hymnal committee that did not limit us to what we already knew! That committee provided us with sound pastoral care. They gave us not simply what we wanted but what we needed.

Selection committees are making a decision that will shape the church's ministry to future generations of worshipers. Consider the range of pastoral and social need represented by the users of a hymnal: people in grief reaching for assurance, people filled with joy eager to sing God's praise, people in doubt seeking faith, people in moral confusion seeking clarity. Choosing a hymnal is an act of ministry that extends over time to hundreds, even thousands, of people. Like all acts of ministry, our decision requires a keen self-awareness, the ability to distinguish between personal desires and the needs of others.

It is essential to remember that our decision must allow not only for individual needs but for the corporate need of the church, especially as this is expressed in its liturgical life. Does your congregation follow the church year closely? Then a hymnal that adequately represents the liturgical year will be essential. What sacraments or ordinances are of central significance to you, and what hymnic resources do you need for them? What is unique about your local congregation? Do you want to use this hymnal at church suppers, weekday prayer meetings, or other special events?

In responding to these liturgical questions, do not limit yourself to current or past practices. One of the exciting things we have discovered in working in a highly ecumenical setting and in workshops on worship renewal with many denominations is that there is an increased openness to sharing the treasures of other traditions. Also, there has been a profound impact on many Reformed and free churches through the use of the ecumenical or common lectionary and through the scholarship of liturgical renewal. For example, we know many free churches that have started to celebrate the season of Advent as a way of countering the over-commercialization of Christmas. They now find themselves wanting more Advent hymns. In a similar fashion, many churches have begun to celebrate the Lord's Supper more frequently, or they are holding services of baptismal renewal. These are not worship fads that will quickly disappear. Rather they are substantive shifts in liturgical life that are founded upon the best scholarship and creative thinking about worship. Before choosing a hymnal, it would be helpful to research these matters through your pastor or someone from a seminary or denominational office. In this way, your choice of hymnal can become an occasion for renewing your congregation's spiritual and liturgical life.

By striving to achieve historical, pastoral, and liturgical breadth, we make a faithful witness to the fullness of God. We do not constrict ourselves to the perceptions of our era, the desires of our heart, or the limitations of our current worship practices. Instead, we draw on a spectrum of resources, moving beyond the idolatries of our subjectivity to consider the vast treasures of Christian faith through the ages.

Language: Reverent, Relevant, and Inclusive

The language of the church is always in tension with the surrounding culture. But in recent years this tension has nearly reached the breaking point. Under the stress of psychological and individualistic values, popular culture has replaced the language of transcendent values with the language of self-actualization.

So in the list of words deliberately missing from expressions of the current dominant ideology we'll find, for example, *absolutes, humility, transcendence, truth, wisdom, wonder, soul, sin, grace, gratitude,* and *God.* We've seen many of the specific ways that such words are kept out of our currently dominant discourse: the way *absolutes* are scorned by *relativist* lines, the way *wisdom* and *truth* are displaced by *opinion* and *consensus,* the way *humility* is lost sight on in *systems* thinking, the way *transcendent purpose* is rendered inoperable by *self-fulfilling evolutionary development.* . . . Nor is there any place for *sin* in a positive self-image permitting only *good feelings;* and the very concept of *soul* is lost in a psychology which, though coming in name from the Greek word (*psyche*) meaning both *self* and *soul,* confines its attention now to *self.* (Peggy Rosenthal, *Words and Values* [New York: Oxford University Press, 1984], 256)

The rampant psychological nature of our language and the attendant values that such language expresses create complex problems for the church's language. On the one hand, we need to use language that connects with people's experience and how they express themselves in daily life. On the other, we cannot afford to lose the gospel by overadopting the language of our society. For example, hymnic language that relies excessively on the first person singular—I, me, mine—tends to reinforce the self-centered values of the culture. We believe it is appropriate to have some first person singular hymns,

because hymnals are often used for private devotion as well as corporate worship. But avoid any book that is preponderantly individualistic in its theology.

To sing in the vernacular does not mean we must stoop to slang and the passing fashions of common speech. In looking at contemporary hymns in any collection, the committee needs to ask: Does this represent the way we speak and think about reality without replacing essential Christian theology and values? In short, is the language simultaneously reverent and relevant?

Any talk of relevance in the closing years of the twentieth century will inevitably lead to the issue of inclusive language: that is to say, language which does not discriminate against people on the basis of gender, race, or handicap. To call a mute person "dumb," to use "black" as a symbol of evil or to assume that "men" refers to women strikes increasing numbers of people as offensive to the wonderful news that all of us are created in the image of God. Even if we are not personally offended by this language, we need to consider those who are, and the coming generations who will be using the book we choose. Their consciousness will be even more sensitive on these matters for there is no way that the movements for civil rights and liberation are going to fade away. Whatever our politics, whatever our position in society, whatever our personal preferences, forces have broken loose that will not die and that the church's hymnody must recognize.

Generally speaking, this shift in consciousness is easier to accommodate at the level of language about humanity than about God. For many Christians language about "Our Heavenly Father" awakens and expresses the joys and yearnings of their hearts. What we need to remember is that the desire to balance such imagery with feminine language about God is in fact an effort to be faithful to the fullness of who God is and often grows out of a profound pastoral need in the human soul. This is a perspective better shared through a story than rational argument: We recall a motherless child who had been beaten by his father with a two-by-four and was subsequently taken from the home and raised by an aunt. In teaching him the Lord's prayer in Sunday School, we discovered it was impossible for him to say the words "Our Heavenly Father." He was terrified by the language. So he learned the Lord's Prayer, "Our Aunt, who art in heaven." The whole church cannot rewrite the words of Jesus' prayer to fit the experience of any one individual, but this is not the point of the story. We believe the story illustrates the exciting pastoral and theological possibilities for a church that is open to the holy and gracious power that breathes more freely through inclusive hymnic language. There are people who will be reached by the grace of God in new ways through the use of inclusive language. No major hymnal that adequately represents the church's history will be entirely inclusive, but any new hymnal that will stand the test of future generations must envince an openness to inclusive language. There are many contemporary hymn writers who are drawing more completely on the range of biblical imagery for the divine and who are developing metaphorical speech that is faithful to the Spirit and substance of God's Word. Look for their work in the books you consider.

Tunes: Singability, Enduring Quality, Variety

If it is difficult to speak about our preferences in the poetry and language of hymns, it is even more complex when it comes to their musical settings. It may seem initially that it is entirely a matter of subjective taste. But in fact there are some clear standards that can make our discussion more precise.

The first and most obvious one is that the music should be singable by the congregation. As an organist friend of ours has said, "Hymns are the congregation's chance to get in there and to sing the praise of God that is in their hearts." Singability means a maximum range of about an octave. The rhythm must not be too complex or tangled looking when it is printed on the musical staff. Remember: many congregation members do not read music or read it minimally. The melody itself must be memorable—not just a string of notes that have been chosen to go along with a progression of chords. A good melody is marked by the sequential development of a musical idea which brings satisfaction to our ears, mind and heart. Afterwards, we may find ourselves humming it repeatedly without growing tired of its progression of sound. As distinct from a merely "catchy tune," a good melody is one that grows on us. It holds up over time.

And yet this does not mean that every tune will have the same quality. That would be deadly for the spiritual life of the congregation and would completely negate our earlier goal of being pastorally inclusive. A well balanced diet is a useful analogy

for thinking about the variety of musical styles (as well as the range of texts). Most people love sweets, but we know that our health requires that we limit our intake of sugar. There is a need for protein, vitamins, and minerals in order to build up our bodies and maintain our health. The same is true of our hymnody. Chorales, broad unison tunes, meditative hymns, rousing, march-like declarations, plaintive spirituals, metrical psalms, lyric folk-like songs, carols, sturdy hymns and other styles make up the musical diet of a healthy congregation. The variety involves forms of spirituality and faith that are not constricted to a single idiom of speech and music. The variety helps to keep the soul open to the sovereign wind of the Spirit and stretches the spiritual imagination of the congregation. Therefore, do not settle exclusively for what is immediately liked by people. To do that is to leave them spiritually malnourished on a diet of "sinfully undemanding" hymnody (Erik Routley, *Christian Hymns Observed* [Princeton: Prestige Publications, Inc., 1982], 84).

Technical Considerations: Layout, Arrangement, and Service Materials

All of your work will amount to little if the worshipers must struggle to read the words and the notes. This is a book for people to use in concert with everyone else in the congregation. It is not like the book they read in their favorite easy chair where they can adjust the light or re-read what they missed. Those words and notes must be instantly available while they are standing and looking at the page in your church.

Are the words clearly and easily placed under the melody notes? We are aware of the great debate about the effect of this upon the poet's work. As creators of new hymns, we treasure language, but we still want to have the words directly under the notes. After all, the purpose is to *sing* the hymn, and everything that facilitates the heartfelt and enthusiastic singing of the congregation moves us closer to our ultimate goal of corporate worship.

That goal will be even more fully realized if there are complete and practically organized indices to the hymnal. Worship leaders are always seeking to find hymns that match the theme of the sermon or the theological emphases of the liturgical year or the pastoral needs of the congregation. Imagine yourself seeking for a particular theme: grace, comfort in time of grief, the struggle with doubt, recommitment to Christ, ecology, peace, marriage, and so on. Can you find what you need by using the index?

Furthermore, are the service materials you need in the book? Depending on tradition, people may expect to have responsive readings, sacramental rites, creeds or affirmations of faith, and psalms in their hymnal. Are these available and are they laid out in a way that makes them easy to use without intrusive instructions from the worship leader about which prayer is to be read or which response is to be offered?

Finally, how does the book feel in the hand? Is it too heavy? How does it open? Are the binding, cover and paper of sufficiently high quality? This book will get heavy physical use. It will be taken out of a pew rack and opened thousands of times over the years. Is it pleasing in appearance and format, a hymnal that invites you to sing with joy to your Lord?

The Hard-Detailed Work of Final Decisions

When you have narrowed your selection down to about three hymnals, you will need to do a thoroughly systematic analysis of each of those volumes you are considering. Every text and every tune must be evaluated. Make a chart based on the principles we have laid out in this article. Examine each hymn and decide which of the criteria it fulfills and place its number under the appropriate heading on the chart. Do not hurry to your decision. You would not buy a house without examining every room and all of the mechanicals. Surely your church's praise of God deserves equal attention. If substantial areas are not covered, these weaknesses will be visually apparent on the chart.

No hymnal will be perfect. There will be complex judgments and tradeoffs in any final decision. That is why you must take the time to make a complete assessment.

More Than a Book: The Necessity of Education and Spiritual Leadership

Because a hymnal is such a central resource for a congregation's corporate life, it is not enough simply to make a decision and present the final choice. The principles of theology and liturgical and pastoral practice that we have described here must be interpreted to the people. This education must go on during the selection process and after the book arrives. Look at this as an opportunity to revitalize your congregation's life, as a way to examine and expand their relationship to Jesus Christ, to each other, to the larger church and the world. It will never be possible to please everyone, but in our choosing a new hymnal and learning to use its resources with grace and joy we grow in Christian maturity. We are preparing for the ultimate goal of all human existence: to know and enjoy God forever.

Carol Doran and Thomas H. Troeger[24]

216 • THE RISE OF THE SCRIPTURE SONG

The Scripture song is one of the most popular musical forms used in worship today. Although scriptural texts have been the basis for the church's music throughout its history, recent historical developments have led to unprecedented use of songs based on short fragments of scriptural texts.

During the last several decades the Christian community has witnessed a vast explosion of hymnody. Some of these new songs are produced by gifted authors, people like Timothy Dudley-Smith or Margaret Clarkson, who write hymns that build on the heritage of Christian hymnody. But a larger part of this "hymn explosion" is Scripture songs—actual scriptural texts or paraphrases of Scripture set to music, often in a popular style.

Such Scripture songs are now used in almost every Christian church. You'll hear them in the "upstairs" church during worship, at church society meetings of young and old, in church concerts, and certainly at Bible-study meetings. Scripture songs have become an integral part of Christian worship.

Long Roots

Actually, the "new" Bible song is not new at all; it has long historical roots. For centuries Christians have been singing both the Psalms and other portions of Scripture. Probably most familiar of the traditional Scripture songs are the four canticles from Luke:

- Luke 1:46-55 (Song of Mary, the *Magnificat*)
- Luke 1:68-79 (Song of Zechariah, the *Benediction*)
- Luke 2:14 (Song of Angels, the *Gloria in Excelsis*)

- Luke 2:29-32 (Song of Simeon, the *Nunc Dimittis*)

The following Old Testament "lesser" canticles were also accepted by both the Eastern and Western churches during the medieval era:

- Exodus 15:1-18 (Song of Moses)
- 1 Samuel 2:1-10 (Song of Hannah)
- Isaiah 12 (First Song of Isaiah)
- Isaiah 38:10-20 (Song of Hezekiah)
- Daniel 3:52-88 [apocryphal text] (Song of the Three Young Men)
- Jonah 2:2-9 (Prayer of Jonah)
- Habakkuk 3:2-19 (Prayer of Habakkuk)

The Reformation, with its emphasis on the Word of God and on worship, produced a flood of new church songs. Many of these were psalms and Bible songs. Most of today's Christians know various hymns from this Reformation period, although they may not recognize immediately that some of these "hymns" are really old Scripture songs:

- "While Shepherds Watched Their Flocks by Night" (Luke 2:8-14—sung to a British psalm tune)
- "Comfort, Comfort Ye My People" (Isaiah 40:1—sung to a Genevan psalm tune)

After the hymns of Watts and Wesley became popular in the first half of the eighteenth century, psalm singing went into a decline in all but the most severe Reformed communities. Even during that time, however, some older Scripture songs survived, and some new ones were freshly set. In fact, the Scottish kirk produced a collection of almost seventy paraphrases of biblical texts in 1781. A number of these Bible songs still appear in modern hymnals. The following selections, for example, are included in *Rejoice in the Lord,* Erik Routley, ed. (Grand Rapids: Eerdmans, 1985):

- "O God of Bethel, by Whose Hand" (Genesis 28:10-22)
- "The Race That Long in Darkness Pined" (Isaiah 9:2-7)
- "Come, Let Us Return to the Lord Our God" (Hosea 6:1-3)

- "Behold, the Best, the Greatest Gift" (Rom. 8:31-39)
- "Ye Who the Name of Jesus Bear" (Phil. 2:5-11)

Almost a hundred years later (1880) the Irish also published a book of paraphrases. But in most countries and churches Scripture songs were no longer popular. In North America, for example, some of the storytelling black spirituals seemed to fit into the Scripture song category, but most effort was concentrated on versifying the Psalms and on writing gospel hymns and Sunday school songs.

Recent Revival

Four phenomena since 1950 have been major factors in the recent revival of Scripture songs. The first of these was the rise of the Jesus people, especially in California. The Jesus movement resulted from evangelistic work among the "hippies" of the sixties. Adherents of the movement liked folk music and had a fervor for Bible study—hence, the setting of short biblical texts to choruses and other simple verse/refrain songs, often by amateurs. The entire enterprise of Maranatha! Music is representative of this movement.

The second phenomenon is Neopentecostalism, or the charismatic movement. Less colorful but more controversial than the Jesus people, the charismatics gained influence in almost all Christian denominations (including the Roman Catholic church). Their emphasis on renewal of worship and on the use of believers' gifts produced a great host of songs, again frequently composed and written by amateurs. Important on a worldwide scale, the charismatic movement has produced some gifted musicians: David and Dale Garratt in New Zealand of *Scripture in Song* fame; and Betty Pulkingham, Jeanne Harper, and Mimi Farra, leaders of the British group Celebration Services.

The evangelical revival in the parish churches of British Anglicanism is a third factor that influenced the re-emergence of Scripture songs. Initially focused on youth, this revival movement now dominates among the lower-ranked clergy and, as such, is influential throughout the Church of England. The texts for Scripture songs contributed by this group are often cast in hymn-like metrical forms. (See the texts of Christopher Idle and Michael Perry, for example.) The musical styles range from solid hymn tunes to the British pop styles. This group's repertoire currently is becoming better known in

North America through the publication of _Hymns for Today's Church._

The Second Vatican Council, which opened the door to vernacular liturgies in the Roman Catholic church, is the fourth factor that encouraged renewed interest in Scripture songs. Shortly after the council's decision, some well-trained composers, along with various Roman Catholic priests and nuns, began writing hymns, paraphrases of biblical texts, and liturgical music with English texts, some of it in decidedly popular styles. Willard Jabusch and Ray Repp are older representatives of this tradition, which has produced Scripture songs that range from chants to folk songs. Many of these songs are also being used in Protestant communities today.

——— Evaluating Scripture Songs ———

The current revival of singing Scripture songs is certainly healthy for the Christian church as a whole. The strength of such songs is found in their biblical lyrics (is there any better way to know the Scriptures than by singing the words?) and in their emphasis on praising God in song. When used in conjunction with other psalms and hymns from the Christian tradition, such Scripture songs have their rightful place in Christian worship and nurture. And it is quite easy to point to all kinds of evidence of how God has used such a repertoire for his glory and for the edification of his people.

However, it is important to be aware of some inherent problems in Scripture songs. First of all, because these selections are often short, they usually contain only one verse of biblical text—a shortcoming that may lead to ignorance of the context of that single verse in Scripture. In the oral tradition from which many of these Scripture songs come, that problem is remedied by adding additional stanzas. Thus, the well-known ''Trees of the Field'' (with music by Stuart Dauermann) might receive the following second stanza:

> The fir and cypress trees will grow instead of
>   thorns;
> the myrtle will replace the briers and nettles:
> this will be a sign, a sign of God's mighty
>   name
> that will not be destroyed. (Isaiah 55:13,
>   versified by Bert Polman)

Other Scripture songs may have language problems: ''Thou Art Worthy'' is obviously based on the

The Symbol of St. Peter. _One of the many symbols of St. Peter shows a cock recalling his denial of the Lord._

King James Version and, as a result, incorporates language that most people do not use in conversation and worship today. The obvious solution is to update the language, making the song more meaningful to contemporary Christians. Yet many Christians will resist singing the updated version of the song: ''You Are Worthy.''

Finally, because many Scripture songs are the work of amateurs, some of them do not stand up well to repeated use. One tires easily of poorly composed tunes and trite patterns of syncopation. Songs that feature descants, rounds, or longer verse/refrain forms tend to live longer because they require more effort from the performers. Other songs are best sung once or twice—with thankfulness!—and then discarded.

Bert Polman

217 ✦ SINGING THE SONG OF POPULAR CULTURE IN WORSHIP

The growth of a huge body of contemporary songs and choruses for worship challenges each congregation to evaluate their musical repertoire and the criteria by which they

*select it. This article describes some of the theological per-
spectives important in this process and then describes many
of the types of songs and choruses that have been composed
in recent years.*

There is a growing sense among congregations
that if we are to continue as faithful stewards of the
gospel, some worship practices must change. Both
churched and unchurched persons have become
increasingly responsive to contemporary worship
music (music written in the styles of the popular
culture), and to culturally relevant worship (worship
in which words, visual images, and music stem from
the mainstream of the worshipers' experiences, in
any given culture or environment). Even so, most
congregations remain reticent to offer overtly contemporary, or even alternative worship. (Alternative
worship attempts to provide a change from what
has been done in the past, but is not necessarily
contemporary or culturally relevant.) Why the reluctance? The first part of this article will examine this
reluctance in light of our heritage, with the hope
of motivating worship leaders to consider adding
contemporary worship in their churches. The second part will discuss some criteria for using contemporary music in worship.

The Road to Recovery

In order to understand the role of contemporary
music in worship, we must first recover a full understanding of our heritage. The fact that worship leaders even question using contemporary worship
music reveals that we have lost touch with important
aspects of who we are. Our heritage is not one of
loyalty to certain types of music, but instead to the
theological commitments that guide, rather than
preserve musical developments. These commitments reflect our identity as redeemed people—
people of a new creation—people in renewal. Renewal is a process, a transforming of the old into the
new by a daily experience of the Gospel, and it
tempers everything we do. Our heritage is an orthodoxy of renewal in Christ, who calls us to disciple
all people into his renewing love. Fully recovering
this heritage will move us beyond some mindsets
about contemporary worship music that stand, like
roadblocks, in the way of the renewal process. By
identifying and examining four of the most troublesome barriers, we can begin to reclaim our heritage

of renewal as it relates to worship music and the
Gospel.

Roadblock 1: *It is the depth and complexity of music that give it meaning.* Most worship leaders are
clergy and musicians who have been trained in or
sensitized to formal music, and who generally think
of formal music as having depth and complexity. We
in this group have for the most part grown up in the
church, and this music is meaningful to us because
the gospel, with all its freedom and creative power,
was communicated through our relationships with
those who taught us the music, and through our
public experiences of the music in worship. But just
as Latin, though meaningful to a certain echelon of
clergy and scholars in 1517, was not relevant to
the mainstream German experience, formal music,
though meaningful to some of us today, is not relevant to the mainstream American experience. Large
portions of our society, both churched and unchurched, have no significant experience with the
language of formal music. Since language apart from
experience has no meaning, the use of formal music
as a conduit of the gospel is therefore limited. When
we proclaim the gospel in the musical vernacular of
those who have gathered to worship, we recover
the heritage of Martin Luther, who translated the
Bible into the language of the people because he
understood the power of the vernacular—language
that is not apart from, but related to experience. In
our zeal for the rich body of music that is meaningful to us, we must take care not to presume that
it has meaning because it has musical depth and
complexity. When music has meaning, it is because
it has been linked, in some way, with experience.

Roadblock 2: *Using popular musical styles in worship means lowering our musical standards.* We
have dubbed contemporary worship music "sentimental," "schmaltzy," and "trite," and have dismissed it because it is not "good" music. Perhaps
that is an appropriate response to some 90s music,
but certainly not to all of it. Contemporary music,
like any other genre, has its spectrum of quality.
In classical music the years have served as a sieve,
separating the poor from the best. To draw from
today's store, one must discern for one's self what is
poor and what is good. We can still apply basic
standards of composition to contemporary music,
but we must do so within the framework of popular
styles. Our reforming ancestors were open to new
styles and idioms, and unique among them, the Lu-

theran reformers respected all quality music. When we do not do the same, we close avenues of renewal. Instead of dismissing contemporary worship music, we ought to embrace it in a spirit of discernment. Rather than asking, "Is it good music?" try asking the question, "Does it have artistic and theological vitality?" This approach will better facilitate choosing contemporary music to suit the high standards of worship.

Roadblock 3: _Contemporary worship music is entertainment and therefore not worthy to communicate the Gospel._ When we use worship music written in popular styles we are not necessarily putting on shows in our churches. Music is a tool. Musicians can use it to glorify themselves, or to glorify God. Music as entertainment is a function of the musicians' intent, not a function of the musical style itself. For generations, most churches have used formal music, that music we describe as "art," or "serious" music, as a main musical diet in worship. But have we forgotten that some formal music used widely in churches was composed specifically for entertainment? Consider Handel's _Water Music,_ first performed as background music for King George's parties on the Thames River. Certainly we use it in worship with a much different focus than was originally intended! This is the transformation of secular music for sacred purposes, a process employed regularly by our reforming ancestors. It is not our heritage to disregard some music simply because it has been entertainment based, or because its style might have developed in secular arenas.

Looking back, I now realize that for some time I basically believed that one kind of music (formal) was more gospel-worthy than any other. After many years of talking to and worshiping with friends whose churches were offering alternative and contemporary worship, I finally saw that God was working in great and glorious ways in their worship experiences—without formal music! I realized I had locked the gospel in a box, along with "legitimate" music, where it was only available to those who wished to learn the combination. But all the while God was loving everywhere outside my box and moving the hearts of hurting people with music I'd dismissed as somehow cheap. God has spoken to people in a variety of ways since the beginning of creation. Why should it be any different with music, which is after all, a language of the soul?

Roadblock 4: _Adopting a contemporary sound in worship means abandoning both the liturgy and the rich musical traditions that have given it expression._ The central and distinguishing feature of liturgy is that it communicates the gospel. We gather weekly and participate in the drama of our salvation through prayer, praise, confession and pardon, and sharing Word and sacraments. These experiences are the essence of liturgy and are expressed through language. That language may be the ancient Mass sung in plainsong, or it may be colloquial English sung in popular styles. It might be contemporary praise choruses, chosen to engage us in confession and prayer, or it might even be movement and dance. (A praise chorus is a short refrain or simple song, often with a biblical text, used as the main body of music in most contemporary worship services throughout the country; praise choruses are particularly easy to sing, and often have accompaniments idiomatic to popular stylization.) Whatever the language, it must be relevant to the experience of those worshiping, so they can fully participate in the action of liturgy—the communication of the gospel. Adopting popular styles in worship does not mean we have to abandon liturgy. Quite the opposite: it means that liturgy, because it is expressed in relevant language, will be open to more people as the living, dynamic, public experience of the gospel that it is meant to be.

What, then, of our rich musical traditions? I am not even remotely suggesting that we abandon our musical traditions. Where traditional worship is reaching people, it should continue. I am, however, suggesting that churches offer culturally relevant worship in addition to traditional worship. Because they were committed to renewal, our reforming ancestors both developed the music of their past and embraced the music of their time. They were also committed to the ultimate function of music as the proclamation of the gospel. This, more than any other value, invites us to share the Good News in the widest possible variety of musical styles, both past and present. Victor Gebauer stresses the importance of just such a variety: ". . . we need each other's songs in a sinful world if we are to piece together even a few shreds of our various, tattered perceptions. . . . Church music, then, will embrace all these songs if its own voice is not to be so particular that it becomes bound to a single cultural imperative" ("Seeking Common Roots Amid Diverse Expressions and Experiences," a lecture given at

Lutheran School of Theology at Chicago, October 1991). If we are bound to anything, it is to the gospel, which in turn frees us through the renewal process. It's time to recover that renewal process in our approach to worship music. Christ will transform our ways and make a new creation—for all people.

New Songs for Worship: Do They All Sound Alike?

It must be emphasized that planning and sustaining contemporary worship is more than simply using new music. It involves a commitment to discussion and decisions about such things as preaching style, the visual aspects of a service, the style of transitions within worship, how a congregation does and does not use ritual, the physical layout of worship space, the design and verbiage of the bulletin (if one is used), and the language used throughout the service. Congregations who wish to add alternative worship will need to experience it in other places, and then begin to develop a style and approach that will be the best proclamation of the gospel for their particular area, given their particular resources. One of the first steps in that process is understanding the important role that music plays in worship, and knowing how to judge which music is most suitable and why.

The most significant musical differences between contemporary and traditional worship are those involving instrumentation and song selection and style. In the mainstream of contemporary worship practice, core instrumentation most often involves electronic keyboard, electric guitar and bass, acoustic guitar (usually amplified), acoustic or electronic drums, and a mixed vocal ensemble of two to eight singers. The vocal ensemble is vital, because it leads the congregation in contemporary worship just as a skillful organist leads the congregation in traditional worship. In this sense, the vocal ensemble is part of the instrumentation. If you hope to use the musical language of the unchurched people in your area, then it is important to achieve an instrumental sound which speaks that language. Again, mainstream practice points to a light pop or pop-rock style. The degree to which we experience this style will depend upon things like the intensity of the drums, whether we hear acoustic or electric guitars (and their complementation of effects), the notation of the electric bass (for example, whole notes vs. driving eighths), and so forth. Using these and other

principles, one can stylize songs in many ways and develop variety even within a particular song genre.

Although song literature will vary some, praise songs tend to be the main musical diet in congregations that are highly sensitive to unchurched visitors. There are many moving praise songs for use in worship, and they can be variously stylized. There are also some new varieties of songs available, which congregations are using increasingly.

Praise Songs. Across denominational lines, praise songs account for most of the music used in contemporary worship, and it is this body of songs that classically trained musicians tend to find least palatable. Praise songs are short, and musically simple, often with a Bible verse as text. If we are willing to adapt ourselves to the use of praise songs, we will discover that there are some well crafted pieces with artistic and theological integrity. It is true one must look diligently to find such songs.

Praise songs can function in a variety of ways, most obviously, for congregational praise singing. In the absence of a sung liturgy they are powerful when integrated into the liturgical structure of a service. They are effective in moments of entrance, meditation, introduction (for instance, before a sermon or message), confession, pardon, prayer, affirmation of faith, and blessing. At first hearing we may say, "But they all sound ALIKE!" I remember saying the same thing in the eighth grade when my piano teacher played a recording of Chopin's nocturnes for me. After learning several of them, and listening to the recording over and over, my opinion changed. Suffice it to say that experience with music, and continued exposure to it, hone the skill of discernment.

In order to use praise songs well, we need to understand their limitations—one of which is the lyrics. There are more praise songs on Old Testament texts than on gospel centered texts, which presents a particular challenge if we are to keep the communication of the gospel as the central feature of liturgical worship. Musicians and pastors often express a concern over a tendency within praise song literature toward "glory theology": the exuberance expressed in many lyrics does not embrace the whole of the human experience and the need for Christ's saving power. Addressing this concern is simply a matter of finding those praise songs expressive of the gospel. Also, images for God are limited. God is most often a King on a throne, to whom we bow down. It is rare to find lyrics describing God with the many other rich images in Scripture, such as servant, midwife, or mother hen. Ironically, many newly composed songs use old King James texts. If one is trying to use relevant language in worship, then songs with the pronouns like thee and thyself, and verbs with -*est* endings automatically confuse the issue of relevant language.

Another concern is lack of inclusivity. God is usually a *him,* and has come to save *man.* It is possible to contact the copyright holders to inquire about changing pronouns and nouns to be inclusive. They are usually agreeable to it as long as the general meaning of the phrase does not change. Should you desire to make such a change, you must obtain permission in whatever manner each copyright holder requires. Several of the companies that are currently publishing volumes of praise songs are Maranatha! Music, Word Music, Mercy Publishing, and Hosanna Integrity.

Songs of Christian Artists. In the worship planning process, songs of current Christian artists are often chosen for congregational singing. Depending upon the song, this may or may not be a good practice. In each case we must ask ourselves if the song allows the congregation to sing easily together. Many such songs are born of a soloistic practice, and although wonderful for their stylistic relevance and powerful lyrics, do not particularly enable group singing. When that is the case, it is better to use a soloistically styled song with a soloist, and honor the ministry of congregational singing with songs that a large group can truly sing. In some songs, the refrain may be well suited to congregational singing, while the verses are better suited for a soloist or small ensemble. This type of musical dialogue can be uniquely effective in worship. In order to choose songs of Christian artists that are best for congregational singing, we need to first consider the nature of the music and then ask the question, "To what type of singing does this music lend itself?"

Worship Songs: Light Pop-Rock Style. There is a new body of worship songs now available in several collections. These songs differ from classic praise songs in significant ways. They tend to be more complex than praise songs, although they are singable and easy to learn. They are in a light pop style (both fast and slow tempos), and melodies are creatively diverse and catchy, with accompaniments using a broad harmonic vocabulary. Many have a

stanza/refrain form, and others are through-composed. They are liturgical in the sense that they not only invite, but enable the congregation to sing. Among many other things, repetition and sequence are often used brilliantly. A melody with a somewhat complex rhythmic structure will be repeated in a way that the worshiper "gets it"—but without suffering artless reiteration!

Lyrics are poetically expressive, cover a wide spectrum of images, describe the breadth of the Christian experience, and have become increasingly inclusive. There are songs to work within every aspect of a worship service, since many of them have been written in liturgically oriented congregations. Their use is by no means limited to liturgical churches, however. Some fine examples of the work described above are the songs of Handt Hanson and Paul Murakami, available through Prince of Peace Publishing, Burnsville, Minnesota, and the songs of Larry Olsen and David Brown, available through Dakota Road Music, Sioux Falls, South Dakota.

New Hymns. A new style of hymnody began to develop in the early seventies that has come into full maturity over the past twenty years. The music does not draw upon the idioms, motifs, and sonorities of light pop-rock, but instead evokes a sense of updated folk music, with layered vocal harmonies and long lyrical melodies adding an almost classical feel. Although these hymns do not sound like the many classic hymns the church has sung for generations, their function in worship is the same—thus their categorization as hymns instead of songs. Again, most of these pieces were written for use in liturgical churches, and for that reason, there are new hymns to suit a broad range of worship needs. There are many new psalm arrangements available for congregational singing as well. They are often designed for a soloist (or small ensemble) and congregation to sing in dialogue. Lyrics are poetic and widely descriptive. Many of the new hymns call for optional solo instruments, always with flexibility in instrumentation. This body of music is particularly useful in helping congregations who wish to add alternative worship, but are skittish about change because of strong traditional practices. In one sense, these hymns are a kind of musical middle ground. Although they are widely singable, many are composed in triple meter. This is a challenge if you choose to use a drummer, as it takes a highly skilled percussionist to play triple meter without creating a feeling of a beer garden omm-pah-pah. Several of the many fine writers whose work defines this genre are Michael Joncas, Marty Haugen, Daniel Schutte, and Carey Landry. Sources for new hymns are GIA Publications of Chicago, and North American Liturgy Resources, to name only a few.

Combining New Sounds with New Songs and Octavos. There are plenty of ways to use new worship songs and praise songs with culturally relevant instrumentation. For instance, a slow worship song with an underlying pop rhythm and chordal structure could be offered in worship with a saxophone on melody, perhaps while the offering is being received. Once the offering is received and dedicated, the congregation then joins in to sing the song before prayer. Or, a praise song may be introduced with lead guitar on melody, using distortion effects. In any case, one must plan instrumentation with great care. It is the structure and style of the music, the worship moment, and the area in which you are ministering that determine the sound which is most appropriate at any given time.

Increasingly, companies are producing octavos which lend themselves to this type of varied use. Such pieces are not necessarily suited to congregational singing, but provide wonderful special music for contemporary (and even traditional) worship. Many moderate tempo pieces are enriched by adding a synthesizer using strings on sustained inverted triads (which the keys player could improvise), and an amplified acoustic guitar picking eighth note subdivisions in the score. In more upbeat music, the guitar may sound better strumming, with a synthesizer set on an electric piano sound, playing the score as written. Such attention to instrumentation can produce beautiful results that are also very expressive of popular styles. When expanding instrumentation from a piano score, it's important to communicate with the copyright holder. In some rare cases they may consider it an arrangement, and set a fee.

Companies are also producing more arrangements which solidly combine old texts (and often tunes) with new musical styles and structures. These are particularly conducive to the type of creative approach described above. For example, "All Good Gifts," by Lon Beery, Beckenhorst Press, is a song with many pop elements in its sonorities and rhythmic structure. Yet its classic words ("We plow the fields and scatter . . .") and sturdy through-composed nature give it added integrity. Another example, "Praise to the Lord," arranged by Tom Anderson, Word Music, begins with the Doxology in slow tempo and moves into a fast paced version of the hymn with an arpeggiated, rhythmically varied accompaniment, reminiscent of George Winston or David Benoit. It works well on the piano, but the nature of the arrangement begs for synthesizer. It is a brilliant and creative blending of a wonderful, timeless hymn with new musical motifs. Two more terrific octavos are "Shout For Joy" by Stan Pethel, Hope Publishing, and "Let There Be Praise" by Dick and Melodie Tunney, arranged by Sheldon Curry, Laurel Press. These and many others like them represent contemporary music that is well crafted in every way, and that lends itself to a variety of uses in worship.

Going Forward . . .
The Holy Struggle

It's easy to avoid thinking about contemporary worship simply because the amount of printed songs is so overwhelming! But getting started is a matter of doing several basic things. Get a variety of song books and resources and begin reading through them over and over. Visit as many churches offering alternative worship as you can. Listen to tapes of the above resources, and begin to open yourself up to the style and expression of the music. Attend a major church conference with workshops on alternative worship (this is a tremendous help). And most importantly, own the struggle. There are many questions, concerns, and polarities in views about worship practice and theology, but they indicate exciting opportunities for growth, renewal, and refreshment. I am convinced that like Jacob wrestling the angel, if we are willing to wrestle honestly and humbly with the worship issues that are before us, God will bless that struggle to both affirm and renew the church.

Dori Erwin Collins

218 • How to Use Scripture Songs in Traditional Worship

Scripture songs may be integrated into traditional approaches to planning a worship service in ways that will enliven the service without disrupting its logical order and flow.

The suggestions that follow may help you make Scripture songs a more meaningful part of your worship liturgy.

1. Use a short Scripture song as a "frame" around another psalm or hymn, similar to the alleluia frames found in Psalms 103–106.

The following Scripture songs also make good "frames":

- "He Is Lord"
- "Rejoice in the Lord Always"
- "Our God Reigns" (refrain only)

Be sure that the Scripture song and its companion psalm or hymn are in the same key or in a suitably related key that permits direct transition from one song to the other; transpose one of the songs if necessary.

2. Choose a Scripture song just as you choose other psalms and hymns—paying careful attention to its place in the liturgy and to the season of the church calendar. Note how the following songs fit into the liturgy:

- "This Is the Day"—at the beginning of worship
- "Arise, Shine"—at the Service of the Word (or during Epiphany)
- "Jesus, Remember Me"—as a response in a litany-style prayer
- "The Lord Bless You and Keep You"—at the close of worship

3. Add more stanzas, particularly to songs in which there is already some repetition of text. For example, add a second stanza to "I Will Sing of the Mercies," or add other first lines to "Those Who Wait upon the Lord," as follows:

Those who love the God of grace shall renew . . .
Those who love a life of love shall renew . . .
Those who die on the march shall renew . . .
   [funerals]
Those who offer gifts of praise shall renew . . .
Those who grow in his ways shall renew . . .
   [profession of faith]
Those who pray "Come Quickly Lord" shall
   renew . . . [Advent]

4. As with all other church music and congregational song, bring creativity and variety into the singing of Scripture songs. Make full use of musical features such as descants or rounds. Occasionally sing select songs in a medley style. And, if the group sings the same Bible song several times in sequence, introduce different levels of dynamics (louds and softs) and provide occasional changes in harmonization and/or accompanying instruments (including Orff instruments and folk instruments in smaller settings).

The contemporary revival in singing Scripture songs is a powerful sign that the Holy Spirit is still making fresh the meaning of the inspired Scriptures to the lives of God's people. When the pitfalls of amateurism, poor leadership, and undue commercialization begin to loom larger, then a simple but well-crafted and wisely used Scripture song may help all of us: "Seek Ye First the Kingdom of God."

Bert Polman[25]

219 • INVOLVING THE CONGREGATION IN PRAISE AND WORSHIP

Worshipers need to learn how to praise God in the freedom of the Spirit. Reflecting the insights of the charismatic tradition, this article directs the church musician toward a number of different ways to lead the congregation in the praise of God.

As we move our congregations into higher and deeper times of praise and worship, there are a variety of types of scriptural songs we can sing to the Lord. These various songs will help keep our times of praise and worship refreshing and avoid lapsing into "rut-routines." Our job as Christians is to maintain good communication and a pure walk with the Lord. Let's remember that God is looking for consecrated vessels that are continually able to abide in his power and anointing for the edifying of his church.

Praise and Worship as a Lifestyle

Don't ignore the obvious. The most common type of singing to the Lord is maintenance of a lifestyle of praise and worship. It is a life full of singing praises and worship that last throughout the day. These songs may be Scripture songs, choruses, or hymns, but they should give expression to that which is flowing from our heart. Psalm 22:3 (KJV) says, "but thou art holy, O thou that inhabitest the praise of Israel." As we sing to the Lord, we create a flow with the Holy Spirit, a time of intimate communion with him that transcends our normal prayers. There is the element of having a song sung continually from our mouth.

David encourages us to worship the Lord often: "Seven times a day" he says he praises God (Ps. 119:164). As I pondered this Scripture a thought came to me of how this could work. Praising God seven times a day could effectively be done in the following manner:

1. Before breakfast
2. Mid-morning
3. Before lunch
4. Mid-afternoon
5. Before dinner
6. Mid-evening
7. Before bed

By taking regular praise breaks during our day we would become more aware of God's direction in our lives. The more we acknowledge what God has done for us, the more we realize how great God is, and the more we praise him. It becomes a constant cycle.

It isn't only individually that we need time in the secret place. We also need a meaningful family worship time that is set apart from everything else. Additionally, joining in corporate worship in a local church is a scriptural priority.

Singing in the Spirit

Psalm 33 says, "Rejoice in the Lord, O ye righteous: for praise is comely for the upright. Sing unto him a new song: play skillfully with a loud noise" (vv. 1-3).

Singing in the Spirit is a natural part of our worship time as a church. Tongues are edifying whether spoken or sung. Singing a new song can also be done "with understanding," that is in one's native language. Both of these types of songs to the Lord take an unction of the Holy Spirit. They flow out of our inner person unto the throne of grace.

Singing Meditation

While the musicians play a simple chord progression, encourage the congregation to take a favorite Bible passage, a psalm, or a verse that is important to them, and then begin singing it over and over again. It might be chanted by some. This is much like regular biblical meditation only you are singing.

You can do this for 5 to 15 minutes at a time even in a public meeting. Start with a musical foundation of three or four chords like C-F-G. Then with this "musical bed" have the congregation begin singing over it.

Afterwards ask for people to come up and share what they experienced. Many have said that they've never had such revelation about a verse as during this time. Psalm 4:4 (KJV) says, "Commune with your own heart upon your bed, and be still," which encourages us to meditate. This time can yield beautiful moments of corporate expression.

Singing Intercession

While singing in the Spirit or while singing the words of a song, cease using those familiar words and begin to intercede using the same music. Call upon the Lord and ask him for help for other people's situations. Sing out healing for them or for their families—whatever the needs are that you know about.

Music alone can be intercession. Prayerful musicians can break the yoke of bondage, just as David did for Saul (1 Sam. 16). As they play, the anointing on their music can be the power that breaks down the gates of brass. Music in praise and worship can cause people to be brought to salvation, even without an altar call. Without any preaching, music—through anointed musicians and singers—has drawn people out of their seat and up to the front. It is a powerful influence. Allow time for the musicians to play as they are led. Healings, too, have resulted from anointed worshipful music. This is true musical intercession.

Singing Songs of Deliverance

Psalm 32:7 (KJV) says, "You compass me about with songs of deliverance." The power of God's unction and anointing is in our mouths. We need to learn to sing deliverance from our bondage as we mature in the Lord. The songs of deliverance are twofold: (1) for yourself and (2) for others. They can be sung either corporately or individually. "You compass me about" gives us the faith promise that we are surrounded by God and can expect protection from our enemies.

You can sing for deliverance as David did, or rejoice after deliverance, as did Deborah and Barak (Judges 5). Our songs of praise cause the devil to flee. Mature Christians can sing their own freedom from bondage. A young believer should call upon others to help.

Singing the Pastor's Message

The minstrels and song leaders sit up front where they can concentrate on what the pastor teaches. As they listen to the message, they write a song containing an abbreviated version of the message. At the end of the sermon, they sing the new melody and words to the congregation. One thing you can do to teach the new songs is to have the singer sing a line and the congregation repeat it. This responsive type of song helps get the Word into their hearts. Then the people can go home and sing the message all week long.

When you first implement this songwriting concept be sure to have a system of checks and balances. A potential song may be checked after the meeting but does not have to be performed. At the beginning many of the songs may be unusable in their original form but can be reworked for future use. Through experience the songwriters will develop a greater ability to write a quality spontaneous song which encapsulates the pastor's message.

Singing Famous Songs of the Lord

This approach is specifically for the trained singer or musician. Take the songs right out of the Bible and let the musicians make up melodies to the words, then sing them. Some examples are the songs of Moses, of Deborah, and of Barak, and songs of David. Some of the songs are really long so they can be in parts. Develop these and have the people meditate on them.

Songs of communion with the Lord are biblical expressions of our spiritual walks and should be entered into freely. It's time we tore down the walls and barriers that limit us. We must embrace reality. We are the sons and daughters of God; we have the privilege to come before his throne in lamentation, intercession, deliverance, and victory!

Let's praise him!

Kent Henry

220 • THE FUNCTION OF PRAISE SONGS IN AFRICAN-AMERICAN WORSHIP

The praise song is integral to worship in the black tradition, expressing Spirit-filled praise and demanding the full participation of the worshiping community. Black praise singing is also expressive of themes important in black Christian experience and in the theology that has been formed out of this experience.

Black religious music and black theology are correlative in meaning. From the beginning, black music has sprung from black theology as a meaningful and life-affirming medium in black experience. This article intends to take a brief look at this interplay between music and theology as revealed in the black Pentecostal praise song.

Luther Gerlach and Virginia Hine have studied Pentecostalism as a mode of social transformation involving a seven-step commitment process required to recruit, convert, and maintain members. The two steps most germane to the Pentecostal praise song are the original commitment event and the orientation process that features group support for modified cognitive and behavioral patterns (Luther P. Gerlach and Virginia H. Hine, _People, Power, Change: Movements of Social Transformation_ [Indianapolis: Bobbs-Merrill, 1970], 110).

Pentecostals call the most significant event effectuating commitment "baptism of the Holy Ghost." Following the acceptance of Christ as their personal Savior, believers are encouraged to seek this experience by prayerfully petitioning God to "fill them" with the Spirit. As recorded in the Book of Acts, the initial sign of Spirit baptism is "speaking with other tongues" (glossolalia; cf. Acts 2:1-13).

In addition to expecting new members to be Spirit-baptized, the established Pentecostal community maintains a strict code of personal conduct. One of the traditional ways black Pentecostals communicate this expectation to new members is through their praise songs. New members do more than simply learn the words of praise songs by joining the community in choruses of faith affirmations; they also learn by rote the theological meanings of the songs and the behavioral expectations of their new religious community. Gerlach and Hine claim that the popular aphorisms contained in black Pentecostal songs are "conceptual models which spring into life and take on deep meaning" (Gerlach and Hine, _People, Power, Change,_ 162). Aphorisms such as "I have crossed the separating line," which abound in praise songs, are not mere pat phrases. They represent the "cognitive building blocks" of Pentecostal belief because they are saturated with theological meaning (ibid.).

In part, what new members in the black Pentecostal church are oriented to is the black religious worldview and the theological reflection that sustains it. Black theology is a defiant act of faith and human will. When black people decided to interpret the Scriptures so that the words would speak to their particular experiences, they concluded that God had not intended for them to be slaves (James H. Cone, *God of the Oppressed* [New York: Seabury Press, 1975], 8). Black religious music is a fascinating artifact of this theological dynamic because it demonstrates how black people, for the purpose of their liberation, reinterpreted their religion designed to reinforce white supremacy. Born in black people's struggle for survival and liberation, the theology of the black worldview continues to transform the meaning of songs black Pentecostals adapt from the white religious tradition.

Conversely, members of other denominations, black and white, have hardly begun to appreciate the musical contribution black Pentecostals have made to the Christian hymnic tradition. Like other denominational groups composing the black church, black Pentecostals have long sung hymns by white hymnists, but the praise songs were created out of the Pentecostals' own unique style of worship. Improvisatory in nature and simple in structure, these songs of praise are rendered differently each time they are sung. Black Pentecostals sing their praise songs in a way similar to the way jazz musicians play their instruments. Just as jazz musicians have an inventory of jazz riffs and chord progressions to call upon, so have the Pentecostal praise leaders an inventory of familiar calls at their disposal for leading the singing of praise songs. Black Pentecostals learn their praise songs by rote via the medium of oral transmission, and it is the spiritual mood of the moment that determines what is sung or played. Walter Hollenweger asserts that black Pentecostals are duplicating the way primitive Christians transmitted theology, through oral channels ("Creator Spiritus," *Theology* 47 (1978): 35).

An integral aspect in the improvisatory singing of the praise song is call and response, the African-derived pattern that survived the cultural transition to America. Jack Daniel and Geneva Smitherman define call and response as

the verbal and nonverbal interaction between speaker and listener in which each of the speaker's statements (or "calls") is punctuated by expressions ("responses") from the listener. As a fundamental aspect of the black communications system, call-and-response spans the sacred-secular continuum in black culture. . . . More than an observed ritual in Church services, call-and-response is an organizing principle of black Cultural Reality which enables traditional black folk to achieve the unified state of balance or harmony which is essential to the Traditional African World View. (Jack L. Daniel and Geneva Smitherman, "How I Got Over: Communication Dynamics in the Black Community," *Quarterly Journal of Speech* 62:1 (1976): 26–39)

In black Pentecostal praise songs, the very act of punctuating the singer's call with a unified response instills a forceful sense of allegiance to the theology of the song being sung. Call and response binds all participants together in meaning and purpose. Observe, as an example of call and response, the following words of a favorite black Pentecostal praise song, "On My Way to Heaven and I'm So Glad":

> Goodbye, goodbye, I've left this world behind.
> I've crossed the separating line.
> I've left this world behind.

In the call and response mode, the song is sung like this:

Leader:	Goodbye
Congregation:	Goodbye
Leader:	Goodbye
Congregation:	Goodbye
All:	I've left this world behind.
	I have cross the separating line.
	I have left this world behind.

The following are the words of another favorite praise song. As in the previous song, the worship leader calls out various verses to which the congregation responds:

Leader:	I'm a soldier.
Congregation:	In the army of the Lord.
Leader:	I'm a soldier.
Congregation:	In the army.
Leader:	If I die, let me die.
Congregation:	In the army of the Lord.
Leader:	If I die, let me die.
Congregation:	In the army.

As these examples illustrate, praise songs are meditations on simple theological themes which help orient new members to the worldview and theology of black Pentecostalism. Praises to God for salvation, explications of Christ's atonement, and pledges of determination to continue the Christian life are among the familiar themes in these songs. So simple are the songs, and so familiar are their themes to Pentecostals, that the creative worship leaders can "call" a medley of songs on a particular theological theme without even breaking the tempo between songs. This makes the worship leader an important factor in the instruction and orientation of new members—a teacher of sorts.

How does the praise song serve black Pentecostal theology? The praise song was never intended to be an exhaustive explication of Christian theology. It is a song that thanks God for the salvation promised to those believers who are faithful and Spirit-filled. In this regard, the praise song is more concerned with rejoicing over salvation than with plotting out the salvation process. The latter—the more in-depth doctrinal aspects of black Pentecostal theology—are taught to members in the contexts of Bible study, Sunday school, and preaching. But the praise song has prepared the way for this more formal instruction. The praise song, then, can afford to concentrate on worshipful acts and on orienting new members (and reorienting old ones) to the more common tenets of Pentecostal belief: the praise of God and human submission to the indwelling Holy Spirit.

Black Pentecostals transmit their theology through the oral channel of praise songs to communicate group values and expectations to individual members. Using song to teach group expectations and to engender worshipful solidarity is an aspect of communal life that has been maintained in black culture from its traditional African religious roots.

Michael G. Hayes[26]

221 • THE BIBLICAL CANTICLES IN WORSHIP

Canticles (from the Latin canticum, _song) are biblical poems with powerful imagery and heightened emotional content. They are similar to psalms but are taken from other books of the Bible. Canticles formed the backbone of the daily office and have often been set to music. Indeed, they are among the richest repertories in all of music._

Canticles are divided into two groups. The three "greater" or gospel canticles are all taken from the Gospel according to St. Luke. They are the _Magnificat anima mea Dominum,_ also called the Canticle of the Blessed Mary; the _Benedictus Dominus Deus Israel,_ also called the Canticle of Zachariah; and the _Nunc Dimittis,_ also called the Canticle of Simeon. (Canticles are still customarily referred to by their traditional Latin titles even when the texts are given in English.) In the Roman monastic hours these formed the climax of Vespers, Lauds, and Compline, respectively. In liturgical denominations today they may be found in Morning and Evening Prayer. The fourteen so-called "lesser canticles," such as the _Jubilate_ and the _Benedicite, omnia opera Domine_ are taken from the Old Testament and the Apocrypha. In the Roman church these were sung at Lauds, one set of seven reserved for the weekdays through the greater part of the year, a second set of seven to be substituted during Lent. The Anglican and Lutheran usage has assigned most of the lesser canticles to Morning Prayer. While any canticle may be sung at Evensong or Vespers, the Canticles of Mary and of Simeon are usually reserved for evening. Nowadays other traditional songs of praise, such as the _Gloria in excelsis_ with its biblical textual elements, or texts from the Orthodox liturgy may be included among the canticles.

Musical settings of the canticles range from simple formulaic music such as plainsong or Anglican chant (indeed, the same music as for the psalms is suitable) to compositions of considerable length and complexity, many accompanied only by organ, still others by orchestra. Among the largest and best-known examples of the latter are the two related settings of the Magnificat by J. S. Bach using the Latin text. There are countless other settings from all periods and in all styles. When sung to simpler settings an antiphon is often used. This is an appropriate and relevant text set to contrasting music which frames the verses of the canticle.

From the sixteenth century on, canticles have often been composed in a complete set (sometimes with the music required for the Holy Eucharist) called a _service._ (In the sixteenth and seventeenth centuries a "short service" was one which was more brief and in a syllabic style while a "great service" was more extended, richer, and more contrapuntal. An _evening service_ consists of musical settings of the _Magnificat_ and the _Nunc Dimittis._ A complete service includes most of the items required for an entire day. Often all of these are in the same key, and the service is, for example, commonly referred to as "Stanford in C." In the twentieth century, especially in the United States, it has been more usual to compose single canticles rather than complete services. Composers of our century have tended to produce musical settings of canticles which are rather extended and suitable for festivals, often with the accompaniment of a very large orchestra. Benjamin Britten's *Te Deum* and William Walton's Coronation *Te Deum* are typical.

Canticles are among the most appropriate texts for the worship service even when there is no prescribed order. Since, traditionally, canticles follow Scripture readings, it is particularly effective to accompany a reading from the Old Testament with the singing of one of the lesser canticles, and a New Testament text with a gospel canticle.

Perhaps it is worth adding that the Song of Solomon or Song of Songs is sometimes called the Book of Canticles. Historically, it was an important source of texts for musical setting, most notably motets from the later middle ages and the Renaissance.

Canticles form a truly substantive repertoire of service music of great variety, power, and beauty.

Philip Beggrov Peter

222 ✦ The Anthem in Worship

Anthems sung by choirs and soloists have a long history in Christian worship. Many of the world's finest composers have written anthems for use in worship. Yet the best anthems are those which unite such musical genius with concern for the text that is sung and the function of the anthem in the context of the entire worship service.

Choral music is used in worship by choirs of all sizes and in almost all denominations. Many churches have a long-standing tradition of thoughtfully prepared anthems contributing to the worship service, while others approach choral music as an afterthought. The goal of all worship leaders should be the former; with planning, this is a goal that can be achieved in churches with even limited resources.

Before discussing the role of choral anthems in worship, it might be helpful to understand the long history of choirs contributing to worship.

—— History of the Anthem in Worship ——

Church musicians and publishers today use the term *anthem* in a general way to mean choral music

of many different voicings and accompaniments, but the term *anthem* does have a specific historical meaning. The anthem had its origin as English choral music used in the Anglican church nearly from its inception. These anthems, in turn, were based on the Latin motet used in the Roman rites. The Latin motets were one of the earliest forms of polyphonic music (*c.* 12th cent.), and they originated as a polyphonic interpretation of the chants which they were used with. In the 1400s, the Latin motet became more a choral composition on a scripturally based text, and was often written with four, six, or more voice parts.

In the Reformation brought about by Henry VIII, the language of worship was brought into vernacular English. This necessitated a change from the Latin both in Scripture and song, and thus the anthem was born. Actually, there are a few examples of English choral music before the Reformation, but liturgical change was the prime impetus for the outpouring of compositions known as anthems. Tye and Tallis were two of the first composers to write what we are referring to as an English anthem. Their compositions are typically rather rhythmically square and conceived more by their harmony than their melody. Some of this can be attributed to the style of the time, but much of it is also due to the spaces in which these anthems were sung: cathedrals with a very live acoustic and long reverberation. The earliest writers began by giving a great deal of consideration to the sound of sung text and its pronunciation, and this emphasis is one we would do well to consider in the performance of choral music today.

The choral tradition was pushed forward by the Reformation, especially in the Lutheran tradition. Luther loved the historic church's music, and choirs in the early Lutheran churches began to sing the main parts of the service, the Mass, though once again in the vernacular. This provided an opportunity for composers of the day to provide new music for the church.

J. S. Bach became one of the greatest forces in church music through his compositions, and even his church compositions were all composed out of need (without denying his inspiration). Church music is a practical matter of facilitating worship, and the history of the church in the last several centuries is full of compositions and choirs meeting the needs of the people and serving the focus of worship. The gospel hymns of Sankey, and the evangelistic focus of the Wesleys and their hymns fit the needs of a particular style of worship. The same is also true for spirituals, whose spontaneity and simplicity were required by the style of worship of the slaves: they often worshiped in the fields with their singing and improvising.

Eighteenth-century America saw the publication of many collections for use in worship beyond the metrical psalters that had long been in use. Tunebooks such as *Kentucky Harmony* (1816) and *Sacred Harp* (1844) provided for all the musical needs of a congregation, both congregational and choral. It must be understood that singing was a primary form of entertainment among people of all social situations during this time, and the interest in singing was not limited to the church, as it often is today. Even the secular collections from the New England singing schools contained many anthems with scriptural basis. In the United States before the turn of the twentieth century, there were many publishers producing traditional anthems and others publishing gospel music for use in churches, and everything in-between.

The publishing of anthems as we know them and refer to them today basically began with Novello and Company in London in the 1940s. They began the publishing of octavo choral music to allow choirs to purchase individual titles. This had the effect of making the music sometimes more disposable in nature, and pieces were more able to exist on their own merits. Oxford University Press is another example of a notable publisher involved for well over a century in the publishing of choral music used for worship.

The twentieth century has seen the flourishing and demise of many publishers of choral music for the church. Much of this is due to changes in society and worship, yet diminishing musical literacy has also played a part. And still, there are denominational publishers such as Augsburg/Fortress, Concordia, and GIA; long-lived, independent publishers such as Hope Publishing Co., Lorenz, Oxford University Press, and Sacred Music Press; the praise-and-worship publishers typified by Word, Inc.; and the newer independent publishers such as Randall Egan, Hinshaw, MorningStar Music Publishers, and Selah Publishing Co.

—— The Role of the Anthem in Worship ——

This article is not the place to define what the act of worship should or could be, but it must be clear that choral music can contribute to the experience of worship. Unfortunately, it can just as easily distract the worshiper.

Church choirs offer singers an opportunity to make an offering of their gifts. What choir members need to understand beyond that offering is the role that they can play in worship. They have the opportunity to add a great deal of meaning to worship through their presentation of choral music.

If anthems are to contribute to worship, they must not distract from worship. And if worship is communal, then the choral music must not be seen as entertainment, with the congregation given a passive role. A congregation worships to experience God's presence in their lives, and choral music can give them an opportunity to view the beauty of God. It can help them in giving glory to God. And it can provide a sensory experience of God's grace. The anthem does not need to be the climactic portion of the service, and in fact rarely should be.

When choosing music for a church choir, a director may face some obvious limitations in resources. The skill of the accompanist or the number in the choir might diminish the choices somewhat. There is quality music that will fit nearly every situation, but a director should choose substantive music that he or she would feel comfortable performing over and over. There is not much sense in putting work into a disposable piece of music. Catchy music has its place in advertising, but there must be more to anthems used in worship than a fancy rhythm or memorable tune. Consider the pastoral role you play when looking at music for your choir: the anthems can illumine and interpret Scripture, a sermon, the church season, or an important current event or change in the life of the church. You have the opportunity to expose the congregation to a variety of music, music sung throughout the centuries in the church, and music that could only be sung in our present latter-day twentieth-century situation.

Choose anthems that aid the flow of worship. For liturgical churches, this might mean finding an anthem that is based on one of the lectionary readings or highlights one of the themes of the scripture passages. For others it might mean an anthem that illumines that worship's theme or focus. It is not necessary to repeat what is being read in Scripture or taught in a sermon, but the anthem can give insight by approaching the subject from a different angle or by infusing the emotional power that the music carries.

It is not harmful to look for innovative ways of using the choir to facilitate worship. Churches in the liturgical tradition might have the service music or setting of the Mass sung solely by the choir. Anthems might take the place of a hymn or be used as a gradual between readings. The appointed psalms might be sung by choir or cantor. Responses can be choral, and through singing the Mass and responses, choirs are given the role as leader of congregational song. These ideas might be beyond the role of the traditional anthem, but there is good choral music available for all of these situations.

Those congregations in the free-church tradition do have flexibility in the role a choir might take in the worship service, from the leader of congregational song to the presentation of Scripture in song. But look for new places in worship where an anthem might be effective, not necessarily where it always has been done.

The practical considerations to keep in mind when choosing anthems include the range of your singers, the balance of parts throughout a piece, and the difficulty of a piece. It is good planning to stretch the limits of a choir, but it is not always appropriate for every occasion. Choose music that is within the singers' grasp. Choirs with limited resources can often use hymns, old or new, as simpler anthems, and yet these can be as effective as an eight-part motet.

There is an art and a craft to singing choral music. Choral music done well requires much attention to vocal production, pronunciation, dynamics, breathing, phrasing, attacks, balance, and so on. One must study and live with the music to find those areas where particular attention must be paid. It is in the interpretation where the art of choral music lies and where we can give glory to God. Those involved in leadership should take every opportunity to improve their understanding of the subtleties of choral music and its performance. Listen critically to recordings or live performance of choral groups. Many publications such as *Choral Journal* publish articles with practical advice on performance practices. Associations such as the American Choral Directors Association or the American Guild of Organists sponsor workshops and conferences where one can view respected directors rehearsing and directing a choir. The insight gained from such observation cannot often be taught. In all of this,

the desire to improve oneself and offer a better gift to the glory of God should be sufficient motivation.

Those who direct church choirs and sing in those choirs are given an opportunity to lift worship to a level where we can experience God more fully, a truly awesome responsibility. And it is through the grace of God that we can do so.

David P. Schaap

223 • Gospel Song

Gospel music is a specifically American genre that has undergone many changes since its inception in revivalistic camp meetings during the mid-nineteenth century. This development has informed both worship style and musical roles within churches across denominational lines. Current trends in gospel music suggest that the influence of general public musical taste may be stronger than that of theology.

——— Historical Orientation ———

Gospel music is a genre of popular Protestant worship-song specifically American in its origins. Traceable to the rural revival camp meetings of the South (1830–60), it later expanded in the major Northern urban revival campaigns of the last third of the nineteenth century. Its practice among both black and white evangelical communities has resulted in two definable styles of performance and sound-aesthetic, despite the amount of material shared in common. Stylistic relations to Tin Pan Alley during the first thirty years of this century, and to definitive black influence from the 1940s onward, are well documented among popular culture historians. As a result, contemporary listening habits in gospel music are basically the same in breadth and type as those of the pop music constituency, notwithstanding the primacy of the medium in the evangelical church. Current uses include structured congregational singing, spontaneous sing-along sequencing, choral settings, solos, duets, trios, ensembles, along with the workplace contexts of all-night music broadcasting, program tags, fillers, and service vamps, but also strategic evangelistic-concert programming, street-witnessing, shut-in or prison visitation, background music for the headphones, Sunday school programming, and a wide variety of youth, collegiate, radio, and TV programming.

Gospel music focus is on the person and work

of Christ, in all contexts. Some constant thematic emphases have remained throughout the over 160-year history of gospel: the grace of God; eternal life and resurrection; the cross; redemption; and faith, hope, and love. On the other hand, there have been some interesting thematic shifts over the years that are discernable and that may have contextualized connections. From 1830 to 1865, these themes included the Last Day, judgment, God the Father, the death of the believer, and the pilgrim's journey; through 1900 and the Sunday school movement, the focus was on prayer, obedience in faith, the prodigal son, solace, and clouds of witnesses; from the 1940s to about 1960, popular themes included soldiers for Christ, victory or witness, and rescue; from the 1970s to the present, music focused on God's attributes, family membership in Christ, fellowship with Jesus, or again, attitude of the worshiper.

In addition, psalm paraphrase is central to gospel music settings. This source links the medium to nearly all Western hymnody in the generic sense, although its styles, uses, and methods of transmission have made it a distinctive body. Because the music traditionally is learned by youth group rote-memorization (and hence liable to all kinds of individual rearrangement and improvisation), it is important to realize that most of the songs are in fact composed pieces. Essentially it is folk music which has a long line of publication in a spectrum of hymnals and softcopy, crossing virtually all Protestant denominations and currently entering ecumenical circles.

Recent popular worship songs appearing in such Roman Catholic sources as *Worship II* or *Worship III* or in the folk-hymn output of the Weston Priory in Vermont have demonstrated (since Vatican II) the existence of a notably charismatic repertory resembling the service methods of gospel music. However, contemporary liturgical worship song is distinguishable from gospel song in two ways: (1) liturgical worship song has Gregorian stylistic roots (both in melody and in formatting), and (2) it adheres to sacramental theology, especially as it pertains to the Lord's Supper.

Varieties of Gospel Music

At present, five distinct repertories are identifiable in gospel music.

Rural White (1830–1865). This is the "shape-note" music of the South and Midwest during the revivals of the antebellum era. The shapes refer to the reading system in which variants of the circle, diamond, square, and triangle form the noteheads, and become pitch-equivalents relative to each line and space of the music staff. "Wondrous Love," "When I Can Read My Title Clear," and "Amazing Grace" are all members of this song-body—all known popularly today as "Early American Folk-Hymnody."

Rural Black (1830–1900). These are call/response songs and soliloquies referred to as spirituals, which have been romantically rescored in a considerable number of choral settings. This type also is deeply related to the history of the rural blues of the Deep South.

Northern Urban White (1875–1975). This is the core repertory popularly called "gospel music." Three identifiable generations of composers/evangelists have contributed to this movement.

The first published hymnals using the term *gospel* as such were P. P. Bliss's *Gospel Songs* (1874) and Bliss and Sankey's *Gospel Hymns and Sacred Songs* (1875), recently reprinted in facsimile in the A-R Editions of the University of Wisconsin (Madison). Aimed at the Sunday schools via the Baptists Robert Lowry and W. H. Doane, these songs moved almost simultaneously into the Chicago-based ministries of D. L. Moody and the Y.M.C.A. Christian-founded secondary schools (e.g., Mt. Hermon, Northfield, Massachusetts) also used the music, as did participants in the British revival movement during the same era. This fact—plus the Anglo-Celtic roots of many of the first-generation composers/evangelists—has secured the core repertory (1865–1975) a solid status in the specifically Anglo-American history of modern evangelism.

The second generation was one that stylistically modeled much of its music on Tin Pan Alley. Flourishing from about 1910 through 1945, it persisted through the successors of the central figures to about 1965. Focusing on figures such as Archer Torrey, Charles Gabriel, Homer Rodeheaver, and Merrill Dunlop, it also included singers such as Esther Hauser (from the Churchill Tabernacle, Buffalo, New York), and up to the early years of George Beverley Shea and the black gospel singers Mahalia Jackson and Ethel Waters. By the end of this period (the late 1950s) gospel singers ranged from Ed Ly-man and Frank Boggs to the operatic bass Jerome Hines.

The third generation is transitional, picking up much of the idiom and ethos of black rhythm and blues and the adaptation of "R&B" during the early 1950s into rock and roll. Thus this generation considerably overlaps the later figures of the second style-period, but by the time it entered the 1970s it merged with the Southern gospel strain of white gospel music (the Gaithers, singer Doug Oldham, and others) and also generated numerous "genre-groups" modelled after the specific personal styles of individual evangelist/composers (e.g., The Great Commission Company of Campus Crusade for Christ, and its bright, upbeat albums of the early 70s and the street sounds incorporated into the musical of John Giminez concerning converted drug-addicts, released in a song-album by Word, Inc.). This period included hit songs from the Billy Zeoli productions of Gospel Films, Inc. It also was the period of a major breakthrough of black gospel, by then a jazz/blues-based practice within the black church, into the secular arena as top-rated hit music (e.g., the Famous Ward Singers, Aretha Franklin, and Sam Cooke, who originally was with the Soul Stirrers).

Urban Black (1900–1945). This music was closely linked to the New Orleans and Chicago jazz and blues scenes and lasted from the era of ragtime, two-steps, and quadrilles through the 1940s. It is the era of Sister Rosetta Tharpe, Thomas A. Dorsey, the Dixie Hummingbirds, the Golden Gate Quartet, and the Sensational Nightingales. It was the sacred counterpart, stylistically, to rhythm and blues and immediately preceded the crossover of R&B to rock and roll through such catalyst figures as Little Richard and Elvis Presley.

Urban Commercial Synthesis (1970–Present). This is a genuinely new musical body, influenced by technological innovation in all audio/visual media, by global marketing networks, by technomusical influences on form, style, and sound, and by maturation of the music industry as an international agent in worship trend awareness, taste formation, marketing patterns, copyright legalities, and public relations within the evangelical culture.

This music body has at least two identifiable subdivisions, the first of which may be called traditional gospel music (including classical sacred songs updated stylistically and technically in the interest of a new sound, a trend represented to some degree since the early 1960s). The second subdivision is largely comprised of the Scripture chorus (or the praise chorus), a genre that is bound to nearly all contemporary movements in worship and to its own Pentecostal origins in the 1970s. This genre has a number of features separating it from the older material. Most important, it has come from an unusually large and active number of composer/performers, many of whom are professional, but even more of whom represent a virtual wave of locally active "neo-troubadours." These musicians are persons who are sufficiently literate in digital sound production to compose and produce their own praise-and-worship songs without necessarily having had formal training in traditional vocabulary and theory of music. Also distinctive is the tendency toward complex vocal rhythm. The syncopations and word displacements of this music effectively alter the traditional listener's aural sense of expectation. It is an issue of music that is simple in structure but subtle in detail.

The Scripture chorus has grown in prolific numbers. At present more than 100,000 individual titles of these songs are listed with Christian Copyright Licensing, Inc. This organization provides semi-annually to its constituent churches a "Top 25" list as a public relations service. Such songs are closely linked with the contemporary Christian music scene and are listed in ratings charts published by Sparrow Corporation, Word, Inc., and *Billboard* magazine. As of 1992, CCLI had provided to more than 43,000 churches internationally fee-based copyright-license issuances (permitting churches to legally duplicate published/protected song material for congregational use). CCLI requests from member churches reports that describe the songs used in worship. Using this information, CCLI can accurately survey trends in song choice and track the current practices of worship leaders.

Contemporary Issues

The Role of the Music Director. In the last decade, growth of the Scripture chorus paralleled a shift in the role of music director. The traditional positions of choir director and organist were replaced in many churches with positions containing more comprehensive descriptions, such as Fine Arts Minister, Pastor of Celebration Arts, Minister of Worship, or Worship Leader. Part of the new emphasis is on intensified stewardship to the congregation, a spiritual responsibility to the assembled body via the acts of worshiping God. This role implies mentoring others in a worship team. With the new modes of contemporary Christian music expression, it is possible for an astute leader to discern and guide emotive progress within the service, partly because the Scripture chorus itself often has tag lines and small segments of words that can be repeated sequentially, thereby creating a connective design throughout the service. This feature is also found in many of the new worship-oriented tapes designed for congregational participation or home use (e.g., Integrity's Hosanna! series *All Nations Worship,* the Kingsway series *Worship Leaders from Around the World,* or the Maranatha! Music's series *Songs of Hope*). These presentations are new models of singalong. They feature professional compilations of soloists, background vocals, percussion, acoustic and electronic instrumentation, and prominent, ongoing participation by the worship leader. In this context Scripture choruses show a flexible modularity and intense expressiveness that has become a hallmark of the Willow Creek seeker-sensitive service.

Decline of Gospel Songs. In contrast, traditional gospel songs in general are showing signs of declining use. In churches where both traditional and newer songs coexist, the hymnal is often complemented by the overhead projector. In other instances, congregations trying to attract the unchurched seeker have completely eliminated the hymnal to promote a wide variety of contemporary, pop-based musical expressions. These range from Top 40 secular selections (with new texts) to TV theme songs or solo and group improvisations. The music staff of Eastside Foursquare Church, Seattle Washington, currently writes more than half of all the choruses sung in their services. This explosion of composition is significant; creative options both for music staff and for individual congregational members are currently more available locally than in recent decades. The Scripture chorus seems to have provided the catalyst for this activity.

Seen in the larger context of the seeker-sensitive movement in worship, the traditional gospel song—while remaining vital in some conservative churches and in specific, targeted radio broadcasts such as *The Morning Chapel Hour* or *Bible Tract Echoes*—may become irrelevant, or at least rare, within the next decade. Two factors appear to reinforce the trend: (1) the listening habits of recent generations raised on the dominant influences of rock and country-western music; and (2) increases in indigenous popular worship music in the Third World countries where major revival is presently active. Immigration has allowed Third World music to find its way into the American experience, particularly through the growth of ethnic churches in which the traditions of the homeland are carried on.

Continuation of Gospel Tradition. Notwithstanding the force of current trends in worship music, there are several factors that still show continuity in traditional gospel music. First, the enormous repertory and practice of Southern gospel, both as a musical style linked to its secular counterpart in country-western music and as a living tradition unbroken since the 1940s to the present, continues through such composer/arrangers as Mosie Lister, the Gaithers, Joseph Linn, Carl Perkins, Elmo Mercer, Dottie Rambo, and other key figures in the movement.

Second, hymnals are still being published that feature gospel music as part of eclectic surveys in a conscious effort to both inspire and educate congregations; such hymnals include Genevox's *The Christian Praise Hymnal,* or Lillenas Musicreation's *Worship in Song.* A similar effort, combined with dramatic landscape views, is Steve Green's album/video, *Hymns: A Portrait of Christ.*

Third, programming on many conservative broadcasting stations (such as the USA Radio Network) continues to feature music that prevailed during the transitional era 1950–1970. One may still hear the songs of John W. Peterson, the arrangements of Paul Mickelson or Ralph Carmichael, or vocals from George Beverly Shea, Claude Rhea, and the operatic duo Dean Wilder and Robert Hale.

Pluralism of Styles. The pluralism of current gospel music practice is apparent in several ways that go beyond the earlier discussion. These matters merit some attention. A growing number of churches are currently reevaluating the purposes and structures of worship (such as open worship or the seeker-sensitive Vineyard Fellowship style) and the impingements these matters have on the worship arts. First Presbyterian Church of San Mateo, California, offers a comprehensive philosophy of worship leadership training that has earned this church a reputation as being a resource center, especially for charismatically oriented mainline churches on the West Coast. This new style is essentially a call for interdisciplinary approaches to worship leadership training. Apart from an assumed biblical and theological growth goal, it exemplifies trends in worship music that are simultaneously more specialized (to the locale) and generalized (in aesthetic stance). An open question is the extent to which such views are currently relevant to small churches or to churches where worship may be more Word-based or informal in strategic planning.

In Christian liberal arts and Bible colleges there is increasing difference between student music preference and the music provided by the institution when the service is not student-controlled. In other terms, comparison can be drawn between formal chapel hymn-scheduling and the private listening habits of Christian undergraduates or their enjoyment and physical participation at contemporary Christian artist concerts. Faculty members and administrators may not be familiar with top singers and the contexts surrounding them, whereas students will know current music through experience and by talking with peers. In short, gospel music may be experiencing a generational culture gap.

Changes in Christian Music Making. Christian musicians, on the other hand, have dealt with change in various ways.

Choirs vs. ensembles. The continuing central focus on the choir, especially in Southern Baptist churches and in urban liturgical churches, stands in contrast to a more variable status of the choir in free churches as a whole. Although the place of choirs traditionally has been most variable in rural churches, the growing prominence of the worship team changes the choral role to some extent even in larger churches where choirs remain important. If anything is perceptible in popular-culture listening habits, it is the preference for the electronically mixed ensemble—not the massed choral effect associated with something like the Robert Shaw Chorale or a college-town community chorus. Choirs are still vital to many urban black churches, where they are deeply integrated into the total service format.

Modernizing Gospel music. There is also the practice of resetting older gospel songs in redefined harmony, updated rhythm, and rescored arrangement as a countercurrent within contemporary preferences. For instance, the orchestra and piano setting of "Guide Me O Thou Great Jehovah" is fused with passages from Mozart's *Eine kleine Nachtmusik;* and "We've a Story to Tell to the Nations"

has been set in syncopated rhythm with orchestration and keyboard backdrop.

Classicism. A fusion style in gospel music persists, largely for piano solo or easy-choir. Such pieces are usually traditional gospel tunes set in textures or idioms borrowed from classical masters, particularly Romantic-era figures such as Liszt or Rachmaninov. A type of pseudo-classicism, it also picks up idioms of J. S. Bach and the late baroque, using them as a novelty sound within a larger frame of unrelated style (e.g., Mosie Lister's "When Christ Was Born in Bethlehem" from his 1986 cantata *Everlasting Lord,* or the Rachmaninov-style piano settings of popular worship melodies by Dino Kazenakis in his concerts of the 1960s). These fusions are popular today as dinner-hour music on certain conservative-taste broadcasts (e.g., Moody Radio Network), where they are designated "sacred stylings."

There is also a type of fusion in the opposite direction—gospel song to classical composition—that is not so well known to the church but which is quite important to the music world. A small number of composers have pursued this practice and have produced major symphonic or vocal works that use gospel tunes as a main source. Examples are in Charles Ives's Symphony No. 1 and his piece "General William Booth's Entrance Into Heaven"; or the *Wondrous Love Variations for Organ Solo* by Samuel Barber. Russian composer Alexander Glazunov also wrote a lively orchestral essay, *Triumphal March* (1893), as a contribution to the World's Columbian Exposition in Chicago in that year, using *The Battle Hymn of the Republic* as the main material. Works of this sort are important primarily to classical music lovers but speak also to theologically trained historians of national culture and its interface with religion.

From Scripture song to lyric solo. Another development is an amplification of the Scripture chorus into the lyric solo song. This slightly formalized variety really traces back to the earlier models in context of Malotte's "The Lord's Prayer" or some of the church songs of Clifford Demarest. Contemporary styling is the main difference (especially from black gospel); often a simplified version of the same song is published for congregational use. Examples include Keith Green's "O Lord, You're Beautiful," or Lanny Wolfe's "More Than Wonderful." Similarly, Word, Inc., puts out a 3-volume *Song Book* (Cason and Green, compilers) featuring contemporary

Christian songs for solo voice and piano based on recorded versions by top artists (e.g., The Imperials, Leon Patillo, Sandi Patti, Randy Stonehill, and others).

Changes in instrumentation. Another move has been to change the sound color of instrumentation and vocalists. This reflects aspects of changing fashion in gospel music aesthetics and merits future study in its own right. One example is changing sound scoring in men's vocal quartets from traditional close harmony (barber shop) with equal parts, with a lead singer in either baritone or shared among the others, toward a soloist format, where the first tenor takes the lead while the others form a backdrop with occasional secondary leads.

Another major change is taking place with regard to the role of the pipe organ in worship contexts. Both theater and classical instruments are affected; the sounds of Harold DeCou at the "Mighty Wurlitzer" are really part of pre-1970 preferences of taste, and are largely heard at present on conservative-taste radio broadcasts. There are some major exceptions, such as the televised performances on the classical instrument at Crystal Cathedral, or the contributions of organist Diana Bish in the Church Music Explosion conferences in Florida. On the other hand, the trend has become more multimedia tolerant, with greater inclusion of electronic band, percussion, and digital keyboards.

Increased rhythmic complexities. Musicians trained in the formal classical method often find this rhythmically complex music hard to sight-read—an unpleasant surprise. On the other hand, persons born since 1960 readily learn the rhythmic licks by ear and internalize them unconsciously. The notated material is genuinely challenging to those who have studio training in worship music and should be regarded with respect by persons working toward any serious commitment as worship leaders. There is also the matter of improvisation in worship music and its growing importance both to amateurs and professionals within the church. The remarkable work of Ken Medema has shown a wide spectrum of style awareness. Medema's ability to modify his singing quality and to improvise in styles ranging from paraphrases on Bach or Bartok on the piano, to tour-de-force rhymed soliloquies that are made up on the spot has set a standard for educated ministers of worship arts—the ability to use spontaneous creativity in worship that is simultaneously based on historical context and situational awareness.

—— Creation, Production, Distribution ——

Publishing and Awards. At present 104 publishing houses furnish gospel music as a service to churches and the public. Of these publishers, four are in the United Kingdom, one each in Australia and New Zealand, two in Canada, and the remaining ninety-six in the USA. Fifty firms alone are in California and Tennessee. Many of these houses provide gospel music that has strong affinities to popular country and western music and is marketed toward such audiences.

Closely tied to this industry are the national awards ceremonies, which are important to composers, arrangers, singers, producers, publishers, and rating-agents. Gospel music has the American Gospel Association's Dove Awards (commenced in 1969) for both black and white music categories. Other honors for artists include the Gospel Hall of Fame and the Grammy Awards in gospel music.

Gospel music's primary publishers currently include The Benson Co. (Nashville, Tennessee), Gaither Copyright Management (Alexandria, Indiana), BMG Music Publishing (Beverley Hills, California), the Roman Catholic F.E.L. Publications (Las Vegas, Nevada), Lorenz Corporation (Dayton, Ohio), Maranatha! Music (Laguna Hills, California), Lillenas Publishing Co. (Kansas City, Missouri), Sparrow Corporation (Brentwood Tennessee), and Word, Inc., (originally Rodeheaver Co.), of Irving, Texas. Many of these publishers of worship music maintain a stable of the best-known gospel composers and arrangers as resident composers. Creative artists in their own right, they also work under the auspices of a publishing house, in effect producing works for specific, perceived marketing needs and/or ministerial goals among churches and worship leaders. Lillenas, for example, retains figures such as Linda Rebuck, Lawrence Enscoe, Joseph Linn, and Mosie Lister, among others. In this respect—much like the popular music industry—gospel music is composed, arranged, and recorded in a broadly networked but tightly coordinated marketing system by which national tastes and trends of taste can both be met and proactively influenced. Media produced through this network include cantatas, sheet music, song anthologies, children's dramas and pageants, praise-song hymnals, traditional hymn collections, demo tapes of choir anthologies and cantatas, accompaniment tracks for solo and choral singing, and instructional media relevant to the music ministry.

Among top-rated singers and recording artists at present are such figures as Ed Curtis, Steve Green, Nancy Honeytree, Susan Ashton, Connie Scott, Cynthia Clawson, and the duo Steve and Annie Chapman. Additional writers and arrangers include figures such as Camp Kirkland, Doug Holck, Dick Bolks or Tom Fettke; much of the material is intended for particular age levels or in some way fashioned for the size and limitations of choirs and accompanists.

Theological and Denominational Differences. There are theological and denominational backdrops to the development of gospel music that merit a few remarks at this point. In the earliest period the conceptual sources were in two main contexts: Congregationalist (Puritan dissenter), and slightly later, Anglican (through the Wesleys, into Methodism). On the other hand, the Northern Urban repertory (1870 to *c.* 1930) tends to be influenced by Baptists, both compositionally and in social usage through the Sunday schools and revivals. Recent eclectic hymn collections prevalent in Christian colleges and certain collegiate Christian fellowships (such as the ones produced by InterVarsity Christian Fellowship) have, since the 1960s, taken on one of three orientations: (1) British (via the hymn-writing movement of the 1960s and 70s, e.g., Eric Routley and Timothy Dudley-Smith); (2) Presbyterian/Reformed, and since the 1980s (3) multicultural ecumenism, such as the songbook of the Madison Campus Ministry at the University of Wisconsin. In contemporary Christian praise/worship repertory, the main roots (also visible in the song lyrics) are Pentecostal, through the Assemblies of God. The influence of this contemporary material on other churches and denominations (including those not sympathetic with Assemblies of God views on spiritual gifts) is well-established, and the acceptance of such songs continues, suggesting a general popularity that may be independent of theological concerns.

Stephen Cushman

224 • AFRICAN-AMERICAN SONG

There are considerable resources for black song among African-American denominations and churches that are now widely available for churches in every tradition. This article is especially helpful in describing the different types of songs that have developed from the black worship tradition.

Black Methodists, Baptists, Holiness, and Pentecostals, as well as black Episcopalians and Catholics, have each produced their own hymnists and hymnody. Among nineteenth-century black clergy who were also hymnists are Bishop Daniel A. Payne of the African Methodist Episcopal Church and Rev. Benjamin Franklin Wheeler of the African Methodist Episcopal Zion Church. Among early twentieth-century hymnists were Charles Albert Tindley of the Methodist church, Rev. F. M. Hamilton of the Colored Methodist Episcopal Church, William Rosborough of the National Baptist Convention, USA, and Charles Price Jones of the Church of Christ (Holiness), USA.

The Episcopal church has to its credit such contemporary black hymnists as David Hurd and William Farley Smith. In addition to singing the hymns of the traditional black churches, black Episcopalians have at their disposal complete musical settings of the Communion service by black hymnists. Smith's setting in the black Episcopalian hymnbook, *Lift Every Voice and Sing* (New York: Church Hymnal Corp., 1981), is entitled "Communion Music for the Protestant Episcopal Church." Its eight parts include the Introit, Gloria in Excelsis, the hymns "Hungry and Thirsty" and "Lord, We Come," Doxology, Sanctus, Agnus Dei, The Lord's Prayer, and Benediction.

African-American Catholics have at their disposal a distinctive body of hymnody composed by black Catholic hymnists. Included in the hymnal entitled *Lead Me, Guide Me: The African American Catholic Hymnal* (1987) are not only the standard favorites of the traditional black church, but also Edward V. Bonnemere's jazz-styled "Christ Is Coming: Prepare the Way'" (complete with guitar chords) and Fr. Clarence Joseph Rivers's "Mass Dedicated to the Brotherhood of Man" (1970). Other black Catholic composers represented in this hymnal are Edmund Broussard, Marjorie Gabriel-Borrow, Avon Gillespie, Rawn Harbor, Leon C. Roberts, Grayson Warren Brown, and Edward V. Bonnemere.

Black Methodists, Baptists, Holiness, Pentecostals, Episcopalians, and Catholics also share a body of hymnody that is hardly differentiated doctrinally or denominationally, namely the spirituals and gospel music. The antebellum spirituals may still constitute the largest body of black sacred music in this consortium of black Christians known as the black church. Among the several thousand spirituals handed down to the present generation of black worshipers, spirituals often found in black denominational hymnbooks, are songs reminiscent of the wide range of sentiments felt by the enslaved. There are songs of joy such as "Every Time I Feel the Spirit," songs of thanksgiving such as "Free at Last," and songs of praise such as "Ride On, King Jesus." The spirituals also expressed with unyielding faith the belief that God would repeat on behalf of the Africans enslaved in America the liberating act performed for the biblical Hebrews subjugated in Egypt. Spirituals of this mood include "Didn't My Lord Deliver Daniel," "Freedom Train A-Comin'," "Go Down, Moses," and "Joshua Fit de Battle of Jericho."

Also among the spirituals are the "sorrow songs." These songs, which seem to be individual rather than communal expressions, include "I Been in the Storm So Long," "Nobody Knows the Trouble I Seen," and "Sometimes I Feel Like a Motherless Child." Many of the sorrow songs, illustrating the unyielding faith of the enslaved, commence on a low note of dejection but conclude on a high pitch of praise. Two of the very few exceptions to this characteristic are "Were You There" and "He Never Said a Mumbling Word," both of which show no glimmer of hope. Today, spirituals have been arranged in hymnic, anthemic, and soloistic forms to be sung by congregation, choir, and trained soloist, respectively. Among the musical arrangers are such historic figures as H. T. Burleigh, R. Nathaniel Dett, and John Wesley Work, Jr., and such contemporary musicians as Verolga Nix and Roland Carter. In whatever form spirituals are arranged—as hymns, anthems, or solo songs—they can be used to complement every phase of the church year.

Complementing the spirituals in the folk, hymnic, and anthemic repertoires of the black church are the songs of racial pride and liberation. The most important song of racial pride is the "Black National Anthem," J. Rosamond Johnson's setting of his brother James Weldon Johnson's poem, "Lift Every Voice and Sing." The principal song of liberation, made popular during the civil rights movement, is "We Shall Overcome." Like numerous civil rights songs, this historic piece is a synthesis and adaptation of extant hymnody. Combining the tune of the old Baptist hymn, "I'll Be Alright," and the text of

the Methodist gospel hymn, "I'll Overcome Someday," the anthem of the civil rights movement is emblematic of how the black oral tradition adapts extant hymns to meet new social and religious needs.

The composer of "I'll Overcome Someday" is the great Charles Albert Tindley, the creator of such well-known gospel hymns as "We'll Understand It All By and By." Many black hymnologists have considered Tindley, a Methodist minister from Philadelphia, to be the most important, if not prolific, hymn writer in the history of the black church. Actually, the most prolific, and certainly one of the most significant, is Charles Price Jones, the founding bishop of the Church of Christ (Holiness), USA. While Tindley composed approximately forty gospel hymns, Jones composed over one thousand hymns (including anthems). Among his hymns is the resplendent "I Will Make the Darkness Light."

Following the Tindley and Jones era of the gospel hymn (1900–1930) arose what has been called the "golden age of gospel" (1930–1969). This period is represented by the "gospel songs" of such black composers and arrangers as Doris Akers, J. Herbert Brewster, Lucie E. Campbell, James Cleveland, Thomas A. Dorsey, Theodore Frye, Roberta Martin, Kenneth Morris, and Clara Ward. Two of the most famous gospel songs of this period are Campbell's "He Will Understand and Say 'Well Done'" and Dorsey's "Precious Lord, Take My Hand." Together, the musicians of this era transformed the congregational gospel hymn of the Tindley and Jones era into the solo, quartet, and choral gospel song of the "golden" period.

Succeeding the golden age of gospel is the modern gospel era. This has been, from its inception in 1969, dominated by black Pentecostal artists of the Church of God in Christ. Among these artists are Walter Hawkins, Edwin Hawkins, Andrae Crouch, Sandra Crouch, and Elbernita Clark (of the Clark Sisters). Among the popular pieces of this period that have been sung by young adult "inspirational choirs" in the black church are Walter Hawkins's "Be Grateful" and "He's That Kind of Friend," Andrae Crouch's "Through It All," and Sandra Crouch's "Come, Lord Jesus." Some of their songs have appeared in the black denominational hymnals published since 1980.

Christian hip-hop is the newest form of gospel music. Similar to modern gospel, Christian hip-hop (orginated *c.* 1989) began as concert rather than liturgical music; it too will likely find its way into the black churches that are seeking to speak to today's youth. Among hip-hop gospel singers are PID (Preachers in Disguise), ETW (End Time Warriors), SFC (Soldiers for Christ), DC Talk, Witness, D-Boy Rodriguez, Helen Baylor, Michael Peace, and Fresh Fish. These groups often have a message that is experientially oriented. For instance, PID addresses such issues as homelessness, sexually transmitted disease, and racism, and does so in a language that today's inner-city youths speak and relate to.

The music that falls into the gospel hymn, gospel song, and modern gospel eras still coexists in the black church, and it is unlikely that even the rise of gospel hip-hop would ever change this inclusive nature of the black church music ministry. These three kinds of gospel that continue to co-exist in the black church generally fulfill the three principal liturgical functions in black churches—testimony, worship, and praise. The testimony hymns are used by worshipers to commence their "testifying" during the testimony service, a ritual practiced especially in black Holiness and Pentecostal churches. In testifying, a worshiper stands, sings a verse or two (or the chorus) of a favorite hymn, and then gives her or his spoken testimony. Using the theme and language of the song, the speaker tells the story of how God has worked positively in their lives during the past week. The fact that testimony typically begins with and is thematically built upon a hymn illustrates that these songs have been an essential source of theology for black worshipers over the years of social, political, and economic struggle. One of the favorite testimony hymns of the black church is "Jesus, I'll Never Forget What You've Done for Me."

The worship and praise songs have a close kinship. The worship hymns do not focus on individual experiences like the testimony hymns, but specifically on the worship of Jesus Christ. Familiar examples of worship songs are "We Have Come Into This House" by Bruce Ballinger and "Bless His Holy Name" by Andrae Crouch. The kindred praise songs are cheerful declarations of exaltation to God, which welcome God's presence in the life of the believer. Among the best known songs of praise are "Yes, Lord" and "My Soul Says, 'Yes.'" Both of these were composed by Charles Harrison Mason, the founder of the Church of God in Christ, and are published in that denomination's first and only hymnal, *Yes Lord!* (1984). Either during or following the singing of worship and praise songs, Holiness and Pentecostal worshipers may engage in giving the Lord a "wave offering" by means of the "lifting of hands," or by giving "hand praise" (applause in gratitude for the Lord's blessings).

Much of the music that is sacred to the tradition of black worship can be found in hymnals compiled by black denominations. Among the most recent and historically important are the American Methodist Episcopal Church *Bicentennial Hymnal* (1984); *The New National Baptist Hymnal* (1977) of the National Baptist Convention; *His Fullness Songs* (1977) of the Church of Christ (Holiness), USA; and *Yes. Lord!: The Church of God in Christ Hymnal* (1982). Among the important hymnbooks published by the black constituencies of predominantly white denominations are *Songs of Zion* (1981) from the United Methodist Church; *Lift Every Voice and Sing: A Collection of Afro-American Spirituals and Other Songs* (1981), from the Episcopal church; and *Lead Me, Guide Me: The African American Catholic Hymnal* (1987) of the Roman Catholic church.

Jon Michael Spencer

225 • Hispanic-American Song

Recently published hymnals have included a wide variety of congregational songs from Hispanic churches. This article describes the experience of Hispanic Christians in America and the music that is often used in Hispanic-American churches.

Like other minorities in the USA, Hispanic congregations have been known for the manner in which they worship God by singing their favorite hymns. In order to understand this, one must go to the roots of Hispano churches all over this country. In the Southwest, which includes California, Arizona, Colorado, New Mexico, and Texas, the Mexican-Americans, which constitute most of the Hispanic people, trace their history back to the days when this territory used to be part of Mexico. Contrary to popular opinion, Protestants did not start their work in the Southwest by sending Anglo missionaries to convert the Catholic Mexicans. By the time the mainline denominations sent their missionaries, there were already evangelical cells functioning in private homes—the result of religious persecution in Mexico, and of the work of the colporteurs who traveled north from south of the border.

Because of this, one finds a lot of strong feelings against the Catholic church, feelings which have survived in many cases up to this date. The Protestants coming to the USA from Mexico brought with them similar feelings to those brought by the religiously persecuted Pilgrims who came in the _Mayflower_.

Since they were in quite a few cases running away from intolerance and prejudice, they wanted to do away with anything related to the Catholic church, including worship practices. Thus, one can understand the rejection today in Hispanic evangelical churches of such things as Gregorian chants, kyries, classical music from the Middle Ages, and even those seventeenth- and eighteenth-century hymns that in any way reflect values and theologies that may sound similar to those they knew from the Roman Catholic tradition.

The mainline denominations in the USA have tried, in some cases with a degree of success, to incorporate in their worship directories quite a few elements that could be characterized as "high church." Such elements are frowned upon, however, by such denominations as the Assemblies of God, the Church of God, Southern Baptists, and other fast-growing independent or nondenominational churches. Hispanic styles of worship, therefore, tend to do away with acolytes, candles, crosses, collects, robes, and kneeling (except at the front of the sanctuary), and the singing of anything that may sound Catholic.

The fast growing barrio churches reflect the culture of those they serve. In quite a few churches, the congregation will include recent arrivals from Mexico or other Central American countries, plus the Mexican-Americans who can trace their roots to the days when the Southwest was Spanish. Most of these congregations include a high percentage of people from the lower socioeconomic classes who prefer _coritos_ to hymns and who favor charismatic-oriented liturgy. The seventeenth- and eighteenth-century hymns they use have been translated to Spanish by missionaries and hymnologists who did their work at the turn of the century. A few hymnbooks were produced by the mainline denominations using some Spanish melodies and indigenous compositions, but seldom to the exclusion of "the great hymns of the church," as understood by their Anglo spiritual mentors. Only recently has a distinc-

tive effort been made by both mainline churches and others to produce hymnbooks and collections of hymns that characterize the Hispanic tradition or reflect its values.

Some of the Hispanic hymns have the "South American Sound." But this sound has been traditionally associated with a lifestyle that is not acceptable to the pietistic values of many Hispanic churches. New compositions, widely used by charismatic Hispanic churches, reflect the contemporary music and words also used by the charismatic Anglo churches.

One of the most widely used Hispanic hymnbooks was produced in the early 1960s by COHAM (at that time COSAW), an interdenominational council that included both mainline churches and sects, and even at times liberal Roman Catholics. The hymnbook _El Himnario_ is mostly a collection of traditional hymns and old time favorites, translated into Spanish by one of the most prolific translators and composers, a Presbyterian missionary, George Paul Simmonds. But it also includes the work of both Mexican-American and Mexican hymnologists, plus a few indigenous works from south of the border.

Hispanic composers known to most Hispanic Protestants include names like Vincent Mendoza, J. B. Cabrera, Abraham Fernandez, Epigmenio Valasco, E. Martinez-Garza, Pedro Castro, E. A. Diaz, Marcelino Montoya, Jose de Mora, Sra. S. Venecia, and of course George Simmonds. These are the better known composer-authors, but there are many others.

Hispanic congregations, like any other congregation in any culture, will sing what the pastor will choose. And the pastor, in most cases, selects what his or her favorites are. The young new pastors are heavily favoring contemporary music and words, either compositions imported from Latin American countries, or produced in the Southwest, Florida (owing to its large Cuban population), and other areas with heavy concentrations of Hispanic parishioners, such as Chicago, New York, Philadelphia, and so forth. Hymns are also selected because of either the music or the words. Favorite hymns become favorite because the music is easy to learn and the words easy to remember. _Coritos_ are popular. Their theology usually is shallow, but there are exceptions. One finds many mainline denomination Hispanic churches using guitars and singing _coritos_ these days. This goes hand in hand with a return of emotionalism and preaching on moral issues, emphasizing conversion experiences. It is "the Old Time Religion," all over again.

Those Hispanics who prefer to follow the lectionary and to use hymns related to the theme being developed find themselves in a minority and not gaining many members. But they are not alone. Many also try to include what is considered as "ethnic hymnody," provided it is a valid contribution to the total worshiping experience. The issue remains whether Hispanic congregations are playing the numbers game, and therefore, attempting to be popular and fill churches, or whether they are trying to proclaim the gospel in a relevant and meaningful manner. By and large, the socioeconomic factor is determinative. The level of education and the degree of sophistication of the congregation must be considered, but not at the expense of excluding others from coming to join the brotherhood of believers.

Service books can be helpful, limited by the fact that, if they were as comprehensive as needed, they would be too hard to handle, and too bulky. But Methodists, Episcopalians, and Lutherans, among others, do use them every Sunday, in Hispanic churches as in any other ethnic or Anglo church. One of the all time favorites with Hispanic congregations is the hymn "Jesus es mi rey soberano," with words and music by Vincente Mendoza, a prolific author and composer of Hispanic hymns. The words were translated to English (a welcome change!) by George P. Simmonds in 1966, and have been used occasionally by Anglo congregations at special times. Another favorite all over the world is "Santa Biblia Para Mi," in English in *The Hymnbook*, number 131.

Carlos A. Lopez[27]

226 • Asian-American Song

According to this author's view, there is no distinctive hymnody that prevails in Asian-American churches, but there are certain characteristics and trends that typify these congregations. In providing detailed distinctions among the various Asian groups, this article does give some perspective on the music used in Asian-American churches and challenges that these churches are facing.

Background of Asian-American Groups

The Chinese were the first to come to the United States over a century ago. Since most of their churches continue to be affected by immigration and are mainly immigrant (first-generation) churches, the worship services are in Cantonese and/or Mandarin. A sizable group of Chinese born in the U.S. are English-speaking members of the Chinese churches, and a few hold English services.

The Japanese, whose immigration to the U.S. basically stopped in 1924, are composed of second to fifth generation English-speaking congregations, with a smaller group of immigrants worshiping in Japanese.

The Koreans are the largest Asian Presbyterian group. Immigration from Korea is resulting in a great increase of Korean churches. Today there are approximately 250 churches, and the number is still increasing. These churches worship in Korean, mainly with ministers who were trained in Korea.

The Taiwanese, Vietnamese, Cambodian, and Laotians are all mainly first-generation persons who worship in their native tongue, with the exception of the Filipinos, who use English.

Types of Worship Services

In the early years, the worship services were essentially informal, patterned more on the synagogue style (simple structure with emphasis upon teaching) rather than the temple style (formal worship utilizing more rituals). We must remember that there is little in the way of history and tradition to give shape to their liturgy and music, for the heritage of these ethnic groups is non-Christian. For example, in Japan, where the religious philosophy is predominately Buddhist and Shinto, only one-half of one per cent of the population are Christian. Since most Asian-American Christians are first-generation converts, there has been no pressure for a traditional formal worship or cherished rituals.

In recent years, Asian churches have developed a slightly more formal style of worship, following the denominational lead in liturgy.

The Need for Bilingual Hymns

Worship serves are often bilingual in order to accommodate the immigrant native tongue and second generation English-speaking persons. Hymns, prayers, Scripture readings, and sermons are in both languages. Sometimes there is a repetition of everything, and in other cases, only selected items are translated. This bilingual worship service may take place every Sunday or only on special occasions. In the latter case, there are two worship services held on Sundays: one in the native Asian tongue, one in English for the second- through fifth-generation members.

The impact of bilingual services on congregational singing is felt in several ways. Hymns must be provided in both languages. Some have published their own bilingual hymnbooks that include most of the familiar and basic hymns. Others use hymnbooks published in their native countries. We can see that because new hymns need constant translating, this poses a predicament for first-generation churches wanting to sing current hymns.

Further problems arise in hymn selections that are limited to hymns which are published in both languages. On special Holy days and Communion, when bilingual services are usually held, finding hymns in both languages utilizing the same tunes and text is difficult. This lack of a full range of hymns to enrich a special worship service acts as a restrictive force in Asian congregations, and worship becomes static because of limited hymn selection.

Bilingual services also mean that the congregation sings in both languages at once, often confusing the worshiper because translations are not directly word for word. These words are not heard as one uniform sound, diminishing the power of the hymn. In spite of this, music continues to be a very important part of their churches, for they all come from cultures that love music and, more importantly, that love to sing.

Most of the hymns sung are those which were taught by the nineteenth- and early twentieth-century missionaries who ministered to the Asian people, both here and abroad. Many hymns are tied in with their life's struggles upon leaving their homes for a strange land. Hymns such as "What a Friend We Have in Jesus" and "The Church's One Foundation" have found deep-rooted meaning.

There is also a small core of original hymns that were written by persons in their native country, most of which are in the style of our missionary hymns. Others are based upon old folk tunes with newly written text.

The Need for Trained Leadership in Music

There is very little trained leadership for music in the church. Pastors need to provide leadership, but for the most part, their seminary training does not prepare them in music, and often very little in the way of liturgy. The instruments with which they work are usually minimal. Pipe organs are rare and unaffordable and very little is directed towards the development of music. Thus, in our churches, we find very few trained Asian church musicians, namely, organists, choir directors, and ministers of music.

It is my opinion that as this development takes place in the ethnic churches, the possibility of developing music which may be distinctively Asian-American will emerge. For there is a vast richness in the Asian musical and historical tradition that could be utilized to direct our Christian worship toward a higher realm of consciousness.

Possible Future Directions for Asian Ethnic Hymns

Many of the tunes used in the *Hymns from the Four Winds* are folk songs set to Christian texts (Nashville: Abingdon Press, 1983). The problem we face here is that these traditional and popular songs are rooted in the common experience of the people. Can the text of the hymn rise above the claims which the tune will be making upon the minds and emotions of the people? Can Christian affirmation come out of a musical setting which is heavily non-Christian in its background? Many great hymns have come out of symphonies (e.g., "Joyful, Joyful, We Adore Thee" and "Be Still, My Soul") and some out of love songs (e.g., "O Sacred Head, Now Wounded") but the cultural setting from which these tunes came is essentially Christian. This is not the case with Asian tunes. They evoke feelings which may have consciously dissociated Christianity from the tune. Thus, no matter how beautiful and appropriate the tune may be, the more familiar you are with the culture from which it comes, the harder it is to allow the tune to carry you into Christian worship.

Perhaps an alternative may be found not in using Asian tunes, but rather Asian musical forms which have been written down in the Western mode by Asian musicians or ethnomusicologists. We find that the basis of music, scales, harmony, rhythm, notation, forms, and styles are very foreign to the Western musician, for the subtleties of Asian music include use of quarter-tones and use of ornamentation and improvisation. This may be the providential task for the Asian American: that they find their forms of expression in hymnody for they are the unique ones that merge the Eastern and Western and upon whom rests the name *Asian-American.* They are challenged to slowly break the boundaries that limit the East and West, and to cross the line to new frontiers:

> Everything which I have said about crossing the frontier is true too for crossing the line which is today hardest for the Western world to cross, the frontier toward the East. It is wrong when the Western people are prevented by education, literature, and propaganda from crossing this frontier. . . . We must also see what is going on in depth over there and seek to understand it. (Paul Tillich, *The Future of Religions* [New York: Harper and Row, 1966], 56–57.)

May Murakami[28]

227 • Shape-Note Singing

Shape-note singing was an important part of the social and religious life of rural America before the Civil War. Entire communities gathered for all-day singing. Some of these gatherings, called conventions, *lasted several days. In some parts of America, these shape-note singing festivals are held yet today, offering a very unique and vibrant style of music that could well be sung in churches of many traditions.*

> Beyond the singing and related activity, a real sense of fellowship is evident at the singings, an emotional bond compounded of mutual affection and appreciation and the knowledge that all are joined in a common cause. (Buell E. Cobb, Jr., *The Sacred Harp: A Tradition and its Music* [Macon: University of Georgia Press, 1978, 1989])

> If these people were not happy, in the best and fullest meaning of the word, then I have never seen human happiness. (George Pullen Jackson, *White Spirituals in the Southern Uplands* [Chapel Hill: University of North Carolina Press, 1933])

These quotations from two of the classic works on shape-note singing give some insight into the survival, virtually intact, of an American hymn singing tradition which dates back nearly 200 years.

Its name is derived from the notation system that associates four different shapes with notes in the scale. This system first appeared in *The Easy Instructor; or a New Method of Teaching Sacred Harmony,* a song book published in 1801 and used by itinerant singing masters in New England to teach sight reading and other rudiments of music. With the urbanization of New England, wider use of pipe organs in churches, and with the ascendant influence of Lowell Mason and others who favored music imported from Europe, the singing masters carried their music and teaching methods to the South and West, settling in areas which remained rural. Their singing schools became an integral part of community life in these places, creating a heritage which survives to this day.

As interest in this music grew in the south during the nineteenth century, several new hymnals were published, including *Southern Harmony, New Harp of Columbia, Missouri Harmony, Kentucky Harmony,* and the one which, after several revisions, remains in widest use today, *The Original Sacred Harp.* Contemporary editions preserve the fuguing tunes and anthems of William Billings (1746–1800) and hymns of his fellow New Englanders Justin Morgan and Daniel Read along with ancient folk tunes and works added by more recent composers. NEW BRITAIN, to which the text "Amazing Grace" is set, and "Wondrous Love" are shape-note tunes which have become familiar to the general public.

Most tunes in contemporary editions of the hymnals are arranged in four parts, with the melody in the tenor. Each part is written out on its own staff, highlighting the linear or contrapuntal nature of this music. Harmonies result from the interplay of these horizontally conceived lines, making music which sounds quite different from that having a soprano melody supported by a predictable progression of chords. The frequent occurrence of fourths and fifths has more in common with music of the Middle Ages than with the close harmonizations of conventional hymn tunes and gospel music.

The fact that many shape-note tunes are based on ancient modes or "gapped" scales instead of the more familiar diatonic (major and minor) scales also contributes to its distinctive character. George Pullen Jackson, whose 1933 work *White Spirituals in the Southern Uplands* was the first serious study of the shape-note tradition, points out that many of its practitioners in the period 1800–1860 were of

Celtic origin. The melodic characteristics of their ballads, fiddle tunes, and dance music are reflected in their hymns.

What distinguishes the singing of these hymns from other kinds of musical experience is its strongly democratic, participatory nature. In its traditional stronghold in the South, shape-note singing is practiced by everyone from pre-schoolers to the most senior of citizens—no one who wants to sing is excluded. Shape-note singing is not a performance for an audience, but is done for its own sake.

Singers are divided into four sections: treble, alto, tenor, and bass. In the treble and tenor sections men and women sing together, each in his or her own octave. Singers are seated with trebles facing the basses and altos facing the tenors, forming a hollow square. They take turns choosing and leading the songs—there is no conductor and no accompanist. The leader or someone in the front row chooses the starting pitch in a range that is comfortable for all the voice parts. No pitch pipe is used.

To begin a song, the leader steps to the center of the square, calling out the number of the tune ("Number 49 on the bottom," for instance). Holding the hymn book in one hand, the leader directs with the other using simple up-down motion. The shapes (fa-sol-la) are always sung first, helping the singers to learn or to recall their parts. The leader decides how many verses will be sung and what repeats will be observed; it is considered bad form to request all the verses of a hymn at a large singing where many will want to take a turn leading.

The sound of shape-note singing bears little resemblance to conventional choral singing. Most of the singers are going "hellbent-for-election," singing the words with deep feeling, not creating an effect to please an audience. Because there is no accompaniment, the music is not tied to equal temperament, and singers are free to tune their intervals as they wish. The level of sound is generally loud—subtlety of dynamics is not a part of this tradition.

The only place where the effect of shape-noters in full cry can really be felt is in the center of the hollow square, the place reserved for the leader. The person who stands there is surrounded by all four voice parts and hears them in balance, a phenomenon which is physically impossible from any other location (and which explains the generally disappointing character of recordings of this music). Newcomers to a singing are sometimes invited to come and stand next to the leader in order to share in this remarkable experience.

Certain themes recur in the texts of shape-note hymns. The transient character of life on earth, the soul's longing for its destiny with God and its dread of separation from him, the sorrow of parting and the hope of eternal happiness are ideas that show up again and again. Isaac Watts and Charles Wesley are among the English writers of the eighteenth century who are most frequently represented in shape-note hymnals. The fervent texts that appealed so greatly to the rural Southerners who formed the shape-note tradition are finding an appreciative new audience in the present generation.

Shape-note groups are springing up all across the country among people who value not only the music and the words but also the fellowship and camaraderie of the singing. Many who would not consider participating in Christian worship can be found on Sunday afternoons singing with full hearts "Shout on, pray on, we're gaining ground . . ." (No. 277, _Original Sacred Harp_) or "Death, 'tis a melancholy day / To those who have no God . . ." (No. 29 on the bottom, _Original Sacred Harp_). In a letter to the _Chicago Sacred Harp Newsletter,_ a singer identifying himself as an Orthodox Jew ("Sephardic, for that matter") writes, "The music means a great deal to me . . . each time I walk away with a tremendous sense of peace and spiritual fulfillment."

Singings begin and end with prayer, and most incorporate a memorial service. Names of those who have died in the year since the last singing are read, as are the names of shut-ins who are unable to attend this day's event. Someone from the memorial committee may offer a brief reflection, and usually a hymn or two will be sung in commemoration of those who are bound for glory.

All-day singings in the South have traditionally been held in rural churches during the summer and early autumn when the crops are "laid by," the interval between the final cultivating and the beginning of the harvest. Dinner on the grounds follows the morning singing, featuring the specialties of local kitchens and gardens and plenty of homemade lemonade and iced tea to soothe the throats of the singers. After socializing over lunch and perhaps walking down a shaded road to spend a reflective moment in the adjoining cemetery, the singers reassemble to sing until the end of the afternoon. A hundred or more hymns may be sung by the end of the day, at which time there may still be a barbecue or other social gathering to look forward to.

The accessibility of this experience to people of varying religious persuasions, all ages, varying educational and cultural backgrounds, and different levels of musical proficiency is genuinely amazing. For Christian believers, it can offer a new dimension to the concept of community. It is best sought out in its homeland, the South, where those who have been brought up in the tradition still gather to sustain it. To be enfolded in this deeply felt music and gracious hospitality has inspired more than one Northerner to join a shape-note group at home or to found a new one.

Johanna B. Fabke

228 • MUSIC OF THE WORLD CHURCH

Recent hymnals have included a wide variety of congregational songs from around the world. These provide new styles of music for use in worship and new ways of expressing the unity of the worldwide church.

A new phenomenon is appearing in denominational hymnals published in the past five years. An example of this is found in hymns like "Asithi: Amen" or "Tu has venido a la orilla," or "Jesus A, Nahetotaetanome." (All the songs, hymns, and tune names listed in this article are found in *Hymnal: A Worship Book,* prepared by Churches in the Believers Church Tradition (Elgin, Ill.: Brethren Press; Newton, Kans.: Faith and Life Press; Scottdale, Pa.: Mennonite Publishing House, 1992). There has always been a sprinkling of Latin and German words in hymnals, at least with familiar phrases as "Gloria in excelsis Deo" and "Stille Nacht, heilige Nacht!" or in tune names such as EIN' FESTE BURG, ABERYST-WYTH, DEUS TUORUM MILITUM, and so on. Yet we have not always acknowledged the culture and language diversity in our midst beyond Western European traditions, nor have we recognized the variety of ways Christ has made himself known to Christians around the world.

At the arrival of the twenty-first century, an age of high technology and global awareness, the North American church is comprised of a mixture of cultures and languages, more so than at any time in its history. For many generations, members of a local congregation have likely been basically of one or two races, Caucasian, and perhaps African-American. But today worshipers are likely to find themselves sitting next to someone of another color, another culture, another language. Such a phenomenon is challenging the church to broaden its perspective, its style of hymnody, and its language in liturgy and hymns.

No longer can an English-speaking congregation assume that English is the only language represented among its worshipers; no longer can the small town or city church demand that all worshipers sing only in English, whatever their background. No longer can those who speak only English refuse to at least try singing in another language. As the world gets smaller, the church must get bigger, more inclusive.

Several new hymnals have provided an important model to worshipers by incorporating languages other than English, and by introducing texts and tunes from churches around the globe. Through this witness, the North American church is becoming sensitized, educated, and appreciative of the hymnody of Christian sisters and brothers of many different cultures and languages. In addition, worshipers are discovering the delight in singing new types of hymns. Take, for example, "Asithi: Amen," a South African hymn that is sung over and over again, as a praise hymn or as a recessional hymn at the end of worship. Its driving rhythms and easy-to-learn Zulu words make it sheer fun to sing! God's people are uplifted in joyful praise. God certainly must be enjoying it too!

Nigerians are incorporating in their worship services their own religious songs, rich with complex rhythms, alongside gospel songs taught them by missionaries from the United States and England during the early part of the twentieth century. One song is a rendition of the Lord's Prayer ("Our Father, who art in heaven"), in which each phrase is first sung by a leader, then by the congregation. Originally written in Hausa, this prayer hymn can be easily learned in English and sung by North American congregations. It is accompanied by African drums, gourds, and cowbell, or similar rhythm instruments that are available.

Since the days of slavery, the North American church has sung the spirituals and black gospel songs of African-American people. However, white and biracial congregations are now being challenged to include a wider selection of authentic African-American music in worship, songs like "Lift Every Voice and Sing" (the official song of the National Association for the Advancement of Colored

People), "I Am Weak and I Need Thy Strength," "When Storms of Life Are Raging," "I Want Jesus to Walk with Me." Such songs speak poignantly to the pain of injustice, alienation, and despair of a people who daily feel the sting of discrimination. All congregations need to sing such heart-wrenching songs, slowly, rhythmically, passionately, in _a cappella_ voices or accompanied by strong, pulsating piano and/or organ arrangements.

Spanish is the second most commonly spoken language in the United States today, and Hispanics are the fastest growing ethnic group. If the North American church wants to reach and fully welcome Hispanics into the church, it is challenged (possibly even compelled before too many years) to include worship litanies and hymns in Spanish. Command of the language is not necessary at all in order to sing. Even a bumbling attempt at pronunciation of an unfamiliar language shows a willingness to step into the culture and language of another person because of Christian concern and love. A congregation might begin learning a Spanish hymn text slowly, with a soloist or quartet first singing it, then the congregation. An exciting hymn to try is "Cantemos al Senor," which repeats the opening phrase on each verse and ends with "Aleluya!" At least, such an attempt shows a willingness to try another language. At most, it shows respect for the language in which a hymn was originally written. Congregations are encouraged to ask a member who is proficient in Spanish to pronounce the words of the text before all join in singing it, possibly even to direct the hymn. A guitar and several rhythm instruments, such as maracas and bongo drums, help the congregation experience the hymn as authentically as possible.

The Taizé community of eastern France, to which thousands of young people from all over the world travel each week, joins in worship three times a day. Imagine hearing the gospel read in ten different languages; a psalm chanted in Swedish, German or Portuguese; and musical refrains sung in French, Polish, English, or Italian. No one language dominates. Latin, no longer anyone's language, becomes everyone's language as it is used in many of the sung prayers. The beauty of the simple music, often accompanied by instrumental obligatos while being sung repeatedly, leads one into deep communion with God. The haunting melodies and harmony "remain alive" within the worshipers long after they leave worship.

Singing in the Taizé service evokes within the worshipers a sense of the church's unity in Christ amidst the diversity of cultures and languages, and it honors the universality of the church.

Taizé music, published throughout the world, has found its way into most of the recently published hymnals. The words may be in Spanish, Latin, German, Polish, and English—many different languages that congregations are finding they learn quite easily because of a song's shortness and repetitive phrases.

Represented in current hymnals is music of Chinese, Japanese, Korean, Indonesian, Latin American, native American cultures. All cultures bring the beauty of their own uniqueness in melody, rhythm, and texts that enrich the church and its members wherever they are located. The Psalmist summons the worshiping community to

> Sing to the Lord a new song
> Sing to the Lord, all the earth (Psalm 96:1)

The Christian church can best do that by singing together each other's songs of faith, in various languages and rhythms that, in their diversity, make a very joyful noise to the Lord!

Nancy Rosenberger Faus

229 • ROMAN CATHOLIC SERVICE MUSIC SINCE VATICAN II

Roman Catholic liturgy, like that of many of the more liturgical churches, features texts that are sung in each liturgy or service. These are called the ordinary _texts. Often these texts are sung. Settings of these texts, and other frequently used texts, are called_ service music _or_ liturgical music. _This music is part of the liturgy itself, not something that interrupts or is added to the liturgy. Since the Second Vatican Council in the early 1960s, Catholic churches have had more freedom in choosing service music. This has resulted in vast numbers of new compositions, many of which are valuable for churches in many worship traditions._

The repertoire and use of ritual music within the English-speaking Roman Catholic church today cannot be fully understood without understanding that, since the reforms of the Second Vatican Council in the mid 1960s (when liturgy moved from Latin to the vernacular), there has been no "official" national hymnal for the United States churches. This is a unique situation, unlike that in the English-speaking Canadian Roman Catholic churches, which have published two versions of the *Canadian Book of Worship,* and the Australian Roman Catholic church, which also published a national hymnal in the mid-1970s. The General Directives within the Roman Missal provide instruction regarding the structure and elements of the Mass, but the only musical settings provided in the Missal are chant melodies for the eucharistic prayer and its acclamations, melodies which are not widely used.

This means that the publication of new music and worship books for U.S. Roman Catholics has been determined by publishing houses that are largely independent of the church and in competition with each other. Today there are a number of independent publishing houses in the United States associated with Roman Catholic worship, including GIA Publications (GIA), Pastoral Press, J. S. Paluch Company, and North American Liturgy Resources (NALR). Other companies that are affiliated to an archdiocese but that retain a good deal of publishing independence include Liturgy Training Publications, Chicago (LTP), and Oregon Catholic Press, Portland (OCP).

When a church as large as the English-speaking Roman Catholic church, with a rich liturgical tradition, changes from Latin to the vernacular in all the components of its ritual, a huge increase in the amount of new music generated is inevitable. This growth is only strengthened when combined with competition between independent publishing houses. Thus, it is not surprising that over the past 25 years music has been written and published that represents all manner of styles, quality, and appropriateness. The lack of an "official" worship book and the resulting eruption of new compositions has also meant that the United States Catholic church today utilizes a repertoire of bewildering complexity and uneven quality. A myriad of settings of the various parts of the Ordinary are currently in use in Roman Catholic churches across the United States. (One difficulty in an article such as this is the definition of terms across denominations. The Ordinary of the Mass refers to those parts of the liturgy which Lutherans and other Protestant groups often refer to as service music, that is, those parts of the ritual that are normally used each week, or at least whenever Eucharist is celebrated.) The evolution of the various weekend liturgies within one parish into organ masses, guitar masses, traditional masses, folk or contemporary masses, and silent masses (meaning the absence of music) has further aggravated this confusion. Another factor is the wide diversity of ethnic expression within the Roman Catholic church in the United States. There are many parishes today that have at least one weekend liturgy in Spanish, and there are also a growing number of parishes that primarily reflect African-American culture in their liturgy.

Until now the choice and use of music within an individual parish has depended mainly upon the particular missalette, hymnal, or songbook which that parish uses and upon the liturgical style and interest of the clergy and musicians. In addition, it is not uncommon today for a parish to supplement published music with unpublished compositions by musicians within the parish. Musical settings of the Ordinary of the Mass consequently become nationally known through grass-roots acceptance rather than because of any official mandate. This acceptance-by-acclamation system has allowed and encouraged the composition and distribution of many more settings than would otherwise have been available. While it could be argued that the number and diversity of these settings has provided for a good deal of creative interchange, the situation has also created a somewhat fragmented English-speaking church, in which neighboring churches or even the various liturgies within one parish have such different repertoires that they often can find no common eucharistic settings.

There are currently nine English-language texts of the eucharistic prayer approved for use by the Bishop's Committee on the liturgy (BCL), the official committee that oversees and approves the publication of musical settings of those texts. For seven of the texts the congregational responses consist of the Holy, the Memorial Acclamation (with four optional responses) and the Great Amen. Two of the prayers, both intended for use with children, include additional acclamations for the congregation. Because of the length of the Roman Catholic eucharistic prayer texts (some of which can easily run for 5 minutes), there has been an increasing desire over the past ten years among composers, liturgists, and parish musicians for permission to publish musical settings that provide additional sung acclamations for the congregation.

Beginnings of Liturgical Renewal

In the early days of the liturgical renewal, the division into "organ-based" and "guitar-based" acclamations in settings of the Ordinary was very clear and distinct. The first guitar-based acclamations were very much like popular folk songs that utilized ritual language. Settings such as the "Missa Bossa Nova" (Peter Scholtes) published in the *Hymnal for Young Christians* (FEL, 1966) were widely used. Little thought was paid at this time to the connection between sung acclamations and the eucharistic prayer, or for the need to sing all the congregational parts within the prayer. The most popular of the early "organ-based" acclamations was "Mass for Christian Unity", composed by Jan Vermulst and published by World Library Publications (in 1964) for their *People's Mass Book.*

With the North American Liturgy Resources (NALR) publication *Neither Silver or Gold* (1974), a group of Jesuit priests calling themselves the St. Louis Jesuits introduced an influential body of guitar-based music written for liturgical use. Their compositions marked a shift toward music based more directly on scriptural texts, specifically texts from the Sunday Lectionary. *Neither Silver Nor Gold* also contained a number of eucharistic acclamations written in a through-composed form (similar in form to settings written for organ at that time). A "Holy, Holy, Holy" and a "Doxology—Great Amen" written by Daniel Schutte, S.J. and Robert Dufford, S.J., became immensely popular throughout the English-speaking Roman Catholic church at that time (and continue to be widely used today). As guitar-based eucharistic acclamations, these settings were a step forward. However, in their initial form, the acclamations provided no option for keyboard or other instruments and lacked a memorial acclamation, insuring that musicians would not for some time have a complete set of eucharistic acclamations that were nationally known and could be easily accompanied by either guitar or keyboard.

Also in 1974, an English translation of *The Performing Audience* by the Dutch composer, Bernard Huijbers, was published in the United States. This book greatly influenced the way that liturgical music in general and eucharistic acclamations in particular would be composed. In *The Performing Audience,* Huijbers describes the concept of elemental music as a model for good liturgical compositions. Elemental music consists of simple, diatonic melodies and intervals that are mainly step motion. Leaps are to be predictable and limited in range, mainly thirds and fifths. Together with Huub Oosterhuis, a Dutch priest and textwriter, Huijbers composed a number of "Tableprayers" utilizing elemental music. These were through-composed, musical settings of alternative eucharistic prayer texts. While the prayers themselves were not widely used in the English-speaking church, they helped to influence a number of other composers in the creation of later eucharistic prayers.

The "Community Mass" by Richard Proulx, which became known throughout the English-speaking world through the GIA Publications' hymnal, *Worship II* (1977), set a new standard for quality eucharistic acclamations. Singable, elemental melodies, well-crafted keyboard accompaniments, and a wide variety of instrumental parts made the acclamations very useful for liturgical celebrations accompanied by the organ. Unfortunately for guitarists, Proulx's "Community Mass", as well as his "Festive Eucharist" and Alexander Peloquin's popular "Mass of the Bells" were not well-suited for guitar accompaniment. It was (and still remains) very common within the same parish for one or more weekend liturgies to utilize the St. Louis Jesuit acclamations on guitar while other liturgies use the "Community Mass" on organ.

Also at the same time, Fr. Michael Joncas composed a musical setting of the Institution Narrative in his collection of music, *Here in Our Midst* (NALR). Although the composition did not include the entire eucharistic prayer, it served as a beginning effort pointing toward a sung eucharistic prayer setting.

More Recent Developments

Marty Haugen's "Mass of Creation" (GIA) was published in 1984. This was the first published Mass in the United States that attempted to provide a setting of the Ordinary that could be accompanied either by organ, piano, or guitar. It sought to begin the process of breaking down the divisions between guitar and organ repertoire. One of the factors that helped in the popularization of "Mass of Creation" was the inclusion of a sung setting of Eucharistic Prayer III.

In 1986 Sr. Theophane Hytrek received permission from the BCL to publish the "Mass for St. John the Evangelist" (GIA). This was the first set of eucharistic acclamations published in the U.S. that included additional optional sung acclamations for the congregation within the eucharistic prayer. The approval of this Mass led to the composition and publication in the United States of many similar settings by other composers.

The past ten years have seen an enormous increase in the number of musical settings of the Ordinary, reflecting a wide variety of styles. The popularity of these settings has to a large degree been dependent upon the use of the hymnal or missalette in which they appear. GIA Publications' hymnals, *Gather, Worship,* and *Lead Me, Guide Me,* have popularized Proulx's "Community Mass," Haugen's "Mass of Creation" and "Mass of Remembrance," David Haas' "Mass of Light" and Michael Joncas' "Psalite Mass." The Oregon Catholic Press missalette *Breaking Bread* has exposed congregations to Owen Alstot's "Heritage Mass," eucharistic acclamations by Bernadette Farrell and Paul Inwood, and, more recently, Bob Hurd's Spanish-language setting "Missa de Americas" and gospel-style setting "Alleluia, Give the Glory." The most popular acclamations from North American Liturgy Resources' songbook *Glory and Praise* continue to be those of the St. Louis Jesuits.

Prospects for the Future

Twenty-five years ago, no one would have predicted the amount and diversity of music that would be in use within Roman Catholic parishes today. It is therefore entirely speculative to suggest what might be the sound of Roman Catholic worship in the next century. However, there are a few tantalizing developments that might suggest the future evolution of liturgical music.

In 1992, a study group of composers, textwriters, liturgists, and theologians convened by Archbishop Rembert Weakland produced the *Milwaukee Report.* Among other things, the document called for an increased understanding of the nature of "Christian ritual music" by all those involved in the creation, publication, and use of worship resources. Composers were called to fashion music that is "embedded within the rite," music that finds its meaning and full expression as ritual. If this call is taken seriously, it will mean the creation of ritual music in musical forms that are more sensitive to the structure and dynamics of the liturgy, forms that are flexible, elemental, and dialogical. Some examples might be "gathering rites" that offer the option of conjoining a hymn or song with a kyrie or sprinkling rite, or "Communion rites" that yoke a fraction song (possibly an adaptation of a "Lamb of God") with a Communion song. Rather than moving seemingly from one disjointed element to another, such a model creates (in the words of liturgist Ed Foley) a seamless "macro-rite." Another recommendation of the *Milwaukee Report* was that composers, publishers, and parish musicians begin to discern which settings of ritual music have won widespread grass-roots recognition, and seek to give those settings quasi-official status, so that a universal repertoire of ritual music can begin to evolve. Naturally, there is little clarity and much debate about how and to what degree such a move should happen. The Milwaukee group called on composers and publishers to "flesh out" existing ritual music publications rather than create endless new settings. This might mean setting a number of the eucharistic prayer texts to the same congregational acclamations.

Over the past six to eight years there has been a significant increase in the sharing of music between liturgical publishers. A notable result of this sharing is that a number of musical settings of the Ordinary are now appearing in all the major publications and becoming more widely known. As this trend continues, it is likely that an unofficial national repertoire of service music will evolve.

International, Interdenominational, and Multicultural Cross-Fertilization

The North American Roman Catholic church has reaped enormous benefits from its interaction with Protestant composers and text writers, and from the contributions of artists in other English-speaking countries. In the past few years, Lutheran composer Richard Hillert, English composers Bernadette Farrell, Paul Inwood, and Christopher Walker of the St. Thomas More Group, and Tony Way of Australia have all contributed settings of the Ordinary to the North American Catholic church repertoire. Liturgical compositions from such Protestant composers as Hillert, John Bell (of the Iona Community in Scotland), Carol Doran, Hal Hopson, Austin Lovelace, Don Saliers, and new settings of texts by such Protestant text writers as Timothy Dudley-Smith, Fred Pratt Green and Brian Wren (all of Great Britain), John Bell and Graham Maule (of the Iona Community), Ruth Duck, Sylvia Dunstan, Tom Troeger, and Jaroslav Vajda have all been published by unofficial Roman Catholic publishing houses such as GIA Publications and Oregon Catholic Press.

In seeking models for dialogical ritual music, many U.S. and Canadian composers have looked to the music of other cultures. The music from the

Taizé community, music collected and written by John Bell and Graham Maule for the Scottish community of Iona, and the South African music in the collection _Freedom is Coming_ have been especially popular. The use of such music will certainly influence the musical forms and sounds of future North American liturgical compositions.

The number of Spanish-speaking Roman Catholics has been increasing dramatically in recent times. Publishers have done an uneven job at best in addressing the needs of Catholic parishes with Spanish-speaking liturgies. At the present time, composers and publishers are beginning to become more aware of the need for a more extensive and useful liturgical repertoire in Spanish. Hispanic composers Donna Pena, Lorenzo Florien, and Cuco Chavez and the Anglo composer Bob Hurd have been providing significant music for Spanish-speaking parishes.

Marty Haugen

230 • THE MUSIC OF THE IONA COMMUNITY

From its location on an island off the coast of Scotland, the Iona Community has done much to influence the music of the world church, especially in North America. They have done this by providing the music used in their own worship services and by collecting songs from the church on every continent.

— The History of the Iona Community —

The Iona Community was founded in 1939 by George MacLeod (later Lord MacLeod of Fuinary), a prophetic minister of the Church of Scotland from both aristocratic and ecclesiastical stock.

At the time when the church, as much else, was in the doldrums due to mid-war depression, he tried to engage the worship of the sanctuary with the life of the street. After a successful church and community experiment in rebuilding a disused mill to become a children's holiday center, he was motivated to embark for the island of Iona with 12 men, half of them trainee clergy and half unemployed workers. Thus, the Iona Community is _not_ a monastic order. Members, with very few exceptions, do _not_ live on Iona. And music and liturgy is not its primary focus.

Iona was the place to which, in 563, Columba came to start a new missionary movement, the ripples of which extended far beyond the shores of Scotland. This evangelistic enterprise, undertaken by Celtic monks, was in due course replaced by the more contemplative monastic life of the Benedictines, who built their abbey in the thirteenth century where Columba had built his in the sixth. Like many Roman Catholic sites, during the Reformation, the abbey settlement was despoiled and vandalized.

The local landowner, the Duke of Argyll renovated much of the sanctuary at the end of the nineteenth century, requiring that its use should not be the preserve of one single Christian denomination. But this ecumenical gesture bore little fruit, partly as ecumenism was not a favorite pastime of nineteenth-century Scots and partly because the remoteness of Iona and the lack of any living accommodation made regular worship in the sanctuary a virtual impossibility.

In 1939, George MacLeod went to Iona to rebuild the other parts of the monastic settlement associated with the common life: the refectory, the chapter house, the infirmary, the library, the chapels, the cloisters, and the bedrooms. It was his hope that the buildings might house an alternative kind of seminary. But over the summers in which rebuilding took place with an ever-increasing and ever-international group of volunteers, the seminary notion was replaced by the idea of the abbey becoming a center for reconciliation, a place of meeting opposites—rich and poor, Catholic and Protestant, faithful and faithless, Germans and British, Third World and First World. During the rebuilding, those most closely involved in the process became convinced of certain aspects of Christian discipleship which, for long, the churches had failed to attend to—personal devotions, the ministry of healing, claiming the political realm for Christ, acknowledging the potential for global annihilation epitomized in the atom bomb, opposing the seduction of materialism.

In time, some of these concerns were framed into discipline or rule that is still the basis of membership of the Iona Community. This rule with its five commitments is kept by members whether they live in island or urban settings, whether they are Catholic or Quaker, male or female, lay or ordained, hospital consultants or domestics.

At present, the Community has over 200 members throughout Great Britain, with a few who have had residency in Scotland living abroad. There are over 1,000 associate members who keep some sections of the rule. What enables members to call themselves a community when they live far apart is both their adherence to the rule and their meeting with each other monthly in regional groups and four times yearly in plenary events.

It may fairly be said that in the fifty-four years of its existence, the Community has had an effect on the life of the church, especially in Britain, out of proportion to its membership. This is in no small way due to the charismatic leadership and personality of MacLeod, its founder who, though a holder of the Military Cross from World War I, became a tireless campaigner for peace and a thorn in the flesh of denominational protectionists by his unrelenting ecumenical enthusiasm. Bishop John Robinson called MacLoud one of the main inspirations for the controversial best seller, *Honest to God*. Having spoken convincingly to thousands of Christians and skeptics throughout the English speaking world about the social and political imperatives of the gospel, MacLoud was awarded the Templeton Award for Progress in Religion towards the end of his life.

But the Community had other pioneers. Much of the initial development work in industrial mission, the healing ministry, mission in areas of urban extension and ecumenical ministry in Scotland, was initiated and advanced by people who were either members of the Iona Community or who came under the inspiration of its founder. The proof of this lively and valued legacy is perhaps best illustrated by the fact what when, during the recession in the late 1980s, the Community decided to replace decrepit wooden huts that masqueraded as a youth camp with center suitable for young people, families, and the disabled. The project, which was the subject of an international architectural competition, was opened debt-free in 1988. The public enthusiasm for its construction was in no small way a gesture of gratitude for the Community and its founder, after whom the MacLeod center is named.

The Music of the Iona Community

There was nothing particularly innovative about the music of the Community for most of the first forty years.

When members were at home, they used the hymnody of their denomination. There was no Iona Community religious song book. When members met in plenary on the mainland or when worship was offered in the abbey in Iona, use was made, in the main, of the 1650 *Scottish Psalter* and the 1929 *Revised Church Hymnary*. This latter was a Presbyterian production, used by the Church of Scotland and its sister churches throughout the British Isles

and the Commonwealth. As most members in the beginning were Presbyterians, and as Iona was within Scotland, its hymnody was that of the majority church culture.

But there were some areas of distinctiveness.

In the first place, the abbey did not have a pipe organ, the perceived norm of ecclesiastical buildings of distinction. For reasons of atmosphere as much as cost and maintenance, it was decided not to install such an instrument, but instead to have two grand pianos positioned in the area known as the musician's gallery, a loft to the left of the chancel. Those who know the abbey would vouch for the sufficiency of the piano to provide keyboard accompaniment where required; few, if any, would wish a pipe instrument in the precincts.

Secondly, the acoustic of the abbey is very good for unaccompanied singing that most ancient Scottish modes of congregational comprise. This form of song long predominated both inside the abbey and outside at several open air ceremonies marking various stages of completion.

Thirdly, during the 1950s, when the youth contingent coming to camps run by the Community increased, musicians of stature were recruited to take charge of the leadership of congregational song, to provide service music, and to encourage vocal and instrumental ensembles among the visitors. Two notables of this era were Reginald Varret-Ayres, a composer and for some time senior lecturer in music at the University of Aberdeen; and Ian MacKenzie, previously and severally assistant organist and assistant minister at St. Giles' Cathedral, Edinburgh. Ian MacKenzie was to become head of religious broadcasting for BBC Scotland and, most recently, delivered the prestigious Baird Lectures, subsequently published, in which he took an overview of music in the church and acknowledged his own indebtedness to his time on Iona.

Away from the island, members of the Community were unwittingly chiseling out a niche for themselves during the 1960s in the development of church music. Ian Fraser, then warden of Scottish Churches' House, Dunblane, cajoled by the late Eric Routley and in the company of other British writers and composers (including Sydney Carter), began a series of hymn-writing encounters which, in the view of many, started the chain reaction leading to the "hymn explosion" in Great Britain. Songs of this era are found in such publications as *Dunblane Praises* and *Songs of the Seventies* (St. Andrew

Press). Undoubtedly, some of this output or its antecedents were being used in worship on Iona long
before they filtered through to parish churches.
"Lord of the Dance" was such an early firm favorite
in Iona, and George MacLeod structured a Communion order in keeping with its sentiment.

Further afield yet, Tom Colvin, a member of the
Community working in central Africa, began to collect tunes from Ghana and Malawi to which he set
either original texts, in keeping with the indigenous
prototypes, or to which he set metrical translations
of the original words. All through the world the
Malawian hymn "Kneels at the Feet of His Friends"
is now well loved and sung, the result of the efforts
of a member of the Iona Community.

There were also other members, such as Ian
Cowie, formerly the director of the Scottish
Churches Healing Center in Edinburgh, and Douglas Galbraith, presently chaplain of St. Andrews University, who were in their own spheres of activity
generating interest in musical development: Ian
wrote words to traditional melodies, while Douglas
pioneered instrumental ensembles at a time when
they were most suspected in Presbyterian parishes.

Contemporary Developments

It is, however, in the last decade that particular
interest in the music emanating from the Iona Community has been raised.

The reasons have little to do with the antecedents
mentioned above and little to do with the island of
Iona.

In the early 1980s youth work within the Church
of Scotland began to change gear with the appoint-
ment in 1978 of Ian Galloway to the post of National
Youth Adviser, based in Edinburgh, and John Bell as
Glasgow Presbytery Adviser in the West of Scotland.
Galloway was a member of the Iona Community;
Bell scarcely knew about it.

Among some of the initiatives they developed was
a biannual youth festival on Iona for young people
of all denominations and even those without affiliations. The experience of the first festival in 1980
made quite clear the paucity of musical and liturgical resources the churches had to capture the imagination and concerns of contemporary young adults.

Later, in Glasgow, John Bell was joined in his work
by Graham Maule (another outsider to Iona) and
began monthly youth events called "Last of the
Month" which over five years attracted up to 500
young people per evening, most of whom had never

been to church in the morning, all of whom were
prepared to stay for worship at the end of the evening.

The Iona Community also sponsored the formation of a cadre of full-time volunteers. These young
adults were prepared to go on the dole for a year or
more, live in areas of urban deprivation, and try to
understand the life of such communities and discern ways of serving the people and the local
churches. This group, which numbered almost
sixty individuals over a five year period, reflected
regularly on their life and faith. They experienced
the inability of traditional religious language and
hymnody to reflect the reality of the life of the
streets as they encountered it or the conflicting
emotions in their own souls.

These experiences—the biannual youth festival,
the monthly youth events, and the experience of
unemployed young people engaging, under the gospel, in the life of impoverished neighborhoods—
these and not quiet monastic surroundings, poetry
prep-schools or circles of gifted musicians—provided the seedbeds for the music now associated
with the Iona Community.

What immeasurably aided the process were two
distinctive areas of liturgical development.

Ian and Kathy Galloway moved from Edinburgh
in 1983 to become joint wardens of Iona abbey.
They went, with among other things, the burning
conviction that worship mattered. Within a short
while, they had used the flexibility of the worshiping space in the abbey to develop morning and evening liturgies. Their robust enthusiasm for
communal singing deepened their commitment to
find musicians appropriate to the task of leadership.
This commitment resulted in the creation of the
post of abbey musician. Instead of being a hit or
miss sequence of six-week volunteers, this position
became a permanent job, perhaps the first full-time
post for a church musician in any Scottish religious
establishment except for the Cathedrals.

In Glasgow, for those who came to the Last of the
Month events, Bell and Maule brought together a
group of young adults who were disquieted with
the predictable and failing patterns of church worship and were keen on investigating other potential
liturgies. From a Lenten study group, which did
little more than reflect, argue, and dream, there
emerged the Wild Goose Worship Group.

This group, begun in 1984, has never had more
than 18 members and has never had any more than

a quarter who can read music proficiently. They range in occupation from a prosthetist (artificial limb maker) to a child-care officer. They do not perceive themselves as a choir and have no intention of emulating a traditional choral sound. From October to May they meet once a week for practice, planning, and worship and all year round lead workshops and worship in churches or at conferences throughout the British Isles. Their liturgical interest is not restricted to song. They devise workshops and methods enabling people to develop skills in corporate prayer, use of Scripture, environment, personal spirituality, and drama.

The group has made seven cassettes and appears regularly either live or on tape in radio and television broadcasts both in Britain and beyond. They have been unilaterally acclaimed as one of—if not *the* most—innovative liturgical groups in Britain today. None of them has ever studied church music and only one of them holds a degree in theology.

— The Process of Musical Development —

To understand the music of the Iona Community (apart from recognizing that its roots are deeply in urban experience rather than island soil), it is perhaps important to know how the original compositions in the published volumes came about.

It was—and continues to be—a very corporate effort.

The origination of words and music is largely the work of John Bell. Prior to any composition, however, the seed for such music begins with conversations within the group or at seminars and workshops where life, faith, and the Scriptures are discussed. Bell works on a first draft of text and music which, most frequently, Maule amends or comments on.

A second draft is then shared with the Worship Group. They have to decide whether the text makes sense and the melody and harmony is singable. If they express strongly negative feelings, the work is discarded. If they suggest alterations in word, melody, or harmony, these are taken on board and produced in the third draft. This is what may be shared with a bigger group in church or at conferences. Again, if it falters or detracts from the act of worship, it will be amended or discarded.

Only after a song, hymn or chant has gone through these processes will it be considered—when the time is right—for publication.

Behind this lies the conviction that hymns are destined to become public property. If the public has no possibility of influencing them, if they remain the precious possession of an obsessive writer who fears criticism, it is better that they be aborted at conception. A hymn is not a private expression of highly personal piety or emotion. A hymn is for public use to express a shared response to the Word, Spirit, and will of God. The more corporate its formation and nurturing, the more likely it is to be apposite, meaningful, and singable.

———— Wild Goose Songs ————

The name, for convenience alone, comes from the original title of the two volumes published in 1987 and 1988, subsequently printed under more descriptive titles.

The Wild Goose is a Celtic symbol for the Holy Spirit as well as being the name of the Worship Group. It is also the name associated with Iona Community Publications.

To date there have been six published collections:

* *Heaven Shall Not Wait* (1987)—fifty songs plus chants on Creation and on the birth and life of Jesus. (Hereafter referred to as *HSNW.*)
* *Enemy of Apathy* (1988)—fifty songs plus chants on the passion, death, and resurrection of Jesus and on the coming of the Holy Spirit. (Hereafter referred to as *EOA.*)
* *Love From Below* (1989)—fifty songs plus chants on stages of discipleship and on the sacraments and ceremonies of the Christian life. (Hereafter referred to as *LFB.*)
* *Many and Great* (1990)—twenty-five songs from the world church, with a slight preponderance of African songs. (Hereafter referred to as *M&G.*)
* *Sent By the Lord* (1991)—twenty-five songs from the world church, with a slight preponderance of Central American songs. (Hereafter referred to as *SBTL.*)
* *Innkeepers and Light Sleepers* (1992)—17 carols for Advent, Christmas, and Epiphany. (Hereafter referred to as *I&LS.*)

Also published in September 1993 was a collection of psalm settings in metrical, chant, and antiphonal styles entitled *Psalms of Patience, Protest, and Praise.*

Stylistically the songs fall into seven nonexclusive

categories which are, in no small way, evocative of the Community's earlier musical styles.

1. Psalms and Paraphrases.

Through a series of conversations about the Psalms—especially the "avoided" ones—and through personal and public attesting of the worth of these ancient biblical expressions of praise, wonder, anger, contrition, and despair, there emerged a desire to have at least some psalm texts both translated into contemporary language and also set to styles of music that would evoke the original intention and intensity of the words.

The misconception of psalms as being solely "praise songs" is something that the Worship Group often has had to counter. Many people who have been saturated with vapid, easy-listening religious music often fail to grasp that the psalms Jesus used express the whole gamut of experience. The collection, _Psalms of Patience, Protest, and Praise_ illustrates the variety of styles which have been found suitable to convey the force of the texts. Some are new metricizations; some are set as chants with more by way of melody than traditional Anglican chant might afford; some use the favored Roman Catholic form of shared antiphon and solo or choral verse; and some are paraphrases in blank verse or rhyme. Previously published examples include "How Long, O Lord?" a bluesy lament found in _Heaven Shall Not Wait_ based on Psalm 13, and "Thirsting for God," a modal four-part metrical setting of Psalm 42 found in _Love From Below._

There have always been attempts to put Scripture into verse by paraphrasing it. This is an ancient as well as a contemporary educational tool. It exposes some people to passages of Scripture that they might never stumble over by casual reading or ever take note of through dull public expounding.

Of continuing popularity are "Sing Praise to God on Mountain Tops" and "Dance and Sing All the Earth," both paraphrases of Genesis chapter 1. "A Woman's Care" (_HSNW_) is based on verses from Isaiah and Romans and has been found very helpful in its allusion to God's self revelation as a being who encompasses motherly as well as fatherly qualities. "Though One with God" is a direct paraphrase of Philippians chapter 2 and, being set to JERUSALEM affords Scottish worshipers the rare opportunity of singing a grand tune they enjoy without the intrusion of patriotic English sentiment.

2. Hymns in Traditional Meters.

One of the realizations of the Worship Group early on was that what people sing has a great effect in shaping their faith. If all one ever sings is four-line choruses about God being wonderful, then faith will find it hard to cope with days when God seems absent or with experiences in contemporary life that have no immediate biblical proof text.

There is, therefore, a value in using CM, 8787D, or 8686 and chorus forms where over the space of four or five verses, a life experience, a theological insight, a musing of some kind on a personal or global dilemma, or the call and response to discipleship can be represented with an economy of words but without the dearth of linguistic expression which inhabits many worship songs from both sides of the Atlantic.

"Jesus Calls Us" (_HSNW_), "Darkness Is Gone" (_EOA_), "We Who Live by Sight and Symbol" (_LFB_), and "Funny Kind of Night" (_I&LS_) are all examples of hymns that would not look out of place in most denominational hymnals. They are there as tributes to the fact that solid stanzas of hymnody shape faith and enlarge our understanding of God. Frequently they will employ traditional tunes such as HYFRYDOL and "Praise My Soul" to accompany the words.

3. Contemporary Songs.

It would be blind and naive to imagine that hymnody cannot be affected by types of popular music, be it ballads, blues, rock, or whatever. Such effects may be seen in the style of writing (such as contemporary choruses or charismatic songs), in the content of the songs themselves (discussion of contemporary realities such as homelessness, AIDS, and so on), the musical expression (composed for guitars or instrumental ensembles rather than the piano or organ), and the tempo (upbeat, syncopated, etc.). Undeniably, while the Iona Community books have a number of songs in what could be called a contemporary style (good examples are "We're Going to Shine like the Sun," "Lord of All," or "Take This Moment"), it is not the predominant type or form of expression. That is partly because of the limitations of the composers, partly because the focus has been on what the voices can do rather than what instruments can do, and partly because there is plenty of such material already available from other sources.

4. Hymns Reflecting the Celtic Expression of Christianity.

Iona was one of the cradles of the ancient Celtic church. Saints such as Patrick and Columba or their amanuenses produced hymns that are still sung today, such as "I Bind unto Myself" or "O God, Thou Art the Father." But the Celtic church did not begin and end with the notables. Long after the Celtic church's official demise at the Synod of Whitby in A.D. 644, the expression of spirituality engendered by the early saints and missionaries was kept alive and developed by communities of people living in remote parts of Scotland, Ireland, Wales, and southwest England.

This tradition of orally transmitted prayer, poem, and song provided fertile soil for Scottish writers of more contemporary years who have drawn on the theological and devotional insights of the Celtic peoples regarding their fundamental belief in the Incarnation, their appraisal of Creation as being God-filled, their affection for the Scriptures, their close alliance of work and worship. Perhaps the most famous example of relatively recent Celtic song is the Christmas carol "Child in a Manger," written by a woman from the Isle of Mull, which lies between the mainland of Scotland and Iona.

Songs published by the Iona Community such as "Today I Awake" (*EOA*), based on the form of St. Patrick's breastplate, "Praise to the Lord for the Joys of the Early" (*HSNW*), "Torn in Two" (*EOA*), and "Hush a Bye" (*I&LS*) are examples of contemporary verse which find their inspiration from the Celtic tradition. In particular, the ancient runes and poems that appear in the Carmina Gadelica collection gathered and translated by Alexander Carmichael have been a rich source for Community songs.

5. Folk Hymns. This category subsumes both songs which are linguistically in a folk style and hymns that are set to folk tunes. It would be fair to say that both these types of songs are closely identified with the Iona Community and have proved to be significant. Folk-style words are more suited for celebrating the humanity of Jesus and the intimacy of the risen Christ than is the case either with grandiose Victorian melodies or with contemporary choruses.

Christ chose not to remain isolated, but to come close in order that he might share our industrial and domestic life. That he calls us by name and engages us in ordinary conversation is seldom reflected in the hymnody of the church. Folk-style words and folk tunes enable this reality to happen comfortably. Thus a line such as "Christ it was who said to Martha, 'listen first, then make the tea'" ("God It Was," *LFB*) would seem extraordinary in a classical hymn set to a churchy tune. But in a song about the kinds of people Christ called, set to an island tune from Skye, there is no irregularity or conflict. Examples of this genre may be found in "Sing Hey for the Carpenter" (*HSNW*), "I Will Give What I Have" (*EOA*), "Jesus Is Risen from the Grave" (*LFB*) and "O Sarah, She Was Ninety" (*I&LS*). In each case the words were accompanied by a composed tune written in a folk style.

When words are set to traditional tunes, something else is in play. Here one of the most ancient Jewish and Christian traditions is continued. (Some of the Psalms were first sung to Jewish folk tunes.) But more than that, the use of folk melody both ensures singability, and allows the gospel to be incarnated, cradled, and clothed in the culture of the nation. It might well be argued that where indigenous cultural expressions have been disdained in favor of a high-church culture—as has been the case in Britain—the notion of God and the things of God as being the prerogative of some kind of religious intelligentsia is reinforced.

Some of the most frequently requested of the Community's songs, for radio and television use and for reproduction in publications or hymn sheets, are those set to Scottish folk tunes, of which the following are typical:

- "The Strangest of Saints" (*HSNW*)
- "Will You Come and Follow Me?" (*HSNW*)
- "The Servant" (*EOA*)
- "Paul's Song" (*EOA*)
- "A Touching Place" (*HSNW*)
- "We Cannot Measure" (*LFB*)
- "Hush a Bye" (*I&LS*)

6. Chants. Like most religious communities, Iona has been aware of the work of Taizé, and many people are familiar with its music. The form of a repeated chant is not something that endears itself immediately to a land where the majority of Christians have been bred on psalms or multistanza hymns. And seldom does the climate allow one to sit in the open air or in enclosed spaces on a balmy night, singing "Ubi Caritas et Amor" for twenty minutes on end.

Yet the value of the meditative chant as an aid to worship or as a response to prayer, preaching, or the proclamation of Scripture has not gone unnoticed. Thus in each of the songbooks of original material there are a number of items in this genre. Some are unison or canon, e.g., "Be Still and Know" (*LFB*), some are straightforward SATB harmony, e.g., "Dona Nobis" (*HSNW*), while others may have some choral interest that is easily within a congregation's grasp, e.g. "Here I Stand" (*EOA*).

7. **World Church Songs.** If folk hymns constitute one style immediately identifiable with music from the Iona Community, the other style must be world church songs. To date, two collections of twenty five songs have been published, nearly all of which were gathered from natives of the countries concerned. This does not mean the compilers traveled worldwide. Within all European and North American countries are the representatives of other nations, yet seldom are their liturgical insights or musical gifts used in local churches.

Sometimes it has been from overseas nationals living in Britain that songs have been collected, and sometimes from church delegates at international conferences and conventions. The Wild Goose Worship Group has sung these songs extensively throughout Great Britain, often—as in the case of South African songs—at open air demonstrations, at Third World conferences, and particularly in local churches. Despite what might be presumed to be an awkwardness in using a non-European language or a difficulty in singing a Southern Hemisphere melody, the published songs offer few difficulties to users. In the selection process, only those which could be sung comfortably by Western voices were chosen.

Wherever possible, the traditional harmony or arrangement has been retained, even though transcribing it was sometimes an adventure, as in the case of "Amen Alleluia" (*M&G*). Where no harmony has been available, sometimes a harmonization has been devised keeping as near as possible to similar material from the same area (see "Imela" [*M&G*] and "Sent by the Lord" [*SBTL*]). In other cases, a harmonization has been made which, while not like the indigenous variety, is different from the domesticated harmonies that previous Western composers inflicted on overseas melodies, making them lose their sparkle and sound neo-Victorian. "Many and Great" (*M&G*) and "Somos Pueblo" (*SBTL*) are two examples of this process.

The songs are sung partly as a means of widening our experience of the witness to the internationality of the Christian community; partly to increase our understanding of God who, when worshiped only in the mother tongue, can become a national idol; and partly as an act of intercession and solidarity, especially at times when nations whose songs have been published are in situations of peril or war.

Use and Acceptance

All published songs from the Iona Community were never intended initially for publication or circulation. They were produced to answer a local need, to fit a particular situation or liturgy, to express a shared discovery. It was never the intention of their writers that they should be gathered into volumes in Britain, let alone published in new editions in the USA and be distributed throughout Australia.

Yet this has happened and there have been fulsome reviews and testimonies from high and humble places. Some critics are appreciative of the style of harmonization, some of the melodic line; some appreciate songs that can be sung a cappella; some express gratitude for material that can be of immediate use to a youth choir or adult ensembles with limited experience.

Many of the correspondents are particularly appreciative of the words, claiming that their freshness and directness communicates in a way that traditional hymns or contemporary choruses do not. This may be associated with the range of subject matter as much as the use of everyday or domestic vocabulary.

It has been interesting to note the appreciative comments of skilled performers, liturgists and musicologists, and at the same time to discover many lay Christians, long sickened by trite rhymes and predictable chord sequences, warming to something which, in their eyes, has both simplicity and sophistication.

In recent years the songs have been represented in a lunch-time recital in Westminster Abbey, used by the World Council of Churches at its Canberra Assembly, featured in television programs in Britain and Germany, and included in the major denominational and commercial hymn collections published or in preparation on both sides of the Atlantic.

Wild Goose Publications of the Iona Community remains the copyright holder and British publisher, with Willow Connection its distribution agency for Australia and New Zealand. In the USA, a very happy relationship exists with GIA Publications of Chicago, who have reinscribed and published the books and are copyright administrators in North America.

John Bell

231 • THE MUSIC OF THE TAIZÉ COMMUNITY

Taizé is a worship renewal community in France that has developed a style of music and Scripture song for all parts of worship. The article below introduces the community, its worship, and song.

In a tiny village in the south of France lies a religious community that has become a focus of spiritual renewal of the young and a center of reconciliation among Christians. A young Protestant lay person had the vision of a community where one's denominational identity would not matter. What would matter would be one's ability to welcome the stranger and pilgrim, no matter who they were, in the name of Christ. Initially a refuge, sanctuary, and shelter for those burdened with the horrors of World War II, the community under the leadership of Brother Roger nearly a half a century ago began welcoming others who would help establish communion amidst division.

Today people come from every corner of the world to irenic Taizé. Three times a day the pilgrims join the brothers in common prayer in order to deepen their inner lives so as to live in solidarity with the whole of humanity. Simple accommodation and food is the venue, with Bible study and questions and answers completing the day's activities.

A week at Taizé reflects the themes one finds in the celebration of Holy Week—the suffering, passion, death, and resurrection of Jesus. At the foot of the cross, prayers and chants flow for the wounded people and places of the world. The sheer numbers of worshipers and their youthful vitality create a spirit of prayer that brings one in touch with the heart of God.

In such a diverse group—usually in the thousands—it was thought necessary to bring a unity to the worship. Jacques Berthier, a trained musician and member of the ecumenical order, developed a style of ostinato chant (repetition of a persistent phrase of music and text) that was simple, short, and direct. Various languages are used because the worship is always international. Most often Latin is used as a "common expression and liturgical language."

The result is a style of sung prayer that can transform and inspire worship. Translated to the local church situation, it is particularly suited for the Communion service. The actual distribution of Holy Communion, whether formally at an altar rail or served in the pew, can be a time of awkward silence or scattered wanderings of mind and eyes. Looking at people coming to the rail or watching deacons collect empty cups hardly makes for a worshipful experience. Rather than dealing with a complete hymn text, choir anthem, or solo, the use of these chants can capture the solemnity and intimacy of meeting the Lord in Holy Communion through their haunting repetition. The use of these Scripture phrases and liturgical prose forms the chants that are sung repeatedly. Using a simple music line (though often four-part harmony), the worshiper can fix his or her heart and mind on such phrases as

Jesus, remember me when you come into your kingdom
   or
Bless the Lord my soul, and bless his holy name

Bless the Lord my soul, he rescues me from death
   or
O Lord Jesus Christ (*O Christe Domine Jesu*)
   or
We adore you Lord (*Adoremus te Domine*)

At Taizé, with its hillside scenery, all join in such sung prayer; it is simple, easy to remember, and lends itself to a focus that is shaped in prayer and meditation rather than complication. It is an acquired taste that can become a powerful expression of prayer in any gathering large or small.

The music is substantive; for most chants there are cantor parts using psalms and canticles for the text set to easy-flowing melodies with parts provided for a host of instruments including oboe, guitar, piano, organ, strings, flute, and brass. Because many classify Taizé music as "modern," they in turn forsake the use of the organ. This is most unfortunate. A well-registered organ can be a perfect way to keep the ostinato going. The initial chant can be sung by a cantor, repeated by the choir, and then joined by all in singing (praying). After the ostinato is firmly established by the assembly, a cantor and/or instruments can augment the prayer with an obligato text, litany, descant, or instrumental embellishments.

There are also chants for the ordinary (unchanging parts) parts of the Eucharist rite, *Kyrie* ("Lord, have mercy"), *Gloria* ("Glory to God"), *Sanctus* ("Holy, Holy, Holy") and *Agnus Dei* ("Lamb of God").

Monks at Taizé come from Anglican, Lutheran, Reformed, and Roman Catholic backgrounds representing twenty nations of the world. Since its founding in the 1940s, popes and archbishops of Canterbury have been among the visitors. The ministries of prayer and reconciliation override the need for strict denominational labels. Brothers also live in North and South America, Africa, and Asia. They live on the income from their work alone; they do not accept donations. Pilgrims from Western countries, by the fees asked for accommodation and board, help pay for visitors from poorer parts of the world. The common prayer of Taizé is one of the gifts the young take home with them wherever they happen to live. Prayer cells and groups are often established at home to maintain a connection with the order.

Each Christmastide an international Taizé gathering is held in a major city, with usually over 50,000 attending. No one Christian tradition can claim this unique musical offering as their own; it belongs to the worshipful Christian willing to use it.

James Rosenthal

232 ✦ PRAYER CHANTS

Like the music from Taizé described earlier, prayer chants may be comprised of one textual and musical phrase that is repeated. This kind of chant focuses the attention of the worshiper and allows the worshiper to experience God's presence without the need to be concerned about the mechanics of the music.

——— Using Chants in Worship ———

Prayer chanting—a musical form in which complete concentration is given to a repeated word or phrase—can be a useful meditation technique. This form is similar in style to the Jesus prayer: "O Lord Jesus Christ, Son of God, Savior, have mercy on me, a sinner."

Prayer chants are also beginning to be used in liturgical (communal prayer) settings. Liturgists and musicians are learning that this short ostinato form complements hymns, songs, responsorial psalms, litanies, and acclamations. The prayer chant experience is somehow different from that found in other musical forms.

But what connection exists between the chanting experienced seated alone in a room before crucifix and candle, and the chanting experienced in St. Paul Church among hundreds of parishioners?

The Mystical Body. What happens in liturgy when an assembly worships by singing a prayer chant?

Since the chant is easy to learn and enter into, the assembly is joined together by high-level participation. As they repeat the chant and become one breath of song, their concentration becomes more and more focused. Finally, they experience the true Christian identity—not in a better way than in other sung forms, but in a different way.

A worshiping assembly has a sense of being the body of Christ through chanting. But this identity is best explained by first exploring the notions of breath and focus in prayer.

Breath and Spirit. Awareness of breath is key to prayer chant for both physiological and biblical reasons.

In Hebrew Scriptures, the word for "breath" or "wind" is *ruah*. This is the same word used for the "spirit of Yahweh" (*ruah YHVH*) or the "spirit of God" (*ruah elohim*). In the Hebrew mind, breath signified life, and the absence of *ruah* was the absence of the life force. The presence of *ruah* meant the presence of God's power.

The notion of God's Spirit as a power is continued in the Christian Scriptures, except that for the first time spirit is revealed as the person, Spirit of God. This pneumatology is highly developed in the Gospel of John and climaxes in 19:30 when Jesus *breathes* forth his own Spirit as he dies on the cross, and in 20:19-23 when Jesus *breathes* the Spirit onto his followers after the Resurrection.

With such awareness of the possibility of connecting one's own breath with the power and very Spirit of God, let us turn to the Hesychist prayer tradition. Hesychasm grew out of the teachings and experience of the early Greek fathers and flourished in the monastic centers of Mediterranean and Eastern Europe. Hesychasm taught a prayer form that connected one's breath and heartbeat with the repetition of the name of Jesus—the Jesus Prayer. Years of practice led to a continual sense of prayer since one's most natural bodily functions became a vehicle for an awareness of communion with God. A Hesychist learned to breath in and out the Spirit of God.

In the Hesychist tradition, the physical is not shunned, but embraced as an aid to prayer. Prayer chanting is similarly holistic. The singing allows for the natural rhythm of one's breath to aid one's awareness of the natural presence of God's Spirit.

Does not *ruah,* the breath of God, bind us as one when we allow the *ruah* to flow in and out of our bodies as we chant together? Just as the Spirit brings relaxation and peace to the Christian, so too the Spirit enlivens, unifies, and empowers the whole body in communal worship. In fact, the Spirit connects us into one body during liturgy. *Lumen Gentium* teaches that when Christ gave forth his Spirit, he made all his disciples mystically into his own body.

Concentrated Focus. In using a prayer chant, you use an apophatic prayer technique of focusing on one phrase, melody, attitude. Your busy, scattered mind becomes single-minded by turning from all other thoughts and attitudes not of the prayer chant. Your whole being focuses upon the prayer chanting as a way to realize God's presence. This continual flow of sound, meditative in nature, makes the heart receptive to the holy.

Although much of what has been said applies to mantras, a prayer chant is not a mantra. The East and West have different conceptions of consciousness, cosmos, deity, and salvation. Using the terms as synonyms is careless. Mantras often have specific hand gestures and visualizations that accompany them. Mantras correspond to "mental vibrations" which are projected upon the centers of consciousness in the body (*chakras*). So a mantra, properly understood in the Eastern religious sense, is more than a prayer chant.

The concentrated focus of the chanting may lead to a sense of timelessness. Often the moment between ending one repetition and beginning another is a blessed encounter with sacred silence. This "indivisible moment of infinite duration" confers the greatest stillness and peace.

In liturgical settings, when the whole assembly is taken up in worship and prayer, a similar "timeless" experience may occur. Through the intensity of the repeating chant, some of the participants may sense an uplifting that imparts a vision of eternal worship.

This grace of being so lost in the singing and prayer is a momentary eschatological glimpse of all renewed creation worshiping in the glory of God's light and love.

A Christian, through prayer chanting, also gains a new awareness. For Christians, this gift is a grace of light, and this light is Jesus.

Using the tools of rhythmic breath and concentration, a prayer chanter sees himself or herself and all else through the eyes of God. An assembly, also worshiping in this way, begins to see itself in the light. This light reveals to the people that they are the body of Christ.

The prayer chant is not magic; it is one form of many. Yet the rhythmic breath and concentrated focus of the chant can bind the assembly and offer it an opportunity to experience its true identity, as the body of Christ.

Where to Use Chants in Worship

Liturgical Music Today speaks of two functions of song: (1) to support the action and (2) to be part of the constituent element of the action. These two functions of song together with different styles of texts give rise to three types of liturgical prayer chants: *processional, intercessory,* and *devotional.*

A *processional* chant supports the action of liturgical ministers or assembly. The two processions in liturgy take place during the Entrance rite and Communion rite. Prayer chants are extremely practical during these times because the form is easily used and repeated, freeing people's hands of songsheets or hymnals. Hands are then free to be held together or to hold banners in an Entrance procession. Hands are free to receive Communion in the hand and to take the cup.

An *intercessory* chant is unlike a processional chant in that it supports some action of the assembly. An intercessory chant is the specific action of the worshiping body, usually during the penitential rite or during the general intercessions. The text of the chant expresses a spirit of petition or contrition. Additional phrases may be added by a singing or speaking soloist over the singing voice of the assembly.

A *devotional* chant is similar to the intercessory chant in being a specific action of the assembly; nothing else goes on while the chant occurs. Use of the devotional chant depends upon the formality, environment, and size of the assembly. One possible use is during the Liturgy of the Word. However, the Judeo-Christian tradition of extending God's Word in the first reading with God's Word in the responsorial psalm should be respected. Hence, substituting a chant for the psalm is not advised. Similarly, the specific texts of the eucharistic prayer acclamations usually would not be substituted with a prayer chant. A prayer chant by its repetitive nature would interrupt the flow of the eucharistic prayer. Post-Communion time is best for devotional chant. Texts expressing oneness with God or the body of Christ would be appropriate.

Whatever type of chant is used, usually only one should be included in any Mass. The intense nature of the chant could make the liturgy too burdensome if several are included in the same service. Liturgy planners should not use a prayer chant every Sunday, but should insert them for variety in much the same way they would use an instrumental or a solo piece.

Rufino Zoragoza

233 • Bibliography for Singing in Worship

———— Hymnody ————

General Resources and Hymnal Companions. James Rawlings Syndor, *The Hymn and Congregational Singing* (Richmond: John Knox, 1960), is an overview of the nature of hymns, hymnals, and the task of leading hymns in worship. The poetic aspects of hymnody are covered consisely in Austin Lovelace, *The Anatomy of Hymnody* (Chicago: GIA Publications, 1965). The nature of hymn tunes is consisely described in John Wilson, *Looking at Hymn Tunes: The Objective Factors* (Croydon, England: The Hymn Society of Great Britain and Ireland, 1985.)

For general hymn resources, companions and studies, the following are of current value:

- In the **Episcopal** tradition, see Raymond F. Glover, *A Commentary on New Hymns* (New York: Church Hymnal Corporation, 1985), giving essays on 77 hymns from the Episcopal *The Hymnal 1982*. Background on text and tune.
- In the **Lutheran** tradition, see Marilyn Kay Stulken, *Hymnal Companion to the Lutheran Book of Worship* (Philadelphia: Fortress Press, 1981). A comprehensive introduction to the various traditions of Lutheran hymnody, thus updating and broadening the monumental pioneer work of Zahn.
- In the **Reformed** tradition, see the handbook for the *Psalter Hymnal* (Grand Rapids: CRC Publications, forthcoming).
- In the **Mennonite/Brethren** tradition, see the accompaniment handbook to *Hymnal: A Worship Book* (Elgin, Ilinois: Brethren Press; Newton, Kans.: Faith and Life Press; Scottdale, Pa.: Mennonite Publishing House, 1993). For historical reference, Alice Leewen, Harold Moyer, and Mary Oyer, *Exploring the Mennonite Hymnal: A Handbook* (Newton, Kans.: Faith and Life Press, 1992) and a companion volume *Exploring The Mennonite Hymnal: Essays* (Newton, Kans.: Faith and Life Press, 1992) jointly study the contents of the hymnal: the *Essays* giving an in-depth study of thirty-four selections, and the *Handbook* commenting more briefly on the remainder.
- In the **Baptist** tradition, see the *Handbook to the Baptist Hymnal 1991* as well as Hugh Martin, et al., *A Companion to the Baptist Church Hymnal* (London: Psalm and Hymns Trust, 1953) and William J. Reynolds, *Companion to Baptist Hymnal* (Nashville: Convention Press, 1976).
- In the **Methodist** tradition, see Diana Sanchez, ed., *Introduction to the Hymns, Canticles, and Acts of Worship* in the 1989 United Methodist Hymnal (Nashville: Abingdon, 1989).

Other handbooks include J. Irving Erikson's *Sing It Again: A Handbook on the Covenant Hymnal* (Chicago: Covenant Press, 1985); Charles W. Hughes, *American Hymns, Old and New* (New York: Columbia University Press, 1980), while a glossary-type companion is in Donald P. Hustad, *Dictionary-Handbook to Hymns for the Living Church* (Carol Stream, Ill.: Hope Publishing, 1978). Also useful are Albert C. Ronander and Ethel K. Porter, *Guide to the Pilgrim Hymnal* (Philadelphia: Pilgrim Press, 1966) and Samuel J. Rogal, *Guide to the Hymns and Tunes of American Methodism* (New York: Greenwood Press, 1986).

The *Hymn Society Book Service* of the Hymn Society of America (HSA) handles nearly every hymn book on the market; the Society's journal *The Hymn* is of primary importance (see also the bibliography of the preceding chapter).

Resources for Hymn Selection and Evaluation. Resources for choosing hymns, evaluating or critiquing hymns are among the most practical tools for worship planning, and include the following:

- Harry Askew and Hugh McElrath, *Sing With Understanding* (Nashville: Broadman, 1980), a comprehensive look at historical, musical, theological, and practical aspects of plainsong, the chorale, metrical psalmody, and recent hymns.
- Austin C. Lovelace, *Hymn Notes for Church Bulletins* (Chicago: GIA Publications, 1987). Brief paragraphs on the history of more than 400 hymns for insertion in a church bulletin.
- S. Paul Schilling, *The Faith We Sing* (Philadelphia: Westminster/John Knox, 1983). Occasionally used as a textbook in church music courses, this is an evaluation and interpretation of theological convictions voiced in representative hymns.

For guidance in hymn choice or planning (including festival preparation), the following are of value:

- Donald Spencer, *Hymn and Scripture Selection Guide: A Cross Reference Tool for Worship Leaders* (Grand Rapids: Baker, 1993), indexes a variety of hymnals used in many evangelical churches, cross-referencing them with allusions to biblical texts.
- Marion Hatchett, *A Guide to the Practice of Church Music* (New York: Church Hymnal Corp., 1989), gives numerous suggestions for music for each Sunday of the year and other occasions, based on the revised rites of the Episcopal church (*Book of Common Prayer* [1979] and *The Hymnal* [1982]).
- Charles Robinson, ed., *Singing the Faith* (Norwich, U.K.: The Canterbury Press, 1990) includes essays on a wide range of subjects related to hymnody, including several essays on the use of hymnody in various liturgical traditions.
- *Hymnal Studies II* (New York: Church Hymnal Corp., 1985). An excellent guide for selecting hymns for every Sunday of the church year.
- *Hymnal Studies V* (New York: Church Hymnal Corp., 1985). A planning tool for all those involved in the musical life of the church. Hymn suggestions for all years of the lectionary cycle.

A brief study of hymn festival history, together with instructions for putting one together is Austin Lovelace's *Hymn Festivals* (Fort Worth, Tex.: Hymn Society of America, n.d.).

Hymn Pedagogy. Aids for hymn-teaching or pedagogy vary in function from activity-type workbooks for children to worship leader-oriented guides, and are represented as follows:

- Mary Nelson Keithahn, *Our Heritage of Hymnals* (New York: Church Hymnal Corporation of America, 1985). A learning activity workbook on the *Hymnal 1982* that is designed for all age levels, but especially directed at children.
- Mary Nelson Keithahn and Mary Louise Van Dyke, *Exploring the Hymnal* (New York: Church Hymnal Corporation, 1985) is an intergenerational instruction book on skills for using a hymnal. Since hymnals employing liturgical rubrics are in more than one format, e.g., congregational and accompanimental (such as *Lutheran Book of Worship*), they are often difficult for practitioners coming out of independent free-church backgrounds. Hence instructions of this sort are quite important. Leaders should be aware of similar orientation requirements for *Worship II* and *Worship III* (Chicago: GIA Publications, n.d.) when approaching these post–Vatican II hymnals.

See also the bibliography to Chapter 9 on music leadership in worship, under the category of leading congregational singing.

───────── **Psalmody** ─────────

The following are a variety of musical settings of the Psalms in very diverse musical styles:

- *Anglican Chant Psalter,* ed. by Alec Wyton (New York: Church Hymnal Corp., 1987), a performing edition setting each of the Psalms to at least two chants: one for congregation, one for choir.
- *Gradual Psalms, Alleluia Verses and Tracts,* 5 vols. (New York: Church Hymnal Corp., 1980–1986), No. 6 in the Church Hymnal Series; the

first three volumes are arranged to the three-year lectionary cycle:

- Pt. 1: *Year A,* comp. by Richard Crocker
- Pt. 2: *Year B,* comp. by Richard Crocker
- Pt. 3: *Year C,* comp. by Richard Crocker
- Pt. 4: Pastoral Offices and Episcopal Services
- Pt. 5: *Lesser Feasts and Fasts,* comp. by Ronald V. Haizlip

- *The Grail Gelineau Psalter: 150 Psalms and 18 Canticles,* ed. by J. Robert Carroll (Chicago: GIA Publications, 1972). In the chant format developed by Joseph Gelineau, this collection presents settings of the complete biblical psalm and canticle repertory—the latter traditionally including material from the Apocrypha. See also the *Guide to Gelineau Psalmody,* published by GIA Publications.
- *A New Metrical Psalter* by Christopher L. Webber (New York: Church Hymnal Corp., 1986) is a words-only modern version of the Psalms, poetically set in common hymn-tune meters.
- *The Plainsong Psalter,* ed. by James Litton (New York: Church Hymnal Corp., 1988). A collection of Western-chant psalm tunes and texts.
- *The Plainsong Psalter: 150 Psalms and 18 Canticles* (Chicago: GIA Publications, n.d.). Based on the Gregorian tradition.
- *Psalm Praise* (Chicago: GIA Publications, 1973). A collection of contemporary psalmody by the likes of Michael Baughen, Norman Warrem, Geoffrey Beaumont, Timothy Dudley-Smith, Michael Perry, and Christopher Idle, among others.
- *Psalter Hymnal* (Grand Rapids: CRC Publications, 1987). This collection comes from the Christian Reformed Church. Many other metrical settings of the Psalms can be found in *Rejoice in the Lord* (Grand Rapids: Eerdmans, 1985) and *The Trinity Hymnal* (Philadelphia: Great Commission Publications, 1990).
- *Scriptures to Sing,* compiled by Ken Bible (Kansas City, Mo.: Lillenas, 1977). A collection of 123 songs of which 40 are psalm-based. Not an historical study, but a practical, varied collection for active use.
- *Psalms for Praise and Worship: A Complete Liturgical Psalter* (John Holbert, S. T. Kimbrough, Jr., and Carlton R. Young, eds.; Nashville: Abingdon, 1992) presents all of the Psalms along with 127 musical responses or antiphons

appropriate for a variety of psalms and occasions in the church year. See also Hal H. Hopson's *Psalm Refrains and Tones* (Carol Stream, Ill.: Hope Publishing Company, 1988).
- *The Celebration Psalter* (Betty Pulkingham and Kevin Hackett, eds.; Pacific, Mo.: Cathedral Music Press, 1991) provides contemporary settings for responsorial psalmody.
- *Ways of Singing the Psalms* (Robin A. Leaver, David Mann, and David Parkes, eds.; London: Collins, 1984) provides many musical examples in styles of psalmody.
- *Psalms for Today* and *Songs from the Psalms* (London: Hodder and Stoughton, 1990) provide settings of each psalm in a variety of contemporary styles.

Bible and Scripture Songs

Scripture Song and Praise Chorus. For helpful performing resources in Scripture chorus or praise chorus music, the following materials are of current value, usefulness, and popularity:

- Frank Garlock and Shelley Hamilton, *Praises I, II, III* (Majesty Music). A mixed-style collection composed by staff members of Majesty Music.
- John Mays, comp., *Best of the American Country Hymns Book* (Word). 4 vols. A series of over 100 Southern gospel classics, both old and recent.
- *One Hundred Hymns, One Hundred Choruses* (Majesty Music). The greatest hymns and praise choruses of yesterday and today.
- Jesse Peterson and Mark Hayes, comps., *Worship Him, I, II* (Tempo Music).
- *Praise and Worship Songbook* (Integrity). 3 vols. (I: 1–103; II: 104–190; III: 191–271). Selected from America's best-selling praise and worship material.

Marantha! Music's *Praise Chorus Book* (1993) is a collection of the 300 most popular praise and worship songs.

Service Music

For guidance in liturgical elements and representative repertory for the Mass, the following citations are of value:

- *The Book of Canticles,* Church Hymnal Studies, 2 (New York: Church Hymnal Corp., 1979; Singers' Edition and Accompaniment Edition). Plainsong and Anglican chant settings for all invitatories and canticles of the *Book of Common Prayer.*

- *Introits and Responses for Contemporary Worship* (Paul A. Hamill, ed.; Cleveland: Pilgrim Press, 1983). Contemporary introits and responses designed for choir and congregation. Inclusive language.

Several Church Hymnal Corporation publications are available for seasonal planning, such as *Gradual Psalms, Alleluia Verses and Tracts* (New York: Church Hymnal Corp.): Pt. 1: *Year A,* comp. by Richard Crocker (1981); Pt. 2: *Year B,* comp. by Richard Crocker (1981); Pt. 3: *Year C,* comp. by Richard Crocker (1980); Pt. 4: *Pastoral Offices and Episcopal Services, Holy Days and Various Occasions;* and Pt. 5: *Lesser Feasts and Fasts,* comp. by Ronald V. Haizlip (1986). All citations are concerned with antiphonal psalmody.

In the Orthodox liturgy of St. John Chrysostom there is an excellent English-language revised-rite series of the New Skete Community texts and music: *Liturgical Music:* Vol. 1, *Selections for Vespers, Matins, and Liturgy;* Vol. 2, *Dogmatica and Other Selections.* Includes the incarnation hymns of the eight tunes (*echoi*), and thirty-seven selections from the great feasts, Vespers, Matins, and Divine Liturgy. The material is set in contemporary musical style for contemporary American Christians.

- Liturgical Music, Series I: The Great Feasts (7 vols).
  1. Transfiguration of Christ
  2. Dormition of the Theotokos
  3. Birth of the Theotokos
  4. Exaltation of the Holy Cross
  5. Entry of the Theotokos
  6. Pascha: The Resurrection of Christ
  7. The Birth of the Savior
- Liturgical Music, Series II: Divine Services (2 vols.)
  1. Services for the Dead
  2. Vespers and Matins

Musical settings of service music are vast in number and are representative not only of contemporary materials written over the last three decades but also of the huge, 500-year legacy of the great European masters ranging from the Franco-Flemish figures, the Counter-Reformation Italian masters, the figures of the French and German Baroque, the English Catholic lineage, to the works of J. S. Bach and the later classical/romantic figures. Much of this repertory is available in collected editions of nearly all of these figures; however, practical performing editions may be obtained through publishers such as Barenreiter, E. C. and G. Schirmer, Novello, Universal Edition, Peters, Kalmus, Eulenberg, Schott, or H. W. Gray. Readers should consult catalogues of these publishers to access works of Bach, Handel, Haydn, Mozart, Beethoven, Brahms, Palestrina, Victoria, and the many, many other figures of this vast sacred repertory.

Gospel Music

Sources in contemporary gospel and praise music are often found in current-events literature, commercial music publications, mission reports, news releases, interviews, and (significantly) in positional job descriptions, church worship bulletins, workshop packages, publisher-based choir seminars, publisher catalogues, copyright-law publications, and all audio/video release reports.

Christian radio and TV programming require careful tracking; often the target patterns of repertory and performing media are discernible only after three or four months' monitoring. Ultimately the historical logs of individual evangelists and evangelistic associations will reveal detailed evidence of long-range music usage. Historical monographs and textbooks (though helpful for the years prior to the 1960s) do not really have much to say about the practices, assumed values, or the repertory of the scope of Christian broadcasting. Scholarly researchers need to have ongoing contact with publications of the Hymn Society of America and to be aware of the institutional repositories of hymn and sheet-music collections.

General Sources in Gospel Music. *Christian Copyright Licensing, International* (Portland, Oreg.) is a semiannual issuance listing all authorized publishers of gospel and praise music, together with all code catalogues (subsidiary firms) of each parent company.

- *Contemporary Christian Music Magazine* (Boulder, Colo.). Probably the most important monthly coverage of popular-culture aspects in the Christian music world. It presents interviews, concert schedules, video and CD reviews, radio airplay charts, ratings, and gives strong emphasis on personalities and lifestyles.

- Tony Heilbut, _The Gospel Sound: Good News and Bad Times,_ 2d ed. (New York: Limelight Editions, 1987). A detailed integrative study of black gospel music and its overall influences on the mainstream.
- _The New Grove Dictionary of Music and Musicians_ (London: Grove's Dictionaries: 1980). Vol. 7, pp. 549–558. The article on gospel music is a comprehensive historical survey of the medium; white repertory treated by Harry Askew, black by Paul Oliver. Not geared to method or practical use, the article is valuable only to the early 1970s and must be supplemented by more recent publications.
- _Worship Leader_ (Nashville, Tenn.). First issued in 1992, this periodical closely watches trends in worship formats and music usage. Issues of leadership, service strategies, theological contexts, Scriptural bearings on music and worship, and coverage on technological music states-of-the-art are prominent.

Black Gospel Music. In gospel music there are a number of organizations that act as liaison agencies for persons in the field of black gospel music.

- _Afro-American Music Hall of Fame and Musicians, Inc._ (P.O. Box 390, Youngstown, Ohio). An archive designed to preserve works of black figures in gospel music, rhythm and blues, and jazz. An excellent resource for identifying important persons in the art.
- _Gospel Music Workshop of America_ (P.O. Box 4632, Detroit, Mich.). This is a liaison office networking performing artists in gospel music. It currently has 184 chapters in the USA, with more than 18,000 members.
- _National Black Christian Education Resources Center_ (475 Riverside Drive, New York, NY). Associated with the National Council of Churches, the organization is an source for accessing all types of materials in Christian education involving the black experience.

Other important works include Michael W. Harris, _The Rise of Gospel Blues: The Music of Thomas Andrew Dorsey in the Urban Church_ (New York: Oxford University Press, 1992); Jon Michael Spencer's _Protest and Praise: Sacred Music of Black Religion_ (Minneapolis: Fortress, 1991); Don Cusic's _The Sound of Light: A History of Gospel Music_ (Bowling Green, Ohio: Bowling Green State University Popular Press, 1990); and Paul Oliver, Max Harrison, and William Bolcom, eds., _The New Grove Gospel, Blues, and Jazz_ (New York: W. W. Norton, 1986).

White Gospel Music. On the earliest historical type of white gospel music, shape-note singing, the two best-established older sources are George Pullen Jackson, _White Spirituals in the Southern Uplands_ (Hatboro, Pa.: Folklore Associates, Inc., 1964; reprinted from the original edition, University of North Carolina Press, 1933); and Gilbert Chase's well-documented study _America's Music: From the Pilgrims to the Present,_ 3d ed. (Champaign, Ill.: University of Illinois Press, 1992). However, the most important bibliographical tool is that of Richard J. Stanislaw, _A Checklist of Four-Shape Shape-Note Tunebooks_ (Brooklyn: Institute for Studies in American Music, 1978), a tool for locating composers/compilers, titles, dates of first printings, locales of accessibility. Other sources include Buell E. Cobb, Jr., _The Sacred Harp: A Tradition and Its Music_ (Athens, Ga.: University of Georgia Press, 1989); Dorothy D. Horn, _Sing to Me of Heaven_ (Gainesville, Fla.: University of Florida Press, 1970); and Irving Lowens, _Music and Musicians in Early America_ (New York: W. W. Norton, 1964). _The Sacred Harp Hymnal,_ McGraw revision, 1991 edition, is available from Sacred Harp Publishing Company, P.O. Box 551, Temple, GA 30179.

For information on where and when to find shape-note singings, see Buell Cobb's _The Sacred Harp,_ which includes a directory of Sacred Harp singings in the South. The _Chicago Sacred Harp Newsletter,_ 1807 West North Avenue, Chicago, IL 60622, is published several times a year by the Chicago Sacred Harp Singers. It is an excellent source of information about related events in the Middle West. Sacred Harp Publishing Company also prepares annually _The Directory and Minutes and Names and Addresses of Sacred Harp Singers Throughout the U.S.A.,_ which includes a listing of all the previous year's singings.

Black Choral Music. Choral sources in black gospel music have certain publishers of note: Martin Morris

Music, Inc. (Chicago); S.R. Music Publishing Co. (Hayward, Calif.); Savgos Music Inc. (Elizabeth, N.J.); Rev. Earl A. Pleasant Publishing (Thousand Oaks, Calif.); and Bridgeport Music, Inc. (Detroit, Mich.). Worship leaders should request catalogues from the above-listed choices and be aware of the following important composers/arrangers: Walter Hawkins, Andrae Crouch, Danniebelle Hall, Larry Farrow, James Cleveland, Doria Akers, Mattie Moss Clark, Margaret Douroux, and Steven Roberts.

SEVEN

Instruments in Worship

Instrumental music was an essential feature of Hebrew worship. The early Christian church, however, rejected instrumental music, largely because of the pagan associations of many instruments. Thus, its church music consisted of exclusively unaccompanied singing. Later centuries again saw the use of instruments in worship, especially the organ. In the twentieth century, music for worship has been accompanied by the widest variety of instruments playing in a wide variety of styles. This chapter will catalogue many of the instruments used in worship today, giving both historical perspectives and practical suggestions regarding their use. In each case, emphasis is given to how given musical instruments can contribute to, instead of interrupting or dominating, the liturgy of various worship traditions. Particular attention is given to how musical instruments can enhance texts that are spoken and sung in worship.

234 ◆ HISTORICAL AND THEOLOGICAL PERSPECTIVES ON MUSICAL INSTRUMENTS IN WORSHIP

The use of instruments in worship has engendered great controversy throughout the history of the church. The following article describes the most important issues at stake in these controversies, highlighting important principles that can guide our use of instruments in worship today.

The Psalms contain numerous statements urging God's people to praise him with instruments. The classic passage of this sort is the catalogue of instruments contained in Psalm 150.

> Praise him with trumpet sound;
> praise him with lute and harp!
> Praise him with timbrel and dance;
> praise him with strings and pipe!
> Praise him with sounding cymbals;
> praise him with loud clashing cymbals!

A person knowing this and similar passages from the Psalms but not knowing anything of the history of the church would not be surprised by what he or she observed at most worship services in Western churches today. Whether Catholic or Protestant, just about any service this visitor wandered into would include the use of musical instruments. At a minimum he or she would hear an organ or a piano or a guitar accompanying singing. But it would not be unusual to encounter churches where large ensembles not only accompany singing but also play alone before or after or during any number of other liturgical acts. Knowing the Psalms but not church history, this visitor would likely assume that the congregation being observed was simply following a mandate given in its sacred book, doing a normal Christian act of worship.

But, of course, there is a long history between the Psalms and the church today, and through most of that history the church has been very reticent about using instruments in worship. From the New Testament through the patristic era, the Middle Ages, and the Renaissance, the use of instruments in Christian worship was highly exceptional. And even after instruments found their way into worship on a more regular basis after 1600, there continued to be questions about their proper use, and always there continued to be a few voices calling for their exclusion. Even today, despite the increasingly warm welcome instruments have received in many churches, there are still a few bodies of Christians who worship without them and others that do not go much beyond instrumental introductions to and accompaniments of congregational singing. Donald Hustad summarizes the situation as follows:

> Eastern Orthodox worship for the most part continues to use only vocal music. In the Western church as well, the use of instruments has been opposed from time to time, both before and since the 16th

century Reformation. Until recently, a fairly large number of evangelical groups in America (e.g., the Free Methodist Church, primitive Baptists, old Mennonites, and certain Presbyterian bodies) perpetuated the "no instrument" practice, but the antagonism is waning. At the present time, the prohibition is most conspicuously continued and defended by certain Churches of Christ, whose leaders argue that they must adhere strictly to what the New Testament authorizes. (*Jubilate! Church Music in the Evangelical Tradition* [Carol Stream, Ill.: Hope Publishing, 1981, 42])

Obviously the matter is not a simple one of literally following the injunctions of the Psalms. Just as obviously, there is no universal agreement among Christians as to how, or even whether, musical instruments are appropriate in worship.

The history of the church's various and varying attitudes towards musical instruments in worship is long and complex. But the big picture is clear. Our current situation in which there is a widespread and often unquestioning acceptance of instruments in worship is "a minority position in the church's whole history" (Paul Westermeyer, "Instruments in Christian Worship," *Reformed Liturgy and Music* 25:3 [Summer 1991]: 111). The majority position over the whole history of the church can be summed up in the words of Rev. Joseph Gelineau: "vocal praise is essential to Christian worship. Instruments are only accessory" (Joseph Gelineau, *Voices and Instruments in Christian Worship: Principles, Laws, and Applications,* trans. Clifford Howell, S.J. [Collegeville, Minn.: The Liturgical Press, 1964], 155).

I cannot trace here the long and complex history of musical instruments in Christian worship. Rather, I will focus on two instances in the church's history when instruments were not used at all. Though I am not advocating a return to that extreme position (nor, on the other hand, objecting to any who would), I think the extreme position presents the clearest view of certain principles that should be in effect when we admit instruments into our worship. The two instances I am referring to are the patristic era and the Calvinist Reformation. But before turning our attention to these, we need to look briefly at Jewish worship before and at the time of Christ to see what light it might shed on the Psalm references to instruments. For that same purpose we will also look briefly at what the New Testament says about instruments.

Little is known about the origin and early history of the Psalms. Tradition long ascribed the Psalms to David. But although it is likely that some go back to him, it is impossible to determine with certainty which are of his making. During the centuries following David, and probably under his influence, psalms continued to be composed, edited, and compiled until by the third century before Christ the 150 Psalms stood together as a canonical Jewish hymnbook.

If the early history of the Psalms is obscure to our view, so is their function. Were they composed originally for liturgical purposes and were the instruments mentioned involved in the liturgy? Scholarly opinion is divided. Most scholars agree, however, that whatever their original functions might have been, the Psalms, in the process of being collected and compiled, were adapted for liturgical purposes—in particular, for singing at the sacrificial rites carried out in the temple.

There is scanty information about how the Psalms were used in temple worship. The few references in the Old Testament historical and prophetic books do not go very far towards giving us ideas about what music in temple worship was like. But we can be fairly certain that, at least for the second temple, the singing of Psalms at the sacrifices was quite an elaborate affair, performed by the Levites, that is, by highly trained singers and instrumentalists.

We have a somewhat clearer picture of temple worship around the time of Jesus owing to some fairly detailed description found in the Mishnah, a redaction of the Talmud from about the year 200 A.D. Every day of the year there was a solemn sacrifice in the morning and another in the afternoon. On sabbaths and feast days there were additional sacrifices. With regard to instruments we learn from the Mishnah that services began with the priests blowing three blasts on silver trumpets. Later in the ritual, trumpets again gave signals as did clashing cymbals, and the singing of psalms was accompanied by stringed instruments, the *nevel* and the *kinnor.* (See James McKinnon, "The Question of Psalmody in the Ancient Synagogue," *Early Music History* 6 (1986): 162–163.)

It is significant that stringed instruments accompanied the singing. These were softer instruments that could support the singing without covering the words. This is an indication of the logocentric nature of Jewish temple music, a characteristic that set it apart from the music of the sacrificial rites of the

Israelites' pagan neighbors. Pagan sacrificial music typically featured the frenzy-inducing sound of the loud, double-reed instruments and the rhythms of orgiastic dancing. Words were superfluous. Temple music differed radically in each of these characteristics of pagan music. Words were primary and governed the musical rhythms. Instrumental accompaniment was by stringed instruments that supported the monophonic vocal line, perhaps with some heterophonic embellishments, but never covering or distracting attention away from the words. Instruments were used independently only for signalling purposes. Trumpets and cymbals signalled the beginning of the psalm and the places at the end of sections where the worshipers should prostrate themselves.

Music in Jewish synagogues was very different from that in the temple. The gatherings in the synagogues were not for sacrifice and did not require the priestly and Levitical classes. Their music, therefore, was not part of elaborate liturgical ceremony and was not in the hands of specially trained musicians like the Levites. It must have been simple and it definitely did not make use of musical instruments. Like temple psalmody, it was logocentric, but unlike temple psalmody, it did not make use of any instruments, not even those that could support singing without obscuring it.

Interpretations that read Psalm references to musical instruments as referring to Jewish worship practices receive little support from what we know of Jewish temple and synagogue worship. Furthermore, they receive little support from the New Testament. References to instruments in the New Testament are few and can easily be summarized. They are mentioned "in connection with pagan customs (Matt. 9:23; 11:17; Luke 7:32; Apoc. 18:22), or explanatory comparisons (1 Cor. 14:7-8; Matt. 6:2; 1 Cor. 13:1; Apoc. 14:2), [or] in an apocalyptic context where they have a symbolic value. . . ." (Gelineau, _Voices,_ 150). There is no evidence that the earliest Christians adopted a different attitude toward instruments in worship. They certainly did not read the Psalms as giving directives to use instruments in worship.

The indifference of the New Testament toward musical instruments does not, however, extend to song. Song, one can say, frames the New Testament. The birth of Jesus brought about an outburst of four songs recorded in the first two chapters of Luke. The second outburst occurs in Revelation when the song to the Lamb is picked up by ever-widening circles until the whole cosmos has joined (Rev. 4). In between Luke and Revelation, the New Testament says little about music. What it does say, however, unquestionably has a positive ring, as in the following familiar passages:

> Let the word of Christ dwell in you richly, as you teach and admonish one another in all wisdom, and as you sing psalms and hymns and spiritual songs with thankfulness in your hearts to God. (Col. 3:16)

> Is any one among you suffering? Let him pray. Is any cheerful? Let him sing praise. (James 5:13)

But it is song, not "pure" music, that the New Testament speaks of so warmly. From its inception, the church, like its Jewish forebears, eschewed music separated from word. Without word, music is too vague, too mystifying. As P. Lasserre put it:

> Music expresses the sentiments, but is not capable of defining them, and without the commentary of words, which are absent from instrumental music, the hearer always remains somewhat vague about the nature of the object of the sentiment by which the musician is inspired. (Quoted in Gelineau, _Voices,_ 148)

For that reason Christian musical thought has always insisted on the importance of _logos_ for keeping music from drifting into vague and undefined spiritual territory. As Fr. Gelineau has put it, only singing, "because of its connection to the revealed word," combines "explicit confession of faith in Christ with musical expression" ("Music and Singing in the Liturgy," in _The Study of Liturgy,_ ed. Cheslyn Jones, et al. [New York: Oxford University Press, 1978], 443). Word, he says elsewhere, "demystifies by naming." Gelineau adds that "when word intervenes . . . the object of the lament is designated; the praise names its intended recipient" ("Path of Music," _Music and the Experience of God,_ ed. Mary Collins, et al. [Edinburgh: T. and T. Clark, Ltd., 1989], 137–138). Christian musical thought has always been at odds with the Romantic notion of a "pure" music "which is all the purer the less it is dragged down into the region of vulgar meaning by words (which are always laden with connotations)" (_Allgemeine musikalische Zeitung,_ 1801; from Dahlhaus, _Esthetics of Music,_ trans. William Austin [New York: Cambridge University Press, 1982], 27).

Against this background, the negative attitude of the early church toward musical instruments makes sense. In fact, as James McKinnon pointed out, the non-use of instruments in early Christian worship was not because instruments were banished. Rather, because they were irrelevant to the logocentric musical thought and practice the Christians inherited from the Jews, they simply did not enter the picture (see "The Meaning of the Patristic Polemic Against Musical Instruments," *Current Musicology* 1 (1965): 78).

A logocentric music need not, of course, totally exclude instruments. Instruments that could support singing were used in the temple and most contemporary Christians would likely attest from experience that instruments can indeed lend support to singing without obscuring or engulfing the words. But that danger and others connected with the use of instruments are always lurking, so throughout much of the church's history leaders have thought the dangers outweighed the potential benefits.

The fathers of the first centuries of the Christian era and John Calvin in the sixteenth century are perhaps the best known of those who decided not to risk the dangers. So they rejected all use of instruments in worship. Involved in both rejections was the principle just discussed: Christian music, like its Jewish ancestor, is logocentric. One indication of how thoroughly logocentric was the early church fathers' thought on music is their vocabulary. McKinnon points out that they rarely used the term *music;* instead, their normal terms were *psalms* and *hymns* ("Patristic Polemic," 79).

Central to both the fathers' and Calvin's logocentric ideas on music, and hence to their rejection of instruments, was the importance they placed on understanding in worship. The apostle Paul stated the principle simply and directly: "I will sing with the spirit and I will sing with the mind also" (1 Cor. 14:15). So, following Paul, St. Basil urged worshipers, "While your tongue sings, let your mind search out the meaning of the words, so that you might sing in spirit and sing also in understanding" (McKinnon, *Music in the Early Christian Literature* [New York: Cambridge University Press, 1987], 66). Centuries later Calvin was particularly explicit in relating the need for understanding in worship to Paul's instructions to the Corinthian Christians.

For our Lord did not institute the order which we must observe when we gather together in His name merely that the world might be amused by seeing and looking upon it, but wished rather that therefrom should come profit to all His people. Thus witnesseth Saint Paul, commanding that all which is done in the church be directed unto the common edifying of all . . . For to say that we can have devotion, either at prayers or at ceremonies, without understanding anything of them, is a great mockery. . . . And indeed, if one could be edified by things which one sees without knowing what they mean, Saint Paul would not so rigorously forbid speaking in an unknown tongue . . . . (Foreword to the *Geneva Psalter,* in *Source Readings in Music History,* trans. Oliver Strunk [New York: W. W. Norton and Co., 1950], 345–346)

In his commentary on Psalm 33, Calvin connected instrumental music and speaking in tongues.

The name of God, no doubt, can, properly speaking, be celebrated only by the articulate voice; but it is not without reason that David adds to this those aids by which believers were wont to stimulate themselves the more to this exercise; especially considering that he was speaking to God's ancient people. There is a distinction, however, to be observed here, that we may not indiscriminately consider as applicable to ourselves, every thing which was formerly enjoined upon the Jews. I have no doubt that playing upon cymbals, touching the harp and the viol, and all that kind of music, which is so frequently mentioned in the Psalms, was a part of the education; that is to say, the puerile instruction of the law. . . . For even now, if believers choose to cheer themselves with musical instruments, they should, I think, make it their object not to dissever their cheerfulness from the praises of God. But when they frequent their sacred assemblies, musical instruments in celebrating the praises of God would be no more suitable than the burning of incense, the lighting up of lamps, and the restoration of the other shadows of the law. . . . Men who are fond of outward pomp may delight in that noise; but the simplicity which God recommends to us by the apostle is far more pleasing to him. Paul allows us to bless God in the public assembly of the saints only in a known tongue. (*Commentary on the Book of Psalms,* vol. 1, trans. James Anderson [Grand Rapids: Eerdmans, 1948], 538–539)

Calvin's implication is clear: instruments speak in an unknown tongue.

Moreover, in this passage, in addition to expressing the ideal of logocentric music, Calvin gave an explanation of why God allowed instruments to his Old Testament people: it was a concession to their spiritual immaturity; it was "puerile instruction" that, after the coming of Christ, became as unnecessary as the other "shadows of the law." Calvin's thought here is precisely in line with that of the church fathers. St. John Chrysostom put it as follows:

> . . . in ancient times, they were thus led by these instruments due to the slowness of their understanding, and were gradually drawn away from idolatry. Accordingly, just as he allowed sacrifices, so too did he permit instruments, making concession to their weakness. (McKinnon, _Music,_ 83)

The primacy of understanding through words, then, was fundamental in causing the early church to continue to practice a logocentric music like that which it inherited from its Jewish forebears; it was also fundamental to Calvin's rejection of instruments in worship. But for both there was another reason almost as powerful. It is incapsulated in the phrase _una voces dicentes,_ "singing with one voice."

In his letter to the Romans, Paul wrote, "May the God who gives endurance and encouragement give you a spirit of unity among yourselves as you follow Jesus Christ, so that with one heart and mouth you may glorify the God and Father of our Lord Jesus Christ" (15:5-6). Although "with one mouth" does not here refer exclusively to singing, there can be no doubt that it articulated a principle that the early church took very seriously for its singing. The importance of singing "with one voice" is a frequent refrain among the early Christian writers. Listen to some of its variations over the first few centuries of the Christian era.

> Let us consider the entire multitude of his angels, how standing by you they minister to his will. For the Scripture says: "Ten thousand times ten thousand stood by him and a thousand times a thousand ministered to him and cried out, 'Holy, holy, holy is the Lord of Sabaoth, the whole creation is full of his glory'" (Isa. 6:3). Let us, therefore, gathered together in concord by conscience, cry out earnestly to him as if with one voice, so that we might come to share in his great and glorious promises. (Clement of Rome; trans. McKinnon, _Music,_ 18)

And so more sweetly pleasing to God than any musical instrument would be the symphony of the people of God, by which, in every church of God, with kindred spirit and single disposition, with one mind and unanimity of faith and piety, we raise melody in unison in our psalmody. (Eusebius of Caesarea; trans. McKinnon, _Music,_ 98)

> [A psalm is] a pledge of peace and harmony, which produces one song from various and sundry voices in the manner of a cithara. . . . A psalm joins those with differences, unites those at odds and reconciles those who have been offended, for who will not concede to him with whom one sings to God in one voice? It is after all a great bond of unity for the full number of people to join in one chorus. (Ambrose; trans. McKinnon, _Music,_ 126–127)

Unity was an important matter to the early Christians and almost from the beginning, as these quotations show, singing "with one voice" became an expression of, a metaphor of, and even a means toward unity.

Calvin's return to unison, unaccompanied, congregational singing was also spurred in part by his recognition of singing as an expression of the communal dimension of worship.

> Moreover, since the glory of God ought, in a measure, to shine in the several parts of our bodies, it is especially fitting that the tongue has been assigned and destined for this task, both through singing and through speaking. For it was peculiarly created to tell and proclaim the praise of God. But the chief use of the tongue is in public prayers, which are offered in the assembly of believers, by which it comes about that with one common voice, and as it were, with the same mouth, we all glorify God together, worshiping him with one spirit and the same faith. (_Institutes_ [III, xx, 31], 894–895)

The twin concerns for keeping the church's music anchored in the Word (and hence in words) and for maintaining a liturgical activity that "touches on the essential mystery of the church as _koinonia_" (Gelineau, "Music," 441) are the primary roots of the early church's and Calvin's avoidance of instruments. For the early church fathers there was a third concern, a concern that had to do with association or context.

James McKinnon began his article on the church fathers' attitude towards musical instruments with this striking observation: "The antagonism which the Fathers of the early church displayed toward instruments has two outstanding characteristics: vehemence and uniformity" (McKinnon, "Meaning,"

69). One need not read far to notice the vehemence, and no matter how far one reads, he will not encounter a significantly different view on the subject. It is hard to understand this vehemence and uniformity simply on the basis of the two concerns we have already discussed. After all, Calvin held those concerns as strongly as the early fathers did, but he does not display their vehemence. He objected to instruments in communal worship but his objection did not go beyond that. In his commentary on Psalm 33 he merely remarked that "if believers choose to cheer themselves with musical instruments, they should, I think, make it their object not to dissever their cheerfulness from the praises of God." That is a long way removed, for example, from the fourth-century Alexandrian canon, which legislated: "When a reader learns to play the cithara, he shall be taught to confess it. If he does not return to it, he will endure his punishment for seven weeks. If he persists in it, he must be discharged and excluded from the church" (McKinnon, *Music,* 120).

Such legislation is likely to strike us as unimaginably harsh. Perhaps it was. But as one reads the fathers more broadly and begins to understand something of the context within which they wrote, their vehement and uniform denunciations of musical instruments become more understandable. The early church, we must remember, had a music that was sufficient for its needs and for which instruments were superfluous. We must also remember that she found herself surrounded by a decadent pagan culture and, after Constantine, filled with people only recently turned from that culture. The music in that culture made prominent use of instruments, both in the sacrificial rites of pagan religions and in many morally degenerate activities common in the late Roman Empire. Invariably it is with specific reference to the religious or social context that the church fathers made their denunciations of musical instruments. Specifically the church fathers' statements about musical instruments come in the context of pagan cultic practices, the theater (often closely related to the cultic practices), pagan banquets, weddings, or, more generally, drunken carousing and sexual immorality. The following quotations are typical:

> You will not honor these things, but rather despise them . . . and those castrations which the Phrygians perform, bewitched at first by the *aulos*. . . . (Gregory of Nazianzus; trans. McKinnon, *Music,* 71)

As the tragic actor loudly declaims, will one reflect upon the exclamations of a prophet, and as the effeminate tibicinist plays, will one call to mind a psalm? . . . (Tertullian; trans. McKinnon, *Music,* 44)

The irregular movements of *auloi,* psalteries, choruses, dances, Egyptian clappers, and other such playthings become altogether indecent and uncouth, especially when joined by beating cymbals and tympana and accompanied by the noisy instruments of deception. Such a symposium, it seems to me, becomes nothing but a theatre of drunkenness. (Clement of Alexandria; trans. McKinnon, *Music,* 32)

It is not the marriage of which I speak—one would hope not—but what accompanies it. Nature indulges in Bacchic frenzy then, those present become brutes rather than men; they neigh like horses and kick like asses. There is much dissipation, much dissolution, but nothing earnest, nothing high-minded; there is much pomp of the devil here—cymbals, *auloi,* and songs full of fornication and adultery. (John Chrysostom; McKinnon, *Music,* 85)

Therefore not without justification [does Isaiah say] woe unto them who require the drink of intoxication in the morning, who ought to render praise to God, to rise before dawn and meet in prayer the sun of justice, who visits his own and rises before us, if we rise for Christ rather than for wine and strong drink. Hymns are sung, and you grasp the cithara? Psalms are sung, and you take up the psaltery and tympanum? Woe indeed, because you disregard salvation and choose death. (Ambrose; McKinnon, *Music,* 128–129)

Similar quotations could be multiplied several times over. What they all point to are religiously repugnant and morally degenerate activities in which instruments were an inextricable part. The early Christians hardly knew any other use of instruments than in the music associated with objectionable pagan religious and social activities. Such close identification of instrument, music, and activity is what made the church fathers so uniformly and vehemently opposed to instruments, not only in worship but in all of Christian life.

Two principles—the primacy of words and the importance of community—led the early church Fathers and John Calvin to renounce the use of musical instruments in worship. A third principle—the need to keep free from inappropriate associations—reinforced the fathers' position. Although conditions change from time to time and from place to place, the three principles that undergirded the fathers' and Calvin's renunciation of instruments in worship are relevant at all times and places. But none of the principles, nor all taken together, necessarily leads to a total renunciation of instruments in worship.

The principle of avoiding unwanted associations is, of course the one whose application is going to be the most fluid. Suffice it to say here that in late twentieth-century Western culture the church should be wary of instruments, or at least the styles of playing them, that are inextricably involved in popular culture. The moral degeneracy of so much in that culture should make Christians today as wary as the church fathers were in the late Roman Empire.

With regard to the principle of "with one voice," it should be obvious that the principle is most clearly practiced in unison singing and that it becomes successively less clear as part-singing, traditional instruments, and finally electronic instruments are introduced.

> From the moment human beings started to "train" their voices . . . there was the potential for driving a wedge between the song of the trained singer *and* the song of the rest of humanity. That potential took a large leap when instruments were introduced, because now sounds were made by mechanisms different from that of the voice. The potential took a quantum leap, however, with the advent of electricity. Instruments severed sounds from the voice, but they still were forced to restrict themselves to acoustic boundaries. Amplification by electricity took away the acoustic boundaries and created sounds even further removed from the voice. (Westermeyer, "Instruments in Worship," 114)

To this I would add that the use of prerecorded music totally violates this principle. It is not the voice of any one of the gathered worshipers.

Finally, even the primacy of words need not necessarily negate the use of instruments. Although they can easily become distractions and overwhelm or obliterate words, if care is exercised, instruments can support and enhance singing in many ways. But even if this is granted, the question remains whether this principle negates the use of purely instrumental music. Again, not necessarily. Even the early church left an opening for wordless music. St. Augustine gave the classic description of the *jubilus,* the outpouring of joy beyond words.

> One who jubilates (*iubilat*) does not speak words, but it is rather a sort of sound of joy without words, since it is the voice of a soul poured out in joy and expressing, as best it can, the feeling, though not grasping the sense. A man delighting in his joy, from some words which cannot be spoken or understood, bursts forth in a certain voice of exultation without words, so that it seems he does indeed rejoice with his own voice, but as if, because filled with too much joy, he cannot explain in words what it is in which he delights. (Trans. McKinnon, *Music,* 361)

However, Augustine does add that proper jubilation ought to be "in justification" and "in confession," which I take to mean in a specific context. In any case it is worth noting that the closest music came to being wordless in the medieval liturgy was in the highly melismatic chants like the Graduals and Alleluias and even more so in the organa of Leonin and Perotin. But this music always had as its context the words of the liturgy. In fact its context was not just words but the Word; it was always sung in the context of the Scripture lessons. If, as Augustine and medieval practice require, wordless music is kept in touch with words and the Word, instrumental music can have a place in Christian worship. But it must never be allowed to suggest that its beauty has some kind of spiritual efficacy. The ease with which Romantic thought about "pure" music slipped into a religion of music should serve to warn us about music's seductive power. We must remember, as Fr. Gelineau's memorable formulation puts it, that its beauty, indeed any perceptible beauty, "can be a sign of grace, but never the source of grace" (*Voices,* 26).

Calvin Stapert

235 • INSTRUMENTAL MUSIC IN SERVICE TO THE TEXT

A wide variety of musical instruments can be used effectively in accompanying hymns and anthems. Creativity in the use of instruments should always seek to reflect and illuminate the text that is sung. The following article gives suggestions for how a variety of instruments can be used to proclaim the text.

Music Proclaims the Word

As a church musician I am vitally concerned about, almost obsessed by words. This is because I believe strongly that music in worship, and by extension a musician making music for worship, is a servant of the Word assisting in leading God's people in prayer and praise, Word and sacrament. The musician encounters text, be it biblical, prose, or poetry, and responds to it. Thus the music, its style, character, timbre, and spirit has evocative power to communicate a sense of the text's focus. The musician (composer or performer) functions exegetically to proclaim and, in the process, to interpret the text.

Instrumental Color in Proclamation

One of the most creative ways a parish musician can enter into this exegetical world of musical proclamation is to be aware of the possibilities for instrumental color. Most of us are not composers or arrangers, but we all can be alert to possibilities for the addition of instrumental color to the song of the congregation and choir. In a way we are like a cook who imparts a distinctive personality to a common recipe by choosing to modify the proportions of certain spices. Instrumental color provides spice for vocal music.

Creative use of instrumental color is most helpful in hymn singing. It is easy for us and the members of our congregations to get into a rut as hymn singers. This is especially true for those familiar texts and tunes used so often that they have lost some of their power to speak to us. If indeed the hymnal is a kind of theological handbook for the people, then we must be ever alert for ways to challenge our congregations to sing with understanding as well as spirit.

The Organ as Primary Instrumental Color

In most churches, the pipe organ continues as the primary instrument for the leading of congregational song. It is ideally suited for this task, able to produce a rich quantity of sound—complex and colorful sound—a sound still controlled and played by one person. No other *single* instrument (not even the wonderful synthesizers and samplers available today) can begin to equal the organ in its versatility and quantity of sound. In addition the pipe organ is wind driven—its pipes sing, supported and energized by air, just as the human voice is. This shared energizing source explains in part why a well-played pipe organ works so well in leading vocal song.

Unfortunately, many organists have not considered the remarkable color possibilities of their instrument, especially in relation to leading congregational song. It is not enough to play through the hymn, perhaps with a louder combination for the last stanza. Gentle reed stops add excitement to a hymn stanza. A solo trumpet soaring out on a hymn melody provides a heightened level of leadership. Gentle flutes 8 and 4 with a soft manual 16 create a warm, dignified, solemn sound. The absence of a pedal on a stanza, the absence of the organ on a stanza (unaccompanied singing is wonderful both in harmony and sturdy unison) provides the opportunity for an instrumental punctuation when the organ returns.

To devise a registrational strategy for each hymn, *carefully read the text* to see what it has to say and consider registrational enhancements that support the message. Some hymns are strong statements of praise, while others are more introspective and contemplative. Some hymns can be envisioned as a crescendo from beginning to end. Others function in just the opposite way. (Interestingly, Wesley's magnificent text, "Love Divine, All Love's Excelling," will work either way.) Some hymn texts reach a climax in the middle. Skillful use of organ registrations can encourage a congregation to begin to sing with varied dynamics if the choir is encouraged to be sensitive to these changes and sing accordingly. If the organ is quiet, we sing more introspectively; if the organ is full and rich, we sing with greater intensity.

While the organ is the primary and most important single source of instrumental color in most churches, it should *not* be the only one. My ideal collection of instruments for worship leadership would include a good piano, handbells, Orff instruments, a good synthesizer with its own high-quality audio system, plus an ever-expanding group of instrumentalists who could be called upon to add the sounds of orchestral instruments to the congregation's song.

Handbells as Punctuation

In many churches no resource is more underutilized than the handbell. Many churches have bell choirs, but few use the bells other than for the performance of set pieces as adornment to the service. Although such contributions are fine and to be encouraged, they only scratch the surface of what bells (or choirs for that matter) can to do assist in propelling the flow of the service and enhancing our encounter with the Word.

Handbells are marvelous pitch pipes. A simple bell tone, or a short cluster of pitches can establish tonality for an a cappella anthem or give the pitch to a worship leader about to sing a psalm. In the hymn "O Come, O Come Emmanuel," bells E4, B4, E5, B5, E6, played in order from bottom to top, provide ample accompaniment for the congregational singing of the hymn. Play the pattern in the speed of the eighth notes of the tune: twice before each stanza and once every time the melody ends on an E or G during the stanza. Free, random ringing of a cluster of bells (or a triad doubled in additional octaves) makes a fine accompaniment for the chanting of a psalm. The refrain to "Angels We Have Heard on High" takes a new spirit of joy with free-ringing bells added. A repeating pattern of E-B alternating with D-G, one pair per bar, works wonderfully to accompany "What Wondrous Love is This." Handbells in slightly more elaborate patterns provide a marvelous accompaniment for a choir (see my arrangement of _Let All Mortal Flesh Keep Silence_ [Augsburg 11-2517] or _Ding Dong Merrily on High in Two Carols_ [Augsburg 11-2080]). Because they are portable, bells work wonderfully to provide pitch for a choir in procession (consider the Boyce _Alleluia Round_ [GIA G-2494] for Easter and the Dufay _Gloria ad modum tubae_ for Christmas [GIA G-2150], the former with free-ringing bells, and the latter substituting bells for the suggested trumpets).

Limitations of space preclude spending more time on handbells. The church musician interested in devising bell patterns for use with choir or congregation is encouraged to experiment at the piano with the damper pedal depressed to simulate the decay of bells. Sound patterns built upon intervals of fourths work especially well (remember bells sound one octave higher than written). Also do consider investing in these two useful resource books: _Tintinnabulum: The Liturgical Use of Handbells_ (Richard Proulx, GIA Publications, G-2358) and _Handbells in the Liturgical Service_ (John Folkening, Concordia Publishing House).

Orff Instruments

The German musician Carl Orff devised an approach to music for children which included a collection of instruments that now carry his name. Some were untuned percussion (various hand drums, miniature timpani, etc.) and others were tuned instruments (xylophones, glockenspiels, and metallophones). All were designed using quality materials to assure good sound but in miniature size for young people. (For example, an Orff xylophone uses the same rosewood bars to produce the sounds made by a regular xylophone.) The pitched instruments were designed so that bars not needed could be removed to minimize the chance for wrong notes.

Orff instruments lends themselves to ostinato ("repeated") patterns which work well in accompanying certain hymn tunes, especially pentatonic folk melodies such as HOLY MANNA or BEACH SPRING. A minimum collection of Orff instruments for church use would include bass and alto xylophones, alto metalophone and glockenspiel.

Such an ensemble can work well to accompany a reasonably large congregation. Since adults enjoy playing these instruments just as much as children do, members of the choir singing a given service could accompany a hymn with Orff instruments. Often it is good to add a treble instrument (flute, recorder, synthesizer, or even organ) to double the melody with the congregation. The collection of hymn arrangements _Take a Hymn_ (Augsburg 11-2172) includes arrangements of hymns with Orff that would work well for congregational or choral song. My arrangement of the hymn _All Things Bright and Beautiful_ (GIA G-3104) calls for Orff alto and bass xylophone with piccolo and works as a choir anthem or as a congregational hymn, the congregation joining the choir each time on the refrain. A good resource book to consider is McRae's _Celebrate: A Practical Guide for the Use of Orff Techniques and Materials in the Church_ (Augsburg 11-5328).

Orchestral Instruments in Worship

Of course everyone loves brass with organ on hymns for festival Sundays. The quartet of two trumpets and two trombones works especially well: the four instruments can play four part harmony from the hymnal, and their principle of construction is similar, so they produce a seamless, blended sound together. There are many published versions of hymns for organ, brass quartet, and congregation, often with special choir parts as well. Another option is the single trumpet. Vocal descants sung by choir sopranos are wonderful but if the congregation is really singing out, the descant is rarely heard. A solo trumpet, lyrically "singing" the descant will be heard and save rehearsal time for the choir director as well.

It is wise to come to know the band director in the local high school who could provide suggestions for instrumentalists. Even better is a nearby college. College instrumentalists have a bit more experience and will be more secure than many high school players. I know of some churches that have established resident brass ensembles, thus assuring a supply of players who have worked together and are readily available when needed. One congregation provides free rehearsal space for an area brass ensemble and free use of facilities for concerts in return for appearances of the brass ensemble a few Sundays each year. Another congregation has established a scholarship program with an adjacent university underwriting music lesson fees for members of their brass ensemble, all music students selected and coached by the trumpet professor, who is a member of the church. Church musicians need to be creative in exploring ways to identify a cadre of instrumentalists ready to play when needed. Most communities have a wealth of talent; we need to find it and harness it.

The flute is an especially useful instrument to use in hymn singing. Since it is rather weak in its lower register, transposing up an octave is often necessary. When played an octave higher than the written melody, its sound soars above a congregation providing ample leadership for the unaccompanied singing of a stanza. Children's choirs are given confidence by the support of a flute or recorder, doubling their melody especially if the accompaniment is for Orff instruments, which do not reinforce the melody. Another possibility is an ensemble of flutes; six or more flutes playing together producing a rich, warm sound that works well on many hymn tunes (have most play at written pitch, one or three an octave higher). In this context it is well to consider Ferguson's first rule for soprano instruments; one or three on the top part, never two. When two play together on the same part, slight imperfections of intonation result in "sour sounds" but the imperfections of

three players cancel each other out producing a "warm ensemble sound."

Clarinets are often overlooked as a useful color, perhaps because we all have heard beginning players squeaking away. The lower registers of a clarinet well played provide a rich mellow sound. Clarinets are transposing instruments so the director must be ready to cope with the special needs of these players. Again, having a cadre of instrumentalists ready to play helps because everyone knows what to expect.

One other observation about wind instruments needs to be made. Do encourage players to slur some intervals. Instrumentalists will tongue between each written note unless instructed otherwise. At the very least, any notes which encompass one syllable should be played slurred just as they are sung. Careful consideration of this dimension of the wind players performance will result in smoother, more elegant sounds from wind instruments.

String instruments also provide lovely additions to our palate of instrumental color, even though they are not quite as useful since they are not strong enough individually to lead a congregation (with the exception of the violin soaring above the congregation, much as a flute can do). Strings are especially painful when not played well, so again it would be important to identify players and nurture them so that they gain experience and poise. There are a few choral octavos for solo string instrument and choir which would provide a special punctuation to a service (for example, my setting of *Ah, Holy Jesus* for choir and viola [Morningstar MSM-50-3012], exploring the mournful sounds of the viola as a color for this passion text). When using a single solo instrument for an anthem in a service, be sure to find other ways to use that instrument as well. A solo instrument can provide a fine introduction to a hymn. If the player is gifted, ask him or her to play alone, melody only, to introduce a more lyrical tune. On a gentle text and tune, solo cello, viola, or violin could be heard joining with the congregation, especially if you encourage the soloist to play out even though choir and congregation will sing rather gently.

Synthesizers and Samplers

No discussion of instrumental color for worship would be complete without some mention of those wonderful, provocative, upsetting instruments made possible by the remarkable technology of our age. A synthesizer makes sound by the manipulation of basic electrical patterns (for example a sine wave is a very pure, flute-like sound). This basic sound or wave is then processed and mutated electronically by the synthesizer, adding additional character to the sound. A sampler begins by taking an electrical picture or "sample" of a real sound (any sound can be sampled—one note of an instrument, a waterfall, a dog bark), which can then be manipulated and processed somewhat like the basic sound waves of a synthesizer. Neither should be considered as replacements for real instruments, but rather as resources which do things real instruments cannot do.

For example, very "windy" sounds can be made that complement wonderfully the profound concept of the Incarnation—the breath of God upon Mary. Or such sounds might work as part of a reading of the biblical story of the coming of the Holy Spirit on Pentecost. Published examples of such creative use of these instruments are beginning to appear (for example, GIA recently published a version of the Genesis creation story, appointed for the Easter vigil with parts for reader, organ, percussion, and synthesizer) and more are bound to come. Anyone doubting the powerful, evocative, colorful possibilities of these instruments to exegete text need only listen to the gifted use of synthesized sound as accompaniment for some of the songs in _The Broadway Album_ of Barbra Streisand (Columbia). I am especially taken by the accompaniment using only electronically generated sounds for the Leonard Bernstein song "Something's Coming" from _West Side Story._ The sounds of the accompaniment evoke the excitement, the anticipation, the impatient waiting that is reflected in the text and tune—a kind of Advent feeling if you will.

No clearer demonstration of the remarkable power of musical color to enhance a text can be cited than this setting of the Bernstein song. Martin Luther is often quoted as saying that the devil didn't need to have all the good tunes. Neither does our secular society need to frighten us away from the many wonderful ways instrumental color, from piccolo and drum to synthesizer, can enrich our worship. Just like Luther, we must be ready to adapt and modify in creative ways and not merely copy things done in secular musical contexts. Here is a challenge worthy of us all.

John Ferguson[29]

236 ✦ THE HISTORY OF THE ORGAN IN THE CHRISTIAN CHURCH

The honor accorded the pipe organ in Christian worship represents a curious paradox. On the one hand, the Christian church through most of its history has had an abiding antipathy toward instruments; on the other, the organ (together with bells) has, since the late Middle Ages, become so identified with the church that it embodies the very essence of "churchliness." How could this have happened? This article traces the history of the organ in worship in order to answer this question.

The early church's rejection of instruments in worship and its mistrust of instrumental music of any kind is well known. In particular, the Roman _hydraulis_ or water organ, a predecessor of the medieval church organ, was linked with pagan rites, games, and the theater. The early church writers had no more use for the organ than for any other pagan instrument. St. Jerome (fourth century) spoke out sharply against the organ, warning that Christian virgins should be deaf to its music (Johannes Quasten, _Music and Worship in Pagan and Christian Antiquity,_ trans. Boniface Ramsey [Washington, D.C.: The Pastoral Press, 1983], 125; 112, n. 128). The Eastern Orthodox churches have never included instruments in their liturgies. In the West, the use of instruments in worship did not become commonplace until the Renaissance, and Roman Catholic ecclesiastical authorities remained somewhat averse to them until well into the twentieth century.

A Gift to Pepin

Yet in spite of its general hostility toward instruments, the Western church accepted the organ into its worship at a relatively early date—perhaps at some point during the tenth century, far in advance of any other instrument except bells. The normal explanation for this paradox begins with the gift of an organ from the Byzantine Emperor Constantine Copronymus to Pepin, king of the Franks, in 757. The gift evoked great curiosity—a fact mentioned in many contemporary chronicles—not only because all knowledge of the organ had died in the West but also because of the organ's imperial connotations. The instrument played a central role in ceremonial occasions at the Byzantine court; indeed, the organ had become the unmistakable symbol of the emperor's imperial majesty.

Pepin's organ was later destroyed, but in 826 there arrived at the court of Louis the Pious (Pepin's grandson) a Venetian priest, Georgius, who was trained in the art of organ building. At Louis's behest Georgius constructed an organ to replace the earlier instrument. A contemporary poem indicates just how significant the organ was to the self-esteem of the Frankish monarchs:

> Thus, Louis, do you bring your conquests to
>   Almighty God
> and spread your aegis over noble kingdoms.
> The realms your forbears could not gain by
>   force of arms
> Beg you of their own accord to seize them today.
> What neither mighty Rome nor Frankish power
>   could crush,
> All this is yours, O Father, in Christ's name.
> Even the organ, never yet seen in France,
> Which was the overweening pride of Greece
> And which, in Constantinople, was the sole
>   reason
> For them to feel superior to Thee—even that is
>   now
> In the palace of Aix [the Frankish capital].
> This may well be a warning to them, that they
> Must submit to the Frankish yoke,
> Now that their chief claim to glory is no more.
> France, applaud him, and do homage to Louis,
> Whose valor affords you so many benefits.
>   (E. Faral, *Ermold le Noir* (Paris, 1932), 2515–
>   2527, in Jean Perrot, *The Organ from Its
>   Invention in the Hellenistic Period to the End
>   of the Thirteenth Century,* trans. Norma Deane
>   [London: Oxford University Press, 1971], 213)

It is generally assumed that the adulation accorded a distinguished Eastern court instrument by the more primitive Western court and church led to its eventual admission into the liturgy of the Western church. There may be some truth in this statement, for church and state were much intertwined during the Middle Ages. But the assumption does not suffice to explain why the Western church should so summarily dismiss its centuries-old prejudice against all instruments and so wholeheartedly embrace an instrument with hitherto unmistakably secular connotations—an about-face reflected in the fact that the most recognized early medieval experts in organ building were monks, e.g., Gerbert of Aurillac (later Pope Silvester II, reigned 999–1003) and Constantius of Fleury. Nor does it explain why

early medieval accounts place organs in churches but do not link them with liturgical functions.

An Embodiment of Cosmic Harmony

These curious inconsistencies are perhaps best explained by understanding the organ of that time as an embodiment of cosmic harmony and a means of manifesting and teaching basic Neoplatonic doctrines associated with the classical educational curriculum, the *quadrivium,* and the medieval cosmic worldview.

The traditional Christian worldview, inherited from ancient Greek philosophy—especially from Plato—understood the cosmos as pervaded by *harmonia,* a quality that caused all things to be related and interconnected, and manifested to humans particularly through music. In his *Timaeus,* Plato, following Pythagoras, asserted that God constructed the universe according to specific proportions or ratios that were none other than those of the perfect musical intervals: the octave (2:1), the fifth (3:2), and the fourth (4:3). For Plato and for medieval Neoplatonic thinkers following Augustine, music was of divine origin. It was the means by which humans could contact and absorb into their souls the balance and perfection of cosmic harmony.

Platonic teachings on music won Christian support not only because they were embedded in the *quadrivium* but also because they were sympathetic to the suspicious attitude toward the sensuous enjoyment of music voiced by most of the church writers. That attitude insisted on strict regulation and restraint in musical expression and eventually fostered a "Christian" music with specific characteristics: ascetic severity, subtlety, rhythmic reserve, serene balance, and repose. The Christian cosmic worldview persisted throughout the Middle Ages (indeed, here and there until the eighteenth century), governing and energizing all facets of musical activity.

The evidence for understanding the organ as a symbol of cosmic harmony is scanty and inconclusive, as is much source material from the early Middle Ages; yet we can trace a slender thread of support for this view. The evidence begins with a statement by the early Christian writer Tertullian (third century), proto-Puritan who, it seems, would be least likely to approve a pagan instrument such as the organ.

Look at that very wonderful piece of organic mechanism by Archimedes—I mean his hydraulic organ, with its many limbs, parts, bands, passages for the notes, outlets for their sounds, combinations for their harmony, and the array of its pipes; but yet the whole of these details constitutes only one instrument. In like manner the wind, which breathes throughout this organ, at the impulse of the hydraulic engine, is not divided into separate portions from the fact of its dispersion through the instrument to make it play: it is whole and entire in its substance, although divided in its operation. (Tertullian, _De Anima_ 14; translation and commentary in Robert Skeris, _Musicae Sacrae Melethmata_ 1 [Altötting, W. Ger.: Coppenrath, 1976], 43)

Tertullian goes on to say that precisely like the wind blown in the pipes throughout the organ, the soul displays its energies in various ways by means of the senses, being not indeed divided but distributed in natural order. Behind Tertullian's words, one can detect not only an assumed Christian monism but also the Greek, Neoplatonic presupposition of a harmonically ordered cosmos.

Some early medieval writers merely hint at this interpretation, as if they take it for granted. Thus St. Aldhelm (ca. 639–709), English poet, scholar, and teacher, wrote:

If a man longs to sate his soul with ardent music,
And spurns the solace of a thin cantilena,
Let him listen to the mighty organs with their
    thousand breaths,
And lull his hearing with the air-filled bellows,
However much the rest [of it] dazzles with its
    golden casings
Who can truly fathom the mysteries of such
    things,
Or unravel the secrets of the all-knowing God?
    (_De Virginitate;_ trans. in Perrot, 224)

And in 873 Pope John VIII charged Anno, Bishop of Freising in Bavaria, "to send us, for the purpose of teaching the science of music, an excellent organ together with an organist capable of playing upon it and drawing the maximum amount of music from it" (_Monumenta Germania Historica,_ Epist. Merov. et Karol Aevi. V, anno 873, p. 287; trans. in Perrot, 222).

Baldric, Bishop of Dol, is much less ambiguous in his estimation of the organ. In a letter written to the people of Fécamp sometime between 1114 and 1130, he says:

For myself, I take no great pleasure in the sound of the organ (_ego siquidem in modulationibus organicis non multum delector_); but it encourages me to reflect that, just as divers pipes, of differing weight and size, sound together in a single melody as a result of the air in them, so men should think the same thoughts, and inspired by the Holy Spirit, unite in a single purpose. . . . All this I have learned from the organs installed in this church. Are we not organs of the Holy Spirit? And let any man who banishes them from the church likewise banish all vocal sound, and let him pray, with Moses, through motionless lips. . . . For ourselves, we speak categorically—because organs are a good thing, we regard them as mysteries and derive from them a spiritual harmony; it is this harmony that the Moderator of all things has instilled in us, by putting together elements entirely discordant in themselves and binding them together by a harmonious rhythm. . . . As we listen to the organ, let us be drawn together by a two-fold charity. (_Patrologiae latinae_ clxvi, 1177–1178; trans. in Perrot, 220–221)

Even in such a late source as the _Syntagma Musicum_ of 1619, Michael Praetorius implies a similar attitude toward the organ: a respect for the instrument's paradigmatic perfection, evident above all in its complex and ingenious mechanism:

Almighty God alone can never be given sufficient thanks for having granted to man in His mercy and great goodness such gifts as have enabled him to achieve such a perfect, one might almost say the most perfect, creation and instrument of music as is the organ . . . in its arrangement and construction; and to play upon it with hands and with feet in such a manner that God in Heaven may be praised, His worship adorned, and man moved and inspired to Christian devotion. (Michael Praetorius, _Syntagma Musicum II: De Organographia,_ trans. W. L. Sumner (Wolfenbüttel: Elias Holwein, 1619), 117–118)

The early appearance of organs in churches, then, may well not have been so much for practical music-making as for symbolic and didactic ends: symbolic in that the instrument was the material embodiment of cosmic harmony, and didactic in that it provided a visible, tangible "sermon" on that harmony. Together with the complex astronomical clocks still extant in some of the medieval cathedrals, organs may have witnessed to the divine basis for the _quadrivium_ and its underlying worldview. The clock represented divine order evident in the heavens, while the organ represented it in music; mathematics and geometry, the other disciplines of the *quadrivium,* were represented by the architecture of the cathedral church itself. (See Otto von Simson, *The Gothic Cathedral* [New York: Harper & Row, 1962], 43.)

The Later Middle Ages

Organs in the earlier Middle Ages normally consisted of a single rank of pipes. At some point during the later Middle Ages, however, the organ underwent a new development in which each key began to control a number of pipes sounding intervals of fifths and octaves above a fundamental pitch. Thus the instrument became, in effect, a single large mixture—a *Blockwerk,* to use the proper German term. This development was most likely brought about by the perception of the overtone series on the part of an organ theoretician or builder. Given the medieval preference for theory over practical observation, however, such an advance was probably grounded in a desire to make the organ embody even more perfectly the Pythagorean proof of cosmic harmony.

Had the medieval organ possessed a sensuous, affective tonal quality, no amount of praise for its perfect structure would have won it the church's approval. Like Bishop Baldric, who was quoted above, the church hierarchy prized the organ not for its sound but for its symbolism. Indeed, the very quality of sound produced by the medieval organ had an affinity to the Christian ideal of cosmic harmony and to the objective, nonaffective music produced by that ideal. The sound had practically no expressive qualities, only the slightest capacity for nuance, little variety in tone, very limited rhythmic capabilities and no potential for crescendo and diminuendo. The medieval organ was remote in its playing mechanism, remote from its listeners (organs were often set in a balcony or "swallows nest" high up on the church wall), and was situated in a remote, mystic and awe-inspiring acoustical environment. Its most unique musical characteristic, the ability to hold a tone at a static dynamic level for a theoretically endless period of time, was distinctly superhuman. If one assumes, as the Middle Ages did, that variation and fluctuation belong to the human sphere, while awe, remoteness, and constancy are characteristic of the divine, the mysterious, the holy, then the qualities enumerated above would

seem to render the organ a peculiarly hieratic musical instrument.

Whether or not the organ gained entry into the church because it was the embodiment of cosmic harmony, it seems fairly certain that the organ was not brought in at first to aid in the conduct of the liturgy. Again the sources are few and inconclusive, but the gradual incorporation of organ music into liturgical celebrations seems to parallel the rise to prominence of polyphony (see Peter Williams, *A New History of the Organ* ([Bloomington, Ind.: Indiana University Press, 1980], 47ff.)—a development that may also have gained impetus from Neoplatonic musical speculation. Since the organ's mechanical advances succeeded in keeping pace with the demands placed on it by musical developments, the instrument became capable of performing intellectual, contrapuntal music as that music evolved in the church. Thus with the support of both speculation and practice, the organ gained a firm foothold. By the thirteenth century, most major churches in Europe—abbeys and secular cathedrals—possessed an organ, and by the fifteenth century many of them had two: one for solo performance and a smaller one to accompany and support choral singing.

Papal and Conciliar Decrees

By the same conservative process that granted approval to other previously foreign elements after long-established use, the Roman Catholic church hierarchy gradually sanctioned the organ's official use in the church's liturgy. This process is best traced through papal and conciliar decrees that include statements on the organ. The only instrument mentioned in the decrees of the Council of Trent is the organ; its playing had to be free from any element that might be considered "lascivious or impure." Other sixteenth-century ecclesiastical ordinances likewise mention no instrument other than the organ (St. Charles Borromeo, Council of Milan in 1565; *Ceremoniale Episcoporum,* 1600). By the eighteenth century, the use of the organ in churches was almost universal, yet Pope Benedict XIV was less than enthusiastic about it, a view shared by his successors up through the early twentieth century. As Benedict wrote in the eighteenth century:

Thus use of the organ and other musical instruments is not yet admitted by all the Christian world. In fact (without speaking of the Ruthenians of the Greek rite, who according to the testimony of Father Le Brun have neither an organ nor any other musical instruments in their churches), all know that Our Pontifical Chapel [the Sistine Chapel], although allowing musical chant on condition that it be serious, decent and devout, has never allowed the organ. . . . In our days we find in France renowned churches that use neither the organ nor figurative chant [i.e., polyphony] in sacred functions. . . . (Pope Benedict XIV, Encyclical _Annus Qui,_ February 19, 1749; trans. in Robert F. Hayburn, _Papal Legislation on Sacred Music, 95 A.D. to 1977 A.D._ [Collegeville, Minn.: The Liturgical Press, 1979, 96])

Benedict's successors wrote in the nineteenth century:

Figured organ music ought generally to be in accord with the grave, harmonious and sustained character of that instrument. The instrumental accompaniment ought decorously to support and not drown the chant. In the preludes and interludes the organ as well as the other instruments ought always to preserve the sacred character corresponding to the sentiment of the function. (Congregation of Sacred Rites, _Encyclical Letter,_ July 21, 1884; in Hayburn, 141)

And so wrote the three popes who bore the name Pius in the twentieth century:

15. Although the proper music of the Church is only vocal, nevertheless the accompaniment of an organ is allowed. In any special case, within proper limits and with due care, other instruments may be allowed, too, but never without special leave from the Bishop of the Diocese, according to the rule of the _Ceremoniale Episcoporum._

16. Since the singing must always be the chief thing, the organ and the instruments may only sustain and never crush it.

17. It is not lawful to introduce the singing with long preludes or to interrupt it with _intermezzi._

18. The music of the organ in the accompaniment, preludes, interludes, and so on must be played not only according to the proper character of the instrument, but also according to all the rules of real sacred music. (Pope Pius X, _Motu proprio tra le sollecitudini,_ November 22, 1903; in Hayburn, 228–229)

There is one musical instrument, however, which properly and by tradition belongs to the Church, and that is the organ. On account of its grandeur and majesty it has always been considered worthy to mingle with liturgical rites, whether for accompanying the chant, or, when the choir is silent, for eliciting soft harmonies at fitting times. In this matter also, however, it is necessary to avoid that mixture of sacred and profane which through the initiative of organ builders on one hand, and the fault of certain organists who favor ultramodern music on the other, threatens the purity of the holy purpose for which the church organ is intended. While safeguarding the rules of liturgy, We Ourselves declare that whatever pertains to the organ should always make fresh development. But We cannot refrain from lamenting that, just as formerly, in the case of styles of music rightly prohibited by the Church so today again there is a danger lest a profane spirit should invade the House of God through new-fangled musical styles which, should they get a real foothold, the Church would be bound to condemn. Let that organ music alone resound in our churches which expresses the majesty of the place and breathes the sanctity of the rites; for in this way both the art of organ builders and that of the musicians who play the organ will be revived and render good service to the sacred liturgy. (Pope Pius XI, apostolic constitution _Divini cultus,_ December 20, 1928; in Hayburn, 331)

These norms [against exaggerated, bombastic music] must be applied to the use of the organ or other musical instruments. Among the musical instruments that have a place in church, the organ rightly holds the principal position, since it is especially fitted for the sacred chants and sacred rites. It adds a wonderful splendor and a special magnificence to the ceremonies of the Church. It moves the souls of the faithful by the grandeur and sweetness of its tones. It gives minds an almost heavenly joy and it lifts them powerfully to God and to higher things. (Pope Pius XII, encyclical _Musicae sacrae disciplina,_ December 25, 1955, #58; in Hayburn, 353)

In the Latin Church the pipe organ is to be held in high esteem, for it is the traditional musical instrument, and one that adds a wonderful splendor to the Church's ceremonies and powerfully lifts up man's mind to God and to heavenly things. (Pope Pius XII, encyclical _Musicae sacrae disciplina,_ December 25, 1955, #58; in Hayburn, 353)

Changing Tastes

The organ experienced its golden age during the Renaissance. By that time, its mechanism was much refined and improved, and sixteenth-century writings attest to the high proficiency level attained in organ performance. Most of the art from this period is unfortunately lost to us, since it was largely improvised—the extant compositions represent only a minute fraction of its glory. There was enormous activity in organ building at this time; ordinary parish churches as well as prominent ones acquired organs. By the time of the Reformation, the organ's place in worship was so well established that its use continued undisturbed among Lutherans and Anglicans, even though Luther and others were in fact less than enthusiastic about it.

> Luther rarely mentioned organ playing, but occasionally he did express an opinion against it, reckoning it among the externals of the Roman service; on the other hand, he was also musician enough in this area to appreciate and praise the art of a Protestant organist like Wolff Heintz. . . . Most Lutheran church regulations, at least in the Reformation period, paid no attention to the organ, a few left it as "adiaphorous" (neither forbidden nor approved) as long as "psalms and sacred songs" rather than "love songs" were played upon it, and as long as the organ playing did not, through its length or autocracy, encroach upon the principal parts of the service. (Friedrich Blume, *Protestant Church Music* [New York: W. W. Norton, 1974], 107)

The growth of *alternatim praxis* (chants divided into versets for choir and organ in alternation; the term is also applied to the Lutheran chorale) continued to insure an important role for the organ in worship. By this means the organ was raised to a prominence equal to the pastor or priest, congregation and choir, since it could "sing" an entire segment of chant or stanza of a chorale, leaving the people to meditate on the text (which they usually knew by heart).

The baroque era witnessed a decline in enthusiasm for the organ in southern Europe. Its mechanical development was arrested, less and less music was written for it (and what was written was of lesser quality), and there were fewer well-known organists. Calvinism stifled organ music in Switzerland, and Puritanism inflicted mortal wounds on it in Great Britain. The Ordinance of 1644 mandated

> the speedy demolishing of all organs, images and all matters of superstitious monuments in all Cathedrals, and Collegiate or Parish-churches and Chapels, throughout the Kingdom of England and the Dominion of Wales, the better to accomplish the blessed reformation so happily begun and to remove offences and things illegal in the worship of God. (1644 Ordinance of Lords and Commons; quoted in William Leslie Sumner, *The Organ, Its Evolution, Principles of Construction and Use* [London: Macdonald, 1962], 135)

> The use of organs in the public worship of God is contrary to the law of the land, and to the law and constitution of our Established church [of Scotland]. (Presbytery of Glasgow, Proceedings [1807]; see Ian Crofton and Donald Fraser, *A Dictionary of Musical Quotations* [New York: Schirmer, 1985], 107:15)

In the early seventeenth century, however, Protestant north Germany found a new purpose for the organ: to accompany congregational singing. Thus the organ continued to be assured a secure place in the church, not only for philosophical or theological reasons but also for practical ones. The instrument reached another mechanical and artistic high point in middle and northern Germany during the seventeenth and early eighteenth centuries, as Michael Praetorius's enthusiastic affirmation quoted above indicates. More than coincidence explains the fact that the authors who furthered ideas about world harmony during this period are the same ones who showed the greatest interest in the organ: Praetorius, Kircher, Werkmeister. Indeed the organ has flourished wherever the Neoplatonic worldview has been cultivated. The seventeenth-century English poets who eulogize the Neoplatonic concept of world harmony praise the instrument:

> Ring out, ye crystal spheres,
> Once bless our human ears,
> (If ye have power to touch our senses so)
> And let your silver chime
> Move in melodious time;
> And let the Bass of Heav'ns deep Organ blow,
> And with your ninefold harmony
> Make up full consort to th' Angelick symphony.
>   (John Milton, "Hymn on the Morning of
>   Christ's Nativity" [1645])

> But oh! what art can teach,
> What human voice can reach
> The sacred organ's praise?
> Notes inspiring holy love,
> Notes that wing their heav'nly ways
> To mend the choirs above. (John Dryden, "A
>   Song for St. Cecilia's Day" [1687])

When the full organ joins the tuneful choir,
Th'immortal Pow'rs incline their ear.
  (Alexander Pope, "Ode for Musick on St.
  Cecilia's Day" [*c.* 1708])

J. S. Bach's music represents the final glorious flourish, both for the concept of cosmic harmony in music (see Timothy Smith, "J. S. Bach the Symbolist," *Journal of Church Music* 27:7 [September 1985]: 8–13, 46) and for the organ as a vitally important factor in the music world; even during Bach's lifetime, the organ was being relegated to the fringe, where it has remained. Yet by that composer's time, the interplay of sacred and secular ideas made paradox the order of the day: it is a measure of Bach's profound synthesizing genius that he made the organ "dance"; a less likely instrument for dancing can hardly be imagined!

The pressure of the radically new Enlightenment ideas about music, such as the idea that its primary function consisted of expressing human emotion or providing entertainment and relaxation, had an enormous impact on the status of the organ and its music. The latter half of the eighteenth century witnessed a rapid decline and trivialization of the organ and its music, a trend that prevailed through the first half of the nineteenth century. The instrument could not compete with the new intimate, affective gestures, the rapid shifts of mood and emotional range of preclassical and classical symphonies and secular keyboard music (e.g., the works of the Mannheim School, or of C. P. E. Bach and Haydn). Compared with them, "the organ quite naturally was thought of as a clumsy, screeching, dynamically monotonous instrumental monster" (Arnfried Edler, "The Organist in Lutheran Germany," in Walter Salmen, ed., *The Social Status of the Professional Musician from the Middle Ages to the 19th Century* [New York: Pendragon, 1983], 89).

If it were to be asked what instrument is capable of affording the greatest effects? I should answer, the Organ. . . . It is, however, very remote from perfection, as it wants expression, and a more perfect intonation. (Charles Burney, *A General History of Music* [London, 1776–89], quoted in *Dictionary of Musical Quotations,* 107–113)

[Organ playing] in France was generally irreverent, although once in a while a significant talent came to my attention within this irreverence. Not rarely is a gay pastorale heard during a church service which turns into a thunderstorm before closing with a sort of operatic grand finale in free style. Given that this is untenable from the German religious point of view, it must be admitted that such things are often done quite talentedly. A requiem mass for Lafitte in the church of Saint Roch gave me the opportunity to hear one M. Lefébure-Wély play in a solemn, appropriate manner, whereas he worked up a tremendous gay mood during the mass on Sunday. In response to my astonishment over this I was told that the clergy as well as the congregation expect light-hearted music. (Adolph Hesse, "On organs, their appointment and treatment in Austria, Italy, France and England" [observations on a trip made in 1844], *Neue Zeitschrift fr Musik* [1853]: 53; trans. in Rollin Smith, "Saint-Saëns and the Organ," *The American Organist* 20:4 [April 1986]: 190–191)

In spite of this decline, however, the organ continued to solidify its position as the musical instrument of the church. By the nineteenth century its sound had come to be regarded as the epitome of churchliness; even those church bodies whose Puritan heritage had hitherto rejected the organ now began to embrace it. Yet significant composers of the period between 1750 and 1850 wrote little or nothing of note for the organ, and no organist of this period was accorded the degree of international recognition granted to the premier violinists, pianists, and singers of the time. This held true even until the present day.

The Modern Revival

The mid-nineteenth century marked the beginning of attempts to rescue the organ from neglect and trivialization; for example, the outstanding work of Mendelssohn in Germany; S. S. Wesley in England; Cavaillé Coll, Hesse, and Franck in France. These attempts were essentially within the framework of the church; the corresponding ground swell to restore the organ to a position of prominence in the world of secular music never attained the same degree of intensity. The revival of the organ within the church was bound up almost entirely with efforts toward church renewal after its first disastrous encounter with Enlightenment ideas. Revival was largely fueled by Romantic sentiments, especially those of historicism (e.g., the revival of gothic architecture and the music of Palestrina and Bach) and aestheticism (the devotion to and cultivation of beauty). As neither of these movements had a firm theological basis, the organ's continued existence in the church came to rest on its practical usefulness as a means of supporting large-group singing and on the increasingly unshakable conviction among the majority of Christian worshipers that the organ is the church's instrument. (The latter notion has at times created problems for the organ, as well as discomfort for organists, especially those who do not wish to be associated with the church.)

Nineteenth-century attempts to make the organ conform to the new taste and the new "enlightened" worldview included enclosed divisions with swell shades and devices for rapid change of registration. These were quite clumsy, especially when compared with the flexible expressivity of the orchestra or piano, and they were only partially successful. Thus there arose in the early twentieth century a countermovement (the *Orgelbewegung* or Organ Reform Movement) that did away with the questionable "improvements" and once again built organs that were in greater conformity with older musical ideals—and inevitably with the old worldview. The revival of older organ building techniques and concepts has only exacerbated the antipathy of those increasingly prevalent forces in the twentieth-century church that promote the ideal of a popular, intimate, and human-scaled church and worship.

The demise of the antique and medieval worldviews has relegated the organ to the fringe of the post-Enlightenment musical scene: to the degree that the modern instrument participates in the characteristics of the medieval organ, it evokes and espouses by the very character of its sound the medieval worldview. The notion that the organ is the church's proper instrument is still strong in many quarters, but the idea has powerful detractors. The rise of styles of worship that deemphasize or exclude the organ while featuring the use of other instruments underlines the gradual dethronement of the organ as the special instrument of the church.

Quentin Faulkner

237 • THE ORGAN IN WORSHIP

The organ is a very complex instrument both to describe and to play. The following article defines many of the terms used to describe and distinguish organs and identifies important issues in playing them in worship.

The organ was an invention of the Eastern empire early in the Christian era, where it was associated with court entertainment and was as a result never employed in church. When imported into the West about the eighth century, it was embraced by the church and became the archetypal instrument for the accompaniment of worship. Fully developed, the organ was, until relatively recently, the most elaborate mechanical device ever created, constructed by the cooperative act of numerous artisans, designed to be a worthy complement to the architecture and adornment of the worship environment.

The latest generation of instruments provides a summation of the best of the past and enables performance of a wide variety of musical styles for a multitude of uses. A single performer, playing authoritatively, can provide both introductory, bridge, and closing music, accompany soloists and choirs, as well as play in concert with other instruments. Most importantly, the organ can lead congregational singing, a fundamental element in corporate worship.

The organ depends greatly for its effectiveness on the resonance of the building in which it is housed. The same acoustic environment which favors the organ aids singing, since singers feel more secure in a resonant building than in an acoustically dry space which results in vocal timidity and fatigue. Thus, it is best to avoid surface treatments that are overly absorbent of sound, such as ceiling tile and carpeting.

Pipe Organs

The pipe organ is custom-designed by definition. It is expensive but can last for centuries. A pipe organ can be impressive visually, displayed sculpturally or enclosed in a sound-focusing case. Considerable space is needed for the largest instruments. Where an elaborate musical program is projected, a pipe organ is ideal. A small chapel might be well served by a small pipe instrument despite its limited power and colors. For the most sensitive performance of early music, a tracker organ might be desirable, despite its higher cost. Naturally, only the most experienced builders should be considered if a sizable expenditure is to be made on a pipe organ.

Electronic Organs

The most recent electronic instruments, those in which the sounds of actual pipes are recorded digitally and stored in a computer, are sonically impressive. These can be of custom design, and vary from modest instruments, appropriate for a small church and congregation, to very large and complex ones. They may include useful features such as the ability to record complete selections using a computer sequencer and instantly alterable tunings. Naturally, since they are a product of the most recent electronic technology, it is impossible to predict their longevity with certitude, though it is probably considerably less than an instrument with actual pipes. Electronic instruments, providing substantial quantity of varied sound at a price more modest than the pipe instrument, are a good value and musically effective.

——— Purchasing or Restoring Organs ———

Nowhere is there such a variety of issues to be faced as with providing an organ for the church. The cost of the instrument, the nature of the worship, the present and anticipated size of the congregation, the extent of the music program and number of choirs, and the amount of music which is actually used in a service are all factors to be considered. A large and expensive instrument is appropriate for a church with a professional-calibre organist and an extensive music program.

The restoration of older pipe organs should be decided on and undertaken with care. Some organs (despite sentimental attachment to them) were built at a time in the first decades of this century when organ design had descended to its worst. The advice of trained and impartial specialists is needed to appraise accurately whether such an instrument is worthy of preservation.

Often, for sentimental reasons money is repeatedly spent on organs which have in truth served their purpose and outlived their usefulness. They may never function adequately, either tonally or mechanically. Sometimes some pipe work can be saved and revoiced and accompanied by new pipes, but this work should only be undertaken with a full awareness on the part of the church administration of what is involved. Having made such a decision, the church should only use a builder fully qualified to perform this work.

——— The Inner Workings of Organs ———

Organ _stops,_ sets of pipes or groupings of sounds, are designated by the approximate length of the pipe needed to produce their lowest tone. Thus 8' represents the pitch of the piano. The pedal division is usually based on a 16' principal, the next important keyboard or manual on 8', the subordinate manuals on 4' and 2'. Those stops with numbers less than eight, such as 4' and 2' are designed for what is called _upper work,_ which gives brightness and carrying power. _Off unison ranks,_ designated 1²/₃', and so on, are called _mutations_ and are used to color the unison stops. All stops should have individual character but should also blend into a cohesive ensemble.

Organs depend on a variety of sounds that have been produced historically by pipes of differing designs. The foundation is made up of the _principals_ or _diapasons,_ pipes of moderate size and scale, pipes of narrow scale. _Flutes,_ open or _stopped_ (closed), are stops of wider scale. _Hybrids_ are tapered pipes such as the **Gemshorn** which have a multipurpose use. The _reeds_ have a vibrating tongue not unlike a party horn and provide colorful solos or more full sounds used in climaxes. _Mixtures_ are complex stops with more than one rank or sound per note and are used to blend the ensemble, giving brightness to the lower notes and added weight to the upper. Various percussive sounds such as chimes, bells, or harpsichord (in some of the electronic instruments), are also available, though not essential.

Registration is the art of combining stops appropriately, which constitutes a special demonstration of the organist's refined ear for sound. The organist should avoid using numerous stops of 8' or unison pitch, but selectively add upper work, especially when leading the congregation's singing. It is best to rely on principal tone with sufficient upperwork to produce a bright sound. The organ should be of sufficient power to support and envelop the voices. Most inexperienced organists play too softly for proper support of congregational singing. Further, softer voices of the organ should be dropped as louder ones are added to retain clarity. It is better to add upper work than more and more stops of unison pitch.

Inexperienced organists often make excessive use of the **tremulant** (or _vibrato_ in certain electronic instruments). This device produces an undulation in the tone of the instrument. Normal organ tone is without it. It may properly be used to provide warmth and contrast either on a soft solo voice, or a soft accompaniment. It should be avoided on louder combinations. [In black gospel worship, however, organists have long used vibrato as a coloristic device, bringing the vibrato to a stop, which functions as an expectant pause, then pushing it to a progressively faster rate as the next musical phrase begins. This kind of use of the organ had a great influence on the use of electronic keyboards in rock music.]

Organists

Most organists start their organ training after studying the piano, when they are able to read music well and play the simpler works of composers such as Bach, Mozart, and Schumann, and have a moderate degree of facility in scales and a basic understanding of harmony. While it is a keyboard instrument like the piano and harpsichord, playing the organ requires its own technique, not withstanding the addition of performance on the pedal board. The organist, having at his or her disposal an instrument which sustains tone, must learn to provide finger movement which connects tones smoothly, a technique called *substitution,* and to carefully articulate repeated notes. While formal instruction is desirable, a pianist who has been called to serve as organist in a small church can profit immensely from working through a good organ-method book. Churches might consider offering partial scholarships for organ lessons to young performers to ensure a supply of properly trained musicians and to relieve the regular musician of the feeling of being chained to the organ bench.

Organ Music in the Worship Service

In the use of solo organ music for the worship service, repetition and routine in registration and in the character of the music selected is to be avoided. Each service should be musically unique and the works to be played chosen carefully. It is best to begin by selecting hymns and anthems that reflect the topics or themes of the appointed scriptural texts and then choosing organ music to complement them. Often these can be an effective treatment of one of the hymn tunes to be heard in the service or one of the many organ works inspired by a line or two of Scripture.

The organ prelude, which prepares for the mood of the service, can be quite short. Prefacing a service with the common fifteen minutes of featureless and forgettable background music should be avoided. Postludes too can be quite short and varied in character. There are many ways of designing the musical

architecture of the worship service. Sometimes, for example, the most substantial use of the organ might be in the center of the service, especially if the end suggests something more introspective.

For most churches the more extended works of Bach, for example, may be too long and grand; in all but the largest churches the congregation may have already left before the conclusion of the piece. An occasional "recital postlude" might prove welcome. For someone of moderate organ technique the so-called *Magnificat* fugues of Johann Pachelbel might serve as excellent postludes. Preludes and postludes based on hymns selected for the core of the service are especially good.

The amount of worthy organ music is vast, from all periods. It ranges through all degrees of difficulty from the simplest (much worthy music having been written for the hands alone) to the most virtuoso. Almost all major composers are represented as well as some lesser known who have made an especially great contribution to the instrument.

In order to avoid the inevitable sense of isolation and enervation that develops when one plays week after week, the solitary organist should avail himself of the opportunity of growth through membership and participation in the many events sponsored by the American Guild of Organists and various other organizations devoted to church music. In addition, listening to recordings of all kinds of music, not just those for their instrument and for the church, is desirable. Attendance at services and musical events sponsored by other churches will provide positive experiences. Hearing performances of symphonies and opera will also stimulate an awareness of the varied power of music. Ongoing musical, liturgical, and theological inquiry is essential. Churches should encourage this through affirmation and budgetary support. The organist is a privileged minister able to proclaim the gospel powerfully.

Philip Beggrov Peter

238 • Designing the Organ for Leading Congregational Song

The primary purpose of the church organ is to lead and accompany congregational singing. This article argues that the highest priority in organ design and construction in churches should not be to produce an impressive organ for recitals, but rather to construct an organ to meet the unique needs of congregational singing.

The organ is not placed in church for recitals, nice as they may be. The organ is not placed in church as a tourist attraction, although some wonderful instruments have resulted from a desire to make a statement and attract people. And especially, the organ is not placed in church for the amusement and delight of organist, builder, or enthusiast. I believe the pipe organ still finds a welcome place in the church because it remains the single best instrument at which one person can lead a variety of styles of congregational song.

Some of you reading this article may be a bit upset with me because you like to use other instruments to lead congregational song. So do I. I have used guitar, synthesizer, piano (I like this one a lot), handbells, flutes, brass ensembles, even full orchestra and band for the leadership of congregational song. All of these possibilities work well if employed creatively and with a good understanding of their musical potential and limitations. But the organ remains as the best *single* musical resource capable of producing an ample quantity, quality, and variety of sound useful for leading many styles of song.

Others may be upset because my original statement implies that I consider the organ's reason for being in a space for worship in relation to its role in leading the song of the assembly. They believe that I am not interested in the organ per se, its repertoire, its history, its lore. Of course I am interested. The organ is my instrument of choice as a performer, and my degrees are all in organ performance. I'm intrigued by its history and perpetually amazed by the incredible variety of organs built over the years. Organs are like people; they come in all shapes and sizes and are fascinating to study. They are complex machines, and many individual examples are marvels of engineering and artistic excellence. But, all the lore, all the questions posed by enthusiasts when visiting a new organ (for example: What kind of key action does it have? Is it suspended? What kind of woods are used in the music rack? Does this organ have flexible winding? How much lead is in the principal pipes?) can obscure or distract us from the real issue. Organs, with few exceptions, are placed in churches for the purpose of leading the song of the assembly. Organs are servants to and energizers of this song. This mission is primary and all other considerations are secondary. With this basic affirmation in mind, let's now look at concepts that should influence the design of organs for spaces where people gather for worship.

Physical and tonal properties need to be considered. Organs are large pieces of furniture, and care must be taken in placing them in a worship space. Since the church organ is not primarily a solo instrument, it must be designed in such a way that organ and organist can interact well with other musicians. The musicians include instrumentalists and especially choir and congregation. Both aural and visual concerns must be remembered when considering this interaction. Will organist and other musicians be able to hear each other with some reasonable feel for balance? Will they be able to see each other? Frankly, this makes it difficult to propose attached-console, mechanical action instruments for any but the smallest instruments. (Please understand I appreciate and affirm such a style of building, but my responsibility as a church musician is to consider the organ not in isolation, but in relation to its servant role in the life of the parish. Citing European examples of such an approach to organ building is not all that helpful either since church music practice there is so different from American practice.) Of course, detached-console, mechanical-action instruments are an option, and I hope more work is done to perfect this style of building. Some fine instruments with wonderful, sensitive key actions have been done. Some horrible examples can be found as well. We need to cautiously and conservatively design and build more good ones.

Console design is another concern. Consider the question of the combination action and layout of stop controls. Small, two-manual instruments don't require combination actions. Larger instruments do (say twenty to twenty-five or more stops). If one is to be free to utilize color possibilities inherent in larger instruments, one needs the flexibility provided by a reliable combination action. The larger the organ, the more efficient and practical the entire console design should be. A few large drawknobs can be placed conveniently close to the manual keys. Thirty or more of the large drawknobs to be found on some organs begin to present problems which are made worse by the use of name plates for the stops placed adjacent to but separate from the knobs. It gets hard to find a single stop quickly in a forest of knobs, and since the addition of a single stop is less noticeable in the total ensemble of a larger instrument, the addition of three or four at once is not all that easy and disrupts one's musical and rhythmical concentration. Simple stop tables placed above the top manual are easier to find and see. Of course, they don't look as elegant, but they do the job more efficiently.

While good physical and visual design is important, good tonal design is vital. The ultimate usefulness of the organ depends primarily upon its aural qualities. So let's consider some basic concepts in tonal design for church organs.

Good, warm singing sounds are the ideal. The assembly sings best when it is invited to join and blend with the organ in song. This invitation is not by a gesture or the singing into a mike by the organist or cantor, but by the very nature of the organ's sound—a sound which inspires participation. This sound requires adequate amplitude (loudness), character, and warmth. It needs a good bottom to lead, support, and undergird the assembly's song (the bass voice is the primary energizer of rhythmic pulse in music). It needs to be clear with some brilliance to communicate the melodic line. The sound must not be so forced or distinctive that the amateur singer is frightened or awed into silence. Aural assault is not the preferred way to encourage congregational song! Rather, the singer must feel surrounded and supported by the sound of the organ, drawn into participation by the very quality and personality of the organ tone.

As the stoplist is determined, certain concepts must be remembered. The organ is an ensemble instrument, not a collection of favorite solo stops gathered willy-nilly into an instrument. A "buffet table" approach to organ tonal design never results in a good organ. Rather, a concern for blend and cohesion of stops, an ensemble approach, is essential, especially in smaller instruments. A large instrument can afford to have a few unique, solo stops that are rarely used. If an organ has only twenty stops, all must work well together. Fortunately, blending and ensemble stops can have character and distinction. Please understand, I'm not arguing for a tonal palate akin to cream of rice cereal. Rather, I am proposing that the ensemble concept in organ tonal design works somewhat like the blend of a choir or congregation in song. All are group activities which work best when no single performer stands apart from the ensemble.

This ensemble concept is at work both within each organ division (say great, swell and pedal) as well as in the relationship between divisions. First, let's look at the concept at work within a division. Most organ ensembles are created by combining stops of different pitches much like rungs on a ladder—8′, 4′, 2′, and so on. And like a ladder, it is better—and safer—not to omit a rung along the way. Within a reasonably complete manual division may be found more than one ensemble: a principal chorus, a flute chorus, and perhaps even a reed chorus. The most important of these ensemble combinations is the principal chorus which, when complete, is "crowned" by a mixture. This ensemble is the backbone of the organ and the critical ingredient in good hymn combinations.

Not every principal chorus begins with a principal at 8′ pitch. It is possible to have a "principal chorus" using flute (usually stopped) registers as long as the combination has a principal on top. The well-designed two manual is likely to have such a hybrid ensemble in the swell with its principal chorus being built upon a Rohrflote or Gedackt 8′ and the principal register being at 4′. Such a chorus will not be quite as broad in tone as one which includes a principal 8′. Flute and reed choruses are often less complete and not as important to hymn playing, although a chorus trumpet on the great and a reed chorus (16′ and 8′ with perhaps a 4′) on the swell is especially useful in hymn combinations.

Each division should have its own principal chorus with secondary flute and reed components. (For service playing, a complete, independent principal chorus in the pedal is not essential, although desirable.) These divisions should be designed to sound good and complete alone but also work well when coupled together. Divisions should complement and enhance each other as they are combined. Since an organ crescendo works best as an increase of brilliance and not just loudness, it is best that secondary divisions have choruses which add brilliance to the primary (great) division. Thus the mixture, or crown, of the swell would be higher than the great so that an increase in brilliance is noted when swell chorus is added to great chorus. While it is true that a crescendo works through an increase of brilliance, not the addition of more and more 8′ and 4′ stops, it is important to remember that as the sound grows brighter, more 16′ and 8′ foundation (especially pedal foundation) must be provided as well. Brilliance does not imply screaming, harsh sounds! No one likes to hear people or instruments shouting for very long.

Now, this discussion of organ tonal design could go on longer, and I could become more specific about choice of appropriate registers for individual divisions. But specific choice of stops is secondary to the primary consideration that basic, good organ design is built upon each division as a complete ensemble working alone or in combination with other divisions. Since congregational song is an ensemble activity, the organ interacts with and leads ensemble singing best when its individual divisions are used together. Thus, my hymn combinations always begin by engaging the couplers. Ensembles in each division are then selected. A more gentle hymn might be played upon a combination of great 8′ and 4′ with swell 8′, 4′, and 2′. A more majestic text might call for complete principal choruses from both manual divisions. The opening hymn on Easter Day would call for chorus reeds added to the ensemble. In each case, a pedal ensemble to support and undergird the manual ensemble would be important, although from time to time it is good to give the feet a rest and lead a stanza with manuals alone. But no matter what the specific combination may be, the goal is always warm, blending sounds from the organ.

A delightful by-product of such a design approach is an organ well suited for the classic core of its own repertoire. Thus good church organ design is not at all in conflict with good organ design for the repertoire, provided one is interested in a reasonably eclectic, middle-of-the-road approach to an instrument for the literature. Good news! We can have our cake and eat it too.

John Ferguson[30]

239 • THE PIANO IN WORSHIP

Many congregations are discovering the piano as an excellent instrument to lead congregational singing. This article informs the reader about the intelligent use of the piano in worship.

Rate in the order of appropriateness for public worship:

a. accordion
b. guitar
c. organ
d. piano
e. zither

Asked this question, my hunch is that the majority who are reading this would put the organ in first place, the piano in second. (Actually, all the instruments have been used.) We'd answer that way because of what we've experienced; in our churches, the organ has long been the instrument most used in worship.

But for a number of reasons, that prominence may be waning. Many congregations are discovering that the piano provides an excellent alternative to the organ. Some use it only to provide variety and to give the organist a break. Others, especially smaller congregations, have consciously decided to use the piano instead of the organ on a regular basis. They have discovered that piano accompaniment is not only suitable but preferable to organ music for their style of worship.

Strengths and Weaknesses

Whether a pianist can successfully accompany hymns and provide service music for worship depends on a few key factors: the acoustics of the church, the quality of the instrument, and the performance ability of the musician. Although a good instrument under the hands of a competent pianist can produce marvelous orchestrations of tone and articulate, crisp rhythms, the piano has neither the sustaining power nor the instrumentation possibilities of an organ.

However, often the problems people face when using a piano in worship have less to do with the instrument itself than with the apparent lack of appropriate literature: unlike the organ, the piano has no rich heritage of repertory explicitly composed for use in worship. This gap can partially be filled from other sources. For example, pianists have discovered that many classical piano compositions may be appropriately adopted for worship. Musicians need only make judicious choices on the basis of length and style, avoiding pieces that are very familiar and thus easily associated with experiences outside of the worship service.

Other pianists have discovered a wealth of material usable in worship services in the repertory of organ music written for manuals only. This music maintains the dignity of a tradition, creates no tension by association with other styles, and generally supports the aim of worship. Only the sound itself is different: the pianist must decide whether a particular work is too idiomatic for the organ to be used effectively on the piano.

Apart from these two sources for piano worship—judicious selections from classical literature and from organ music for manuals only—pianists face an inadequate supply of commendable material suitable for worship. During the past century, composers in the American popularist tradition have attempted to create a body of sacred piano literature, most of it based on hymn tunes. But without the advantage of historical precedent available to the organ, pianists have adapted various models of piano style that may not be appropriate for the worship service: nocturnes, etudes, concertos, and cocktail music have all had an influence.

Most of these efforts at adaptation are unsatisfactory because they are obvious imitations, conjuring up associations outside of worship traditions, calling attention to themselves, forcing hymn tunes to be something they are not, and in effect intruding on worship. If a model for piano style in worship is required at all, a more effective one is organ literature associated with worship. However, due to the inherent differences between the two instruments, this model also has problems.

A most helpful source of suggestions for piano music suitable for church (unfortunately never published and therefore not conveniently at hand) is Richard Cole Shadinger's dissertation "The Sacred Element in Piano Literature: A Historical Background and Annotated Listing" (Southern Baptist Seminary, 1974).

Another helpful source now available is a ten-volume anthology, compiled and edited by Dr. William Phemister, Chairman of the Piano Department of the Wheaton College Conservatory of Music, released by the Fred Bock Music Co. in May 1987. The multivolume collection is comprised primarily of music originally composed for the piano. (Exceptions include three organ chorale preludes by Brahms.) Six volumes are devoted to individual composers: Mendelssohn, Brahms, Schumann, Liszt, J. S. Bach, and Beethoven. Of the four remaining volumes, two include seasonal music (Christmas and Lent/Easter), another is a collection of duets (four hands, one piano), and the final volume contains selections by twentieth-century composers. These last two volumes also include some organ transcriptions. While this ten-volume work is designed for church pianists, it also of value to student pianists.

——————— Selecting Music ———————

As with any genre of music, church music's quality or lack of it is associated with the names of publishers. Their boards establish the standards, which, if consistent, are of great assistance to the individual musician who faces a market of very uneven quality. The Lutheran publishing houses, Concordia and Augsburg, offer an outstanding selection of music for the piano, much of it published as organ music for manuals only. Other very reputable companies include Oxford University Press, Harold Flammer, Inc., and Peters.

In selecting music the musician should take into consideration principles of quality, moderation, and appropriateness. Some more specific, but not exhaustive, suggestions include the following:

1. Do not choose music that is too difficult. Unless you can play the music well, you should not play it at all.
2. Avoid obvious virtuosity. The music should assist worship and never be confused with a recital performance.
3. If the music is based on a hymn, be sure its arrangement does not injure the original character of the tune and associated texts, either by excessive chromaticism or technical demands.
4. Avoid any style that has strong associations with music outside of the context of a worship service.
5. Avoid banality. Regard the music as an offering to the Lord, and make it the best in style, content, and rendition. Avoid obvious "formulas" for accompaniments, figurations, and modulations.
6. Giving careful thought to the place of the music in the liturgy will help you decide whether to choose something quiet and meditative or festive and celebrative. The mood and associated text, if there is one, should be compatible with the church season and/or worship theme.

Noel Magee

240 • ELECTRONIC KEYBOARDS AND THE CHURCH MUSICIAN

Recent technology has generated a wide variety of electronic keyboards available to the church musician. This article defines many of the technical terms that are used to distinguish the varieties of keyboards available and provides guidelines for their use.

The word *keyboard* has taken on new meaning the last decade or so. Most of us think of keyboards in the context of musical instruments, especially the piano, we have experienced all our lives. These instruments have evolved over some 500 years, and with the appearance of the piano in the eighteenth century, have remained essentially unchanged.

Today the word *keyboard* describes a bewildering variety of instruments. Keyboards are everywhere: small, mini-instruments that fit into a backpack, semi-portable "electric pianos," keyboards stacked one upon another like some sci-fi organ, and especially keyboards of all types as the instrument of choice for the teenager. In fact the keyboard has replaced the guitar as the instrument of the younger generation. But what about the church?

Electronic keyboards are now found in churches and have potential that is just beginning to be explored. Yet most of us are a bit uncomfortable about these new instruments, wondering how to use them and even if we should use them. Before exploring these questions, it is helpful to define a few terms which will give some perspective for any discussion of the use of electronic keyboards in church. Let's begin with general terms that may or may not apply to any specific electronic keyboard.

A Glossary of Terms

MIDI. MIDI is an acronym for *musical instrument digital interface.* It is an international standard, agreed upon by manufacturers in the industry, a "language" which enables any MIDI-equipped device to communicate with any other MIDI-equipped device. Computers can "talk" to electronic keyboards; a synthesizer can be played from a guitar or organ console. MIDI technology has revolutionized the commercial music industry and is beginning to impact music publishing. MIDI will touch almost all musicians of the future.

Sequencer. A *sequencer* electronically records all information (pitch, rhythm, key velocity, and duration) while an instrument is played and then plays it back through that instrument or another MIDI-compatible instrument. The recorded information is stored digitally in computer memory and during playback the instrument is activated from this memory. Thus a sequencer is more like a player-piano roll than a tape recorder, since the sequence is played back through the instrument, not as an audio recording. Computers can have a sequencer program. Sequencers are a part of some electronic keyboards or can stand alone as a separate little "box."

Track. *Track* is the term used in sequencing when the performer plays once through a song using a particular sound (e.g., piano). This track can then be replayed while another is "laid down" (e.g., a percussion part). Both could then be played back while a melody line is performed on the same keyboard. Thus it is possible to be a one-person band! Of course there are some problems here; if the first track does not slow down for a cadence, the subsequent tracks must not slow or the ensemble will collapse. Singing with such tracks must be rhythmically perfect without extra time for breathing or expression. This is one reason why such sequenced tracks work better for pop music, which tends to have a more stable pulse than traditional concert, choral, or congregational music.

Touch Sensitive. Keyboards can be made to respond to the most subtle degrees of touch. As varying pressure is applied, loudness could increase or decrease or vibrato could change in intensity or depth. A fast stroke could result in a sharp beginning for a sound, a gentle stroke the opposite. A piano has a touch sensitive keyboard, but the best electronic keyboards are, in their own way, more touch sensitive than an acoustic piano. (To refer to an instrument as *acoustic* implies that it is a real one rather than an electronically generated imitation of a real instrument).

Polytimbral. Keyboards can be designed so that they produce more than one sound simultaneously. For example, keyboards can be split, with the lower half providing one sound (e.g., string bass) and the other half another (e.g., piano). Many polytimbral keyboards are such that different sounds occur simultaneously, some via a previously prepared sequencer track and some live, played by the performer. Thus one can play a duet (or trio or quartet) with oneself.

Electronic Keyboards

Now, what about the keyboards themselves? Before examining the various types available, a bit of history would be helpful. Early in this century, the new technology of electronically generated sounds made possible the first electronic organs as well as a few other instruments, specifically the Ondes Martinot and Theremin. They produced undulating, spooky sounds that were employed by a few composers of the time.

In the 1960s rapidly evolving electronic technology made possible much more sophisticated, synthesized sounds. Instruments called synthesizers (remember the famous Moog synthesizer?) began to appear. By the 1980s, electronic keyboards had become much more sophisticated and at the same time affordable and user-friendly. These electronic keyboards have been around long enough that various categories or types seems to be emerging.

Portable Keyboards. These instruments range in size and quality and tend to have a few pre-set sounds. Most have a small amplifier and speaker system "on board" and are relatively inexpensive. They are practical, easy to use and move about, and do offer the advantage of staying in tune (assuming they are in tune from the beginning).

Electronic Keyboards. These instruments are somewhat more sophisticated than their portable cousins and are designed to imitate an acoustic piano. Some do quite well, complete with weighted, touch-sensitive keys. Some offer optional sounds (e.g., harpsichord, concert grand, barroom upright). While still portable, they are more expensive than the simplest electronic keyboards and usually require a separate audio system. Most have their sounds permanently stored in memory that is largely unchangeable.

Samplers. Samplers and synthesizers are more complex than the keyboards above and at the same time more flexible. A sampler takes a digital "picture" (a short recording) of a real sound which then can be played back at any pitch level. Any sound can be sampled and played back: rain, thunder, water running, voices, birds, instruments. Special aural effects as well as reasonably realistic acoustic instrumental sounds are possible. Electronic modification or change of sampled sound is also possible. Unfortunately, real, high-quality, musically satisfying samples of acoustic instruments are very difficult to achieve because instruments produce complex sounds, sounds which change in timbre as the pitch range changes. While simple in concept, the process of sampling quickly becomes complex and requires voluminous data storage (computer memory in other words). Quality samplers are expensive ($2,000 and up!) and always demand quality external audio equipment.

Before rushing out to purchase a sampler instead of finding four good brass players for Easter, it is well to remember that what makes individual, live music-making exciting to experience is its imperfection and infinite variety. Samplers are too perfect, lacking the incredible subtlety of even amateur-level performers, to say nothing of really fine performers. It is one of the amazing ironies of all electronically produced sounds that they tend to be too perfect and our ear hears perfection as sterility—a kind of strange, unreal, boring flavor to the sounds. To produce musically convincing imperfections—the infinite variety of subtle changes in articulations and quality of tone that a real instrument can achieve—is the great challenge facing any attempt at electronic generation of an acoustical sound. To create electronically the effect of an ensemble (a group of acoustical instruments, each with its own imperfections to give life and interest to the composite sound) is an even greater challenge.

All of the above notwithstanding, a good sampler can do a fine job of sounding like an acoustic piano and will do certain other instruments (tuned percussion instruments being one example) with astounding fidelity. Single musical lines also tend to come off better than complex sonorities, because the individual line can be mutated somewhat through the use of the touch sensitive keyboard and other controls that most samplers and synthesizers include which allow the performer to instantly modify a specific sound. But it is important to remember that the more subtle the acoustic sound, the more difficult it is to reproduce it via sampler, since its many nuances are impossible to program.

Synthesizers. A synthesizer combines and manipulates individual dimensions (parameters) of a sound, generating it electronically. The skilled synthesist can produce a wide variety of interesting and useful sounds, many of which are remarkably like acoustic instruments. A recent development has seen the inclusion of some sampled sounds from acoustic instruments in the data base or memory of the synthesizer. These sounds can then be modified and combined with synthesized sounds for remarkable results. Good quality synthesizers (in the same general price range as samplers) also require external audio equipment, and just like samplers vary widely in price depending upon features and degree of flexibility. (Features can include, but are not limited to, an on-board sequencer, polytimbral capability, and touch sensitivity.)

Since the skills to produce good sampled or synthesized sounds are very complex, most users rely upon previously derived collections of "sounds" that can be purchased as floppy disks or cartridges and "loaded" into the memory of the instrument. Many synthesizers come with a number of pre-engineered "sounds" stored in their memory, ready to be used by the performer. Thus it is not necessary to know how to program a synthesizer to produce sounds in order to use it.

Audio Equipment. Most of the better-quality electronic keyboards require separate audio equipment. It is important to remember that these instruments are designed to produce, not reproduce, musical sounds. Most have a wider pitch range than most pipe organs. Typical church PA systems are totally inadequate for these instruments. Most home stereo systems are also inadequate and in fact can be damaged by the wide dynamic and pitch range of even a medium-quality electronic keyboard. Any consideration of a keyboard also must include consideration of an adequate audio system to project the sound. Small, portable, and reasonably effective systems are available for modest cost. More extensive, perhaps permanent installations, will be required if the better keyboards available today are to sound at their best, especially in larger worship spaces.

As this discussion makes clear, the amazing world of the electronic keyboard can be quite complicated. However, it is not to be feared. Almost every congregation has someone (usually a high school or college student) who is "into" electronic keyboards. These people are enthusiasts who would be happy to share their knowledge. After a basic session with an enthusiast (a good way to begin might be to take this article along and ask that each term defined be demonstrated for you), it might be helpful to go to a music store for additional information. If you can find one, the best resource is a business dealing exclusively in electronic keyboards. Often the employees are more knowledgeable than those in a general music store, and you will not be distracted by clashing cymbals or wailing guitars. The best time to visit is earlier on a weekday; in other words, never go when school is not in session, unless you want to compete for attention with all the young enthusiasts. Upon visiting such a resource, make clear your interest (church, not rock band!) and how much experience you have had to date. Don't be afraid to ask questions. If you feel that your needs

are not being met, the specific store visited may not be the place where you should purchase equipment. After all, you will need some help and advice after the purchase as well.

Electronic Keyboards in the Local Church

A few applications in the musical life of the local congregation are immediately obvious. Convenient, always-in-tune keyboards are now possible for the church school or the choir room; in fact anywhere in church where a simple accompanying instrument is needed. While these keyboards may not replace a good quality grand piano, they are better and more flexible in many situations, if only because of their size, than the typical old upright piano which is so common in choir rooms and church-school rooms.

Once one moves beyond the use of a keyboard as replacement for an acoustic piano, things become more complex. Sequenced accompaniments or adjunct parts for accompaniments are possible but do raise musical problems since the potential for spontaneous addition of rubato is destroyed if one must stay synchronized with the previously sequenced accompaniments. Sequenced tracks for leading of congregational song present special problems. One's best notion of the perfect tempo for a hymn may change between Saturday, when the sequenced tracks were done, and Sunday morning, when the congregation attempts to sing with them.

There is also the question of musical ethics in using sampled or synthesized sounds to replace or in place of live instrumentalists. Is it morally correct to use synthetic devices, especially in church where honesty is proclaimed as a virtue? On the other hand, is it better to use a few sequenced tracks done well than a live performance so poor that it gets in the way of the music and our worship? Since there is no single or easy answer to these questions, it is important to explore and discuss how these new instruments can best contribute to the musical life of the congregation. My own conviction is that their greatest possibilities lie in their ability to create new sounds; sounds that real instruments cannot make. In this way we find additional expressive possibilities for singing new songs to the Lord as well as enriching our singing of the old songs.

John Ferguson[31]

241 • THE SYNTHESIZER IN WORSHIP

The synthesizer is one of the most versatile yet affordable instruments a church can purchase. It can contribute a variety of sounds and accompany a variety of musical styles.

The Synthesizer's Impact on Worship

The development and utilization of the synthesizer as a musical instrument has had a revolutionary impact on the music community worldwide. The electronic music industry as a whole, integrating technologies involving computers, synthesizers, software, and advanced networking and communication interfaces, has left an indelible and immensely significant impression on the historical record of musical development. The full impact of this electronic music revolution is yet to be determined but is sure to be monumental.

Let us begin with some definitions. For our purposes, a synthesizer is a musical instrument which produces sound through the physical (analog) or computer-induced (digital) manipulation of electrical current. The parameters of the nature and extent of the electronic manipulation must be programmable by the operator of the instrument (or the musician operating the instrument). So, these two factors are necessary for an instrument or electronic hardware implement to be considered a synthesizer: electronic tone production and human programmability.

The Synthesizer in Worship

How does this development of electronic music technology apply to worship in the church? Biblically and historically, God's people have sanctified and incorporated contemporary technologies into the life of the community of faith. King David sanctified and utilized instruments that were in common usage in other cultures and invented some new instruments in addition. Throughout church history, developments in musical instrument technology have been sanctified (sometimes reluctantly) and used in Christian worship. For example, the pipe organ, now one of the most commonly found instruments in Christian churches, was developed by Egyptians and Greeks for secular usages. The electric guitar, bass, and drums, which, along with the piano, comprise the contemporary rhythm section, have come into common usage in worship after achieving success in the jazz and rock idioms (al-though many churches still consider the rhythm section to be anathema). To ignore the development of musical synthesis and its potential use in worship would be tantamount to our predecessors in church worship direction ignoring the development of the pipe organ.

The Synthesizer in Place of Acoustic Instruments. The synthesizer is utilized in two often overlapping ways in contemporary worship settings. First, the synthesizer is used to imitate or replace acoustic instruments. Since the extent of its tone production capabilities are so vast, the synthesizer can effectively imitate strings, woodwinds, brass, percussion, or other keyboard instruments (even ancient keyboard instruments). It can fill in the gaps in typical church orchestra settings where instrument groups are often missing. In churches where budgetary restrictions disallow the purchase of an organ or a good piano, the synthesizer can be a feasible, affordable substitute.

However, this application of the synthesizer as an imitating or replacing instrument is limited by the very nature of the instrument. Digital reproduction of sound can never exactly imitate real sound, although it can come very close. The playing of an acoustic instrument is characterized by an investment of a human factor which is not comprehensively reproducible electronically. Also, the sound produced by the synthesizer must be run through a sound system, which tends to further limit its range of harmonic richness. In spite of these limitations, the synthesizer can be effective in filling in instrumental gaps or replacing a piano or organ.

The Synthesizer as a Unique Instrument. The second and possibly more definitive use for the synthesizer is as a unique and distinct musical instrument. It can produce a multitude of sounds and effects

Worship Candles. Candles have always been used to symbolically represent the presence of God in worship. Three candles represent the Trinity, two the humanity and divinity, and one the unity of the godhead.

that no other instrument is capable of producing. This distinctive character of the synthesizer not only makes for it an irrefutable place in the history of musical instruments, but also provides for it a contemporary application as a member of the rhythm section of an orchestra.

Along with the use of sequencers and other electronic gear, the synthesizer makes such areas as recording and orchestrating much more accessible to the average church musician. As equipment becomes more sophisticated as well as more reasonable in cost, the God-given creative potential in musicians can be nurtured and released, resulting in new ways to communicate and express praise and worship to the Lord.

James R. Hart

242 • ARRANGING MUSIC FOR INSTRUMENTS

Writing music for orchestral instruments requires knowing about the unique design and sound of each instrument. This article examines each major type of orchestral instrument, outlining the basic features of each and suggesting ways of effectively arranging music for each.

——— Brass Instruments ———

Fear not! Band and orchestral instruments can be understood by the church musician. Here are some brief discussions and examples of what the brass instruments can do. Of course, there is plenty of good published music. And, of course, not every church musician is an arranger, but there are occasional times when a special hymn or piece of music without published parts needs some instrumental parts. Here's how to do it.

Brass Groups. Having secured enough funds for a good ensemble, you need to know exactly what forces are available to you. The most common brass ensemble is the brass quartet. This ensemble usually consists of two trumpets and two trombones. A less common grouping uses two trumpets, horn in F (French horn), and trombone. If you are buying parts, be careful! Some arrangements use the trombone on the tenor line, some use the horn on the tenor line. Many arrangements come with a part for horn and the exact same part transposed for trombone. (More about transposition later.) If you hire a quartet that plays regularly as a group, make sure you find out what instruments they use. You

can be sure they will have a sufficient amount of material for preludes and postludes. Most liturgical publishers have a good selection of hymn concertatos and service music using brass instruments. Don't be surprised if a musician walks in with a tuba. A tuba or a bass trombone can play the second (lower) trombone part.

A brass quintet consists of two trumpets, horn in F, and two trombones (or trombone and tuba). Although music exists for brass sextet and brass choir, this article does not have sufficient space for a discussion of this group. So, if this Easter is your first attempt at using brass, start small!

Individual Instruments. The trumpet works well as a solo instrument or in an ensemble. Most trumpets are B♭ trumpets. Like many band-orchestra instruments, the B♭ trumpet is what is known as a transposing instrument. Rather than attempting to explain why some instruments are transposing instruments and some are not (like flute, violin, and oboe), it is important to explain only how they work. Think of it this way: when a B♭ trumpet player sees treble clef middle A on the music, and presses the proper number of valves to play treble clef middle A, what really sounds is treble clef middle G. Likewise, if you want the trumpet to play C, you must write D. Technically, we say a B♭ trumpet sounds a major second lower than written.

Just when you thought it was safe to start writing parts, be aware that occasionally you may buy a set of brass parts that includes C trumpet parts. The C trumpet is a nontransposing instrument. When the organ plays G, the C trumpet also plays G and the pitches match. If you find yourself with C trumpet parts and a B♭ trumpet player, you will have to transpose the part as mentioned above. There are professional musicians who own C trumpets. Once again, if you are hiring a professional brass group, ask if the trumpets prefer B♭ or C parts. Professional trumpet players may frequently play B♭ trumpet parts on their C trumpet (or vice versa), transposing at sight. If your trumpeters are not comfortable doing that, make sure the music matches the trumpet!

Don't forget key signatures. An organ part in the key of F major means the B♭ trumpet must play in the key of G major. Never use a transposed part in a liturgy without rehearsing it first. When writing trumpet parts, use the soprano voice as a guide. Trumpet parts are always written in the treble clef. Think of your choir sopranos—high F and G start them shaking, high A and B are pretty chancy, and high C and above are best left to the professionals. A good, competent professional trumpet player is expected to play high F, G, A with no problem. High school players may find this a bit challenging. Likewise, sopranos and trumpets should stay away from notes much below middle C. The lowest possible note on a B♭ trumpet is low F♯. The very bottom notes should be avoided. The following diagram shows the possible range and the desired range:

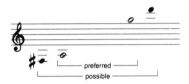

The trombone presents fewer problems. It is a nontransposing instrument. The bass clef note on the organ is the same bass clef note for the trombone. Trombone parts should always be written in bass clef. Just as the trumpets correspond to the soprano and alto voices, the trombones are the tenor and bass voices of the brass ensemble. As with all brass instruments, there is no limit theoretically to the uppermost note they can play. But once again, think of your choir tenor section. It is best

not to write trombone parts higher than 𝄢

The lowest possible note is 𝄢 but should be

avoided. Some trombonists play a bass trombone. A bass trombone has the added possibility of playing lower notes due to the addition of a special attachment to the instrument. Tuba parts can be played on the bass trombone; you may need to alter a few pitches below. Here are the possible and desired ranges of the trombones:

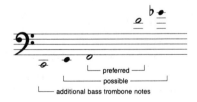

The French horn, or horn in F, is a transposing instrument. The horn sounds a perfect fifth lower than written. When the horn sees and plays middle G, what really sounds is middle C. In order for a horn to sound middle F, you must write high C.

The horn is usually assigned the tenor line in brass music. Horn parts are always written in treble clef. Remember your key signatures again when transposing! When the organ is in the key of C, the horn is in the key of G. The horn has a wide range, but sounds best in parts written from low F to high E.

As a special aside to those directors of music more comfortable with brass instruments, a French horn quartet is a marvelous alternative to the traditional brass quartet. There are plenty of published fanfares, preludes, and postludes.

As a review, let's take the tune DUKE STREET as found in any SATB setting and arrange it for a brass quartet of two B♭ trumpets, horn in F, and trombone. The two trumpet parts become the soprano and alto parts. In treble clef we use the key of E major (one whole step up from the organist's D major). We transpose up a whole step, or a major second. Thus the organ copy looks like this 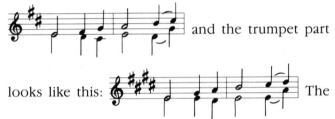 and the trumpet part

looks like this: The

horn plays the tenor line. Although the organist's copy is in the bass clef, we need to write the horn parts in treble clef. Think of adding one sharp to or subtracting one flat from the key signature when transposing horn parts. The key of D (two sharps) becomes the key of A (three sharps) for the horn. Thus  for the organ

becomes for the horn.

The trombone is a nontransposing instrument and plays the bass line exactly as it appears in the hymnal:

Do not feel that the brass must play on every musical item within the liturgy. At least you now have the capability of providing music for every acclamation and hymn . . . and perhaps a recessional; since the players are there, you might as well use them.

Woodwind Instruments

If brass instruments provide power and strings add warmth, the woodwind family of instruments can be thought of as adding color and agility to the overall sound of the choir and accompanying instruments. The woodwind family is a large one, and like most families, contains some strange relatives and adopted members. Here is an overview of the woodwinds:

- FLUTE and piccolo, alto flute and bass flute
- CLARINET (B♭ Soprano) and E♭ clarinet, alto clarinet, bass, and contrabass clarinets
- OBOE and English horn, bassoon, and contrabassoon
- SAXOPHONE (soprano, alto, tenor, and baritone)
- RECORDER (soprano, alto, tenor, and bass)

Upon viewing the list, one notices not all the instruments are wood; however, early versions of the instruments were wooden. Later additions (i.e., saxophones) were placed in the family because of similar properties they share.

Woodwinds have become increasingly popular in liturgical music due to the ubiquitous "C instrument part" found in so many folk/contemporary arrangements. Furthermore, there is an abundance of woodwind players because flute and clarinet tend to be the most frequently chosen instruments by grade school and high school instrumentalists. They are relatively easy to play, and a competent high school player should be able to play most published parts found in octavos and song collections.

Before we look individually at instruments, let us take another look at that generic C instrument. The C instruments are so named because they are non-transposing instruments. An A on a piano is an A on a C instrument. The C instruments are flute, piccolo, oboe, soprano recorder, and also violin and orchestra bells. A synthesizer can also play a C instrument part. Be judicious in assigning instruments; what is appropriate for an oboe is frequently not appropriate for orchestra bells. Some C instruments are bass and tenor instruments (cello, bass, trombone, bassoon). These instruments use the bass clef and may not use treble-clef parts.

The Individual Instruments. The flute may be the most popular woodwind instrument. Like all woodwinds, it displays the ability to be acrobatic when called for, yet is capable of sustaining a legato tone of great warmth and color. When not playing its own parts, it may be helpful to have the flute play the soprano line or melody of a hymn or song. This is exceptionally helpful on descants, and the flute can also help center the pitch if singers are instructed to tune in to the flute sound. The flute has a range of over two-and-a-half octaves, but the bottom octave should not be used with large forces—it will be inaudible. However, this bottom octave is very lovely if only the solo flute is playing. Some flutists may own alto and bass flutes. They generally should not be used for ensemble playing, but in solo performances. Their sound is quiet and haunting and best suited to meditative moments. The piccolo is one octave higher than the flute and has been neglected by many music directors. Piccolos need not always conjure up images of "The Stars and Stripes Forever." The piccolo in its bottom register has a "chiffy" sound, to borrow from organ terminology. The piccolo works well on folk or "rustic"-sounding music; imagine it playing a tune like ASH GROVE or HOLY MANNA. Its upper limits should be avoided. The flute and piccolo play in the treble clef and ranges are given below:

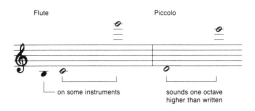

The oboe, bassoon, and their siblings are double-reed instruments, called so because the reed is two pieces of cane (reed) tied together. The reed on woodwind instruments vibrates and produces what is called a *crow,* similar to the sound made by placing a blade of grass between your thumbs and blowing.

The oboe sound can be described as plaintive and melancholy. (Remember the duck of Peter and the Wolf? If you are not familiar with that piece, then think of the old snake charmer song, a favorite of fourth-grade oboists.) Unlike the flute, the oboe has a bottom range capable of piercing through a heavy ensemble sound. In some instances, the bottom octaves may be too pronounced for use with choir.

The oboe and flute work well together. The flute should always take the higher part if you are using a part for two C instruments. Likewise, when doubling choral parts, it is advisable to assign the alto part to the oboe. Be aware that some alto notes fall below the oboe's possible range. Much rehearsal time for choir can be saved by use of flute and oboe and other instruments (for example, during a carol sing-along before Christmas masses when part singing can be made easier by have choir sections focus in on specific instruments). The oboe has a very distinctive sound for the choir altos on which to isolate. Of course, the oboe can also be used on soprano parts. A wonderful sound is produced by having the flute and oboe playing melody, with the flute playing the melody an octave higher.

The English horn is a peculiar relative of the oboe. As the old quip goes, it is neither English, nor a horn. (The name may be a derivative of "angle," relating to the slight bend of the thin metal tube at the top of the instrument.) If you are lucky enough to have access to one, it likewise should be used only as a solo instrument. Its tone is deeper than that of an oboe. If trumpets remind you of Easter morning, the English horn may remind you of Good Friday. It is a transposing instrument. Its G sounds like a C. In order to sound a G, you must write D.

The bassoon is the bass clef member of the double-reed family. Although its strength lies in its role as an ensemble instrument, it can provide a unique solo sound. The bassoon is a C instrument and may play the tenor or bass part when doubling choral parts. There is little need to use the contra-bassoon. An interesting combination (perhaps for Epiphany) would be a double-reed quartet—two oboes and two bassoons. A very limited amount of music is published for this exotic grouping. The oboes would play the soprano and alto parts and the bassoons would play the tenor and bass parts. The possible and preferred ranges for the double-reed instruments follow.

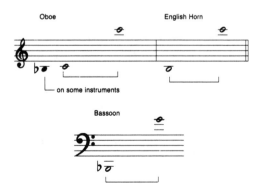

The clarinet is marked by its warm, mellow sound. Beginning clarinetists are asked to think of a "chocolatey" sound. The range of the clarinet is

over three octaves. The typical clarinet is a B♭ clarinet. (A thorough explanation of transposing instruments was given in the section on brass instruments.) When the clarinet plays a D, what really sounds is a C. Likewise, in order for the clarinet to play a G, you must write an A. If you wish to use a C instrument part with a clarinet, the part must be transposed up one whole step. The clarinet possesses different characteristics in its different ranges. The bottom range is dark and warm. The mid-range is frequently thin and breathy. The upper range gets increasingly shrill as the notes get higher.

The clarinet is suited to the soprano, alto, or tenor ranges. Distant relatives in the clarinet family include the little E♭ clarinet, which has a thin, piercing sound. The alto clarinet has the ability to play lower notes than the regular B♭ soprano clarinet. Its only use now seems to be in music for clarinet choir. The bass clarinet is the second-most-used clarinet. Its curved neck and bell give it a resemblance to the saxophone. The bass clarinet uses a treble clef. It transposes at the range of a ninth; thus, a written D sounds like a C. In order to sound a D, you must write an E.

The bass clarinet (and contrabass clarinet) have their best use in the clarinet choir. *Clarinet choir* is a name given to anywhere from four to eight or more clarinets, with five and six being the most common groupings. There is an abundance of clarinet choir music for purchase. When writing your parts, or adapting a hymn, the B♭ soprano clarinets should take the soprano and alto lines, a bass clarinet may take the tenor line, and a contrabass clarinet may take the bass line. Note that some contrabass clarinets are in B♭ and some are in E♭. Check in advance with the player. All clarinet parts are written in treble clef.

The saxophone has had an image problem among "serious" musicians because of its association with jazz and its lack of use in the standard orchestral repertoire. The saxophone was a favorite instrument of French composers in the early part of this century, so it is not surprising to learn that there is no shortage of music for saxophone quartet. The unique feature of a saxophone quartet is that it is comprised of four distinct instruments—soprano, alto, tenor, and baritone. Each instrument has its own unique sound. The ranges of all saxophones are the same. The alto and baritone are E♭ instruments; a written F-sharp sounds an A on the alto saxophone and an A an octave lower on the baritone. Note that although it is the bass voice, the part is still written in treble clef. The soprano and tenor saxophone are B♭ instruments; thus, a written D sounds a C on a soprano saxophone and a C an octave lower on a tenor saxophone. Tenor saxophone is likewise written in treble clef.

Although they are not a band or orchestra instrument, the recorders are the predecessors of modern woodwind instruments. Recorders are found in SATB voicings with soprano and tenor being C instruments and the alto and bass recorder being F instruments. Their ranges are two octaves. Note that they sound an octave higher than written. A G on soprano recorder really sounds like a G an octave higher. If a part is marked recorder, flute is an adequate substitute. The lower recorders possess a haunting sound, much like the alto and bass flutes. The recorder is well suited to Renaissance pieces as well as newer folk/contemporary pieces.

Other Ensembles. Another ensemble for which music exists is the woodwind trio in various forms, including two flutes and clarinet, or oboe, clarinet, and bassoon. The woodwind quintet consists of flute, oboe, clarinet, horn, and bassoon. This combination can produce a number of colors and moods. It may be the most common of all woodwind groupings. For hymns and liturgical music, you may want to arrange parts in this manner:

Voice Part	Instrument
Soprano	flute (one octave higher)
	oboe
Alto	clarinet
Tenor	horn
Bass	bassoon

Remember to transpose accordingly!

Too often our creativity is limited to trumpets on Easter and strings on Christmas. The woodwinds provide a wide range of color and expressiveness. Explore the unique sounds of the woodwind family. It just might add a little more excitement to your musical program.

String Instruments

Stringed instruments in this article refer to those found in the orchestra—violin, viola, violincello (cello), and contrabass violin (bass or string bass). They all have four strings and may be played by bowing (drawing the bow across the strings) or by plucking the strings. In our previous two articles, we mentioned that brass instruments provide power and woodwinds provide agility to the choral sound. Strings, of course, provide a lush warm sound—if played well and in tune! We have also previously noted that a good high school player can frequently satisfy your needs for woodwind or brass parts; be careful, however, when recruiting string players from your congregation. Strings tend to be a little more difficult to play in tune than wind instruments. (There's nothing quite like the sound of a violin just slightly out of tune.) Ideally, you should be able to hire competent professional musicians for feast days. My former pastor frequently reminded me that the electric bill alone for our parish complex was $2500 a month; spending several hundred dollars (if not close to a thousand) for musicians on a feast day was certainly within the budget line. After all, what are our priorities?

Having laid that last line on your pastor, you are either looking for a new job or you have a budget with which to work. How many strings should you get? The standard string ensemble is the string quartet. It consists of two violins, a viola, and a cello. The violins play the soprano and alto line, the viola takes the tenor line, and the cello provides the bass part. Publishers have plenty of choral music with string parts. If you are blessed with an abundance of good string players or funds, you may want to increase the size of your string ensemble. There is an unwritten law of strings that states that two players on one part is trouble. It is advisable to have three violins on a part if you are using a larger ensemble. Why? Because two players playing ever so slightly out of tune will produce a spine-tingling sound. However, three or more players tend to "cancel out" out-of-tune notes, and a fuller, richer sound is produced. Once again, avoid having two violins playing the same part. The ideal ensemble to accompany an organ, large congregation, and choir would be three first violins, three second violins, three (maybe two) violas, and a cello with a string bass. True, it is a pretty large and expensive ensemble, but for something as important as midnight Mass or the Easter vigil, it is very justifiable.

Another problem with a large string ensemble is the amount of space it will need. Bows sailing through the air and large instruments like cellos and basses require space. Of further concern is the direction the players are facing. Those squiggly little f-shaped holes on the instruments (called the f holes) are where the sound comes out. Putting the violins on the "wrong side" of the conductor is like having the stereo speakers facing the wall instead of the room. A final concern deals with baton technique when conducting. Yes, baton technique. Orchestral players are accustomed to following a baton. Furthermore, it just may wake up your choir a bit: "What is that thing in the directors hand?" Be aware of a little delay at first when conducting. Orchestral players tend to play a little "behind" the beat; you may give a downbeat and the strings may come in "late." Simply ask them to anticipate the beat and stay with the choir. They will adjust accordingly.

Writing Your Own Parts. There may be instances when you will have to arrange music yourself for the string quartet or ensemble. Here is an overview of the individual instruments.

The violin, as noted earlier, plays the soprano and alto lines in SATB music. The practical range of the violin is three octaves, and it uses the treble clef.

The viola is the tenor of the string quartet/ensemble. The most troubling aspect of part writing for the viola is feeling comfortable writing in the alto clef.

Once again, higher notes are possible but not advisable. What about that funny clef? When using the C clef (alto clef in this instance), remember that the line found at the middle of the lines is C. In this case, the third line is C. This C is middle C on a piano, or the C at the very bottom of a soprano's range. Note that the viola can play one octave below that C and many notes above that C. The cello and the string bass use bass clef and take the bass line.

Let's look at arranging a hymn to reinforce these concepts. Taking the standard SATB setting of "Silent Night," we give the melody to the first violin. If you are using a string quartet, it is advisable to write the soprano line one octave higher so the sound can carry through the organ/choir/congregation texture. It will get "lost" in the octave as written. If you have a string ensemble, perhaps have one violin play the melody up an octave and keep the other first violins down the octave as written.

The second violins will play the alto line. Once again, alter the parts as suggested above. The violin parts project better when used in the upper octave.

The viola plays the tenor line. Ready to use the alto clef? What looks like

in the hymnal should look like

on the violist's page.

Finally, the cello (and bass) play the bass line directly out of the hymnal. Note that the bass sounds an octave lower than written. It is desirable for the bass to provide this lower octave.

When examining published parts, or when writing your own parts, there are two terms that appear occasionally. *Arco* means bow the notes; *pizz.* (short for *pizzicato*) means pluck the notes. Pizzicato, when used sparingly, is a wonderful sound. Before singing "God Rest Ye Merry, Gentlemen," have the strings play it once pizzicato.

This brief article is only a starting point for understanding the band and orchestra instruments. Along with a sacramentary and lectionary, every church musician should have a copy of an orchestration book on their shelves. For a more detailed explanation of ranges, transposition, and characteristics of individual instruments, consult either of the following two books, both of which are recognized as authoritative treatments of orchestration: Kent Kennan, *The Technique of Orchestration* (Englewood Cliffs, N.J.: Prentice Hall, 1952, 1970) and Walter Piston, *Orchestration* (New York: Norton, 1955).

Michael Silhavy[32]

243 ✦ Brass in Worship

Brass has enjoyed a long use in worship, beginning in Old Testament times and continuing into the present. This article describes where and how brass may be used in worship.

Brass Instruments

Brass-like instruments have been used as instruments of sound production for many centuries. Some have been constructed of metal, while others have been constructed of wood, animal horns, or conch shells. Most have been made so as to produce specific musical pitches (i.e., pitch-oriented) while some others have not (i.e., nonpitch-oriented).

A brass instrument may be defined as any instru-

The Trumpet. *The trumpet has always been a symbol of the day of judgment. It also symbolizes the call to worship.*

ment configured as an open tube which produces sound when the player blows air through his compressed lips placed against one end of the tube. As the lips vibrate, the column of air within the tube is vibrated at the same frequency, producing a musical pitch. The tightness of the lips (i.e., the embouchure) and the length of the tubing determine the pitch that is produced. The instruments usually have a cup-shaped mouthpiece that facilitates lip vibration and a flared bell on the opposite end which amplifies the produced pitch and helps to tune that pitch. Modern brass instruments, which are primarily made of brass or other metal, also have valves or slides for chromatic pitch production. Chromatic tone production was achieved on older instruments either by using tone holes, crooks (added lengths of tubing), or just by manipulating the lips.

Trumpets in Scripture

In biblical usage there were two kinds of trumpets. The most common, mentioned over seventy times, is the *shofar*. The shofar, also called the *jobel* (*yovel*) or *keren* (*qeren*), was made from the hollowed-out horn of a bullock or ram. It is translated as "trumpet," "ram's horn," or "cornet." The shofar was a nonpitch-oriented instrument used for signaling or announcing. It was played in the Year of Jubilee on the Day of Atonement (Lev. 25:9). It also was used for leading in warfare, particularly at the Battle of Jericho (Josh. 6:5-20, Num. 31:6, Judg. 3:27; 6:34), for sounding an alarm (Joel 2:1, 15), and in the procession of the ark of the covenant to Zion (2 Sam. 6:15). The shofar is used to describe the sound of God's voice in Exodus 19:16, 19 and 20:18 (sounding from Sinai) and in Zechariah 9:14.

The *chatsotserah* (or *chatsotser* or *chatsorer*) were the silver trumpets which the Lord commanded Moses to make in Numbers 10:2. These instruments, mentioned more than thirty times in Scripture, were pitch-oriented and shaped like a long straight slender tube with a flared end (the bell). They were constructed of one piece of beaten or hammered silver. According to the historian Josephus, Solomon is said to have had as many as 20,000 of these trumpets. The term *chatsotserah* is usually translated "trumpet" in English translations of Scripture. These instruments were used in numerous ways: to call an assembly or congregation; to break camp; to call to war; in rejoicing; at various feasts; especially the Feast of Trumpets (New Year's Day—now *Rosh Hashannah*); at the beginning of months; when offering burnt offerings or peace offerings; at the dedication of Solomon's temple; and to minister regularly before the ark of the covenant (see Num. 10; 29:1; 1 Chron. 15:28; 2 Chron. 5:12-13; 7:6; 13:12, 14; 15:14, 28).

Modern Brass Sections

Today's brass section consists of one or more of the following: trumpet, cornet, flugelhorn, French horn, alto horn, trombone, baritone horn, euphonium, and tuba. All the instruments have a cup or funnel-shaped mouthpiece with a flared bell at the opposite end. Almost all have some means of altering pitch to achieve chromatics—either a group of valves or a slide (or a combination of both). Many of the brass instruments are keyed differently from the written pitch, making them transposing instruments (i.e., the parts they play are written in a different key from what is actually sounding when played).

Many of the instruments are keyed to B-flat (their fundamental pitch). The most common exceptions are the French horn and alto horn. Of the B-flat instruments, the trumpet, cornet, flugelhorn, and treble-clef baritone horn are transposing (e.g., a C is played but a B-flat is sounded), and the trombone, bass-clef baritone horn, euphonium, and tuba are not transposing (e.g., a C is played and a C is sounded). The French horn and alto horn sound down a perfect fifth from where they are written (e.g., a C is played but an F is sounded). Some of the instruments, particularly trumpet and tuba, are commonly constructed in other keys (e.g., C trumpet and double-C tuba).

The instruments with more cylindrically shaped tubing (e.g., the trumpet and trombone) sound brighter and edgier than the instruments with more conical tubing (e.g., the French horn and flugelhorn), which sound more mellow. The tone of all brass instruments can be altered by using any one of a variety of mutes. A mute will alter the instrument's timbre and often decrease its volume.

Brass Instruments in Worship

Brass instruments have been used in Christian worship most prominently since the sixteenth century. In the early church, brass instruments were not utilized in worship since the volume of the instruments was inappropriate for small and sometimes clandestine meetings. Also, the use of brass in Roman festivals, some of which incorporated Christian torture or martyrdom, created an associational stigma that was undesirable for those believers. The Council of Laodicea in the fourth century disallowed instrumental music altogether in worship.

It was not until the sixteenth century that brass was prominently restored to the church as a legitimate means of worship. The writing of tower music (brass music performed from a church tower) and brass accompaniment for choirs (usually doubling choir parts) gave impetus for the church to receive brass instruments back into an important worship role.

Today, brass can significantly enhance the worship of any congregation. They can be used as they were in biblical times, to signal or announce an event (like a call to worship or an opening hymn). They can accompany and help lead the congregational worship or add an element of pageantry to a processional. They can spice up a rhythm section when used in a contemporary "horn section" style employing idiomatic stylized contemporary or jazz writing.

Since brass instruments blend very well with organs, they can be used in worship to help a congregation accept the idea of adding instruments to the traditional organ worship leadership. They can be used in outreach to the community, particularly in the genre of the brass quintet or the brass quartet.

Setting Up a Brass Section

When starting a brass section in a church, several items should be kept in mind: the composition of the brass section; how to write for brass players; and how to encourage players' improvement through practice.

Listed below are several example brass section setups. A music minister should have a goal in mind for his section composition.

A. Symphonic
   1. 4 horns
   2. 3 or 4 trumpets
   3. 3 trombones (1 bass)
   4. 1 tuba
B. Studio
   1. 2 or 3 horns
   2. 3 or 4 trumpets
   3. 3 or 4 trombones (1 bass)
   4. Optional tuba
C. Jazz
   1. 4 or 5 trumpets
   2. 4 or 5 trombones (1 bass)
D. Quintet—2 trumpets, 1 horn, 1 trombone (or 2 trombones), 1 tuba (or bass trombone)
E. Quartet—2 trumpets, 1 horn, 1 trombone (or 2 trombones, or 1 trombone and 1 tuba)

When writing for brass, one must avoid being overly idiomatic, particularly with fanfarish brass licks. The writing should display a wide range of styles stretching the capabilities of the church's players. Utilizing a wide range of stylistic elements in different pieces keeps the music sounding fresh.

Players should be encouraged to practice and improve. Some books which can be suggested as resources are

A. For beginners—the Rubank Series
B. For more advanced players—Arban's *Complete Conservatory Method*
C. Other etude and technique books as time permits

One final word of warning: due to the volume of sound brass instruments are capable of producing, "bleeding" from the horns into other sections' microphones is an ongoing and challenging problem. Brass should be kept somewhat isolated from other instrumental sections.

James R. Hart

244 ◆ THE ORCHESTRA IN THE PRAISE-AND-WORSHIP TRADITION

The orchestra has found a significant place in the worship of Pentecostal, charismatic, and praise-and-worship churches. This article describes the use of the orchestra in this worship tradition.

The special kind of orchestra known as a worship orchestra is very different from any other kind of musical group used in churches. Consequently, there are many different concepts of what it is and of its role in the church.

The Orchestra as Accompaniment

At the outset, it will help if the role of the worship orchestra is identified as an accompanying role. "Then David spoke to the leaders of the Levites to appoint their brethren to be the singers accompanied by instruments of music, stringed instruments, harps, and cymbals" (1 Chron. 15:16).

Although there are times when the worship orchestra may have a SEL + AH (a musical interlude when the orchestra worships or performs unto the Lord), it is basically an accompanying group as distinguished from a performing group. In any case, the orchestra's audience is the Lord himself. Figuratively, I see the orchestra and singers standing side by side, both groups facing the Lord, and helping one another to worship him.

It is also very important for worship leaders to see the orchestra, not just as a random collection of instruments, but as _an_ instrument—one instrument in the hands of a director or conductor. It may be even more important for the orchestra members to see themselves in this light.

Spontaneity and Flexibility

With the new emphasis on worship instead of the standard song service has come a new emphasis on instrumental worship. But new challenges for instrumentalists have come out of this development. These challenges center around two basic features of the worship movement—spontaneity and flexibility. Spontaneity is a feature of the style of worship

leading itself; flexibility expresses the necessary response of the musicians to this style.

A spontaneous worship service may appear to be free-flowing and unplanned; songs of praise and worship flowing from one to another without interruption. I say "appear" because there is usually prior planning and a listing of songs to be sung in a certain order. Rarely, however, is this order followed exactly, and it may be dispensed with entirely after the first song. Then everybody is on his or her own. This is in contrast to the denominational church's "song service," where all songs used are decided well in advance. There are few surprises in this kind of service.

The Flexible Accompanist. As a pianist who has accompanied spontaneous worship for over twenty years, I have had to work out a lot of solutions to problems raised by this apparent spontaneity and lack of planning. A worship pianist should be ready to play any song he or she knows (and some he doesn't) in any key on the piano and be able to modulate back and forth at a moment's notice. He should be ready to repeat back to any spot to which the worship leader feels led.

Over the years, I have tried to coordinate such things with a number of organists. We have had to develop a number of signals with each other and the worship leaders in order to work together effectively in this kind of highly unstructured setting— that is, unstructured by us prior to the event. We always hope that the end result of what we are doing represents the structuring of the Holy Spirit. Let me emphasize that I believe the Holy Spirit can and does reveal His intention to leaders of worship services ahead of time as well as "on the spot." We should seek the guidance of the Holy Spirit and plan accordingly, but we must be flexible enough to be able to make a change right in the middle of our well-laid plans, if the Spirit so directs.

The Orchestra and Flexibility. Accompanying this kind of worship with a piano, an organ, and perhaps a rhythm section is one thing. When other instruments are added, often problems can arise. This is especially so if the other instrumentalists are unable to play by ear or improvise and must depend upon written parts. The piano, because of its clarity of attack and pitch, can be important here as a center around which the other instruments rally.

Ten years ago, I was the pianist at a national convention on the Holy Spirit held in Kansas City. The night sessions were held at Arrowhead Stadium. I was on the stage in the center of the field with my organist and a thirty-five piece orchestra directed by someone else. The orchestra was using written arrangements for the worship songs we had planned to sing. An immense amount of preparation had gone into these "spontaneous" worship services. The orchestra leader, my organist, and I were connected to the worship leader by means of an intercom system. One night, as the spirit of the worship service was at an extremely high peak, I heard the worship leader inform the orchestra leader about a song he wanted to sing just then that was uniquely appropriate. The orchestra leader either didn't have the music for that particular piece or it was going to take a while to get the all the players involved in it. Suddenly, the worship leader's voice crackled in my headset, "Frank, can you get us started on this one now?" Bang! I struck the opening chord on the big grand instantaneously. The attack and the pitch of the notes ricocheted off the walls and seats of the stadium, and off we went.

The orchestra found the music after a while, came in, and no one was the wiser. After the service, the worship leader came back and told us how reassuring it was to know that in a tight spot like that, someone would come through.

This story illustrates the problem of orchestral inflexibility in this kind of setting. It also shows how various accompanying instruments can work together in such a setting so that the flow of the Spirit may be unhindered.

Playing by Ear and Improvisation

Some groups deal with the problem of inflexibility by having only musicians who can improvise or play by ear. But this approach has its own drawbacks. First, it rules out many fine musicians who simply cannot play without written music. Second, many groups using this approach wind up sounding like a giant Dixieland band.

I have tried to play in groups like this in which everyone not only had his own notion of a supporting part, but also had his own notion of the correct chord pattern. I don't mind dissonance occasionally, but chaos is another matter. Third, most orchestras that improvise cannot play with sectional unity or with many of the other features of true orchestral sound. There are no solid chordal backgrounds from the horn section or the trombone section. There are no unison and octave contrapuntal lines

from the strings, nor are there any nice rhythmic accents from the trumpet section as a unified whole.

The chief objection to playing by ear or improvising (which is different) in this kind of setting is that they both are essentially techniques used by soloists. This works against the principle stated earlier that the worship orchestra is basically an accompaniment orchestra. This means that a different approach must be taken to the whole matter of improvisation. I call it *responsible improvisation.* That means that the individual instrumentalist must learn to improvise in some sort of coordination with other players in the orchestra, especially with those in his own section. It is not something that can be learned overnight, but it can be learned.

I also use responsible improvisation to describe the ability to play based on knowledge of music theory and harmony. Such playing is never irresponsible (that is, having no regard to what others are doing around you). It is not some sort of stream-of-consciousness playing either. Let me hasten to add, however, that there are times when the whole musical group (singers, instrumentalists, etc.) will be caught up and directed by the Spirit. I have been a participant in such events. Unfortunately, this doesn't occur as often as we would like. Aside from that, the most responsible and spiritual approach is to prepare oneself technically as well as one can, then to be sensitive to the leading of the Spirit. This allows the Spirit more to work with when he does come with power and anointing.

There is an alternative to orchestral improvisation that may be a more viable option for most church orchestras. It is the use of a special kind of written arrangement.

Written Arrangements

The most common objection to the use of written arrangements by the kind of orchestra we have been describing is that it does not allow the orchestra to be very flexible in a spontaneous worship setting. I have been dealing with this challenge in developing church orchestras and have recently developed a type of arrangement for worship orchestras which I call a *resource arrangement,* as opposed to a set arrangement. A set arrangement is the ordinary arrangement in which one must pretty well use the instrumentation called for and must play the arrangement as written. By contrast, a resource arrangement is extremely flexible. If you have three instruments besides the rhythm section, it sounds well. If you have fifteen, it sounds better. If you have fifty, it sounds even better (i.e., more combinations of sound colorations, contrasts, breadths of tone, etc.). In this arrangement, each instrument has two or three versions of the song written on his part. For most instruments, this will consist of a melody version and a chordal version; trumpets may have an accented rhythmic pattern of trumpeting or "shots." Thus, the director of the orchestra has at his command an almost infinite number of combinations from which to select an orchestration during worship.

Another feature of these arrangements is that they feature words on every part, even those that are playing a sustained background pattern. This does two things:

1. It allows the player to find his or her place in the music instantly when the worship director decides to sing something not on the "list," requiring the player to find the song in his alphabetically arranged loose-leaf folder;
2. It keeps the instrumentalist constantly aware of the spiritual message being expressed by the notes he is playing. This makes the instrumentalists more a part of the worship team, since orchestral members tend to get wrapped up in the notes and musical phrases.

Other features of these arrangements include:

1. more emphasis on the horizontal movement (counterpoint or melodic interest in the inner parts) than on the vertical (chordal backgrounds, etc.);
2. melodic modulation rather than just harmonic (congregations can hear and act upon the former more easily, which is important since they need to participate and not just listen);
3. and the usage of "strong lines" and "broad strokes."

This last feature uses a lot of doubling of the parts and does not concern itself with delicate little phrases and intricate technical passages that characterize performance arrangements for an audience that is just listening to the orchestra. Similarly, a pianist playing for worship with an orchestra should not spend a lot of time with intricate finger patterns. In the first place, they won't be heard, and in the

second place, they won't add anything particularly helpful to the accompanying role in worship.

Space does not allow us to deal with the many other features of this kind of arrangement, but it should be emphasized that such arranging requires a different emphasis and approach.

The Worship Orchestra Director

I use the term _director_ because _conductor_ is more of a description of the leader of a performance group. Who is the director? He may be the worship director, if he knows something about instrumental music and the group is fairly small. He may be the worship pianist if he has the same qualifications. Ideally, the orchestral director should be someone other than the worship leader or pianist, mainly because these people have all they can handle in the carrying out of their basic responsibilities. The director should be someone who understands the technical requirements of the various instruments of an orchestra, but more important, he should be a person who is a worshiper himself. The technical aspects of music should never have to conflict with the spiritual considerations, but if they do, the director should come in on the side of the spiritual.

There are other differences between the director of a worship orchestra and a conductor of a performance orchestra. For one thing, the worship orchestra director may not even beat time on a continuous basis except to start off a song in proper tempo or to change or correct tempos after starting. Some of his more important tasks are

1. to indicate the desired sound levels to the various instrumentalists and sections (many groups I hear are completely overwhelmed by the electric bass and percussion);
2. to indicate by certain signals the part each section is to play at any given time from the special worship arrangement (for instance, he might signal: "Reeds, you play the first time through; strings, you come in the second time; and brass, you come in the third time with trumpets playing the lead");
3. to indicate the various repeats desired by the leader;
4. and to give advance notice of modulations and specific keys during improvisation.

These are just a few of the specialized tasks of the director of a worship orchestra. As a suggestion, I believe the director, if he is capable, is the best person to be on the synthesizer. This places him in the position to add whatever parts are missing, to strengthen certain sections, and to use that versatile instrument in many other applications. In any case, the best people to use synthesizers in this setting should be arrangers at heart. They should have an understanding of orchestral sound and the various instruments in the orchestra.

Although the pianist works very closely with the worship leader and usually takes the lead in beginning a new song (especially if a modulation is involved or the orchestra is going to have to look up the written part), he or she should be under the general supervision of the orchestral director. The pianist's style of playing should complement that of the orchestra, not compete with it. In fact, every instrument should be in this position, including the electric bass player and the drummer! Unless the director has some control over every instrument that contributes to the volume and the style and feel of the arrangement, sonic chaos will eventually result.

The Anointing

Finally, I want to make it clear that none of the material in this article is of much use without the anointing of the Holy Spirit. In dealing with the practical aspects of making music, it is easy to give the impression that "getting the sound right" is all that is required to be successful in worship. Nothing could be further from the truth. While technical excellence of itself will not bring us into the presence of God, the results of neglecting the pursuit of excellence can be a distraction and an outright hindrance. The musicians who ministered in the Tabernacle of David were said to be "skilled" or "practiced." Likewise, we need to offer our very best to the Lord by striving to perfect the gifts He has placed in us. Then we should look for the anointing of the Spirit to activate it all. God was pleased with this approach in that day; I believe He will be pleased with it in our day.

Frank Longino

245 • The Band in the Praise-and-Worship Tradition

Music in the praise-and-worship tradition is often accompanied by a small consort or band of instruments. Precedent for the band in worship goes back to the foundation of the

Salvation Army in the nineteenth century. This article describes this history and suggests how the contemporary worship band can be used as a means of musical leadership.

Using Contemporary Instruments and Music

The worship band may be defined as any ensemble of musical instruments with a rhythm section foundation. The rhythm section is comprised of drums, bass, and one or more of the following: piano, guitar, organ and/or synthesizer, and percussion. Other instruments in the worship band may include woodwinds, brass, or strings. (Sample instrumentations will follow.) The repertoire of the band generally consists of contemporary music in the pop, jazz, rock, or Latin idioms. (These are general categories. Other ethnic styles may be prevalent in some churches, particularly in areas with non-Western ethnomusicological influences.)

Although the worship band is a fairly new development in Christian worship, the concept is not a new one. Throughout biblical and church history, elements of music which were labeled as secular by some were sanctified by others to sacred uses. Although King David created many of the instruments used in worship during his reign, he also utilized instruments that had been invented by other cultures. All these instruments were sanctified for the worship of Yahweh.

Likewise, the pipe organ, which was developed by the Egyptians and Greeks, has been used by Christian churches for centuries to aid in leading congregational worship. Martin Luther often used secular melodies when he reestablished congregational singing because lay people were not musically capable of reproducing the intricate chanting which had dominated church music for centuries, sung only by clergy. Luther assigned or wrote godly texts to well-known secular melodies. Thus, the congregation didn't need to know how to interpret musical notation in order to enter into corporate worship. One of the prominent Mass-writing styles of the Renaissance period, the *cantus firmus* Mass, combined what was often a secular melody (the *cantus firmus*) with the sacred text of the Mass. One great example of this is the *Missa l'Homme armé,* based on the secular tune "*l'Homme armé.*" There are over thirty known Mass settings of this tune by such composers as Josquin, Dufay, Obrecht, and Palestrina.

Establishing Cultural Relevance

With almost every great reform or revival movement in church history there has been an associated musical movement toward cultural relevance. In other words, the music of the common people becomes the worship music of the church. For musicians and theologians as well as lay people, the struggle with this trend has been, and continues to be, balancing cultural relevancy of musical style, instrumentation, and so on, with the attempt to reveal God's transcendence in the worship of the faithful. Both elements of relevancy and transcendence are vital to the Christian worship experience. There must be an openness to culturally relevant musical styles and instrumentations and so on, while making certain those relevant musical elements are sanctified by prayer, sacrament, and the Word of God to God's transcendent nature.

The worship band began to be utilized in the late 1960s as an attempt to make Christian worship relevant to the young and unchurched of that generation. It continues to help fulfill that need cross-denominationally and cross-culturally. When sanctified to the Lord's purposes, the worship band significantly aids a congregation to relate to the more contemporary elements of both the congregation and the societal environment. It can provide some familiarity for those who are unfamiliar or uncomfortable with formalities of traditional or liturgical music, while simultaneously providing those same people the opportunity to enter into the relationship of worshiping God. Or for those who just prefer that musical style, it can provide for them a relevant worship experience. There are a number of musicians who desire to use their talents to lead others in worship but do not fit in instrumentally with more traditional musical offerings. The worship band can provide opportunity for these musicians to offer their talents to the Lord in corporate worship leading.

Instrumental Music in Scripture

Instrumental music is well founded in Scripture as a means for worship expression. One of the seven Hebrew words for praise is *zamar,* which means to praise the Lord upon musical instruments (Ps. 33:2, 3; 98:4-6; Isa. 38:20). Scriptures contain many promptings and much precedence for believers to praise God on musical instruments (1 Chron. 16:5-6; Ps. 150). In a number of Old Testament references, instruments are mentioned as being used to inspire and accompany prophecy (1 Sam. 10:5; 2 Kings 3:15; 1 Chron. 25:1). David played his harp so that Saul would be relieved of the evil spirit which had beset him (1 Sam. 16). Instruments, particularly trumpets, were used in warfare (Josh. 6:1-20; Joel 2:1; Num. 10:9; 31:6; Judg. 7:16-22). They were played in times of great celebration (2 Sam. 6:5, 15, 1 Chron. 13:8; 15:16, 19-22; 2 Chron. 5:11-14; 20:28).

In David's tabernacle, the most comprehensive scriptural paradigm of spiritual worship, priests were assigned to play instruments in worship to the Lord regularly and continually in the house of God. While sin offerings, burnt offerings, and peace offerings were made in the temple, instrumental music played (Num. 29:1, 2 Chron. 29). The Psalms were written to be accompanied by instruments, often specific instruments. *Selahs,* which occur throughout the Psalms, are instrumental interludes during which the reader, listener, and/or writer reflects on what has just been stated in the previous passage. Trumpets were used to assemble the congregation of Israel, break camp, signal a specific message, and announce feasts, particularly the Feast of Trumpets. There are approximately 195 instances in Scripture that pertain to using instruments in the worship of God.

Although instrumental music is not specifically mentioned in English translations of the Bible, the Greek words *psalmos* (found in 1 Corinthians 14:26, Ephesians 5:19, and Colossians 3:16) and *psallo* (found in Romans 15:9, Ephesians 5:19, and James 5:13) both denoted singing a sacred song with stringed instrument accompaniment. Several passages in Revelation indicate the existence of instruments accompanying the worship of heaven (5:8-10; 14:1-5; 15:2-3).

The scriptural precedent for worship with instrumental music is clear as well as prevalent. The role of the band in worship should be based on that precedent. The band should accompany and help to lead the musical worship of the church. It should inspire and, at times, accompany the God-breathed prophetic Word as it is presented in the congregation. Instrumentalists should assist in the relief of oppression and lead in times of worshipful celebration. They should help believers to enter fully into God's manifested presence and lead them to reflect on the great attributes of God.

─── Biases Against Musical Styles ───

In many churches there exist some biases against certain styles of music due to the aesthetic nature of the music or its association with forms of immorality. Those biases are often aimed particularly at contemporary styles of music most prevalently played by worship bands. While we must be diligent in sanctifying styles of music for the Lord's purposes, we must also deal with the biases that exist in the church against those styles. Instrumental music often has a definite aesthetic value, and, sometimes, detrimental associations. It is the job of the church musician or minister of music to exploit musical aesthetics for the kingdom of God; i.e., use the aesthetic value of music to draw people to a place of encounter with the Lord. He or she must also either avoid music with detrimental associational value or gradually re-educate the congregation to receive it. The ministerial effectiveness of music is dependent upon the pure heart of the ministering musician and the receptivity of the listener.

─── Instrumentation ───

The instrumentation of a worship band can vary from a small rhythm section up to a full orchestra with rhythm. (Many principles covered in the article on "The Orchestra in Worship" apply here and vice versa.) Below are listed some sample instrumentations:

A. Rhythm section only:
  1. Piano/Keyboard
  2. Guitar
  3. Bass
  4. Drums
  5. Additional keyboard—e.g., organ or synthesizer
  6. Percussion
B. Rhythm section with horns:
  1. Rhythm
  2. Trumpets—1 or 2
  3. Saxes—1 or 2
  4. Trombones—1
  5. Flute
C. Studio Orchestra
  1. Rhythm
  2. Woodwinds
    a. 4 or 5 players doubling on sax, clarinet, flute, and double reeds
    b. Flute

  3. Brass
    a. 3-4 trumpets
    b. 3-4 trombones (bass trombone doubles on tuba)
    c. 2-3 horns
  4. Strings
    a. 3 (at least) Violin I
    b. 2 (at least) Violin II
    c. 1 (at least) Viola
    d. 1 (at least) Cello
    e. Double bass optional
  5. Harp

The attempt should be made to accommodate as many players as possible while taking into account musical and spiritual standards for personnel and available space and instrumentation. It is possible and quite probable that the band could have more players than needed for a certain instrument. For example, there are often too many guitarists. So the players should be rotated, so long as consistency and quality are not sacrificed. Keeping as many players involved as possible helps to keep interest and excitement up when working with volunteers. It also creates resources for additional groups or backup players when needed.

─── Musical and Spiritual Unity ───

It is recommended that the band learn to read *charts,* or musical arrangements. Using written arrangements can significantly improve the musical quality of the group and make them more effective in leading worship.

Live sound mixing should be utilized in rehearsal so the band can work with the audio crew to achieve a quality house and monitor mix. This would be facilitated by allowing the band to rehearse where they play during services, if possible. The sections of the band should be congregated to avoid "bleeding" between sections; i.e., try to keep instruments of one kind together and somewhat separated from other sections to avoid microphones picking up too much sound from those other sections. However, segmenting the orchestra too much should be avoided as well. Maintaining eye contact for signals is crucial. One person should be designated to give signals.

Because the rhythm section is improvisatory by nature, musical responsibilities must be delineated and accompaniment patterns simplified so as to avoid musical confusion and cacophony (noise).

The goal of every worship band or orchestra is to achieve a concerted symphonic (sounding-together) sound musically as well as spiritually. That is, to be in such musical and spiritual unity that the congregation is led into worship rather than distracted from it.

James R. Hart

246 • THE GUITAR IN WORSHIP

The use of stringed instruments in worship goes back into the Old Testament and has a history of its own in the Christian church. In recent years, the guitar has been frequently used to lead music for worship. This article explains where and how to use the guitar.

The use of the guitar in praise of God is founded solidly on biblical precedent. The Psalms come immediately to mind with their frequent mention of instrumental praise (e.g., Ps. 33:2; 71:22-23; 92:3; 144:9), and even a cursory reading of the history of Israel reveals the regular use of stringed instruments in worship.

Today, the re-emergence of stringed instruments (specifically the acoustic guitar) can be traced back to the 1960s, an era now famous for its proliferation of folk music, the *vox populi.* Popular singers like Peter, Paul, and Mary, and Joan Baez (to name a few) captured the public imagination with their simple, immediate, troubadour style, reflecting the concerns of the day in song. The drug culture, the sexual revolution, and protest against the war in Vietnam were all critical elements in the formation of a new counterculture.

The nearly simultaneous appearance of the Jesus Movement, so prevalent among youth of the day (a *counter*-counterculture) and the beginning of the charismatic renewal converted much of this dynamic energy and brought it, often through the popular Christian coffeehouse venue, into the more formal church environment.

——— The Guitar in Corporate Worship ———

The reintroduction of the guitar into corporate worship has not been without difficulty, but this has not negated its usefulness to the people of God in the offering of praise. As the church finds its life expressed in settings other than the traditional church building (e.g., house churches, prayer groups, cell groups), many will find the guitar, portable in a way that the organ and piano are not, to be the instrument of choice.

Two different approaches are possible when using the guitar in worship: as an accompanying instrument in an ensemble to support corporate song, or as a principle leading instrument in the hands of a worship leader. As an accompanying instrument, rhythm and harmony are the primary contributions the strummed (or folk) guitar gives to instrumental texture.

Classical Style. The classical style of guitar playing is suitable for a wide range of music; repertoire is limited only by the player's ability. Its inclusion in an ensemble can provide a pleasing textural element. As a lead instrument, the classical guitar is less effective, except in the most intimate settings, because of its lack of natural aural presence.

Leading Corporate Song. Using the guitar to lead corporate song requires an understanding of the ethos of folk-worship leadership. The roots of this type of leadership are found in the tradition of the troubadour (the storyteller) and the accompanying characteristics of interaction and spontaneity. The guitar is eminently well-suited to be a vehicle for allowing the worship leader to relate back and forth with the people who are gathered, to manifest that ingredient unique to folk-worship leadership: interaction. In Judeo-Christian worship, the use of responsorial psalmody reflects this tradition: a cantor/soloist/storyteller sings the verses of a psalm, and the people respond with a simple memorable refrain or antiphon. This verse/refrain structure remains an effective song form in sacred and popular music alike.

Visible presence makes interaction easier. However, in circumstances where this is not possible, folk leadership can be effected through audibility alone. This technique, common in African music and discernible in American spirituals, employs the call-and-response form, a variation of verse/refrain. Either visible or audible presence alone can be effective, but clearly both are desirable.

The guitar's usefulness can be increased by the development of a variety of strums to interpret different musical moods. The use of a pick (or plectrum) will not only make playing more audible but will add rhythmic clarity as well. (See *Leading Worship with the Guitar,* a teaching video produced by Celebration, P.O. Box 309, Aliquippa, PA 15001.)

It should be noted that the folk guitar is not suited to all idioms found in today's corporate worship. This is especially true with traditional four-part hymnody. However, since many enduring and endearing hymn tunes find their origins in folk melody, a unison rendition of the tune, accompanied by harmonies idiomatic to the guitar, can add a new dimension to one's experience of familiar hymns.

Choosing a Guitar for Worship. The choice of an instrument will depend on the player, the circumstance in which it will be used, and the musical material to be played. The most commonly used steel string guitars are the six-string and twelve-string. Either is suitable for leading corporate song.

The six-string guitar provides a well-defined sound for crisp, articulate playing. The twelve-string guitar provides a cushion of sound, rich in harmonic texture, with octave strings creating its characteristic "ring." Those same octave strings, however, increase the challenge of maintaining a well-tuned instrument.

A nylon string guitar is meant to be plucked or strummed with the fingertips. The use of a pick produces a muffled tone, and as was noted above in the discussion of the classical style, its usefulness is limited to very intimate settings of worship.

The electric bass guitar, while itself not an acoustic instrument, can be extremely useful in an acoustic ensemble, providing both rhythmic stability and harmonic foundation.

Amplification. Finally, mention should be made of sound reinforcement, an ingredient that is often critical to the success of the acoustic guitar in corporate worship. There are various ways to amplify the guitar other than a factory-installed design. The most successful method is with either a flexible strip microphone, which is attached directly to the body of the instrument, or with an internal pick-up placed in the sound hole. The player thus has freedom of movement which is not possible when playing before a stationary microphone, and the actual resonance of the wood body is transmitted with less "air noise."

The acoustic guitar can be quite versatile in the hands of a sensitive worship leader and continues, as it has for centuries, to be a fitting instrument to make music in praise of the Most High God.

Bill and Mimi Farra

247 ◆ HAND-HELD PERCUSSION IN WORSHIP

The history of percussion instruments is traceable to the Old Testament. These instruments, used on only a limited basis throughout the history of the church, have re-emerged in contemporary worship. This article describes various hand-held percussion instruments and their usage in Christian worship.

Rhythm is an essential element in all music. Be it plainsong or jazz, pulse is present. Percussion instruments, identified by the way in which they are struck when played, can enhance the inherent rhythms found in music. From the subtle strike of a triangle or clicking of claves to the flashing roll of a tambourine, percussion instruments have added flavor and excitement to worship since biblical times.

— Hand-Held Percussion Instruments —

Hand-held percussion instruments are those that are small enough to be held in the hand when played. Some common instruments include tambourine, claves (wood sticks), triangle, finger cymbals, maracas, castanets, cabasa shaker, guido, and all manner of small drums. It is also important not to overlook the instruments we all carry with us— our hands that can clap, and our fingers that can snap. For purposes here, we will discuss three of the most common instruments: tambourine, claves, and triangle.

Tambourine. The tambourine, most often referred to as the *timbrel* in Scripture, is an ancient instrument, popular in many cultures throughout the world. It is a round, shallow drum with jingling metal disks fitted into the rim that is shaken with one hand and struck with the other, producing a shimmering ring. It may or may not have a drum head. In more recent years a "half-moon" shape variation has evolved offering a bolder, more aggressive sound. The tambourine's primary use is for colorful rhythmic accentuation. There are various ways to play the tambourine: by tapping the rim; by swinging back and forth with a measured pulse: or by shaking continuously with strikes on accented beats.

Claves. Claves consist of two round hardwood sticks that are struck together. One is cradled in the hand, forming a resonating chamber, while the other is used to strike against it. Hardwood (rosewood, ebony, walnut) is the material of choice. It produces the characteristic chirp, sounding very similar to a cricket. Claves should be played lightly, not banged together, as the sound of good quality wood carries easily. They are usually played on the off-beat.

Triangle. The triangle is a length of steel tubing bent to form a triangular shape open at one corner. It is usually suspended from a cord of leather or string, and played with a metal striker. Triangles are of indeterminate pitch, and the size and gauge of tubing affect the tone. Too large a gauge will give a "dinner bell" sound, while too small a gauge will give a thin, weak sound. The triangle can be played effectively with a single strike as musical punctuation; it can be played by rapidly striking two adjacent sides, creating a "roll"; or it can be played with a specific rhythmic pattern.

Reinforcing the Rhythm of an Ensemble

Physical proximity to the primary music ensemble is crucial when using these percussion instruments. This is particularly true with respect to the tambourine, which has a critical effect on rhythmic stability. It is important with any of these instruments to play a pattern that is sympathetic to the music and that reinforces the rhythmic thrust of the rest of the ensemble.

Consistency with the pattern is desirable. A rhythmic motif should not change every other measure, but should repeat a pattern that will increase rhythmic stability. It is good to begin with a simple rhythmic motif and develop the pattern further as the song continues. In a song or hymn with a verse-refrain form, it is sometimes effective to play only on the refrain. In a strophic song or hymn, it is best to wait until the piece is firmly established before adding the ornamentation of percussion. Care must be taken to remain faithful to the idiom, to the rhythm inherent in the music, and to the rhythmic patterns played by the whole ensemble.

Enhancing the Worship Experience

In psalms, hymns, and spiritual songs, hand-held percussion can add a joyful presence, a spark of new interest and excitement. One recalls Miriam playing her timbrel in jubilation after the Hebrews' safe crossing of the Red Sea, or the priests of Levi sounding cymbals in temple worship at the time of King David. Tambourine and drum can give the feel of a Renaissance dance to an old familiar hymn that has its origins in folk song. The influence of percussion in popular music can be utilized in contemporary sacred song, as well as the snapping of fingers to a swinging "blues" tune or the clapping of hands to a rhythmically compelling song.

The Lord gives many instruments to praise his name, all of which can add to the worship of the people of God. As the psalmist exhorts, "Praise him with tambourine and dancing, . . . praise him with resounding cymbals. Let everything that has breath praise the Lord!" (Ps. 150).

Bill and Mimi Farra

248 ✦ BELLS IN WORSHIP

Bells have long been employed in worship. In contemporary use one can find large bells used for calling to worship, carillons or chimes, small Sanctus bells used during liturgy, and handbells, which are covered in the next article.

Bells appear in the instructions for the furnishing of the priest, Aaron, in the tabernacle:

Make pomegranates of blue, purple and scarlet yarn around the hem of the robe, with gold bells between them. The gold bells and the pomegranates are to alternate around the hem of the robe. Aaron must wear it when he ministers. The sound of the bells will be heard when he enters the Holy Place before the LORD and when he comes out, so that he will not die. (Exod. 28:33-35)

Unauthorized entry into the holiest portions of the tabernacle carried the promise of death to the intruder. The bells, then, were a sign to the Lord that it was the consecrated priest who was entering the Holy Place. In the only other mention of bells in Scripture, Zechariah prophesied that at the day of the Lord, even the bells on the horses would bear the inscription HOLY TO THE LORD. This was the same inscription that God commanded to be put on a gold plate bound to the priest's turban (Exod. 28:36). Thus to the Israelites bells betokened the sacred in formal worship and, in the vision of the perfected Israel communicated by the prophets, the sacredness of ordinary life.

Church Bells

The earliest church bells were hand-held, crafted of brass or bronze sheet metal, and struck with a mallet. St. Patrick's bell, which is of this sort, is enshrined in Dublin. Cast bells mounted in church buildings are first attested by Gregory of Tours around 585, although legend attributes their first use to Paulinus of Nola in Campania around 400. From Campania we get the word *campanile,* which usually refers to a detached bell tower common in Italy from the sixth century on, of which the Leaning Tower of Pisa is one. The first bells in England came from Italy in 680 according to the ecclesiastical historian Bede.

The earliest church bells were rung by striking them manually. The invention of the clapper, however, made it possible to ring bells by ropes suspended to a floor below the bells. The further development of the wheel and slide enabled the bells to be parked upside down between peals. In England this technology led to the development of one of the most characteristic of English arts, change-ringing. Change-ringing is a rigorously mathematical art which has achieved the status of a folk art, now preserved by societies and devoted groups wherever a set of bells is still to be found. Most of us have heard the changes rung on occasions of great festivity, such as the end of war or royal weddings when all the bells of London sound together in a jubilant cacophony.

In Europe, particularly Germany and the Low Countries, development of bells went in the direction of chimes and carillons, which feature stationary bells rung by levers controlled from a keyboard or by hand. These arrangements had the advantage of being able to play tunes. The great clock-builders devised mechanical means to encode and play back these tunes on chimes. The popularity of chimes and carillons has spawned electronic imitations that are found in many small towns and cities in the U.S. Often inferior equipment, especially speakers, renders these chimes more offensive than pleasing, a fact which should be considered by any church planning to install them.

It is traditional to name bells, not only in Catholic, Anglican, and Lutheran churches, but also in Reformed churches. In high liturgical churches bells are "christened" or "baptized" in a rite of consecration that involves sprinkling with holy water and censing, with dedicatory prayers. In Reformed churches they are simply dedicated. It is also the custom to add a name or names when an old bell is acquired by a new church. Some bells are inscribed with a line of verse suggesting their purpose. Church bells range in size from the relatively small treble to the large tenor. The largest bell is reputed to be one in the cathedral at Cologne, made from French cannon and weighing 27 tons.

The primary use of church bells today is as a call to worship. Even where a church has only one bell, rhythmic peals may be used, such as three triplets plus nine as a call to worship, or a double pattern repeated for solemn assemblies such as Good Friday. Other occasions likewise have distinct peals: in earlier days, the "passing bell" was rung as a parishioner was dying, and the death knell when they died. In England the death knell was a single bell tolling or a muffled peal. Baptisms and weddings were also times for celebratory bells. In Roman Catholicism, the *Angelus,* a prayer in memorial of the Incarnation consisting of three Ave Marias with a versicle and a collect, was rung three times a day, with three rings for each Ave and nine for the collect. In a more civic function, bells have often been used as alarms, usually with special patterns such as the backward peal. Church bells are sometimes used in place of sacring or Sanctus bells during the Eucharist. Some old English and colonial churches have special bells for this purpose housed in Sanctus bell turrets.

Contemporary churches need not have a bell tower to house bells. Even a single bell, such as those found in many early American churches, can add a vigorous public dimension to the call to worship and to great celebrations. In earlier days church bells stirred the whole community, and those still lying in bed when the church bell rang on Sunday morning at least knew that they were choosing not to be a part of the assembly. We no longer live under the power of Christendom as a social force; but if, as Alexander Schmemann insists, the liturgy begins when one rises from bed with the intention of going to church, then the church bell can still be powerful evidence of the act of assembly.

The greatest occasion for the ringing of bells is the moment in the Great Vigil of Easter when the Alleluia, which has not been said throughout Lent, returns to the lips and hearts of the congregation. As the minister proclaims, "Alleluia! Christ is risen!"

and the people shout in response, "The Lord is risen, indeed! Alleluia!" the bells burst forth in jubilation at the great news. In this case the adage "the more the merrier" rings particularly true; many churches encourage the people to bring small bells to the vigil so they can join in the festivities.

Sanctus or Sacring Bells

Sanctus or sacring bells are usually a handheld set of bells mounted on a handle. Their sound is characterized by high clear tones and a long persistence of ring. Some churches use gongs or orchestral chimes as Sanctus bells. Sanctus bells have long been used in Eastern churches, and in Western churches since the Middle Ages, to call attention to certain points in the liturgy. As the name implies, they have been rung traditionally at the Sanctus (Holy, holy, holy) and also at the elevation of the host in celebrant. The ringing at the elevation was an innovation in twelfth-century France, where it signalled the assembly to look to the altar. The presumption, evidently, was that, for the common folk, seeing the sacrament was as good as partaking of it. In any case that is as close as some parishioners got to the bread. Because of this taint of superstition, Sanctus bells have largely fallen out of favor in Catholic parishes since Vatican II. The practice is retained, however, along with the use of incense, in high Catholic and Anglican churches (hence the phrase "smells and bells" to describe such worship). Eastern Orthodox churches also sometimes attach small bells to the chains of the thurible (censer), which jingle every time an object or person is censed.

The use of Sanctus bells is a matter of the individual parish's conscience. There is little danger today that the superstition of the past will live on in the minds of the people. Where that problem persists, it may be best to dispense with them. It is advisable, however, to limit their use to accompanying the Sanctus, signalling the completion of the consecration of the elements (not the _moment_ of consecration), and perhaps at the invitation to Communion.

Larry J. Nyberg

249 • Handbells in Worship

Handbell ringing is an English art that has made a phenomenal appearance in American worship in this century. This article explains the various kinds of handbells, how to organize a handbell group, and how and where to use handbells in worship.

History

Since about the fourteenth century, handbells have provided tower ringers with the opportunity for practice for ringing a peal of bells in changes, or mathematical sequences until all conceivable combinations are exhausted. If you lived near a peal of bells, you would be most grateful that ringers practice with handbells and not the bells in the tower! It was natural that these ringers should experiment with harmony on their practice bells, and thus the handbell became a new musical instrument, playing simple tunes with simple harmonies.

Mrs. Margaret Surcliff, who organized a band of ringers in Boston in 1923, is given credit for introducing the handbell to America. My own introduction to the instrument occurred some thirty years ago, when as dean of our local chapter of the American Guild of Organists, my program committee invited Doris Watson from the Brick Church, New York City, to present a workshop on handbells for our members. I attended with less than enthusiasm, sure that next we would have a workshop on the musical saw. But I was pleasantly surprised, and once I had the opportunity to ring a bell, I was "hooked." I saw the possibilities for a real contribution to our worship and to the music program for our young people. And so the bells were purchased. Until they arrived, I attended several workshops so that I would be prepared to begin rehearsals immediately (our young people practiced by blowing small organ pipes to get a head start).

During those early days, everyone who worked with bells was an expert. With the founding of the American Guild of English Handbell Ringers in 1954, an accepted standard playing technique and notation began to develop. The range of bells increased to five octaves and beyond. Today the number of ringers in our country is estimated at 75,000. With encouragement from the Guild, composers began writing for this new instrument. Workshops and conventions were held, bringing together directors with great experience and those just beginning. Choirs as well as directors began to share their techniques and expertise and repertoire with each other. Now hundreds of ringers join together in massed choir concerts, and the fellowship and fun are grand. It is true, as the Guild phrases it, that bells unite "people through a musical art."

Two Types of Bells: English and Dutch

Today, one has a choice of several companies from which to purchase bells. But still there are basically two distinctive bells, the English and the Dutch. The prominence of the various overtones determines the timbre of the bell, the English with a prominent twelfth and the Dutch with a prominent minor tenth. With the Dutch bells, the presence of a strong minor tenth can cause harmonic problems, particularly in massive chords, since this overtone introduces foreign pitches into the simple chord. Judicious scoring and arranging can do much to alleviate this dissonance.

In the past few years, several American companies have begun casting handbells, so that the long waiting period once common after the placement of the order until the delivery of the bells is no longer necessary. American bells are tuned to the English timbre. And while all bell ringers have their own preference, American bells seem to be well accepted and valued by directors and ringers.

Inappropriate Bell Music

But with the ready availability and proliferation of bells, something else happened. The simple melodies and harmonies that were so effective were replaced by complicated and intricate arrangements and a maze of chromaticism. Choirs ring everything from "The Flight of the Bumblebee" to the *1812 Overture*. Composers anxious to provide arrangements for concert choirs and directors demanding complex, challenging music have forgotten the bell.

A bell is a bell is a bell, and would seem to have at least two distinct characteristics: (1) it sounds only one basic pitch, and (2) once struck, the sound continues indefinitely until it is artificially dampened or diminishes beyond the level of audibility. Today, to counteract the "unbell" arrangements, directors resort to dampening the bell at each harmonic change, a practice which destroys one of the unique characteristics of the instrument, the period of sound decay. Some seem to believe that music, if it has been composed, should be playable on bells—but should it?

It is possible that "Swanee River" could be played by two piccolos, a schalmei, and an electric bass, but should it? To be able to compose or arrange for

mixed voices or organ does not guarantee that same ability to compose or arrange for bells. They are a collection of different instruments and demand a different skill, a different understanding in writing. If you write for bells, please remember the old acronym K.I.S.S.—Keep It Simple, Stupid! That axiom should apply to bell composers and arrangers simply because the bell tones are complex and continue their resonance long after being struck. Do you put catsup on your steak? I hope not. The heavy flavor of the condiment wipes out and destroys the subtle essence of the juicy morsel. Artificial dampening during ringing can make a composition squeaky and antiseptically clean but wipes out and destroys the true flavor of the bell. Skeletal chords and slowly changing harmonies sound best. Bells seem to favor, especially, music of the classical period.

A wealth of material is available for bell choirs from most music publishers, but careful selection is required. Many choir anthems are published that incorporate bells effectively, and a few organ compositions are available with bell arrangements. Some composers publish compositions that require the bell choir to sing as well as ring. I find it impossible, however, to perceive that both voice and bell are presented at their musical best in such compositions.

Is the Ability to Read Music a Necessity?

For me, it seemed a shame that participation in a bell choir was limited to only those who could read music; in other words, those who already played a musical instrument. It just was not fair! So, to open our group of ringers to all who wanted to play, I devised a method of counting and marking the notes on each individual sheet of music. At the top of each copy of music I place a preprinted sticker on which are noted bells later needed and the bells first used. Music is marked for each person. Notes for which the ringer is responsible are circled with red or green pens, depending on which hand is to ring that assigned bell. A ringer is alerted to the change of a bell in a hand by an arrow on the circle following the use of that hand before the change. The preparation of the scores takes much time, but the rewards are great. It has worked beautifully. Some of our young people who could not read a note of music have become excellent ringers and have even learned to read notation. They were able to have a musical experience as well as enjoy the fun and fellowship of the ringing group.

I find that the basic problem in bell ringing is not the inability to read music, but readiness—the readiness of coordination, which seems to develop at different times in each child's life. Coordination is needed between the eye and the arm and the wrist muscles. While some directors have had success with bell choirs in the primary and junior grades, it has been my experience that these younger children are not yet ready. They are not sufficiently developed and coordinated to warrant the time and effort. Rehearsal becomes a chore rather than a fulfilling musical experience. For this reason, while I do allow fourth, fifth, and sixth graders to try the bells, I attempt no serious work with them. I realize this seems to contradict the experience of many instrumental teachers, namely, the Suzuki method of instrumental pedagogy. However, youngsters can practice the violin, flute, or trumpet at home. This is impossible for a ringer. A ringer plays only two or three tones or bells. His or her work is "fitting in," inserting these tones into the fabric of the composition with other members of the choir. This makes ringing a different kind of musical experience. Ringing is a physical act of waiting, and then striking, perhaps only a single tone.

In assigning bells, a frequent mistake is having too many ringers so that one person has only one bell. This leads to boredom, inattention, and the eventual demise of a ringer's interest. To each person, I assign two bells, their accidentals, and "occasional" bells as needed. This provides the necessary challenge. Membership in each choir is limited to eleven ringers, and is adequate for most music. Occasionally, an extra person, usually an "alumnus" or capable junior ringer, is asked to join the group for a special presentation. Beginning in a kind of junior high training choir, these ringers, who on occasion perform or play in public, graduate into the senior high handbell choir. On occasion I have organized an "alumni" choir of graduates who practice and ring for the fun of it and play for a specific occasion. For several years an older adult choir met and practiced, again ringing primarily for fun and fellowship. All this takes my time, and with added responsibilities, something had to give. I believe that a rehearsal of less than 1½ hours is a waste of everyone's time. Little is accomplished since part of the rehearsal time is consumed by getting, arranging, and returning bells.

Corporate Aspects of Bell Ringing

Bell ringing is a team sport. A basketball player may practice dribbling and shooting baskets and may be consummate at each, but until he or she is in and with the others on the team, sensing their moves, positions, and speed, his or her talent is of little value. Every voice is valued (usually!) in a singing choir, but a missing alto can be "covered for" by the rest of the group and the integrity of the performance preserved. That can't happen in a ringing choir. Shall I tell one player to ring a little louder because we have a member of the choir missing today?

Bells command and demand discipline and dedication. Rehearsals are important and attendance is essential if the team is to win. Most of us are not able to have the luxury of a second string and even so, each position is so specialized that a substitute is not usually available. In our own church, we've found that Saturday morning is the best time to schedule rehearsal. Prior to the first rehearsal of each season, parents and ringers meet, and the expectations of each are shared. I have been very fortunate that both the young people and their parents take the opportunity to ring bells seriously. It had become a badge of merit to attend rehearsal following a Friday night (all night) prom without even going home first. I once learned that a ringer had stayed home rather than miss a rehearsal and concert when the rest of her family went to Disneyland. This is devotion beyond the call of duty!

Why will people make such commitment? Because ringing is an opportunity to make a significant contribution to worship. Bells enrich our worship just as voices do. Our bell choirs ring to God's glory as an offering of their time and talent in praise and thanksgiving with the worshiping community. Their possibilities in worship are vast and are limited only by the creativity of the director.

Special Uses for Bells

Two special uses for bells I have found effective involve random ringing. First, using small bells as a pseudo-zimbelstern adds harmonics and excitement to the climax of both organ and choral passages. Second, a slow random ringing, but with large bells, proves very effective and provides a certain "monastic" background for Gregorian chants and composed music of a similar style.

I hesitate to use bell descants for congregational

hymns. Many find it distracting. Concentration on the words and music by the congregation is sometimes interrupted by not only the sounds of the bells, but also by the sight of the ringers. Bell choirs are a visual experience as well as an aural one.

If you are really interested in bells, first join the American Guild of English Handbell Ringers (AGEHR), whose publication *Overtones* provides a wealth of information and suggestions. In it you will learn what is happening in the world of bells. Secondly, find a good handbell choir in the area and sit in on a few rehearsals. See how it is done. Maybe they'd even let you ring with them. Thirdly, from *Overtones* magazine, find workshops sponsored by the AGEHR. Classes and help are always available for the beginner. Lastly, decide if you have enough time to put into a bell program. If you haven't or are not sure, stay away. It does take time! Nothing sounds worse than an inadequately prepared bell choir directed by one who "loves" bells, but has been very busy—nothing sounds worse except a piccolo octet.

Donald L. Clapper

250 • Drums in Worship

Every style of music embodies certain rhythmic features, many of which can be clarified, enhanced, or emphasized by percussion instruments. This article outlines the historical use of percussion instruments and discusses their function in the praise-and-worship tradition.

The Vital Role of Percussion in Worship

One of the three major components of music is rhythm (the other two being melody and harmony). Rhythm is the organization of music notational values into a pulsated time continuum. Rhythm includes such factors as beat (pulse), meter, tempo, and patterns of notes of varying lengths.

The percussion section of an orchestra or band plays a major role in helping to establish, maintain, and control the rhythmic motion and timing in the music that the ensemble performs, particularly in contemporary styles of music centered around a rhythm section. Within the contemporary rhythm section, the drummer traditionally has the primary responsibility for the establishment, maintenance, and control of the "groove," which involves the

combination of tempo and style. The groove forms the rhythmic foundation upon which most contemporary music is built.

Percussion instruments may be defined as musical instruments that produce tones when they are hit, scraped, rubbed, shaken, or whirled. There are two categories of percussion instruments—those with definite pitch (such as the timpani, xylophone, marimba, vibraphone, bells, or chimes) and those of indefinite pitch (such as drums of various types, cymbals, claves, castinets, triangle, woodblock, tambourine, or gong).

Sound can be produced in percussion instruments in two ways. Idiophones, or self-sounding percussion instruments, produce sound when the main body of the instrument is hit, scraped, rubbed, shaken or whirled. Cymbals, gongs, mallet instruments (chimes, bells, marimba, xylophone), and Latin hand percussion (such as cabassa, gourd, claves, vibraslap, castinets) are examples of idiophones. Membranophones are percussion instruments which have a skin or other membranous material stretched over a hard hollow body. Sound is produced by striking the stretched membrane with the hand or with a beater. Most of the drum family falls into this category of instruments.

— Percussion Instruments in the Bible —

Three categories of percussion instruments are specifically mentioned in the Bible—cymbals, sistra, and timbrels.

Cymbal. There were apparently two kinds of cymbals. The single cymbal, or the *tselatsel,* was a rattling, tinkling, or clattering cymbal that was possibly struck with some kind of implement (like a stick or rod) or clanged together with another cymbal. The double cymbal, or the *metselath* (double tinkler), was probably a pair of cymbals that could either be clanged together or struck with some kind of hard implement, much like the contemporary high hat (sock cymbal).

Sistrum. The sistrum, or the *menana,* was an instrument constructed of metal rings which moved freely on metal rods mounted on a loop-like frame with a handle. The instrument made a rattling sound when shaken, similar to our contemporary rattles, shakers, tambourines, and the like.

Timbrel. The timbrel, or *toph,* is variously translated as timbrel, tabret, or tambourine. It was a hand drum with a hard, hollow body (either open on one end or both ends) and a membranous head stretched over one open end. The timbrel head was struck either with the hand or a beater, similar to our contemporary tambourines and members of the drum family. In addition to these categories of percussion instruments mentioned in the Bible, a drum, or _tympana,_ is mentioned in the Book of the Maccabees 9:39. This was probably a single-headed drum struck with either the hand or a beater.

History of Percussion in Worship

Rooted in the Hebraic worship found in the synagogues at the time of Christ, early Christian worship did not make use of instruments. Also, due to the intimate and sometimes clandestine nature of early Christian gatherings, instrumental music was deemed unnecessary or inappropriate. During the persecution of the church in the early centuries, musical instruments, particularly brass and percussion, were employed during the execution of Christians and the performing of pagan rituals. Therefore, because of their pagan associations, instruments were disallowed from use in worship at the Council of Laodicea in 367. An exception to this rule, however, was the worship of the Ethiopian church, which from the beginning featured drums, sistra, and sticks as well as dance.

Percussion instruments were not used in Christian worship until the seventeenth century. During the seventeenth and eighteenth centuries, only timpani (kettledrums) were prominently used in church music and only in the performance of large scale sacred choral works such as oratorios, masses, requiems, magnificats, cantatas, and coronation anthems. During the Romantic period (_c._ 1825– _c._ 1900), other percussion instruments were added to the orchestration of major choral works. However, these instruments continued to be generally absent from congregational worship, even well into the twentieth century.

Rhythm Section in Praise Worship

With the development of jazz in the United States in the early 1900s came a new role for the percussionist. The core of the jazz band (later, the dance band, swing band, or swing orchestra) was, and still is, the rhythm section, comprised of piano, bass, drums, and guitar. The drummer plays on a drum set made up of a battery of drums, cymbals, and other percussion instruments. Slowly, as churches in the late twentieth century began to incorporate orchestral instruments into worship, the drum set began to be employed in churches desiring a stylistic slant that used pop-rock and jazz idioms and contemporary praise music. Since the late 1960s and early 1970s, there has been an explosion of interest in praise music based in the contemporary rhythm section.

The Drumset

A basic drumset (also called trapset, traps, or drum kit) includes a bass drum (kick), a snare drum, one or more tom-toms, a high hat (sock cymbal), and two or more cymbals of varying weight and shape. The bass drum is usually muffled and often has either a partial front head or no front head. This provides a good, nonreverberating sound when the foot pedal strikes the back head. The high-hat cymbals are manipulated also by a foot pedal.

Tom-toms can be double headed (for a more contained, controlled sound) or they can have a top head only (for a louder, less contained sound). The smaller tom-toms are attached to the drumset, while the larger ones, called floor toms, sit on the floor next to the drummer.

The largest cymbal is the ride cymbal, which is used to help keep time. The medium-sized cymbals are crash cymbals, and the smallest are splash cymbals, all of which are used either for accent or color (musical mood setting). The drummer can also have an array of percussion instruments at his disposal, such as cowbells, woodblocks, inverted cymbals, wind chimes, shakers, and others. Drummers also carry a variety of sticks, mallets, and brushes to achieve a wide spectrum of effects.

The Drummer

The drummer is the rhythmic leader of the rhythm section. He is responsible for establishing a groove appropriate to the music being sung or played and for keeping the time, or tempo, very consistent. All tempo changes are led by the drummer.

When writing for the drummer, the composer/arranger must take care to not overwrite for the drums (unless the composer is the drummer) but also not to ignore the drummer. Simple parts indicating the general rhythm pattern (at the beginning and at change-of-feel points) for one or two bars along with a brief explanation of style is almost always sufficient. Specific notation is rarely needed.

Miking a drumset is a significant challenge. Care must be given to accurately reproduce the drum sound in the audio system while containing the sound enough so that the drums do not bleed into other microphones. Most professional drummers and sound men are familiar with this challenge and can be valuable resources.

—— Further Developments in Drums ——

The development of electronic music has opened new vistas for drummers. Drum sets can now be partially or totally electronic using either synthesized drum sounds, sampled drum sounds (i.e., real sounds that are digitally recorded and reproduced) or a combination of the two. Electronically produced percussion sounds can be accessed from the drum set, allowing the drummer to be essentially an entire percussion section. These electronic digitalized sounds do not replace the live percussion sounds, but rather add to the enormous array of sounds and effects that are at the disposal of the drummer.

James R. Hart

—————— Drum Machines ——————

The way you use a drum machine in a service will depend upon the coordination of the main keyboard player. The drum machine is going to have to be controlled by that person, whether that person is the worship leader or not. Since the lead keyboard player must start and maintain the proper tempos and styles of the songs, it is his or her responsibility to program the drum machine and know where the appropriate patterns are. The main keyboard player will have to have some idea of how drums should be played or how they should sound in order to program the drum machine. With this basic knowledge, the rest can be learned somewhat simply. If all else fails, ask a real drummer to help you create all of the different drum patterns that can accompany the different song styles that you sing.

As the worship leader, it is imperative that you are comfortable with the operation of all of the equipment you are using. You must be able to flow in praise and worship and not be distracted by the starting, stopping, and changing of drum patterns (if that is necessary). What this means is many hours of practice! You will only flow comfortably in the sanctuary if you are comfortable at home or in your practice time at the church. As a musician accompanying the worship leader, you will have to stay tuned in to all that the leader wants to do even more intensely than if you were leading.

When you start out using the drum machine in church, start using it only on the fast songs. Prepare a 16-beat pattern to help keep a steady tempo with the congregation. The beat may be most appreciated on fast songs to add excitement to the music. The next step is to use it on medium tempo songs that have a basic 4/4 tempo. By now you and the congregation will become more comfortable and familiar with the drum machine.

As you get acquainted with the use of the drum machine, I am sure that you will realize that having the proper volume settings is an important factor in the flow of the praise and worship. Once you and the congregation are really comfortable with the use of the drum machine in church, you can program very simple patterns to accompany the slow worship songs. Simple means using only the kick drum and high hat, or adding rim shots to those. Believe it or not, the Holy Spirit will still operate in your services, and the anointing will still be evident.

I have found that the drum machine can be a very useful tool to any musician who will take the time to learn how to make it do what he or she wants it to do. I use it in all of the services in which I minister all around the world. Sometimes when I take my church worship team out to minister at special functions, I will use the drum machine rather than trying to take an entire drum set.

The instruments that are being created with this new MIDI (musical instrument digital interface) technology are to be used for the glory and honor of God. I believe it is our responsibility as Christian musicians to study them to show ourselves approved, a Christian rightly dividing the Word of God through music.

David Lawrence

251 • Churches that Refrain from Use of Instruments in Worship

A small minority of churches today are opposed in principle to the use of instruments in worship. The following article outlines a typical argument for this position. It is written by a leader in the Reformed Presbyterian Church, one denomination that refrains from the use of instruments in worship.

Music is one of the arts that God has given for man's expression and joy. Scripture records the origin of instrumental music; in Genesis 4:21, we read that Jubal was "the father of all who play the harp and lute." The use and appreciation of instrumental music should be encouraged among the people of God.

While most people would agree that a capella singing is the best expression of the human voice, there is not unanimity when it comes to the use of instrumental music in worship. There are those who believe that an organ sets an atmosphere for worship and that musical instruments help people to worship.

The worship of the early Christian church was patterned after the synagogue, where instruments were not used in worship. It wasn't until the eighth century that instruments were generally used in the Roman church. The Eastern church never did introduce them. At the time of the Reformation, Reformed and Presbyterian churches removed instrumental music from their churches; early Methodist, Congregational, and Baptist churches had a strong position against the use of musical instruments in worship. It has been in comparatively recent years that many churches have departed from that historic position.

There are still churches who do not use musical instruments in worship. The Reformed Presbyterian Church is one of them. Our reasons are summarized briefly as follows:

1. We are committed to the Bible as the inerrant Word of God and the only infallible guide for faith and life. In this context of the authority of Scripture, we believe that God, who is the object of worship, has revealed to us in his Word how we are to worship Him. In contrast to those who worshiped other gods, and in order that God's people would not be ensnared in false worship, God said, "See that you do all I command you; do not add to it or take away from it" (Deut. 12:32).

2. This regulative principle is stated in the Testimony of the Reformed Presbyterian Church as follows: "Worship is to be offered only in accordance with God's appointment, and in harmony with the scriptural principal that whatever is not commanded in the worship of God, by precept or sample, is forbidden."

3. Instruments were used in Old Testament worship by the command of God in direct connection with the sacrificial offerings of the ceremonial law. "As the offering began, singing to the Lord began also, accompanied by trumpets and the instruments of David, king of Israel. The whole assembly bowed in worship, while the singers sang and the trumpeters played. All this continued until the sacrifice of the burnt offering was completed" (2 Chron. 29:27-28). Back in verse 25 we see that this use of instruments was commanded by God. Its integral relationship to the ceremonial law is articulated clearly since the instruments began when the sacrifice began and stopped when the offering was completed.

4. The typical nature of the use of instruments in the Old Testament is evident in the fact that their use was the special prerogative of the Levities, and that they were used almost exclusively in connection with the offering of sacrifices and burnt offerings.

5. It would seem clear that the music of the Levitical choir accompanied with instruments was designated to portray the joy and gladness which should characterize God's covenant people as they come into his presence (2 Chron. 29:30).

6. There is neither command nor example given by Christ or the apostles of the use of musical instruments in worship. The Old Testament types of Christ are fulfilled in His coming. Our joy in Him is complete. Musical instruments are no longer needed nor are they appropriate.

7. Everything necessary to bring us into the presence of God has been accomplished by the finished work of Christ. The simplicity of New Testament worship makes this clear. We no longer need a priest to burn incense, for Christ is our great High Priest who hears our prayers. We no longer need to bring sacrifices for offerings, for Christ our Passover has been sacrificed for us. We no longer need the Levites to sing praise for us with the accompaniment of instruments; God has made us all priests before Him, and has given to each of us an instrument which only He can teach us to play—namely a heart overflowing with the thankful song of salvation (Heb. 13:15).

Bruce C. Stewart[33]

252 ✦ Bibliography for Instruments in Worship

For general information on instruments and instrumental classes themselves, a primary reference is the Diagram Group's illustrated encyclopedia *Musical Instruments of the World* (New York, 1976), a massive presentation that also includes a listing of major museum instrumental collections in an appendix.

Bibliography on instruments in worship is best approached via the individual instruments.

Organ

The American Guild of Organists, the Organ Historical Society, and the Canadian Royal College of Organists are the fundamental professional organizations for the instrument in North America, and provide the journals *The American Organist* (New York), a monthly journal, and *The Diapason* (New York), also monthly. John Fesperman's *Hymnal Studies IV: Organ Planning: Asking the Right Questions* (New York: Church Hymnal Corporation, 1985), provides a comprehensive and step-by-step process for acquiring an organ suitable for the worship practices of a given community; the issue of hymn-playing at the organ is faced by Austin C. Lovelace in *The Organist and Hymn-Playing*, rev. ed. (Carol Stream, Ill.: Hope Publishing, 1981), a step-by-step analysis of techniques needed for good hymn accompaniment.

For a bibliography of music for organ based on *Psalter Hymnal* tunes, see Joan Ringerwale, *Bibliography of Organ Music* (Grand Rapids: CRC Publications, 1994). Other valuable works include Joy E. Lawrence, *The Organist's Shortcut to Service Music* (Cleveland: Ludwig Music, 1989; supplement 1, 1988; volume 2, 1992) and Daniel J. Werning, *A Selected Source Index for Hymnal Choral Tunes in Lutheran Worship Books* (St. Louis: Concordia, 1985). For a complete survey of organ literature, see Corliss Richard Arnold's *Organ Literature: A Comprehensive Survey* (Metuchen, N.J.: The Scarecrow Press, 1984).

Advanced-technique organists should consult the catalogues of G. Schirmer, C. F. Peters, Kalmus, and Schola Cantorum. Library copies of the publications of Durand et Cie of Paris may also be available. These publishers feature music of the great classical composers in organ: J. S. Bach, Buxtehude, Franck, the Couperins, Brahms, Durufle, Dupre, and many others. Numerous American figures of the mid-twentieth century (e.g., Carl McKinley, Leo Sowerby, Samuel Barber, Bruce Simonds) are represented through the specific series of publishers: *E. C. Schirmer Organ Library* (Boston), edited by Victor Mattfeld, and the H. W. Gray *Contemporary Organ Series* (New York), edited by William Strickland. Representing European composers is the series *Musik für Orgel* of B. Schott (Mainz, Germany). There is also the *St. Cecelia Series of Compositions for the Organ* (H. W. Gray), which is an international survey in composers from the Baroque to contemporary times and includes some transcriptions.

Guitar

For guitar, the following citations are useful:

- Mimi Farra and Wiley Beverage, *Leading Worship with the Guitar* (Pacific, Mo.: Cathedral Music). A VHS videocassette that teaches Fisherfolk style in a 28-minute demonstration.
- Larry Folk, *Worship with Guitar* (Phoenix: North American Liturgical Resources). A collection of practical theory and performance tips, with information regarding use of the guitar in community worship. More than 130 exercises, 70 figures and illustrations, and many musical examples.
- *Glory and Praise* (Phoenix: North American Liturgical Resources). Hymns and songs for contemporary worship. Three volumes. I: 1–80, guitar accompaniment; II: 81–173, guitar accompaniment; III: 174–275, guitar accompaniment.
- Betty Pulkingham: *Mass for the King of Glory* (Chicago: GIA Publications). SATB choir, congregation, keyboard and guitar; other instruments optional.

Piano

Numerous piano collections are available for worship leading and playing. The North American Liturgical Resource's *Glory and Praise* series, 2 vols., and a large listing from Lillenas, including collections by Don Phillips (*Devotional Piano*), Myra Schubert (*Give Him Glory*), Margaret Bos (*Classic Praise*), John Innes (*Carols for Keyboard*), and Ken Bible (*Contemporary Classics*) are good starting points. William Phemister offers a 2-volume instructional series called *Contemporary Keyboard Styles* in video format. Phemister is also editor of the *Masterworks Piano Library* (Fred Bock Music Co.), 10 vols. The first three volumes are currently available; the remaining are in process. Another piano repertory collection is that of David N. Johnson, *Free Hymn Accompaniments for Manuals* (Minneapolis: Augsburg), 2 vols. Suited for pianists, it is also appropriate for organists who do not use pedals or for manuals-only organ use. Similarly, organ music transferable to piano with some success is found in Hermann Keller's edition of *Eighty Chorale Preludes* (New York: C. F. Peters) and in C. H. Trevor's edition of *Organ Music for Manuals* (New York: Oxford University Press). Repertory drawn from classical compositions includes a generous number of superior works: Brahms's *Intermezzi;* Franck's *Forty-Six Short Pieces for Piano* as well as his *Prelude, Chorale, and Fugue;* J. S. Bach's *Little Notebook for Anna Magdalena;* certain of Liszt's *Consolations,* his *Four Short Pieces,* and his *Pater Noster.* The well-known Pachelbel's Canon can be played effectively on piano. Hope Publishing Company (Carol Stream, Ill.) provides two excellent piano collections: *Piano Preludes on Hymns and Chorales,* arranged by Reginald Gerig; and Jack C. Good's *Piano Hymns for the Church Year,* a strongly contemporary and moderately challenging anthology.

Handbells and Orff Instruments

The American Guild of English Handbell Ringers is the primary source for material on handbells. Also worthy of attention are John Folkening, *Handbells in the Liturgical Service* (St. Louis: Concordia, n.d.) and Nancy Poore Tufts, *The Art of Handbell Ringing* (Nashville: Abingdon, 1961). For Orff instrument resources, see the catalogs of the American Orff-Schulwerk Association, Dept. of Music, Cleveland State University, Cleveland, Ohio, or *Magna Music Baton,* published in St. Louis. Helpful background to the concepts and practice of Orff instruments can be found in Bridgett Warner's *Orff-Schulwerk* (Englewood Cliffs, N.J.: Prentice-Hall, 1991).

EIGHT

Planning Music for Worship

With the great variety and sheer quantity of music available for use in worship, one of the greatest challenges for worship planners is selecting music for use in worship and deciding how it will be used. These decisions must be based on a variety of factors: musical—music for worship should be well-crafted music; textual—the texts chosen should be faithful to the Bible and communicate their message well; pastoral—selections should be made with sensitivity to the spiritual needs of individual worshipers; and liturgical—choices should be made so as to complement, not destroy the logical flow of the worship service. The following chapters offer advice on how to make thoughtful choices based on these factors.

253 • MUSIC FOR THE FOUR ACTS OF WORSHIP

Music is integral to each of the four basic acts of worship. Music sets the tone or mood for what takes place in each act. It is also a means by which the unique aspects of each part of the service many be expressed. The process of planning music for worship should always take into account the function of music in relationship to the structure of the worship service.

Music has the power to express the various moods of each part of worship: the Entrance employs joyful music; the Word, instructive music; the Table, celebrative music; the Dismissal, triumphant music. This is equally true of the various seasons of the church year: Advent music expresses the longing of the heart as it awaits the coming of Christ; Christmas, the joy of his appearing; Epiphany, the stirring command of the missionary advance; Lent, the quietness of the inner journey; Holy Week, the sobriety of death; Easter, the joy of resurrection; Pentecost, the excitement of the coming of the Holy Spirit. Music captures and expresses all of these moods in the four acts of worship.

——— Music for the Acts of Entrance ———

Gathering Music. Music during the gathering can create either a mood of reverence or of joy. Traditional worship will use an organ prelude or instrumentation or both to reach the hearts and allow people to meditate before the service begins. Today many churches, desiring to create a mood of joy and celebration, will sing praise songs as the people gather, then move to a traditional Entrance hymn to

signal the procession and the beginning of the various parts of Entrance into the presence of God.

Many churches are using praise choruses for the gathering. Praise choruses constitute a new musical form which found its origins in the Jesus movement of the early 1970s and in the rise and spread of the charismatic movement. In the praise-and-worship tradition, choruses are often sung for the entire acts of Entrance.

Praise choruses are also being integrated into a more traditional form of worship in two very effective and helpful ways. First, some churches have a time of praise choruses during the gathering, followed by an Entrance hymn that signals the beginning of the more formal worship. In these churches the praise choruses replace the more traditional organ prelude and prepare the people for worship through joyful singing. Second, praise choruses are very effective during the Communion as an expression of praise and adoration to God for the work of Christ experienced at the Table.

Entrance Music. Careful consideration needs to be given to the mood of both the Entrance hymn and the act(s) of praise. The Entrance hymn should be joyful, familiar, and capable of accompaniment with organ and brass. Coming into the presence of God is a festive act, which, if not expressed by the music, probably will not be experienced by the people.

A hymn is the most appropriate expression of Entrance, especially if it is used with a procession. A hymn, as Augustine stated, is "the praise of God in song." So convinced was he of this truth that he went on to say that the praise of God not sung is not a hymn.

It is generally thought that Ambrose, the fourth-century bishop of the church in Milan where Augustine was converted, is the father of ancient hymnody. Although a number of hymns were written in the ancient and medieval church, few melodies are found before the twelfth century, and not until the twelfth century were hymns officially admitted into the Mass, although they were used extensively in the divine offices.

Hymn singing in the vernacular was promoted in the fourteenth century in the worship of the Bohemian brethren led by John Huss. During the sixteenth century the Reformers introduced more hymns which were to exert a lasting influence on the people. Hymn singing was popularized by John Wesley in the eighteenth century and through revivalism in the nineteenth century.

Today there is a considerable amount of hymnal updating and many new hymns are being written. Nearly every denomination around the world is producing new hymns and new hymnals. This is a sign of the vitality hymn singing brings to worship and the importance of hymns that support the action of worship.

Praise tradition groups that have neglected the hymn in worship are now reconsidering, recognizing that they have cut themselves off from the rich treasury of hymn material available to the church to support and intensify its worship.

The act of praise is addressed to God and extols God's worthiness of praise. The ancient _Gloria in Excelsis Deo_ is the traditional act of praise sung here. There are numerous musical settings for the Gloria, ranging from formal to folk or praise tunes. While the Gloria is really the most appropriate act of praise, other hymns or praise songs extolling God's worth can be used. Because the mood is one of joy and adoration, the musical expression should be fast and upbeat. Numerous instruments or combinations of instrumental music are appropriate for the Entrance.

A canticle may also be sung in the Entrance, especially when sung to a metrical tune as in the _New Metrical Psalter._ In Christian worship a canticle is a song from the Bible other than the book of Psalms. Canticles, originally sung at morning and evening prayer, are now sung in worship on special occasions. For example, the gradual alleluia, not sung during Lent, may be replaced by a canticle.

The most often sung canticles are the _Benedicite,_ a song of Creation which comes from the Apocrypha; the _Benedictus,_ the song of Zechariah (Luke 1:68-79); the _Nunc Dimittis,_ the song of Simeon (Luke 2:29-32) and the _Magnificat,_ the song of Mary (Luke 1:46-55). A good translation of these and other canticles can be found in _The Book of Common Prayer._

Music for the Service of the Word

In the Service of the Word the act of worship shifts from Entrance into the presence of God to hearing God speak. Consequently, the musical shift is from voices raised in praise to ears attentive to the Word of God read and preached. Music must serve that shift and assist the congregation in hearing the Word.

Music of the Word can include

1. The singing (chant) of the Scripture lessons (this form of music was used in the synagogue and passed down to the early church). Chant fixes the words in the mind better than reading.
2. Sung responses such as the responsorial psalm and the gradual alleluia; the form of music that best expresses an attentive and listening mood is chant in one form or another. Some churches will sing the psalm to a metrical tune. Although metrical music is not as conducive to listening, it may be used for congregations not accustomed to chant.
3. The singing of the Apostles' Creed. A number of chants, modified chant, and melody tunes are available.
4. Singing the prayers. Chant best expresses the mood of prayer.

It is also appropriate to speak all of the above since the spoken word serves well the mood of attentiveness. Generally instrumentation for music in the Service of the Word should be used sparingly, and almost never with chant. One exception might be the use of an organ accompaniment to the monotone chanting of the Apostles' Creed. These usually are subtle modulations and harmonizations on the chant tone that reflect the emotional or dramatic contour of the creed.

What is used most often in the Service of the Word is the psalm. The oldest form of music in the

Christian church is psalm singing, a form rooted in Hebrew worship.

The earliest form of psalm singing was chant. The early church developed what has come to be known as the Gregorian chant. In the Reformation era John Calvin introduced metrical psalm singing, and in 1719 Isaac Watts introduced a Christianized version of the psalms in *The Psalms of David Imitated in the Language of the New Testament and Applied to the Christian State and Worship*. For example, "Jesus Shall Reign Where'er the Sun" is his rendition of Psalm 72, and "Joy to the World" comes from Psalm 98. In contemporary worship renewal, psalms have been recovered in all three styles—chant, metrical, and translation.

Chant is rooted in the biblical tradition and has been used in worship throughout history. Although Protestants have seldom used chanting in worship, this musical form is undergoing a renaissance today, especially in prayer. Because chant is given to the repetition of a word or phrase, it is highly useful as a form of meditation, a way of centering in worship. Chanting the Psalms has the advantage of singing the actual text rather than a paraphrase of the text. Psalm chants are used primarily in the responsorial psalm in the Service of the Word, located between the Old Testament reading and the Epistle, and in the gradual, the singing before the reading of the Gospel. In the Catholic church the psalm must be sung by chant and not meter because chant, it is argued, fits the mood of hearing the Word and concentrating on it better than does meter.

There are a number of chant patterns. One of the most widely used is the antiphonal chant. The soloist or a choir sing the psalm refrain or an alleluia. Then the congregation repeats it. The entire psalm is sung this way with the cantor chanting the verse and the congregation responding. This is a very beautiful way to sing a psalm and an effective one for hearing the Word. A more simple form of congregational chant is the pattern found in the *Lutheran Book of Worship*. In this form the entire congregation sings the psalm together. Although the chanting of the psalms is used primarily in liturgical churches, nonliturgical churches should consider its occasional use. The best time for nonliturgical churches to use chant psalms is during Lent and Holy Week.

The metrical psalms originated among the English Protestant exiles who fled the persecution under Queen Mary to reside in Geneva. These psalms were popularized by Calvin and have been used in Reformed churches with continuing adaptation and change to the present.

In contemporary worship renewal metrical psalm singing has enjoyed a renaissance. Many denominations already have, or are in the process of creating, new Psalters for congregational singing. While metrical psalms may be sung as Responsorial Psalms, they are more appropriate in the Gathering, in the Entrance, and as Communion Songs. This is particularly true of those psalms that are joyful in nature, offering praise to God.

For example, a number of churches now sing a psalm or two as the people gather to worship. These psalms create a mood of joy and reverence and prepare the people for the Entrance song and rites that bring them into the presence of God. The Entrance song itself can be a psalm or a psalm can be used as an act of praise where the traditional *Gloria in Excelsis Deo* appears. Because many psalms are joyful and express high praise for the deeds of God, they are quite appropriate as acts of praise during Communion. These are the major places in worship where a metrical psalm can be used effectively.

Music in the Service of the Table

The shift that occurs at the Table moves people from attentive listening to active involvement once again. The focus, which shifts from the Word to the Table, from our encounter with Christ in the preached Word to our encounter with Christ at the Table, needs the assistance of music that will support the text and convey the mood of what is actually occurring.

Setting the Table. Here people of the congregation bring the bread and wine and place it on the Table. Here an anthem can be sung, the congregation may sing, or both may occur. It is best to do both. If a choice has to be made, sing a hymn. People have been sitting and listening to the Word; they now need to express their faith.

The Prayer of Thanksgiving. In high liturgical churches the Prayer of Thanksgiving is sung in a chant tone. The people respond at the appropriate point in the prayer with the *Sanctus,* the eucharistic acclamation, the Great Amen, and the *Agnus Dei.* Even if the text is read, at least the responses should be sung. Here is the great commemoration of the mystery of the incarnation, death, resurrection, and return of Christ. Music is a much better way to express mystery than speech alone. It communicates the meaning of the gospel to deeper levels of the personality and allows for a response from the hearer that comes from deeper than the intellect. Of course, to accomplish this the liturgy must be sung as a prayer and sung in faith. A mere rote recitation of the words without adequate intention or reverential awe, which this great mystery should inspire, will fall flat and be uninspiring.

Communion Song. What is said above is equally true of singing during the reception of Communion. This is no time for soft organ music, for instrumental performance of any kind. It is time for the corporate singing of songs of joy. Here praise music of the Taizé or Maranatha or Fisherfolk varieties fits well, as do great ancient hymns regarding the meaning of the Eucharist. It is a celebration of the Resurrection, not a sober reflection on the death. Communion is also enhanced with the use of chants, acclamations, litanies, and refrains or antiphons.

Besides psalm chant, there are at least three other uses of chant: processional chant, intercessory chant, and devotional chant. The _processional chant_ is best used as the people are processing to the Table to receive Communion. One Scripture chant made famous by the Taizé community in France is the phrase of the thief on the cross, "Jesus remember me when you come into your kingdom." These words, sung over and over again, allow a scattered and busy mind, body, and spirit to focus on the meaning of Christ's death and participation with him in the kingdom. As the congregation chants this Scripture and joins together in song and centering, a sense of God's spirit can be felt and experienced intensely.

The _intercessory chant_ is sung with penitential prayers (usually during Lent) and with the general prayers of intercession. The chant tone supports the action of the community, its penitence or its petitions.

The _devotional chant_ has a strong likeness to the intercessory chant except that nothing else is going on in worship at that time. It supports personal devotion and is therefore best done as a post-Communion song, allowing worshipers to express their devotion in an intense way.

Acclamations may also be sung in Communion. An acclamation is a short burst of praise that may be said or sung as a response to a divine action occurring in worship. Examples are

1. The gradual alleluia
2. The Sanctus (Holy, Holy, Holy) in the prayer of thanksgiving
3. The memorial acclamation in the prayer of thanksgiving
   - Christ has died
   - Christ is risen
   - Christ will come again.
4. The Great Amen in the prayer of thanksgiving

While these acclamations are used primarily in the liturgical church, there is no reason why they cannot be used as effective congregational responses in a nonliturgical church as well.

Litanies are also often used in Communion. A litany is a form of song or prayer that builds through repetition. A litany such as "Lord have mercy" or "Lord, hear our prayer" is often sung or said in the intercessions at the end of each prayer.

In the Communion the _Agnus Dei_ ("Lamb of God that takes away the sin of the world have mercy on us") is frequently used. This phrase is repeated twice and then the third time the congregation sings "Lamb of God that takes away the sin of the world, grant us your peace."

A refrain or antiphon is not nearly as "explosive" as an acclamation. It is a response that is more subdued and subtle, a meditative response that echoes and re-echoes in the heart.

A refrain may be used after the responsorial psalm or it may be used in the Communion time. Communion refrains such as "Taste and see that the Lord is good" or "Ubi caritas" ("Where charity and love are, there is God") have been widely used throughout the centuries at Communion.

Music for the Act of Dismissal

The recessional hymn, usually the only music in the Dismissal, maintains the upbeat mood of the Table. Here a gospel song may be sung. Gospel songs that speak of God's touch or the mission before the church are appropriate ways to be sent forth.

Gospel songs, which are also called witness music, have their modern origins in the music of the Wesleyan revivals. The texts of these hymns shifted from a vertical focus on God and God's character to a more horizontal approach, a concern for the human person before God. Attention was paid to sinful conditions, to the need for salvation, to God's offer of salvation in Christ, and to the change in heart and life that comes through conversion and restoration with God.

Most hymn books contain many gospel songs from the pen of John or Charles Wesley, Fanny Crosby, and others. While these gospel songs are not generally fitting for an Entrance hymn, they may be used effectively as response to the sermon (in churches that do not use creeds), and as a concluding recessional hymn.

In summary, all forms of music may be used in any given service—chant, ancient hymns, psalm singing, praise music, gospel, and more. All of these musical styles create an environment, a mood that carries the community into an experience of heaven. Consequently renewal worship draws on all the traditions of music and does not adhere, or should not adhere to one single style.

Robert E. Webber

254 • THE LECTIONARY AS A GUIDE TO PLANNING MUSIC FOR WORSHIP

One type of tool that pastors often use to select Scripture readings for a service is known as a lectionary. Although not well known to church musicians in some traditions, this tool can be very helpful in assisting the church musician to select music that is appropriate for a given service. The following article suggests why this is so and then lists resources that can assist church musicians in working with the lectionary.

Imagine yourself as the minister of music. The previous pastor has relocated to another church and the new preacher has just arrived. Often these are periods of transition and confusion. You worked well with the previous person, and both understood each other. However, the new leader has announced that his or her sermons will be based on the lectionary. The pastor urges you to likewise observe the lectionary in selecting the music for worship. While you have heard the term once or twice before, you are not at all clear what a lectionary is or how it can assist you in your weekly responsibility.

A little background can clear the confusion and reveal the numerous benefits that come from utilizing this resource. Very simply, a lectionary is a collection of "lections" or readings, specifically the readings of Scripture. How does the pastor choose

which passage to use on any given Sunday? By what method are those readings selected week after week, year after year? Since the beginning of the church, two systematic approaches have gained popularity. *Lectio continua* is the practice of beginning at the first verse of a designated book, for example Philippians, and reading it continuously from week to week, verse by verse, chapter by chapter, until you reach the end of the fourth chapter. Conversely, *lectio selecta* is the random selection of a text that resembles the movement of a grasshopper. The Scripture will vary from book to book each week, depending upon the topic selected by the preacher.

It was based on these two versions of Scripture selection that the lectionary arose. Worship scholars insist that the roots of the lectionary reach back to the early Jews before the time of Christ. When Jesus read from the prophet Isaiah during his visit to the synagogue in Nazareth, he turned to the designated passage for the day (cf. Luke 4:17-19). By the ninth century after Christ, the church had established a standardized collection or lectionary of readings for each Sunday.

Today there are four lectionaries in use: the Roman Catholic, Episcopal, Lutheran, and Common (finalized in December 1991) which is employed by many Protestant denominations. While diversity obviously exists between these four variations, there is much that is held in common. All lectionaries are built around a three year cycle known as Year A, B, and C. The three-year focus enables a different synoptic gospel (Matthew, Mark, or Luke) to be read each year. In addition to the weekly gospel lesson, all lectionaries contain an Old Testament, Psalm, and New Testament/Epistle reading. Further, it should be noted that these passages are organized according to the church year. That is to say, Scripture for December will reflect the Advent themes of prophecy and expectation of Jesus Christ as the promised Messiah who has come and will return again. Readings during Epiphany, the season which follows Christmas, will manifest the nature and ministry of Jesus Christ as God's Chosen One. The longest period of the church year, known as ordinary time, follows Pentecost. It is during this segment one will find the greatest divergence among the various lectionaries.

Your pastor asserted there were numerous benefits to using the lectionary. Indeed there are. For the preacher as well as congregation, it ensures they will hear a broad cross section of Scripture. Some critics of this approach maintain employing the lectionary restricts one's freedom in selecting the Sunday text. However, the opposite is more likely to be true. Lectionary preaching challenges and guides the preacher in more fully exploring the entire range of God's revelation to us.

As minister of music, you can perceive some valuable benefits from following the lectionary. Perhaps you recall times when you have worked with a pastor who was never sure until the preceding week what he/she would preach upon the following Sunday. Repeatedly you asked the preacher for the sermon themes for the next three or four months so you could order, practice, and adequately prepare music with your choirs. Using the lectionary greatly increases the opportunities for planning worship that is unified and cohesive. Remember, the specified passages for each week of the lectionary have a common theme which is woven throughout the other Scriptures. This unity also exerts an influence on crafting worship that is unified. Rather than allowing three or four disjointed themes to arise, which may not reinforce each other, you can create a common thrust which will greatly assist the worshipers in focusing on God and being more clearly challenged to a proper response. Always, our goal should be to coordinate music which complements the Scripture as read and preached.

A related aspect of planning pertains to hymn selection. Approaches differ from place to place. Some preachers choose hymns because they feel they have a more accurate sense of the worship theme. Other pastors expect or invite the minister of music or organist to select hymns. If the latter is your experience, once again the lectionary will greatly enhance and simplify your task. Most hymnals provide indices which suggest suitable hymns for a given text of Scripture. Further, many helpful resources are now being produced that aid in the selection of hymns according to the lectionary. Some of these are listed in the resources below. In such situations, the minister of music or organist is not at the mercy of another person, but can choose and practice in advance music which will be appropriate to the Scripture of the day.

Employing the lectionary for music planning offers the further benefit of increased dialogue. Using a common, agreed upon selection process for Scripture and song enlarges the opportunity for cooperation between pastor and musician. Additionally, it provides you, as the church musician, with a unique resource. It is likely that numerous other churches in your community are following the lectionary. Many pastors participate in small groups which gather to study and discuss the given texts for the next Sunday. This holds the potential to stretch their minds and gain insights from others to improve their preaching. Likewise, musicians can form similar groups to assist them in reviewing and selecting music from the varied options available to them.

The strengths of the lectionary actually exert a dynamic, silent force. The more Christians gather around the Scripture, the stronger they grow in Christ. As more pastors and musicians gravitate toward the lectionary approach, there is an increased strength within the church, not just isolated and scattered congregations, but in the church as the body of Christ. While initially this trend may not be easily detected, with time it will disseminate a formative influence much like yeast does to a piece of dough. Anything that can foster broader dialogue with Scripture and about our triune God should be strongly encouraged.

The challenge of planning for music in worship is a huge responsibility. Selecting and coordinating hymns, songs, anthems, preludes, and postludes can be a challenging task. However, the lectionary can provide helpful and practical support to guiding you in your weekly ministry. The following sources are useful tools for lectionary planning of music.

Resources

Books

Bower, Peter, ed. *Handbook for the Common Lectionary*, developed by the Office of Worship of the Presbyterian Church (USA). Philadelphia: Geneva Press, 1987.

Doran, Carol, and Thomas H. Troeger. *New Hymns for the Lectionary: To Glorify the Maker's Name.* New York: Oxford University Press, 1986.

Laster, James, comp. *Catalogue of Choral Music Listed in Biblical Order.* Metuchen, N.J.: Scarecrow Press, 1983.

Periodicals

In issues of *The American Organist* (magazine of the American Guild of Organists, 475 Riverside Drive, Suite 1260, New York, NY 10115; [212] 870-2310), Marilyn Kay Stulken has assembled a most helpful collection of prelude, offertory, postlude music, and hymn selections generated from all four lectionaries. Listings for Year A are printed in issue 23:11 (November 1989): 58–75; for Year B in 24:11 (November 1990): 107–123; and Year C in 25:11 (November 1991): 72–89.

Church Music Calendar (available from Augsburg Fortress, 4700 Wissahickon Avenue, Philadelphia, PA 19144-4280; 1-800-367-8737) provides prelude, postlude, and anthem suggestions for Year A, B, and C. *GIA Quarterly* (7404 South Mason Avenue, Chicago, IL 60638; [708] 496-3800) provides hymn and choral suggestions for Year A, B, and C of the Roman Catholic lectionary.

Reformed Liturgy and Music (published by the Presbyterian Church [USA], Theology and Worship Ministry Unit, 100 Witherspoon Street, Louisville, KY 40202-1396; [502] 569-5289) provides prelude, postlude, hymn and anthem suggestions for Year A, B, and C of the Common lectionary.

Worship Arts (published by the United Methodist Church, P.O. Box 24787, Nashville, TN 37202; [615] 340-7453) provides hymn suggestions for Year A, B, and C.

Tom Schwanda

255 ◆ Planning Psalms for Singing in Worship

Building on centuries of tradition, churches in almost every worshiping tradition are rediscovering the value of singing the Psalms in worship. The following article describes several possibilities for the inclusion of the Psalms in worship. The article is especially concerned with planning worship in the Reformed tradition, which has always placed high value on singing the Psalms, but the ideas it presents can be easily applied to worship in any tradition.

The Psalms have been used in numerous ways in Christian liturgy, at least three of which are familiar to congregations in the Reformed tradition. First, and perhaps most familiar to most of us, is the use of psalms as expressions of the congregation's successive acts of praise, penitence, dedication, and thankfulness. For example, a congregation might begin a service by reciting the votum ("our help is in the name of the LORD") from Psalm 124:8. The minister continues with the greeting and blessing, and the congregation responds by singing a psalm of praise, perhaps Psalm 95 or 150. The service of penitence includes a general confession of sin

and/or a penitential psalm, possibly Psalm 51 or 130. Following the declaration of pardon comes the reading of the Law, which may be followed by a sung selection from Psalm 119. And so on throughout the service.

A second way of using the Psalms—linking psalms to Scripture text and sermon—is also familiar to Reformed Christians. Though not every text and sermon can be matched precisely with an appropriate psalm, often a minister can find a few verses that will echo something in the text. For example, a congregation might sing Psalm 82 in conjunction with a reading from Amos, where the common emphasis is on doing justice to the poor and weak. A third way is to choose both psalm and text to reflect a particular season or feast of the church year (e.g., Advent, Christmas, Epiphany, Lent, Easter, Pentecost). This third way of using the Psalms is closely related to the second and is frequently practiced in our churches. Both of these can be grouped under the broad heading of a "psalm-of-the-day" approach.

A variation of this third way comes with the use of a lectionary oriented to the church year. In recent years many denominations have begun to use the three-year *Common Lectionary* or some variation thereof. This practice has had the effect not only of increasing the amount of Scripture heard and preached in such churches but also of reviving the liturgical use of psalmody.

Those churches who follow the lectionary read three biblical passages each Sunday, one from the Old Testament, one from the New Testament epistles (including the Acts or the Revelation), and one from the Gospels. Between the reading of the Old and New Testament lessons, a Psalm is appointed to be said or sung, one that generally relates in some way to one or more of the lectionary texts. For example, on Christmas Day the appointed Psalm will be either 96, 97, or 98 depending on whether it falls in year A, B, or C in the three-year cycle. On Ash Wednesday Psalm 51 is read every year, as is Psalm 22 on Good Friday. On the first Sunday in Lent Psalms 130, 6, and 91 are read during years A, B, and C respectively.

In adopting the new lectionary, many churches that have historically been weak in the singing of psalms have now made the Psalter an integral part of their liturgies. The lectionary has transformed Roman, Anglican, Lutheran, and other churches into psalm-singing churches. It is becoming increasingly less probable that one can attend to the liturgy of these churches without hearing at least one psalm. The lectionary is not, of course, the only way to revive the liturgical use of psalmody, but it is a significant means to this end. Moreover, unlike the first way of using the Psalms, the "psalm-of-the-day" approach ensures a place for at least one psalm in the liturgy. Those congregations that are weak in psalm-singing would do well to consider the use of some variety of the three-year lectionary.

Which of these ways of using the Psalms is the best? The "psalm-of-the-day" approach? Or the approach whereby several psalms are used in the course of the liturgy? I would suggest that neither of these is any more Reformed than the other and that, furthermore, both are mutually compatible and ought to be put to use. One can easily envision an Easter Communion liturgy in which Psalm 118 is sung as the appointed psalm in accordance with the lectionary and Psalm 103 is sung after the reception of Communion. Both of these ways of using the Psalms work well together and have a long tradition within the Christian church as a whole.

David T. Koyzis[34]

256 • COMMUNION SONG IN WORSHIP

Singing during Communion is an ancient practice that has been restored in renewal worship. This article presents common guidelines for the restoration of Communion song.

There is evidence that Christians sang hymns and song refrains during Communion from the earliest days of Christianity. St. Augustine mentions that the singing of psalms during Communion processions was introduced in North Africa in his time.

In time, however, this ancient custom changed in the West, although Orthodox Christians have retained this custom to the present day. Many parts of the liturgy—gestures, actions, and prayers—were taken away from the people and placed with the clergy. Congregational singing, too, was given to the _scholas,_ which were choirs made up of men in minor orders.

The time has come to restore these elements to the churches in the West, so they may celebrate their faith in as many different ways as possible.

Serious obstacles can stand in the way of restoring congregational singing during Communion. The most common objection is that people "do not want to sing" because they perceive receiving Communion as a "private time." There is a lack of awareness among people, including many priests and liturgical musicians, that liturgical services are not private functions, but are celebrations of the church, which is the sacrament of unity. (This is stated in paragraph 26 of the _Constitution on the Sacred Liturgy._) The same document terms the Eucharist "a sacrament of love, a sign of unity, a bond of charity," and says: "Christ's faithful, when present at this mystery of faith, should not be there as strangers or silent spectators." The Mass is a public and social event, and failure to understand this must be dealt with through great patience, consideration, and education.

This does not mean, however, that we must wait for the whole church to understand that the Communion rite is not a private happening before we can introduce congregational singing at this time. Rather, Spirit-filled prayer, expressed in song, provides good liturgical prayer experiences that can do much to help people to accept the above truths.

The document _Music in Catholic Worship_ provides us with some guidelines for the reestablishment of congregational singing at Communion.

1. The Communion should foster a sense of unity. It should be simple and not demand great effort. In essence, we violate this principle many Sundays by asking our people to sing the wrong songs. We expect them to carry a hymnbook, watch where they are going, receive Communion in the hand while holding a hymnbook, and still sing a Communion hymn. This is patently impossible. Responsorial songs, in which a cantor or choir sings the verses while the people join in on a refrain, are the best types of music to use during Communion. The text should be short, not too long to remember, and the melody should be easy to sing. Whether the verses are sung by a cantor or choir, there should always be someone up front to bring in the congregation when it is their turn to sing.

2. The Communion gives expression to the joy of unity in the body of Christ and the fulfillment of the mystery being celebrated. Communion songs can do this best when they speak of praise and thanksgiving and are joyful in nature. No dirges here!

3. Most benediction hymns, by reason of their concentration on [private] adoration rather than on Communion, are not acceptable [during Communion].

4. In general, during the most important seasons of the church year (Easter, Lent, Christmas, and Advent) it is preferable that most songs used at the Communion be seasonal in nature. Finding good responsorial music which speaks of Communion in a congregational way and yet is also seasonal is often difficult to do. Sometimes the best we will be able to do is to use songs that fit the "sound" of a particular season. However, by studying the Communion antiphons in the Sacramentary, one can often obtain some help in choosing music to fit the season.

5. During the remainder of the church year, however, topical songs may be used during the Communion procession, providing these texts do not conflict with the paschal character of every Sunday.

Among the most appropriate texts for general Communion songs are some of the psalms. Lucien Deiss, in his *Spirit and Song of the New Liturgy,* lists a number of the Psalms that have eucharistic themes: Psalms 23, 34, 42, 43, 84, 104, 116, 128, 136 145, and 147 (common numbering). However, Marian hymns and patriotic songs certainly do not express the paschal mystery. Pastors and liturgical musicians would do well to correct these abuses immediately.

Although Communion music should begin when the priest and other ministers communicate, this does not necessarily mean that the congregational song must begin. We all know that there is an unavoidable awkwardness at the beginning of Communion, as people stand and turn and move forward. This is not at all conducive to singing. The liturgical musician should consider starting with a short choir piece or organ piece and begin the congregational song after the procession is well established.

Plan the music during Communion time as carefully as a recital program, balancing choir anthems with congregational songs and organ or other instrumental interludes. The congregational songs should be long enough to enhance the moment's unity. Avoid music that is too complicated or showy early in the procession as this can easily be distracting.

Avoid elaborate commentaries explaining why a song was chosen. If a song is sufficiently vague or strange as to require an explanation, then it should not be done at this time. Ministers of music should realize that while it is important for them to play, sing, and lead with skill, they are there to help the congregation pray, not to indulge in musical performances for an audience. "The Eucharist is (designed to promote) the unity of the Body of Christ, Christians loving Christ through loving one another" (*Ministries in Catholic Worship,* paragraph 48).

Each parish will need to explore the best time for the music ministers to receive Communion without disturbing the flow of the music. The choir or cantor might receive at the very beginning, while the organ is playing, or might elect to wait until the end, right before the period of silence.

It is important for liturgical musicians not to intrude in the silent time after Communion. Sacred silence is provided for not only in the *Constitution on the Sacred Liturgy,* but also in the revised Order of Mass. The Communion vessels may be set aside or returned to the sacristy to be purified later, so that the celebrant and other ministers can participate in the silence without interrupting the flow of the service.

We have only begun to touch the surface of human experience in prayer. Singing together is one central action which, when done in the context of the blessing, giving thanks, breaking and sharing food, has the capacity to elevate our human spirits and unite us with our Lord. We must care enough about this kind of prayer to try harder.

Helen Marie Hunt

257 • How to Select Hymns

The choosing of hymns relevant to worship requires thoughtful planning and creativity. Here are several principles of hymn selection and use that contribute to an enriched experience of worship.

Choosing music for the worship service is both a privilege and a challenge. The first step is the selection of hymns that reflect the assigned Scriptures. Hymns are the "propers" of the service, textual and musical selections that are appropriate to the scriptural message and to their place in the liturgical year. The first principle of hymn selection is relevance.

Hymn selection requires ongoing Bible study, a

thorough knowledge of the hymnal, and an appreciation of and commitment to the task. The process of hymn selection is made simpler for those using the *Common Lectionary* as the texts are then known in advance. In other cases, however, where the clergy customarily select texts for the service, consultation between the musician and clergy is absolutely essential.

Many hymns have phrases directly quoted from the Bible and their choice is obvious. Beyond that, the Scriptures will suggest certain major themes or topics and these should be reflected in the hymns. The process will be aided by a good commentary and dictionary of the Bible. The hymnal will probably contain useful appendices and indexes, and there are also separately published commentaries which are helpful. Even if your church does not use the *Common Lectionary,* published guides will help, though ingenuity will be required. Whatever aid these materials may give, there is, however, no substitute for the musician's own study and inspiration. The hymns for each service should not be a miscellany, and relying on a few quickly chosen "old favorites" results in something much less than satisfactory. Unifying the Scriptures and the music, however, produces a worship service of great emotional power.

Hymns should be chosen to allow maximum contrast. It is not wise to consistently program a loud and vigorous opening and closing hymn. The climax of the service, its emotional power, volume, etc., should be shifted occasionally so that those participating in worship are never able to give in to routine. Palm Sunday, for example, might begin with a big joyous hymn like "All Glory, Laud, and Honor," echoing the acclamation accorded Jesus' entrance into Jerusalem, and close with a solemn hymn performed softly in anticipation of the events of Holy Week, even omitting an organ postlude. Nearly every church uses a fairly predictable order of worship; this should not be an excuse for dull routine.

The character of the hymns in each service should be varied. Unison hymns, those in which the melody is the strength accompanied by an interesting organ part, should be mixed with those which are harmonic. Hymns of different metric character should be alternated; a hymn which is more free in meter-like chant might be contrasted with one in a regular duple or triple meter. It is best to avoid triple meter when a choir is processing, however. Narrative hymns, powerful hymns of praise, and prayerful hymns all need to be included in their appropriate place.

Usually all verses should be used so that the entire textual message is conveyed. In earlier times hymns often had a dozen or more verses but today hymnals limit most to four, five, or at times six. Occasionally it may make a telling effect to use only one or two verses. For example, for a hymn before the gospel there may be a portion of a hymn that is particularly relevant to the gospel text.

A pace that is perfunctory, whether routinely fast or slow, should be avoided. While many hymns should be vigorous, others should be measured and solemn. It is imperative to read the words and listen to the heart and let this be reflected in appropriate performance.

Avoiding routine with well-known hymns gives them new impact. The hymn "Holy, Holy, Holy" sung to the tune NICAEA is usually used as a vigorous processional. The text suggests, however, that it is really a prayer, and it will gain fresh impact if used softly at a reflective moment in the service. Conversely, a hymn that is usually sung in a meditative fashion may gain power through the use of a more full accompaniment. Every effort should be made to reexamine the character of the best-known hymns.

While it is not absolutely necessary, with familiar hymns the accompaniment might be varied, especially in the final verse. There are published varied accompaniments if the musician does not feel comfortable devising one. It might be effective occasionally to use a change of key at the end of a hymn verse, transposing up a half or full tone (using the transposition device on certain instruments or writing the hymn out in the new key if needed). The use of the piano, especially for hymns from the praise tradition, is perfectly proper and affords a good contrast.

It is well to plan on introducing new hymns often. The musician should, however, first thoroughly familiarize himself with the new text and music. A new hymn might be introduced with a brief rehearsal after the prelude, before the service. This moment also provides an opportunity for the musician to explain why the hymn is particularly suitable and provide information about the text and tune. It is then wise to repeat the new hymn again as soon as it is appropriate to the worship context. A record of when each hymn is used should be kept. Often it will take quite some time before it becomes familiar, especially for those people who do not attend regularly each Sunday.

Finally, the technique of leading hymns properly on the organ is not at all obvious and should be studied carefully. Since music for worship begins with the congregation, every effort should be expended on choosing the hymns carefully and leading them authoritatively.

Philip Peter

258 • How to Plan a Hymn Festival

A hymn festival is a worship service devoted especially to congregational singing. It is a type of service especially well suited to the celebration of important events in the Christian year and in the life of the congregation. This article provides information on how to plan a hymn festival for your congregation.

Planning a special service for your church community? Consider a hymn festival, a blending of song and readings, often from Scripture, that appeals to people of all ages.

The apostle Paul urged the people of Ephesus to sing the words and tunes of the psalms and hymns when they were together, and to go on singing and chanting to the Lord in their hearts, "always giving thanks to God the Father for everything, in the name of our Lord Jesus Christ" (Eph. 5:20).

The hymn festival is an excellent framework for responding to Paul's advice—gathering with other Christians to sing praises to the Creator.

Why a Hymn Festival?

The hymn-festival format is wonderfully flexible and elastic. It can be organized to challenge the gifts of a cathedral-sized congregation or structured to meet the needs of the twenty families who gather in an inner-city chapel. A hymn festival can involve the leadership of only two people (minister and musician) or many people (choirs, readers, vocal and instrumental soloists).

Basically, a hymn festival is a worship service in which most of the service is music. Usually such festivals are constructed around a single theme to add unity and meaning to the service. Themes might include hymns on the work of Christ, hymns on the work of the Holy Spirit, hymns on one of the church seasons (e.g., Advent, Lent), or hymns of one particular hymn writer. Since it is generally better to

leave people wanting more than to supersaturate them, hymn festivals should generally not exceed an hour and a quarter.

Forming the Festival

Choosing the theme should be the planning committee's top priority. After they have agreed on a unifying concept, the group should either look for a published hymn festival on this subject or begin to carefully study hymn texts, select appropriate hymn texts and Scripture, and add litanies, prayers and other parts of the liturgy that will unify the whole with a common message and purpose. The next priority should be choosing a variety of ways in which members of the congregation will interpret the hymns. Consider the following possibilities, all of which have been used with success by other congregations:

Use a Concertato. The catalogues of Augsburg, GIA, Hope, Coronet/Presser, and Concordia all contain numerous hymn settings that involve instruments, congregations, and a variety of choir voicings.

Highlight Individual Stanzas by having them read in unison instead of sung, sung by a soloist, sung by a choir, interpreted by the organist or another instrumentalist, sung by men or women alone, sung a cappella, sung as a canon, interpreted by movement and/or drama, or accompanied by descants/ instrumental obbligatos over the melody.

Use Varied Introductions and Some Interludes to set the mood of the hymn or to bridge from a prayerful, introspective stanza to one of festive acclamation (or vice versa).

Have the Choir Sing a Hymn-Anthem to give the congregation a break.

When selecting hymns for the festival be sure to use a combination of favorite hymns in conjunction with newer, less familiar hymns. If you want to avoid the "congregational rehearsal" often held at the beginning of such a festival, have soloists or choirs sing through two or three stanzas of an unfamiliar hymn before inviting the congregation to join in. As the adage goes, "We like what we understand, and we understand what we like."

Whether you come from a large or small congregation, be sure to involve as many people as possible. Include readers, choirs, instrumentalists, and soloists. Use rhythm instruments, handbells, strings, woodwinds, and guitar. If possible invite brass players from a local high school to join in with fanfares, or ask community performing groups to add festive descants. The more people you involve, the better your support and attendance are likely to be.

And remember, when considering which members of your congregation have talents to offer to the hymn festival, don't call only on musicians and good speakers. Consider the talents of business people, men and women whose knowledge of publicity (the local newspaper) and printing (programs, posters, and brochures) can be of great assistance. Use the artistic talents of members to design program covers, posters, and banners for the hymn event. Ask retired members to address notices and telephone each member of the congregation with a personal invitation; have them arrange carpools for members who are unable to drive. And seek out recording buffs to tape the festival for those who were unable to attend or would like to relive the festival and "continue singing."

Planning Countdown

Planning a hymn festival takes time—about three months is reasonable. It's very important that all key participants in the festival are comfortable with the flow of the program. All instrumentalists should rehearse in the room to get a feel for the acoustics and the ensemble balance. The choirs should be very familiar with all the texts so that they can assist the congregation. All readers should be familiar with their texts and should be given time to work with the amplification system. If everyone understands and is comfortable with these intricate details, the pace of the festival will be relaxed and poised and will proceed with confidence and great success.

Finally, as Dr. Paul Manz suggests, make your hymn event a "Te Deum" (the Latin title of the hymn "We Praise You, O God") and not a "tedium!" Careful planning and your own personal enthusiasm have much to do with the success of the program. The most wonderful hymn services and festivals are the result of thoughtful, conscientious effort.

Sue Mitchell Wallace[35]

259 • CONCERNS ABOUT COPYRIGHT

Music for worship, like any other music, is copyrighted material and must be used with the proper consent of the composer and text-writer. This article answers many of the questions concerning the copyright law.

Those of us who are concerned about the function and use of music in the life of a church need a basic understanding of the copyright if we are to do our job properly. The responsibility for the selection of hymns, anthems, and the other music used in public worship goes beyond that simple act. As worship leaders we must authorize or provide the books or the sheets from which the song is sung.

Many honest, God-fearing people presume that the copyright law is so unfathomable that they close their eyes on the problem. After all, they reason, they work twelve hours a day, seven days a week, and still cannot tend to all the problems that need their attention. If someone in the parish runs off a few copies of a hymn they wish to sing on Sunday— why not? If the soloist arrives with her only copy of Malotte's "Lord's Prayer," why would anyone object if the organist runs off a copy to use at the console? If the church school class would like to use the Avery and Marsh doxology the following week, why not? Would they not love to have their hymn sung?

This is not meant to be facetious or to indict the whole of Christendom. All of us have experienced similar examples, and a better understanding of the copyright law and permission policies of publishers can help your church operate within the law without having to resort to something illegal.

First let us look at what copyright is and is not. Then we shall get more specific as to what is legal and what is not, and what you can do in the future to be sure that you observe the copyright laws, and by so doing, protect the rights of others.

What Is Copyright?

The framers of the Constitution established copyright as the principal legal tool for ensuring that creators have first and primary rights to exploit their works. In 1790, the first U.S. Copyright Law was enacted. This provided for 14 years of protection with a 14 year renewal term. There have been several major revisions of the copyright laws since then, two of which occurred in this century. On January 1, 1978, the Copyright Act of 1976 (Title 17 of the U.S. Code) Public Law 94-553 came into effect. This general revision of the copyright law took two decades to accomplish and was the first such revision since 1909.

Basically the old law crumbled before the onslaught of technology. Even the new law is sadly deficient in several areas. The problem of videotaping television programs for private use was a matter that the Supreme Court just recently sent back to Congress, saying in effect, your law is silent in this matter. Therefore home taping is legal until the law says otherwise.

You composers will be interested to learn that any work created after January 1, 1978, is your property when you raise your pen for the final time. You now have a fixed work and, for all practical purposes, copyright has already commenced. Be sure to add a notice that contains three elements to the bottom of the page. The first element is the © symbol for the word copyright. The second states the year and the third item is your name. The notice should, therefore, read as follows: © 1984 by Jane Doe

Nothing else needs to be done until after the work is published. At that time two copies of the first edition should be submitted to the Library of Congress with a Form PA and a $10.00 fee. Forms and additional information may be obtained from the Register of Copyrights, Library of Congress, Washington, D.C. 20559.

Duration of a Copyright

The most dramatic change in the new law is the method of figuring the duration of a copyright. The renewal period has been scrapped and we have adopted the British system of life of the author plus an additional 50 years of protection after the author's death. In the case of a joint work prepared by two or more authors, the term lasts for 50 years after the last surviving author's death. Works copyrighted prior to 1978 continue under the provisions of the old law in that they will have a 28 year original term and a 47 year renewal term for a total of 75 years of protection. This means that all songs written in 1909 will go into the public domain on January 1, 1985. Anything originally copyrighted prior to 1909 is already in the public domain and may be used by anyone in any way they wish without obtaining permission from anyone.

Fair Use of Copyright

The new law also adds a provision of the statute specifically recognizing the principle of "fair use" as a limitation on the exclusive rights of copyright owners. Fair use is basically a doctrine of reason. To me it says: use your own common sense. Some of the highlights of this section include

A teacher may make a single copy of

1. A chapter from a book.
2. An article from a magazine or newspaper.
3. A short story, cartoon, or picture from a book.
4. A short excerpt (up to 10 percent) from a performable unit of music such as a song movement or section for study purposes.

A teacher in a classroom may make multiple copies for classroom use only of

1. A complete poem if less than 250 words.
2. A story, essay, or article if less than 2500 words.
3. One illustration, chart, diagram, graph, drawing or cartoon per book or periodical.
4. Up to 10 percent of a performable unit of music (song, movement, section) for academic purpose other than performance.
5. A single recording of student performances.
6. An emergency replacement copy to substitute for a purchased copy that is not available for an imminent musical performance.
7. Opaque projectors in a classroom situation.

However the law does not permit the making of a transparency. Also spelled out are guidelines which teachers may not do. These include

1. Copies to replace anthologies or compilations to substitute or replace them.
2. Copies from works intended to be consumable.
3. Copies to substitute for purchase of books, periodicals, music or recordings.
4. Copy music or lyrics for performances in or outside the classroom, with the emergency provision noted earlier.

Let us now turn from this short and general discussion of the new copyright law to more specific questions concerning the use of music in the church.

- May I make copies of a public domain hymn from our hymnal?
- May I make copies of a public domain hymn from someone else's hymnal?

- May I make copies of an anthem already ordered but not received in time for the performance if I destroy them when the ordered copies arrive?
- May I print the words to an anthem in the bulletin if copies have been purchased for the choir?

The answer to all of the above questions is YES. The words of an anthem in the bulletin technically does require permission, but I know of no publisher who would charge for this and all with whom I have spoken encourage the practice.

Printing the words to a copyrighted hymn in the bulletin for use by the congregation is, of course, a different story and does require permission. Most such permissions can be obtained with a note or a phone call and the fees required usually are minimal.

Finally, what should I do if the church or school in which I work is guilty of negligence in some of these areas? Usually a gentle reminder is all that is necessary. There are very few who flagrantly break the copyright laws and flaunt such conduct. Copyright owners do, from time to time, receive letters with copies of illegally produced products from guilt-ridden church members who know better.

Such cases are often referred to attorneys for settlement. It is surprising how quickly illegally reproduced copies disappear the day after a registered letter from a law firm is received.

Those desiring further help with a copyright problem should seek help from the publisher involved. They might also consult a local copyright attorney and obtain a free copy of the new statute by writing directly to:

Copyright Office
Library of Congress
Washington, DC 20559

requesting a copy of Title 17—Copyrights—Public Law 94-553—October 19, 1976.

It should be remembered that copyright is a legally granted property right. It should be respected just as we respect the rights of others. The copyright owner, by contract, is probably acting as the representative of the author and/or composer, many of whom depend for their livelihood on their musical, God-given gifts.

George Shorney[36]

NINE

Music Leadership in Worship

Music is such a powerful force because it is created and recreated in the midst of a group of people who join together to express common thoughts, emotions, and prayers. In addition to careful planning, the use of music in worship requires skilled and sensitive musical leadership. The persons who fill this role should be both trained and well-rehearsed musicians, able to lend confidence to the singing of all worshipers and also spiritual leaders in the community, able to lead in worship by example. The following articles use these twin ideals to describe the various ministries of musical leadership in the church, including the roles of the music director, composer, cantor, and choir.

260 • PERSPECTIVES ON MUSICAL LEADERSHIP IN THE CHURCH

Musical leadership is a great challenge, with musical and pastoral demands. It is also a great privilege, with opportunities to celebrate the gospel and work among God's people. This article describes the practical life of the church musician in terms of these challenges and privileges.

Church musicians are all too typically regarded as those who sustain the church by providing musical services. This view has them responsible for creating fellowship and good feeling in the congregation—dispensing services that keep everybody happy, entertaining the troops, and giving everybody warm fuzzies.

This job description creates two intolerable tensions. First, if a congregation is even in the remotest sense Christian and not totally a reflection of the culture, its church musicians feel the gnawing sense that simply meeting people's needs is wrong. Church musicians are not trained to be theologians so they cannot always articulate this feeling, but it is there and it can be downright painful.

The second tension comes from the pressure of trying to satisfy the desires of everybody in the congregation. It can be difficult to try to meet what are often competing demands: some people want gospel hymns, some want rock, some want Lutheran chorales. Still others don't want to sing at all and expect the choir to do it. Some want the choir to sing sixteenth-century motets, others want it to sing only nineteenth-century music. One group wants nonsexist texts when referring to humanity; others want non-sexist terms for both humanity and God; others insist one should never alter the original text. The musician is supposed to meet all those requests. The musician is not expected, however, to think, make judgments, ask questions, or have a dialogue with anybody. The congregation wants the musician simply to satisfy its wants, no matter how contradictory and confusing those may be.

Defined this way, the life of a church musician is a nightmare indeed. Musicians in this situation not only sense that something is wrong at the heart of things, but that they can never do anything right. They do not know what to plan and practice, or what demands to heed. They receive no direction except for the worst sort of consumerism. This makes them always look over their shoulders, worried that they did something wrong or that one group will be offended when another faction gets its way. Ultimately, what Stanley Hauerwas and William Willimon refer to as the "voracious appetites" of demanding people can devour the musician. So, to avoid being devoured, musicians seek to manipulate tastes and needs. Some use commercial television as a model, offering cute and contrived jingles (I have heard these called "teeny hymns"). Others push for high taste or for their personal tastes. These approaches inevitably lead to frustration because they focus on power. The musician's work gets reduced either to obvious power plays and outright war or to subtle forms of control, which are the antithesis of freedom.

I cannot begin to count the number of church

musicians who have told me about the despair they have experienced in churches where they are regarded merely as need-fillers. Not all have articulated the problem in just this way, but it is suggested in many of their comments. Many of these musicians have continued to struggle in spite of the problems because of their grit, determination, and sense of faithfulness; many have switched churches; too many of them have left their musical posts altogether. The most tragic result is that countless young people who have sensed the despair of the musicians in their churches have never considered a career in church music even though in other respects it appeals to them.

There is an alternative to this situation, an alternative that can emerge when the church affirms some fundamental aspects of the faith. First, the church must acknowledge that it is not sustained by the services it provides or by anything it does. As the community of the baptized, the church is sustained by God's grace. God creates the church, and God will sustain the church—with us, without us, and in spite of us. Our continual errors are eloquent enough testimony to that. If the church were supported only by human efforts, it would have disappeared long ago. So let us keep our priorities straight: the place to begin is with baptism; God's grace drives and sustains the church and our works, not the other way around.

Second, if the church is attentive to the New Testament, Justin Martyr and Hippolytus, the Eastern church, the Western Catholic tradition, the Anglican tradition, the Lutheran tradition, the Calvinist intent (and practice, if not in Geneva then in places like John Robinson's Leiden), the Wesleyan intent and that of the early Methodists, then its worship on every festival of the Resurrection—that is, on every Sunday—will include both Word and Supper, not one or the other. Our Protestant heritage has gotten derailed in the last several centuries. We have legitimately objected to the medieval practice of celebrating the Supper without the Word, which is a replication of the Old Testament practice of sacrifice. But we have substituted Word without Supper, which is a replication of synagogue worship minus the joy of the Resurrection. If we are serious about our worship and our responsibility as worshiping Christians, we will be faithful to Christ's command and to our heritage by celebrating Word and Supper every week.

While worship seems to be what we do, it is actu-

ally what God does. It looks like our praises, our prayers, our words, our bread and wine, but it is really God addressing us in our weak human words and giving us life in the messianic banquet. It looks as if God is our audience, but we are the audience and the object of God's grace, love, and care. That is true at all times and all places, of course, but in our worship it is uniquely and profoundly so.

Worship belongs to the people. It is not the sole property of the clergy, the musician, or any other church leader. The Reformation taught us that worship is not the precinct of the priests. We Protestants forget that and deny it every time we shut the people out and turn worship into entertainment by clergy or musicians before silent congregations. Worship belongs to the whole people of God, not to any individual or group.

Worship is profoundly related to both the past and the present. We did not invent it. Virtually all people have worshiped. For us Christians worship is derived from Hebrew sources, radically controlled by the Christ event and edited by the church from generation to generation. Worship is also profoundly contemporary. It relates precisely to the here and now and flows into our culture in the most priestly way while at the time bringing to bear on us the prophetic demands of justice and peace. For in worship God always calls us to a radically new and responsible life together. Worship is probably the most powerful engine for justice and peace because in it God's call, which stands behind and before us, cannot be denied, will not let us rest and drives us into the world on behalf of the downtrodden and the oppressed.

All of this means that worship has a rhythm about it that is bigger than our individual rhythms. It relates to a story that is far larger than our individual stories, even as it encompasses those stories. To sense the big rhythm and the big story we need to be attentive to the church year and the lectionary. They protect us from being confined in out pet likes and dislikes.

What is the role, then, of church musicians? They are fundamentally responsible for the people's song, the church's song. That's why the term _cantor_ is so helpful in describing the church musician. Church musicians are the chief singers, the leaders of the church's song. They are responsible for singing the congregation's whole story. That means knowing the local stories and traditions of the particular parish they serve, and it also means relating those local stories to the catholic fullness of the whole story, and doing that with pastoral sensitivity.

If these affirmations are correct, then the church musician's practical life grows out of the nature of the church. It is driven by the grace of God, not by our sinful needs. This view resolves some of the conflict church musicians so often sense, for it defines the church musician's duties by the logic of the community he or she serves, not by the claims of the surrounding culture. It also provides a sense of direction. With this understanding, musicians do not have to look over their shoulders, wondering if one or another group is satisfied. Nor will they try to manipulate taste or people. They should and can operate in freedom and with purpose.

This purpose might be described under five headings: Sunday morning worship, the church year, planning, practice, and relationships.

1. The Practical Life of the Church Musician Is Controlled above All by Sunday Morning. Each Sunday is a little Easter, the celebrating of the Resurrection and the time therefore for Word and Supper. The pastor, on behalf of the host who is Christ himself, serves in Christ's stead. The musician leads the people's song at this banquet. So, at the appropriate points—and there are many—the pastor relinquishes leadership to the musician. Church music has the capacity to give something of the fullness of the people's song each Sunday because it can put into context and pull together themes through the richness of poetic and musical imagery in a way that the spoken word cannot.

2. There Is No Way to Sing the Fullness of the Story on Any Given Sunday Morning. The only way to sing the fullness of the Christian story is over many Sunday mornings. Since we are all tempted to sing only our favorite parts of the story, we need some way to protect the people and to protect us from ourselves. The church year gives us that way. Over a year's time we recount Christ's advent, birth, epiphany, passion, death, resurrection, and ascension; then we celebrate the church's birth at Pentecost and reflect on the results of our life together and in the world. In the three-year ecumenical lectionary we get the richness of *lectio continua* and *lectio selecta*. (It is tragic that these readings do not always coincide among denominations. That not only destroys their purpose and makes denominational and

ecumenical resources less useful, but it also prevents opportunities for interaction in marriages and families whose members represent different traditions and attend different churches.)

Unfortunately, church musicians often merely go through the motions of Sunday mornings and the festivals of the church year without sensing their order and relationship and without drawing on their tremendous potential. The weekly festival of the Resurrection and the celebrations of the church year are the fecund soil from which the craft of the church musician grows. We need to see these festivals for what they are and for the discipline and tremendous aid and direction they provide.

3. Observing the Church Calendar Requires Planning and Practice. Both need to be structured into the musician's routine because they are among the most critical things that happen in a local church. While no one formula will work in all churches, planning has to involve both pastor and musician. Otherwise the confusion that characterizes worship in so many churches is inevitable. It is possible to assign most of the planning to one person; if both agree on that arrangement, trust each other, and the planner communicates instructions to the other, that approach can work. It is possible to assign responsibilities and then meet briefly, even by phone, to make sure there is coherence. That too will work if both parties agree on the system, trust each other, have a common sense of direction and know each other well.

My preference, however, is for weekly meetings at which pastor and musician plan together and for regular planning meetings held weekly, monthly or seasonally with lay people. Since worship is communal, to plan it alone always seems to miss the mark, no matter how able one person is. The planning needs to reflect the communal nature of what is being planned.

There should be a discipline to this process. Nobody gets to choose his or her own few favorite hymns. Hymns have to fit the occasion. What we do has to make sense for the people of God in Chicago or New York or Springfield or wherever we are, in the late twentieth century, with the themes of Pentecost VI or Advent I or whatever the occasion is, with all the resources that are available to us within the confines of our capabilities: old hymns, new hymns, music from various periods and of various styles, old translations, new translations, the same and different ways of doing things, and so on.

4. For Musicians to Do Their Jobs, They Must Practice. Not to practice is to regard the people with contempt. Musicians must practice far enough ahead so things are ready when they need to be, and they must practice up to the last moment so that they will be fresh for the service.

This is difficult, particularly for those whose positions are part-time. While full-time church musicians find their hours consumed by paper work and phony administrative duties (not the legitimate ones), part-timers have a more difficult time finding practice time because they usually also hold full-time jobs and are tired at the end of the day.

There is no single solution, but it is possible to work practice into our days. It takes some imagination and some discipline, like the organist spending a few minutes every day at a piano keyboard and reserving certain times of the week, like Saturday mornings, for practice at the church. For the choral conductor, time with a score at a desk on a lunch break is possible, along with time later at a keyboard. The singer simply has to find times and places to sing: sometimes in the car, with the windows rolled up, on the way to and from work will do nicely. If we do not practice, we render our planning useless and deny our vocation.

5. Underneath All This Is the Church Musician's Relationship with Parishioners and with God. Because church musicians operate within a community of grace that is sustained by God, they do not have to try to manipulate people or their tastes. The musician is free to take risks, to fail and succeed, because sustenance is not the musician's concern; faithfully singing the song with the people is. That means knowing the big story, knowing the people's stories and their capacities, and then serving them with care.

Like all worthy crafts people, church musicians have their own disciplined inner peace. But that peace is not generated simply by the craft of church music. The practical life of the church musician is the outcome of a vocation—a calling—that serves God and the people of God with the unique gift of music.

Paul Westermeyer[37]

261 • COMPOSING MUSIC FOR WORSHIP

Excellence is not a negotiable quality for church music: our worship of God demands our very best. This premise extends to the complex art of composing music for use in worship. This article outlines liturgical, textual, and musical guidelines for composers who seek excellence in composing music for the church.

Quality music for the church is a little like a "good Christian chair." If such an entity as a good Christian chair existed, it would first of all be a well-designed, well-built chair; a cross carved into its back would not, by itself, make it "good". The analogy breaks down fairly quickly but perhaps serves to clarify what, for me, is a basic premise: church music of quality is first of all music of quality: compositionally solid, well-crafted, written with an understanding of the performing medium. Sincerity and zeal, while desirable, cannot substitute for well-honed compositional skills and a well-developed musical imagination.

But the modifier *church* does add another dimension—that of function—to the definition and to any assessment of quality. Music is indeed a gift of God, to be enjoyed for its own intrinsic values; but music in worship is neither concert nor entertainment. Church music properly functions to assist and support the congregation in worship. (The congregation includes choirs, organists, and other musical leaders, as well as those who "sit in the pew.") In this capacity, it assists and supports most effectively when it relates to other aspects of worship on a particular day. The most tangible connection between music and worship themes is, of course, text. When a music text, whether congregational song, choral response, or anthem, relates to other texts for the day, its potential for supporting, enriching, and enlivening worship is greatly increased. Even instrumental music, if hymn-based, can relate via text, especially if the hymn tune is a familiar one.

A good text, like good music, has integrity. Texts selected for church music should have theological grounding; they should be well-written and, whether Biblical or non-biblical, they should help the listener understand and relate to theological truths. A general, all-purpose text, such as "sing, sing, sing and rejoice," will seldom move anyone to "a more profound Alleluia" (F. Pratt Green, "When in Our Music God is Glorified," stanza 2, Oxford University Press). To borrow an analogy from C. S.

Lewis: A general anthem is "like a hall out of which doors open into several rooms. . . . [While a hallway is all right for waiting], it is in the rooms, not in the hall, that there are fires and chairs and meals" (C. S. Lewis, *Mere Christianity* [New York: Macmillan, 1981], xliv). Lewis was here describing general, nondenominational Christianity. Texts that warm the spirit, or rest it or feed it, will usually be created "in the rooms."

A text will reach more listeners if its language is up-to-date and inclusive. Use of the generic "he" and words like "whither" and "mayest" promotes the notion that the church is out of touch with reality, ready to be filed on the shelf as historical reference material. A number of excellent contemporary poets are writing new and vibrant texts for the church. Composers might also look for—or create, if they have the skill—up-to-date translations of older texts. Some favorite old texts are mediocre English translations of old-fashioned German translations of Latin paraphrases of original Hebrew! The original meaning is often compromised when filtered through so many layers.

Not only do the music and text need to have integrity: the two together must have integrity. "Amazing Grace," for instance, simply doesn't sing well to the tune of "Joy to the World" (ANTIOCH), even though it has the right number of syllables in each line. In setting a text, a composer must be sensitive to everything the text conveys and seek ways in which the music can convey, non-verbally, the same message. The joint integrity of text and music is fragile and sometimes difficult to balance. While imagination is vital to the creation of good church music, cleverness is an attribute to be applied sparingly. In the same way that a witty story can upstage the focus of a sermon, musical cleverness can easily overshadow the idea it is intended to illuminate. When it is the composer's ingenuity that is remembered and not the message of the text, the composer has done a disservice to both the text and the listener.

Church music exists in a world of nonprofessional musicians and short rehearsals. A composer can gain valuable insights by observing, or participating in, actual rehearsals. It becomes clear, for example, how much rehearsal time is saved and uncertainty averted when tempos, mood, dynamics, and hoped-for subtleties are indicated in the score. "Gently moving" (=84) will convey much more than simply "Moderato." The musicians may have

ideas to contribute but should not have to guess at the composer's intentions.

A typical church choir rehearses once a week, perhaps for an hour, often at a time when voices, minds, and bodies are tired. This does not mean that the singers enjoy learning banal music. On the contrary, many church choir singers have an artistic and spiritual sensitivity that makes them highly responsive to the power of theology in music, and they often bring to their music-making a depth of personal commitment almost unknown in professional circles. To write artistically and imaginatively for non-professional musicians, inspiring their sensitivity and commitment, is indeed an exciting challenge.

Excellent writing for non-professional singers— whether congregation, choir or soloist—begins with, and is very nearly encompassed in, good vocal writing. The distinctions between writing for trained and untrained voices, or adult and children's voices, are shades of the same color when compared to the distinctions between writing for voices and writing for instruments. An understanding of the human voice—the original, natural instrument—informs and enlightens the whole compositional process.

Singers live their musical lives melodically even when they are not singing the melody. Lacking visual or tactile reference points on their instruments, they find pitches principally by relating them to a previously sung pitch. While all performers enjoy a melody, singers "need" them. A melodic line that has no horizontal logic—that moves, for instance, from F to B to E♭ to G♯ to C—will not sing well, regardless of its context or the amount of rehearsal time devoted to it. A good vocal melody will move logically and gracefully from note to note and will give the singer time to breathe without gasping. The principals of good part-writing apply to vocal writing with a particular urgency, since going against the grain usually violates melodic principles as well as harmonic ones.

It is generally understood that singing ranges are more limited than most instrumental ranges; but even more than range, it is tessitura—the area where a large share of the notes lie—that makes passages singable or awkward. An awkward tessitura may be one that lies very high or very low for long stretches, or one that consistently sits at the vocal "break": the point at which singers adjust between their two "voices," head voice and chest voice. The very existence of text, which is so important in church music, creates complications that instrumentalists never experience. The ease with which a given pitch is sung may relate as much to the vowels and consonants of the word as to the pitch itself; and the way in which the note is approached melodically will also affect its singability. A phrase like "Despair engulfs earth's frame" (Norman O. Forness, "Rise Up, O Saints of God!," stanza 2, _Lutheran Book of Worship_, 1978) combines consonants in a way that is extremely disruptive of the musical line; singing the phrase quickly would be impossible. Generally the music should allow the text to flow as naturally as possible, with important words highlighted by length and rhythmic placement within the phrase.

Vocal intonation is affected by many factors, including tone production, tessitura, and simply not hearing where the next note should sound. While a clarinetist may play one note out of tune and be back in tune on the next, a singer, relying on each pitch as a guide to the next, loses that point of reference after singing a note out of tune. Even repeated notes with a changing text, as in a vocal pedal point, are difficult to sing in tune, since vowel changes can affect the pitch. Once again, a melodic line that is logical and graceful, easy to sing, will help singers achieve good intonation naturally.

In writing for instruments in the church, composers do need to be aware of the differences between experienced and inexperienced players. In many published instrumental settings, the music is not too difficult per se but too difficult to be performed reliably by inexperienced players without repeated rehearsals over a long period of time. A high school trumpeter, for instance, may be able to perform a high A (B on the instrument) in a school band concert, after practicing the piece three times a week for six weeks, but may not be able to negotiate the same note reliably in a hymn setting on Sunday, after only two rehearsals. Inexperienced instrumentalists respond similarly to music in a difficult key. The key of D major, for instance, which is simple for singers and C instruments, requires trumpeters to play in the key of E, with four sharps, a much more difficult key. The result may be on-the-spot lapsed memory, even if the trumpeter can play the notes correctly in scale warm-ups at school. Rhythms that are unnecessarily complicated will also cause problems for inexperienced players.

Quality is not defined by complexity, and music

for the church need not be music for posterity. A unique contribution is made by the composer who composes for a specific tenor section that has a range of five good notes, a specific children's choir that is just learning to sing in parts, or a specific young trombonist who is wearing braces. Nonprofessional musicians, when singing or playing music they can handle with confidence, can contribute immeasurably to worship. Theirs is an extraordinary gift, worthy of a composer's finest efforts.

One of the most controversial topics in the church today is style, and music—rightly or wrongly—appears to be at the center of the debate. While no musical style is intrinsically appropriate or inappropriate for worship, styles carry with them strong associations. The musical style itself may not be problematic, but the association—for instance, with promotion of violence or chemical abuse— may be. In each generation composers must find their own musical and personal integrity and write in a style consistent with that integrity. And the finest music from each period and style will continue to transcend century and place, enriching the communion of saints across time, denominations, races, and cultures.

Carolyn Jennings

262 • THE ART OF ORGAN LEADERSHIP OF CONGREGATIONAL SONG

Accompanying congregational singing is an extraordinary challenge, requiring careful practice and disciplined creativity. The following article outlines many of the musical matters that every organist must consider, along with suggestions for the creative interpretation of the texts that are sung.

The organist can be a catalyst, an energizer, for congregational song. Where one finds a good organ and sensitive leadership, things can and do happen. The organ works well as a medium for inspiring congregational song, surrounding the assembly with sound. This sound need not be overbearing or excessively loud, rather, it should be rich, full, and warm, assisting the singer to feel encouraged to participate. The organ supports and undergirds the singer with its sound, thus diminishing their feeling of being alone. Of course, other instruments can work well too, but the organ is unique in that one player can produce enough quality, range, and variety of sound to lead a large congregation. To be a good leader of song at the organ, three qualities are essential: the organist must be trustworthy and predictable, the organist must be sensitive to interact with other leaders of the assembly, and the organist must lead in creative ways. Let us take a look at each of these considerations.

Musical Trustworthiness

First, the congregation must trust the organist. As Robert Batastini writes, "The *last* thing the average congregant wants to do is sing a solo." If the organist is unstable rhythmically, if the organist is timid, or if the organist is unpredictable, members of the congregation will withdraw; they will be subconsciously afraid to participate fully for fear they will be left alone, singing a solo. Thus the major considerations for the organist become: (1) rhythmical and metrical stability, (2) control and accuracy of notes, and (3) sensitivity to the needs of the singers in such areas as tempo and key.

The organist must strive to achieve rhythmical and metrical stability. Each musical selection for a given service needs to be examined to determine the appropriate metrical feel and tempo. This decision is made by *singing,* not playing, the selection since we are concerned with song. Often a selection notated with a meter signature of 4/4 really moves and feels as if it were 2/2. In other words, the half note is the real energizer of the music. If the piece is played feeling the half note, the music has a better flow and feel of forward momentum. If the piece is played feeling the quarter note, the music often seems to drag. Many times, pieces in 3/4 should be felt in one beat per measure. An example of a 3/4 tune that works in one is "Holy God, We Praise Thy Name" to the tune GROSSER GOTT. Examples in 4/4 that move in two include "O God, Our Help" (ST. ANNE) or "Joyful, Joyful, We Adore You" (HYMN TO JOY). This feel of a larger unit of measure as energizing pulse does not imply that a piece should go faster. Rather, it means that the music will take on greater energy and vitality; it will have forward momentum. This momentum will draw the congregant into more vigorous participation.

Once this concept of the energizing pulse as a larger value is established, one must then work on rhythmical and metrical control and stability. Notes must be given correct value, tempo must be stable, pitches of a given vertical sonority must sound together. All of these things seem so obvious, yet will

not happen without careful, meticulous practice. At workshops in hymn playing, I often play a hymn for us to sing, shortening last notes of a phrase, rushing or delaying the start of a next phrase, missing a few pedal notes, playing vertical sonorities a bit out of line or not maintaining a stable tempo. We all agree (after a good laugh) that our first and intuitive reactions as singers was *withdrawal*. My inconsistent playing did not lend confidence, and as a result, we didn't want to sing. After all, who wants to follow a leader who communicates a confused lack of direction?

The matter of breathing, both within stanzas and between stanzas of a hymn, is of great importance. Organs can go on and on; people need to breathe. As much as possible, breathing should be within the metrical structure of the song. For example, in a phrase ending with a half note, this note is shortened to allow time to breathe, the next phrase beginning on the beat and in time. Usually, this shortening should be done rhythmically. In other words, a half note would become a quarter note with a quarter rest to breathe.

In the case of strophic compositions—including most hymns—think of each stanza as a related but independent musical entity. Play to the end of the stanza, perhaps broadening just a little bit, hold the last chord full written value, stop, breathe in the tempo of the tune, and begin the next stanza. It is dangerous to generalize about these things, but this is the basic strategy I pursue. While I believe in maintaining a stable tempo, there are some tunes that demand the addition of a bit of time at certain spots to give room for a breath. Other tunes demand a subtle bit of rubato to make them sing well. Yet, these are exceptions to the basic principle that stability of tempo is essential. Perhaps the single greatest reason that these ideas work for me is that I try to be consistent in applying them. When the organist is predictable, the congregant begins to trust the organist, relaxes, and enters into the singing. Consistency is the most important single consideration.

Another thing to consider is the treatment of repeated notes. Vocal music with many repeated pitches is a challenge to play well at the organ. Many hymns written in four-part vocal style, especially nineteenth-century tunes like HYMN TO JOY ("Joyful, Joyful") or AURELIA ("The Church's One Foundation," or "O Christ the Great Foundation") have many repeated chords. Of course, the melody must be played exactly as written. The other voices, especially the bass, benefit from selective repeating of the pitches, lifting before strong beats. For example, if one considers a 4/4 melody as moving in units of half notes, then repeated notes in the lower voices would be tied together and played as half notes.

My great emphasis on stability and control does not mean to imply that I advocate inflexibility in leading congregational song. Predictability and consistency should be tempered by a sensitivity to the needs of the congregation as well as the character of the music to be sung. Choice of tempo is influenced by text and melodic structure of tune as well as by size of the congregation. The text plays a large role in determining appropriate tempo; singers need time to encounter the text, not just mouth words. The melodic contours of a tune may suggest that a slower or faster tempo would work better. While it is true that large congregations cannot move as rapidly as a chamber choir, they do not need to drag through music which begs for vitality. "Joy to the World" (ANTIOCH) can be sung briskly by an assembly of 4,000 (I've experienced it), but the rapid tempo cannot be as fast as 16 professional singers could use. More time will be needed by the larger assembly for breathing.

Sensitivity to the needs of the congregation also includes choice of key. Some tunes have a very wide range and must not be played in a key too high. Some tunes have a smaller range but the tessitura is high or low and could influence choice of key. People can sing higher with great ease later in the day, so I might play the same tune lower at 8:00 A.M., higher at 11:00 A.M. In general, I do not advocate transposing melodies radically lower (down a third) and in some more recent hymnals would transpose them back up, closer to the keys in which they were originally written. A few hymnal editors have transposed some tunes too low and some new tunes have been notated too low. The best part of our voice, the most vibrant part, is not at the bottom of our tessitura. We must encourage our congregants to relax and discover their entire vocal range by selecting keys that encourage using the most resonant part of their voice.

Teamwork

Even after we have learned how to play hymns well, how to lead well, there is more to do. We must consider our relationship to the other leaders of worship. Organists need to understand their leadership role and dialogue with other leaders in worship

to be sure that all comprehend their differing responsibilities. Then we will be much less likely to send confusing signals to the congregation. When the singing of a song leader or cantor of the hymn competes with the organ sound or dominates the sound of congregation and organ, the congregants become confused and withdraw from participation. Things don't go well when it is unclear who is leading. The congregation needs to sense and see a logical sharing of leadership depending upon what is happening in the liturgy. The cantor, song leader, or minister must move away from the microphone during congregational song. If this is not possible, the cantor must mouth the words without singing the congregant's part so the confusion of the two leadership sources is removed.

Another dimension of shared leadership is advanced planning and practice so that each leader has sufficient time to prepare and is comfortable in shared situations. The organist needs to practice each week with cantors and even with presiders. As we become comfortable and secure in what we do, we communicate that poise for the assembly. When we feel secure, they will feel secure and become more willing to participate.

As we feel comfortable technically and evolve good relationships with others leading worship, we are ready for the best part of our role as catalyst for congregational song. We are ready to provide encouragement and leadership in such a way that the level of involvement for all begins to grow. Good leadership of congregational song is more than encouraging enthusiastic participation. Congregational song should involve the head and heart as well as the body of each participant.

Creativity in Accompanying Congregational Singing

Creative use of the organ, careful choice of registrants, and use of alternative harmonizations all lead to better singing. For me, leading a congregation in song is a challenging responsibility. It is also fun! It is a joy to read the text and ask myself how my musical skills can be employed to assist us all to proclaim the text through intelligent, vital song. Which stanzas should be loud, which more gentle, which reharmonized, which a cappella, which without pedals? Variety based upon creative encounter with the text is even better, as it increases understanding and never bores.

So then, how do we lead a congregation with

musical and theological creativity? First, we must consider again that a hymn is words—poetry set to music. A hymn (or any liturgical music) must be considered as text first. In some ways a hymn is like the program for a tone poem. The text gives us some sense of how the music is to be perceived.

Nevertheless, the music selected as companion for the text plays an immense role in communicating the spirit, the essence of that text. Consider how our perception of the text "Amazing Grace" changes if it is sung to the tune ANTIOCH ("Joy to the World"). The different spirit of ANTIOCH changes our response to the text of "Amazing Grace." Try this switch some time with your choir and note the reactions. Music has enormous communicative power of its own and will influence, sometimes radically, sometimes subtly, the intrinsic, inherent message of a text. Music is not neutral. Music is exegetical; that is, it interprets and amplifies the meaning of any text it accompanies.

Some organists believe that when leading hymn singing it is wise to be neutral. One plays the notes on the page, well and with rhythmical discipline, but does little more. Registrational changes, harmonic changes, or whatever are not in order for fear they will get in the way of and distract from the text. There is much to be said for such an approach, for it is preferable to flamboyance for flamboyance' sake. But I believe that such an approach, while acceptable, is not adequate. Such neutrality can communicate in ways unintended.

It is as if a computer were programmed to read out loud. The pronunciation is perfect, the accent superb, but the computer does not understand the language. It communicates no *Geist,* no spirit, just perfectly formed sounds. A hymn tune is not absolute music; it is the vehicle for the proclamation of text. Consequently one must encounter, respond to, and be influenced by the meaning of the text.

As one examines the text in relation to a given tune, one moves past just playing the notes to considering how variety in the playing of introduction and subsequent stanzas can enhance the meaning and support the spirit of text and tune. To encounter a text and tune is to begin a creative process exploring options for playing the hymn so that the congregation is inspired to sing with greater understanding and spirit. The practical outcome of such a process is that any two adjacent stanzas are rarely played the same way or with the same registration.

I use the term *alternation* for this variety between stanzas. Part of my preparation of any hymn for congregational singing is to devise an alternation scheme for the hymn. Creative alternation can encourage a congregation to remain more engaged, more involved in singing. Alternation between subgroups of the congregation (men and women, congregation and choir, etc.) provides vocal rest as well. Members of the congregation do not have a vocal warm-up before plunging into the typical multistanza opening hymn of praise and after a few stanzas may become vocally fatigued and cease singing. A planned stanza of rest (always reading the text while others sing it) allows individual singers to re-enter, renewed and inspired (we hope) by hearing the singing of others. An alternation approach to hymn singing could be structured as follows: each hymn is examined and a scheme prepared (for example, stanza 1—all; stanza 2—women; stanza 3—harmony; stanza 4—men; stanza 5—all). Such a scheme is printed in the worship folder so that all are aware of the performance plan for the hymn.

After vocal alternation is considered, musical color can be factored into the mix. A registration scheme for each hymn should be prepared (for example, stanza 1—principals and reeds; stanza 2—remove reeds; stanza 3—flues 8 & 4; etc.), written down on a piece of scratch paper and placed beside the music for quick reference when playing. The vocal alternation scheme may also result in changes of color. The sound of men's voices or women's voices alone is very distinctive. Organ registrations could complement these sounds.

Many times specific ideas for alternation and registration come through study of the text. Some hymns (for example, "Love Divine, All Loves Excelling") lend themselves to a gradual crescendo, first stanza to last. Others can be envisioned as a gradual diminuendo, beginning forte, decreasing during the middle stanzas with the organ vanishing during the last, allowing the people to finish unaccompanied. ("Love Divine" can work this way as well.) Adopting such approaches would be determined by the place and function of the hymn in a specific service as well as the text itself.

Of course most hymns do not lend themselves to dramatic changes. Even so, the contrast between accompanied and unaccompanied singing, the absence or presence of reed stops, gives a flavor to a stanza, impacts our response to it. Over time and with gentle encouragement, a congregation learns to respond to aural signals from the organ and will crescendo or diminuendo with it. Thus, congregational dynamic changes become an addition to our palette of color possibilities.

Another alternation technique is to vary the musical setting of a tune. Melodies soloed out (in soprano, tenor or even bass voice) provide interesting variety. Filling in leaps of thirds and fourths in alto, tenor or bass is another. Judicious use of pedal point or other musical, rhetorical devices can provide a fresh flavor for a stanza. Complete reharmonizations (improvised, written in advance, or played from the many published sources) are the ultimate examples of modified musical settings.

A choral or vocal solo stanza is an especially useful alternation possibility. Choral stanzas could be as simple as a careful rendering in harmony of a stanza from the hymnal to the excerpting of a unique setting of a stanza from one of the many hymn anthems or concertatos in print. An organ stanza is another alternation device when the organ "sings" while all listen and read the text. Short settings of the tune from published, hymn-based repertoire are possible sources for such organ stanzas if one is not ready to improvise them.

Another variant is alternation between two hymns. The congregation sings one hymn (with help from choir and organ) and the choir (or soloist) sing stanzas of a second interspersed between those of the first. Both musical and theological relationships need to be considered in selecting two hymns for such alternation.

Still another area that begs for careful consideration is the introduction for each hymn. Here the organist can be quite creative since the congregation is not yet singing. The hymn introduction provides starting pitch and tonality, gives time to find the page in the hymnal, communicates the spirit of text and tune, and if necessary, reminds the singers of the melodic structure of the tune or introduces a less-familiar tune. Again, it is important to let textual as well as musical considerations inform one's creativity. A gentle, whispering introduction, no matter how well it sounds from a musical perspective, will not prepare a congregation for the singing of a favorite, powerful hymn of praise. There are many interesting introductions (or intonations as I like to call them) in print, but ideally the organist should learn to improvise these. This is a good place to begin as improviser. No one is singing yet, so there is no need to worry about leading the congregation astray when an improvisation takes an unexpected turn.

Intonations can be brief, which minimizes the single greatest challenge to the improviser, the maintenance of formal coherence over time.

Any attempt to deal comprehensively with the many possibilities for creativity in hymn playing is beyond the scope of any single article. All that can be accomplished here is to offer a few basic concepts and encourage their implementation. As these ideas are put into use, it is essential to be in dialogue with clergy colleagues and worship boards, encouraging them to help by making sure that congregational music for worship is selected early enough to provide for adequate preparation. Also, it is important to solicit their support and cooperation in informing the congregation about the role of congregational song in worship. Articles in the parish newsletter and brief paragraphs in the weekly service folder will contribute to the growth of a congregation's understanding of their song. Supportive comments from clergy colleagues and worship boards will do much to encourage greater participation in congregational song and affirm the leadership role of the organist in nurturing that song.

And, of course, as in any artistic endeavor, a little bit goes a long way. It is possible to do too much in any one service (normally a worship service is not a hymn festival) or try to do more than we are ready to do well. But as we grow as leaders of congregational song, we discover a rich and challenging way to utilize our musical abilities, a rewarding way to serve as church musicians.

John Ferguson[38]

263 • THE ROLE OF THE CHOIR IN WORSHIP

The choir does not participate in worship for its own sake, but rather for the sake of the whole of the worshiping people. It leads the worshiping people in their song and contributes additional music as the liturgy or pattern of worship requires. Ideally then, a choir should be a group of facilitators, not performers, a role defined in this article.

The choir has more to do with a pastor's ministry than is often acknowledged. Historically speaking, the choir has always been the minister's right hand. Yet few pastors currently reap the fruit of such a partnership.

Billy Graham on occasion has termed the music department the war department of the church. It is a designation not without justification. Almost everyone in the pastoral ministry has at one time or another been at odds with music or musicians.

It is said that the pastor's job is to preach, the choir's to sing special music—each in its own place in a mutually beneficent but separate endeavor. We smile at such a naive perception of the role of the pastor. But in the case of the choir we grant the fact that special music is what it is all about. Quite frankly, the ministry of the choir goes far beyond the singing of special numbers. It reaches down into the very heart of church life. It finds its center in being one with the pastoral leadership of the worship of the church. To put it succinctly, the choir's job is to support the pastor's parish ministry.

Biblical Background

Historical precedents of such partnerships are well documented (as are occasional cases of adversarial relationships). Some of the most compelling of these are found in the Bible itself.

The Old Testament documents an organized, well-conceived plan for providing worship leadership. The musicians were part of that plan, being given the specific task of ministering to the Lord in music. They were of the priestly tribe of Levi. Each son of Levi (Gershom, Kohath, and Merari) was represented throughout succeeding generations by those specifically appointed to be musicians and music leaders.

By the time of the building of the second temple (c. 515 B.C.), there had emerged a threefold sacerdotal order—high priest, priest, and Levite. It is striking to note that the Levite musicians, no less than the priests, were set aside and consecrated as part of the tribe of Levi to do the work of the Lord in the temple and were supported materially in their ministry by the other eleven tribes. They were "called-out" ones who shared a common spiritual responsibility. Indeed, the musicians were minor clerics.

It is this clerical role which must be reemphasized in our time, not by titles, papers, or ordination, but by the power of regeneration through the blood of our great High Priest, Jesus Christ. We are a chosen generation, a royal priesthood, a holy nation, a peculiar people (1 Peter). Having received new life, we are all, simply put, ministers.

The choir stands in the gap between people and pastor. It has a ministerial function in the leadership of worship but is congregational in its makeup. It follows in the great Levitical tradition, having a role to play which cannot be duplicated by any other ministry—it is unique.

Responsibilities of the Choir

The choir's potential will not be realized unless both pastor and musicians are aware of the purpose of such a body. To use the choir well first means to understand its function.

The following list is not exhaustive, but it will give a new direction from which can develop those particularized rubrics to fit the individual needs of each pastor, congregation, and choir. Specifics here are less important than the trend which is established.

Pastoral responsibilities of the choir are:

1. To maintain a Christ-like attitude in all things. This is the choir's first priority. It is the thing which more than anything else determines success in ministry. One must have a right attitude toward God, congregation, pastor, music, and musicians.
2. To be responsible for lifting up the pastor in prayer, word, and deed.
3. To enter into worship wholeheartedly and with enthusiasm. A dead choir will elicit a dead reaction from the congregation.
4. To listen and respond to the worship leader of the moment, to be attentive to everyone and everything. During prayer the choir members should earnestly pray; during worship they should visibly worship.
5. To lead in the congregational singing of hymns, choruses, and spiritual songs. Such leadership should be with faces, eyes, and hands as well as voices. Any other service music, such as calls to worship, benedictions, responses, etc., will be well prepared and rendered.
6. To be helpful in giving prayers, testimonies, tongues, interpretation of tongues, words of edification, and scriptural admonitions, especially when a general invitation has been given without any ready congregational response. The choir should act in the role of icebreaker and leader.
7. To listen attentively and visibly respond to the ministry of others: soloists, musical groups, evangelists, and pastor.
8. To open up personally to the preached word

modeling the sought-after congregational response. Nothing will aid a pastor's sermon communication with the congregation more than the example of a choir hanging on his every word, obviously being edified and lifted up. The congregation will tend to imitate the listeners they see in front of them. A choir of disinterested, unenthusiastic, unresponsive, sleepy individuals, who feel that because they have finished singing their "special music" they have no further responsibility, is grossly missing the point of its ministry. In such a case it would be better to do away with the choir.

9. To be available to do altar work, giving prayer support and general encouragement to those who respond to the invitation after the sermon. It is distracting to have the choir in a hurry to leave. It must use its influence to help open the congregation to the gentle and unhurried moving of God's Spirit.
10. To sing any additional music deemed appropriate for the service.

The choir is a facilitator of worship. It seeks to show the congregation (under pastoral guidance) the way to extend beyond the temporal and reach, if only briefly, a taste of the worship of heaven. It exhibits a worship in spirit and in truth which encourages the congregation to do the same.

One can readily see then that the main function of the choir is to be the "show and tell" of worship. It takes the initiative, it inspires, it helps, and it leads.

Individuals in the choir must be carefully and systematically taught their role. Such teaching is most effective when paced with the developing experience of the choir as a whole. One must avoid the pitfall of believing that giving information will automatically make the right things happen. The priorities and attitudes we wish to foster must be made to be routine and are best learned as the music director shepherds the choir, carefully and consistently, into maturing patterns of behavior.

Pastoral Responsibility

The pastor needs to nurture his relationship with the choir. They are co-workers, yet with his calling as chief pastor, it falls to him to gently establish the expectations he has for the choir's ministry. He can do this, of course, through the music director. But what cannot be delegated is his personal rapport

with the choir, most notably in the area of a shared ministry. The choir, as congregational/ministerial helper, needs to shoulder with the pastor responsibility for the spiritual growth of the congregation. Having a common spiritual goal which goes beyond mere music-making will cause the choir to blossom and flourish.

To the end of a mutual sharing of and identification with such a common spiritual goal, it is important that regular times of intercessory prayer, with the pastor, especially prior to the service, be part of the Sunday routine. It is also beneficial to engage in conversational dialogue concerning items of mutual interest and concern.

Living life in a caring relationship will heighten the corporate sense of togetherness that nourishes true community. Nothing will so inspire the choir to do its best as the "esprit de corps" generated by a pastor who demonstrably loves his choristers, listens to them, and expects them to shake the rafters of heaven in their mutual quest for the spiritual advancement of the congregation.

Conclusion

The choir is responsible for more than making music. It has potential for being a dynamo of spiritual energy in the worship life of the church. Under pastoral guidance it can be a visible microcosm of God's dealings with the whole church, a channel of his grace and glory, and a corporate respondent in the call to holy living and fuller commitment.

Let there be no misunderstanding. Hosts of musical things must be addressed by a prophetic music ministry. But they all stem from a churchly orientation, quite apart from that of the stage and concert hall.

A shift in priority from musical performance to corporate worship leader will give a perspective to church music-making that frees it from an uncompromising aestheticism and from a nihilistic pragmatism. That is not to say musical ministry ought to silence criticism, but rather that church music creativity ought to arise out of the ashes of musical pride and conceit. A disciplined washer of feet makes the best church musician. And when coupled with a like attitude on the part of the pastor, the combination is hard to beat.

Pastor and choir together are co-workers, a model of how the body of Christ operates. When the choir is used to its fullest potential in support of the pastoral ministry, only the Kingdom gains.

Calvin M. Johansson

264 • CLASSIFYING CHURCH CHOIRS

Choirs play very different roles in various denominations and traditions. This article describes three different types of choirs based on their role in the worship service, commending an approach that integrates the choir's contribution within the structure of the whole worship service. Although written from a Reformed perspective, the insights found here have applications for all traditions.

Choral Society

The first type of choir is what I'll call the "church choral society." This group works on some big anthems or on a cantata for special occasions. At first they sing only after the evening service in a special program; later, as part of the evening service; and perhaps eventually as part of a special service in the morning. The choral society is not so much a church choir as a choir made up of members of the same congregation who love to sing together.

Anthem Choir

The second type is the "anthem choir." This group works faithfully on anthems, which are from time to time inserted into the Sunday liturgy. Usually the anthem does not replace an item in the liturgy; rather, it is an addition to the order of worship. A large and well-developed choir prepares an anthem every Sunday, learning several new ones each year and recycling favorites. In our congregations, by far the most church choirs fall into the anthem choir category.

In borrowing the idea of an anthem choir from churches of other traditions, however, most of us ignored a few things. In Catholic, Lutheran, and Anglican churches, anthems were chosen and composed to relate to the Scripture of the day. Many times the words of the anthem were taken directly from Scripture. In other words, the anthem was an integral part of the liturgy. Because most of these churches followed a lectionary, the choral director knew the Scripture passages for a given service far in advance.

If our choirs ignore that integration between Scripture and anthem, they borrow only part of a

The Descent from the Cross (Zaire). The removal of Jesus' body from the cross was originally depicted by artist Kafusha Laban in resin on glass. It appears in a Methodist church in Africa.

tradition; the other part goes begging for attention. When it has no relationship to what precedes and follows in the order of worship, the anthem becomes "special music," an intrusion in worship. It may be a beautiful intrusion, but it is an intrusion nonetheless.

Service Choir

I'll call the third type of choir a "service choir." This group sings service music. In other words, it participates in worship by taking over one of the liturgical actions that were going to take place anyway. For example, the service choir may sing a call to worship, a call to confession, or a prayer for illumination before the sermon. Or it might augment congregational song with descants and special accompaniments. The music a service choir sings may be either short and simple or long and substantial (including anthems); whatever its length, it is meant to carry liturgical action.

Many Calvinists might point out that the service choir concept brings the priestly function of the choir into question. What about the Reformed principle that the people should do their own worship? Interestingly we have had no problem with the minister switching roles between proclamation and response; no one I know has argued that the congregational prayer should be voiced by the entire congregation. But when it comes to the choir performing a similar role, many Reformed Christians have expressed doubts.

Some of those who hesitate do so because they fear that the more active the choir becomes, the less active the congregation will be. But that should not and need not happen. Actually, by having the choir sing a call to worship or to confession we are moving toward, not away from, the idea that worship belongs to the people. And we are moving toward the concept that a choir sings on behalf of the congregation as all together bring their worship and adoration to God; away from the idea that the choir brings something to the congregation that was not there before.

A good way to start transforming an anthem choir into a service choir is by selecting music for particular liturgical actions. The bulletin then lists the selection as part of the order of worship (Call to Confession: title) rather than as an addition (Anthem: title). And the text is printed in the bulletin so that all the people can understand every word.

When such a change is made, choirs will begin to find their rightful place in Reformed worship. Choral music will no longer intrude or merely decorate but will enrich our worship with that marvelous power that Calvin also recognized: music can "move and inflame the hearts of men to invoke and praise God with a more vehement and ardent zeal." A service choir will enrich our liturgy as we seek to worship the Lord not only in the beauty of holiness but also in holy beauty.

Emily Brink[39]

265 • CHILDREN'S CHOIRS AS LEADERS OF WORSHIP

Children's choirs need not be relegated to simply providing entertainment in worship. Instead, they should function as important worship leaders. The imagination and energy that children are capable of bringing to this role will enrich the service and challenge them in their own spiritual journey.

The moment has arrived: Sunday morning; public worship; the youth choir anthem. With precision,

the children, music folders in hand, rise in unison from the pew and walk to the front of the sanctuary. They stand along the top step—lined up according to height—and turn toward the congregation. The director steps forward and faces the choir. All eyes focus on the director; hands open the music folders; heads and shoulders straighten. The accompaniment begins as the director raises a hand to indicate the entrance of singing. The congregation sees focused faces, hears the melodious music, and well articulated text. At the anthem's conclusion, the choir, the director, and congregation quietly beam. The choir methodically returns to their pew, for they have completed the "presentation" of their anthem within the context of worship.

Unfortunately, the children have fallen prey to "presenting" or "performing." In fact, this performing mode often appears to be an assumed expectation because of the nature of a children's choir. Congregations look forward to the children's singing because of their spontaneity and charm; their faces and voices evoke positive, lighthearted feelings. Worshipers unconsciously receive them as entertainers, a brief relief from confessions, affirmations, and Scripture. The children thus become a highlight of worship, rather than an integral part. Directors, parents and members of the congregation need to ask the following questions:

- In what ways does the youth choir experience themselves as worshiping members _of_ the congregation, rather than performers _before_ the congregation?
- In what ways does the youth choir's offering of music complement if not enhance other elements of worship?
- In what ways does the youth choir's offering of music communicate importance and leadership within worship?
- In what ways does the youth choir's offering of music interact _with_ the congregation?

Youth choirs can be integrated into corporate worship, not as presenters or performers, but as participants, just as any other serving member of the community of faith.

In order for a children's choir to experience themselves as worshiping members on an equal par with adults, a fundamental understanding of worship must be acknowledged. Throughout the services, people offer praise and prayers and hear the Word.

Worship becomes a corporate event—a faith-shaping event. The church embraces corporate worship as the central, constituting act of the community of faith gathered in the name of Christ. Worship provides the setting where our identity is shaped, and we are one—a reconciled community of all sizes, shapes, colors, and ages. Together, at the table of the Lord and through the work of the Holy Spirit, both children and adults of all ages and stages become one. The gift of the Spirit binds the church together as one family. The response to this gift manifests itself through weekly celebration (i.e., worship). On the Lord's Day, this *oneness* is exalted through active participation, by responding to God's gifts and God's call. Children may not fully comprehend either why we respond or celebrate, but through their participation in choirs and corporate worship, children can sense they are an important, equal, contributing member among the people of God.

How the Youth Choir Can Become Participants in Worship

Children as well as adults learn through multisensory experiences. What multisensory learning could a child experience in worship—especially singing in a youth choir? Consider sight, sound, touch, and taste.

Sight. When the choir arrives before the service, they put on their robes and an appropriate colored stole to match the liturgical season or day (e.g., purple for Lent, white for Easter, red for Pentecost, and green for ordinary time). Among the commotion of dressing, one always hears the question, "What color are we today?" The children know that a particular liturgical color matches the day or season. In the sanctuary, they encounter that same color in banners, paraments, and tablecloths, as well as stoles worn by liturgical leaders and adult choir members. The simple act of matching of colors communicates consciously and unconsciously to children a sense of *belonging* to the whole worshiping community and its environment.

Upon entering the sanctuary, each choir member receives from an usher his or her own order for worship, just like everyone else who comes to worship. The children hold it, read from it, sing from it, pray from it, just like everyone else sitting in the pews around them. To some people, distributing orders for worship to each chorister may seem unnecessary or useless. After all, some children cannot even read, others scribble or draw pictures on it, or even leave it behind on the pew. What the critics fail to realize is that this order for worship tells the children *they are significant, contributing members of the church,* their presence and participation in the service is wanted, needed, and valued. Children observe others with the same papers. Whether young or old, tall or short, they see themselves as part of a family. They are brothers and sisters in Christ, accepted and loved.

Sound. Listening to the tone and tempo of service music throughout the service, children differentiate among the various components of worship. An opening hymn of praise such as "Joyful, Joyful, We Adore Thee" (HYMN TO JOY, *Presbyterian Hymnal* #464, sounds radically different from a Kyrie Eleison ("Lord, have mercy") sung after a prayer of confession. HYMN TO JOY sounds lively, expectant, and optimistic, and is played and sung as such. The Kyrie, on the other hand, frequently conveys a slower, somber, penitent mood that follows a corporate confession of sin.

These auditory shifts in the service signal to the choir that something different is happening in worship, and that we as a congregation are responding accordingly. Children cannot rationally explain how what they hear affects them, but they do *experience* the changes in sound. It may not be obvious, however, to the average adult how many times the tone and tempo of what we say and sing is directly related to a particular component of worship.

Taste and Touch. Youth choirs have another opportunity to experience the *oneness* of a church family through celebration of the Eucharist. During the distribution and serving of the elements, allow the children to serve each other just as the adult members do. (If younger children are present, it might be a good idea for "choir parents" to be interspersed among the group.) Let each child hold the bread or plate, and offer it to whomever sits beside him or herself. Allow them to speak to one another, offering words of care and friendship. Encourage the children to serve their neighbor before themselves, proclaiming a simple act of servanthood. Let them eat the bread and drink the wine as a celebratory meal that we share as the body of Christ—a meal that might be served differently from that at home, and a meal that satisfies us though we do not feel stuffed. As a choir, they are introduced to a new concept of being "fed" within the family of God, and not by their nuclear family in their home.

Most of the time, children do worship while in a pew with their nuclear family. How does attending worship with your family differ from sitting together as a youth choir? If one constantly sits with his or her parents and siblings, a constant tension and confusion exists about the concept of family. The child may wonder, "What is this family of God? I have a family; I don't need another one." Sitting together as a choir gives them the opportunity to serve someone other than their immediate family and to experience a bond outside of their home—a bond that exists because of being called together as the body of Christ.

A choir can experience this _oneness_ with the congregation if we allow members to be present and to be _participants,_ not performers. As adults, we need to recognize and encourage these nonverbal mysteries of worship (sight, sound, touch, and taste) that shape the liturgy and give it meaning to our children.

How the Youth Choir Can Enhance Other Elements of Worship

Most directors spend time planning appropriate music to complement the Scripture or liturgical season. But often the offering of music still looks and feels like an intrusion on the normal flow of worship. Consider the following placements and purposes of an anthem:

1. Normally anthems are sung during a traditional "offering of music" slot. Consider shifting the anthem to a different element of worship. For example, let the anthem serve as the psalm or scripture reading. On the Day of Pentecost, they could sing Hal H. Hopson's version of Psalm 104, "O Lord, Send Down Your Spirit" (from _Ten Psalms_ [Carol Stream, Ill.: Hope Publishing Company, 1986], 12–13).

- The choir introduces the antiphon by singing it alone.
- The choir and congregation repeat the antiphon.
- The choir alone sings each stanza, followed by the congregation singing the antiphon.

Singing the Psalms with the youth choir as leader is a welcome relief to the commonly spoken responsive readings or even to adults who sing the stanzas as cantors. The Psalms come alive, take on new meaning, and give the children a feeling of importance because they _are_ the psalm reading for the day.

Allow the youth choir to sing a Scripture reading for the day, as an alternative to hearing just the spoken Word and, again, to give the choir a purpose for singing other than entertaining. "The Song of Mary" (MORNING SONG, _Presbyterian Hymnal_ #600), tells the story in Luke 1:46-55. A lector can read Luke 1:39-45, introducing Mary's visit to Elizabeth, followed by the choir singing her song. What an effective way to actually hear the _sung_ "song of praise" and to interweave an anthem into worship. The choir then becomes _leaders_ of worship by offering the Scripture and, at the same time, learns the words and stories of the Bible. Learning occurs as a by-product of proclaiming to others.

2. Music supplemented with instruments can also enhance worship. A hymn sung by the choir can radiate new meaning if accompanied by an instrument. "Cantad al Senor" ("O Sing to the Lord") (_Presbyterian Hymnal_ #472) clamors for maracas or sand blocks to impart the Brazilian folk melody. It is a rare organist who can play this hymn with its natural Brazilian beat and aura that surround this type of folk music. Let the children's choir, with all of their innocence and spontaneity, expand the horizons of hymns.

Handbells also can enliven hymns—not played as a handbell solo but as a complement to the anthem. Children in youth choirs are very capable of playing handbells, with proper handling and ringing instruction. What better way to accentuate the anticipated joy of a Christmas Eve service than for the children to sing _In Bethlehem a Babe was Born_ (DISCOVERY, _Presbyterian Hymnal_ #34), supplemented by a simple handbell arrangement for the refrain. The combination of music and children possesses a power beyond explanation which greatly invigorates the liturgy. How adults employ this power to broaden and strengthen worship remains a challenge to us all.

3. A choir can participate in worship without offering music. For example, during Lent, worship assumes a more solemn, contemplative atmosphere. So refrain from singing joyous, resounding hymns accompanied by trumpets. Suspend shouting

praises and loud alleluias. In fact, on the Sunday of the Transfiguration of the Lord (immediately prior to Ash Wednesday), let the choir creatively design and decorate their own individual alleluia posters or banners. During the concluding hymn of corporate worship, the choir then carries their alleluia posters or banners to the front of the sanctuary, places them in a box or cabinet labeled "alleluia chest," and literally "locks up" the alleluias for Lent. After this time and all through Lent, no alleluias are spoken or sung in church, at choir practice, or at home. The children will truly more fully experience and understand the mood of the season of Lent. As a choir director, try rehearsing your Easter anthem with the choir refusing to sing alleluia! It's no easy task! With the alleluia chest "locked up" and visible in the sanctuary for all of Lent, both choir and congregation are reminded that worship in Lent assumes a unique tone. The youth choir in this example has taken on a leadership role by teaching and showing a different way of living during Lent.

How the Youth Choir Can —— Communicate Importance and —— Leadership Within Worship

One elementary way is through the simple act of wearing choir robes. The robes mark the choristers as leaders, particularly in that they visually match and equal the robed adults who have a special role Sunday after Sunday. Occasionally, plan a joint children's and adult anthem to provide an experience for the young choristers to look, feel, and sound like one of the major contributors to worship. Again, the children also will experience the *oneness* of the worshiping community.

Another way to link their offering of music to their role of leadership can present a real challenge to the director. Utilize your hymnal to its fullest. After all, hymns teach the children (and us adults) the church's song and theology throughout all the ages. So, take a break from printed sheet music and sing a hymn for each offering of music. Hymn singing introduces the children to the hymnal and allows them to feel comfortable using it, for they can recognize and sing with fervor the hymns they know well.

It is the responsibility of pastors, musicians, and worship planners to offer opportunities for our children for ongoing nurture in the faith—to tell them the story through words, actions and music. Hymns offer such opportunities in that they are sung repeatedly throughout the church's life and liturgy. The church's song will never disappear; it continues month to month, year to year, and from generation to generation. Hymns provide a portable foundation for everyone's journey of faith. Let us not underestimate the lifelong power of text and tune.

Moreover, through the singing of hymns, the choir can teach themselves—as well as the congregation—hymns that are new to the hymnal or seldom sung. This is hardly a novel idea, for on 16 January 1537, William Farel and John Calvin laid before the Council of Geneva their *Articles on the Organization of the Church and its Worship at Geneva*. Their recommendations are modest at first appearance, but far-reaching in their implications. For instance:

> worship should include the congregational singing of psalms, so as to give fervor and ardor to the prayers which otherwise are apt to be dead and cold. Since, however, neither tunes nor words are known to the congregation, many of whom are probably illiterate, there shall be a children's choir which shall sing clearly. The people for their part shall listen "with all attention" and gradually pick up the words and music." (T. H. L. Parker, *John Calvin: A Biography* [Philadelphia: Westminster, 1976], 63)

By teaching the congregation new tunes and texts, the youth choir then becomes a leader in worship. In the community of faith of all ages and stages, we frequently become both teachers and learners with one another. This *oneness* continues when the youth choir's anthem encourages an interactive role with the congregation.

—— How a Youth Choir Can Interact —— *with* the Congregation

In what ways can all choirs complement the choir of the congregation? When the children offer a hymn, invite the congregation to sing alternate stanzas or join in on the refrain (given the citation or printed material from which to sing). The anthem then becomes a corporate congregational (concertato-like) anthem where all participate and no one performs.

For the benediction, let everyone sing "Go With Us, Lord" (TALLIS' CANON, *Presbyterian Hymnal* #535). The children can sing it themselves the first time, with everyone joining in the second time; the third time, divide the congregation into three sections and sing it as a canon. The tune will surround the entire community, again making it a corporate contribution of music.

Choir and congregation can interact musically not just with their voices but also with their bodies. During the Christmas season, sing "Angels We Have Heard on High" (GLORIA, _Presbyterian Hymnal_ #23). Let the choir come forward, dance to the stanzas, and sign the words with their hands and arms on the refrain. The congregation, seated, can mimic the signing so they too can respond to the music and experience text, tune, and movement.

The purpose of worship is for _all_ to come together to respond and to receive. This togetherness can happen only if the choir's role becomes one of participant rather than performer. Let their music involve and interact with the congregation. Let their music relate to and enhance the total worship experience. Let their music emanate leadership within the body of Christ. When this happens, worship helps us catch a glimpse of the kingdom to come, where all are one.

Youth choir rehearsal begins. The children eagerly arrive, having just enjoyed refreshments with the adults. Susan wants to show you the Noah's ark she created in church school; Joseph wishes to tell you about his vacation; and Ezra thanks you for the choir's note he received in the mail acknowledging the day of his baptismal anniversary. All are settled. The piano music introduces the warm up song, Psalm 118, "This is the Day the Lord Has Made," sung with crescendos and decrescendos. The psalm is followed by the choir's favorite, "Come, Christians, Join to Sing" (MADRID, _Presbyterian Hymnal_ #150), sung in ascending keys. Rehearsal continues with action songs, "silly song," and worship responses. Today the children concentrate on "I Danced in the Morning" (SIMPLE GIFTS, _Presbyterian Hymnal_ #302). The choir discusses the text and the importance of clearly communicating this story through their singing. They listen intently to the tune and then respond to the text _and_ tune through dance and body movements. Next Sunday, they will offer this hymn during corporate worship. They shall stand tall and sing joyously (with no printed music) as they offer this music to God on behalf of the congregation. They shall contribute to the service not by entertaining or through their

"charm," but as active, participating members of the worshiping congregation.

Molly M. Macaulay[40]

266 • THE PLACE OF THE VOCAL SOLO IN WORSHIP

A vocal soloist can function in much the same way as a choir, leading the people's song and presenting additional music that may be required by the structure and theme of a given order of service. This article addresses several practical concerns related to this role.

Do solo singers have a place in our worship services today? In recent years many Christians have struggled with that question. Some insist that soloists are superfluous, unrelated to the heart of true worship. Others are convinced that soloists call attention to themselves rather than lead the congregation in worship through music. Still others believe that all parts of the worship service should be marked by participation rather than observation and that hymns, which involve the worshiping people directly, are therefore more appropriate than solo numbers.

All these objections have validity. But they reflect the need not to rid our services of soloists but rather to find ways to use them more appropriately.

The chief vocal music used in our worship services should be congregational, but a choir can also fill an important role in worship. Congregational singing, of course, is an integral part of every worship service we attend. Not so with choral music. Sometimes a choir is not available. At such times one can view the solo singer as a "one-person choir" (C. Halter and C. Schalk, _A Handbook of Church Music_).

Of course, our worship should never be interrupted by solo singers singing "special music"—solos that call attention to the singer and add nothing to the fabric of the liturgy. The solo singer, like the choir, has an obligation to lead the congregation in worship, directing thoughts toward God, building up the body of Christ. If a vocal solo is chosen carefully, performed well, and integrated into the service, it can be a valuable addition to the worship service, providing variety when choral music is not available or even, on occasion, used in addition to choral music.

Important Considerations

Placing the Musicians. Deciding where to place musicians can have an impact on how the congregation views their contribution to worship. For example, placing the organist and soloist in the balcony, out of view of the congregation, tends to focus attention on the music itself rather than on the musicians.

If a singer must sing from the front of the church, it is important that personal appearance in no way distract from the dignity of the service or bring undue attention to the singer. Some churches provide a robe for soloists to discourage the congregation from focusing on appearance and behavior.

Selecting Music. It is also important for soloists to choose material that is well within their range of expertise and for the songs to be well prepared and rehearsed with the accompanist before the service. Furthermore, soloists should keep in mind the congregations for which they are singing. A simple but well-chosen hymn may be best for a congregation whose accompanists have limited skills and whose members are not familiar with more complex styles of sacred music. Poorly performed music or material that upsets the congregation calls attention to the singer and does not contribute to the worship of God.

In his book *The Practice of Sacred Music,* Carl Halter suggests three considerations that musicians should keep in mind when selecting music for the worship service:

1. Its value for the praise of God; since worship is God-centered, not people-centered.
2. Its suitability for the particular service in which it is to be used.
3. Its ability to communicate to the hearers.

Halter sees the third consideration as a problem of language rather than quality since "not every group of people will be able to understand every worthwhile musical language [or style]." He continues, "It is the duty of the musicians patiently and lovingly to develop the needed understandings by the use of the best examples of whatever language is employed" (Halter, p. 37).

Conscientious singers will find material that is not too ornate. If a composition is filled with operatic tendencies toward virtuosity, the singer, rather than the message of the song, again becomes central.

Deciding on a Text. A song has two parts: text and music. The text of a song is extremely important and must be consonant with Scripture in order to belong in a worship service. Perhaps the best texts come from Scripture itself, but versified Scripture or well-crafted poetry that is in harmony with Scripture may also be very edifying to a congregation and worthy praise of God. In *Music and Worship in the Church* (p. 126), Lovelace and Rice mention four tests for determining whether a text is appropriate for worship:

> It is necessary to study the text of every anthem, even it is scriptural, to determine if it is theologically acceptable, profound in its message, beautiful in its expression, and meaningful to the listener of today.

These tests apply not only to anthems but also to every hymn, psalm, and Bible song—to any words that are sung during worship, by congregation, choir, or soloist.

Evaluating Music. It is more difficult to formulate tests to evaluate the music we use in worship. In his preface to *A Well-Appointed Church Music* (pp. 12–13), Howard Slenk writes,

> In church music more than any other facet of worship, the idea of entertainment or performance has done the most damage. "Play what the congregation likes" is only one of the frequent comments that shows the encroachment of the entertainment world into worship. The idea of word and music as an offering to God rarely exists. We forget that worship is not entertainment but participation. Worship requires an active congregation, not an audience. The question "Will they like it?" must be replaced by "Will he accept it?" The question "Does this music please me?" is not as important as "Is this music worthy of God?"

Appropriate for the Occasion

The soloist who chooses excellent music and fitting language for the congregation will have done much to ensure that his or her offering is a meaningful addition to worship. But fine music and a pleasing text are not the only considerations the musician must keep in mind. It is equally important that each selection is appropriate for the occasion and fitted into the worship service so that it does not appear extraneous.

Several possible positions for a solo are the call to

worship, response to Scripture reading, call to prayer, response to prayer, or benediction.

Soloists may also contribute to the liturgy of other services, such as weddings, funerals, and prayer services as well as to more informal programs and meetings in the church. Although the music used at weddings, funerals, and other services should be subjected to the same tests that we use for music in our Sunday services, selections sung for more informal and nonliturgical gatherings need not be evaluated by such rigorous standards.

For example, although I often sing Max Reger's "The Virgin's Slumber Song" for adult fellowship groups at Christmas time, I would never sing that song for a public worship service. Why? Because I judge that this text, while poetic and devotional, is merely a lullaby to baby Jesus and, as such, is not suited to a liturgical setting.

Special problems may arise for the solo singer at weddings and funerals. Often the family has certain preferences for music, and many times their choices are not appropriate liturgically. It often takes a great deal of tact and firmness to refuse to sing songs that are either inferior in quality or inappropriate for the setting. Some churches wisely have attempted to eliminate this problem and to preserve the dignity and liturgical nature of weddings and funerals by setting guidelines and rules for the music used in these services.

Sources for Solos

In choosing vocal music for worship, the soloist can use a wide range of sources. First is the hymnal, which can often provide meaningful and useful music for the service (and can also help the congregation learn new and unfamiliar hymns). Other sources include vocal solo repertoire with sacred text, written originally as independent solos; the large repertoire of oratorios and cantatas that sometimes provide movements which can be used separately; and the unison anthem, which frequently makes an excellent vocal solo.

Trudi Huisman Huizenga

267 • THE PLACE OF THE CANTOR IN WORSHIP

The cantor played an important role in biblical and ancient worship. The role of the cantor is being recovered in contemporary worship. This article explains how and where to use the cantor in the liturgy, with reference to Roman Catholic liturgy in particular.

The cantor is becoming an integral role in our worship. With that trend comes important questions. Who should these persons be? How can we find them? And what should they do?

Qualifications of a Cantor

The cantor should be a person who has a good voice and who is able to carry a tune. Asking for such persons through the parish bulletin is not recommended; you'll likely get some very well-intentioned people who cannot sing. It is better for you to approach candidates who have proven they can sing in one of the parish music groups.

The cantor should be someone who feels comfortable standing in front of the assembly and leading the people in song. For some, this comes naturally. Others will need to work on this skill.

Cantors need to understand their role in the celebration and have an understanding that they are leading the people in prayer. Encourage them to study liturgy and the role that music plays in our celebrations.

Also, encourage the cantor to take voice lessons. The parish might subsidize this study or hire a voice teacher to work occasionally with all of the cantors in the parish.

The Cantor's Role

For the eucharistic liturgy, the cantor should sing the verses to the responsorial psalm, lead the refrain to the responsorial psalm, lead the singing of the gospel acclamation. In addition, the cantor can lead the antiphonal song for the Communion processional, assist in the singing of the penitential rite, intercessions, Lamb of God, and possibly the Gloria.

For Morning and Evening Prayer, cantors can lead the singing of the Psalms. They can also lead music at penance celebrations, baptisms, funerals, and weddings—although few parishes have taken advantage of a good cantor's ability to draw forth a music response from the assembly on these occasions.

The cantor can introduce and teach new music. Most cantors should be able at least to introduce a new refrain for the psalm responsorial, but not all should be expected to have the ability to introduce a new hymn.

Parish cantors should meet regularly to learn the music. This would also be the time for the cantors to learn how to use the parish sound system properly, to critique each other, and to further study liturgy and the Psalms.

If your parish has not yet explored the ministry of cantor, I strongly urge you to do so. Seek out parishes who use cantors and see what has worked for them.

John Kubiniec

268 • THE CANTOR'S TOOLS OF COMMUNICATION

A cantor or lead singer must master more than simply the music of the liturgy. For as worship leader, the cantor has important responsibility for making worshipers feel welcome and comfortable in their role in the service. Nonverbal communication by gestures is one important aspect of the cantor's task.

Gestures come in many forms of nonverbal communication such as eye contact, decorum, posture, facial expression, and actual arm and hand gestures.

In the 187 Catholic dioceses of this country, hundreds of women and men enter into the eucharistic celebration of their parishes each Sunday and lead the gathered assembly in sung prayer. By right of their baptism, and because they have the gift of singing, cantors serve the people of God, motivating them to "full, conscious, and active participation" in the liturgies as expressed by the Second Vatican Council (*Sacrosanctum Concilium* #14).

As cantors, we are keepers of the Psalms, the song of the church. We lead, inspire, and serve as models by which the whole community can identify the Gospel, but we do not live in a vacuum. There are many other demands placed upon our daily lives. All of us at one time or another are overwhelmed, and we seem to be pulled in so many different directions. The desire to become more involved in this ministry (improving one's cantoring skills, deepening our knowledge of Scripture, and taking stock of the quality of service given to the assembly) gets placed on a back burner, and we can begin to lose sight of our purpose. We tend to fall into ruts, or into repeated bad habits, and our cantoring becomes "second nature" to a fault. If we are not careful, our work may turn out to be musically haphazard and our ministry spiritually unfulfilling both for ourselves and for our assembly.

From the experience in my own parish of being a cantor and of training cantors, I am continually reminded that in order for one to be effective in the Sunday assembly it is absolutely necessary to examine his "cantor conscience" on a regular basis, while asking some hard questions about attitudes and talents. Just what are the pitfalls and what are these bad habits that plague us, these habits that keep us from being truly effective leaders of prayer?

If given the chance, surely all of us could write a list! Here are three considerations: (1) the role of cantor in relationship to the singing assembly, (2) gestures, and (3) the use of microphones. As each is discussed here, it is my hope that each of us would make an examination of our own cantor conscience, discover what skills need to be revised or revived (each of our styles have their own creative challenges), and allow ourselves to play and set goals, so that with renewed vision, we can be well on our way towards excellence in this ministry.

It goes without saying that the assembly exercises the primary ministry of music within the liturgical celebration and, as stated before, there are those of us who have proven musical talents and a specific call to use these gifts on behalf of the parish community. To assume this position of leadership, we need always to remember that we ourselves are first and foremost members of the assembly. We belong. We are musicians that are working *with others,* not doing something *for others.*

Our duty is to *support* and *encourage* the song of the people of God *as far as needed.* This is an issue of hospitality, trust, and great expectations. The Notre Dame Study on Catholic Parish Life (report #5, Mark Searle and David C. Leege) notes that "where the cantor sings less than 70 percent of the music, congregational participation rises sharply above that attained with any other kind of musical leadership." I find in my experience that cantors are afraid to let go, they don't trust the assembly to sing. Our role is neither to overpower the assembly nor do the work for them, and liturgy is certainly not a forum for our vocal performance. Yes, we intone melodies, lead responsorial singing, and sing psalm verses and litanies—that is our service to the people. During the hymns and acclamations, why not give the other instruments (organ, contemporary ensemble, and so on) the opportunity to lead the assembly? We might be surprised at what we hear if we step back and blend our voices with those we serve. Our leadership should always come out of the knowledge that this ministry is one which is life-giving to the assembly and reaches its fulfillment when we take the assembly beyond the music and into the prayer itself.

The second consideration is the use of gestures. Gestures take practice. They have become basic to the cantor's craft when inviting people to sing. They come in many forms of nonverbal communication such as decorum, posture, facial expression, eye contact, and the actual arm and hand gestures. In order to be effective, cantors need to consider how comfortable they are in their own bodies.

We are highly visible in this ministry, and we must be at ease when standing in front of large crowds. Being at ease with one's appearance, well rehearsed with the other musicians, vocally warmed-up, and prepared (having all material in order beforehand) certainly minimizes any feeling of stage fright. People sense nervousness and are less likely to follow a leader who communicates a lack of confidence or experience. Our facial expressions and eye contact are also important as these help us to maintain our rapport with the people.

Hand and arm gestures are the physical communications that motivate the assembly to sing. These are not abstract movements. Rather, they are visual cues for the people, cues that are united to the rhythm and tempo of the music, cues which take into consideration the space in which we are singing and the size of the assembly. Cantors should always stand with good singing posture: erect and comfortable, stable head, shoulders relaxed, hand at sides, knees bent, feet slightly apart but planted firmly on the ground. Do all of this while presenting yourself to the assembly with dignity and confidence. When the people are ready to sing, cue them by rhythmically breathing with them, raising both arms just about to shoulder height, with palms facing upward. Once the assembly begins to sing, slowly return your arms to hang at your sides. Do not leave your arms in the air! Once the assembly is in, get the gesture out of the way!

Also be willing to modify these movements according to the space and the size of the group. At times, eye contact and a nod of the head will be adequate gestures for the assembly's participation. Perhaps there will be time when it is necessary to hold the music. In this case, one would have to adjust or alter the gestures using only a hand position (with a slightly rounded hand, fingers together with the thumb separate, extend the arm and turn the hand upward), breathing with them, and inviting the assembly to sing. Personal practice and consistency is all that's required!

The use of microphones is the next consideration. How we love to hear ourselves sing through these little electronic miracles! In listening to many cantors, it is my experience that this is exactly what is happening—cantors are hearing themselves sing, and they are loving every minute of it! But what has happened to the assembly—what about their song? In most cases, the voice of the people is being over-powered, drowned out, and reduced to nothing-ness! Should we wonder why they are not singing?

My first suggestion is to see if you can do your work without using the microphone. The natural sound of the human voice is most desirable. If you cannot do it without amplification, find an honest friend who will listen to you practice with the sound system of your church. Have your friend tell you whether or not you can be clearly understood and heard, if you are too loud or too soft. Know that the microphone will be used differently for speaking and for singing. Perhaps you will have to move closer to the microphone for singing; therefore, practice speaking into the microphone as you will be using verbal communication for teaching music to the assembly. Too often, we rely heavily on this electronic voice to carry our voice and become lazy, and this results in poor vocal production, poor diction, and poor breath control. This is disastrous for vocal soloists, for there may come a time when they really need good vocal techniques and will discover that a lot has been lost. Each of us is created differently, so when using a microphone it is important to discover what is most comfortable and what sounds good within the space.

Do we always need the microphone? I don't think so. The use of good judgment prevails here. I repeat, be willing to let go, to modify those practices which are second nature. If the size of the gathered assembly is only thirty-five people, turn the microphone off! Also, move away from the ambo or lectern. It is not always necessary to stand behind or lean on a lectern when cantoring. Sing with the people to whom we belong, leading them when necessary while fulfilling our liturgical role as cantor.

Nevertheless, the microphone has become a part of our work as cantors, and most of us will use one at times during the liturgical celebration. How we work with these amplification systems is key to our musical leadership, the assembly's participation, and the preservation of our vocal techniques.

As ministers of music, our commitment and responsibility is to lead the people of God into the prayer of the liturgy by seeking to help them learn both to sing prayer and to pray by singing. To achieve this, we need to let go of practices that hinder them from singing their song. Let's inform ourselves about the practices of our field, start approaching our skills with new insight, and begin to make a difference with those we serve and to whom we belong!

Rosemary A. Hudecheck[41]

269 • BIBLIOGRAPHY FOR MUSICAL LEADERSHIP IN THE CHURCH

—— General Reference Works ——

Papale, Henry. *Handbook of Musical Terms*. Phoenix: North American Liturgical Resources, n.d. Alphabetical listing gives precise, insightful definitions to a wide range of nearly all musical terms.

Poultney, David. *Dictionary of Western Church Music*. Chicago: American Library Association, 1991. Contains definitions of terms and genre, biographies of composers, and lists of publishers, societies, organizations, and periodicals.

Schalk, Carl. *Key Words in Church Music*. St. Louis: Concordia, 1978. Essays on important terms and concepts in the history and practice of church music.

Schalk, Carl, and Carl Halter, eds. *A Handbook of Church Music*. St. Louis: Concordia, 1978. Articles on practical problems facing the church musician.

—— The Minister of Music ——

Bauman, William A. *The Ministry of Music: A Guide for the Practicing Church Musician*. Washington, D.C.: The Liturgical Conference, 1979. An overview of the various roles of the church musician, along with advice about liturgical and pastoral judgments that must be made in the practice of church music.

Delamont, Vic. *The Ministry of Music in the Church*. Chicago: Moody, 1980.

Lawrence, Joy E., and John A. Ferguson, *A Musician's Guide to Church Music*. Cleveland: Pilgrim Press, 1981.

Funk, Virgil C. *The Pastoral Musician*. Washington, D.C.: Pastoral Press, 1900. A collection of 10 essays that describe both a vision for the role of the musician in the worshiping community and practical suggestions for how to achieve it. Some essays are directed primarily to the Roman Catholic tradition, but the volume as a whole could (and should!) be profitably read by musicians in any Christian tradition.

Funk, Virgil C., and Gabe Huck. *Pastoral Music in Practice*. Washington, D.C.: Pastoral Music Press and Chicago: Liturgy Training Publications, 1981. A collection of several of the best liturgical and practical articles published in *Pastoral Music* magazine.

Orr, N. Lee. *The Church Music Handbook*. Nashville: Abingdon, 1991. A recent handbook that describes many of the practical challenges facing the contemporary church musician.

Patterson, Keith L. *Evaluating Your Liturgical Music Ministry*. San Jose: Resource Publications, 1993.

Routley, Erik. *Music Leadership in the Church*. Nashville: Abingdon, 1967. Perspectives on the primary goals of the musical leadership in the church.

Schalk, Carl. *The Pastor and Church Musician: Thoughts on Aspects of a Common Ministry*. St. Louis: Concordia, 1984. Discusses the importance of the relationship of the pastor and church musician, with helpful advice for fostering the positive growth of this relationship.

Westermeyer, Paul. *The Church Musician*. San Francisco: Harper & Row, 1988. A widely received handbook for choir directors, organists, ministers of music, song leaders, soloists, pianists, choir members, pastors, music committees, and all in the ministry of music.

———, ed. *The Parish Education Series*. St. Louis: Morning Star Publications, n.d. Articles on the practice of church music in the Lutheran tradition.

—— Leading Congregational Singing ——

Lovelace, Austin. *Hymn Notes for Church Bulletins*. Chicago: GIA Publications, 1987. Brief descriptions of the background to several hundred commonly sung hymns.

Parker, Alice. *Creative Hymn Singing*. Chapel Hill, N.C.: Hinshaw, 1976. Ideas for invigorating congregational singing, along with specific discussion of twenty hymns from various periods in the history of the church.

Schmidt, Orlando, ed. _Hymn Singing._ Newton, KS.: Faith and Life Press and Scottdale, PA.: Mennonite Publishing House, 1981. Five essays that defend the importance of creative, energetic, and thoughtful congregational singing and describe how to promote it.

Sydnor, James. _Hymns and Their Uses: A Guide to Improved Congregational Singing._ Carol Stream, IL.: Hope Publishing, 1982. A very helpful book for any church musician concerned about congregational singing. The book describes musical and textual features to which the church musician must attend and provides many helpful suggests for invigorating singing even in small parishes.

Sydnor, James. _Introducing a New Hymnal._ Chicago: GIA Publications, 1989. Ideas about the process of introducing a new hymnal, along and extended section on ways of improving singing the local congregation.

———— Solo Resources ————

For resources for solo voice in worship, the following citations provide a good general approach to acquiring a balanced repertory:

The publisher G. Schirmer provides collections compiled by W. Kirby (_Seventeen Sacred Songs_), Ruth Michaelis (_The Church Year in Song_), and Lloyd Pfautsch (_Solos for the Church Year_ and _The Church Soloist_), all of these being multiple-composer collections.

PGP Publishing, Inc. features Joan Welles's _Soloists' Guide to Selecting Sacred Solos_ (1988), a checklist of more than 650 solos, indexed by title, composer, biblical reference, range, and publisher. Similarly, James H. Laster's _Catalogue of Vocal Solos and Duets Arranged in Biblical Order_ (Metuchen, N.J.: Scarecrow Press, 1984) is an excellent collection according to scriptural theme or context. See also Noni Espina, _Vocal Solos for Christian Churches,_ 3d ed. (Metuchen, N.J.: Scarecrow Press, 1984). The second edition is _Vocal Solos for Protestant Services._

Other publishers who have extensive solo vocal listings in worship music are H. W. Gray, Concordia, Lawson-Gould, Boosey and Hawkes, Stainer and Bell-Galaxy, and Augsburg. All of these publishers specialize in works of standard classical repertory; for praise-song solos and gospel settings one must turn to the main gospel distributers such as Presser, Word, Lillenas, Zondervan, or Maranatha! Music.

Index